Gun Digest®

39th Anniversary
1985 Annual Edition

EDITED BY KEN WARNER

D1609461

DBI BOOKS, INC., NORTHFIELD, ILL.

ABOUT OUR COVER

For 1985, the familiar Sturm, Ruger logo and superb cutaway art is found on the covers of this, the 39th Annual Edition of GUN DIGEST.

At the top you'll see a cutaway of the popular Ruger "Red Label" 12-gauge shotgun. In the center is a rendering of the Ruger Mark II, 22-caliber semi-auto pistol. The Mark II is the offspring of the tried and true Ruger Standard Auto, the gun that made the name "Ruger" one of the most recognized names in American gun-making history. At the bottom is the Ruger Redhawk, a double action, large-framed revolver that's available in 357, 41 or 44 Magnum.

Ruger products have graced the covers of a number of GUN DIGESTS over the past four decades. As most of you know, many of those Ruger covers have featured cutaway artwork. Because of the letters we've received over the past years, we thought you'd be happy to know that Ruger is finally offering reprints of some of the cutaway art so synonomous with that company's well-known line of products. Limited Edition sets of full-color lithos by artist James Kritz are available directly from Sturm, Ruger. Each set contains four cutaway prints, one each of the M-77, the No. 1, the Mini-14 and the Red Label Over & Under.

GUN DIGEST STAFF

EDITOR-IN-CHIEF
Ken Warner
ASSISTANT TO THE EDITOR
Lilo Anderson
SENIOR STAFF EDITOR
Harold A. Murtz
ASSOCIATE EDITOR
Robert S. L. Anderson
PRODUCTION MANAGER
Pamela J. Johnson
CONTRIBUTING EDITORS
Bob Bell
Dean A. Grenell
Rick Hacker
Edward A. Matunas
Layne Simpson
Larry S. Sterett
Hal Swiggett
Ralph T. Walker
D. A. Warner
J.B. Wood
EUROPEAN CORRESPONDENT
Raymond Caranta
EDITOR EMERITUS
John T. Amber
GRAPHIC DESIGN
Mary MacDonald
Jim Billy
PUBLISHER
Sheldon L. Factor

DBI BOOKS INC.

PRESIDENT
Charles T. Hartigan
VICE PRESIDENT & PUBLISHER
Sheldon L. Factor
VICE PRESIDENT — SALES
John G. Strauss
TREASURER
Frank R. Serpone

Copyright © MCMLXXXIV by DBI Books, Inc., One Northfield Plaza, Northfield, Illinois 60093. All rights reserved. Printed in the United States of America.

No part of this publication may be reproduced, stored in a retrieval system, or transmitted in any form or by any means, electronic, mechanical, photocopying, recording, or otherwise, without the prior written permission of the publisher.

The views and opinions contained herein are those of the authors. The editor and publisher disclaim all responsibility for the accuracy or correctness of the authors' views.

Manuscripts, contributions and inquiries, including first class return postage, should be sent to the Gun Digest Editorial Offices, One Northfield Plaza, Northfield, IL 60093. All material received will receive reasonable care, but we will not be responsible for its safe return. Material accepted is subject to our requirements for editing and revisions. Author payment covers all rights and title to the accepted material, including photos, drawings and other illustrations. Payment is at our current rates.

CAUTION: Technical data presented here, particularly technical data on handloading and on firearm adjustment and alteration, inevitably reflects individual experience with particular equipment and components under specific circumstances the reader cannot duplicate exactly. Such data presentations therefore should be used for guidance only and with caution. DBI Books, Inc. accepts no responsibility for results obtained using this data.

Arms and Armour Press, London, G.B., exclusive licensees and distributors in Britain and Europe; Australia; Nigeria, South Africa and Zimbabwe; India and Pakistan; Singapore, Hong Kong and Japan.

ISBN 0-910676-75-5   **Library of Congress Catalog #44-3588**

The NRA Some More

It's more alarums and excursions. After losing at Phoenix last year, Neal Knox—or somebody—managed things so he got thrown off the Board of Directors over the winter, presumably over a major—and public—disagreement with NRA's—read Harlon Carter's—legislative posture. So they went to the mattresses again at Milwaukee in May, 1984. Neither side distinguished itself with the quality of its rhetoric, but in the end Harlon Carter got yet another vote of confidence.

The Milwaukee meeting saw more new shooting stuff shown than has been lately usual:

Ruger had a Single Six in 32 H&R Magnum and Federal had a second 32 Magnum load, a jacketed hollow point.

Marlin had its Model 9, a blowback semi-auto carbine for the 9mm Luger. Its magazines are, cleverly, S&W magazines; the gun is appealing to the 9mm boy in all of us.

Colt showed its Officers ACP, a chopped and channeled Government Model in 45 with 3-dot sights. It's all steel, too.

Ruger also showed over-under 12s with stainless receivers, and a stainless version of the Ruger 22 auto pistol.

Special Guns Everywhere

This was the year when it seemed there were as many special firearms

S&W donated their first 45 autoloader to the cause of Olympic shooting.

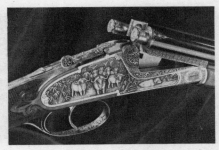

Heym's rendition of a 375 H&H double rifle was No. 3, the buffalo, in the SCI Big 5 series. It brought $65,000 at auction.

The 3,000,000th 1100 was a Premier Skeet gun donated toward the cause of Olympic shooting by Remington.

as there were press releases. Several of the former may be seen here.

Covering Ourselves

Our splendidly compact catalog section is growing again. For 1983, it ran about 193 pages; for 1984, about 214; and here it is in this edition over 230. And that's despite Harold Murtz's massaging the copy and photos tighter and tighter. So we've decided to set it off with its own cover and you'll find it on page 263.

Shot Show Numbers

These are very interesting. In contrast to numbers everywhere, SHOT Show numbers only go up. They did in Dallas in 1984; they will in Atlanta in 1985. In 1986—any bets?

Merwin Hulbert Fans

Art Phelps at P.O. Box 672, Rough and Ready, CA 95975 (916-273-7593) feels somebody knows where Hopkins & Allen production records are for the years (ca.1880-1896) when H&A produced Merwin Hulberts. He needs, besides, catalogs and other good stuff for a book.

NSSF Marches As Before

It's hard to beat those National Shooting Sports Foundation guys. When they're not promoting Hunting and Fishing Day, they're backing Ducks Unlimited, and while they're

resting, they get up programs like a national target shooting qualification for anybody 8-18: A kid gets an adult to supervise shooting 10 shots at (safely, of course) a single target and signs it and that and a buck gets the kid a pin. That's good stuff.

The Simmons Collection

Regular readers will recognize Donald M. Simmons' name. A longtime regular in these pages, Simmons specializes in all-out wall-to-wall collector coverage, particularly of the world's autoloading pistols. The 1000-piece collection on which much of his research has been based may now be seen in its own museum at Old Tucson, a famous movie location in Tucson, Arizona.

N. B. Fashingbauer, we report with regret, died in July, 1983, at the age of 69. A stockmaker with an early national reputation, Fashingbauer served in World War II and in Korea.

Norman Hoss, whose career as Editorial Director of Outdoor Life Book Club had its special impact on GUN DIGEST, died November 18, 1983. He will be missed by those who make this book.

With his impact on the U.S. firearms market yet unmeasured, Hubert Zink of Heckler & Koch returned to Germany in early 1984 for another H-K job elsewhere.

CONTENTS

DEPARTMENTS

Guns and Gunfire

Here is the legendary Gary Cooper in a scene from Warner Brothers hit SERGEANT YORK which has all the compromises that didn't keep the picture from being a great classic: First York was a corporal at the time of the fight, and he had a mustache. Second: the gun York used in his famous sweep-up of Germans was a Colt 45 M1911 automatic which will not work with blanks, and not the 9mm Luger shown which will.

on TV Tube and Movie Screen

by KONRAD F. SCHREIER, JR.

LIKE THOSE legendary words: "quiet — lights — sound — camera — action —," guns and gunfire are one of the parts of movie and TV magic. They were a big part of the first movie which told a story: Thomas A. Edison's 1903 western THE GREAT TRAIN ROBBERY. The guns were real, and the blanks were the regular factory kind loaded with extra fine black powder, and they worked out just fine since movie making was still in the primitive stage.

It wasn't until the making of the D. W. Griffith-Mutual epic THE BIRTH OF A NATION in 1915 that movie-guns and gunfire came of age. BIRTH OF A NATION was the first show in which special effects, costumes, props and all the technical aspects of production received close and careful attention. Most of the prop guns were real ones, many purchased from the legendary Francis W. Bannerman. Believe it or not, many of those same guns can still be found in various prop gun collections around Hollywood.

Since BIRTH OF A NATION, the guns used to make movies and TV shows have either come from collections owned by the studios, or from prop houses like Stembridge Gun Rentals, Joe Lombardie's Special Effects Unlimited, or Ellis Mercantile Company, all of whom are in the business of renting guns to the people who

make the shows. The goods and services of these prop houses are only available to recognized movie and TV production companies, and they will not do business with the public.

Of course, most of the guns used in movie and TV production are the real thing. Manually operated revolvers, lever-action rifles, bolt-action rifles, and pump shotguns are used just the way they were made. In recent years, many of the older guns have become very valuable, and the prop houses have replaced them with modern reproductions.

When it comes to semiautomatics and machine guns, the guns must be modified.

The Hollywood special effect gunsmiths have a practically standard modification: They fit the gun with a "bore restrictor" which lets the gas pressure from the blank make the gun function. One common method is to thread the inside of the bore at the muzzle so they can screw in an Allen head screw. This screw has a hole drilled the right size to make the gun work the way they want it to.

While the bore restrictor will work with most automatic pistols, submachine guns and machine guns, there are exceptions. One of these is the good old U.S. Army Colt Model 1911 automatic pistol which nobody, not even the Army, has ever been able to

make work with blanks. The special effects gunsmiths' way around this is to use 9mm automatics like Colt copies made in Spain. They look real on camera, and work well with blanks and a bore restrictor.

Another gun which won't work with a bore restrictor is the Johnson semi-automatic rifle of World War II. This rifle has a unique recoil system of operation, and to make it work for theatrical use it has to be converted to a simple blowback operated gun and have a bore restrictor installed. Then it works just fine. Of course, the gun would blow sky-high if it was fired with a real live cartridge, but so would any automatic with a bore restrictor. Since live ammunition is very seldom used in movie and TV production, they have a rule that ball ammunition is *never* allowed around movie guns. This rule is so carefully enforced that accidents with ball ammunition are unheard of.

When it comes to scripts which call for muzzle-loading guns, the special effects gunsmith has his job cut out for him unless the producer or director decide to take the shortcut of using breechloaders in hopes the audience will not know the difference. If they decide they will use muzzleloaders, they will use real ones for close-up scenes by firing them with simple blank charges. Then for long shots

Sixty years of faking it provides the techniques to make it all as real as the audience can stand.

In this Civil War film Universal Pictures' SHENANDOAH made in 1965 it looks as if Jimmy Stewart and his supporting cast are carrying Henry rifles, but look again—they are nothing but the ubiquitous Winchester '92s used in so many Hollywood epics with their fore-stocks removed to make them look like Henrys.

Here are the classic veterans of the thousands of movie and TV westerns: The '92 lever action Winchester and the single action Colt, and a bunch of the special 5-in-1 theatrical blanks they both fire. The Winchester was nicely refinished after it was sold off, but the Colt is a very worn out gun.

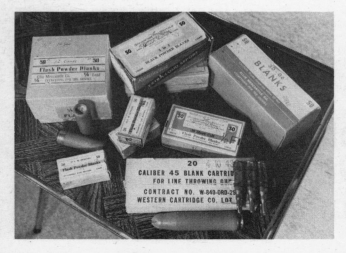

These are all typical movie and TV theatrical blanks—12 gauge shotgun, 5-in-1, 30-06 Springfield, 38 Short Colt, 45-70 line throwing gun blanks which were reloaded for movie use, 7.62mm machine gun blanks, a 20mm anti-aircraft gun blank, and several boxes of 22 rimfire blanks for special effects use.

they will use guns modified to fire blanks, whether long guns, pistols or revolvers. It is also possible to use breechloaders like the trap-door Springfield with simulated flint locks if the camera doesn't get too close. They also convert modern reproduction Colt and Remington cap-and-ball revolvers to fire cartridge blanks.

Shotguns present a special problem since it is not practical to make auto-loaders function with blanks. The big wads will jam any bore restrictor. The way around it is to use doubles or pump guns which will work perfectly with blanks. If somebody insists on an automatic shotgun, they simply cut the film. The gun fires one shot and by using this cut over and over they make it look as if the semi-auto is firing normally.

When it comes to a picture like 20th-Century Fox's THE LONGEST DAY where it takes enough guns to arm an army, the studios hire an army and rent its guns. Then blanks are provided, and they are fired with the regular military blank adapters. If an old-time army is required, like in John Melius's THE WIND AND THE LION, the movie people hunt around until they find enough guns to arm the troops.

When the action of a show requires actors or stunt men to do something dangerous with a gun, the gun is usu-ally a rubber prop. The action may be

In this shot from the D. W. Griffith-Mutual epic BIRTH OF A NATION the troops are properly uniformed in Bannerman-supplied gear, but the rifles are trapdoor Springfields instead of the muzzleloaders they should be. This is typical of the liberties which are taken to make it possible to produce movies—teaching all the extras how to fire muzzleloaders would be impossible.

something like a fall from a horse or building, and it's so fast that a good rubber prop gun won't look wrong. The molds for these rubber guns are made with real guns, and a soft metal tube armature makes them rigid so they look real up very close. If lots of guns are needed in a scene without shooting, the same kind of props can be used, or there are prop guns cast in something like rigid fiberglass.

There are situations and places where production companies cannot get permission to bring along real guns, so they have ways around this problem. They can use the cast prop guns. They can convert the pot-metal nonguns to fire harmless pyrotechnic theatrical blanks, which they can sometimes arrange to use. They can also use cast-metal solid dummy guns—anything from a handgun to a heavy machine gun—set up to fire with a "gas gun" special effect.

The movie gas gun is a tricky little special effect device originally devised for use in miniature work — things like sea battles done with model ships floating in a studio tank. Since the part that goes "bang" is not much bigger than a king-size cigarette in most cases, adapting it to fit in a cast gun is easy. Of course, the electrical valves for the tanks of gas and compressed air, the hoses between them and the gas gun, the wire for the igniter, and the control system

A 45-70 trapdoor Springfield carbine, a 7.65mm Walther pocket automatic, and a 38 Smith & Wesson—all foolers. The Springfield is a rubber prop, the Walther a non-gun, and the S&W a solid cast aluminum prop. All these and more are used in movie and TV work to save wear and tear on the real thing.

This is a scene from Warner Brothers THE FIGHTING 69TH where both actors are armed with Colt 45 automatics. Dennis Morgan, the actor on the left, doesn't fire his regular U.S. Army 45 Colt, but George Brent, the actor on the right, does fire his Colt Model 1905. The M1905 Colt can fire blanks, but the M1911 can't, so the switch was made to be sure to have a gun which would shoot blanks.

In this shot from 20th Century Fox's ZARDOZ science fiction movie the pile of guns in the foreground is typical of what a prop house can supply when asked for "a pile of assorted guns"—right off the top there is a double barreled shotgun, a Luger, a U.S. Army M16, a Sterling submachine gun, a British Enfield rifle, another shotgun or so—you name it.

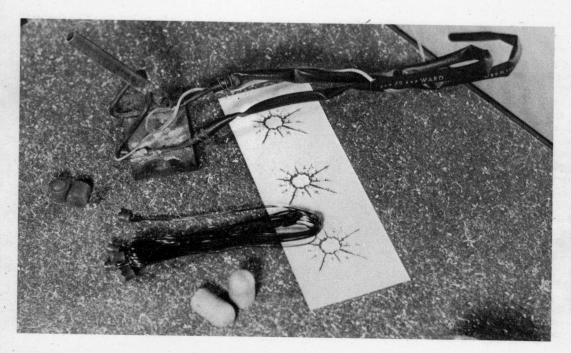

These are all special effect gunfire items. The odd thing on the top is a gas gun, and just to the left of its base are a couple of wax bullet hit effects. The wires are all attached to bullet hit special effect squibs, and below them are a couple of dust capsule bullet hit effects for use in air guns. The sheet of three bullet hit effect decals are actually very real looking if they are applied properly.

all have to be hidden from the camera. There are complete gas gun rigs which an actor can wear, and they are hitched up so they don't show, and the gun effect can be pretty realistic. The best gas gun effects are usually done with a mixture of gasses including butane and propane.

That brings up another point — how they get the sound of gunfire for movies and TV. The gas gun just described makes a noise, but any resemblance between it and the sound of gunfire is accidental. No theatrical blanks make noises like the real thing, and even if the noises were right, the kind of recording gear which picks up dialogue won't pick up gunfire. So they put the gunfire sounds into the film later on, and they use sound effects which have been recorded to satisfy the director and sound editor on the film. These sound effects are so perfectly synchronized with the film that nobody in the audience can tell they are not the actual noises the prop guns made when they were fired for the camera.

Another thing which has to be set up so the camera will see it right is blank cartridge firing. The problems with the camera getting a good shot of a gun going off are numerous, but probably the most critical is that the cameras take 24 frames — individual pictures — a second. That means that the exposure time for each frame is about 1/48th of a second, and the rest of the time is used to move the film. In order for the camera to see it properly, it is necessary for the gun flash to be seen on several frames of the film. The flash time of real cartridges is often too fast to be seen on several frames for a good camera effect.

Filmmakers solve this problem with theatrical blank cartridges loaded with special compositions. They mix very fine black powder and aluminum, iron, magnesium and other metal powders. Sometimes the pyrotechnic effect is enhanced by the addition of a little strontium nitrate or other chemicals. The make-up of this theatrical blank cartridge — it's usually called flash-blank composition — depends on the special effects man who makes up the blanks, and it can be varied to suit both the gun it will be fired in and the conditions under which it will be fired.

Another way the theatrical blanks are adjusted to suit the filming situation is by varying the charge strength. They are made in quarter charge, half charge, and full charge loadings. The closing wad is marked with the blank's strength as ¼, ½, or full. Typically, quarter charge loads

would be used in night shots, half charge in poor light, and full charge in daylight. Light charges are also usually used inside the studio or other interiors.

Once it comes to shooting guns in scenes with actors, a lot of things happen in the special effects category. One of the simplest of these is when the special effects man pulls the hard cardboard wad out of a theatrical blank and replaces it with a wad of facial tissue so it can safely be fired at an actor from close range — say five or so feet.

When the action calls for an actor to be "shot" at very close range — perhaps even with the gun touching him — he must wear heavy leather armor and have his skin coated with thick flash-and-burn-resistant make-up. Often, particularly with the gun very close, a special effects gun with its muzzle plugged and sideways gas exit ports just back of the muzzle will be used. Then a special soft theatrical blank, often a 22 rimfire, which makes smoke and flash without much more than the pop of a capgun can still make the effect very realistic.

The 22 rimfire theatrical blanks are also used in special miniature guns fired on models, and a number of other special effect devices. Most military blank cartridges work quite well for the camera. Movie and TV production companies buy them from special effect companies who either buy them on the surplus market or direct from the makers. Shotgun blanks used in the movie and TV business are practically all 12 gauge, and are specially loaded with theatrical flash-blank composition. There are also special effect shotshells loaded with things like smoke puff bombs. These are seldom encountered outside the hands of special effects men.

The most famous movie blank of all is the "5-in-1", invented for the movies in the 1920s. The 5-in-1 is basically a blank loaded in a 38-40 WCF shot case, and it functions in the five revolver calibers most used in western movies: 38-40 WCF, 44-40 WCF and 44 S&W and 44 Colt, and 45 Colt, and it will feed in 38-40 WCF and 44-40 WCF caliber lever-action rifles and carbines. While most 5-in-1's have been loaded in brass cases headstamped "REMINGTON 5-in-1," in recent years they have been loaded in plastic cases which cost less than the brass ones. A lot of people in the movie and TV business like the new plastic blanks in many calibers — they don't look like the real stuff.

Once a gun is fired for the camera, there have to be bullet impacts, and

the special effects men have a bunch of ways of simulating them. The simplest is to use a special effects air rifle which fires capsules loaded with dust for impacts on hard things, wax for impacts on glass or things like cars which can't be damaged by the hit, and other things. These air guns have magazines which hold up to a hundred hit effects, and they fire with a bottle of compressed gas anything from single shots up to machine gun bursts. Any special effects marksman using one of the guns is highly trained and proficient, and knows how to keep an actor out of danger as he fires his air gun from where the camera can't see him.

The way hits on actors' bodies are handled is by the use of a little special effect "mortar" attached to the leather armor. This mortar is a little flat metal gadget in which a special effects squib is fired to give the bullet hit effect. A bag of prop blood is often used in this special effect, and the whole thing is fired electrically.

Like a lot of special effects, these bloody body hit effects can be very realistic. In fact, well-managed and executed movie and TV gunfire can be frighteningly vivid, though no one ever gets hurt. When people who know the effects of real gunfire see action on the screen which isn't realistic — it's usually too realistic — they should blame the director and production staff of the show who insisted on having it done that way. The special effects man's gunfire has to be done the way these people want it.

Gunfire is just a part of a special effects man's job, but it is an important part. It takes training and knowledge and years of experience to make a good special effects man. There aren't more than a dozen or so in all Hollywood who are well and truly qualified to handle movie and TV guns and gunfire. As in most areas of the movie and TV business, it is very difficult, in fact, almost impossible, to join this exclusive group at the present time.

Despite the limited number of special effects men, movies and TV are still done with guns and gunfire, and they probably always will be. There is a lot more to doing the job than is explained in this article, but these are the basics. Firearms special effects are something no untrained person should try. Even if somebody has a few special effect theatrical blanks, they shouldn't be fired in a gun because the fouling from the flash-blank composition is very corrosive, and could ruin a gun.

As they say in the movie and TV business, "that's a wrap" . . . this time. ●

Getting a
GRAND SLAM
ON TURKEYS...

The author, using this wingbone caller, has called all five birds of the Royal Grand Slam to within easy shotgun range.

... an idea whose time has come.

by DWAIN BLAND

ON A STILL spring morning, in late March, or early in April, if you could hear far and wide across this country, you would be darned well surprised at what a ruckus the yodeling of a wild turkey hen can cause. The pink blush of coming day is faintly washing the horizon off to the east, and from her roost branch, she stirs, head turning slowly at first, and then, moments later she stretches, a leg and wing on one side, then the other. She shakes like a wet dog, then stands alertly, eyes searching the treetops.

'Kyawk, kyawk, kyawk, kyawk,' she calls, the talk of spring love drifting across America.

'GOBBLE-OBBLE-OBBLE.' Far to the south, deep in Southern Florida, a great black ghost listens, and toasts her from where he's spent the night hours, from high in the crown of a giant cypress, boughs caressed by tresses of Spanish moss. Far below, dark waters beckon the unwary. The grand chimera lays like a water-logged tree trunk, eyes studding the quiet waters, as the swamp alligator endlessly waits to kill.

The hen yelps again, and all across America's heartlands she is heard, north to Vermont's hardwoods, down the eastern seaboard through the Virginias and the Carolinas, across the Deep South, up into Arkansas, and drifting among the Ozark ridges, her hen talk is answered by the gobbles of thousands of wild gobblers. Wherever the dogwood blooms splash white on rocky ridges, the Eastern turkey reigns as King.

Further west, the hen's calling falls on other ears. Rio Grande gobblers wait coming day on broad branches of sky-scraping cottonwoods. Redbirds lilt their lovesong, and the creek bottoms are aglow with the blooming of the chickasaw plum thickets. Out on the high prairie, the shinoak clumps are wreathed in gold as new leaves bring life to the gnarled branches.

And as the hen calls once again, even further to the west and north a fourth gobbler kingdom awakens. Astraddle high mountain ridges, where gobblers strut on thick horizontal branches, ponderosas stand straight and tall, spires in the giant cathedral of the Rocky Mountains. The hen is answered by black and white Merriam's turkeys from Arizona north to Montana and the Dakotas, on Indian reservations in Utah and New Mexico, from the ski slopes in Colorado, and across and down to the lower mesa country in the Oklahoma Panhandle.

Osceola; Eastern; Rio Grande; Merriam: Those are the four kinds of wild turkey which make up a Grand Slam turkey hunters can dream of.

These four sub-species are all found within the United States, predominantly across the southern half of the country. Whereas several decades ago, it would have been difficult to take specimens of all four within a period of months, today's transportation allows the serious hunter to kill all four during a single season. Of course, it can't be done without study, planning, and the ability to follow through with seasoned decisions and hunting methods.

The hunter who intends to kill the Grand Slam of turkeydom probably has taken birds of at least one sub-specie. Perhaps he's not a turkey hunting veteran, but he does have turkey hunting experience. He has a fair to middlin' knowledge of how to hunt the birds, both during the spring and the fall seasons, is experienced in using one or two kinds of turkey calls, and we'll have to presume he has patterned old Sue Betsy.

The first step towards rounding out his Grand Slam will be to decide which bird he wants to hunt next, but this can't be done until he looks over the options, as various factors could cause him to change his mind. Many of these do not come to light until the hunter has written the state game departments of possible areas he would like to hunt, and in studying the rules, he will find things which he hadn't counted on.

Here are some:

Will he be allowed to hunt all day? If the hunter hasn't got but a couple or three days, he wouldn't want to travel any distance to be allowed to hunt only until noon.

License cost might be a factor. A few states sell short-term licenses for a small sum, while others require a yearly non-resident license costing up to and above a hundred dollars. For instance a hunter can take two gobblers during a spring hunt in my home state of Oklahoma (in specified counties) for a sum of $62.25. To the West, in Arizona, the hunter is allowed but a single bird, license fees totaling $109. Arizona also requires special permits for all spring turkey hunting, so the hunter must get his name in the hat early, or else he'll not hunt there.

(Wherever the hunter chooses, he should buy his license and tags prior to traveling to the area, if at all possible. There is nothing worse than driving from town to town with a buddy trying to locate a non-resident license, while everyone else is in the woods giving them fits.)

What about a place to hunt? Does the state you've chosen have large tracts of hunting grounds open to the public? Or is it largely private lands?

Anyone wanting to hunt the Osceola turkey must hunt in Florida. The bird isn't found anywhere else. But, while Florida does have a good number of public management areas, pressure is heavy on them during turkey season, for much of Florida's cattle country allows little hunting. Again, the finest Osceola area, Fish Eating Creek, requires a special permit, which must be applied for months before the hunt dates. The hunter who decides at the last moment to hunt Osceola must settle for other management areas which allow spring turkey hunting, which is on a daily basis, the permit available at the access points during season. Florida's wild turkey populations are adequate, though below those of states like Missouri or Virginia. But you hunt a turkey where a turkey is, and Florida is where you hunt Osceola.

What about pay hunting for wild turkeys?

The hunter who wants to be virtually guaranteed a shot at a Rio Grande gobbler can do just that by paying to hunt ranches in Texas. The great majority of Rio Grande range found in Oklahoma and Texas is on private lands, the bulk of which will not give permission to hunt. Pay hunting hasn't come to Oklahoma, so even money won't get him in the gate. West Texas ranchers long ago realized there is money in the hunters' pockets, so the turkey hunter who will shell out the coins can kill turkeys. Many of the ranches have excellent populations of Rio Grandes. It's all-day hunting too.

Should the hunter plan on being at the chosen area on opening day?

The average hunter has the mistaken conception that if he isn't there for the opener he'd might as well stay home. Very often, that's exactly what he should do. Opening day has its bad points.

Look at it this way. *All* of the serious turkey hunters, plus all of the I'll-go-once-and-quit hunters are out on Opening Day. Turkeys are jittery critters at best, and with the woods trembling from the pounding of footsteps, hunting conditions are at the very worst.

Actually, with spring turkey hunting, there is an even greater factor to consider: Are the turkeys into the prime gobbling season? Are the hens nesting, laying, and incubating? Or are they with the gobblers all day long?

Take the Florida hunt, for an instance. In Osceola country, the season is long, if you consider the dates allowed in the Fish Eating Creek, as well as other areas. The February dates could be well advanced of the prime gobbling season, whereas a hunt in late March could find the turkeys past the prime hunting conditions. Oklahoma has a month-long spring hunt, but on an average, where I hunt in western Oklahoma, hunting is best during the last half of the season.

Fall and winter hunts depend as heavily on the hunter studying the dates prior to planning a hunt, if he is to kill turkeys. The early fall hunt will find the birds slightly younger, in smaller groups, easier to call when scattered, and besides, the weather will be more enjoyable. For the hunter who wishes to hunt Eastern Wild Turkeys in the deep woods, leaf fall has a tremendous bearing on an early fall

hunt, so it must be considered. Has the area had a dry summer? This will affect both food supplies for wild turkeys and their water.

The turkey hunter who wants to kill the four sub-species found in the Lower Forty-Eight very often has his sights set on killing what he considers a trophy gobbler of each. He has hopes of bagging four long-whiskered turkeys. Good for him. To the serious turkey fanatic, this is the name of the game. It also requires a hunter who is planning a hunt into strange and new country to allow additional time if he is hunting the bird during the fall and winter hunts. Adult gobblers ordinarily have been afflicted with a sure case of shutmouth by October, and have little to say or to do with man or turkey for the remainder of the winter. My advice to the Grand Slam hunter is to stick with spring hunting.

My number one priority when traveling for wild turkeys is in how many birds I am allowed. I shudder at the thought of moving my carcass up-

wards of a thousand miles to hunt one bird. So I plan with the intention of hunting two states, if possible, from one camp. I've done it many times. The greatest advantage to this is when you are one of a party of hunters. Any one who makes a kill, continues to hunt, merely by crossing the state line. You will want to study the game laws of each intently before the hunt, for one may allow baiting, and the other allows roost shooting. And you don't condone either.

There are turkey hunters who cannot enjoy a hunt if rifles are permissible within the state being hunted. I haven't made a study on the percentage of turkey hunters who are shot each year, nor how many were downed with rifles. I doubt seriously it can be measured because the bulk of riflemen are shooting with scopes, which should help them in making identification before shooting. Too often, the turkey hunter who is fired on is shot at from close range in heavy woods, and when there is little light, such as at dawn or dusk. Too, most wounded hunters were calling with a turkey call when shot. They are shot with shotguns. Several states allow rifles in hunting wild turkeys. A great number of states have regulations on the size shot for shotgunning turkeys, which is advisable. There are folks who would hunt turkeys with buckshot, or BBs and #2s, none of which are good turkey killers. Such loads only encourage long-range blasting, the equivalent of sky-busting geese.

Other considerations the gypsy turkey hunter must remember is that he will need heavier clothing in mountainous regions, binoculars in certain parkland areas in rugged terrain, and he should never forget to carry special medicines on trips far from home. The big country hunter should never leave camp without a compass, a sharp knife, and a match-safe filled with dry kitchen matches.

Many hunters will travel to country far from home with no knowledge of what hazards might await them deep in the woods. Rattlesnakes are found in a great part of turkey country, many of them in striking moods during a spring hunt, and also still about during fall seasons. Snakes hunt during the dawn and dusk hours, particularly if the afternoons are hot. Copperheads are abundant too. Turkey hunters in Florida should keep in mind the giant Florida Diamondback, a nasty monster which has been known to curl on top of palmetto clumps. Insects of all sorts can cause misery if they bite. Mosquitoes are the least worrisome, buffalo gnats

A wild turkey gobbler is a trophy to most hunters, but all the more so if it is a sub-specie they have not killed before. This is Cecil Andrus, former Secretary of the Interior, with a Rio Grande gobbler.

The author studying a map before planning a hunt in strange country for wild turkeys. Such preparedness makes the actual hunt a lot simpler.

sting like tiny branding irons and fire ants feel much the same; while chiggers and ticks dig in to delay anguish until later. Poison oak, poison ivy, poison nettles, and poison sumac can cause you troubles about the time you get back home from having so much fun.

If you have a habit of drinking from spring branches, you should be aware that the bulk of all water nowadays is contaminated in some form. Keep an eye on "wild" dog packs in the woods. These free-to-roam bunches of household pets have seriously injured hunters. Folks who don't know cattle should be watching those mean looking brahmas in Florida, and steer wide of all black-and-white Holstein bulls. These devils have seriously gored two men I know.

Thorns, sandburrs, cactus needles, all of these can create problems. I've had to forget hunting after driving chickasaw plum thorns into an eyeball, and let me tell you, a long drive home with a patch on a bad eye will make you wish you had a buddy along. Far back in the mountains of Old Mexico's Sierra Madre, I cut an artery in one leg when I fell backwards onto the spears of a huge maguey plant. I found the pressure point, and stopped the blood flow, but not before my right shoe had filled with blood.

A gobbler track made after you have driven a back country road means but one thing: "Turkeys are here, NOW."

One winter afternoon while hunting easterns in the Ozarks, I'd backed in against the trunk of a large oak to wait out a windy shower. The wind dislodged a huge dead limb, a widow-maker, which dropped me to my knees when it hit. For a moment I thought the sky had fallen, and broken my neck.

The hunter in strange terrain should be aware in mountain country of abandoned mine shafts, natural caves, sudden changes in the weather, and should take compass readings before leaving his vehicle. Unexpected clouds, fog, wind shifts, and countless other conditions can cause a veteran hunter to become disoriented in moments. Sure, I know, you're one of those folks who just don't get turned around. There's a few just like you buried in every cemetery in the West. Not all of them are buried in town, though, for some have never been found.

I was gallivanting around some mountains down in the Gila country in New Mexico one cold April afternoon, when it was clouded over solid, and chill winds were knifing through heavy clothes. I'd cranked up an old

gobbler far up on the face of a mountain, but it became obvious very soon that he wasn't going to come down to me. Any hen worth his stuff would have to come up there.

I said to myself, "Well, you old bastard, if you don't think it ain't hot enough to trot down here, I'll come up there, and we'll see who has the last say."

So, I sneak around into an arroyo, break into a saddle, and slip uphill, breaking out on the same knifeback ridge he's on. Dropping over the backside of it, I walked upright until I felt I was opposite him, and just behind him up and over the mountain behind his location at a distance of maybe 50 yards. I eased up to the crest, sneaked in behind a big pine which had some ground clutter around its base, slid the gun out alongside the trunk, and from a standing position, made a call with the wingbone.

The setup was much like one I'd encountered two days earlier, in the Blue Range, on top of the "rim," over Arizona. I'd come in above an old gobbler there, made one call, shot the old turkey when he strutted uphill to me, and that was that.

The spur is the true indicator of a wild turkey gobbler in the trophy class.

But, this time there was no answer. I called again. No gobble.

What the hell. Now, I mean this turkey was cranked up good. He had been gobbling at the slightest sound of my hen calls earlier. I waited a few moments, and then eased out to where I could study the steep slope flowing down towards where I had been calling. He wasn't there.

Disgusted, I headed downhill. I couldn't understand why he'd left all of a sudden. A couple hundred yards later I realized there didn't seem to be anything which resembled the area where I'd been calling. Never having set foot on the mountain before, I didn't give it much thought, but began looking around for anything familiar. Even the horizon didn't seem right.

Hauling out the compass, I stood and stared at the bearing. I laid down the gun, and carrying the compass to a rock, stood back, and looked at it again. It was lying.

Compasses don't lie, so I had to force myself to walk away from where I *knew* the truck had to be parked. Sure enough, the truck was in the direction the compass said it was.

Before I got there, though, I headed back to where I'd left the old turkey. Maybe in all my sashaying around, he hadn't seen me. Could be he was still waiting for the hen to call.

Nope. Couldn't raise him. But while I was at it, I couldn't pass up the opportunity to try and learn where I'd went wrong. It was easy to understand: Once I'd dropped over onto the backside of the ridge and began following it around to where I presumed I was opposite the turkey, I had unknowingly branched out onto a side ridge which I hadn't known cut in on a level with the top of the hill. Once I had cut onto it, I then began walking away from the turkey. I'd been calling into an empty basin.

It isn't the first time I've been lost, confused, turned around or, as I've heard some of my friends say, on returning to camp hours after sundown "Heck, no, I wasn't lost. I just decided to look at some strange country."

In the *dark?*

Some of us hope to get lost. We'll at least get away from the crowd. But don't do it if you don't carry a compass.

Killing the Grand Slam of Wild Turkeys isn't difficult if you've planned the trips methodically, and done your homework. Study the subspecies as thoroughly as possible. Write the game department of the state you've chosen to hunt, ask them for any available material concerning the turkey you wish to hunt. Hunters' dollars have paid for these studies; you are entitled to them. Subscribe to that state's monthly game department publication. You'll learn no end of facts about wildlife in its game woods.

Though there are vast differences in the homeland terrains of the four sub-species, the lifestyles of all are alike. All roost in trees, fly down at daybreak, mosey around for a short spell, perhaps gobble if it's springtime, then wander off to feed. Towards noon they'll lollygag for a while, then again hit the feeding trail. Come dusk, they'll find a place to put up for the night, and at dawn do it all over again. The true difference in hunting the various kinds of turkeys is in the change of the terrain. The turkeys have adjusted to it, so the hunter will have to do the same if he wants to be successful.

Throughout the travels required in hunting the birds of the Grand Slam, the hunter will cover ground from slightly above sea level, to those where the Rocky Mountain Merriam's turkey lives, varying from 4000-foot levels to up around 9000 feet.

Across the old historic ranges of this bird, which includes areas in Arizona, New Mexico, Colorado, and into the far western end of the Oklahoma panhandle, the Merriam turkey leads a gypsy way of life, traveling back and forth as the weather dictates. Sudden snowstorms can push them to lower levels, but again, if the storm is not of long duration, the birds will stick it out and, once the storm has abated, go back to a normal life. This migrating back and forth — and up and down — can create problems for a hunter not acquainted with this habit.

The Merriam's turkey is certainly worth the hunter's efforts, and to the first-time hunter, initial impressions of an adult gobbler will be "a large black and white bird." The white tipped lower rump feathers, along with the white tail band and the abundance of white on the wings, in contrast to the black feathering of the back and breast is what causes this appearance. The hens are drab, with no sheen as is found on an Osceola hen, and the heads look black due to black hairs scattered over the bare skin area of the head. Merriam's turkeys have large feet, though spur development is very poor. Beard growth seems also to be minimal, though this bird lives much of its life in cold and snow, icy region, and could lose some beard length to these conditions. Too, the Merriam's does not have long legs, which allows the beard to wear on the

ground. The average Merriam beard will be small in circumference too, so while the bird is a beautiful turkey, it does come up short in the trophy adornments.

Merriam's terrain varies from rolling hills studded with pines, juniper, and stunted oak, to high mesas, steep mountain sides, open park-like mountain meadows, and knife-backed ridges atop the continental divide. Thankfully, throughout much of the historic ranges, a tremendous amount of lands are open to public hunting. Due to the ruggedness of the country, human populations are low, so hunter pressure is all but nonexistent.

To the hunter who has never hunted Merriam's turkeys, unless he has been told where birds are, his number one problem will be to locate them. The Rocky Mountains are not the kind of ground where a hunter can simply set out, hoping to walk into turkeys. Of course, today's hunter can write game agencies for reports of best areas and, since many states conduct hunter surveys quite often, the results of these will point out areas of high kill.

A hunter who knows he is within

the general area of Merriam's turkeys should then look for sign along old logging roads, listen for gobbling birds from high points, and use binoculars to watch open meadows near timber. A hunter accustomed to hearing numerous gobblers sounding off at a single location in Eastern turkey-range should not be disappointed in hearing but a single bird at most locations in Merriam country, as these turkeys scatter to a much greater extent than do others, even several miles apart. The hens are likewise scattered, and are seldom seen.

Calling is often excellent for spring gobblers. Stalking and bushwhacking are not easy in much Merriam range. The understory growth is often scant, allowing the birds good visibility. This also makes scatter-and-call hunts tough during the fall seasons. A busted drove can regroup by sight too easily.

The bulk of Merriam's turkeys taken during winter hunts are by rifle, often by a hunter whose primary game is deer or other big game. Full camouflage is a must for the shotgunner, as the lack of understory permits the turkey good vision. Otherwise,

Turkeys of the Merriam and Mexican sub-species have much white on the lower rump, and a white tail band.

the hunter will be faced with some long range shots, which is certainly to be avoided.

Downhill to the southwest of the Rockies, out on the rolling grass-covered prairies, is the home of the Rio Grande Wild Turkey. This medium sized turkey, with big feet and buff-tipped rump and tail feathers, is found along tree-lined creek bottoms, in cedar-choked canyons, and out on the high plains, dotted with hackberry, where the bird's brownish feathering permits it to fade-in with the dull grey of the sandsage brush covered hills. Much Rio Grande range is abundant in stunted oaks of varying kinds, and almost all of it is fenced lands. Gaining permission to hunt is the number one problem for a traveling hunter. The problem is compounded in that the ranches and farms are large, which results in a hunter spending a good deal of time in locating landowners. Roost shooting and baiting are both practised widely in Rio Grande country, and a good part of the birds that are not killed in these ways are shot from pickup windows along ranch roads.

Rio Grandes are what I call "noisy" drove turkeys, and as they wander throughout the range, feeding, the birds often yelp and chatter back and forth among the bunch. These birds often gang together in the fall in large numbers, which causes problems in busting the birds apart. Once a drove is well scattered, calling is often excellent, but the hunter may need to hunker in small cover, instead of sitting back against a large treetrunk. Very often I will stretch out on my belly in stunted oak clumps, or in sagebrush, and once the bird has been called into short range, stand up and kill it as it flushes or runs.

Stalking can be good, once a drove is located, and all Rio Grande hunters should carry binoculars. Ground cover can be used in stalking, but in many instances, once a hunter is within 100 yards of a bird he is hoping to waylay, he may have to finish the sneak on hands and knees or belly-crawling. A trophy gobbler is worth a few sticker-burrs, and some cowpie on the elbows of your camo shirt. Bearded hens are numerous among Rio Grandes. Beard growth on adult gobblers is average, when compared to Eastern gobblers in Pennsylvania, Virginia, Georgia, and Mississippi or Alabama. Spur development is not near that found in Osceola, yet it beats that of Merriam. Beard length is shy of twelve inches, a length not extremely rare in the East.

This is probably due to the Rio Grande having shorter legs, much like Merriams, and also due to abrasion on coarse groundcover such as bluestem grass and sagebrush. Texas, parts of western Oklahoma, and southwest Kansas are where to find Rio Grandes. (The traveling hunter can't hunt Kansas, for although all the birds they have restocked are from other states, and originally brought about through the dollars of hunters everywhere, Kansas does not allow non-resident turkey hunting, a shameful attitude. If all game departmens should take this stand, there would be no grand slam for turkey hunters.)

From eastern Oklahoma to the Atlantic seaboard, north to Vermont, and south to Florida, are the homelands of the Eastern Wild Turkey. Perhaps 95 percent of all that has been written about wild turkeys has been based on this bird, so we won't dwell long on it. Due to the leafy ter-

Primary wing feathers from an Osceola gobbler (right), and an Eastern gobbler (left) are much smaller than one in the middle from the wing of a Mexican gobbler.

rain where the bird lives, calling is exellent, as the bird must walk nearer to be able to see what it is hearing. Of course, locating a position to call from requires careful thought, for if the turkey can see to where the calling is coming from at a distance, it could "hang up," and not come any closer. I steer clear of calling from large open park-like flats, long rolling hillsides, and other areas devoid of groundcover.

Stalking, and still-hunting, do not work well in Eastern range due to walking noises on leaves, sticks, rocks, and what-have-you. I've walked into easy gunshot of numerous Easterns but very often only wind or rain-dampened leaves made this possible. During the spring season, the gobblers will often sound off to "owling," or owl hooting, as done by the hunter. The eastern turkey is far more apt to do this than any of the other sub-species. Also, many eastern gobblers will gobble at length in the late afternoon, a trait not so common with other wild turkeys.

The size of this turkey is as varied as its habitats. The birds further south, towards the Gulf of Mexico, are small, as are those found in the northeastern states. Missouri boasts the largest of the race, as each spring a good many birds will be checked there topping 25 pounds. Beards on some of these look much like a black whiskbroom. In comparison to the feet of the birds further west, the feet of the Eastern strain are small. Spur development is good, and beards range upwards of 12 inches.

The Osceola turkey was named after the famous chief of the Seminoles and, like him, reigns over southern Florida. A beautiful bird, the gobbler has long legs, long slender toes, gives the impression of "black," when first seen, and due to its long legs, seems to strut "tall." The ordinary wild turkey appears to be much nearer the ground than these while in full strut. This could explain the brooming in the secondary wing feathers, near the body, on many of these black swamp turkeys. I've killed two adults on which these feathers were worn until a slender spike protruded from the main shaft of the feathers. Endowed with excellent beard growth, these birds have perhaps the finest spurs of all wild turkeys. The hens, when viewed in Florida's sunshine, have a burnished brown sheen.

Like the Rio Grande, the Osceola's range is largely on private lands, the bulk of it cattle ranches. The terrain is very flat, swampy, and what isn't covered with palmetto, will be oak hummocks, cypress swamps, creek swamps, and cabbage palms. Calling is excellent, as is still-hunting and stalking. A blind can be built in a moment or two, for the large fanlike leaves of the palmetto and palm are everywhere. Florida will hide a fully camouflaged hunter easier and quicker than any state in the Union. Green face paint makes it perfect.

Florida's fine weather far outdoes any other state for turkey hunting, but it is offset by such things as cottonmouths, alligators, mosquitoes, and, in addition to too many people, it also has high prices. Even worse is the 1:00 PM curfew for spring hunting.

The trophy hunter who wants to take outsized specimens of all four of this country's wild turkey gobblers should be well-heeled with three commodities: time, physical and mental strength, and lots of money. Simply taking a legal bird of each will require much less.

Which one is the easiest to kill? Hardest?

All four. The same answer to both questions.

I've hunted all four on lands where they were highly protected, and all were a pushover. I've also hunted all four on terrain where each had been hunted hard for days and weeks, and it would be a tossup as to which would be the most difficult to put shot into at 25 yards. I will say there is one turkey who is always tough and, for my game, is the joker in the deck.

The WILD, wild turkey that I'm speaking of is the tremendous turkey found back in Mexico's Sierra Madres, the Mexican wild turkey. *Gallapavo mexicana* in scientific lingo or, as it's also known, *gallapavo mexicana Gould*. These birds live in the higher elevations of the Sierra Madre Occidental range which is a continuation of the continental divide extending into northwestern Mexico. The Mexican turkey is found in the pine-oak-juniper zone, in areas from 6000 feet upwards. These turkeys have been hunted since man came on the scene thousands of years ago, and throughout its range are shot at to this day anytime the opportunity arises.

I have never found the birds in large numbers, though I am told there are tremendous ranches in the mountains where can be found good populations. It is reported that these birds are well protected, and should also be much easier to hunt. In the areas where I have hunted *mexicana*, the sites of summertime campfires can be found on the edge of summer grazing pastures, and careful searching will very often result in finding turkey bones. The birds are killed and eaten by the summer herdsmen. But, before you begin criticizing, you should know that these people do this as a way of life, for their ancestors, and those people's ancestors, taught them these things. Man is a meat eater, and for these hardworking mountain people, if they want meat, they must kill javalina, deer, turkey, or beef. The beef brings money, so the choice falls with the wild meat.

The Mexican turkey is big, a gorgeous black and white bird. Total length, total wingspan, the length of tail and wing feathers, and the size of feet, completely dwarf other wild turkeys. Spur growth is not good, and beard development is on a plane with Merriams. The birds eat manzanita berries, several kinds of acorns, grass seeds, juniper berries, grasshoppers, and an endless variety of foods. Feeding conditions are excellent. Water is often scarce, and is a limiting factor in keeping down turkey numbers in the High Sierras. Predator populations are not high, and unless critter numbers are exceptional, these animals do not have a great effect on turkey populations.

Terrain in Mexican turkey range is rugged, rocky, and always mountainous, dry and hot in summer, and dry and cold in winter. The summer rainy season is in late July and August, and therefore the prime gobbling season is in early May. The poults are hatched so they will begin life when the mountains have rain in August. Tree forms are Chihuahua and Apache pines, Mexican blue oak, Fremont oak, alligator bark oak, and junipers. The understory consists of madrono, manzanita, wild cherry, Johnny-jump-up, and others. Yucca spires dot the mountains, along with the always present maguey plant, from which mescal, pulque, and tequila are made. Numerous cactuses dot the barren landscapes, and when these bloom, bring color to the drab mountainsides.

Hunting methods back in the High Sierras are much like what would be utilized in hunting Merriams, or any mountain turkey. The number one thing to remember is to get above the bird. Calling is good in spring hunts and also scatter-and-call fall hunting. Presently Mexico has put an end to fall and winter hunts, but in time that could return. The spring hunt lasts for ten days.

My advice to anyone wishing to hunt this wild turkey is for them to contact an outfitter, or guide, who hunts Mexico, and let him make all the arrangements. Lifestyles are exceedingly different. What we soft gringos take for granted is but a dream for the average Mexican citizen.

Osceola; Eastern; Rio Grande; Merriam: four of a kind that can make the turkey hunter's Grand Slam. You could add a Mexican wild turkey and call it a Royal Grand Slam. ●

The Miquelet Lock

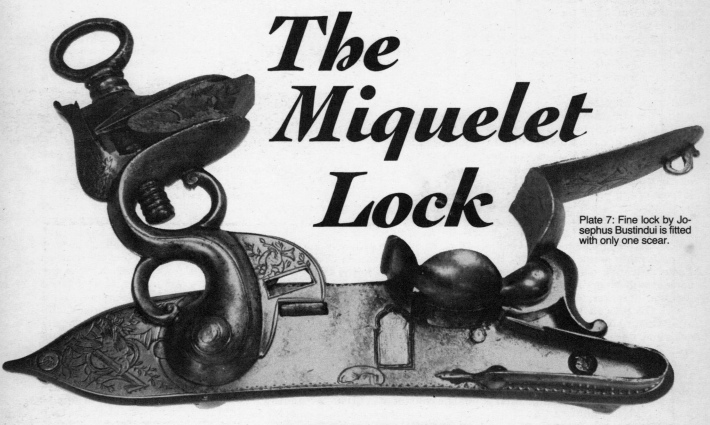

Plate 7: Fine lock by Josephus Bustindui is fitted with only one scear.

by **MAJOR NOEL CORRY**

Interesting and decorative, it follows its own rules.

In 1588, King Philip II of Spain sent his Armada to invade England and, as every British schoolboy learns, a great storm blew up and the Spanish ships were blown northwards to be wrecked on the shores of Scotland. Many members of the crews managed to scramble ashore, and amongst these unfortunate invaders there must have been at least one trained armourer on each ship. Doubtless, when captured, several were made to work at their trade in return for their keep. They must have had a hand in producing some of the very earliest Scottish pistols — rare early examples exist which are fitted with miquelet locks of the general types we show here.

How else can one explain the geographical gap? While this form of lock was probably invented in Spain during Philip II's reign (1556-1598), it is virtually never found on any English or French flintlock arms. In any event, the lock was rapidly superceded in Scotland by the English type of flintlock action.

The name probably originates from a diminutive of the Spanish Christian name Miguel. It was to spread from Portugal, along the north coast of Africa into Southern Italy, and much further East into Turkey, Persia and Southern Russia. The miquelet lock is to my mind by far the most interesting and decorative of all the gun locks made after the wheel-lock and nearly to the breechloader.

I imagine it is safe to say that the majority of gun collectors think of the miquelet lock as easily recognizable because it alone has an outside mainspring. This is not the case.

Actually, conventional flintlocks are to be found with the mainspring outside the lockplate. This sometimes occurs on multi-barreled sidelock arms where there is not always room to fit the mainspring in the conventional inside position.

The real definition of a miquelet lock to my mind is "a lock in which the scear(s) operate at right angles to the barrel, through the lockplate." The important word in this definition is "through." Miquelet locks have one or two holes in the lockplate, through

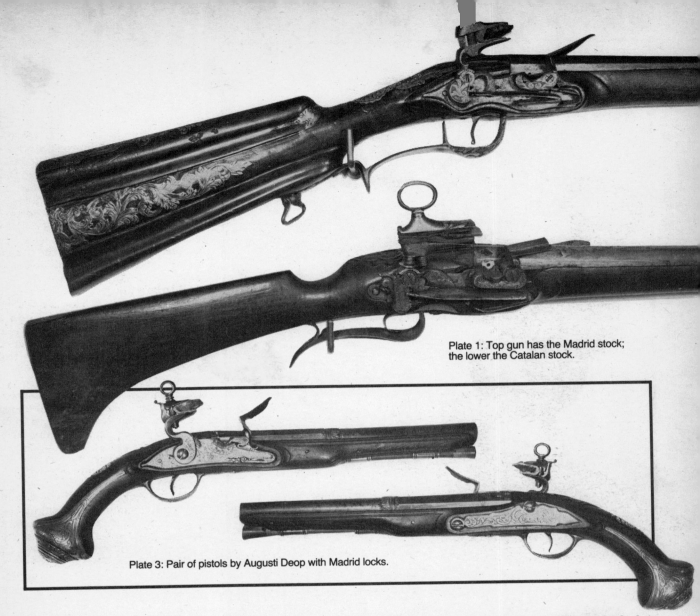

Plate 1: Top gun has the Madrid stock; the lower the Catalan stock.

Plate 3: Pair of pistols by Augusti Deop with Madrid locks.

which the scear(s) operate. The scear itself may be defined as "the part which comes into play when the lock is cocked and which the trigger presses up against when it is required to fire the gun." Normally in a miquelet lock the secondary scear holds the hammer at half cock, and the primary scear holds it at full cock. The trigger in a miquelet lock always presses the tail of the scear backwards and not upwards, as is the case in an ordinary flintlock. (Editor's Note: "Scear" is a spelling for the word "sear" which American editors permit English writers to use.)

Plate 1 shows two typical Spanish shotguns, the upper has a barrel over 43 inches long. It is fitted with engraved brass mounts which include a grotesque mask beneath the triggerguard. The lock is marked CARLA; the stock is the Madrid type. The lower gun is shorter with a barrel of

29 inches and was made by Francisco Anuada and is dated 92 (1792). Its stock is the Catalan type. I believe these stock classifications are from W. Keith Neal's book, *Spanish Guns and Pistols*. Both guns are fitted with the commonest type of miquelet lock with two scears operating on the toe of the hammer. Both are 16 bore.

Plate 2 shows the action of a Portuguese flat-stocked miquelet lock arm which may date as early as 1650. The stock is more reminiscent of a wheellock cheek stock, but the gun can in fact be fired from the shoulder. The 21-inch barrel is of 5½ bore. The rare feature on this lock is that the outside mainspring operates downwards on the toe of the hammer, in the same way as an ordinary flintlock mainspring does. The weapon is shown at half cock, the second scear, consisting of a steel rod, has popped out through its hole in the lockplate, below the

toe of the hammer. When the lock is fully cocked, the first scear slips out just above the hammer heel and holds it down until the trigger is pressed. This first scear is made in the shape of a small rectangle. The pierced steel bridle covers up both these scears and it is not possible to photograph them. The scears are pressed through the lockplate by two long straight springs. This rare lock is in some ways similar to a commoner type of Italian miquelet lock. When the trigger on this specimen is pressed, the action is as smooth as that on many rifles in use today. The lock embodies a typically Spanish feature — the large ring in the top jaw screw, which allows the flint to be replaced without the use of a screwdriver, since any suitable rod or large nail can be inserted into the ring and used to unscrew the top jaw.

The frizzen or feather spring in

Plate 4: Top lock is on full cock; the middle is on half cock; the lower is seen from the inside.

Plate 2, it will be noted is straight for half its length and then curves slightly under the toe of the frizzen. The method of attaching the hammer to the lockplate, with a pin which goes through the square at right angles to the hammer, avoiding the need for a hammer screw is also typically Portuguese. It was most interesting to me to discover this after many trips to Spain followed by two visits to Portugal in search of antique weapons.

In Plate 3 we see a fine pair of brass-mounted "Madrid" lock pistols. Made by Augusti Deop *circa* 1750, the escutcheons and grotesque masks of the butt caps are of silver. The frizzen springs are typically conventional flintlock. At a casual glance, this appears to be a flintlock, but in fact, it is a true miquelet lock. This can best be explained by reference to Plate 4 which shows the two locks from these pistols detached, together with a third from another similar pistol by the same maker, shown from the inside.

In the Madrid lock, the mainspring is on the inside but the scears operate through the lockplate. The hammer has a small spur sticking out in front and another behind, both being flush with the lockplate. The top lock in Plate 4 is at full cock, the rectangular first scear has come through the lockplate and has engaged above the spur behind the cock. In the middle lock of three, the round scear is holding the hammer at half cock. The second scear is sticking out in front of the hammer, and fits under the spur on the front of the latter. The bottom lock in Plate 4 has been photographed from the inside and the scear, scear spring and bridle have been removed. The scear is below on the right, the toe which is pressed back by the trigger is pointing towards the bottom of the photograph. The middle projection on the top side of the scear holds the weapon at full cock, while the projection at the top left end of the scear controls the half cock position. The scear is lying on its side here, but when in position the toe will stick out towards the reader. The small curved spring seen on the left of the scear is screwed into position through a hole at the right end of the scear, and this spring presses down on the center projection which comes through the lockplate when the hammer is fully cocked. The screw referred to holds the spring, and the scear in position. The piece right at the bottom of the photograph is the bridle and screw, which fits over the scear in the same way as a bridle operates on a conventional flintlock. Today, the Madrid lock is exceedingly uncommon.

Plate 5 illustrates the inside of a detached conventional miquelet lock (flint), removed from a good quality pistol. The arrangement of the two scears, which are quite separate, is described below. The top of the frizzen is in this case rounded, though a flat top is much more commonly found. The two round ends of the short arm of the mainspring may be seen (given a close look) projecting through the inside of the lockplate below the pan. The projection on the left just below the screw head and slightly to the right of this screw is held in position with a small steel pin. This screw head referred to holds the first scear in position. The pin is missing from the projection on the right. The screw in the right end of the lockplate holds the second scear in position.

Incidentally, this straight first scear spring is kept under constant strain when the weapon is uncocked and often becomes weak through the years, so weak the weapon appears not to be in working order. This can very often be remedied by removing both scears and giving the inside of the lockplate a good clean. The spring should then be carefully bent by holding one end in a vise and gently pressing the other end.

Another typical feature of the miquelet lock is clearly seen in Plate 5. That is the serrations cut down the inside of the frizzen. These enable almost any flint picked up from the road to be used, there thus being no need to carry a supply of specially knapped flints.

Plate 6 illustrates a small Spanish pistol fitted with steel mounts and inscribed in silver on the barrel "Ano d 1821." The lock on this pistol is probably the final development of the miquelet before the percussion era. I say *probably* as it is always possible that another variation of this fascinating lock may be found. The screw holding the hammer and the frizzen in position are inserted from the inside of the lockplate, the frizzen spring itself has become completely visible and is not covered up by the box cover over the pan. Also, there is a spur running up behind the hammer jaw.

In Plate 7 we see a detached lock that is a real gem. I was lucky to find this in the Rastro in Madrid one Sunday morning and believe the shopkeeper must have been slightly hungry. (The Rastro is a large antique market where there are literally dozens of small shops massed into one area. They normally do not bother to open except on Sunday mornings, and then as a general rule the prices are

Plate 8: Roman locks fit close to their barrels and require less wood to be cut away from the stock.

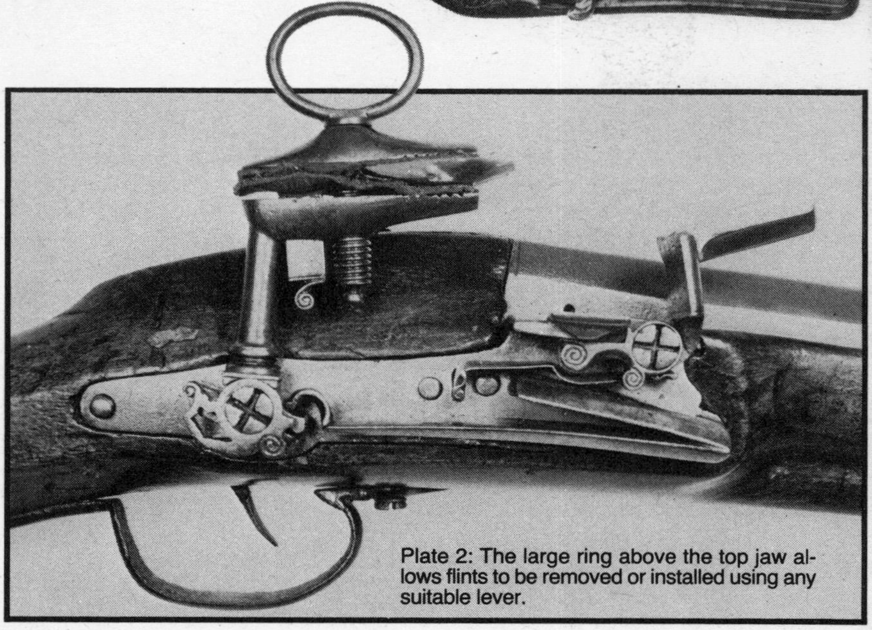

Plate 2: The large ring above the top jaw allows flints to be removed or installed using any suitable lever.

very high, unless, as I was, one is lucky.) This lock was made by Josephus Bustindui, one of a very famous family of Spanish gunmakers. It is in some respects similar to that in Plate 6, but was made some 50 years earlier. Bustindui obviously had seen examples of locks made in France. There is a rainproof slot cut into the rear end of the pan, but the really interesting feature is the fact that there is only one scear. This may be seen holding the hammer on full cock, while the hammer itself has a slot cut into it through which the scear slides when the lock is on half cock. Bustindui's

gold *poincon* may be seen on the lockplate.

The two locks illustrated in Plate 8 are both made in what is termed the Roman form, and were in fact made in Italy. The top one from a gun is inscribed Vinovio Sagnollis and is dated 1735, while the delightful little pistol lock beneath it is signed C.A. on the inside. Both scears operate through the lockplate, half cock holding the projection on the front of the hammer whilst full cock is maintained by the square projection which holds the tail of the hammer down. A feature on all miquelet locks that have their main-

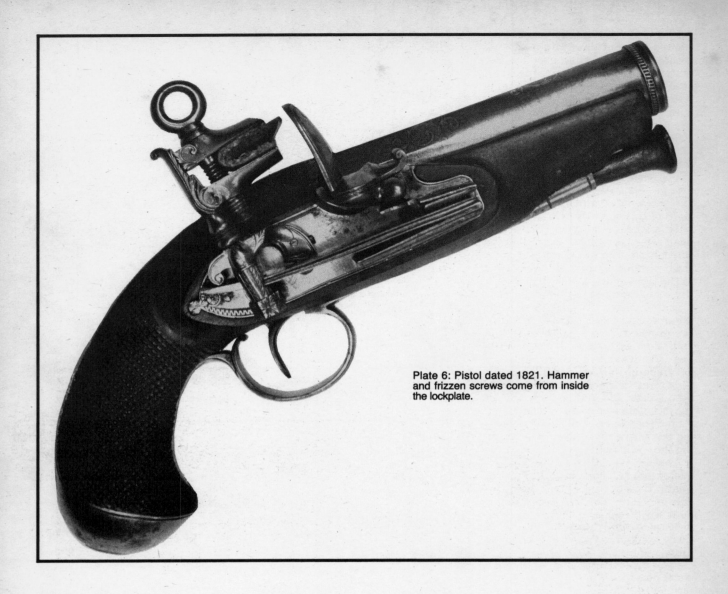

Plate 6: Pistol dated 1821. Hammer and frizzen screws come from inside the lockplate.

springs on the outside of the lockplate is, of course, that they can be more easily positioned right up against the touchhole, without cutting away anything like so much of the stock, as is the case of a lock with the mainspring inside the plate.

We now turn to the percussion era in this description of the miquelet lock.

The pistol shown in Plate 9 is a brass-mounted Spanish arm, originally a Madrid lock holster pistol made about 1750. The maker's name as usual appears in a gold *poincon* on top of the barrel, but, as is often the case, it is not possible to make it out. The gunsmith who converted it to percussion has made a very interesting job of it. The considerable amount of filing necessary to remove the pan left the front half of the lockplate blank; to counteract this blank patch he left the flat side of the engraved percussion hammer head blank. The pistol mea-sures 16½ inches over-all; the forward half of the 17-bore barrel is 16-sided.

Plate 10 shows a single-barrel 16-bore shotgun made by Ybarazabal in Eibar. The lock is signed "ORTIZ" in gold and there is much gold inlay. The hammer takes the form of an animal eating the nipple; he has an elaborate tail which is of course used as the thumb piece. The heel of the hammer is fitted with a roller wheel which reduces friction to a minimum. Only the very highest quality Spanish firearms were fitted with these roller bearings; even in really good quality guns, they are scarce.

Plate 11 illustrates a pair of Spanish percussion pistols with lion's head hammers. The upper one is on half cock and the lower on full cock. These pistols are of 16-bore and have on the barrels, inlaid in gold, "En Eibar Ano 1856". The barrels are 8½ inches long and the over-all measurement is 13 inches. The lion was the commonest of all the animals utilized when the early percussion gunmakers made their hammers so decorative.

The pair of pistols illustrated in Plate 12 are fitted with barrels signed by Jacob Kuchenreuter, who was one of a famous family of German gunsmiths and worked, according to Gardner, from about 1740-1770. It is very unusual to find arms made in Spain without Spanish barrels. The tendency was distinctly for Spanish barrels to be exported to other countries, and not German barrels to Spain.

The locks on these pistols are signed F.B. and the mounts are of silver. These fine pistols were made in the period 1830-1840. It is difficult to say whether they, and the hosts of European pistols of a similar type, were made with duelling or target shooting

Plate 5: Note serrated frizzen which does not require a specially knapped flint.

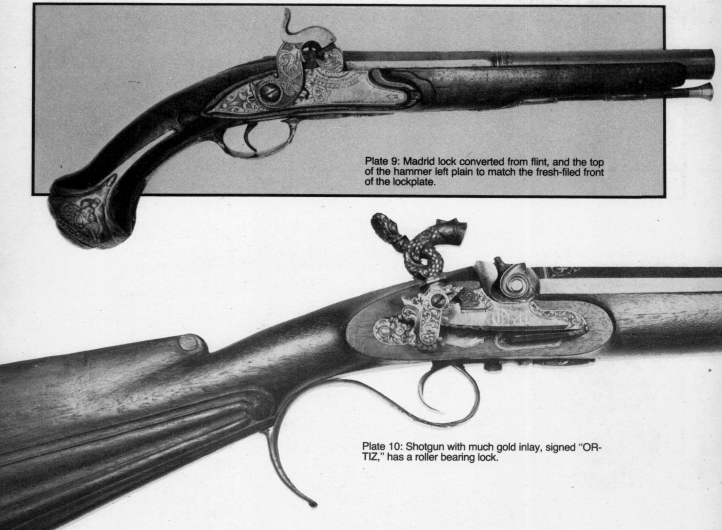

Plate 9: Madrid lock converted from flint, and the top of the hammer left plain to match the fresh-filed front of the lockplate.

Plate 10: Shotgun with much gold inlay, signed "OR-TIZ," has a roller bearing lock.

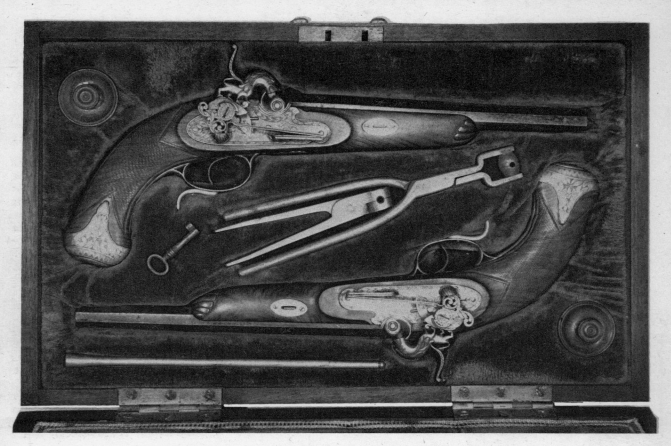

Plate 12: Cased pistols with German barrels by Kuchenreuter.

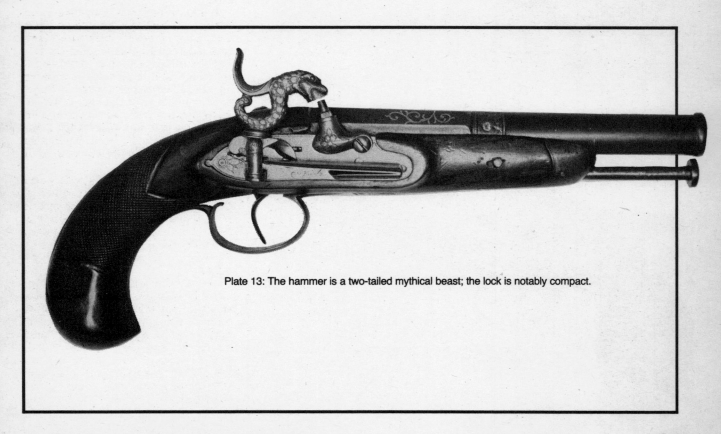

Plate 13: The hammer is a two-tailed mythical beast; the lock is notably compact.

Plate 11: Pistols made in Eibar in 1818 with lion's head hammers.

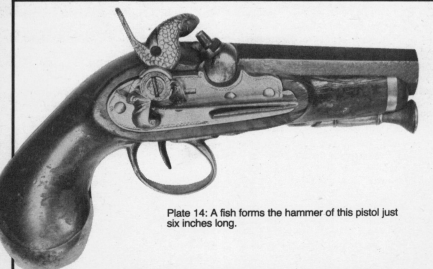

Plate 14: A fish forms the hammer of this pistol just six inches long.

in view. The trigger guards are fitted with spurs intended for the second finger to counteract "jump" at the shot. The pair are fitted in a blue velvet-lined case with two bullet moulds, steel ramrod, and two turned wood boxes, one for caps and the other for bullets. There is no provision for a powder flask in the case. The lid is elaborately carved with the initials C.P. Cased pairs of Spanish pistols are rare items.

An interesting Spanish pistol is seen in Plate 13. It has been converted from flintlock, being most probably of the usual style of miquelet lock. It will be noted, however, that the hammer is secured by a screw from inside the lockplate. The animal forming the hammer is very unusual, though these animals or grotesques form an interesting study on their own. The portion holding the nipple fits over the lockplate as seen, and the screw on the right of this piece must be removed before the barrel can be tapped out. The barrel must be lifted clear before the lock can be withdrawn. The barrel is inlaid with a quantity of silver wire.

My last photo, Plate 14, illustrates yet another hammer, this one made in the form of a fish. This little 24-bore pistol is only 6 inches over-all; it has no markings or decoration other than the brass strip near the tip of the stock.

It is of course quite impossible in an article of this length to show more than a few of the different types of miquelet lock. However, I must try and put one misconception right: Poor little Albania, a mountainous country on the Adriatic coast, south of Yugoslavia and north of Greece, is even today credited with having made an enormous number of rat-tailed miquelet lock pistols by most top British auctioneers. It is not the source of those pistols.

Several years ago, my wife and I tried to get into Albania to check this, hopefully to find piles of such pistols all going for a song. Of course, it was not to be. In those days tourists were only allowed to make a brief visit if in a group of 20 and accompanied by guides.

Later, on a visit to the Military Museum in Istanbul, what I then knew was the real truth about "rat tailed pistols" was confirmed in no uncertain terms. They are, of course, Turkish. In the Museum, there are considerable numbers of figures in the traditional dress of various periods; each has a rat-tailed miquelet pistol in its belt. ●

BEAR RIFLES

by **RAY ORDORICA**

Bear cartridges against Kiavak Bay, Kodiak Island. Left to right: 338 OKH; 340 Weatherby; 350 Remington Magnum; 404 B-J Express; 470 Nitro, 510-gr. bullet.

Bigger is always better, this writer believes.

A SLIGHT breeze blew through the mountains on the south end of Kodiak Island and came sweeping down Kiavak Bay, bouncing off the ocean and the mountainsides that jump directly out of the ocean. It swirled in and out of the deep cuts in the mountainsides, then came whistling past us, a typical erratic Alaskan breeze, It swept our scent down toward the great bear and ruffled his long fur until it looked like wheat in the wind. Too late, he was alerted to our presence. Canadian hunter Mark Cooke was already putting the final ounces of pressure on the trigger to send the bullet on its way.

It was really good shooting. The 24-year-old Cooke placed four shots well on the Kodiak bear, all inside 15 sec-onds, shooting his custom 340 Weatherby at 200 yards from the prone position. His first two shots hit within three inches of each other on the shoulder of the bear, ranging into the vitals. However, the bear *did not fall* to the first shot. It took two to deck him, and he was down only for about a second. Then he was up and running. Cooke's fifth hit on the bear broke the spine and put him down for good.

Even before the last echoes of the last shot had quit bouncing off the hills around Kiavak Bay I asked myself, "Was this really adequate performance for a bear rifle?"

Here we had a bear hit hard with 250-grain premium-brand bullets handloaded carefully, yet the bear was able to run along the beach with a broken shoulder. I wondered if one could have successfully prevented the bear from closing with the hunter if the bear was determined to do so?

On a guided hunt, one can use just about any rifle, action, and cartridge one can shoot well. If all does not go well, your friendly guide will take over with his pet bear buster and prevent bruin from getting away. With a guide to back you up, you could even choose a single-shot rifle for your bear gun with no misgivings.

If you are hunting alone, you may find you need all the stopping power you can get some day. To my way of thinking, the true bear gun must be capable of such backup work and I would never choose anything less than a rifle capable of such backup work for my own bear hunting. I started wondering more and more about bear rifles at Kiavak Bay.

A couple of weeks later I was to see the demise of a second bear. I was the guest on Kodiak Island of Mr. Andy Runyan, holder of Alaska's #2 Master Guide's license. Andy had graciously invited me down so I could get some firsthand insight into the hunting of the great bears. In return I was to be his "camp boy" for a month.

The second bear was taken after 11 days' hard hunting in the rain. This hunter, 21-year-old Mario Garcia of El Salvador, used a factory 338 Winchester Magnum with factory 300-gr. soft nose bullets. He hit his bear well with three out of four shots, all at about 50-70 yards, including his first shot which took the bear in the center of the chest and ranged back into the paunch. *Not one of his shots put the bear down!* This bear got into the alders, and Runyan said, "Now I've got to earn my salary."

So saying he loaded up his 404 Barnes-Johnson Express (bulletmaker Fred Barnes' old Oberndorf Mauser) and proceeded to stalk the wounded bruin—very carefully.

We finally caught up with him in some of the thickest alders the bear could find. Using 400-gr. bullets, Runyan punched one into the alder thicket at the bear. Out came bruin, going away, with a 400-gr. bee in his bonnet, so to speak. He lit out up a small rise and as he topped it Runyan busted him through the hump with another 400-gr. bullet. The bear took two running steps, then went down, rolling down the hillside. He got to his feet again, but was too far gone to go far and we found him a short distance away down the hillside. It must be noted that the cal. 411 rifle throwing a 400-grain bullet was capable of putting the bear down even though the bear was wounded, his adrenalin was up, and he was fully capable of running.

We finally came up to the bear and Mario put the final shot into him. Just before we "skun him out," as Runyan says, I noticed the bear's nose still twitching. Runyan asked me to kindly put a sixgun slug down through his spine, please. I pulled my 4 inch M29 Smith & Wesson loaded with Keith 250-gr. cast slugs in front of 22 grains of 2400, the old Keith load. While watching bruin's eye, I felt with my hand until I had the center of the spine located, and punched one down through it. Then we proceeded with the skinning job.

Runyan says, "Sometimes I'm not really sure these fellows are dead until we get the hide off them."

Sad to say we were unable to do a really adequate autopsy on this second bear. It was late in the day on the last day of the season, it was drizzling rain, we had lots of work still to do in camp and a plane to catch in the morn, so we did not have a good chance to dig into the bear as we would have liked. We did recover one of the 300-gr. 338 bullets, mushroomed perfectly against the hide. I do know that Runyan's second 400-gr. 404 bullet went through the bear near the top of the back, for I heard it howling off down the hill. It missed the spine.

The toughness of these big bears is truly remarkable. You read over and over about just how tough a wounded Alaskan Brown bear can be, but until you witness this firsthand you will not realize the meaning behind the words.

These bears squared about 7½ feet, by no means the largest on Kodiak Island. Kodiaks sometimes—rarely—square over 10 feet—the average of width across front legs, and length from tip of nose to tip of tail on an unstretched hide. They get tougher as they get bigger.

Two bears do not an expert make. However, bear hunting was by no means new to my host, Andy Runyan. Andy has been a bear guide in Alaska since 1951. He was the youngest registered guide in the Territory back

Mark Cooke (left) with Andy Runyan and the bear. Mark's custom 340 Westherby made five good hits at 200 yards.

Three real bear rifles. Top to bottom: Fred Barnes' old 404 B-J Express, now Andy Runyan's personal bear stopper; writer's best quality Churchill 470 double rifle; Jay Frazier's personal 375 with claw-mounted scope.

then. He has hunted bear from the Panhandle to Point Barrow, and has witnessed the demise of approximately 300 bears of all types—blacks, grizzlies, brownies, and polar bears. It is his opinion that all grizzlies and brownies are pretty tough customers.

Andy has used or seen used various 33-caliber rifles, 35s, 375s, 40s, 429s, 450 Alaskans, 458s and the 450 Watts against bears. The smallest rifle he had seen used against the great bears was a 243. That client killed his bear with three well-placed shots. There is no question that just about any rifle will kill the bears; it is just a matter of how quickly they will do the job. According to Andy, the only way to put down bruin for good with one shot where he stands is to sever the spine near the shoulder bosses, or to put one into the brain.

Runyan used to use a 458 for his work on Kodiak. He has used 510-gr. soft-nose, and said that each good hit would put the wounded bear down and this gave him time to put in additional, more careful, hits. In time he came to favor handloaded 350-gr. bullets after he had to lob 510-gr. bullets into an escaping bear that a client had wounded. The wounded bear got out to very great range, apparently over 500 yards. As Andy put it, "I had the second round in the chamber before the first one got to the bear!"

After that he used the 350-gr. 458's with every satisfaction.

Andy eventually abandoned the 458 for a wildcat called the 429, which took .429″ bullets in full-length cylindrical belted brass cases, which are somewhat longer than 375 H&H cases, necked to accept the 429 bullets. This proved to be a very good tool although recoil was pretty severe, as the rifle was built very light for easy carrying up and down the hills of Kodiak Island. Andy told me this 429 would " . . .back you right out from underneath your beanie!"

The 429 was stolen, and Andy replaced it with his 404, which is a shortened 375 case necked up to take .411″-dia. bullets. At 338-458 length, the 404 is fire-formed to give straight walls. The cartridge gives a 300-gr. bullet some 2800 fps. Andy chooses the 300-gr. bullet over the 400 for most of his work, when he has to be able to hit the bear at extreme range. But if he has to go in the brush after bruin he uses the 400-gr. bullet in preference to the 300.

When asked what he considers the minimum caliber for backup work on the big bear, Runyan named, somewhat to my surprise, the 350 Remington Magnum. Andy has a Remington 700 BDL for that cartridge with 24-inch barrel. He has used this rifle on occasion and reports very good results even on wounded bear. He prefers the 200-gr. factory load. However, he does not use this rifle himself today, preferring his larger 404.

I was and remain somewhat surprised at Runyan's recommendation of light bullets in his big rifles—300-gr. in the 404, 200-gr. in the 350, 350-gr. in 458 rifles, and so on. His reason is quite simple: They worked for him better than anything else. A lot of practical experience will often lead one to draw strong opinions contrary to generally-touted views. I might add that Runyan is not the only guide who has noticed that the 200-gr. bullet in the 338 Winchester Magnum seems to kill faster than heavier ones on the big bear and moose.

One of Andy's assistant guides is riflemaker Jay Frazier of Birdcreek, Alaska. Jay showed up in camp with one of the finest 375's I've ever seen, built by himself on a Mauser action. This had a claw-mounted scope that Jay had tested by firing a shot, removing and then replacing the scope, firing another shot, and so on. He showed us the target, and the rifle had shot into an inch at 100 yards with the scope replaced for each shot. I asked Runyan what he thought of the 375 for a bear gun. He told me he used to use one but got something bigger when he once had a hard time stopping a mad wounded bear with his old 375. Since this man makes his living by shooting wounded bears when necessary, he figured he'd better get some bigger "life insurance."

In any discussion of bear rifles one must consider the terrain. On Kodiak

Island and the Alaska peninsula, much bear habitat is relatively open, grassy slope, often jutting nearly vertically out of the ocean and rising to a height of 1500 to 2000 feet. These mountains break into jagged valleys in which one might hide a dozen bears and a hamburger stand to boot. Where the mountains meet the ocean there are shale beaches where bruin often prowls. A brown bear crossing such country might offer you only a relatively long-range shot, and will be putting a lot of this rugged terrain between you and him as fast as he can if he's wounded.

In the valleys lie the alder patches, twisting mazes of gnarled moss-covered shrubs with branches often as thick as a man's leg. In the springtime when the alders have no leaves at all, a bear in them can be totally invisible at a distance of 15 feet. The backup rifle must keep the bear from reaching these alder thickets if at all possible. Once in the alders, a wounded brown bear becomes what many consider to be the most dangerous game animal on earth. Invisible at close range, capable of closing with the hunter in a split second, and more than willing and able to inflict terminal damage to the hunter following him up, a wounded brown or Kodiak bear is a terrifying proposition for the guide who must by law follow him up into these dense alders. Small wonder the knowledgeable bear guide will start shooting when the bear heads for the alders.

So the bear rifle for such country must be relatively flat shooting, to make hitting easier at long range, and still have enough power left to do some good when the bullet meets the bear. There should at least be a good blood trail to help in tracking.

One may also hunt big bears on the Alaskan panhandle, in terrain very like a rain forest or jungle. Ranges may be short, and the brush only a jump away from bruin. Here it is very rare to get a shot at over 100 yards, 50 being about average. The best backup rifles for this country are probably large-bore double rifles, throwing heavy bullets capable of stopping bruin with any good body hit, and giving time to get in a more carefully placed killing hit. Runyan once had a chance to buy Mr. Pulitzer's (of Pulitzer Prize notability) 50-caliber double for backup work when he used to guide on the Panhandle, in southeastern Alaska. He passed it up, and has regretted it ever since.

What, then, are the criteria for the backup rifle? How do we define the real thing?

Andy Runyan is just 15 feet away from the camera in the alders. A bear at such distance may be totally invisible, with fur exactly the color of the brush. When they run in this stuff they go over it.

The need for a flat-shooting rifle may be seen in this broken country, where you may not be able to get much closer than 200 yards. Runyan of course recommends getting as close as possible, but it could still be 200 yards.

Ordorica finds that easy handling is high on the list of bear rifle necessities. Here he manipulates Runyan's 404 stopper.

sult in a dandy rifle for bear work, offering fast repeat shots, but it would be strictly a custom job and one would have to use fairly low pressures, nowhere near as high as one could use in a bolt action, I suspect.

I feel the need for ultimate reliability rules out the auto-loading rifle, at least for me. If one were to use the Browning 338 or a custom rifle based on that action, one could have just about all the power one would need in the autoloader. However, I for one would wonder just what the salt air was doing to my rifle's action during the course of the day's hunt.

The trombone or pump action is not available in any adequate caliber on today's market. I feel the time and money necesary to come up with something like a custom-built slide-action 458 could be better spent elsewhere.

This leaves us with two serious contenders for the throne, and there is a place for both: The bolt action and the double rifle.

For its ability to handle long range, high pressures, great demands on accuracy, telescope sights, and light weight in a custom rifle, the bolt action is supreme as a bear gun.

For the ultimate in dependability and speed for two shots, handiness in the brush, no openings to trap rainwater which will squirt into your eye when you pull the trigger, and for the ultimate in balance, grace, and beauty, no rifle beats the fine, well-cared-for double rifle. With ejectors, one can reload very fast.

To choose the caliber of the bear rifle, we must say that the smaller one's rifle the more one must rely on perfect bullet performance and placement, with certain restrictions. It is not responsible to state that with a smaller rifle one can shoot more accurately than with a big one and hence can "make do" nicely with a smaller rifle. Tell that to the bears. If you think a small rifle can be used to shatter a shoulder and hence stop a charge, you are very badly mistaken. I saw a small brownie running very fast along a beach, doing rather well, in fact. His shoulder was powdered bone fragments at the time.

Muzzle energy is not the answer. That is too theoretical an idea. The answer seems to be big heavy bullets, say caliber 40 minimum, *and* 300 grains at over 2500 fps minimum. As does Runyan, I'd feel better with more of both caliber and bullet weight at close range.

• It must be able to knock down a wounded brownie with every good hit to give you time to reload and carefully place your succeeding shots on the bear, specifically to sever the spine.

• You may have to place hits on a wounded bear at extreme range.

• The rifle must be a repeater to allow fast follow-up shots when needed.

• It must be totally reliable.

• It ought to be handy and light for brush use and long hours of carrying.

• Since much of Alaskan bear hunting takes place in close proximity to salt water one should give thought to rust-proofing.

A thorough consideration of that list leads us, perhaps with some prejudices, to several conclusions:

One can rule out single shot rifles for serious consideration as backup rifles for the big bear. There are better, faster, choices. And one can rule out commercial lever rifles since none offers a flat-shooting big caliber. One could, of course, have a custom rifle made up, like the 450 Alaskan, which is the 348 case necked up to caliber 458, but on what action? Perhaps one could use a Marlin lever action and make up a custom 40 cal. based on the 45-70 case blown out. This might re-

I have already told how two small bears acted when shot with 250-gr. and 300-gr. bullets out of 338-caliber rifles. In the case of the 250-gr. bullet out of the 340 Weatherby there was some question about the performance of the bullets. With the 300-gr. bullets out of the 338 Winchester Magnum there was none. These did all they could have done. These bears did not fall with every good hit from these rifles. Perhaps they were exceptions. If so, they are the exceptions that prove the rule for me, that leads me to believe 338 is not big enough for my own uses on the great bear. Andy Runyan had reasons to doubt the ultimate stopping performance of his old 375, so he went to a bigger rifle. There are limits, of course. One could carry a 460 Weatherby or a 600 Nitro, but these must by their very nature be very heavy weapons. If made light enough for all-day carry, who would want to shoot them?

It is interesting to question a man such as Andy Runyan, who has spent his entire adult life in the pursuit of Alaskan game, including the great bears, and who is also interested enough in rifles and their performance to have made a careful study during his life of the performance of various calibers in actual game-shooting experience from his own shoulder. In their own way, his experiences are similar to those of men like John Taylor, who studied the old British calibers on the game of Africa. So perhaps we can learn something from a close perusal of his personal rifle.

I have already told you it is a 404 Barnes-Johnson Express on a very smooth Mauser action. On it he has, in Redfield mounts, a Leupold 1.5x-5x variable set on the lowest power setting. There are no iron sights. He had Jay Frazier cut the stock to fit him and install a Pachmayr Old English pad, and Frazier also refinished the wood and applied one of his fine cold rust blue jobs. The rifle weighs 8½ pounds fully loaded. Andy had it Mag-Na-Ported in order to reduce muzzle jump. He says the Mag-Na-Porting helps him keep the animal in the scope's field while the rifle is in recoil. Barrel length is 22-inch. It has a Canjar nonsettable trigger, and the bolt knob is checkered for a good grip when wet.

The one problem with his rifle is the bore. It is hard to keep it from rusting in the saltwater and rainy atmosphere on Kodiak Island.

Andy and I compared notes and we came up with the outline for the ultimate bolt action bear rifle. It will have either a fine commercial Mauser action or a pre-'64 Winchester M70, standard length. A third possibility is the Ruger M77 action. Caliber will be 411, the cartridge identical with the 404 B-J Express as detailed above, basically a 338 necked up to take .411″ bullets. Only difference will be that one of the factories will hopefully hear me and come out with a commercial cartridge. It could be designated the 10mm Remington Magnum or the 404 Winchester Magnum—I wouldn't care.

Our ultimate custom bolt action rifle will use this new commercial cartridge, but it must have the full-length reliable Mauser-type extractor. It will also have a stainless barrel, Mag-Na-Ported, of 22-inch length. The action will have Armoloy or some other rust-proofing on it. The stock will be fine wood to suit our sense of aesthetics, although we did consider a plastic stock because rifles get very wet while bear hunting. The rest of the rifle will be nearly identical with Andy's 404 Express as to weight and details.

Individuals could modify this rifle to suit their whims. I prefer auxiliary iron sights on all my hunting rifles, while Runyan does not want them on a scoped rifle. Andy wants the stainless barrel ironplated and blued, while I would just as soon leave it bright but sandblasted to cut glare. And so it goes.

I don't know if there is a market for 40-caliber rifles. However, with all the new cartridges being brought out to increase interest and sales, we might as well have a legitimate 40 on today's market. To me this makes for more interest than the multiplicity of 7mm's and so on being brought out like so many flapjacks in the morn.

This discussion would be incomplete if I did not also give my opinions on the ultimate double rifle for bear hunting. Granted the double is mostly a close-range affair, yet if I can see a bear at 200 yards I am sure I could kill him cleanly with a good iron sighted double. And if I have to crawl down a bear trail through the alders after a wounded bear I will take a big double over any and all bolt action rifles, thank you.

I feel that one of the best double rifles for such work would be a 400-3-inch (400 Jeffery) Westley Richards with hand-detachable locks. I am, in fact, starting my search for just such a rifle. The cartridge throws a 400-gr. bullet at around 2125 fps. The rifle should be an ejector for fastest reloading. The hand-detachable locks are to be used for daily removal, inspection and oiling in a rainy saltwater environment. Other makers offered hand-detachable locks, but only Westley offered metal-to-metal detachable locks. I prefer double triggers. Barrel length ought to be 24 inches to no more than 26 inches.

The outside of the rifle will have to be something less than perfect, although I will insist on very good bores and a tight action. I carried my best quality Churchill 470 double rifle out in the rain on the bear trails. Its finish is nearly perfect and I confess I was not too happy about all that water on the big rifle. So the exterior finish on my ultimate bear double will have to be something less than perfect, strange though that may seem.

It turns out, you can see, that rifles for big bear should be big rifles. I'm sure of it. ●

WHAT CAN YOU learn about a rifle's accuracy if you only have one box of cartridges to shoot?

This is an important question to the hunter who is not a handloader. With prices as they are today many might justify one extra box of cartridges for sighting-in a new rifle and to determine its potential, but draw the line at that point.

The question is also important if you have just one box of a particular cartridge to test for accuracy. This happened to me recently and was what started me on the way to writing this article. I was rearranging things in my gun cabinet and ran across a box of Norma 22-250 50-grain soft point ammunition that was at least 12 years old. I thought it would be interesting to find out how well it would shoot after sitting on the shelf that long. My varmint rifle, a Remington Model 700 with 26-inch Douglas premium heavy barrel, a Canjar set trigger and Redfield 12x scope was clearly the perfect test instrument. The real problem was to get the most information from this very limited supply of ammunition.

My first inclination was to fire four 5-shot groups. But then I got to thinking about the hunter with his single box of ammunition. He really has only 15 cartridges available for accuracy testing because it will probably take two shots to be sure he is hitting the target more or less where he wants at 100 yards. After firing 15 cartridges for accuracy and making final sight adjustments this leaves three shots for a final group to check that the center of the bullet pattern is where he wants it.

So what to fire? One 15-shot group, three 5-shot groups or five 3-shot groups? A little more thought showed that I could do all of these! The trick is to have three targets, one behind the other, with the edges carefully lined up. This presents the view of a single target to the shooter. All 15 shots are fired at the front target. However, the back target is changed after every three shots and the middle target after each fifth shot.

The single 15-shot group is particularly useful in determining the center of impact of the bullet pattern. The 3-shot and 5-shot groups give a good estimate of the relative accuracy of the rifle/cartridge combination compared to other rifles for which groups of the same number of shots have been fired.

For the hunter the most important thing is to know the center of impact and how far his bullets disperse around it. After all the name of the game is to hit the game, not to make neat patterns in the thin air. As you will see from the groups I shot—and may well have realized from your own shooting experience—the center of impact of each of several 3-shot (or 5-shot) groups are at quite different locations on the target. The smaller the number of shots in the group, the

This is the author with a new rifle, discovering

Author spends two hours on a 15-shot session at Fairfax range.

more varied is the position of the center of impact.

I now knew exactly what to do. But did I just take my varmint rifle and the old ammunition out to the range and proceed? Well, yes, I did. But I was getting so interested in the problem of the hunter with his new rifle that in the interests of ballistic science I went out and bought one of the new Winchester Model 94 Angle Eject rifles in 307 Winchester.

The 307 Winchester cartridge is clearly capable out to at least 200 yards. Therefore, I opted for a four-power Redfield Widefield scope and counted on the Widefield feature for adequate field-of-view close-in. After mounting the scope, I went out one weekday morning to the Fairfax Rod & Gun Club ranges. No one else was there, so it was no problem to take all those walks down to the 100-yard target frame to change the middle and back targets.

The first thing I did was cover the whole cardboard target backer with

Figure 1

WHAT ONE BOX OF AMMUNITION CAN TELL YOU

by **DAVID LEESTMA**

brown wrapping paper to avoid confusion with all the existing bullet holes. Then I mounted the sighting-in target. The first bullet through the rifle was fired from 25 yards. The bullet hole was above the target and I sure was glad I put the brown paper up or I would never have been able to figure where that first shot went. After adjusting the sights the next shot was fired from 100 yards. It hit the target reasonably close to where I wanted it, so I proceeded to fire for accuracy.

The weather was hot, but I had the whole morning. To avoid shooter fatigue or the effects of a hot barrel, I allotted two hours to shoot the 15 shots, all fired off the benchrest. Since the

center of impact was one of the things to be determined, I held the rifle quite like I would if I were hunting. My left hand gripped the forend and the back of that hand rested on the sandbag. The butt of the rifle was pulled tightly into my shoulder. The rear of the stock did *not* rest on a sandbag, but my right elbow did rest on the bench. I've found that this technique not only gives me a center of impact corresponding to what I'd get from normal hunting positions, but also gives very good accuracy.

Now for some heresy. I found that this technique also works for the light kickers like my varmint rifle. With my favorite varmint load—53-grain

Sierra benchrest bullet, 35 grains 4064, Remington 9½ primers and Norma brass loaded with one of the old Lee Target Loaders—I consistently get 5-shot groups at 300 yards under two inches. The only rifle I've ever had which did not work best with this method was a Shilen heavy varmint rifle in 222 Remington. It worked best with the classic technique of sandbag support fore and aft and a very light hold. With the classic technique it gave groups around 0.3 inches at 100 yards, while with my usual technique it gave groups around 0.6 inches.

One other thing worth mentioning: Recoil from the Model 94 in 307 Winchester is not bothersome from normal hunting positions, but it is noticeable when shooting off the bench. Since I was looking for the best possible group rather than to prove I was macho, I folded a towel and placed it between the rifle butt and my shoulder. This eliminated any recoil problems as far as I was concerned.

Having done all this, the shooting conditions were ideal. I decided not to allow any alibis. Each shot fired—even if it looked like a flyer—would be part of the group because such a flyer probably would also happen in a hunting situation.

Now let's look at the results. Figure 1 shows the 15-shot group. Figures 2 and 3 are the 3-shot and 5-shot groups, respectively. Things start to get revealing when figure 4 is examined. It shows how the center of impacts of all the groups are distributed.

Determining the center of impact of a group is quite simple. Measure the vertical distance from the bottom edge of the target to the centers of all the bullet holes—that is, from the center of the bullet hole straight down to the bottom edge—and add these numbers together and divide by the number of shots in the group (for a 15-shot group divide by 15, for a 5-shot group divide by 5, etc.). This gives the *average* vertical distance of the group from the bottom edge of the target. It is the same as the vertical measurement of the center of impact of the group.

Now choose one side of the target and measure the horizontal distance from that edge to the centers of all the bullet holes—from the center of the bullet hole straight across to the edge. Proceed exactly as before to obtain the average horizontal distance. Table 1 shows these measurements for the 15-shot target. They are listed in the order in which they were fired.

To locate the center of impact of the group just draw a line parallel to the bottom edge of the target at average vertical distance, and another line parallel to the side of the target to the average horizontal distance. Where the two lines cross is the center of the group.

To know the true center of impact of a rifle/cartridge combination would involve firing a group with an infinite number of shots. This could get to be expensive, to say nothing about it taking an eternity to finish all the shooting. However, the center of impact of a 15-shot group gives a pretty good estimate of where the center of impact of a rifle/cartridge combination is really located.

By using statistical techniques involving what is called Chi-Square distribution, it turns out that to a high degree of confidence the true center of impact is located within a box centered on the 15-shot center of impact and with sides equal to 1.5 times the standard deviation in the vertical measurements and 1.5 times the standard deviation in the horizontal measurements. For a 5-shot group the factor is 4.6 instead of 1.5. For a 3-shot group the factor is 12.2

It is relatively easy, though somewhat tedious, to obtain the standard deviations. A hand calculator which takes square roots makes things manageable. Let's look at how to get the standard deviation of the vertical measurements for the 15-shot group in Table 1. Start by taking the first vertical measurement (1.27) and subtracting from it the *average* vertical measurement (2.34). The answer is −1.07. Now square this number, i.e., multiply it by itself. This gives 1.1449. Write this number down. Repeat this process for the remaining 14 vertical measurements. When you are finished, add the numbers you have written down. This gives 15.4984. Now divide by one less than the number of shots in the group. (15.4984 divided by 14 gives 1.1070285) Finally take the square root of the result. To two decimal places this gives 1.05. This is the standard deviation of the vertical measurements. The standard deviation in the horizontal mesurements is obtained in the corresponding way.

Table 2 shows the vertical and hori-

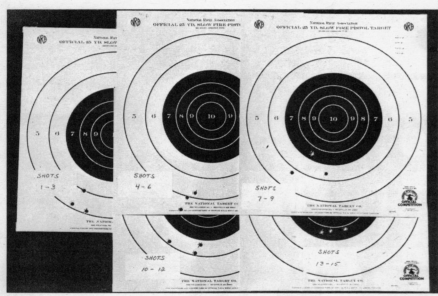

Figure 2

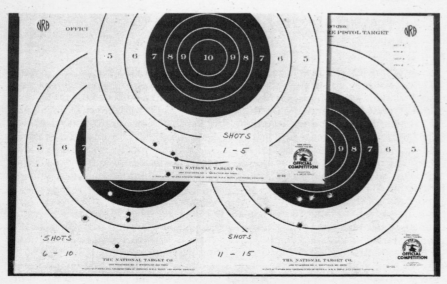

Figure 3

zontal standard deviations obtained by this method for all groups. Table 3 displays the dimensions of the box which contains—with a high degree of confidence—the true center of impact of the rifle/cartridge combination.

Note how large the uncertainty in the location of the true center of impact is for a single 3-shot group as compared to the 15-shot group. That's why shooting a 15-shot group is so valuable. It gives a very good approximation of the true center of impact. The hunter can then adjust his sights based on the 15-shot center of impact and have high confidence that he has put the true center of impact where he wants it.

Now let's examine how the bullet holes are dispersed about the center of impact. To do that we need to know the distance of each bullet hole from the center of impact of the group. This is easily found using the information in Table 1. Pick one of the shots. Subtract the *average* vertical measurement from the actual vertical measurement and square the answer. Now subtract the *average* horizontal measurement from the actual horizontal measurement and square this answer. Add the two squares and take the square root of the result. This is the distance of the bullet hole from the center of impact of the group. The results for all 15 shots are shown in Table 4.

Note that 13 out of 15 shots (87%) are within nearly 1½ inches of the center of impact at 100 yards, and all the shots are within 2¼ inches.

All the above gives, in my estimation, the really important information about the accuracy of a rifle/cartridge combination. However, since most people are used to thinking in terms of group size, it is useful to present that information. I've included the group size information on that 22-250 Norma ammo in case you are curious. The results are given in Table 5.

The really surprising thing to me was how well the Model 94 grouped. Average 3-shot groups under 1½ inches at 100 yards from a lever action rifle was not what I expected, but I surely was pleased. This is as good or better than the groups I have obtained from many bolt action rifles which have passed through my hands over the years. This particular Model 94 will take a prominent place in my gun cabinet.

As you can see, I like accurate rifles. Having a rifle which groups tightly means that as practice improves my holding ability from a field position, I will increase the consisten-

cy of my hitting small targets.

But to put things in perspective, consider the problem of hitting a deer in the kill zone at 100 yards. The kill zone of a deer is about 10 inches in diameter, which is pretty big. If from a field position I can shoot a 15-shot group at 100 yards which is 10 inches in extreme spread, then I have a very high confidence that I can put a shot in the kill zone of a deer when shooting from that field position.

The group shot from field position can be considered to consist of two parts: (1)) the rifle's contribution, i.e., the group that would be obtained shooting that rifle from benchrest, and (2) the shooter's contribution, i.e., the size of the group the shooter would get using a perfect one-holer rifle

Figure 4

TABLE 1

Shot	Vertical	Horizontal
	Location of Bullet Holes in 15-Shot Group Fired From Model 94 in 307 Winchester (180 grain)	
1	1.27	3.81
2	1.65	3.03
3	2.44	3.65
4	0.31	3.63
5	0.99	3.97
6	1.26	4.40
7	2.50	3.00
8	2.47	4.91
9	3.66	4.08
10	2.72	4.86
11	2.23	4.56
12	2.92	3.12
13	3.48	4.55
14	3.55	5.08
15	3.65	5.91
Average	2.34	4.17

Note: All measurements are in inches. Horizontal measurements are from left edge of target. Measurements made with vernier caliper.

TABLE 2

Standard Deviations
For 307 Winchester (180 grain)

Shots	Average Vertical	Average Horizontal	S.D. Vertical	S.D. Horizontal
1 - 3	1.79	3.50	0.60	0.41
4 - 6	0.85	4.00	0.49	0.39
7 - 9	2.88	4.00	0.68	0.96
10 - 12	2.62	4.18	0.36	0.93
13 -15	3.56	5.18	0.09	0.69
1 - 5	1.33	3.62	0.79	0.36
6-10	2.52	4.25	0.86	0.78
11-15	3.17	4.64	0.60	1.02
1 -15	2.34	4.17	1.05	0.83

TABLE 3

| | Dimensions of Box | | Center of Box | |
Shots	Vertical	Horizontal	Vertical	Horizontal
1 - 3	7.3	5.0	1.79	3.50
4 - 6	6.0	4.8	0.85	4.00
7 - 9	8.3	11.7	2.88	4.00
10-12	4.4	11.3	2.62	4.18
13-15	1.1	8.4	3.56	5.18
1 - 5	3.6	1.7	1.33	3.62
6 -10	4.0	3.6	2.52	4.25
11-15	2.8	4.7	3.17	4.64
1 -15	1.6	1.2	2.34	4.17

Location of True Center of Impact For 307 Winchester (180 grain)

TABLE 4

Distance of Bullet Holes From Center of Impact For 15-Shot Group with 307 Winchester (180 grain)

Shot	Vertical minus Avg. Vert.	Horizontal minus Avg. Horiz.	Distance
1	−1.07	−0.36	1.13
2	−0.69	−1.14	1.33
3	0.10	−0.52	0.53
4	−2.03	−0.54	2.10
5	−1.35	−0.20	1.36
6	−1.08	0.23	1.10
7	0.16	−1.17	1.18
8	0.13	0.74	0.75
9	1.32	−0.09	1.32
10	0.38	0.69	0.79
11	−0.11	0.39	0.41
12	0.58	−1.05	1.20
13	1.14	0.38	1.20
14	1.21	0.91	1.51
15	1.31	1.74	2.18

TABLE 5

Group Sizes

Shots	307 Winchester	22-250 Norma
1-3	1.18	1.02
4-6	1.22	0.52
7-9	1.91	1.05
10-12	1.74	0.70
13-15	1.37	0.40
Average 3-shot	1.48	0.74
1-5	2.13	1.06
6-10	2.42	1.15
11-15	2.88	0.70
Average 5-shot	2.48	0.97
1-15	4.04	1.41

from the field position. The field group size is just the square root of the sum of the squares of these two parts. Table 6 illustrates some combinations which can be expected to produce a 10-inch field group.

Note that if I can hold well enough to shoot a 4.4-inch group at 100 yards with a perfect rifle, I would still have a very high confidence of killing a deer if I used a rifle that was only capable of 9-inch groups at 100 yards! Also it is evident from Table 6 that a shooter has nearly the same confidence in hitting the kill zone of a deer with a rifle which shoots 5-inch groups as with one that shoots 1-inch groups. This is because the shooter's holding ability needed to get a 10-inch field group is about the same in both of these cases.

Still and all, I subscribe to Townsend Whelen's comment, "Only accurate rifles are interesting."

A final word in closing. Throughout this article I have made some assumptions about the statistical nature of the groups produced by shooter and rifle. Principal among these assumptions are that for both the rifle's contribution and the shooter's contribution the distributions in the horizontal and vertical directions are independent and that these distributions are normal (or Gaussian). In most cases these are pretty good assumptions. Even if for your rifle or holding ability they are not completely accurate assumptions, nevertheless the results obtained by using them are a good guide to the accuracy of your rifle.

Now go out and buy a box of cartridges and learn and have fun! ●

EDITOR'S NOTE: When a physical scientist and serious computer user like this writer uses words here like "confidence," he is using them in the same statistical sense he used them in examining and reporting on heavy weapons systems for our government.
K.W.

TABLE 6

Combinations Producing A 10-Inch Group From Field Position

Rifle's Contribution	Shooter's Contribution
1.0	9.95
2.0	9.8
3.0	9.5
4.0	9.2
5.0	8.7
6.0	8.0
7.0	7.1
8.0	6.0
9.0	4.4

Larry Lalouette twisting standing blanks using a Ruger "funny gun" and Sidewinder rig. The gun was fired with the muzzle at the front lip of the holster, follow-through carried it to the position shown.

The Funny Guns and Gear of the Western Fast Draw Game

by BOB ARGANBRIGHT

THE SPORT OF Western Fast Draw burst upon the scene 25 years ago as a by-product of the popularity of the many new TV "adult western" series. And at the beginning, shooters used the Colt Single Action Army revolver or the Great Western copy with Hollywood fast draw rigs—gunbelt and holster—by such makers as Arvo Ojala and Andy Anderson. Those guns and rigs evolved into today's "funny guns" and "funny rigs," analogous to drag racing's "funny cars."

Initially, fast drawers used the thumb-cocking style introduced by Hollywood fast draw coach Arvo Ojala. Called "hammer slapping," Ojala's style had the shooter's thumb slapping the hammer to full cock position *before* the gun left the holster. The stiff holster was fitted to let the cylinder revolve.

The Colts preferred by most were generally 45 caliber with 4¾-inch barrel. Modifications were few. They lightened the action by grinding the mainspring narrower or thinner, and replaced the fragile bolt and trigger spring with one made of music wire. Action parts were honed for smoothness and hammer spurs were modified by removing all checkering and polishing them smooth. Some shooters removed the front sight, though it is doubtful this affected the speed of the draw.

Possibly the greatest influence during the first 10 years of Fast Draw was Hollywood holster maker Andy Anderson. Anderson had started as foreman in the Ojala holster shop, influencing the quality and appearance of the Ojala rig. A short time later, he opened his legendary Gunfighter shop, developing his line of Gunfighter rigs, including the famous Walk and Draw (W&D) Western rig as used by Clint Eastwood in all of his Spaghetti Western movies.

Anderson also did custom gunsmithing on fast draw guns. An example is the unique "Big Iron", originally built by Anderson on a reject Great Western frame, with 44 Special cylinder and a 44-40 Model 1892 Winchester rifle barrel cut down to 12 inches. It didn't end there.

Early live ammunition fast draw top gun Walt Ivie purchased the custom Buntline type and obtained an oversize cylinder in 44 Magnum from Great Western. Ivie replaced the frame with a post-war Colt frame and replaced the backstrap and trigger guard with an original rare all-steel Colt 1860 Army unit with beautiful one-piece grips made of Alaskan ram's horn, supplied by Anderson.

Because all competition fast draw required point shooting, Ivie shortened the barrel a little at a time until his big sixgun pointed instinctively for him, ending with a 9⅝-inch barrel. Country-western superstar Marty Robbins met Ivie in the Gunfighter shop and was infatuated with the big 44. A few days later, one of the first 45 RPM records of Robbins new hit single "Big Iron" arrived at the shop. Anderson and Ivie both feel that their 44-caliber Big Iron was Robbins' inspiration.

Walt Ivie won the first fast draw contest in which he used the Big Iron, a live ammunition contest with nine-inch balloon targets at 21 feet, best two out of three elimination. Walt defeated the last three shooters with a total of six shots.

Many shooters found the grip frame on the single action revolver to be too short. Their little fingers wrapped around the bottom. Anderson then produced a very limited number of extended backstraps and matching

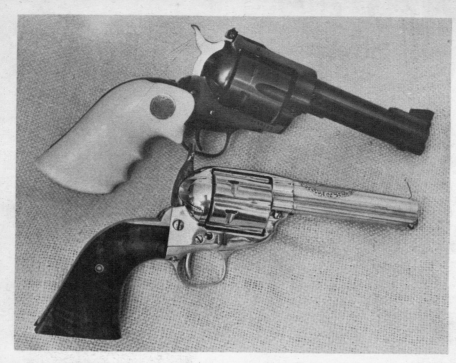

Top—Ruger 357 Blackhawk with custom Hogue Monogrips. Bottom—Ruger 45 "funny gun" has steel-lined aluminum barrel, reshaped frame, shaved trigger guard, full fluted cylinder, fanning hammer and Martin twisting stocks.

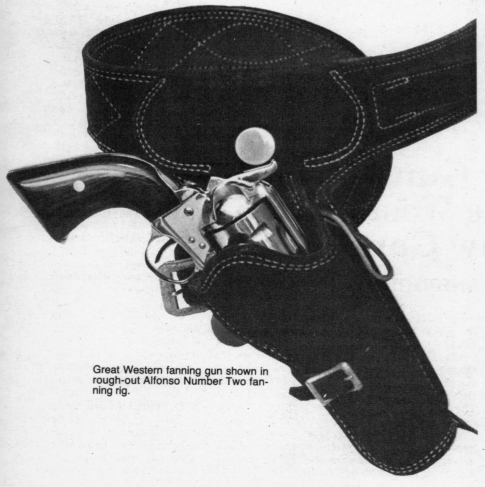

Great Western fanning gun shown in rough-out Alfonso Number Two fanning rig.

stocks on a custom basis. The bottom flat was replaced with an "S" curve that properly mated with the un-altered trigger guard assembly. This curve provided a rest for the little finger and added to the racy lines of the Colt single action.

I bought such a backstrap and matching walnut stocks at a gun show in St. Louis recently. The stocks are signed in ink "STYLED BY ANDY ANDERSON/4715 LANKERSHIM/N. HOLLYWOOD." Correspondence with Andy revealed that this is the only set he produced in walnut and is one of two sets made for movie star Steve McQueen. McQueen used a set made of sheep horn in the movie "Nevada Smith." His stuntman double wore the walnut set now in my collection.

The Anderson W&D rig mentioned earlier was the best of the rigs used for the thumbing draw. It included a steel lined holster with a steel lined hip plate on the back side of the gunbelt which anchored the rig in place on the shooter's hip without a tiedown strap. All Anderson rigs had a muzzle forward angle—called the muzzle rake—which prevented the gun muzzle from crossing any part of the shooters' body during the draw. This greatly increased safety.

One of the sport's better thumbers, Bill Corbin, produced an interesting action modification on the Colt. As we used our Colts harder and faster, they began to "skip"—the cylinder revolved so fast the bolt misses and the cylinder is out of time when the hammer falls, causing a misfire. Corbin modified the hand, so it acted as a secondary cylinder lock, much as in Colt's 1878 D.A. Frontier revolver.

The sport and spectacle of Fast Draw changed dramatically in the late 1950s with the introduction of the Walk and Draw event. Prior to this, all shooting was with the shooter stationary. The W&D event represented Hollywood's version of the classic western gunfight. Two shooters faced off at a distance of 120 feet, walked toward each other upon command, and drew and fired their blank-loaded single actions upon a visual start signal. Electronic fast-draw timers indicated the winner and the winning time in hundredths of a second. This event became very popular with spectators and was the basis for the Las Vegas National Championships sponsored by Colt Firearms and the Sahara Hotel in 1959, '60, '61 and '62.

W&D, however, created serious problems for the competitor. That little hammer spur was very evasive when it was swinging from the shooter's moving hip. Soon, many were fanning their sixguns. While not as fast as thumb cocking in the holster, fanning was much more consistent for the W&D.

Finally, a West Coast shooter found the answer. Curt Blakemore developed the "twist fan" draw, in which he fanned the gun while it was still holstered. This twist draw has the shooter squeezing the trigger at first hand contact and twisting out the sixgun clockwise so it is on its side with the muzzle just above the face of the holster, as the fanning hand sweeps by to hit the hammer spur and fire the shot. This is the fastest way known to draw and fire a single action revolver.

Blakemore dominated the sport with his new draw for two or three years. Drawing times for the W&D dropped from 44/100ths of a second for fastest shot of the 1959 National Championships, shot by new National Champion Gary Freymiller thumbing, to 31/100ths of a second in the 1962 Nationals, by National Champion Vance Anderson, twist fanning.

This constant fanning soon took its toll, as the Colt would not stand this abuse. It required constant tuning and repair to prevent the dreaded skipping. One obvious alternative gun was the new Ruger Blackhawk. The 357 Magnum Blackhawk was used by removing the rear sight and extending the hammer spur. The action was modified by clipping coils off of all the springs. The locking notches in the cylinder were deepened to prevent skipping and the guns lasted almost indefinitely. They were, however, too heavy for the super fast times. Enter the "Funny Gun."

We found that the Blackhawk cylinder diameter permitted boring for the 45 Colt cartridge. We shot only wax bullets with no powder charge and/or blanks, so there was no need for the strength of a steel barrel. The first aluminum fast draw barrels had rifled steel liners, but it wasn't long until a few shooter-machinists were turning out rifled aluminum barrels.

Once balloon targets were added for the blank shooting events the 45 Colt cartridge became the standard. Its greater powder capacity was an advantage when breaking four-inch diameter balloons at eight feet with nothing but burning powder. These early Rugers had steel ejector rod housings, which most shooters replaced with aluminum.

In a short time the standard fast draw funny gun had become an old model (three screw) 357 Ruger Blackhawk converted to 45 Colt caliber, with a 4⅝-inch rifled aluminum bar-

An Anderson Walk-and-Draw holster, showing the high plate behind the drop shank. Fast-draw Colt has custom Anderson backstrap and stocks and smooth hammer spur for thumb cocking while in the holster.

Author's 45 "funny gun" with Lalouette stocks in Ernie Hill "Sidewinder" rig. Extra steel shield in face of holster is to protect holster from the hot handloaded blanks.

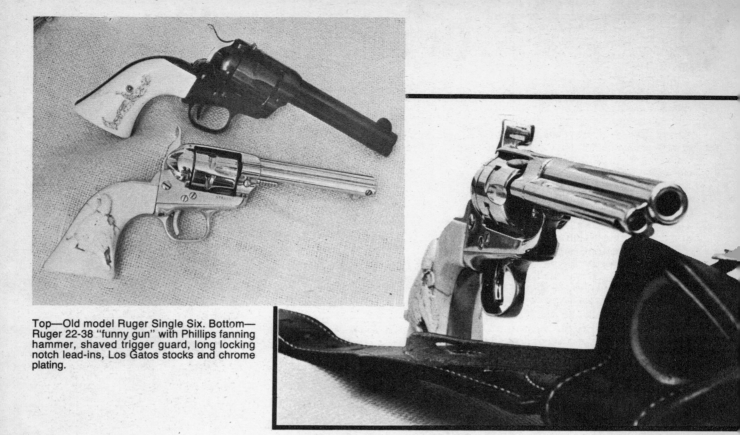

Top—Old model Ruger Single Six. Bottom—Ruger 22-38 "funny gun" with Phillips fanning hammer, shaved trigger guard, long locking notch lead-ins, Los Gatos stocks and chrome plating.

The Ruger 22-38 "funny gun." Chrome-plated with Phillips wide-spurred fanning hammer, long locking notch lead-ins and shaved trigger guard for right-handed shooter. Holster in foreground has a teflon liner to reduce wear.

Interior of a Ruger "funny gun" frame, showing hammer, trigger, locking bolt, coil locking bolt spring and steel filler block to right of the locking bolt.

rel, no sights, the topstrap of the frame ground down and rounded to resemble the traditional Colt and further reduce the weight, the cylinder notches deepened and the cylinder leades lengthened, the hammer spur extended upward not to exceed ½-inch above the topstrap, and the front of the trigger guard bow narrowed for faster trigger access.

Action modifications include cutting six coils off the mainspring for easier cocking, as well as placing a hardened steel block in the base of the backstrap. This block acts as a stop for the mainspring strut, preventing overtravel of the hammer. A steel block is also placed in the frame to prevent the locking bolt from battering its opening in the frame oversize. This would allow the locking bolt head to develop a sloppy fit in the frame which could cause skipping.

A unique funny gun was developed by one of the top shooters in the state of Texas. This Ruger's cylinder had been shortened from the front until it would just accept a cut-off 45 Colt case. The barrel had then been set back in the frame to match the short cylinder. Revolver barrel length is

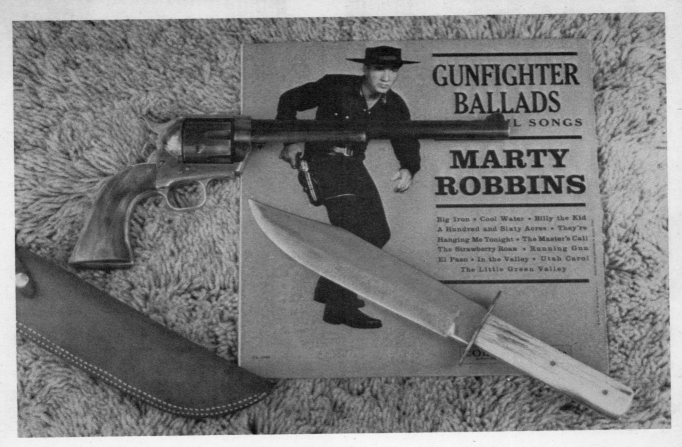

The Andy Anderson-Walt Ivie custom Big Iron seen here with Ivie's Bowie knife and Marty Robbins' album including the song "Big Iron."

correctly measured from the face of the cylinder. This "funny gun" technically had a barrel which met the minimum length of 4⅝ inches, yet the barrel projected from the frame the same as a four-inch barrel. This gun was barred from competition and soon reappeared with a standard aluminum barrel and the short cylinder lengthened to standard size with an aluminum spacer. This two-piece cylinder was the rage for a while, offering steel locking notches with minimum weight. It was the immediate predecessor of the current all-aluminum cylinder.

New heat treating technology has allowed the development of aluminum cylinders which withstand the pounding of constant fanning. Today's funny gun looks a great deal like the traditional Colt SAA, but except for the steel frame and action parts, it is constructed of aluminum. Most funny guns are chrome-plated, for ease of maintenance, especially when using black powder in the blanks.

Jim Martin, active in fast draw for 25 or 30 years, recently developed custom stocks to increase the twister's speed. Martin's stocks have flat sur-

The Big Iron mainspring, as reshaped by Andy Anderson for easier thumb cocking.

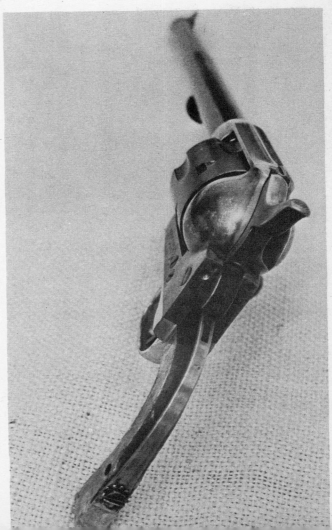

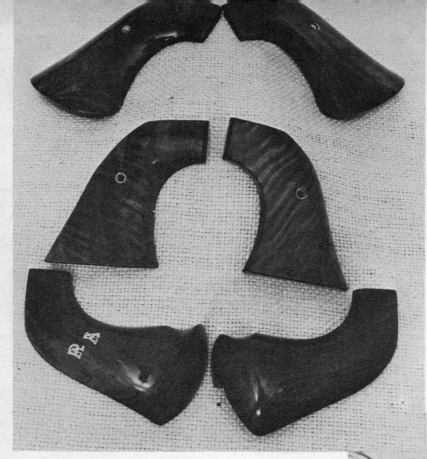

Custom fast draw stocks: Top—Set of extended stocks made for twisting by Larry Lalouette, finished by the author. Center—Jim Martin fancy walnut "funny stocks" for twist fan. Bottom—Extended stocks by the author. Bell-shaped contour provides palm swell and rest to anchor the hand.

Custom-extended backstrap and matching right-side stock panel as made by Andy Anderson.

Phillips fanning hammer with decorative file work by the author. Steel block in grip frame prevents overtravel of the hammer when it is fan-cocked.

Where Fast Draw started: Crosman 22 pellet gun was a trainer for many in the late 1950s. It was packaged with "Rules and Regulations For Fast Draw Competition."

faces on the rear of the right panel and the leading edge of the left panel. These opposing flats cant the six-shooter to the left as much as 15-20 degrees. When twisted into firing position, these stocks cause the shot to go higher, allowing the shot to be fired a few thousandths of a second faster and still have the muzzle elevation to break the balloon target.

Larry Lalouette, one of the best twisters in the sport, is currently producing extended stocks with a flat leading edge on the left side only, using the finger tips to flip the gun muzzle up for maximum elevation. Most of the fastest shooters in his home state of Kansas are using these beautiful stocks.

While the 45 Colt funny gun may be used for shooting wax bullets or blanks, a special wax bullets-only variation, the 22-38, was developed in the Midwest. Originally developed for economic reasons—a hobby gunsmith converted my first Colt Scout to 22-38 for $10.00—it has become recognized as the finest wax bullet fast draw gun available. This gun starts life as a three-screw Single Six in 22 Long Rifle. The action gets a standard fast draw tuneup and the hammer is modified for fanning. John Phillips, former fast draw gunsmith, manufactured a beautiful fanning hammer by cutting the original spur off, then dovetailing and silver soldering a new one on the top of the hammer body. The new spur projects straight up a half-inch above the topstrap, and a half-inch to the left of center for a right-handed shooter. These are the maximum dimensions allowed by the rules of the World Fast Draw Association.

Being meant for wax bullets, the 22-38 has a 38-caliber barrel in either steel or aluminum. The cylinder is what makes this funny gun different. It is bored out to accept front-loading of 38-caliber wax bullets, while the chamber end is 22 caliber for blanks, hence the 22-38. In use, the cylinder is removed for loading. Winchester or Remington blanks are fired in competition, and cheaper imported crimp blanks in practice. This is the fastest load available for the wax shooter. When one may lose the World Championship by a difference of 1/1000th of a second for the total contest, that's important and worth the trouble.

The ultimate extension of the 22-38 is two-time World Fast Draw Champion Ron Phillips' wax gun. Starting with a 22 Single Six, the firing pin was modified for centerfire and a second cylinder was made and chambered for the 9mm Luger cartridge.

Phillips uses the gun with 38 Red Jets powered by shotgun primers in the 22-38 cylinder in fast draw competition, and shoots in some of the Arizona live ammunition combat matches using the 9mm cylinder.

With the advent of the digital fast draw timer displaying times in thousandths of a second, all elements of the fast draw equation became critical. This includes hand-loaded blanks used to break the four-inch balloons at eight feet. The old standby load of a case full of 1F black powder wasn't good enough. Shooters experimented with different powders and combinations of powders. Today's funny blanks consist of a fast burning "kicker" used to achieve maximum velocity of the burning powder, a 1F black powder main charge, and a topping of slow-burning rifle powder in case of a windy day. My personal load consists of 2.5 grains Bullseye and 2.5 grains 3F black powder as the kicker, 25 grains of 1F black powder tamped lightly, with the remainder of the 45 Colt case filled with 4831 rifle powder. A thin card wad is seated on top and sealed with water glass. This mixture will break the most stubborn of balloons, and reaches out to eight feet faster than the all-black powder load.

The extent to which the Ruger funny gun is used is shown by professional exhibition shooter Joe Bowman. Bowman shot competitively in fast draw approximately 20 years ago. Since turning professional shooter he has appeared at numerous functions for Sturm, Ruger & Co., using a matched pair of Ruger fast draw funny guns which look more like Colts than like Rugers.

Just as twist fanning caused major changes in fast draw guns, it caused the development of new twisting rigs. Alfonso of Hollywood, another former Ojala employee, developed a line of fast draw holsters just for the fanner. For many years, the Alfonso Number Two was the standard twisting rig. It raised the gun higher, positioned it farther forward and out from the body, making it easier to reach the fanning hammer with the off-side hand. Holster angle was increased with the gun muzzle angled forward for speed and safety. All fast draw rigs have steel lined holsters as this is necessary to allow the revolver cylinder to revolve freely while the gun is being cocked in the holster.

Once the average shooter was using the twist fan draw, we all started looking for ways to make it faster. The holsters before the Alfonso were made to precisely fit the gun they

held. But now we wanted to twist the gun, and if the holster was oversize the gun could be twisted as it was drawn, rather than the slower draw-twist-fan sequence. It soon became standard proceedure to order a rig made for a Ruger Super Blackhawk with 4⅝-inch barrel, even though the gun to be used was a Ruger Blackhawk with ground-down topstrap. The smaller gun could be easily twisted clockwise while still in the oversize holster.

Two basic rules limit the speed possible in shooting blanks. These set a maximum holster angle of 45 degrees and the height of the adjustable balloon stand can not be below the buckle on the shooter's gunbelt. Current rules state that all of a 4⅝-inch barrel must be covered by the holster, so the holster fronts are cut down to expose all of the funny gun's topstrap.

Ernie Hill, of Phoenix, Arizona, has been shooting fast draw since he was three years old and currently holds the World Record for the fastest single standing reaction blank shot of .208 second. Ernie produces fast draw rigs (Ernie Hill Speed Leather) and recently developed his "Sidewinder" rig, which I prefer to call with all respect, the "Rule Beater." Hill claims that his rig allows a shooter to use the twist-fan style and shoot a reaction shot as fast as if he had the gun in his hand and fanned it. The "Sidewinder" takes advantage of the holster angle and balloon height rules. The holster pouch is 4½-inches front to back measured at the top. This permits the gun to lie at an angle of 60 degrees, although the face of the holster, where holster angle is measured, never exceeds 45 degrees. This extreme gun angle, combined with the low cut holster front, allows shots that clear the holster with almost no gun movement.

In order to get the balloon lower, where the super speed shots most often go, the gunbelt is cut on a special contour which places the belt buckle lower than the rest of the belt. With this new rule beater, today's top shooters are able to twist fan and break the balloon in times, including reaction, consistently under .250 second.

Just as the drag racer of the 1980s pulls to the start line in a fiberglass shell funny car that looks sort of like a family sedan, the Fast Draw shooter of the 1980s comes to the firing line wearing an aluminum funny gun in a steel lined funny holster which resembles the traditional Colt SAA revolver in a Hollywood rig, but not too closely. ●

THE EXTRAORDINARY
P.O. ACKLEY...

... the gunsmith who showed them how.

by LESTER WOMACK

WHILE COOLING my heels in an Army camp in 1944, I fired a letter off to P.O. Ackley. I apologized for writing at such a time but gave him some thoughts on a rifle I wanted to make up after the war. I promptly received a lengthy answer detailing the possibilities within my limitations—straightforward and no hard-sell. Highly impressed, I promised myself to meet this remarkable man some day. We have since visited and corresponded for many years.

Parker Otto Ackley was born in Granville, New York, on the 25th of May, 1903. He grew up on the family farm and hunted in the nearby woods, as did all the farm boys of the period. I asked him once when he first became interested in guns.

"When I was born, I guess. At least I never remember *not* being interested," he replied.

It was in those tender years that he started reworking guns. He decided his little Stevens Crack Shot 22 was in need of a new stock and built it a full length Mannlicher type.

"That was the first and about the *last* stock I ever made," he said.

Since then his interest in guns has been devoted to the metal work, leaving the wood to others.

Ackley graduated from Syracuse University in 1927, magna cum laude. He majored in Agriculture and took a number of engineering classes, along with the R.O.T.C. program. He returned to the family farm to apply his newly acquired knowledge and the first year produced a bumper crop of the finest potatoes known in the country. Times were bad, however, and there were no takers—even at ten cents a bushel.

The country was on a downhill skid into the Great Depression, and eastern states were the first to feel the pinch. Then the stock market crash of 1929 brought down the few small farmers that were left. Ackley managed to hang on a few more years, but he finally decided farming was a losing game.

It was about this time that he noticed an ad in the Arms Chest in the classified section of the *American Ri-*

fleman. Ross C. King had placed his gun shop on the market in Roseburg, Oregon. Ackley thought it over until a late spring freeze finished off his crop. That did it—he took the plunge. King wanted $2,000.00 for the whole set-up; half down and "the rest when you can." It didn't take long to settle affairs in New York. Ackley loaded Ma and the kids into the old Oldsmobile on Memorial Day, 1936, and headed West—never looking back.

Oregon may not have been exactly the land of milk and honey, but the little gun shop kept the wolf from the door. The Depression years never laid as heavily on the West as they did in the East. Guns in Oregon were working tools, and a lot of repair work was required to keep them functioning.

Ackley had always wanted to make rifle barrels, and he soon contacted an old friend by the name of Ben Hawkins who had been in the gun business nearly fifty years.

"Come on back to Cincinnati," Hawkins said. "Work for me and we'll teach you something about barrel making."

With the family taken care of in Oregon, Ackley headed back east. He began working with Hawkins' master barrel maker, a German who had begun his apprenticeship at the age of twelve in the Old Country. Seizing the bull by the horns, Ackley worked day and night, seven days a week, to learn as much as possible in the least amount of time. It was a golden opportunity and within a year he felt confident to go it alone in the barrel business.

Back home in Oregon, he started building a hand powered deep-hole drill and rifling machine. With his limited funds he could only tool up to bore one caliber, and he chose the 22. For larger calibers he could ream the 22 bore out. About this time he recieved an order from U.S. Hubble, an old Army Indian scout in Tensleep, Wyoming, to rebarrel a '98 Mauser action to 257 Roberts. After several days and a few sleepless nights, he turned out a barrel.

"Everything on that thing was wrong. I never saw a barrel warp as badly as that one," Ackley says today.

He threw it in the corner and tried to forget the whole thing. There it lay until a letter came from Hubble telling him in no uncertain terms to, "Git that barrel job up here!"

In desperation, Ackley finished the job and sent it off, fearing the repercussion that was bound to come.

The old timer went to rail-head to pick up his express package. Not one to put things off, he put a target up on a pile of cross ties in the railway yard and proceeded to shoot a pinwheel the

first time around. He sent this target and a glowing report off to Fred Ness, at the time Editor of the Dope Bag section of *The American Rifleman*.

"I never got caught up after that," P.O. says.

About the time he had worked the bugs out of the process and Ackley barrels were coming into good supply, World War Two threw a monkey wrench into the works, so to speak.

Without priority status, he was left high and dry without critical materials. Since he couldn't fight them, he decided to join them.

His R.O.T.C. commission from Syracuse came in handy here. He was sent to the Ogden Ordnance Depot in Utah to set up a repair program, which soon developed into a full arsenal overhaul facility. Here he worked with civilian gun-nuts such as Fred

P.O. Ackley in his Salt Lake City, Utah, shop late in 1977.

Barnes, the bullet man; Elmer Keith, the gun writer; and Ward Koozer, noted gunmaker of the period.

While repairing the Army's weapons, typewriters and what not, Ackley and Koozer decided to go into partnership after the war. They contacted George Turner in Cimarron, New Mexico, who had a gun shop to sell. By 1944, Ackley had enough points for an Army discharge, a deal was closed

ple, many of whom were gun-nuts. What better way for a gun lover to spend his time than visiting a gun shop? Since these people had time on their hands, the problem to the Ackley shop was obvious, a perplexing problem to any gunsmith. It was decided the best way to cope with the situation was to move out of town, and they built a shop several miles away. Suspecting the answer, I once asked

trainees, P.O. took a proposal to Dean C.O. Banta, head of the vocational school at Trinidad State Junior College. Banta was enthusiastic about a gunsmithing curriculum. The new president, Dwight C. Baird, soon had Ackley on the staff to head up the department. A flurry of activity produced enough space and machine tools to start the course, and January, 1947, saw the first students arrive on

Office and shop crew of P.O. Ackley and Company in front of the first Trinidad, Colorado, plant in early 1946. The boss is the only one with a necktie.

with Turner, and they were on their way to New Mexico.

The isolation of Cimarron was soon felt, and Ackley convinced the Ration Board of their need to move to a town with rail service. This proved to be Trinidad, Colorado. They were provided with gasoline ration stamps, and away they went.

They settled in downtown Trinidad and began producing the Turner mount (now the Ackley Snap-In Mount), Ackley rifle barrels, and custom built rifles. It was soon discovered that they were within walking distance of a great number of retired peo-

P.O. if this move solved his problem.

"Nope," he said ruefully, "They just brought their lunches!"

By 1946, Ackley was receiving letters in every mail from men wanting to work for his firm to learn the gun building business. Within a two-year period he received more than 4,000 letters, mine among them, from men eager for hands-on training in the industry. Most were ex-G.I.'s and wanted to take advantage of the G.I. Bill with its provision for on-the-job training.

Since the Ackley shop couldn't begin to accommodate such a number of

campus, and the first gunsmithing school with an academic background was under way. It continues to flourish, as popular as ever.

I got to Trinidad in 1949, and never have I seen a more enthusiastic group of people. Everywhere we went it was "gun talk;" students, instructors, even the townsmen, and P.O. Ackley was the center of it all. Machines in the shop classes were always filled. If for any reason a regular student was absent, someone was there to take his place. This was encouraged by the school and embraced wholeheartedly by the students. The place was a beehive of activity from before eight in the morning until after ten in the evening when they had to chase us out to lock up for the night.

Ackley's years of association with the students of Trinidad Junior College was a two-way street. With an inquisitive mind and a bent to experiment, he now had lots of enthusiastic help. All he had to do was suggest an experiment, and everyone was ready to go. It was at this time that we ran a series of blow-up tests on military rifle actions to determine their strength and suitability for sporter conversion. This was an eye-opener and remains the only scientific approach made to the subject.

Ackley had been making up wildcat cartridges for many years, and now he encouraged students to experiment with most anything within the limits of safety. He had developed many of his line of "improved" cartridges by altering the shoulder angle to 40° and reducing the taper to give the case greater powder capacity. In some instances the shoulder was also moved forward to take advantage of an overlength neck, producing an entirely new cartridge. Some were not necessarily improved by this treatment, and Ackley was the first to admit it if a cartridge turned out to be a turkey. To keep a damper on the students' heady enthusiasm, he insisted on a chronograph report before accepting any ballistic data. Figures don't lie, but liars do figure. The chronograph is an impartial judge.

Now and then someone mentions that he knows Parker Ackley personally, to which I can only reply: Not very well! To his friends he has always been known only as "Pee Oh." It seems that the Parker handle was hung on him when he was young and defenseless. It was simply his mother's family name and he acknowledges it with indifference.

Adulation of one's professor is nothing new, but in Ackley's case the students at Trinidad felt it was more than justified. In spite of his 16-hour days, he was always available to anyone in need of help. He gave freely of any information he might have. He used to say that anybody in the gun business who thought he had a trade secret wasn't kidding anyone but himself. He was always quick with a joke and could see the humorous side of most any situation.

We soon found that he was a man of firm convictions with a couple of favorite expressions for any occasion. Any item of less than the highest quality was "Just a total loss," and anything showing poor worksman-

ship was "Rougher than a boar's ass sewed up with a log chain."

Early in the course, Ackley pointed out to the students that gunsmithing wasn't necessarily a road to riches. Since a gunsmith must be proficient at machine work, wood work, heat treating, and a myriad of other skills, was the student also prepared to equip a shop? If not, did he have assurance of employment in an estab-

lished shop upon graduation? Even if he had his own shop and equipment at the time, was he willing to put in long hours at low pay in order to make a living?

A simple love of firearms wasn't enough to pull one through as the public wasn't disposed to pay a premium price for a man to work long hours on their weapons. As a hobby, you could take all the time you wanted, but gun work was done on a flat rate basis, and one must do the job as quickly as possible when your bread and butter depended upon it.

"If my wife hadn't had a good job, I

would have starved to death long ago," Ackley used to say, only half in jest.

The attrition rate among new gunsmiths has always been appalling. Thinking back, I can count all the men from my class still in the gun business on one hand—and have a few fingers to spare. In this manner, he tried to prepare us for the real World when we got out of school.

Turning the contour on one of his barrels, P.O. Ackley looks up from his lathe at P.O. Ackley, Inc., in February, 1950.

The 1939 catalog of Stoeger Arms Corporation listed a new self-loading rifle of the most advanced design. Built by the German firm of Heinrich Krieghoff, this weapon resembled a sexy over-under shotgun more than a rifle and was available for any rimless cartridge. The gas cylinder was about the same size as the barrel and extended to the muzzle. Gas was tapped from the barrel under the front sight and drove a piston rod back to operate the action. Ackley acquired one of these rifles in 8×60mm Magnum shortly after World War II. While I was at Trinidad, we admired this masterpiece of engineering often.

One day he said, "I'm going to fit another barrel in 7mm to that Krieghoff.

"Why!," I said astonished, "That 8×60 is perfect."

"Just a project." he said, and added, "The barrels will be completely interchangeable."

After burning a suitable portion of midnight oil, he came up with a dead ringer for the original barrel and no alteration of any kind was made on the rest of the rifle. Very few of the Krieghoffs were ever made and this is the only one I have ever heard of in

About the time I left Trinidad, Ackley and a number of students were pursuing an interesting ballistic venture. Since the Japanese Arisaka Type 38 (M1905) rifle is super strong, and the price was right—Arisakas sold for around ten bucks at the time—it was decided to see what would happen when a 6.5mm was rechambered to 7mm Mauser. Chambering reamers were re-ground with 6.5mm pilots and throating reamers made to cut the throat for the 175-gr. 7mm bullet. No alteration was made to the bore. Several rifles were rechambered in this manner and fired

dangerous to fire through the old J bore (.318″) Mauser rifle. All this is well and good for the keen experimenter, but many remain skeptical.

In 1951, the stockholders of P.O. Ackley, Inc. decided to sell the firm to Easton Engineering Company of Salt Lake City, Utah. Ackley taught his last class at Trinidad State Junior College and moved with the shop to the new location. He worked with the new owner for a short time to fulfill a contract obligation of sale. He then re-established his own shop and happily continued his experimenting. He has been in Salt Lake City ever since.

P.O. Ackley, right, and the author discuss a project early in 1950. This is the second location in Trinidad, called P.O. Ackley, Inc.

the United States. Shortly after finishing the 7mm barrel job, Ackley traded this rifle off to his good friends at the H.P. White ballistic laboratories. It does surface from time to time as it goes to a new owner. Each time I see a listing it always has a notation: "Extra 7mm barrel by P.O. Ackley."

For a number of years following World War One, Springfield rifle blow-ups were reported around the country. Many of these incidents were dismissed with a notation to the effect that the accident was no doubt caused by someone shooting "souvenir 8mm Mauser cartridges brought home from Europe by American servicemen." Ackley felt there were other valid reasons for these rifles coming un-glued since there is much evidence that oversized bullets do not necessarily increase chamber pressures.

from a test stand with factory loads. Only one showed any sign of excessive pressure and this was traced to a reamer cutting a chamber with undersized neck area. This was corrected with a proper reamer and it wasn't long before these rifles were being shot from the shoulder with no problems—except some said they kicked like a Government mule! Accuracy was good with all weights of bullets and cases indicated no more pressure than those fired in standard 7×57 rifles.

After moving to Salt Lake, Ackley built up pressure equipment and worked with different calibers. He found that oversized bullets had little effect on pressures *when* the bullet was free to leave the case mouth of the cartridge. He also exploded the myth that 8mm S bore bullets. (.323″) were

Now that he had complete control of his shop once again, he plunged into even more activity. He became the gunsmith editor of two national periodicals and began amassing material for a book. The first edition of *"Handbook for Reloaders and Shooters"* was published in 1962, Volume II appeared in 1966, and he is today preparing Volume III. These books contain a veritable treasure trove of technical gun lore, sure to excite and please any true gun-nut. In addition to articles by many authors, it gives information and loading data for most every wildcat cartridge in captivity. More than 50 of these cartridges have been developed by Ackley himself, with more to come.

Over the years Ackley has been in constant demand to serve as expert witness in court cases involving gun accidents. He avoids this dubious distinction like the plague.

"People can pull the dumbest stunt in the world with a gun and then want to sue someone when they get hurt," he says and feels that in our liberal society the cards are stacked against the manufacturer.

Recent cases throughout the country bear this out. When approached by a defense attorney to testify, he stated: "I'm no expert on the subject."

To which the lawyer replied, "You are just the man we want because everyone else *is*."

Ackley then begged off on grounds

There's valid reason for such a testimonial.

Men work in another's shop for two reasons: they love guns and they want to go into their own business. Ask any about pay and working conditions. They will tell you that each leaves a lot to be desired but they are willing to endure all this until they can start their own firm. The average gunsmith shop today is little more than an on-the-job training program for a never-ending line of aspiring gunsmiths. Since they are gun-nuts, they invariably have a pet project of their own under the bench, or in a drawer,

many in the custom gun business today.

Since moving to Salt Lake City, Ackley has sold his business twice, only to build it up again. Now that he is pushing 80, he says he has to slow down a bit. He does all the bench work himself and his daughter takes care of the office.

"Don't want to build it up again where I can't do the work myself and get into the hired help hassle," he says.

He has paid into the Social Security fund since its inception, and I asked him recently if he had considered re-

P.O. Ackley looks on, and perhaps kibitzes a bit, while Florence Conti operates a deep-hole drill. She will turn that bar into a famous Ackley rifle barrel in the Salt Lake City shop, 1977.

of poor hearing and let it go at that.

As he built up his shop to take care of the increased business, Ackley once again faced the old problem of competent help. To solve this, he took a bold step for the gun business; he hired women bench employees. Women had done a good job for him in the office and shipping departments, so why not hire them for the actual shop work? With proper training, he reasoned, they could do anything a man could do. Florence Conti was his last full-time shop employee, and I asked him one time how she worked out.

"Great," he said, "She puts in an hour's time for an hour's pay. She has eagerly learned to do every job and do it well. She isn't interested in going into business for herself. Best of all, I can leave the place and be assured the work goes on as if I was here."

that can be quickly retrieved when the boss steps out. Supplies mysteriously melt away via these personal jobs.

I asked Florence Conti what brought her into the gun business.

"I wanted a job," she said simply.

Taking another tack I said, "Do you do any shooting?"

"Only in test-firing shop guns," she said, and added, "I don't own any guns."

How many shop owners, I reflected, have dreamed of such an employee and never thought of hiring a woman?

Ackley views with dismay the recent encroachment of the lunatic fringe on the gun scene. He feels the para-military and survivalist mentality can do nothing to enhance the image of gun owners in the eye of the public. This thought is shared by

tirement. Apparently it hadn't even entered his head.

"Got too many things to do to even think of that nonsense," he snorted.

Over the years Ackley has had little time for hunting or shooting in general. The intriguing technical aspect of firearms has been his driving interest. He has had a passing interest in automobiles and still likes to travel occasionally. These trips usually take him and Mrs. Ackley into the open country of the West to poke into old mining camps and do a little rock-hounding. He enjoys taking his dogs for a romp on these outings. Still, the gun is his great interest, and the gun has treated him well. It has been his engrossing curiosity for these many years, and he has been able to make a comfortable living from it. Not everyone could. ●

Ye Olde Gunsmithing Tools

by M. L. BROWN

The tools tell the story almost as well as the guns.

TOOLS ARE THE cornerstone of human achievement and the craftsman is the catalyst using them to transform abstract concepts into reality.

Many common hand tools currently employed were conceived in prehistory. They were significantly improved with the advent of the Bronze Age, *circa* 4000 BC, and reached a higher plateau of sophistication as ferrous metals imparted more durability and strength in the Iron Age, *circa* 3000 BC. During the early Hallstatt period in western Europe (*circa* 800-500 BC), Celtic artisans introduced an astounding variety of innovative hand tools little altered at present from those original designs.

With the emergence of the Renaissance, *circa* AD 1325, and the introduction of gunpowder and guns, the venerable armorer of antiquity began to diversify and was gradually transformed into the gunfounder and the

gunsmith. By the late fifteenth century specialization was already evident in the European gunsmithing craft, exemplified by the introduction of rifled firearms in Germany *circa* 1460-1475 and the development there and in Italy of the complex wheel-lock ignition mechanism. It was also then that primitive machine tools were introduced for making guns and gunpowder.

In 1492, an unprecedented epoch of colonization and commerce began as the full impact of the Old World invasion fell on North and South America. As England, France, Holland, Spain, and Sweden bitterly confronted each other as well as hostile Indians in the savage struggle for ascendancy in North America there was an inordinate demand for cannon, firearms, gunpowder, and related ordnance; all had to be imported from Europe at considerable expense and great risk.

"The Colonists in America," as Charles W. Sawyer sagaciously re-

marked in *Firearms in American History,* "were the greatest weapon-using people of that epoch in the world."[1]

As such, they required skilled craftsmen to make and repair their arms. And of all the creative craftsmen identified with colonial America, the gunsmith was foremost among them. He frequently labored with crude hand tools under the most primitive conditions to fashion or mend a complex and vital commodity needed for survival. The influence of the gunsmith and the production of firearms on nearly every aspect of colonial endeavor cannot be overstated, and that pervasive influence continued beyond the colonial period.

The earliest American gunsmiths were trained as apprentices at the bench and forge of Old World masters, bringing to the New World specialized skills, hand tools, and the crude, manually operated machines affiliated with the craft.

In colonial America the flow of fire-

Table 1

Fig. 1: Wood auger
Fig. 2: Pointed awl
Fig. 3: Rat-tail rasp
Fig. 4: Spring compass
Fig. 5: Multi-sided barrel breach reamer
Fig. 6: Marking gauge
Fig. 7: Marking slate
Fig. 8: Chisel
Fig. 9: Cleaning rod
Fig. 10: Bore scraper
Fig. 11: Stock template
Fig. 12: Carbine barrel
  (1) cross-section
  (2) breech plug
Fig. 13: Barrel components
Fig. 14: Fish-tongue chisel
Fig. 15: Offset stock-inletting chisel
Fig. 16: Offset ramrod groove gouge
Fig. 17: Crow bill scraper
Fig. 18: Plane blade, stock inletting
Fig. 19: Plane blade, ramrod rounding
Fig. 20: Plane blade, rounding forestock
Fig. 21: Two-piece lockplate alignment template
Fig. 22: Single hole alignment template
Fig. 23: Cherry, with bow drum
Fig. 24: Taphandle (see Fig. 35)
Fig. 25: Bow drill pressure plate (see Figs. 23, 26, and 27)
Fig. 26: Bow, of bow drill
Fig. 27: Drill, of bow drill
Fig. 28: Offset file
Fig. 29: Stamping die
Fig. 30: Scriber
Fig. 31: Mainspring vise
Fig. 32: Grinding wheel bit, attached to bow drum (see Fig. 23)
Fig. 33: Countersink, bow drum
Fig. 34: Bevelling vise
Fig. 35: Tap, internal threads
Fig. 36: Die (screwplate)
Fig. 37: Bullet worm
Fig. 38: Double calipers

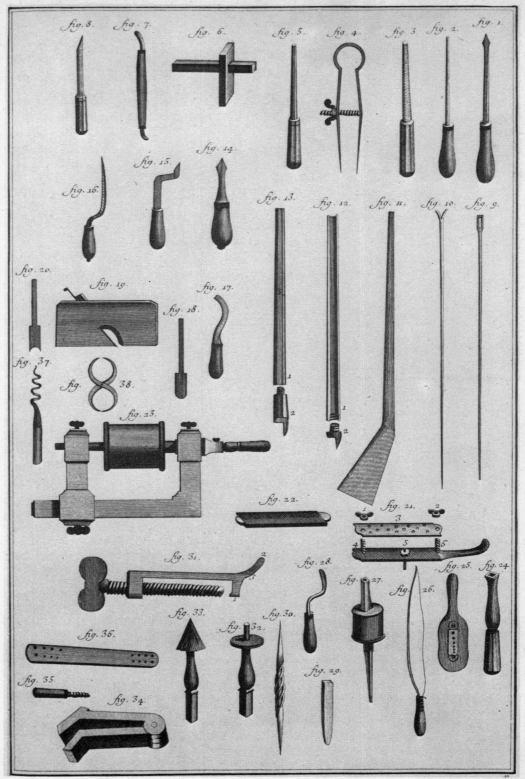

Arquebusier Plate IV from Vol. 1, *Recueil de Planches Sur Les Sciences et Les Arts* (The Collection of Plates Pertaining to the Sciences and the Arts) of the eleven volume supplement to Denis Diderot and Jean La Rond d'Alembert, *L'encyclopédie, ou Dictionnaire Raisonné des Sciences, des Artes et des Métiers* (The Encyclopedia, or Analytical Dictionary of the Sciences, and the Arts and Crafts), Paris, 1770. Courtesy of the Special Collections Library, University of South Florida, Tampa.

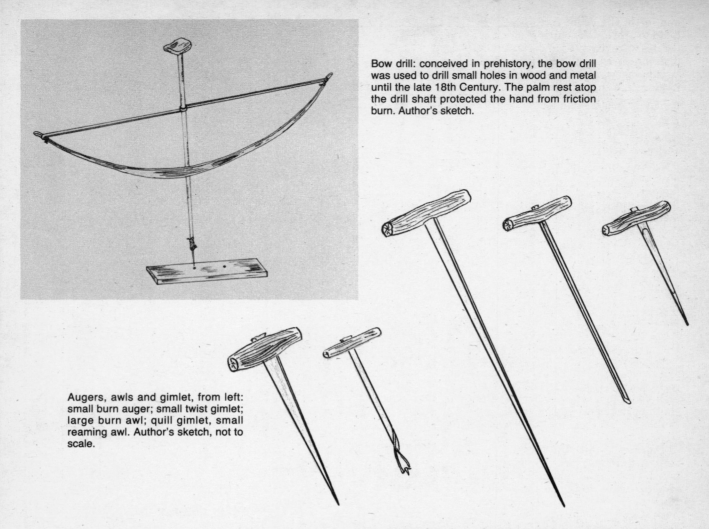

Bow drill: conceived in prehistory, the bow drill was used to drill small holes in wood and metal until the late 18th Century. The palm rest atop the drill shaft protected the hand from friction burn. Author's sketch.

Augers, awls and gimlet, from left: small burn auger; small twist gimlet; large burn awl; quill gimlet, small reaming awl. Author's sketch, not to scale.

arms, firearms components, and the other requisites of the gunsmithing craft was initially tenuous at best, often interrupted by European wars and the long, perilous journey across the capricious Atlantic. Consequently, the gunsmith was given the alternatives of making what he needed or cannibalizing damaged and obsolete firearms for their parts. As a result the early gunsmith became a creative, self-reliant artisan usually working independently in what was a simple household enterprise often established on the knife-edge of civilization, where the guns were needed most.

Table 1 is a list of common 18th-century French gunsmithing tools. The Table is keyed to the illustration captioned *Arquebusier* (Gunsmith), the numbers reading right to left. The hand tools depicted are similar to those utilized throughout Europe *circa* 1770 and they are representative of the gunsmithing tools available there two centuries earlier as well.

A hand tool commonly used by the early gunsmith was the bow drill, its origin traced to the innovative fire-making implements of prehistory (*q.v. Arquebusier,* figs. 23, 25, 26 and 27). The bow drill was used to bore small holes for pins employed to attach the barrel to the stock, for lockplate and sideplate screws, for the breech vent (touchhole), and any others required. Not until the late 18th century was the venerable bow drill entirely supplanted by the bitstock (brace).

Boring holes in gunstocks was also early accomplished with plain awls, small hand augers, the quill and the twist gimlet, and "burn" awls; the points of the latter heated in the forge and pressed into the wood with a twisting motion.

The innovative brace was introduced during the late 17th century, its frame initially made of naturally shaped, seasoned hardwood. The handgrip (elbow) freely rotated around a palm rest and, as the chuck was integral with the elbow, it turned the bit when rotated. The iron bit with its steel cutting edge was secured in the chuck by a lead collar.

By about 1700 wrought iron braces emerged, utilizing interchangeable bits fixed in a stationary chuck by a wedge or lock screw. Some bits had wedge-shaped butts corresponding to the chuck recess. The steel edge of the bit was forged integral with the helical (spiral) body; the steel was folded into the iron in a method then commonly used to make axe blades.

Used in conjunction with the bow drill and the brace was the gunsmith's cherry. The French specimen depicted (*q.v. Arquebusier,* fig. 23) extends from the right side of the bow drill drum. The cherry was made of steel, its head displaying a series of cutting edges; its shape gave it its name. The date the cherry first appeared remains disputed, though it was known in the 17th century.

The cherry was used for rounding the priming pan cup, beveling (chamfering) the internal circumference of a gun muzzle, and in shaping bullet mould cavities. As seen in fig. 23, the cherry was fixed in the bow drum with the bow string looped around the drum. As the bow was "sawed" back and forth, the drum reciprocally rotated to provide the cutting action.

Files were the most important hand tools employed by the early gunsmith because they were the most versatile implements then available for shaping and removing the hardest of metals. Introduced by Celtic craftsmen during the early Hallstatt period, files were handmade until the late 19th century.

Files were utilized by the gunsmith for many purposes, among them shaping and smoothing breech and barrel flats, tapering barrels, shaping and smoothing the lockplate and its small components, and finishing the rough castings of brass and iron buttplates, sideplates, trigger guards and the like.

The early American gunsmith exhibited a virtuosity with the file unknown to his modern counterpart accustomed to using sophisticated machine tools, and in the colonial period there were a greater variety of files in general use than at present. A 1739 inventory of the hand tools needed to equip a Hudson's Bay Company trading post gunsmithery lists 29 files ranging in size and cut from a large "ruff" (rough) to a small, half-round bastard.[2]

The files in the 1739 inventory are similar to those retrieved in September, 1964, by a Canadian-U.S. archaeological team diving in the Granite River at Horsetail Rapids on the Minnesota-Ontario border. They recovered intact a bundle of 30 files lost when a fur trader's canoe capsized. The files were made between 1774 and 1797 by Nicholas Jackson who was active from *circa* 1758 to 1828 in Sheffield, England.[3]

In addition to files, abrasive stones were used to smooth and polish cast furniture and lock components. Applied wet or dry, emery powder was used to lap and polish bores or to bring a lustre to wrought or cast firearms components.

Barrel lug pins, lock pins, trigger pins, sling swivel rivets, and brads were handmade by the gunsmith from suitable wire, most of it imported during the colonial period. Coin silver, sheet silver, German silver, and brass wire used for ornamentation were formed and sized with a wire-drawing tool.

One of the most difficult problems encountered by the early gunsmith was making screws. Breech plug tang screws and lockplate screws used in early firearms were more akin to the modern threaded bolt than the common, helical woodscrew introduced during the 17th century. Screw-mak-

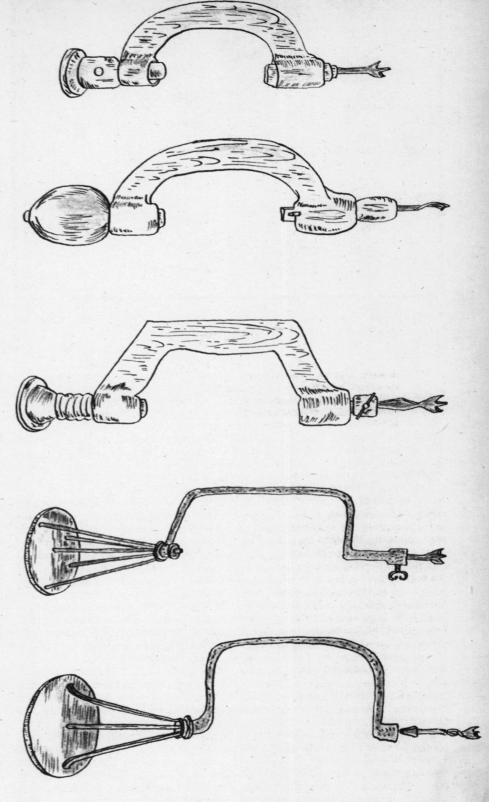

Braces or bitstocks, top to bottom: All wood New England-style brace with steel-tipped iron bit held by lead collar, 1690-1725; all wood pumpkin-handle New England-style brace with bit held by lead collar and wedge, 1715-1730; all wood Pennsylvania-style brace with bit held by turnscrew, 1765; wrought iron brace, New England, with bit held by turnscrew, 1700; wrought iron brace, Pennsylvania, with bit held by wedge-shaped chuck. Author's sketch, not to scale.

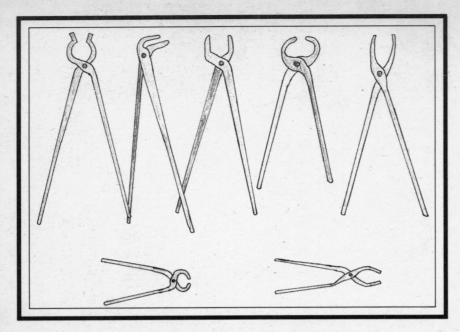

Tongs, from left: hammer tongs; offset barrel skelp tongs; flat bit tongs; large pincers; hammer tongs. Small pincers and small hammer tongs shown below. Author's sketch, not to scale.

ing was a time-consuming task with problematic results.

During the early colonial period in North America most gunscrews were imported; however, by the beginning of the 18th century, the innovative screwplate was commonly encountered. Precisely when the screwplate emerged in Europe remains conjectural though it was probably in the early 14th century (*circa* 1325). The screwplate continued to be employed until the early 19th century when it was rendered obsolete by the invention of screw-turning lathes.

The steel screwplate served as a die; its surface perforated with a series of holes corresponding in diameter to the desired screw thread size, and each hole featured a sharp, internal edge. Suitable wrought iron round stock, softer than steel, was forced through the hole with a twisting motion; the sharp die edge cut the male thread.

Equally innovative taps *(q.v. Arquebusier,* fig. 35) were used to cut the corresponding female threads in the screw hole. The tap, also made of steel and resembling the gunscrew, was forced into the screw hole with a twisting motion; the sharp, external edges forming the threads. Large taps, often tapered, were used to cut the female threads in the breech of the barrel when a threaded breech plug was used.

Lock components and mountings were nearly always cast prior to the mid-19th century when machine

swedging became popular. Bullet moulds and component moulds differed in design though they were both made of various materials including brass, iron, soft stone like soapstone or sandstone, and occasionally wood. Large components like patchbox covers and sideplates, buttplates, and trigger guards were usually cast in sand moulds.

Thin sheet brass and silver used for some mountings and ornamentation like stock inlays or signature plates were cut to shape with shears or formed by a swedge, an implement made of hardwood or metal in a single or two-piece unit and employed in conjunction with hammering.

The single swedge was male or female, *i.e.* the male displaying a raised design and the female an incised pattern of the desired object such as a ramrod guide. The gunsmith hammered the sheet metal in or around the single swedge to form the object. With the two-piece swedge, the thin metal was inserted between the halves and then hammered.

A variety of swedges were also used to shape wrought iron taken from the forge, among them hammer swedges. Hammer swedges, known also as rounding tools, came in various sizes with the head displaying a groove. They were generally employed by the gunsmith for rounding the roughly forged barrel skelp (blank) or strengthening the longitudinal or helical seam resulting from either of the barrel-making techniques then em-

ployed. The swedge head groove corresponded to the barrel diameter and the groove cut into the face of the barrel anvil.

Other hammers were used by the gunsmith, primarily distinguished by weight and the face and peen design of the head. Forging hammers had flat head faces and a sharp peen for creasing or notching when it was desired to fold the iron as when forging skelps. Hammers with non-ferrous heads of brass, copper, and lead were used in barrel-straightening or on other finished iron work to prevent marring the surface because they were softer than wrought iron or steel.

Mallets with leather or wooden heads were generally used when working non-ferrous sheet metal for ornamentation and mountings or for driving brads as in attaching the patchbox sideplates to the stock, the soft heads protecting the metal surface.

An assortment of tongs and pincers were employed by the gunsmith for grasping and bending the charcoal-fired wrought iron worked on the anvil. Tongs are identified by the bit (jaw) design; barrel-forging tongs displaying a short, flat upper bit and a longer lower bit which was slightly rounded; thus making it easier to turn and press the heated barrel skelp around the mandrel during the barrel-making process.

The mandrel was a long iron rod occasionally provided with a T-shaped handle and it was used by the gunsmith when forging the skelp into a tube (cylinder) to form the barrel. Depending on the required length, two or more skelps were needed to make the barrel. Inserted in the roughly forged cylinder the mandrel, slightly smaller than bore diameter, prevented the barrel from collapsing as it was worked on the grooved anvil.

The early gunsmithery often featured two kinds of anvils, one a common blacksmith's anvil with a flat surface and the other a barrel-making anvil with a grooved surface; the semi-circular grooves varying in width to correspond with the desired barrel diameters. The grooves simplified controlling the shape of the skelp as it was forged around the mandrel. On the early 19th-century American frontier the barrel anvil was often referred to as a buffalo head.[4]

Another indispensable gunsmithing tool was the bench vise, a practical way to secure large objects when working on them. The bench vise featured iron or wood jaws; the latter usually found faced with iron. To prevent damage to the work surface, the vise jaws were normally covered with brass or lead plates. When, in 1794, South Carolina gunsmith John Milnor died in Charleston, he bequeathed to his son ". . . my Smiths pair of Bellows, an Anvil & Vice [sic]."[5]

Hand vises were used to hold or clamp small firearms components, the most common variety known as the mainspring vise. The mainspring vise compressed the flat, powerful leaves of the spring which simplified removing or replacing it in the lock. During the French and Indian War (1754-1763) colonial militia sergeants carried a mainspring vise and an assortment of springs in the event one had to be replaced in the field; a practice also encountered during the American Revolution (1775-1783) and thereafter.

Also considered tools are the gunsmith's workbench and charcoal-fired bellows forge. The large wood workbench was conveniently located near a window for light and the space beneath it was used for storage. During the early colonial period the brick or fieldstone forge was often as not separate from the gunsmithery; however, it was usually covered for protection from the elements. Interior forges had a chimney for draught and exhaust. In small forges a hand bellows fed oxygen to the fire, increasing the temperature when required. In large forges the leather bellows was usually attached to a flue leading to the firebox and it was pumped by a foot treadle or a pole-and-chain arrangement operated manually.

The early gunsmith was also an adept wood-worker, using a variety of tools for making stocks. Gouges, chisels, awls, augers, planes, clasp knives, spokeshaves, saws, slickers, draw knives (snitzels, the so-called Pennsylvania-Dutch called them), rasps, and various grades of sandpaper were employed to cut, shape, and mortise the stock for the barrel, lockplate, trigger plate, trigger guard, patchbox, breech plug tang, inlays, signature plates, band springs, buttplates, and other furnishings.

The previously cited 1739 inventory listed, besides the files, five kinds of rasps: (1) Large, fine, half-round; (2) Small, fine, half-round; (3) Small, half-round; (4) Small, coarse; and (5) Coarse.

The forestock and the belly and the comb of the buttstock were rounded with a hollow (rounding) plane. The forestock interior, where the barrel was bedded, was roughed out with gouges and chisels and then smoothed with a bedding plane. The hollow

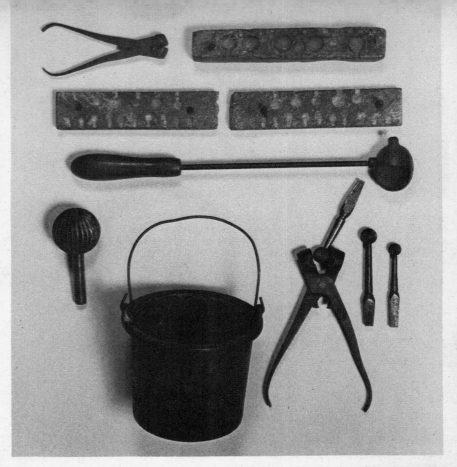

Tools and accessories: Top left—34-cal. iron bullet mould, ca. 1835; top right—single half of rare multiple cavity soapstone bullet mould casting 67- and 34-cal. balls and assorted bird shot sizes, 18th Century; immediately below—soapstone mould casting 30- and 32-cal. balls and assorted birdshot, back of one half marked SHENANDOAH, other engraved with sunburst, 18th Century; center—ladle with pour spout and wood handle, ca. 1840; center left—large cherry for wall gun, 18th Century; center right—68-cal. cherry with 68-cal. bullet mould, ca. 1850, and two cherries, calibers 65 and 45, ca. 1845; bottom—pot for melting lead, 19th Century. Courtesy, Eagle Americana Shop and Gun Museum, Strasburg, Pa. Charles L. Maddox, Jr. photo.

Gunsmithing/blacksmithing forge, 17-18th Century: author's sketch from an exterior forge reconstructed at Colonial Williamsburg, Williamsburg, Va.

Gunsmith's bench, bench vise, and barrel anvil with mandrels: Bench vise (left) has partially formed barrel section (skelp) fastened in jaws. Barrel anvil (right) has five grooves, concave side for making ladles; mandrels rest against anvil. Courtesy, Pennsylvania Farm Museum of Landis Valley, Lancaster, Pa. Charles L. Maddox, Jr. photo.

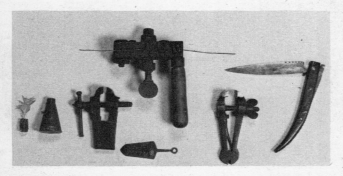

Gunsmithing tools and accouterments: Top—wire-drawing tool, 19th Century. Center, from left—tin oil can with cork stopper and feather applicator, 18th/19th Century; mainspring vise, ca. 1795-1815; mainspring vise, ca. 1800-1840; handmade clasp knife, ca. 1815. Bottom—small screwplate, ca. 1795-1810. Courtesy, Americana Shop and Gun Museum, Strasburg, Pa. Charles L. Maddox, Jr. photo.

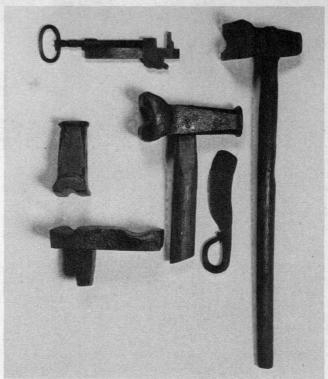

Gunsmithing tools: Top left—mainspring vise, ca. 1720-1750 (note similarity to vise in *Arquebusier,* Fig. 31); right—hammer swedge, 19th Century; center—hammer swedge (short handle) with flint striker adjacent (knapping tool for making gunflints), 18th Century; far left—hammer swedgehead, 19th Century; bottom left—anvil swedge, bottom projection fits hole in blacksmith's anvil, 19th Century. Courtesy, Eagle Americana Shop and Gun Museum. Charles L. Maddox, Jr. photo.

Stocking planes: Left—bedding plane for inletting forestock, ¾-in. cut, 19th Century; center—rounding plane for forestock, ¾-in. cut, 19th Century; right—*Snitzel* (draw knife) for shaping stock, 19th Century. Courtesty, Eagle Americana Shop and Gun Museum. Charles L. Maddox, Jr. photo.

Gunsmithing tools and accouterments: Top left—small grease horn for lubricating rifle ball patches, 18th Century; top right—hand-carved barrel plug (tompion), 18th Century; upper center—two braces, 19th Century; center—iron ladle, 18th-19th Century; lower center—stock inletting tool for bedding, 19th Century; bottom left—handmade awl or scriber, 18th-19th Century; bottom right—handmade saw, 18th-19th Century; bottom—handmade punch with corncob handle for removing pins, 18th-19th Century, and handmade hammer. Courtesy, Mercer Museum, Bucks County Historical Society, Doylestown, Pa. Charles L. Mattox, Jr. photographer.

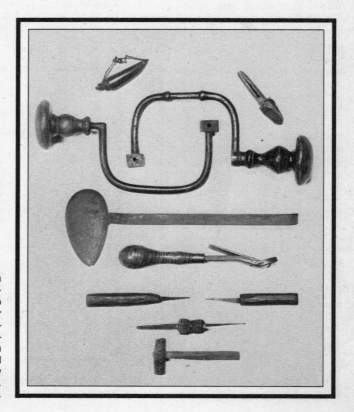

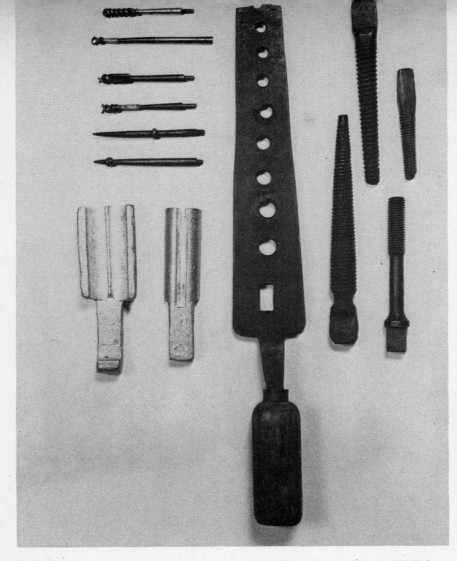

Gunsmithing tools: Top left—ball screws (worms) and wipers, for extracting lead balls from the barrel and for cleaning, 19th Century; bottom left—two-piece swedge for shaping sheet brass to form forestock cap for Pennsylvania-Kentucky rifles; raised center and corresponding groove provided ramrod channel, 18th/19th Century; center—large screwplate, rectangular recess near wood handle served as tap wrench, 19th Century; right—group of four taps, three tapered, used for cutting threads in breech, 19th Century. Courtesy, Eagle Americana Shop and Gun Museum, Strasburg, Pa. Charles L. Maddox, Jr. photo.

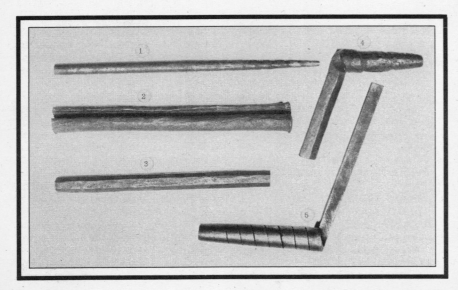

Mandrel and barrel sections, 18th and 19th Century. (1) Barrel mandrel. (2) Partially formed barrel skelp with longitudinal seams; a technique used in making musket and fowling piece barrels. (3) Partially formed barrel skelp with flats file-formed. (4) Partially formed barrel skelp with helical (spiral) seam; a technique used in making fowling piece barrels. (5) Partially formed barrel skelp with helical seam; seams were hammer-welded with the mandrel inserted to prevent the cylinder from collapsing. Courtesy, Eagle Americana Shop and Gun Museum. Charles L. Maddox, Jr. photo.

plane produced a concave cut and the bedding plane a convex cut. The sides of the buttstock were curved with a *snitzel* or a spokeshave — the latter a wheelwright's tool — and the rough surface was removed by sandpapering.

After linseed oil was hand-rubbed into the stock as a preservative, the wood swelled slightly and it was simultaneously smoothed and polished by forcefully rubbing it with a "slicker" in a process called "boning." Slickers were simply hard beef bones though some early gunsmiths preferred turkey wing bones because of their natural curvature.

The most difficult problem confronting the gunsmith was whether the barrel, rifled or smoothbore, was as absolutely straight as he could make it; a crooked barrel was inaccurate no matter how precise it was bored or how perfect the rifling.

In rifled firearms the barrel was straightened before the rifling was cut, the former process evolving in the late 15th century though not applied to smoothbore firearms until the sport of shooting birds in flight became popular during the early 17th century. A time-consuming chore mastered by few gunsmiths, barrel straightening is one of the earliest forms of specialization identified with the craft and it is currently employed by a select handful of master gunsmiths creating custom shotguns, gun factories apart. Not until the late 19th century were machines designed for straightening barrels.

The initial step in barrel straightening was to polish the bore. The bore was then scrupulously cleaned and transversed with a fine silk thread stretched taut between the ends of a wooden bow. With the bow held to prevent the thread from touching the bore surface, the barrel was raised to a natural light source. Casting an easily observed shadow on the polished bore surface, the thread revealed any irregularities if its shadow deviated from a straight line.

Where deviations were found, the barrel exterior was chalk-marked at those points corresponding to the interior, the thread removed, and the barrel placed in an anvil groove where the marked areas were tapped sufficiently hard with a "soft" hammer to bring them in alignment. The process was repeated until no irregularities could be detected.

During the early 19th century an alternate method of barrel straightening known as "truing by shade" was introduced for smoothbore musket barrels in the U.S. national armories at Springfield, Mass., and Harper's Ferry, VA.[6]

In the "truing by shade" process, employed during the War of 1812 and thereafter, the barrel straightener peered through the polished bore at a diagonal line applied to a window pane or a framed glass; the line corresponding to the thread used in the bow method. Irregularities were corrected in the same manner.

As the century progressed, small arms bores were substantially reduced and smoothbore muskets were replaced by breech-loading rifled firearms; however, at Springfield Armory as late as 1880 it was considered an outstanding day's work if 40 to 50 barrels had been straightened using the shade-truing techniques.[7]

That barrel straightening was a crucial technique can be successfully argued by an incident which transpired during the Civil War (1861-1865). The Confederate Ordnance Department experienced a production loss of 360 rifles a month at the Richmond (Va.) Armory because barrel-straightener and militiaman John Jones was killed defending the city during Col. Ulrich Dahlgren's raid of March 3, 1864.[8]

The colonial gunsmith generally made his own tools during his apprenticeship and thereafter repaired or replaced them when necessary; however, by about 1750, as specialization in manufactured implements increased because of mechanization and the proliferation of machine tools fostered by the advent of the Industrial Revolution, the gunsmith frequently purchased tools as well as many of the firearms components formerly made by hand. As early as 1755, Pennsylvania riflesmiths in the Reading vicinity bought pre-bored barrels from the forging, boring, and grinding mills active along Wyomissing Creek.[9]

The inordinate demand for firearms during the American Revolution saw the number of barrel-forging mills escalate in the colonies and there was a commensurate increase in the use of water-driven boring and grinding machines. By 1785 there emerged in France a revolutionary concept in arms-making pioneered by Parisian musket maker Honoré Blanc who introduced the radical technique of producing firearms using interchangeable components made entirely by machine.[10]

Before the turn of the century Blanc's concept was applied to firearms manufacture in the infant U.S. by Eli Whitney and Simeon North and by 1824 it had been perfected at Harper's Ferry Armory by John Harris Hall. Therafter the innovative concept was rapidly accepted by other arms-makers in the private sector who employed numerous workmen in factories expressly designed to manufacture firearms; thus, by about 1835, the character and the complexion of the gunsmithing craft as an individual enterprise gradually diminished in the United States.

Nevertheless, it cannot be disputed that the independent, self-reliant gunsmith working with a wide variety of hand tools in his small shop made a major contribution to our unique technological history. Nothing speaks more dramatically or eloquently about his skilled craftsmanship than the raw metal and wood now transformed into one of the many firearms that have survived to remind us of our rich and colorful cultural heritage. ●

Notes

1 *Op. cit.*, 29.
2 S. James Gooding, *The Canadian Gunsmiths 1608 to 1900* (West Hill, Ontario: 1962), 32-33.
3 Robert C. Wheeler, et al., *Voices from the Rapids: An Underwater Search for Fur Trade Artifacts 1960-1973* (Archaeology Series No. 3, Minnesota Historical Society, St. Paul: 1975), 23-25, 59-61, 95.
4 Charles E. Hanson, Jr., *The Plains Rifle* (Harrisburg: 1960), 16.
5 Henry J. Kauffman, *Early American Gunsmiths 1650-1850* (New York: 1952), 67.
6 Felicia Johnson Deyrup, *Arms Making in the Connecticut Valley* (York, Pa: 1970), 204.
7 Ibid.
8 Frank E. Vandiver, *Ploughshares Into Swords: Josiah Gorgas and Confederate Ordnance* (Austin: 1952), 235.
9 M. L. Brown, *Firearms In Colonial America: The Impact on History and Technology, 1492-1792* (Washington: 1980), 272.
10 Ibid., 380-381, 383, 386.

Bibliography

Brown, M. L. *Firearms In Colonial America: The Impact on History and Technology, 1492-1792.* Washington, 1980.
Deyrup, Felicia Johnson. *Arms Making in the Connecticut Valley.* York, Pa., 1970.
Farnham, Alexander. *Tool Collectors Handbook, 2nd ed.* Stockton, N.J., 1972
Gooding, S. James. *The Canadian Gunsmiths 1608 to 1900.* West Hill, Ontario, Canada, 1962.
Gunnion, Vernon, and Hopf, Carroll. *The Blacksmith: Artisan Within the Community.* Harrisburg, 1972.
Hanson, Charles E., Jr. *The Plains Rifle.* Harrisburg, 1960.
Hindle, Brooke. *Technology in Early America.* Chapel Hill, 1966.
Kauffman, Henry J. *Early American Gunsmiths 1650-1850.* New York, 1952.
———, *The Pennsylvania-Kentucky Rifle.* Harrisburg, 1959.
Sloan, Eric. *A Museum of Early American Tools.* New York, 1964.
Smith, Elmer L. *Early Tools and Equipment.* Lebanon, Pa., 1973.
Vandiver, Frank E. *Ploughshares Into Swords: Josiah Gorgas and Confederate Ordnance.* Austin, 1952.
Wheeler, Robert C., et. al. *Voices From the Rapids: An Underwater Search for Fur Trade Artifacts 1960-1973.* St. Paul, Minn., 1975

Acknowledgements

The author expresses his gratitude to the Smithsonian Institution Press, Washington, D.C., for permission to use material from his *Firearms In Colonial America: The Impact on History and Technology, 1492-1792* upon which this article is partially based. Further, he thanks for their co-operation the directors and staffs of the Mercer Museum, Bucks County Historical Society, Doylestown, Pa., and the Pennsylvania Farm Museum of Landis Valley, Lancaster, Pa. In addition, he appreciates the assistance of Vincent Nolt, Owner/Curator, Eagle Americana Shop & Gun Museum, Strasburg, Pa., and photographer Charles L. Maddox, Jr., Doylestown, Pa.

This relic of African days still does the job. From Ken Waters, its owner, we learn . . .

THE STORY

The hardware at the receiver ring shows this to be a takedown. From Westley Richards in 318, it belonged first to a British officer.

OF A RIFLE

THIS IS THE story of a rifle, but it must commence with a tale about a man, a man of action to whom big game hunting was a way of life and the rifle an extension of his will. Together, they went repeatedly in harm's way.

For a British officer in India in late 19th Century, leaves long enough to permit going to England were seldom and the abundance and variety of hunting within the sparse limits of military pay provided an altogether satisfying alternative. To a young lieutenant of the 2nd Bengal Cavalry, Himalayan bear and ibex along the Northern Frontier, Indian deer and goural in the lower hill country, and best of all, the great striped tiger must have been powerful lures. For relatively few rupees, he could organize his own hunting party.

That was true for hundreds of officers in the old British Indian Army who chose big game hunting as a principal form of recreation. I've chosen to write about a man with the unlikely name of Vesey Mangles Stockley who successfully combined vocation and avocation.

As a subaltern under General Wolseley in 1882, he had helped defeat the forces of Arabi Pasha at Tel-el-Kebir. Then came orders to India where a series of duty assignments kept him until the end of the century. In 1900, Captain (or perhaps it was by then

Major) Stockley was in China as part of the multi-national force putting down the Boxer Rebellion. Then, he returned to India where, at some undetermined point in time, he was appointed to command the 16th Cavalry, Indian Army, with the rank of colonel.

Polo after five when the day's heat had subsided provided active sport for the young cavalrymen, but the month's leave that came once a year was the best time for hunting enthusiasts, and Colonel Stockley was no exception. Less usual for those days, his wife accompanied him on several of those trips afield.

A careful study of the game animal species of India together with an incisive knowlege of the native population were undoubtedly instrumental in his repeated successes as a hunter, enabling him to offer sound advice to younger followers. For example, he said men purporting to be *shikaris* were often frauds. Instead, he urged picking guides from amongst intelligent villagers.

As to the selection of a proper rifle for taking large and sometimes dangerous game, Stockley gave it as his opinion that the hunter should choose the most powerful rifle he could carry and shoot well, explaining that it wouldn't always be possible to pick one's shots in bush or jungle, especially if following-up a wounded animal. Further, under such conditions a

heavy bullet might prove necessary to stop a charge at close quarters.

English gunmakers did a thriving business between 1870 and 1914, providing sporting arms for wealthy Britons and for military and civil servants at Empire posts. For the less well-heeled there were rugged falling-block single-shot rifles, and there were big double rifles for those willing and able to pay. Before 1900, both were blackpowder arms. Ammunition was sent out from England in sealed tins as protection from humidity and were opened only as needed.

Stockley appears to have been able to afford some of the better rifles, even in his early days in India. He began with a battery composed of a Westley Richards 577 Black Powder Express and an 8-bore for a second rifle, both doubles. Of these he preferred the 577 because of its lighter recoil, but probably also because of a pair of unfortunate accidents suffered while using the 8-bore.

In one instance while cocking the 8-bore a hammer slipped from under his thumb, causing the rifle to fire and driving the action lever back into his right hand between thumb and forefinger—"the lock-jaw place," as he called it because of the grave danger of tetanus from such an injury.

Another episode with that hardkicking 8-bore saw both barrels fire together, he having cocked both hammers before firing. Whether this was due to inadequate sear contact, or simply caused by his finger slipping off the front trigger onto the rear trigger under the jarring shock of recoil, he didn't say. Whichever it was, the simultaneous discharge of twenty drams of black powder driving a pair of two-ounce balls must have left a lasting impression!

Thereafter, Stockley adopted a double 500 Black Powder Express as a second rifle, using copper-tubed express bullets on the lighter non-dangerous game, but also with satisfactory results on Himalayan brown bear.

The 577 Express remained his favorite, especially for tiger. For those hunts he told of making crude night sights by sewing a band of white cloth around the barrels behind the front sight, and another close to the rear sight.

With the arrival of smokeless powder however, and still convinced of the superior effectiveness of the 577 bore, he obtained a new double rifle proofed for smokeless powder in that caliber, firing 650-grain soft nose bullets loaded over 90 grains of cordite. This second 577 appears to have been the rifle chosen for use on his trips to Somaliland after lion, that country being then under the control of the government of India and requiring the shortest travel to reach from the sub-continent. Whilst the abandoned 8-bore might have been stronger medicine for elephant and rhino, he found the 577 to be a better lion gun.

His method of hunting the big Somali cats was to locate a lion kill and from there take up the spoor on foot in daylight, followed by horsemen whose job it was to gallop ahead, cutting off the lion and (hopefully) bringing him to bay. Some of the maned heads thus obtained by Colonel Stockley were presented to the 16th Cavalry Officers Mess.

The cordite 577 proved so successful for this hunting that Stockley ordered a new matched pair of 577 double rifles regulated for a heavier charge—750-grain solid or soft-nosed bullets driven by 100 grains of cordite—which he referred to as 577 H.V. (high velocity) rifles. So far as I was able to ascertain, these were his final pair of double rifles and the last of the big bores.

As a military man he was naturally exposed to the ubiquitous 303 effective on men, but not so effective on big game animals. Stockley's distrust of the 303 shows through in a remark he made concerning the pursuit of Himalayan black bear, in which he said that he had decided to use "a good

heavy bullet" (from the big double rifle) for the first shot, the 303 to be employed for a follow-up shot if necessary.

Still, the 303 offered a trio of features which were bound to impress even the most devoted big bore shooters, namely a flatter trajectory, longer range and far lighter recoil. While Stockley's thoughts on these matters weren't recorded, some logical deductions can be made from his final acquisition—a Westley Richards magazine rifle in 318 Express.

The designation "318" for this cartridge is unfortunately misleading in that actual bullet and barrel groove diameters were .330 in. Furthermore, the 318 drove longer and heavier 250-grain solid or Westley Richards capped bullets at about the same velocity as a 174-grain from the 303, and some 350 fps faster than the 303's 215-grain round nose. From these ballistic considerations he may have reasoned that with the 318 it was possible to combine the 303's advantages with the heavier bullets in which he placed so much faith.

Introduced sometime around 1910 to provide a general purpose medium-bore cartridge suited for use in standard length bolt actions, the 318 had become enormously popular in Africa, possibly *the* most popular of all mediums. Offering an adequately flat trajectory, the long straight-sided 250-grain solids gave deep penetration, earning for the caliber a quite marvelous reputation. For thin-skinned animals there was also the special Westley Richards "capped" bullet—a 250-grain copper-capped round-nose that provided expansion for lion and gained a creditable reputation when properly used, plus a 180-grain pointed cap hollow-nose fit only for non-dangerous lighter game.

With his long years of experience and preference for heavy bullets, it is most unlikely that Colonel Stockley experimented with these lighter bullets, but his faith in Westley Richards products may have influenced him to rely overmuch on the 250-grain capped bullets. Following service in command of the 21st Northumberland Fusiliers during the Great War of 1914-18, he had moved to East Africa, still pursuing his favorite sport of big game hunting.

No details are available as to the type of bullet Stockley was using in his 318 on that fateful day in early March, 1921, when he undertook to shoot a Ugandan buffalo. Nor do we know why he used that rifle on such heavy and dangerous game. Had he abandoned the 577s entirely, or were

they simply not at hand when he needed them? Again, we don't know.

What *is* known is that he failed to stop the buffalo's charge, and the animal got to him with fatal results. The *London Times* in its edition of April 21, 1921, announced the death of Colonel Vesey Mangles Stockley, killed in Uganda by a buffalo and buried on March 9th in the King's African Rifles Cemetery at Kampala. He had written *Big Game Shooting in India, Burma and Somaliland,* published in 1913.

For the colonel, life had ended. Not so for his rifle which stands today in this writer's gun cabinet, the initials "VMS" still clearly visible in the tarnished silver oval stock plate. The bluing is much the worse for wear, but the rifle is otherwise undamaged except for the usual stock dings. And the old Westley Richards continues to participate in hunts.

Where it was and what it did during the three decades following Colonel Stockley's death, I've been unable to learn. Undoubtedly, viewing its badly worn bore, it saw much use, suffering the usual effects of cordite powder and corrosive primers, so it is interesting to speculate on the variety of game it may have taken.

Some way or other, the old rifle found its way to Kenya, and there we pick up its trail when in the course of the Mau Mau insurrection of 1952-56 it was swept up by the British authorities, crated and shipped out of the country. I found it languishing amongst a group of second-hand rifles in a dealer's racks during the 1960s, forlorn in appearance but as sound mechanically as the day it left London. The extra large band of steel surrounding the receiver ring identified it as a takedown—the first such I had encountered in a bolt action—and the engraved inscriptions were equally interesting. *(EDITOR'S NOTE: From the same dealer, I bet, I got a Charles Jefferies 256 Mannlicher magazine rifle. I still have it. KW.)*

On the left side of the out-sized receiver ring are the words "Westley Richards .318 Accelerated Express," and just forward of that on the barrel breech section, "Square Shouldered Case Patents 2762-4661 II." Test-firing the rifle with British Kynoch cartridges, I soon found out what was meant by "square-shouldered case." The cases emerged with the sharpest, almost right-angled, shoulders ever seen on any cartridge, factory or wildcat.

A parade of five open V-sights from a standing leaf marked 100-yds, followed by four folding leaves successively identified to 500-yds, are mounted on a quarter-rib in best English fasion. Up front, a large squarish block contains a standard steel bead and a folding ivory-faced night sight. Barrel length is 26 inches, which somehow doesn't seem at all clumsy on this rifle.

My first move after test-firing was to have my old gunsmith friend Floyd Butler (now retired) refinish the stock, a job he executed with consummate skill leaving the rifle as originally finished with subdued patina over the French walnut graining. No rebluing was allowed as it was desired to retain the evidence of its many years of service.

Of course, that didn't help the way its worn rifling tended sometimes to scatter shots, so the barreled action was shipped off to re-boring specialist J.W. Van Patten in Pennsylvania with instructions to re-bore the barrel to 35-caliber, but without altering that unusual square-shouldered chamber except, of course, to open the neck area to accommodate .358 in. bullets.

It was an altogether pleasing restoration, made the more so when I discovered that it would now group five shots in two inches or less at 100 yards, and that cases could readily be formed from 30-06 brass, thereby ridding me of the necessity to use Berdan primers.

After some experimentation, I found that 250-grain Hornady round-nose soft points loaded over 54 grains of IMR-4320 gave me the accuracy I sought with close to original ballistics; that is, a 250-grain bullet at 2450 fps. It is, if you will, an Anglicized version of our respected 35 Whelen

cartridge, but with squared shoulder.

When an opportunity arose to hunt wild boar at the Hall Brothers Lodge in Georgia while attending the 1982 Shot Show in Atlanta, the Westley 35/318 was the rifle I selected to take along. I wanted a rifle that was both powerful enough to penetrate from any angle, and yet capable of being packed in a standard suitcase. I was confident I could count on its meeting the first requirement, and its takedown feature admirably took care of the second.

It was freezing cold in Georgia that January, with skim ice on the waterways of that old rice plantation below Savannah, and I evinced a desire to try stalking a boar rather than shooting from a stand or hunting with the pack. I hoped for a more challenging shot. Jack Douglas, my guide, couldn't have been more understanding or accommodating, and I seriously question whether any boar hunting guide knows his game and their habits better.

By the end of the second day he had located for me an old settler who was obviously the patriarch boar, driving off younger rivals with raking tusks. We immediately named him "Old Ugly."

Misjudging the range in the fading late afternoon light and turning up wrong sight leaf, my first shot merely creased the back of the feeding boar,

and he broke into a flat-out run. Here was the shot I had hoped for, and with the correct sight leaf now turned up, I swung ahead of the running boar and touched off the shot.

If you've never heard a fatally hit boar bellow and seen him switch ends in midair and collapse in a heap, you can't know how spectacular it can be!

The 250-grain Hornady round-nose soft point penetrated clear through, smashing both shoulders, tearing up the tops of the lungs, and expanding to leave an exit hole resulting in an enormous and very rapid loss of blood for a clean, quick kill. This was the sort of performance which earned the 318 its great reputation; I was happy the new bore played up to standard.

Measuring a full six feet in length with little or no fat, Old Ugly was judged worthy of a head mount, created by taxidermist Charles Douglas. As I write this, the boar looks down on me from my gunroom wall with baleful glare and exposed tusks, a memento of yet another chapter in the life story of a grand old rifle. •

Waters and his 318/35 Westley Richards with "Old Ugly." One 250-grain Hornady round nose was all it took.

Would you believe that before World War I there was a long-range single shot handgun? It was . . .

FRED ADOLPH'S GEM

by R. P. STEPIEN

ABOUT 1910, Fred Adolph, a remarkable master gunsmith from Genoa, New York, designed, developed and offered a single shot long range 22-caliber pistol on a custom-made basis. Its action is a modified Martini, the lever in the back of the handle.

The barrel of my Adolph pistol is ten inches long and is made of Poldi Anticorro Steel. The Poldi Steel Works of Vienna developed their version of what we now call stainless steel shortly after the turn of the century.

The grip style may be seen in the illustration. The walnut is nicely inletted into the frame and carries fine, 24 l.p.i. checkering. The forend is a matching fine grained piece of walnut with an ebony buffalo horn forend tip.

The weight of the trigger pull is regulated with a set screw directly above the trigger. The trigger itself is nicely curved and grooved.

The front sight base is slotted for the sight with a screw keeping it in place. Thus the front sight may be changed to a different height, width or shape at one's pleasure.

The pistol's rear sight is "the famous Fred Adolph micrometer pistol sight." It has twin micrometer screw adjustments for windage and eleva-

tion. One turn moves the impact of the bullet ¼-inch at 50 yards. There is a crisp and distinct click for each point marked on the scales.

The 22 centerfire cartridge for the Long Range Pistol was designed by Adolph's long-time friend and associate Charles Newton, the well-known Buffalo, New York, rifle manufacturer. Newton took the Stevens 28-30-120 rimmed rifle case, cut it down and necked it to fit the then widely acclaimed Savage 22 Hi-Power soft nosed copper-jacketed bullet.

A powder charge of 17 grains of Lightning, we are told, developed 2000 fps with a striking energy of 632 foot pounds. This is pretty good by today's standards, and back in 1910 was in a class by itself.

This performance put the Adolph pistol close to the then-popular 32-40 rifle cartridge. The Fred Adolph 22 Long Range Pistol cartridge we are again told, had power enough for an effective range of 500 yards and was equal in accuracy to a rifle, providing one could hold accurately enough.

There were several variations of this single shot long range pistol. Being custom-made throughout, it could be ordered to satisfy the buyer's individual desires, particularly in ornamentation.

Many testimonials were written ex-

tolling the merits of Fred Adolph's new development. One famous contemporary, Charles Askins, Sr., said in 1912:

"The most cleverly designed single shot pistol that the writer has seen is the hand-made weapon of Fred Adolph. We have probably all had occasion to admire the writing of some man who put into words just what he had been thinking of for a long time, and I like Adolph's weapon because I built it in imagination a long time ago.

"This pistol being hand-made can be varied in length of barrel, weight, shape of grip and trigger pull to suit the user. In fact, as I understand it, it can be built to order and every specification fulfilled. The man who is desirous of owning the very best target pistol made, should be able to get it here, though what it will cost him is more than I can say.

"Naturally, being built to order, this Adolph pistol can be constructed to go into either the one or two-pound class. In a weight of about a pound and a half it would make a mighty handy belt gun, to be carried in connection with a hunting rifle or the shotgun, and its shape and balance are such that it is a very superior weapon for snap and wing shooting after pistol fashion." ●

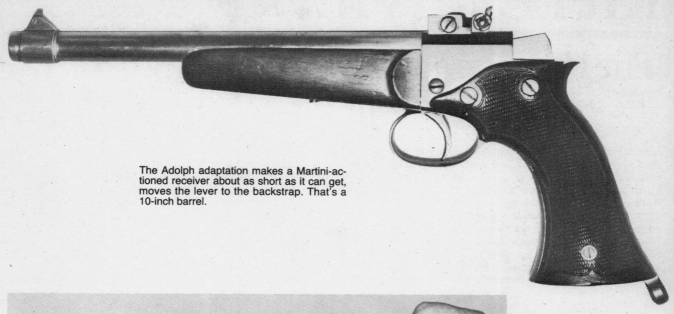

The Adolph adaptation makes a Martini-actioned receiver about as short as it can get, moves the lever to the backstrap. That's a 10-inch barrel.

Nothing finicky about chambering the Newton-designed 22-caliber neckdown of a shortened Stevens 28-30 case loaded to a claimed 2000 fps with the .228-inch Savage Hi-Power bullet.

Bragging-size groups were all the rage back then, as this Adolph publicity demonstrates. It was all just 60 years too soon to make a big splash.

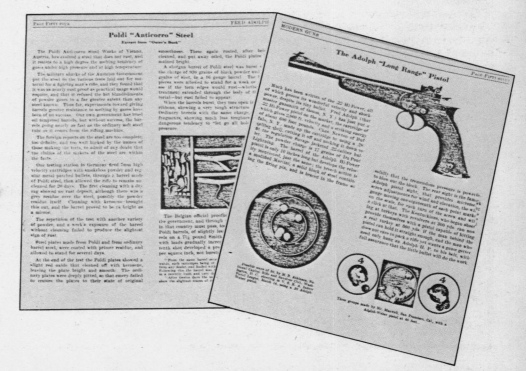

RIFLE REVIEW

by LAYNE SIMPSON

They're giving us what they think we want.

CONTACTING various companies last year for updates on their wares was depressing. Many told tales of glum and gloom. Thank goodness, I listened to happier tunes in early 1984. With few exceptions, '83 was a good year with sales forecasts projecting an even better dozen months ahead. Why is this?

For one thing, our overall economy is enjoying a slight upturn and for an-

quickly respond if the demand is thought to be there will continue to lead the pack. In other words, if we shooters ask for something loud enough and long enough, they'll make it available.

Our rifle manufacturers have a tough job, there's no doubt about it. We consumers tend to be a whimsical and fickle lot. Sometimes we cry long and loud in our demand for something

idea will fly and what won't. If my crystal ball were 100 percent accurate, I'd shut down this typing machine, hire out to Remchester Firearms as a consultant and spend the other six months each year knocking off big game around the globe—but it isn't. On the other hand, sometimes when it's accurate I tend to ignore its message.

For example, that same crystal ball tells me that in order for a 7mm cartridge to be successful, it must either produce magnum velocities or fit into a short action and yet I tell the world a midsize 7mm is the thing to have. Of course, the world pays this message

For 1984, Browning will build 1,000 high grade Model 1895s (shown) and 9,000 standard grades, all in 30-06.

other, more rifle companies are taking note of consumer demand and planning the development of new product accordingly. Time was when the American shooter got nothing more than what our gun companies wanted him to have, regardless of what he asked for. In most cases it's different now because competition in the rifle market is much stiffer. Companies that sit on their laurels with deaf ears fall behind, while those who seriously evaluate new trends and

and then turn away with a yawn when it does become available. The 17-caliber cartridge comes to mind, as does a modern lever-action rifle. A manufacturer's timing has to be dead on the money too or his R&D and advertising dollars will be spent for naught. Twenty years ago, one of the best bolt action carbines ever made got the cold shoulder from the hunting majority, but just take a look at what's hot now.

Purely and simply, it's all a big gamble and none of us can always predict with unfailing accuracy what

no mind. It also tells me that shiny stocks, shiny metal and whiteline spacers sell more rifles than satin hues, matte finishes and conservative styling, but I switch the ball off and keep on typing in my opinionated direction.

As compared to a bombardment of new choices in 1983, our 1984 rifle shopper will mostly be faced with choosing between modifications of existing models, but even this is exciting. Two of our manufacturers who in their own times, have created bandwagons of their own and launched

Marlin's Model 1894 is now available in 41 Magnum, as Model 1894S.

All Model 94s now have Angle Eject, like this standard model with optional scope. New calibers include 44 Magnum, 444 Marlin, 45 Colt and 7x30 Waters.

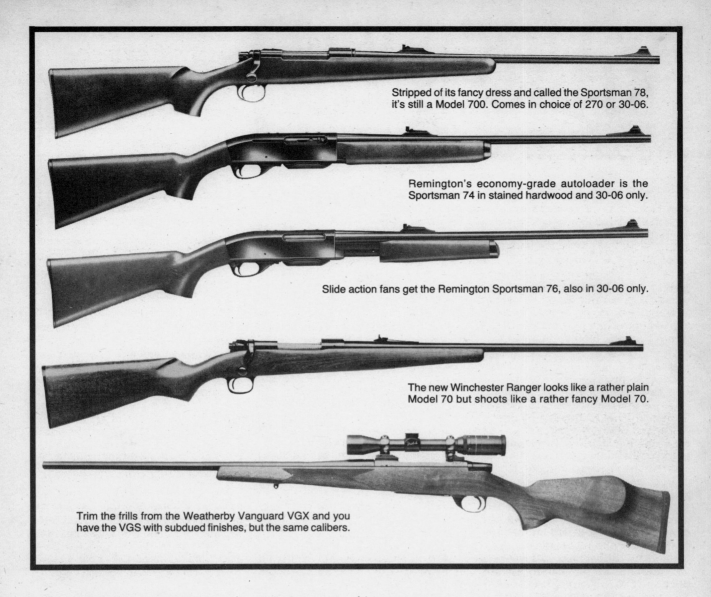

Stripped of its fancy dress and called the Sportsman 78, it's still a Model 700. Comes in choice of 270 or 30-06.

Remington's economy-grade autoloader is the Sportsman 74 in stained hardwood and 30-06 only.

Slide action fans get the Remington Sportsman 76, also in 30-06 only.

The new Winchester Ranger looks like a rather plain Model 70 but shoots like a rather fancy Model 70.

Trim the frills from the Weatherby Vanguard VGX and you have the VGS with subdued finishes, but the same calibers.

them down the bumpy road to successes have hopped aboard the bolt action carbine express for '84.

We'll see two rifles booted farther into the 20th century—one an old bolt action with a new short throw and a lever action woods rifle in 7mm caliber. Not since the 1930s, when Colonel Whelen suggested to Remington that their new 257 Roberts be named after its creator have we had a commercial cartridge with an individual's name stamped on its base—and on rifle barrels—but we'll see one about July of '84.

Our smaller shops and companies continue to fill slots and demands that are too small for the big boys to sell at a profit; a high grade, lightweight single shot rifle; takedown rifle conversions; double rifle conversions and rifles for cartridges like the 17 Hornet, 218 Bee, 6×47mm, 25-284 and 7mm TCU. Synthetic stocks just won't go

away so one company has one out while two others stand awaiting in the wings.

Charles Newton's sweet little 250-3000 cartridge is back in style and Teddy Roosevelt, wherever you are, what do you think about that big lever action from Utah? And, finally, we have an American-made bolt gun with its action scaled down for the 222 Remington family of cartridges—and it's pretty too.

The year also brings its share of sad news, with a shocking announcement from our largest maker of rifle scopes. Since I'm trespassing onto Bob Bell's stomping grounds and am sure he'll cover it with his usual thoroughness, I'll say no more than: Unless the cavalry galloped quickly to Texas, a big chunk of Americana has become history.

Now let's take a close look at good things in store for us.

Alpha Arms

The standard Alpha I has been discontinued with a new high grade rifle now being offered. The Custom Alpha differs from its predecessor with a classic-style stock, replete with fancy hand-finished wood and cut checkering. It also has a checkered bolt knob, engine turned bolt body and deluxe metal finish. Calibers available are: 243, 7mm-08, and 308 with 20-in. barrel and, at 21 in., the 284 Winchester and, shades of the 1960s, the 25-284. The 358 Winchester will also be added to the list if enough of us ask for it.

I've been working with a prototype in 284 and had forgotten what a fine cartridge this is. It has about as much soup as the 280 Remington; more than the 7mm-08 and yet it works in short actions. As a bonus, the Alpha I's medium length action keeps bullets out of the powder cavity. Old

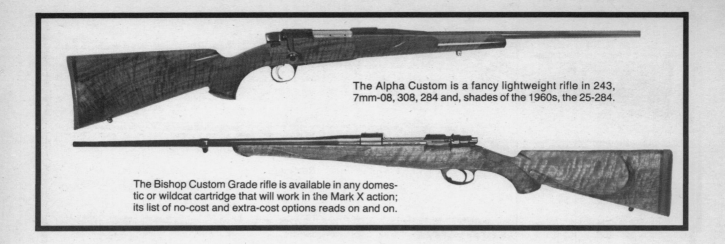

The Alpha Custom is a fancy lightweight rifle in 243, 7mm-08, 308, 284 and, shades of the 1960s, the 25-284.

The Bishop Custom Grade rifle is available in any domestic or wildcat cartridge that will work in the Mark X action; its list of no-cost and extra-cost options reads on and on.

number P5 likes to shoot into tiny groups with the 130 Speer loaded atop WW-785. I've got to have one.

Bishop

During 1983, the gun stock people introduced completed rifles in three grades: Model Ten, Model Ten Custom and Masterpiece. The standard rifle is available in 25-06, 270, 7×57mm, 7mm Remington Magnum, 30-06 and 300 Winchester Magnum for $400. For another $100 you can get the Custom with all sorts of no-cost options; cheekpiece styles; length of pull; comb height; recoil pad or steel buttplate; schnabel, plain or contrasting forend tip, etc., etc. The list goes on and on but other options will cost you extra. At $1000 and up, the Masterpiece is more of the same thing. Any caliber that will work on the Interarms Mark X action is available, including any wildcat ever dreamed up. Next year I'll let you know how my 35 Whelen performs. Stacks of brochures are sitting out in Warsaw, awaiting your query. You order the rifle from your local dealer, though.

Browning

The first repeating sporting rifle chambered for the then-new 30-06 was Winchester's John Browning-designed Model 1895. It was discontinued in 1931 but the Browning Arms Company has breathed new life into the big lever action for 1984. Actually, it's a limited edition as only 1,000 high grade rifles and 9,000 standard grades will be built in 30-06. If Browning continues the program, next year's caliber will be the 30-40 Krag and who knows, they might eventually get around to the 35 and 405 Winchester. A splendid little program, you could say.

Chipmunk

How do you spoil a child? Well, first of all you spare the rod and give him everything he wants, including a deluxe grade Chipmunk with engraved receiver, fancy wood and hand cut checkering, all for $500. Or, you could wield the rod, keep the Chipmunk for yourself and give him everything else.

Custom Gun Guild

I've long had a soft spot for good single shot rifles and one of the nicest I've seen lately is Frank Wood's little Number 4 falling block. Its one-piece, classic stock is of fancy claro walnut, accented by either of three different checkering patterns, all cut 22 or 24 lines to the inch. Among other nice things, it has all machined parts; rotary tang safety; skeleton or solid steel grip cap and buttplate; right or left hand stock and tapered octagon barrel, 20, 22 or 24-in. long. It has engraving too.

At a nominal 5½ pounds, the Number 4 is a lightweight and can be had in several calibers: 22 LR, 22 WMR, 22 Hornet, 218 Bee, 223, 22-250, 243, 257 Roberts, 7×57mm, 308, etc. The price tag I saw read $2975 but by late '84 a standard grade priced competitively with other single shots is slated to appear.

Backpackers will like the CCG Ruger 10-22 takedown conversion while world travelers will go for the same conversion to various bolt action centerfires. You can send, say, a Rem-

Above—The Kleinguenther K-15 (top) has spawned the K-22 (bottom). The same fire control system is used in both rifles. The K-22 is shown with the optional double-set triggers. Right—K-22 has both dovetails and tapped holes for scopes; its bolt has front locking lugs.

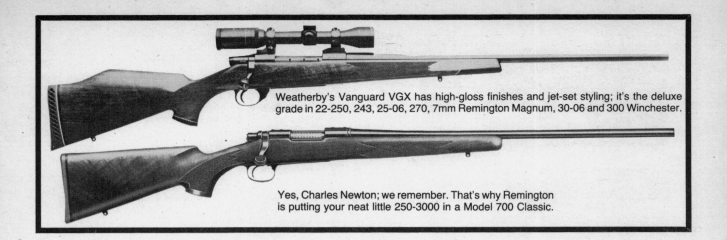

Weatherby's Vanguard VGX has high-gloss finishes and jet-set styling; it's the deluxe grade in 22-250, 243, 25-06, 270, 7mm Remington Magnum, 30-06 and 300 Winchester.

Yes, Charles Newton; we remember. That's why Remington is putting your neat little 250-3000 in a Model 700 Classic.

ington Model Seven to Georgia and the work will cost $550, or, you can just send $650 and no rifle and they'll ship you a complete Model Seven with fiberglass stock. Since the Editor will probably discuss his Model Seven, I won't thump this tub any longer.

Kendall

Importers of Lapua ammunition, high quality shotguns and air rifles, Kendall International is now offering Lothar Walther button-rifled barrels from Koenigsbronn, West Germany. They're available in chrome moly and stainless steel, chambered or unchambered and in various American and European rifle and handgun calibers from the 22 Hornet to the 9.3×62 to the 460 Weatherby Magnum. Also available are blanks for muzzleloaders (stainless, too) and 177-caliber for air rifles. I have a blank in 224 caliber and will report on its performance when there is some.

Kimber

The innovative and creative folks out in Clackamas have been busy during the past twelve months. A wildcat cartridge called the 17 Kimber R2 is under development, while the Model 82 Custom Classic Grade rifle with select claro walnut and ebony forend tip was introduced in late '83. With the Custom Classic came a new more natural finish, and all Kimber rifles now have it, including the top-of-line Super America. Another change made in all Kimber rifles is a tapered tang.

My pick of the most exciting rifle news for 1984 is Kimber's new rifle in 223 Remington. Listed among its credentials are twin front locking lugs; box magazine with hinged floorplate; Mauser-type extractor and Model 70 ejector. Otherwise, it's much like the Model 82. Kimber is also taking a hard look at a Model 84 single shot with solid bottom receiver as well as other chamberings: 17 Rem., 219 Fireball, 6×47mm and 7mm TCU.

Also new for '84 is a fixed version of Kimber's Brownell-designed side lever scope mounting rings. Like their quick-detach mates, these fit the grooved receiver of Kimber rifles and they're also available with bases for other rifles like the Remington Model 700, '98 Mauser, Model 70, etc., etc. You Kimber collectors who bought a Kimber rifle sling and Leupold-built scope with the Kimber logo, hang onto them—there will be no more.

Kleinguenther

Kleinguenther's K-15 centerfire rifle has spawned a 22 RF mate called the K-22. In a nutshell, the K-22 feels and handles like a big game rifle built for grownups; shoots like a target rifle and looks like it ought to cost more than it does. I'll save the rest of the good news for my Testfire Report. (See page 222.)

Marathon

This firm opened its doors in 1983 with an economy grade single shot bolt action in 22 rimfire for $74.95 or for do-it-themselvers, the same rifle in kit form for $15 less. The rifle is said to weigh 4.9 pounds with a 24-in. barrel rifled with, interestingly enough, a 1-12.6-inch twist.

Also available from Marathon is a Mauser action repeater in both kit and finished form for $258 and $380, respectively. Its advertised chamberings include 243, 270, 7×57, 7mm Remington Magnum, 308, 30-06 and 300 Winchester Magnum.

Both rifles are a bit unique in that their barrels are cold formed by an extrusion process with steel tubes, as they are called, drawn between an external die and internal mandrel—simultaneously. According to the manufacturer, barrels made in this manner have longer life and much smoother lands and grooves. Marathon also offers barrel blanks in various calibers, including 177 air rifle. (When we can, we'll shoot some of these and let you know about them.)

Left—The Ruger Red Label is fun to shoot, especially if it has two 375 H&H barrels.

Below—At top is Marathon's Mauser centerfire rifle and below, their single shot rimfire. Both are available as shown or in kit form.

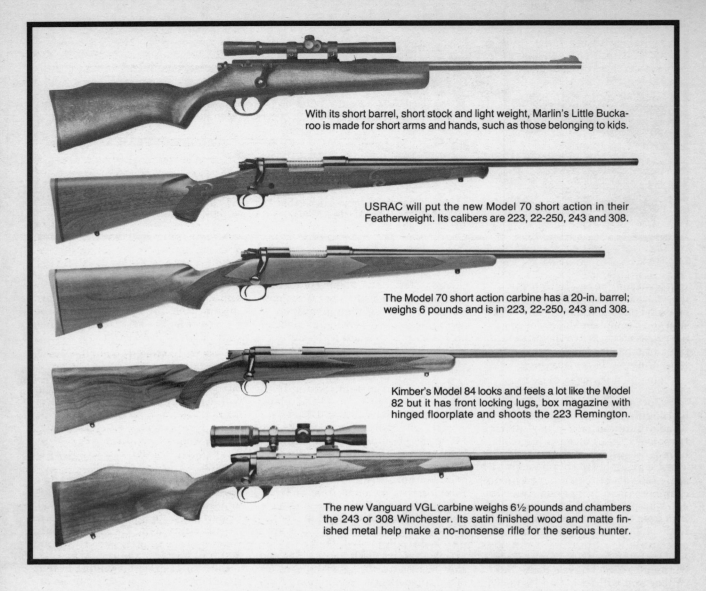

With its short barrel, short stock and light weight, Marlin's Little Buckaroo is made for short arms and hands, such as those belonging to kids.

USRAC will put the new Model 70 short action in their Featherweight. Its calibers are 223, 22-250, 243 and 308.

The Model 70 short action carbine has a 20-in. barrel; weighs 6 pounds and is in 223, 22-250, 243 and 308.

Kimber's Model 84 looks and feels a lot like the Model 82 but it has front locking lugs, box magazine with hinged floorplate and shoots the 223 Remington.

The new Vanguard VGL carbine weighs 6½ pounds and chambers the 243 or 308 Winchester. Its satin finished wood and matte finished metal help make a no-nonsense rifle for the serious hunter.

Marlin

Marlin has now passed the two million mark with their Model 39s and Model 60s and the three million level with Model 336s. That's a lot of bad news for big game, small game, paper targets and tin cans. Marlin is said to be our largest rifle maker. They're quite generous too; the 2,000,000th Model 39, a beautiful custom rifle, was donated to NSSF for education.

Handgunners who have longed for a companion rifle to their 41 Magnum revolvers will welcome this cartridge in the short, light Model 1894. According to Marlin, the 1894S packs only slightly less punch than the 44 Magnum version with only a bit more recoil than the 357. Sounds like a pretty good deal to me.

Kids need 22 rimfire rifles, too, with adult supervision of course. Now the little fellows have another choice; the Model 15Y is made just for them. Marlin has modified their faithful old Model 15 bolt action single shot by shortening its Micro-Groove barrel to 16¼-in. and shrinking its buttstock to where short arms and little hands can reach the trigger. The Model 15Y weighs a nominal 4¼ pounds and measures a mere 33¼-in. long. Its firing pin cocks when the bolt is opened; it can be opened with the safety on, by the way. Open sights are there and a scope mount for the grooved receiver is included in the package as well. Marlin calls it the Little Buckaroo; little buckaroos will call it a dandy.

Although announced in early 1983, the Model 336ER (Extended Range) did not become available until a year later. It's now available in 307 Winchester with a 22-in. barrel and with 20-in. barrel in 356 Winchester. Both are fine candidates for whitetail hunters who don't like to follow long blood trails or moose and elk hunters who like to tiptoe through the thickets.

Remington

The fine but obviously neglected Model 788 is gone. What more can I say? Other victims of the grim reaper's swing are the entire line of baby 788s in 22 RF; Models 581, 582, 541-S and the poor boy's favorite target rifle, the Model 540-XR. And, after struggling along for but a few short years, the mighty 8mm Magnum has died in its infancy. The 17-cal. Remington is also in its death throes and may feel the axe's sharp bite before we meet again. Ignore the fellows who know nothing about this neat little cartridge except what they heard or read and buy one quick while there's still time.

Now for the good news.

Remington calls their new line of rifles the Sportsman Series. Actually, they're nothing more than time-proven models with the frills trimmed away. With its stained, hardwood stock, sans checkering and sling swivels, along with no-shine metal, the Sportsman 78 is the Model 700 in country boy's clothing. I've examined the 78 and whether you buy the 270 or 30-06, you get a lot of rifle for the money. The Model 7400 autoloader and Model 7600 slide action have plain vanilla cousins too; they're called the Model 74 and Model 76, both in 30-06.

Connoisseurs of fine rifles should write to Remington and request a catalog from their custom shop. Those fellows are producing nothing less than works of art and delivery time is surprisingly short. Back in November, I looked over several examples on display at the new products seminar held at Remington Farms. They were most handsome. Grades 1, 2, 3 and 4 will set you back $1100, $2000, $3000 and $4000, respectively, but the sky and pocketbook are the limit.

Some of them used to do it but it's been a long time since a gun company offered exotic elixirs for protecting guns from the ravages of time, element and wear. Remington has brought back an old name bearing a space-age product and called Rem Oil. They've been using it for quite some time in their repair shop and now we can too. DuPont Teflon is one of its most important ingredients.

Ruger

Although it was announced and shown in early 1983, I've yet (February) to see a Model 77/22 production rifle, nor do I know anyone else who has. Why do they do that? During this past deer season, I used, among other rifles, a Model 77 Ultra Light in 270. It carries light; comes to shoulder in a flash and shoots three shot groups smaller than skinny barrels are alleged to. Even with the long action it weighed but 6 pounds, 2 ounces fresh from its box. I like this little carbine. I don't see the No. 1AB listed in their '84 catalog so it must be gone.

Sako

Several prototype hunting rifles with McMillan fiberglass stocks were on display at the '84 SHOT show but none of the Sako people would say whether they are scheduled for production or just there to attract attention. They certainly looked good. Perhaps of greater interest were wood-stocked rifles with a pleasingly subdued no-gloss finish.

Searcy Guns

I've been shooting a double rifle built on the Ruger Red Label shotgun frame and am quite pleased with it. Gunsmith Butch Searcy (5801 Stevenson Dr., Farmington, NM 87401) is offering this conversion in any caliber up to 458 Winchester. Mine is in 375 H&H and with factory equivalent handloads consistently puts two overs and two unders into four inches at a hundred yards. It has Shilen barrels with a quarter rib holding the fixed rear sight and Kimber side-lever scope rings. Searcy also converts the Winchester 101 and Ruger Red Label to combo guns, most any caliber with most any gauge. Another neat thing in his bag of tricks is shortening the actions of bolt guns.

Thompson Center

The T.C.R.'83 has undergone a few minor internal modifications since its introduction. Most would go unnoticed to the average shooter but later production runs are said to have slightly smoother triggers. I have T.C.R. number 25 and don't see how its trigger could be improved but that's the way the T/C crew operates, constantly trying to improve on a good product.

USRAC

When Winchester introduced their series of short cartridges back in the 1950s, a short action Model 70 was lurking just around the corner, or so the rumors flew. Finally it's more than a rumor; U.S. Repeating Arms has unveiled the Model 70 Featherweight with a short bolt throw and 22-in. barrel in 223, 22-250, 243 and 308 Winchester.

The short action is also utilized in one of two new Model 70 carbines with 20-in. barrels. It's available in the same calibers as the Featherweight and rated at a nominal six pounds. The other Model 70 carbine is offered in 270 and 30-06, longer cartridges requiring the standard length action. It weighs a quarter-pound more than its short-throw mate.

Also new for '84 is the Model 70 Ranger, a no-nonsense, economy grade with stained hardwood stock and no checkering. All Model 94s now have the Angle Eject feature incorporated into their design. This includes the standard, XTR, Wrangler and Trapper versions. New chamberings for the 94 are 44 Remington Magnum (also takes the 44 S&W Special), 444 Marlin, 45 Colt and 7×30 Waters. Created by gunwriter Ken Waters,

the 7×30 is to be introduced in a special version of the Model 94. According to Ken, the reason behind this cartridge is increased performance at 30-30 chamber pressures. I am told that the 7×30 is simply the old 30 WCF necked down with a few other changes, possibly a shorter neck. More information was not available prior to deadline time. Federal plans to load the ammunition with a special Hornady flat-nose, 140-grain bullet to about 2600 fps. To get this velocity, the Model 94 in this caliber will have a 24-in. barrel.

Commemorative buffs should be scampering for the new Winchester-Colt matched pair. Both carbine and revolver are chambered to 44-40 WCF with only 4,440 being made. Each of the pair will bear the same serial number (1WC-444OWC) and a fancy display case goes along with the deal.

Weatherby

Now we have three Vanguard models to suit the tastes of jet-setters as well as those of a more conservative nature. The VGX is the deluxe grade with high gloss finish on wood and metal; cut checkering; rosewood tip and cap, all wrapped around the time-proven Vanguard barreled action. It's available in 22-250 with number 2 or 3 barrel contour as well as number 2 only in 243, 25-06, 270, 7mm Remington Magnum, 30-06 and 300 Winchester Magnum. The 22-250 and 243 are on the short action.

Strip the frills from the VGX and you have the VGS. It has a satin-finished, cut-checkered stock with not a white spacer, grip cap or forend tip in sight.

The VGL is a new lightweight carbine with 20-in. barrel. Rated at 6½ pounds, its an abbreviated version of the VGS except it's available only with the short action in 243 and 308. It's neat. All Vanguard models are guaranteed to put three shots into 1½-in. at 100 yards.

Have you tried a Fibermark lately? My test rifle, a 240 Magnum with the 26-in. number 2 countour, doesn't take kindly to factory loads but H-4831 pushes the 100 Sierra into 1 MOA with boring regularity. I suppose, because of its fiberglass stock, this rifle is thought of as a lightweight but this is not exactly true. The 'glass stock does trim away a few ounces but in this case it is not Weatherby's intent; they're thinking about stability, or a rifle that will maintain yesterday's zero today, just as it will tomorrow. The Fibermark works. ●

BLACK POWDER REVIEW

by RICK HACKER

LIKE A FREE trapper from the fur trade era emerging after a long winter, the muzzleloading industry has weathered the storms of the recent recession and has stepped out into the sunlight of the latter half of the 80s leaner and stronger. Giving impetus to this strength are whole new ranks of black powder shooters.

The Civil War skirmishers and Revolutionary War historians that boosted muzzleloading in the '60s and '70s are still with us, and thousands of hunters are entering the frontloading ranks each year. Thirty-one states now offer separate black powder seasons for deer hunting. Adding to this new wave of enthusiasts are weekend plinkers and collectors. Certainly the new black powder products this year reflect these new trends.

Allen Fire Arms Co.

In addition to the Uberti replicas, Allen offers the Tryon Rifle, Brown Bess Musket and LePage pistol, all of which are made by Davide Pedersoli in Italy and which have popular models for other firms such as Dixie Gun Works, Navy Arms and Trail Guns Armory. Two new rifles to be sold exclusively by Allen this year are Pedersoli's Kentucky Carbine and Pennsylvania Rifle.

The carbine features a 28-inch blued octagon barrel with fixed sights and is available in 38, 45 and 50 calibers. The longer Pennsylvania Rifle has a 4½-inch browned octagon barrel with adjustable buckhorn sights and is bored for 32, 38, or 45 round ball. Both rifles are available in either flintlock or percussion, with the caplock guns employing a brass flash cup, which helps protect the shooter's hand and eyes from flying cap fragments. The locks on both models are nicely polished and blued, while trigger guard, patchbox, buttplate and ramrod thimbles are brass.

To complement their extensive line of handguns, Allen has brought out an array of holsters handmade in Santa Fe from original patterns of the 1850s and '70s. Available in plain leather or carved, these military flap and civilian-styled belt holsters come in a variety of styles and sizes for the Colt 1860 Army and 51 Navy, the 36 and 44 Remingtons, and even the hard-to-find Walkers, Dragoons and 1862 belt pistols as well as the Colt and replica single action cartridge revolvers.

Navy Arms

After being relatively quiet on the new products scene, Navy Arms has come forward with two new products and a reincarnation of a popular collector's favorite.

First is the long-awaited sidehammer small game hunting rifle. The sidehammer was popular during the 1850s due to its fast, short-throw hammer and comparatively positive ignition, where the nipple screws directly into the barrel. Modern shooters might also prefer the sidehammer due to its "cleaner" lines in the breech area and the fact that there is no thick hammer spur looming up near the shooting eye; all the action takes place along the right side of the gun. The Mountainman's Squirrel Rifle, as Navy calls their sidehammer, has adjustable sights, brass furniture and is available in 32, 36 and 45 calibers, either finished or kit.

Another new rifle is the Navy Arms Cub, a scaled down boy's rifle which looks somewhat like a miniaturized version of their Mark I Hawken. I have long advocated muzzleloaders designed for the smaller reach and stature of children in the 8 to 12-year old group as one means of perpetuating family interest and growth of our sport. With the Traditions, Inc. Scout reported here last year and now the Navy Arms Cub, perhaps a much-needed trend is starting. The Cub is a halfstock percussion rifle in 36 caliber. Over-all length is only 27 inches and the rifle sports a 22-inch barrel, which is just about long enough to completely burn a powder charge of 30 to 35 grains, thereby keeping recoil down for such a light 4½-pound gun. Sights are adjustable buckhorn. Val Forgett is to be commended for taking this step towards helping to preserve muzzleloading among our nation's youth.

In addition to the two new guns mentioned above, Navy Arms has brought back their 1836-era replica Paterson. The Paterson was Sam Colt's first commercial attempt at producing a revolving pistol for the mass market. The well-made replica of this gun was originally brought out by Navy a few years ago but was limited to just 500 of the standard version and 50 engraved guns. This 36-caliber five-shot revolver with its folding trigger quickly sold out; even at gun shows they are rarely seen for sale. Now the Paterson replica is to become a regular part of their line in a standard, non-engraved version.

CVA

For the outdoorsman, CVA has made 1985 the year of the southpaw

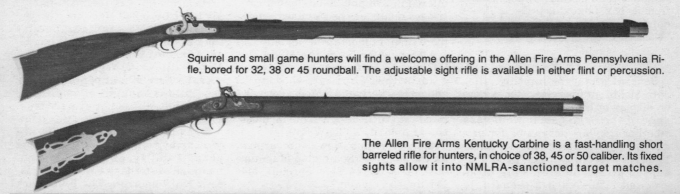

Squirrel and small game hunters will find a welcome offering in the Allen Fire Arms Pennsylvania Rifle, bored for 32, 38 or 45 roundball. The adjustable sight rifle is available in either flint or percussion.

The Allen Fire Arms Kentucky Carbine is a fast-handling short barreled rifle for hunters, in choice of 38, 45 or 50 caliber. Its fixed sights allow it into NMLRA-sanctioned target matches.

Above—Navy Arms now produces the first replica sidehammer action for today's black powder shooters.

After an absence of many years, Navy Arms now brings back their replica Paterson revolver.

To carry their complete line of cap and ball revolvers and early-style single actions, Allen Fire Arms sells authentically-styled handmade holsters.

CVA salutes southpaws this year by introducing left-handed versions of their Squirrel Rifle and their Frontier Rifle.

This flintlock blunderbuss by CVA has a brass smooth-bore barrel capable of handling either shot or round ball.

Oregon Trail Riflesmiths is offering a handbuilt replica of the Leman Trade Rifle for the discriminating shooter-hunter-collector.

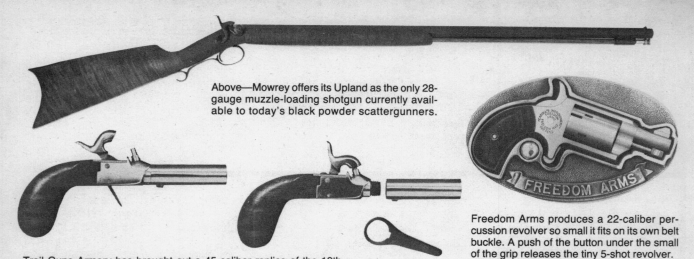

Above—Mowrey offers its Upland as the only 28-gauge muzzle-loading shotgun currently available to today's black powder scattergunners.

Freedom Arms produces a 22-caliber percussion revolver so small it fits on its own belt buckle. A push of the button under the small of the grip releases the tiny 5-shot revolver.

Trail Guns Armory has brought out a 45-caliber replica of the 19th Century muff pistol. Called the Liege Derringer, each gun comes with a wrench for unscrewing the barrel.

by producing lefthand versions of their 50-caliber Frontier Rifle and their 32-caliber Squirrel Rifle. For the casual upland shotgunner and "mail coach guard" who wants something a little different, CVA has brought out their version of the Blunderbuss, a flintlock, brass-barreled smoothbore with a traditional flared muzzle.

Handgunners will find interest in CVA's brass-framed version of the New Model Remington. This five shot, spur triggered revolver is the most visually interesting new member of CVA's growing line of percussion revolvers and is the best-selling new gun in their handgun display.

Trail Guns Armory

This Texas firm has built its reputation largely on its side-by-side muzzle-loading double rifle, The Kodiak. Mike Powasnik is now branching out and TGA is carrying the Brown Bess Musket and Mustketoon and Pedersoli's LePage pistol. And there are two new black powder guns unique to TGA.

First is their Leige Derringer, a little 45 caliber single shot percussion pistol styled after the muff pistols of the 1840s. These tiny close range guns were the forerunners of today's backup guns and off-duty snubbies. Their small size made them convenient to tuck into boot or muff; hence, the nomenclature. TGA's muff pistol comes with a leather case, powder flask and barrel wrench. A folding trigger pops down when the hammer is cocked. The muff pistol comes in two versions: plain blued with walnut grips or engraved with imitation ivory grips.

TGA's second new offering is aimed towards the commemorative market

and is the second Paterson pistol to appear this year. Unlike Navy's blued version, however, TGA's Texas Paterson will be left "in the white" and shall be limited to only 150 guns, in celebration of the 150th anniversary of Texas independence. This Paterson will feature special engraving along the top barrel flat, with a Texas star etched in the right side of the frame and one piece handcarved ebony grips. According to Powasnik, this limited edition cap and ball will be "made in Texas by Texans!"

Pecos Valley Armory

John Goodwin might be a name familiar to readers who like to read gun writers' bylines. However, John has given up gunwriting to join up with Chester Berry and produce an attractive Halfstock Pennsylvania Rifle. This is their only product and it is hand assembled from top quality parts. Barrels are by Montana Barrel, the Durs Egg-styled percussion lock is by L&R, the double set triggers are by Davis, brass furniture is by Tedd Cash and the richly figured stock has an authentic handrubbed satin finish. With a somewhat short 13½" length of pull, this rifle, which is available in either 36 or 45 caliber, would make an ideal hunting gun for anyone with a non-husky stature, including women and teenagers. I have seen the prototype of this rifle and it is extremely well finished and attractive, although as of this writing I have yet to give a thorough field test to one of the regular production pieces.

Oregon Trail Riflesmiths

Remember the old Green River Rifle Works and their much admired Leman Trade Rifle? The Green River firm, during its brief existence in the

late 1970s, produced an excellent version of this short-barreled, big bore hunting rifle. Unfortunately, GRRW fell on hard times and faded from the gunmaking scene, but their legend lives on. And so does some of their machinery.

Ted Holland and Lloyd Helms have acquired the authentically-styled furniture that Green River used and have paired it up with Montana Barrels and Davis or Ron Long locks to produce a finely crafted semi-custom trade rifle. This sturdy rifle is available in either flint or percussion and can be ordered in 45, 50, 54 or 58 caliber. Right- or left-hand versions in halfstock or fullstock models are available, as are a variety of custom options, such as special wood or sights or fancy engraving. You may have to wait from three to six months to get your gun, but such is the tradeoff of ordering a semi-custom gun from these dedicated folks.

Mowrey Gun Works

This is the company that has used Ethan Allen's basic 1836 rifle design to create their popular 32 and 36 Squirrel Rifle as well as their 50 and 54 Plains and Rocky Mountain Hunter rifles. They have now carried this design one step further by introducing a lightweight 28-gauge upland shotgun. Because a 28 gauge translates approximately into a 54-caliber smoothbore, the Upland might also be of interest to deer hunters in states like Massachusetts, where an unrifled bore is the only legal muzzle-loader to use during their black powder season.

Freedom Arms

Although announced last year, these miniature muzzle-loading revolvers are finally into production. Made entirely of stainless steel (except for the grips, which may be ordered in black plastic, rosewood or ivory), these spur trigger five-shot wheelguns use #11 caps and fire a soft lead 22-caliber conical bullet available from the firm. Each chamber in the cylinder holds about 10 grains of black powder and the manufacturer recommends using 4F priming powder. To load, the cylinders must be removed from the gun, which comes with a handy and necessary pliers-type loading tool.

All revolvers are supplied with 20 rounds of .22 conical bullets (a package containing 100 of these 29-grain conicals may be ordered from Freedom Arms for only $2.29), and a soft, zippered pouch for carrying and storage. Three versions of these mini-guns are available: bird's head butt with 1-inch barrel, bird's head grip with 1¾-inch barrel and a flat-bottomed grip version, called a Boot Gun, with a 3-inch barrel.

The two smallest guns can easily be concealed in an empty pack of cigarettes and the boot gun can be ordered with an optional leather holster that hooks over the top of your boots. I suspect it would even work well attached to a garter belt. Another intriguing accessory is an oval belt buckle with a recess for the 1-inch barreled revolver to snap into. A push of a button and the tiny five-shooter pops out into your hand . . . or onto the floor, if you're not fast enough!

Accessories

Most professional gunmakers have their own "secret formulas" that they covert away in the dark recesses of Michigan. Normally, most muzzle-loading rifles have only the halfcock notch of their hammer to serve as their safety. With the Silent Safety, however (a lever and sear arrangement which must be installed on the lock), the hammer can be kept at full cock without danger of it being tripped by the trigger. When ready to shoot, a safety lever on the side of the lockplate is silently released and the gun can be fired in a normal manner. Especially useful for hunters, the Silent Safety eliminates the sound shattering "click-click" of cocking the hammer and does away with the danger of walking around with a cocked rifle. Currently, Silent Safety is only available for Thompson/Center rifles but a new version for CVA rifles is coming out soon.

Another innovative design for hunters is the Buffalo Bullet, a pre-

Blue and Gray's Cap Guard is a waterproofing plastic ring that slips over the capped nipple on percussion rifles and pistols.

Squirrel rifle maker Ted Hatfield has bottled his various "secret formulas," each capped with red sealing wax.

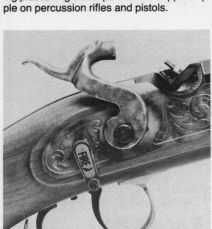

Silent Safety is a device which, when properly installed on the lock of a Thompson/Center or CVA rifle, effectively locks the hammer at half cock. (Tony MeDina photo)

their workshops. But Ted Hatfield, maker of the finely-crafted Hatfield Squirrel Rifle, has decided to package his firm's gun care products and market them. Available to the public for the first time this year are Hatfield's Warranted Gun Stock Stain, Gun Oil, Browning Solution, Gun Stock Finish and Black Powder Solvent.

Blue & Gray Products has come out with a simple yet effective plastic ring called Cap Guard that slips over a capped nipple, thereby providing a truly watertight seal that literally blows away when the gun is fired. This innovative firm also has a complete new line of muzzleloading shotgun wads in gauges ranging from 8 to 20. K&M Industries now has a brass screw-top waterproof container for #11 percussion caps.

One of the most novel new accessories is a device called Silent Safety, developed by Joseph Cott of Warren, lubed, conical hollow point bullet that provides a better gas seal with heavy hunting loads and improved expansion on game animals. Currently, Buffalo Bullets are available in 45, 50 and 54 caliber, which I will be testing on my next big game hunt this fall. Finally, Pyrodex has been improved! Not only is it easier to ignite and burns with a more consistent pressure, but it now comes in a wide mouth plastic moisture-inhibiting jar. And for ease of pouring, Butler Creek has come up with their Gunpowder Pour Spout, a snap-in plastic funnel that fits securely over the mouth of the Pyrodex container. Two sizes of pouring funnels are available; one fits the old-style cylindrical cardboard containers and the other snaps onto the new jar-shaped plastic container. Looks like things are continuing to improve for muzzleloaders each year! ●

The Gun That Followed the Famous Webley .455

by WILFRID WARD

DURING THE year 1921 Messrs Webley and Scott of Birmingham submitted to the War Office an experimental revolver and 200 rounds of ammunition. In outward appearance, the pistol seemed to be a scaled-down version of the Webley Mk. VI (.455) which had been the standard sidearm for a high proportion of British officers during the recent conflict. Despite its 38½ oz. weight the Mk. VI had been highly successful; the idea behind the change was to seek a .38 pistol with the stopping power of a .455. The consideration of the matter was in the hands of the Small Arms Committee under the Chairmanship of Colonel Lord Cottesloe.

This story is essentially a British one. Readers must not think that in treating this as such I have forgotten the great debt of gratitude which my country owes to the United States, nor the vast number of American handguns which came to us in the dark days of the 1940s. It is just that the 38 calibre selected became a peculiarly British one, and the American arms which came in it did so by virtue of the previous British decision. Accordingly I shall be looking at the history of this changeover almost exclusively in terms of Enfield and Webley revolvers.

The first of the many. Dated 1929, this was Serial No. 1. Note the marks on the various component parts. (Photo courtesy RSAF Enfield)

Destined to be the last of the great battle revolvers, the Enfield Mk. I .380 fell short.

This rather posed-looking scene makes it clear the No. 2 Mk 1* was in Australian hands at an early stage of the North African Campaign. (Photo courtesy Imperial War Museum)

The decision to change from one revolver to another, rather than to an automatic pistol had its origins in the trenches of 1914-18. There the Webley Mk. VI (.455) had proved its worth as a close combat arm. Its reliability was, perhaps, its greatest claim to fame, though its accuracy and easy double action pullthrough were high on its list of merits. Trench warfare made speed of fire with officers' personal weapons vital for survival. (The early automatics *did* jam and mishandle. Even so, many supported them.)

Because of this, a high proportion of ordinary officers and N.C.O.s became first-class double-action revolver shots. Examination of the two classic works on the subject, written by active officers, reveal Tracy (*Revolver Shooting in War*) and Pollard (*The Book of the Pistol*) both advocating pulling through on the "Trigger Action" and doing so in the fastest possible time *without pause*. The adoption of this method was an anticipation of the system with which McGivern was to work his wonders nearly twenty

years later. On a lower plane it made the British Army an early home of double action shooting. Although the double action pull on the Webley Mark VI was some three pounds heavier than that of its .38 successor it was probably less noticeable because of the greater weight of the Webley.

Thus, the new pistol was being considered by those who had this kind of practical experience at their disposal, which would have been shared by the Instructors from the Small Arms School at Hythe, many of whom actually conducted the trials of the pistols. Such decisions are not reached lightly. When we consider the whole story it is proper to remember that the idea behind the change can be likened to trying to get something for nothing. It sometimes works, but not often. When we look at the trials we can ask ourselves to what extent this result was achieved.

The tests carried out at Hythe in September, 1921, prior to the submission of the new revolvers to the Small

Arms Committee, were thorough. The improvements claimed by Webleys were examined and the shape of the butt criticized. Perhaps the most significant part of this report, in light of later events, was that the bullet was said to be still too light and it was thought that a longer cylinder was needed. In conclusion, there was a recommendation that information be sought as to the stopping power of the bullet compared with .45 revolvers and automatics.

The earliest trials were on the two revolvers supplied by Webleys. They comprised not only tests on these pistols, but comparisons with the *.455* Colt automatic and 9mm. Parabellum as well as the .455 Webley Mk. VI. In each instance, the two .38 Webleys (5-in. and 3-in. barrels) obtained the lowest muzzle velocities with the .455 Webley rather ahead. Both the Colt and the Parabellum readings were considerably higher. Roughly the same order was maintained with muzzle energy and striking energy. Penetration tests at 50 yards left the

En route for Norway, this officer wears the webbing holster, remarkably practical, and far superior to those used with the Sam Browne of the 1914-18 war. (Photo courtesy Imperial War Museum)

two .38s with penetrations of 1⅓ and 1 boards respectively, as against 2¼, 3 and 6 boards for the Mk. VI, Colt and Parabellum.

On the other hand the laurels in matters of weight and general handiness went unquestionably to the two new Webleys. Accuracy between the .38 and the .455 appeared to be roughly equal. Having examined the report, the Committee concluded that the saving of over a pound in weight was of the utmost importance, and decided that the stopping power of the new pistols should be investigated, but that preliminary shooting trials should be held before the "stopping" trials took place.

The performance of various American cartridges convinced the Committee that the .38 was capable of doing a satisfactory job at "pistol" distances, but at that stage no decision was reached as to which particular bullet was to be used.

It is of interest that at the same time as the .38s were under consideration the Enfield Factory (wishing to provide work for its skilled men) was producing an Enfield version of the Webley Mk. VI. This was designated the Pistol Revolver No. 1 Mk. VI .455. Thought was also being given as to whether this design could be simplified, the production cheapened, and the highest possible level of interchangeability of parts attained. No final decision was reached at that stage, (April, 1922) but proposals were invited from the factory with this end in view. When, by December, 1922, the tests on the .38s had progressed further, it was decided that the .38 should receive precedence.

In April, 1922, after further deliberations, the Commandant of the Small Arms School had reported his conclusion that, subject to certain provisos on "stopping power" and the shape of the grip, the new .38 referred to him would be a more suitable service weapon than the Mk. VI Webley. The report was particularly concerned with the grip, trigger release, and balance as well as accuracy and sights. In the view of the writer these points are all highly relevant to the question what kind of pistol the army wanted and why. Even at this early stage all indicators pointed to a *primarily* double action pistol with a single action capacity.

On the receipt of this report, the one matter outstanding was that of the stopping power of the new revolvers. Initially it was proposed to ask Webleys if they could arrange trials on this aspect of their pistols. In September, 1922, discussions were arranged, and after hearing General Pilcher's report it was decided that the stopping power of the pistol was adequate. The bullet in the Webley cartridges was a high shouldered 200-gr. bullet loaded into a .38 S&W case, and in July, 1923, it was decided to prepare designs for a cartridge loaded with such a bullet propelled by neonite.

By March, 1924, two revolvers were made by Webleys, incorporating the modifications suggested by the Small Arms School, together with cartridges loaded with 200-gr. and 145-gr. bullets. Further tests were carried out. These confirmed that the accuracy of the .455 and the .38 was roughly equal, and that as between the 5-in. and 6-in. varieties of barrel on the .38 there was also little to choose. After a number of minor details had been disposed of, the issues outstanding had been resolved into the grips and the weight of the trigger pull. The latter was agreed to have been too light and after experiments in August, 1925, it was decided that six sample pistols should be prepared.

In October, 1926, the .38 revolver was approved and all was set at Enfield to prepare for its manufacture there. The approval of the specifications of the new round then became of high priority. Further tests took place to determine between a lead-tin and a lead-antimony bullet. It was concluded that there was no material difference between the two. Penetration trials held in September, 1928, revealed that at ten yards the new .38 cartridge penetrated three boards whilst the *specification* for the .455 was only that it should penetrate two.

The end of the first stage of this story comes in February, 1929. The first production models of the new pistols were expected immediately and 20,000 rounds of ammunition were ordered for them.

Thus, after a great deal of experimentation, a new revolver design was arrived at. It was essentially a smaller version of the .455, but a great deal lighter. Its designers had also had in mind pointability and speed shooting in its design. Whilst Winans and Fairburn (the latter of the Shanghai police) had advocated fast shooting with the automatic, the Committee had placed its faith in the revolver, and had envisaged its users shooting double action and finding the target by instinct pointing. They did not, as their successors were to do, go the whole hog, and cut off the hammer spur, but they had gone a surprisingly long way along the road to total double action shooting.

The shape of bullet used was partially an innovation, but not entirely so, since there was a definite resemblance to the .455 Mk. l (Eley) "Manstopping" bullet. In light of the criticisms which were to be leveled against the cartridge with its later jacketed bullet, we are fortunate to have access to an almost contemporary expert criticism of the cartridge. This comes from Major (later Major General) Julian S. Hatcher in his *Textbook of Pistols and Revolvers* (Samworth 1935). There, the round is examined in the form of the .38 S&W, Super Police.

The cartridge in question was made by the Western Cartridge Company for solid frame revolvers chambered for the .38 S&W. Instead of the 146-grain bullet usual to that round, a high shouldered round-nosed bullet, apparently identical to the British 200-gr. bullet was loaded. The ballistics of the two rounds were identical. Western produced theirs in February, 1929, whilst the Webley version, as we have seen, was available in prototype form from about March, 1924. Commercially the latter was known as the ".38 Webley and Scott Special loaded with 200-gr. bullet" and Hatcher so describes it. (op. cit. p. 89)

It is interesting that in that passage he has high praise for the Webley which he says was designed to meet the demand for a lighter gun than the .455 Service arm, "Which would combine perfect balance and great accuracy *with exceptional stopping power*." He goes on to compliment the design of the grip (the obviation of need for a filler) refers to it as "this excellent revolver" and finally notes the exceptionally light trigger pull.

The ballistics of the Western and the Webley cartridges were, as we have seen identical. If there is a distinction in bullet shape it is not discernible to the naked eye, yet in his description of the Western cartridge (op.cit. p. 346) he goes on to say that a number of tests, which he had conducted on this "Low velocity heavy bullet" to see whether it had greater

This picture illustrates the great difference in bulk between the Webley Mk VI and the .38 Enfield. The latter appealed to the Small Arms Committee once they felt it had adequate stopping power. This .380 started life as a standard Mk 1, later despurred. (Photo courtesy B. E. Chaplin Ltd., Winchester)

.38/200 demonstration round compared with the later jacketed round shows the shape that might have made the difference in battle. (Photo courtesy RSAF Enfield)

stopping power than the regular load, were "inconclusive."

In a robust passage quoted from the company's letter to him, Hatcher gives us what I regard as conclusive evidence in favour of the *lead 200-gr.* bullet in either British or American cartridge:

"A policeman shot a holdup artist in East St. Louis the other day with this Super Police. Hit him square in the center of the back at 75 yards which was a darn good shot. When the coroner dug the bullet out of the crook he found it half-way through him and flattened on the point to about the size of a quarter."

As Hatcher goes on to advise against the use of the cartridge in tip-

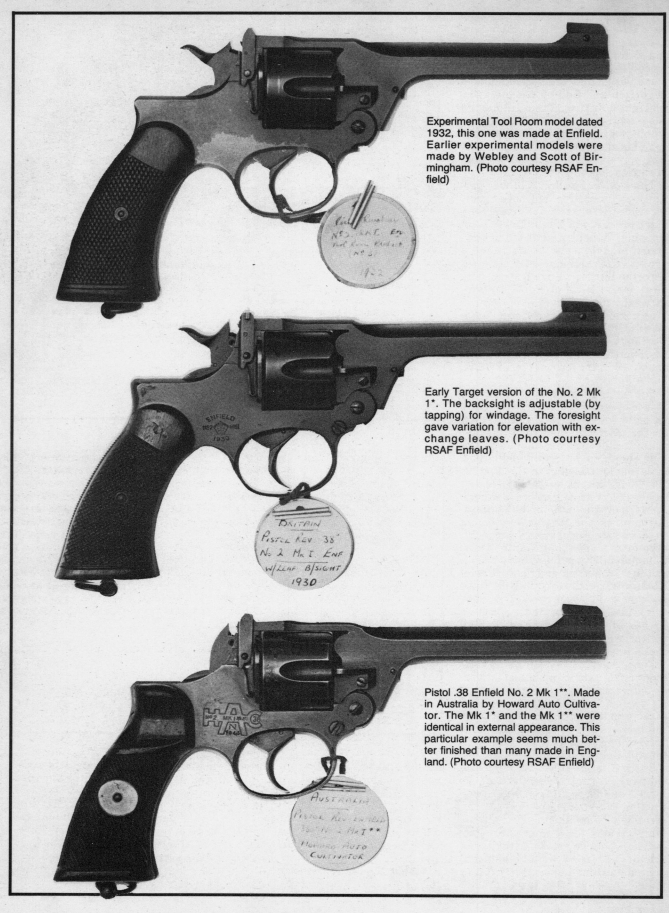

Experimental Tool Room model dated 1932, this one was made at Enfield. Earlier experimental models were made by Webley and Scott of Birmingham. (Photo courtesy RSAF Enfield)

Early Target version of the No. 2 Mk 1*. The backsight is adjustable (by tapping) for windage. The foresight gave variation for elevation with exchange leaves. (Photo courtesy RSAF Enfield)

Pistol .38 Enfield No. 2 Mk 1**. Made in Australia by Howard Auto Cultivator. The Mk 1* and the Mk 1** were identical in external appearance. This particular example seems much better finished than many made in England. (Photo courtesy RSAF Enfield)

The probable choice 1914-1918—the Webley Mk VI or the Webley automatic. Officers provided their own pistols and the latter was a popular choice in France. (Photo courtesy B. E. Chaplin Ltd., Winchester)

up revolvers it could be that the American version was more potent. I do not think this to have been the case however, rather that the problem had been anticipated in the alteration of the latch of the Webley and Enfield. (Note: There were, of course, a great many lightly constructed tip-up revolvers in use here. Editor.)

By the end of 1929, therefore, it seems reasonable to conclude that the British forces were being re-equipped with a worthy new revolver. Although doubtless many then, as today, would have preferred to have had an automatic, this was a debatable issue. The chosen weapon had been well designed by a highly experienced firm and improved on by tests by experts. Looking back it seems that even the recurrent doubts about stopping power on balance were not justified in relation to the 200-gr. lead bullet. Yet it was this wisp of cloud on the horizon in the late 1920s which was to turn into a thunderstorm and would eventually destroy the reputation of this finely planned pistol during the 1939/45 war.

In service terms, there was never any accuracy problem with the new pistols. Some users thought that the 200-gr. bullet kicked even more than the .455. It is probable that this impression arose in part from the lightness of the pistol and the different shape of the grips. As far as one can see, however, these were probably the sum of the complaints. Although

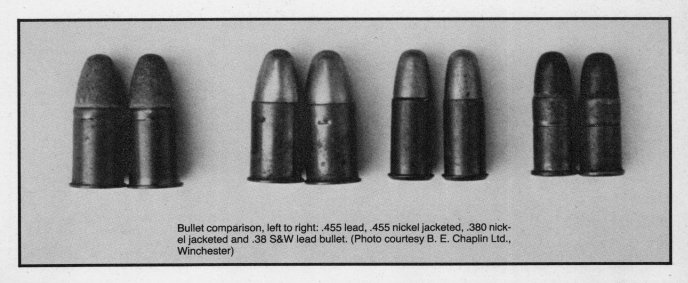

Bullet comparison, left to right: .455 lead, .455 nickel jacketed, .380 nickel jacketed and .38 S&W lead bullet. (Photo courtesy B. E. Chaplin Ltd., Winchester)

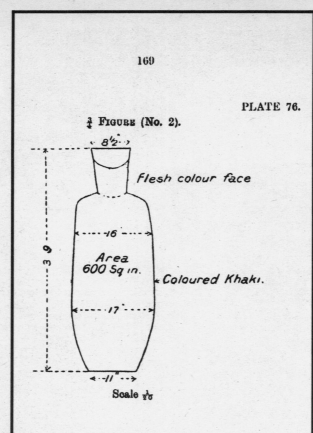

169

PLATE 76.

¾ FIGURE (No. 2).

8'2"

Flesh colour face

16

Area
600 Sq in.

← Coloured Khaki.

3 9

17

11"

Scale 1/10

Revolver target, *circa* 1925. (Courtesy Imperial War Museum)

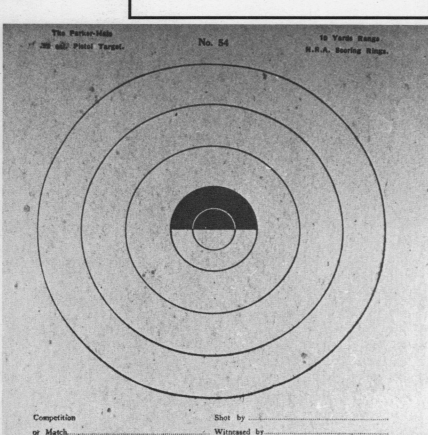

This is the 10-yard N.R.A. Target. The other targets were identical but larger according to distance.

there had been a mention of a lighter bullet for target shooting, this suggestion was never followed up.

For service training purposes, outline silhouettes were used, with a central rectangle 12 × 16-in. and a 1-in. square at the center. The purpose of these courses of fire was to teach the user *adequate* accuracy coupled with speed. It was all realistic shooting aimed at producing effective revolver shooting rather than pursuing unnecessary accuracy at the cost of speed.

The targets used at Bisley were the standard N.R.A. (of G.B.) one of which I illustrate. The only military feature, if it can be so termed, was the semicircular aiming mark. This was black on a grey ground, the rings scoring 5, 4, 3, 2, with one point for a hit anywhere else. The black portion was intended to represent a tin helmet projecting over the top of the trench.

The shoots were held at 50, 20 and 10 yards with six-shot strings. Timings were 2 minutes (50 yds.), 1 minute (20 yds.), 15 seconds (20 yds.), and 10 seconds (10 yds.). This course of fire had existed since the early 1920s, the figure targets used by Winans and his contemporaries having been abandoned earlier. The course had a lot of double action in it, but the 50-yd. string called for slowfire accuracy, as did that at 20 yds. At 10 yds. there was the nearest thing to quick shooting. What was needed was a combination of accuracy and speed.

In the latter days of the competition, most competitors fired all the rapid strings double-action. Those who were using the hammerless version of the Enfield had to pull through. When I shot this competition, it was still theoretically possible to use a .455 though few, if any, were seen apart from that used by our team. Ours fired jacketed bullets and was wildly inaccurate.

For the most part it was won by the Royal Air Force. They used .380 Smith & Wessons with 6-in. barrels. Bisley did not change very quickly in those days (late 1950s) as was evidenced by the fact that the use of the Webley Fosbery Automatic revolver was still precluded by the rules—though I doubt whether anyone had thought of using the weapon for the previous twenty years or more. The R.A.F. held the trophy for a number of years, this was I think, because of the actual shooters in the respective teams rather than any superiority of weapon (until they got K 38's chambered for the service cartridge.)

Some quite outstanding performances were put up with Enfields, particularly in the 10-second series

These two revolvers from the Editor's collection are what might be found in the U.S. The No. 2 Mark I at top is dated 1933, has the later bulky Bakelite grips. The war-finish model below has the slim wood grips.

where possibles were by no means unheard of. One trouble which reflected the difficulties in the early days of the jacketed cartridge was that sometimes a bullet would stick in the barrel. With all the noise a competitor would quite often not notice this. The result was a barrel with six bullets in it and a bulge as well. On the occasion that I did this I found that there was little or no difference in the later performance of the pistol despite the bulge, but I got another barrel just to be on the safe side. Though there may have been cases of this with Webleys and Enfields, I do not remember coming across one. The popular belief was

that it did not happen with the 5-in. barrels, only occasionally with Smith and Wessons, and not the British revolvers.

Although the 200-gr. bullet worked reasonably well as far as one can tell, trouble was at hand for the Enfield pistol. It came from an unexpected source—The Hague Convention. During the 1914 War revolver bullets had been either lead or a lead/antimony mixture. They were not jacketed. Whether a plain lead projectile was prohibited under the terms of the Hague Conference of 1899 was (and is) debatable. Then, the use of bullets "which expand or flatten easily in the

human body, such as bullets with hard envelopes which do not entirely cover the core, or are pierced with incisions" was prohibited. This declaration was ratified in Article 23 (a) of the Hague Regulations of 1907. Regulation 23 (e) particularly forbade the use of arms, projectiles or materials calculated to cause unnecessary suffering, specifying, amongst other items, bar shot, hot shot and chain shot.

During the 1914 conflict the British and American view was that this article did not prohibit the use of lead shot in shotguns. Indeed, these continued to be used both in Malaya and

Vietnam. In the 1930s Germany, whose 9mm Parabellum pistols happily handled jacketed bullets, maintained that the prohibition extended to all lead bullets. There was perhaps some plausibility to this argument, since the theory behind the big slow moving bullets of both .455 and .380 was that they toppled on hitting the target thus causing a much bigger wound internally. The broad striking surface also increased the impact.

Whatever the legal arguments on this point may have been, in 1937 Britain gave way and the .380 Mk. II cartridge was approved on October 22nd of that year.

Extensive trials had, of course, been carried out before this bullet shape and weight was adopted. Bear-

side causing a good deal of logistic confusion with the arrival of .38 Specials under Lend Lease, was to reveal a lamentable lack of killing power when put to the ultimate test of wartime use.

It is not the wish of the writer to criticise the designers of this round, but it is quite clear that in the jacketed form it was not suited for use in most revolvers with 6-in. barrels, even though they were chambered for .38 S&W. Moreover, even in the Enfield for which it was designed, it suffered severe limitations. If proof of the former be needed it exists at the Imperial War Museum, where a Colt is to be found with the last two inches of its barrel bored smooth. This was to prevent the bullets from sticking. As-

It was strongly rumoured during the 1940s that .455s were being called in so that they might be sent from European theatres of war to the Far East. A comparison of the relative stopping power of the .38 and the .455 (and perhaps some confirmation for the rumour) can be had from the singular adventure of Subadar (later Captain) Lal Bahadur Thapa V.C. 2nd Ghurkas. When faced with a German patrol, he shot five of them with his .455 Webley Mk. VI using his right hand, then disposed of the remaining three with his Kukri, which he had in his left hand. If there were any more one would feel that they had already left. According to surgeon Rear Admiral Beadnell R.N. (Rtd) the striking velocity of the .455 was 210

In the Long Range Desert Group, this belt carries a .45 1917 S&W. There seems to have been widespread distrust of the stopping power of the .38 cartridge. (Photo courtesy Imperial War Museum.)

ing in mind the extent of the earlier trials, one can only assume that within the predetermined limits of the pistol and the need for a jacketed bullet the round produced was as good as the circumstances permitted. It is only sad that the fighting years of so excellent a revolver should have been marred by cartridge troubles which rendered it unreliable to say the least of it.

The new bullet weighed 178 grains and was cylindro-conoidal in shape, whilst its predecessor had a hemispherical nose and a cylindrical body. The jacket was cupro nickel or gilding metal (from March, 1941, onwards) and the core a lead alloy of 2% antimony. It was this cartridge which, be-

suming that the bullet left the barrel satisfactorily, it was by no means certain that even a whole cylinder-full of cartridges would stop one's opponent.

Whilst researching for this article, I have heard two examples of this. In the first instance a friend of mine made up a dummy in a service greatcoat and fired his revolver at it. The bullets did not penetrate far enough to wound. In the second case, my informant discharged all six shots at an oncoming Japanese. The latter fell to the ground, only to get up immediately to return to the attack, though all 6 shots were in his chest. It was only the intervention of a soldier armed with a rifle, who dispatched the Japanese, which saved the officer to tell the tale.

ft. lbs. as against 155 ft. lbs. for the Mk II .380 cartridge.

Though the change of bullet was not a success, there came in 1937 a further series of experiments which was to make this ill-fated pistol one of the most interesting to come from the service of any country. This was the Pistol Revolver No. 2 Mk.1* in experimental form. Though popularly referred to as the "Commando" Enfield I have found no evidence to imply that this pistol was in any way particular to these crack troops. If anyone was specially considered it was the tank drivers and those likely to be using the pistols in confined circumstances where the hammer might snag clothing on the pistol being drawn. Doubtless Commandos and other special groups received preferential treatment as to *all* their requirements, but I think that the designers felt the improvements would be beneficial to everyone equipped with a revolver.

Basically it was an ordinary .380 Enfield with the spur of the hammer cut off and the single-cocking notch eliminated. At that stage the butt was still unaltered. In the trials the old shape of butt was criticized and the distinctive and fatter style illustrated was eventually adopted. With this total commitment to double action there was inevitably some heart searching. As already noted, the authorities regarded a double action shot as the ideal response to an emergency. This was, it was said, particularly important as this style of shooting produced greater efficiency *in the hands of less experienced shots.*

Though utterly true, one expects such a lesson to be propounded more in the hills of Montana than in Whitehall. Yet was it quite unconnected? Was it pure coincidence that in McGivern's *Fast and Fancy Revolver Shooting* (published in 1938) all of the twenty exercises for *trainee* police officers involve double-action shooting at distances up to 45 yards? We shall never know; but not to have considered the theories of the world's fastest revolver shot when deciding what to do to the world's only service revolver might be thought remiss.

The basis of the tests was a comparison between the two versions of the Enfield. The new version was less accurate in many of the tests, but only in the grouping was there much in it. On the other hand the hardest test of all—three shots from the left hand in three seconds—was won by the new pistol by a modest margin. Both in the duelling phase and the dummy trench users preferred the hammerless version. The same was true of the loophole shot where the smoother action of the latter also found most favour, though the accuracy was about the same. In concluding with its preference the report gave four good reasons for their choice all of which ring true today:

1. It was easier to fire, needing only one identical manipulation.
2. It gave greater confidence. Accidental discharge was less likely. (A real point with a conscript army.) Particularly suitable for use from loophole, horse, or cycle (mechanization was not then completed).
3. Only the first shot tended to inaccuracy, especially at speed.
4. Finally, and probably most appealingly to the authorities, it represented a simplification of training.

The question of new shape to the grips was referred to the Small Arms School; also serrations were to be applied to the back strap despite an intimation that their omission would cheapen production. The wooden grips, so well made in early specimens, were to be replaced by Bakelite grips for *gas proofing*. The new shape also helped to get a good grip for instinct shooting. The two deep cuts acted as thumb rests (right- or left-handed) and assisted both consistency and speed. This is how the penultimate version of the pistol came into being. The final version was the Pistol Revolver No 2 Mk.1**. In appearance this was identical to the Mk.1*, but the hammer safety stop had been removed. This modification was not a success and in most instances was cancelled by the re-installation of the stops after the war.

The Army had designed the new modification. Again the merit of handiness played a big part in the new shape. After two sets of trials and subsequent alterations, the final shape of the pistol was probably as good a factory-made shape for a double-action revolver as could be designed. The actual operation was easier than any competitor, and the top break frame made for quick loading. In other words, the final version of this pistol was just about as good as any revolver could be until one came to remember that it was a service pistol with a cartridge which was just not up to service requirements.

How does one look at such a pistol? It cannot be dismissed as useless. Those who planned it did so with the utmost care. In its early form it probably was all that Webleys and Enfield hoped for it. Factors beyond their control overtook it. Wartime conditions would have given opportunity to test the new cartridges in action; yet as it was adopted in 1937, the opportunity did not exist.

In the early days with the 200-gr. bullet, the pistol was as good a revolver as could be hoped for. By seeking to reduce weight and keep stopping power, the designers had sailed dangerously close to the wind, but they had got away with it. Whether they should have foreseen what happened is not for us to speculate. In light of the very long development period it is probably too much to demand of them.

What we do know is the weakness which the jacketed bullet, lighter and without the more lethal hemispherical nose, showed up in the pistol. Good design and perhaps a touch of good luck had saved it once. It did not do so the second time. From the viewpoint of the student it is only sad that the hammerless version was not thought of ten years earlier. Then we would have seen what a good double action revolver shooting its proper cartridge could do. This was not to be.

Perhaps the lesson for the future is that one should beware of changes which appear too easy. Had the original weight been less and the chosen calibre larger things might have worked out differently, but that is speculation, too! ●

Postscript

The Enfield .380 revolver was declared obsolete in 1957. It was succeeded by the 9mm Browning which had first been used by British troops in its Canadian version during the war. The .380 continued to be used in some parts of the Commonwealth. The last news which I had of it came through the Editor. He had, he tells me, discovered a substantial quantity of .38/200 cartridges and contemplated a purchase. When he returned to make this they had all gone. The war in Afghanistan had just started. It was probably just a coincidence, but if it was not, it just might be that someone who loved Freedom more than the provisions of the Hague Declaration shared my view that the 38/200 was an effective cartridge after all.

Acknowledgements

I wish to acknowledge the very considerable help which I have received from the Royal Small Arms Factory at Enfield especially from Mr. H. Woodend, to the Trustees of the Imperial War Museum Lambeth Road, London SE1 and particularly my friend David Penn, Keeper of the Firearms, for his assistance. I am indebted to both of these establishments for the opportunity to take photographs of their exhibits. Readers wishing to make further study are referred to the *Webley Story* (Major W.C. Dowell) and *Pistols of the World* (Hogg & Weeks). Finally I am especially indebted to Mr. Owen of W & C Scott, Ltd. of Birmingham for his assistance in many aspects of this article. He had the distinction of testing the last Webley Mk. IV produced by that firm.

SCOPES AND MOUNTS

The world without Weaver

by BOB BELL

THE MOST shocking scope news to come along in years is that the W.R. Weaver Co. has gone out of business. I had trouble believing it when a friend phoned from El Paso, though I knew the company had been for sale for upwards of a year. In January, 1983, I was writing a story on their 50th anniversary. Now, as of January 1984, the company which did more than any other to help the average shooter get a scope on his rifle is out of existence.

The official explanation is that it became impossible to compete economically with the Japanese-built imports. Perhaps that's so. But I have a hunch that if Bill Weaver were still alive, the company would still be churning out scopes by the boxcar load and shipping them around the world. Some companies are essentially one-man operations, even when they employ hundreds, and I think that's the way it was with Weaver. Well, maybe by the time you read this, some other individual will be making Weaver work. I hope so. Weaver had some interesting stuff on tap for announcement this year.

Meanwhile, other companies are busily supplying scopes. Let's look at the situation.

Bausch & Lomb, after a long absence, got back into hunting scopes a year ago with the introduction of the 3-9x and 4x we described last year. The variable has been in use on a M700 Remington 7mm Magnum for quite a while now, and it's an impressive item. It's bigger than I like, but that's a factor that doesn't seem to bother most users.

New this year there's a pair of variables that bracket the conventional powers. First is a 1.5-6x big game model, while the second is an action-mounted 6-24x apparently intended for varmint shooters. The smaller model has a 60-foot field at bottom power, which means it is suitable for moving game at brush ranges, or for dangerous game if the rifle is properly stocked. At top power, it will provide all the aiming precision needed for shots at the longest range most anyone should be trying. At 11 inches and almost 14 oz., this is neither a small nor light scope, but as with other B&Ls from years gone by, we expect it will be durable. At bottom power, it

Shepherd 3-9x Dual Reticle scope, here mounted on Bob Bell's Featherweight M70 30-06, is a highly sophisticated design for long range shooting. Covered fully in last year's GD, its qualities can be summarized as: one-shot zeroing, parallax elimination, and a range-compensating reticle which permits dead-on aiming to extreme range. Lenses are multi-coated for light transmission well above 90% according to designer Dan Shepherd. (Bob Haines photo)

has a 14mm exit pupil, which will make rapid aiming easy.

The 6-24x is 16.5 inches long and weighs 21.1 oz. Its objective unit focuses for range, with the lens having an unobstructed diameter of 40mm. This is about as large as you can go and still use conventional mounts, and it's big enough to transmit plenty of light at most powers.

Both B&L variables mount solidly. As with the two earlier ones, they have multi-coated lenses and thick-walled mono-tube construction machined from a single section of air-craft-grade anodized alloy. The internal adjustments are valued at ⅓-MOA on the 1.5-6x, ¼-minute on the 6-24x. The manufacturer states that point of impact changes resulting from changing power are nonexistent. We haven't had a chance to test that yet, so far as we could tell it was true on the earlier 3-9x. Fixed elements are secured and sealed with anaerobic adhesives, which is said to result in waterproof and fogproof scopes.

In case you hadn't noticed, both of these new scopes give a power spread in which the top magnification is four times the lowest. That's unusual, the usual ratio is 3:1. Except for the B&L 6-24x introduced in the mid-'50s, it would be awfully hard to name another scope offering this range. Thirty-some years ago, B&L was intending to introduce two variables, a 6-12x for varmint hunting and a 12-24x for target work, but they managed to put it all into one model, the BALvar 24, with a new optical principle developed during work on that early scope.

Apparently the same principle is incorporated here. The BALvar 24 has been gone for 15 years, but anyone who wants a new B&L of the same power can now have it . . . . at a list price of $399.95. The 1.5-6x retails for $299.95.

Bushnell also has a number of new scopes this year. As a followup to the 4x and 3-9x Banner Lite-Sites introduced in 1983, there is now a 1.5-6x Banner Lite-Site. Somewhat smaller than the B&L described above—9.8 inches, 12.4 oz.—it obviously has similar application for hunters. There is one important additional feature—a center aiming dot created by a battery. Or more precisely, by two alkaline A76 "button" batteries located in a rectangular housing atop the ocular bell. When switched on, a bright red dot is projected onto the recticle intersection, making it possible to aim accurately at any target which can be seen at all. New batteries are capable of powering the dot for six hours of continuous use, which should translate into weeks of actual field use. Price, $219.95.

For those needing a high-power variable, there's now a 6-18x Banner. Lenses of course are fully coated, and the power change system is sealed with O-ring moisture barriers. To make things easier for the silhouette shooters, heat-treated steel adjustment screws are encircled with sharp-edged serrations. Spring-loaded plungers of hardened steel give ⅛-MOA clicks which can be both felt and heard. Screw-on caps protect the adjustments when not in use.

This 6-18x is 14.5 inches long and weighs 16 oz. The objective unit focuses as close as 10 yards, which means it could be used for some indoor shooting. Price, $179.95.

In response to the needs of serious hunters who long have complained about the shiny finish of most scopes, Bushnell now is offering black matte finishes on two of their top-of-the-line Scopechiefs, the 4x and the 2.5-8x. I doubt if the average buyer will go for these—most seem to prefer glistening guns and glass sights to match—but I hope Bushnell will keep them in the line for the guys who need and want them. I gotta admit they have a more professional look than I reach with my can of flat black spray paint.

Bushnell's Sportview line has been expanded to include two Rangemaster variables, a 3-9x and a 4-12x. They use the Multi-X reticle plus a stadia wire paralleling the horizontal cross-wire to form a range finding unit. At low power, the space between these subtends 14 inches at 115 yards, 18 at 150, and 24 at 200—the approximate withers-to-brisket measurements of pronghorns, deer and elk. In use, the animal is bracketed between the wires by turning the power adjustment ring. The ring has color-coded range numbers for each animal. The distance is then dialed onto the numbered elevation drum, which permits a dead-on hold.

These scopes come with three elevation drums, one of which will correlate closely with the bullet path of most any load. After sighting in at 150 yards, the elevation drum is removed and replaced with its 150-yard marking positioned next to an index dot on the turret housing. This puts everything into synchronization, assuming those distant animals are actually the size you expect, etc., etc. But that's an assumption most so-called rangefinding scopes make nowadays, so this system doubtless works as well as all the rest.

The 3-9x, which has a 32mm objective, lists for $79.95, the 4-12x 40mm at $99.95.

Bushnell also has some new mounts this year. For handgunners, extruded alloy bases are available for numerous Colt, Smith & Wesson, Ruger, Dan Wesson and Thompson/Center models. They have male dovetails to accommodate rings which are recessed around their full circumference to hold neoprene bushings that cradle the scope. These improved gripping surfaces help to eliminate the forward creep of the scope on hard-kicking combinations.

Buehler's new M83 handgun mount has a recoil shoulder to catch the rear of this Blackhawk's top strap — a good idea.

Left — In addition to their extensive gun mount line, Williams now markets mounts for installing scopes or iron sights on bows. Who says archers are neglected? Below — Williams has taken a different approach. They put irons on top instead of providing a tunnel to view barrel-mounted sights.

Below — Bushnell Lite-Sites, here in 1.5-6x, have battery-supplied center aiming dot of light which makes exact aim possible in the dimmest ambient light.

Matte finish is now offered on several Bushnells, including 2.5-8x Scopechief. This is an improvement for serious hunters.

A new Bushnell rifle mount is offered in one height, designed so that a 40mm objective bell will clear the barrel. It will fit most standard rifles including the Browning BBR, Remington M700, Ruger 77, Savage 110, Weatherby Mark V, and Winchester 70. Bottom sections of the rings are integral with the bases, eliminating the usual joint here. Made of extruded alloy, the ring tops are secured with two #6 screws which fit into counterbored recesses.

Also new is a see-thru mount with a wide V beneath the scope to permit instant use of iron sights. The units are angled rather than vertical, so they can be installed in swept-back or swept-forward configuration, to clear enlarged objective or ocular bells or

the adjustment turret. Or the scope can be mounted farther forward than normal for extra eye relief on heavy recoiling rifles.

Burris continues to expand their line of scopes with two new Intermediate Eye Relief (IER) models for 1984 and one 4-12x Mini for the guy who wants a small scope with a lot of power. The latter is only 11.2 inches long and weighs 15 oz., which means it is almost four inches shorter than the standard Burris 4-12x and 3 oz. lighter. You have to pay for the size reduction some way, so field is noticeably smaller at bottom power, 19 ft. vs. 27, but at the top end you lose only 2 feet, 8 vs. 10. On the other hand, you gain a half-inch of eye relief, with 3.75 inches in the Mini. Either Plex or dot

reticle is available, the latter varying from 2 inches down to 0.7 at 12x.

The IER models are intended for handgun use. A new 7x has an adjustable objective to allow precise focusing for range and parallax elimination. Target knobs with click adjustments are standard. Eye relief is 10-16 inches, weight 11.5 oz. and length 11.5 inches. Field, 6½ ft.

The second IER is a 10x. At 13.6 inches, it requires a barrel length of at least 14 inches. Eye relief is 9-14 inches, and the objective unit is adjustable. At 14 oz., this is neither a light nor small scope, as handgun models go, but I'm sure many hotshots will grab it for the extra power. It wasn't long ago that any scope on a handgun was an oddity; now there are shooters using scopes of more power than many riflemen prefer—and hitting targets that a lot of us long-gunners would miss. This 10x IER-PA has only a 4-foot field, so it's not for the beginner. As with the other two new models, it's offered with either Plex or center dot.

Prices: 7x IER-PA, $189.95; 10x IER-PA, $199.95; 4-12x Mini, $249.95. Dots are extra.

Also new this year are 1-inch "22" steel scope rings to fit grooved rimfire receivers, in medium or high heights. And if you want engraved rings for the high power mount, they're now offered in low or medium versions. The pattern atop the rings is a gold pigment-filled starburst. $79.95 per pair.

Leupold has boosted the power choice in their Vari-X II line by adding a 4-12x this year. This range of course accommodates for most big game and varmint shooting, handling what might be called average-type shots in either field. With a field just under 23 feet at 4x, it isn't really a brush gun, but most of the guys who hunt such cover are specialists who know what they need without any advice from me. Leupold's small variable or 2½x Compact can handle all such chores, of course. This 4-12x is intended for those who usually work at longer distances but want a fairly small scope for all the obvious reasons.

The 6x Compact announced a year or so ago is now also made with an adjustable objective for those who want this refinement. This power apparently is gaining converts again—it was reasonably popular with varmint shooters in the late '40s and early '50s, 'til the magnification mania took over—with mountain and plains hunters turning to it now. At the distances they work, field is no problem and the extra power, compared to the long-popular 4x, can be helpful. Twenty-some years ago, when I spent a few days with bulletmaker Fred Barnes, I noticed that he had 6x's on all his long range hunting rifles, and no one can deny he knew what shooting was about. Maybe we're coming full circle in this area too. This 6x Compact is only 11 inches long and 10 oz., with 33mm objective lens. Personally, for big game use I'd pick the original model with solid objective—it offers less opportunity for leakage on a rough hunt and parallax is insignificant. For varmint use, the adjustable objective will make exact focusing easy.

The 3-9x Compact is now made with a matte finish. It weighs only 9.5 oz. Leupold also has a new mount base for the Thompson/Center T.C.R. 83 single shot rifle.

Lyman is now offering their bench-rest scope in 35x as well as 25x and 20x, the top power listing at $399.95. I haven't used this high-magnification entry, but years ago did considerable shooting with a 20x Lyman—which we felt was a lot of magnification at the time—and liked the scope a lot. Lyman's bench models can be had with standard (.0005) or extra fine (.0003) crosswires, or ¼- or ⅛-minute dots.

In the hunting line, Lyman now has a straight 4x, 2-7x and 3-9x variables, and three Silhouette models (which

Top — New Mini model from Burris is the 4-12x with range focusing unit. It's the sort of scope the pronghorn and prairie dog shooter will like on a 243-class rifle. Middle — Burris' 7x IEZR-PA (parallax adjustment) means handgunners can have high power glass and focus precisely for range. Bottom — For those who want to aim at a bullet mark on their silhouette targets, this new 10x Burris IER-PA should make it possible.

Last year Bausch & Lomb re-entered the scope market with a big 3-9x and a straight 4x. This year they lengthened the line by bracketing the variable with this 1.5-6x (top) and the 6-24x. One or the other ought to solve most hunters' sighting problems. All mount solidly and have multi-coated lenses.

also double for varmint shooting) in 6x, 8x and 10x.

Redfield is celebrating its 75th anniversary this year, the company having been founded by John Redfield in 1909. A peace officer, government hunter, scout and inventor, Redfield reversed Greeley's advice and went east—well, southeast—from his Glendale, Oregon, birthplace to Denver, hoping the Colorado gold and silver miners would have need of a rock drill he had invented. The mines were petering out when he arrived, so he turned his attention back to the gun field and founded the Redfield Gunsight Co.

There was almost no popular demand—or even knowledge—of scopes in those days, and no Redfield scopes existed. The famous No. 70 and No. 80 Redfield iron sights were early prod-

Left — Cincinnati Cinova 80 milling machine helps Conetrol maintain same-day shipment policy. That's boss George Miller himself at the wheel. Below — Fluted Conetrol bases are new this year, give a custom look to a factory product. Now available for M70 and large ring Mauser; others take a few weeks.

Leupold 4x Compact will fit on Ruger 77's integral mounts, but short tube length allows no possibility of fore-and-aft movement to adjust for eye relief. Still, it should work for most shooters.

2½x Leupold Compact looks right at home on S&W 1700 270, gives big performance out of a small unit.

ucts and led to an extensive line of hunting and target sights.

He designed the efficient and now worldwide-used Redfield Jr. and Sr. scope mounts, featuring the rotary dovetail which made proper zeroing easy even with scopes that had no windage adjustment, as was common in those days. Other Redfield company developments have included the constantly centered nonmagnifying reticle, the Accu-Range rangefinder reticle, the Widefield concept which increases horizontal field dimensions, and the Accu-Trac trajectory compensating system.

Currently, the top of the Redfield line is the 3-9x Illuminator, which features an unusually sophisticated objective unit and is made in both Traditional (round eyepiece) and Widefield versions. Other traditionals are offered in 2½x, 4x (two models, one being a ¾-inch tube with enlarged lenses for rimfires), 6x, 2-7x, 3-9x (two versions), 4-12x and 6-18x. Then there are a half-dozen Low Profile Widefields, which have flattened objectives to allow lower than normal mounting; three are straight and three variable. There are also three Tracker models, 4x, 2-7x and 3-9x. Though lower priced than the traditionals and LPWs, the Trackers retain the one-piece tube construction. Trackers are now available with matte or polished finishes. Three SR bases (for the FN, 70A and 700) are made with a dull finish.

Weatherby started his rifle business in 1945 and brought out his first scope line, the Imperials, in 1953. These were not adaptable to the image-moving principle which permitted constantly centered reticles, so were replaced by the Premier line. Now, there is a new Weatherby scope line, the Supreme. It consists of five models, a 4x44 and 3-9x44, the latter number indicating the diameter of the objective lenses—44mm; a 4x34 and a 2-7x34; and a 1.75-5x20. The latter three are more compact and thus more suitable for normal or thick-cover use.

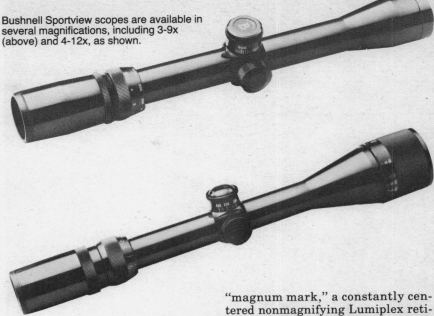

Bushnell Sportview scopes are available in several magnifications, including 3-9x (above) and 4-12x, as shown.

These Supremes have multi-coated lenses, for superior light transmission and color rendering. This process, which is an improvement over the conventional single magnesium fluoride coating, was developed by Zeiss and has been in use on certain camera lenses for some time, as well as on Zeiss scopes. Burris and Bausch & Lomb are the only other American scope companies I can think of which use multi-coating. Whether they all have the same number of coatings, I can't say.

The Supremes have binocular-type focusing for the eye, a neoprene eyepiece ring to reduce the chance of a

Leupold 6x Compact has already found following among mountain and plains hunters.

Leupold's 3-9x Compact sits low on gun, provides top optics in a reasonable-size package.

"magnum mark," a constantly centered nonmagnifying Lumiplex reticle which appears black against light backgrounds and seems to lighten against dark ones, and the Autocom system which is designed to automatically compensate for trajectory without making elevation adjustments.

Zeiss announced their C-Series of scopes in 1981, and these four models—4x, 6x, 3-9x and 10x—continue to be available. They were created for the American market, and thus have one-inch tubes, centered and nonmagnifying reticles, reasonable-size objectives, one-piece tubes with integral adjustment turrets, and accurate internal adjustments. In addition, the oculars have diopter adjustments for fast easy eye focusing, cushioned eyepieces, and multilayer coating that boosts light transmission. Eye relief on all four scopes is 3½ inches, with the full field available from that distance.

B-Square continues to expand their line of no-gunsmithing lightweight mounts—2½ oz. or so in most cases. The Model Seven Remington unit is interesting in that the rear scope ring is situated about midway of the action opening, allowing a forward position of the ocular on this short action. The front ring sits ahead of the receiver ring on the extended one-piece base which of course utilizes the factory-drilled holes.

The Lightweight Mount is now also made for the Ruger 10/22, 77, and TCR-83, Heckler & Koch sporting rifles, Winchester, Remington and Savage bolt guns. There are also versions for various shotguns using conventional scopes or Aimpoints, high-grade airguns, and many handguns.

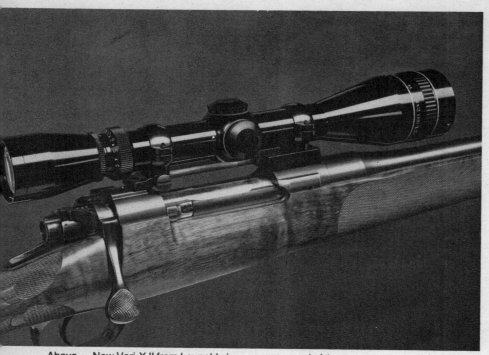

Above — New Vari-X II from Leupold gives power spread of 4-12x, so will cover all hunting situations except brush shooting — and many will use it there, too. Mount base is relieved to clear power adjustment ring if stock-crawler needs to move scope ahead.

Redfield's Tracker line can be had with dull matte finish, making these reasonably priced scopes even better for hunters.

Redfield has produced a special, very valuable, 75th Anniversary hand-engraved rifle and scope set. There's a one-of-a-kind gold medallion inset in the turret, while the Weatherby Mark V has extensive engraving, gold overlay and an exceptional walnut stock. The set, in a walnut and glass display case, has been donated to the National Rifle Association and will be sold to the highest bidder to assist in financing the new NRA Museum.

B-Square has many other scope-related items, including machined wrenches for tightening Redfield-type windage screws and Weaver-type base-locking screws. They beat hell out of screwdrivers and coins.

Buehler's new M83 handgun mount, crafted of aircraft aluminum alloy, is available in either black or silver finish, and is designed for calibers up through the 357 Magnum. It is currently available for the S&W K, L and N models, Dan Wesson, Colt Python, Trooper Mk III and V, Ruger Blackhawk, Single Six and Security Six. Others soon. Price, $68.25 to match stainless guns, $57.25 blued. The mount sits on the topstrap and has a recoil shoulder at the rear to catch the upper frame. Hex-screw-fastened sideplates help secure the base to the gun, and two rifle-type rings attach the scope to the base.

Buehler offers over 100 different mount base combinations—they can solidly attach a scope to most anything. And they'll custom make bases for rifles not now covered.

Clear View See-Thru Mounts now are also available in a broad-view version, which means the bottom holes through which the iron sights are used have been widened considerably to increase field. This can be a help on running shots. Their M101 fits Weaver-type bases, and since these are made for practically everything, the Clear View mounts can be used on most any rifle. Side-mounted versions are made for the M94 Winchester, including the Big Bore variation, utilizing factory screw holes. There is a rimfire version for grooved receivers. It will accept one-inch tubes and can be had with inserts for 7/8- or 3/4-inch scopes.

New from Clear View this year are thirteen scopes, including two handgun models. There are three Standard grade rifle models—4x32mm, 3-9x32mm and 3-9x40mm—and eight Prestige grades—2.5x32mm, 4x32mm, 4x32 with adjustable objective 4x40mm wide angle, 1.5-5x32mm, 2-7x32mm, 3-9x40mm wide-angle and 3-9x with range adjustment. The handgun models are 1.5x20mm and 4x32mm, with long eye relief. All Clear View scopes have duplex reticles, quarter-minute internal adjustments, nitrogen filling, and coated lenses.

Conetrol has refined the bases of their popular mount by fluting the top outer corners to give a look which formerly was available only on custom designs. The new design is currently in production for the standard M70

Winchester and large ring military Mauser actions, in the white at $49.98 or satin finished and blued at $74.97. Bases for other popular actions take 2-3 weeks for delivery. This fluting is a nice touch for a mount which has long been recognized as one of the sleekest available anywhere.

Conetrol recently increased their productive capacity by installing a Cincinnati Cinova 80 horizontal milling machine, which helps them maintain same-day shipping on most items. It is also Conetrol policy to allow an automatic 1% discount on every sale to an NRA member.

J.B. Holden's Ironsighter mount, which mounts directly over the bore except on the models intended for the 94 Winchester, now has a 34% wider opening for factory sight use. Introduced in 1967, the Ironsighter is available for most centerfire rifles, muzzleloaders, shotguns, pistols, and 22-cal. rifles with grooved receivers. Slanted risers permit adapting to scopes which have long enlarged tube sections, power selector rings or unusually placed adjustment turrets. Ironsighters are now available for the TCR-83.

New within the past few months is what Holden calls the Model 50 Portable Bench Rest, but which is really a rifle/handgun rest for use on a bench. Interestingly, it is made of wood. Three adjustable metal legs support a triangular wooden base which at the front has a padded fore-end support which can be adjusted vertically via a springloaded stem. Dovetailed guideways at each end of the rest are intended to keep things in alignment. We've been using one of these M50s for some time, and find it more than adequate for zeroing in hunting or varmint rifles. It's also light and conventient enough to use for varmint shooting where a lot of walking isn't done, as it has a hand-hole for easy carrying. However, the dovetail clearance necessary for easy vertical adjustment permits more movement of the fore-end rest than competitive benchresters will tolerate. That's okay. It wasn't designed for those specialists.

S&K Insta Mounts still make it possible to quickly install scopes on many military rifles without drilling or tapping. In addition to the obvious convenience, such installation does not alter the rifle in any way, thus does not affect possible collector value. The Insta Mount is made for many autoloaders such as the AR-15 and FN FAL, as well as for older bolt guns such as the '03 Springfield and 1917 Enfield. S&K conventional mounts are also available for factory drilled rifles.

Wally Siebert, whose conversions were instrumental in convincing manufacturers to build high-power, action-mounted scopes for benchresters, still is kept busy boosting the power of some varmint and target types. Those in the 8x to 12x range can usually be increased by 100%, while the 20x to 36x can go up to 30x or 45x, depending upon various things. Wally converts only the Lyman AA line with Perma-Center reticles, certain Leupolds, and the Unertl BV-20, Ultra Varmint and 2-inch Target. He can also go the other way with power, essentially cutting it in half, which then increases eye relief to the 10-20-inch bracket for handgun use. Assorted Leupolds and the 12x Redfield can have this operation.

Kimber of Oregon has for some time been manufacturing the double lever scope mount designed by Len Brownell shortly before his death. Originally this mount utilized a set of dovetail blocks having serrations along one edge to engage matching teeth inside the lever-movable locking unit which attached the rings.

Now, in addition to the blocks, quarter ribs are manufactured for certain rifles. Either way, this is a handsome, high quality, quick detachable mount. In addition to the standard units made by Kimber, Billingsley & Brownell make custom bases as needed. These can be had for doubles, overunders and combination rifles.

Williams Gun Sight Co. has taken a different approach to the dual-sight approach this year. Whereas numerous other manufacturers have been raising the scope higher to permit iron sight viewing beneath it, Williams decided to keep the scope low and raise the iron sights. They called the resulting design the S-O-S (Sight-Over-Scope), and brought it about by integrating a front sight on top of the forward scope ring, an adjustable aperture sight on the rear ring. The front sight can be moved sideways in its dovetail slot for further windage, if desired. Because of the small sight separation, any imperfection of aim is magnified far more than it would be with a front sight at the muzzle, but for the purpose intended—emergency use at short range—the S-O-S should serve very well and is an interesting concept.

The S-O-S top ring will work with any Williams mount having the two-piece one-inch rings. It is now available for a large number of popular rifles, including some muzzleloaders and rimfires. The front sight normally comes with a $3/32$-inch fluorescent orange bead, but white or gold is optional. The rear sight is the Williams Guide Receiver, with Twilight or regular aperture.

For archers, Williams also has two new bow mounts, one utilizing rifle-type front and rear sights with adjustments, the other accepting any one-inch pistol scope. Each fits on a two-way adjustable bracket that is screwed to the bow. ●

Weatherby's new scope line, the Supremes, are represented by the 3-9x shown on this Mark V Lazermark. Its 44mm objective gives good light transmission and resolving power. Also made in 4x, 1.75-5x, and 2-7x.

HOW TO LOVE A 22

Hunting need not stop in early winter when a shooter has a 22 and a cottontail season, as Greg Thompson knows.

by **SAM FADALA**

"YOU COULD MAKE a living with this little rifle," the man said, as he patted the well-used wood of the forearm. "In fact, I nearly did back in Louisiana when I was a kid."

He rolled the tiny Model 4 Remington rolling block single shot in his hands as he added, just for the sake of accuracy, "Along with a fishing pole, that is. You'd need a fishing pole, too."

Some scenes remain sharp in the mind no matter how many years intervene, and I can still see Mr. Mullens fondly handling that 38-inch, four-pound 22 rifle as he spoke. He'd ear back the hammer and the block, reach into his pocket, slip a 22 Short hollow-point cartridge down the breech, move the hammer to half-cock and declare he was ready to look for food. Food meant cottontails mostly.

And if you didn't place the 27-gr. bullet in the head of your edible target, a head no more than a couple inches wide, you missed the mark according to Mr. Mullens. We would slow-pace the banks of the little canal outside Yuma, Arizona, slip down the earthen side to a miniature jungle of undergrowth, working side by side separated by 30 or 40 yards, and then a hand would go up, usually his hand, and that meant "Stop, game sighted."

The little rifle was mounted to his shoulder the way a painter strokes his brush over the canvas. There was never any force in the motion, just one graceful sliding of the arms upward, the comb of the butt settling against his face, the tiny "Spttt!" of the 22 Short, and another edible was ready for field-dressing. He made running shots, too. It always seemed to me the target would be well out of sight before the man got a shot off, he was so deliberate. But when the 22 barked its little bark, more often than not there would be another one for the pot.

Even that little 22 Short bullet seemed to zap from the muzzle to the target faster than a light ray, at least to the eyes of a boy. I had no 22 rifle, and the little 17-caliber pellet from my air rifle waltzed away from the muzzle totally without fanfare — no crack to split the air, no projectile breaking the sound barrier. Still, I collected a few rabbits anyway, up close, sitting shots only. Mostly I waited for the day when I would move up to a 22 rifle and in the meanwhile I listened to the man and watched him hunt and I learned. I learned a lot about the value of hunting and why a man would bother to go at all and how to take care of the most important part of the hunt, the meat, the food.

Thinking back, I realize that the man was offering a special favor to an untutored kid. He wanted to see me get started right.

I still love a 22. I've never outgrown that. No shooter does. And no other caliber replaces the simple 22 rimfire round and all that it can do for just plain shooting enjoyment. The mundane 22 stays foremost in the lineup. It stays number one for important duties aside from the fun.

I love a 22 for getting started. How many of us can remember those first days of shooting? All of us right? And the great bulk of today's marksmen will recall a 22 rifle that was the teaching tool. It's almost always that way. I remember my first rifle that actually fired a cartridge, and of course that cartridge was the 22 rimfire. I bought my own first 22 rifle, saving for a long time. When I opened the box, the little Model 61 pump seemed twice as shiny as when I had handled it in the store and the action worked smoother, too, and the sights lined up a lot better than I'd remembered.

every time through careful aim, interest in smooth function and handling of the firearm, interest in being careful. Instead of having to learn to handle the more stringent aspects of big bore shooting, the rimfire eliminates all of the more trying aspects of shooting, leaving only the enjoyment, and the concentration needed for trigger squeeze, sight picture and firearm control.

I love a 22 for hunting. When the big game seasons are closed, and often in spite of the fact that they are open, I'll grab a 22, slip a box of ammo into my pocket, a jackknife and maybe a sandwich and I'm all set to hunt for some small game meat. Small game hunting with a 22 keeps the eye sharp and it also keeps the hunter sharp in terms of seeing game and working the field. There's a lot to be learned about hunting which can be accomplished on rabbits using a 22 rifle.

My partner and I like to slip out on a weekend morning, leaving early, catching the sunrise, especially on winter days when in our country the

You just don't outgrow a 22

Before sighting in, I carefully filled the tubular magazine with what seemed an awful lot of 22 rimfire ammo and I shot the magazine dry, just to get the feel of the rifle and its action and to watch it perform in its flawless way. And when I did get her sighted in just right, I marveled at how accurate the rifle really was and how those bullets obeyed a good aim and sliced through the bull's eye every time when the shooter did his part.

Yes, a 22 rimfire is just right for getting started with a cartridge gun because it does a lot more than teach the basics. Sure, the recoil is nil and the noise level immaterial and with a decent backstop there is a strong safety factor in the 22 rimfire round. But more than all of these things, the 22 is just right for getting started because it instills the right kind of interest in a shooter, interest in hitting the mark

air is cold but the sun is still warm. We share the field and we never hunt very far apart so we can stop, reach into the small packs we carry and pull out a snack or a small vacuum bottle of hot coffee or tea. Sitting on a down tree, being in the outdoors, having good conversation and still putting some small game in the bag — it's not a bad way to spend some time. Leaning there in the security of a limb crotch there is sure to be a 22 rifle. Quiet and economical, as well as plenty efficient, it's that 22 rimfire which is just right for small game hunting.

I love a 22 on the trail. A very short time ago as I write this, I was enjoying a special deer hunt in an area where big western mountains meet the plains country. This was a black powder deer hunt, but of course a 22 rimfire was still allowed for small game, and the area was replete with cottontails and a few squirrels. I had a

This replica 22 copies the old Remington rolling block rifle. Sold by Allen Fire Arms Company, the 1871 carbine model is very small and light, a close copy of the Remington Model 4.

base camp. From that camp, I would take a trail and work around in a big circle, toting my 54 caliber caplock for deer, but ready for a little meat with a 22 pistol holstered on my hip.

I only took what I could eat, except for the last day when I bagged a couple extra rabbits to take home with me. If the occasional "Pop! Pop!" of the little 22 harmed my big game hunting I couldn't tell it, for a nice buck was harvested all the same and I'll remember that. But I won't forget the work accomplished by the accurate little pistol either. The evening campfires threw light on my smaller cooking fire and in the skillet the fine white meat of the rabbit fried up golden brown, lightly embraced with flour, a harvest brought to bag with the 22.

On the high country trails where I live, there are also grouse, and these mountain grouse are legal game for a 22 rimfire, as they should be. And so these trails are also vastly improved by having a little 22 rimfire along. One season in Idaho a hunting friend and I decided to backpack into the country. We had food in our packs, but fresh meat in the form of mountain cottontail rabbits and grouse was provided once again by the 22 rimfire. On the trail, I can't think of another cartridge that could do a better job of providing small edibles. I love the 22 along the trial.

I also love the 22 for camp. I don't believe in a constant shootfest in a hunting camp, though it is hard to prove that the shooting of a 22 rimfire will drive big game into the hinterlands. However, hunting camps should be somewhat on the quiet side, I think. So a constant "Splat! Slpat!" of shooting is out. However, there are many camps well-suited to having a safe little range set up with a good backstop and then there is nothing wrong with one and all enjoying some informal shooting.

Also, there is a more serious side to having a 22 rimfire in camp, and one is the small game aspect. Camps may be set in tree squirrel country, for example, or where the camper may obtain other small game edibles in open season. And once in a while, a 22 rimfire is called upon to dispatch an unwanted camp guest in the form of a rattlesnake or other dangerous visitor. I'm not in favor of smacking every poisonous snake I run across; however, right in a camp or close by, a person may have to elect to put down a dangerous animal. When it is a small thin-skinned dangerous animal, such as a snake, the 22 rimfire is perfect for the job.

A very short time ago, my wife and four-year old daughter shared a camp with me in some brushy hills which marked the beginning of a big mountain range. Although it was October in Wyoming, the sun was doing its usual October work and the ground it-self was very warm. My wife walked a few yards from camp and in front of her by one more single pace was a rattler poised with head held high. He was on a small rise she was walking toward and there is no doubt that she would have stepped right into the snake, at which point he probably would have struck, which certainly would have been the natural thing.

I would have liked to back off or to have found a way to put the rattler on some other terrain, but the camp was semi-permanent and our little girl would be walking over the grounds for the next two days. The 22 rimfire was called upon and the snake was dispatched. So I love a 22 in camp. It can come in handy for practice or fun, and for more serious work if need be. Sel-

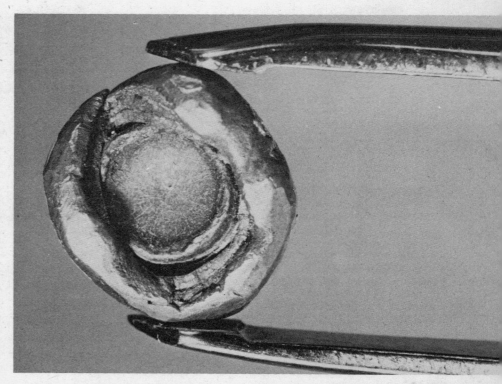

This 22 Short hollow point shows excellent mushrooming. It's the author's favorite cartridge for taking edible small game. Some will argue a Long Rifle hollow point is needed and if the shooting is going to be at longer ranges, 75 yards and up for rimfire work, this could be right. But Fadala has never lost any small game properly hit with the 22 Short hollow point.

dom do we set up a camp without a 22.

I love a 22 for plinking. Jerry Rakusan, editor of *GUNS*, told of a very famous plinker in his December, 1983 column. Said Jerry, "Legend has it that Abe Lincoln was a plinker. The story goes that Christopher Spencer went to the White House to show his repeating rifle to the President, and rather than turn the gun over to the military, Abe took it to the garden and plinked!" I don't know if the story is true about Abe plinking, but I can guarantee that a whole bunch of us less famous folk enjoy the sport.

Plinking, of course, has been a grand teacher as well as fun-maker. As the newcomer to shooting learns

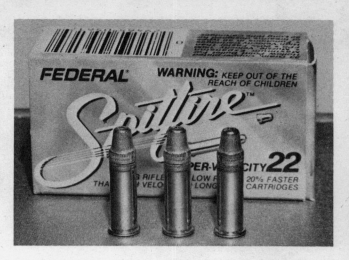

Federal's Spitfire 22 LR cartridge is an example of the newer hyper-velocity ammo available to rimfire fans. Used on pests and vermin, the hyper-velocity cartridge is an excellent addition to the long rimfire line of loads.

From left to right we have: The 22 Short CB Cap; the 22 Short; the 22 Long CB low velocity; the 22 Long; the standard velocity 22 LR; the high velocity 22 LR; the HV 22 LR hollow point; the 22 Long Rifle shot cartridge; the Spitfire, a hyper 22 Long Rifle round; the solid or full metal jacketed 22 WMR along with the 22 WMR hollow point.

his craft, usually with a 22 rimfire, of course, he tends to want to see targets which react to his firing. Up against an earthen bank, tin cans are sent rolling and jumping into the air like spawning carp. My brother and I used to invent all sorts of plinking games for the 22 rifle. Our best one, I think, was a circle scratched into the ground with a stick. Into the circle we placed several tin cans , the object being to see who could send the greatest number of tin cans flying out of the circle. Incidentally, let it be known that the rim shot is the best for this work. A direct strike on the rim of a tin can will send it up against the backstop with one mighty jump.

I love a 22 for practice. Although we

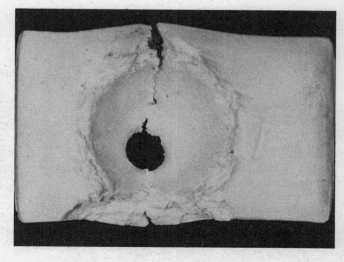

The exit hole created by the 22 WMR hollow point jacketed bullet is quite impressive in this bar of soap. There is also a solid bullet for those who use this cartridge for small game hunting, wild turkeys, javelina or fur-harvesting.

Author loads the magazine of his old Model 12 Remington pump gun. The joys of the 22 lie partly in the fact that this little round offers so many different chamberings in both old and new arms. (Nancy Fadala photo)

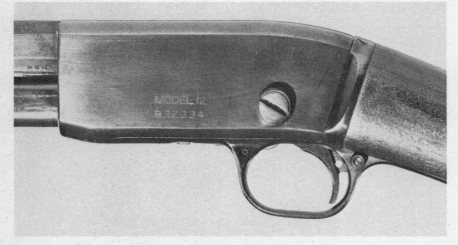

The receiver of the long-out of production Model 12 Remington pump 22 rifle shows the takedown bolt and the safety. That small hole behind the trigger accepts a tiny lock to render the rifle inoperable.

have been talking around this particular aspect of enjoying a 22 rimfire, I think it bears mentioning that a 22 rimfire is great as a serious tool for keeping sharpened up. At the beginning of any hunting season, a fellow who grabs his 22 rimfire and a couple boxes of ammo is a wise shooter, for he can tune up at the range or in some informal place where a backstop presents itself.

I also love a 22 for owning. There are really no more interesting firearms than 22 rimfires, with the exception of course of some very unique period shooting pieces of historical significance. A single big game rifle, however, is sufficient, truth be known. And one shotgun, especially with a variable choke device, is plenty for hunting quail to geese, though it is always nice to have more than one. But I can't see how a shooter could get by with only one 22 rifle.

There are 22 rifles made for serious competition shooting for those who love that sport. And there are tiny single-shot rifles, such as the Chipmunk, which are just right for starting that young shooter. There is the semi-auto rifle for fast action among the small game fields. And there is the single shot for that deliberate one-shot, careful-aim approach. Lever actions and repeating bolt-actions abound. And the older 22 firearms are quite different from the newer models. We have expensive near-custom 22s and we have custom 22s, as well as used 22s that cost no more than a tank of gasoline. I like them all. I love a 22.

It's also easy to love a 22 because all good 22s, and most 22 rimfires are good, come with an array of sights which lead to successful shooting. I decided a long time ago that I could not get by with only one 22 rifle, and I even have a couple 22 handguns. On the rifles, I rely mainly upon the standard iron sight for my shooting because my small game hunting and informal firing is mainly close-range. But when I get very serious about putting the holes close together on paper, I turn to a scope sight, leaning more in the direction of the full-sized "big game" scope than the 22 style scope, though I have had success with the latter, too.

The iron sights, then, are fine for the informal work and close-up shooting of small game. They are also nice for running shots on rabbits, though a wide-field scope sight is also good in this department. But small game means a small target, too, and there is nothing like the scope sight to make that two-inch wide head shot on a cottontail rabbit a reasonable one. There is also long range to consider. Long range? Well, long for a 22 rimfire. I get a great deal of pleasure out of setting up tin cans at 125 yards, even 150 yards with the intent of picking them off with a scope-sighted 22 rimfire rifle. What I happen to know of wind drift I learned here, with a 22 rifle. What I happen to know of holdover, I learned here, with a 22 rifle. Naturally, when a shooter turns to larger-bore firearms he must adapt his knowledge of drop and wind drift. But on a miniature scale, the 22 Long Rifle round is a grand teacher when those targets move out to 125 or 150 yards.

As for the 22 handguns, I only ask one thing, target sights, fully adjustable. I have no interest at all in the simple "point at 'em" sights which are in fact a front sight coupled with a notch in the topstrap of the handgun, or something similar. A friend has a smaller 22 rimfire revolver he likes to carry in the field as a small-game-getter, but I was on one hunt with the fellow when he shot over a half box of 22 ammo to come off with two cottontail rabbits, and these were very unsophisticated bunnies atop the far reaches of the western mountains.

My own 22 handgun which sees a lot of use is a Ruger Mark II with a bull barrel. Naturally, the sights are fully adjustable. This means that a shooter can sight the piece in, first of all, and it also means that he can gain a good sight picture, hitting a target with groups rather than a random scattering, which is usually what point-at-'em sights offer.

Most of all, for some of us, the 22 rimfire rifle harvests edible small game. When other hunts are closed down, we still have rabbits and squirrels open and available to us.

Only a year ago as I write this, a friend of mine joined me for a week of hunting "out West." He enjoyed his antelope hunt. He especially liked our sage hen hunt. But after our time was spent, he admitted that the simple hunting of cottontail rabbits with 22 rimfire rifles was perhaps the most rewarding part of his trip. We went about our small game hunting seriously, but without any pressure at all.

I scouted around before the season to make certain that the rabbits would be in the field when my friend arrived. The first morning out, we parked a few hundred yards from the beginning of our rabbit area, loaded up a couple 22 rifles, and began a leisurely stroll, walking about 30 or 40 yards apart, crossing paths for easy

converstaion from time to time and ever on the lookout for our quarry, trying to spot the sedentary ones which we could stalk for a clean harvest. It turned out to be one of those

days you didn't know you deserved.

Over the first little rise, there were two bunnies just moving out from the shade into the sun. They were probably 30 yards away, and since we had

Fadala starts his daughter on her shooting lessons by simply showing her a little Chipmunk rifle which will be hers one day. A little at a time, the new shooter is introduced to the art. Early introductory experiences help build interest as well as a sound basis of safety attitudes. (Nancy Fadala photos)

Keeping the firearm under complete control, the author shows his daughter how to take a sight picture through the Chipmunk rifle, a scaled-down model meant for the young shooter.

The fast-handling Browning 22 lever-action rifle requires a mere flick of the wrist in order to eject the spent cartridge and chamber a fresh round. The rifle is fitted with a 4x Redfield ¾-inch scope.

Bill Fadala takes fast aim with a Weatherby 22 semi-auto rifle, another of the high quality full-sized rifles available today. The Weatherby makes a fine rifle for shots at jumped jacks and fast-moving cottontails.

The sophisticated Weatherby 22 semi-auto rifle wears a Weatherby scope on an integral mount. With 10-shot clip, this fast-shooter delivers superb accuracy.

approached quietly and had not burst over their horizon, they went on chewing up the edge of a small field. "Pop! Pop!" We had two, and as if the shooting were a signal call for more rabbits, two more broke from the edge of the field and headed for the rocks we were perched on. We took both of them. Two each already, and I was beginning to worry about the bag limit of five being filled almost too fast.

We carried the four to a clean grassy spot and quickly field-dressed them, using a few splashes of water from my canteen to wash the meaty morsels before placing them into the clean plastic bag. After washing my hands and drying them on the towel I always carry out rabbit hunting, I glassed the field. "I see a couple cottontails by that old machinery over there," I said after a few minutes of observation. We planned a stalk as if the rabbits were big game animals and we soon had two more for the fry pan.

Fortunately, we missed our next shots. I'm glad we did. Things were going too well, too easy. The cards seemed to be stacked too much in our favor at first. But things evened a bit, and I missed a fairly easy shot on a rabbit that darted from his secret rock to his burrow like a sparrow getting out of reach of a hawk's talons. I chuckled to myself. Mr. Mullens would have made that shot, I said half-aloud. By middle morning my friend and I had a grand total of 10 rabbits.

We took our prize bag home, cut the meat into serving pieces, washed the seprate hunks in cold water, soaked them out in a mild salt water for a couple hours and then placed them in a marinade of milk and eggs with spices added. That night we floured the pieces straight out of the marinade. The meat was white as clean snow. The golden-fried pieces were tender and good.

That's how to love a 22 rifle—with an open mind. The 22 rimfire round is one of those small things in life which accomplishes many and varied tasks. And the rifles (and handguns) that shoot the little round are just as varied, just as useful. Out-of-date or as new as the latest model, 22 rifles keep on serving their owners, teaching them, keeping them in practice, entertaining them, removing a few varmints when necessary and perhaps best of all, providing delicate edibles, all without requiring much attention and without more than a little bit of noise to announce the accomplishment. I love a 22. ●

A shooter never outgrows the 22 rifle. There is so much that can be done with the 22, not only in the rifle but the handgun. In fact, many shooters consider the 22 rimfire a lifelong challenge, for it takes skill to gather small game limits with this caliber. Fadala never hesitates to shoot from a rest. (Nancy Fadala photo)

John Fadala takes a bag of cottontail rabbits with a scope-sighted Winchester Model 69 bolt action rifle. John uses the 22 Short hollow point for rabbits.

Modest pest control is one of the many functions of the 22 rimfire rifle. This prairie dog village near a ranch house furnished a hunt to Bill Fadala. When the "dogs" get too heavily populated on such ranch areas, they are often poisoned extensively. Hunting will not remove a prairie dog population; however, a mild control measure is possible through a shooting program.

Lefthander bangs away at African turtle doves, piling them up as can be seen, which is the only way to learn to shoot.

by **STUART WILLIAMS**

YOU CAN SHOOT 90% ON WILD BIRDS . . . SOMETIMES

THE MARKETING researchers at the Big Three ammunition companies tell me that the ordinary American birdhunter expends about two boxes of shotshells a year. With the firing of those 50 rounds, he bags about 10 birds—an average of one bird for each five shells. Certainly, that's not very impressive shooting.

Mike Fontana, winner of the 1983 North American Field Shooting Championships, former All-American international Skeet shooter, and guide at the best duck hunting club in Washington State, confirms that ratio. He says that his average client, taking all shots offered within reasonable range, will average about one bird for four shells when shooting over decoys, but will only average about one bird for five or six shells when pass shooting.

Harvey Fisher, retired sales representative for Federal Cartridge Company and a former All-American trapshooter, guides duck and goose hunters on Sauvie Island, Oregon, one of the waterfowl hotspots of the West Coast. Harvey says that his hunters will, when taking all shots offered within 40 yards, average about one bird for five shots. Furthermore, he says that after more than 50 years of upland gunning and observing upland gunners, he has concluded that the average hunter will require three shells per pheasant shot over dogs, and *seven* or *eight* shells for each dove killed in the wind.

Mike Fitzgerald, president of Fish and Game Frontiers of Wexford, Pa., a specialty travel agency that arranges superb (and expensive) birdshooting worldwide, has had the opportunity to observe hundreds of his clients in action all around the world. He estimates their birds-to-shells ratio as follows: one for three on driven pheasants in Denmark and Hungary; one for four on driven pheasants in England, where the terrain is more irregular; one for four on whitewing doves in Mexico, eared doves in Colombia,

This kind of morning's bag makes a soft-shooting autoloader like the KFC-250 appreciated and sharpens the eye for the afternoon shoot.

mallards in Denmark, driven red-legged partridge in Spain, and passing geese in Argentina; one for five on driven Scottish grouse; and one for *seven* or *eight* on the wicked wind-blown doves of Morocco and Botswana.

Robert Brand, a genial Texan who owns two luxury shooting resorts in Mexico, has the opportunity to observe over a thousand of his countrymen shooting every year. He says that on whitewing doves they will average about one for four, and on mourning doves about one for five. If there is a wind blowing these averages will go

way down. Jerry Crider, another enterprising American who offers superb duck and dove shooting out of his Mexican resort, says that over the long run, wind or no wind, his clients will average about 15%, i.e., slightly less than one bird for six shots.

Why does the ordinary two-boxes-a-year birdhunter shoot so poorly? The obvious answer is lack of practice, but that is only a superficial answer. The real reason is lack of self-confidence. A man who addresses each bird that approaches him with the unshakeable confidence that he is going to kill that bird will certainly kill it far more often than not. However, such confidence is born only of years and years of practice, to the tune of thousands of rounds fired at live birds each year.

I have observed many British shooters—as a nationality the British are certainly the best wingshooters in

These strings of Moroccan doves—one morning's shoot for one happy sportsman—could have burned up 300 shells.

the world—who were the very picture of self-confidence as they addressed each bird and stroked it out of the sky. Little wonder they are so self-confident—many of them will fire over 5000 rounds a year at live birds, and some of them will fire as many as 20,000 rounds a year. Virtually all of them will, before the start of the season, attend a shooting school. There they will fire 500-1000 rounds under the watchful eye of an expert instructor.

The lack of wingshooting opportunities in this country begets three ills that plague the huge majority of Americn wingshooters. First, they tend to shoot at excessively long ranges. Stimulated by the competitiveness of public hunting areas and by shotshell advertising claims of hyper-range killing power, many hunters will blast away blithely at birds far beyond the reach of their shooting skills—even though the gun-choke-load combinations they are using may be quite adequate to kill at such ranges. Their rationale is: what the heck, I get so few shooting opportunities I'm going to give every one a try. The ultra-smooth, self-confident, and lethal British shooter will very seldom shoot beyond 40 yards. He knows full well that there are very few men who can consistently hit beyond that range, regardless of the gun-choke-load combination they may be using.

Then there is the tendency to shoot

unselectively. The shooter has not been born who is equally deadly on all types of shots presented. For example, I am sudden death on incoming and high overhead and right-to-left crossing birds, but there are days when I can't *buy* a high left-to-right crossing bird. I simply pass up all left-to-right crossing birds on those days.

Every really good field shooter that I have ever observed does the same. He shoots to his strengths and avoids shooting to his weaknesses. In that manner he maintains a very high birds-to-shells-expended ratio. He also puts to work *for* him—rather than *against* him—what I call my theory of psychological reinforcement.

EDITOR'S NOTE:

The writer here is Stuart Williams and his credentials are:

He has fired 15,000 or more shotshells at wild birds in each of the past 16 years, traveling from the goose marshes of Argentina to Hudson's Bay in the Americas and from Morocco to Denmark in the Old World.

He once killed 90 ducks with 100 shells in one day's memorable shoot in Yucatan. He says they decoyed beautifully.

He thinks a case of shells a day is about right, but if you're not up to excellence on a given day you should quit shooting.

He's a good shot.

That theory posits that when you hit a bird that hit creates a positive reinforcement in your mind, i.e., it increases the chances that you will hit the next bird. However, if you miss a bird that miss creates a negative reinforcement in your mind, which increases the chances that you will miss the following bird.

The usual two-boxes-a-year bird-hunter, who gets very few shooting opportunities, is going to take all opportunities presented, be they near or far, flying to his strengths or to his weaknesses. The result is a high incidence of misses, and the theory of psychological reinforcement working against him more surely with each miss.

Another result of too few shooting opportunities and too little shooting practice is that most American wingshooters shoot far too consciously and deliberately. They try to calculate leads as they shoot, a usually futile endeavor. To be done well, shooting must be done without deliberate and conscious effort. In fact, it must be done with the greatest of ease. In this respect, shooting is like skiing or ice-skating or roller skating. These are sports that must be done without conscious effort to be done well. When you start making a conscious effort is when you make mistakes. Shooting is furthermore like those sports in that when you make a mistake you pay the price immediately, i.e., you miss or you fall.

Another very common fault of American birdshooters is that they tend to mount their guns prematurely. They get their guns up on their shoulders when the bird is 80-100 yards away, and then wait for it to come within range. In so doing they rob the gun of all its momentum, or even bring it to a total stop on the shoulder. The result is a miss behind the bird every time. My guess is that most shooters who commit this common error do so because they have received all their early shooting instruction with rifles, wherein a great emphasis is placed on immobilizing the gun. Alternatively, they may be shooters of American-style trap or Skeet, in which the bird is called for with the gun mounted to the shoulder. British shooters—who have little or no experience with rifles, and who only shoot international or low-gun Skeet if they shoot it at all—seldom evince this error. They wait until the very last instant, then mount, swing, and shoot in one swift, continuous motion.

As Macbeth said in a rather different context: "If it were done when 'tis done, then 'twere well/It were done *quickly*." Mounting a shotgun is perhaps the only area of endeavor in which it is better to be late than early.

Another problem created by the skimpy bag limits imposed in this country is that on any given day no shooter gets to fire enough shells to really develop a rhythm. Every really good field shot that I have spoken with says that he has to fire a certain minimum number of shells to "warm up" and to establish a shooting rhythm. With some it is only about a box, with others it is about 1½ boxes, with still others it is about 2 boxes. I don't really get in the groove until I have fired about two boxes. Furthermore, the shots should not be spaced more than one minute apart. Needless to say, it is seldom possible to get a proper shooting rhythm established during a day's shooting in this country.

So far we have established that the ordinary two-boxes-a-year American birdhunter is a duffer with the shotgun. He raises the gun to his shoulder and hopes for the best. The best, however, he seldom achieves; generally he pokes about. Despite such pitiful performance, however, I am convinced that the great majority of such shooters—given reasonably good coordination and fast reflexes—have the potential to shoot much better, in fact, to shoot extremely well. Most of them would be astounded at how well they could shoot given the proper conditions.

All they need is the opportunity to shoot and shoot and shoot and then shoot some more, day in and day out, week after week, month after month. As Macdonald Hastings writes in his excellent book, *The Shotgun*: "The secret of the best shots in England was that they scarcely did anything else but shoot from August to January."

If we can believe the accounts of the old market hunters such as Fred Kimble, those men shot with a hitting percentage of over 90% every day—and that is because they *shot* every day, for 4-5 months of the year.

I have observed many of my countrymen shooting abroad in some of the great gamelands of the world, and the typical pattern of their shooting performance is as follows: on the first day they will generally shoot fair to poorly, averaging one bird for each four or five shells, about what they would do at home. On the second day they will do better, averaging one bird for each three or four shells. On the third day they will do better still, averaging about one for three. (During this time they will have been shooting anywhere from four to twenty boxes of shells per day.) At that point they reach a plateau above which few of them will rise because they must quit and go home, usually after four or six days shooting.

In confirmation of my observations, outfitter Alberto Lleras of Colombian Hunting, Ltd.—which offers unquestionably the finest dove shooting in the world—tells me the following: on the first day, newly arrived shooters average about one bird for five shells; on the second day they average about one for four; and on the third and final day they average one for three. They routinely fire a case of shells a day each. These averages are confirmed by a very precise count of birds killed and shells expended. When the shooters come back the following year, they

Truckloads of geese are what it takes, the writer says, to make a world-class game shot. This truckload was dropped in one day in Argentina.

start out with one-for-five again.

On the big estate shoots for mallards and driven pheasants in Denmark the shoot operators keep a very precise count of shells fired and birds killed. They use large squadrons of black Labs, so they have about a 99% recovery of downed birds. Moreover, on many shoots there stands behind each shooter a man who punches a digital counter in his right hand each time the shooter fires, and one in his left hand each time a bird falls. This removes all the lying about shooting performance (and a lot of the fun too). Consequently, the shoot operators know precisely how well each man is shooting, and how well the group is shooting.

They indicate that on the first day a typical American group will average one for four on mallards or driven pheasants, and that by the fourth (and final) day they will be averaging one for three. Each man will fire 150-250 rounds per day. Occasionally a group will come along that will—under favorable circumstances—shoot a fantastic one-for-two average on driven pheasants on the final day. This is really brilliant shooting by anybody's standards.

I shot with just such a group in No-vember, 1983. On the third day of the shoot, at the famous Frisenborg Estate, we set a new Danish one-day record of 1249 pheasants. This group of eight outstanding shooters had been coming to Denmark to shoot driven pheasants every year for the past eight years. In the interim they would travel individually to many of the great wingshooting venues of the world—Colombia, Argentina, Mexico, Hungary, Botswana, Morocco. Each man would fire a minimum of 10,000 rounds a year at live birds. None of these men was endowed with extraordinary coordination nor lightning-fast reflexes, and none was young, but all were plenteously endowed with that one commodity important to becoming an outstanding wingshooter—money.

There, of course, is the rub. Most of us will never have the funds to be able to develop our shooting skill to its fullest potential, and therefore most of us will never know how well we might really shoot. The goal must remain purely ideal and theoretical.

Now that we are discussing the purely ideal and theoretical, what level of shooting performance could one achieve, given the ideal circumstances of unlimited time and money and birds to shoot at, and excellent co-ordination and reflexes? That is a very difficult question to answer because few or no shooters have ever enjoyed such an ideal set of circumstances.

Fred Kimble claimed to shoot 90% on ducks consistently, but that figure seems superhumanly high to me, even for a man who shot about 100 ducks a day for four or five months a year. Mike Fontana, winner of the 1983 North American Field Shooting Championships, says that he shoots about 40% on decoying ducks and on passing ducks up to 40 yards, but that he only shoots about 20% on really high passing ducks, ducks over 50 yards distant. However, he says down in Colombia, when he is really hot and picking and choosing his shots, he can average 400 doves with a case of shells, or 80%. Normally, he figures he averages about 300 doves with a case, taking all shots offered within reasonable range. These figures are confirmed by the outfitter, Alberto Lleras, who says that Mike is the best shooter that he has observed.

Then there is the singular case of Lord de Grey, later Marquis of Ripon, who was accounted the greatest ga-meshot of his time (ca. 1867-1915), and who many serious students of the shotgunning sport consider to have been the greatest shot of all time. The Marquis of Ripon kept detailed records of his daily kills, and they were prodigious. Blessed with immense wealth, he shot, in the period 1867-95, 316,999 birds, including 111,190 pheasants, 84,491 partridges, and 47,468 grouse. In his lifetime he accounted for well over half a million birds.

Nevertheless, that eminent British student of shotguns and shotgunning, Macdonald Hastings, doubts that the Marquis of Ripon or that other great Victorian shooter, Lord Walsingham, averaged better than one bird for each four shells. With all due respect to Mr. Hastings' expertise, I cannot accept that figure. I would certainly think that both men must have put up much better performances.

In conclusion, and at the risk of being somewhat arbitrary, I would say that any man who can average 40%, i.e., 2 birds for 5 shells, day in and day out on all species of birds, driven or shot over dogs, passing or shot over decoys, in wind or in calm, taking all chances offerred within 40 yards, is an extremely good shot. The number of shooters I know that can shoot so well can be counted on the fingers of one hand, with a couple digits to spare. ●

Shooting outfitters the world around see very individual styles, but agree unanimously that one bird for three shells is good shooting for the usual dude.

THIRTY MILLION HANDGUNS

Over a dozen autoloading and revolving pistol designs have sold over 1,000,000 copies each.

by L. R. WALLACK

IN THE 37TH GUN DIGEST, "SIXTY MILLION GUNS" was all about U.S.-made long guns that had exceeded the million mark in unit sales.* That leads naturally to a similar story about handguns. There are important differences, however, since handguns are more difficult to list as individual models in most cases and because the largest single number of revolvers are those used in law enforcement.

By way of background, it's interesting to note that while the numbers of handguns made and sold today are very large, this is by no means anything new. For example, Smith & Wesson made more than two million top-break revolvers, in all calibers, from 1870 until 1912 when they were discontinued. To help fix this number of guns in your mind, U.S. Census figures for 1870 show 40-million population; in 1910 we had more than doubled to 92-million; today we're at 230-million or so. Though today's handgun numbers are indeed impressive, you must conclude that the 40-year production life of S&W's top-breaks also saw an awful lot of revolvers made, sold and used.

It is also of interest to note that all manufacturers but one freely gave me totals produced. The cagy one was Smith & Wesson. However, since the 1968 Federal law, manufacturers are required to report production figures to BATF. Under the Freedom of Information Act, the figures are available. If the powers at S&W don't think the anti-gun people have these numbers they are living in a make-believe world. The figures I've given for S&W therefore are based on BATF reports plus standard references published and available to anyone. The major source, in addition to the federal reports, was *History of Smith & Wesson* by Roy Jinks; another was "100 years of Gun Making," an address by then-president Carl R. Hellstrom to the Newcomen Society on the occasion of S&W's anniversary.

It is also interesting to note that some of the more famous guns in American history never achieved the million mark. Colt's great Single Action Army for example only reached the half-million mark despite its popularity, and despite the later success Ruger has had with a similar revolver.

Of considerable importance today is that great numbers

*An update on the long gun story: Ithaca has made more than a million Model 37 pump shotguns and Ruger more than a million and a half Model 10/22s.

EDITOR'S NOTE: The late L. R. Wallack put this together in the year prior to his death. Bob watched the gun business for forty years, at least, so his conclusions were often accurate. For example, he wrote during 1982; as we go to press in 1984, there are indeed great numbers of handguns in dealer showcases.   K.W.

of sportsmen are shooting revolvers and pistols for pure sport. The 1980 Department of the Interior Survey of Fishing and Hunting, which is done every five years, showed a total of 1.3 million handgun hunters, a truly impressive number. Moreover, there are many thousands of handgun silhouette shooters; you might say with considerable accuracy that the experimenters who gave us modern bench-rest shooting a generation ago have now turned their attention to the handgun. They have developed new cartridges, new guns, new accessories and have succeeded in coaxing a whole new degree of accuracy out of the one-hand sporting firearm. A lot of this activity has resulted in new markets, but there also remains basic law enforcement—you need more cops for a population exceeding 200-million than the nation needed for 1870's 40-millions—and the basic need for citizens to protect home and family.

In the long gun survey, I eliminated those guns which were military, but you can't do that with pistols and revolvers. Wartime needs produce huge numbers of side-arms, guns which are perfectly suitable for civilian use, and so you will find the Colt 45 automatic listed because vast quantities of them are in civilian hands either for target shooting, personal defense or just collecting.

Additional interesting numbers are that in 1978 domestic production of pistols and revolvers had risen to slightly more than one-third of the U.S. total production of fire-arms. By 1981 it had jumped to nearly one-half by U.S. government figures. There have been monumental changes in the handgun market. Before World War II for example, there were two major producers—Smith & Wesson and Colt. There also were the smaller well-known makers—High Standard, Harrington & Richardson, Iver Johnson plus a few specialized types. Among the imports were Walther, Luger, Mauser and the English Webley. Today, it's next to impossible even to count the makers.

Today's leaders are Smith & Wesson and Sturm, Ruger. In marking the company's centennial, S&W President Carl Hellstrom stated: "In the last decade we have made more arms than in the entire previous existence of the company, and our capacity right now is larger than the combined revolver manufacturers of the world" (October 21, 1952). In the period 1973-1981 S&W produced nearly six-million handguns of which a half million were pistols (BATF).

Sturm, Ruger began in 1949 in a little building in Southport, CT. Today the company also operates a huge complex in New Hampshire and has been the aggressive force behind expansion of the handgun business with innovative products and manufacturing techniques. Another old firm, Harrington & Richardson which began in 1871, has also maintained pace with the times with a new plant and modern tooling. H&R has strengthened its leadership in its particular market niche—moderate and low-price revolvers. Charter Arms, not an old-timer, should have its million seller soon.

What are the reasons for the enormous sale of handguns during recent years? A corollary to that question might be "Is there really an escalation in sales of handguns?" As previously noted there were astronomical sales of revolvers in the 1870-1912 period approximately. During the '20s and '30s sales were very slow by comparison and they began to escalate again in the '50s, '60s and '70s. Today, sales have nearly come to a screeching halt, perhaps due to the current problem economy.

There is no way to determine at this late date the reason for such big sales in the early period but we can pinpoint a number of reasons for the big sales that began in the late 1950s and extended through 1980. (The slowdown began in 1981.) First, there were a number of new cartridges that spurred interest; among them the 22 WMR, 41 and 44 Magnums and just lately the 357 Maximum from Remington and Ruger that may again spur sales. Interest and participation in handgun hunting has escalated considerably plus such target shooting activities as combat courses and metallic silhouette. Handgun scope development has widely expanded the use and flexibility of such sidearms. It is important for gun people to note that a considerable amount of this increased proliferation lies in sporting uses. Those who think all pistols and revolvers are intended to kill people are wrong.

There has been a vast increase in law enforcement staffing and every cop carries a sidearm. Finally, the rise in criminal activity of all kinds has led to an increased arming by the public for self-protection, an increase aided and abetted by the increased legislation against the handgun—worded "better buy now while we still can."

COLT

Colt 45 Auto Pistol Model 1911: More than 3 million

Quite possibly the most famous automatic pistol ever developed, the 1911 was invented in 1905 by John Browning, has been the official U.S. military sidearm since 1911. Under wartime demand, many thousands were made by manufacturers other than Colt, most notably by Remington Arms, Ithaca, and Remington Rand. According to a Browning source, this was the first small arm ever tested by Army Ordnance that went through all its trials with a perfect record. Two world wars and many lesser skirmishes have proved the 45 auto a reliable and virtually indestructible sidearm.

Colt has for years sold a civilian version of this pistol which is still listed. Other Browning-designed Colt auto pistols have approached the million mark. The well-known Model 1903 pocket pistols in 32 and 380 calibers were finally discontinued in 1946 after production of 900,000 units. And the vest pocket 25 Auto Model 1905 totaled over a half-million by Colt. It was also manufactured in Belgium by FN (Fabrique Nationale) and the combined total is more than 1,750,000.

Colt Detective Special Revolver: More than 1½ million

In 1926, Colt fitted out the Police Positive Special with 2-inch barrel and called it Detective Special. In 1933 they rounded off the butt corners for better carrying ability. The Police Positive was brought out in 1905 and chambered for 38 Special two years later when the word "Special" was added to its name.

Colt's Official Police and Police Positive revolvers were very popular with law enforcement officers though, according to Colt, never achieved the million mark. Collectively, these revolvers were pretty much the cops' standard up until World War II when the market turned to Smith & Wesson.

Colt was purchased by Fairbanks Morse, a holding company which promptly sold off most of the assets including much valuable real estate in downtown Hartford where Colt had been located for many years. Later the name was changed to Colt Industries. The part we're interested in is now known as the Firearms Division. Soon after the takeover, Colt elected to sell directly to dealers, eliminating the wholesaler. Upsetting this traditional distribution system proved a costly error. Moreover, Colt appeared more

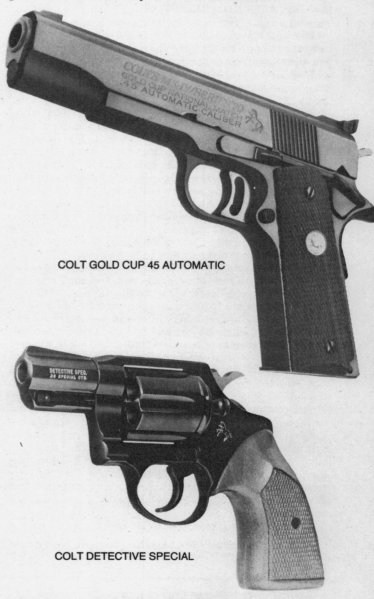

COLT GOLD CUP 45 AUTOMATIC

COLT DETECTIVE SPECIAL

interested in manufacturing war rifles (the Viet Nam M16 for example). The result pretty much left the market open to a vigorous Smith & Wesson and an ambitious newcomer to the market — Sturm, Ruger.

Colt Python & Trooper:
More than 1 million (combined)

According to Colt, these models combined exceed a million in sales. The Python, introduced in 1955, is quite possibly the most expensive factory produced revolver available. Colt consistently calls it "the world's finest revolver;" in all honesty it is a fine revolver but I've never heard anyone outside of a Colt employee who was willing to make that claim. It is available only in 357 Magnum caliber; has a wide range of barrel lengths.

Trooper, a much plainer gun, was originally introduced in 1953; improved in 1969; subsequently remodeled. It is now available as MK III in 357, 22 and 22 WMR. As MK V it is only in 357 Magnum. You could say the early Trooper is a slightly lower priced Python although that isn't completely accurate. Python is also made in Silhouette and Hunter styles complete with Colt/Leupold scopes, mounts and aluminum case.

COLT PYTHON 357

According to BATF, Colt made more than a half-million 357 revolvers in the 1973-81 period which tends to confirm the Colt figures.

STURM, RUGER

Ruger Standard Auto: 1.1 million

Young Bill Ruger had an idea. He had designed a neat little 22 auto pistol that could be manufactured inexpensively and yet had wide appeal. He tried to peddle it to any number of gun manufacturers but there were no takers. Too bad for them. Ruger got together with Alex Sturm who provided the meager capital for a startup, and who tragically died a couple years later, and began the manufacture of the Ruger Standard pistol in 1949.

In slightly more than 30 years, this gun has broken the million barrier, more units sold than the famous Colt

**RUGER MARK I
TARGET 22 AUTOMATIC**

**RUGER NEW MODEL
SINGLE SIX 22 REVOLVER**

woodsman or the High Standard auto. Why? The reason would seem to be that the Ruger went on the market at $37.50, and the price held for over 15 years until 1965! Not only was it less costly than its competitors, but it proved just as satisfactory. In 1952, Ruger introduced a target model with crisp trigger, heavy barrel and target sights. It has been and still is used by many top pistol shooters.

You might say that the similarity of the name Ruger with that of George Luger was a fortunate happenstance. At least that got the name on the tongue where it rolled around familiarly. But what kept it there was excellent design and the introduction of manufacturing techniques, all innovative, that helped keep costs down and profits up.

Ruger Single Six: 1.5 million

With his 22 auto pistol a marketing success and generating generous profits for the company, Ruger turned to the single action revolver. Popularized long ago by Colt as the gun of the cowboy, frontier marshal and western bad man, there was an awful lot of romance associated with the old design. The Ruger Single Six is frankly patterned after the old Colt but it has Ruger refinements which produced a better action. It also lent itself to the Ruger methods of manufacture which meant it could be produced at far lower cost while still returning a decent profit to the company.

The Single Six is a 22 and very soon after its 1953 introduction Winchester produced the 22 WMR, the Winchester Magnum Rimfire. While the new cartridge was considerably more powerful than existing rimfire 22's, it also used a jacketed bullet .002-inch larger than the Long Rifle. Ruger quickly found you could employ a .224" barrel for both cartridges with equal success and added an extra cylinder chambered for the other cartridge. Thus was born the "Convertible," a revolver with two cylinders.

It's true that Ruger copied the basic Colt pattern but you have to add that Ruger has made almost three million single action revolvers in the past 30 years. Colt made a little more than a half million from 1873 until the Colt Single Action Army was finally dropped in 1982.

Ruger Blackhawk: More than 1.3 million

With the Single Six firmly established, Bill Ruger moved into the centerfire single action market with his Blackhawk in 1955. Produced in various calibers and in several configurations over the years it is well established as the most popular gun of its type in the world.

Early on Ruger believed that any firearm ought to be able to be dry-fired (snapped without cartridges) without damage. At many early shows (my first NRA show was in 1952) the Ruger exhibit featured a single action revolver set up in a machine that cycled the action hour after hour. Snap, snap, snap for hundreds of thousands of times, perhaps millions for all I know. That this helped make shoot-

ers aware Ruger guns were rugged is undeniable; that it was reinforced by actual field use is fact.

Ruger's latest Blackhawk is chambered for the 357 Remington Maximum, a longer cartridge than the standard 357. At the 1982 Remington's writer seminar held in Pincher Creek, Alberta, we were told about the new cartridge. When I arrived home from Alberta, there was a Ruger release on my desk; a phone call to Ruger advised that guns would be available "in ten days." The sample gun arrived about two weeks later.

SMITH & WESSON

This company is the world's biggest producer of revolvers, or if you prefer the term, "handguns." It is still the number one. S&W alone among all manufacturers refused to quote exact numbers of guns produced but there are sufficient other sources available that have been used and the numbers given are very close.

During the approximate 40-year period from 1870 to 1912 when they were dropped, S&W produced more than two-million top-break revolvers. This includes both double and single action guns and various calibers from 44 Special, Russian and American down to the smaller sizes.

That's an awful lot of guns; especially when you consider that few of them were military* because the U.S. Army favored the Colt single action over the S&W because the Colt used a more powerful cartridge.

It wasn't until 1957 that S&W began using model numbers and this makes exact classifications difficult so I have used another method for this article. It may not be as precise as the system used for long guns, but it was essential to do it this way.

*Total production for the Russian government approximated 150,000 revolvers.

SMITH & WESSON MODEL 10
MILITARY & POLICE REVOLVER

Smith & Wesson 38 Military and Police: More than 6 million

A former S&W sales manager once told me: "I don't know what retired cops do with their guns, they must take them with them because all new cops buy guns."

This refers to such departments as New York City where officers buy their own; some cities furnish guns. It does give you an idea of how many guns are made and sold because there are an awful lot of cops in America.

The 38 Special M&P is built on the K-frame at S&W and I have included the rest of K-frame guns in this total because there is no way to separate them. Both the cartridge and M&P revolver were introduced in 1899; the first million mark was reached in 1942. Today the basic M&P revolver is known as Model 10 and it is the most popular revolver in the world. It is not inaccurate to say this is the standard law enforcement revolver. It also is the bread and

butter model at the S&W factory. Annual production of 38 Special revolvers at S&W, mostly Model 10s, run between 200,000 and up to more than 300,000. It doesn't take many years to reach a million guns at that rate.

Ever since Carl Hellstrom took over the reins at S&W just before World War II—he was made president in 1946—the company made progress from near-bankruptcy to a solid financial future. S&W's modern business was based on the Military & Police revolver.

Smith & Wesson 357 Magnum revolvers: More than 1 million

The 357 Magnum cartridge was developed during the 1930s. The first model was delivered in April, 1935 and presented to J. Edgar Hoover. While it met with instant success and achieved worldwide publicity only slightly more than 6,000 were made by 1941 when production was temporarily halted for the war. Reintroduced in 1948, sales were strong. This cartridge was made for use in N-frame S&W revolvers, a frame model which had been introduced originally in 1908 for the 44 Special cartridge. It now is used for 357, 41 and 44 Magnums. Today's Model 27 is considered the oldest N-frame still in production.

S&W also makes 357s on the K-frame, Models 19 and 66 for example, and they are included here because I have no way of separating them from the N-frame 357s.

This "first of the Magnums" was a profound publicity success. One of the original "tests," or stunts if you prefer, was that it would shoot through a car's engine block and that was the talk of all gunners of the day. Exactly what it might have proved was never told but it sure equated the cartridge with power. It still has power although it's been shadowed by the 44 and 41 Magnums.

Smith & Wesson J-Frame Revolvers: More than 2 million

S&W's J-frame was developed at the urging of company president Carl Hellstrom in 1949 to present a new small frame revolver to handle the 38 Special cartridge. The first gun was produced in 1950, a five-shot cylinder contributing to its smaller size and lighter weight. It was promptly named Chief's Special, a name chosen at a meeting of police chiefs in 1950.

Using a special aluminum frame and cylinder, a new model known as Chief's Special Airweight made its appearance in 1952. Designed to be used with standard ammunition only, many complaints were made to the factory about the aluminum cylinders with heavy loads so the cylinders were later changed to steel.

SMITH & WESSON
CHIEFS SPECIAL REVOLVER

Model 60, a stainless steel version of the Chief's Special, was authorized by William G. Gunn, president after Carl Hellstrom's death in 1963, and marked the company's (and the industry's) first stainless steel revolver. It has proved extremely popular. J-frame guns are all small sidearms designed for off-duty law enforcement use and the use of stainless steel for firearm manufacture has escalated substantially since 1963.

HARRINGTON & RICHARDSON

H&R started business in 1871 just after the Rollin White patent, held by Smith & Wesson, for revolver cylinders with bored-through charge holes expired. Many companies started then, for this patent had strangled the market. Only two of them remain in business as major manufacturers — the other is Marlin which began with revolvers but dropped them long ago. While H&R has made many extremely fine firearms, the company is best known for a line of low-priced revolvers and this has been true since 1871.

In a long conversation with Harrington & Richardson's president, C. Edward Rowe, Jr., it became obvious that there is no way on earth to estimate closely how many guns the company has made over the years. H&R made guns for many other firms, and they were stamped with the customer's names. These include other firearms' companies as well as such hardware wholesalers as E. K. Tryon of Philadelphia. Moreover, many of the older guns were not serial numbered and even when they were, there are discrepancies. For example, Mr. Rowe told me that he

had several examples of the same model, all of which were stamped with the serial number "1".

One reference I have indicates that H&R produced more than 2-million revolvers of the types known as "H&R American" and "YOUNG AMERICA" — I have combined the two since they are nearly alike; they were made from 1883 until 1940. And a total of 1.3 million Automatic Ejection top break revolvers from 1887-1940.

It is also virtually impossible to categorize H&R's revolvers since model numbers are "all over the place" and there is considerable overlapping. In my talk with Ted Rowe we elected to simply separate them by caliber; 22, 32 and 38 S&W for the simple reason there was no other way to do so. It may be surprising that there is still a demand for 38 S&W but Mr. Rowe advises that they drop it occasionally but every time they do a new demand comes along.

Over the past more than a hundred years H&R has made millions of revolvers — the exact number will never be known.

Harrington & Richardson 22 Revolvers: More than 6 million

The illustration shows Model 999, the top of the line. It's a top break model and the only top break being made anywhere. While there have not been a million 999s made they are very popular among sportsmen.

Currently, H&R makes vast numbers of 22 revolvers, in a wide variety of styles. Among them are western style convertibles which handle both 22 Long Rifle and WMR cartridges, swing-out cylinder models and so-called solid frame models in which the cylinder pin is pulled out to remove the cylinder for loading.

Despite the long and colorful history of this company and its impressive record lasting many years there is little or nothing known of its early records or history. It's too bad collectors have never paid attention to this company which I suspect is because the numbers made are so huge, the variations so frequent and the values so low.

Model 999 was designed by the late Walter Roper in the 1930s.

Harrington & Richardson 32 Caliber: More than 3 million

You would think the ancient 32 S&W Long cartridge ought to be obsolete by now. It was developed in 1903 for the Smith & Wesson First Model solid frame hand ejector. The same cartridge is also called 32 Colt New Police and is considered the smallest cartridge adequate for police use. It was relatively popular for years before the introduction of small, lightweight 38 revolvers.

Made for many years as a top-break model, the 32 H&R revolvers were available in various barrel lengths, blued and nickel finishes. Today, H&R 32 revolvers are still in demand and are available in swing-out and solid frame styles.

Note: Illustration shows 22-caliber Model 929; same gun is available as Model 732 in 32 S&W Long.

Harrington & Richardson 38 S&W Caliber: More than 1 million

Here's another old-timer that defies obsolescence. According to H&R president Rowe it is dropped from the catalog frequently but then a new demand for it keeps cropping up. Currently it has been dropped again but it will probably be added once more if history repeats itself.

H&R 38 S&W revolvers were available in much the same styles and models as those in 32 caliber. The 38 S&W is an old favorite however, and it's an around-the-world one at that. Developed in 1877 for S&W top-break revolvers, it was especially popular in England prior to World War II where in a 200-gr. loading it was the official service cartridge. It was well distributed through English-speaking countries.

Both the 38 and 32 S&W cartridges were most popular during the days when they were primarily used for light weight pocket guns. Maybe that's why they still enjoy an occasional run of popularity.

HARRINGTON & RICHARDSON MODEL 999 22 REVOLVER

HARRINGTON & RICHARDSON MODEL 929 22 REVOLVER

HARRINGTON & RICHARDSON MODEL 935 38 S&W REVOLVER

OTHERS

Iver Johnson, like Harrington & Richardson, started business in 1871 and made huge quantities of revolvers during the late 1800 to early 1900s period. Mostly these were inexpensive, mass-produced guns which have never had any collector interest. As a result of this lack of interest there is almost nothing known about them. IJ moved from Fitchburg, Mass. to a New Jersey location a few years ago; the company is still in business but now in Arkansas. It is safe to say Iver Johnson guns were made in the million category in that early period but none of those guns remains in the line today and so in not within the subject matter of this article.

It should be noted that **RG Industries** of Miami has made about ¾-million 22-caliber revolvers. If market conditions remain strong they will achieve the million mark in a couple years. Including 25-caliber pistols and 38-caliber revolvers RG has made more than a million guns. ●

BIG GUNS and SMALL GAME

THE BIG GRAY danced across the beech log, unsure where the noise had come from. He stopped at the end of the log, balanced himself with his fluffy tail, then turned toward the sound of dry branches cracking underfoot. His sharp eyes were unable to pick out the hunter just 45 yards away.

Slowly, I took a cartridge from the breast pocket of my jacket, without looking away from the squirrel. This cartridge was unlike the one in the chamber of the Ruger No. 1, and had been specially prepared for such an occasion.

I was hunting black bear, but for three days monster gray squirrels threatened to devour me. I had to defend myself against their attacks, but 180-grain Nosler bullets seemed inappropriate.

I worked the lever and let the long 300 Winchester magnum cartridge fall to the ground, then tilted the rifle barrel down. The heavy black cartridge slid into the chamber of the single shot rifle with a metallic clink.

The crosshairs of the Jason variable wandered on, off, then on target as I squeezed off the shot and hit. Two more grays fell victim to the Ruger that afternoon, each shot was little more than a pop in the woods of Maine's north country.

This unique cartridge was not a special handload, concocted for small game, but an arrangement of sorts, provided courtesy of the Winchester Cartridge Company, and Harry Owen, president of Sport Specialties.

Using Winchester-loaded 32 ACP

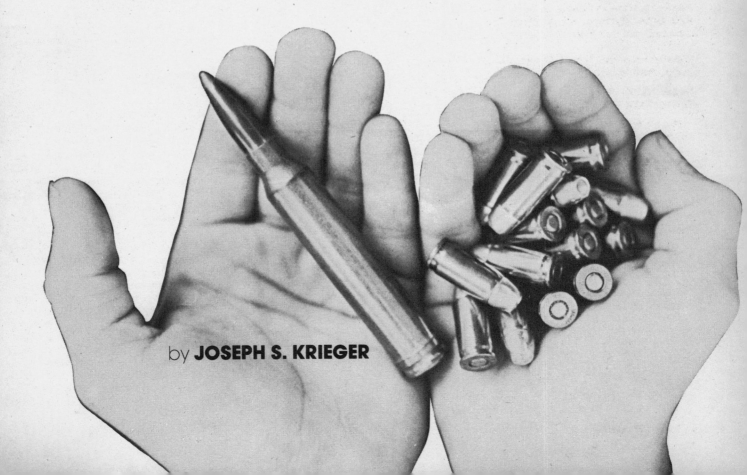

by **JOSEPH S. KRIEGER**

cartridges in a sub-caliber insert marketed by Sport Specialties, I was able to collect those three squirrels without frightening other game in the area. My Ruger is chambered for the huge 300 Winchester Magnum, but this arrangement let me load down the big gun *without* handloading.

Even for the hunter who does handload, this method is much easier than coming up with a reduced load in the magnum case. For one thing, loading down makes the cases used unsuitable for heavy, game loads. Since the cartridge case is the most expensive component, wasting cases for reduced loads is not economical. Considering the low cost of the inserts, ($16.95 for the centerfires, and $25.00 for the rimfires), they pay for themselves in 50 to 100 rounds, depending on the caliber.

For your $16.95, Harry Owen supplies a rugged, reusable cartridge, machined to fit the chamber of your rifle. This insert is, in turn, chambered to hold a sub-cartridge, smaller, but of like caliber.

The rimfire inserts are more complicated, therefore their higher cost. Still, at $25.00, they're quite a buy. The rimfire inserts come complete with an integral, rifled barrel, 1¼" long, to guide the 22-caliber bullets, and a steel base plug that acts as a

A handload 30-06 is at right; at center is an Owens adaptor, which may be had for either 32 ACP or 30 Carbine, both shown; at right is another Owens adapter for rimfire cartridges, shown with the choice of Long Rifle or WMR cartridges, and with the insert's base plug.

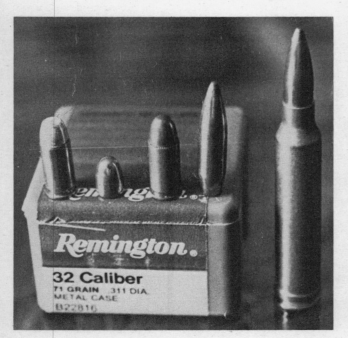

The use of the 32 ACP, in a 300 Winchester Magnum, puts less strain on the shooter's joints, as well as his wallet. Three 32s can be fired at the same cost of one full-house Magnum load. When used on small game, the Magnum borders on useless, considering its recoil and the disintegration of the target.

Owen's rimfire inserts are more complex, carry their own rifling and require a separate base plug as shown.

striker to fire the rimfire cartridge. The rifle's firing pin punches the base plug, and the blow is transmitted to the 22 rim.

The base plugs are fitted with neoprene O-rings, and the tight fit allows the rimfire units to be cycled out of the action of *any* firearm. Their overall length does not allow these inserts to be fed from the magazine; they must be hand-fed into the chamber. The same hand-feeding is necessary when chambering the 30 Carbine, and the 32 ACP inserts because of the loose fit between the insert and the sub-cartridge. While the Sport Specialties inserts must be loaded singly, they can be used in *any rifle,* single shot or repeater.

After the shot, the insert, with spent case in place, is ejected from the action. I use a short length of wooden dowel, or the tool marketed by Sport Specialties, to get the fired case out of the insert. Cleaning the insert with Hoppes will keep it rust-free, and in good working order. Being made entirely of steel, the insert will, unless lost, probably outlast both the gun and the shooter.

Accuracy in reduced loads is difficult to find at times. This is especially true in a case like the 300. The use of the Sport Specialties' insert eliminates the use of lead bullets and the messy bullet lube, in addition to providing the accuracy necessary. While there are many who consider bulletmaking a pleasant offshoot of reloading, I'd rather bathe the dog than work with lead bullets in a rifle. It just doesn't seem to be worth the effort.

The use of factory loads is more practical in the case of the 32 ACP, which is the sub-caliber I use in the Ruger. There are few bullets available to the handloader that are compatible with this case. Factory loads from Winchester and Remington seem more varied than anything the handloader could put together.

Of the four 32 ACP loads fired in the Ruger, the Silvertip hollow points offered by Winchester were the most accurate. They are no more destructive on game than solid high velocity rimfires. On animals the size of squirrels and cottontails, there is not enough body to disrupt the bullet, it simply passes through the animal without expanding. In effect, you can have your game and eat it, too.

When used on woodchucks, the bullet is explosive. On these tough-bodied animals, there is sufficient body to cause bullet expansion. A solid body hit puts a woodchuck down for good. The Silvertip can thus be an all-

around bullet; at least it has worked that way in two 30-caliber rifles I carry.

A variety of inserts available from Sport Specialties allow a progression downward. In the Ruger, the shooter can step down from the full magnum case to a 30 Carbine cartridge, then to the 32 ACP, then to the 22 WMR, and finally to the standard 22 rimfire, all without handloading, or modifying the rifle in any way.

Energy Progression, 300 Winchester Magnum

300 Winchester Magnum,	
180-grain Nosler:	3500 ft. lbs.
Insert, 30 Carbine:	850 ft. lbs.
Insert, 32 ACP:	140 ft. lbs.
Insert, 22 WMR:	175 ft. lbs.
Insert, 22 LR:	100 ft. lbs.

Levels of accuracy vary with the four inserts I have used in the 300 Winchester Magnum. Beyond 30 yards, the rimfire accuracy deteriorated to a point where 50% of the shots taken were misses on a target the size of a cottontail. Out to 50 to 60 yards, the 32 ACP was accurate and had enought zap to drop the target. Stretching the yardage farther makes this setup marginal.

When the range exceeds 60 yards, the 30 Carbine in the appropriate insert is better suited for the shot. Out of the Ruger barrel, the Carbine cartridge was more accurate than it ever was in a number GI autoloaders I've fired. In spite of the accuracy, this cartridge should not be used on big game; it's inadequate at best. Its usefulness on smaller game beyond 90 yards is also suspect.

Inserts for the 22 rimfires, the 32 ACP, and the 30 Carbine, are offered in several other 30-caliber cartridges, including 30-30 Winchester, 308 Winchester, 30-06 and 300 Weatherby Magnum.

In 30-06, all but the Carbine insert were used in a Remington 760 pump, with results similar to the Ruger's. Again, the Winchester Silvertips in 32 ACP, were the most accurate of the reduced ammunition fired in the Gamemaster. The 22 rimfires worked well out to 20 yards. Beyond, more misses than hits occurred.

In my rifles, both 30-caliber insert cartridges show a tendency to center bullets horizontally on the target. The rimfires, on the other hand, tend to print groups not only low, but right or left from center, depending on the gun and the ammunition. This is the result, I believe, of the relatively short,

rifled section of the insert that guides the bullet. The 30-caliber sub-cartridges are launched, of course, through the gun's barrel.

It would be informative and extremely helpful if I were able to tell you just where the bullets will hit, but that's impossible. To discover the correct trajectory for your rifle and the ammunition you'll use, it's necessary to *shoot* that combination. Start with the target 10 yards from the muzzle, and increase the yardage until you find it difficult to keep the majority of your shots on the bull.

Be sure to log the different points-of-impact for reference in the field. During a big-game hunt, you have only to refer to this listing. Holding off is a better idea than making a change in scope or sight setting. You don't want to blow a shot on a bear or an elk just to pot a rabbit or squirrel. During the off season, there's nothing wrong with adjusting the sighting equipment to zero the sub-caliber, but leave yourself with the time needed to realign the sights with game loads before the season sneaks up on you.

Small game hunting is just one of the many uses for Harry's inserts. These inserts provide a means that is much less costly, and less punishing than the standard chambering. In the 300 Winchester for instance, battering yourself senseless is hardly the best way to get acquainted with your rifle. Firing 50 rounds of 32 ACP through the barrel is not likely to bruise your budget or your shoulder.

As a teaching aid, the inserts are invaluable. A flinch, once ingrained, is difficult to correct. Even a caliber like the relatively mild 308, has more recoil than many shooters can tolerate and still concentrate on the shot. Starting out with the inserts and mild loads will allow the shooter to learn without frightening him, (or her). Heavy loads can then be worked up to after the shooter has had some experience with the rifle.

Sport Specialties' inserts also allow for practice without bringing down the neighbors, or an irate farmer, who have been bothered by the noise of the big gun.

Harry Owen can ship inserts in an almost endless number of calibers, and combinations, including one that allows the use of a 25 ACP cartridge in the 25-06, and another that uses a 9mm in a rifle chambered for the 35 Remington. There's also an insert that fires a 22 rimfire in the 375 H&H Magnum. If you own a rifle, there's probably a sub-caliber insert made for it and I think the insert will let you make better use of the gun. ●

HANDGUNS TODAY:

SIXGUNS AND OTHERS

by HAL SWIGGETT

Hal Swiggett shoots the 454 Casull; claims he didn't flinch — his eyes are still open, anyway.

LAST YEAR was rough on handgun manufacturers. At the 1984 SHOT Show many seemed to be simply hanging on. Slight modifications were the most several major companies had to offer but—and there are always one or two willing to step forward and be counted—there are two new revolver calibers and new guns to shoot them. The 32 H&R Magnum made its debut along with the 450 Magnum Express, this from North American Arms. And the Goliath promised in last year's report made it and I have been shooting two 454 Casull single actions.

Let's talk about one of those new revolvers first. Harrington & Richardson teamed up with Federal Cartridge Corporation to produce the H&R 32 Magnum. Featuring a lead semi-wadcutter 95-gr. bullet at 1,030 fps, the 32 H&R Magnum produces 225 ft-lbs. of energy at the muzzle or, put another way, gives a 12.5% increase over the standard 158-gr. 38 Special lead semiwadcutter. The 32 H&R 95-gr. bullet thumps its target with only 7.5% less energy than does the hot 110-gr. 38 Special +P. Mid-range trajectory over 50 yards is 1.1 inches. These figures were developed through a 4⅝-inch test barrel.

The guns are available in three models, plus one variation. The Model 586 H&R is a Western-style 5-shot (all H&R 32 Magnum revolvers are 5-shot). The finish is antique and barrel lengths of 4½, 5½, 7½, and 10 inches are available. Model 504 is blue with swing-out cylinder and with two butt configurations. Square butt 504s are in 4 or 6-inch barrel lengths. Round butt versions of the same model feature 3 or 4-inch lengths. Model 532 is a solid frame, blue, with round butt, and with 2½- or 4-inch barrel. Model 586 and 504 wear adjustable sights; Model 532 has fixed sights.

The 32 has not been popular lately and I'm not at all sure why. Accuracy is tops—at least equal to the 38. As a target shooting, plinking, small game handgun load it should be ideal since there is little noise and even less recoil.

I've been guilty, too, but intend to fix that soon as my test H&R Model 504 with 6-inch barrel gets here. I've already researched loads, have bul-

lets on hand, and just maybe will find the centerfire I've been looking for, that one to use instead of a 22 rimfire. I've tried, for many years off and on, using 38 Specials with light wadcutter loads. They do a good job, too, but I seem always to go back to the 22. This new H&R Magnum could well be the cartridge that weans me away from the 22 as my small game, rock busting, plinking, "let's see if we can hit that little tiny rock way out yonder" gun. Loaded to around 700-750 fps with wadcutters, cottontails and squirrels—eatin' game—should be ideal targets. Full magnum loads would easily handle most small varmints and as a medium to long range jackrabbit cartridge might be near perfect.

The other new revolver is North American Arms single action 450 Magnum Express. Based on the 45 Winchester Magnum case it is ⅛-inch longer. Naturally the parent cartridge can be fired in the 450 Magnum Express.

The N.A.A.-SAS (North American Arms Single Action Stainless) is all stainless steel and offered in two barrel lengths. The 7½-inch length lists at 52 ounces and the 10½-inch at 56 ounces. The 450 Magnum Express is a 5-shot single action. Three finishes will be available—high polish, semimatte, and black chrome. Sights are fully adjustable. A scope mounting system is also to be had.

Everything concerning this new powerful 45 single action is being done by the numbers, so to speak. North American Arms is part of a huge company specializing in highly technical aerospace equipment so all that expertise is brought into play in developing both the revolver and ammunition. H.P. White Laboratories are, as this is written, working on pressure tests with all current 45-caliber bullet weights so nothing will be left to chance.

The revolver is in production. A major company is ready to start loading ammo soon as those pressure tests are completed. My only concern, and I hope they read this, is that they don't get overly excited about velocity with light bullets. This has the makings of a highly potent cartridge easily capable of taking on anything that walks, but to do this it has to have a bullet of at least 300 grains weight and 320 to 350 might be better. Only thorough testing will determine that point. I'm certain that's what handloaders will do, but the factory should offer such loads for those not wanting to brew up their own ammo.

Last year this section could only announce the long-heralded 454 Casull marketed by Freedom Arms along with Wayne Baker's promise it would be in production later in the year. It was. I shot their Number 12 revolver for several months, returning it only when told to do so because an adjustable sight version was on the way. The fixed-sight five-gun (it's a five-shooter, not a six-shooter) went out one day and its replacement arrived the next.

Dick Casull has been working on this big revolver a long time, a very long time. Though barrel lengths of 4¾, 7½, 10 and 12 inches are available I chose 7½ and have not regretted that decision. Factory specs list the revolver at 50 ounces. The fixed sight gun weighed 51 and the just-arrived adjustable sight model weighs 52.5 ounces.

Constructed from 17-4 PH stainless steel 454 Casull single actions are built to handle loads that would turn other single actions into scrap metal immediately if not sooner. In fact, shooting North American Ammunition (NAA) 225-gr. JHP loads, I get the feeling the heavily constructed revolver can take more punishment than a man can.

NAA 454 Casull cases are ⅛-inch longer than 45 Colt brass. Regulation 45 Colt ammo can of course be shot in the 454 Casull, but not the other way around.

Factory ammunition sent with the first gun is topped with 225-gr. JHP bullets listed at 1,800 fps. That's a right smart listing. Federal 45 Colt 225-gr. loads are listed at 900 fps. Federal loads the only 220-gr. 44 Magnum bullet, nearest to compare with the Casull, and lists it at 1,390 fps.

Shooting those 225-gr. loads is a pleasure, with nowhere close to the excessive recoil I'd been led to expect. The load is light, I think. Cases eject with ease and are smoked along almost the entire length indicating they are not even close to maximum.

My only problem came with the

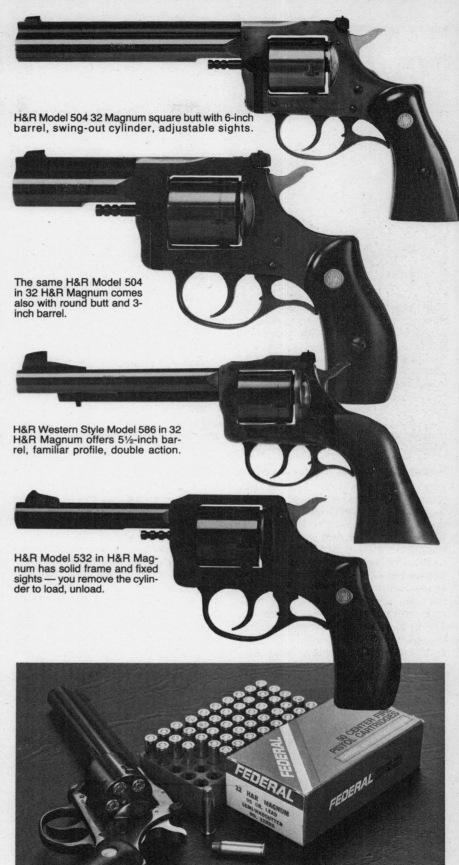

H&R Model 504 32 Magnum square butt with 6-inch barrel, swing-out cylinder, adjustable sights.

The same H&R Model 504 in 32 H&R Magnum comes also with round butt and 3-inch barrel.

H&R Western Style Model 586 in 32 H&R Magnum offers 5½-inch barrel, familiar profile, double action.

H&R Model 532 in H&R Magnum has solid frame and fixed sights — you remove the cylinder to load, unload.

Federal's 32 Magnum 95-gr. lead semi-wadcutter cartridges for the new Harrington & Richardson revolvers.

Right — 454 Casull with 7½-inch barrel in fixed sight style is all stainless steel.

Left — J. D. Jones with a Corsican ram taken on the Y.O. Ranch with the 454 Casull.

fixed sight. Literature sent with the gun said to file the front sight down to sight in. This was a loan gun and I couldn't convince myself anyone would seriously want to shoot light 225-gr. bullets, so "Kentucky windage" became the order of fire. Rocks were shattered at varying distances out to 150 yards. J.D. Jones, long-time friend and handgunner of note, dropped a fine Corsican ram with it by holding up about ⅛-inch of the front sight.

With this adjustable sight edition that's just arrived came a box of Dick Casull's personal 454 loads. Loads topped with 300-gr. bullets cast from a mixture including 11% antimony and 5% tin. I'm not going to tell you the load, but Dick said it was turning out over 1,900 fps. That's more than 100 fps faster than NAAs factory 225-grain load.

I wouldn't go so far as to say those first light loads rate as "pussycat" but would hesitate to rate them higher than maybe half-grown bobcat. These 300-gr. "personal" loads at more than 1,900 fps—they are as close to tigers as you are going to find and definitely not for the average handgunner.

I'd go so far as to say the 454 Casull is not for the average handgunner. The majority of 44 Magnum shooters will back off after a few rounds of full-power loads. The 454 Casull is a man's gun and no others need apply.

Sure, I know what's going to happen, and so do you. Shooters will buy 454 Casull revolvers then load light or shoot 45 Colt ammo, yet throw back their shoulders and say "I'm shooting a 454 Casull!"

However, for the serious handgunner, the handgunner who has trained himself to handle heavy recoil, the

454 Casull will kill anything that breathes air on the face of this earth and it is the only single action at the moment capable of such a feat. Near as I can tell it outclasses the 44 Magnum by at least the same percentage the 44 Magnum outdoes the 38 Special.

Besides all that power, the 454 Casull is a beautifully built single action. Every piece fits. Wood, metal, sights—nothing has been spared to make the 454 Casull very good.

Sturm, Ruger & Co. dropped the biggie on us last year when they and Remington introduced the 357 Maximum single action and 158-gr. cartridge. Federal jumped in with both feet by adding the heavier 180-gr. load. Almost before the ink was dry, Ruger pulled the New Model Blackhawk-SRM, their 357 Remington Maximum single action, off the market. When that happened Federal immediately stopped releasing their 180-gr. load. Remington, however, kept the thing going by seeing that dealers had plenty of their 158-gr. load, the one introduced with the revolver. And Federal came back.

Several other companies got on the 357 Maximum bandwagon and so far as I know are still producing guns. We'll get to them later, right now we are talking about Ruger. As I write this, I know of no Ruger 357 Remington Maximum New Model Blackhawk single action revolvers being released, but it does get a half page in their new catalog. Whether this is to just save face or there really is to be such a revolver in the future only time will tell. Hopefully the erosion problem will be solved for Ruger's sake as well as those wanting to try the new cartridge in a Blackhawk.

The 454 Casull adjustable sights look like this.

The 454 Casull cases carry their own headstamp.

I wasn't a 357 Remington Maximum fan when it was announced and absolutely nothing has happened this past year to change my mind. It maybe does well on steel/iron targets for those not up to shooting full grown guns on silhouette ranges. That's where it got started and if we are lucky that's where it will stay. It is definitely not a big game caliber and that will be borne out when those who have killed their one or two animals start counting those that didn't drop where they could be found and how many shots it took to keep the few dropped on the ground. I come from an

Charter Arms Bulldog 44 Special has 2½-inch barrel, full length ramp front sight and pocket or chopped hammer.

Charter Arms Off-Duty 38 Special has 2-inch barrel, is all stainless steel.

Charter Arms got a revolver set up for 32 H&R Magnum right away.

Colt MK V Troopers with 6-inch barrel come nickel or blue.

Colt Commando Special has non-glare combat finish, 2-inch barrel, fixed sights and Colt's new recoil-absorbing rubber grip.

Colt MK V Lawman with 4-inch barrel and fixed sight, a simple and effective belt gun.

Left — Richard Mertz with the latest M.O.A. "Maximum" single shot pistol.

Above — A set of working Dan Wesson stainless 6-inch revolvers in 44 Magnum, 41 Magnum, and 357 Magnum, all with Pachmayr grips and yellow insert front sights.

Left — United Sporting Arms, Inc. (of Arizona) all stainless Seville 41 Magnum with 7½-inch barrel.

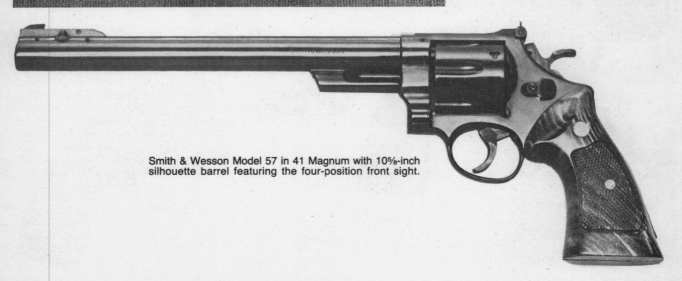

Smith & Wesson Model 57 in 41 Magnum with 10⅝-inch silhouette barrel featuring the four-position front sight.

era where one, two, or three of anything didn't prove anything. Let's see what time does to the cartridge and where it gets placed over that long run.

Ruger added 5½-inch barrels to the rugged Redhawk along with the addition of 357 Magnum and 41 Magnum chamberings. The Redhawk is big, rugged, dependable, just like the Blackhawk and Super Blackhawk. Shorter 5½-inch barrels will undoubtedly add to its popularity, maybe even more so than those additional calibers. The Redhawk is a proven gun—period—added calibers and choice of barrel lengths just make it better.

With the 357 Maximum fresh in mind let's get on to Dan Wesson and how they are handling the problem.

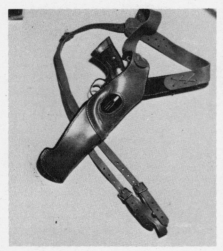

"Dirty Harry" shoulder holster from Cattle Baron Leather.

Uncle Mike's nylon shoulder holster for hunting handguns.

DW labels their offering 357 Super Mag—that's the handle IHMSA put on Elgin Gates' cartridge which started this string of events. Sensing more cylinder length might be advantageous, DW made theirs 150 thousandths longer than the Ruger, but it hasn't seemed to help with that erosion problem. It is still there and in fact, DW ships two (2) barrels with each Super Mag along with a discount certificate for a third when it's needed. That's not a solution to the problem per se, but a definite help towards keeping the shooter in business. Dan Wesson revolvers are big and heavy and the extended cylinder length and all that went with it put the gun overweight for IHMSA. The fix was two slots in each side of the shroud.

There is another DW caliber, though I'm not supposed to mention it because it can be bought only through IHMSA. Please do NOT call Dan Wesson Arms trying to buy a 375 Super Mag. For IHMSA, 375 Super Mag revolvers shoot a 375 Winchester case shortened to 1.6 inches, same as the 357 Maximum. The only way you can get one is to join IHMSA, which by the way would be a good idea too.

Smith & Wesson held tight for this year by adding only a 10⅝-inch barrel to their Model 57 41 Magnum. This is their big N-frame revolver identical to the Model 29 44 Magnum except for caliber. This additional barrel is of course the Silhouette four-position front sight barrel announced last year.

Colt introduced the no-frills lightweight Agent last year and it was so successful they have added a no-frills Commando Special for this go-round. Finished like the Agent, it is the Detective Special built for the budget-conscious shooter wanting Colt quality. The Commando Special is six-shot with two-inch barrel wearing Colt's new recoil-absorbing firm rubber grip.

I've been shooting a Python stainless steel 357 Magnum for almost a year, off and on, and it is a jewel. Long the top of the Colt line—and worthy of that recognition—the stainless Python has been altered by me only in front. I did put one of Larry Kelly's Magnum Sales Limited "C More Sights" up front replacing the black Colt sight. These are tough, damage resistant Du Pont Acetal. A packet of five colors—pink, orange, blue, yellow, and green—is available for all three barrel lengths of Ruger's Super Blackhawk and the Colt Python. Larry suggested I try green. Long a fan of yellow front sights I followed

his suggestion and though it has been referred to as "bilious green" by several it's still there and mighty easy to see, too—in all light conditions.

Charter Arms lists three new goodies; their Undercover series 6-shot 32 S&W Long revolvers are now chambered for the new 32 Magnum introduced this year by Harrington & Richardson and Federal. This makes the first 6-shot revolver chambered for the new 32 Magnum round.

Charter's popular 44 Special Bulldog is now cataloged with 2½-inch bull barrel featuring a full length ramp front sight, a "pocket" hammer for snag-free drawing from a pocket yet with the hammer serrated for cocking. It wears the famous Bulldog grips, is 5-shot, of course, and weighs 19½ ounces.

There is also a new Off-Duty 38 Special from Charter. It's a 5-shot with a 2-inch barrel. Sights are fixed and there is a red dot in the front sight. There are two finishes: matte black is the new non-glare finish; then there is a stainless version. The black one weighs 16 ounces; the stainless 17.

M.O.A. Maximum—the single-shot falling block pistol announced here last year—is going great. I took one to Kansas on a prairie dog hunt during early summer. Chambered for the 223 cartridge it was topped with a 4x Weaver scope. Shooting Federal 55-gr. boat-tail hollow points it was very efficient out to 250 yards as could be testified to by numerous prairie dogs except that they were beyond possible repair by even the best of veterinarians. Changes in the lock-up and extraction system have been made.

The M.O.A. Maximum is chambered for 18 calibers starting with 22 Hornet and stopping with 44 Magnum with all sorts of in betweens including such rifle cartridges as 22-250, 243, 308 and 358 Winchester.

High Standard is hanging on, determined to stay in the gun manufacturing business. To do so, they have branched out into aircraft parts manufacturing. That's not a new combination for a gun company — another does exactly this same routine except that their gun business came as a sideline to their enormous aircraft parts business. High Standard is an old name in handguns. I'm glad they have found a way to stay with us.

Thompson/Center Contender single-shot pistols, long famous for barrel interchangeability, were chambered for the 357 Remington Maximum instantly. The Contender is the only 357 Maximum handgun to

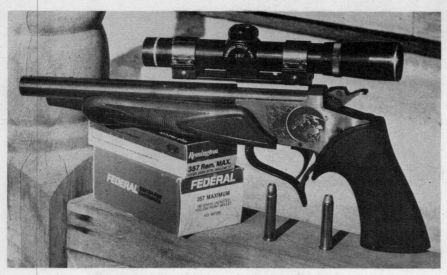

Thompson/Center Contender 357 Maximum with 10-inch barrel and T/C's 3x RP scope in Weaver rings and base.

Power Custom Combat — 5½-inch barrel, Millet sight, Hogue custom grip, is made from a Ruger Redhawk.

go merrily on its way with *no* problems whatever. With the cartridge chambered directly in the barrel it harbors no erosion problem. I've been shooting a 10-inch topped with T/Cs 3x RP scope since last summer. It is literal death on 150-yard jackrabbits and proved lethal to three South Texas coyotes and a single javelina. I've shot only Federal 180-gr. ammunition. One coyote was dropped at 110 steps when he balked at coming closer to the call. The others were inside 50 yards. The javelina was only a little over 50 yards.

In my opinion the 357 Maximum is a top coyote/javelina/jackrabbit caliber and one to be highly considered by

any long range (meaning 150 or so yards) shooter for critters near this size. It ought to be near perfect to anchor eastern woodchucks that are known to crawl off from lesser bullet weights. Could be Remington's 158-gr. load would be ideal for this, maybe better than the Federal 180-gr. but I haven't tried it on game of this size.

I did try the Federal 180-gr. load in this 10-inch T/C on a whitetail buck at about 60 yards. I put the shot on the heavy bone directly over the heart in an effort to knock out that organ, but the buck was lost. The deer was trailed 3½ hours and seen twice, but with no chance for another shot, and finally lost. The only blood found was

where the buck stopped and stood still. One bullet, I'm the first to admit, proves nothing.

United Sporting Arms of Arizona is again under new ownership turning out those great Seville single actions. It was sold to a trio of businessmen and will be operating under the name United Sporting Arms, Inc. New owners are: William Maley, J.C. Munnell, and Harry Moore. Maley serves as President and General Manager, Moore as Vice-President of Sales. Their address remains the same. Their current hottest chamberings (in sales) are the 357 Super Mag (357 Maximum) and 375 USA Mag (375 Super Mag). This latter is the 375 Winchester case cut to 1.6 inches, same length as the 357 Maximum, then loaded with the 375 bullet.

Pachmayr, well known for the autoloading pistol conversions, is offering a unit so new not even a photograph is available at this writing. I did see it at the SHOT Show however so know it exists. Would you believe a single shot on an autoloader frame? That's it. Strip off the slide and ejector of a 45 semiautomatic, install Pachmayr's single shot conversion unit, available in most any caliber you might think of including 308 Winchester, and you have a single shot rifle.

Remember the Glaser Safety Slug? Invented by the late Colonel Jack Canon it was the most devastating cartridge ever produced. Instant death to whatever it hit. Colonel Jack is gone, but his Glaser Safety Slug is alive and well—maybe even better. Jack's son Kurt is continuing the business and building those slugs on modern equipment thereby producing a fine looking product. Colonel Canon's were made one at a time, by hand, and no two were alike.

The "slug" consists of #12 shot Teflon coated so they won't stick together and stuffed in a bullet jacket. On hitting the target they penetrate far enough to get inside before rupturing and dispersing all those tiny pellets throughout the body cavity. I've killed game so dead it never knew what hit it with chest shots. Many years ago, I was the first writer ever to put the Glaser Safety Slug into print. I've shot it a lot.

It comes in six-round packages and can be had in 25 ACP, 380, 9mm, 38 Super, 38 Special, 357 Magnum, 44 Special, 44 Magnum, 45 ACP, 45 Colt, 308 Winchester, and 30-06 Springfield. It isn't inexpensive—$18.60 suggested retail for six rounds of 44 Magnum—but it is the best at stopping something instantly. ●

HANDGUNS TODAY:

AUTOLOADERS

by J. B. WOOD

J. B. Wood, firing the Steyr GB pistol. (Mike Schmidt photo)

LOOKING AT this year's pistols of new design and at the new versions of older designs, I've noticed one thing about all of them: Quality is greatly improved. This reverses a trend that prevailed just a few short years ago, and it's a welcome change. No one, these days, is making or importing anything that could be called junk. It would seem that everyone has discovered one of the Great Truths of Gundom: Serious shooters will gladly pay more, if the pistol is made *right*.

Among those who favor combat-styled arms, it's as if a fine dividing line has been drawn. On one side, it's single action, cocked-and-locked, and nothing less than 45 caliber. On the other side, it's 9mm Parabellum, double action, and 15 to 18-round magazines. Between these groups, the only point of agreement seems to be that stainless steel is nice. This divergence of opinion is a good thing, though, because it has engendered the design of a lot of interesting pistols. In random order, let's check over the new offerings:

Colt

With a nod toward the burgeoning trend of customizing their GM-pattern pistol, Colt recently introduced a Combat Grade version of their Mark IV/Series 80 pistol. As standard equipment it has a higher undercut front sight and a taller white-outline rear sight. The ejection port is opened, and the magazine entry is beveled. A long trigger and a flat mainspring housing are used, and the wrap-around rubber grip is specially made for Colt by Pachmayr. The buyer of the Colt Combat Grade thus has several of the expensive custom alterations already done. The pistol has, of course, the new automatic firing pin lock safety of all the Series 80 guns.

I haven't fired the Combat Grade yet, but I have put quite a few rounds through the new Colt 380 pistol. A true pocket pistol, it's smaller than today's average medium-frame 380, but it's pleasant to shoot. Fit, finish, and performance are just about perfect.

Smith & Wesson

With their neat little Model 469 well-launched, the S&W engineers have turned their attention to a new project—a double action pistol in 45 Auto. So far, only one finished gun exists, a beautiful, extensively embellished pistol that was auction-sold early in 1984 to benefit the U.S. Olympic Shooting Team. Regular production of the Model 645 will begin sometime in 1985, we're told.

The pistol has the bushingless muzzle of the Model 469, and a similar hooked-and-checkered guard, but otherwise its external lines are very similar to the Model 59. It's larger, of course. By the time the Model 465 appears, there's sure to be a long waiting list.

Arminex

Slowly but surely, the first of the Trifire pistols are coming out of Arminex, Ltd., in Scottsdale, Arizona. For those who came in late, the gun has a general external similarity to the classic Government Model, but there are many differences. As its name implies, the Trifire is convertible from 45 Auto to 38 Super and 9mm Parabellum, and this is done without changing slides. A slide-mounted manual safety blocks the firing pin, but does not drop the hammer. Trifire has a wide, smooth trigger, a specially-contoured one-piece backstrap insert, and no grip safety. I fired one of the first assembled guns early in 1984, and it performed very well.

Randall

This popular all-stainless GM-pattern pistol has been available in four models, and now they have added three more. The three new pistols are all true mirror-image left-handed guns! Not only are the controls and the ejection port reversed, but even the internal parts and the twist direction of the rifling in the barrel. The Service Model and a shortened version, the Raider, are now offered in left-hand configuration, along with a lightweight model of the smaller gun. This will be great news for the more than ten percent of shooters who are left-handed, and who are tired of dodging ejected cases.

Detonics

At the time this is written, I haven't fired the little 9mm double action from Detonics, but I have put a few rounds through their first "big gun," the 45 Scoremaster. This one was obviously designed with competition in mind, as it has several nice features that are the sort of thing added in custom pistol work. The "coned" shape of the forward portion of the barrel adds diameter and weight that give a "bull barrel" effect.

Beretta

Last year, the question on the little Beretta Model 20 was: When would we see a 22 Long Rifle version? That question has now been answered, and it's called the Model 21. I've handled the prototype, and it offers the same features as the 25-caliber Model 20, including double action and an eight-round magazine. The size and weight are the same.

There are one or two small differences. The smooth walnut grips are retained by two screws on each side, and the frame forms a solid backstrap at the rear, with more curve at the lower end. The push-button magazine release is moved slightly upward.

By now, nearly everyone knows how I feel about Beretta quality and performance, so I'll restrain the superlative adjectives—but it's not easy. Meanwhile, in the Beretta big-gun department, the Model 92SB has been adopted as the sidearm of the Connecticut State Police.

Interarms

There is a long list of fine automatic pistols in the Interarms catalog. They have Walther, Bernardelli, Astra, and the marvelous Star Model 28. And, of course, the entire line of SIG/Sauer pistols. A recent addition is the beautiful 380 SIG/Sauer P230 in stainless steel. Another is the SIG/Sauer P226, a full-sized 9mm with a 15-round magazine and a reversible push-button magazine release. Except for these two important features, and a subtle change in the grip shape at the rear, it has the same handling qualities as the well-known P220. I have fired a regular-production P226 extensively, and it's superb.

Dornaus & Dixon

When they made the expensive Jeff Cooper Commemorative version of the Bren Ten, some skeptics ventured the opinion that this was all we'd ever see of the pistol and its new high-performance 10mm cartridge. Well, Tom Dornaus and Mike Dixon are having the last laugh, because now there's the Standard Model, a smaller Pocket Model (for large pockets!), a dark-finished Military/Police Model, and a new addition, a compact Special Forces Model. Along the way, a push-button firing pin block safety was added to the design.

Production of all models is under way, and Norma is loading the 10mm cartridge. Conversion units for 45 Auto will be available. If you want a Bren Ten, better let them know now—there's a long list of back-orders.

Auto-Ordnance

The Auto-Ordnance version of the Government Model design was intro-

The Colt Government Model in "Combat Grade."

The Randall mirror-image left-hand Government model.

The innovative Trifire, from Arminex, Ltd.

The Thompson from Auto-Ordnance, now available in 38 Super.

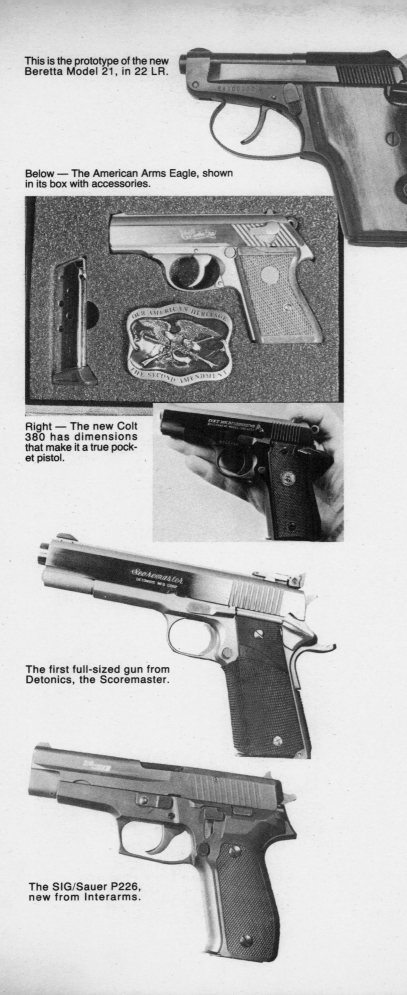

This is the prototype of the new Beretta Model 21, in 22 LR.

Below — The American Arms Eagle, shown in its box with accessories.

Right — The new Colt 380 has dimensions that make it a true pocket pistol.

The first full-sized gun from Detonics, the Scoremaster.

The SIG/Sauer P226, new from Interarms.

duced in recent years as a good, dependable, no-frills pistol. The 45 was soon joined by a 9mm Parabellum chambering, and now they have the pistol in 38 Super.

Considering the lower price of these Thompson guns, they are remarkably well-fitted. Also, they do have one little "custom touch"—a long-style trigger with an adjustable stop screw. These guns have the look and feel of a standard Government Issue piece, but they shoot a lot better.

American Arms

The saga of the Indian Arms 380 stainless pistol continues: Five years ago in this space, I reported that the Indian was gone, and spoke too soon. This fine little pistol, which greatly resembles a Walther PPK, was picked up by Michigan Armament, Inc., and they announced plans to produce it as the "Guardian."

Meanwhile, in Garden Grove, California, American Arms, Inc., has apparently gotten there first. Early in 1984 I examined several production samples of this neat little pistol, and their version, called the "Eagle," looks very good. A 22 LR model is also planned. I'm looking forward to trying it in both chamberings.

Fraser

Over the past 14 years, the Bauer stainless-steel version of the Browning Baby has been made by R. B. Industries, Ltd., in Fraser, Michigan. A year or so back, some sort of disassociation occurred, and since that time the pistol has been made, by the same firm, as the Fraser. I recently tried to contact the Bauer company, and was unable to reach them. As near as I can determine, they are no longer in business.

Meanwhile, at Fraser Firearms, they are offering more than plain stainless steel. There's a new black nitride finish, the QPQ process developed by Kolene Corporation, and, for those who may want to impress a lady, a version of the gun in 24K gold plate in a fitted "book" case.

I've tried the Fraser, and the pistol is the same as it has always been, but with a different name. The new black finish seems to be extremely tough, and it has a nice appearance.

Heckler & Koch

During the U.S. Military Test Program, H&K modified their P7 pistol to take a stagger-type magazine, and created the experimental P7A13. In addition to the 13-round magazine, there were several other modifications, and some of these (but not the magazine) have now been used to produce the P7M8.

There's an ambidextrous magazine release, located at the lower rear of the trigger guard. A plastic heat shield is above the trigger, and the trigger itself is covered with the same material. The trigger guard is slightly enlarged, to comfortably admit a gloved finger. The extractor now serves as a loaded-chamber indicator, and the firing pin retainer is knurled and removable without tools.

The P7M8 has been adopted by the New Jersey State Police as their standard sidearm. At this time, it is not available on the civilian market.

Steyr

Make no mistake—this is not the ill-fated U.S.-made version you remember from a few years ago. This is the real thing, made in Austria with typical Steyr precision. It's the 9mm Steyr GB, and its unique gas-locked system allows a solidly-mounted barrel which delivers amazing accuracy.

With my GB pistol, one 25-yard group from a casual rest measured just seven-eights of an inch. Other features of the GB include an 18-round double-feed magazine, a three-dot luminous sight system, and an automatic firing pin block safety. The handling qualities are excellent, and the felt recoil is very light. So far, I've put around 500 rounds through mine, and I can find nothing to criticize.

Browning

Yes, the rumors are true—there will soon be a regular-production double action version of the venerable Browning Hi-Power. You may recall that during the government test program, two modified versions of the Hi-Power were tried, one an unusual "Fast Action" model, and the other a double action. FN has decided to produce the DA Hi-Power, and Browning will be importing it into the U.S., sometime in 1985.

It's not definitely decided, but it's possible that 1984 may have been the last production year for the single action Hi-Power. At the time this is written, there's not even a photo of the new DA version, so the details will have to wait for the next edition. I'll bet, though, that the new pistol will stay very close to the configuration of the original Hi-Power.

Auto Nine Corporation

Five years ago, the little 22 Auto Nine made its first appearance. Designed and made by John Ray Wil-

The Fraser 25 is now available in a new black finish.

The new 22 Auto Nine from Parma, Idaho.

The Steyr GB pistol: 18 rounds and a unique gas locking system.

The F.I.E. TZ75 pistol, a fine copy of the famed Czech CZ75.

The new AMT Lightning pistol, this one with a 6½-inch bull barrel.

The Taurus PT-99, a modification of the Beretta M92 design.

Above — The Raven MP-25 is now available in a black Teflon finish.

Below — The new 223 Bushmaster, redesigned and reliable.

kinson, it was sold by FTL Marketing Corporation. Ray's genius packed nine rounds into a tiny precision-made package, and like everything else made by Wilkinson Arms, it worked perfectly.

Now, we can refer to that discontinued pistol as "Model I," because "Model II" is here. Ray Wilkinson is now located in Parma, Idaho, and the new pistol is being marketed by a new firm, Auto Nine Corporation.

The pistol is closer in design to Ray's "Diane" 25 Auto of a few years ago. There's a larger ejection port and a pivoting internal hammer. The gun is all in blue and black, very small, very flat, and my new Auto Nine will even shoot the CCI Stinger. Ray has done it again.

Bushmaster

Until this year, my only contact with the formidable 223 Bushmaster pistol was an occasional repair of one of the early guns by the original company. In recent months, I've been trying out a current-production Bushmaster, as made by the new company. I can report that they've corrected all of the problems. Parts that were of marginal size and strength have been beefed-up, and the rather flimsy safety lever by the trigger is now a substantial part, located on the left side of the lower receiver. And, everything *works*. The muzzle flash from that short barrel is awesome, but the gun is pleasant to shoot and totally reliable. My gun is in electroless nickel with a non-reflective matte surface, an optional finish offered.

Taurus

Before the Beretta Model 92S and Model 92SB, there was, briefly, the plain Model 92. Some shooters preferred its frame-mounted sear-block safety. Whether the Model 92 is still being made by Beretta is uncertain, but one thing is sure: The Model 92 has not been imported by Beretta for more than three years.

Meanwhile, in Brazil, the Taurus company has a Beretta-built factory that is making an almost identical pistol in two models. The PT-92 is almost exactly the same, except for a "hook" added to the shape of the trigger guard. The PT-99 has the added advantage of a fully-adjustable rear sight. The grips are a smooth, light Brazilian walnut with a beautiful grain pattern.

In addition to standard blue, a finish option is a polished alloy frame, and the slide and barrel in satin nickel. My own PT-99 is in the latter fin-

Above — The sleek Solokovsky Automaster, a unique 45 target pistol.

Right — An all stainless DA in 22 LR, the "Double Deuce" by Steel City Arms.

STEEL CITY ARMS, INC.
PITTSBURGH, PA. U.S.A.

ish, and it looks handsome and performs accordingly.

F.I.E.

From Firearms Import & Export, the big news is the arrival of the TZ75 from Italy. Made in Brescia by Tanfoglio Giuseppe, it's an almost exact copy of the famed (and very difficult to obtain) Czech CZ75. The principal difference is in the safety systems, and in my opinion the one on the TZ75 is better than the frame-mounted sear-block of the Czech pistol. When turned downward and toward the rear, the TZ75 safety first pulls the firing pin well inside its tunnel, then locks it in place, and finally drops the hammer. The sights of the TZ75 are also better, with a white-bracketed rear and a white-stripe front.

I've fired both pistols, and I prefer the F.I.E. TZ75. Its good points include a 15-round magazine, all-steel construction, and an ultra-smooth double action trigger system. Also, its price is about one-third the cost of a Czech 75.

Beeman/Agner

Formerly known as an airgun company, Beeman is now very much into firearms. On their impressive list of imports is an absolutely marvelous 22 LR target pistol, the first of its type to be made entirely of stainless steel. Designed by Bent Agner and made by Saxhoj Products of Denmark under his personal supervision, the Agner M80 has numerous outstanding and innovative features.

There's a single control on the left side that is a safety, magazine release, and a removable locking key. A dry-firing device allows endless practice without stressing the firing system parts. Its balance and performance are, for this casual target shooter, amazing. The Beeman/Agner M80 is quite expensive—and worth it.

Sokolovsky

While we're in the expensive category, I'll mention Paul Sokolovsky's beautiful, hand-built Automaster, which is the sleekest 45 pistol I've ever handled. It has no obvious external controls, and no screws or pins.

The safety, magazine release, and barrel latch are operated via "sub-triggers" that are on each side of the firing trigger. The barrel is removable without complete field-stripping, and the main parts are made of stainless steel.

The pistol has a Millett adjustable

rear sight, and the instruction manual firmly states that the Automaster is a target pistol, not a combat or service model. I haven't had an opportunity to fire the gun, but it has superb balance, and is one of the best-looking pistols I've ever seen.

AMT

In addition to Harry Sanford's Hardballer in Standard and Long Slide versions, and the excellent 380 and 22 Back-Up, AMT now has a sleek, new stainless-steel creation called the "Lightning." Essentially, it's a customized version of the Ruger Standard Auto, made entirely in stainless by AMT. Among other special features, it has a Clark trigger, a hooked guard, a wrap-around rubber grip, and an external bolt latch. The receiver sides are flat, and the top is grooved for scope mounting. Barrel lengths from 5 to 12½ inches are offered. Recently, I've been shooting a 5-inch bull-barrel Lightning, and its performance is outstanding.

Steel City Arms

Four years ago, when I examined the prototypes of Chuck Bailey's neat little "Double Deuce," the plans were to offer it in regular steel, with blue or chrome finish. By the time production got rolling in 1984, the tiny 22LR double action pistol was of all-stainless construction. The standard grip panels are rosewood, but other exotic woods are available at extra cost. The "Double Deuce" is very flat, just seven-eighths of an inch in width, and the firing pin block safety is ambidextrous. The over-all look is quite Walther-ish. I'm looking forward to trying it.

END NOTES

Wildey Moore is no longer associated with Wildey Firearms, the company that was originally formed to produce his gas-operated 45 Winchester Magnum pistol, and the future of that particular gun is uncertain at this time. Wildey does, though, have other endeavors in the works. One of these is an entirely new gas-operated design that externally resembles the old Auto-Mag, but is entirely different inside. Another project of Wildey, Incorporated, is a gas/roller unit that will convert 1911-pattern pistols to a fixed barrel.

In Texas, the Lone Star Arms recreation of the 380 Browning Model 1910 began production. This modern version of a very popular pistol should do well. In California, Raven Arms is still quietly making the most reliable low-priced 25 Auto on the market.

An Unmatched Pair . . .

. . . for a study in double rifles.

THE DOUBLE RIFLE is an idea whose time has come and gone and come again and gone again for just about 300 years, give or take. The concept is so simple and elegant as to be irresistible, the mechanics so complex as to be nearly impossible.

But we try and I'm not sure why. Certainly I have given the *idea* a go, now and again. Only the lack of $100,000 and a couple of free years has kept me from really wringing out the guns in the field.

by KEN WARNER

Two double rifles, each with a set of shotgun barrels, is a respectable pile. The case is for the Chapuis.

Here's what I did with the last try and what I wanted to find out:

Without getting into a big testing program which wouldn't solve anything, I wanted to compare the two basic double rifle systems. I was not trying to decide between sidelock and boxlock, or between single and double triggers, or extractors and ejectors, or even outside hammers versus hammerless. I wanted to compare the side-by-side to the over-under.

So I got one of each in the same caliber, and just for the fun of it. I got models that came with spare 20-bore barrels as well. For a while there I bet your reporter was the only fellow in North America with such a pair—one over-under in 9.3x74mm and 20-gauge; one side-by-side ditto.

Getting the side-by-side was pretty simple. Chapuis of France catalogs such a combination, so one simply ordered and waited. This was a couple-three years ago and I used it around and liked it a lot.

Actually, in user terms, I thought the Chapuis system would be pretty hard to beat. The "handles just like a shotgun" double rifle is a rare bird, regardless of the name on it, but this Chapuis actually is a quick and very comfortable companion.

With the shotgun barrels in place, in fact, the Chapuis is lively. You really couldn't find a quicker bird gun. So the side-by-side was a pretty

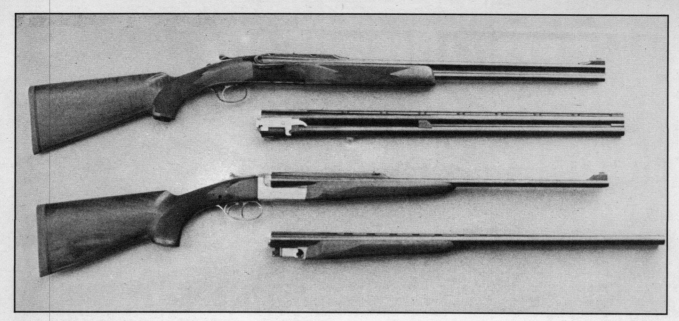

The Ruger/Francotte is at top; the Chapuis below it. Unusually, both are easy-carrying pieces, quick to the shot.

good set-up before I started to complete the pair.

The over-under started to happen when Jay Hansen, the Connecticut entrepreneur, suggested that he might get Francotte (of Liege) to "transform" my Ruger 20-gauge Red Label shotgun into a double rifle. So we went for it in 9.3x74mm. (That's my preference. Mostly they make 30-06s and such. Given a choice, I want

rims on the cartridges I stuff into double rifle chambers.)

The process involves shipping the Ruger to Belgium and waiting. What you get is your original Ruger and an extra set of barrels that fit the original forend. It is hand work, and it is nicely done. Hansen gets the headaches, and there are some—among other things, the Belgians seem very sensitive to the relative value of the

dollar and so prices keep changing.

Sure enough, a little cartouche set into the quarter-rib of the rifle barrels reads "Transforme par A. Francotte et Cie," so it is indeed a transformation. Perhaps more important is the fact that the quarter-rib accepts the Ruger scope rings, so scope-mounting is easy.

I was happy to discover that this

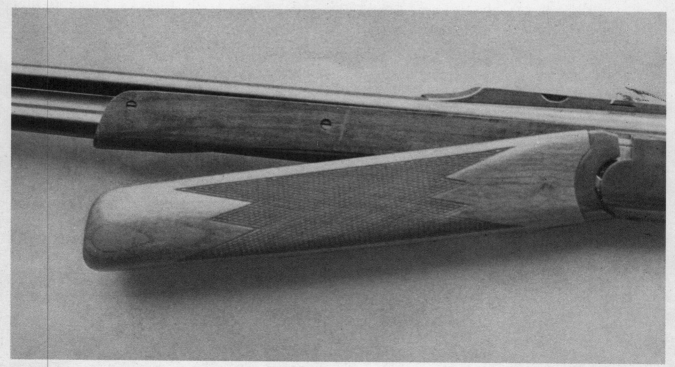

Francotte avoids making a new forend iron and new wood by splicing wood about the rifle barrels. Note Ruger scope mount dovetail in quarter rib.

combination of Ruger and Francotte, which is certainly the long way around to get a double rifle, is also a handy, lightweight "handles like a shotgun" hunting tool. The Ruger Red Label 20-bore handles like a shotgun, perhaps because it is one.

So there it was. The whole set assembled, the two systems matched against each other, and altogether not as big an investment as a Diesel pickup truck, maybe even as little as a medium-sized American car. They were not, however, exactly *equal*, though I got lucky and 9.3x74 cartridge cases fired in one were not ruined for the other. I did not need two separate batches of ammo.

The Ruger 20 has 3-inch chambers; the French shotgun barrels are for 2¾-inch shells. The Ruger has a selective single trigger; the Chapuis has double triggers. The Ruger easily mounts a scope; the Chapuis does not. (Although the factory would do it, which is another thing.) The Francotte iron sights are quite small, though quite good; the Chapuis iron sights are bold and visible.

Nevertheless, the guns were simply equal, though separate. That sounds like a cop-out, but I bought and paid for the guns to find out and that's what I found out. I could not choose between them on either a rational or a subjective basis.

Each would shoot two rights and two lefts into a fist-sized bunch at 40 yards offhand, into about twice that size at 80 yards. Benched, the Chapuis, shot carefully, was a 150-200-yard deer gun (and an all-ranges *big* game rifle, if the power is sufficient).

With the scope, the Ruger would hold better out to 200 yards, and shot very well indeed with the lower barrel only. That is how it should be set up, I figure—as a scoped single shot—for the long ranges; up closer, bang-bang works fine, scoped or not. (Understand, these are this writer's results. There are many better shooters around.) Recoil was not bad with either gun, any time.

Theoretically, the Ruger-Francotte might be just a bit more versatile, given the scope potential and the 3-inch shotgun chambers. Certainly it carries very well, grasped about the breech. The Chapuis is very likely a little quicker to the shot, and a bit more friendly to the hand over a long day's walk.

I'm satisfied with my answer which is: Essentially, the two systems are about equal in use, which means a fellow with a preference one way or the other can suit himself. Probably you all knew that in the first place. ●

Both rifles have this Continental muzzle protection, rather a good idea.

The 9.3x74 is big enough to deserve a double, small enough to shoot a lot.

(Above and right) In contrast to some over-under rifles, the Francotte transformation of the Ruger is genuinely light and trim. It also shoots. The Red Label butt is straight enough for ease in scope use.

MANAGING THE MUZZLE-LOADING SHOTGUN

This writer does it all with front-stuffers, from rabbits to geese and turkeys.

by TOBY BRIDGES

A limit of bushytails and the Navy Arms Classic. The powder flask is an old English-made original; leather shot pouch is available from Dixie.

AN EVER-GROWING number of hunters have turned to muzzle-loading guns of late. Since shooting black powder first began to draw a lot of shooter interest during the early 1960s, muzzle-loading rifles have reigned in popularity and hunting game, especially deer, with front-loaders has become so popular that many states now offer a special muzzle-loading season.

The rifles still hold that number one spot, but recently there has been a real surge of interest in shotguns. Nearly every major black powder arms importer/manufacturer currently offers at least one model. If you're now faced with limited hunting time, perhaps you should take a serious look at a muzzleloader for at least some of your shotgunning. Properly stuffed these scatterguns can almost keep pace with modern breechloaders. And they're a heck of a lot more fun to hunt with, a lot of us think.

Most original 19th century guns and a majority of modern reproductions currently available have cylinder bore barrels. Choking a shotgun barrel that must be loaded through the muzzle more often than not results in difficult loading. Some of the old guns were built with jug-choked barrels. The choke was located as much as several inches below the muzzle, and the bore flared back out to true bore size or even a little larger. The funnel effect allowed the shooter to load tight-fitting card and felt wads. I've loaded and shot several of these and found them about modified choke. I used one old Belgium-made double so choked to down quite a few ducks and geese over a period of several seasons.

The strangest muzzle-loading shotgun barrels I've ever seen were found on an original John Manton percussion double I once owned. At the muzzle, both barrels were 10 gauge, measuring .775-in. However, when I loaded it for the first time, I was amazed when 10-ga. wads simply dropped down each tube and the bores were as good as the day the gun had been made, just as was the outside condition. I was puzzled and when a gunsmith friend of mine offered to pull off the breechplugs, we did it.

We discovered the gun was built with fully tapered bores, measuring right at .810-in., or slightly larger than a 9 gauge, back at the breech. Apparently, this Manton was designed for loose wadding, tamped into a compressed layer over the powder charge with the button of the ramrod. So loaded, I found it would produce tight 80% patterns at 30 yards but even with light 80- and 90-gr. charges in the 11-pound double recoil was very noticeable.

Ideally, wads for a muzzle-loading shotgun should fit just snug enough in the bore that they stay in place if downward pressure on the ramrod stops. Wads that fit so loose they practically fall onto the powder charge when inserted through the muzzle won't properly seal the gases of the burning black powder. Blow-by will blow open patterns and leave huge areas void of shot. Also, much needed power is lost. On the other hand, a wad that must be driven into the muzzle and down the bore will normally shoot well enough, but once the bore begins to cake with fouling, loading becomes next to impossible. Herein lies the trouble with choking a muzzle-loading shotgun barrel. Once a proper diameter over-powder wad is inserted through the constriction of the choke it no longer fits the bore tight enough to insure a proper gas seal and once the shotgun has been fired several times loading becomes even more difficult.

The secret to getting the cylinder bore barrels (that are thus almost a necessity on a muzzleloader) to perform acceptably lies in loading near-equal volumes of powder and shot. The volume of one should never be greatly out of proportion to the other. A 75- to 80-gr. charge of FFg works well with 1 and 1⅛-oz. shot charges; 90 grains of the propellant is nearly equal volume to 1¼-oz. shot; 1½-oz. of shot should be teamed up with a powder charge of at least 100 to 110-gr.

Each and every time you load a muzzle-loading shotgun you can have a custom reload. This is one of the real beauties of hunting with a frontloading smoothbore—its versatility. The same shotgun can be stuffed with 75 grains of FFg black powder and 1⅛-oz. of No. 7½ shot and used to take quail or dove, then loaded with 85 or 90 grains of black powder and 1¼-oz. of No. 4s for big ducks and pheasants. If the weight of the shotgun permits it, it could handle a really heavy charge of 100 grains of FFg behind 1½-oz. of No. 2s for geese or turkey.

One of my favorite reproduction muzzle-loading doubles is the big percussion 10-gauge side-by-side from Dixie Gun Works. Although listed in the catalog as a 10 gauge, the big boomer is actually an 11-bore and measures right at .751-in. in my sample. This 30-in. gun weighs 8½ pounds and can handle light, medium and heavy charges with authority. It's the do-it-all model of the current muzzle-loading smoothbore lineup.

An 80-gr. charge of FFg behind 1⅛-oz. of No. 6 or 7½ shot has put all kinds of upland game on our table. This particular load is about equal to the standard 3-dram load commonly used in modern shotshells. Muzzle velocity is right at 1,000 fps.

During a Kansas combination quail and pheasant hunt several years ago I used the Dixie 11 gauge. Early in the morning we hunted the wide open milo fields of north central Kansas for pheasants. With a 90-gr. charge of FFg and 1¼-oz. of No. 5 shot, I found I could maintain pace with my breech-loading hunting partners. Most of the shots were at 25 or 30 yards, a distance at which the Dixie double performs its best. Over the powder charge, I put a heavy .125-in. thick card wad, followed by a half-inch fiber cushion wad. Next, I loaded a shot cup trimmed from one of Remington's 12-gauge Power Piston one-piece plastic wad units. Over the shot, I put a .030-in. card wad. This load, even though fired from a cylinder bore barrel, is capable of keeping approximately 65% of the pellets inside a 30-in. circle at 30 yards.

About midday we hunted the brushy draws and along the small creeks that broke the otherwise rolling prarie, primarily for quail. We occasionally jumped a cottontail or flushed a pheasant, so I loaded the left barrel with the 90-gr. charge, but with No. 6 shot. The right barrel carried an 80-gr. charge of FFg and 1⅛-oz. of No. 8 shot, and no plastic shot cup. This opens up patterns considerably. The Dixie prints about 50% at 30 yards when loaded without the shot cup. The gun dropped a number of birds at distances up to 30 and 35 yards with the left barrel and heavier load on follow up second shots. It was so effective several companions on that hunt now use muzzleloaders some of the time.

Larger than 12 and smaller than 10, this gun can't use one-piece wad units. The load with the shot cup is one thing; the shotgun performs poorly when the entire plastic wad is used.

There is a gun that performs adequately in upland gunning when loaded with a full plastic wad column. It's the Classic side-by-side from Navy Arms Company. This is a true 12-bore with 28-in. cylinder barrels. I shot one for years. It performed best when loaded with a heavy card and fiber over-powder wadding, but it shot well enough with about any 12-ga. one-piece wad unit to warrant their use when loading was likely to be fast and furious, such as over a hot dove field. The one-piece plastic wads fit the bore snugly, but can be pushed with the ramrod.

I used the Navy double when hunting with a group of modern shotgunners for big swamp rabbits in southern Illinois. Now, this was a group of hunters that didn't feel like waiting for anyone, especially a slowpoke with a muzzleloader. Once their beagles had one of the oversized cottontails on the run, it was every man for himself. Fortunately, I was able to keep up with the entire group all day, thanks to the one-piece plastic wads.

Navy Arms' 7½-pound English style smoothbore is capable of 60% or better patterns when loaded much the same as the Dixie double described earlier, especially when a plastic shot cup is used in conjunction with a heavy .125-in. thick card and .500-in. thick fiber over-powder wad. The Classic double I've been shooting for the past couple of years performs best when stoked with 90 grains of FFg and 1¼-oz. of No. 6 shot. For some reason, it prefers 6s over all others. I've taken quite a few pheasants and a variety of decoying waterfowl with this load. Although I've never used it with lighter loads, I have stoked it up with as much as 100 grains of FFg behind 1½-oz. of No. 2 shot for geese. Recoil was a little on the painful side; the shotgun proved capable and took the big birds at 30 to 35 yards.

Euroarms Magnum Cape Gun is a well-built muzzle-loading smoothbore that performs nicely, however, some hunters might find a single shot not sufficient. Percussion doubles are much better suited for some hunting, especially for waterfowl and even turkey where a second shot is occasionally an absolute necessity.

Author calling Canadas within range of his old Belgian double. A heavy load of FFg and healthy charge of No. 2 shot will easily down the big birds out to about 30 or 35 yards.

Euroarms of America's Magnum Cape Gun performed well with the homemade shot cup load described in text. The gun easily produced 75% patterns at 30 yards, nearly as good as the modern full choke.

Bridges used Dixie's percussion 10-gauge to take this big Missouri gobbler, which shows that this time he did everything right.

There aren't many flint smooth-bores available to today's black powder burner. Dixie Gun Works currently markets an 11-gauge flint smoothbore they refer to as the Indian Gun. The big flinter is basically a modified Brown Bess with a short 30-inch barrel. The gun is an attempt to offer a copy of the Indian Trade musket at a reproduction price. The only other firm offering a suitable flint smoothbore that can double as a flint fowler is Northstar Enterprises, of Dayton, Ohio. This firm offers a kit of the Indian Trade musket, available in 12, 20, 24 and 28-gauge with barrel lengths from 30 to 41 inches. When properly assembled, the Northstar kits make a very authentic copy of this historical flintlock smoothbore and a fine shooting flint fowler.

The card and fiber muzzle-loading shotgun wads I've mentioned are available from Butler Enterprises, R.R. 2, Box 284, Lawrenceburg, IN 47025. The firm packages the .125- and .030-in. thick card wads 1,000 to the box, while the half-inch thick fiber cushion wads come 500 to the box. They are $4.50 postpaid per box, and available in sizes from 8 to 28 gauge.

I think the greatest challenge the muzzle-loading hunter faces is on wild turkey. The 50 to 60% patterns thrown by the cylinder bores barrels perform nicely for upland game and waterfowl shooting, but they're a little sparse for 40-yard shooting on turkeys. A gobbler may seem a sizeable target, but the effective kill zone is just the head and neck, roughly two to three inches wide and no more than eight inches tall. It takes a fairly dense pattern to get even as few as four or five hits with No. 4 shot in this small an area at 40 yards.

While getting ready for an Arkansas turkey hunt several seasons back, noted primitive shooter Bill Kriemer, of Sunman, Indiana, showed me how to make any muzzle-loading shotgun print full-choke patterns at the longer distances. Bill hunts turkey with a 20-ga. flintlock Indian trade gun and has taken several of the big birds at ranges well over 30 yards. In fact, he shoots nearly 1½-oz. of No. 2 shot in the small bore scattergun, and has learned to obtain near 80% patterns at 30 yards!

He makes special shot cups from plastic 28-ga. shotshell hulls. Bill fills an empty with sand, then crimps it. Next, he cuts off the base and dumps the sand. He slices two narrow (¼ inch wide by ½ inch long) wings—on opposite sides so they'll fold out. The idea of the two wings is to slow the cup shortly after it leaves the muzzle of the shotgun, letting the shot column continue.

This very successful muzzle-loading hunter places one of the heavy card wads over the powder charge, followed by a fiber cushion wad. He then thumbs his homemade plastic shot cup into the muzzle, making sure they fold back into their cuts. He then pours in the shot charge and seats the cup over the two over-powder wads. He then seats a .030-in. card wad over the entire load.

I've found that a 16-ga. hull fashioned in the same manner works well in several percussion 12-gauge doubles I hunt with regularly. However, I've been able to get the best performance with the winged shotcup when loaded in one of the 32-inch Magnum Cape Guns offered by Euroarms of America. In this 12-ga. single-barrel I've modified Bill's loading technique slightly. In addition to the card and fiber wads directly over the powder charge, I also place a second cushion wad inside the homemade shotcup. There is still plenty of room for shot charges of up to 1½ ounces.

At 30 yards, the cylinder bore Magnum Cape Gun will keep up to 75% of the load inside the 30-in. circle customarily used to determine pattern density. At 40 yards, I've found I can keep an average of six hits on a 2½ by 8-in. strip of red construction paper, duplicating the kill zone on a turkey. With 90 or 100 grains of FFg, the gun and load would be deadly on turkey and could prove equally effective on geese and other waterfowl that refuse to decoy close enough for more open patterns. I've used the 16-ga. hull shot cups in the Dixie 11-ga. double to take a beautiful Missouri gobbler at about 35 yards.

It takes a little practice to become really proficient at handling a muzzleloader in the field. Modern reproduction locks have both a half-cock and full-cock notch. During loading — with caps off the nipples — the hammer should be at half-cock. This lets air out the nipple port and allows the shooter to check visually to be sure the nipple is clear. A muzzle-loading shotgun should be carried with the hammers on half-cock. And the cap should always be removed from the nipple of the second barrel of a double before reloading a fired barrel. No use pointing a loaded gun at yourself!

Most states now consider a muzzleloader "unloaded" if the cap has been removed from the nipple or priming powder dumped from the pan. However, it would be wise to double-check your

With a trio of cottontails hanging from his belt, the author gets on another running ahead of a pack of beagles.

Bridges used a modern front-loading smoothbore to take this pair of Tennessee ruffed grouse.

Dixie's percussion 10-bore took this pair of beautiful pheasants; author feels it's a very versatile gun.

state. At the end of a day's hunt, the loads can be pulled with a worm or fired out. If the smoothbore has been fired at all, it will have to be cleaned before being put away.

These frontloaders clean easier than rifles. Most come with hook-breeched barrels so they can be quickly removed for easy cleaning. Several soapy water-soaked patches through each bore will normally break down and remove fouling from an entire day of gunning. A couple of dry patches remove moisture from the bore and several oily patches put a rust preventive coating of lube on the inside barrel walls.

Triggers on most reproduction side-by-side muzzle-loading smoothbores are positioned the same as often found on modern doubles. The front trigger drops the right hammer, the rear trigger the left hammer. On a goose hunt years ago, I drew both hammers to full cock when a dozen or so Canadas began working our shadows. As the big birds set their wings and sailed into the plywood cutouts, I mentally locked on and had already decided which two I'd take to fill my limit. As the first goose touched ground, my partner and I rose out of the pit and quickly sighted in on the back-pedaling geese still suspended in midair. The bead of my William Moore ten-bore swung on the first of "my" geese and I smoothly slid my trigger finger rearward. The jolt I received nearly knocked me back to the rear wall of the pit. I didn't need to check if both barrels had shot at the same time — two 110-grain charges of FFg behind twin 1½-ounce loads of No. 2 shot had already let me know. I got one somewhat shot-up goose.

Recoil from a heavy charge can commonly cause the second hammer on a double to fall. For that reason, I now only cock the barrel being fired. It takes a little practice, but a shooter can easily learn to cock and fire, then cock the other hammer and fire again nearly as fast as if both hammers are cocked. And there's very little chance of double ignition when one barrel is brought to full-cock at a time.

Hunting with a muzzle-loading smoothbore may sound troublesome to anyone who never hunted with a muzzle-loading rifle but once the shooter gets the hang of loading the frontloader he can easily stuff in the right combinations in seconds. Perhaps these black powder scatterguns won't work quite the same as sophisticated pumps or autoloaders, but when properly loaded they are definitely game getters. What some call a slow-poke form of shotgunning surely won't appeal to everyone. However, it takes a lot more personal involvement and those that do give it a try are likely to enjoy it. ●

Dixie Gun Works 10 gauge side-by-side.

This hefty built percussion double is available through Connecticut Valley Arms.

Navy Arms' Classic double 12-bore.

THE MODIFIED AIR GUN

Galan has just assembled his trusty Jackal-modified BB gun in preparation for a "hit," probably on a pesky lizard.

by J. I. GALAN

The mission is possible, often fun, occasionally impractical.

AT FIRST thought the idea seems a bit incongruous. Why on earth modify something which is so splendidly versatile and, at the same time, low-key? Perhaps if we looked at a definition of the verb *to modify*. Webster's dictionary tells us that *to modify* means "to make less extreme: moderate."

Now, I can't think of anything in the shooting sports in general that's less extreme and less in need of moderation than airguns. They produce little or no smoke, no deafening noise, no harsh recoil, no fouling, and are rarely lethal to humans. They perform a variety of jobs very well, from Olympic-style target shooting to small-game hunting.

In comparison to firearms, then, it may even be said that airguns *are* the ultimate modification in and of themselves, without going any further. There is more truth in that statement than it appears at face value, as we slowly come to the realization that in the world of airguns, the term *modification* has a severely restricted connotation, far more so than with firearms. We shall soon see why.

Despite the limited range of modifications that can be performed on airguns in general, the fact remains that airguns are highly interesting mechanical devices. Couple that with our basic tinkering nature and sooner or later you are going to have a modified airgun. Practicality sometimes takes a backseat when it comes to airgun modifications, though, and not all airgun modifications are necessarily meant to improve the performance of a particular gun.

Cosmetic modifications are rather more common in this field than anything else. It is essentially up to the manufacturers to modify basic models to improve performance. When this is done, the company usually renames the gun and brings it out as a totally new model. They do the same thing with even greater frequency when the changes are only superficial; but that's the nature of business.

A few years ago Millard Brothers, Ltd. (Milbro) of Scotland introduced the Cougar air pistol into the British market. Large, even for an air pistol, the Cougar was supplied with a somewhat flimsy wire shoulder stock, standard open rear sights and a removable scope ramp that also accepted a micrometer sight. The Cougar never really caught on, despite its competitive price, adequate power and accuracy. Milbro took the basic Cougar and replaced its conventional sights with a novel reflex sight. The wire shoulder stock was replaced with a sturdy skeletonized metal stock with rubber recoil pad, and a black web sling was added to match the new pistol's all-black finish. The redecorated Cougar became the Black Major, which was shortly thereafter imported into the United States by Barnett International as the "Hellfire" air pistol!

In any event, modifying an airgun to the point where it becomes something radically different from its original shape entails a great deal of highly skilled work. In many cases, it takes much more work and knowledge than it would take to effect the same general changes in a firearm. Even highly skilled gunsmiths come up short when asked to repair or upgrade the powerplant of a modern adult airgun, and the average airgunner wishing to modify his piece in some way is severely restricted in what he can do.

Airguns, in truth, permit fewer modifications than firearms. This stems from the basic fact that airguns carry their own powerplants within themselves, while firearms do not. An airgun, with some exceptions, is a to-tally self-contained unit utilizing only a minute portion of that free commodity we call air, in order to launch a projectile. A modern firearm is merely a launching pad for a projectile propelled by a chemical reaction that is quite independent from the firearm itself. Indeed, modern firearm cartridges are self-contained units that carry their own powerplant.

The incredibly complex relationships involved in a spring-piston powerplant are the first hurdle for anyone other than engineers or factory-trained technicians to tinker successfully with this type of airgun. Even seemingly innocent changes, no matter how flawlessly executed, can have disastrous results.

I was asked some months ago to modify a high-quality magnum air rifle as a survival or backpacker's rifle. The end product was to retain a high degree of usability, accuracy and power, at an absolute minimum of weight and bulk. Quite frankly, such an air rifle would be a worthwhile undertaking for any manufacturer to play with. The problem is that for an individual to pull this project off successfully, there would have to be a substantial expenditure in time as well as money.

Take a magnum spring-piston rifle, for instance. Most of these brutes generate a great deal of vibration in addition to their sometimes harsh "double recoil." They have fairly massive stocks for precisely those reasons, and any attempt to lighten the stocks can spell disaster for the gun. A backpacker's rifle should have a skeletonized folding stock. Such a thing in a high power spring-piston rifle would play havoc not only with the rifle's accuracy but with its powerplant effectiveness as well. Excessive vibration would literally shake the gun apart after a few hundred rounds. It would be almost impossible to keep a telescopic sight zeroed on such a modified rifle due to constant slippage.

How about cutting down the barrel in order to economize on weight and length? Not so fast. If the rifle in question is a barrel-cocker, any significant reduction in barrel length will augment the cocking effort tremendously. As they come from the factory, most barrel-cocking magnum air rifles require over 30 pounds of pressure to compress their stout mainsprings. Reduce the length of the tube by just a few inches and the cocking effort could literally double.

A sidelever or an underlever cocking mechanism, on the other hand, would not be so affected by cutting

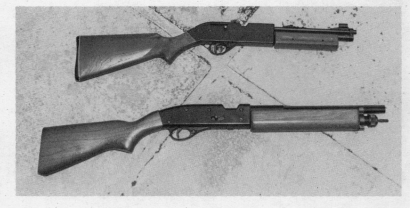

Author's modified Crosman 760/BB pellet rifle (top) is a handy fun-gun. Below is the sawed-off Crosman 1100 CO_2 shotgun, deadly poison for any small critter.

Author's chopped-down Crosman 760 pneumatic rifle has taken its fair share of undesirable critters at home and elsewhere.

Don Nygord took the Gold at the 1981 World Championships shooting his chopped FWB 65 MKI. Beeman now has a factory-modified version, the Beeman/FWB 65 MKII.

down the barrel. Accuracy may suffer a bit, but that's all. In spring-piston airguns, maximum compression takes place while the pellet is still travelling through the first five or six inches of the bore. Beyond that point, no further energy is imparted to the pellet. As a matter of fact, a short barrel in an airgun may generate a slightly higher muzzle velocity, due to reduced friction. This situation is just the opposite of that encountered in firearms.

One good example of the above could be found in one of the air rifle models produced by the now defunct Sussex Armoury of England. Their 22-caliber Model AR-7 sidelever cocking rifle had only an 8-in. barrel, yet it produced a MV of 580-600 fps. Their standard barrel length model, utilizing the same powerplant as the AR-7, produced only around 570 fps. Beeman's C1 carbine produces a smashing 830 fps in 177 caliber and 670 fps in 22 caliber, yet it sports a mere 14-in. barrel. The recently introduced carbine version of the powerful RWS Model 45 air rifle is an example of a factory-shortened barrel without any loss in power.

Pneumatic rifles offer the individual bent on modification a few more options than do spring-piston rifles.

To begin with, modern pneumatic rifles (both single-pump and multi-pump) do not generate recoil or vibration during the firing cycle. Thus, it is quite possible to trim down their stocks to a bare minimum, or to replace them altogether with a suitable skeletonized stock. Cutting down barrels, however, is impossible in most cases. The design of most pneumatic rifles dictates that the barrel be positioned directly atop the pump housing tube. Benjamin, Crosman, Sheridan, and other brands have traditionally utilized this arrangement. Usually, the barrel runs the full length of the pump tube, so there is no point in shortening it. Trying to modify the pumping mechanism itself, or the release valve of these guns, is definitely verboten unless you are an engineer or otherwise technically qualified to work on airguns of this type.

Some pneumatic rifles (carbine-sized to begin with) can be successfully converted into practical little mini-carbines by the average person with just a bit of judicious work and a few common tools. I have a spare Crosman Model 760 pump up rifle that got the short-barrel modification. Its thin, solid steel barrel was cut all the way down to its retaining collar in front of the pump mechanism tube. The re-

sulting 10½-in. barrel gives me a piece that's only 27-in. over-all. A hooded post front sight was epoxied behind the new muzzle, giving a sight base of only 6-in. that can still produce enough accuracy to hit a mouse dead-center at 15 yards. As a BB/pellet plinking gun, my chopped-down Crosman 760 has few equals. It can be tossed in a canvas bag and placed in the trunk of the car. On a few occasions it has come in quite handy in eliminating small marauding pests around the backyard.

In essence, a modified airgun is any airgun which has had anything added to it or taken from it for whatever purpose. Usually, a specialized application is associated with the modification of any sort; however, in the case of some airguns the modification could mean just the opposite: to make the piece in question usuable in a wider range of applications. If you have followed the airgun scene at all during the last five years or so, you must have noticed a proliferation of shoulder-stocked air pistols. In fact, hanging a shoulder stock on an air pistol is probably the number one modification currently in vogue.

There are good, solid reasons for this particular alteration. Adding a shoulder stock to any handgun adds to

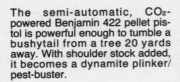

The semi-automatic, CO_2-powered Benjamin 422 pellet pistol is powerful enough to tumble a bushytail from a tree 20 yards away. With shoulder stock added, it becomes a dynamite plinker/pest-buster.

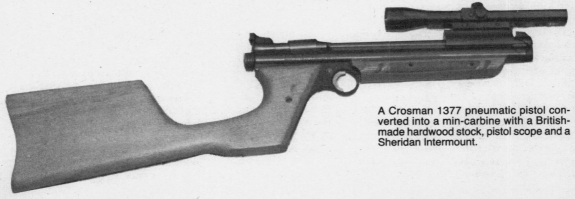

A Crosman 1377 pneumatic pistol converted into a min-carbine with a British-made hardwood stock, pistol scope and a Sheridan Intermount.

The Benjamin 3030 before and after modification.

Author plinking with his highly modified Benjamin 3030 CO₂ BB gun.

The Jackal-style BB gun has tubular aluminum stock that slips over gun's end cap and secures via grub screw. Large aluminum trigger is pinned to sear bar and folds flat against receiver bottom.

the distance at which the weapon can be fired accurately. The steady support which a shoulder stock affords can turn any handgun into a highly concealable miniature rifle, and is one of the principal reasons that most modern cartridge handguns are illegal when a shoulder stock is attached to them. Fortunately, the same restrictions do not apply to air pistols.

Beeman's was the first airgun outfit in the U.S. to offer optional shoulder stocks for some of the air pistols they sold back in the mid-70s. They even offered the highly popular Diana Model 5 air pistol with a folding paratrooper stock in those days! Seeing the handwriting on the wall, especially from the airgun market in Britain, Crosman decided in 1980 to produce a plastic shoulder stock that would fit their 1377 and 1322 air pistols and all of the various vintage Crosman pneumatic and CO₂ pistols having a similar grip configuration. This particular item was very well received by owners of those Crosman pistols because it enabled them to convert their hard-hitting pellet handguns into terrific mini-carbines. The Crosman shoulder stock is still available and comes with a peep sight element for when the stock is installed. This year Crosman

has added a pistol scope with mount to their accessory lineup, which can be attached to their highly successful Model 357 CO₂ revolver *and* to the 1377/1322 pneumatic pistols as well.

Daisy Manufacturing Co. was a bit late jumping into the shoulder-stocked air pistol act, but they too finally took the plunge in 1984. Their popular Model 717 pistol is now modified to accept their new wire frame stock. In addition, they have marketed a similar wire frame stock that fits their Model 1200 CO₂-powered BB pistol.

For years, BSA (Birmingham Small Arms) has resisted modifying their ponderous Scorpion air pistol to take a shoulder stock. They, too, have seen the light and come up with a one-piece, synthetic thumbhole stock that makes the Scorpion look like a shrunken version of BSA's own Buccaneer carbine. Last, but not least, Dynamit Nobel introduced last year an adjustable, all-steel shoulder stock for their RWS Model 5G air pistol.

Ridiculous, you think? Not at all, judging by the way in which these accessories add versatility to already highly recreational and practical guns. Modification, then, is the name of the game when it comes to air pistols.

In the world of airguns, the most eminently modifiable type is unquestionably the CO₂ gun. Because these guns rely partly on an outside power source (liquid carbon dioxide in a small metal bulb), they can be designed to look like, and even duplicate, the repeating actions of real firearms. Crosman Air Guns has for years dominated the CO₂-powered look-alike gun market. About 15 years ago, they introduced a CO₂ 38-caliber shotgun patterned after the well-known Remington Model 1100 scattergun. In fact, Crosman named their model the Trap Master 1100. As sad fate would have it, the Crosman CO₂ shotgun was way ahead of its time. The American shooting public wasn't "airgun-sophisticated" enough at the time to see and appreciate the excellent features and comparatively high craftsmanship of this gun. The result was that the Crosman CO₂ shotgun disappeared some two years after its rather unsuccessful debut.

Over the years, I have owned several of these Crosman CO₂ shotguns. One of the early ones was soon "customized" by reducing its long, slender barrel down to 15 inches (quite legal, since this is not a firearm) and cutting off a section of the stock to wind up with a piece only 32 inches in over-all

Dynamit Nobel modified their RWS Model 5 air pistol by adding a muzzle weight and telesight. The result is an excellent all-purpose fun gun.

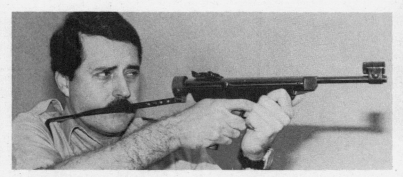

This RWS Model 6G air pistol from Dynamit Nobel has that company's adjustable shoulder stock attached.

An example of factory-implemented cosmetic modification: BSA produced 1,000 of these highly customized Airsporter-S air rifles to commemorate the factory's 100th Anniversary.

length. This short beauty has accounted for a fair share of mice and other miscellaneous nasties. The short, unchoked 38-caliber barrel puts out a nice, wide pattern of approximately 55 #6 shot pellets at 10 to 15 yards that can quickly end the earthly aspirations of even the nimblest suburban rat. A few misguided pigeons intent upon messing up a corner of my roof have from time to time flown into a terminal dose of CO_2-powered #6 shot from the relatively quiet-spoken modified Crosman shotgun.

In his best-selling novel *The Day of the Jackal,* Frederick Forsyth had his chillingly professional hit man come up with a one-of-a-kind, custom-made sniper's rifle to use against French President De Gaulle. The Jackal's rifle could be concealed within an ordinary aluminum crutch and assembled in a matter of seconds. I was fascinated by the concept of such a highly specialized gun and decided to modify one of my airguns to resemble as much as possible the Jackal's rifle. Spring-piston and pneumatic rifles were ruled out from the start, due to their inherent bulkiness. Eventually I chose a Benjamin Model 3030 CO_2-powered BB repeater. Although a smoothbore, the Benjamin 3030—no longer in pro-

duction—can propel an ordinary steel BB at over 650 fps of muzzle velocity, with creditable accuracy to boot. Quite hot for a BB-gun, by any standard, and certainly powerful enough to carry out quiet "hits" against the local rodent leaders.

The wooden stock of the Benjamin was replaced with a two-piece tubular aluminum stock that slips over the end of the gun and is secured via a grub screw. The trigger was cut off flush with the sear bar and a new, folding aluminum trigger pinned to the sear. A Beeman pistol scope base was epoxied to the receiver and a 4-power airgun scope mounted on it. I decided to leave the gun's simple, yet adequate open sight for greater flexibility, in case the scope could not be used for some reason.

The resulting combo is as deadly-looking, and just as concealable, as the Jackal's imaginary rifle. It can be hidden inside a tube only 22-in. long by 2-in. in diameter, if necessary, along with an ample supply of BB's and several 8-gram CO_2 bulbs; plenty for an afternoon of plinking activity. The modified Benjamin 3030 still prints 1¼-in. groups at 15 yards, which is accurate enough to "terminate with extreme prejudice" any wayward mouse. To complete the

look-alike effect, a plastic "silencer" from a toy cap gun can be slipped over the muzzle, although it doesn't really do anything to reduce the fairly low report of this gun.

From a legal standpoint, there is absolutely nothing to restrict or dissuade the enthusiast from modifying a suitable airgun. Barrels can be sawed off, rifle stocks can be shortened or replaced with folding stocks. It is even possible, under federal and most state and local laws, to own a fully-automatic *airgun* without any bureaucratic red tape or special tax stamps whatsoever. In sharp contrast, the average law-abiding citizen cannot tamper with, or possess certain modified firearms so freely, because there are severe penalties in store for him at federal, state and local levels. In this regard, the sky is practically the limit when it comes to altering airguns by individuals as well as manufacturers.

The potential airgun tinkerer should always remember the special prayer that will hopefully guide his actions. To paraphrase a famous prayer: "May I be granted the courage and technical savvy to modify the airguns I can; the serenity to accept those that I can't; and the wisdom to know the difference." ●

Aerial Targets —Safe Again

The good old days return on the wings of plastic bullets that won't go 50 yards.

Tossing the oil can, gun in left hand uncocked, but with thumb on the hammer.

As the can climbs, the hammer is cocked while raising gun to follow target.

EVER SINCE I first read Ed McGivern's *Fast and Fancy Revolver Shooting,* I've been an ardent enthusiast of aerial target shooting. It takes more space than most shooting, so I haven't often had a chance to practice. Thanks to some new short-range ammo I've discovered, that's about to change.

In a Dynamit Nobel ammunition brochure a while back, I discovered that the firm manufactures plastic "training" cartridges in 9mm Luger and 38 Special. Performance is amazing, to say the least. The 6.2-grain plastic bullets leave the muzzle at about 3,000 feet per second (fps) but lose velocity rapidly, and travel less than 50 yards. The ballistic table, reproduced here from RWS data, tells the story.

Intriguing as the information in the brochure was, there were some unanswered questions. How accurate would the plastic bullets be at aerial target ranges, and how close would they shoot to the sights? Typically, light weight, high velocity projectiles shoot low, and these are very light, very HV. The only way to find out was to get some and try 'em. An order was placed at once.

Most of my aerial target work has been with double-action revolvers. DA shooting permits rapid fire, either for multiple targets or several shots at a single target. The long trigger pull seems to stabilize the gun and help hold sight alignment.

Single action revolvers work well enough if only a single shot is to be fired. Few shooters can cock a single action rapidly enough to fire twice at

by DAVE REYNOLDS

a single target, certainly not yours truly.

I have seldom tried auto pistols of any kind for aerial work, mainly because it's so easy to lose cartridge cases out in the pasture. For this project, though, an auto was included be-

On target, just before the shot, everything focused on the target.

A hit on lower edge of can bounces it up and spins it around.

cause of the 9mm ammo. I suspect that there are lots of 9mm shooters who may not own revolvers. Since these cases are not reloadable, it doesn't matter if they get lost.

The guns I used included: two 357 revolvers—a S&W Model 27 and a Colt Single Action Army; two 9mm revolvers—a S&W Model 547 and a Ruger Old Model Blackhawk; and the S&W Model 39 auto pistol.

I determined the performance capabilities of each of the gun/cartridge combinations on our 10-meter indoor airgun range. Number one son, JD, was most anxious to find out if the 9mm plastic develops enough momentum to work the action of the Model 39. It doesn't, which makes the gun a pump instead of an auto. The Model 39 produced tighter groups at 10 meters than any of the other guns, and the S&W 547 was next. All of the revolvers shot low, but the auto printed almost exactly to the sights. For indoor shooting, ear protection was necessary. Recoil was almost non-existent.

The 9mm round was chronographed, fired from the 547 and the 39. Velocities recorded were substantially lower than published data, as would be expected. The ballistic table shows that velocity drops from 3440 fps at the muzzle to 1475 at 10 yards. Using 5-foot spacing on our Oehler 33 Skyscreens, with the front screen 5 feet from the muzzle, we were recording the velocity at about 7½ feet out. The revolver averaged 2346 fps and the auto clocked 2696, 350 fps faster. These figures seem to validate the published data reasonably.

We then headed for the outdoors. We could, of course, shoot this ammo into the air safely at our range. Quart oil cans (with paper walls) and aluminum drink cans were used for targets. We soon discarded ear muffs. Without walls for the sound to bounce around on, the report is very mild.

Because the Model 39 performed best on stationary targets, it was tried first, with poor results—no hits in a couple of clips full of ammo.

Switching to the revolvers, I started hitting the oil cans, then graduated to the drink cans with reasonable success. At the time I assumed that it was because I'm more accustomed to working with revolvers, but that probably isn't the whole story. Unpracticed shooters tend to shoot high at aerial targets, and I'll admit to being a bit rusty. Because the revolvers all shoot low with the plastic, perhaps my sighting error was compensated for by the guns.

If you haven't tried aerial targets,

Plastic training cartridges are made in 38 Special and 9mm, with bullet and case molded in one piece. Bullet tears off when fired. There is a powder charge; these are not powered by primers.

These guns proved the best of five: Colt Single Action Army in 357; S&W Model 547 in 9mm; S&W Model 39 in 9mm. The 9mm training ammo will not cycle 39.

Ballistic Table
GECO Plastic Training Ammo

Caliber	Velocity (ft./sec.)				Energy (ft./lbs.)			
	Muzzle	10 yds	25 yds	50 yds	Muzzle	10 yds	25 yds	50 yds
32 ACP 3.1-gr. bullet	2625	900	290	—	52	6	0.6	—
9mm 6.2-gr. bullet	3440	1475	750	—	170	32	8	—
38 Spl 6.2-gr. bullet	2660	1015	360	—	97	14	2	—

32 ACP is not available in US. Data included here for reference only. Cartridges manufactured by GECO Division of Dynamit Nobel, available from Dynamit Nobel of America, Inc., 105 Stonehurst Court, Northvale, NJ 07647. Like all ammunition, the GECO plastic is available only through dealers. Have your dealer contact Dynamit Nobel. Retail prices of both 9mm and 38 Special were $10.80 per box of 50 at the time of this trial.

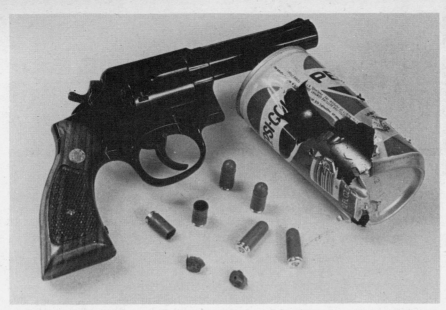

All hits on Pepsi can were made with S&W 547. Hits are hard enough so you know you hit, and the bullets are soft enough to deform.

This target shows several rim hits. When your targets look like this, you need to concentrate on smaller groups because most of these would have missed the drink can.

S&W 547 shot small groups four inches low at 10 meters. The Colt also shot very low but with slightly larger groups.

S&W 39 produced tightest groups, shooting almost exactly to the sights. Group shown would scale under two inches at 25 yards.

but would like to, a few tips are in order:

Begin with a target that is large enough to hit. If you miss, you have no positive frame of reference to tell whether you are shooting over, under, or to the side. Empty gallon plastic milk jugs will do for most folks. Practice a few times with an empty gun to get the feel of what you are doing. Gently toss the jug up at about a 60 degree angle so that it goes up 10 or 15 feet before it starts to fall.

The closer the jug is, the easier it is to hit. When you start hitting consistently, begin throwing the jug higher, and/or at a shallower angle, so you'll have to hit it farther away.

Pay particular attention to where your hits land on the target. Are they solid center hits, or are you just dusting the edges? Are your dusters at the top, bottom, or side? These represent sighting errors that must be corrected before you move to smaller targets. When you are satisfied with your performance on gallon jugs, move down to quart cans and start over.

Do not try to shoot at the instant that the target "stops" at the top of its arc. At that instant it stops climbing and starts falling, but unless it was thrown straight up and falls straight down, it doesn't stop moving. In any case, it will have moved by the time the bullet gets there. The best method is to align your sights on the target while it is climbing, then start squeezing the trigger as it begins to fall. Keep the target floating above the sights all the time.

It is better, at the start, to throw your own targets. With your non-gun hand, using a gentle underhand motion, pitch the target up and out. As you toss the target, bring the gun up and follow the target's movement over the sights. Be particularly careful about horizontal alignment. You should not have to move the gun laterally to stay on target, because the target will be moving straight away from you, not to the side. You want to make what McGivern described as a perfect line shot. This simplifies the problem of lead to a single dimension. Later, after you have it down pat, you can apply the same principles to crossing targets.

At this point I don't know how small a target can be used with the plastic ammo. On the day of our field test, there was a gusty wind that precluded targets much smaller than the aluminum drink cans. But I'm looking forward to calmer days and more practice with the Model 39. It should be able to pop 35mm film cans, if I can learn to do my part.

HAND LOADING UPDATE

by DEAN A. GRENNELL

As FOR THE past several years, handloading continues to remain an important branch of the shooting sports, commanding the intent interest of many different manufacturers. The present discussion concerns itself with handloading equipment and allied topics, rather than with new components such as bullets and primers, covered elsewhere. Let's take the manufacturers with new products and list their new offerings for the past year in alphabetical order:

BBM Corporation

I think BBM's 45 ACP Hardcap load is a major and possibly significant breakthrough. It's a shot cartridge capable of reliable cycling through an autoloading pistol. I mention it here because the maker hopes to offer the needed components for assembly by handloaders at some future time. They are now at work developing a 9mm Luger version of the Hardcap and, simultaneously, are trying to improve production of the 45 Hardcap to lower the cost of firing it below the current tab of about a buck and a half per shot.

To the present, the cartridges vary in their performance, depending upon the gun. A Colt Combat Government handles them quite effectively. A Model 25 S&W disperses them very rapidly, while an aging Model 1917 S&W, with its barrel trimmed back to four inches, delivers marvelously tight patterns. A Ruger Blackhawk with 45 ACP cylinder installed does quite well but a Thompson/Center Contender carrying a ten-inch bull barrel (now discontinued) performs disappointingly. So it goes.

The Hardcap loads closely resemble 230-grain military hardball loads. I have yet to experience a stoppage with them in any 45 ACP autoloader. A cylinder or magazine full of the Hardcaps leaves the target area looking impressively shopworn.

C-H Tool & Die Corp.

If you find yourself motivated to reload the spent cases from a caliber 50 Browning machine gun, C-H can supply the dies, shell holder and an oversized inside/outside case neck deburring tool large enough to handle that size or even a bit bigger.

What's more, they offer their new C-H hydraulic loader to ease the effort of working those big cases. It has a six-inch stroke, a one-horse motor, a foot switch and a price tag of $995. It handles all the smaller cartridges too, of course.

If you fancy something a little more sophisticated, there's the new C-H Manmatic press, fully automatic and operating at a production rate of 2400 rounds per hour. Perhaps I should say that's the cyclic rate, because it shuts down automatically if it runs out of cases, primers, powder or bullets. Even so, that's 40 rounds a minute or one every 1½ seconds. Suggested list price for the Manmatic is $12,990, making it an item of sharp interest only for those with a fairly prodigious appetite for ammo.

Corbin

The Corbin Bullet Press has been given several refinements in recent times, starting with its redesign from a C-type to an O-type by inclusion of an upper frame member.

A few months back, Corbin went back to the old drawing board and emerged with what he now calls the Model CSP-1 press. Both the frame and handle are machined from castings of a remarkable alloy called Ampco 18 which has a yield strength of over 100,000 p.s.i. The bare metal is an attractive dull bronze in color. The handle is longer for increased leverage and the ram stroke is a full two inches. Like the earlier unit, the Model CSP-1 requires specialized bullet swaging dies available from Corbin, as are other bulletmaking needfuls such as jackets, lead wire, core cutters and the new Model HCT-1 hand cannelure tool that applies a professional cannelure to all calibers in a matter of seconds. (There's also the Model PCM-1 power cannelure machine with a production rate of 100 cannelures per minute.)

There are now six other Corbin presses in addition to the Model CSP-1. Two are powered by compressed air and the other four are hydraulic. Prices range from about $200 for the CSP-1; $650 and $2250 for the air-

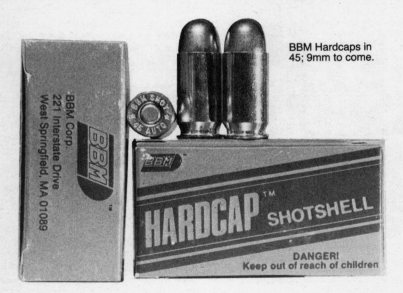

BBM Hardcaps in 45; 9mm to come.

Corbin Manufacturing produces seven different models of hand and power presses. Shown above is the CHP-1 Mark III Corbin Hydro-Press, capable of reloading, bullet swaging, lead wire extrusion, and jacket forming.

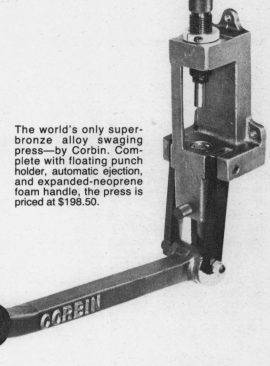

The world's only superbronze alloy swaging press—by Corbin. Complete with floating punch holder, automatic ejection, and expanded-neoprene foam handle, the press is priced at $198.50.

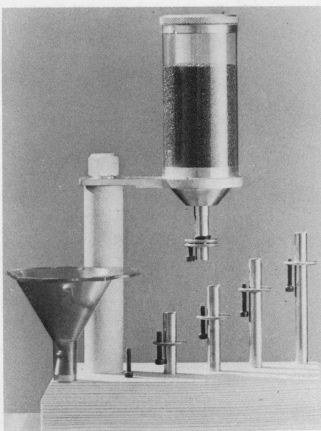

The Francis Quick Measure for rifle cartridges is elegantly machined from brass, very accurate, very sturdy.

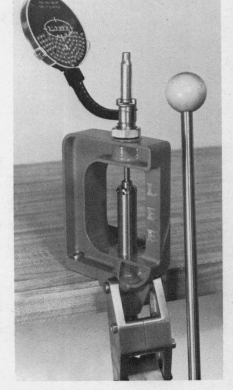

Lee Precision Model 2001 carries an impressive guarantee and even more impressive linkage.

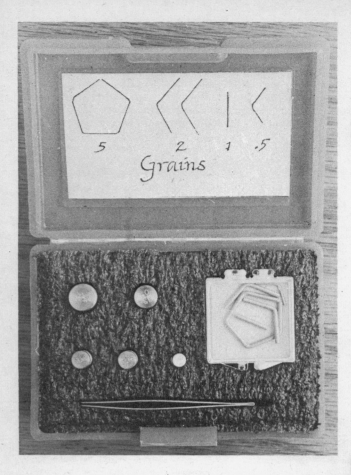

Test your scale? Sure. Lyman's new outfit handles a full range of weight tests.

This is Lee's Turret Press with both Auto-Index and Auto-Disk powder measure installed.

Hornady's well-thought-of 366 shotshell loader is now available for the Skeet shooters' 2½-in. 410 shell.

Corbin CHP-1 Hydro-Press equipped with Corbin LED-1 Lead Wire Extruder. Kit comes with all parts necessary to extrude four standard diameters covering 22-45-caliber bullets.

powered and $3250 to $4500 for the hydraulics. At $10,000, there is the ASP-1 Model 2400, a full-automatic bullet swaging machine that turns out lead (not jacketed) bullets at 2400 per hour, 40 per minute. Obviously, some of these are for bulletmakers bent upon business, not for the casual weekend plinker.

Quite recently, I had a need for some 41-cal. jacketed bullets in weights heavier than usually available in that diameter, for use with the 411 JDJ cartridge discussed elsewhere here. I used a squeeze-down die and punch in the RCBS Big Max and A-2 presses to draw down some 44 jackets to 41 size, going on to add cores that were cast bullets that had been lube/sized in the usual manner in various designs and weights. I also drew down some .7-inch length 45 jackets and found they also worked well. I was able to produce 41-cal. bullets from about 100 grains to a bit over 300 grains and several of them grouped well in the 411 JDJ.

One of the more successful approaches involved remanufacturing some jacketed 44 bullets from Hornady, Sierra and Speer. I used the squeeze-down die and punch, having first rolled them across a pad to which Corbin Swage Lube had been applied. That got them down to .410-inch, but left the jacket in no more than casual contact with the core. A pass through the 41 point-forming die in the CSP-1 press restored their neat appearance and intimate contact between core and jacket.

I also performed an operation I call "reverswaging" on some of Sierra's nice 220-grain 41 silhouette bullets by putting them base-first into the 41 point-forming die and stroking the handle to a careful adjustment of the die. That resulted in a conical-pointed FMJ bullet that seemed to group just a little better in the longer cartridge than did the original bullets as they came from Sierra.

Within a short time, I had 40 or more batches of bullets in assorted shapes and weights to try out in the 411 JDJ and could have produced a great many more.

It seems that every time I start puttering with the CSP-1 press, it's a wrench to have to stop and go on to load the bullets and try them out. It puts a bullet factory on your bench and that can be at least much fun as a tiger in your tank.

Francis Tool Co.

Long noted for their admirable line of chambering reamers and similar precision tooling, this firm recently brought out a novel, innovative and efficient powder measure. Called the Francis Quick-Measure, it is primarily designed for dispensing charges for rifle cartridges. The smallest obtainable charge is about 24.0 grains of IMR-4198, or its equivalent in bulk with other powders.

As with any volumetric powder measure, a dependable powder scale must be used to determine the weight of the charge dropped, during and after adjustment. Once adjusted, the typical uniformity with most powders is on the order of plus or minus 0.1-grain.

All of the metalwork is brass, machined to a beautiful finish. It comes without a stand, but it's easy to fashion one, or you can use it handheld quite conveniently. Four brass powder tubes of varying length are supplied with the measure and a longer fifth tube is available. A 6-40 screw is threaded through a collar on each tube to facilitate fine adjustment of the charge weight.

The Francis Quick-Measure will dispense powder into the pan of a scale for individually weighed charges or you can use the specially modified funnel supplied with the measure to drop the charges directly into the cases. The funnel has a rod with a hemispherical dome at the tip to stop up the lower end of the tube during measurement. When using the funnel, you get about 0.8-grain less than when measuring against a flat surface.

Due to the ingenious design, powder granules are never sheared during measurement, even with the coarsest extruded powders. Largest of the four tubes supplied gives about 72 grains; up to 85 with the fifth, optional tube.

Freechec'

The cost of gas checks for cast bullets has gotten downright substantial in recent times, in case you hadn't noticed. And if you ever tried it, you learned a bullet designed for gas checks doesn't shoot at all well without them. Comes now one Pack Kelly, with a solution.

Kelly has developed a neat little rig he calls the Freechec', consisting of just three pieces to the set. There's a hardened steel cutter, a forming punch and a knockout punch. Your raw material consists of cut-apart and flattened-out aluminum beverage cans.

In use, you cut the ends off the can, slit it down one side, straighten its curvature by drawing across a straight edge and cut the small discs from the metal by rapping the outer body of the Freechec' against a flat surface with a mallet. Take one or two discs—as required—and insert them into the inverted cutter body, followed by the business end of the inner punch and give the assembly a few crafty whacks. Insert the knockout punch into the larger punch and use that to dislodge the completed gas check.

They hold securely and seem to work as well as the "store-boughten" kind. Do your forming so as to have the painted surface on the inside and bare aluminum on the base and exposed skirts. Price for the Freechec' set in one caliber is about $40, postpaid.

Hodgdon

The twenty-third edition of the *Hodgdon Manual* appeared in 1978 and Number 24 recently made its appearance. Of special interest to shooters of high-powered rifles, it carries a complete listing of loads for Hodgdon's H4350 powder. Hitherto, there was little choice except to dispense H4350 in loads recommended for Du Pont's IMR-4350.

As it turns out, H4350 is rated slightly faster in burning rate than IRM-4350, so that loading the former on a grain-for-grain basis is not a good idea. To cite but one example: In the 300 Winchester Magnum cartridge, 74.0 grains of H4350 is the listed maximum charge for use with a 150-grain bullet, delivering 3244 fps at a peak pressure of 53,000 CUP. According to Du Pont's recommendations, 76.0 grains of IMR-4350, in the same load, puts out 3335 fps at 53,900 CUP. The Du Pont data was developed in a 24-inch barrel, while a 26-inch barrel was used for the load listed in the Hodgdon Manual.

At $10.95 a copy, the new Hodgdon Manual offers a great deal of helpful guidance, including specific load recommendations for the other Hodgdon powders having designations with numbers that coincide with Du Pont powders, such as 4895 and 4831, both similar but not necessarily identical to Du Pont's.

Hornady/Pacific

A shift of emphasis is being made with Hornady over the Pacific brand names. Their Pro-7 progressive reloader for metallics, introduced last year, is unabashedly the Hornady Pro-7, with the Hornady name cast into the frame. Other equipment still carries tags that say Hornady Pacific

Reloaders, with the Hornady in substantially larger type. The current catalog heads the sections as Hornady Metallic Reloaders, Hornady Shotshell Reloaders, Hornady dies and so on.

The top-of-the-line Model 366 shotshell reloader, once set up and operational, has but three manual operations: insert an empty shell into the proper station, insert a wad into the swing-out wad guide and work the handle down and back up. The shell plate advances automatically, primers are fed automatically and the loaded shell is ejected automatically. It turns out a complete shell with each cycle of the handle and has three-stage crimping featuring Taper-Loc for factory tapered crimp. It has been available with die sets for 12, 20 and 28-gauge, at a suggested retail price of $445. New this year is a Model 366 to handle the standard 2½-inch 410-bore shotshells at a suggested retail of $525. Conversion sets are available to load either 12 or 20-gauge three-inch shells, but not as yet for the 410.

Huntington Die Specialties

Fred Huntington has made further useful improvements in his little W-type Decker press. The ram stroke now goes over top dead center in the manner of most reloading presses and the handles have been rounded off for greater operator comfort. It's still about the smallest, most compact press capable of full-length resizing the larger rifle cases without undue effort.

HDS has another new item, called Huntington Die Lubricant. It's one of the new synthetic lubricants and it is the best stuff for resizing cases I've encountered thus far. As the hair-glop commercial used to say, "A little dab'll do ya." When working with clean, new cases, merely touch one fingertip ever so lightly to the surface of the lube in the jar and rub it beween that fingertip and the nearest thumb. Hold the head of the case in the other hand and rotate the body lightly between the lubed fingertips, also applying a dainty wipe to the case neck; none at all to the shoulder. It sizes with delightful ease, putting no dents in the shoulder at all.

The stuff is likewise effective for general lubrication such as application to the closely fitted parts of a loading press. At last report, a two-ounce jar was retailing for $3.50, postpaid and I'd guess I might use up a jar of the stuff in five years or so. It doesn't leave your fingers feeling sticky and has no obnoxious odor that I've noticed. I like it; use it all the time.

Lee Precision

In last year's edition, I noted the coming appearance of Lee's Auto-Index and Auto-Disk systems but had not yet checked them out. Since then, both items have appeared and I can note they perform in fine fashion. They are intended for use with Lee's turret press.

The Auto-Index moves the turret one-third-turn at the completion of the handle stroke, eliminating the need to rotate the turret manually. The Auto-Disk is a powder measure for installation in place of the usual mouth-expanding die and it dispenses the charge at the same time the case mouth comes up beneath the hollow expanding collar to which the measure is mounted. If there's no case in the shellholder, no powder is dispensed. Each Auto-Disk comes with four charge disks and each disk has six cavities, thus providing 24 different charges for any given powder.

The Lee turret press takes one fired case at a time to fully reloaded status. With the press set up for the 9mm Luger cartridge—not the easiest round to load—and the Auto-Index operating, I found it completed a reload in about 15 seconds. With the Auto-Disk measure added, the time was shaved to more like 12 seconds per round, and that without making any special effort to do it quickly. Call it five rounds per minute.

Soon due off Lee's production line is their Model 2001 press, a single-station, O-frame design with compound leverage and a choice of four different systems for seating the primers. Retail price is reported to be in the mid-$30 brackets.

(Continued on page 152)

FAIRLY NEW CARTRIDGES

I will not take oath that each and every one of the rounds about to be discussed came into bud and bloom since the previous edition came off the press, hence the cautiously qualified title. These are some I've been working with for the first time in the past year and my comments and impressions are offered for such interest as they may stir.

7mm International Rimmed (7-R)

This cartridge was developed by the IHMSA as an alternative to the 7mm Thompson/Center Ugalde or T/CU. The 7-R is quite easily produced by running a 30-30 WCF case up into the full-length resizing die of the three-die set made by Redding, which includes a seating die and a neck-sizing die. After the first firing, its shoulder squares out perceptibly and, presumably, it can thenceforward be reloaded with the neck-size die.

Hornady ran up some load data for the 7-R, based upon their range of bullet weights, from 100 to 154 grains and held to a peak-pressure ceiling of 40,000 CUP. The fur-

This is the 30-30 at left; the new 7mm International Rimmed at center; the popular 7mm T/CU at right.

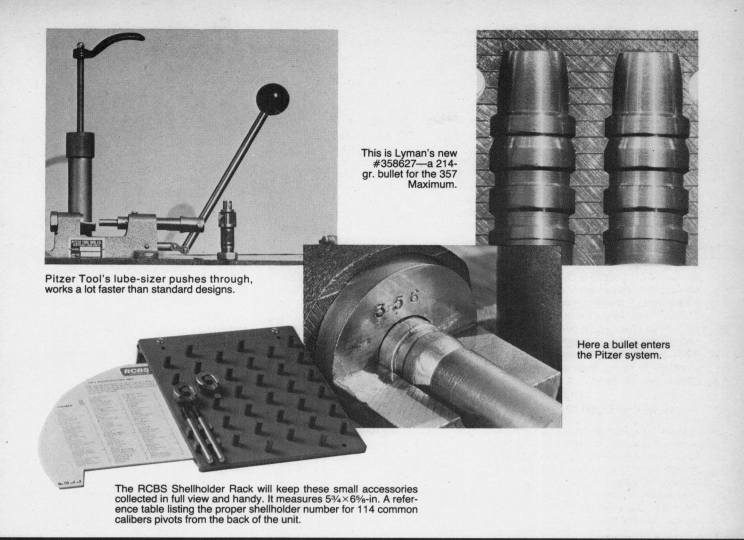

This is Lyman's new #358627—a 214-gr. bullet for the 357 Maximum.

Pitzer Tool's lube-sizer pushes through, works a lot faster than standard designs.

Here a bullet enters the Pitzer system.

The RCBS Shellholder Rack will keep these small accessories collected in full view and handy. It measures 5¾×6⅝-in. A reference table listing the proper shellholder number for 114 common calibers pivots from the back of the unit.

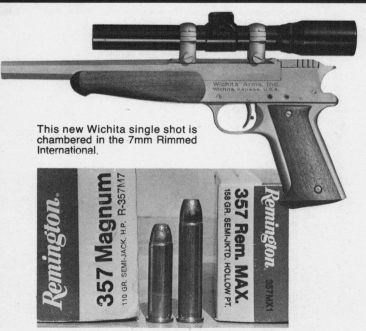

This new Wichita single shot is chambered in the 7mm Rimmed International.

The 357 Remington Maximum (here with 357 Magnum) satisfies Grennell with heavy bullets in single shots, whatever its fate in revolvers.

nished data did not go on to cite the foot-pounds of muzzle energy, but it was a simple matter to calculate that by way of establishing an evaluation of net performance. The greatest amount of muzzle energy is generated by Hodgdon's H335 behind the 139-grain Hornady boat-tail soft point for 2040 fps and 1285 ft. lbs.

Hornady worked up their data in a 10-inch T/C Contender barrel and it's the unanimous consensus that 40,000 CUP is the absolute maximum for this cartridge, to be approached with due caution. That is dictated by the fact that the parent 30-30 case has a fairly large head diameter: .506-inch, with an area of .201 square inch.

Break-action single shot pistols are acutely sensitive to the head-area of the case. Reduce that figure, and they can cope with substantially higher peak pressures.

The 223 Remington case that serves as parent brass for the 7mm T/CU has a head diameter of .378-inch and an area of .112 square inch; about 55.7% as much as the 30-30 head. That gives the smaller-headed case the ability to work and cope with substantially higher peak pressures.

Back in late 1981, the Speer Labs worked out some suggested loads for the 7mm T/CU for use with their bullets, most if not all of which are of slightly differing weights from the Hornady numbers. The maximum foot-poundage figures for the 7mm T/CU, as suggested by Speer, come out to 1486 fpe for their 115-grain bullet; 1601 for their 130-grain; 1638 for their 145-grain; 1543 for their 160-grain

Lyman

This maker has a whole raft of new items for the handloader this year. There is a much larger version of the Turbo Tumbler, available for either 120 or 220 volt operation, with a capacity of 1000 38 Special cases or the equivalent in other sizes and they now offer a Turbo Sifter to separate the polished cases from the medium as well as a Turbo Charger for reactivating the medium.

Then there's their Formula 1 Degreaser, handy for removing lubricant or rust-preventive from the cavities of mould blocks and similar uses. There's the Turbo Case Cleaner, a liquid pre-cleaner for cases in advanced stages of fouling and corrosion. It's non-etching and can be used as a wet cleaner and followed by a session with the dry medium for final finishing.

They've also turned some attention to cleaning/trimming/preparing cases, with three different items added to the catalog. There's the Ream/Clean accessory set for the Lyman universal trimmer to offer easy and quick cleaning of primer pockets, removal of military stamped crimps, along with much the same facilities for use by hand in the Lyman Case Preparation Kit. The latter includes inside/outside case neck deburring tool and three case neck brushes.

The Lyman Universal Drill Press Trimmer converts any drill press into a high-volume case trimmer. Lyman's patented chuck head bypasses the need for holding collets, accepting any and all case head dimensions. It needs only the Lyman pilot to work with any given case neck diameter or caliber.

Then there's the Lyman Dial Caliper, accurate to .001-inch, supplied in a sturdy protective case, complete with a leaflet giving the trim lengths for all of the popular cartridges.

The Lyman Safety Kit can be used advantageously for handloading and for many other shop activities, as well. It includes a pair of sturdy leather gloves, safety glasses with safety strap, face mask respirator, ear plugs—helpful when worn while running power saws and many other noisy shop tools!—as well as a heavy-duty shop apron and a copy of their new Cast Bullet Users Guide.

If you've ever wondered about the innate, pin-point accuracy of your loading scale—as what handloader hasn't?—Lyman now has a Scale Weight Check Set to verify the ongoing reliability of scales that are older, heavily used or suspected of possible damage.

Add to that their Magdriver with seven interchangeable bits, magnetically held in the business end of the handle and the Lyman Organizer, which serves as a sturdy work station, adjustable for mounting nearly any loading press, sizer, lubricator or other gear, available in your choice of unfinished kit or ready to use at a useful saving for the former.

Lyman has four new moulds shown in their latest catalog. Three may seem familiar to oldtime Lyman fans: the 225438 44-grain gas check in 22; the 257420 65-grain gas check in 25 and the 287346 135-grain gas check in 7mm. The 358627, at 214 grains, is utterly new, never before seen. A gas check design, it offers a choice of two grooves for crimping and looks like a natural for the new 357 Remington Maximum cartridge for use in revolvers or the more charitable and easygoing single-shots such as the T/C Contender.

Four pistol bullets and one rifle bullet can now be had in single-cavity blocks for casting hollow-point bullets. They are the 356156, 358429, 429244, and 429421 in handguns, along with the 457122 for rifles. As always, the first three digits of the designation indicate the aproximate diameter in the convenient Lyman system.

MJL Industries

In last year's edition, I noted that a liquid called Rust Free seemed most helpful in removing light coatings of oxide and general crud from the inside of bullet mould cavities, being gently and patiently applied with a Q-Tip swab or similar applicator. If the rust has eaten a bit deeper, it will still remove it, but cannot fill in the resulting pits. Unlike any other such com-

---

and 1657 for their 175-grain. This is lots better than the 7-R.

It isn't too hard to understand why the 7mm T/CU cartridge has taken the ram-slamming world by savage storm and won a lot of fanatic users. It is probably the most runaway-popular wildcat of recent years and its transition into a sanctioned factory load may not be much farther down the road. I say that without benefit of inside knowledge, solely on a basis of logical expectation.

Meanwhile, the 7-R is a bigger cartridge, with more room for powder charges, but it is painfully hamstrung by that large head area that limits its peak pressures. Whether it can surmount that handicap is a moot point and time alone can tell. Rechambered 7mm T/CU barrels are available in 7-R, as is a new break-action pistol going into production by Wichita Engineering. The latter is heavily reminiscent of the Merrill Sportsman design, complete with an action locking bar that has to be dragged to the rear to let the action break. The Wichita has the basic hold and feel of the hallowed M1911 Colt and an external hammer. You can snap the action shut as heartily as you wish and the hammer will still drop when the trigger is pulled. It has, however, the same in-built sensitivity to slightly longer than standard cartridges as the Contender and, if the fit is a tad too tight, the round won't fire, although a faint dent will be seen in the primer.

Early examples of the Wichita design allow a lot of flow-

The 411 JDJ at left has considerably augmented potential over the potent 41 Magnum revolver round.

Lyman is not bashful about their dispenser.

Grennell really likes this goop from Huntington—best yet, he claims.

Hornady's universal loading tray offers something for nearly everyone who reloads.

pound of which I'm aware, Rust Free will not attack the blued surfaces of firearms, nor will it harm nickel plating, color case-hardening or other finishes. It loosens and dissolves rust and that's its only prey.

Rust Free is made by MJL Industries, P.O. Box 122, McHenry, Illinois 60050. Suggested retail price is $3.98 for a two-ounce bottle, $11.98 for the eight-ounce size. If not obtainable locally, they will send it direct for the quoted price plus an additional $1 for postage and handling. I'm not sure if that applies to overseas addresses.

Omark/CCI

CCI introduced their Collector's Cartridge Display board, with mounted (presumably inert) specimens of 52 different cartridges they market. Acquire one of these and keep it in good condition for a given number of years and you have a guaranteed collector item potentially saleable at an indeterminate margin of profit. Meanwhile, you can put eye-tracks across it, yourself.

Omark/Outers

Newest cadre of the Good Ol' Boys fraternity, Outers offers at least one new product of potential interest to handloaders. It's a pressurized spray can of some stuff they call Crud Cutter, subtitled a metal degreaser.

If you use bullet moulds with ferrous blocks, there seems to be no known practical way to protect them

The steps in making a 300-gr. 41 bullet on the Corbin press, drawing a 44 jacket to 41 and using a #358415 Lyman cast bullet as the core are clear here.

A reswaged Hornady bullet in 411 JDJ at 50 meters for five shots shown against a 1¼-inch paster.

back into the firing pin port, contributing to difficulty in getting the action broken open. I'm told that this situation is under rectification and I hope that's true.

The .284-inch diameter seems to be a heavily popular choice for silhouette work in handguns, as well as for general hunting applications. Whether the 7-R is going to be able to carve itself out a significant portion of the overall action or not is a matter that remains to be resolved at this given moment.

357 Remington Maximum, aka 357 Super Magnum

Back in 1935, the 357 Magnum set the handgunning world back on its collective hunkers with fantastically augmented performance based primarily upon its ability to work at higher peak pressures than any prior contender of the same girth, including the ephemeral 38-44 round. Nonetheless, they didn't elongate the cylinder, and as a result, the promising cartridge spent the next many years in a really deep quandary. If you wanted to use a heavier bullet, you had to pack it deeper into the neck of the case, so the bullet nose wouldn't protrude from the front of the cylinder and hang up its rotation.

If, on the other hand, you wanted to burn more powder, you had to use a shorter, lighter bullet to make room for it. Cylinders for the 357 Magnum were still about the same length as for the 38 Special and therein lay the problem. The Ruger Blackhawk, as made for the 357 R-Max, has a

between casting sessions except to give the cavities a fast wash with a good rust preventive. So you need a fast and effective way to remove every last bit of the protective coating and that's where the need for an effective degreaser comes in.

Omark/RCBS

New for this year is a rotary cartridge case tumbler known as the Sidewinder, with durable ball bearing motor and a 12-hour, auto-off timer for added convenience. It's rated to handle up to 150 30-06 cases or 300 38 Specials at a batch and can be used with either wet or dry media.

Soon to appear is a long-awaited *Cast Bullet Manual* with full details and specs for loading the many bullets RCBS moulds will make into all of the myriad cartridges they fit; or most, at least.

RCBS now has a line of five sizes of plastic ammo boxes for rifle and pistol loads, featuring anti-rattle bullet tip protection. And an RCBS Beginner's Reloading Kit includes a Reloader's Special-2 press, a 505 scale, *Speer Reloading Manual,* case lube kit, case-loading block, primer tray and powder funnel. Price is said to be attractive and there will be a $10 factory rebate on it.

Another neat and handy item is the new RCBS rack to hold and keep track of shell holders, each of which rests on its own little numbered peg,

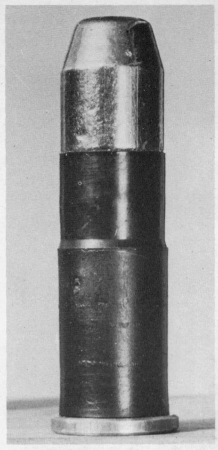

The new United States Ammunition Co. plastic 38s are reloadable, given the unique heeled bullets; can be returned to original dimensions by boiling. Other calibers expected.

cylinder 1.938 inches long, as compared to about 1.600 inches for a typical 357 Magnum.

Thompson/Center brought out Contender barrels for the 357 R-Max in lengths of 10 and 14 inches. The Contender barrels would accept bullets of any over-all length, so long as the bullet permitted the round to chamber fully. I dug out an old set of blocks for a gas-checked round nose weighing about 245 grains. That was the heaviest bullet I tried in the R-Max, but never did succeed in getting them to tumble, even at moderate velocities. Any lighter bullets performed superbly, including Speer's discontinued 220-grain JSP rifle bullets. With scope sights on the Contender barrels, accuracy was well beyond hopeful expectations. Groups with all holes touching at 25 yards were quite common.

411 JDJ

This is another J. D. Jones development, available as an SSK barrel for use in the Thompson/Center Contender receiver. The one I used measures 12½ inches, with SSK's T'SOB scope mounts and rings to hold a 4x Redfield.

The 411 JDJ is made by means of a two-die set available from RCBS. It's based upon the 444 Marlin case and case-forming is just a simple matter of lubing the case and running it up into the regular full-length resizing die. You use large rifle primers and Jones counsels against use of the #215 Federal large rifle magnum primer, noting it

The Olsen Invicta cartridges—.257" bullet in 357 and .358" in 44 Magnum—are not, Bob Olsen says, wildcats.

with a swing-out chart that tells which number goes with what cartridge. Then there's the Accessory Base Plate, which can be temporarily C-clamped to any work surface or permanently screwed to the bench. Precision tapped holes mate perfectly with a variety of RCBS bench tools and the appropriate screws and bolts are supplied.

Eleven new designs are added to the listing of RCBS bullet moulds for this year. Two of them are 98-grainers for use in cartridges such as 32 S&W Long or the upcoming 32 H&R Magnum; a wadcutter and semi-wadcutter design, signalling some amount of renewed interest on the part of the handloading public in these petite revolver cartridges.

Pitzer Tool Co.

The new Pitzer bullet lubricator and sizer is a push-through design, rather than the usual in-and-out concept and, as a result, operates faster and with greater convenience. All of the seals are O-rings to minimize lubricant seepage and migration.

With lubricant added to the vertical reservoir, the reservoir handle is turned down to put the lube under pressure. The bullet is placed in the semicircular groove of the loading platform, with the base going into the die and the operating handle is stroked forward to the limit of travel, then pulled back to the other limit. At that time, grease is forced into the groove of the sized bullet. As you cycle the next bullet, the lower plunger is drawn rearward to act as a valve, cutting off the flow of grease until it is pushed forward again as the operating handle is drawn back. That strikes me as downright ingenious.

For the present, tooling is available for handgun bullets from 9mm to 45-cal. sizes and dies as well as nose punches for rifle bullets are scheduled to follow shortly. Current retail prices are $120 for the unit complete with one die and nose punch; $20 for additional dies and $7.50 for extra punches. If you have more than one style of bullet in a given diameter, you only need to obtain another nose punch, provided both bullets have the same number of lube grooves.

Saeco

This maker of bullet moulds, lube/sizers, melting pots and hardness testers has added four new mould designs since last year. All are of the truncated-cone nose shape. Three are in .358-inch diameter: a 180-grain gas-check, #399; a 200-grain plain-base, #402; a 240-grain gas-check, #404; and the fourth is in .41-inch, a 210-grain plain-base, #413.

United States Ammunition Company, Inc., (USAC)

Another new company with a bright idea, USAC is starting out with 38 Special ammunition in plastic cases with brass heads. These are reloadable, unlike the aluminum-cased Blazer cartridges from Omark/CCI, but they require a special bullet with a stepped heel, somewhat in the manner of the old 41 Long Colt, only more so.

A side benefit of the new system is that the cases can be reloaded with the use of a compact squeezer-device powered by the user's hand grip and small enough to carry in the pocket. Seating the primer is performed with a separate device, such as the Lee Auto-Prime, as is dispensing the powder charge.

After some given number of firings—with no need for case resizing or neck flaring—the plastic case mouth loses its elasticity to the extent it will no longer grip the heel of the bullet properly. The tight fit can be restored by boiling the deprimed case in water for about five minutes.

The bullets are of lead, electroplated with copper. That's an approach that has been explored with a marked degree of success by Omark/Speer with some of their new bullet designs. USAC will also offer a line of bullets made by the same basic process to conventional shapes for reloading the familiar brass cartridge cases. ●

---

tends to develop too much pressure with his suggested 411 loads. I used Federal 210M and CCI BR-200, both of them match-type primers of standard power.

Most of Jones' data covers bullets weighing 210 grains or more. I tried Hodgdon H4227 powder behind the 170-grain Sierra JHC bullet and got 2204 fps. I scrounged up some of the old 44 half-jackets Speer used to make, drew them down to 41 size and created a cute little slug weighing just 114 grains to find that H4227 could send them screaming forth at 2726 fps. Curiously enough, they seem to group fairly well.

Sierra's 220-grain silhouette bullet, with its non-expanding JHP format, proved to be an excellent performer in the 411 and it's about the heaviest bullet readily available in .410-inch diameter. I managed to produce some 240-grain and 265-grain bullets by drawing down and reswaging some 44 bullets. Both performed well.

The pistol, as set up, weighed 4¼ pounds. With one of Steve Herrett's Handgun Hunter stocks installed, it was not as punishing to fire as you might suppose. Recoil was more of a determined shove than a stinging slap.

257 and 358 Invictas

Bob Olsen, developer of these innovative cartridges, registers mild annoyance if anyone terms them "wildcats." The Invicta system is based upon the ready ease of rebarreling the Dan Wesson Arms revolvers. The 257 Invicta is essentially a 357 Magnum case, slightly modified by means of a special resizing die to carry a Lexan adapter in its mouth to hold a bullet of .257-inch diameter.

The 358 Invicta operates upon the same principle, with a 357 bullet in the Lexan adapter at the front of a 44 Magnum case. The barrels are of suitable dimensions to accept bullets of .257 or .358 diameters. The Lexan adapter moves forward upon firing to obturate or seal the juncture between the front of the cylinder and rear of the barrel, thus eliminating the gas leakage that has been a problem with revolvers since time immemorial.

Olsen has experimented with a number of other materials for the adapters but has settled upon Lexan as by far the most satisfactory for the purpose. He notes that it's possible and practical to load two 148-grain wadcutters into each round of the 358 Invicta, thereby doubling the number of shots per loading and providing about 38% more frontal area than the 44 Magnum; other tandem combinations of bullets are likewise feasible.

If these interest you, write Olsen Development Lab, 307 Conestoga Way #37, Eagleville, PA 19403; 215/631-1716.
Dean A. Grennell

The Mountain Rifle Question

This Remington 700 30-06 has Six Enterprises stock, turned down barrel, scope in claw mounts, weighs under seven pounds as you see it on a Colorado ridgetop.

by KEN WARNER

THE MOUNTAIN RIFLE as a design format means, and has meant, different things to different people. Those who conceived mountain shooting as long-range stuff used to build long and heavy sniping guns; nowadays, we're looking for short and light rifles that still shoot well. And we're willing to depart from tradition, it seems.

Having seen several mountains on one or two occasions, this editor votes the lightweight ticket and if all else were equal would also go for the least length possible. Best of all would be a reliable gunbearer, but the price of them went out of sight lately.

Of recent years, dealing with the mountain rifle problem has forced your reluctant reporter into the design and acquisition of several somewhat special projects to try to solve the problem. The time has come to speak of these.

A while ago I achieved a sensible and functional lightweight rifle by taking what I didn't want off a standard Model 600 Remington in 308. It was called, thereafter, "Ugly Gun" for good reason. It weighed 6 lbs., 6 oz., scoped and loaded; it moved a 200-

Right now, the answer is glass.

grain handload at over 2400 fps; it could be packed in two 26-inch pieces in a duffel bag and upon reassembly still hit game; I liked it.

That was one solution. It seemed to me there might be some slicker ways to go. And about then I had a chance to try out a Six Enterprises fiberglass stock for a Remington 700 *and* a

chance to get a set of German claw mounts designed for the 700—supposed to be bolt-ons. So I bought a barreled action in 30-06 and went for it, with the help of Chuck Lanham and—later—Ben Toxvard.

Chuck did the basic work, including a lot of remachining of those $90 bolt-on mounts. I wound up with a scoped 30-06 at just a bit over seven pounds that could shoot better than I could. It has a 2¾x Bear Cub scope that pops on and off slick as anything. It's sort of split pea soup-green and I learned a lot from it.

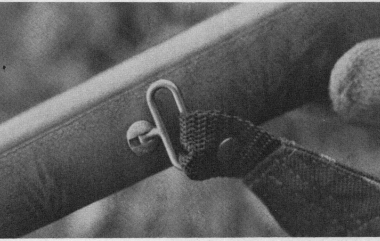

The side-mounted Pachmayr swivels provide this comfortable secure carry muzzle up or muzzle down. You carry mountain rifles a lot more than you shoot them.

With a pair of light rifles in 308 and 222, one can be benched for fun; Burris 2x-7x Mini Scope in Burris mounts looks just right.

Those who knew it in the old days won't recognize Ugly Gun now—all work on the pair by Brown Precision; weight at just six pounds each.

This is Dave Petzal's 280 on a Remington 700LH by David Gentry of Bozeman. Dave says it will put three factory rounds under an inch at 100 yards and weighs 6¾-lb. as you see it.

Garrett Accur-Light stock designs offer Mannlicher styling in short-action rifles like the 600 and Ruger 77, get the gun below five pounds before scoping.

Because Remington 788s shoot so well, Brown Precision offers stocks for them—you can use the pigmented ones as they come from the mold.

The first thing was that very few factory actions and barrels are light and in a 1½-pound glass stock they don't balance well. The eventual cure was to get Ben Toxvard of Shenandoah Guns (Berryville, VA) to turn down the barrel. He took it right down, then screwed the factory iron sights right back in the same holes, which is a stunt I asked him to try, though neither one of us knew it would work. Sure made a slick article—like transforming a discount store pump gun into a Purdey—for balance and took half a pound off.

Learned some things about claw mounts, too, but I still like them for some guns. They limit the scope choices *severely*. If you want a low scope, you have to have a short straight tube. The first morning I hunted with the rifle, it was wet snow, at first, and then it got colder and started to blow a little. When I decided to take the scope off and go up through the brush iron-sighted, the fool thing was frozen up, literally. It was full of frozen water and wouldn't work. The zero stays close enough and I love the convenience, freezing up excepted.

The best thing was that assembly was as good a carrying and shooting outfit as anybody needs. I got Chuck to put the Pachmayr studs on the left side of the stock and favor that. That's the way the M1 Carbine and the Kar. 98 were set up and it suits me. In contrast to all the skinny little wood lightweights, a glass stock can be full-sized and you can both hang onto it and lean into it. And I believe the glass stock makers when they say the character of recoil is different with glass.

Certainly this 30-06 of mine is a very well-behaved accurate rifle. I have carried it up, down and along quite a few ridges and it's a joy. I recommend the procedure. I believe you'll like it.

Not too long ago, an elderly gent of my acquaintance named Pete Petrola came up with an old Model 600 Remington in 222. Actually he had two, but I just bought one. And I conceived the idea of a pair—Ugly Gun and this one. There was a period of negotiation, this time with Chet Brown of Brown Precision, Inc., and I finally shipped the two Model 600s off to him on a Friday.

On Sunday, two days later, at a Remington seminar, I was among the first to learn of the new Model Seven rifle. That's one way to get a mountain rifle that's easy to carry and shoots well—just buy a Model Seven.

Indeed, I considered calling Brown Precision and cancelling, but I didn't. And I'm glad of it because the new pair are splendid little machines of some distinction.

They match so closely I have to look at the muzzle to see which I have. Each has a Burris mini-scope, the 2-7x. The metal is dull nickel plated and the stock is camouflage green, so they're very noticeable. And they are very well-made and very accurate, and light, and easy to carry. They are so much all those things I lost them to my wife Deborah immediately. She's rather taken with the idea she can shoot the 222 for practice, the 308 for real.

Brown can take the fiberglass idea in more directions than most shops that work in glass. Their finishes seem to me to be about as good as you'll get.

Now I know a percentage of fellows just snort at the idea of fiberglass stocks because they really prefer walnut and blue steel. And they know a good man can make a real light stock out of wood. The problem with that is they can't do it for a lot less than $4,000 and I only know so many fellows who go to the hills with $4,000 rifles—three, to be exact, and two of them make their own.

Now you might say it would be different if I owned a couple of good rifles, but you'd be wrong. I've had 'em and I got 'em. I sold a couple once I was satisfied with these, true enough, but there are still a couple of nice custom-stocked rifles in the larder. They're gorgeous, but if you try for minimum weight in wood and steel you get minimum bulk as well and I've grown to like the full-sized stock.

Well, the truth is that, like you, I like 'em all, but for the special problems involved in hard hunting in the hills when you're a sure-enough dude, I think the glass stocks are the best solution for now.

Of course, the commercial trend is toward the slimmer, lighter, shorter rifle. They're looking at glass stocks real hard, the factories are. If they make 'em as good as these I've been shooting, we'll all be better off. ●

The nickeled surfaces of the Brown Precision 600 in 308 are a lot less obvious than a blaze orange cap or a high polish blue finish. Dave Gentry's own 338 is all silvered up, including a Leupold 3x9 scope, weighs six pounds plus scope.

The New Takedown

by KEN WARNER

Above — The Model Seven is a trim little gun and altering it to take down easily doesn't change that. Right — It takes several seconds, perhaps five to get the gun apart, or put it together.

THIS is just for the record: The Custom Gun Guild takedown system for modern rifles works and works fine.

I couldn't think of a way to improve my new Remington Model Seven until Frank Wood volunteered to take it apart and put it together so I could take it apart and put it together over and over again. I have now done that many times and it still shoots right where I zeroed it,

It also rides inside an ordinary suitcase, takes apart simply for cleaning and fascinates most shooters who see it. I hunted it through two days of hard rain, and got it clean and dry in three minutes each night.

Getting the job done costs about as much as a new rifle. There's no getting around that, though the work is first class. While you're at it, you can have a second barrel fitted in a second caliber.

They say both barrels will zero if you give them the actual load you're going to use. Here's how the job is done:

Your rifle is gauged, then taken apart. An inside-threaded insert is screwed into the receiver. It's flanged to full diameter of your stock. Your barrel is re-threaded in the interrupted-screw pattern of the insert. Your buttstock is cut and fitted to the receiver flange, while your forearm has a spring-catch installed behind another flange.

From then on, you just push the catch forward to loosen a ball detent in the faces of the opposing flanges, turn the barrel a quarter-turn, and your rifle is in two pieces. I never tried it, for safety reasons (that is, I don't *need* to mess around), but I bet you could do it while the chamber is loaded.

I know a fellow who stopped by the Custom Gun Guild shop recently. It was full of these takedown conversions waiting their turn. It doesn't have to be a Remington — almost any good modern rifle is a candidate.

My rifle in my hands shot 3-shot clusters of about an inch or a little over out of the box and it still does. I don't believe I'll ever have an accuracy complaint on the job.

The main thing for me is convenience. It's easier to travel with, easier to clean and someday, maybe, I'll get that second barrel. A man should always have a good goal. ●

This little outfit will fit into some attache cases; the system is precision-fit and both shoots well and holds zero.

The Hornady Pro-7, 5-station, progressive re-loading press is remarkable in that it is capable of handling all popular rifle and pistol calibers with only a change of dies and shell plate. The Pro-7 seen here has been outfitted with a Hornady Deluxe powder measure and has been set up for 38/357. Output is an amazing 400-500 rounds per hour. The Hornady Pro-7 features full-auto priming and full-auto advance with each pull of the handle. It's well suited for those reloaders needing high-volume production.

SCHRADE USA

Schrade has been providing hunters and outdoorsmen with top flight knives for 80 years. Seen here are four well-known Schrade blades. At the upper left is the Uncle Henry 164 UH; at the lower left is Schrade's Old Timer "Sharpfinger"; at the bottom is the Old Timer 34-OT pocket knife; and, to the right, is Schrade's Uncle Henry Lock-Back 7. All Uncle Henry knives are guaranteed against loss for one full year from date of registration. Write them for your free copy of the SCHRADE ALMANAC.

UZI

IMPORTED EXCLUSIVELY BY

action arms ltd.

Action Arms, the importer of the well-known UZI Carbine (top), now imports the latest offering from IMI-Israel — the UZI Pistol. The UZI Pistol is a much-scaled-down version of its big brother. Both UZIs are semi-auto and chambered for the 9mm Parabellum. Also seen is a supply of Action Arms "Samson" 9mm Parabellum ammo. Both UZIs are notable for their exceptional compactness and reliable operation.

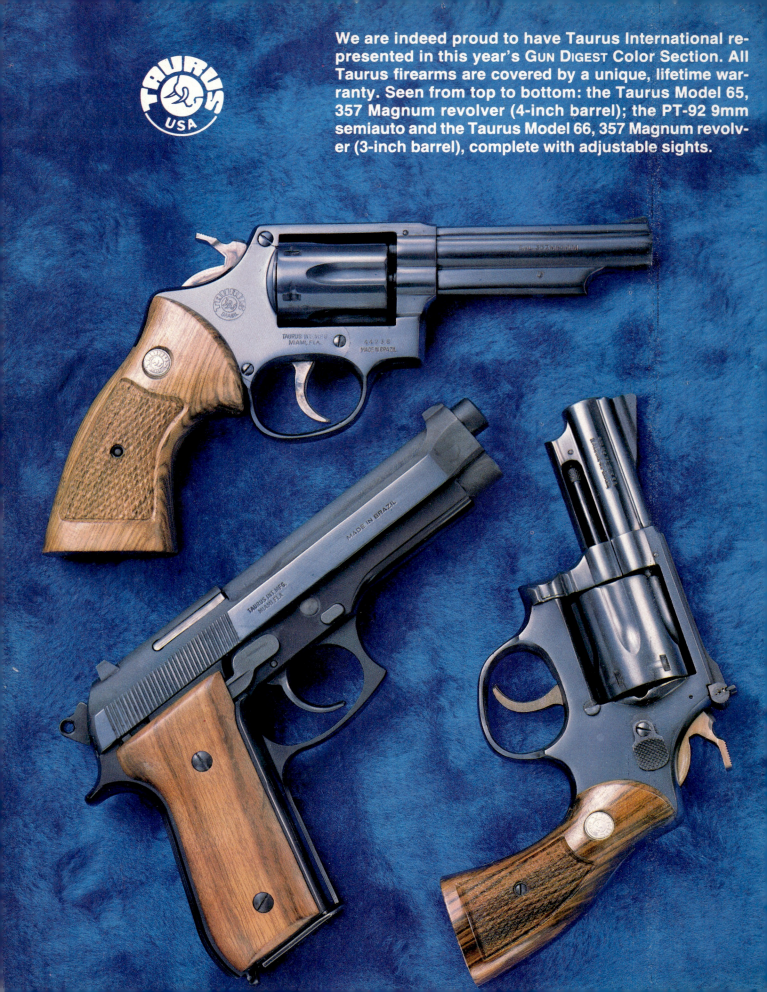

We are indeed proud to have Taurus International represented in this year's GUN DIGEST Color Section. All Taurus firearms are covered by a unique, lifetime warranty. Seen from top to bottom: the Taurus Model 65, 357 Magnum revolver (4-inch barrel); the PT-92 9mm semiauto and the Taurus Model 66, 357 Magnum revolver (3-inch barrel), complete with adjustable sights.

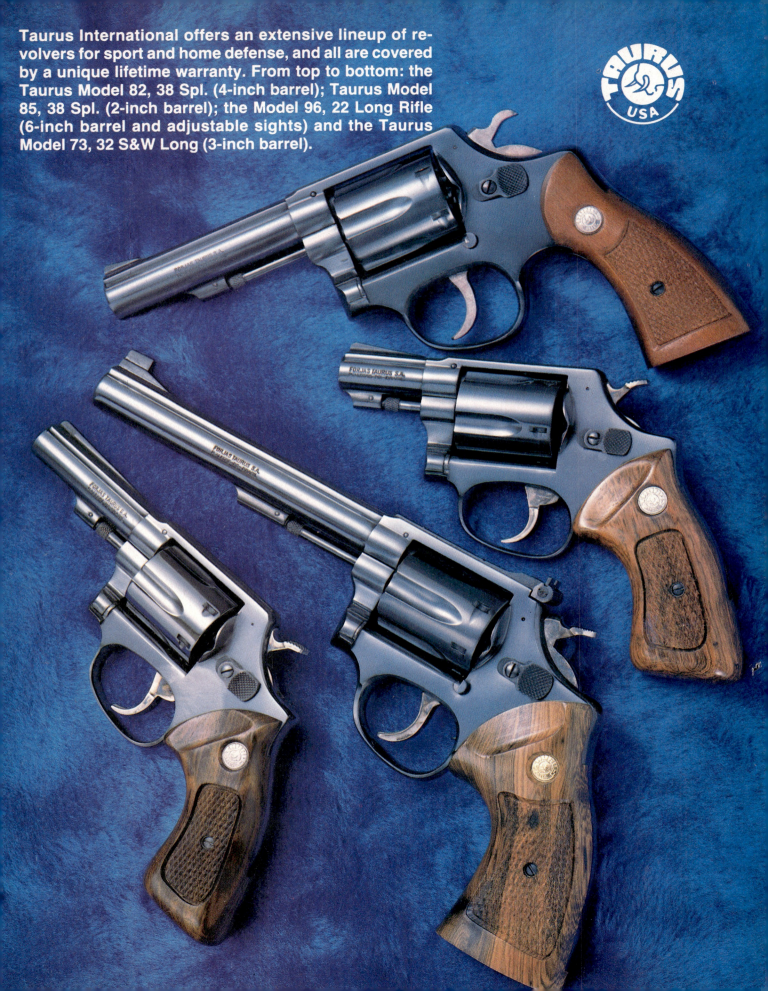

Taurus International offers an extensive lineup of revolvers for sport and home defense, and all are covered by a unique lifetime warranty. From top to bottom: the Taurus Model 82, 38 Spl. (4-inch barrel); Taurus Model 85, 38 Spl. (2-inch barrel); the Model 96, 22 Long Rifle (6-inch barrel and adjustable sights) and the Taurus Model 73, 32 S&W Long (3-inch barrel).

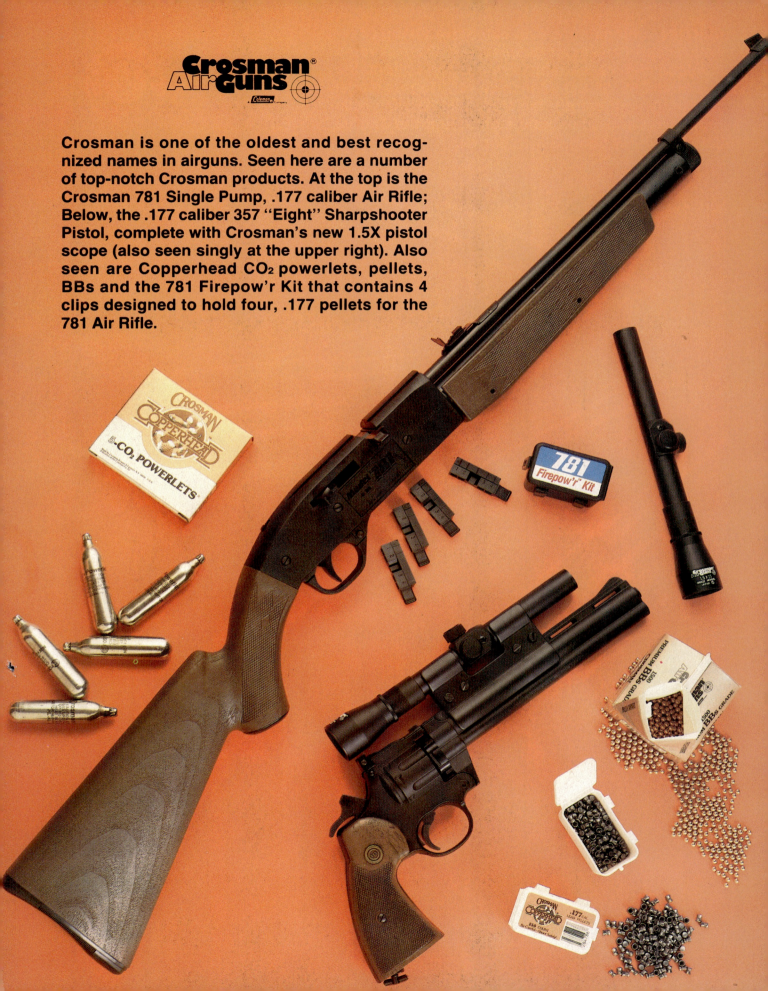

Crosman AirGuns

Crosman is one of the oldest and best recognized names in airguns. Seen here are a number of top-notch Crosman products. At the top is the Crosman 781 Single Pump, .177 caliber Air Rifle; Below, the .177 caliber 357 "Eight" Sharpshooter Pistol, complete with Crosman's new 1.5X pistol scope (also seen singly at the upper right). Also seen are Copperhead CO_2 powerlets, pellets, BBs and the 781 Firepow'r Kit that contains 4 clips designed to hold four, .177 pellets for the 781 Air Rifle.

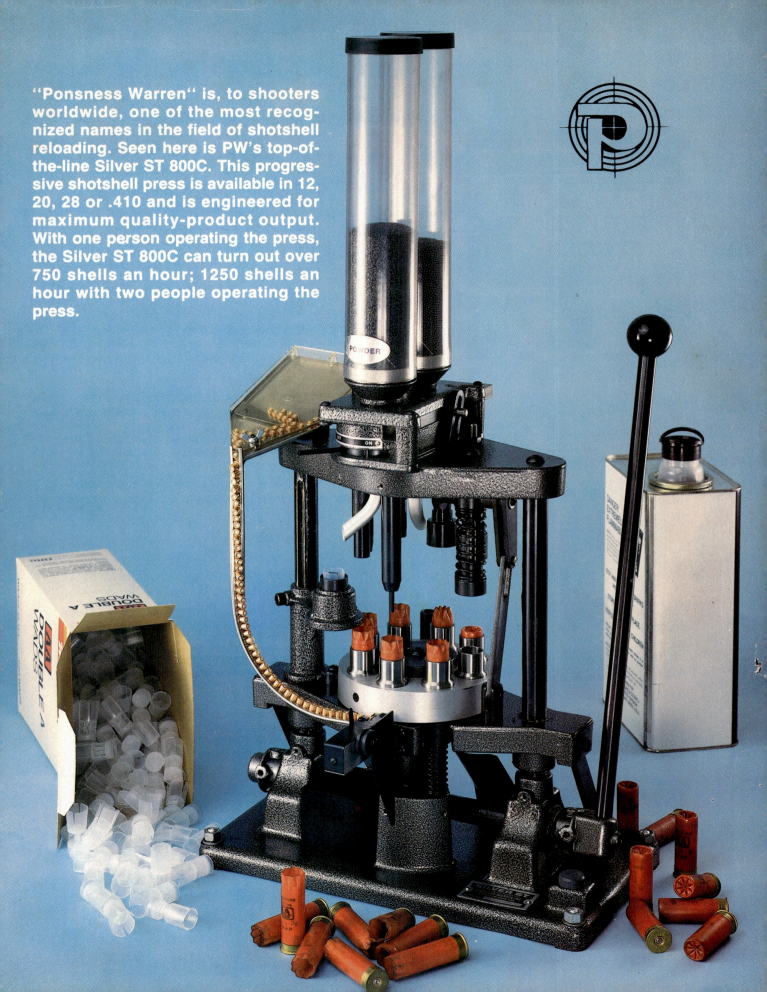

"Ponsness Warren" is, to shooters worldwide, one of the most recognized names in the field of shotshell reloading. Seen here is PW's top-of-the-line Silver ST 800C. This progressive shotshell press is available in 12, 20, 28 or .410 and is engineered for maximum quality-product output. With one person operating the press, the Silver ST 800C can turn out over 750 shells an hour; 1250 shells an hour with two people operating the press.

IVER JOHNSON

Iver Johnson, one of the country's oldest and best-known producers of sporting firearms, currently offers an excellent selection of handguns. Seen on this page, at the top is the PO 380, a semi-auto 380 ACP pocket pistol; at the bottom right is the new TP 22 D/A semiauto pocket pistol. In the center is Iver Johnson's newest offering, the design of which should be familiar to GUN DIGEST readers. It's the new Iver Johnson Trailsman, a 22 caliber semi-auto designed for hunting and plinking.

Little-Known **22 Pistols** of the Post-War Era . . . .

a new collectors' specialty.

by CHARLES E. PETTY

WHEN THE technology for repeating pistols was developed, the single shot pistols and double-barrels quickly went the way of the horse and buggy after the automobile. With the exception of a few specialized guns, the single shot pistol had all but disappeared from the scene by the 1930s.

Then, rather suddenly in the early '50s, a whole new generation of single shot 22s appeared. This was not a giant backward leap of technology but rather a response to major advances in manufacturing methods and the application of principles used in automatic pistols. For the most part, these new guns were practical, inexpensive, and intended for use either in the field or on the plinking range.

In the past, the majority of guns had been made by gouging their shapes out of solid hunks of steel, an expensive and wasteful process. Most of the steel became chips in a trashcan, and the machining that produced them was done on expensive equipment using expensive tooling by expensive labor. In order to remain competitive manufacturers had to find ways of reducing costs, and one of the best was to avoid all those expensive chips.

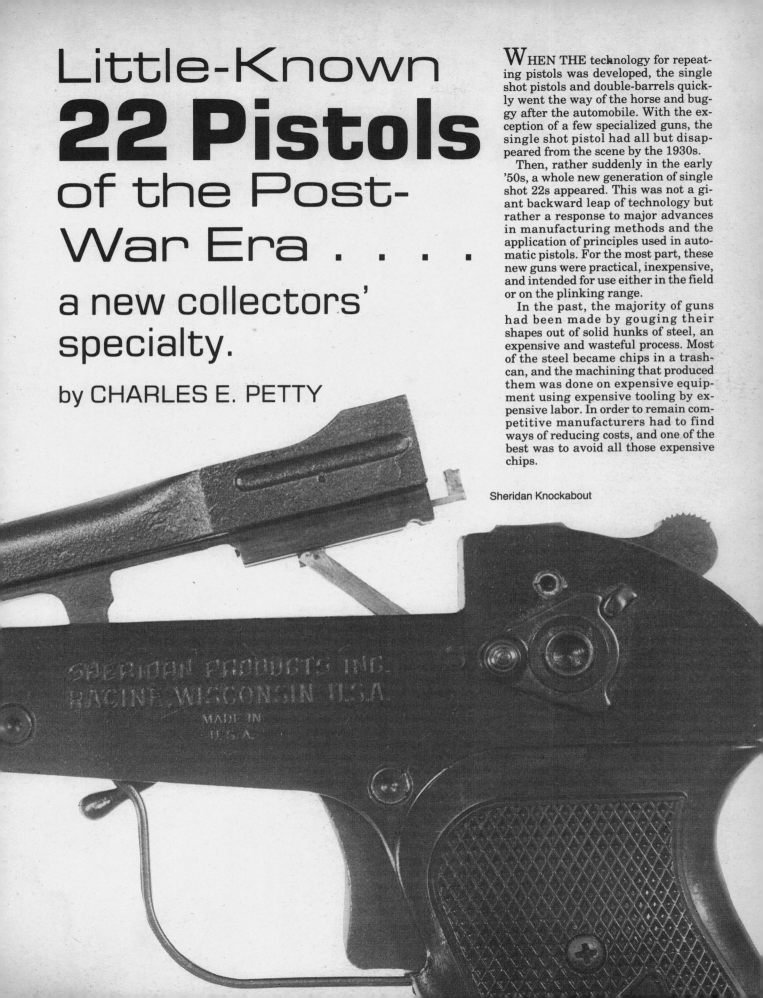

Sheridan Knockabout

This new crop of single shots proved a good place to try manufacturing methods which emphasized the use of castings or stampings to take the place of machined parts. Castings were especially appealing because they could often be used with little additional machine work. This was made possible in part by an alloy called Zamak; a zinc-based metal with good casting properties and strength. Stampings had been used successfully in World War II firearms and were quick and inexpensive to produce.

These new methods were combined, in some guns, with blowback operation to give shooters nearly automatic pistols. Three new guns appeared in rapid succession. Two used the blowback principle, but the most successful didn't. It was a neat little gun called the Sheridan Knockabout, which made good use of stampings—and rivets.

The name of Sheridan Products of Racine, Wisconsin is well known for the air rifles they still produce. The Knockabout was their first—and only commercial—venture into cartridge arms. When the Knockabout was introduced in April, 1953 it was intended to be, as the name implies, a gun that could be left in the tacklebox, cabin, backpack or wherever. It sold for the modest price of $17.95.

The Knockabout was simply but ruggedly built, with a minimum of machined parts. It has a tip-up action with only two main components. The barrel is a steel casting, used with little exterior finishing, and the surprisingly large and functional sights were cast right in. It locks into the tip-up action with a locking lug that is also a part of the casting. The frame is a sandwich of two stamped halves which enclose the few internal parts. The whole thing is held together by six large rivets.

Operation is really quite simple. The action is opened by pressing the barrel release in front of the trigger guard; the spring-loaded barrel pops right up. The safety on the left side of the frame is large and easy to operate. It blocks the hammer but does not interfere with the trigger or action. Since engaging the safety actually moves the hammer back a little, the design encourages the shooter to put the safety on, for if he doesn't the extractor will catch on the firing pin and prevent the gun from opening fully. I don't know if it was an intentional design feature or not, but it makes good safety sense. As with all exposed hammer guns the Knockabout should never be carried with the hammer down

on a live round, for a sharp blow to the hammer could cause an accidental discharge.

It is surprising, in a gun of this type, to find a good trigger pull, but most of the Knockabouts I have examined had good pulls. Most are fairly heavy—around six pounds—but they are crisp and appear to be lighter than they really are. Accuracy with the Knockabout is also quite good. The large sights are easily aligned, and the 5-inch barrel is long enough for decent accuracy. Since the design is tip-up, the over-all length is only 7 inches, so it is a compact little gun. The frame partially shrouds the hammer which makes it suitable for carrying in the pocket of a hunting coat.

If this sounds like a commercial for a gun that has been discontinued since 1960, perhaps it is, for the Knockabout strikes me as decidedly practical. Unfortunately, the $17.95 price is long gone. Decent specimens are offered for around $100, with some hopeful dealers asking much more. Collector interest is also gaining which may account for the prices.

Statistically, production began in April, 1953, at serial number 01000 and continued to October, 1960, where it ended at serial number 16309. Total production is given by the factory as 10,759 with no explanation for the gaps in numbering. No variations are known or reported by the factory.

Since the Knockabout was intended for a rough life, collectors may have to hunt a bit to find a nice one. Rarest of all would be to find one in the original red box. The box, by the way, has exceptionally good instructions printed inside the lid, and there is also an insert, "Suggestions on Shooting Your Knockabout," with pointers on safety and basic marksmanship.

While the Sheridan was successful, another gun that came along at about the same time didn't fare so well. The S-M Sporter was designed by the late W.H.B. Smith and he and Sydney Manson had it manufactured by the Richmond-Parke Co., of Springfield, Mass. Distribution was through the S-M Corp. of Alexandria, VA.

The S-M Sporter was the first of this generation to apply the principle of blowback operation to a single shot pistol. As with any pioneering venture, it was not without its problems. The design combined the blowback principle with economies of manufacture. There is a simple tubular receiver, to which the barrel is silver-soldered. The action consists of a bolt, spring and cocking handle which all slide within the tube of the receiver.

To the receiver is silver-soldered a stamped housing to hold the trigger mechanism, safety and bolt latch.

To operate the gun the shooter must pull the cocking piece fully to the rear where it is caught and held by the bolt latch. When the round is loaded in the chamber, the bolt latch is released to close the bolt, and the gun is ready to fire. When the shot is fired, the bolt is left open for the next shot, the chamber ready to load, and manual cocking is not required for subsequent rounds.

There is no grip frame, as we usually think of it. Instead there is a long screw attached to the trigger group with a pin. The large molded plastic grips are attached by this screw, and form the bulk of the frame. According to Mr. Manson, the grips were the weakest area in the design, primarily because the molded plastic was not strong enough and often broke. Manson believes the gun would have been a success, had the plastic manufacturer been able to come up with a stronger material for use in the grips.

The grips were not the only weakness however. I have examined a number of S-M Sporters, and found several with broken parts. The bolt latch must take a terrible beating since it has to catch the bolt and hold it open against the rather strong main spring. The safety is a very small stamped lever which must be rather fragile, for I've seen a couple of guns where it was broken off. I have heard rumors that the S-M Sporter failed because of mechanical problems that caused many of the guns to be returned. In our conversation, Mr. Manson confirms this, although he feels that the major problem was the grips.

The S-M Sporter died a quick death, and of such deaths are collectors' items born, for production is sure to be low, and this is no exception. Total production can only be estimated, since the records are long gone, but based on serial numbers known it is likely that the total is around 600 guns. In the August, 1963, *American Rifleman,* the late M.D. Waite answered a reader's question about the S-M with perhaps the most concise history of a gun ever written, for in less than a single column he told almost everything there was about the S-M.

Although there are no known major variations, there are a number of serial number ranges which will add a little spice to the collectors' search. First production was serial numbered from 1 to 50, and these guns were reserved for employees and promotion. The second series runs from serial number 2000 to 2165. A third begins

Sheridan Knockabout

Whamo Powermaster

S-M Sporter

Savage 101

Whamo Powermaster

S-M Sporter

Savage 101

at serial number 3000 and runs to 3190. These were all that Waite reported, but thanks to my friends in The National Automatic Pistol Collectors Association I have been able to confirm a fourth serial number series. These began at around 6000 and run to a little over 6200.

An exact count of this last group is not possible, for it is based on serial numbers reported by other collectors, but probably accounts for around 200 guns. Adding this to Waite's total of 397 leads me to the 600 figure. Regardless of an exact count, be it 400 or 600, the S-M Sporter is a rare gun. A collector wanting to get one from each

serial number series is sure to have his work cut out for him.

The only known variation is in the color of the grips. The majority of guns have black plastic grips, but I have observed a couple of pair of brown grips, and Mr. Manson confirms this. He explained that the problem with breakage led the plastic manufacturer to try other materials, and believes that the brown color may have been a part of those attempts.

The S-M Sporter is one of those guns that are hard to appraise, but I would consider a nice one for less than $100 to be something of a bargain. If it had the original blue and white box,

it would be a steal.

Another gun using the blowback principle came along a little after the S-M, and was much more successful. The Whamo Powermaster, made by Whamo Manufacturing Co. of San Gabriel, CA, was another venture into firearms by a company best known for other things. *(Editors Note: Whamo today has no records and no interest whatever in exploring its past in the gun business. K.W.)*

The design of the Powermaster is novel, and combines unit assembly with castings in a manner that was different. The appearance of the gun would suggest that it was made of two

Whamo Powermaster, action open to show ejector spring.

Savage 101 extractor system.

Whamo Powermaster

S-M Sporter barrel latch is in front of safety.

castings held together by screws. It is, but the casting encloses a steel unit comprising the barrel and action. The two castings are Zamak, and mark one of the earliest uses of the alloy.

The Powermaster has a target pistol look, and their advertising called it one, but that may have been a little generous. The Powermaster would make a dandy plinker or training gun, but lacks the refinements of sights and trigger necessary in a true target pistol. Operation is not complicated, but takes a little getting used to. The bolt slides back and forth within the frame, and when it is retracted the gun is cocked and the

chamber is exposed as is the ejector spring. It was this spring that drew the criticismn of the NRA's technical staff when they reviewed the Powermaster in July, 1956 *American Rifleman*. They commented that the spring interfered with loading. The spring projects from the bottom of the receiver and extends well above the chamber, and must be pushed down before a round can be loaded.

On reflection, I wonder if this might not have been intended as a safety measure since it takes a deliberate action to load the gun. The NRA technical staff also criticized the lack of a separate safety system. In their ad-

vertising Whamo said that safety was accomplished by simply opening the bolt, and that the gun would not fire if the trigger were pulled with the bolt open. On my guns it won't but it seems a rather risky thing and I would prefer not to give Murphy's Law a chance. The best safety feature is a bright red ring painted around the striker which lets you know that the gun is cocked.

There is no factual production information available, and repeated efforts to get information from the factory have proven fruitless. Since the Rifleman's evaluation appeared in July, 1956, it seems likely that the gun was introduced early that year. It would appear that serial numbers began at 000100 and continued to just over 004400. This would suggest a total production of perhaps 4000 guns—not a particularly large number, but one subject to revision if better information becomes available. No major variations have been observed other than a few with ivory-colored plastic grips instead of the more common brown. The original price was $19.95, but the current prices are in the range of $75 to $150.

A good many years ago, at an Ohio Gun Collectors show in Columbus, Ohio, I happened across a gun with a small tag that said 'High Standard." Although it did have a High Standard front sight (it also had a M1911A1 rear sight), the only thing I was sure of was that it wasn't a High Standard. As I examined it I noticed some remarkable similarities with the Powermaster. The price was reasonable, so I brought it home for study and speculation.

Side by side comparison with a Powermaster convinced me that what I had was either a homemade copy or a prototype. The more I thought about it, the less likely it seemed that anyone would go to all that trouble when a Whamo could be bought for $19.95. The frame is an aluminum casting, and the barrel began life as a 38 but was sleeved down to 22. The method of assembly is identical to the Powermaster, and even uses the same type screws. Unfortunately there are no markings other than F&S at appropriate places around the safety (a feature the Whamo doesn't have). If I ever track down who designed the Powermaster you can be sure I'll ask about it. I may find out I'm wrong, but I don't think I'll mind, for I have had more than my money's worth of fun speculating about it.

There was a gap of several years before another single shot appeared on the market, but when it did, it was from a famous manufacturer and was destined to become the most successful of the types. In 1959, Savage Arms Co. resumed production of pistols after a near-thirty-year layoff.

Their new gun was the product of the inventive mind of Robert L. Hillberg, and made the maximum use of castings and powdered metal parts. The Savage 101 was a lookalike of the Colt Single Action Army, and was one of a pair of guns designed by Hillberg with a specific market in mind. Hillberg believed, and still does, that children should be taught to shoot with the safest possible guns and that, be-

cause of their simpler actions, single shots are best for that use. (The other gun of his pair was a scaled-down version of Winchester's famous Model 94. It was produced by Ithaca as their Model 94 and was also a great success.)

Hillberg's pistol is faithful to the single action in appearance only, for the mechanical function is entirely different. There is a barrel/cylinder assembly which pivots to the right to expose the single chamber. An ejector rod is used to remove fired cases, but it operates a really massive extractor instead of entering the case mouth as it does on the Colt. The barrel is conventional and is attached to the cast steel cylinder. The cylinder casting faithfully reproduces the single action appearance even to the extent of appearing to have bullets in the non-existent chambers. The frame is a one-piece Zamak casting, but the casting simulates a separate backstrap.

As with the other single shot pistols of this period, collectors are getting interested in the Savage 101, perhaps for its association with that famous company's other handguns. There is quite a contrast in a collection of Savage automatic pistols with a 101 included.

The Savage 101 sold in 1959 for the popular price of $19.95, and today they are offered in the range of $75 to $125. Production began early in 1959 at serial number 1 and continued to number 30999. At this point a small change was made in the design of the cylinder gas port clearance cut and a new serial number range began. The second range began in 32000 and continued to 54816 when production was halted in 1968. Total production is given as over 53,800 guns.

Aside from the small design change there were no major variations in the gun, but there are a couple of different boxes if the collector should want to get really picky—and could find them. The first box used was brown cardboard embossed to resemble leather. Later, this was changed to white cardboard.

One interesting variation, and impossibly rare, is a model made up at Hillberg's request. It is a completely faithful, but non-functional, version with a solid barrel and cylinder. It was marked "DUMMY" and Hillberg had perhaps a dozen made for a special group of friends . . . a few of the kids in his neighborhood.

Although there are now a few single shots available, none are intended for the uses that the guns of the '50s and '60s were. The current offerings

Acknowledgements: The author wishes to thank Mr. Bob Greenleaf of Savage, Mr. Wm. Bach of Sheridan, and Mr. Bob Hillberg for their invaluable assistance.

References

The American Rifleman, August, 1963.

The American Rifleman, July, 1956.

Byron, David; *The Official 1982 Price Guide to Antique and Modern Firearms;* The House of Collectibles, 1982.

Stebbins, Henry M.; *Pistols: A Modern Encyclopedia;* Stackpole, 1961.

Sell, DeWitt E.; *Collector's Guide to American Cartridge Handguns;* Stackpole, 1963.

Smith, W.H.B.; *Book of Pistols and Revolvers,* Seventh Edition; edited by Joseph E. Smith; Stackpole, 1968.

Bach, Wm. C.; personal communication.

Greenleaf, Robert; personal communication.

Hillberg, Robert L.; personal communication.

are, for the most part, specialized target arms and there is a gap for a kid's or beginner's gun. While we have no way of knowing whether Bob Hillberg's idea for a kid's first gun was the reason for the success of the Savage 101, I, for one, believe it must have been. The ready availability of another shot is of little value when we are trying to teach our kids basic marksmanship and safety principles. I suspect that many of us use our expensive repeaters as single shots when we take our children out for their first handgun lessons. I know I did, and perhaps the next time mine want to go shooting I'll drag along that old Knockabout, and maybe the Savage, and perhaps . . . the Whamo? ●

Sheridan Knockabout ejector.

Sheridan Knockabout, grips removed to show rivets.

Possible prototype Whamo Powermaster in Petty's collection.

IN 1961, reflecting on the problem of the proper deer rifle for various ranges, I wrote an article for GUN DIGEST titled *The 10% Deer Rifle*. Now, after 20 years more deer hunting, if I were retitling that particular piece of gun enlightenment, I would call it *The 1% Deer Rifle*. That rifle was designed to take care of those long range shots across West Coast logging slashes or on the open mule deer ranges of Eastern Oregon.

It's still in my gun rack, a 300 Short Ackley Magnum, 24-inch barrel, Husqvarna Swedish action, topped by a 3-9x variable power Bushnell scope. I have killed only three deer with it during the past 20 years. For my deer hunting, I prefer a middle ground rifle.

Closely duplicating the ballistics of the 300 H&H Magnum, my long range rifle has plenty of reach. Pushing a 180-gr. bullet at 3000 fps, I would place its sure hitting range on deer at around 450 yards, if properly sighted in to take full advantage of its flat shooting. As for killing power, it was adequate for anything on the North American continent, to say nothing of the larger share of African game.

The recoil of this 300 Short Ackley Magnum was more than I, an experienced rifleman, cared to handle, off-season and on. It wasn't a pleasant rifle to shoot, making it less than fully compatible.

It is typical of all too many deer rifles taken afield by the average once-a-year deer hunter—well beyond his handling ability. Deer hunters, without exception, it seems to me, are better served with a rifle in the middle ground—such as the 30-30, 35 Remington—for all ranges this side of 200 yards where 99% of all deer are killed. Where more open shooting is obtained the 250 Savage, 243 Winchester and 6mm Remington, 257 Roberts and 7mm Mauser are the best choices.

Les Bowman, who once ran a packing and guiding outfit in Wyoming, is

MIDDLE GROUND

It's what's up close that counts for over 90% of deer hunting.

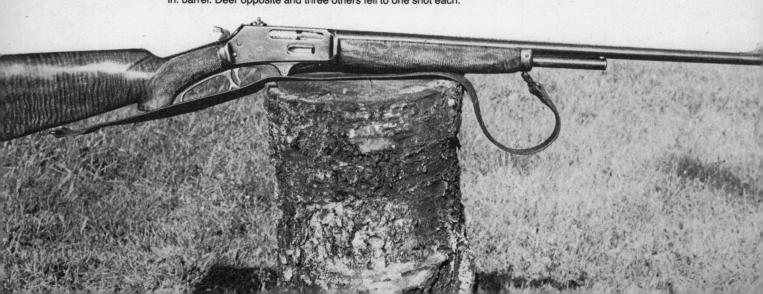

The 25/35 Tomcat handles a 117-grain 257 bullet at 2575 fps MV, weighs 7⅛ lb., has 24-in. barrel. Deer opposite and three others fell to one shot each.

on record as saying that most of his clients were buffaloed by the magnum rifles they carried. When they showed up with a hot shot magnum, planning on taking everything from deer to elk, they immediately came under Bowman's suspicion about their rifle handling ability. Put to the test on pre-hunt targets, about 9 out of 10 flinched, and had hard jobs keeping their bullets even on the paper at 100 yards!

When Les Bowman persuaded a hunter to use one of his lesser powered rifles, business picked up at once. For antelope and deer he armed them with the then-new Winchester 243.

ing on rifle shooting. But, despite all of this missionary effort, the 30-30 is still a top choice of the majority of deer hunters, along with the 35 Remington caliber—mostly in lever actions.

Let's examine that 35 Remington in detail. This cartridge was first brought out by the Remington Arms Company in 1906 for their Model 8 autoloader. Later, Remington brought out a pump-action for the 35 Remington caliber in 1912. At present it is made in a lever-action by Marlin, and a limited edition in pump-action by the Remington Arms Co., who also made some Model 600 bolt-action carbines in 35.

able in factory ammo—a 150-gr. round nose bullet pushed at about 2350 fps, and a 200-gr. bullet at 2100 fps. These two bullets are both good deer killers. The 200-gr. bullet arrives at the 200-yard mark about 12 inches below line of sight of a 100-yard zero. So, actually it is at its best within 150 yards. These 150 yards of killing range are the most important of deer hunting distances. It is here that almost all deer are killed.

At present, in the 35-caliber Remington lever-action Marlin, there is another important deer killing factor. Properly loaded, it is an excellent small game rifle for squirrel, rabbit, or what have you! I use it that way.

DEER RIFLES by FRANCIS E. SELL

With all this in mind, let's examine some of those middle ground deer rifles. First, I doubt if more than 10 out of 100 deer hunters can handle the recoil of the 30-06. This opinion, it seems to me, is endorsed afield by the persistent popularity of such old-time favorites as the 30-30 which has been condemned by all the experts punditting on rifle shooting.

Stevens once made a lever-action in this caliber. It also appeared as a gas-operated autoloader under the name of Standard—the first gas-operated autoloading rifle on the American scene.

To survive since 1906, a deer rifle cartridge must have plenty of ball afield. Two bullet weights are available in factory ammo.

Speer's Reloading Manual lists a 125-gr. jacketed hollow point 357 load for the 35 Remington caliber. Using 42 grains of DuPont 3031, the muzzle velocity is 2500 fps. There's also a 158-gr. jacketed soft point, with 36 grains of DuPont 3031 for a muzzle velocity of around 2100 fps.

This is my off-season plinking and

small game loading. I adapted it because I found it shooting to the same point of aim as the regular 200-gr. deer bullet. In many ways, the ability to adapt a deer rifle to off-season shooting is the most important factor in autumn deer shooting. Obviously, a deer hunting rifleman of the present day cannot hope to shoot enough deer to become expert in the full sense of the word. Though I hasten to add that a rifleman who has taken four or five deer offhand has a confidence and ability much beyond the skill developed by shooting the same number of shots at a target.

I do plenty of off-season shooting—pest control—all shots taken offhand. Where a middle ground rifle is used, instead of an out and out sniping rifle, it puts the hunt back in the hunting. This, too, has plenty of autumn payoff, once a deer trail is underfoot.

The 375 Winchester is an excellent middle ground deer rifle. It has a bit more delivered energy than the 35 Remington. But the difference is not great. Both are at their best in that all important deer range bracket, this side of 150 yards. These two calibers are at their best, it seems to me, as lever-actions. Winchester fanciers can have the 375 Winchester in the Model 94 carbine. It is also available as a Marlin lever-action.

Before considering other middle ground deer rifles, I want to review the 30-30 or, rather, review its critics.

There are several statements current that summarize the collective attitude of the 30-30 critics. They go very much like this, "The 30-30 was a good deer rifle in its day—it is still popular because the average deer hunter is totally ignorant of the superior ballistics offered by the more modern rifling—the 30-30 has wounded more deer than any other caliber—so . . ."

Some present day pundits claim modern hunters are playing Western hoss opera. Actually, those hunters prowling the woods of Maine, Wisconsin, Michigan and other deer-producing sections use lever-action Marlin or Winchester carbines because they are among the best designs for their purpose. This is just as true of the short range West Coast and northern deer hunting territory.

These deer hunters take most of their deer at 50 yards or less. A long shot is 100 yards. And, let it be whispered, the modern lever-action 30-30, with a 170-gr. round nose soft point bullet, delivers more energy to the 50-yard target than many of the rifles more favored deliver out there at 300 yards and more.

Bullets from the fabulous old 30-30 are very effective because it is a very

simple matter to make bullets that expand beautifully at 30-30 velocities. When you begin pushing game bullets at 3000 to 3500 fps you are on debatable ground. Quite often there is a lack of expansion at the maximum ranges, too much blowup at the shorter ranges—even with partitioned bullets.

This bullet problem is more or less endemic to the magnums, but it is much less a problem with the smaller high-velocity calibers, such as the 6mm. A 6mm 100-gr. bullet, such as the Hornady Interlock, or the Remington Core-Lokt, gives very good expansion at a muzzle velocity of around 3000 fps.

The so-called wounding potential of the 30-30 and its 170-gr. round nose soft point raises several questions in my mind. Prowling the wilderness for the past 65 years, seeing hundreds of deer killed cleanly with the 30-30 and similar calibers, I am of the opinion that the 30-30 is a clean killing deer caliber at all average ranges. It seems obvious to me that if the 30-30 was a wounder, it wouldn't have survived and kept growing in popularity.

Attributing the continued popularity of the 30-30 as a deer rifle to the fact that its ammo can be obtained at any crossroads store is the old chicken and egg question all over again. Which came first? Obviously the popularity of the 30-30 as a deer rifle created the demand for the ammo before

The 35 Remington in the Marlin works all seasons, with 200-gr. deer load at left or the 158-gr. small game load next to it. Bullets are a 200-gr. Hornady, a 158-gr. soft point, and a 200-gr. bullet after expansion.

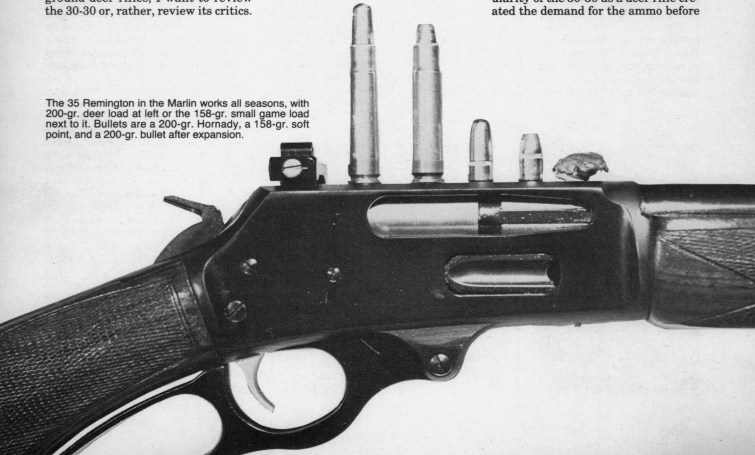

Here is the 6.5x5mm deer rifle stocked for offhand snapshooting mentioned in the text. It killed nine deer with ten shots.

it was stocked by all the country trading posts.

When the magnum fanciers say the 30-30 was a good deer rifle in its day, but now there are superior calibers, they are dabbling in rather muddy ballistic waters. When the 30-30 was introduced, it managed a 165-gr. soft point bullet at a modest 1900 fps at the muzzle. Over the years since 1894, there has been updating and today that 170-gr. bullet is pushed at 2200

fps MV and meets more deer rifle range and killing potential than most rifles taken afield each autumn.

Some of the popularity of the 30-30 as a middle ground deer rifle can be attributed to the popularity of the lever action. The Winchester Model 94 Carbine is a good example of the well-crafted rifle for offhand deer shooting, though it has been cheapened by stamping instead of milled parts during the past several years.

The Savage Model 99 lever action, no longer made in 30-30 caliber, is still a popular choice in the backwoods among knowledgeable deer hunters, and a Model 90 30-30 commands a premium price.

Probably the best of the present-day lever-actions is the Marlin Model 336. This action is very strong, smooth in operation, and the trigger pull is capable of very critical adjustment. The average Marlin 336 comes from the factory, usually, with a very acceptable pull.

How about the actual accuracy of the 30-30? More to the point how about the accuracy of the lever action compared to the bolt action? Out of the box, I would say that the Marlin 336 is just as accurate as the average bolt-action rifle. In sighting in my own Marlin 30-30, a 35 Remington, and an updated wildcat 257 Tomcat of my own design, I have no trouble keeping a 3-shot, 50-yard hunter group within ⅝″.

Long ranges have been over-emphasized by the magnum rifle fanciers. This over-emphasis is underscored by the muzzle-loading, black powder deer hunters. It is also underscored by the bow hunters. There are several factors more important than extended ranges in deer rifles. One is portability—where the lever-action carbines, Winchester or Marlin are tops. Another important detail I have belabored previously—recoil. In many ways, it is more important to match deer rifles to deer hunters than it is to match them to deer killing.

One caliber I have often played around with is the 6.5mm. In this case, a 6.5x55mm, the Swedish Army cartridge. I once made up such a rifle for my deer hunting in the middle ground.

I had a Husqvarna bolt-action, one merit of which was its shotgun-type safety that made the first shot as fast as one from an exposed hammer lever-action. The late Bliss Titus made me a fairly heavy 20-inch barrel for this action. Then I stocked it Mannlicher-style with a beautiful piece of myrtle. The custom stocking is worth the

Sell doesn't say it here, but his 25/35 Tomcat is a recreation of a long-ago time when he fed people with a 25-35 on contract.

telling. I glass bedded it full length, barrel and action, to suit the wet West Coast forests I prowl. I worked the stock down to proper offhand dimensions with the help of the deer in the old orchard around my wilderness cabin.

As I sanded and rasped, I snapped the rifle to my shoulder, time and again, my eyes on the vital area of a deer in the orchards, range about 50 yards. When the rifle invariably came up with the sights always on target, I had my proper dimensions. Not once during the stocking adjustments did I measure. The only two dimensions I measured to start with were pull length and pitch, taken from my wing shooting shotguns.

I killed nine deer with this rifle in heavy cover, using 10 cartridges. All shots except one were within 50 yards, the exception being a deer at about 150 yards. The one shot missed was at a running deer at about 45 yards, an over shot as I tried for a neck shot, and I connected on the second try. All deer killed, moving or standing, were shot through the neck, something achieved because I got a fraction more time because the sights came up ready aligned.

How about the more open ranges? Not all those chances come at 400-500 yards even in the long range sections of deer cover in the West. The majority of "long range" shots are at 250 yards or less. Out around 350-500 yards, successful hits are usually the product of a barrage.

Several seasons ago, while hunting Canada geese in Oregon's beautiful Warner Valley, I had the nice task of recommending a rifle for mule deer hunting. My rancher friend had a son who was ready for his first deer rifle. The quarry here, aside from antelope, was open country mule deer. The boy, 14 years old, was rawhide tough, riding all summer and handling range cattle in the high desert country, but he wasn't a heavyweight. I recommended the scoped 243 Winchester bolt-action and the 100-gr. bullet.

Next season when I returned, Johnnie brought a beautiful mule deer steak to my trailer. And in five years since, he has killed his mule deer each season, almost all one-shot kills. The last time I talked with his father, he was mulling the notion of selling his 30-06 and getting a 243 for his own use.

The 6mm Remington, 257 Roberts, 250 Savage, are all powerful enough, and flat-shooting enough, middle ground rifles to cover the more open ranges. So's the new 7mm-08, or the old 7x57mm, for that matter.

At maximum ranges, if the bullet is well placed, they all have sufficient killing power for the more open ranges. Anytime a rifleman delivers 900-1000 foot pounds of energy to the vital area of a deer, it is meat in the pot, uphill or down. This energy must be delivered accurately, it goes without saying. This, in turn, means a deer rifle that doesn't have the hunter buffaloed. This means a bullet delivered from a middle ground rifle, capable and compatible to the point that the rifleman doesn't flinch or subconsciously dread the opportunity for a shot.

Using such a rifle puts the hunt back in deer hunting, which is another way of saying that it puts the pleasure back in the hunting. ●

This is the target, Sell says, and it's usually close, far inside a magnum's usefulness.

Sell's 308 Short Ackley Magnum at left is a 1% rifle, he now believes, and is outclasssed by a 35 Remington Model 336 Marlin.

A grouse moor in Yorkshire, in the north of England, with a row of stone butts.

THE UNHAPPY HUNTING GROUND

REMOVE SIX thousand square miles from Illinois, and add about forty million people—and you get England. Don't forget the class system, in existence for a thousand or so years and still a poignant reality, if in somewhat altered form. Britain was the first to make the Industrial Revolution, and so offers some centuries of pent-up class resentment. A victim of its own history, today there is an atmosphere of general hostility, and a pathological fear that the guy next door might have a bit more cooking in his pot. This requires the English to observe their neighbors' pots carefully, even at the expense of their own.

What's it all got to do with hunting? Considerable when you consider it works out, on average, that there is one acre of England per Englishman, and there are 900,000 Britons with shotgun certificates (issued by the police) who would like to get on the land. Since Britain is a coun-

try where prestige is important—only slightly less so than air—and hunting long the prerogative of royalty, the nobility, and the upper class generally, it is understandable that those still on the lower rungs of the social ladder would have a strong desire to emulate their social betters, given money to do so.

It is not necessarily the urge to hunt that is the primary motivation; an odd day on a moor, after driven grouse, projects an image obtainable in no other way. The only place on earth one is likely to find the red grouse is the northern part of Britain, and Ireland. It is a bird few British hunters will ever have the opportunity to see driven to them. Possession of the moor, providing there are a sufficient number of grouse on it, could warrant an invitation to the Prime

by SIDNEY DU BROFF

Minister, who will no doubt be pleased to accept, if he—or she—happens to be a Conservative. If Labour is in office, the Prime Minister might be forced to turn down the invitation, however reluctantly, since there are elements within the Labour Party who would like to stop all forms of "Blood Sport," as they call it. Nevertheless, members of the Royal Family are amenable if a big enough kill can be assured.

What is sufficiently large? Well, in the county of Lancashire, eight guns accounted for 2,929 grouse. That was back in 1915. Up in Yorkshire, in one day on Blubberhouse Moor, Lord Walsingham, all by himself, killed 1,070 grouse. He did it, on that August day of 1888, to prove a point. He had hoped to entertain Prince Albert, the future King Edward VII, on his moor, but the Prince, a keen shot, felt there were not enough grouse to make the trip worthwhile. So the good Lord felt compelled to have the birds driven back and forth over him, until the bag did mount. Some grouse were picked up intact, suffering from exhaustion rather than gunshot, but nonetheless were counted.

Things have been on the decline ever since, however, and a bag of a couple hundred would be considered a very respectable day. The cost of producing a *brace* (two birds—the term is used for counting unless there is an odd one, which is called half a brace), is about equal to a full day's pay for many people. What do they do with all those birds? Eat a few and sell the rest.

If one can't actually have the prestige of being there on the "Glorious 12th" (of August—Opening Day), then the next best thing is to be in a restaurant that serves grouse on Opening Day, which suggests affinity with the moor. The birds may have been flown down that very day, or taken from the freezer, where they have lain in wait for the best part of the year. The red grouse, feeding on heather and the odd berry, is, incidentally, the worst-tasting bit of flesh I have ever been forced to consume. But no one knocks a bird which, except for its taste, is representative of the aspirations of all high achievers.

A good host will provide his guests with loaders, unless a guest prefers to bring his own, usually his game keeper. The loader is, as the term implies, the chap who does the loading. After the gun has been fired at the fast, incoming birds, disturbed by the advancing beaters (doubles only, please, definitely no autos or pumps), the empty gun is handed over the shoulder (without turning around) and the second and loaded gun accepted. It must be done swiftly, deftly, with no false movement, since, in these circumstances, seconds count.

A good loader can make a difference, which is why people do bring their own, having, usually, a good working relationship with him. It will be understood how in these conditions a matched and consecutively-numbered pair of doubles is essential. In halcyon times, now long passed, sportsmen brought up to four guns, and had as many as three loaders.

Pheasant hunting is more universal, practiced everywhere in the Kingdom on small acreages and large. The delineation here is between rough shooting and driven shooting. Shooting driven birds, as anyone who does it will be quick to point out, is the only way to do it. Many would agree. It is not without prestige; one could reasonably expect

A certain amount of muddling is inevitable in England whilst in search of shooting or the shot.

a royal guest if the shooting were good enough. On one shoot, seven guns killed 2,937 pheasants, though that was 1913. Today, to show the extent of British decline, it is possible for ten guns to take a day on Lord Somebody's Estate, paying the equivalent of about $240.00 each, and hope to bag in the neighborhood of 100 pheasants. Being able to discuss the shoot afterwards, even if no shot is ever again fired, should elevate the participant considerably on the social scale.

Driven shooting is not hunting; if, in a Briton's breast, there exists the urge to *find* something before actual-ly firing upon it, that urge must be resolutely repressed. Finding, in fact, isn't the problem. Everybody knows where the birds are; they have been put there. It's only a question of shooting them.

Conditions and situations vary. The "Gun," as the hunter is called, tries to become a part of a shoot that provides the maximum of satisfaction. Though in the words of one shooting sage, "There is no such thing as a perfect shoot."

Saturday is the traditional day. Shooting on Sunday is forbidden. Some shoots are on Wednesday, which carries a prestige all its own—a hunter able to get away during the week is required.

The group of hunters, known as a syndicate, will generally shoot every two weeks. They have banded together for expedience, like sharing the costs, which could easily work out to something like three thousand dollars each for the season. The land has to be leased, a keeper or two employed to

In the Lake District of Northern England, spotting for deer sometimes offers problems.

feed the pheasants and discourage the poachers (a pheasant sells for as much as ten dollars) though keepers, themselves, are known as the most enthusiastic poachers, being already on the scene, and who's doing the counting when there are a thousand or so pheasants milling around demanding dinner?

Shooting starts October 1st, but might be delayed by an individual syndicate if the birds haven't grown to maturity. It ends on February 1st, or sooner, if the syndicate runs out of pheasants. The "Guns" stand now at numbered posts, and wait for those few minutes when the birds will be flying over their heads.

The beaters are approaching slowly, banging sticks against the ground, and crying out the familiar wail, "Eye, Yii Yii, Eye, Eye, Yii, Yii, Eye . . . ."

Whether these words are more effective in compelling pheasants to rise up has never been determined. But, hopefully, some will rise up, and not just sprint ahead, because it would be considered extremely bad form to be seen shooting a pheasant running on the ground.

The pheasants take to the air. The "Guns" get off their shooting sticks. The birds fly overhead, hopefully

thick, and not too fast. Guns along the whole line roar. Pheasants drop, cock and hen alike. The survivors sail away to be, hopefully, targets on another day.

The first drive is over. The drivers appear—farm workers, locally-recruited boys, sometimes the odd girl—and the more of them there are, the happier the Guns will be, not just because they can beat more of the ground, but because more servants on a shoot must elevate the status of the shoot, and, hence, the shooters. The general atmosphere is one which attempts to convey conviviality between served and servers. But beaters, having plowed through bramble, are cut up from the thorns and nursing their wounds, and become a disgruntled lot, exacerbated by the facts that they have five more drives to endure, and are unlikely ever to have three thousand dollars so that they can do the shooting instead of the beating.

Now the picker-uppers move in—people with Labrador retrievers sufficiently well-trained to gather up the fallen, which is their entree to the shoot. They aren't paid for their efforts, or those of their dogs, except in satisfaction, which includes the satisfaction of being in relative proximity to those who can pay three thousand dollars to belong to this shoot.

The Guns may bring their own dogs, and the keeper might have several. But the Gun is spared from having to bend down to pick up his dead birds, or to carry them. They and the Guns will be loaded on to a Land Rover, or a more prestigious Range Rover, and transported to the next stand, where they will wait with eagerness

and anticipation for the next drive. And so it will be during the course of the day.

At the end of the day, it's a brace for each Gun and the rest off to market, unless a Gun would like some extras, available at prevailing prices.

With only derision from driven bird shooters, and commanding false respect from those who don't shoot at all because they don't know the difference between the two forms, are the rough shooters. Superficially, from a view high up on a hill, a rough shoot resembles some American shooting, as a number of men with guns walk through a field. But that's where the similarity ends, particularly when up to ten guys are doing the walking; the more guns, the more the cost can be reduced by sharing it out (which includes leasing the land).

This was the kind of shoot I had come to know, and eventually to hate. Every two weeks we appeared through the season with about ten shoots anticipated. Usually it was a waste of time toward the end of the season because there was nothing to shoot. We put down the pheasants—modern agriculture makes natural breeding impossible in most of the country—and then we tried to find them again. It worked out all right for a couple of years; we had a driven shoot as our neighbor. They kindly, if unintentionally, drove their birds onto our land. This made it possible to harvest more birds than we put down.

Things changed in the world, when the Arabs put up the price of oil, and our neighbors ceased to be casual about the pheasants that wound up on our land. The keeper conditioned his birds to come and feed when he blew his whistle. Not only did he get his birds back, but all of ours.

We lost the lease to that land—somebody else offered more money—and remained with about 500 acres of stubble some distance away. Here we could occasionally view the fleeing hare. We marched around on these barren fields most of the day, saving the good bit for the end—a wood that followed a creek, which harbored our pheasants.

Here too we had a neighbor with a driven shoot, whose presence we deemed an asset, particularly when his birds insisted upon flying over our guns. Unwilling to be our benefactors, the keeper put his dogs through our wood, scattering our birds, the majority of whom took refuge in his standing corn. This was particularly unfortunate, since we had spent the spring and summer building a release pen, from which the pheasants we had

Driven shooting is all right, but waiting is such a bore.

bought could have a refuge until we were ready to go hunting for them. But a nearly inevitable fact of life is that English neighbors have a falling out eventually.

The other kind of hunting is what they do from the back of a horse, in pursuit, hopefully, of a fox. It isn't really hunting; it's a bunch of people out for a ride, and sometimes, if they can find one, there is a fox involved. It costs around six hundred dollars to get kitted out with clothes, including the red coat; on some hunts, green or other colors are acceptable.

There are something over 200 hunting packs in the country. Their primary function appears to be occupying the interest and attention of various anti-hunting groups, some of whom drag huntsmen from their horses when they can, and administer sharp kicks to the ribs. The hunters are vulnerable because they assemble on public roads, and often proceed along

them from one field or another.

The cost of keeping a horse, and feeding the approximately 8,000 hounds that make up the grand total, prohibit many from joining in the hunt. Farmers do much of the fox hunting. They already have the horses, the facilities for housing them, and are able to deduct much of it as business expense.

Through their efforts they eliminate between 15,000 and 18,000 foxes each year. The anti-hunters are less concerned about the foxes than the fact that there are still people about who can afford to chase them.

Fox hunters are not overly popular with shooters, either, when they share the same domain. When perhaps 39 hound dogs (to which a huntsman would refer as 19½ couple) spread over a field in search of a fox and proceed to scatter every pheasant in the vicinity, for instance. The hunt people diminish their popularity still

further by bringing foxes into areas where they want to chase them, an act they deny, but which everyone knows to be the way it is.

It costs in the neighborhood of $200 a day to hunt the fox, with twenty days afield considered normal. One might rent a horse in order to participate, which the occasional huntsman might do—price about $130.00.

They hunt, in some cases, by Royal prerogative, and no law can prevent them from going through a field, which they may well subject to serious damage. It is just one more manifestation of the conflict between the wishes of one group and another in a country too small to accommodate them all.

This was demonstrated with exceptional clarity a short time ago when it was discovered that the man designated, in a keen fox-hunting district, as the Conservative candidate for Parliament, was found to have a wife who was a member of the League Against Cruel Sports. Hers was an expression of betrayal his supporters could not endure, and they proceeded to withdraw their support from the man.

"High water mark" is the term that engenders a further delineation between Britain's social classes, particularly amongst those who shoot, or want to. Traditionally, the area below which the high tide reached—the marshes and wastelands around the coast—were open to whoever had the desire to venture forth into it in pursuit of ducks and/or geese—"wildfowl," as they are collectively known in Britain. Clearly, those who did the venturing were not gentlemen, so the prohibition on Sunday shooting did not apply.

The season is from September 1st to February 20th, and there is no bag limit. What you can find, you can kill, on the water, in the air, over decoys made of wood, or live ones that quack at the appropriate time, using any scattergun of your choice, including a four-gauge, if you have one. You can chase them in a power boat, and sell them after you've caught up to them and killed them.

This domain below high water mark attracted the ever-increasing numbers who had guns, and nowhere to use them. They shot at whatever they could find which could include a sea gull or the odd song bird, and became known as "marsh cowboys."

The Local Authority is the body responsible for the administration of local government. It consists, far too often, of those not known for their competence. They are able to exact large amounts of money in the form of taxes from defenseless householders, and feel it incumbent upon themselves to squander it. Consequently, they have an insatiable need for more. It was seen by many such authorities that these marshes would provide it, and they proceeded to take over their administration, leasing to clubs and individuals areas that had been available previously to all without cost.

The basic British attitude towards waterfowl is that if Nature creates it, grab it, or somebody else will. Now wildfowl shooting has been stopped on Sunday, not particularly as a conservation measure, but as an expression, typical of Britain, and much of Europe, that says if somebody wants something, try to avoid letting him have it as a matter of principle. The various anti-blood-sports groups

Wildfowlers hunt below the high water mark. These have a gray goose.

would stop it altogether if they got their way.

Above high-water mark, on ponds, marshes, and in open fields, wildfowling ends on January 31st, with the same lack of restrictions, though, in many cases, the ducks have been raised and while they may be *fowl,* they are decidedly not wild. The land above high-water mark is as inaccessible as any other, and gaining entrance is probably even more difficult because there is less of it. Navigable waterways—rivers, canals—have the same status as the Queen's highways, which makes it illegal to fire a gun across either of them.

In a country where an acre of land costs about four thousand dollars, more in some places, the chances of earning it back by what's grown or raised on it appears to be rather unlikely in the course of a single lifetime. But land-hungry Europeans are almost always prepared to mortgage

their future, as well as that of future generations, in order to acquire a couple of more acres. The average farm is only 160 acres, with 300 acres considered a big one.

Rabbits were, decades ago, the quarry for many a hunter, and farmers gave access to a few people whom they knew, to clear what are termed "vermin" from their fields. But a more efficient method of clearance was developed, called myxomatosis, a disease developed in a Swiss laboratory, and introduced into the fields, where in due course the rabbits of Europe became virtually extinct, and so did hunting for them.

It took about 20 years for the rabbits to have made a comeback; the disease, caused by a tick, killed the animal slowly, blinding it, distorting its body. It did its work when the rabbit was in its burrow below ground along with the rest of its family. It spread from one rabbit to another. Far from having run its course, the disease is still about. While it is now illegal to introduce myxomatosis, those farmers who prefer it as their method of clearance will obtain a diseased rabbit and introduce it onto their land.

Hare, who don't burrow and live their lives atop the ground were not affected by myxomatosis. They are of the same family as our jackrabbits, but in Britain they are highly regarded, sell in the shop for five or six dollars. In some places in Europe they have as much status as pheasant, largely because as a creature that weighs in the neighborhood of nine pounds, there is a considerable amount to eat on them.

The wood pigeon is the game bird of the lower English social order. It, in fact, is not a game bird, but classified as vermin, has no protection in law, and can be shot at any time in any quantity. Loved deeply by many a gunner whose gun would otherwise fall silent, it evokes great passion in hearts attuned to it.

Pigeons earn the ire of farmers when they swoop down in waves to eat grain. It is then that the farmer frantically phones the "Clearance Society," if he doesn't have anybody else available for the job. The "Clearance Society" is the euphemistic name of those who have banded together as an organization to kill pigeons, and who, as individuals, would probably not have any shooting otherwise.

On a good day it is possible to knock off 50 pigeons, and sell them, if one choses. The going rate is about a dollar apiece retail, approximately half of it to the hunter.

For no apparent reason collared

doves moved into England; probably they expanded their habitat and, needing more room, found suitable conditions here. They stay the winter, particularly in the south, where the weather is usually not too severe. They have, in some areas, even pushed out the earlier-established pigeons. Though some of the other dove species are regarded as songbirds and have full protection, the collareds have none, and may, at least for the moment, be shot without restriction.

Most people are not aware of the invasion and are unable to distinguish between the dove species. English pigeon gunners remain largely indifferent, preferring the larger pigeon, an easier target that they have come to more fully understand. But it is only a question of time before a group of people, hearing that collared doves have been shot—the bird of peace—will form themselves into a Collared Dove Protection Society, and agitate for a complete ban.

While there are squirrels, there is no squirrel hunting, but a considerable amount of squirrel killing. The English feel great hostility towards the grey squirrel, regarded as being of North American origin. It has devastated their indigenous red squirrels. The greys are classed as rodents, and would be eaten with equal alacrity. It would be interesting to note the reaction were I to tell my English guests that the game casserole I had served to them consisted in part of squirrel.

That an English shotgun is a joy to hold and behold is undeniable. It also bestows upon its owner a status higher than if it were a gun of some other national origin. To derive full benefit, the gun, made largely by hand and almost always a side-by-side double, should be created to order, the man having been measured for fit. It should also be a sidelock; a boxlock will never carry the same kudos. The differences seem to be slight, there being none in the functioning. The sidelock is supposed to be stronger, some people claim, and hence costs more to create. But its real benefit is in the showing.

Britons claim not to be competitive, but are probably the most competitive people alive, their need to win surpassing even their need for food. Consequently, just prior to the beginning of the hunting season, many surreptitiously return to shooting school for a day of instruction so that they won't "blot their copy books" on opening day; others go unsurreptitiously.

A man on our shoot, the owner of a pair of doubles originally made for his father and worth roughly $20,000,

Du Broff at a manor house in Scotland, where it's wet. (Nedra Du Broff photo)

they can't look good, at least they hope to be able to make someone else look bad. They aspire to the "magic" guns, usually over-and-unders, the Belgian Brownings and the Italian jobs, which, if they don't improve their shooting, will certainly enhance their status.

To buy a shotgun you have to get police permission, with the application form to be signed by the doctor, minister or magistrate of your choice, any of whom might disapprove of guns and hunting and refuse to sign. The police, particularly in some districts where they have taken it upon themselves to limit the number of guns in their constabulary, exceeding their authority, may bury the applica-

The lack of forest in Scotland is, one way or another, the fault of the English, who cut them down. The Scots insist the English did it to deny the Scots sanctuary during the time they were at war with each other. The English said they did it because they wanted the timber to make some ships. This was happening in the late 18th Century, just about the time England was battling its thirteen rebellious North American colonies. They are still arguing over the real motive behind the destruction.

And so now, denied the concealment offered by what would, by this time, be some very big trees, you go up the bare mountain, hugging the ground. Don't worry about the rifle;

wanted an arm of his own choosing. His choice happened to be a French-made autoloader, which sometimes fired without resort to the trigger. Once it went off on impact, when its owner jumped over a ditch. On another occasion, the circumstances were not too clear, and the owner refused to elucidate. It was already dark, and we were in the process of returning from field to vehicle, when the shot was heard, the flash observed.

The owner, a lawyer and otherwise responsible man, was asked to return to either of his doubles. He refused, regarding the request as an impingement of his fundamental liberty and a denial of his basic freedom as an Englishman. Since all involved were extremely eager to curtail his freedom in the interest of continued good health, it was firmly establlished that the French autoloader would no longer be welcome on the shoot. Whereupon neither of them ever returned, the man remaining true to his firm English conviction—love me, love my shotgun.

Few in Britain find it easy to love a shotgun that doesn't break open, particularly when in the hands of another. In fields that are small, with as many as ten men walking abreast, sometimes only feet apart, it creates a feeling of confidence and well-being, when, upon reaching the end of that field, guns are broken open and are observably safe, however one felt whilst walking.

Clay shooters in the UK are out for blood to a greater extent even than game shooters—each other's. Here, if

Hunter and guide approach a downed roe deer, in the south of England. (Nedra Du Broff photo)

tion in the hope of permanently discouraging the applicant.

To own a rifle one has to have a place to use it, and satisfy the police that it is both safe and available—because they check. You want to go deer hunting? Don't try to borrow a rifle in England; that's against the law. But in Scotland it's okay. The red deer in Scotland are close cousins of our North American elk. Essentially forest animals, they wander about on the deforested Highlands, trying to grow decent antlers but not often succeeding. Twelve points make a Royal, not all that common. On the Continent, where there is forest in which to roam, 20 points are frequent enough, with antlers as big around as your wrist.

you're not carrying it. Your stalker is. Even if you wanted to carry it, he wouldn't let you. He claims it's his job, but, in fact, holding your gun—call it a rifle; in Britain, a "gun" is a shotgun—gives him complete power over you, which is precisely what he wants.

You make it up somewhere near the top, and there's your deer. If a hind—a female—doesn't happen to spot you from a distance and bark a warning, you could get in a shot. The stalker, when he determines it to be the appropriate moment, removes the rifle from the rifle bag and hands it to you, allowing you the privilege of pulling the trigger. And don't forget the tip—the usual is $12.00 per point.

In Scotland, out after roe deer once, we encountered a red deer with a reasonable rack. He was some distance away, but his bulk made him an easy target.

"How much for him?" I asked my Forestry Commission stalker.

The deer obligingly remained motionless while the stalker made his calculations and named the figure. By today's exchange, it would have been a thousand dollars.

"Too expensive," I said, and settled for lining him up in my scope, just for the view.

Down in England the roe deer are more numerous than they have ever been, invading and denuding gardens in the outer suburbs. The Forestry Commission created new forests, since a Britain without an indigenous supply of wood presented a considerable number of unsolvable problems, particularly during the last war. The roe deer then moved into the woods, and did what roe deer do to trees, particularly the small trees. Having had little experience with either trees or roe deer, and wanting the trees and not the deer, the decision was taken to kill off all the deer.

The pheasant is England's primary game bird. (Nedra Du Broff photo)

The roe, not a party to the decision, in no way concurred and managed to survive, despite the official onslaught. In one area inhabited by 13 roe, 12 were killed, the 13th managing to elude the Forestry Commission guns. The next year 13 roe deer were back in the same area.

The Forestry Commission ultimately concluded, if somewhat late in the day, and taking into consideration the experiences of the rest of Europe which they had previously ignored, that if they couldn't kill 'em, they could join 'em. Co-existence, rather than elimination, became the policy. Deer, they said, as if nobody had ever thought it or said it before, were also a resource.

Limited hunting was made avail-

able, with 70 percent of those who do it coming from outside Britain, mainly Germany, France, Belgium, and Holland. The harsh conditions imposed on rifle ownership on the native population made it extremely difficult for Englishmen, who might otherwise have done so, to acquire the arm and the experience the Forestry Commission demanded in order to go deer hunting. Foreigners are also better tippers, having had more experience of what was expected of them.

You pay for the forester to go out with you and act as your guide; pay again for the antlers, based on their size; and pay a third time if you want any of the deer meat to take home—at market price. It would otherwise be sold to the local hotel, or shipped over to Belgium or Holland for consumption there.

The roe is a small deer that lives over most of Europe. Highly adaptable, it has not changed at all in its entire evolutionary development. It weighs 50 to 60 pounds, is about 26 inches high at the shoulder, and carries a pair of not-very-impressive antlers that may reach eight or ten inches in length, sometimes with a couple of points.

On Forestry Commission land you take a test before the commencement of hunting. You might then sit in a high seat, walk, or both. The forester gives you a mark for your performance that goes on your permanent record, which is earned by the way you follow his instructions. If you miss a deer he doesn't think you should have shot at in the first place, or wound one that he did, you might

as well not bother applying to come back, because you got a "C," and they're not going to let you.

But for this, if you insist, they will allow you to carry your own rifle. You can only use it on the land where you have permission; you can carry it there and back; and nowhere else. In some instances, an "open" certificate will be granted, which means that the holder can take his rifle where he likes—and has access—to go deer hunting.

Besides roe, there are sika deer, introduced from Japan in the 19th Century, and doing well. They now live in about half of the British counties, and in Scotland are hated because sika will mate with the red deer hinds. The resultant offspring is felt by the Scots to be something less than desirable.

The Romans, it is thought, brought over the fallow deer, a handsome animal, bigger than a roe, but smaller than a red, with an impressive rack of palmated antlers. And now there is the muntjac, a small deer of Oriental origin, with not much by way of antlers, who used to be just decorative, adorning the grounds of Woburn Abbey, the property of the Duke of Bedford. The muntjac chose freedom, and now breeds in the wild in all of the surrounding counties, and can be spotted 25 miles from London.

Britain is old and tired, its people squabbling over a small pie. It has become the Unhappy Hunting Ground. You can't exactly say 50,000,000 Britons can be wrong about hunting and shooting, but it's starting to look that way. ●

Pheasants and pigeons for sale at a London butcher shop.

Shotgun Review

by RALPH T. WALKER

THE HEAVY competition in shotgun sales plus the state of the economy has resulted in a scramble for every available sale. The public has the attention of the gun manufacturers, and the new shotguns incorporate features more attuned to practical use and increased versatility. It is a situation where everybody wins. The shooters have what they want and demand. The manufacturers that made changes find their sales are on the upswing.

The increased practicality and versatility blue ribbon should go to Smith & Wesson. While I personally would question the accuracy of the model designation "SUPER GUN," there is no doubt the new S&W is one of the best designs to come down the

power, these solutions would be simple. As they are not, adjustments must be made in design that will allow function and cycle with low, standard and high-powered ammunition. The usual gas-operated gun could handle anything in the 2¾-inch case, but the 3-inch magnum shell required another gun. The standard gun could not handle the long shells nor could the magnum guns handle the full range of standard cartridges.

Even in the standard 2¾-inch guns, gas pressure differences from low to high power created problems. Most designs had ways of bleeding off enough excess gas from the high power shells to allow the gun mechanism to cycle at about the same speed. Probably the best design was or is

them equally and cycle at the same rate of speed.

As ice cream on the cake, the Smith & Wesson Super gun also includes their screw-in interchangeable choke system termed the Multi-choke. Three choke tubes come with the gun—improved cylinder, modified and full—which makes the gun even more versatile.

Rifle ammunition, for all practical purposes, had made the switch from black powder to smokeless powder by 1912 or so with resulting changes in barrels and such. Not so with the shotshells, due to a problem with the primer providing ample ignition of the powder charge. Black powder shotshells were still quite common in the 1920s and 1930s. Black powder re-

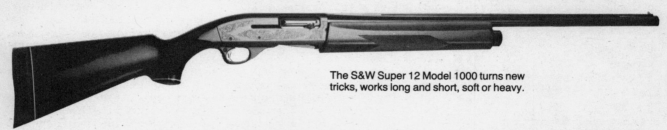

The S&W Super 12 Model 1000 turns new tricks, works long and short, soft or heavy.

pike in a long, long time. To appreciate the design and the gun, a wee bit of technical history is necessary.

In the late 1950s Remington, for all practical purposes, ushered in the age of the gas-operated semi-automatic shotgun and still dominates the field in units sold. Other manufacturers quickly jumped in with their own designs. A latecomer, Smith & Wesson eventually introduced their Model 1000. From a practical point of view, all gas-operated shotguns delivered the same performance and selection became more a matter of personal choice rather than innovative design.

They all utilized gas ports drilled into the bore of the barrel with the gas from the shell exiting into some form of chamber. The gas was put to work there to cycle the action and make the gun self extracting-ejecting and to move a fresh shotshell from magazine into chamber. This requires very careful placement of carefully designed gas ports and good management of the weight of the moving parts and other technical considerations.

If all shotshells were of a standard

that used by Winchester in their Model 1400-1500 semi-autos—a needle valve with a spring provides closure on standard or light loads, and opens when a heavy load is fired to vent excess pressure.

Question: Why didn't they simply provide porting to allow one gun to handle both shell lengths? One company did—SKB in their 20 gauge, but it required a switch mechanism that worked fine as long as the gun was loaded with one or the other shells. And SKB has long parted the scene. The question is simple; the answer is complex, very complex.

However, the question has now been answered and the gun is available from Smith & Wesson in a redesigned Model 1000 that they call the Super 12. It will handle 2¾-inch shells from light to short magnum and will also handle all the versions of the 3-inch magnum. This would have been a breakthrough even with a switch à la SKB. No switch is necessary with this design and this is extremely important. The shooter can *mix* the shotshells, lightest to heaviest together and the gun will digest

quires a long barrel to burn, hence shotgun barrel lengths of 36 and 34 inches were quite common, and 30 inches was a standard.

The change to smokeless powder and the subsequent change in the general public's mind did not take place at the same time. The demand for a long shotgun barrel from the general public dictated a slow and gradual change to shorter barrel lengths. The evolution has resulted in the 26- and 28-inch length becoming the accepted standard, although most knowledgeable shooters were aware that even shorter lengths were more in line with modern shotshell development.

Several years ago, Remington led the pack by introducing a shorter barrel length of 24 inches and offering everything from full to improved cylinder choke. This, to my understanding, was a test run to determine public acceptance. It soon turned to an overwhelming demand and necessitated standard production to meet consumer requests. In summation, the day of the short barrel length had dawned and other companies rapidly followed

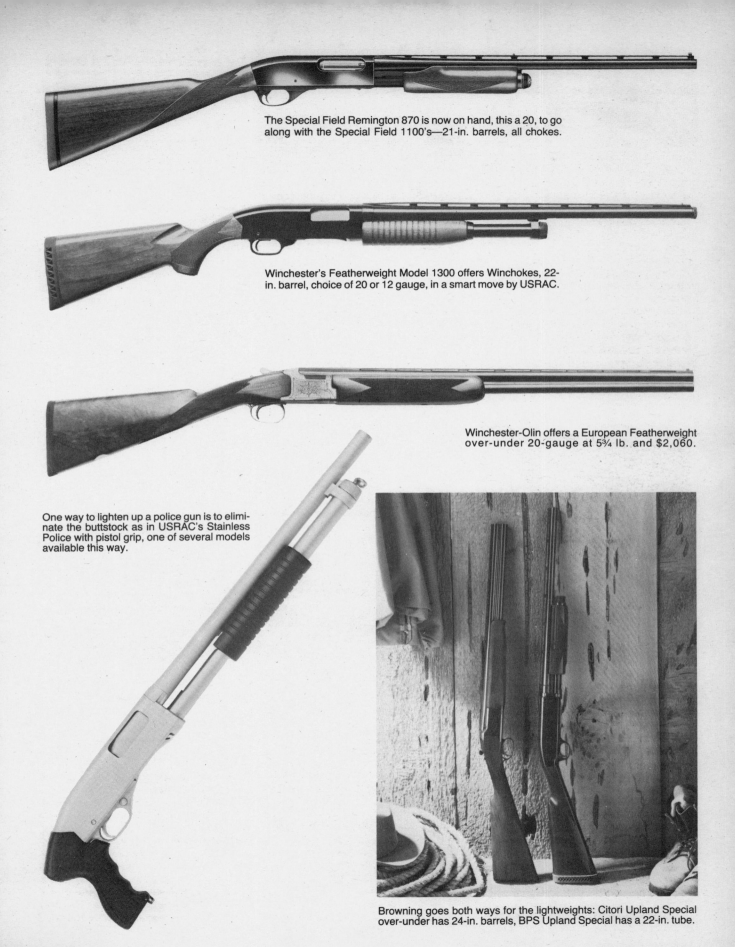

The Special Field Remington 870 is now on hand, this a 20, to go along with the Special Field 1100's—21-in. barrels, all chokes.

Winchester's Featherweight Model 1300 offers Winchokes, 22-in. barrel, choice of 20 or 12 gauge, in a smart move by USRAC.

Winchester-Olin offers a European Featherweight over-under 20-gauge at 5¾ lb. and $2,060.

One way to lighten up a police gun is to eliminate the buttstock as in USRAC's Stainless Police with pistol grip, one of several models available this way.

Browning goes both ways for the lightweights: Citori Upland Special over-under has 24-in. barrels, BPS Upland Special has a 22-in. tube.

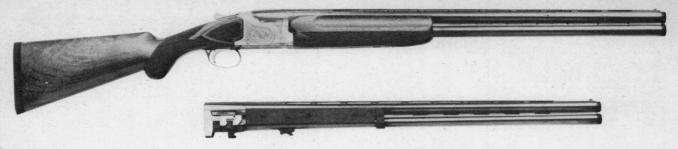

Winchester of Olin here puts together something really special: The Two Barrel Hunting Set offers 12- and 20-gauge (28 and 27 inches) barrels and a total of 10 Winchoke tubes.

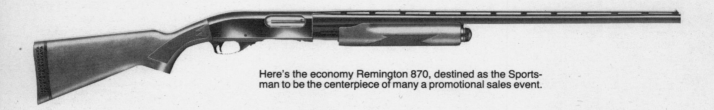

Here's the economy Remington 870, destined as the Sportsman to be the centerpiece of many a promotional sales event.

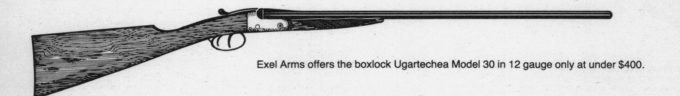

Exel Arms offers the boxlock Ugartechea Model 30 in 12 gauge only at under $400.

The Clayco Model 6 over-under 12 is made in China, originally imported to sell at $295.

MARBLE'S Poly-Choke®

Two familiar names now to be together: Marble's bought Poly-Choke.

A Parker again, this time by Winchester, will be made in Japan, but the parts will interchange with the originals.

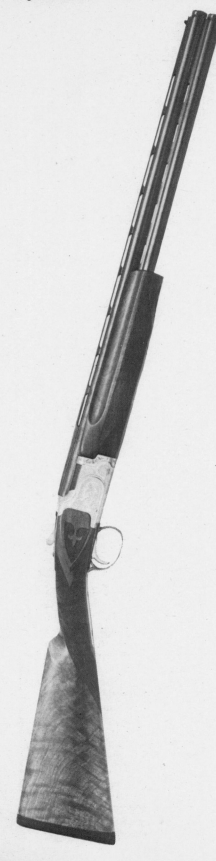

This Quail Special by Winchester-Olin is a 25½-in. 20-bore with Win-Choke and a price tag under $2,000.

Remington's lead, notably Browning and Ithaca.

Remington has even gone back to 21-inch barrel this year in some of their guns and they are finding wide acceptance. Several other companies now offer a short barrel length in various models.

A modern shotshell, depending upon the individual shell, will reach maximum acceleration (velocity) at around a 26-inch barrel length and there is little loss in shortening. Nothing except weight is gained with a barrel length in excess of 25-26 inches. Velocity and pellet weight determine energy or "power" at the target. Pattern density is controlled by the degree of choke. A 25-inch full choke barrel will give the same pattern and striking energy as a 45-inch full choke barrel or any length in-between.

The short barrel is quicker on target under field hunting conditions and a heckuva lot easier to carry through heavy brush. For long range shooting, the only advantage of a longer barrel is the optical impression given by the longer barrel, and a narrow or decreasing-width rib will give the same optical impression. There is no practical advantage to a barrel length in excess of 25-26 inches and thankfully the general public is becoming aware of this and so are the gun manufacturers.

The third advantage of the new breed of shotguns is weight. Until recently if you wanted a 12 gauge under seven pounds, the only choice was a double of non-U.S.A. manufacture. Ithaca introduced the ultra-light pump several years ago and its acceptance has dictated similar action on the part of other gun manufacturers. Remington has not been asleep and has combined light weight with the shorter barrel that has their guns selling like cold Coke on a hot day. Winchester has also brought out several lightweight versions as has Smith & Wesson and Browning and others have such in the works.

There are people out there who could not care less if the bluing is less than state of the art or if the stock is genuine walnut. They are the type who toss a shotgun in the back of a pick-up, pile ten dogs on top and drive like mad down a dusty road or through a heavy rain.

This year, gun manufacturers have given more thought to this market and placed plain-Jane versions of their standard models on dealer racks. There is no loss of internal quality, only a lack of cosmetic goo-

dies. Remington, for example, introduced their Sportsman series aimed for the economy market. Among the offerings is the well known 870 pump in 12 gauge three-inch chambering and with factory rib and recoil pad. Winchester also has an economy version known as the "Ranger" series. Marlin, Mossberg and Savage all have similar offerings.

Light weight, shorter barrel length, interchangeable choke tubes, and the ability to function with 2¾-inch or 3-inch shells mixed in the magazine tube are the dominating news in the repeating shotgun market for this year plus the addition of no-frills versions of proven models.

The introduction of Browning's over-and-under fitted with the Invector screw-in choke tubes now makes three over-and-under shotguns with this feature. The first was Winchester's Model 101; second Lanber's Model 2004 LCH; and now Browning. The Lanber tubes are similar to the Winchoke but of metric persuasion. The Invector tubes, incidentally, will interchange with Winchoke tubes, the difference being that the Winchoke tubes have the knurled tube section visible, the Invector is within the barrel and removed via several notches in the front end with a special wrench.

Most European shooters, with the English predominating, have always maintained that a twin triggered shotgun is the fastest method of barrel selection. One simply pulls the trigger of choice and then moves that finger to the second trigger to fire the second barrel. When Browning first introduced the Superposed, they marketed a version equipped with twin triggers. The shooter selected the trigger to fire a barrel with desired choke and after firing, simply pulled that same trigger again to fire the second barrel. The design left a lot to be desired in mechanical reliability as the component was extremely complicated in abundant parts. Laurona has a reliable version in the same theme, i.e., pull a trigger of choice and then pull the same trigger. It is extremely fast once you get used to the system and faster than the normal single selective trigger. Their gun is imported and marketed by Exel Arms.

Valmet, noted for the seemingly endless choice of over-and-under shotgun barrel selection with fitting of barrels not requiring a trip to the factory, totally redesigned or "Americanized" their buttstock and forend and now calls it the 412S model. I fired one several hundred times, and it is a welcome change and bound to be more acceptable to the general public. The new stock is interchangeable with the older 412K. Most important, the stock length or pull can be altered to suit the shooter at the store with various width spacers secured to the stock with *machine* screws, not wood screws. You can even change the pitch up or down with available angled spacers. This little goodie allows the stock to be altered to fit the shooter and not the shooter altering himself to fit the stock.

The big news in side-by-side doubles is the introduction—reintroduction—of the well-known Parker shotgun. It is not a new or revised design, as each and every part and component will fully interchange with the original Parker that exited the market in the late 1940s. The new Parker is being built by Winchester's plant in Japan under exclusive contract. A Mr. Tom Skeuse, president of Reagent Chemical and an ardent Parker collector, is the prime mover behind this endeavor. As I understand the story, he carried several of his personal collection over to the factory for blueprinting. The gun will sell for about $2,800.00 with all other extras such as a fitted case adding to the tab. It's a beautiful gun and the new company should recoup its initial investment in nothing but new parts and components for all of the original Parkers still floating around.

The English W & C Scott guns are now available through the L. Joseph Rahn company, who also markets the Italian Garbi. The Garbi is about as close as you can come to the old English Best Guns nowadays at anything resembling acceptable price. The same firm can furnish top quality oak and leather shotgun cases produced in Italy.

Another interesting side-by-side shotgun is the Spanish Ugartechea from Exel. The sidelock version retailing for just under $600.00 is reminiscent of the old L.C. Smith in both over-all appearance and feel although it differs considerably internally. The upper-priced grades have such goodies as engraved receivers, automatic ejectors, etc., all fitted with twin triggers. I shot a test loaner gun with the auto ejectors during dove season and it functioned flawlessly.

Few shooters have ever bothered to pattern their shotguns and one reason is the lack of a good target. Finding the necessary paper and then drawing a 30-inch diameter circle around the pattern can be a hassle. Hunterjohn (P.O. Box 477, St. Louis, MO 63166), under the Winchester name, now

markets a patterning target that is both interesting and practical. Basically, it's an aiming point with the 30-inch circle predrawn around the aiming point. It differs in that there are four additional circles slightly off center to compensate if the shot pattern goes high, low, left or right of the aiming point. Packed three per container, the pattern sheets also offer a wealth of necessary information printed right on the target.

Anyone who does a lot of shotgun shooting is always interested in some way to cut costs. Reloading is an obvious step, but with the high cost of shot, the savings is reduced. Now you can make your own shot. The original design of the unit came from Scotland (where else?) and has been through

The pattern target of the future? Maybe. It's from Hunterjohn, with Winchester's name on it.

several design changes. My original test was with one of the earlier versions, but it was very successful. Basically, a heating unit melts the lead which in turn flows through special sized nozzles. The exiting molten pellets fall into a closed container of liquid and are cooled. It's actually an old process known as the short drop. The end result is fully usable shot pellets of preselected size with price dependent on the lead supply. The unit sells for $134.95 from Shannon Associates (P.O. Box 32737, Oklahoma City, OK 73123), and is fully guaranteed to perform.

One of the tools quite often sought by shotgunners deep into choke and bore dimensions is a bore micrometer. Stan Baker of Seattle now markets

one in 12 gauge under the name "bore reader." Quite recently a new firm, Custom Shooting Products (8505 K Street, Omaha, NE 68127) has brought out a similar version with interchangeable heads for 12, 20, 28 and 410 gauge at $339.00 for the four-gauge unit which includes a fitted case.

Poly-Choke was recently purchased by Marble Arms (P.O. Box 111, Gladstone, MI 49837) who is moving the whole operation from Connecticut. They will continue to market the PolyChoke and Polyrib. Incidentally the old firm also sold a bore micrometer suitable for 12, 16 and 20 gauge with current availability unknown, but worth the try.

An item worth repeating is that Diana Import (842 Vallejo St., San Francisco, CA 94133) has parts and accessories for the Breda shotguns as well as the shotguns themselves. For those trying to locate independent felt and nitro wads for shotshell reloading, which virtually disappeared with the advent of the one-piece plastic wad, Diana is the source.

Pennsylvania Arms Co. (Box 128, Duryea, PA 18642), produces custom shotgun barrels that are rifled to exactly take a slug. Accuracy is exceptional and of high interest in those states that require shotgun slugs only for deer. This firm walked away with the Diana Grand Championship which is a match held in New Jersey in which only shotgun slugs are used. ●

Some Selected Shotguns

The New Stuff is Good Stuff

The sleek Special Field 1100 is a good gun for a 5-ft., 4-in. woman like Deborah Warner or any other shooter.

It USED TO BE there was a new shotgun now and another again, spaced through the seasons, if not the years. Now they seem to come in bunches from all directions, and that's how I'm going to have to report on several I've seen lately.

Before we get into it, let me say that any man who cannot find a shotgun to suit him or his intended quarry in the United States today would complain about the character of new money. They are *all* out there, men. As always, rarefied tastes require the soothing touch of lots of money, but there remains a lot of stuff for us working folks.

The big guy in American shotguns is Remington Arms, so the big autoloader is the 1100. And what they've been doing with that lately has been hard to keep track of. There are just all kinds of 1100s these days.

You know there are Model 1100 standards and magnums, and then there have been special lightweights, and lots of Skeet and trap models. Here lately, they offered 26-inch full choke barrels on magnum 12s which, this writer is happy to report, work very well in the field.

Having thus demonstrated a perfect willingness to experiment, Remington went not quite as far as they can go and introduced the Special Field 1100—a straight-gripped short magazine, short-barreled delight of a shotgun in 20 and 12 gauges.

When we say short-barreled, we mean 21 inches. When we say "not quite as far as they can go" we mean that about all that's left to try is the interchangeable choke tube and that's probably next.

The Special Field models are going to tickle shooter fancies. They are also going to work just fine in the field. Your reporter has 20 years' experience with short-barreled Remingtons, has been shooting an 870 with three barrels—a 20-inch slug barrel, a 20-inch (original factory) full choke barrel and a 20-inch Poly-Choked barrel—since the early '60s. Don't hesitate if you like the idea—it works.

By the way, you can't just buy the 21-inch barrel to fit to your gun. The Special Field magazine tube and forend are shorter than standard, so the barrels won't interchange with other 1100s.

On the dramatic side, it seems to this writer that Remington has gotten very close to the mythical all-around shotgun this time. To put that another way, a fellow who had a special Field bird gun sure would not have a need to own a riot gun as well.

There's considerable literature on behalf of the double guns, some of it even true. They are slick, friendly, simple, deadly and—if they're all those things—generally expensive. Mostly, the ones they write about are *very* expensive.

That's a $400 28-gauge Armas Erbi wand the editor is wielding over the brush pile.

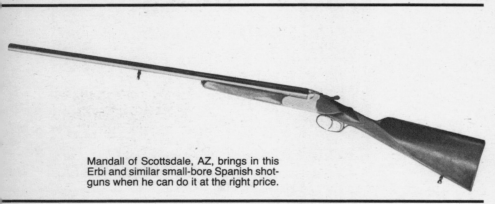

Mandall of Scottsdale, AZ, brings in this Erbi and similar small-bore Spanish shotguns when he can do it at the right price.

The Lanber 844ST Magnum is a sensible wildfowler and turkey gun that shoots where it looks.

However, there are a few rays of light. In fact, there seem to be doubles of some virtue under $500 and I have two at hand.

The cute one was the best of three smallbores—a 410 and two 28s—Marty Mandall sent along. He tells me he keeps an eye on Spanish makers, and brings in good stuff when he can do it at the right price, under $400 for these.

These are mighty nice, and the one I picked to keep has a bunch of stuff going for it: It's nicely made, adequately engraved, and you'd be astonished how long a set of 27¾-inch 28-gauge barrels look. Armas Erbi made it.

It's a real nice plain gun—two triggers, extractors, straight grip, light straight-grain walnut, enough checkering in a point pattern. It shoots where it looks and weighs about six pounds.

For me, this little Erbi takes the place of some other doubles, some expensive ones. It has the looks, the handling—you shoot it like a double.

Bad points? I guess so, but to find any big ones I'm going to have to shoot it a long time. I've decided I like the sling swivels, and that I don't care that the black plastic buttplate is held on by Phillips-head screws. The action fences are filed out so nicely I just never look at the butt.

The other double at hand is from the other end of the field spectrum— it's a 3-inch 12-gauge over-under. This one is a Lanber, and it's a healthy, robust specimen, but without extreme weight.

There are a couple of nice touches. I like the flared forend, sort of a schnabel, and I like the way the heel of the factory recoil pad is rounded off—it looks good and it mounts correctly with no catching. It's a sober specimen, this gun, generously equipped with working class checkering and a single selective trigger.

At $499 or thereabouts, this Model 844ST field grade magnum gun actually comes in at a deluxe autoloader price. Its plain extractors pull the empties up far enough for quick reloads and it shoots where it looks, which is what I say about any field 12 that lets me break 22 birds or so at trap the first time I shoot it, as this one did.

It seems obvious to me that a fellow who wants a double can have one. In fact, as I said at the beginning, an American who can't find a shotgun to suit him these days is too picky to go out where he might get his shoe soles dirty.

Ken Warner

JOHN M. BROWNING: THE MAN AND

The inventor with his Auto-5 above; the patent drawing for his wildly successful Model 1911 pistol at right.

HIS PATENTS

by D. A. TOMLINSON

As I walked through the small museum in Ogden, Utah, I was awestruck by what I was seeing. Only a small fraction of John M. Browning's life's work is on display there, but that small part is enough to astound anyone who knows what he's seeing.

No gun designer in the history of the world approaches John Browning; his guns have stood the test of time, the test of war, the test of customer tastes, and the tests of increasing pressure in more modern cartridges. He died on the 26th of November, 1926, over a half-century

ago, but many of his guns are still in production.

For anyone interested in guns, the story of John Moses Browning holds fascinating information.

Are you an IPSC shooter? Browning designed both the 45 Colt and the Browning Hi-Power 9mm: the two pistols most commonly used in your sport.

Are you a World War II vet? John designed the 30-06 and 50-caliber Browning machine guns and the Browning Automatic Rifle (BAR). That means that every standard-issue machine gun used by the U.S. Army, Navy, Marines, and Air Corps in that

war was designed by him. So were the 303-cal. machine guns that won the Battle of Britain from the wings of the Spitfire and Hurricane fighters of the Royal Air Force.

Are you a gun collector? John designed the Winchester High-Wall, Low-Wall, 1886, 1887, 1890, 1892, 1893, 1894, 1895, 1897, 1906 and more, all the basic Colt automatic pistols, and many other fine collector's items.

I am a Canadian, and I'm astonished at the American neglect of John M. Browing. What you're reading is just a sketch of the life and work of the American who became The Master, the greatest gun designer the world has ever known. It isn't enough. There should be books, copies of all his patents gathered together into one volume, research . . . such material would be most valuable in the library of any arms designer, and an object of long study for anyone interested in fine guns, or in American military history. There should be commentary on his guns and on the production history of his guns. There should be research, collecting, and study.

The importance of this man, both to the firearms world and to the cause of freedom, can't be seen in scattered bits. It is only by taking it step by step, patent by patent, that we can see the sheer size and importance of his work. He was such a quiet man, so reasonable and unpretentious, that his accomplishments are often unrecognized and unremembered. Perhaps if he had been as flamboyant as Samuel Colt, he would be better remembered by those of us who owe him so much.

John's father was a Mormon, a gunsmith and an inventor named Johnathan Browning. Johnathan invented and built repeating cap-and-ball rifles, both in revolver and in the seldom-seen harmonica type. His revolving rifles were fine specimens, and the harmonicas were cheap, effective, and easy to repair; ideal for the early Mormon settlers of the 1830s and 40s. Like most working-class percussion rifles, few of Johnathan's making survived into the 20th century.

Johnathan brought 11 children with him to Utah in 1852, and sired 10 more after he arrived. The story deals with the younger, Utah-born family.

As John grew up, he worked with his younger brother Matt, and his four half-brothers. The oldest of the group, he was the leader and always the senior, even with Matt. The sign over the door of their business seems to indicate the relationship; though all six worked there, it said: "J. M. Browning & Bro."

Johnathan's inventiveness may have started John as an inventor, but Johnathan's trade certainly made John a craftsman. John first realized this at the age of 13 when a wagon freighter gave him a crushed and broken caplock shotgun. He disassembled it, and realized that there was no part, except the barrel, he couldn't make himself. The barrel was almost the only undamaged part, and the boy soon had the gun repaired, re-stocked, and shooting again.

At the tender age of 15, John was advised by the local schoolteacher

that he'd graduated; he'd learned all that the teacher had to teach. He became a full-time gunsmith, but business was bad and the shop was run down. John built up the business, and gradually became the gunsmith in residence as his father gradually retired.

A remark by his father caused the next major shift in his life; John was cussing at a single shot rifle he was working on because it was complex and badly designed. He growled that he could design a better rifle himself. Old Johnathan calmly replied, "I know you could, John Mose, and I

In July of 1896, Browning showed this gun and three others to Colt. Patent 580,923 (opposite) was granted April 20, 1897. It's gas-operated.

wish you'd get at it. I'd like to live to see you do it."

During that year of 1878, John built his first two Browning guns, both single shot rifles for metallic cartridges.

One of the rifles (unpatented?) had a reversed lever that lay under the rear of the forearm, and was pulled back and down to load; the other (U.S. Patent 220,271) is familiar to anyone who has ever handled a Winchester Hi-Wall, a Winchester Lo-Wall, or an FN/Browning B-78 single shot rifle. He applied for a patent on this one in May of 1879, and U.S. Patent 220,271 was his first.

Another important aspect of his career began here. He didn't design guns on paper; he built working firearms and then patented them by making the drawings from the guns. Bear it in mind, because each "design" I will talk about was a working, shooting, well-made and durable custommade firearm.

Winchester, at this time, was in trouble. The Model 1873 repeater was selling well, but the '73 wasn't strong enough for heavier cartridges such as the 45-70. Winchester had no good single shot rifle for these heavy cartridges, either.

John was also in trouble; he disliked the dogwork of business, but he was ambitious. He'd bought a little five-horsepower steam engine, and set up a miniature arms factory. Matt and the four half brothers were his workers. He also employed Frank Rushton, an English Mormon who'd arrived on the day they began setting

up the factory. Rushton had worked in the big English gun factories, and he knew machine tools and gunmaking. John hired him and learned from him.

Their Browning Single Shot, today a collector's item, was a good seller. It sold as fast as they could make it, which wasn't very fast. On a good day, they could make three rifles. The brothers also ran a sporting goods store in the front room of the little arms factory, and they sold their rifles there.

As the rifles spread around the area, the inevitable happened; early in 1883, a Winchester representative bought one second hand and sent it to the Winchester factory for their examination. If it was wise of Andrew McAusland to send it, it was doubly wise of Thomas G. Bennett, Winchester's General Manager, to recognize what it implied. The serial number, 463, was not too impressive; but it was a production gun. Somewhere, out in the wilds of Utah Territory, there was a new competitor—it said, "BROWNING BROS. OGDEN UTAH" on the barrel of the best single shot rifle he'd ever seen.

Bennett was an active man. He boarded a train for Ogden. On arrival, he found the factory and the 25-year-old inventor. He promptly bought the patent for $8,000 and a promise to put J. M. Browning & Bro. on Winchester's jobber list.

The deal was a happy one for both sides. For Bennett, it was an important new product for Winchester; for John, it was a lump sum of much-

chester's jobber list, became a major sporting goods store, employing three of John's half-brothers, partly run by Matt, John's only full brother.

Bennet had taken a train back east on the same day he arrived in Ogden, but with John's comments about a heavy cartridge repeater design stirring his interest in the young inventor. Bennett's day in Utah was in the spring of 1883; in October, 1884, John was ready with the rifle some call the finest lever action of them all—the smooth, slick action that was to become the Model 1886 Winchester (306,557) and later the Model 71.

fed a fresh cartridge, as smoothly as sliding cold butter on a hot stove. There were other lever-action repeaters on the market, but none were in the class of John's design for strength, smoothness of action, and simple beauty—the beauty of a well-designed machine with perfect functioning.

John and Matt went east for the first time in October of 1884, taking the prototype of the Model 1886 with them. They stopped off in New York, partly to see the sights, and partly to visit Schoverling, Daly, and Gales, the jobbing house that was their chief supplier of sporting goods. They toured the city with a Schoverling salesman whom they knew from his visits to Ogden, then returned to their hotel.

To Matt's surprise, John invited the salesman up to see the new rifle. John figured that the salesman knew guns, and he knew the gun business; his opinions could be a valuable clue to the importance of the new design. After handling it, the salesman pronounced it the finest rifle he'd ever seen, and commented that John probably held the future of the Winchester company in his hands. The worry that he was bringing a design already surpassed by someone else faded from John's mind.

Partly as a result of the salesman's comments, John felt free to ask for a steep price for the design. It is believed that he got $50,000 for it—and Winchester got a bargain. Some 203,261 rifles were made under this patent as the Model 1886 and the Model 71, a slight redesign introduced in 1935. It was in production for 71 years.

As a result of the new way of making money (selling guns to Winchester), a design team was assembled in Utah: John, the designer and inventor; Matt, the businessman; and half-brother Johnathan Edward (Ed), the machinist and model maker.

John would make sketches and sheetmetal models of parts to study working relationships. Once the relationships were clear in his mind, Ed would be brought in to do the heavy machining of parts for the working firearm, under John's direction. Later still, he and John would do the fine fitting and trimming. Once the firearm was complete, working, and ready to patent, Matt Browning would handle the paperwork and financial end of the business.

Winchester's Bennett was a man who liked to control his business. He bought John's patents outright, for flat sums. John got no royalties on

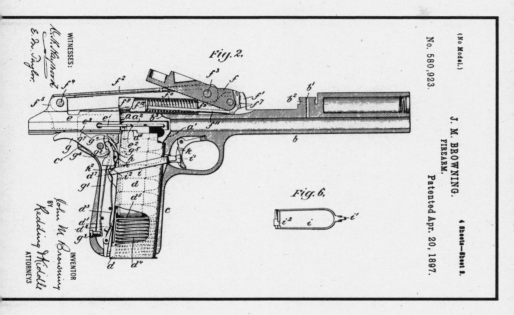

needed capital, and some hope of earning important money by his brains instead of by production and administration.

It is probable that Bennett saw two more guns of John's design, because Browning had already patented two repeaters. One was a bolt action with a tubular magazine (261,667), which does not survive; the other was a very simple lever action repeater, also with a tube magazine (282,839). That one may rank as the simplest lever action repeater ever constructed. It was probably intended for production in the little factory, and it's now in the Ogden museum. While it may have been suitable for small scale production, John was apparently unsatisfied with it; he had a better design in mind, and Bennett asked to see that when it was ready.

Relieved by Bennett's $8000 of the daily business of running a factory, John radically revised his business. The store in Ogden, thanks to Win-

John applied for the patent on the new repeater himself, on May 26, 1884. He didn't take it east to Winchester until the patent was actually granted, in October, 1884. While waiting for the patent, he designed and built two attractive lever-action repeating rifles, one in 38 caliber (312,183), and one recorded by Browning and Gentry as in 30-40 Krag (324,296). This second caliber seems dubious, as 1884 is very early for it, but may be correct. The rifle is still in existence, in the Winchester museum, so I hope someone will check it. Personally, I'm dubious about many of the calibers attributed to Browning prototypes, as little hands-on research has been done in the last 50 years.

The 1886 was a beautiful piece of design. The lever pulled the twin locking bars down, while pivoting on its front end; then it pivoted on its middle and racked the bolt back to cock, extract and eject. Snapping the lever up

the firearms he sold to Winchester, which was a pity. With royalties, the returns would have been slower but much greater. In the end, this system led to his final break with Winchester, but for the first 16 years of his career, all his long arms were sold to Winchester on similar terms.

When he bought the Model 1886, in late 1884, Bennett asked for a lever-action shotgun design. John proposed a pump action as better adapted to the larger shotgun shells, but Bennett felt that the public associated Winchester with lever actions. That's why John's next production design was the lever-action shotgun now known as the Winchester Models 1887 and 1901 (336,287). The request was made in October, 1884, and the patent was applied for (by Winchester!) on June 15, 1885. Bennett also bought the two rifles (324,296 and 324,297) mentioned above in 1885.

The patent procedure was worth noting: John designed and built firearms, but the company which bought the design often arranged for the patent in his name. This was apparently a convenience step, as the companies had legal departments and draftsmen and engineers, while John disliked paperwork. He used this system with several companies. He supplied working, tested firearms; they made production and patent drawings from the guns.

Bennett was a shrewd businessman. He bought all of John's long arm designs, some for production and others, apparently, to prevent his competitors from buying them. These patents for firearms that weren't manufactured also made it more difficult for lesser designers to design new firearms without infringing on patents owned by Winchester. As you'll see when we get to 1900, gun makers may be missing a bonanza by not studying the patents for John's guns, both produced and never produced. He was so productive that many excellent designs were never made, simply because they could only have competed with the ones that were produced; and what maker competes with himself?

The effects so far were incredible. In 1885, Winchester announced the Single Shot; in 1886, the heavy caliber Model 1886 repeater; and in 1887, the Model 1887 lever-action shotgun. These were the best available firearms in three widely differing fields.

In 1886, John sold Bennett three more designs, in the form of five working guns. There were two versions of one design of pump-action shotgun (356,271), two versions of the com-

pletely different pump-action shotgun (345,882), and a 22-caliber rifle (385,238). The shotguns were never produced, but the 22 became the first really successful 22 repeater. Issued by Winchester as the Model 1890, it became famous for rugged durability. It was the common rifle found in public shooting galleries for decades for that reason. Re-issued as the Model 06 and 62 and 62A, the total production reached 2,106,475 from Winchester alone. I have no way of totalling the numerous copies made by other makers, such as Rossi.

The success of the 22 must have been embarrassing for Winchester's

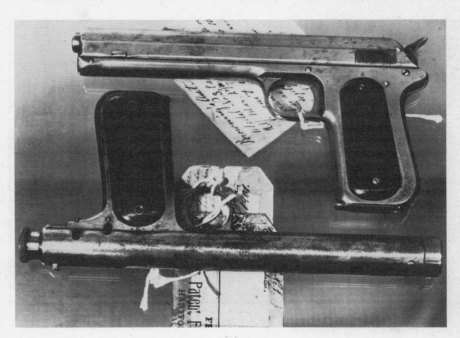

in-plant experts. It was a design requested by Bennett, and, pushed for time, John sent drawings instead of a working model. The experts told Bennett the design could not possibly work, and he notified John. John made a rifle and sent it in; the rest is history.

John sold no guns to Winchester in 1888. He was out on the road, drafted as a missionary by the Mormon church. He was 32 and married; today, the church selects only unmarried men for this duty, but in the 1880s John was eligible, and he was called. On his return, he went back to work.

In 1889, he sold Winchester only one design, in the form of two working rifles. It was an unusual repeater (428,887) that held its cartridges inside a one-piece breech block lever magazine, nose down. John often used one piece to do several jobs,

which accounts for some of the simplicity of his works, but this seems to be going a bit too far—having all three major components of a lever-action repeater in just ONE piece!? One suspects that the design was a bit tongue-in-cheek, but the two rifles made to this patent (a 45-70 and a 44-40) are not at all odd-looking.

In the autumn of 1889, a minor event stirred Browning into a new path. At a shoot of the Ogden Rifle Club, he noticed that the weeds in front of a competitor's rifle swayed away from the muzzle when he fired. Probably already thinking about automatic firearms (the Maxim ma-

chine gun became available in 1888), he immediately gathered Matt and Ed and headed for the shop. There, he fired a 44-40 1873 Winchester through a hole in a bit of two-by-four. As the muzzle blast hit its rear suface, the wood was thrown violently forward, away from the muzzle.

By the next day, the same rifle had had its lever shortened, its trigger lengthened, and a crude "flapper" attached to the muzzle. In action, the flapper swung down and away from the muzzle when hit by muzzle blast. Actuated by the flapper's movement via a thin rod running from flapper to lever, the lever worked as though a hand had moved it. This extracted and ejected the empty. A spring returned the flapper to the pre-blast position, moving the lever to feed another cartridge. At the moment of final bolt closure, the short lever contacted the trigger, and the piece fired again. The work, from initial concept to a working 44-40 black powder machine carbine firing about 1000 cartridges per minute, had taken one day.

On January 6th, 1890, he applied for a patent (417,782) on the first gas-operated automatic firearm in the world. By that time, he had made several working automatic guns, of which only two survive. They are in

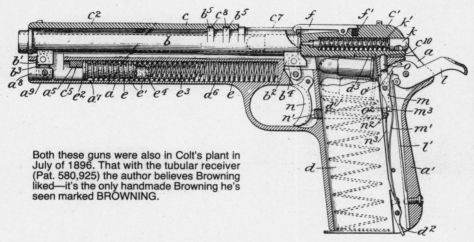

Both these guns were also in Colt's plant in July of 1896. That with the tubular receiver (Pat. 580,925) the author believes Browning liked—it's the only handmade Browning he's seen marked BROWNING.

the Ogden museum. Automatic arms now began to play an increasing role in the Browning story.

He did not stop his work for Winchester; the automatic arms were not ready to be considered for sale or production. In June of 1890, he sold Bennett the design now known as the Winchester Models 1893 and 1897 pump-action shotguns (441,390). The Model 1893 was replaced in the line by the Model 1897, in 1897. Total production ran to 1,274,750. It was discontinued in 1957 after a 64-year run.

In 1890, Bennett requested a design for a small rifle, as similar as possible to the Model 1886, but for the 25-20, 32-20, 38-40, and 44-40 family of cartridges. Winchester had tried to miniaturize the Model 1886 in the plant, but had failed. Impatient for once, Bennett offered $10,000 for a design delivered in three months, or $15,000

for one delivered in two months. Browning, wanting to see the look on Bennett's face, offered to have the rifle in Bennett's hands within thirty days for $20,000, or give it to him for nothing. This would give him six days to get back to Ogden by train, 18 days to design and build the rifle, and six days to get it to Bennett in New Haven, Connecticut. A contract was drawn, citing the three possible dates and corresponding fees, but with the gift idea omitted. Browning collected the $20,000. It was another bargain for Winchester; the Model 1892 Winchester (465,339; 499,005; 306,577) had a production run of 1,034,687. It was put back into production as the B-92 by FN of Belgium and Browning Arms a few years ago. It was also widely copied elsewhere, as the El Tigre and under other names.

Examination of the prototype in the Ogden museum startled me; knowing the history of its incredibly rapid development, I did not expect to see any major change from the Model 1886, but there is one. The prototype has the locking bars hidden under the top surface of the bolt, so the bolt top is smooth. Winchester deleted this feature on the production guns.

If this feat wasn't enough, John sold Bennett two more rifle designs in 1891, a 22 pull-apart rifle (465,340) (sort of a reverse direction pump-action), and a lever-action hammerless box magazine rifle (465,339) in 45 caliber. This rifle is stocked in military fashion, and may have had something to do with the trials that led to the adoption of the 30-40 Krag by the U.S. Army in 1892.

Now, let's back up a year. This was a busy time for John, who was branching out. On November 22, 1890, Matt wrote to Colt's Patent Firearms Mfg. Co., and informed them that the Browning Bros. had a 40-pound machine gun (471,783) in 45-70 caliber, capable of firing government black powder cartridges at the rate of six shots per second. Was Colt's interested? Colt's replied that they had been making and selling Gatling hand-cranked machine guns, but Gatlings were expensive and sales were poor. They would, however, like to see the gun. They would also like to meet the inventor of all those superb Winchesters, if he cared to come to Hartford.

John and Matt arrived in early 1891. The gun they took to Colt's still exists in the Ogden museum. It bears the marks of the forge and is highly unattractive to the eye, but the visit was not an attempt to sell a finished design. John just wanted to know if he was completely wasting his time in the machine gun area. Kindly received by John Hall, the President of Colt's, the brothers asked for a place to demonstrate the gun. They had four belts of fifty each, and the gun hammered them all through without a hitch.

The talks with Hall after the demonstration were inconclusive; Colt's was interested, but, lacking a war, the market for a new type of machine gun did not exist. Hall showed them a Colt's-made Gatling, and John and Matt surprised him when they admitted that it was the first machine gun they'd ever seen, except for their own.

During this visit, John's reticence was bypassed by Matt's cheerful explanations of John's history and inventions. A shrewd businessman, Hall decided that this young inventor should be encouraged to develop his connection with Colt's. It was the beginning of a relationship that made both Colt's and the Brownings much wealthier. It seems probable that the patenting of this machine gun (471,783) was the first of many patents secured via the Colt's legal and drafting departments for the Brownings, as it was applied for in August of 1891.

Hall arranged an unofficial military test later in 1891, and John returned alone with the gun. The Naval Ordnance Department wanted to see the gun try for three minutes of continuous fire. They thought that ships in battle might get within small arms range of one another for up to three

melting in the barrel! Shoot, change belts, shoot . . . The barrel turned blue. Then it turned red. John thought about the tiny extractor, touching that red-hot barrel 600 times a minute. It would soften and break, he knew it . . . silence. For a moment, he thought the extractor had broken, but the smoke dissipated and he became aware that the belt was empty and there were no boxes left. He'd done it!

I doubt that anyone can watch three minutes of uninterrupted fire roaring through a machine gun without being impressed. Browning was using 45-70 black powder loads, so it must have been really spectacular, especially to men who had never seen a fully automatic weapon in action before.

Hall took Browning and the Naval officers to dinner that night, and John had his first-ever glass of champagne. Colt's signed an agreement

fle, or was Browning just jumping on the bandwagon of the next U.S. military cartridge?

Still in 1892, John sold Bennett a rifle (499,005) which was a minor variant on the Model 1892 patent in 44-40 caliber. He patented, but did not sell, the simplest 22 single shot rifle ever made, with ONE spring and ONE moving part. We will return to it later—in 1900.

In addition, he applied for one more machine gun patent. It covered a machine rifle (502,549) of small size, low power and light weight which was never produced.

In 1892 and 1893, John applied for four patents (544,658; 544,659; 544,660; and 543,567) for the machine gun now known as the Model 1895 Colt "Potato Digger." It was later manufactured in 30-40 Krag, 30-06, and 236 Lee Navy by Colt's.

This gun used a development of

This is the inventor's original Browning Superposed.

The 1887 shotgun design for Winchester—this is the original gun—was made to order for T. G. Bennett.

minutes, so that was their test. John was appalled; he had the gun firing at 600 cartridges per minute, and he knew that the heat effects would be terrific. It was a lot to ask of a crude prototype, and he didn't really expect perfect success. Hall, however, said that the point had been made that the gun was not fully developed and the officers would be forgiving of small failures.

Late one afternoon in 1891, John sat down behind the gun. He had nine boxes, each with a 200-round belt. He sat on a bicycle seat he'd attached to the gun's tripod. Earnestly watched by Hall, two Navy officers, and the works manager, he fed in the first belt and worked the action once. Twenty roaring seconds later, he tossed off an empty box, slapped a fresh one on, and started another belt. He lost count of the boxes very early, and swore as the flapper fanned droplets of molten lead back in his face. The bullets were

with John; he was to make a finished gun for them to try to sell. The contract included a generous royalty for John on production guns. Up to this time, all his design sales had been to Winchester, and there had been no royalty provisions. This deal probably started John and Matt (who was the businessman of the family) thinking.

In 1892, John sold Winchester two pull-apart rifles (486,273) in 30-40 Krag, a pull-apart shotgun (487-659), two lever-action rifles (486-272 and 492-459) in 30-40, and an odd rifle with a lever that swung back and down (499,007) instead of forward and down, also in 30-40.

1892 was the year that the U.S. Army adopted the 30-40 Krag rifle. Three of these rifles had military style stocks, and the two pairs were a full-stocked rifle and a carbine (for cavalry?) each. Were Browning and Winchester competing against the Krag to supply the next U.S. Army ri-

John's early "flapper." Gas was tapped from a port in the bottom of the barrel to push a swinging lever downward. The lever gave the gun its name, for it would dig dirt if the gun was mounted too low on the tripod. This swinging lever deserves more attention than it ever got; its action is excellent for a machine gun, because its initial movement is mostly down but slowly to the rear, providing enormous strength for the crucial initial movement of the bolt, followed by speed for the rest of the travel, and slow, positive closure on return. The prototype preserved in Ogden is one of the smoothest firearms I have ever handled, and swinging that big lever is like operating a well-oiled 1886 Winchester.

Belt-fed, and quite reliable, the Colt 1895's were bought by the U.S. armed forces in small numbers. They were used in the Spanish American War, and also in the Boxer Rebellion in China, where they were credited with saving the foreign legations from massacre.

Only a few thousand M1895's were ever made, but Marlin made some with conventional fore-and-aft pistons during the First World War, for use in aircraft and tanks. Though this redesign is usually credited to the Marlin factory, it was actually present as a possible variant in Browning's original patent.

For serious students of firearms design, it should be noted that a frequently-used photograph of the M1895 is in error; properly, a belt enters the gun below the breech from the left, and exits, empty, from a short slit on the right. Ejection is from the right rear of the breech. The photograph shows a short, loaded belt stuck into the ejection port from the wrong side of the gun!

A fluke of timing and a lot of hard ate smokeless without a murmur. John always designed for both durability and strength. In fact, none of his black powder guns were rendered obsolete by the coming of smokeless powder. The extra stress of doubled pressure was within Browning's designed-in safety factors, without any modifications being required.

In 1894, the design of the Model 1895 Winchester (549,345) was completed and sold to Winchester. It was the first production lever gun with a box magazine, which made it suitable for sharp-nosed hardpoint ammunition of military type. Made in 30-40 Krag, 30-06, and 405 Winchester (among others), it was produced from 1895 to 1931 for a total of 425,881.

Patented in 1894 were also: a pump-action shotgun (552,864), sold to Winchester, and a small automatic rifle (544,461), never sold and apparently made only to test and demon- with outside hammer, detachable magazine in the butt, and locked action.

2. A hammer-fired dropping barrel-locked action pistol (580,924), with similar magazine, obviously the prototype M1900 Colt, and the direct ancestor of the M1905 and M1911 Colts.

3. A striker-fired, rotating barrel-locked action pistol (580,925), with similar magazine and a grip safety.

4. A hammer-fired blowback pistol (580,926), with similar magazine, obviously the direct ancestor of the M1900 FN pistol.

One may be forgiven for taking a serious look at recognizing him as The Master, a title given him later by the workers of FN, when one realizes that the patented features included in this lot include the grip safety, the slide, the dropping barrel lock, the detachable magazine in the grip and the slide return spring placed under, over, and

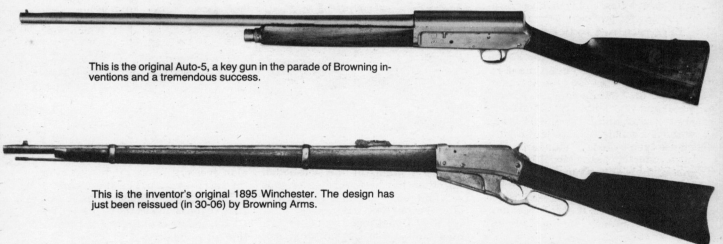

This is the original Auto-5, a key gun in the parade of Browning inventions and a tremendous success.

This is the inventor's original 1895 Winchester. The design has just been reissued (in 30-06) by Browning Arms.

work led to the large number of patents applied for in 1892. They came in two lots, one early in the year and one quite late. He applied for few in 1893, but in that year he designed the most famous lever gun of them all—the Model 1894 Winchester (524,702), still in production.

Designed for the family of black powder intermediate cartridges, the 32-40 and 38-55, the Model 1894 was immediately adapted to the 30-30 Winchester. The designation stood for 30 caliber and 30 grains of SMOKE-LESS powder. It was a revolution. The big 45's and 50's thinned out quickly, as the superior ballistics and power of the world's first sporting smokeless powder cartridge rendered them, and the heavy rifles they needed, obsolete. It is noteworthy that the Model 1894 required *no* changes in the action design to withstand the doubled pressure of the smokeless loads; designed for black powder, it strate some ideas for automatic arms. Also in 1894, he designed and tested a gas operated semi-automatic pistol with a potato digger-type swinging lever which swung upward instead of downwards.

In 1895, John sold Winchester another pump-action shotgun (550,778) which externally resembles the Stevens Model 520, a gun he designed for Stevens in 1903. In 1896, he sold Winchester another (577,281), externally similar but internally quite different. He also designed and made several more semi-automatic pistols.

Sometime during or before July of 1896, John arrived at the Colt's plant with four semi-automatic pistols. There were a few semi-auto pistols on the world market in 1896, but only the 1896 Mauser and a heavily modified version of the 1893 Borchardt are still remembered (as the Luger or P.08) as successful designs. He had:

1. A gas-operated pistol (580,923) around the barrel!

Try and think of a semi-auto pistol that does not use at least one of these key patented features.

John signed an agreement (24 July 1896) with Colt's which licensed Colt's to produce his pistols and promised licenses for any improvements to come, in exchange for royalties. It included Colt's being responsible for patenting the four pistols, at Colt's expense.

In 1896, he built a modified version of the blowback pistol (#4), and patented it (621,747) via Colt's.

A chance meeting with Hart O. Berg at Colt's in 1897 proved a major turning point in John's life. Berg was a representative of Fabrique Nationale d'Armes de Guerre of Belgium, a large plant originally set up to make M1889 Mauser rifles to re-equip the Belgian Army. With the Army contract fulfilled, they had nothing to make!

Ludwig Loewe and Co., a German firm, had sold FN their Mauser manufacturing tooling. By 1896, Loewe owned DWM, Mauser, the big Steyr plant called Osterreich Waffenfabrik (probably; this relationship is unclear), and Fegyver es Gepgyar of

that moved with the lever like a modern Browning BLR.

In 1899, Bennett requested a single shot 22 to compete with the cheap European Flobert rifles then flooding the U.S. market. John designed the bolt-action Model 1900 Winchester

onto the trigger guard. Push a 22 shell into the open breech, aim, and pull the trigger. This unhooks the block. The spring tosses the block upward, behind the shell, and the trigger vanishes upward. Disconcerting at first, no doubt! As the block gets to the top of its travel, a fixed firing pin digs in and fires the shell. Push the block down, and pluck out the empty. Why no enterprising small business-

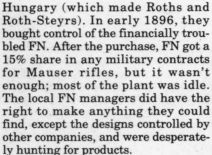

Hungary (which made Roths and Roth-Steyrs). In early 1896, they bought control of the financially troubled FN. After the purchase, FN got a 15% share in any military contracts for Mauser rifles, but it wasn't enough; most of the plant was idle. The local FN managers did have the right to make anything they could find, except the designs controlled by other companies, and were desperately hunting for products.

Berg returned to Belgium with John's modified blowback pistol (621,747) and a license for FN to make it for the European market. Smaller than the 1896 type. it was in 32 ACP or 7.65mm caliber, pocket sized, and very slim. The FN managers tested it, and it fired 500 rounds without a bobble, an excellent performance even by today's standards. Put into production as the Model 1899 and immediately slightly modified, it was renamed the Model 1900 (to take advantage of the turn of the century?), it sold like hot cakes. It also gave a new word to the French language: browning—an automatic pistol.

There was a complex Browning-Colt-FN agreement, dating from July, 1897, which gave the European market to FN, the Americas to Colt, and shared the British areas; John licensed each of them to make his designs, and each decided what to produce. They paid each other royalties for sales infringing on each other's exclusive territories. This agreement, with minor modifications from time to time, ran at least to the start of World War I, and probably later. The two companies co-operated and communicated, as we shall see.

In 1897, John sold Bennett a box magazine lever-action rifle (599,595) in 236 Lee Navy caliber. It had an incredibly short receiver. He sold Winchester another (619,132), in 30 caliber, in 1898. There were two differing rifles made to this basic design, one with a one-piece stock and the other with a flush magazine. Both had extremely short receivers, and triggers

This is Lt. Val Browning posing, in 1917, with an early BAR. The modified 1892 Winchester above, probably a 44-40, was originally a full-auto potato-digger, now is semi-auto.

(632,094) for him, the only bolt-action gun, other than his first repeater, that I can find record of him designing.

Remember the ultra-simple 22 (511,677) I mentioned as being patented, but not sold, in 1892? John did. It was even simpler than the hinged breech Flobert—so John sold it to Bennett. He knew that Bennett would not make it, because it was a mechanical joke, and Bennett took his company's prestige seriously. Equally, he knew Bennett would have to buy it—if someone else started producing it, nothing could be made cheaper or easier. There were four working rifles of this design, with minor variations in the extraction method. They are now in the Winchester museum, and the patent has expired. Does anyone want to produce the world's cheapest 22?

This tiny rifle worked like this: The rifle has no trigger in the trigger guard, so put your thumb on top of the breech block and push it down against spring tension. As it slides down, the apparently missing trigger (which is just a section of the block) appears, coming downward into the trigger guard. Fully down, the block hooks

man ever put it into production after the patent expired, I can't imagine!

The bolt-action Model 1900 22 sold well, reappearing as the 02, 04, 99, 36, 58, 60, and 68 over the years. Production hit 1,458,606.

By March of 1899, John had a semi-automatic shotgun ready for Winchester. While no one else had figured out how to make an auto shotgun, John had made two! One is now known as the Browning Auto-5 (659,507; 689,283; 710,094; and 812,326), the Remington Model 11, and under several other names; the other was never produced, but used a Luger-style toggle action.

A large caliber semi-auto rifle (659,786) was patented at this time too, probably through Winchester. Its history is a bit obscure; patented in 1900, it did not appear as a commercial production gun until 1906, when it became the Remington Model 8, in 25, 30, and 35 Remington; in 1936 it became the Model 81. Remington halted production in 1950. It was also produced by FN, but did not prove popular in Europe. Its relationship to the Auto-5 quarrel are obscure.

The Auto-5 was the cause of the

break with Winchester. Bennett was, apparently, afraid of it. He wasn't sure that automatic firearms were here to stay, and he stalled for two years. He refused to buy it or produce it, and he refused to state definitely that he would not buy it or produce it. The prototypes were kept at Winchester for trials and patenting.

One day in 1902, an angry John Browning stalked into Bennett's office, determined to force a showdown. He demanded a huge fee for the Auto-5, but the killer was that he demanded royalties as well. Bennett stated that Winchester didn't pay royalties, and John stated that he no longer sold without getting royalties. John picked up his prototypes from the drafting room and left.

Winchester did the patent work (in John's name) on the Auto-5, but hadn't bought it, so John went to Remington to try and sell it. On January 8th, 1902, while he was waiting

FN-Browning manufacturing and selling business partnership that brought America so many fine firearms.

Interestingly enough, the Auto-5 was so good that no other really successful semi-auto shotgun design appeared until 1957, when the first gas-operated shotguns hit the market. The two keys to this situation were the bronze friction brake he invented, which handled the heavy recoil forces by dragging on the magazine tube, and the cocking handle. It was the only really good place to put a cocking handle, and he not only patented that point, he patented nearly every other place one *could* put it!

The Auto-5 has been made by FN, Remington, Savage, Daiwa, and, with minor modifications, by many others. It is still in production, and likely to stay in production. Millions have been made, in Belgium, America, Italy, and Japan.

This design was simultaneously produced as the Colt 32ACP and (later) 380ACP pocket pistols, based on a smaller handmade prototype. The pocket Colts were more successful, about 572,215 being made in 32 and about 150,000 in 380, with production running from 1902 to 1945. In 1903, John sold a pump shotgun (781,765) to Stevens, who produced it as the Model 520 for many years.

In 1904 or 05, John designed a really small pistol; the 25ACP Colt or 6.35mm FN. It was patented in Belgium through FN in 1905, and production began there in that year. From 1905 to 1940, some 1,080,408 6.35mm FN's were made in Belgium.

Colt decided to produce a 25 in 1906. American patent laws did not allow patenting John's design for FN in the U.S., since it had been patented elsewhere. This prevented a cottage industry in re-patenting foreign patents, but left the 25 unprotected in the U.S. FN provided drawings and a sample pistol to Colt's, and we have a problem. Colt's made a toolroom prototype with a hammer instead of a striker firing system like the FN; we know that, but was this John producing another type for Colt's, or Colt's re-doing the 25 nearer to the 32 by themselves?

In any case, Colt's actually manufactured a duplicate of the FN, starting production in 1909. Three patents were listed on the slide, but none of them are relevant to the pistol; it was an attempt to pretend it was covered by U.S. patents, apparently. In 1910, a real U.S. patent was applied as well; it covered John's new safety catch (947,478) for the 25, which doubled as a takedown latch. The 25 Colt was discontinued in 1946, after 500,000 had been made.

The series of heavy caliber Colt Brownings began with the original four from the 1896 contact. The M1900 38ACP (a longer and more powerful cartridge than the 380ACP) with two-link dropping barrel lockup was disappointing in commercial sales, but it was sold in small test quantities to the U.S. Army and Navy in 1900. Complaints about the 38-caliber and design problems led to John's patent 708,794 for a slide lock to hold the pistol open when empty, and to experiments in 41 and 45 calibers.

The 41 experiments died out, but John designed a 45 pistol (808,003) in 1905, and Colt's produced it. A hammerless (internal hammer) example of this pistol still exists.

The U.S. Army insisted on using a heavier bullet than the M1905's 200-

Here's the Hi-Power, handmade, and its 1923 patent profile; both are slimmer than the production models of 1935.

to see Marcellus Hartley, President of Remington, Hartley dropped dead of a heart attack. This resulted in John making a trip to Belgium, where he arranged for FN to produce the Auto-5. He also signed a contract to purchase 10,000 Auto-5's marked "Browning Automatic Arms Company" for the American market, which he reserved for his own company. This was the real start of the

It seems probable that John also took to FN, on this trip, the large prototype of the pistol (747,585) that became the 1903 FN in 9mm Browning Long caliber. It was a partial success as a military pistol. The FN version was adopted by seven countries, but only about 150,000 were ever made, and more than half of those were made by Husqvarna in Sweden for the Swedish armed forces.

grain, so the pistol was beefed up for the trials of 1906-07. It did well enough to be bought in test quantities for 1908 field trials, but Browning wasn't happy with it. He produced an almost totally new pistol (984,519) for the tests of 1909. This pistol, never produced, is basically an M1911 with the grip at 84 degrees to the slide instead of 74 degrees, and no manual safety. Complaints about grip angle caused John to make his 1910 version, recognizably an M1911, but still with no manual safety. The 1910 prototype is in Ogden.

The final, triumphantly successful M1911 I will leave to others to sing about; Lord knows there were enough people doing it, and have been for the last 70-plus years. I will add, however, mention of two little-known pistols from this series. There was a hammerless prototype of the 1909, and it's in Ogden. It looks just like a giant version of the Colt 32ACP pocket pistol, with an external slide locking lever added to the left side, and a safety catch. Even the grip safety looks like the 32ACP's.

There was also a 9.8mm toolroom version of the 1910 design fabricated at Colt's. It had features from both the 1910 and the 1911 prototypes, and wasn't quite either. Eugene Reising of Colt's claimed to have demonstrated it in Rumania, Serbia, and Bulgaria in 1911 and 1912. It probably died because Colt's had their plate running over, mass-producing M1911s for the U.S. armed forces.

Now, we back up a tad to 1910. John designed a 32ACP and 380ACP pistol for FN that year. It went into production as the M1910. With extended slide, barrel, magazine, and butt, it later became the military and police version, the M1922. About 572,590 M1910's and 396,865 M1922's were made by FN; there were the usual unlicensed copies everywhere, and a true copy made by DWM in Germany. Several European forces were equipped with the M1922, including the Yugoslav and Dutch armies, and the Belgian, Danish, French, Swedish, and Czech police. FN's still making M1910s.

In late 1912, Browning patented a lovely little takedown 22 semi-auto rifle. It was produced by FN, and by Remington as the Model 24 and 241, for many years. Barely a yard long, it breaks into two parts of equal length for storage and backpacking. It also had the best takedown system ever devised; it was adjustable. The chief fault of takedown rifles is that they get loose in their old age, but the Browning has an adjustment that

takes up the slack. It's nearly impossible to wear one out. Its only fault is its bottom ejection; I hate those hot cases entering my cuffs.

A request from the U.S. Army for a practice pistol in 22 caliber caused Colt's to try a 22 conversion unit for the M1911, but it was not a success. No records survive, except for a 1911 letter from Colt's, stating that a 22 version had proved impossible, and they were trying a 25ACP version of the M1911. As this would have defeated the purpose of cheap practice with rimfire cartridges, we understandably know of no further developments in this line. We don't know if John was involved; Colt's had other inventors in its string.

Springfield Armory did make a prototype M1911 look-alike in 22 Short rimfire, but it also died very young. Browning may have produced a 22 rimfire pistol in 1911, or did he? Bady has a photo (Fig. 91) of a pistol that is clearly a Browning handmade; he labels it as an internal bolt 22, and he's

The handmade Colt automatic pistol that became the "Woodsman."

wrong. That prototype is in Ogden; it's related to the first prototype of the Browning Hi-Power, and it probably dates from about 1923. It isn't a 22; it's probably in 9mm Luger.

The Master did produce a 22 prototype in 1915, Bady's Fig. 92, and it was tested and rejected by the U.S. Army in 1916. He made several other 22 pistols in 1914 and 1915, but only one (1,276,716) made it into production. That one was to become known as the Colt Woodsman, and it was made from 1915 to the late 1970s with minor variations. Some 540,000 were made. It was also copied, as in the Tala from Argentina.

By this time, World War I was raging, but the U.S. wasn't in it—yet. John knew that the U.S. might get in,

and then there would be a mighty rush to make arms. He already had a better machine gun (678,934) than the M1895, patented in 1900. The war in Europe, plus his own inventiveness, had spurred him to make improvements which were patented (1,293,021) in 1916. Tested at Springfield Armory in May, 1917, the water-cooled Browning in 30-06 fired 20,000 rounds without a malfunction or a broken part. It was then fired for a further 20,000 rounds, with the same result.

The test was so spectacularly successful that there were murmurs of disbelief; was the test gun rigged in some way? Ignoring the silliness of that idea, John felt obliged to answer it. A second toolroom gun was brought out, and it not only duplicated the performance of the first one, it actually fired a continuous burst lasting 48 minutes and 12 seconds. This incredible burst ended when the supply of available belted ammunition gave out. Such a phenomenal burst could, of course, only be fired with a water-cooled gun.

A second gun, first made by John in 1910 and also improved as the war loomed closer, was tested during the 1917 trials. This was a 15-pound light machine gun, in 30-06, with a 20-shot magazine. It was gas operated, and became known as the Browning Automatic Rifle (BAR). It served the U.S. through the 1950s.

Both guns were later manufactured in quantity by FN and others; for example, the BAR became standard in the Swedish army, and FN-made 30's are still used by the Israeli army.

Although it is not generally recognized, the FN General Purpose Machine Gun, now standard for many armies including the British, is a heavily modified, belt-fed BAR.

In late 1917, an American Army officer called on Browning to settle details of the government's rights to produce the M1911 Colt pistol, the BAR, and the M1917 machine gun for the duration of the war. The chief detail was the price; the officer made one bid, a flat cash sum for all rights. He stated that he knew the sum offered was only a fraction of what would go to John if he wanted royalties on the guns, even if only those already ordered for production were considered, so negotiations would probably be necessary. Browning didn't hesitate; he simply said: "Major, if that suits Uncle Sam, it's all right with me."

John M. Browning deserves to be remembered for that moment of patriotism. He actually received $750,000 for that contract; if he had insisted on the standard royalties he could have had for the asking, he would have received $12,704,350.

In 1917, John took an apartment in Hartford, and supervised the making of drawings and toolroom models of his guns. He checked the work of all the factories making his pistols, BAR, and M1917 machine guns (Colt in Hartford and Meriden, Conn; Westinghouse in Springfield, Mass; Marlin-Rockwell and Winchester in New Haven, Conn; and Remington in Ilion, NY). He cut red tape and worked quiet miracles, but there was a lesson to be dearly learned. The U.S. went to war with exactly 1100 obsolescent machine guns on hand; and it took time to tool up and produce all the guns that were needed. That war was over before the Army could be fully equipped with Browning guns, but they were ready for World War II.

General Pershing, commander of the U.S. Army in France, was faced by the first primitive German tanks. He promptly requested a gun, firing bullets of 670 grains minimum weight at a velocity of 2700 fps minimum. Springfield Armory tried and failed to produce such a gun, so John was called in. He made the 50-caliber Browning machine gun, and had it firing by September, 1918. It was scheduled for formal government acceptance trials on 11 Nov 1918. The armistice delayed the tests until the 15th, when John fired bursts of 100 to 150, and had no malfunctions in 877 rounds.

The 50 looks like a scaled-up 30-06, but it's more than that. It incorporates a hydraulic buffer to handle the massive recoil of the 50 BMG cartridge.

Both the 30 and the 50 developed into weapons systems as time rolled on. Water-cooled and air-cooled, light-barrelled and heavy-barrelled, one side feeding or either side feeding, slow fire or rapid fire, bipod, tripod, pedestal, or turret mounts, in aircraft at 30,000 feet and 40-below temperatures, in the mud of Viet Nam, in the

desert of North Africa, the Brownings went with the troops and the Brownings worked.

In one interesting area, the 50 was scaled up to become a 20mm aircraft cannon. Unfortunately, it was the Japanese who did this, and 20mm Brownings (which American experts said couldn't be made) were used against America from the wings of Japanese fighters. That was much later.

In 1918, somehow, Browning found time to prepare a little-known firearm, the Browning 30-18. It looked like an infantry rifle of the period, with a long stick magazine hanging out the bottom. From the magazine size, I think it may have been a development spurred by the idea of the Pedersen device. The Pedersen device temporarily converted the Springfield bolt-action rifle into a semi-auto firing a cartridge like a long 32 pistol cartridge. The 30-18 is associated with FN, and the action reappeared in a line of French (MAS 38, etc.) submachine guns. The action used a bolt that moved at a slight angle to the bore to retard the bolt opening by friction.

By 26 July 1919, John was back at his normal trade. He applied for a patent (1,424,553) on a pump-action 22 rifle, and FN produced it for many years.

In the years 1920 through 1923, he had a big project; the U.S. Army had been asking him for a 37mm machine cannon. They had been trying to produce one for several years, with no success, and General C.C. Williams, Chief or Ordnance, finally decided only Browning could do it. John begged off, pleading that his work on sporting arms had him tied up. In 1920, though, he finally agreed, mostly because he knew he could do it. He also knew he'd never make a dime out of it in peacetime.

The Army sent him a few dummy cartridges, and noted that it would have to make up some solid-projectile ammunition; the only ammo they had on hand had explosive projectiles. John finished the gun in three months; the ammunition wasn't ready yet.

The 37mm was as usual a reliable, strong, and workmanlike gun. The Army promptly asked if it could be made more powerful, as the muzzle velocity of 1400 fps was a bit pathetic. John pointed out that that was the cartridge they supplied and asked to have the gun made for, then made a gun for 37mm cartridges producing 2000 fps, as requested. He then made another, for 37mm cartridges produc-

ing 3050 fps, again on request. The patents (1,525,065 to 1525,067) date from 1923 and 1924, but the guns did not go into production until 1935, nine years after John's death.

As the M4 and M9, the 37mm machine cannons were used in the Bell P-39 Airacobra and a few other planes. The Russians used the high velocity M9 in Lend-Lease Airacobras as a tank destroyer. Today, it would be an excellent weapon for Armored Personnel Carriers.

In 1923, the Superposed shotgun (1,578,638 and 1,578,639) was patented. Also in 1923, Browning patented the Hi-Power pistol (1,618,510). This final development in a line from the Colt M1900, M1905, M1911 family featured a double column magazine, cam unlocking, and a tangent elevating rear sight. It may have been designed to cash in on the lucrative Chinese market for shoulder-stocked pistols with large magazines, the result of Chinese laws banning ownership of rifles, but silent on pistols. Mauser, Astra, and others were selling well there; probably FN wanted a piece of the action. One feature in the patent drawings for the Hi-Power that doesn't appear in the finished gun is a trigger safety; the pistol could be put on safe by swinging the trigger forward and up. It was his last patent, and it's still in production.

John Moses Browning died of heart failure in the office of his son, Val Browning, at FN on the twenty-sixth of November, 1926. The Master is gone, but his guns still proclaim his mastery. No one has taken his place. It is unlikely anyone ever will. Honor his memory; we owe him much. ●

Editor's Note: GUN DIGEST thanks the Browning Arms Co. for the photos used here. K.W.

BIBLIOGRAPHY

John M. Browning, American Gunmaker; Doubleday & Co. Inc; John Browning and Curt Gentry, 1964

Handguns of the World; Stackpole Books; Edward C. Ezell, 1981

Colt Automatic Pistols; Borden Publishing Co; Donald B. Bady, 1973

The World's Assault Rifles; TBN Enterprises, Daniel O. Musgrave and Thomas B Nelson

The World's Machine Pistols and Submachine Guns, Vol IIa; TBN Enterprises; Thomas B. Nelson and Daniel O. Musgrave, 1980

Mauser Bolt Rifles, Third Edition; F. Brownell & Son, Publishers, Inc; Ludwig Olsen, 1976

Like son, like father . . .

Another Browning's Rifle

by ROBERT K. SHERWOOD

Johnathan Edmund Browning and his great great great-grandfather's rifle. This Ed Browning does airplanes, not guns.

SOME PORTION of genius seems to be a genetic entity. The genius behind the Browning name is well known in our world of firearms and most of us have a reasonable knowledge of the life and achievements of John Moses Browning, the famous Ogden, Utah, designer of firearms.

Certainly possessed of the spark that made the flame was his father, Johnathan Edmund Browning. He had his genius and it showed up in some early inventions, chiefly his harmonica rifle. When we consider why he designed his rifle and what he executed it with and for, it's plain to see.

There have been other Johnathan Edmund Brownings—three of them. Two of them were gunsmiths, but the one that lives across town from me expresses his talents down other avenues and hasn't much to do with ri-

fles. He did construct and sponsor aircraft in certain races that set speed records as yet unbroken. He and his Red Baron team put a jet racer in the air in 1977 that set a still-standing blowtorch speed record and in 1979 his much modified F-51 set a propdriven record, likewise still standing out in front. With typical Browning persistence this Johnathan Edmund Browning would like to break his own records before someone else does.

He does have to do with one rifle, and I will travel quite a way before I find another rifle that fascinates me quite as much. It is a brass-framed slide or "harmonica" rifle that has been in the ownership of one Browning or another since the original Johnathan Edmund Browning constructed it.

This Browning is a five-shot repeat-

er, with a five-shot chamber bar that slides through the frame horizontally. The chambers have a capacity of about 70 grains of FFg; its caliber is about 45. The nipples are milled into the chamber block, each offset to the right of the chamber it fires. It uses #11 caps.

The chamber bar is moved manually through the frame and that makes it one of the first he made.

In later underhammer slide rifles, the raising and returning of the camming lever supposedly repositioned the chamber bar for the next shot. Most of this type that Browning made were underhammer and the tempered trigger guard was used as a hammer mainspring. These also had 40¾-inch barrels while this overhammer measured 30¾ inches in tube.

All his slide rifles had brass frames, and this factor constituted their only real weakness. Brass was much used in mid-19th century firearms, but it does tend to stretch under repeated recoil, so the heavy use most firearms got precluded long service life. The good condition of Ed's rifle is accounted for by the fact that the original JEB was never allowed to go to war, being kept so busy he had little time for hunting, except on his brief trip across the plains from Council Bluffs to Ogden.

The rifle has no serial number, no date and no name stamped on it. There is a feathery design stamped on the barrel just ahead of the receiver, which may be a code marking; more of the reasons for this later. Had the piece not always been in the possession of the original JEB or in that of one of his direct descendants it would

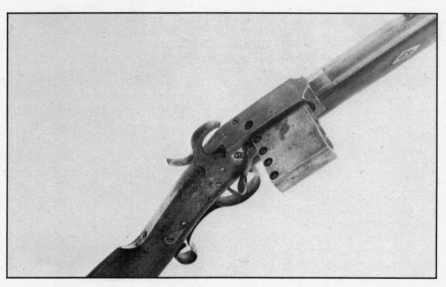
Lever on side of receiver cams magazine forward; releases it to slide to next chamber.

be impossible to identify it as an authentic Browning. Throughout his life Johnathan evidenced small concern for such matters, and there was a part of his life when prudence might have dictated guns to go unsigned.

To understand the history of this rifle and of its type, we must consider the history of Johnathan Edmund Browning and his chosen church that had such a profound influence on his life and the course of it.

Johnathan Edmund Browning was born in Tennessee on a Brushy Fork of Bledsoe Creek about 30 miles south of Nashville, on October 22, 1805. He grew up on a hard-luck farm there, and his talents were turned to mechanical repairs at an early age. He once was paid an unserviceable flintlock rifle for farm work he had done

for a neighbor. He repaired the rifle to serviceability and sold it back to the neighbor for $4.00. After that, he worked for some time at gun repair in a blacksmith's shop, and by the time he turned 19 he was known as the local gunsmith.

At that time he traveled to Nashville, finding work and training in the shop of Samuel Porter. At the end of three months, young Browning was making rifles from scratch, constructing and finishing barrels and all, without assistance. His industry and ability so impressed Porter that the smith offered him a share of the business, but Browning declined. He had a girl back in Brushy Fork, and, as we shall see, women were to be important entities in his life, several of them, anyway.

He returned to Bledsoe Creek, bearing gifts of tools from Porter, and located a shop near Gallatin, Tennessee, where he turned out single shot muzzle-loading rifles and shotguns. Some sources call these early Brownings models of function, but note they usually bore some tool marks and hammer dents. None of these guns survive today, or if they do, their origins are not known. Not many bore a stamp. Some were used in the Seminole war, and certainly in the Blackhawk War.

Westering fever was epidemic in the late 1820s, and the Browning family as a group had had enough of trying to make a living on farms in Tennessee. Several other family members went to the then-new territory of Illinois, and in 1832 Johnathan received word from a relative that there was an excellent location for a gunsmith at Quincy, Illinois. He closed his

Brushy Fork shop and wagoned his family and his possessions, arriving in Quincy early in 1834.

The demand for gun manufacture and repair in this town of 734 souls was high indeed. Here, in what was shortly a better-equipped shop than the one in Tennessee, Browning began experimenting and inventing repeating rifles. The first he made were something like Colts, except that they were sidehammers and the cylinders were turned by hand. He made some revolving pistols on the same principle; later he would copy Colts more closely. And he continued to make rugged conventional muzzle-loading rifles.

It was in this period of his life, incidentally, that he made the acquaintance of and was friendly with an obscure traveling lawyer named Abraham Lincoln. Lincoln is known to have been a guest of Browning's on several occasions.

The revolving rifles taxed Browning's resources, although he could and did make them. The precision of chamber spacing and position in the cylinder made making a revolver slow. Browning turned to the straight feed principle and made his slide rifle. If a chamber varied a bit in its distance from one neighbor and from that to the next, it made little difference, and it was easier to drill them exactly spaced in a horizontal line than it was in a circle anyway. It was also simpler to lock them into battery position than it was in the wheel guns.

The lever that locked the individual chambers into firing place also cammed a flanged extension of each chamber into a tapered recess in the barrel breech, making a better gas seal than any revolver possessed at the time, and better than most of them have today. This not only improved velocity and reduced backspit, it rendered far less likely the multiple discharges the big Colt rifles were infamous for.

Most of these rifles were of five-shot capacity, but Browning advertised and undoubtedly made some 25-rounders, although none survive today. Each rifle was sold with two slides or magazines and these, when fully loaded, gave the shooter 10 fairly rapid shots without reloading. The larger the slide the more unwieldy the rifle had to be, and indeed less bulk was the only advantage of the revolving rifle over the harmonica gun.

The slide rifle was a simple thing to manufacture; it could be hammered out in a fraction of the time required to produce a revolving rifle; and its simplicity and ruggedness was less liable to parts breakage. The one weakness was the brass receiver. I have seen a copy of this rifle with an iron frame and changeable nipples that screwed into threaded vent holes in the magazine.

For six years Browning designed and built rifles and built a good name as a craftsman thereby. He attracted a lot of attention, being the only good gunmaker for many miles. Quincy was the focal point of the Mormon settlement as these persecuted folk were driven out of Missouri; many of Johnathan's customers were Mormons; and he was converted to that faith in 1840. The exact circumstances surrounding his conversion are not known today, but certainly the need of the Latter Day Saints for weapons of war had something to do with their recruiting zeal as they sought the conversion of the inventor-smith.

The formational history of this radically different religious group had been marked with strife and violence. They had been subjected to riot violence and farm burnings in Missouri and Ohio, and on October 25, 1883, three companies of Mormons under a Captain Patten attacked and routed a force of Missouri State Militia commanded by a Captain Bogart at Crooked River. The militia lost one killed, six wounded, and the Mormons two dead and nine wounded. The militia retreated in some disorder.

Governor Boggs of Missouri issued his famous extermination order on October 27 of that year and on October 30, Missouri State Militia commanded by Col. William O. Jennings slew 17 and severely wounded 12 at Haun's Mill, near Far West, Missouri. Some of the casualties were children as young as 10; some were women. This small action fueled Mormon hatred and reprisals. They had earlier formed a counter-terrorist group called the Danites and these did some looting, burning, and a few sporadic killings.

The Mormon arrival in Illinois was marked by severe riots and mob violence and they fought back on several occasions. It should be noted that the hatred with which the Mormons were greeted had less to do with their religious beliefs and practices than it did with the rapidity of the group's growth and the fact that they constituted a solid and formidable voting bloc which could well affect such issues as state's rights and slavery.

Joseph Smith, styled the Prophet by his followers and the founder and leader of the Mormon Church, was a militant. He recruited and trained the

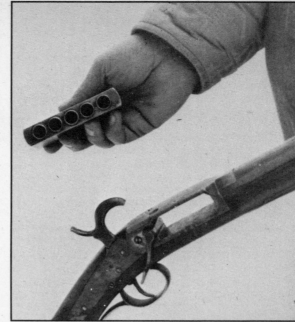

Five-shooter was apparently the best compromise between portability and firepower.

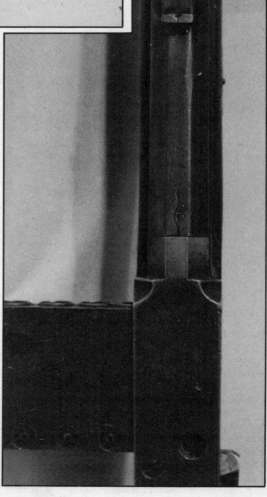

The device on the top barrel flat may be what distinguishes this Browning harmonica rifle from all the rest.

Nauvoo Legion in 1841. This body of troops was entirely Mormon and was nominally a component of the Illinois State Militia. By 1842, the group numbered 1600 foot and 400 horse soldiers and was a force to be reckoned with. Joseph Smith held the rank of Lt. General; at least he professed and uniformed for it.

The Legion furnished some of its own rifles and carbines, and some were made by Browning, but a good part of the unit's armament, including cannon, was furnished by the State of Illinois. It was, in fact, the simplest way to train and equip Mormons for wars to come. Some slide rifles were furnished to selected riflemen in the Legion; however only about 400 of all types of this rifle were made, at least by Browning, so the claim of some Mormons that he armed the Legion is wishful thinking.

Smith's power and following was growing rapidly, and the idea that such a leader had a maverick unit of well-trained and well-armed militia was not one some factions liked. The building of the Mormon capitol at Nauvoo was viewed with further apprehension.

Johnathan moved his shop to the rapidly growing city of Nauvoo in 1842, building there a house and shop of handmade bricks that still stands today. His production was relatively high for the next two years. Armed men often guarded Joseph Smith, even in the Mormon stronghold, and

the state all the cannons and muskets it had furnished the Legion and began the retreat across Iowa in the winter of 1846. This was a hard trek.

Thus it is seen that to stamp one's name on a rifle that was to be carried by combatant Mormons might lead to serious reprisal when the rifle was found with a Danite or Legionaire corpse. This might well account for Johnathan's increasing reluctance to put his name on a rifle or pistol of his manufacture.

He arrived at what is now Council Bluffs in the spring of 1846 and set up shop on Mosquito Creek, 8 miles south of Kanesville. In the summer of 1846, he attempted to volunteer for the Mormon Battalion, to fight against Mexico under General Winfield Scott, but was forbidden to do so by Brigham Young. He was the best and perhaps the only gunsmith and artisan in metal they had and Young was not about to let him march off to Mexico.

Browning resumed the production

Mormons remaining at Nauvoo. In three days of fire exchange, the Mormons lost four and the Guerrillas seven. The wounded were not recorded. Certainly, Browning rifles were used in this last episode in this region.

Browning did not go to the Mormon capitol at Salt Lake City, but settled instead in Ogden, twenty or so miles to the north. There he reassembled his shop and began the manufacture and repair of practically any and all hardware used by the colony. He still made some guns and repaired many, but he did not invent any new types. He was literally spread too thin, for the rest of his productive life. He did marry two more women, after the Mormon fashion of the day, and, in all, he fathered 22 children. John Moses Browning was the first born of his union with Elizabeth, his second wife.

In 1853, the settlers fought the Walker War; this one lasted until May of 1854, and something over 50 Mormons and an undetermined number of Ute Indians were killed. The

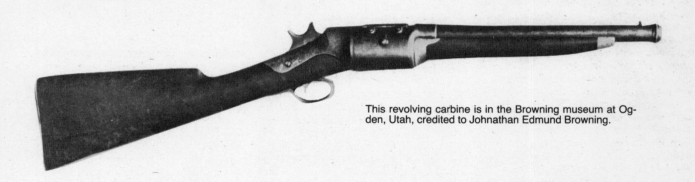

This revolving carbine is in the Browning museum at Ogden, Utah, credited to Johnathan Edmund Browning.

supplementary weapons were needed by the Legion. Then on June 25, 1844, Joseph Smith and his brother Hyrum were imprisoned, though left with small arms, in the Carthage, Illinois, jail, on a charge of treason against the state of Illinois. On June 27, they were murdered by a mob that stormed the jail.

Then began the Mormon exodus from Illinois, under the leadership of Brigham Young, and Johnathan went with it, with what he could salvage from his shop. Young wisely decided that though the Legion was a considerable force and could whip much that might immediately be brought against it, they would eventually be overwhelmed by the state and Federal forces that might ultimately infest the area. He gave up to

and repair of guns in his shop and, by order of Young, broadened his activities to any hardware fabrication and repair needed by the Mormons for their westward migration. Young was convinced that they could find no peace in lands governed by the United States, and he proposed to locate New Zion far to the west, in lands nominally owned by Mexico.

To move thousands of Mormons from Iowa to what is now Utah was a big task and no one had more to do with the logistics and ordnance of it than Johnathan Browning. He earnestly desired to go, but Young kept him at the staging area at Mosquito Creek until 1852. He missed, of course, the final Midwestern battle of Mormon and "Gentile," when 800 Illinois Carthage Guerillas attacked the

slide rifles gained a reputation in this conflict; often the Indians would draw the first volley of the Legion at extreme range and then rush in, trying to catch the militiamen before they could reload. The rapid fire of the slide rifles was enough usually to back off those it didn't kill.

Johnathan is reputed to have made some Colt Dragoon copies to arm the officers of the Nauvoo Legion when they set out to oppose the invasion of Utah by General Albert Sidney Johnston in 1857. He did not stamp any of these, but finely crafted copies of the big Colt have turned up around Ogden through the years. They cannot be verified as Brownings, but who else could have made them?

This "conflict" was a sparring and cattle-stampeding exercise; there was never an exchange of gunfire between the Legion and Johnston's soldiers. But September 7 of 1857 saw a much bloodier fray begin. Mormons allied with Indians surrounded a wagon company of Missourian emigrants in southern Utah at the Mountain Meadows, fighting with them until September 11, when the emigrants surrendered, only to be slain by their captors. In all, 120 men, women and children were killed by the joint efforts of Mormons and Indians. The church and Brigham Young disavowed any connection with the massacre, but the participants in the slaughter were Nauvoo Legionaires. It is late now to assign blame, perhaps, but it is one the Mormons will not quite live down. And Browning's guns were surely used then.

And there were further Indian fights. The Sanpete County War saw the defeat of the Utahs by the Mor-

Johnathan spent his last days in the shop, marveling at the work accomplished by John and three brothers. He died in 1879; to the end of his days he evidenced great pride and affection for his own mainstay, the slide rifle.

Ed Browning and I regard his slide rifle with great curiosity. We cannot find a date on it, but it was most likely made in the Quincy shop. It is 10 inches shorter in the barrel than the underhammers. I have never seen another overhammer, so I know not if this one is unique. There were so few of the overhammers made, we're told, that they are each unique. The underhammers were obviously simpler to make and speed of fabrication was JEB's goal in producing the type anyway.

It is Ed Browning's supposition that this particular rifle was never sold, that it was kept as the personal rifle of the original Johnathan Edmund

from Utah, saying that it was made by and had belonged to *his* grandfather, the old patriarch, the first gunsmithing Browning.

In summary, I have concluded it would be a lot easier to cut a phony name and date on a fake than it would be to get a lie out of Ed Browning. Were the piece in the possession of a non-Browning, its authenticity might be discussable, but considering the fact that it has been handed down from one JEB to another through the years and has never gone anywhere else leaves me with no choice but to call it authentic. The Brownings claim it and I don't know of anyone qualified to argue with them.

Ed thinks a museum ought to have it. He says that way people to whom this bit of history means more to than it does to him might see and perhaps handle the firearm. Me, I hope it is a nearby museum. ●

This underhammer boot pistol from the Ogden museum is unmarked, but may very well be another Johnathan gun—it's of the right era.

mons. Losses of the Saints in killed were 55, and the number of Indians killed though much greater, is not known. This brief and bloody action took place in April of 1865. And there were two short sharp fights near Spanish Fork with Shoshones in 1863; about 30 Saints were killed in the two actions.

The end of the conflicts spelled the end of Johnathan's work with rifles. He was employed on Young's command to make mills, wagons and any hardware needed by colonists as they went out to found new communities; he had to salvage metal from burned Army wagons; and he barely found time to make smiths of his sons.

Smiths they became, obviously, and

Browning. The inventor never fired a recorded shot in anger in his life, but certainly the possibility that he might have to was a tangible thing for much of his time. Did he fancy that he might carry it as he marched away with the Mormon Battalion? He did intend to do this, and carrying someone else's rifle would have been virtually out of the question.

Records show that when Johnathan joined the western movement of Mormons he was appointed captain of 10 wagons in the company commanded by Henry Miller. He was also the primary meat hunter for Miller's company, shooting buffalo and antelope to feed the migrants. He gained a reputation as an unerring shot at this work. Was this the rifle he used? Considering his pride in and liking for the slide rifle, it is likely, and if not this one, another like it. Neither family or historical records mention another.

Some might challenge the authenticity of the piece because it bears no name. I have scrutinized the Browning family genealogy and our Johnathan Edmund Browning IV, known as "Ed" here in Idaho Falls, is a direct descendent of the Brushy Fork gunsmith, Johnathan Edmund Browning. He has told me often how his grandfather, Johnathan Edmund Browning III, brought him this rifle

Bibliography

Allen, James B. and Glen M. Leonard; *A History of the Church of The Latter-Day Saints*, Deseret Books Company, Salt Lake City, Utah, 1976.

Bancroft, Hubert Howe; *The History of Utah*, The History Company Publishers, San Francisco, California, 1890.

Browning, Johanathan E. "Ed" in conversation; Idaho Falls, Idaho, 1983, 1984.

Browning, John and Gentry, Curt; *John Browning, American Gunmaker*, Doubleday and Company, Inc., Garden City, New York, 1964.

Roberts, B.H.; *A Comprehensive History of the Church of Jesus Christ of the Latter Day Saints, Century I in 6 Volumes* (vols I & II), Deseret News Press, Salt Lake City, Utah, 1930.

Russell, Carl P.; *Guns on the Early Frontier*, University of California, Berkeley, California, 1957.

Sharpe, Phillip Burdette; *The Rifle in America*, 4th Edition, Funk & Wagnalls, New York, New York, 1958.

Wadsworth, Nelson; "The Guns of Johnathan Browning," in *Guns Managzine*, August, 1967.

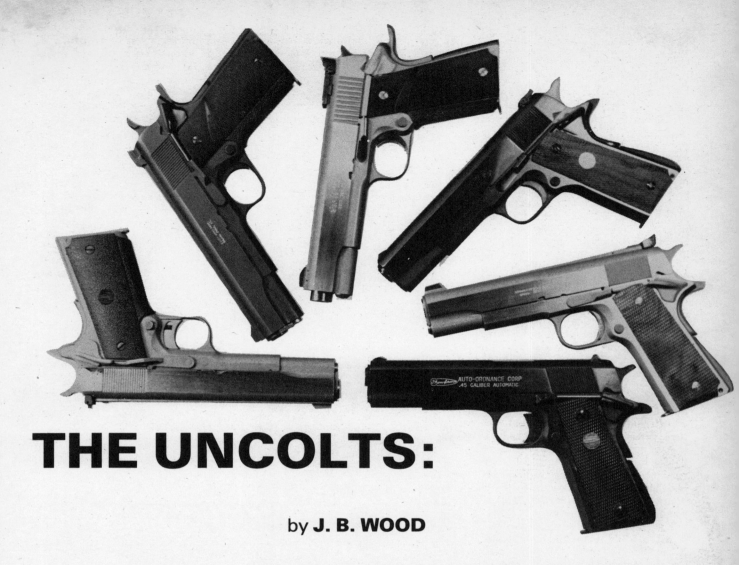

THE UNCOLTS:

by J. B. WOOD

IF JOHN MOSES Browning were alive today, he might be pleased to see how his design of 75 years ago has lasted and, in recent years, proliferated. In his own time, he saw his 1911 U.S. Government Model pistol produced in a commercial version by Colt, and made for military use by Colt and several other government contractors. In Norway, a slightly-modified version was made under license as their Model 1914, and numerous unlicensed copies were made in Spain and elsewhere. A licensed copy was also later made in Argentina for military use.

Down through the years, the Colt company has continued to make the pistol. Along the way, they have made several modifications to the original design, but the basic pattern has been unchanged. In addition to the original 45 Auto chambering, the pistol was made available in 38 Super, and later in 9mm Parabellum. A shortened version in all three calibers was offered as the Commander, with a choice of frames in steel or lightweight alloy. A target model of the full-sized gun, the National Match, later evolved into the excellent Gold Cup.

Inside, the Colt engineers have made some subtle changes. Lately, a collet-type muzzle bushing grips the barrel for more consistent position-ing, and the introduction of this feature gave the pistol a new designation, "Mark IV/Series 70." More recently, the addition of an automatic internal firing pin block safety system created the "Mark IV/Series 80." Last year, Colt introduced their "Combat Grade" model, with special sights and ejection port, a wrap-around Pachmayr rubber grip, a longer trigger, and a beveled magazine entry, among other features.

Meanwhile, since the basic design has long been out-of-patent, others have wisely decided to make their own versions of the old war-horse. These range from virtually identical copies to very innovative extensions

U.S.-Made Pistols of 1911 Pattern

of the pattern. One stainless-steel copy, the Vega, was short-lived, but the rest are doing quite well. Over the past few weeks, I've tried seven of them, and all are a credit to the original Browning concept.

AMT

The first successful stainless-steel version, Harry Sanford's AMT Hardballer, is presently offered in both a standard size and a Long Slide, the latter with seven-inch barrel. Other features of both models are extended safety and slide latch levers, fully adjustable rear sights, and skeletonized triggers with adjustable stop screws. The grip is a wrap-around rubber type by Supreme. A raised and ribbed sighting plane runs the full length of the slide top.

The mainspring housing is straight, with vertical serrations, the one favored by many serious shooters. Firing the Long Slide model was, for me, an interesting and educational experience. Up to now, seeing photos of some of the custom long slide pistols, I had always wondered . . . well, now I know. The recoil and muzzle whip are reduced, and the sight picture, because of the extended radius, is enhanced. The extra two inches of barrel length give a slightly higher velocity, and the accuracy is absolutely deadly. Finally, I expected the handling to be a bit awkward, and it wasn't.

The AMT guns have matte finishes on all surfaces except for the side flats of the slide, the magazine, the barrel, and the plug and bushing. The overall fit and finish are excellent. At the range, the functioning was perfect.

(I'll note here that I fired all of the guns with regular 45 full-jacket rounds by Federal and Hornady/Frontier. I was firing them for functioning and accuracy, and not as combat pieces, so I didn't try hollow points. Remarkably, even though most of these guns were in-the-box new, there was not a single incident of misfeeding or incomplete ejection—tribute to Mr. Browning's design, and good ammunition.)

Detonics

Another stainless-steel entry has been around for a while in abbreviated form—the Detonics. The finely-made small guns have now been joined by the Scoremaster, a full-sized 45 that has several special features. Starting from the top, there's a fully-adjustable Bo-Mar rear sight, and a double-pinned ramp front sight with an inset orange "T" in its rear face. The barrel is pure Detonics design,

The Thompson by Auto-Ordnance carries the old bullet logo, true-to-type fit and finish.

The Arminex Trifire, long slide version, has all the tricks, can go to all three: 45, 38 Super, 9mm.

The Randall Service Model is all stainless steel, has surface differences, but runs mostly true to 1911 form.

The new Detonics Scoremaster is the firm's first full-size 1911. Barrel and allied parts are different.

The MS-Safari Arms Enforcer is the small one; they make them big, too, with a wide array of options.

The slide and frame are by Essex, the rest from assorted sources; it works really well, Wood says.

with a coned front section that is hand-fitted to the slide interior, so there's no bushing. The buffered recoil spring system is also of Detonics design.

A graceful full-beavertail extension tops the grip safety, to eliminate any chance of hammer-bite. The manual safety is of standard design, but is ambidextrous, and the opposite unit on the right side is a beautiful piece of engineering. The grip is wrap-around rubber by Pachmayr, and the rear of the straight mainspring housing is also checkered rubber. The magazine entry is beveled, and the release button is high-profile. The vertically-grooved trigger has an Allen screw for stop adjustment.

This pistol was obviously designed for serious competition, not casual shooting, and my range-testing methods sometimes border on plinking. Even so, it performed beautifully. The unique "coned" effect at the muzzle results in an external diameter of .695", a little over $11/16$ of an inch, and this gives the effect of a "bull barrel"—a slight muzzle heaviness and reduced whip during recoil. Accuracy was outstanding. The fit and finish are up to Detonics standards—impeccable.

Randall

A newcomer to the stainless-steel 1911 group is the Randall, and from the start this California firm has concentrated on one of the old design's main points, reliability. This is not to say, though, that they have neglected other important features. The Randall is made 100% of stainless steel, a special alloy, and the barrel has ten-groove rifling. A solid recoil spring guide is used. The ejection port is opened, and the magazine entry is beveled. The gun is available with either fixed combat-style sights (stainless, but black-finished), or with fully-adjustable Millets. Long or short triggers are optional, and both have a stop-screw.

On the Service Model, Randall stays very close to the original pattern, except for the special recoil spring guide and a combat safety that is slightly extended at the front of the lever. The Randall has the arched mainspring housing of the 1911A1, with vertical grooving. The finish is satin, slightly brighter on the sides, but still not highly reflective. The grips are checkered walnut, and on my Randall they have a nice grain pattern. The fitting of the steel parts is precise, and all lines and flats are very clean.

At the range, I found that the Randall performed as well as it looked. I didn't fire from a rest at formal targets with any of the pistols, but some of my casual targets were smaller than the standard center bull, and the pistol hit them with regularity. Later, when there's time and the weather is better, I'm going to find out if that ten-groove barrel is as superior as they claim. For now, it's enough to say that it will consistently nail a soft-drink can at 25 yards, and that's very good. In addition to the Service Model, there are five others, including lightweight and shortened versions, and this year they introduced a true mirror-image left-handed model.

Auto-Ordnance

Moving out of the stainless-steel group, there's a pistol that probably comes closest to the military-issue Government Model, and it's the Thompson by Auto-Ordnance. If the name is familiar, it's because they're also the makers of the modern-day version of the famed Thompson Submachinegun and the Thompson Semi-Auto Carbine. In fact, the pistol carries the well-known bullet/signature trademark on its slide and on the grip medallions. The Thompson is supposed to be a Spartan, no-frills gun, and it costs somewhat less than the others, but there are a few surprises.

As standard equipment, it has a long-style trigger that is screw-adjustable for over-travel, and an arched, checkered mainspring housing. The hammer is the old, comfortable wide-spur model with fine checkering, and I'd swear that the smooth magazine is original military issue from a high-quality supplier. For a pistol that's intended to be utilitarian, the fit and finish are surprisingly good. The surface is a nice blue, matte on the top and undersides, and a medium polish on the sides of the slide and frame.

The sights are the standard fixed military type, and on my pistol they were perfectly aligned for a center hold at 25 yards. For those who are afflicted with World War II nostalgia, the Thompson will have a magical effect—it feels exactly like a GI-issue 45, and to a great extent also looks like one. It does, however, shoot much better than most of them did. Auto-Ordnance also offers the same gun in 9mm Parabellum and 38 Super.

Essex

The next one on our list is not available as a finished pistol. The Essex Arms Corporation of Island Pond, Vermont, makes a nicely-finished frame and slide, for the shooter who

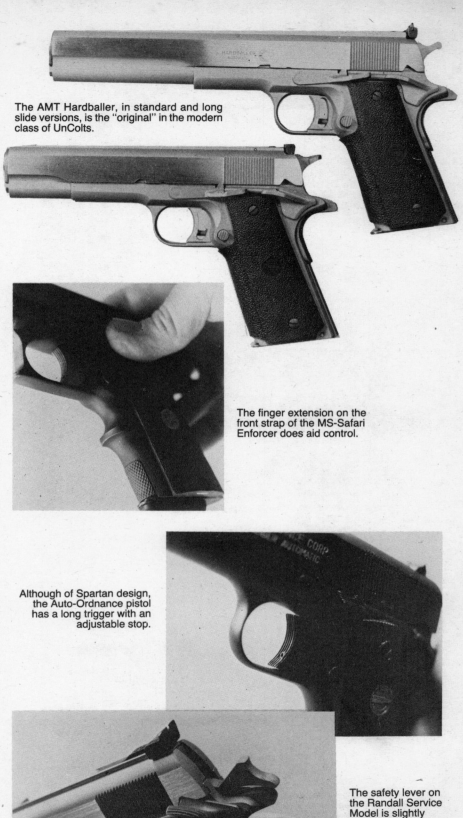

The AMT Hardballer, in standard and long slide versions, is the "original" in the modern class of UnColts.

The finger extension on the front strap of the MS-Safari Enforcer does aid control.

Although of Spartan design, the Auto-Ordnance pistol has a long trigger with an adjustable stop.

The safety lever on the Randall Service Model is slightly extended; the sight is by Mitchell.

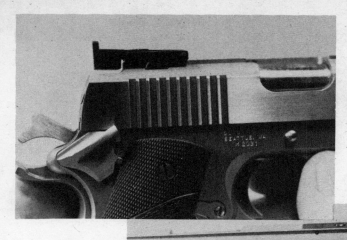

The ambidextrous safety on the Detonics Scoremaster is especially well-designed.

The slide latch and the safety are both extended on the Hardballer.

prefers to build his own gun. A while back, a friend gave me an Essex frame and slide, and over a few months time I gradually put together a 45 Auto that has proved to be both dependable and accurate. The finish on my Essex is either a matte blue or very smooth Parkerizing, I've never established which. A wide raised solid rib extends the full length of the slide top, and it has five deep grooves.

The front sight cut and aperture were there, but the rear of the rib was left uncut, to allow the individual to decide what type of rear sight was wanted. I chose an MMC combat-style with white outline, and a matching bar-cross front blade. An old-style wide-spur hammer was installed, and a standard safety. All of the smaller internal parts were standard, either U.S. surplus or Colt. The stainless magazine originated from the now-departed Vega.

Rubber wrap-around grips from Pachmayr were used. The barrel bushing, recoil spring unit, slide latch, and one-piece solid backstrap were from Arminex, Ltd. I beveled the magazine entry. Except for that and the mounting of the sights, no other gunsmithing was done. By fortunate accident, the safety and the sear engagement were perfect as installed, and the barrel required no fit-ting. When one of these Frankenstein jobs is assembled, that's not always the case. By now I've probably put at least a thousand rounds through my Essex, and it has given me no problems with any type of factory ammo.

MS-Safari Arms

Long before I actually fired one, I looked at the photos of the MS-Safari Arms Enforcer, and wondered about the "hump" on the frontstrap, between the second and third fingers. Was it comfortable? Did it have any real purpose? Now that I've fired an Enforcer extensively, I have the answers: Yes, and Yes.

MS-Safari makes several models, including full-sized and special target/competition versions, but the one I have is their smaller gun. The barrel is 3 $\frac{15}{16}$ inches, and the height is 5¼ inches, with the shortened magazine holding six rounds.

On an MS-Safari pistol, you can choose the features you want, such as an extended slide latch, ambidextrous safety, or other items. My gun has both these. The fully-adjustable rear sight is similar to a Smith & Wesson revolver sight, but somewhat heavier. The trigger is long-style, stop-adjustable, and the grips are rubber with a pebbled surface.

The handling qualities are excel-lent, and the reliability and accuracy were above reproach. I found that the "hump" on the frontstrap gave a more secure grip, and it was a definite help in controlling muzzle whip.

Arminex Trifire

I will admit to a certain amount of non-objectivity in regard to the Ar-minex Trifire. When it was just in the planning stages, I had many long con-versations about it with my good friend Jim Mongello and, by sugges-tion at least, I had a small part in its design. When it emerged, the Trifire had several distinctive features. As its name suggests, it is convertible from 45 Auto to 38 Super and 9mm Parabellum, without changing the slide.

While it has the "classic cosmetic configuration" of the Government Model, it abandons the frame-mount-ed sear-block safety in favor of a slide-mounted firing pin block type that does not drop the hammer. The firing pin can be manually locked during loading, and the pistol can be carried cocked-and-locked. It can also be dry-fired forever with the hammer never touching the firing pin.

The Trifire has an Arminex self-contained recoil spring unit and a sol-id one-piece backstrap. Both are available as separate accessories for use on other 1911 pistols. The solid backstrap has a subtle shape that is exactly right, and the absence of a grip safety is welcome.

A fixed combat-style rear sight or a fully-adjustable target sight installs in the same milled space at the rear of the slide, and the retaining cross-pin is extra heavy. The ramp-style front sight is double-cross-pinned to the slide rib. The rib is low and wide, with lengthwise grooving. The hammer is a ring-type, and the slide latch is slightly extended. An ambidextrous safety system is available.

The trigger is beautiful. Wide and glass-smooth, it's made of beryllium alloy. At the range, the Standard Tri-fire performance and handling quali-ties were outstanding. The external-ly-mounted pivoting extractor and wide ejection port put the fired cases neatly in a group for retrieval.

I was favorably impressed with all these pistols. Once, more than 30 years ago, I spent an afternoon shoot-ing a government-issue 45 at reason-ably-sized targets, and my abysmal scores engendered a long-lasting dis-like for the 1911 design. If that pistol had been one of the modern versions described above, it would have been a different story. ●

Author and Mahongo, Norman Sparrow's head tracker, with Cape buffalo bull taken near Mozambique border in 1978.

Make Mine a Sidehammer Rifle

The old design is functionally superior for the serious big game hunter.

by JACK LOTT

FROM HUMBLE beginnings as a "serpentine" or "cock" to hold the match of a matchlock, on up through the wheellock, snaphaunce, flintlock and percussion sidelock, the external sidehammer is indelibly associated with the muzzleloader. It may surprise many readers, but it is fair to state that during the breechloader era, probably more sporting guns have been made with external hammer sidelocks than all other types. This production continues apace in Europe, Asia, Africa, and the Western hemisphere, in shops from the crudest native village smith in Africa, the Liege makers of "trade guns," U.S. replica muzzleloaders, on to exquisitely crafted Italian double-barreled hammer shotguns.

My interest in outside hammer guns is 25% aesthetic and 75% practical, and limited mainly to double rifles of "double screw-grip" underlever action, but also W. W. Greener's famous "Treble Wedge-Fast" sidelock shotgun action. For certain forms of hunting big game in close cover, experience has taught me that no other action compares functionally with this double screw grip in a double rifle action.

The main reason for the continued demand for outside hammer shotguns and rifles long after the advent of Anson & Deeley's hammerless action was convention. The double screw grip gun had achieved perfection after a long evolution. The only "improvements" were top levers and ejectors, which complicated and weakened the bar of the action with cuts and slots for under bolts and cocking levers, as well as eliminating the unique solidity of this design. Such "improvements" mainly involved shotguns since double rifles of large caliber required more action strength and outside-hammer double rifles therefore are normally of extractor-only conventional underlever design.

Such great shotgunners as Lord Walsingham, the Marquis of Ripon and King George V were superb shots, all brought up with sidehammer guns. They amassed unbeaten shooting records of game with them. To them and their peers, the hammerless action was an effete heresy and needless fad like Harlequin spectacles on Tarzan.

For many gunmakers, the continued demand for sidehammer double rifles in cordite persuasion, was welcomed for two reasons; it held the increased pressures of smokeless better than the new hammerless designs and required no design or tooling changes, which in turn kept production costs low. In addition, the Indian school of big game hunting regarded this design as a *sine qua non* for dangerous game in thick jungle. Right up to 1920 there are extant many photos showing elephant, buffalo and lion or tiger with both a modern Mauser and a heavy hammer rifle leaning against the trophy.

Sentiment and aesthetic considerations aside, there are technical advantages to the screw-grip hammer action not found in other designs. First is the absolute tightness of the screw-grip action. This is because it is the *only* action which tightly locks the barrels down against the action bar. In all other double or single, hinged drop-barrel actions, such as the popular top lever hammerless types, the locking system must have ample clearance all around the locking members so that the gun opens easily by turning the top lever or other release. These tolerances are closer in best quality guns, due to careful hand fitting, but cheaper hammerless guns have just enough tightness to permit opening and closing minus obvious clatter that might spoil a sale.

Once slight wear occurs, all this inherent looseness can result in an ac-

cumulated headspace on firing, which in the case of shotguns isn't serious until it becomes flagrant, but with rifles, the same headspace can cause head separations. This slight clearance, needed in even the finest hammerless double guns for easy opening, acts as a sort of head start, when full pressure takes up all gaps and the top of the standing breech opens in a hinging action away from the barrels. This is called "going off the face," and is why so many double shotguns and rifles have extra bolts at the top of the standing breech, intended to preclude or limit this tendency. I have examined more loose fine used English shotguns than tight. Most hammerless double rifles of quality are tight, due to the lesser number of rounds fired, and the extra bolting and reinforcement of the action bar as compared to shotgun actions.

The screw-grip sidehammer action on the other hand, is a much stronger proposition than *any* hammerless action, because the barrels are clamped down tightly to the action bar's "water table" so that no gap occurs at the instant of firing. This not only eliminates the springing of the action bar and bolts, as with hammerless guns, but on firing, all elements of action and barrels hold tightly together as if a unit.

With my best Holland 577 screw-grip underlever sidehammer rifle I have yet had to size a case, and have

been reloading the same eight cases over and over, with only crimping after firing. The cases fall out of the chambers like new ones. Part of this is, of course, because the 577 3-inch case is a straight taper, which causes less side pressure case expansion than a bottle-necked design. Mostly it is due to the absence of stretching from that action/barrel flexing.

The manual cocking and plain extractors eliminate internal action cuts for the cocking levers, and with a back action design, there are no cuts in the action bar for the main springs. This action bar is more rigid and creates a shallower profile than hammerless types of identical calibers, as well as providing a lighter gun.

In the early stages of Anson & Deeley and hammerless sidelock action development, after the advent of cordite, there were many actions fractured at the angle of the standing breech and water table, until reinforcing bulges and internal web thickness increases were incorporated, plus the diverse third fasteners or rib extensions, such as the dollshead.

This great action was the most popular design for black powder double rifles made in Great Britain during the latter third of the Victorian era and was the only external hammer design to make the transition to smokeless. It required no design changes other than thicker barrels at the breech end, shallower rifling for

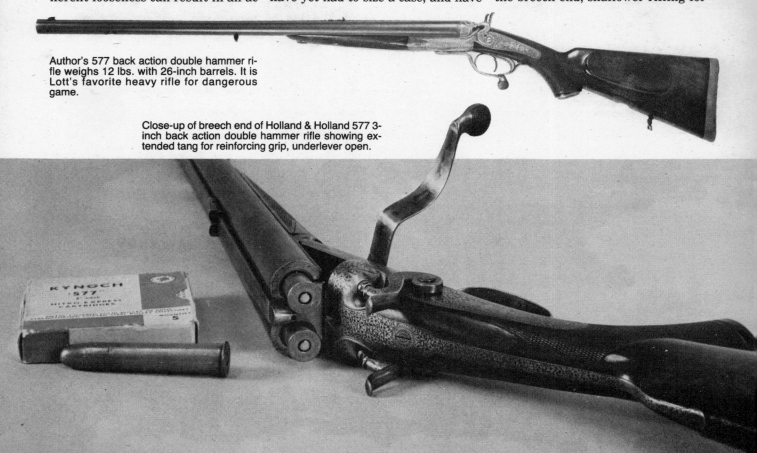

Author's 577 back action double hammer rifle weighs 12 lbs. with 26-inch barrels. It is Lott's favorite heavy rifle for dangerous game.

Close-up of breech end of Holland & Holland 577 3-inch back action double hammer rifle showing extended tang for reinforcing grip, underlever open.

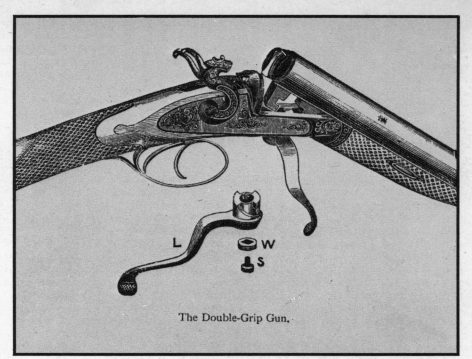

Line engraving of Henry Jones' double-grip underlever action as widely produced in Britain from about 1870 to 1930. It was the tightest hinged barrel action because it screwed the barrels tight to the action body. From W.W. Greener's "The Gun, and Its Development."

The Double-Grip Gun.

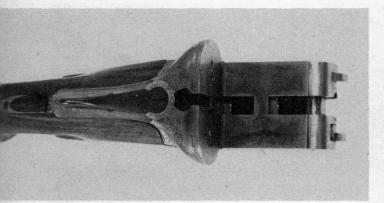

Anson & Deeley boxlock action of 12-bore "Jungle Gun." Bar is undercut for sliding Purdey underbolts and knuckle has large cuts for cocking levers. In addition, the action body is hollowed out for the lock mechanisms.

Greener Treble Wedge-Fast bar action sidehammer top lever action. Action bar is strong for weight since no cuts exist for ejectors, but internal slots for sliding underbolts weaker bar.

Bar action sidelock of Rigby 450 best quality sidelock ejector has bar undercut for sliding underbolts and knuckle cut out for cocking levers. Action is stronger than boxlock, but theoretically weaker than a back-action hammerless sidelock.

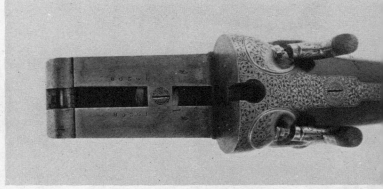

This rebounding hammer back-action is strongest of all, since the action bar has no slots for underbolts or mainsprings. When locked, barrels are clamped tightly.

jacketed bullets and higher sights. The action's inventor did not receive public credit for his outstanding conception, yet it, almost alone, required no modification to hold the much increased pressures of cordite. This design is called "inert," one in which the barrels drop via hinge, but locking, or bolting is accomplished without internal mechanism by a manually operated lever.

It was invented by Henry Jones, a Birmingham gunmaker, and patented in 1859 as No. 2040. Unfortunately, Jones did not profit from his extremely popular invention because he let his patent lapse on September 19th, 1862, by failing to pay a 50-pound stamp duty to keep it in effect for another 4 years. Sadly, it is probable that Jones, an independent soul, could not afford it, since it is known that he went bankrupt four years later and the contents of his home at Key Hill House, Hockley, were sold.

Such a celebrated gunmaker as W. Greener, who also was a prolific popular author on guns and gunmaking, disposed of Jones' contribution thusly in his fifth edition of *The Gun and Its Development,* stating, "This important improvement was effected by a Birmingham gunmaker who omitted to patent this modification."

Greener was not given to more than faint praise for another maker's work and tried to prove that Jones' action was unnecessarily strong because the line of force from the explosion was was in line with the bore thereby not requiring the tight clamping-down effect of the double screw-grip action. Greener overlooked the downward flexing of action bars and the many failures of hammerless actions at the angle in the early days of cordite. He also overlooked the plain truth that the in-line thrust transferred from cartridge head to breech face is reciprocated by a tendency to open the action due to the hinging of action with barrels. This effect is secondary to the in-line thrust, but demands a strong action bar to keep flexing to a safe minimum, which again is a virtue of Jones' solid steel action bar.

Jones apparently lived to be 100 or more and upon achieving his "century" did receive recognition in the press and the gift of a "purse of gold," containing 21 sovereigns, subscribed to by Birmingham's gunmakers, including W. W. Greener. Readers interested in learning more about shotgun and double rifle action development should read Ian Crudgington and D. J. Baker's fine book, Volume One of *The British Shotgun,* Barrie & Jenkins, Ltd., London.

Such ultra-fine external hammer shotguns as the Famars Castore 270 cock on opening via the top lever and are ejector guns. Such guns are as strong, no more or less, than hammerless guns of equal quality and metallurgy. This is because the hammers must be cocked exactly like those of a hammerless gun, with all the internal

Cape buffalo taken by author in 1974 near Chiredzi River, Rhodesia, with 577 back-action Holland & Holland hammer rifle. First shot with 750-grain steel jacket solid wounded buff in raking shot through left flank and into right shoulder muscle. Buff downed with shot in right flank through left shoulder as he turned to charge.

parts and milling of slots and drilling of holes this requires. However, such guns, aside from their obvious beauty, do have one mechanical advantage over hammerless guns, in that they can be uncocked by hand, then silently cocked at will, and when cocked, the hammers are visible cocking indicators.

Loaded hammerless double guns cannot normally be carried uncocked, so are invariably carried loaded, cocked and safety on. By loading when the gun is disassembled, most hammerless guns can be loaded uncocked, but having no hammer blocks as with rebounding sidehammer locks, they can conceivably fire if jarred enough to overcome hammer and/or firing pin inertia. The rebounding hammer lock of the sidehammer gun can however be carried uncocked, the safest condition of all, and the condition of the locks, cocked or uncocked, is always visible or can be felt at night. No doubt, rebounding sidehammer guns have been fired "accidentally," but no gun is foolproof. Regardless of safety features, it is the cocked gun which poses the greater danger of accidental discharge. The sidehammer gun can be carried loaded and closed, whereas hammerless guns should really be carried broken *for equal safety*. As the uncocked hammer gun is mounted, the right hammer is cocked. This takes practice, but so does working a bolt at shoulder or flipping coins.

Naturally, the *uncocking* of a hammer gun requires care so that the releasing thumb doesn't slip, but when the uncocking is done as it should with action broken open, the process is entirely safe. Earlier types of hammer actions did not have rebounding hammers and were less safe. The better British pre-rebounding hammer types did have safety bolts for each hammer, which must be pushed into place for safe carrying of this type of gun when loaded. Other external hammer guns with no such hammer safety slides, no rebounding hammers, and only half-cock notches are definitely unsafe to carry loaded and action closed, since a fall or a slip while cocking or half-cocking can easily result in an accidental discharge. The only remedy for those who intend shooting such inherently unsafe hammer guns is to carry them broken and loaded until ready to use. Such guns with worn sears and cocking notches are ready for repair or retirement as decorators.

Some instances have been reported of uncocked outside hammer guns and rifles accidentally firing when a hammer has caught on some object such as a fence rail, wire or a branch. With rebounding hammer actions which have steel blocking bars to block hammer fall unless the triggers are pulled, such a thing would be almost unheard of. There are many non-rebounding hammer guns around of poor to mediocre quality, mostly cheap European shotguns such as were imported by the thousands during the 50-year period before World War I. Hammer guns by their nature demand more of the shooter, both in cocking and in handling. The shooter must thread his way through thick cover, and if in doubt about it, should carry the loaded gun broken. Carrying the gun with the muzzle always elevated will not only be the safest position, but will make the barrels and undersurface of the gun a solid barrier to any object coming in contact with hammers, cocked or not. In case of a fall, a loaded and uncocked rebounding hammer gun is safer than a cocked and loaded hammerless gun with safety on.

More often than not, silence is more important than rapid fire in close cover hunting since the hunter normally approaches concealed and upwind so only a foreign sound can give him away. With a hammer gun, one can silently cock one or both hammers, by holding back the trigger as the hammer to drawn back, then easing the hammer forward against the released trigger to engage the cocking notch. If the game still runs off, the locks can be uncocked, and then the hammers are in a rest position, well above the firing pins and blocked from forward movement. This is the only external hammer system to be considered in this context of safety, called "rebounding hammers," as most breech-loading hammer guns will have. Regardless of what type of gun one carries, the usual safety rules apply, and then, despite an accidental discharge, the muzzle is pointing up and/or away from others.

Many European hammerless shotguns and rifles have cocking indicators so that even in the dark the condition of the locks can be felt. With hammer guns, the hammers themselves are the cocking indicators, and in addition, these "rabbit ears" are easily cocked in cold weather. The opinions of experts such as the late Major Sir Gerald Burrard, Bart., D.S.O. and John Taylor are worth repeating. Burrard in his classic *Notes On Sporting Rifles* said, "There is only one snag about the safety mechanism on hammerless actions, apart from the liability of the rifle being jarred off by a fall, and this is the slight "click" made when pushing the safety slide forward. I have already mentioned the manner in which wild animals can hear and locate some very slight metallic sound which would be almost inaudible to humans. This is probably because it is a new or strange sound, since no sudden contact with metal occurs either in the jungles or on the mountain side except through the agency of man. This

This 19th century Belgian bar action top lever opening shotgun has long "gone off the face." Such looseness is the result of poor fitting, poor material and an action bar undercut for sliding bolts.

slight "click" may be just enough to warn an unsuspicious animal or provoke a wounded one to charge."

Burrard fails to mention another source of alarming noise from the hammerless double rifle. When you have fired your first barrel at an animal it is essential to reload the fired barrel before moving from the spot. When opening a hammerless double rifle with one or both chambers fired, the "ping" of the ejectors or in the case of a non-ejector rifle, the "click" of the tumblers in cocking as the barrels are dropped, is more than enough to reveal one's position to a wounded animal. At best this will warn the animal and at worst, it will enable a sharp-eared tiger, lion, leopard, elephant, buff or gaur to locate and charge his hunter.

John "Pondoro" Taylor, in his classic work *African Rifles & Cartridges* commented; "I am very fond of the double hammer action because of the absolute silence with which it can be loaded and cocked. I know of more than one man sitting up at night for man-eating tiger who scared off his beast by the 'click' of the safety as he prepared to shoot with a hammerless rifle. If you draw back the hammer on a hammer rifle while holding back the trigger and then let the trigger go; you will have cocked without a sound of any sort. Then there is the delightful ease with which the breech opens; powerful double rifles are fitted with powerful main springs to obviate any possibility of a misfire; those springs have to be compressed as the breech of a hammerless action is opened and the locks cocked. There is nothing of that with the hammer rifle — you cock with your thumb, one lock at a time. I would happily finish the remainder of my career with nothing but best-grade double hammer rifles. Incidentally, such weapons can occasionally be picked up second hand at very low prices, not because the hammer action is no good, but simply because fashion favors the hammerless. If you get such a chance, provided the weapon is in good condition, you need not hesitate. It will satisfactorily answer any questions you are ever likely to ask it."

Taylor, like many hammer gun users, disliked cocking both hammers, based on a false belief that hammer guns are more prone to double discharge than hammerless guns. Hammer guns have cocking notches and sears just like hammerless guns. If the cocking notches or sear surfaces are worn or poorly fitted, then any type of gun is capable of being "jarred off." I have never experienced a double discharge with hammer guns, but have with two double hammerless rifles of good make. Underlever guns are fast to reload with minimal practice, since the barrels are cammed down as the underlever is pulled out, and there are no mainsprings to compress as the barrels are dropped, and closing is aided by a final camming action.

Not long ago, I enjoyed an extended trip to Southern Africa, and during a Rhodesian safari, used my Holland 577 3-inch underlever hammer rifle on Cape buffalo near Mozambique. Ranges were all under 25 yards in thick mopani and thorn bushveld, where only a slight foreign sound can give away the hunter. I was accompa-

nied by Norman Sparrow, professional hunter, and Mahongo, the head tracker, a Shangaan. After a long spooring-up of three big bulls from where they had rolled in a mud wallow, and after losing the spoor several times, we arrived to within some 20 yards of their resting place. It was an overcast day with intermittent drizzle, and about the ugliest possible atmosphere to seek battle with that tank of the bushveld, the Cape buffalo. We had crawled some 25 yards to a dubious screen of bush that concealed us only when our heads were down. I could see the tremendous spread of one bull's horn tips extending from either side of a small mopani which he was shaking violently to remove mud from his head, but I couldn't see anything else. I refused to guess at the rest of his body nor whether his boss was hard.

To his right was another huge bull with shoulders and head visible broadside. Norman told me to take him, so I eased back the right hammer of the big Holland, then the left, while holding back the triggers. The 577 was cocked without a sound, which at that range, no matter how slight, would have sent them away at a gallop. Slowly I eased myself into a kneeling position and aimed the Holland at the shoulder, then with a roar, the cordite flash blurred a final glimpse of the buffalo thundering to the left out of sight.

We jumped up and ran to the departing spoor, then slowed to a careful crouching walk looking for telltale blood spoor, but it was nowhere to be seen. A sickening feeling of failure came over me as I contemplated how I could have missed so big a target at 20 yards. Just then we hear a bovine cough ahead and left. Norman and Mahongo signalled me to follow in a running crouch to the left of the sound and off the spoor. You don't follow a wounded buffalo's spoor right past his place of ambush unless you enjoy Cape Buffalo Roulette. We dropped flat and began a slow crawl towards the direction of the cough, Norman creeping with his 404 Mauser, Mahongo carrying my 450 Rigby double sidelock ejector and myself like a four-legged crab with the 577 in one hand.

I was signalled down flat as Norman watched for the bull, then he motioned me forward and, still crawling, up to a low bush ahead of him. I had previously reloaded the Holland, and painfully raised up on my knees with the 577 pointing ahead, until but 30 feet away I could see the blackness of the bull's head and neck extending from his ambush hide, facing away on

his trail in the direction from whence he had come. In a flash my mind returned to thick bush off the Revui river in Mozambique, September 18, 1959, when a wounded buffalo bull ambushed me, tossing me three times. That bash-up required four 458s and seven 375s before the furious beast expired.

I was determined to not let that happen again. The front bead nestled down in the wide "V" open rear, and centered the black barrel of his neck when the 577's 100 grains of cordite and 750-grain solid steel-jacketed bullet thundered. Automatically I opened the action in one movement, extracted the empty which fell out, slipped in another 750-grain solid, closed it and cocked again silently. I then rose and ran to the left of the buff's thicket. At the shot he had disappeared from view and I wanted to cut off any retreat to another ambush or break a possible charge, but it was unnecessary.

As I reached a broadside position adjacent to his hide, I saw his black mass stretched out in a disorderly matt of blood and trampled grass. Mahongo's exultant shout of victory came just as I had rounded the corner of bush where he fell. I stood in silent awe of the importance of sound; the buff's cough which told us where he was, and the absence of sound when I reloaded and cocked the big Holland hammer rifle. Despite the enormous wound through the lungs, the bull had not bled at all until arriving at his last stand where those great gouts of lung blood revealed the cause of his cough. This story would probably have ended very differently had I been armed with a hammerless double with its distinct "click" of a safety slide and cocking action.

Norman Sparrow called up the two Africans of our group who had stayed well behind as he, myself and Mahongo spoored up the buff, telling them to bring up the Toyota safari vehicle. As I contemplated the massive, now prostrate but still formidable looking, buffalo. I remembered how when we were close to them before my first shot, that I had handed my fine 450 Rigby double sidelock ejector to Mahongo and taken over the elderly 577 Holland hammer rifle. That Rigby 450 is the finest hammerless double ejector rifle I have ever owned, and its presence as a second heavy rifle increased my confidence in approaching such dangerous game, but I was glad I had taken over the old 577 hammer rifle during the last act of this little bushveld drama. ●

Kleinguenther K-22 Rimfire

Simpson benched the K-22 with his favorite 16x Redfield 6400 scope on top.

Have you ever seen a 22 rimfire rifle with locking lugs at the front of the bolt? I have; in fact, I've been having a ball shooting tiny groups with one for several months now. It's called the K-22 and it's from Kleinguenther, Inc., the folks out in Seguin, Texas who also offer the K-15 centerfire rifle. Both the K-15 and K-22 are made by Voere over in the Black Forest of West Germany.

Like its big brother, the K-22's locking lugs engage abutments milled into a Stellite receiver ring insert. Unlike its big brother, when a cartridge is fired, backthrust does not impinge directly on the bolt face proper but instead, on a nonrotating breech block inside the bolt body. Shear stress is transmitted through the bolt body to the twin locking lugs by an integral shoulder on the breech block. Sounds a bit complicated but it's not. It is, for certain, an extremely rigid lockup system. For now, the K-22 is available in 22 Long Rifle and 22 WMR, with the 22 Hornet a possibility for later on down the road.

The K-22 is a man-sized rifle, yet at 6½ pounds it's not too heavy. The 40 inch length includes a 21½ inch chrome-moly barrel, rifled with four lands and grooves. The fire control system is interchangeable with the K-15 centerfire rifle and has sear engagement and weight of pull adjustments of 0.3 to 0.4mm and 2.5 to 3 pounds, respectively. Optional double-set triggers cost an additional $125. Actually, the list of options is mind-boggling.

At the bottom is the standard grade with stained, cut checkered, beech wood stock and matte metal finish for $227. For accurizing to 1 MOA, we add $139 for a total of $366. From here the sky and your bankroll are the limits, i.e.;

	ADD
22 WMR chambering	$ 99.00
Open sights	28.00
Extra five-shot clip	12.50
Quick-detach sling swivels	18.50
Ten-shot clip	16.50
Trap magazine	129.00
High luster metal finish	50.00

Stock Options

Classic, Thumbhole or Featherweight
American Grade A Walnut
Oil Finish	265.00
High Luster Finish	370.00

American Grade AAA Walnut or Maple
Oil Finish	525.00
High Luster Finish	630.00

Monte Carlo Style
European Grade A Walnut
Oil Finish	105.00
High Luster Finish	210.00

American Grade A Walnut
Oil Finish	210.00
High Luster Finish	315.00

European Grade AAA Walnut
Oil Finish	260.00
High Luster Finish	365.00

See what I mean? And, I left out many possibilities like left hand stock, special select grade wood with 100% coverage and custom built competition rifles. Wow!!

Now let's see how a K-22 shoots. The receiver is drilled and tapped but I used the dovetail grooves for mounting a 16x Redfield 6400. During three different 50-yard test sessions, the K-22 has averaged from 0.40 to 0.60-inch for both five and ten-shot groups with RWS R50, Lapua and Eley Tenex. The smallest five-shot group fired to date measures under 0.20-inch. Darned good shooting for a country boy with a sporter weight rifle.

Like all 22 rimfires, the K-22 has its preferences in domestic ammunition. At 100 yards, five-shot groups with Federal high velocity hollow points average just over an inch when the wind's not blowing, while CCI Green Tag, Winchester Silhouette and Federal Silhouette average close to MOA.

The K-22 has performed without hitch and I can find no fault with it. The trigger is superb; the bolt glides smoothly to and fro and the five-round clip magazine is easily removed and inserted. Wood to metal fit on the standard grade is up to par but the checkering is nothing to brag about, nor is the heavily stained stock finish. The standard grade will get the job done but this is a classy rifle and it needs a classy stock. If it were me, I'd pay more and go with the oil-finished classic or featherweight stock in Claro walnut.

Kleinguenther will sell lots of these rifles.

Layne Simpson

Hacker found the DGW Indian Trade Gun a workhorse smoothbore that shoots well.

It is somewhat paradoxical to call any recreated muzzleloader a "new" gun, but Dixie Gun Works has brought back a flintlock so commonplace in its day that it was often ignored in contemporary writings and consequently, is little known among many buckskinners today. This is the Indian trade rifle, which was called by various other names until approximately 1875.

The French called it a *fusil* and others "fusee." In England, where most of them were made, the popular nomenclature was the Carolina Musket. Early Americans and French Americans called it the London Fusil and Northwest Gun. Because of the large volume of sales it enjoyed with the Hudson's Bay Company and the Mackinaw Company of Canada, the gun was colloquially called the Hudson's Bay Gun or the Mackinaw Gun,

Dixie's Trade Gun

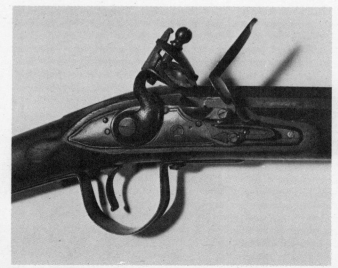

The browned flintlock has the old sitting fox mark; the large bow trigger guard is typical.

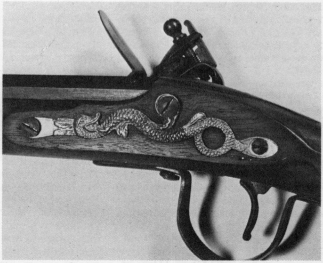

The serpent sideplate is also normal for the type.

depending upon whose inventories were involved. However, today, an all-encompassing term used by collectors, historians and consequently Dixie Gun Works is the Northwest Trade Gun.

Originally, these guns were designed as low cost, yet rugged weapons to be produced in great number and used as bartering items with North American Indians, sold as inexpensive protection to travelers passing through frontier trading posts, and given as treaty pledges to various tribes by the U.S. government. As a result, trade guns saw extensive use throughout the West, Northwest and Southwest by both white men and Indians alike. Their chief attractions were the fact that as smoothbore flintlocks, they could shoot anything from lead balls to pebbles and, in an era when a good quality hunting rifle cost $14 to $18, a new trade gun could be purchased for as little as $5.

The Northwest Trade Gun as offered by Dixie Gun Works is a very close copy of the lightweight, smoothbore flintlock trade gun produced by Robert Wheeler in Birmingham, England, from 1780 until the late 1830s. It has all of the notable characteristics of the originals: a finely detailed brass "serpent" sideplate, flat brass buttplate held to the stock with the appropriate square nails, the "sitting fox-in-a-circle" stamping of the Hudson's Bay Company on the lockplate and the overly large "mitten" trigger guard, which makes it somewhat easier to fire this gun while wearing gloves.

Like the originals, the Dixie trade gun is light, weighing in at a scant 6½ pounds. This and the slim configuration of the stock make it easy to carry over long distances and rough terrain. The 36-inch part round, part octagon tapered barrel is browned and is bored to 20 gauge, or approximately 60 caliber. In true musket fashion, there is no rear sight, only a low brass front sight.

Overall impression of the trade gun is that it is authentically styled and well made. Not only would it be an excellent choice for the fur-trade rendezvous crowd, but for the hunter as well, inasmuch as there are very few reflective parts on the gun. In states such as Massachusetts, where only smoothbores are allowed, the Dixie trade gun would seem to enjoy a welcomed reincarnation in an area it once inhabited 155 years ago.

My test gun was serial #1 and I must admit I was somewhat apprehensive about a lightweight 60-cal. shoulder weapon. However, recoil was not at all unpleasant, even after a half day of firing everything from lead shot to 300-grain lead balls. Moreover, for a smoothbore, the Northwest Trade Gun shot surprising well. Using the manufacturer's recommended charge of 60 grains of FFg black powder, and firing a .590-in. round ball patched with Ox-Yoke's prelubed All-Day Wonder Patch, the trade gun consistently printed six-inch groups at 25 yards, opening up to 12-inch groups at 50 yards. This is unusually good shooting for a smoothbore work gun with no rear sights. It just means that deer hunters will have to be content with lung-heart shots and should forget aiming for the neck.

For shotgunners, Blue & Gray Products and Gary Butler Enterprises both carry 20-gauge over-powder and over-shot wads and I found the gun shot best with 1½ oz. of #6 shot and 60 grains of FFg. In all cases, I primed with FFFF powder.

Unfortunately, the gun was not a consistent sparker, probably due to the fact that I was shooting the first one off of the assembly line. The guns are made up for Dixie in Tennessee, using parts from North Star Enterprises. However, by "breaking in" the frizzen and switching to a better quality English flint, I was able to overcome this problem somewhat.

All in all, the Dixie Northwest Trade Gun is a handsome piece of fur trade history that is every bit as capable of making meat as the originals. It can also be authentically frontierified with brass tacks, perhaps a strip of rawhide around the wrist of the gun. In addition, trade guns often had their barrels shortened to as short as eleven inches for running buffalo.

In ready-built form, the Dixie Northwest Trade Gun sells for $495 and it is also available as a kit for $350. Now, in an era when today's sophisticated Hawken frontloader with its rifled bore, adjustable rear sight, pewter nosecap and coil mainspring is selling for about the same price or maybe a little less, one might wonder why a Chevrolet-styled smoothbore flinter like the Northwest Trade Gun costs so much? Well, it may be a Chevie, but if so, it is more like a '58 Impala. In my part of the country, Impalas are considered classics and are bringing far more than a new Cadillac. Likewise, the Dixie Northwest Trade Gun is a well made, authentically-styled firearm that shows every promise of serving its owner with the same simple, rugged reliability that the classic originals did during the opening of the Far West.

Rick Hacker

From this position, one can shoot the Ruger very well, with very quick repeat shots.

Legal Pistol Stock

Maybe you've seen an ad for this Assault Accessories, Inc. stock for pistols, called a "legal pistol stock." That's just what it is.

It's legal because it doesn't attach to the gun, and it works because in use it doesn't need to be attached to the gun. Right now it's made for Ruger 22 auto pistols.

It costs $45.00, which seems quite a bit of money for eight ounces or so of welded steel wire, but if you want a legal pistol stock I don't think you can beat it. It's very well made and it works very well indeed.

What I mean is you grab this thing and the gun in one hand, rest it on your shoulder, and pull it back with your other hand and your pistol starts shooting like a little rifle. The zero changes, but not much. Squirrel hunting and the like is easy—you carry gun and stock all together as a unit in one hand. Starting with the gun in a holster and the stock in your other hand, I'd judge it would take 5 seconds to get it all together for an aimed shot.

It's worth the money if you like that kind of thing.   *Ken Warner*

Nicely made stock presents rubber surface to pistol and hand, is quite rigid in use, though, of course, completely separate.

Powder-Powered Pellet Rifle

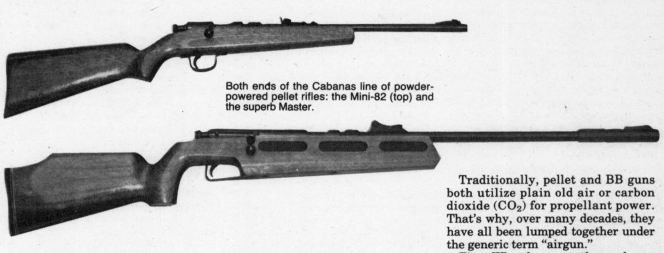

Both ends of the Cabanas line of powder-powered pellet rifles: the Mini-82 (top) and the superb Master.

The Mini-82 quickly became a hit with Mrs. Galan.

Factory-supplied 22 rimfire blanks and .190-inch lead balls.

Traditionally, pellet and BB guns both utilize plain old air or carbon dioxide (CO_2) for propellant power. That's why, over many decades, they have all been lumped together under the generic term "airgun."

Fine. What happens, then, when a confirmed airgun enthusiast like me chances across a couple of new pellet/BB rifles that utilize 22 rimfire *blanks* to move pellets? Well, there is a lot of head-scratching, for one thing, and a great deal of test-firing for another.

The rifles in question are manufactured in Mexico by Industrias Cabañas, S.A., and are imported by Mandall Shooting Supplies, Inc. Mandall's latest catalog reveals he imports seven different rifle models manufactured by Cabañas. All of them are single-shot *177-caliber*, bolt action sporting rifles. At the bottom end of the price and size scale is the Mini-82, measuring a mere 33 inches and weighing nearly 3½ lbs. The top model in the Cabañas line is represented by the "Master," at 45½ inches and 8 lbs.

The Mini-82 retails for a breezy $69.95. It is perfect for youngsters learning the basics of marksmanship (under adult supervision, of course) or for women of small build who can't really handle a heavy magnum air rifle. The hefty Master sells for $149.95, still a pretty good value considering what it has to offer. The remaining five models fall in between these two in price as well as in finish, and differ among themselves primarily in barrel length and stock configuration. The latter, incidentally, is made of nicely grained hardwood with a tough polyurethane finish. The Master model sports a match-style stock that looks just like the stock of the RWS Model 75 match air rifle. I'll bet this is no coincidence, either. All models in the Cabañas line come with 12-groove barrels.

It was these two models, then, that I had the distinct pleasure of wringing out for a few weeks. I found these unique 177-cal. BB/pellet rifles are truly worth having around for a variety of practical applications.

Their single-shot bolt action is straightforward enough — lift up the bolt and pull straight back in order to expose the breech. In the Mini-82, a knurled striker must be pulled back in order to cock the rifle. In the Master, cocking is accomplished automatically as the bolt is closed.

These rifles can shoot slightly oversized lead BBs (approximately .190-in.) supplied by Mandall's, and some — not all — 177 pellets. Regular steel BBs will simply roll out of the barrel and, besides, they are too "bouncy."

The lead balls that came with the rifles weighed an average of 9.7 grains. When regular 177 pellets are used, care must be exercised. Due to the relatively heavy and instantaneous pressure created by the detonation of the propelling 22 rimfire blanks, many standard diabolo-type pellets will simply fall apart. I found that heavy English pellets such as those produced by Webley worked just fine.

The heaviest 177 pellet currently on the American market is the Beeman Ram Jet. These pellets were designed for silhouette shooting and weigh around 9.6 grains. They also have a head configuration that gives them tremendous punch at high velocities.

The booklet that accompanied my test guns indicated a muzzle velocity of 1,150 fps with the aforementioned round lead projectile. One of the sensors in my electronic chronograph was out of order at the time that I was testing these rifles, and I was unable to get accurate velocities; however, the .190-in. lead balls supplied with the rifles had no difficulty at all punching clear through ¾-in. pine boards at 60 feet, then continuing on to bury themselves *one inch* in ballistic putty used as a backstop. Impressive indeed. Beeman Ram Jets usual-

ly bore right through the pine boards, but they did not get far into the ballistic putty. Pointed pellets were far from satisfactory, due to skirt separation in many cases.

I had no difficulty keeping most of my shots inside a ½-in. circle at 60 feet even with the short-barreled Mini-82. Incidentally, this model's trigger can be adjusted by removing the stock, but my test sample had a single-stage trigger smooth as oiled glass, breaking cleanly at 4 lbs. The Master model's adjustable trigger, also single-stage, adjusts from outside. My test sample was a bit rough at first, but after a few dozen rounds and some careful adjustment, it too became silky-smooth.

The Mini-82 comes with a simple front blade on a ramp, and a rear sight with square notch, adjustable for elevation via a disc with engraved numbers and for windage via slotted screws. The Master sports a rather shallow front sight blade that is difficult to pick up in less than ideal lighting conditions. The rear sight is a more elaborate affair, though. It also has a numbered disc for elevation adjustments. Windage is set by first loosening the knurled nut that locks the entire rear sight element in place, then turning the knurled knob on the right side of the sight in the desired direction. There is a choice of two similar (and decidedly small) square notches cut on opposite sides of the rear sight. Personally, I am not too happy with this setup, but fortunately there are grooves cut on top of the receiver for mounting a telesight. Even with its less-than-thrilling open sights, I was able to get ⅜-in. groups

consistently at 20 yards with the Master.

All these models feature a simple extractor for the 22 blank cartridge. A knurled collar that fits around the barrel just in front of the receiver pulls to the rear. Two steel prongs connected to this collar slide out from their recesses at the breech end of the barrel, carrying the blank casing with them.

As far as firing noise is concerned, these guns are perhaps even quieter than some "magnum" spring-piston air rifles. At first, I was concerned that they might be too noisy for use in a suburban backyard, but as it turned out, they are *very* quiet indeed.

These rifles are classified as firearms because they expel a projectile through the action of an explosive mixture; therefore, they must be shipped to an FFL holder just like any other regular firearm. It is interesting to note, however, that in reality these rifles perhaps should fall under the same category as muzzleloaders, because they do not fire a self-contained cartridge. In fact, they cannot chamber even a 22 BB Cap! The 177 pellet or lead ball must be dropped in first at the breech, followed by the 22 blank.

Although the additional expense of buying blank cartridges may turn some people away from these rifles, their hot performance is well worth the slight extra cost. Small game hunting and pest-control are ideal applications. Their truly unique concept is enough to make them extremely interesting to airgun and firearm buffs alike.

J. I. Galan

Kimber's 223: The Model 84

(Once again, Contributing Editor Simpson concocts a conversation that might have taken place between two employees at one of our rifle makers. The next such will appear in the 1995 GUN DIGEST.)

"Have you noticed how the 223 Remington has taken varmint shooters by storm?"

"Yep."

"Let's build a rifle for it."

"You kidding? Everybody builds rifles for that cartridge; ours would be just another 223 lost in the shuffle."

"You're right. We need to offer something different if we're to outsell the competition."

"What you got in mind?"

"Ponder this: no American manufacturer has ever produced a rifle action scaled down in weight and proportion to the 222 family of cartridges, right?"

"Why, I'd never thought about it but you're exactly right. It'll be easy; we'll just take a Model 82 in 22 Hornet, ream out its chamber to 223, lengthen its ejection port and magazine and, eureka, we've developed a new rifle."

"I'm afraid it won't be so simple. This cartridge is loaded to higher chamber pressures and generates more backthrust due to its larger base area so we want an extra margin of strength. We'll have to go to the drawing board."

"What's first?"

"Well, let's make its lockup extremely rigid by positioning twin, op-

net feed properly almost did me in. Hold up a second; we need to plan farther down the road than just one cartridge. This new action would be a perfect home for the 222 and 17 Remington, as well as several wildcats such as the 6x47mm and 7mm TCU. Every time we introduce a new chambering we may have to modify the clip."

"So, how do we avoid that headache?"

"We've stayed with time-proven design details thus far, let's just carry on with the same program. We'll go with a staggered box magazine, replete with steel follower."

"Now we're really cooking but how will the fellows unload?"

"With this cute little hinged floor-

varmint shooters would take to a single shot bolt action with solid bottom receiver, just like the benchrest boys use?"

"Sounds great but first things first."

"We need to test fire it; how do we mount a scope?"

"The scope needs to be low down on the receiver so we'll attach it with dovetail grooves, just like the Model 82. We'll even use our side lever rings because they fit the grooves perfectly."

"Quick-detach rings are fine on rifles with open sights but what about those with naked barrels?"

"That's easy. With the new rifle, we'll introduce a new fixed version of the Brownell-designed side lever and

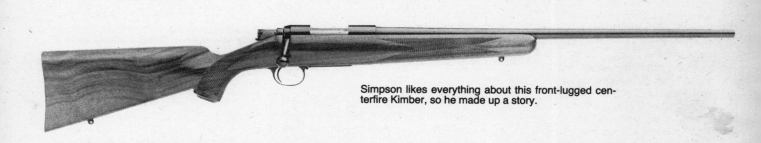

Simpson likes everything about this front-lugged centerfire Kimber, so he made up a story.

posed locking lugs at the extreme front of the bolt, a la '98 Mauser."

"Great idea; here, I've sketched out an extractor that'll fit inside the bolt face counterbore wall."

"Sorry Charlie, but we'll follow Paul Mauser's lead here too; we'll use his yet-to-be-improved-upon, outside, claw-type extractor."

"Why didn't I think of that? It'll be the talk of the industry. Gun writers will cut backflips clean over their typewriters. Oh, well, I'll work on a spring-loaded, plunger-type ejector."

"Wrong again; we'll stay with Mauser there too."

"Ah ha, I gotcha this time; the Mauser ejector design has a flaw—it requires a split in the left locking lug that weakens its shear strength."

"For once you're right. I've got it; we'll modify it just as Winchester's engineers did with the old Model 54 back in the 1920s, virtually the same ejector, in fact, that was carried over to the Model 70 in 1937."

"I believe we've got a winner."

"Yep, but we're not through yet."

"My gosh, I almost forgot about having to make a clip magazine for the 223."

"It'll be a pain; making the 22 Hor-

plate and its spring-loaded latch in the front of the trigger bow."

"The steel floorplate looks great but shouldn't its hinge be a bit more narrow and shouldn't the latch be inside the trigger bow?"

"We'll leave it this way on the prototypes but may change both on production rifles in July."

"How about the bolt release, do we stay with Mauser there too?"

"The Model 82 bolt release is much neater and besides, with our ejector we don't need so much hardware back on the receiver bridge. So, we'll just modify the Model 82 bolt release. Same goes for the fire control system; the Model 82's adjustable trigger would be tough to improve on and its rotary safety is positive, handy and quiet."

"Looking good. Why don't we screw in a 22½-inch barrel and since folks seem to like quicker rifling pitches with the 223, try a 1-12 inch twist in lieu of 1-14 inch? In fact, there are all kinds of possibilities here; we could even eliminate the box magazine and its cut in the bottom of the receiver, use a slightly heavier barrel and semibeavertail forearm and call it the Kimber Varminter. I wonder how

even make them available for other rifles."

"Hey, it's pretty; that ought to make the old cash register sing. Let's mount a 16x Model 6400 and go see how it shoots."

"Ok, you go first."

"Not bad, I didn't know a 6½-pound rifle was supposed to place five bullets into such a tiny cluster so consistently, even with good handloads."

"It's called less than minute of angle by those who are in the know about such things."

"What's left to do?"

"Well, since it's the same size as the Model 82, we'll make it look just as good with pretty wood, cut checkering and nice steel hardware."

"Yeah, yeah; so the boys can have matched sets in 22 Long Rifle, 22 WMR, 22 Hornet and 223. That about takes care of the project, doesn't it?"

"Not quite; we need to come up with a snappy name; got any ideas?"

"Let's see; we arbitrarily added thirty years to 52 and came up with Model 82 but it confused some of the fellows when we unveiled it in 1979. We're introducing the new rifle in '84, sooo . . ."

Layne Simpson

IWA 1984

by
RAYMOND CARANTA

THE IWA-84 Show in Nuremberg was unquestionably once more the most important in Europe. The products of 531 companies from 23 countries were on display in three huge halls. Foreign products from 231 companies located outside Germany (against 208 in 1983) represented 58 percent of all the items offered and professional visitors came from 40 different countries.

Among the major foreign exhibitors, the Italians were first with 56 direct entries (plus 9 manufacturers represented), followed by the United States (41 plus 47), Austria (36 plus 1), Spain (21 plus 2) and France (20 plus 5). The German industry in guns, ammunition and accessories consists now of 30 companies employing 6,000 people. Most imports to Germany come from the U.S. and Italy.

Among the new guns displayed, we noted:

The Anschutz Olympic models and accessories; an Astra 357/9mm Luger revolver with cylinders interchangeable without any tools; the simplified Benelli "Montefeltro" delayed-action automatic shotgun; the Beretta bolt action and express rifles; beautiful engraved rifles of original design from Blaser; the French Bretton ultra-light automatic shotgun; a complete line of new Browning products made in Belgium including the long sought-after double action 13-shot Hi-Power pistol; a set of three ultra-mod-

A Finnish light sniper rifle, fitted with a silenced barrel, was chambered 308 Winchester to fire a special Lapua subsonic round.

Ted Rowe of H&R showed his 32 Magnum revolver at IWA.

Caranta liked this new and extremely compact rifle introduced by Zastava of Yugoslavia.

ern target automatic pistols by Fiocchi for the Olympic, Standard and Centerfire events.

Harrington & Richardson and Federal introduced European visitors to their 32 H&R Magnum revolvers and cartridges in a beautiful booth. The German manufacturer Heym enjoyed a tremendous success with its $65,000 rifle set which was certainly the most beautiful gun of the show.

The streamlined Smith & Wesson 12-shot pistol Model 469 in 9mm Luger attracted many European shooters, even in competition with the lightweight 15-shot Star P30 K and the host of new Brazilian Taurus automatic pistols (among which, a 9-shot staggered magazine 22 LR ultra-compact vest pocket model *made in the United States* seems quite promising!).

The American displays of Colt, Remington, Ruger and Winchester were outdoing one another as did the European stands of Beretta, Dynamit Nobel, Zeiss, Heckler-und-Koch, Steyr, Krico, Voere Erma, Hämmerli and Sauer.

With Hunfishow no longer a factor, the "Comité des expositions de Paris" (7, rue Copernic - 75782 Paris Cedex 16 - France), organized, under the heading the A.N.G.I.C.T., a gun show in Paris from March 3 to March 6, which gathered more than 150 exhibitors and about 20,000 visitors. The SICAT was opened to everybody during two days.

This great success was mostly due to the fact that France is the first European country for hunting with 1.5 million hunters. It's ahead of Great Britain (1.1 million) and Spain (1.05 million). French hunting grounds cover 125 million acres, while those of Spain are of about 106 million, Italy 67 million, and 58 million for Western Germany.

There are approximately 4.5 million shotguns and hunting rifles in France, which means that about 15 percent of all families have at least one. Every year, 200,000 new guns are sold at an average price of $375. The yearly ammunition consumption per hunter is about 100 rounds.

During recent years, antique gun shows have become quite common in Western Europe, but the Saint-Germain-en-Laye show, organized by Mr. Yves de Montais in a beautiful small town near Paris, is still the most rewarding and famous, judged by the quality of the pieces displayed and the crowds of gun lovers visiting. The seventh edition was held from March 24 to March 26 and enjoyed its usual well-deserved success. ●

The most fascinating accessory of IWA 84 may have been the extraordinary Shepherd scope displayed at the Hakko stand (and discussed at length in the 1984 GUN DIGEST).

SICAT 84 in Paris had, naturally, a Bretton display—and also, 20,000 visitors.

The Riding School of the Kings of France provides a fine hall for a regular gun show, pretty much U.S.-style, each year at St-Germaine-en-Laye.

JOSEPH

SAM WELCH

The Art of The Engraver

SAM WELCH

RICHARD D. ROY

FRANK BRGOCH

DENNIS BROOKER

LEONARD FRANCOLINI

BYRON BURGESS

KENNETH W. WARREN

MARTIN RABENO

JOHN M. KUDLAS

BILLY BATES

JOHN R. ROHNER

MARCELLO PEDINI

JOE RUNDELL

H. V. GRANT

JIM KELSO

E.C. Prudhomme's ENGRAVING PROJECT

by SID LATHAM

The master at work—and his own engraving project plate at right—demonstrate that some, at least, can work past 70.

EDWARD CLARK Prudhomme is 72 years of age now. When I visited him in his studio in Shreveport, Louisiana, he was still engraving. He's not as quick as he once was—he began engraving in 1932—but he is as deft as he ever was.

Prudhomme is the author of *Firearms Engraving Review*, Books 1 and 2. These works are the bible for the engraving fraternity. Unfortunately, they went out of print in 1976, but there is high hope of updating them with more modern photographs.

A few years ago in Tulsa, Oklahoma, at the Firearms Engraving Guild meeting, E.C. gave to each member of the Guild at the meeting, a plate measuring 1½" × 4" long. "Do anything you want. But do the very best," instructed E.C. These pictures of the various engravings are going to be used for magazines and articles about the talent of fine engraving.

The plates have been coming in right along. Naturally, not everyone will send a plate in. There are those, quite frankly, who are still untalent-

ed and those who don't want anyone to see what they are doing, sort of secretive I guess. In many more cases, the work has been outstanding.

Out of fifty or more plates, perhaps forty or more have arrived. According to E.C., "There has not been a single disaster of any plates returned and all have been very accomplished indeed."

There *have* been a couple of beginners and naturally they have not been able to compete with the top-drawer talent.

Said Prudhomme, "They probably

George Sherwood chose to treat his plate as a sample of a single project.

Fred Harrington's geese are ambitiously sketched and framed fittingly.

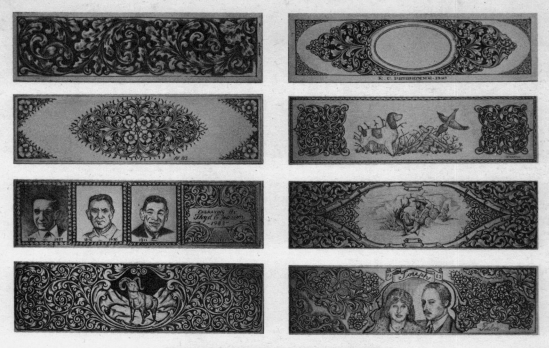

In left column: Ben Shostle, Muncie, IN; Ray Viramontez, Dayton, OH; Floyd Warren, Cortland, OH; Ben Lane, Amarillo, TX. In right column: E.C. Prudhomme; Bob Evans, Oregon City, OR; Ron Smith, Fort Worth, TX; Joseph of New Haven, CT, who uses only one name. At center is Sam Welch, Kodiak, AK.

have been isolated from other engravers, mostly through great distances, and they have not received the proper instruction to seriously advance their own talents."

"Confidence, that is the big word as far as engraving is concerned," says Prudhomme. "If you don't have confidence in this business then you're dead. If you are doing gold or silver inlays then you don't want to make any mistakes, believe me."

The plates went to no foreign engravers, though if overseas engravers had been members of the Firearms Engraving Guild they would have received sample plates.

"But we had had a big enough job as it was just collating the plates that were returned," said Prudhomme.

"This should be an outstanding display of the engraved product," Prudhomme said, "and also a better understanding of what good engraving is all about."

Obviously, Mr. Prudhomme is on the right track. Engraving is an art form and one has to look at the engraving of some foreign engravers to see what it is all about.

Publication of these engraved plates would enhance the art of engraving skills and certainly bring fame and a little bit of money to those not so famed.

The advancement in the performance of engravers themselves, the improvement in their product will, in the long run, bring the buyer of fine engraving something better, too. ●

Mike Dubber chose to display several scrolls—and even oak leaves.

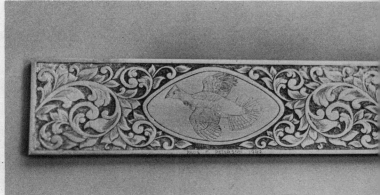

Paul Peterson demonstrated a bold scroll, but had to crowd his grouse a little.

CUSTOM GUNS

AMERICAN CUSTOM GUN GUILD
With Duane Wiebe stock, Pete Grisel metal and Terry Wallace engraving this handsome classic is the first of a Guild series.

MAURICE OTTMAR
Particularly clean lines in a fully realized sporter in Australian walnut, a 220 Swift on a VZ-24 Mauser. (Bilal photo)

STERLING DAVENPORT
Your basic Model 70 338 with a few touches like a deceptively heavy barrel in French walnut. (Int'l. Photographic Assoc. photo)

WAYNE SCHWARTZ
A new look for the Ruger No. 1 takes it back to schuetzen days classically.

R. H. DEVEREAUX
Another 338, this Ruger 77 is in modern mesquite with 20-line point checkering, weighs 8½ pounds.

JERE D. EGGLESTON
This pre-'64 Model 70 Featherweight 243 has an aggressively visual California English stock.

CLASSIC ARMS CORP.
The big scope gives this Mauser 98 a Continental look; the cheekpiece shape helps.

ROBERT M. WINTER
The unusual forearm tip is ebony on this California English walnut stock for a Winchester 70 in 280 Remington.

STEPHEN HEILMANN
Bastogne walnut was chosen for this 270 on a Sako action.

PAUL R. NICKELS
The severe profile disguises the lush surface treatment of a complex checkering job.

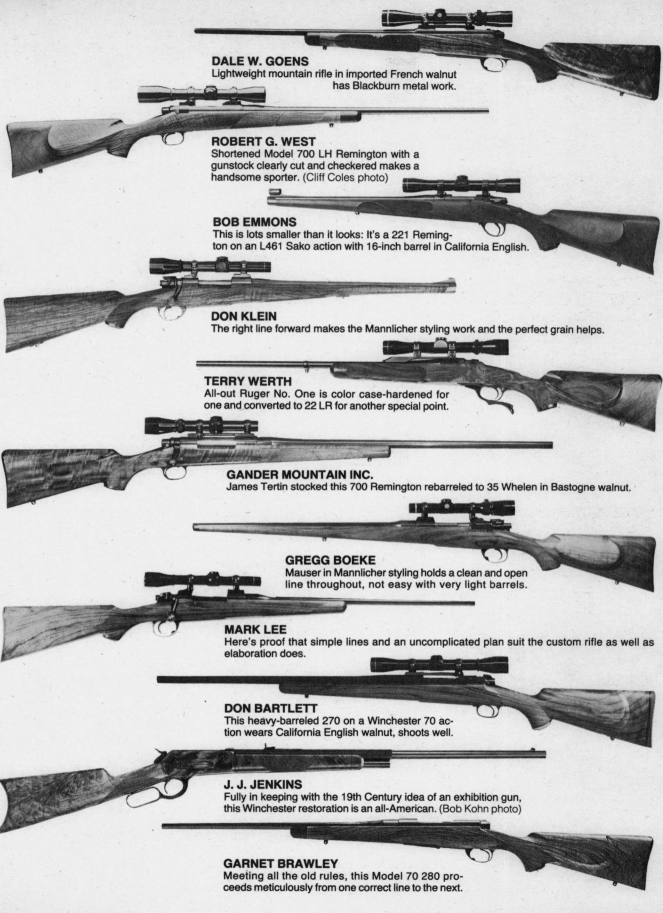

DALE W. GOENS
Lightweight mountain rifle in imported French walnut has Blackburn metal work.

ROBERT G. WEST
Shortened Model 700 LH Remington with a gunstock clearly cut and checkered makes a handsome sporter. (Cliff Coles photo)

BOB EMMONS
This is lots smaller than it looks: It's a 221 Remington on an L461 Sako action with 16-inch barrel in California English.

DON KLEIN
The right line forward makes the Mannlicher styling work and the perfect grain helps.

TERRY WERTH
All-out Ruger No. One is color case-hardened for one and converted to 22 LR for another special point.

GANDER MOUNTAIN INC.
James Tertin stocked this 700 Remington rebarreled to 35 Whelen in Bastogne walnut.

GREGG BOEKE
Mauser in Mannlicher styling holds a clean and open line throughout, not easy with very light barrels.

MARK LEE
Here's proof that simple lines and an uncomplicated plan suit the custom rifle as well as elaboration does.

DON BARTLETT
This heavy-barreled 270 on a Winchester 70 action wears California English walnut, shoots well.

J. J. JENKINS
Fully in keeping with the 19th Century idea of an exhibition gun, this Winchester restoration is an all-American. (Bob Kohn photo)

GARNET BRAWLEY
Meeting all the old rules, this Model 70 280 proceeds meticulously from one correct line to the next.

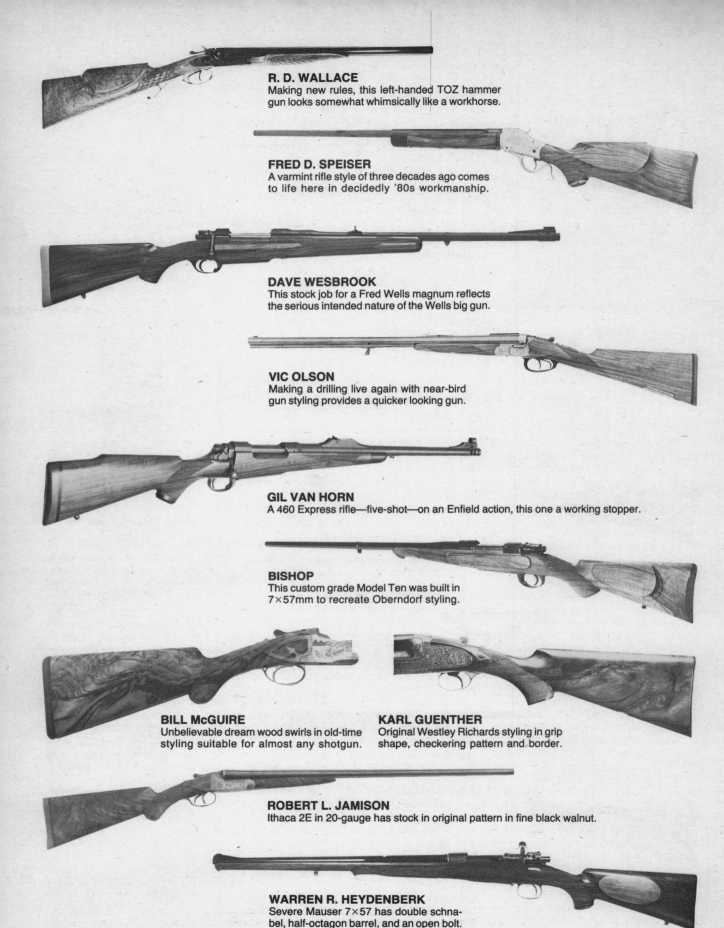

R. D. WALLACE
Making new rules, this left-handed TOZ hammer gun looks somewhat whimsically like a workhorse.

FRED D. SPEISER
A varmint rifle style of three decades ago comes to life here in decidedly '80s workmanship.

DAVE WESBROOK
This stock job for a Fred Wells magnum reflects the serious intended nature of the Wells big gun.

VIC OLSON
Making a drilling live again with near-bird gun styling provides a quicker looking gun.

GIL VAN HORN
A 460 Express rifle—five-shot—on an Enfield action, this one a working stopper.

BISHOP
This custom grade Model Ten was built in 7×57mm to recreate Oberndorf styling.

BILL McGUIRE
Unbelievable dream wood swirls in old-time styling suitable for almost any shotgun.

KARL GUENTHER
Original Westley Richards styling in grip shape, checkering pattern and border.

ROBERT L. JAMISON
Ithaca 2E in 20-gauge has stock in original pattern in fine black walnut.

WARREN R. HEYDENBERK
Severe Mauser 7×57 has double schnabel, half-octagon barrel, and an open bolt.

Ammunition, Ballistics and Components

by EDWARD A. MATUNAS

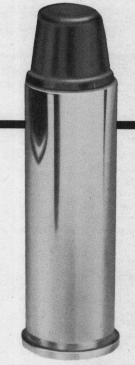

The new Federal 32 H&R Magnum with its 95-gr. semi-wadcutter bullet and a PIR value of 64 is a fine choice for small game hunting and suitable for emergency defense.

THE AMMUNITION and components manufacturers strive to make the consumer aware of their product lines. To gain increased market share, they introduce new products. Sometimes, these are innovative and fill a definite need. Others are only variations of existing items, and sometimes unneeded.

You, the consumer, always make the final decision on any new product, though factory problems can influence the success of any new item. Last year's hot news, the 357 Maximum, has proven somewhat of a headache and at this point its potential for success is somewhat shaky.

Manufacturers and consumers alike often refuse to have their enthusiasm dimmed by either start-up or continuing problems of a special load or component. And perhaps this is how it should be, for without new items things could get a bit dull. So without further delay let's look at the new or sometimes overlooked older goodies of the ammunition and component manufacturers for the next year.

Federal Cartridge Corp.

Federal continues to broaden the types of ammunition they offer to the shooter. They are filling in gaps in their own product line and also anticipating needs not currently filled by others.

A prime example is their newest revolver round. It's sometimes difficult to train new shooters with noisy cartridges or ones that produce even the modest level of recoil of the 38 Special. Too, some need exists for a mild cartridge for the person who would like to keep a gun at home, yet does not have the opportunity to shoot more than perhaps a box of shells per year.

Federal has recognized this need with a new 32-caliber magnum revolver cartridge. Designed for the new H&R Magnum revolver, it gives a 95-grain bullet a muzzle velocity of 1030 fps from a 4⅝-inch revolver. This new load does not have the usual round nose profile, but a well-shaped lead semi-wadcutter which generates 225 foot pounds of energy at the muzzle. That's double the energy of the usual 32-caliber revolver cartridge and greater than some 38 Special loads. With a PIR (Power Index Rating) value of 64 versus the 158-grain 38 Special round nose load's PIR of 56 (4-inch barrel), the new load is well up to the task of emergency defense. Too, it should make a fine small game load.

This new baby magnum round's case length of 1.075 inches precludes it from being used in existing 32 Smith & Wesson Long chambers. When teamed with the new Harrington & Richardson revolver it will prove a fine choice wherever minimum recoil and noise are desirable while affording ample smash to get a lot of handgun jobs done and done well. The accompanying table lists the comparative ballistics of this new round.

Federal's 32 H&R Magnum Comparative Ballistics

Cartridge	Bullet Weight	Velocity at: Muzzle	Velocity at: 50 yds.	Energy at: Muzzle	Energy at: 50 yds.	PIR at Muzzle	PIR at 50 yds.
32 H&R Mag.	95	1030	940	225	190	64	53
32 S&W	88	680	645	90	81	23	20
32 S&W Long	98	705	670	115	98	27	25
38 Special	158	755	723	200	183	56	51

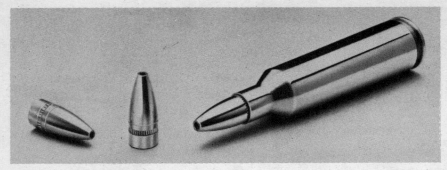

A 40-gr. hollow point bullet turns up a sizzling 4000 fps in the new Federal 22-250 Blitz.

Federal's Hot New 22-250 Remington 40-grain Jacketed Hollow Point Blitz

| | Range in yards | | | | | |
	-0-	-50-	-100-	-150-	-200-	-250-
Velocity (ft/s)	4000	3650	3320	3010	2720	2450
Energy (ft/lbs)	1420	1185	980	805	660	535
Mid-range traj. (in inches)	-0-	0.1	0.3	0.8	1.6	2.8
Drift in 10 mph crosswind (in.)	-0-	0.3	1.3	3.0	5.7	9.3

shot load to suit his needs. Federal's newest additions are 12- and 20-gauge loads using steel shot in No. 6 size. The 12-gauge load is a 1⅛-ounce shot charge and the 20-gauge load is ¾-ounce. Both 2¾-inch loads are light by lead shot standards, thus the hunter should accordingly shorten the range at which he will shoot. When one includes the shot size options, Federal now offers a total variety of 16 different steel shot loads. The nearby table will bring you abreast of all these various loadings. Either the 10-gauge or 12-gauge 3-inch loads will prove the most satisfactory for waterfowling.

Federal has also introduced some new lead shot loads. Waterfowl hunters, turkey shooters and others requiring extra heavy shot loads will find the latest 12-gauge 3-inch loading of particular interest as it has a full 2 ounces of shot for the payload. Up until now the only way to push 2 ounces of shot from the muzzle was to use a 10-gauge 3½-inch magnum.

To accomplish this increase in shot weight, Federal is using a one-piece

In the rifle ammo department, Federal has a new higher velocity 22-250 Remington load that delivers a sizzling 4000 fps (feet per second) muzzle velocity. The load uses a thin jacketed hollow point bullet. It's called Blitz and rapid expansion is assured. Despite the bullet's light weight it maintains flat trajectory and will therefore prove ideal for varminting to 300 yards or perhaps a bit more. As with other Federal varmint loads, great accuracy should be the norm. The accompanying table lists the specific ballistics of this new loading.

Another new rifle load introduced for 1984 by Federal is a Premium load with a Nosler Partition bullet option for the perennial favorite, the 30-30 Winchester. I'm not sure how many 30-30 users will be willing to spend the few extra cents per round to purchase these Premium loads but they are worthwhile and enhance the game-stopping potential of this popular cartridge. Complete data is shown in a nearby chart. Users should keep in mind that although 300-yard ballistics are shown, sportsmen should keep 30-30 shots to a 200-yard maximum.

I guess it's no secret that I find steel shot less than satisfactory for waterfowl shooting. Yet, steel shot has been mandated by law in specific waterfowl hunting areas. Therefore, the more options available the better the hunter will be able to select a steel

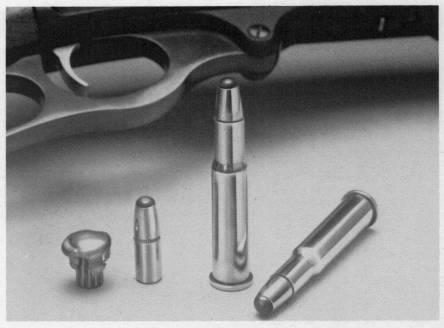

Federal's new Premium 30-30 load uses a 170-gr. Nosler Partition bullet and is sure to increase the effectiveness of this perennial favorite.

Federal's New Premium 170-grain 30-30 Winchester With Nosler Partition Bullet

| | Range in yards | | | |
	-0-	-100-	-200-	-300-
Velocity (ft/s)	2200	1900	1620	1380
Energy (ft/lbs)	1830	1355	990	720

Federal Steel Shot Loadings

Gauge	Shell Length	Drams Equiv.	Shot Wgt. in ounces	Available Shot Sizes
10	3½"	4¼	1⅝	BB, 2
12	3"	MAG.	1⅜	BB,1,2,4
12	2¾"	MAG.	1¼	BB,1,2,4
12	2¾"	MAX.	1⅛	2,4,6
20	3"	3¼	1	4
20	2¾"	3¼	¾	4,6

Above—Mandated by law in many localities, steel shot loads for waterfowling continue to be improved and broadened in scope. Federal is now offering a new No. 6 size steel shot load in both 12 and 20 gauge.

Below, left—Shown on the right is a 10-gauge load in 12-gauge disguise. Federal's new 12-gauge 3-in. load uses a full 2 oz. of shot, a charge weight previously available only in 3½-in. 10-gauge. It's a smasher for long range waterfowling or turkey hunting. The load on the left is Federal's new Heavyweight, a 12-gauge 1⅜-oz. high velocity loading. Below, right—Want to add 5 yards to your buckshot range? Try the new Federal Premium brand buckshot loads: extra hard copper-plated shot with a granulated polyethelene buffer and an elongated shot column.

plastic case that has a very low inner base, affording extra case volume. Available only in Federal's Premium line, it incorporates copper-plated, extra hard shot, granulated plastic shot buffer, and a plastic shot cup; all the good things that make long range shooting practical. Only 35 fps has been sacrificed in muzzle velocity compared to the existing 1⅞-ounce 12-gauge 3-inch load. With a muzzle velocity of 1175 fps and either No. 2 or No. 4 pellets, this load should prove extremely effective in providing dense, long range patterns.

A shot load long removed from factory loads has been returned in the new Federal 12-gauge 2¾-inch Heavyweight load for 1⅜ ounces of shot. Lately, factory ammo has been restricted to a maximum of 1¼ ounces of shot in high velocity loads yet the heavier 1⅜-ounce load is a better choice for large game birds such as pheasant. Federal's Heavyweight is being offered in shot sizes 2, 4, and 6. My choice for pheasants would be No. 4; I've also used 1⅜-ounces of No. 4s for ducks quite successfully when shooting over decoys; and 1⅜-ounces of No. 6s has always been my favorite prescription for crows. Velocity of the Heavyweight is 1295 fps, a scant 35 fps less than the usual high speed 1¼-ounce load. I'm happy to trade this

miniscule amount of velocity for the extra shot pellets.

As most buckshot users know, it is extremely difficult to obtain dense patterns with these giant pellets. Accordingly, when hunting deer with buckshot, the savvy hunter usually restricted his maximum range to 25 or perhaps 30 yards. You now may be able to add another 5 yards or so of practical range to these numbers by using the new Federal Premium buckshot loads, available in 12 gauge 00 and No. 4 buck. The 00 load is offered in a standard 9-pellet round or a short magnum 12-pellet load. Packaged in new 10-round packs, these loads use a higher antimony content lead alloy to insure hard pellets to help resist deformation as they travel

from case to muzzle. The pellets also receive a two-step polishing to help insure roundness and then they are copper plated. Granulated plastic buffer and a full plastic shot cup are used to assemble these rounds, and a unique system of pellet layering is employed to elongate the shot column, a final step to minimize shot deformation at the forcing cone and choke.

Federal is claiming that 90 percent of the pellets in the 00 loads and 80 percent of the No. 4 buck load will be contained in a 30-inch circle at 50 yards, when fired from a full choke. The way I see it, this means an effective pattern (15 inches in diameter) up to about 35 yards. And that indeed is quite a long way for buckshot.

Above—A reusable loading block style tray packs a number of Federal's handgun loads.

Right—Federal is offering the new 357 Maximum both as a loaded round (180-gr. JHP) and as a component case.

Federal 180-grain 357 Maximum in 10½-in. Revolver

	Range in meters:				
	-0-	-50-	-100-	-150-	-200-
Velocity (ft/s)	1550	1305	1135	1030	955
Energy (ft/lbs)	960	680	515	425	365
Mid-range trajectory (in inches)	0	0.6	3.0	7.8	15.5
PIR	357	253	191	157	136

Federal 210-grain 41 Remington Magnum Jacketed Hollow Point
(fired in a 4-in. vented test barrel)

	Range in yards:	
	-0-	-50-
Velocity (ft/s)	1300	1130
Energy (ft/lbs)	790	595
PIR	322	243

Reloaders will be happy to hear that all current production of Federal's 38 Special, 357 Magnum, 357 Maximum, 9mm Luger, 380 Auto, 32 S&W Long and 32 H&R Magnum are being packaged in the "Benchmark" reusable cartridge tray. The folks at Federal have introduced their version of the 357 Remington Maximum. It's a 180-grain jacketed hollow point that reportedly produces 1550 feet per second from a 10½-inch revolver barrel. Shipments were "on hold" for several months but resumed in early 1984.

Federal has gotten into the 22 Winchester Magnum Rimfire business with two 40-grain loads; one a jacketed hollow point and the other a full metal jacket. Both are rated for 1910 fps at the muzzle. Being a big fan of the magnum rimfire I'm looking forward to testing both loads. Federal now catalogs a 41 Remington Magnum 210-grain jacketed hollow point bullet at 1300 fps muzzle velocity. There's also a 95-grain jacketed soft point 9mm Luger round at 1350 fps.

Gone from Federal's newest catalog is the Premium 30-06 load with the 200-grain boattail soft point. No other deletions were noted in the centerfire cartridges. Gone from the rimfire lineup is 22 Long Rifle Pistol Match.

Federal's component line shows some new items. These include the 205M and 210M primers; small rifle match and large rifle match respectively. Also 357 Maximum empty, unprimed cases are listed as well as nickel-plated unprimed match cases for the 222 Remington and the 308 Winchester. All else in the component line seems the same. Some of the aforementioned components have been available previously, but have not, until now, been shown as standard catalog items. All in all it's been a busy year for the R & D folks at Federal.

If you're looking for some very accu-

Federal 22 Winchester Magnum Rimfire 40-grain bullets

Bullet	Velocity (ft/s) at:		Energy (ft/lbs) at:		Traj. in inches (at yards)		
	Muzzle	100 yds.	Muzzle	100 yds.	50	100	150
Jacketed HP	1910	1330	325	155	+1.3	⊕	−6.1
Full Metal Case	1910	1330	325	155	+1.3	⊕	−6.1

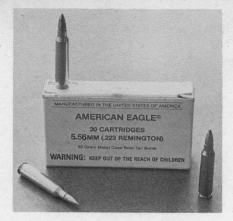

This is the most accurate of all the military style 223 ammo the author used: Federal's American Eagle brand with 55-gr. FMJ bullets.

rate 223, full metal cased ammunition you might want to try some of Federal's American Eagle brand ammo in the plain white wrapper. It is by far the most accurate military style ammo I have used to date. Its accuracy performance has made all other similar ammo very poor second choices in my rifles.

Remington Arms Co.

New product folks at Remington have been busy with quite a few new rifles and shotguns during the past year and hence the ammunition line has remained relatively unchanged. Of course, there have been on-going changes. For instance, depending upon how fast your dealer turns over his shotshell inventory, all of the SP shotshells with their separate asbestos-like base wad are being replaced with a new one-piece all plastic case body.

Last year, I wrote about the then-new Premier Remington shotshells. These shells embodied all of the advances that have, over the years, been made in shotshells. Such aspects as a one-piece plastic wad, extra hard copper-plated shot and granulated polyethelene buffering were used to give the best possible long range patterns. Too, these shells use a very strong one-piece plastic hull which reloaders will find especially well-suited to their needs.

"Copper-Lokt" extra-hard copper-plated shot

Plastic buffer compound

"Power-Piston" one-piece wad and shot container

One-piece plastic hull for extra strength

Remington "Premier" Shotgun Shell 12-Gauge, 2¾-inch Magnum

Above—The author field-tested the 12-gauge Remington 1½-ounce Premier load of No. 2s with obvious success. Premier loads are well-suited, among other things, to long range pass shooting.

Left—A cutaway of the Remington premium grade shotshell called Premier. Extra hard copper-plated shot, granulated polyethelene buffer and a Power Piston wad all add up to a practical extension of maximum range.

The Premier shells did not become generally available, it seems, until quite late in 1983, hence many shooters have not as yet had the opportunity to try them. I was able to use a quantity of Premier shells during the 1983-84 waterfowl season. They are capable of regularly taking ducks or geese at notably longer ranges than

Remington's Power Lokt Loads

Caliber	Bullet Wgt. (grs.)	Velocity (ft/s) at: Muzzle	100 yds.	200 yds.	300 yds.	Energy (ft/lbs) at: Muzzle	100 yds.	200 yds.	300 yds.	Average[1] Accuracy (in inches)
17 Remington	25	4040	3284	2644	2086	906	599	388	242	⅞
222 Remington	50	3140	2635	2182	1777	1094	771	529	351	⅝
222 Rem. Mag.	55	3240	2773	2352	1969	1282	939	675	473	1
223 Remington	55	3240	2773	2352	1969	1282	939	675	473	⅞
22-250 Rem.	55	3680	3209	2785	2400	1654	1257	947	703	1
243 Winchester	80	3350	2955	2593	2259	1993	1551	1194	906	1⅛
6mm Remington	80	3470	3064	2694	2352	2139	1667	1289	982	1⅛
25-06 Remington	87	3440	2995	2591	2222	2286	1753	1297	954	1

(1) Average of five 5-shot groups at 100 yards from a test rifle

Above—Remington Power Lokt loads are something special in the accuracy department without the need to handload. One-inch groups, or less, are not uncommon with these fine shooting bullets.

Above—One of Winchester's newest offerings in target rimfire ammunition is the 22 Super Silhouette round which features a heavier than normal 42-gr. bullet in a truncated cone configuration.

Right—The Super-Max is Winchester's hyper velocity long rifle replacement for the now defunct 22 Xpediter.

any ammo that could be purchased a number of years ago. The hard plated shot and buffering do help patterns considerably.

Most waterfowlers are quick to jump at any shell that offers extended range or pattern improvement, but other hunters can benefit, too. Much of my pheasant hunting is for wild flushing birds often fired on at 40 yards or more. On more than just a few crow shoots, I've seen the closest bird 10 yards above the tree tops which meant 50-to 60-yard shooting. If your shooting is at long range, you might try some of these truly improved shotshells.

If you reload only because factory rifle rounds are not accurate enough for you, perhaps you have not tried the Remington Power Lokt loads. These are available in 17 Remington (25 grain), 222 Remington (50 grain), 222 Remington Magnum (55 grain), 223 Remington (55 grain), 22-250 Remington (55 grain), 243 Winchester (80 grain), 6mm Remington (80 grain), and 25-06 Remington (87 grain). All are hollow-pointed bullets designed for rapid expansion on varmints. These bullets are made by plating the jacket material to a lead core and they are accurate. In my rifles Power Lokt loads shoot as well as my best reloads. For example, in my Remington 222 Model Seven with its lightweight 18½-inch barrel, I consistently get ½-inch to ¾-inch 5-shot groups at 100 yards. And that, my friends is fine accuracy from any hunting rifle with even the best reloads.

Winchester

More 22-caliber rimfire ammunition is fired than any other type. During the past decade or so, manufacturers have tried a number of new Long Rifle variations. Some of these have been successful and others have not. The Winchester Xpediter cartridge, for example, has passed into oblivion. This has, however, not dampened Winchester's spirits and indeed we now have two new 22 Winchester rounds: the new Super Silhouette 22 Long Rifle and the even newer Super-Max 22 Long Rifle.

I have burned up a fair quantity of the Super Silhouette rounds, with their heavier 42-grain bullet. Checked with my Oehler chronograph these loads turned in an average velocity of 1227 fps from several 24-inch barrels. The standard deviation was 18 fps with an extreme variation of 67 fps, and the muzzle energy was 140 ft/lbs. The new round is obviously aimed at rimfire silhouette shooting, be it with rifle or handgun. Acceptance could prove a good thing for Winchester. In my test rifles accuracy has been good, but not great. Accuracy in his own firearm should guide the individual, of course.

The Super-Max round is hyper-ve-

Winchester 42-grain Super Silhouette 22 LR

| Cartridge | Velocity (ft/s) at: | | Energy (ft/lbs) at: | |
	Muzzle	100 yds.	Muzzle	100 yds.
22 Super Silhouette	1220	1003	139	94
T-22	1150	976	117	85

Winchester 34-grain Hollow Point Super-Max 22 Long Rifle

| Cartridge | Velocity (ft/s) at: | | | Energy (ft/lbs) at: | | |
	Muzzle	50 yds.	100 yds.	Muzzle	50 yds.	100 yds.
Super-Max 34 gr.HP	1500	1250	1081	170	118	88
Super-X 38 gr.HP	1280	1107	1015	135	101	85
T-22 40 gr. solid	1150	1055	976	117	99	85

Winchester Ballistics

Cartridge	Bullet Weight (grs.)	Barrel Length (inches)	Velocity in ft/s at:				Energy in ft/lbs at:			
			Muzzle	100 yds.	200 yds.	300 yds.	Muzzle	100 yds.	200 yds.	300 yds.
223 Remington	53	24	3330	2882	2477	2106	1305	978	722	522
30-06 Springfield	165	24	2800	2573	2357	2151	2873	2426	2036	1696

Winchester 38 Special + P 125 gr. Silvertip Hollow Point

Velocity in ft/s at:			Energy in ft/lbs at:			Mid-range Trajectory	
Muzzle	50 yds.	100 yds.	Muzzle	50 yds.	100 yds.	50 yds.	100 yds.
945	898	858	248	224	204	1.3″	5.4″

Ballistics specs for 4-inch vented barrel.

locity, its 34-grain hollow point bullet claimed to produce a muzzle velocity of 1500 fps in a 24-inch barrel. As with similar rounds, Super-Max offers extra energy and more violent expansion up to 50 or 60 yards when compared to the usual Long Rifle high speed hollow point. At the 100-yard mark, ballistics usually fall off enough so that there is no advantage to the hyper-velocity load. I have yet to try the Winchester round.

Another superb Silvertip hollow point handgun load—a 125-grain 38 Special +P load—is now in the Winchester centerfire lineup. Rapid and violent expansion without loss of bullet weight is a characteristic of all the Silvertip hollow point rounds. And also new from Winchester is a 53-grain hollow point load for the popular 223 Remington cartridge. This load uses a very frangible bullet that provides maximum fragmentation at the target. Muzzle velocity is just over 3300 fps from a 24-inch barrel. Then, at last we have a 165-grain bullet in 30-06 from Winchester for the 30-06 Springfield. Ballistics are similar to the already popular Remington and the bullet is a pointed soft point. In the shotshell department, there is now a 20-gauge 3-inch magnum steel shot load with one ounce of No. 4 pellets.

Gone are the Super Target loads which used the paper case. Also gone is the 25-20 lead bullet load (the jacketed soft point load is still listed). The 87-grain 257 Roberts load is also now history. Dropped is the 220-grain loading for the 30-40 Krag as well as the 150 and 220-grain bullet weights for the 300 H&H Magnum. This shooter, who favors the 300 H&H, is sad to see the choice down to just the

180-grain bullet. Also, the 250-grain loading for the 358 Winchester passed into history. In rimfire cartridges the 40-grain Winchester Dynapoint has passed beyond. And the handloader will be finding one of the Ball Powders somewhat difficult to locate—

785. Currently, this powder is in short supply. The last Winchester powder that fell into short supply—630—finally was dropped.

Norma

Norma brass cases are beginning to see, once again, sufficient distribution to make them available to a large number of reloaders. Some hard to get calibers are currently seeing at least limited availability. These include the 22 Savage (5.6×52R), 7.7 Jap, 7.65 Argentine, 308 Norma Magnum, 6.5 Jap, 6.5 Carcano, 6.5×55, 7×57R, 7×64 and 7.5 Swiss. In addition the

Left—Norma's 50-gr. 222 FMC load is a good choice for hunting fur bearers. Below—U.S. Ammunition Co. offers a truly new innovation in commercially available cartridges: a plastic case moulded to a brass head. Shades of the old Dartig 'round! 38 Special only in the beginning, with more to come. It's easily reloadable.

loaded rounds are seeing somewhat increased distribution by the sole U.S. representative, Outdoor Sports Headquarters, Inc.

The loaded rounds include some of the standards such as 222 Remington, 243 Winchester, 270 Winchester and 30-06 Springfield. Plenty of hard to find calibers are also offered including 22 Savage, 6.5 Jap, 7.62×39 Russian and others.

I had the opportunity to shoot some 150-grain 30-06 and some 270 Norma ammo during the past year. While my samples were limited to two boxes of each type, I was favorably impressed with the accuracy of each load. I also got to fire several boxes of 222 Remington loads using a full metal case bullet. Accuracy was good enough to make this load useful on fur bearers such as fox or coyote. With such a non-expanding bullet, shots must be placed precisely in a vital area or your quarry will escape wounded.

The Norma 130-grain 270 load continues to be the most accurate factory load in this caliber based on tests in my various 270 rifles. I have a Remington 700 Classic which will consistently shoot into 1¼ inches at 100 yards with this load.

U.S. Ammunition Company

A new West Coast concern, U.S. Ammunition, has a truly new ammo product—plastic cased 38 Special ammo. Four different loads will be available including a 148-grain wadcutter, 150-grain semi-wadcutter, 158 grain semi-wadcutter and 158-grain round nose. Bullets are lead with a copper plating and USAC refers to them as FMJ bullets.

The plastic cases are fully reloadable on a palm-sized tool offered by this ammo maker. I have been told that about $50 will buy all the tools necessary to load these cases which can be reloaded repeatedly. The plastic case is flexible enough to allow easy seating of the bullet yet rigid enough to hold it securely in place. Because the plastic cases are reported to return to their original dimensions after the expansion of firing, no resizing or trimming of the plastic case should be required. When bullets will no longer seat tight, just boil the empty plastic cases for 5 minutes to obtain a new fit. Those guiding this new ammunition company have indicated that their plastic case (which is moulded to a brass head) offers price advantages as well as some ballistic advantage. Also they indicate that their product line will be broadened extensively as time goes on.

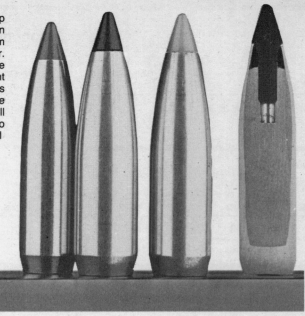

Nosler's new Ballistic Tip bullets are available in three diameters—270, 7mm and 30-caliber. Reminiscent of the Remington Bronze Point bullets, these components feature a polycarbonate color-coded tip which will not become deformed due to rough handling or recoil

U.S. Ammunition is currently moving to new facilities which will be located at 1476 Thorne Road, Tacoma, WA 98421 (206-627-8700). At this time I'm happy to report that this new ammunition company sold an entire year's production at one distributor show. This new product has obviously been well-received. Distribution should be well underway when you read this.

U.S. Ammunition is also offering a wide range of component bullets for standard cases. These are a copper-plated, lead core style and are being offered as FMJ bullets. Included are several 125-grain 9mm, three 38/357 Magnum styles, a 220-grain 41 caliber and a 240-grain 44 caliber, as well as both 200 and 230-grain 45 caliber bullets. And a round ball line with 14 diameters ranging from .310-in to .570-in. will also be available.

Component bullets for the plastic cases are also in the lineup. These cases require USAC heeled bullets which snap into the narrower-than-usual case mouths. Perhaps the most outstanding feature, other than the plastic case, of this ammunition and these components is cost; lower than usual by a notable amount. As a plus, the plated bullets do away with the leading and smoke associated with lubricated bullets.

Nosler

How many times have you dropped, banged or otherwise dinged-up the soft points on your reloaded rifle ammunition? Or perhaps you have had bullet tips damaged in your rifle during recoil or feeding. Well, it need never happen again due to a new style

of expanding bullet being offered by Nosler. It's called Ballistic Tip bullet.

The new projectile features a polycarbonate tip which fits into a hollow point nose; much like the Remington Bronze Point bullet. The exposed lead tip of a normal hunting bullet is completely eliminated. Too, the new bullet will help prevent you from attempting to load the wrong diameter as each caliber is color coded: yellow for 270, red for 7mm and green for 30 caliber.

Ballistic Tip bullets are being offered in both 130 and 150-grain weights for the 270 with 140 and 150-grain bullets available in 7mm diameter, while 30 caliber bullets are available in three weights: 150, 165 and 180-grain. Accuracy and expansion, if up to Nosler's usual standard should prove to be excellent.

Sierra

The Sierra bullet folks continue to expand their bullet line at a very rapid pace, with nine new bullets being available this year. The smallest of the new offerings is a 40-grain hollow point, most similar to that used in Federal's new 22-250 Blitz loading. Other new 22-caliber bullets include 55-grain hollow point boattail and a 60-grain hollow point.

In addition, a 69-grain hollow point boattail bullet has been introduced, although it is going to require a very fast twist rate to stabilize it. My guess is that it will not be suitable in most commercially produced 22-caliber barrels. What's the right rate of twist? I would be inclined to try a 1-8-in. or perhaps even a bit faster. A 1-10-in. twist will probably prove too slow.

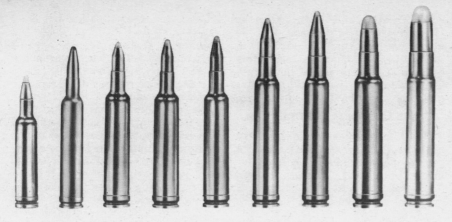

The Weatherby Magnum cartridge lineup is a somewhat overlooked source of beefed-up performance. See Weatherby ballistic table for performance specifications. From left to right: 224, 240, 257, 270, 7mm, 300, 340, 378 and 460.

The Activ shotshell, soon in loaded rounds, uses an all-plastic case with a metal insert in the head and a very low inner base.

This bullet will probably see its greatest use in some of the service rifle matches with barrels specially rifled to handle it.

Target shooters might find Sierra's new 150-grain 30 caliber full metal jacketed boattail bullet of interest. Other new bullets are a 115-grain FMJ 9mm and a 180-grain FMJ Match grade 38/357 diameter bullet. A 250-grain FPJ Match bullet (44 caliber) and a 200-grain FPJ) Match bullet (45 caliber) will become available this year.

PMC

The Patton and Morgan Corporation has moved their headquarters from New York City to Los Angeles. As reported previously in these pages, this outfit has been expanding upon their original line of full metal cased military ammo. The parent company, located in Korea, has added quite a few soft point hunting bullets to the product line.

This year shows no changes in the company's aggressiveness, with a number of new loads being offered to the U.S. sportsmen. The new rounds include a 55-grain soft point and a full metal case load for the 22-250 Remington. The 30-30 Winchester cartridge is now available in both the popular 150-grain and 170-grain bullet weights, both soft points. And the 300 Winchester Magnum cartridge is being offered in 150 and 180-grain hunting rounds.

But perhaps of most interest is the new line of PMC rimfire cartridges: Shorts, Longs and Long Rifles too. High velocity and standard velocity offerings are available and, wanting a complete line of rimfire cartridges, the PMC folks will also be offering 22

Magnum rounds in full metal cased and jacketed hollow point configurations. Obviously, the billions of rounds of rimfire ammo fired annually in the U.S. has become an appealing market to this Asian firm.

Fiocchi

This Italian manufactuer has previously maintained a U.S. based manufacturing facility in Alton, Illinois. Remember the joint Alcan/Fiocchi effort? However, they have been absent from the U.S. market for a long time. Recently Fiocchi management decided to renew their efforts in the U.S. and a new facility is being readied. Their immediate efforts will, of course, be directed at the shotshell market.

Their first price sheets show low prices for 18 different shotshell loads, with several choices of shot size and type in each, covering the full range of U.S. shotgun activity. Also priced are primers, and 10 rimfire 22 loads, and 20 handgun loads in 15 calibers.

Some of those handgun cartridges will be very welcome. They include 38 Automatic; 7.62mm Nagant; 7.63 Mauser; 30 Luger; 9mm Steyr; and 455 Webley (Mk. II).

Hornady-Frontier

This Grand Island, Nebraska firm has announced five new bullets, all handgun items. There is a 71-grain 32 caliber and a 124-grain 9mm, both full metal jacketed round nose styles. In addition, there are a 160-grain 38/357, a 180-grain 38/357 and a 240-grain 44 caliber, each a jacketed truncated cone bullet designed for silhouette shooting. These three all have a flat nosed profile.

Hornady, as you know, loads up

their own bullets into factory shells that are sold under the Frontier brand. Currently there are some 19 different calibers being offered. The newest of these loads are a 60-grain 22-250 Remington, a 154-grain 7mm Remington Magnum, a 180-grain 300 Winchester Magnum, a 124-grain full metal jacket 9mm Luger, a 140-grain jacketed hollow point 38 Special (and 357 Magnum), a 180-grain Silhouette load for the 357 Magnum and a 240-grain Silhouette load for the 44 Remington Magnum.

JCL-Zigor Corp.

Since 1980 Rainel de Puerto Rico has been attempting to market their all-plastic shotshell in the U.S. (This shell has a steel disc moulded into the head.) They have succeeded only in getting a minimum number of cases into the reloading market. Now tactics have changed and the company has opened facilities in Kearneysville, West Virginia to load the Puerto Rican-manufactured case. The new shotshell ammo will be marketed under the ACTIV brand name. Reloaders may not take well to this case as it requires some modification of existing popular loading tools to accommodate its very low inner base wad.

Rumor has it that the company plans to undertake manufacturing at about a 50 million rounds per year level, using components purchased from major U.S. manufacturers. Only time will tell exactly what will occur. In addition I'm told that the new company will be marketing products which will be imported from Spain.

Estate Cartridge of Conroe, TX, has announced it will produce custom-loaded, custom-market cartridges using the ACTIV shell cases.

They begin with eight 12-bore loads and four for the 20, and intend to offer scatter loads, low-recoil loads and other special items. A key to their marketing will be personalized or corporate logos on every shell.

Industrias Technos

This Mexican firm has an ammunition production facility in Cuernavaca in the state of Morelos. A high capacity shot tower is part of the facility as well as machinery ranging from some old Remington equipment to some very modern tooling. They turn out a fine line of 22 rimfire ammunition as well as a broad spectrum of shotshell loads and some metallic cartridges.

Industrias Technos fully realizes that the U.S. sporting market represents the largest single opportunity in the entire world. Hence, they and a number of other worldwide companies are attempting to furnish loaded rounds for the U.S. consumer. There are no new products *per se*, but rather a new source of familiar loads. It's going to be a difficult job for these new companies to compete with the giant U.S. firms. Companies such as I.T. do not as yet fully understand the U.S. market and what motivates shooters to favor specific products, but surely the extra competition will not hurt and might even be stimulating.

Brass Extrusion Laboratories

BELL continues to make empty brass cartridge cases available for a good number of oldie-but-goodies. Included in the BELL line are British, European and American oddities. If you want to load for an old Sharps or a big English double rifle this outfit might just have what you need. Some loaded ammo is also available for the 416 Rigby, 470 Nitro Express, 500/465 Nitro Express and several other similar calibers.

Bumble Bee

Bumble Bee Wholesale in California is currently the sole U.S. agent for a French-made line of personal defense loads that, as a whole, are nonlethal. Cart-A-Buck and Cart-A-Ball are the names of the firm's 12 gauge shotgun loads that feature rubber—that's right, RUBBER—buckshot or a round rubber ball. Meant for crowd control and used by various branches of the French government, these loads are said to be proven deterrents to household invaders.

No toys, they can inflict mortal injury if the range is short enough and depending upon the portions of the anatomy actually struck. Wide distribution is unlikely at this time, but national advertising will make it possible for most dealers to obtain an inventory of these loads.

Sample shells were loaded with black powder but subsequent production is to be loaded with a black powder substitute. 'Tis a pity the black powder loads are not so marked, as a fine shotgun barrel might be ruined for failure of the owner to clean it promptly after firing one of these shells.

Dynamit Nobel

With headquarters in Northvale, New Jersey and a parent company in Germany, this firm is constantly trying to make inroads into the U.S. ammunition market. For a number of reasons their products do not see an overwhelming amount of distribution yet most shooters are at least aware of one item they sell: the famous Rottweil Brenneke shotgun slugs. Also, the R50 brand of RWS 22 Long Rifle ammunition is among the most accurate such ammo manufactured in the world. However, a low marketing profile may keep these and other fine ammunition products in the Dynamit Nobel line from being readily available in your neck of the woods.

At press-time it was learned that **Paul Jaeger, Inc.**, of Jenkintown, PA, will handle RWS centerfire rifle rounds to serve shooters with foreign rifles, selling them through, or delivering them through, local dealers. Jaeger says it will sell as little as one 20-round box at a time in this program.

Israel Military Industries

Not much new to report here other than a name change. As you probably are aware, IMI has been selling ammunition in the U.S. under the Eagle brand. This name has been replaced by Samson; why, for the life of this old marketing man, I can't imagine. Unless all my market savvy has gone sour, "Samson" will not pull as well as "Eagle." Of course, the product itself remains unchanged. The largest volume of Eagle ammo full metal cased bullets has been used for plinking in

The new Cart-A-Buck and Cart-A-Ball 12-gauge loads feature rubber pellets or a rubber ball projectile(s) and are intended for non-lethal crowd control or personal protection.

the military style rifles and handguns. There is no reason to expect any changes. The major appeal of the IMI rounds has been, of course, its low pricing. It's this type of ammo that makes shooting affordable for the majority of us.

The Samson line includes cartridges for the 9mm Luger, 38 Special, 357 Magnum, 380 Auto and the 45 ACP as well as the very popular 223 Remington and 308 Winchester rounds.

Worthy Products

The folks who put together the very accurate Worthy 12 gauge rifled slugs have moved to Box 88, Chippewa Bay, NY 13623. The Worthy slugs are now packaged in a 5-round box instead of the earlier 25-round size.

An increased level of effectiveness has been put into the Worthy Slug with the manufacturer increasing the powder charge by 1½ grains. A recent test of these slugs loaded with the new powder charge showed no deterioration in accuracy levels. Worthy slugs continue to be one of the most accurate big game loads available to those who hunt with a 12 gauge gun.

Omark

The Omark folks have extended the CCI Blazer line of ammunition to include the 25 Auto. This aluminum cased line of ammunition costs from 30 to 50 percent less than brass cased ammo and is ideal for those who do not reload. The new 25 ACP round uses a 45-grain jacketed hollow point bullet at 850 fps.

Also there are some new Speer bullets. These include a 50-grain FMJ bullet for the 25 ACP and a 124-grain FMJ bullet for the 9mm as well as a 230-grain FMJ bullet for the 45 ACP. Also new is a 98-grain lead hollow base wadcutter for 32 caliber revolvers. This bullet is currently available only in bulk quantities. The two new rifle bullets are a 6.5mm 140-grain HPBT match grade bullet and a 9.3mm (.366″ diameter) 270-grain spitzer soft point. For those who need bullets of this diameter, this hard to find selection should be warmly received.

Conclusion

Each year a great many smaller companies try to enter the U.S. market with reloaded, imported or even newly manufactured ammunition and components. Of course, it would be impossible to report on or even be aware of each of these companies. GUN DIGEST strives to report on all

Dynamit Nobel imports the RWS R50 22 Long Rifle cartridges, among the world's most accurate rimfire ammunition.

those whose products are generally available or whose products are unique enough to have interest to our readers. The developments or product lines changes of the big suppliers as well as items such as rubber buck shot, rubber slugs and plastic cased pistol ammunition, are the kinds of ammo products we feel are newsworthy. If we ever miss something noteworthy, let us know. We will give it every consideration for inclusion in the next issue. Ditto for worthwhile components.

Worthy Products newest slug loading has increased velocity and a new 5-round pack. Average group sizes of 2¾ inches for 5 shots were obtained during 50-yard testing.

CENTERFIRE RIFLE CARTRIDGES—BALLISTICS AND PRICES

(R) = REMINGTON; (W) = WINCHESTER-WESTERN); (F) = FEDERAL; (H) = HORNADY-FRONTIER; (PMC) = Patton & Morgan Corp.

Cartridge	— BULLET — Wt. Grs.	Type	Bbl. (in.)	— VELOCITY (fps) — Muzzle	100 yds.	200 yds.	300 yds.	— ENERGY (ft. lbs.) — Muzzle	100 yds.	200 yds.	300 yds.	— BULLET PATH† — 100 yds.	200 yds.	300 yds.	Price Per Box
17 Remington (R)	25	HPPL	24	4040	3284	2644	2086	906	599	388	242	+0.5	− 1.5	− 8.5	N.A.
22 Hornet (R) (W)	45	PSP,HP, OPE	24	2690	2042	1502	1128	723	417	225	127	0.0	− 7.7	− 31.3	*24.50
218 Bee (W)	46	OPE	24	2760	2102	1550	1155	778	451	245	136	0.0	− 7.2	− 29.4	*36.95
222 Remington (R) (W) (F) (H)	50	PSP, SX	24	3140	2602	2123	1700	1094	752	500	321	+2.2	0.0	− 10.0	10.45
222 Remington (R)	50	HPPL	24	3140	2635	2182	1777	1094	771	529	351	+2.1	0.0	− 9.5	N.A.
222 Remington (W) (R) (PMC)	55	FMC	24	3020	2675	2355	2057	1114	874	677	517	+2.0	0.0	− 8.3	10.45
222 Remington (F)	55	MC BT	24	3020	2740	2480	2230	1115	915	750	610	+1.9	0.0	− 7.7	10.45
222 Remington Magnum (R)	55	PSP	24	3240	2748	2305	1906	1282	922	649	444	+1.9	0.0	− 8.5	N.A.
222 Remington Magnum (R)	55	HPPL	24	3240	2773	2352	1969	1282	939	675	473	+1.8	0.0	− 8.5	N.A.
223 Remington (R) (W) (F) (H) (PMC)	55	PSP	24	3240	2747	2304	1905	1282	921	648	443	+1.9	0.0	− 8.5	11.45
223 Remington (R)	55	HPPL	24	3240	2773	2352	1969	1282	939	675	473	+1.8	0.0	− 8.2	N.A.
223 Remington (R) (H)	55	MC	24	3240	2759	2326	1933	1282	929	660	456	+1.9	0.0	− 8.4	11.45
223 Remington (W) (F) (PMC)	55	FMC, MC BT	24	3240	2877	2543	2232	1282	1011	790	608	+1.7	0.0	− 7.1	11.45
225 Winchester (W)	55	PSP	24	3570	3066	2616	2208	1556	1148	836	595	+1.2	0.0	− 6.2	12.70
22-250 Remington (R) (W) (F) (H) (PMC)	55	PSP	24	3730	3180	2695	2257	1699	1235	887	622	+1.0	0.0	− 5.7	11.45
22-250 Remington (R)	55	HPPL	24	3730	3253	2826	2436	1699	1292	975	725	+0.9	0.0	− 5.2	N.A.
22-250 Remington (F) — Premium	55	BTHP	24	3730	3330	2960	2630	1700	1350	1070	840	+0.8	0.0	− 4.8	12.40
220 Swift (H)	55	SP	24	3630	3176	2755	2370	1609	1229	927	686	+1.0	0.0	− 5.6	14.70
220 Swift (H)	60	HP	24	3530	3134	2763	2420	1657	1305	1016	780	+1.1	0.0	− 5.7	14.70
243 (W) (R) (F) (H) (PMC)	80	PSP, HPPL, FMJ	24	3350	2955	2593	2259	1993	1551	1194	906	+1.6	0.0	− 7.0	14.30
243 Winchester (F) — Premium	85	BTHP	24	3320	3070	2830	2600	2080	1770	1510	1280	+1.5	0.0	− 6.8	15.25
243 Winchester (W) (R) (F) (H) (PMC)	100	PPSP, PSPCL, SP	24	2960	2697	2449	2215	1945	1615	1332	1089	+1.9	0.0	− 7.8	14.30
243 Winchester (F) — Premium	100	BTSP	24	2960	2760	2570	2380	1950	1690	1460	1260	+1.4	0.0	− 5.8	15.25
6mm Remington (R) (W) (Also, 244 Rem.)	80	PSP, HPPL	24	3470	3064	2694	2352	2139	1667	1289	982	+1.2	0.0	− 6.0	14.30
6mm Remington (R) (W) (F)	100	PSPCL, PPSP	24	3130	2857	2600	2357	2175	1812	1501	1233	+1.7	0.0	− 6.8	14.30
25-20 Winchester (W) (R)	86	SP	24	1460	1194	1030	931	407	272	203	165	0.0	−23.5	− 79.6	*23.20
256 Winchester (W)	60	OPE	24	2760	2097	1542	1149	1015	586	317	176	0.0	− 7.3	− 29.6	*29.85
25-35 Winchester (W)	117	SP	24	2230	1866	1545	1282	1292	904	620	427	0.0	− 9.2	− 33.1	16.60
250 Savage (W)	87	PSP	24	3030	2673	2342	2036	1773	1380	1059	801	+2.0	0.0	− 8.4	14.50
250 Savage (W)	100	ST	24	2820	2467	2140	1839	1765	1351	1017	751	+2.4	0.0	− 10.1	14.50
250 Savage (R)	100	PSP	24	2820	2504	2210	1936	1765	1392	1084	832	+2.3	0.0	− 9.5	N.A.
257 Roberts (W)	100	ST	24	2900	2541	2210	1904	1867	1433	1084	805	+2.3	0.0	− 9.4	14.50
257 Roberts (W) (R)	117	PPSP, SPCL	24	2650	2291	1961	1663	1824	1363	999	718	+2.9	0.0	− 12.0	14.50
25-06 Remington (R)	87	HPPL	24	3440	2995	2591	2222	2286	1733	1297	954	+1.2	0.0	− 6.3	N.A.
25-06 Remington (W) (F)	90	PEP, HP	24	3440	3043	2680	2344	2364	1850	1435	1098	+1.2	0.0	− 6.1	15.50
25-06 Remington (R)	100	PSPCL	24	3230	2893	2580	2287	2316	1858	1478	1161	+1.6	0.0	− 6.9	N.A.
25-06 Remington (F)	117	SP	24	3060	2790	2530	2280	2430	2020	1660	1360	+1.8	0.0	− 7.3	15.50
25-06 Remington (R) (W)	120	PSPCL, PEP	24	3010	2749	2502	2269	2414	2013	1668	1372	+1.9	0.0	− 7.4	15.50
6.5mm Remington Magnum (R)	120	PSPCL	24	3210	2905	2621	2353	2745	2248	1830	1475	+1.3	0.0	− 6.6	N.A.
264 Winchester Magnum (W) (R)	100	PSP, PSPCL	24	3320	2926	2565	2231	2447	1901	1461	1105	+1.3	0.0	− 6.7	20.05
264 Winchester Magnum (W) (R)	140	PPSP, PSPCL	24	3030	2782	2548	2326	2854	2406	2018	1682	+1.8	0.0	− 7.2	20.05
270 Winchester (W) (R)	100	PSP	24	3480	3067	2690	2343	2689	2088	1606	1219	+1.2	0.0	− 6.2	15.50
270 Winchester (W) (R) (F)	130	PPSP, BP, SP	24	3110	2849	2604	2371	2791	2343	1957	1622	+1.7	0.0	− 6.8	15.50
270 Winchester (W) (R) (H) (PMC)	130	ST, PSPCL	24	3110	2823	2554	2300	2791	2300	1883	1527	+1.7	0.0	− 7.1	15.50
270 Winchester (F) — Premium	130	BTSP	24	3110	2880	2670	2460	2790	2400	2050	1740	+1.6	0.0	− 6.5	16.60
270 Winchester (W) (H)	150	PPSP	24	2900	2632	2380	2142	2801	2307	1886	1528	+2.1	0.0	− 8.2	15.50
270 Winchester (F) — Premium	150	BTSP	24	2900	2710	2520	2350	2800	2440	2120	1830	+1.6	0.0	− 7.0	16.60
270 Winchester (R) (F)	150	SPCL, SP	24	2900	2550	2225	1926	2801	2165	1649	1235	+2.2	0.0	− 9.3	15.50
270 Winchester (F) — Premium	150	NP	24	2900	2630	2380	2140	2800	2310	1890	1530	+2.1	0.0	− 8.2	20.35
7mm Mauser (R) (W)	175	SP	24	2440	2137	1857	1603	2313	1774	1340	998	0.0	− 6.8	− 23.7	15.80
7mm Mauser (F)	175	SP	24	2470	2170	1880	1630	2370	1820	1380	1030	0.0	− 6.6	− 23.0	15.80
7mm Mauser (F)	140	SP	24	2660	2450	2260	2070	2200	1865	1585	1330	+2.4	0.0	− 3.2	15.80
7mm-08 Remington (R)	140	PSPCL	24	2860	2625	2402	2189	2542	2142	1793	1490	+2.1	0.0	− 8.1	N.A.
280 Remington (R)	150	SPCL	24	2970	2699	2444	2203	2937	2426	1989	1616	+1.9	0.0	− 7.8	N.A.
280 Remington (R)	165	SPCL	24	2820	2510	2220	1950	2913	2308	1805	1393	+2.3	0.0	− 9.4	N.A.
284 Winchester (W)	150	PPSP	24	2860	2595	2344	2108	2724	2243	1830	1480	+2.1	0.0	− 8.5	18.35
7mm Remington Magnum (W)	125	PPSP	24	3310	2976	2666	2376	3040	2458	1972	1567	+1.2	0.0	− 6.5	19.25
7mm Remington Magnum (R) (W) (F)	150	PSPCL, PPSP, SP	24	3110	2830	2568	2320	3221	2667	2196	1792	+1.7	0.0	− 7.0	19.25
7mm Remington Magnum (F)—Premium	150	BTSP	24	3110	2920	2750	2580	3220	2850	2510	2210	+1.6	0.0	− 6.2	20.35
7mm Remington Magnum (F)—Premium	165	BTSP	24	2860	2710	2560	2420	3000	2690	2410	2150	+1.6	0.0	− 6.9	20.35
7mm Remington Magnum (R) (W) (F) (H)	175	PSPCL, PPSP	24	2860	2645	2440	2244	3178	2718	2313	1956	+2.0	0.0	− 7.9	19.25
7mm Remington Magnum (F)—Premium	160	NP	24	2950	2730	2520	2320	3090	2650	2250	1910	+1.8	0.0	− 7.7	23.95
30 Carbine (R) (W) (F) (H)	110	SP, HSP, SP, RN	20	1990	1567	1236	1035	967	600	373	262	0.0	−13.5	− 49.9	9.95
30 Carbine (W) (F) (H) (PMC)	110	FMC, MC, FMJ, FMC	20	1990	1596	1278	1070	967	622	399	280	0.0	−13.0	− 47.4	9.95
30 Remington (R) (W)	170	SPCL, ST	24	2120	1822	1555	1328	1696	1253	913	666	0.0	− 9.7	− 33.8	N.A.
30-30 Accelerator (R)	55	SP	24	3400	2693	2085	1570	1412	886	521	301	+2.0	0.0	− 10.2	N.A.
30-30 Winchester (F)	125	HP	24	2570	2090	1660	1320	1830	1210	770	480	0.0	− 7.3	− 28.1	12.20
30-30 Winchester (W) (F) (PMC)	150	OPE, PPSP, ST, SP	24	2390	2018	1684	1398	1902	1356	944	651	0.0	− 7.7	− 27.9	12.20
30-30 Winchester (R) (H)	150	SPCL	24	2390	1973	1605	1303	1902	1296	858	565	0.0	− 8.2	− 30.0	N.A.
30-30 Winchester (W) (R) (F) (PMC)	170	PPSP, ST, SPCL, SP, HPCL	24	2200	1895	1619	1381	1827	1355	989	720	0.0	− 8.9	− 31.1	12.20
300 Savage (R)	150	SPCL	24	2630	2247	1897	1585	2303	1681	1198	837	0.0	− 6.1	− 21.9	N.A.
300 Savage (W)	150	PPSP	24	2630	2311	2015	1743	2303	1779	1352	1012	+2.8	0.0	− 11.5	15.50
300 Savage (W) (F) (R)	150	ST, SP, PSPCL	24	2630	2354	2095	1853	2303	1845	1462	1143	+2.7	0.0	− 10.7	15.50
300 Savage (R) (W)	180	SPCL, PPSP	24	2350	2025	1728	1467	2207	1639	1193	860	0.0	− 7.7	− 27.1	15.50
300 Savage (R) (W) (F)	180	PSPCL, ST	24	2350	2137	1935	1745	2207	1825	1496	1217	0.0	− 6.7	− 22.8	15.50
30-40 Krag (R) (W)	180	SPCL, PPSP	24	2430	2098	1795	1525	2360	1761	1288	929	0.0	− 7.1	− 25.0	16.35
30-40 Krag (R) (W)	180	PSPCL, ST	24	2430	2213	2007	1813	2360	1957	1610	1314	0.0	− 6.2	− 21.1	16.35
303 Savage (W)	190	ST	24	1940	1657	1410	1211	1588	1158	839	619	0.0	−11.9	− 41.4	17.90
308 Accelerator (R)	55	PSP	24	3770	3215	2726	2286	1735	1262	907	638	+1.0	0.0	− 5.6	N.A.
308 Winchester (W)	110	PSP	24	3180	2666	2206	1795	2470	1736	1188	787	+2.0	0.0	− 9.3	15.50
308 Winchester (W)	125	PSP	24	3050	2697	2370	2067	2582	2019	1559	1186	+2.0	0.0	− 8.2	15.50
308 Winchester (W)	150	PPSP	24	2820	2488	2179	1893	2648	2061	1581	1193	+2.4	0.0	− 9.8	15.50
308 Winchester (W) (R) (F) (H) (PMC)	150	ST, PSPCL, SP	24	2820	2533	2263	2009	2648	2137	1705	1344	+2.3	0.0	− 9.1	15.50
308 Winchester (PMC)	147	FMC-BT	24	2750	2473	2257	2052	2428	2037	1697	1403	+2.3	0.0	− 9.1	N.A.
308 Winchester (H)	165	BTSP, SPBT	24	2700	2520	2330	2160	2670	2310	1990	1700	+2.0	0.0	− 8.4	16.58
308 Winchester (W) (R)	180	PPSP, SPCL	24	2620	2274	1955	1666	2743	2086	1527	1109	+2.9	0.0	− 12.1	15.50
308 Winchester (W) (R) (F) (PMC)	180	ST, PSPCL, SP	24	2620	2393	2178	1974	2743	2288	1896	1557	+2.6	0.0	− 9.9	15.50
308 Winchester (W)	200	ST	24	2450	2208	1980	1767	2665	2165	1741	1386	0.0	− 6.3	− 21.4	15.50
30-06 Springfield (W)	110	PSP	24	3380	2843	2365	1936	2790	1974	1366	915	+1.7	0.0	− 8.0	15.50
30-06 Springfield (W) (R) (F)	125	PSP, PSP, SP	24	3140	2780	2447	2138	2736	2145	1662	1269	+1.8	0.0	− 7.7	15.50
30-06 Springfield (W)	150	PPSP	24	2920	2580	2265	1972	2839	2217	1708	1295	+2.2	0.0	− 9.0	15.50
30-06 Springfield (W) (R) (F) (H) (PMC)	150	ST, PSPCL, SP, SP	24	2910	2617	2342	2083	2820	2281	1827	1445	+2.1	0.0	− 8.5	15.50
30-06 Springfield (R)	150	BP	24	2910	2656	2416	2189	2820	2349	1944	1596	+2.0	0.0	− 8.0	N.A.
30-06 Springfield (PMC)	150	FMC (M-2)	24	2810	2555	2310	2080	2630	2170	1780	1440	+2.2	0.0	− 8.8	N.A.
30-06 Accelerator (R)	55	PSP	24	4080	3485	2965	2502	2033	1483	1074	764	+1.0	0.0	− 5.0	N.A.
30-06 Springfield (R)	165	PSPCL	24	2800	2534	2283	2047	2872	2352	1909	1534	+2.3	0.0	− 9.0	N.A.
30-06 Springfield (F) (H)	165	BTSP	24	2800	2610	2420	2240	2870	2490	2150	1840	+2.1	0.0	− 8.0	16.10
30-06 Springfield (R) (W) (PMC)	180	SPCL, PPSP	24	2700	2348	2023	1727	2913	2203	1635	1192	+2.7	0.0	− 11.3	15.50
30-06 Springfield (R) (W) (F) (H) (PMC)	180	PSPCL, ST	24	2700	2469	2250	2042	2913	2436	2023	1666	+2.4	0.0	− 9.3	15.50
30-06 Springfield (R)	180	BP	24	2700	2485	2280	2084	2913	2468	2077	1736	+2.4	0.0	− 9.1	N.A.
30-06 Springfield (F)	200	BTSP	24	2550	2400	2260	2120	2890	2560	2270	2000	+2.3	0.0	− 9.0	16.10
30-06 Springfield (W) (R)	220	PPSP, SPCL	24	2410	2130	1870	1632	2837	2216	1708	1301	0.0	− 6.8	− 23.6	15.50

CAUTION: PRICES CHANGE. CHECK AT GUNSHOP.

Cartridge	Wt. Grs.	— BULLET — Type	Bbl. (in.)	— VELOCITY (fps) — Muzzle	100 yds.	200 yds.	300 yds.	— ENERGY (ft. lbs.) — Muzzle	100 yds.	200 yds.	300 yds.	— BULLET PATH† — 100 yds.	200 yds.	300 yds.	Price Per Box
30-06 Springfield (W)	220	ST	24	2410	2192	1985	1791	2837	2347	1924	1567	0.0	− 6.4	− 21.6	15.50
300 H & H Magnum (W) (R)	180	ST, PSPCL	24	2880	2640	2412	2196	3315	2785	2325	1927	+2.1	0.0	− 8.0	19.80
300 Winchester Magnum (W) (R)	150	PPSP, PSPCL	24	3290	2951	2636	2342	3605	2900	2314	1827	+1.3	0.0	− 6.6	20.30
300 Winchester Magnum (W) (R) (F) (H)	180	PPSP, PSPCL, SP	24	2960	2745	2540	2344	3501	3011	2578	2196	+1.9	0.0	− 7.3	20.30
300 Winchester Magnum (F) Premium	200	BTSP	24	2830	2680	2530	2380	3560	3180	2830	2520	+1.7	0.0	− 7.1	21.40
303 British (R)	180	SPCL	24	2460	2124	1817	1542	2418	1803	1319	950	0.0	− 6.9	− 24.4	N.A.
303 British (R)	180	PPSP	24	2460	2233	2018	1816	2418	1993	1627	1318	0.0	− 6.1	− 20.8	16.00
32-20 Winchester (W) (R)	100	SP	24	1210	1021	913	834	325	231	185	154	0.0	−32.3	−106.3	*23.40
32-20 Winchester (W) (R)	100	L	24	1210	1021	913	834	325	231	185	154	0.0	−32.3	−106.3	*18.90
32 Winchester Special (F) (R)	170	SP	24	2250	1920	1630	1370	1911	1390	1000	710	0.0	− 8.6	− 30.5	13.00
8mm Mauser (R) (W)	170	SPCL, PPSP	24	2360	1969	1622	1333	2102	1463	993	671	0.0	− 8.2	− 29.8	16.00
8mm Mauser (F)	170	SP	24	2510	2110	1740	1430	2380	1670	1140	770	0.0	− 7.0	− 25.7	16.00
8mm Remington Magnum (R)	185	PSPCL	24	3080	2761	2464	2186	3896	3131	2494	1963	+1.8	0.0	− 7.6	N.A.
8mm Remington Magnum (R)	220	PSPCL	24	2830	2581	2346	2123	3912	3254	2688	2201	+2.2	0.0	− 8.5	N.A.
338 Winchester Magnum (W)	200	PPSP	24	2960	2658	2375	2110	3890	3137	2505	1977	+2.0	0.0	− 8.2	24.25
338 Winchester Magnum (W)	250	ST	24	2660	2395	2145	1910	3927	3184	2554	2025	+2.6	0.0	− 10.2	24.25
348 Winchester (W)	200	ST	24	2520	2215	1931	1672	2820	2178	1656	1241	0.0	− 6.2	− 21.9	28.60
351 Winchester S.L. (W)	180	SP	20	1850	1556	1310	1128	1368	968	686	508	0.0	−13.6	− 47.5	40.55
35 Remington (R)	150	PSPCL	24	2300	1874	1506	1218	1762	1169	755	494	0.0	− 9.2	− 33.0	N.A.
35 Remington (R) (F)	200	SPCL, SP	24	2080	1698	1376	1140	1921	1280	841	577	0.0	−11.3	− 41.2	14.35
35 Remington (W)	200	PPSP, ST	24	2020	1646	1335	1114	1812	1203	791	551	0.0	−12.1	− 43.9	14.35
358 Winchester (W)	200	ST	24	2490	2171	1876	1610	2753	2093	1563	1151	0.0	− 6.5	− 23.0	21.95
350 Remington Magnum (R)	200	PSPCL	20	2710	2410	2130	1870	3261	2579	2014	1553	+2.6	0.0	− 10.3	N.A.
375 Winchester (W)	200	PPSP	24	2200	1841	1526	1268	2150	1506	1034	714	0.0	− 9.5	− 33.8	18.90
375 Winchester (W)	250	PPSP	24	1900	1647	1424	1239	2005	1506	1126	852	0.0	−12.0	− 40.9	18.90
38-55 Winchester (W)	255	SP	24	1320	1190	1091	1018	987	802	674	587	0.0	−23.4	− 75.2	17.60
375 H & H Magnum (R) (W)	270	SP, PPSP	24	2690	2420	2166	1928	4337	3510	2812	2228	+2.5	0.0	− 10.0	24.15
375 H & H Magnum (R)	300	ST	24	2530	2268	2022	1793	4263	3426	2723	2141	+2.9	0.0	− 11.5	24.15
375 H & H Magnum (R) (W)	300	FMC, MC	24	2530	2171	1843	1551	4263	3139	2262	1602	0.0	− 6.5	− 23.0	24.15
38-40 Winchester (W)	180	SP	24	1160	999	901	827	538	399	324	273	0.0	−33.9	−110.6	30.20
44-40 Winchester (W) (R)	200	SP, SP	24	1190	1006	900	822	629	449	360	300	0.0	−33.3	−109.5	31.30
44 Remington Magnum (R)	240	SP, SJHP	20	1760	1380	1114	970	1650	1015	661	501	0.0	−17.6	− 63.1	N.A.
44 Remington Magnum (F) (W)	240	HSP	20	1760	1380	1090	950	1650	1015	640	485	0.0	−18.1	− 65.1	11.90
444 Marlin (R)	240	SP	24	2350	1815	1377	1087	2942	1755	1010	630	0.0	− 9.9	− 38.5	N.A.
444 Marlin (R)	265	SP	24	2120	1733	1405	1160	2644	1768	1162	791	0.0	−10.8	− 39.5	N.A.
45-70 Government (F)	300	HSP	24	1810	1410	1120	970	2180	1320	840	630	0.0	−17.0	− 61.4	17.65
45-70 Government (W)	300	JHP	24	1880	1559	1294	1105	2355	1619	1116	814	0.0	−13.5	− 47.1	17.65
45-70 Government (R)	405	SP	24	1330	1168	1055	977	1590	1227	1001	858	0.0	−24.6	− 80.3	N.A.
458 Winchester Magnum (W) (R)	500	FMC, MC	24	2040	1823	1623	1442	4620	3689	2924	2308	0.0	− 9.6	− 32.5	49.40
458 Winchester Magnum (W) (R)	510	SP, SP	24	2040	1770	1527	1319	4712	3547	2640	1970	0.0	−10.3	− 35.6	32.55

*Price for 50. †Bullet Path based on line-of-sight 0.9″ above center of bore. Bullet type abbreviations: BP—Bronze Point; BT—Boat Tail; CL—Core Lokt; FN—Flat Nose; FMC—Full Metal Case; FMJ—Full Metal Jacket; HP—Hollow Point; HSP—Hollow Soft Point; JHP—Jacketed Hollow Point; L—Lead; Lu—Lubaloy; MAT—Match; MC—Metal Case; NP—Nosler Partition; OPE—Open Point Expanding; PCL—Pointed Core Lokt; PEP—Pointed Expanding Point; PL—Power-Lokt; PP—Power Point; Prem.—Premium; PSP—Pointed Soft Point; SJHP—Semi-Jacketed Hollow Point; SJMP—Semi-Jacketed Metal Point; SP—Soft Point; ST—Silvertip; SX—Super Explosive. PMC prices slightly less.

WEATHERBY MAGNUM CARTRIDGES—BALLISTICS AND PRICES

Cartridge	Wt. Grs.	— Bullet — Type	Bbl. (in.)	— Velocity (fps) — Muzzle	100 Yds.	200 Yds.	300 Yds.	— Energy (ft. lbs.) — Muzzle	100 Yds.	200 Yds.	300 Yds.	— Bullet Path† — 100 Yds.	200 Yds.	300 Yds.	Price Per Box
224 Weatherby Magnum	55	PE	26	3650	3214	2808	2433	1627	1262	963	723	+2.8	+3.6	0.0	22.95
240 Weatherby Magnum	70	PE	26	3850	3424	3025	2654	2305	1823	1423	1095	+2.2	+3.0	0.0	22.95
240 Weatherby Magnum	87	PE	26	3500	3165	2848	2550	2367	1935	1567	1256	+2.8	+3.6	0.0	22.95
240 Weatherby Magnum	100	PE	26	3395	3115	2848	2594	2560	2155	1802	1495	+2.8	+3.5	0.0	22.95
240 Weatherby Magnum	100	NP	26	3395	3068	2758	2468	2560	2090	1690	1353	+1.1	0.0	− 5.7	30.95
257 Weatherby Magnum	87	PE	26	3825	3470	3135	2818	2827	2327	1900	1535	+2.1	+2.9	0.0	23.95
257 Weatherby Magnum	100	PE	26	3555	3256	2971	2700	2807	2355	1960	1619	+2.5	+3.2	0.0	23.95
257 Weatherby Magnum	100	NP	26	3555	3242	2945	2663	2807	2335	1926	1575	+0.9	0.0	− 4.7	32.95
257 Weatherby Magnum	117	SPE	26	3300	2853	2443	2074	2830	2115	1551	1118	+3.8	+4.9	0.0	23.95
257 Weatherby Magnum	117	NP	26	3300	3027	2767	2520	2830	2381	1990	1650	+1.2	0.0	− 5.9	32.95
270 Weatherby Magnum	100	PE	26	3760	3341	2949	2585	3140	2479	1932	1484	+2.4	+3.2	0.0	23.95
270 Weatherby Magnum	130	PE	26	3375	3110	2856	2615	3289	2793	2355	1974	+2.8	+3.5	0.0	23.95
270 Weatherby Magnum	130	NP	26	3375	3113	2862	2624	3289	2798	2365	1988	+1.0	0.0	− 5.2	32.95
270 Weatherby Magnum	150	PE	26	3245	3012	2789	2575	3508	3022	2592	2209	+3.1	+3.8	0.0	23.95
270 Weatherby Magnum	150	NP	26	3245	3022	2809	2604	3508	3043	2629	2259	+1.2	0.0	− 5.4	32.95
7mm Weatherby Magnum	139	PE	26	3300	3037	2786	2546	3362	2848	2396	2001	+3.0	+3.7	0.0	23.95
7mm Weatherby Magnum	140	NP	26	3300	3047	2806	2575	3386	2887	2448	2062	+1.1	0.0	− 5.4	32.95
7mm Weatherby Magnum	154	PE	26	3160	2928	2706	2494	3415	2932	2504	2127	+3.3	+4.1	0.0	23.95
7mm Weatherby Magnum	160	NP	26	3150	2935	2727	2528	3526	3061	2643	2271	+1.3	0.0	− 5.8	32.95
7mm Weatherby Magnum	175	RN	26	3070	2714	2383	2082	3663	2863	2207	1685	+1.6	0.0	− 7.5	23.95
300 Weatherby Magnum	110	PE	26	3900	3465	3057	2677	3716	2933	2283	1750	+2.2	+3.0	0.0	23.95
300 Weatherby Magnum	150	PE	26	3545	3248	2965	2696	4187	3515	2929	2422	+2.5	+3.2	0.0	23.95
300 Weatherby Magnum	150	NP	26	3545	3191	2857	2544	4187	3392	2719	2156	+1.0	0.0	− 5.3	33.95
300 Weatherby Magnum	180	PE	26	3245	3010	2785	2569	4210	3622	3100	2639	+3.1	+3.8	0.0	23.95
300 Weatherby Magnum	180	NP	26	3245	2964	2696	2444	4210	3512	2906	2388	+1.3	0.0	− 6.0	33.95
300 Weatherby Magnum	220	SPE	26	2905	2578	2276	2000	4123	3248	2531	1955	+1.9	0.0	− 8.6	23.95
340 Weatherby Magnum	200	PE	26	3210	2947	2696	2458	4577	3857	3228	2683	+3.2	+4.0	0.0	25.95
340 Weatherby Magnum	210	NP	26	3180	2927	2686	2457	4717	3996	3365	2816	+1.3	0.0	− 6.2	40.65
340 Weatherby Magnum	250	SPE	26	2850	2516	2209	1929	4510	3515	2710	2066	+2.0	0.0	− 9.2	25.95
340 Weatherby Magnum	250	NP	26	2850	2563	2296	2049	4510	3648	2927	2331	+1.8	0.0	− 8.2	40.65
378 Weatherby Magnum	270	SPE	26	3180	2796	2440	2117	6064	4688	3570	2688	+1.5	0.0	− 7.3	40.95
378 Weatherby Magnum	300	SPE	26	2925	2564	2234	1935	5700	4380	3325	2495	+1.9	0.0	− 9.0	40.95
378 Weatherby Magnum	300	FMJ	26	2925	2620	2340	2080	5700	4574	3649	2883	+4.9	+6.0	0.0	46.95
460 Weatherby Magnum	500	RN	26	2700	2395	2115	1858	8095	6370	4968	3834	+2.3	0.0	− 10.3	44.95
460 Weatherby Magnum	500	FMJ	26	2700	2416	2154	1912	8095	6482	5153	4060	+2.2	0.0	− 9.8	51.95

†Bullet Path based on line of sight 1.5″ above center of bore. Bullet type abbreviations: FMJ—Full Metal Jacket; NP—Nosler Partition; PE—Pointed Expanding; RN—Round Nose; SPE—Semi-Pointed Expanding.

CAUTION: PRICES CHANGE. CHECK AT GUNSHOP.

NORMA C.F. RIFLE CARTRIDGES—BALLISTICS AND PRICES

Cartridge	Bullet Wt. Grs.	Bullet Type	Bbl. (in.)	Velocity (fps) Muzzle	100 Yds.	200 Yds.	300 Yds.	Energy (ft. lbs.) Muzzle	100 Yds.	200 Yds.	300 Yds.	Bullet Path† 100 Yds.	200 Yds.	300 Yds.	Price Per Box
222 Remington	50	SP	24	3200	2650	2170	1750	1137	780	520	340	+1.6	0.0	− 8.2	$10.75
222 Remington	50	FJ	24	3200	2610	2080	1630	1137	756	480	295	+1.9	0.0	−10.1	10.75
222 Remington	53	SpPSP	24	3117	2670	2267	1901	1142	838	604	425	+1.7	0.0	− 8.7	10.75
22-250 Remington	53	SpPSP	24	3707	3192	2741	2332	1616	1198	883	639	+1.0	0.0	− 5.7	11.75
220 Swift	50	SP	24	4110	3611	3133	2681	1877	1448	1090	799	+0.6	0.0	− 4.1	15.85
22 Savage Hi-Power (5.6 x 52R)	71	SP	24	2790	2296	1886	1558	1226	831	561	383	+2.4	0.0	−11.4	21.00
22 Savage Hi-Power (5.6 x 52R)	71	FJ	24	2790	2296	1886	1558	1226	831	561	383	+2.4	0.0	−11.4	21.00
243 Winchester	100	SP, FJ	24	3070	2790	2540	2320	2090	1730	1430	1190	+1.4	0.0	− 6.3	14.50
6.5mm Carcano	139	PPDC	24	2576	2379	2192	2012	2046	1745	1481	1249	+2.3	0.0	− 9.6	21.95
6.5mm Carcano	156	SP	24	2430	2208	2000	1800	2046	1689	1386	1123	+2.9	0.0	−11.7	21.00
6.5mm JAP	139	SPBT	24	2430	2280	2130	1990	1820	1605	1401	1223	+2.7	0.0	−10.8	21.00
6.5mm JAP	156	SP	24	2065	1871	1692	1529	1481	1213	992	810	+4.3	0.0	−16.4	21.00
6.5mm Norma (6.5 x 55)	139	PPDC	29	2790	2630	2470	2320	2402	2136	1883	1662	+1.8	0.0	− 7.8	21.95
6.5mm Norma (6.5 x 55)	156	SP	29	2495	2271	2062	1867	2153	1787	1473	1208	+2.6	0.0	−10.9	21.00
270 Winchester	130	SPBT	24	3140	2884	2639	2404	2847	2401	2011	1669	+1.4	0.0	− 6.6	15.75
270 Winchester	150	SPBT	24	2800	2616	2436	2262	2616	2280	1977	1705	+1.8	0.0	− 7.7	15.75
7mm Mauser (7 x 57)	150	SPBT	24	2755	2539	2331	2133	2530	2148	1810	1516	+2.0	0.0	− 8.4	16.25
7 x 64	150	SPBT	24	2890	2598	2329	2113	2779	2249	1807	1487	+1.7	0.0	− 7.5	18.00
7mm Remington Magnum	150	SPBT	26	3250	2960	2638	2440	3519	2919	2318	1983	+1.2	0.0	− 5.8	19.50
30-30 Winchester	150	SPFN	20	2410	2075	1790	1550	1934	1433	1066	799	0.0	− 7.0	−26.1	12.50
30-30 Winchester	170	SPFN	20	2220	1890	1630	1410	1860	1350	1000	750	0.0	− 8.1	−29.2	12.50
7.5 x 55 Swiss	180	SPBT	24	2650	2441	2248	2056	2792	2380	2020	1690	+2.1	0.0	− 8.9	22.00
7.62 x 39 Short Russian	125	SP		2385				1580							18.95
7.62 Russian	180	SPBT	24	2625	2415	2222	2030	2749	2326	1970	1644	+2.2	0.0	− 9.1	22.35
308 Winchester	130	SPBT	24	2900	2590	2300	2030	2428	1937	1527	1190	+1.9	0.0	− 8.6	15.75
308 Winchester	150	SPBT	24	2860	2570	2300	2050	2725	2200	1760	1400	+1.9	0.0	− 8.5	15.75
308 Winchester	180	PPDC	24	2610	2400	2210	2020	2725	2303	1952	1631	+2.3	0.0	− 9.4	17.25
30-06	130	SPBT	24	3205	2876	2561	2263	2966	2388	1894	1479	+1.4	0.0	− 6.7	15.75
30-06	150	SPBT	24	2970	2680	2402	2141	2943	2393	1922	1527	+1.7	0.0	− 7.8	15.75
30-06	180	SP	24	2700	2477	2261	2070	2914	2430	2025	1713	+2.1	0.0	− 8.7	15.75
30-06	180	PPDC	24	2700	2494	2296	2109	2914	2487	2107	1778	+2.0	0.0	− 8.6	17.00
303 British	150	SP	24	2720	2440	2170	1930	2465	1983	1569	1241	+2.2	0.0	− 9.7	16.75
303 British	180	SPBT	24	2540	2340	2147	1965	2579	2189	1843	1544	+2.4	0.0	−10.0	16.75
308 Norma Magnum	180	PPDC	26	3020	2798	2585	2382	3646	3130	2671	2268	+1.3	0.0	− 6.1	27.90
7.65mm Argentine	150	SP	24	2920	2630	2355	2105	2841	2304	1848	1476	+1.7	0.0	− 7.8	21.95
7.7mm JAP	130	SP	24	2950	2635	2340	2065	2513	2004	1581	1231	+1.8	0.0	− 8.2	22.50
7.7mm JAP	180	SPBT	24	2495	2292	2101	1922	2484	2100	1765	1477	+2.6	0.0	−10.4	22.50
8mm Mauser (8 x 57JS)	196	SP	24	2525	2195	1894	1627	2778	2097	1562	1152	+2.9	0.0	−12.7	19.65

†Bullet Path based on line of sight 1.5″ above center of bore. Bullet type abbreviations: BT—Boat Tail; DC—Dual Core; FJ—Full Jacket; FJBT—Full Jacket Boat Tail; FP—Flat Point; HP—Hollow Point; MC—Metal Case; P—Pointed; PP—Plastic Point; RN—Round Nose; SP—Soft Point; SPFN—Soft Point Flat Nose; SPSBT—Soft Point Semi-Pointed Boat Tail; SPSP—Soft Point Semi-Point; SpPSP—Spire point Soft Point.

RIMFIRE CARTRIDGES—BALLISTICS AND PRICES

Cartridge Type	Wt. Grs.	Bullet Type	Velocity (fps) 18½" Barrel Muzzle	50 Yds.	100 Yds.	Energy (ft. lbs.) Muzzle	50 Yds.	100 Yds.	Velocity (fps) 6" Barrel Muzzle	50 Yds.	Energy (ft. lbs.) Muzzle	50 Yds.	Price Per Box 50 Rds.	100 Rds.
22 CB Short (CCI & Win. only)	29	Solid	727	667	610	34	29	24	706	—	32	—	$11.95(2)	$4.63
22 CB Long (CCI only)	29	Solid	727	667	610	34	29	24	706	—	32	—	N.A.	4.63
22 Short Standard Velocity	29	Solid	1045	—	810	70	—	42	865	—	48	—	2.28	N.A.
22 Short High Velocity (Fed., Rem., Win.)	29	Solid	1095	—	903	77	—	53	—	—	—	—	2.28	N.A.
22 Short High Velocity (CCI only)	29	Solid	1132	1004	920	83	65	55	1065	—	73	—	N.A.	4.57
22 Short High Velocity HP (Fed., Rem., Win.)	27	Hollow Point	1120	—	904	75	—	49	—	—	—	—	2.41	N.A.
22 Short High Vel. HP (CCI only)	27	Hollow Point	1164	1013	920	81	62	51	1077	—	69	—	N.A.	4.83
22 Long Standard Vel. (CCI only)	29	Solid	1180	1038	946	90	69	58	1031	—	68	—	N.A.	4.83
22 Long High Velocity (Fed., Rem., Win.)	29	Solid	1240	—	962	99	—	60	—	—	—	—	2.59	5.17
22 Long Rifle Stand. Velocity (CCI only)	40	Solid	1138	1046	975	115	97	84	1027	925	93	76	N.A.	5.17
22 Long Rifle Stand. Velocity (Fed., Rem., Win.)	40	Solid	1150	—	976	117	—	85	—	—	—	—	2.59	5.17
22 Long Rifle High Vel. (CCI only)	40	Solid	1341	1150	1045	160	117	97	1150	1010	117	90	N.A.	5.17
22 Long Rifle High Velocity (Fed., Rem., Win.)	40	Solid	1255	—	1017	140	—	92	—	—	—	—	2.59	5.17
22 Long Rifle High Velocity HP (CCI only)	37	Hollow Point	1370	1165	1040	154	111	89	1190	1040	116	88	N.A.	5.73
22 Long Rifle High Velocity HP (Fed., Rem., Win.)	36-38	Hollow Point	1280	—	1010	131	—	82	—	—	—	—	2.87	5.73
22 Long Rifle Yellow Jacket (Rem. only)	33	Hollow Point	1500	1240	1075	165	110	85	—	—	—	—	N.A.	N.A.
22 Long Rifle Spitfire (Fed. only)	33	Hollow Point	1500	1240	1075	165	110	85	—	—	—	—	2.85	N.A.
22 Long Rifle Viper (Rem. only)	36	Solid	1410	1187	1056	159	113	89	—	—	—	—	N.A.	N.A.
22 Stinger (CCI only)	32	Hollow Point	1687	1300	1158	202	120	95	1430	1100	145	86	3.25	N.A.
22 Winchester Magnum Rimfire (Win., Fed.)	40	FMC or HP	1910	—	1326	324	—	156	—	—	—	—	7.00	N.A.
22 Winchester Magnum Rimfire (CCI only)	40	FMC or HP	2025	1688	1407	364	253	176	1339	1110	159	109	6.99	N.A.
22 Long Rifle Pistol Match (Win., Fed.)	40	Solid	—	—	—	—	—	—	1060	950	100	80	5.95	11.90
22 Long Rifle Match (Rifle) (CCI only)	40	Solid	1138	1047	975	116	97	84	1027	925	93	76	N.A.	7.92
22 Long Rifle Shot (CCI, Fed., Win.)	—	#11 or #12 shot	1047						950	—	—	—	5.28	N.A.
22 Winchester Magnum Rimfire Shot (CCI only)	—	#11 shot	1126	—	—	—	—	—	1000	—	—	—	3.95(1)	N.A.
22 Short Match (CCI only)	29	Solid	830	752	695	44	36	31	786	—	39	—	N.A.	4.78
22 Long Rifle Silhouette (Fed. only)	40	Solid	1150	—	976	117	—	85	—	—	—	—	N.A.	6.95
22 Long Rifle Super Silhouette (Win. only)	42	Solid	1220	—	1003	139	—	94	—	—	—	—	N.A.	5.93
22 Long Rifle Super-Max (Win. only)	34	Hollow Point	1500	1250	1081	170	118	88	—	—	—	—	—	N.A.

Please note that the actual ballistics obtained in your gun can vary considerably from the advertised ballistics. Also, ballistics can vary from lot to lot even within the same brand. All prices were correct at the time this table was prepared. All prices are subject to change without notice.
(1) 20 to a box (2) Per 250

CAUTION: PRICES CHANGE. CHECK AT GUNSHOP.

CENTERFIRE HANDGUN CARTRIDGES—BALLISTICS AND PRICES

Win.-Western, Rem.-Peters, Norma, PMC, and Federal

Most loads are available from W-W and R-P. All available Norma loads are listed. Federal cartridges are marked with an asterisk. Other loads supplied by only one source are indicated by a letter, thus: Norma (a); R-P (b); W-W (c); PMC (d); CCI (e). Prices are approximate.

Cartridge	Bullet Gr.	Bullet Style	Muzzle Velocity	Muzzle Energy	Barrel Inches	Price Per Box
22 Jet (b)	40	SP	2100	390	8⅜	$ NA
221 Fireball (b)	50	SP	2650	780	10½	NA
25 (6.35mm) Auto*	50	MC	810	73	2	15.15
25 ACP (c)	45	Exp. Pt.	835	70	2	16.25
256 Winchester Magnum (c)	60	HP	2350	735	8½	29.85
30 (7.65mm) Luger Auto	93	MC	1220	307	4½	24.80
32 S&W Blank (b, c)	No bullet		—	—	—	14.45
32 S&W Blank, BP (c)	No bullet		—	—	—	14.45
32 Short Colt	80	Lead	745	100	4	14.55
32 Long Colt IL (c)	82	Lub.	755	104	4	15.15
32 Auto (c)	60	STHP	970	125	4	18.75
32 (7.65mm) Auto*	71	MC	905	129	4	17.35
32 (7.65mm) Auto Pistol (a)	77	MC	900	162	4	17.75
32 S&W	88	Lead	680	90	3	14.65
32 S&W Long	98	Lead	705	115	4	15.15
32-20 Winchester	100	Lead	1030	271	6	18.90
32-20 Winchester	100	SP	1030	271	6	23.40
357 Magnum	110	JHP	1295	410	4	22.75
357 Magnum	110	SJHP	1295	410	4	22.75
357 Magnum	125	JHP	1450	583	4	22.75
357 Magnum (d)	125	JHC	1450	583	4	22.75
357 Magnum (e)	125	JSP	1900	1001	—	22.75
357 Magnum (e)	140	JHP	1775	979	—	22.75
357 Magnum (e)	150	FMJ	1600	852	—	22.75
357 Magnum*	158	SWC	1235	535	4	19.25
357 Magnum (b) (e)	158	JSP	1550	845	8⅜	22.75
357 Magnum	158	MP	1410	695	8⅜	22.75
357 Magnum	158	Lead	1410	696	8⅜	19.25
357 Magnum	158	JHP	1450	735	8⅜	22.75
9mm Luger (c)	95	JSP	1355	387	4	21.55
9mm Luger (c)	115	FMC	1155	341	4	21.55
9mm Luger (c)	115	STHP	1255	383	4	22.60
9mm Luger*	115	JHP	1165	349	4	21.55
9mm Luger*	125	MC	1120	345	4	21.55
9mm Luger (e)	125	JSP	1100	335	—	21.55
38 S&W Blank	No bullet		—	—	—	17.50
38 Smith & Wesson	145	Lead	685	150	4	16.30
38 Special Blank	No bullet		—	—	—	17.60
38 Special (e)	110	JHP	1200	351	—	20.75
38 Special IL +P (c)	150	Lub.	1060	375	6	17.80
38 Special	158	Lead	855	256	6	16.35
38 Special	200	Lead	730	236	6	17.50
38 Special	158	MP	855	256	6	20.80
38 Special (b)	125	SJHP		Not available		NA
38 Special Match, IL	148	Lead	770	195	6	17.05
38 Special Match, IL (b)	158	Lead	855	256	6	NA
38 Special*	158	LRN	755	200	4	16.35
38 Special	158	SWC	755	200	4	17.60
38 Special Match*	148	WC	710	166	4	17.05
38 Special +P (c)	95	STHP	1100	255	4	21.85
38 Special +P (b)	110	SJHP	1020	254	4	NA
38 Special +P	125	JSP	945	248	4	20.75
38 Special +P	158	LRN	915	294	4	18.15
38 Special +P*	158	SWCHP	915	294	4	17.80
38 Special +P*	158	LSWC	915	294	4	16.70
38 Special +P (e)	140	JHP	1275	504	—	20.75
38 Special +P*	110	JHP	1020	254	4	20.75
38 Special +P*	125	JHP	945	248	4	20.75
38 Special Norma +P (a)	110	JHP	1542	580	6	26.00
38 Short Colt	125	Lead	730	150	6	16.00
38 Long Colt	150	Lead	730	175	6	24.50
38 Super Auto +P (b)	130	MC	1280	475	5	NA
38 Super Auto +P (b)	115	JHP	1300	431	5	21.85
38 Auto	130	MC	1040	312	4½	19.35
380 Auto (c)	85	STHP	1000	189	3¾	18.55
380 Auto*	95	MC	955	190	3¾	17.75
380 Auto (g)	88	JHP	990	191	4	NA
380 Auto*	90	JHP	1000	200	3¾	17.75
38-40 Winchester	180	SP	975	380	5	30.20
41 Remington Magnum	210	Lead	1050	515	8¾	25.60
41 Remington Magnum	210	SP	1500	1050	8¾	29.55
44 S&W Spec.*	200	LSW	960	410	7½	22.55
44 S&W Special	246	Lead	755	311	6½	22.55
44 Remington Magnum*	180	JHP	1610	1045	4	27.10
44 Remington Magnum (e)	200	JHP	1650	1208	—	13.57
44 Remington Magnum (e)	240	JSP	1625	1406	—	13.57
44 Remington Magnum (b)	240	SP	1470	1150	6½	NA
44 Remington Magnum	240	Lead	1470	1150	6½	29.10
44 Remington Magnum (g)	240	SJHP	1180	741	4	NA
44 Remington Magnum (a)	240	JPC	1533	1253	8½	30.50
44-40 Winchester	200	SP	975	420	7½	31.30
45 Colt*	225	SWCHP	900	405	5½	21.90
45 Colt (g)	250	Lead	860	410	5½	NA
45 Colt, IL (c)	255	Lub., L	860	410	5½	23.30
45 Auto (c)	185	STHP	1000	411	5	24.95
45 Auto (e)	200	JHP	1025	466	—	11.87
45 Auto	230	MC	850	369	5	23.70
45 Auto WC*	185	MC	775	245	5	24.90
45 Auto*	185	JHP	950	370	5	24.90
45 Winchester Magnum (c)	230	FMC	1400	1001	5	25.90
45 Auto Rim (b)	230	Lead	810	335	5½	NA

IL—Inside Lub. JSP—Jacketed Soft Point WC—Wad Cutter RN—Round Nose HP—Hollow Point Lub—Lubricated MC—Metal Case SP—Soft Point MP—Metal Point LGC—Lead, Gas Check JHP—Jacketed Hollow Point SWC—Semi Wad Cutter SJHP—Semi Jacketed Hollow Point PC—Power Cavity

SHOTSHELL LOADS AND PRICES

Winchester-Western, Remington-Peters, Federal

Dram Equivalent	Shot Ozs.	Style	Shot Sizes	Brands	Price Per Box	Velocity (fps)
10 Gauge 2½″ Magnum						
4½	2¼	Premium	BB, 2, 4	Fed., Win.	$29.75	1205
4¼	2	H.V.(2)	BB, 2, 4, 5, 6	Fed., Rem., Win.	27.75	1210
Max	1¾	Slug	Slug	Fed.	6.80(1)	1280
Max	Variable	Buck	00, 4	Fed., Win.	5.75(1)	Variable
Max	1¾	Steel	BB, 2	Win.	25.20	1280
4¼	1⅝	Steel	BB, 2	Fed.	25.15	1285
10 Gauge 2⅞″ Magnum						
4¾	1⅝	H.V.(2)	4	Rem., Win.	17.15	1330
4	1⅞	Premium	BB, 2, 4, 6	Fed., Rem., Win.	19.90	1210
4	1⅝	Premium	2, 4, 6	Fed., Rem., Win.	18.60	1280
4	1⅞	H.V.(2)	BB, 2, 4	Fed., Rem., Win.	18.60	1210
4	1⅝	H.V.(2)	2, 4, 6	Fed., Rem., Win.	17.20	1280
4	Variable	Buck	000, 00, 1, 4	Fed., Rem., Win.	4.35(1)	Variable
4	1½	Steel	BB, 1, 2, 4	Win.	20.05	1315
3½	1⅜	Steel	BB, 1, 2, 4	Fed.	20.05	1245
3½	1¼	Steel	1, 2, 4	Rem.	N.A.	1275
4	2	Premium	2, 4	Fed.	21.15	1175
12 Gauge 2¾″ Hunting & Target						
3¾	1½	Premium, Mag.	BB, 2, 4, 6	Fed., Rem., Win.	17.65	1260
3¾	1½	H.V.(2), Mag.	BB, 2, 4, 5, 6	Fed., Rem., Win.	15.55	—
3¾	1¼	H.,V.(2), Premium	2, 4, 6, 7½	Fed.	15.80	1330
3¾	1¼	H.V.(2)	BB, 2, 4, 5, 6, 7½, 8, 9	Fed., Rem., Win.	11.95	1330
3¼	1¼	Std. Vel., Premium	7½, 8	Fed.	11.40	1220
3¼	1⅛	Std. Vel., Premium	7½, 8	Fed.	11.05	1255
3¼	1¼	Std. Vel.	6, 7½, 8, 9	Fed., Rem., Win.	11.15	1220
3¼	1⅛	Std. Vel.	4, 5, 6, 7½, 8, 9	Fed., Rem., Win.	10.20	1255
3¼	1	Std. Vel., Promo	6, 7½, 8	Fed., Rem., Win.	N.A.	1290
Max.	1¼	Slug	Slug	Fed.	4.90(1)	1490
Max.	1	Slug	Slug	Fed., Rem., Win.	3.90(1)	1580
4	Variable	Buck, Mag.	00, 1, 4 (Buck)	Fed., Rem., Win.	3.75(1)	Variable
3¾	Variable	Buck	000, 00, 0, 1, 4 (Buck)	Fed., Rem., Win.	3.40(1)	Variable
3½	1⅛	Int. Skeet	9	Win.	N.A.	1310
3¼	1⅛	Int. Trap	7½, 8	Win.	N.A.	1255
3¾	1⅜	H.V.(2)	2. 4. 6	Fed.	12.95	1295
3¼	1¼	S.P.(3)	7½, 8	Win.	N.A.	1220
3	1⅛	T&S(4)	7½, 8, 9	Fed., Rem., Win.	7.80	1200
2¾	1⅛	T&S(4)	7½, 8, 8½, 9	Fed., Rem., Win.	7.65	1145
2¾	1	T&S(4)	8, 8½	Fed., Rem., Win.	7.65	11.80
3¾	1¼	Steel	BB, 1, 2, 4	Fed., Win.	16.35	1330
3¾	1⅛	Steel	1, 2, 4	Fed., Rem.	15.00	1365
16 Gauge 2¾″						
3¼	1¼	H.V.(2), Mag.	2, 4, 6	Fed., Rem., Win.	15.30	1260
3¼	1⅛	H.V.(2)	4, 5, 6, 7½, 9	Fed., Rem., Win.	11.45	1295
2¾	1⅛	Std. Vel.	4, 5, 6, 7½, 8, 9	Fed., Rem., Win.	10.15	1185
Max.	⅘	Slug	Slug	Fed., Rem., Win.	3.90(1)	1600
Max.	12 pellets	Buck	1	Fed., Rem., Win.	3.40(1)	1225
20 Gauge 3″ Magnum						
3	1¼	Premium	2, 4, 6	Fed., Rem., Win.	15.80	1185
3	1¼	H.V.(2)	2, 4, 6, 7½	Fed., Rem., Win.	14.40	1185
Max.	18 pellets	Buck	2	Fed.	3.75(1)	—
Max.	1	Steel	4	Win.	14.35	—
20 Gauge 2¾″ Hunting & Target						
2¾	1⅛	Premium, Mag.	4, 6	Fed., Rem.	14.00	1175
2¾	1⅛	H.V.(2), Mag.	4, 6, 7½	Fed., Rem., Win.	12.75	1175
2¾	1	H.V.(2), Premium	4, 6	Fed., Rem.	11.30	1220
2¾	1	H.V.(2), Promo	4, 5, 6, 7½, 8, 9	Fed., Rem., Win.	N.A.	1220
2½	1	Std. Vel., Premium	7½, 8	Fed., Rem.	10.00	1165
2½	1	Std. Vel.	4, 5, 6, 7½, 8, 9	Fed., Rem., Win.	9.25	1165
2¼	⅞	Std. Vel., Promo	6, 7½, 8, 9	Fed., Rem., Win.	N.A.	1155
Max.	¾	Slug	Slug	Fed., Rem., Win.	3.60(1)	1600
Max.	20 pellets	Buck	3	Fed., Rem., Win.	3.40(1)	1200
2½	⅞	Skeet	8, 9	Fed., Rem., Win.	7.30	1200
28 Gauge 2¾″ Hunting & Target						
2¼	¾	H.V.(2)	6, 7½, 8	Fed., Rem., Win.	10.60	1295
2	¾	Skeet	9	Fed., Rem., Win.	8.65	1200
410 3″, 2½″ Hunting & Target						
Max.	11/16	3″ H.V.(2)	4, 5, 6, 7½, 8, 9	Fed., Rem., Win.	9.85	1135
Max.	½	2½″ H.V.(2)	4, 6, 7½, 9	Fed., Rem., Win.	8.35	1135
Max.	½	2½″ Target	9	Fed., Rem., Win.	7.15	1200
Max.	⅕	Slug	Slug	Fed., Rem., Win.	3.40(1)	1830

(1) 5 rounds per box; (2) High velocity; (3) Super Pigeon; (4) Trap & Skeet.

CAUTION: PRICES CHANGE. CHECK AT GUNSHOP.

SHOOTER'S MARKETPLACE

HOME GUN SAFES

Omark Industries has added a full line of gun safes to its broad range of products.

Stowline safes bolt to the wall instead of relying on excess weight. 12-gauge steel and 100 percent welded seams add strength but not extra mass. Critical points are reinforced through advanced design, not with unnecessary bulk.

These units are designed to provide maximum protection for your firearms and other valuables. Additionally, Omark provides $1000 of free contents insurance.

Offered under the Outers brand, Stowline products consist of five home models with a variety of interiors for five to ten long guns.

Manufacturer's suggested retail price: $95 to $400.

OMARK INDUSTRIES

1858 PERCUSSION REVOLVER

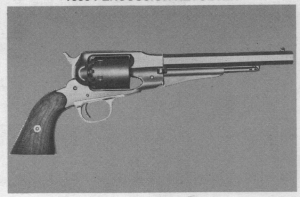

Made in Gussago, Italy, by Pietta, this reproduction of the Remington 1858 percussion revolver is currently being offered by Navy Arms.

This six-shot revolver is available in 44 caliber and has been manufactured as an *exact* reproduction of the original; consequently, this revolver is slightly larger than other reproductions of this type.

Navy Arms' 44 caliber New Army Revolver features a precise copy of the original progressive twist rifling, standard thread screws and a charcoal blue finish.

This Navy Arms reproduction has been imported to meet the needs of black powder shooters interested in hunting, target shooting and period replication. It features a blade front sight and grooved topstrap. Walnut grips. Manufacturer's suggested retail price: $175.

NAVY ARMS

SCREWDRIVER SET

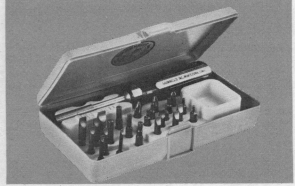

Screwdriver blades must fit screw slot width and length exactly to prevent damaging the slot. Brownells recently designed a Professional Magna-Tip® Screwdriver System that has a handle with fixed shank, but with interchangeble/replaceable blades held in the shank chuck by a permanent magnet, so you only have to change and grind the much less expensive blade.

Unlike "hollow-ground" screwdrivers that are dubbed-off square, Professional Magna-Tip® Blades are made from industrial steels in a true hollow-ground shape to evenly and smoothly transmit power to the screw slot. Set includes: Solid Handle, 24 bits, Bench Tray and unbreakable polyethylene Field Case. Suggested retail price: $24.50.

BROWNELLS, INC.

CLEANING EQUIPMENT

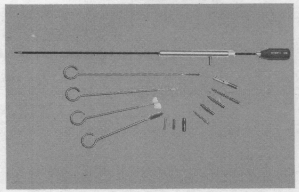

J. Dewey Mfg. offers one-piece, spring steel, nylon coated gun cleaning rods that provide full protection against barrel wear. Now available are stainless and brass cleaning rods, female threaded to accept most American brushes and cleaning accessories. The new line is a mixed combination of loop-style and revolving ball bearing handles. An unbreakable brass patch loop comes with each rod. Dewey rods are available from 4" - 44" lengths, 17 cal. - 12 Ga.

The J. Dewey Bore Saver cleaning rod guide replaces the bolt in your action while cleaning. The guide allows the cleaning rod to go straight into the bore without harming the chamber or throat.

Manufacturer's suggested retail price: Cleaning Rods $6 to $20; Bore Saver, $12.50 to $15.

J. DEWEY MFG. CO., INC.

See manufacturers' addresses following this section.

PREDATOR CALL

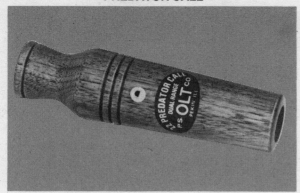

A new dual range predator call has been added to the P.S. Olt Company's line of game and bird calls. The new Olt offering, the Model 22 Dual Range Predator Call, is designed for both long and close range calling with the same call. The Model 22 Dual Range Predator Call contains two separate reeds—one a high-volume voice for calling predators at long distances, the other a low-volume reed for making soft cries and squeaks to bring close-in predators that last few yards into shooting range. The call barrel is turned from American Walnut, and each call is hand tuned to insure proper tone. The P.S. Olt Model 22 Dual Range Predator call was designed for use by experienced or novice hunters.

Manufacturer's suggested retail price: $9.95.

P.S. OLT COMPANY

STAINLESS STEEL LUBRICANT

RIG +P STAINLESS STEEL LUBRICANT is a special blend of RIG Universal, EP additives and a heat stabilizer. This lubricant is highly recommended for the slides on stainless steel automatics. Can be used efficiently on all steel automatic rifles and pistols. This lubricant helps eliminate binding often associated with stainless steel firearms. RIG +P STAINLESS STEEL LUBRICANT can be used on any surface that requires an extreme-pressure lubricant. This specialized lubricant was designed to meet the needs of hunters, shooters and law enforcement personnel who use stainless steel firearms. Available in 2 oz. jars. Made in U.S.A.

Manufacturer's suggested retail price: $3 per 2 oz. jar.

RIG® PRODUCTS

SWAGED LEAD BULLETS

Alberts swaged lead bullets are available in 25 styles and 11 calibers. Alberts currently offers pistol bullets in 32, 380, 9mm (2), 38 (6), 41, 44 (2), 45 (7), 45 Long Colt and 45-70. Alberts is also currently offering belted conicals in 36 and 44 caliber for black powder enthusiasts, and a 30 caliber rifle bullet for plinking. All Alberts bullets come from the factory pre-lubed and ready for reloading. They are subjected to exacting quality control procedures to insure maximum accuracy, something every handloader strives for. The Alberts line of precision swaged bullets is available throughout the U.S., Australia and Europe.

Manufacturer's suggested retail price (100 pack): From $4.27 to $9.13, depending upon the caliber purchased by the handloader.

ALBERTS CORPORATION

PROGRESSIVE PISTOL PRESS

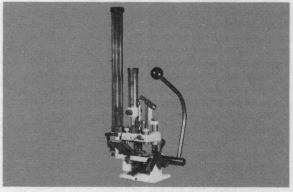

The RCBS Green Machine is designed with an *automatic* case feed from a five-tube magazine with a straight line transfer from there through four die stations. It has a carbide sizing die and automatic primer feed designed to feed primers from a flat magazine to the primer transfer bar without tubes. Powder is charged *automatically* from the Little Dandy powder measure. Then bullets are fed into a window-type seater for crimping. Finished rounds are completed at a rate of about 600 an hour.

Included are the necessary adjustment wrenches and gauges, a cleaning brush, soft dust cover, extra decapping pins and instructions. The Green Machine is available in 38/357, 9mm, 44 Mag/44 Spec., and 45 Auto. Suggested retail price: $600 to $650.

OMARK INDUSTRIES

See manufacturers' addresses following this section.

45 AUTO SCOPE MOUNT

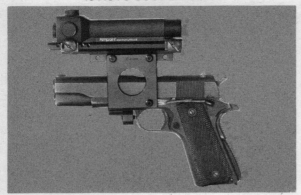

B-Square has a new 45 Auto scope mount that fits on the frame of the gun, not the grip. It has the elevation adjustment provision necessary to zero scopes on 45s. Windage shims are included with the mount's 1-inch rings. The B-Square mount attaches by replacing the gun's slide stop. A Pachmayr extended lever slide stop is furnished with each mount. Aimpoint mounting bases are furnished with each mount.

The new B-Square mount weighs only 5½ ounces complete with rings. A wrench is furnished for easy do-it-yourself installation. The mount is easy off and on and all 45 Auto accessories can be used with mount installed. The mount comes complete with *both* 1-inch rings and Aimpoint base.

Manufacturer's suggested retail price: $69.96.

B-SQUARE CO.

30-ROUND 10-22 MAGAZINE

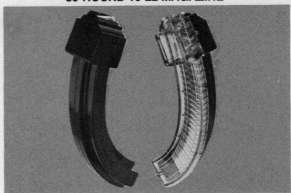

Ram-Line now offers a 30-round magazine for Ruger's 10-22, semiauto, rimfire rifle. This large-capacity magazine is well suited for both small game hunting and plinking. Testing (over 30,000 rounds) has verfied anti-jam functioning even at 20° below zero. A full factory replacement warranty comes with each magazine. Made from a specially engineered resin, these magazines are durable and wear resistant. No modification to the gun is required. The basic magazine is black; however, a clear version, which allows the bullet level to be seen, is also available.

Additionally, Ram-Line makes magazines for Remington, Charter and Colt firearms.

Manufacturer's suggested retail price: Black magazine, $16.75; Clear magazine, $17.95.

RAM-LINE, INC.

CENTERFIRE AMMUNITION

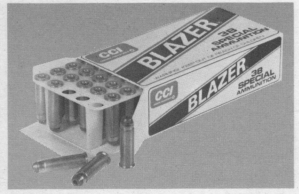

CCI introduced a new line of aluminum-cased centerfire ammunition in 1982.

Blazer centerfire ammunition is made by a unique patented process, performing as well as the best brass-case ammunition. While not reloadable, it sells for an average of 35 percent less than factory new brass-cased centerfire ammunition.

Blazer ammunition is available in a variety of 38 Special, 38 Special +P, 357 Magnum, 9mm, and 25 Auto rounds. The first 45 Auto Blazer cartridge will be available in the fall of 1984. 38 Special and 9mm Blazer is available in 50 or 100 count packages. Blazer handgun ammunition is well suited for target, hunting or home-defense purposes. Manufacturer's suggested retail price: $8.50 to $13.50.

OMARK INDUSTRIES

ELECTRONIC GUN SAFE

Treadlok Models 605 and 757 security chests are now available with the new Electronic Logolok™ feature. The switch of the concealed pushbutton combination lock is hidden within the Treadlok name plate on the door of the chest. There are over 2 million combinations to choose from using any sequence of seven letters in the Treadlok logo. Unlocking is accomplished using the pushbuttons concealed in the logo.

Once the opening sequence has begun it must be completed within 10 seconds or the lock will reset itself. This also means that the safe will *relock* automatically if the bolt operating handle is turned to the closed position. Suggested retail price: Model 605 U $910; Model 757 (13-gun capacity) $1525; Model 757 (26-gun capacity) $1464.

TREAD CORPORATION

See manufacturers' addresses following this section.

OVER-UNDER SHOTGUN

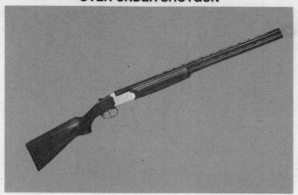

Navy Arms is currently importing an over-under, field grade shotgun.

Made in Italy by ROTA Luciano, the Model 84 Bird Hunter over-under features 28", chrome-lined barrels. The barrels on this shotgun also feature double vent-rib construction. The receiver of the Model 84 Bird Hunter comes fully engraved. The forend and butt-stock are made of European walnut; both the forend and buttstock are hand checkered for a more positive grip. This gun is equipped with gold-plated double triggers, bead front sight.

The Model 84 Bird Hunter comes in 12 or 20 gauge. Choke (for either gauge) is I.C./Mod. or Mod./Full.

Manufacturer's suggested retail price: 12 gauge, $299; 20 gauge, $319.

NAVY ARMS

COMBO CLEANING ROD

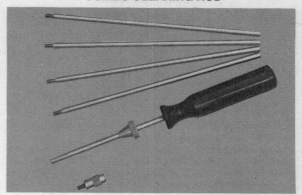

This five-piece stainless steel RIG-ROD can be used for all handguns & rifles of 25 caliber and up. It can also be used on all shotguns with the enclosed brass adapter for brushes and patch pullers. The rod is made of 303 stainless steel, the handle is made of unbreaka-ble Delrin and swivels on the rod. The RR-32-5HD comes packed in a zip-lock plastic carrying case complete with a brass bore guide and a brass shotgun brush adapter.

This rod is ideally suited for bench or camp use. Because RIG's Rifle-Handgun-Shotgun combo cleaning rod is sectioned, it's well suited to those shooting/hunting situations where cleaning-gear portability is an important factor. Made in U.S.A.

Manufacturer's suggested retail price: $19.95.

RIG® PRODUCTS

DRILL & TAP KIT

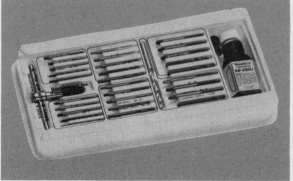

The most common and frequently used drills and taps in any gunshop — large or small — are the ones used by gunsmiths and serious hobbyists to mount sights and scopes. Brownells No. 2 Drill & Tap Kit includes tap-hole and clearance drills, plus the taper, plug and bottom taps needed for these jobs. Included is a professional-type "T"-handled tap wrench, a refer-ence chart giving tap-hole drill and clearance drill size for each tap, and a 2-oz. bottle of Do-Drill. The kit is packed in a durable compact bench box.

The No. 2 Drill & Tap Kit is American-made. Taps are Carbon steel (so when you break one in the hole, you can shatter the stub with a punch and remove the pieces). Drills are made of standard, replaceable, high-speed steel. Suggested retail price: $34.72.

BROWNELLS, INC.

CASE TUMBLER

RCBS has just introduced the *"Sidewinder,"* a case tumbler made for reloaders, by reloaders.

Sidewinder works well with either wet or dry media. RCBS offers both so you can determine which formula works best for you. The liquid cleaning agent removes powder residue and tarnish in as little as 30 minutes. The RCBS Sidewinder also comes with a screen top that separates cases from the media so clean up is quick and easy.

The Sidewinder is built for long-term use, featuring a durable, full ball-bearing motor. The bowl is made of a unique material that absorbs sound, making tumbling a quiet process. A 12-hour auto-off timer is built into each Sidewinder brass tumbler.

Manufacturer's suggested retail price: $135.

OMARK INDUSTRIES

See manufacturers' addresses following this section.

BORE CLEANER

Marksmans Choice is a bore cleaner and conditioner that was originally formulated for competitive bench-rest shooters. Marksmans Choice removes powder and copper fouling, and lifts carbon and lead deposits. It can be left in a barrel indefinitely, will remove rust, and also serves as a lubricant for working parts.

Marksmans Choice removes plastic wad residue from shotgun barrels and works equally well on handgun and blackpowder barrels.

Marksmans Choice is a non-abrasive cleaner that performs the function of two or more existing products. It is formulated to remove residue and fouling without affecting the surface of the bore.

Manufacturer's suggested retail price: $5.95 for a 4-oz. bottle.

MARKSMANS, INC.

AUTO PISTOL

Taurus International is now offering a lifetime warranty on all of its firearm products, including the PT-99 semi-auto pistol seen here.

The 9mm PT-99 features a large capacity (15 round) magazine, double action operation, fully adjustable sights, Brazilian walnut stocks, exposed hammer, chamber-loaded indicator and inertia-type firing pin. Additional features include a grooved fore strap, back strap and combat-style trigger guard.

Introduced in 1983, the PT-99 is available in either polished blue or satin nickel finishes. The Taurus PT-92 is identical to the PT-99 except that it has plastic grips, fixed sights.

Manufacturer's suggested retail price: PT-99 "blue" $419; "Satin nickel" $459; PT-92 "blue" $383.

TAURUS INTERNATIONAL MANUFACTURING

O-FRAME RELOADING PRESS

Recently, Lee Precision, Inc., introduced a new O-Frame reloading press, the 2001 Challenger.

The 2001 Challenger features compound leverage. The mechanical advantage is easily "user adjustable" by simply shortening the lever. The frame is cast from ASTM380 alloy that has 46,000 psi tensile strength; a fatigue strength of 20,000 psi at 500,000,000 cycles.

This new press also has a stress-limiting design (patent pending) that makes the press unbreakable. That same feature also prevents the frame from springing out of alignment. The large O-Frame opening is offset 30° for greater convenience.

Suggested retail price: $39.95; $59.95 (includes press, dies, shell holder, powder measure, load data, powder funnel, ram prime tool and case lube).

LEE PRECISION, INC.

PRIMERS

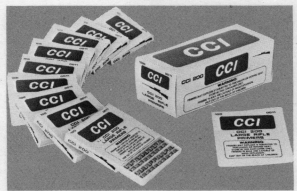

CCI currently offers a line of 14 different primers for reloading. The standard large and small rifle and pistol primers are supplemented with the #11 percussion caps for muzzleloaders and premium Benchrest primers for small and large bore rifles. CCI also offers a variety of primers designed specifically for the reloading of shotshell ammunition.

CCI primers are manufactured by a combination of state-of-the-art technology and quality control. Every CCI primer is charged by hand and then inspected. Their special lead styphnate formula consistently produces a white hot flame for uniform cartridge/shotshell ignition.

Manufacturer's suggested retail price: $1.50 to $3.00

OMARK INDUSTRIES

See manufacturers' addresses following this section.

Shooter's Marketplace

ALUMINUM GUN CASES

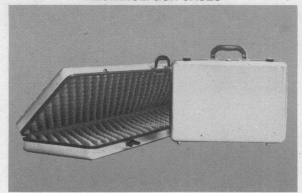

Outers' Silverline aluminum gun cases are rugged, precision built, and designed for convenience and protection. A built-in interlocking feature and an outer formed (not welded) aluminum body with extra thick aluminum exterior adds strength without adding weight. The full-length piano hinge assures permanent alignment. Inside, dense foam holds firearms securely. A continuous rubber gasket seals out dust and moisture. Comes with a free protective silicone gun sleeve. The long gun cases measures 52½″ × 13″ × 4¼″ and accommodates two shotguns or scoped rifles. The handgun case dimensions are 18″ × 13″ × 4¼″ which allows for two large frame or four small frame handguns. Strong tumbler lock. Manufacturer's suggested retail price: $125 and $215.

OMARK INDUSTRIES

GUNSMITH SCREWDRIVER

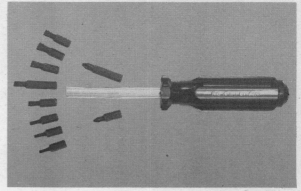

The RIG 10-in-1 Gunsmith is a unique tool designed for the professional as well as hobbyist gunsmith. It contains seven screwdriver blade bits which will fit those common screws normally found on sporting firearms.

The RIG 10-in-1 Gunsmith screwdriver kit also contains one special bit for use on butt pads and two Phillips bits for general purpose use. All blades are especially forged and heat treated to withstand use in power tools. Under normal use, these bits will last for many years. All ten bits fit snugly into the handle. The RIG 10-in-1 Gunsmith screwdriver kit can be conveniently carried in the shooter's gun box or shirt pocket. Made in U.S.A.

Manufacturer's suggested retail price: $19.95.

RIG® PRODUCTS

SPRINGFIELD SCOPE MOUNT

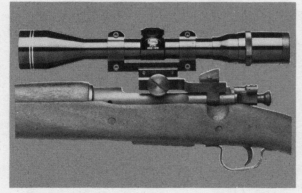

B-Square Company is currently offering a scope mount for all types of 1903 Springfield rifles.

This new mount requires no drilling, tapping, bolt alteration or sight removal when it comes to installation. This new B-Square mount has been specifically designed to eliminate any physical alteration to now-valuable, collectible, 1903 Springfields.

Simply replace the gun's magazine cut-off with B-Square's steel bracket and attach the mount. B-Square's mount is quick off and on without zero change. The new mount has both windage and elevation adjustment. Any 1-inch tube scope may be used in conjunction with this mount. The gun's iron sights can be used with scope installed.

Manufacturer's suggested retail price: $59.95.

B-SQUARE CO.

TARGET PISTOL

The Le Page pistol manufactured by Davide Pedersoli & Co., of Gardone, Italy, reproduces the full characteristics of an 18th century target pistol.

The percussion model (not seen) features a 44 caliber, 9″, rifled, octagonal barrel. The barrel has been finished bright while the European walnut stock has been hand checkered. The lock plate, hammer and trigger guard are engraved. It has a fully adjustable single set trigger.

The flint model seen here, is identical to the percussion model except the barrel is finished in brown. The forward portion of the stock is carved in the shape of a shell and the buttcap is hinged. The flintlock is available with either a rifled or smooth-bore barrel.

Suggested retail price: From $275 to $1,975.

NAVY ARMS

See manufacturers' addresses following this section.

SHOOTER'S MARKETPLACE

PICKUP GUN SAFES

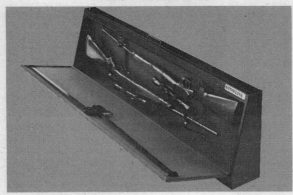

The Outers product line now includes gun caddys and gun safes for pickup trucks. These safes and caddys carry the Stowline name and offer considerable security for valuable firearms.

Omark offers, under the Stowline name, safes and caddys made for a variety of full-sized and down-sized pickups. These units mount easily behind bench seats in Ford, Dodge, Chevrolet and GMC standard cab trucks. The rifle safe shown will fully accommodate two long guns and fits any full-size pickup truck.

Carrying firearms behind the seat instead of in traditional gun racks greatly reduces the risk of theft. The gun safe, and storage caddys are nearly invisible from the outside once they are installed.

Manufacturer's suggested retail price: $95 to $200.

OMARK INDUSTRIES

NYLON SHOULDER HOLSTER

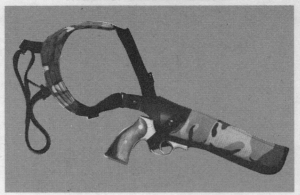

Pioneer Products recently announced their new Sudden Thunder Shoulder Holster System.

The entire outer construction of the Sudden Thunder rig is made of Cordura nylon and is available in four colors: brown, black, autumn camo and spring camo. The holster and harness is foam padded for ease of carry. The interior of the holster is suede lined for a smooth draw and minimal blue wear.

The Sudden Thunder shoulder holster is lightweight, durable, and may be worn inside or outside a jacket. The rig is fully adjustable. Sizes are available to fit medium or large frame revolvers (4" to 10½" barrels), 22 autos (5½" to 7" barrels) and large frame autos and Thompson Contenders (10" to 14" barrels).

Manufacturer's suggested retail price: $32.95.

PIONEER PRODUCTS

STOCK BEDDING COMPOUND

Introduced by Brownells as an update of their well known Acraglas® Stock Bedding Compound, Acraglas Gel® Stock Bedding Compound has a smooth consistency that will not drip, run or leach out from between wood and metal after being put into the gunstock. Acraglas Gel® is formulated with nylon derivatives for greater "thin strength," shock resistance and stability over normal temperature extremes. Shrinkage is less than $\frac{1}{10}$th of 1%. Easy to use 1-to-1 mix gives stable molecular lattice structure that will not crack, craze or "sugar-out." Readily blends with atomized metals.

Acraglas Gel® 2-Gun 4-oz. Kit sells for $7.70. Larger 16-oz. Shop Kit is $23.20. Kits contain two-part epoxy, stock-matching dye, mixing sticks and dish, release agent and detailed instructions.

BROWNELLS, INC.

SHORT-BARRELED REVOLVER

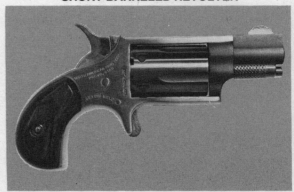

North American Arms line of 5-shot mini-revolvers are lightweight and compact. Each gun has the following standard features: all stainless steel construction; laminated wood grips, polished satin and matte finish. The design of the cylinder is such that the hammer cannot strike the cartridge without perfect cylinder alignment. It also encloses the head of the rimfire cartridge to prevent the possibility of flying particles if a case rupture occurs. In addition to the half-cock safety feature, North American Mini Revolvers have a separate slot between chambers that the hammer blade can rest in. You can safely carry the gun with all chambers loaded with the hammer in the safety slot.

Available in 22 Short, 22 Long Rifle, or 22 Magnum. Suggested retail price: $116 - $137.50.

NORTH AMERICAN ARMS

See manufacturers' addresses following this section.

SHOOTER'S MARKETPLACE

BULLET CASTER'S FLUX

Marmel Products has been offering their Marvelux casting flux since 1971.

Marvelux reduces dross formation and increases melt fluidity. The reduction of dross and the addition of greater fluidity assures a well formed cast bullet.

Marvelux is non-corrosive to iron and steel as this casting flux contains no sal-ammonia. As a result, rust producing fumes are not present, eliminating any permanent damage to molds, pots or other traditionally-iron implements used in the bullet-casting process.

Marvelux casting flux is well suited for any lead-alloy melt intended for the casting of rifle bullets, pistol bullets or swaging cores.

Manufacturer's suggested retail price: 1 lb. $5.85; 4 lb. $12.80; 8 lbs. $20.25.

MARMEL PRODUCTS

AEROSOL LUBRICANT

RIG 2 is a light oil that stops rust, lubricates, penetrates and removes moisture. RIG 2 will neutralize fingerprint acids and harsh residue created by the burning of gunpowders. The oil base of RIG 2 is a high grade mineral oil that is completely free of sulphur. Petroleum wax additives increase lubricity and add to the protective qualities of the oil film. The solvent portion of RIG 2 removes moisture and carries the protective film into the metal. Unique rust fighters are added to increase protection with RIG 2. RIG 2 conforms to, and exceeds the requirements of Military Specification Mil-C-23411. This shooter-oriented product is also being used and specified by major airlines and industry worldwide. Available in 8 oz. aerosol cans. Made in U.S.A. Manufacturer's suggested retail price: $3.

RIG® PRODUCTS

ATTACHE CASE

Wildlife Leather, Inc., is currently offering a wide selection of leather products for hunters, shooters and outdoorsmen.

The attache case seen here has been custom embossed with a gun-club logo and a running whitetail deer. Other available embossings include moose, eagles, rams, wild turkeys, bow hunting, ducks and "Right to Bear Arms."

The embossing seen on the attache case is fully three-dimensional. The embossing is available on a wide variety of Wildlife Leather products. All products are handmade with particular attention given to fit, finish and stitching.

Manufacturer's suggested retail price: Attache case $125.

WILDLIFE LEATHER

RELOADING STARTER KIT

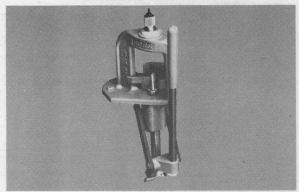

RCBS offers a Reloading Starter Kit that contains almost everything needed to start reloading rifle and pistol ammunition including: Reloader Special-2™ Press, 5-0-5® Powder Scale, Speer Reloading Manual #10 (instructions), Powder Funnel, Case Loading Block, Primer Tray, Case Lube Pad, 2 oz. tube of Resizing Lubricant and two Case Neck Brushes with Handle.

With this kit the new reloader need only buy the proper loading dies, shell holder, powder, bullets and primers to get started in the hobby of reloading. In addition, the price of the RCBS Reloading Starter Kit is 10 percent lower than if the contents were purchased individually.

Manufacturer's suggested retail price: $148.

OMARK INDUSTRIES

See manufacturers' addresses following this section.

RIMFIRE AMMUNITION

CCI offers a full line of 22 rimfire ammo. Their 15 rimfire products include a number of innovations.

An example of this is the CCI Stinger™. It has a 30 percent faster muzzle speed than normal high velocity 22 Long Rifle ammo. This, combined with its unique "Penta-Point" hollow point bullet, makes it well suited for small game and varmints.

CCI Competition Green Tag™ 22 Long Rifle ammunition is designed for use by competitive shooters. Accurate and consistent, this Olympic-quality ammo is equally suited for the taking of small game.

Other rimfire products include a variety of 22 Short, Long, Long Rifle, WMR and even shotshell cartridges.

Manufacturer's suggested retail price: $2.50 to $6.50.

OMARK INDUSTRIES

PIN PUNCH SET

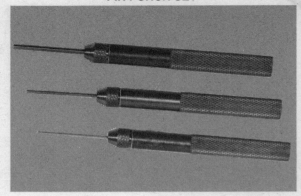

Brownells, Inc., now offers a pin punch set that features instantly replaceable pins.

Handles are made of LaSalle Fatigueproof C.R.S. steel (tensile strength of over 140,000 psi), with a removable, knurled chuck to hold the punch. These bevel-headed punches are designed for tool, die and mold makers as perforators, punches, ejector and core pins. Oil hardened to 58-60 Rockwell "C". Heads are annealed to 42-45 Rockwell "C".

Available in sets of 3 Punches with 2″ Pins in sizes: .039 ($\frac{3}{64}$″), .060 ($\frac{1}{16}$″) and .091 ($\frac{3}{32}$″), overall length 4¾″, $7.14. 2″ Replacement Pins, 2 each dia., $2.65. 2½″ Replacement Pins, 2 at .039″ and 1 each .060″ and .091″, $2.60. 1″ Starter Replacement Pins, 2 each dia., $3.20. All prices are manufacturer's suggested retail.

BROWNELLS, INC.

HARD GUN CASE

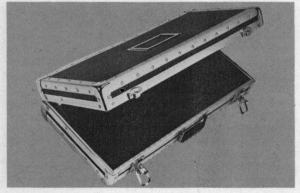

Magnum Firearm Cases, by Wilson Case, are designed to protect firearms during transport or storage. These cases are constructed of ¼″ plywood bonded to a protective outer cover of Kydex®, a material that's both flame and chemical resistant.

The entire body of the case is fully framed with aluminum extrusions, then capped with heavy steel corners and fully machine riveted. The cases are fully hinged, all hardware 100 percent nickel plated.

Each Magnum case is fully lined with shock-resistant foam. Locked closures provide security against theft or tampering. Magnum cases are available in sizes ranging from 54″ × 14″ × 4″ (for the largest of firearms) on down to 14″ × 10″ × 4″ (for handguns).

Suggested retail price: From $99 to $219.

WILSON CASE COMPANY

BARRELS

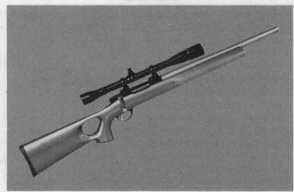

Lone Star rifle barrels provide the full accuracy potential of every caliber suitable for medium and big game. They are offered in 10 calibers from 22 to 458; and in 18 chamberings from 222 to 458 Win.

Handgun silhouette enthusiasts can get Lone Star barrels in 30 caliber or 7mm, and chambered for the most popular competition rounds: 308 Win., 30 IHMSA, 7mm x 08 Rem., 7mm IHMSA and 7mm Rem. BR. Shilen also offers a complete line of Lone Star pistol barrels, from 22 rimfire to 45. All Lone Star barrels are made of 4140 chrome-moly steel, button rifled with eight lands and grooves, and stress relieved. *Match Grade* Shilen barrels of chrome-moly or stainless steel are also available.

Suggested retail price: $164 to $348, installed.

SHILEN RIFLES, INC.

See manufacturers' addresses following this section.

STAINLESS STEEL DERRINGER

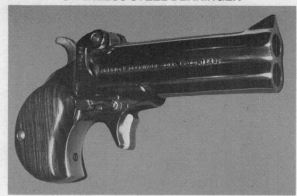

American Derringer is now offering a stainless steel derringer with 4-inch barrel chambered for the 3-inch 410 shotgun shell. This derringer also features a 45 caliber rifled barrel and will also shoot 45 Colt cartridges.

This pistol was developed to provide ranchers, campers, fishermen, and other outdoorsmen with a small, lightweight defensive weapon for killing snakes at short range; 12 feet or less. It can also be used as a survival gun to kill small game at 20 feet or less with the 410. The 45 Colt could be used to shoot larger game in an emergency. The overall length is 6″, weight 16 oz., rosewood grips. Stainless steel construction makes this gun ideal for survival uses.

Manufacturer's suggested retail price: $350.

AMERICAN DERRINGER CORP.

RIFLE & PISTOL BULLETS

Speer's current line up of bullets for reloaders consists of 89 rifle bullets (22 to 45 caliber), 39 pistol bullets (25 to 45 caliber), 13 round lead balls (36 to 58 caliber) and 38, 44 and 45 caliber plastic indoor bullets and cases.

Pictured is one of the most recent additions to the Speer line. It is the 44 caliber FMJ Silhouette pistol bullet. This projectile has a 100 percent copper jacket with no exposed lead. By a new process, the copper jacket is bonded to the lead core resulting in a solid one-piece bullet with a jacket that cannot slip, shear or separate. Accuracy is increased substantially through gyroscopic balancing. This new design of bullet is available in 25, 9mm, 38, 357, 44 and 45 versions.

Suggested retail price: $3.50 to $30.50.

OMARK INDUSTRIES

AMMO CARRIERS

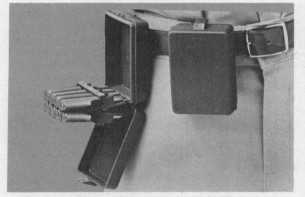

The Case-Gard AMMO HOLSTER™ (illustrated) is part of a product line that includes over 80 models, in almost 30 different styles.

There are 50-, 60- and 100-round boxes for rifle rounds; 50- and 100-round boxes for handgun ammo; "slip top" boxes and AMMO WALLETS™ for both; carriers and AMMO WALLETS™ for rimfire shooters; 100 round shotshell boxes (including 410) and a wide selection of both metallic and shotshell carriers.

Other MTM products include equipment boxes, a new Cartridge Display Board, reloading accessories, carriers for back-up auto magazines, an Adjustable Shooting Rest, a Bore Guide and a clay bird thrower.

Every MTM product is covered by a full 3-year guarantee. Suggested retail, Ammo Holster, $8.98.

MTM MOLDED PRODUCTS COMPANY

BLACK POWDER RIFLE/KIT

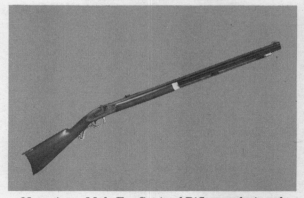

Navy Arms Mule Ear Squirrel Rifle was designed to meet the needs of the modern black powder small game hunter.

Available finished or in kit form, the Mule Ear Squirrel Rifle is available in 32, 36 or 45 caliber. The rifle weighs only 5½ pounds and features fast ignition, the nipple being directly mounted on the barrel. The overall length of the pre-straightened barrel is 26″. Adjustable sights are standard. The stock is constructed of Pennsylvania Black Walnut and comes with solid brass furniture. The name "Mule Ear" is indicative of this rifle's color case hardened side-hammer lock. Given its size and light weight, the Mule Ear Squirrel Rifle is well suited for field use.

Suggested retail price: $184 (finished), $134 (kit).

NAVY ARMS

See manufacturers' addresses following this section.

SHOOTER'S MARKETPLACE

TEFLON AEROSOL

Outers Laboratories has just introduced TR-3™ Teflon lubricant, formulated to assure the maximum friction-free movement of parts. TR-3 also has a strong cleaning action, but still leaves a long-lasting film that prevents rust and corrosion.

The properties of the Teflon additive help protect metal against part-to-part wear. This lubricant also has a solvent action that penetrates, enabling the loosening of frozen/rusted screws. Outers TR-3 is a synthetic lubricant that works within a wide range of temperatures (−65°F. to +475°F.) without gumming up. The formula for TR-3™ Teflon lubricant is not electrically conductive.

Manufacturer's suggested retail price: $2.89, 3 oz. can; $3.78, 6 oz. can.

OMARK INDUSTRIES

AMMO BOXES

RCBS has five new plastic ammo boxes.

Stacking legs are built into each box, the 90-degree angle projections on the top and bottom corners interlocking to prevent any sliding of boxes when stacked.

The one-piece RCBS Ammo Boxes have a positive, flush latch that is easily opened and an integral "living" hinge that will last for thousands of flexings.

These boxes are made of unbreakable, light green transparent plastic that permits the contents to be seen. A compartment for a load description label is in the inside front of the box and can be easily viewed.

The rifle boxes have a raised collar for bullet tip protection in the bottom of each compartment. All boxes are 50 count and available in five popular rifle and handgun sizes. Suggested retail price: $1.60 to $3.40.

OMARK INDUSTRIES

MANUFACTURERS ADDRESSES

ALBERTS CORPORATION
519 E. 19th St., Paterson, NJ 07514
Phone: 201-684-7583

AMERICAN DERRINGER CORP.
127 N. Lacy Dr., Waco, TX 76705
Phone: 817-799-9111

B-SQUARE CO.
P. O. Box 11281, Ft. Worth, TX 76109
Phone: 800-433-2909

BROWNELLS, INC.
200 S. Front St., Montezuma, IA 50171
Phone: 515-623-5401

J. DEWEY MANUFACTURING CO., INC.
186 Skyview Drive, Southbury, CT 06488
Phone: 203-264-3064

LEE PRECISION
4275 Hwy. "U", Hartford, WI 53027
Phone: 414-673-3075

MTM MOLDED PRODUCTS CORP.
8000 Obco Ct., Dayton, OH 45414
Phone: 513-890-7561

MARKSMANS INC.
P. O. Box 598, Chesterland, OH 44026
Phone: 216-729-9392

MARMEL PRODUCTS
8687 Winchester Dr., Sterling Heights, MI 48078
Phone: 313-731-8029

NORTH AMERICAN ARMS
1800 N. 300 W., Spanish Fork, UT 84660
Phone: 801-798-9893

NAVY ARMS COMPANY
Dept. SMP, 689 Bergen Blvd., Ridgefield, NJ 07657
Phone: 201-945-2500

OMARK INDUSTRIES
P. O. Box 856, Lewiston, ID 83501
Phone: 208-746-2351

P. S. OLT COMPANY
P. O. Box 550, Pekin, IL 61554
Phone: 309-348-3633

PIONEER PRODUCTS
P. O. Box "G", Magnolia, AR 71753
Phone: 501-234-1566

RAM-LINE, INC.
406 Violet St., Golden, CO 80401
Phone: 303-279-0886

RIG PRODUCTS
87 Coney Island Dr., Sparks, NV 89431
Phone: 702-331-5666

SHILEN RIFLES
205 Metro Park Blvd., Ennis, TX 75119
Phone: 214-875-5318

TAURUS INTERNATIONAL MANUFACTURING
4563 S.W. 71st Ave., Miami, FL 33155
Phone: 205-662-2529

TREAD CORPORATION
P. O. Box 13207, Roanoke, VA 24032
Phone: 703-982-6881

WILDLIFE LEATHER
321 Wynsum Ave., Merrick, NY 11566
Phone: 516-378-8558

WILSON CASE COMPANY
P. O. Box 953, Hasting, NE 68901
Phone: 402-463-2893

THE

COMPLETE

COMPACT

CATALOG

GUNDEX®

A listing of all the guns in the catalog, by name and model, alphabetically and numerically.

This feature of our catalog speeds up the chore of finding the basic facts on a given firearm for the experienced. And it may make the contents of the catalog far more available to the inexperienced.

That is our intention.

To use it, you need the manufacturer's name and model designation. That designation might be a number, as in Winchester Model 94, or it might be a name, as in Colt Python. And you need to know the alphabet.

The manufacturers are listed alphabetically and the entry under each manufacturer is arranged in the quickest way—numbers are in numerical order, names are alphabetical.

It's all very straightforward. It is all pretty voluminous, as well. There are nearly 1400 entries (1397 to be exact). At 255 lines per page, what with headings and all, the GUNDEX® is nine pages long.

We have tried to make it easy to find, too—just look for the black GUNDEX® label along the edge of the page, flip to there, and get your page number in short order.

GUNDEX

AMT LIGHTNING AUTO PISTOL

Caliber: 22 LR, 10-shot magazine.
Barrel: Tapered — 6½″, 8½″, 10½″, 12½″; Bull — 5″, 6½″, 8½″, 10½″, 12½″.
Weight: 45 oz. (6½″ barrel). **Length:** 10¾″ over-all (6½″ barrel).
Stocks: Checkered wrap-around rubber.
Sights: Blade front, fixed rear; adjustable rear available at extra cost.
Features: Made of stainless steel. Uses Clark trigger with adjustable stops; receiver grooved for scope mounting; trigger guard spur for two-hand hold; interchangeable barrels. Introduced 1984. From AMT.
Price: 5″ bull, 6½″ tapered or bull, fixed sight **$230.00**
Price: 8½″, tapered or bull, fixed sight **$240.00**
Price: 12½″, tapered or bull, fixed sight **$250.00**
Price: For adjustable rear sight add **$21.00**

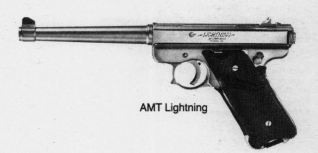

AMT Lightning

AMT "BACKUP" AUTO PISTOL

Caliber: 22 LR, 8-shot magazine; 380 ACP, 5-shot magazine
Barrel: 2½″
Weight: 18 oz. **Length:** 4.25″ over-all.
Stocks: Checkered nylon.
Sights: Fixed, open, recessed.
Features: Concealed hammer, blowback operation; manual and grip safeties. All stainless steel construction. Smallest domestically-produced pistol in 380. From AMT.
Price: 22 LR or 380 ACP **$250.00**

AMT Backup

AMT 45 ACP HARDBALLER LONG SLIDE

Caliber: 45 ACP.
Barrel: 7″.
Length: 10½″ over-all.
Stocks: Wrap-around rubber.
Sights: Fully adjustable rear sight.
Features: Slide and barrel are 2″ longer than the standard 45, giving less recoil, added velocity, longer sight radius. Has extended combat safety, serrated matte rib, loaded chamber indicator, wide adjustable trigger. From AMT.
Price: **$625.00**

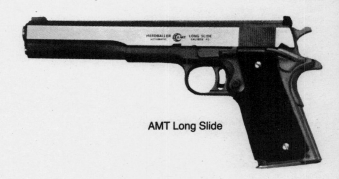

AMT Long Slide

AMT 45 ACP HARDBALLER

Caliber: 45 ACP.
Barrel: 5″
Weight: 39 oz. **Length:** 8½″ over-all.
Stocks: Wrap-around rubber.
Sights: Adjustable.
Features: Extended combat safety, serrated matte slide rib, loaded chamber indicator, long grip safety, beveled magazine well, adjustable target trigger. All stainless steel. From AMT.
Price: **$550.00**
Price: Government combat (as above except no rib, fixed sights) ... **$500.00**

AMERICAN ARMS EAGLE 380

Caliber: 380 ACP, 6-shot magazine.
Barrel: 2½″.
Weight: 20 oz. **Length:** 6¼″ over-all.
Stocks: Checkered walnut.
Sights: Fixed.
Features: Double action, stainless steel construction, firing pin lock safety. Comes with fitted carrying case, belt buckle and one magazine. Introduced 1984. From Wilkerson Firearms Corp.
Price: **$289.00**
Price: As above, except with black rubber grips.................. **$298.00**
Price: With black rubber grips, black Teflon finish **$319.00**

American Arms Eagle

AMERICAN DERRINGER 25 AUTO
Caliber: 25 ACP or 250 Magnum; 7-shot magazine.
Barrel: 2.1″.
Weight: 15½ oz. **Length:** 4.4″ over-all.
Stocks: Smooth rosewood.
Sights: Fixed.
Features: Stainless or ordnance steel. Magazines have finger extension. Introduced 1980. From American Derringer Corp.
Price: Stainless, 25 ACP **$212.00**
Price: Blue, matte finish, 25 ACP **$200.00**
Price: 250 Mag., stainless **$212.00**
Price: 250 Mag., blued **$200.00**

American Derringer 25 Auto

ARMINEX TRIFIRE AUTO PISTOL
Caliber: 9mm. Para. (9-shot), 38 Super. (9-shot), 45 ACP (7-shot).
Barrel: 5″, 6″, 7″.
Weight: 38 oz. **Length:** 8″ over-all.
Stocks: Contoured smooth walnut.
Sights: Interchangeable post front, rear adjustable for windage and elevation.
Features: Single action. Slide mounted firing pin block safety. Specially contoured one-piece backstrap. Convertible by changing barrel, magazine, recoil spring. Introduced 1982. Made in U.S. by Arminex Ltd.
Price: Blue. **$396.00**
Price: With wood presentation case **$452.00**
Price: Target model, 6″ barrel **$424.00**
Price: For 7″ barrel, add **$12.00**

Arminex Trifire

ASTRA A-80 DOUBLE-ACTION AUTO PISTOL
Caliber: 9mm Para., 38 Super (15-shot), 45 ACP (9-shot).
Barrel: 3.75″.
Weight: 40 oz. **Length:** 7″ over-all.
Stocks: Checkered black plastic.
Sights: Square blade front, square notch rear drift-adjustable for windage.
Features: Double or single action; loaded chamber indicator; combat-style trigger guard; optional right-side slide release (for left-handed shooters); automatic internal safety; decocking lever. Introduced 1982. Imported from Spain by Interarms.
Price: Blue. **$425.00**
Price: Chrome **$465.00**

Astra A-80 Pistol

ASTRA CONSTABLE AUTO PISTOL
Caliber: 22 LR, 10-shot, 380 ACP, 7-shot.
Barrel: 3½″
Weight: 26 oz.
Stocks: Moulded plastic
Sights: Adj. rear.
Features: Double action, quick no-tool takedown, non-glare rib on slide. 380 available in blue or chrome finish. Engraved guns also available—contact the importer. Imported from Spain by Interarms.
Price: Blue, 22 . . . . **$299.00**
Price: Chrome, 22 . . . . **$324.00**
Price: Blue, 380 . . . . **$279.00**
Price: Chrome, 380 . . . . **$309.00**

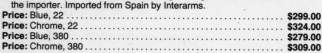

AUTO-ORDNANCE 1911A1 AUTOMATIC PISTOL
Caliber: 9mm Para., 38 Super, 9-shot, 45 ACP, 7-shot magazine.
Barrel: 5″.
Weight: 39 oz. **Length:** 8½″ over-all.
Stocks: Checkered plastic with medallion.
Sights: Blade front, rear adj. for windage.
Features: Same specs as 1911A1 military guns—parts interchangeable. Frame and slide blued; each radius has non-glare finish. Made in U.S. by Auto-Ordnance Corp.
Price: Approximately **$324.95**

Auto-Ordnance 1911A1

CAUTION: PRICES CHANGE. CHECK AT GUNSHOP.

Beeman SP-1 Standard

BEEMAN SP-1 STANDARD PISTOL
Caliber: 22 LR, single shot.
Barrel: 8″, 10″, 11.2″, 15″.
Weight: 50 oz. **Length:** 18″ over-all.
Stocks: European walnut, anatomically-shaped with adjustable palm rest.
Sights: Blade front, notch rear adjustable for windage and elevation.
Features: Two-stage trigger; loaded chamber indicator; grooved for scope mount. Detachable fore-end and barrel weight optional. Imported by Beeman. Introduced 1984.
Price: Right or left-hand **$249.50**
Price: Deluxe (with fore-end), illus. **$299.50**

Bernardelli Model 80

BERNARDELLI MODEL 80 AUTO PISTOL
Caliber: 22 LR (10-shot); 380 ACP (7-shot).
Barrel: 3½″.
Weight: 26½ oz. **Length:** 6½″ over-all.
Stocks: Checkered plastic with thumbrest.
Sights: Ramp front, white outline rear adj. for w. & e
Features: Hammer block slide safety; loaded chamber indicator; dual recoil buffer springs; serrated trigger; inertia type firing pin. Imported from Italy by Interarms.
Price: Model 80, 22 or 380 . . . . **$235.00**
Price: Model 90 (22 or 32, 6″ bbl.) **$275.00**

BERETTA MODEL 81/85 DA PISTOLS
Caliber: 32 ACP (12-shot magazine), 380 ACP (13-shot magazine).
Barrel: 3¾″
Weight: About 23 oz. **Length:** 6½″ over-all.
Stocks: Smooth black plastic (wood optional at extra cost).
Sights: Fixed front and rear.
Features: Double action, quick take-down, convenient magazine release. Introduced 1977. Imported from Italy by Beretta USA.
Price: M-81 (32 ACP) **$408.00**
Price: M-84 (380 ACP) **$408.00**
Price: Either model with wood grips **$425.00**
Price: M-82W, 32 ACP wood grips, nickel, 9-shot mag. **$495.00**
Price: M-85W, 380 ACP wood grips, 9-shot mag. **$495.00**

BERETTA MODEL 950 BS AUTO PISTOL
Caliber: 22 Short, 25 ACP
Barrel: 2½″.
Weight: 8 oz. (22 Short, 10 oz.). **Length:** 4½″ over-all.
Stocks: Checkered black plastic.
Sights: Fixed.
Features: Thumb safety and half-cock safety; barrel hinged at front to pop up for single loading or cleaning. From Beretta U.S.A.
Price: Blue, 22 . . . . **$200.00**
Price: Blue, 25 ACP. **$190.00**
Price: Nickel, 22 or 25. . . . . **$208.00**
Price: Blue with gold highlights **$220.00**

Beretta Model 92 SB Compact

BERETTA MODEL 92 SB, 92 SB COMPACT
Caliber: 9mm Parabellum (15-shot magazine, 14-shot on Compact).
Barrel: 4.92″
Weight: 33½ oz. **Length:** 8.54″ over-all.
Stocks: Smooth black plastic; wood optional at extra cost.
Sights: Blade front, rear adj. for w.
Features: Double-action. Extractor acts as chamber loaded indicator, inertia firing pin. Finished in blue-black. Introduced 1977. Imported from Italy by Beretta USA.
Price: With plastic grips **$600.00**
Price: With wood grips **$620.00**
Price: Compact, plastic grips **$620.00**
Price: Compact, wood grips. **$635.00**

Beretta Model 70S Pistol

BERETTA MODEL 70S PISTOL
Caliber: 22 LR, 380 ACP.
Barrel: 3.5″.
Weight: 23 oz. (Steel) **Length:** 6.5″ over-all.
Stocks: Checkered black plastic.
Sights: Fixed front and rear.
Features: Polished blue finish. Safety lever blocks hammer. Slide lever indicates empty magazine. Magazine capacity is 8 rounds for both calibers. Introduced 1977. Imported from Italy by Beretta USA.
Price: **$274.00**

BERSA MODEL 225 AUTO PISTOL
Caliber: 22 LR, 11-shot.
Barrel: 5″.
Weight: 26 oz.
Stocks: Target-type checkered nylon with thumbrest.
Sights: Blade front, square notch rear adjustable for windage.
Features: Blow-back action; combat-type trigger guard; magazine safety; blue finish. Imported from Argentina by Outdoor Sports Headquarters. Introduced 1984.
Price: Model 225 . . . . **$169.95**
Price: Model 226 (6″ barrel) **$169.95**

Bersa 225

BERSA MODEL 383 AUTO PISTOL
Caliber: 380 ACP, 9-shot.
Barrel: 3½″.
Weight: 25 oz.
Stocks: Target-type checkered black nylon.
Sights: Blade front, square notch rear adjustable for windage.
Features: Blow-back action; magazine safety; combat-type trigger guard; blue finish. Imported from Argentina by Outdoor Sports Headquarters. Introduced 1984.
Price: Model 383 . . . . **$205.00**
Price: Model 223 (as above except 22 LR) **$165.00**

Bersa 383

Bren Ten Standard

BREN TEN STANDARD MODEL
Caliber: 10mm Auto, 11-shot magazine.
Barrel: 5″.
Weight: 39 oz. **Length:** 8.37″ over-all.
Stocks: Textured black nylon (Hogue Combat).
Sights: Adjustable; replaceable, 3-dot combat-type.
Features: Full-size combat pistol, with selective double or single action. Has reversible thumb safety and firing pin block. Blued slide, natural stainless frame. Introduced 1983. From Dornaus & Dixon Enterprises, Inc.
Price: Standard model **$500.00**
Price: Military & Police (matte black finish) **$550.00**
Price: Dual-Master (same as Standard except comes with extra 45 ACP slide and barrel, better finish, engraving, wood grips, wood case) **$800.00**
Price: Jeff Cooper Commemorative (same as Standard except has extra fine finish, 22K gold-filled engraving, details, cartridges, laser engraved Herrett's grips and wood case) **$2,000.00**
Price: 45 ACP conversion kit (4″ or 5″ bbl.) **$125.00**
Price: 22 LR conversion kit (5″ bbl., 13-shot) **$250.00**

Bren Ten Special Forces

Bren Ten Pocket Model
Similar to the Standard Bren Ten except smaller. Has 4″ barrel giving 7.37″ over-all length, and weighs 28 oz. Fires full load 10mm Auto cartridge with 9 round capacity. Has hard chrome slide, stainless frame.
Price: **$600.00**

Bren Ten Special Forces Model
Similar to the Pocket Model except has standard size grip frame with 11-shot capacity; weight is 33 oz. with 4″ barrel. Available in either all black or natural light finish. Introduced 1984.
Price: Black finish **$600.00**
Price: Light finish **$650.00**

Browning BDA-380 Pistol

BROWNING BDA-380 D/A AUTO PISTOL
Caliber: 380 ACP, 13-shot magazine.
Barrel: 3¹³⁄₁₆″.
Weight: 23 oz. **Length:** 6¾″ over-all.
Stocks: Smooth walnut with inset Browning medallion.
Sights: Blade front, rear drift-adj. for w.
Features: Combination safety and de-cocking lever will automatically lower a cocked hammer to half-cock and can be operated by right or left-hand shooters. Inertia firing pin. Introduced 1978. Imported from Italy by Browning.
Price: Blue **$410.00**
Price: Nickel **$455.00**

CAUTION: PRICES CHANGE. CHECK AT GUNSHOP.

Browning Hi-Power Auto

Browning Hi-Power Classic & Gold Classic

Same as standard fixed sight Hi-Power except both editions have game scenes of a bald eagle protecting her young from a lynx on satin grey slide and frame, as well as a profile of John M. Browning. The Gold Classic has the main subjects in contrasting gold inlay. Grips are finely checkered walnut with double border and floral designs. Classic series limited to 5,000, Gold Classic to 500, each with its unique serial number, "1 of 500," and so on. Each gun comes in a velvet lined walnut case.
Price: Hi-Power Classic **$1,325.00**
Price: Hi-Power Gold Classic **$2,800.00**

Browning Challenger III Sporter

Browning Challenger III Pistol

BUSHMASTER AUTO PISTOL

Caliber: 223; 30-shot magazine.
Barrel: 11½" (1-10" twist).
Weight: 5¼ lbs. **Length:** 20½" over-all.
Stocks: Synthetic rotating grip swivel assembly.
Sights: Post front, adjustable open "y" rear
Features: Steel alloy upper receiver with welded barrel assembly, AK-47-type gas system, aluminum lower receiver, one-piece welded steel alloy bolt carrier assembly. From Bushmaster Firearms.
Price: **$439.95**
Price: With matte electroless nickel finish **$479.95**

BROWNING HI-POWER 9mm AUTOMATIC PISTOL

Caliber: 9mm Parabellum (Luger), 13-shot magazine.
Barrel: 4²¹⁄₃₂".
Weight: 32 oz. **Length:** 7¾" over-all.
Stocks: Walnut, hand checkered.
Sights: ⅛" blade front; rear screw-adj. for w. and e. Also available with fixed rear (drift-adj for w.).
Features: External hammer with half-cock and thumb safeties. A blow on the hammer cannot discharge a cartridge; cannot be fired with magazine removed. Fixed rear sight model available. Imported from Belgium by Browning.
Price: Fixed sight model **$535.00**
Price: 9mm with rear sight adj. for w. and e. **$585.00**
Price: Nickel, fixed sight **$610.00**
Price: Nickel, adj. sight **$655.00**
Price: Silver chrome, adj. sight **$610.00**

Browning Louis XVI Hi-Power 9mm Auto

Same as Browning Hi-Power 9mm Auto except: fully engraved, silver-gray frame and slide, gold plated trigger, finely checkered walnut grips, with deluxe walnut case.
Price: With adj. sights and walnut case **$1,530.00**
Price: With fixed sights **$1,460.00**

Hi-Power 88 Auto Pistol II

Similar to the standard Browning Hi-Power except available only with fixed rear sight, military parkerized finish, black checkered polyamid grips, single-action only. Comes with extra magazine. Introduced 1982. Imported from Belgium by Howco Distributors, Inc.
Price: With extra magazine **$499.50**

BROWNING CHALLENGER III SPORTER

Caliber: 22 LR, 10-shot magazine.
Barrel: 6¾".
Weight: 29 oz. **Length:** 10⅞" over-all.
Stocks: Smooth impregnated hardwood.
Sights: ⅛" blade front on ramp, rear screw adj. for e., drift adj. for w.
Features: All steel, blue finish. Wedge locking system prevents action from loosening. Wide gold-plated trigger; action hold-open. Standard grade only. Made in U.S. From Browning.
Price: **$239.95**

Browning Challenger III Auto Pistol

Similar to the Challenger III except has a 5½" heavy bull barrel, new lightweight alloy frame and new sights. Over-all length is 9½", weight is 35 oz. Introduced 1982.
Price: **$239.95**

Bushmaster Auto Pistol

CHARTER ARMS MODEL 79K DA AUTO PISTOL
Caliber: 32 ACP, 380 ACP, 7-shot magazine.
Barrel: 3.6".
Weight: 24½ oz. **Length:** 6.5" over-all.
Stocks: Checkered walnut.
Sights: Fixed.
Features: Double action with hammer block, firing pin and magazine safeties. Stainless steel finish. Introduced 1984. Imported from West Germany by Charter Arms.
Price: 32 or 380 ACP $375.00

Charter Model 79K

Charter Arms Model 40 DA Auto Pistol
Similar to the Model 79K except chambered for 22 Long Rifle, 3.3" barrel, 6.3" over-all length, and 21½-oz. weight. Stainless steel finish. Introduced 1984. Imported from West Germany by Charter Arms.
Price: $299.00

Charter Model 40

CHARTER EXPLORER II & SII PISTOL
Caliber: 22 LR, 8-shot magazine.
Barrel: 8".
Weight: 28 oz. **Length:** 15½" over-all.
Stocks: Serrated simulated walnut.
Sights: Blade front, open rear adj. for elevation.
Features: Action adapted from the semi-auto Explorer carbine. Introduced 1980. From Charter Arms.
Price: Black or satin finish $102.00
Price: Extra 6", 8" or 10" barrel $24.95

Charter Explorer SII Pistol

COLT 380 GOVERNMENT MODEL
Caliber: 380 ACP, 7-shot magazine.
Barrel: 3.29".
Weight: 21.8 oz. **Length:** 6.15" over-all.
Stocks: Checkered composition.
Sights: Ramp front, square notch rear, fixed.
Features: Scaled down version of the 1911A1 Colt G.M. Has thumb and internal firing pin safeties. Blue finish only. Introduced 1983.
Price: $299.95

COLT GOV'T MODEL MK IV/SERIES 80
Caliber: 9mm, 38 Super, 45 ACP, 7-shot.
Barrel: 5".
Weight: 38 oz. **Length:** 8⅜" over-all.
Stocks: Checkered walnut.
Sights: Ramp front, fixed square notch rear.
Features: Grip and thumb safeties, and internal firing pin safety, grooved trigger. Accurizor barrel and bushing. Blue finish or nickel in 45 only.
Price: Blue, 45 cal. $459.50
Price: Nickel, 45 cal. $489.95
Price: 45, Satin nickel w/blue, Pachmayr grips. $488.50
Price: 9mm, blue only $456.95
Price: 38 Super, blue only $464.50

Colt 380 Government

Consult our Directory pages for the location of firms mentioned.

Colt Gov't Series 80

Colt Conversion Unit
Permits the 45 and 38 Super Automatic pistols to use the economical 22 LR cartridge. No tools needed. Adjustable rear sight; 10-shot magazine. Designed to give recoil effect of the larger calibers. Not adaptable to Commander models. Blue finish.
Price: $254.95
Price: Fixed sight version $244.50
Price: 9mm Series 80 Conversion Unit $265.50

Colt Combat Government

Colt Combat Government Model Series 80
Same as the standard Government Model except has a higher undercut front sight, white outline rear, Colt/Pachmayr wrap-around grips, flat mainspring housing, longer trigger, beveled magazine well, and an angled ejection port. Has internal firing pin safety. Introduced 1983.
Price: **$551.95**

COLT SERVICE MODEL ACE
Caliber: 22 LR, 10-shot magazine.
Barrel: 5″
Weight: 42 oz. **Length:** 8⅜″ over-all.
Stocks: Checkered walnut.
Sights: Blade front, fully adjustable rear.
Features: The 22-cal. version of the Government Model auto. Based on the Service Model Ace last produced in 1945. Patented floating chamber. Original Ace Markings rolled on left side of slide. Introduced 1978.
Price: Blue only **$485.95**

Colt Service Model Ace

COLT COMBAT COMMANDER AUTO PISTOL
Caliber: 45 ACP, 7-shot; 38 Super Auto, 9-shot; 9mm Luger, 9-shot.
Barrel: 4¼″.
Weight: 36 oz. **Length:** 8″ over-all.
Stocks: Sandblasted walnut.
Sights: Fixed, glare-proofed blade front, square notch rear.
Features: Grooved trigger and hammer spur; arched housing; grip and thumb safeties.
Price: Blue, 9mm **$456.95**
Price: Blue, 45, Series 80 . . . . **$459.95**
Price: Blue, 38 super **$448.95**
Price: Satin nickel, 45, Series 80 . . . . **$481.50**

Colt Lightweight Commander Mark IV Series 80
Same as Commander except high strength aluminum alloy frame, wood panel grips, weight 27 oz. 45 ACP only.
Price: Blue. **$459.50**

Colt Combat Commander

COONAN 357 MAGNUM PISTOL
Caliber: 357 Mag., 7-shot magazine.
Barrel: 5″.
Weight: 42 oz. **Length:** 8.3″ over-all.
Stocks: Smooth walnut.
Sights: Open, adjustable.
Features: Unique barrel hood improves accuracy and reliability. Many parts interchange with Colt autos. Has grip, hammer, half-cock safeties. From Coonan Arms.
Price: **$595.00**

DETONICS 45 PISTOL
Caliber: 45 ACP, 451 Detonics Magnum, 6-shot clip; 9mm Para., 38 Super, 7-shot clip.
Barrel: 3¼″.
Weight: 29 oz. (empty). MK VII is 26 oz. **Length:** 6¾″ over-all, 4½″ high.
Stocks: Checkered walnut.
Sights: Combat type, fixed; adj. sights avail.
Features: Has a self-adjusting cone barrel centering system, beveled magazine inlet, "full clip" indicator in base of magazine; standard 7-shot (or more) clip can be used in the 45. Throated barrel and polished feed ramp. Mark V, VI, VII available in 9mm and 38 Super; MC1 available in 9mm Para. Introduced 1977. From Detonics.
Price: MK. V, matte stainless, fixed sights. **$626.00**
Price: MK. VI, polished stainless, adj sights **$635.00**
Price: MK. VII, matte stainless, no sights **$635.00**
Price: Combat Master MC1, non-glare combat stainless, fixed sights **$560.00**
Price: MC2, as above with fixed sights, wallet, Pachmayr grips, cleaning kit, extra magazine **$621.50**
Price: OM-3, non-glare finish, fixed sights, polished slide flats **$575.00**

Detonics Auto Pistol

CAUTION: PRICES CHANGE. CHECK AT GUNSHOP.

DETONICS POCKET 9 DOUBLE ACTION AUTO
Caliber: 9mm Para., 6-shot clip.
Barrel: 3".
Weight: 26 oz. **Length:** 5.7" over-all, 4" high.
Stocks: Black micarta.
Sights: Fixed.
Features: Stainless steel construction; ambidextrous firing pin safety; trigger guard hook for two-hand shooting; double and single action trigger mechanism; snag-free hammer; captive recoil spring; "Chamber Lok" breech system.
Price: About **$425.00**

Detonics Pocket 9

Desert Eagle 357

ERMA KGP22 AUTO PISTOL
Caliber: 22 LR, 8-shot magazine.
Barrel: 4".
Weight: 29 oz. **Length:** 7¾" over-all.
Stocks: Checkered plastic.
Sights: Fixed.
Features: Has toggle action similar to original "Luger" pistol. Slide stays open after last shot. Imported from West Germany by Excam. Introduced 1978.
Price: **$216.00**

ERMA KGP38 AUTO PISTOL
Caliber: 380 ACP (5-shot).
Barrel: 4".
Weight: 22½ oz. **Length:** 7⅜" over-all.
Stocks: Checkered plastic. Wood optional.
Sights: Rear adjustable for windage.
Features: Toggle action similar to original "Luger" pistol. Slide stays open after last shot. Has magazine and sear disconnect safety systems. Imported from West Germany by Excam. Introduced 1978.
Price: Plastic grips **$216.00**

F.I.E. "THE BEST" A27B PISTOL
Caliber: 25 ACP, 6-shot magazine.
Barrel: 2½".
Weight: 13 oz. **Length:** 4⅜" over-all.
Stocks: Checkered walnut.
Sights: Fixed.
Features: All steel construction. Has thumb and magazine safeties, exposed hammer. Blue finish only. Introduced 1978. Made in U.S. by F.I.E. Corp.
Price: **$154.95**

F.I.E. TZ-75 DA AUTO PISTOL
Caliber: 9mm Parabellum, 15-shot magazine.
Barrel: 4.72".
Weight: 35.33 oz. **Length:** 8.25" over-all.
Stocks: Smooth European walnut.
Sights: Undercut blade front, open rear adjustable for windage.
Features: Double action trigger system; squared-off trigger guard; rotating slide-mounted safety. Introduced 1983. Imported from Italy by F.I.E.
Price: **$349.95**

F.I.E. "SUPER TITAN II" PISTOLS
Caliber: 32 ACP, 380 ACP.
Barrel: 3⅞".
Weight: 28 oz. **Length:** 6¾" over-all.
Stocks: Smooth, polished walnut.
Sights: Adjustable.
Features: Blue finish only. 12 shot (32 ACP), 11 shot (380 ACP). Introduced 1981. Imported from Italy by F.I.E. Corp.
Price: 32 ACP **$189.95**
Price: 380 ACP **$219.95**

DESERT EAGLE 357 MAGNUM PISTOL
Caliber: 357 Magnum, 9-shot clip.
Barrel: 6", 8", 10", 14" interchangeable.
Weight: 52 oz. **Length:** 10¼" over-all (6" bbl.).
Stocks: Wrap-around soft rubber.
Sights: Blade on ramp front, combat-style rear.
Features: Rotating three lug bolt, ambidextrous safety, combat-style trigger guard, adjustable trigger (optional). Military epoxy finish. Contact importer for extra barrel prices. Announced 1982. Imported from Israel by Magnum Research Inc.
Price: 6" barrel, standard pistol **$699.00**

Erma KGP22 Pistol

ERMA-EXCAM RX 22 AUTO PISTOL
Caliber: 22 LR, 8-shot magazine.
Barrel: 3¼".
Weight: 21 oz. **Length:** 5.58" over-all.
Stocks: Plastic wrap-around.
Sights: Fixed
Features: Polished blue finish. Double action. Patented ignition safety system. Thumb safety. Assembled in U.S. Introduced 1980. From Excam.
Price: **$159.00**

F.I.E. TZ-75

F.I.E. TITAN II PISTOLS
Caliber: 32 ACP, 380 ACP, 6-shot magazine; 22 LR, 10-shot magazine.
Barrel: 3⅞".
Weight: 25¾ oz. **Length:** 6¾" over-all.
Stocks: Checkered nylon, thumbrest-type; checkered walnut optional.
Sights: Adjustable.
Features: Magazine disconnector, firing pin block. Standard slide safety. Available in blue or chrome. Introduced 1978. Imported from Italy by F.I.E. Corp.
Price: 32, blue **$136.95**
Price: 32, chrome **$144.95**
Price: 380, blue **$169.95**
Price: 380, chrome **$179.95**
Price: 22 LR, blue **$129.95**

F.I.E. Titan II Pistol

F.I.E. "TITAN 25" PISTOL
Caliber: 25 ACP, 6-shot magazine.
Barrel: 2⁷⁄₁₆".
Weight: 12 oz. **Length:** 4⅝" over-all.
Stocks: Smooth nylon.
Sights: Fixed.
Features: External hammer; fast simple takedown. Made in U.S.A. by F.I.E. Corp.
Price: Blue. **$64.95**
Price: Dyna-Chrome **$74.95**
Price: Blue, walnut grips **$79.95**
Price: Dyna-Chrome, walnut grips **$89.95**

FTL AUTO-NINE PISTOL
Caliber: 22 LR, 8-shot magazine.
Barrel: 2¼", 6-groove rifling.
Weight: 10 oz. **Length:** 4¾" over-all.
Stocks: Checkered plastic.
Sights: Fixed.
Features: New design internal hammer. All ordnance steel construction with brushed blue finish. Made in U.S. by Auto-Nine Corp. Available from FTL Marketing.
Price . . . . **NA**

Fraser Auto

FRASER AUTOMATIC PISTOL
Caliber: 25 ACP, 6-shot.
Barrel: 2¼".
Weight: 10 oz. **Length:** 4" over-all.
Stocks: Plastic pearl or checkered walnut.
Sights: Recessed, fixed.
Features: Stainless steel construction. Has positive manual safety as well as magazine safety. From Fraser Firearms Corp.
Price: Satin stainless steel, 25 ACP **$129.50**
Price: Gold plated, with book-type case. **$247.50**
Price: With black Q.P.Q. finish **$149.50**

GUARDIAN-SS AUTO PISTOL
Caliber: 380 ACP, 6-shot magazine.
Barrel: 3.25"
Weight: 20 oz. **Length:** 6" over-all.
Stocks: Checkered walnut.
Sights: Ramp front, combat-type rear adjustable for windage.
Features: Double action, made of stainless steel. Custom Guardian has narrow polished trigger, Pachmayr grips, blue slide, hand-fitted barrel, polished feed ramp, funneled magazine well. Introduced 1982. From Michigan Armament, Inc.
Price: Standard model **$330.00**
Price: Custom Guardian **$395.00**

Guardian-SS Stainless Pistol

Consult our Directory pages for
the location of firms mentioned.

HAMMERLI MODEL 212 HUNTER'S PISTOL
Caliber: 22 LR.
Barrel: 4.9".
Weight: 31 oz. **Length:** 8.5" over-all.
Stocks: Checkered walnut.
Sights: White dot front adjustable for elevation, rear adjustable for elevation.
Features: Semi-automatic based on the Model 208, intended for field use. Uses target trigger system which is fully adjustable. Comes with tool kit. Imported from Switzerland by Osborne's Supplies. Introduced 1984.
Price: **$1,180.00**

Hammerli 212

HECKLER & KOCH P9S DOUBLE ACTION AUTO

Caliber: 9mm Para., 9-shot magazine; 45 ACP, 7-shot magazine.
Barrel: 4".
Weight: 31 oz. **Length:** 7.6" over-all.
Stocks: Checkered black plastic.
Sights: Open combat type.
Features: Double action; polygonal rifling; delayed roller-locked action with stationary barrel. Loaded chamber and cocking indicators; cocking/decocking lever. Imported from West Germany by Heckler & Koch, Inc.
Price: P-9S Combat Model $550.00
Price: P-9S Target Model $630.00
Price: Walnut wrap-around competition grips $135.00
Price: Sports competition model with 4" and 5½" barrels, 2 slides . . . $990.00

Heckler & Koch P9S Pistol

HECKLER & KOCH HK-4 DOUBLE ACTION PISTOL

Caliber: 22 LR, 25 ACP, 32 ACP, 380 ACP, 8-shot magazine (7 in 380).
Barrel: 3¹¹⁄₃₂".
Weight: 16½ oz. **Length:** 6³⁄₁₆" over-all.
Stocks: Black checkered plastic.
Sights: Fixed blade front, rear notched drift-adj. for w.
Features: Gun comes with all parts to shoot above four calibers; polygonal (hexagon) rifling; matte black finish. Imported from West Germany by Heckler & Koch, Inc.
Price: HK-4 380 with 22 conversion kit $480.00
Price: HK-4 in 380 only $430.00
Price: HK-4 in four cals. $590.00
Price: Conversion units 22, 25 or 32 cal., each $101.00

Heckler & Koch VP 70Z Pistol

HECKLER & KOCH P7 AUTO PISTOL

Caliber: 9mm Parabellum, 8-shot magazine.
Barrel: 4.13".
Weight: 29 oz. **Length:** 6.54" over-all.
Stocks: Stippled black plastic.
Sights: Fixed, combat-type.
Features: Unique "squeeze cocker" in front strap cocks the action. Squared combat-type trigger guard. Blue finish. Compact size. Imported from West Germany by Heckler & Koch, Inc.
Price: $599.00
Price: Extra magazine $26.00

Heckler & Koch HK-4

HECKLER & KOCH VP 70Z DOUBLE ACTION AUTO

Caliber: 9mm Para., 18-shot magazine.
Barrel: 4½".
Weight: 32½ oz. **Length:** 8" over-all.
Stocks: Black stippled plastic.
Sights: Ramp front, channeled slide rear.
Features: Recoil operated, double action. Only 4 moving parts. Double column magazine. Imported from West Germany by Heckler & Koch, Inc.
Price: $399.00
Price: Extra magazine $27.00

Heckler & Koch P7 (PSP) Pistol

HIGH STANDARD SPORT-KING AUTO PISTOL

Caliber: 22 LR, 10-shot.
Barrel: 4½" or 6¾".
Weight: 39 oz. (4½" bbl.). **Length:** 9" over-all (4½" bbl.).
Stocks: Checkered walnut.
Sights: Blade front, fixed rear.
Features: Takedown barrel. Blue only. Military frame.
Price: 4½" barrel, blue finish $250.00
Price: 4½" or 6¾", electroless nickel $265.00

High Standard Survival Pack

Includes the High Standard Citation pistol (see Competition Handguns) finished in electroless nickel, extra magazine, and a padded canvas carrying case with three interior pockets for carrying the extra magazine, knife, compass, etc. Introduced 1982.
Price: $385.00

CAUTION: PRICES CHANGE. CHECK AT GUNSHOP.

INTERDYNAMIC KG-99 PISTOL
Caliber: 9mm Parabellum; 36 shot magazine.
Barrel: 5″.
Weight: 46 oz. **Length:** 12½″ over-all.
Stocks: High-impact nylon.
Sights: Blade front; fixed, open rear.
Features: Semi-auto only. Straight blowback action fires from closed bolt. Entire frame is high-impact black nylon. Introduced 1982.
Price: About **$449.95**
Price: Extra magazine. **$32.95**

Interdynamic KG-99K Pistol
Similar to the KG-99 except has 3″ barrel, over-all length of 10″, and weighs 44 oz. Standard magazine is 25-shot, with 36-shot optional. Introduced 1983.
Price: **$249.95**

Iver Johnson PO 300

IVER JOHNSON MODEL PO300 PONY
Caliber: 380 ACP, 6-shot magazine.
Barrel: 3″.
Weight: 20 oz. **Length:** 6″ over-all.
Stocks: Checkered walnut.
Sights: Blade front, rear adj. for w.
Features: All steel construction. Inertia firing pin. Thumb safety locks hammer. No magazine safety. Lanyard ring. Made in U.S., available from Iver Johnson's.
Price: Blue. **$260.00**
Price: Nickel **$270.00**
Price: Military (matte finish) **$260.00**

IVER JOHNSON TRAILSMAN PISTOL
Caliber: 22 LR, 10-shot magazine.
Barrel: 4½″ or 6″.
Weight: 46 oz. (4½″ bbl.) **Length:** 8¾″ (4½″ bbl.).
Stocks: Checkered composition.
Sights: Fixed, tagret type.
Features: Slide hold-open latch, positive sear block safety, push button magazine release. Introduced 1984.
Price: Blue only **$160.00**

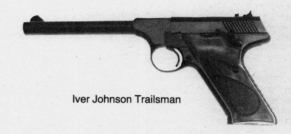

Iver Johnson Trailsman

IVER JOHNSON TP22B, TP25B AUTO PISTOL
Caliber: 22 LR, 25 ACP, 7-shot magazine.
Barrel: 2.85″.
Weight: 14½ oz. **Length:** 5.39″ over-all.
Stocks: Black checkered plastic.
Sights: Fixed.
Features: Double action; 7-shot magazine. Introduced 1981. From Iver Johnson's.
Price: Either caliber, blue **$140.00**
Price: TP22N (22 cal., nickel) **$156.00**

Iver Johnson TP22B

IVER JOHNSON PP30 "SUPER ENFORCER" PISTOL
Caliber: 30 U.S. Carbine.
Barrel: 9½″.
Weight: 4 lbs. **Length:** 17″ over-all.
Stocks: American walnut.
Sights: Blade front; click adjustable peep rear.
Features: Shortened version of the M1 Carbine. Uses 15 or 30-shot magazines. From Iver Johnson's.
Price: Blue finish **$250.00**
Price: Stainless steel. **$281.00**

Iver Johnson Super Enforcer

JENNINGS J-22 AUTO PISTOL
Caliber: 22 LR, 6-shot magazine.
Barrel: 2½″.
Weight: 13 oz. **Length:** 4¹⁵⁄₁₆″ over-all.
Stocks: Walnut on chrome or nickel models; checkered black Cycolac on Teflon model.
Sights: Fixed.
Features: Choice of bright chrome, satin nickel or black Teflon finish. Introduced 1981. From Jennings Firearms.
Price: About **$69.95**

Jennings J-22 Pistol

L.A.R. Grizzly Mag

L.A.R. GRIZZLY WIN MAG PISTOL
Caliber: 45 Win. Mag., 7-shot magazine.
Barrel: 6½".
Weight: 51 oz. **Length:** 10½" over-all.
Stocks: Checkered rubber, non-slip combat-type.
Sights: Ramped blade front, fully adjustable rear.
Features: Uses basic Browning/Colt 1911-A1 design; interchangeable calibers; beveled magazine well; combat-type flat, checkered rubber mainspring housing; lowered and back-chamfered ejection port; polished feed ramp; throated barrel; solid barrel bushings. Announced 1983. From L.A.R. Mfg. Co.
Price: **$749.95**
Price: Conversion units (9mm Win. Mag., 45 ACP, 357 Mag., 30 Mauser, 38 Super, 38 Spec., 9mm Steyr, 9mm Browning Long, 9mm Luger)..... **$169.95**

LLAMA OMNI DOUBLE-ACTION AUTO
Caliber: 9mm (13-shot), 45 ACP (7-shot).
Barrel: 4¼".
Weight: 40 oz. **Length:** 9mm—8", 45–7¾" over-all.
Stocks: Checkered plastic.
Sights: Ramped blade front, rear adjustable for windage and elevation (45), drift-adjustable for windage (9mm).
Features: New DA pistol has ball-bearing action, double sear bars, articulated firing pin, buttressed locking lug and low-friction rifling. Introduced 1982. Imported from Spain by Stoeger Industries.
Price: 45 ACP **$466.95**
Price: 9mm **$434.95**

Llama Omni D.A. Pistol

Llama Large Frame Auto

LLAMA LARGE FRAME AUTO PISTOLS
Caliber: 9mm Para., 45 ACP.
Barrel: 5".
Weight: 40 oz. **Length:** 8½" over-all.
Stocks: Checkered walnut.
Sights: Fixed.
Features: Grip and manual safeties, ventilated rib. Engraved, chrome engraved or gold damascened finish available at extra cost. Imported from Spain by Stoeger Industries.
Price: Blue. **$249.95**
Price: Satin chrome, 45 only **$334.95**

Llama Small Frame Auto

LLAMA SMALL FRAME AUTO PISTOLS
Caliber: 22 LR, 380.
Barrel: 3¹¹⁄₁₆".
Weight: 23 oz. **Length:** 6½" over-all.
Stocks: Checkered plastic, thumb rest.
Sights: Fixed front, adj. notch rear.
Features: Ventilated rib, manual and grip safeties. Model XV is 22 LR, Model IIIA is 380. Both models have loaded indicator; IIIA is locked breech. Imported from Spain by Stoeger Industries.
Price: Blue, 380 .... **$216.95**
Price: Blue, 22 LR **$200.95**
Price: Satin chrome, 380 .... **$249.95**
Price: Satin chrome, 22 LR **$249.95**

MAB Model P-15

MAB MODEL P-15 AUTO PISTOL
Caliber: 9mm Para., 15-shot magazine.
Barrel: 4½".
Weight: 41 oz. **Length:** 8⅛" over-all.
Stocks: Checkered black plastic.
Sights: Fixed.
Features: Rotating barrel-type locking system; thumb safety, magazine disconnector. Blue finish. Introduced 1982. Imported from France by Howco Distr., Inc.
Price: **$375.00**

CAUTION: PRICES CHANGE. CHECK AT GUNSHOP.

HANDGUNS—AUTOLOADERS, SERVICE & SPORT

Turkish MKE Pistol

MKE AUTO PISTOL
Caliber: 380 ACP; 7-shot magazine.
Barrel: 4".
Weight: 23 oz. **Length:** 6½" over-all.
Stocks: Hard rubber.
Sights: Fixed front, rear adjustable for windage.
Features: Double action with exposed hammer; chamber loaded indicator. Imported from Turkey by Mandall Shooting Supplies.
Price: **$350.00**

Manurhin PPK/S

MANURHIN PP AUTO PISTOL
Caliber: 22 LR, 10-shot; 32 ACP, 8-shot; 380 ACP, 7-shot.
Barrel: 3.87".
Weight: 23 oz. (22 LR). **Length:** 6.7" over-all.
Stocks: Checkered composition.
Sights: White outline front and rear.
Features: Double action; hammer drop safety; all steel construction; high-polish blue finish. Each gun supplied with two magazines. Imported from France by Manurhin International.
Price: 22 LR **$340.00**
Price: 32 and 380 .... **$335.00**

Manurhin PPK/S Auto Pistol
Similar to the Model PP except has 3.25" barrel and over-all length of 6.12".
Price: 22 LR **$340.00**
Price: 32 and 380 .... **$335.00**

O.D.I. VIKING COMBAT D.A. AUTO PISTOL
Caliber: 9mm, 45 ACP.
Barrel: 5".
Weight: 39 oz.
Stocks: Smooth teakwood standard; other materials available.
Sights: Fixed. Blade front, notched rear.
Features: Made entirely of stainless steel, brushed satin, natural finish. Features the Seecamp double action system. Spur-type hammer. Magazine holds 7 rounds in 45 ACP, 9 in 9mm. Made in U.S.A. From O.D.I.
Price: **$579.95**

O.D.I. Viking D.A. Pistol

O.D.I. Viking Combat D.A. Auto Pistols
Similar to the standard Viking pistol except 4¼" barrel, weight of 36 ozs. The Viking II Combat has a slide-mounted thumb-activated firing pin safety.
Price: Combat I, 9mm only **$579.00**
Price: Combat II, 45 ACP only **$639.00**

RG 26 AUTO PISTOL
Caliber: 25 ACP, 6-shot magazine.
Barrel: 2½".
Weight: 12 oz. **Length:** 4¾" over-all.
Stocks: Checkered plastic.
Sights: Fixed.
Features: Blue finish. Thumb safety. Imported by RG Industries.
Price: **$64.00**
Price: Nickel **$71.00**

RANDALL SERVICE MODEL AUTO PISTOL
Caliber: 9mm, 38 Super, 45 ACP.
Barrel: 5".
Weight: 38 ozs. **Length:** 8½" over-all.
Stocks: Checkered walnut.
Sights: Blade front, fixed or adjustable rear.
Features: All stainless steel construction, including springs and pins. Standard with ten grooved barrel, patented long recoil spring guide rod, long trigger, extended slide stop and thumb safety, ported slide, beveled magazine well, checkered walnut grips. Available with round-top slide and fixed sights or ribbed-top slide with adjustable sights. Also available left-handed. Made in U.S.A. by Randall Firearms.
Price: With fixed sights, about **$455.00**
Price: Left-handed, with fixed sights, about **$485.00**
Price: Combat version (9mm, 38 Super, 45 ACP), about **$540.00**
Price: Left-handed Combat version, about **$570.00**
Price: With adjustable sights, about **$540.00**
Price: Left-handed, with adjustable sights, about **$570.00**

Randall Service Model

CAUTION: PRICES CHANGE. CHECK AT GUNSHOP.

Randall Raider

Randall Raider Auto Pistol
Same as the Service Model except has a 4½" barrel, 7¾" over-all length, and weighs 36 oz. Same standard features and options. Introduced 1984.
Price: With fixed sights, about.. $455.00
Price: Left-handed, with fixed sights, about........................ $485.00
Price: Right-handed, with adjustable sights, about $540.00
Price: Left-handed, with adjustable sights, about.................. $570.00

Randall Curtis E. LeMay Four Star
Similar to the Service Model except has a 4½" barrel, 7¾" over-all length, 6-shot magazine capacity, and weighs 35 oz. Squared trigger guard, extended magazine baseplate. Same standard features and options. Introduced 1984.
Price: With fixed sights, about................................... $520.00
Price: With adjustable sights, about $610.00
Price: Left-handed, fixed sights, about.......................... $555.00
Price: Left-handed, adjustable sights, about..................... $645.00

RAVEN P-25 AUTO PISTOL
Caliber: 25 ACP, 6-shot magazine.
Barrel: 2⁷⁄₁₆".
Weight: 15 oz. **Length:** 4¾" over-all.
Stocks: Smooth walnut.
Sights: Ramped front, fixed rear.
Features: Available in blue, nickel or chrome finish. Made in U.S., available from EMF Co.
Price: $59.95

Raven P-25 Pistol

RUGER MARK II STANDARD AUTO PISTOL
Caliber: 22 LR, 10-shot magazine.
Barrel: 4¾" or 6".
Weight: 36 oz. (4¾" bbl.). **Length:** 8⁵⁄₁₆" (4¾" bbl.).
Stocks: Checkered hard rubber.
Sights: Fixed, wide blade front, square notch rear adj. for w.
Features: Updated design of the original Standard Auto. Has new bolt hold-open device, 10-shot magazine, magazine catch, safety, trigger and new receiver contours. Introduced 1982.
Price: Blued $168.00
Price: In stainless steel.. $225.00

Ruger Mark II Stainless

SEECAMP II STAINLESS DA AUTO
Caliber: 25 ACP, 8-shot magazine.
Barrel: 2", integral with frame.
Weight: About 10 oz. **Length:** 4⅛" over-all.
Stocks: Black plastic.
Sights: Smooth, no-snag, contoured slide and barrel top.
Features: Aircraft quality 17-4 PH stainless steel. Inertia operated firing pin. Hammer fired double action only. Hammer automatically follows slide down to safety rest position after each shot—no manual safety needed. Magazine safety disconnector. Introduced 1980. From Sile Distributors.
Price: $199.95

Seecamp II Stainless

SIG P-210-1 Pistol

SIG P-210-1 AUTO PISTOL
Caliber: 7.65mm or 9mm Para., 8-shot magazine.
Barrel: 4¾".
Weight: 31¾ oz. (9mm) **Length:** 8½" over-all.
Stocks: Checkered walnut, with lacquer finish.
Sights: Blade front, rear adjustable for windage.
Features: Lanyard loop; polished finish. Conversion unit for 22 LR available. Imported from Switzerland by Osborne's Supplies and Mandall Shooting Supplies.
Price: P-210-1 about (Mandall) $1,500.00
Price: P-210-2 Service Pistol (Mandall) $1,600.00
Price: 22 Cal. Conversion unit (Mandall) $850.00
Price: P-210-1 (Osborne's).................................... $1,850.00
Price: P-210-2 (Osborne's).................................... $1,275.00

CAUTION: PRICES CHANGE. CHECK AT GUNSHOP.

SIG P-210-6 AUTO PISTOL
Caliber: 9mm Para., 8-shot magazine.
Barrel: 4¾".
Weight: 36.2 oz. **Length:** 8½" over-all.
Stocks: Checkered black plastic. Walnut optional.
Sights: Blade front, micro. adj. rear for w. & e.
Features: Adjustable trigger stop; target trigger; ribbed front stap; sandblasted finish. Conversion unit for 22 LR consists of barrel, recoil spring, slide and magazine. Imported from Switzerland by Osborne's Supplies and Mandall Shooting Supplies.
Price: P-210-6, about (Mandall) **$1,750.00**
Price: 22 Cal. Conversion unit (Mandall) **$850.00**
Price: P-210-6 (Osborne's) **$1,580.00**

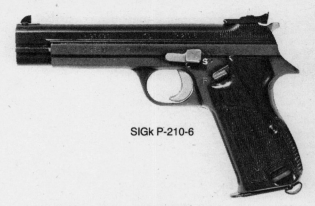

SIGk P-210-6

SIG-Sauer P-220 Pistol

SIG-SAUER P-220 D.A. AUTO PISTOL
Caliber: 9mm, 38 Super; 45 ACP. (9-shot in 9mm and 38 Super, 7 in 45).
Barrel: 4⅜".
Weight: 28¼ oz. (9mm). **Length:** 7¾" over-all.
Stocks: Checkered black plastic.
Sights: Blade front, drift adj. rear for w.
Features: Double action. De-cocking lever permits lowering hammer onto locked firing pin. Squared combat-type trigger guard. Slide stays open after last shot. Imported from West Germany by Interarms.
Price: **$585.00**

SIG-SAUER P-225 D.A. AUTO PISTOL
Caliber: 9mm Parabellum, 8-shot magazine.
Barrel: 3.8".
Weight: 26 oz. **Length:** 7³/₃₂" over-all.
Stocks: Checkered black plastic.
Sights: Blade front, rear adjustable for windage.
Features: Double action. De-cocking lever permits lowering hammer onto locked firing pin. Squared combat-type trigger guard. Shortened, lightened version of P-220. Imported from West Germany by Interarms.
Price: **$615.00**

SIG-Sauer P-230 D.A. Pistol

Consult our Directory pages for the location of firms mentioned.

SIG-SAUER P-230 D.A. AUTO PISTOL
Caliber: 380 ACP (7 shot).
Barrel: 3¾".
Weight: 16 oz. **Length:** 6½" over-all.
Stocks: Checkered black plastic.
Sights: Blade front, rear adj. for w.
Features: Double action. Same basic action design as P-220. Blowback operation, stationary barrel. Introduced 1977. Imported from West Germany by Interarms.
Price: **$445.00**
Price: In stainless steel **$495.00**

SILE-BENELLI B-76 DA AUTO PISTOL
Caliber: 9mm Para., 8-shot magazine.
Barrel: 4¼", 6-groove. Chrome-lined bore.
Weight: 34 oz. (empty). **Length:** 8¹/₁₆" over-all.
Stocks: Walnut with cut checkering and high gloss finish.
Sights: Blade front with white face, rear adjustable for windage with white bars for increased visibility.
Features: Fixed barrel, locked breech. Exposed hammer can be locked in non-firing mode in either single or double action. Stainless steel inertia firing pin and loaded chamber indicator. All external parts blued, internal parts hardchrome plated. All steel construction. Introduced 1979. From Sile Dist.
Price: **$349.95**

SMITH & WESSON MODEL 439 DOUBLE ACTION
Caliber: 9mm Luger, 8-shot clip.
Barrel: 4".
Weight: 27 oz. **Length:** 7⁷/₁₆" over-all.
Stocks: Checkered walnut.
Sights: ⅛" square serrated ramp front, square notch rear is fully adj. for w. & e. Also available with fixed sights.
Features: Rear sight has protective shields on both sides of the sight blade. Frame is alloy. New trigger actuated firing pin lock in addition to the regular rotating safety. Magazine disconnector. New extractor design. Comes with two magazines. Ambidextrous safety an extra-cost option. Introduced 1980.
Price: Blue, from **$388.00**
Price: Nickel, from **$419.00**
Price: Model 639 (stainless), from **$433.00**

Sile-Benelli B-76

SMITH & WESSON MODEL 459 DOUBLE ACTION

Caliber: 9mm Luger, 14-shot clip.
Barrel: 4″.
Weight: 28 oz. **Length:** 7⁷⁄₁₆″ over-all.
Stocks: Checkered high-impact nylon.
Sights: ⅛″ square serrated ramp front, square notch rear is fully adj. for w. & e. Also available with fixed sights.
Features: Alloy frame. Rear sight has protective shields on both sides of blade. New trigger actuated firing pin lock in addition to the regular safety. Magazine disconnector; new extractor design. Comes with two magazines. Ambidextrous safety an extra-cost option. Introduced 1980.
Price: Blue, from **$442.00**
Price: Nickel, from **$474.50**
Price: Model 659 (stainless), from **$449.00**

Smith & Wesson Model 659

Smith & Wesson Model 469 Mini-Gun

Basically a cut-down version of the Model 459 pistol. Gun has a 3½″ barrel, 12-round magazine, over-all length of 6⅞″, and weighs 26 oz. Also accepts the 14-shot Model 459 magazine. Cross-hatch knurling on the recurved-front trigger guard and backstrap; magazine has a curved finger extension; bobbed hammer; sandblast blue finish with pebble-grain grips. Ambidextrous safety an extra cost option. Introduced 1983.
Price: **$399.00**

Star Model 28 DA

Smith & Wesson Model 469

STAR MODEL 28 DOUBLE-ACTION PISTOL

Caliber: 9mm Para., 15-shot magazine.
Barrel: 4.25″.
Weight: 40 oz. **Length:** 8″ over-all.
Stocks: Checkered black plastic.
Sights: Square blade front, square notch rear click-adjustable for windage and elevation.
Features: Double or single action; grooved front and backstraps and trigger guard face; ambidextrous safety cams firing pin forward; removable backstrap houses the firing mechanism. Introduced 1983. Imported from Spain by Interarms.
Price: **$414.00**

STAR MODEL PD AUTO PISTOL

Caliber: 45 ACP, 6-shot magazine.
Barrel: 3.94″.
Weight: 28 oz. **Length:** 7⁷⁄₁₆″ over-all.
Stocks: Checkered walnut.
Sights: Ramp front, fully adjustable rear.
Features: Rear sight milled into slide; thumb safety; grooved non-slip front strap; nylon recoil buffer; inertia firing pin; no grip or magazine safeties. Imported from Spain by Interarms.
Price: Blue. **$339.00**

Star Model PD Pistol

STAR BM, BKM AUTO PISTOLS

Caliber: 9mm Para., 8-shot magazine.
Barrel: 3.9″.
Weight: 25 oz.
Stocks: Checkered walnut.
Sights: Fixed.
Features: Blue or chrome finish. Magazine and manual safeties, external hammer. Imported from Spain by Interarms.
Price: Blue, BM and BKM. **$284.00**
Price: Chrome, BM only **$299.00**

STERLING MK-7 PARA PISTOL

Caliber: 9mm Parabellum, 10-shot magazine.
Barrel: 4″ standard, 8″ available.
Weight: 3.6 lbs. **Length:** 14″ over-all.
Stocks: Checkered black plastic.
Sights: Post front, peep rear.
Features: Helical, self-cleaning bolt; two-stage recoil assembly allows wide range of ammunition to be used. Comes with 10-shot magazine (34-shot optional), sling and manual. Five year warranty. Imported from England by Lanchester U.S.A. Introduced 1984.
Price: About **$525.00**

Star Model BM, BKM Pistol

CAUTION: PRICES CHANGE. CHECK AT GUNSHOP.

Steyr GB

STEYR GB DOUBLE ACTION AUTO PISTOL

Caliber: 9mm Parabellum; 18-shot magazine.
Barrel: 5.39″.
Weight: 33 oz. **Length:** 8.4″ over-all.
Stocks: Checkered walnut.
Sights: Post front, fixed rear.
Features: Gas-operated, delayed blowback action. Measures 5.7″ high, 1.3″ wide. Introduced 1981. Imported by Gun South, Inc.
Price: $595.00

Stoeger Luger 22 Auto

STOEGER LUGER 22 AUTO PISTOL

Caliber: 22 LR, 10-shot.
Barrel: 4½″.
Weight: 30 oz. **Length:** 8⅞″ over-all.
Stocks: Checkered walnut.
Sights: Fixed.
Features: All steel construction. Action remains open after last shot and as magazine is removed. Grip and balance identical to P-08.
Price: $199.95
Price: Kit includes extra clip, charger, holster $241.95
Price: Combo (includes extra clip, holster, charger and carrying case) $249.95

TARGA MODEL GT27 AUTO PISTOL

Caliber: 25 ACP, 6-shot magazine.
Barrel: 2⁷/₁₆″.
Weight: 12 oz. **Length:** 4⅝″ over-all.
Stocks: Checkered nylon.
Sights: Fixed.
Features: Safety lever take-down; external hammer with half-cock. Assembled in U.S. by Excam, Inc.
Price: Blue. $58.50
Price: Chrome. $64.00

TARGA MODELS GT32, GT380 AUTO PISTOLS

Caliber: 32 ACP or 380 ACP, 6-shot magazine.
Barrel: 4⅞″.
Weight: 26 oz. **Length:** 7⅜″ over-all.
Stocks: Checkered nylon with thumb rest. Walnut optional.
Sights: Fixed blade front; rear drift-adj. for w.
Features: Chrome or blue finish; magazine, thumb, and firing pin safeties; external hammer; safety lever take-down. Imported from Italy by Excam, Inc.
Price: 32 cal., blue. $133.00
Price: 32 cal., chrome. $143.00
Price: 380 cal., blue. $159.00
Price: 380 cal., chrome. $167.00
Price: 380 cal., chrome, engraved, wooden grips $214.00
Price: 380 cal., blue, engraved, wooden grips $205.00

TARGA GT380XE GT32XE PISTOLS

Caliber: 32 ACP or 380 ACP, 12-shot magazine.
Barrel: 3.88″.
Weight: 28 oz. **Length:** 7.38″ over-all.
Stocks: Smooth hardwood.
Sights: Adj. for windage.
Features: Blue or satin nickel. Ordnance steel. Magazine disconnector, firing pin and thumb safeties. Introduced 1980. Imported by Excam.
Price: 32 cal., blue. $189.00
Price: 380 cal., blue. $205.00

Taurus PT-22 Pistol

TAURUS PT-22 DOUBLE ACTION PISTOL

Caliber: 22 Long Rifle or 25 ACP
Barrel: 2.75″.
Weight: 18 oz.
Stocks: Smooth Brazilian walnut.
Sights: Serrated front, fixed square notch rear.
Features: Pop-up barrel, blue finish. Introduced 1983. Made in U.S. by Taurus International Mfg. Inc.
Price: Blue only, about $160.00

Taurus PT-99 Pistol

Taurus PT-99 Auto Pistol

Similar to the PT-92 except has fully adjustable rear sight, smooth Brazilian walnut stocks and is available in polished or satin blue. Introduced 1983.
Price: Polished blue, about $385.00
Price: Satin blue, about $400.00

CAUTION: PRICES CHANGE. CHECK AT GUNSHOP.

TAURUS MODEL PT-92 AUTO PISTOL
Caliber: 9mm P., 15-shot magazine.
Barrel: 4.92".
Weight: 34 oz. **Length:** 8.54" over-all.
Stocks: Black plastic.
Sights: Fixed notch rear.
Features: Double action, exposed hammer, chamber loaded indicator. Inertia firing pin. Blue finish. Imported by Taurus International.
Price: About $340.00

UNIVERSAL ENFORCER MODEL 3000 AUTO
Caliber: 30 M1 Carbine, 5-shot magazine.
Barrel: 10¼" with 12-groove rifling.
Weight: 4½ lbs. **Length:** 17¾" over-all.
Stocks: American walnut with handguard.
Sights: Gold bead ramp front. Peep rear.
Features: Accepts 15 or 30-shot magazines. 4½-6 lb. trigger pull.
Price: Blue finish $256.00
Price: Nickel plated finish (Model 3010N) $272.00
Price: Gold plated finish (Model 3015G) $309.50
Price: Black, gray or olive Teflon-S finish $278.00

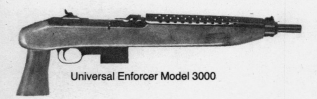

Universal Enforcer Model 3000

UZI PISTOL
Caliber: 9mm Parabellum.
Barrel: 4.5".
Weight: 3.8 lbs. **Length:** 9.45" over-all.
Stocks: Black plastic.
Sights: Post front, open rear adjustable for windage and elevation.
Features: Semi-auto blow-back action; fires from closed bolt; floating firing pin. Comes in a molded plastic case with 20-round magazine; 25 and 32-round magazines available. Imported from Israel by Action Arms. Introduced 1984.
Price: $550.00

UZI Pistol

Walther PP Auto Pistol

WALTHER PP AUTO PISTOL
Caliber: 22 LR, 8-shot; 32 ACP, 380 ACP, 7-shot.
Barrel: 3.86".
Weight: 23½ oz. **Length:** 6.7" over-all.
Stocks: Checkered plastic.
Sights: Fixed, white markings.
Features: Double action, manual safety blocks firing pin and drops hammer, chamber loaded indicator on 32 and 380, extra finger rest magazine provided. Imported from Germany by Interarms.
Price: 22 LR $520.00
Price: 32 and 380 . . . . $500.00
Price: Engraved models . . . . **On Request**

Walther American PPK/S Auto Pistol
Similar to Walther PP except made entirely in the United States. Has 3.27" barrel with 6.1" length over-all. Introduced 1980.
Price: 380 ACP only $459.00
Price: As above, stainless $499.00

Walther PPK/S American

WALTHER P-38 AUTO PISTOL
Caliber: 22 LR, 30 Luger or 9mm Luger, 8-shot.
Barrel: 4¹⁵⁄₁₆" (9mm and 30), 5¹⁄₁₆" (22 LR).
Weight: 28 oz. **Length:** 8½" over-all.
Stocks: Checkered plastic.
Sights: Fixed.
Features: Double action, safety blocks firing pin and drops hammer, chamber loaded indicator. Matte finish standard, polished blue, engraving and/or plating available. Imported from Germany by Interarms.
Price: 22 LR $690.00
Price: 9mm or 30 Luger $650.00
Price: Engraved models . . . . **On Request**

Walther P-38 Auto Pistol

Walther P-5 Auto Pistol

Latest Walther design that uses the basic P-38 double-action mechanism. Caliber 9mm Luger, barrel length 3½"; weight 28 oz., over-all length 7".

Price: **$790.00**

Walther P-5 Pistol

Walther P-38IV Auto Pistol

Same as P-38 except has longer barrel (4½"); over-all length is 8", weight is 29 oz. Sights are non-adjustable. Introduced 1977. Imported by Interarms.

Price: **$625.00**

WILDEY AUTO PISTOL

Caliber: 45 Win. Mag. (8 shots).
Barrel: 5", 6", 7", 8", or 10" interchangeable; vent. rib.
Weight: About 51 oz. (6" bbl.).
Stock: Select hardwood, target style optional.
Sights: Blade front, rear adjustable for windage and elevation.
Features: Interchangeable barrels; patented gas operation; selective single or autoloading capability; 5-lug rotary bolt; fixed barrel; stainless steel construction; double-action trigger mechanism. Has positive hammer block and magazine safety. From Wildey Firearms.
Price: All barrel lengths **$1,295.00**

Wilkinson "Linda" Auto Pistol

> Consult our Directory pages for the location of firms mentioned.

WILKINSON "LINDA" PISTOL

Caliber: 9mm Para., 31-shot magazine.
Barrel: 8⁵⁄₁₆".
Weight: 4 lbs., 13 oz. **Length:** 12¼" over-all.
Stocks: Checkered black plastic pistol grip, maple fore-end.
Sights: Protected blade front, Williams adjustable rear.
Features: Fires from closed bolt. Semi-auto only. Straight blowback action. Cross-bolt safety. Removable barrel. From Wilkinson Arms.
Price: **$463.00**

COMPETITION HANDGUNS

Air Match 500

AIR MATCH 500 TARGET PISTOL

Caliber: 22 LR, single shot.
Barrel: 10.4".
Weight: 28 oz.
Stocks: Anatomically shaped match grip of stippled hardwood. Right or left hand.
Sights: Match post front, fully adjustable match rear.
Features: Sight radius adjustable from 14.1" to 16.1"; easy disassembly for cleaning or adjustment. Comes with case, tools, spare front and rear sight blades. Imported from Italy by Kendall International Arms. Introduced 1984.
Price: **$450.00**

CAUTION: PRICES CHANGE. CHECK AT GUNSHOP.

COMPETITION HANDGUNS

Beeman/Agner 80

BEEMAN/AGNER MODEL 80 TARGET PISTOL
Caliber: 22 LR, 5-shot magazine.
Barrel: 5.9″.
Weight: 36 oz. **Length:** 9½″ overall.
Stocks: French walnut briar; anatomically shaped, adjustable.
Sights: Fixed blade front, rear adjustable for windage and elevation; 8¾″ radius.
Features: Security "key" locks trigger, magazine and slide. Design minimizes gun movement; dry-fire button allows trigger practice. Imported from Denmark by Beeman. Introduced 1984.
Price: Right-hand **$1,295.00**
Price: Left-hand **$1,395.00**

Beeman/FAS 601

Beeman/FAS 601 Match Pistol
Similar to SP 602 except has different match stocks with adj. palm, shelf, 22 Short only for rapid fire shooting; weighs 40 oz., 5.6″ bbl., has gas ports through top of barrel and slide to reduce recoil, slightly different trigger and sear mechanisms.
Price: . . . . **$995.00 to $1,045.00**

Beeman/Unique 69

Beeman/Unique 823-U

BERNARDELLI MODEL 100 PISTOL
Caliber: 22 LR only, 10-shot magazine.
Barrel: 5.9″.
Weight: 37¾ oz. **Length:** 9″ over-all.
Stocks: Checkered walnut with thumbrest.
Sights: Fixed front, rear adj. for w. and e.
Features: Target barrel weight included. Heavy sighting rib with interchangeable front sight. Accessories include cleaning equipment and assembly tools, case. Imported from Italy by Interarms.
Price: With case **$425.00**

BEEMAN/FAS 602 MATCH PISTOL
Caliber: 22 LR, 5-shot.
Barrel: 5.6″.
Weight: 37 oz. **Length:** 11″ over-all.
Stocks: Walnut wrap-around; sizes small, medium or large, or adjustable.
Sights: Match. Blade front, open notch rear fully adj. for w. and e. Sight radius is 8.66″.
Features: Line of sight is only 1¹⁄32″ above centerline of bore; magazine is inserted from top; adjustable and removable trigger mechanism; single lever takedown. Full 5 year warranty. Imported from Italy by Beeman Inc.
Price: . . . . **$1,060.00 to $1,140.00**

BEEMAN/UNIQUE D.E.S. 69 TARGET PISTOL
Caliber: 22 LR, 5-shot magazine.
Barrel: 5.91″.
Weight: 35.3 oz. **Length:** 10.5″ over-all.
Stocks: French walnut target style with thumbrest and adjustable shelf; hand checkered panels.
Sights: Ramp front, micro. adj. rear mounted on frame; 8.66″ sight radius.
Features: Meets U.I.T. standards. Comes with 260 gram barrel weight; 100, 150, 350 gram weights available. Fully adjustable match trigger; dry firing safety device. Imported from France by Beeman.
Price: Right-hand **$799.00**
Price: Left-hand **$849.00**

BEEMAN/UNIQUE MODEL 823-U MATCH PISTOL
Caliber: 22 Short, 5-shot magazine.
Barrel: 5.9″.
Weight: 43 oz. **Length:** 11.3″ over-all.
Stocks: Anatomically shaped, adjustable, stippled French walnut.
Sights: Blade front, fully adjustable rear; 9.7″ sight radius.
Features: Light alloy frame, steel slide and shock absorber; five barrel vents reduce recoil, three of which can be blocked; trigger adjustable for position and pull weight. Can be dry fired. Comes with 340 gram weight housing, 160 gram available. Imported from France by Beeman. Introduced 1984.
Price: Right-hand **$945.00**
Price: Left-hand **$998.00**

Bernardelli Model 100

CAUTION: PRICES CHANGE. CHECK AT GUNSHOP.

Beretta Model 76

BERETTA MODEL 76 PISTOL
Caliber: 22 LR, 10-shot magazine.
Barrel: 6″.
Weight: 33 ozs. (empty). **Length:** 8.8″ over-all.
Stocks: Checkered plastic.
Sights: Interchangeable blade front (3 widths), rear is fully adj. for w. and e.
Features: Built-in, fixed counterweight, raised, matted slide rib, factory adjusted trigger pull from 3 lbs. 5 ozs. to 3 lbs. 12 ozs. Thumb safety. Blue-black finish. Wood grips available at extra cost. Introduced 1977. Imported from Italy by Beretta Arms Co.
Price: With plastic grips $370.00
Price: With wood grips $415.00

Colt Gold Cup Series 80

COLT GOLD CUP NAT'L MATCH MK IV Series 80
Caliber: 45 ACP, 7-shot magazine.
Barrel: 5″, with new design bushing.
Weight: 38½ oz. **Length:** 8⅜″
Stocks: Checkered walnut, gold plated medallion.
Sights: Ramp-style front, Colt-Elliason rear adj. for w. and e., sight radius 6¾″.
Features: Arched or flat housing; wide, grooved trigger with adj. stop; ribbed-top slide, hand fitted, with improved ejection port.
Price: Colt Royal Blue $599.95

DETONICS SCOREMASTER TARGET PISTOL
Caliber: 45 ACP, 451 Detonics Magnum, 7-shot clip.
Barrel: 5″ heavy match barrel with recessed muzzle; 6″ optional.
Weight: 41 oz. **Length:** 8¾″ over-all.
Stocks: Pachmayr checkered with matching mainspring housing.
Sights: Blade front, Low-Base Bomar rear.
Features: Stainless steel; self-centering barrel system; patented Detonics recoil system; combat tuned, ambidextrous safety; extended grip safety; National Match tolerances; extended magazine release. Comes with two spare magazines, three interchangeable front sights, and carrying case. Introduced 1983. From Detonics.
Price: 45 ACP or 451 Mag., 6″ barrel $995.00
Price: As above, 5″ barrel $985.00

Detonics Scoremaster

HAMMERLI MODEL 120-1 FREE PISTOL
Caliber: 22 LR.
Barrel: 9.9″.
Weight: 44 oz. **Length:** 14¾″ over-all.
Stocks: Contoured right-hand (only) thumbrest.
Sights: Fully adjustable rear, blade front. Choice of 14.56″ or 9.84″ sight radius.
Features: Trigger adjustable for single- or two-stage pull from 1.8 to 12 oz. Adjustable for length of pull. Guaranteed accuracy of .98″, 10 shots at 50 meters. Imported from Switzerland by Mandall Shooting Supplies.
Price: Model 120-1 . . . . $995.00
Price: Model 120-2 (same as above except has walnut target grips with adjustable palm-rest RH or LH) $1,195.00

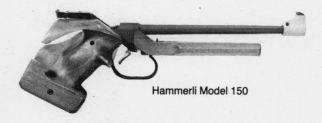

Hammerli Model 150

HAMMERLI MODEL 150 FREE PISTOL
Caliber: 22 LR. Single shot.
Barrel: 11.3″
Weight: 43 ozs. **Length:** 15.35″ over-all.
Stocks: Walnut with adjustable palm shelf.
Sights: Sight radius of 14.6″. Micro rear sight adj. for w. and e.
Features: Single shot Martini action. Cocking lever on left side of action with vertical operation. Set trigger adjustable for length and angle. Trigger pull weight adjustable between 5 and 100 grams. Guaranteed accuracy of .78″, 10 shots from machine rest. Imported from Switzerland by Osborne's Supplies and Mandall Shooting Supplies.
Price: About (Mandall) $1,500.00
Price: With electric trigger (Model 152), about (Mandall) $1,650.00
Price: Model 150 (Osborne's) $1,620.00
Price: Model 152 (Osborne's) $1,720.00

Hammerli 208

Hammerli 232

HECKLER & KOCH P9S COMPETITION PISTOL
Caliber: 9mm Para.
Barrel: 5.5".
Weight: 32 oz. **Length:** 9.1" over-all.
Stocks: Stippled walnut, target-type.
Sights: Blade front, fully adjustable rear.
Features: Comes with extra standard 4" barrel, slide and grips, as well as the target gun parts and tools and is fully convertible. Imported from West Germany by Heckler & Koch.
Price: $990.00

Consult our Directory pages for the location of firms mentioned.

HIGH STANDARD X SERIES CUSTOM 10-X
Caliber: 22 LR, 10-shot magazine.
Barrel: 5½" bull.
Weight: 44½ oz. **Length:** 9¾" over-all.
Stocks: Checkered walnut.
Sights: Undercut ramp front; frame mounted fully adj. rear.
Features: Completely custom made and fitted for best performance. Fully adjustable target trigger, stippled front- and backstraps, slide lock, non-reflective blue finish. Comes with two extra magazines. Unique service policy. Each gun signed by maker.
Price: $714.00

HIGH STANDARD SUPERMATIC TROPHY MILITARY
Caliber: 22 LR, 10-shot magazine.
Barrel: 5½" bull, 7¼" fluted.
Weight: 44½ oz. **Length:** 9¾" (5½" bbl.)
Stocks: Checkered walnut with thumbrest.
Sights: Undercut ramp front; frame mounted rear, click adj.
Features: Grip duplicates feel of military 45; positive action mag. latch; front- and backstraps stippled. Trigger adj. for pull, over-travel.
Price: 5½" or 7¼" barrel $380.00

HAMMERLI STANDARD, MODELS 208 & 211
Caliber: 22 LR.
Barrel: 5.9", 6-groove.
Weight: 37.6 oz. (45 oz. with extra heavy barrel weight). **Length:** 10".
Stocks: Walnut. Adj. palm rest (208), 211 has thumbrest grip.
Sights: Match sights, fully adj. for w. and e. (click adj.). Interchangeable front and rear blades.
Features: Semi-automatic, recoil operated. 8-shot clip. Slide stop. Fully adj. trigger (2¼ lbs. and 3 lbs.). Extra barrel weight available. Imported from Switzerland by Osborne's Supplies and Mandall Shooting Supplies.
Price: Model 208, approx. (Mandall) **$1,295.00**
Price: Model 211, approx. (Mandall) **$1,195.00**
Price: Model 215, approx. (Mandall) **$1,195.00**
Price: Model 208 (Osborne's)................................. **$1,180.00**
Price: Model 211 (Osborne's) **$1,230.00**
Price: Model 215 (Osborne's) **$995.00**

HAMMERLI MODEL 232 RAPID FIRE PISTOL
Caliber: 22 Short, 6-shot.
Barrel: 5", with six exhaust ports.
Weight: 44 oz. **Length:** 10.4" over-all.
Stocks: Stippled walnut; wraparound on Model 232-2, adjustable on 232-1.
Sights: Interchangeable front and rear blades, fully adjustable micrometer rear.
Features: Recoil operated semi-automatic; nearly recoilless design; trigger adjustable from 8.4 to 10.6 oz. with three lengths offered. Wraparound grips available in small, medium and large sizes. Imported from Switzerland by Osborne's Supplies. Introduced 1984.
Price: Model 232-1, about................................... **$1,085.00**
Price: Model 232-2, about................................... **$1,155.00**

H&K P9S Competition

High Standard X Series Custom 10-X

HIGH STANDARD VICTOR
Caliber: 22 LR, 10-shot magazine.
Barrel: 5½".
Weight: 47 oz. **Length:** 9⅝" over-all.
Stocks: Checkered walnut with thumb rest.
Sights: Undercut ramp front, rib mounted click adj. rear.
Features: Vent. rib, interchangeable barrel, 2 - 2¼ lb. trigger pull, blue finish, back and front straps stippled.
Price: $405.00

High Standard Citation II

HIGH STANDARD SUPERMATIC CITATION II MILITARY
Caliber: 22 LR, 10-shot magazine.
Barrel: 5½", 7¼" slabbed.
Weight: 46 oz. **Length:** 9¾" (5½" bbl.)
Stocks: Checkered walnut with thumbrest.
Sights: Undercut ramp front; slide mounted rear, click adj.
Features: Adjustable trigger pull; over-travel trigger adjustment; double acting safety; rebounding firing pin; military style grip; stippled front- and back-straps; positive magazine latch.
Price: 5½" or 7½" barrel **$350.00**

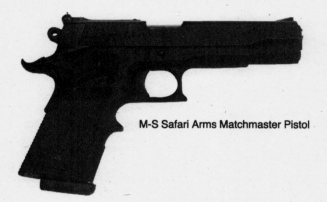

M-S Safari Arms Matchmaster Pistol

M-S SAFARI ARMS MATCHMASTER PISTOL
Caliber: 45 ACP, 7-shot magazine.
Barrel: 5".
Weight: 45 oz. **Length:** 8.7" overall.
Stocks: Combat rubber or checkered walnut.
Sights: Combat adjustable.
Features: Beavertail grip safety, ambidextrous extended safety, extended slide release, combat hammer, threaded barrel bushing; throated, ported, tuned. Finishes: blue, Armaloy, Parkerize, electroless nickel. Also available in a lightweight version (30 oz.) and stainless steel. Made by M-S Safari Arms.
Price: **$681.80**

M-S Safari Arms Model 81 Pistol
Similar to Matchmaster except chambered for 45 or 38 Spec. mid-range wadcutter; available with fixed or adjustable walnut target match grips; Aristocrat rib with extended front sight is optional. Other features are the same. From M-S Safari Arms.
Price: **$868.00**
Price: Model 81L long slide **$995.00**

M-S Safari Arms Model 81BP
Similar to the Matchmaster except designed for shooting the bowling pin matches. Extended slide gives 6" sight radius but also fast slide cycle time. Combat adjustable sights, magazine chute, plus same features as Matchmaster.
Price: **$956.00**

M-S Safari Arms Model 81NM Pistol
Similar to the Matchmaster except weighs 28 oz., is 8.2" over-all, has Ron Power match sights. Meets all requirements for National Match Service Pistols. Throated, ported, tuned and has threaded barrel bushing. Available in blue, Armaloy, Parkerize, stainless steel and electroless nickel. From M-S Safari Arms.
Price: **$868.00**

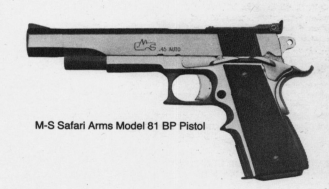

M-S Safari Arms Model 81 BP Pistol

M-S SAFARI ARMS UNLIMITED SILHOUETTE PISTOL
Caliber: Any caliber with 308 head size or smaller.
Barrel: 14¹⁵⁄₁₆" tapered.
Weight: 72 oz. **Length:** 21½" over-all.
Stocks: Fiberglass, custom painted to customer specs.
Sights: Open iron.
Features: Electronic trigger, bolt action single shot. Made by M-S Safari Arms.
Price: **$945.00**
Price: Ultimate model, heavy fluted barrel, shorter action **$945.00**

M-S Safari Arms Enforcer Pistol
Shortened version of the Matchmaster. Has 3.8" barrel, over-all length of 7.7", and weighs 40 oz. (standard weight), 27 oz. in lightweight version. Other features are the same. From M-S Safari Arms.
Price: **$681.80**

MANURHIN MR. 32 MATCH REVOLVER
Caliber: 32 S&W Long, 6-shot.
Barrel: 6".
Weight: 42 oz. **Length:** 11¾" over-all.
Stocks: Anatomically shaped grip for target shooting; supplied shaped but not finished; small, medium and large sizes.
Sights: Interchangeable blade front, adjustable underlying micrometer rear.
Features: Target/match 6-shot revolver. Trigger is externally adjustable for weight of pull, and comes with shoe. Imported from France by Manurhin International, Inc. Introduced 1984.
Price: **$750.00**
Price: Model MR. 38—same as MR. 32 except chambered for 38 Special, 5¾" barrel. **$750.00**

Manurhin MR.32

COMPETITION HANDGUNS

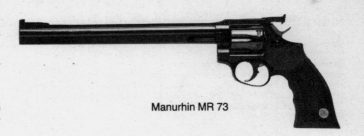

MANURHIN MR 73 LONG RANGE/SILHOUETTE REVOLVER

Caliber: 357 Magnum; 6-shot.
Barrel: 9″ (Long Range), 10¾″ (Silhouette).
Weight: 45 oz. (9″ bbl.); 50 oz. (10¾″ bbl.) **Length:** 14″ over-all (9″); 16¾″ (10¾″).
Stocks: Checkered walnut.
Sights: Interchangeable blade front, adjustable micrometer rear.
Features: Trigger externally adjustable for backlash and weight of pull. Single action only. Comes with trigger shoe. Imported from France by Manurhin International, Inc. Introduced 1984.
Price: **$750.00**

Manurhin MR 73

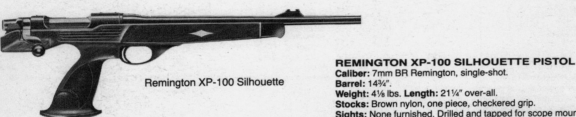

Navy Grand Prix Silhouette

NAVY GRAND PRIX SILHOUETTE PISTOL

Caliber: 44 Mag., 30-30, 7mm Special, 45-70; single shot.
Barrel: 13¾″.
Weight: 4 lbs.
Stocks: Walnut fore-end and thumb-rest grip.
Sights: Adjustable target-type.
Features: Uses rolling block action. Has adjustable aluminum barrel rib; matte blue finish. Made in U.S. by Navy Arms.
Price: **$375.00**

Remington XP-100 Silhouette

REMINGTON XP-100 SILHOUETTE PISTOL

Caliber: 7mm BR Remington, single-shot.
Barrel: 14¾″.
Weight: 4⅛ lbs. **Length:** 21¼″ over-all.
Stocks: Brown nylon, one piece, checkered grip.
Sights: None furnished. Drilled and tapped for scope mounts.
Features: Universal grip fits right or left hand; match-type grooved trigger, two-position thumb safety.
Price: **$393.00**

RUGER MARK II TARGET MODEL AUTO PISTOL

Caliber: 22 LR only, 10-shot magazine.
Barrel: 6⅞″, 5½″ or 10″ bull barrel (6-groove, 14″ twist).
Weight: 42 oz. with 6⅞″ bbl. **Length:** 10⅞″ (6⅞″ bbl.)
Stocks: Checkered hard rubber.
Sights: ⅛″ blade front, micro click rear, adjustable for w. and e. Sight radius 9⅜″ (with 6⅞″ bbl.). Introduced 1982.
Price: Blued, 5½″ or 10″ **$196.00**
Price: Stainless, tapered 6⅞″ barrel **$255.00**

SEVILLE "SILHOUETTE" SINGLE ACTION

Caliber: 357, 41, 44, 45 Win. Mag.
Barrel: 10½″.
Weight: About 55 oz.
Stocks: Smooth walnut thumbrest, or Pachmayr.
Sights: Undercut Patridge-style front, adjustable rear.
Features: Available in stainless steel or blue. Six-shot cylinder. From United Sporting Arms.
Price: Stainless **$400.00**
Price: Blue **$325.00**

Ruger Mark II Target Model

SIG/Hammerli P-240

SIG/HAMMERLI P-240 TARGET PISTOL

Caliber: 32 S&W Long wadcutter, 5-shot.
Barrel: 5.9″.
Weight: 49 oz. **Length:** 10″ over-all.
Stocks: Walnut, target style with thumbrest. Adjustable palm rest optional.
Sights: Match sights; ⅛″ undercut front, ⅛″ notch micro rear click adj. for w. and e.
Features: Semi-automatic, recoil operated; meets I.S.U. and N.R.A. specs for Center Fire Pistol competition; double pull trigger adj. from 2 lbs., 15 ozs. to 3 lbs., 9 ozs.; trigger stop. Comes with cleaning kit, test targets. Imported from Switzerland by Osborne's Supplies and Mandall Shooting Supplies.
Price: About (Mandall) **$1,500.00**
Price: 22 cal. conversion unit (Mandall) **$750.00**
Price: With standard grips (Osborne's) **$1,425.00**
Price: With adjustable grips (Osborne's) **$1,495.00**

CAUTION: PRICES CHANGE. CHECK AT GUNSHOP.

COMPETITION HANDGUNS

SMITH & WESSON MODEL 29 SILHOUETTE
Caliber: 44 Magnum, 6-shot.
Barrel: 10⅝".
Weight: 58 oz. **Length:** 16⅛" over-all.
Stocks: Over-size target-type, checkered Goncalo Alves.
Sights: Four-position front to match the four distances of silhouette targets; micro-click rear adjustable for windage and elevation.
Features: Designed specifically for silhouette shooting. Front sight has click stops for the four pre-set ranges. Introduced 1983.
Price: Without presentation case **$423.50**
Price: With presentation case **$469.50**

Smith & Wesson 29 Silhouette

SMITH & WESSON 22 AUTO PISTOL Model 41
Caliber: 22 LR, 10-shot clip.
Barrel: 7⅜", sight radius 9⁵⁄₁₆".
Weight: 43½ oz. **Length:** 12" over-all.
Stocks: Checkered walnut with thumbrest, usable with either hand.
Sights: Front, ⅛" Patridge undercut; micro click rear adj. for w. and e.
Features: ⅜" wide, grooved trigger with adj. stop; wgts. available to make pistol up to 59 oz.
Price: S&W Bright Blue, satin matted bbl. **$390.00**

Smith & Wesson Model 41

SMITH & WESSON 22 MATCH HEAVY BARREL M-41
Caliber: 22 LR, 10-shot clip.
Barrel: 5½" heavy. Sight radius, 8".
Weight: 44½ oz. **Length:** 9".
Stocks: Checkered walnut with modified thumbrest, usable with either hand.
Sights: ⅛" Patridge on ramp base. S&W micro click rear adj. for w. and e.
Features: ⅜" wide, grooved trigger; adj. trigger stop.
Price: S&W Bright Blue, satin matted top area **$390.00**

SMITH & WESSON 38 MASTER Model 52 AUTO
Caliber: 38 Special (for Mid-range W.C. with flush-seated bullet only). 5-shot magazine.
Barrel: 5".
Weight: 41 oz. with empty magazine. **Length:** 8⅝".
Stocks: Checkered walnut.
Sights: ⅛" Patridge front, S&W micro click rear adj. for w. and e.
Features: Top sighting surfaces matte finished. Locked breech, moving barrel system; checked for 10-ring groups at 50 yards. Coin-adj. sight screws. Dry firing permissible if manual safety on.
Price: S&W Bright Blue... **$573.50**

Smith & Wesson Model 52

TAURUS MODEL 86 MASTER REVOLVER
Caliber: 38 Spec., 6-shot.
Barrel: 6" only.
Weight: 34 oz. **Length:** 11¼" over-all.
Stocks: Over size target-type, checkered Brazilian walnut.
Sights: Patridge front, micro. click rear adj. for w. and e.
Features: Blue finish with non-reflective finish on barrel. Imported from Brazil by Taurus International.
Price: About... **$187.00**
Price: Model 96 Scout Master, same except in 22 cal., about........ **$187.00**

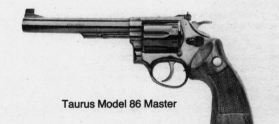
Taurus Model 86 Master

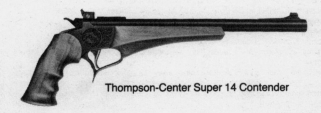
Thompson-Center Super 14 Contender

THOMPSON-CENTER SUPER 14 CONTENDER
Caliber: 22 LR, 222 Rem., 223 Rem., 6.5 TCU, 7mm TCU, 30 Herrett, 357 Herrett, 30-30 Win., 35 Rem., 357 Rem. Maximum, 41 and 44 Mag., 45 Win. Mag. Single shot.
Barrel: 14".
Weight: 45 oz. **Length:** 17¼" over-all.
Stocks: Select walnut grip and fore-end.
Sights: Fully adjustable target-type.
Features: Break-open action with auto safety. Interchangeable barrels for both rimfire and centerfire calibers. Introduced 1978.
Price: **$285.00**
Price: Extra barrels **$125.00**

VIRGINIAN DRAGOON STAINLESS SILHOUETTE
Caliber: 357 Mag., 44 Mag.
Barrel: 7½″, 8⅜″, 10½″, heavy.
Weight: 51 oz. (7½″ bbl.) **Length:** 11½″ over-all (7½″ bbl.).
Stocks: Smooth walnut; also comes with Pachmayr rubber grips.
Sights: Undercut blade front, special fully adjustable square notch rear.
Features: Designed to comply with IHMSA rules. Made of stainless steel; comes with two sets of stocks. Introduced 1982. Made in the U.S. by Interarms.
Price: Either barrel, caliber $425.00

WALTHER GSP MATCH PISTOL
Caliber: 22 LR, 32 S&W wadcutter (GSP-C), 5-shot.
Barrel: 5¾″.
Weight: 44.8 oz. (22 LR), 49.4 oz. (32). **Length:** 11.8″ over-all.
Stocks: Walnut, special hand-fitting design.
Sights: Fixed front, rear adj. for w. & e.
Features: Available with either 2.2 lb. (1000 gm) or 3 lb. (1360 gm) trigger. Spare mag., bbl. weight, tools supplied in Match Pistol Kit. Imported from Germany by Interarms.
Price: GSP $925.00
Price: GSP-C. $1,050.00
Price: 22 LR conversion unit for GSP-C $600.00
Price: 22 Short conversion unit for GSP-C $650.00

Walther OSP Rapid-Fire Pistol
Similar to Model GSP except 22 Short only, stock has adj. free-style hand rest.
Price: $925.00

WICHITA MK-40 SILHOUETTE PISTOL
Caliber: 7mm IHMSA, 308 Win. F.L. Other calibers available on special order. Single shot.
Barrel: 13″, non-glare blue; .700″ dia. muzzle.
Weight: 4½ lbs. **Length:** 19⅜″ over-all.
Stocks: Metallic gray fiberthane glass.
Sights: Wichita Multi-Range sighting system.
Features: Aluminum receiver with steel insert locking lugs, measures 1.360″ O.D.; 3 locking lug bolts, 3 gas ports; flat bolt handle; completely adjustable Wichita trigger. Introduced 1981. From Wichita Arms.
Price: $640.00

WICHITA SILHOUETTE PISTOL
Caliber: 7mm IHMSA, 308, 7mm x 308. Other calibers available on special order. Single shot.
Barrel: 14¹⁵⁄₁₆″ or 10¾″.
Weight: 4½ lbs. **Length:** 21⅜″ over-all.
Stocks: American walnut with oil finish, or fiberglass (yellow or black). Glass bedded.
Sights: Wichita Multi-Range sight system.
Features: Comes with either right- or left-hand action with right-hand grip. Fluted bolt, flat bolt handle. Action drilled and tapped for Burris scope mounts. Non-glare satin blue finish. Wichita adjustable trigger. Introduced 1979. From Wichita Arms.
Price: Center grip stock $750.00
Price: As above except with Rear Position Stock and target-type Lightpull trigger. (Not illus.) $820.00

WICHITA CLASSIC PISTOL
Caliber: Any, up to and including 308 Win.
Barrel: 11¼″, octagon.
Weight: About 5 lbs.
Stock: Exhibition grade American black walnut. Checkered 20 lpi. Other woods available on special order.
Sights: Micro open sights standard. Receiver drilled and tapped for scope mount.
Features: Receiver and barrel octagonally shaped, finished in non-glare blue. Bolt has three locking lugs and three gas escape ports. Completely adjustable Wichita trigger. Introduced 1980. From Wichita Arms.
Price: $1,615.00
Price: Engraved, in walnut presentation case $3,500.00

WALTHER FREE PISTOL
Caliber: 22 LR, single shot.
Barrel: 11.7″.
Weight: 48 ozs. **Length:** 17.2″ over-all.
Stocks: Walnut, special hand-fitting design.
Sights: Fully adjustable match sights.
Features: Special electronic trigger. Matte finish blue. Introduced 1980. Imported from Germany by Interarms.
Price: $1,325.00

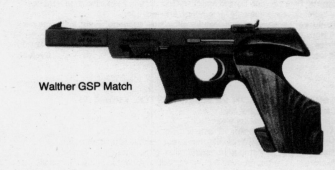

Walther GSP Match

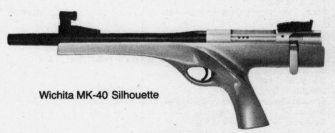

Wichita MK-40 Silhouette

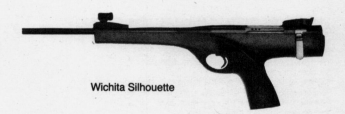

Wichita Silhouette

Wichita Hunter International

WICHITA HUNTER, INTERNATIONAL PISTOL
Caliber: 7mm INT-R, 30-30 Win., 357 Mag., 357 Super Mag., single shot.
Barrel: 10½″.
Weight: International — 3 lbs., 13 oz.; Hunter — 3 lbs., 14 oz.
Stock: Walnut grip and fore-end.
Sights: International — target front, adjustable rear; Hunter has scope mount only.
Features: Made of 17-4PH stainless steel. Break-open action. Grip dimensions same as Colt 45 auto. Safety supplied only on Hunter model. Extra barrels are factory fitted. Introduced 1983. Available from The Silhouette.
Price: International $595.00
Price: Hunter. $595.00
Price: Extra barrels $225.00

ARMINIUS REVOLVERS

Caliber: 38 Special, 357 Magnum, 32 S&W, 22 Magnum, 22 LR.
Barrel: 2″, 4″, 6″.
Weight: 35 oz. (6″ bbl.). **Length:** 11″ (6″ bbl. 38).
Stocks: Checkered plastic; walnut optional for $14.95.
Sights: Ramp front, fixed rear on standard models, w. & e. adj. on target models.
Features: Thumb-release, swing-out cylinder. Ventilated rib, solid frame, swing-out cylinder. Interchangeable 22 Mag. cylinder available with 22 cal. versions. Imported from West Germany by F.I.E. Corp.
Price: .... **$112.95 to $214.95**

Arminius Revolver

ASTRA 357 MAGNUM REVOLVER

Caliber: 357 Magnum, 6-shot.
Barrel: 3″, 4″, 6″, 8½″.
Weight: 40 oz. (6″ bbl.). **Length:** 11¼″ (6″ bbl.).
Stocks: Checkered walnut.
Sights: Fixed front, rear adj. for w. and e.
Features: Swing-out cylinder with countersunk chambers, floating firing pin. Target-type hammer and trigger. Imported from Spain by Interarms.
Price: 3″, 4″, 6″ **$275.00**
Price: 8½″ **$285.00**
Price: 4″, stainless **$315.00**

Astra Model 41, 44, 45 Double Action Revolver

Similar to the 357 Mag. except chambered for the 41 Mag., 44 Mag. or 45 Colt. Barrel length of 6″ only, giving over-all length of 11⅜″. Weight is 2¾ lbs. Introduced 1980.
Price: **$299.00**
Price: 8½″ bbl. (44 Mag. only) **$309.00**
Price: 6″, stainless, 44 Mag. **$329.00**

BEEMAN/KORTH REVOLVER

Caliber: 22 LR, 22 Mag., 357 Mag., 9mm Parabellum.
Barrel: 3″, 4″, 6″.
Weight: 33 to 38 oz. **Length:** 8″ to 11″ over-all.
Stocks: Checkered walnut, sport or combat.
Sights: Blade front, rear adjustable for windage and elevation.
Features: Four interchangeable cylinders available. Major parts machined from hammer-forged steel; cylinder gap of .002″. High polish blue finish. Presentation models have gold trim. Imported from Germany by Beeman.
Price: .... **$1,595.00 to $2,995.00**

Beeman/Korth Revolver

CHARTER ARMS UNDERCOVER REVOLVER

Caliber: 38 Special, 5 shot; 32 S & W Long, 6 shot.
Barrel: 2″, 3″.
Weight: 16 oz. (2″). **Length:** 6¼″ (2″).
Stocks: Smooth walnut or checkered square butt.
Sights: Patridge-type ramp front, notched rear.
Features: Wide trigger and hammer spur. Steel frame. Police Undercover, 2″ bbl. (for 38 Spec. + P loads) carry same prices as regular 38 Spec. guns.
Price: Polished Blue **$190.00**
Price: 32 S & W Long, blue, 2″ **$190.00**
Price: Stainless, 38 Spec., 2″ **$245.00**
Price: "P" model, blue **$193.00**
Price: "P" model, stainless **$249.00**

Charter Arms Undercover

Charter Arms Off-Duty Revolver

Similar to the Undercover except 38 Special only, 2″ barrel, Mat-Black non-glare finish. This all-steel gun comes with Red-Dot front sight and choice of smooth or checkered walnut or neoprene grips. Also available in stainless steel. Introduced 1984.
Price: Mat-Black finish **$149.00**
Price: Stainless steel **$199.00**

Charter Arms Off-Duty

Charter Arms 32 H&R Magnum Police Undercover

Similar to the standard Undercover except chambered for the 32 H&R Magnum (6-shot). Patridge-type front with fixed square notch rear on the 2″ barrel, adjustable rear on the 4″ version. Blue finish only, checkered walnut grips. Also available with Pocket Hammer. Introduced 1984.
Price: 2″ barrel, standard hammer **$192.00**
Price: 2″ barrel, Pocket Hammer...................... **$195.00**
Price: 4″ barrel, standard hammer **$202.00**

Charter Arms Pathfinder

Same as Undercover but in 22 LR or 22 Mag., and has 2″, 3″ or 6″ bbl. Fitted with adjustable rear sight, ramp front. Weight 18½ oz.
Price: 22 LR, blue, 3″ **$200.00**
Price: 22 LR, square butt, 6″ **$215.00**
Price: Stainless, 22 LR, 3″ **$250.00**
Price: 2″, either caliber, blue only **$200.00**

CHARTER ARMS BULLDOG
Caliber: 44 Special, 5-shot.
Barrel: 2½", 3".
Weight: 19 oz. **Length:** 7¾" over-all.
Stocks: Checkered walnut, Bulldog.
Sights: Patridge-type front, square-notch rear.
Features: Wide trigger and hammer; beryllium copper firing pin.
Price: Service Blue $200.00
Price: Stainless steel.. $260.00
Price: Service blue, 2½" $203.00
Price: Stainless steel, 3", neoprene grips $264.00

Charter Arms Bulldog

Charter Arms Bulldog Tracker
Similar to the standard Bulldog except has adjustable rear sight, 2½", 4" or 6" bull barrel, ramp front sight, square butt checkered walnut grips on 4" and 6"; Bulldog-style grips on 2½". Available in blue finish only.
Price: $210.00

CHARTER ARMS POLICE BULLDOG
Caliber: 32 H&R Mag., 38 Special, 6-shot.
Barrel: 4", 4" straight taper bull.
Weight: 21 oz. **Length:** 9" over-all.
Stocks: Hand checkered American walnut; square butt.
Sights: Patridge-type ramp front, notched rear.
Features: Accepts both regular and high velocity ammunition; enclosed ejector rod; full length ejection of fired cases.
Price: Blue.. $195.00
Price: Stainless steel.. $255.00

Charter Arms Police Bulldog

COLT AGENT
Caliber: 38 Special, 6-shot.
Barrel: 2".
Weight: 16¾ ozs. **Length:** 6⅞" over-all.
Stocks: Checkered walnut.
Sights: Fixed.
Features: A no-frills, lightweight version of the Detective Special. Parkerized-type finish. Name re-introduced 1982.
Price: $209.95

Colt Agent

COLT DETECTIVE SPECIAL
Caliber: 38 Special, 6 shot.
Barrel: 2" or 3".
Weight: 22 oz. **Length:** 6⅝" over-all (2" bbl.).
Stocks: Full, checkered walnut, round butt.
Sights: Fixed, ramp front, square notch rear.
Features: Glare-proofed sights, smooth trigger. Nickel finish, hammer shroud available as options.
Price: Blue, 2"... $377.50
Price: Nickel, 2" $414.95
Price: Blue, 3"... $385.50
Price: Nickel, 3" $422.95

Colt Commando Special
Same gun as the Detective Special except comes with rubber grips and combat-grade finish. Introduced 1984.
Price: $249.95

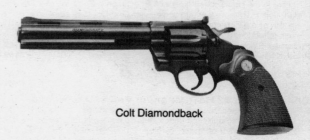

Colt Commando

COLT DIAMONDBACK REVOLVER
Caliber: 22 LR or 38 Special, 6 shot.
Barrel: 4" or 6" with ventilated rib.
Weight: 24 oz. (2½" bbl.), 28½ oz. (4" bbl.). **Length:** 9" (4" bbl.)
Stocks: Checkered walnut, target type, square butt.
Sights: Ramp front, adj. notch rear.
Features: Ventilated rib; grooved, crisp trigger; swing-out cylinder; wide hammer spur.
Price: Blue, 4" bbl. 38 Spec. or 22 .... $396.95
Price: Blue, 6" bbl., 22 or 38................................. $405.95
Price: Nickel, 4", 22 LR $433.50
Price: Nickel, 6", 22 LR $439.50

Colt Diamondback

CAUTION: PRICES CHANGE. CHECK AT GUNSHOP.

COLT PYTHON REVOLVER
Caliber: 357 Magnum (handles all 38 Spec.), 6 shot.
Barrel: 2½″, 4″, 6″ or 8″, with ventilated rib.
Weight: 38 oz. (4″ bbl.). **Length:** 9¼″ (4″ bbl.).
Stocks: Checkered walnut, target type.
Sights: ⅛″ ramp front, adj. notch rear.
Features: Ventilated rib; grooved, crisp trigger; swing-out cylinder; target hammer.
Price: Colt Blue, 2½″ $577.50
Price: 4″ $589.50
Price: 6″ $599.95
Price: 8″ $611.50
Price: Nickeled, 4″ $625.95
Price: Nickeled, 6″ $628.50
Price: Nickeled, 8″ $641.50
Price: Stainless, 4″ $661.50
Price: Stainless, 6″ $671.50

Colt Python 357

COLT TROOPER MK V REVOLVER
Caliber: 357 Magnum, 6-shot.
Barrel: 4″, 6″.
Weight: 38 oz. (4″). **Length:** 9⅛″ over-all (4″).
Stocks: Checkered walnut target-style.
Sights: Orange insert ramp front, adjustable white outline rear.
Features: Vent. rib and shrouded ejector rod. Re-designed action results in short hammer throw, lightened trigger pull and faster lock time. Also has re-designed grip frame. Introduced 1982.
Price: 4″ blue $318.95
Price: 4″ nickel, ... $338.50
Price: 6″, blue $319.95
Price: 6″, nickel $344.50

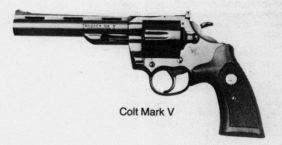

Colt Mark V

Colt Lawman MK V Revolver
Same as the Trooper MK V except has plain bull barrel, fixed sights and is available only with 2″ or 4″ barrel. Blue or nickel finish. Introduced 1982.
Price: 2″, blue $287.95
Price: 2″, nickel $306.50
Price: 4″, blue $287.95

Colt Lawman MK V

F.I.E. MODEL N38 "Titan Tiger" REVOLVER
Caliber: 38 Special, 357 Magnum.
Barrel: 2″ or 4″.
Weight: 27 oz. **Length:** 6¼″ over-all. (2″ bbl.)
Stocks: Checkered plastic, Bulldog style. Walnut optional ($15.95).
Sights: Fixed.
Features: Thumb-release swing-out cylinder, one stroke ejection. Made in U.S.A. by F.I.E. Corp.
Price: Blue, 38 Special $129.95
Price: Chrome, 38 Special $144.95
Price: 357 Magnum $214.95

H&R Model 686

HARRINGTON & RICHARDSON M686 REVOLVER
Caliber: 22 LR/22 WMRF, 6-shot.
Barrel: 4½″, 5½″, 7½″, 10″ or 12″.
Weight: 31 oz. (4½″), 41 oz. (12″).
Stocks: Two piece, smooth walnut-finished hardwood.
Sights: Western type blade front, adj. rear.
Features: Blue barrel and cylinder, "antique" color case-hardened frame, ejector tube and trigger. Comes with extra cylinder.
Price: 4½″, 5½″, 7½″, 10″ bbl. $176.50
Price: 12″ bbl. $195.50

H&R Model 586

Harrington & Richardson Model 586 H&R Magnum
Similar to the Model 686 except chambered for 32 H&R Magnum. Redesigned action, 5-shot cylinder, available with 4½″, 5½″, 7½″ and 10″ barrel. Color case-hardened frame. Introduced 1984.
Price: $195.00

Harrington & Richardson Model 649 Revolver
Similar to model 686 except has 5½″ or 7½″ barrel, two piece walnut-finished hardwood grips, western-type blade front sight, adjustable rear. Loads and ejects from side. Weighs 32 oz.
Price: $152.50
Price: Model 650—as above except nickel finish, 5½″ only $162.50

HARRINGTON & RICHARDSON M622 REVOLVER
Caliber: 22 S, L or LR, 6 shot.
Barrel: 2½", 4", round bbl.
Weight: 20 oz. (2½" bbl.).
Stocks: Checkered black Cycolac.
Sights: Fixed, blade front, square notch rear.
Features: Solid steel, Bantamweight frame; patented safety rim cylinder; non-glare finish on frame; coil springs.
Price: Blued, 2½", 4" bbl. $103.50
Price: Model 632 (32 cal.), 2½" bbl. only $103.50

H&R Model 532

Harrington & Richardson Model 532 H&R Magnum
Similar to the Model 622/632 except redesigned to accept the 32 H&R Magnum cartridge with 5-shot cylinder. Solid frame design. Available with 2½" barrel (round butt), 4" barrel (round butt); blue finish, wood grips. Introduced 1984.
Price: $115.00

HARRINGTON & RICHARDSON M732
Caliber: 32 S&W or 32 S&W Long, 6 shot.
Barrel: 2½" or 4" round barrel.
Weight: 23½ oz. (2½" bbl.), 26 oz. (4" bbl.).
Stocks: Checkered, black Cycolac or walnut.
Sights: Blade front; fixed notch rear.
Features: Swing-out cylinder with auto. extractor return.
Price: Blued, 2½" or 4" bbl. $126.50
Price: Nickel, 2½" bbl. (Model 733) $136.50

H&R Model 732

HARRINGTON & RICHARDSON MODELS 904, 905
Caliber: 22 LR, 9-shot (M904, 905).
Barrel: 4" (M904 only), 6" target bull.
Weight: 32 oz.
Stocks: Smooth walnut.
Sights: Blade front, fully adjustable "Wind-Elv" rear.
Features: Swing-out cylinder design with coil spring construction. Single stroke ejection. Target-style bull barrel has raised solid rib giving a 7¼" sight radius.
Price: 904 . . . . $167.50
Price: M905, 4", H&R "Hard-Guard" nickel finish. $179.50

HARRINGTON & RICHARDSON M929
Caliber: 22 S, L or LR, 9 shot.
Barrel: 2½", 4" or 6".
Weight: 26 oz. (4" bbl.).
Stocks: Checkered, black Cycolac or walnut.
Sights: Blade front; adjustable rear on 4" and 6" models.
Features: Swing-out cylinder with auto. extractor return. Round-grip frame on 2½" only.
Price: Blued, 2½", 4" or 6" bbl. $126.50
Price: Nickel (Model 930), 2½" or 4" bbl. $136.50

Harrington & Richardson Model 504 H&R Magnum
Similar to the Model 904 swing-out except has redesigned action for the 32 H&R Magnum; 5-shot cylinder, wood grips. Available in 3" with round butt, 4" round or square butt, 6" square butt. Blue finish. Introduced 1984.
Price: $185.00

HARRINGTON & RICHARDSON M949
Caliber: 22 S, L or LR, 9 shot.
Barrel: 5½" round with ejector rod.
Weight: 31 oz.
Stocks: Two-piece, smooth frontier style wrap-around, walnut-finished hardwood.
Sights: Western-type blade front, rear adj. for w.
Features: Contoured loading gate; wide hammer spur; single and double action. Western type ejector-housing.
Price: H&R Crown Luster Blue $126.50
Price: Nickel (Model 950) $136.50

H&R Model 504

H&R SPORTSMAN MODEL 999 REVOLVER
Caliber: 22 S, L or LR, 9 shot.
Barrel: 4", 6" top-break (16" twist), integral fluted vent. rib.
Weight: 34 oz. (6"). **Length:** 10½".
Stocks: Checkered walnut.
Sights: Front adjustable for elevation, rear for windage.
Features: Simultaneous automatic ejection, trigger guard extension. H&R Crown Lustre Blue.
Price: Blued, 4". $215.00
Price: Blued, 6" engraved $525.00

H&R Model 999

CAUTION: PRICES CHANGE. CHECK AT GUNSHOP.

HIGH STANDARD SENTINEL
Caliber: 22 LR and 22 Mag. with extra cylinder.
Barrel: 2" or 4".
Weight: 22 oz. (2" barrel). **Length:** 7⅛" over-all (2" barrel).
Stocks: Checkered walnut.
Sights: ⅛" serrated ramp front, square notched rear.
Features: Double action, dual swing-out cylinders; steel frame; blue finish; combat-style grips. From High Standard.
Price: Model 9390 (fixed sights) **$250.00**
Price: Model 9392 (adj. sights) **$250.00**
Price: Model 9360 (2", 4", 22 Mag., fixed or adj. sights) **$235.00**

High Standard Sentinel

HIGH STANDARD DOUBLE-NINE CONVERTIBLE
Caliber: 22 S, L or LR, 9-shot (22 Mag. with extra cylinder).
Barrel: 5½", dummy ejector rod fitted.
Weight: 32 oz. **Length:** 11" over-all.
Stocks: Smooth walnut, frontier style.
Sights: Fixed blade front, rear adj. for w. & e.
Features: Double-action, Western styling, rounding hammer with auto safety block; spring-loaded ejection. Swing-out cylinder.
Price: Blued **$250.00**
Price: Blued, 22 LR, fixed sights **$235.00**

High Standard Long Horn Convertible
Same as the Double-Nine convertible but with a 9½" bbl., adjustable sights, blued only. Weight: 38 oz.
Price: With adjustable sights **$250.00**

HIGH STANDARD CAMP GUN
Caliber: 22 LR and 22 Mag., 9-shot.
Barrel: 6".
Weight: 28 oz. **Length:** 11⅛" over-all.
Stocks: Checkered walnut.
Sights: ⅛" serrated ramp front, rear adjustable for windage and elevation.
Features: Double-action; comes with two cylinders; blue finish; combat-style wrap around grips. From High Standard.
Price: Model 9393 .... **$250.00**

High Standard Camp Gun

HIGH STANDARD HIGH SIERRA DOUBLE ACTION
Caliber: 22 LR and 22 LR/22 Mag., 9-shot.
Barrel: 7" octagonal.
Weight: 36 oz. **Length:** 12½" over-all.
Stocks: Smooth walnut.
Sights: Blade front, adj. rear.
Features: Gold plated backstrap and trigger guard. Swing-out cylinder.
Price: Adj. sights, dual cyl. **$250.00**

KASSNAR-CONCORDE SPECIAL REVOLVER
Caliber: 22 LR, 22 Mag., 38 Special.
Barrel: 3", 4", 6".
Weight: 24 oz. **Length:** 9½" (4" bbl.).
Stocks: Target-type of hand checkered exotic wood.
Sights: Ramp front, fully adjustable rear.
Features: Heavy barrel with ventilated rib, full ejector rod shroud. Imported from the Philippines by Kassnar.
Price: With vent. rib **$199.00**
Price: Model Concorde, solid rib **$189.00**

Kassnar/Concorde

Llama Super Comanche

LLAMA COMANCHE II REVOLVERS
Caliber: 357 Mag.
Barrel: 6", 4".
Weight: 28 oz. **Length:** 9¼" (4" bbl.).
Stocks: Checkered walnut.
Sights: Fixed blade front, rear adj. for w. & e.
Features: Ventilated rib, wide spur hammer. Chrome plating, engraved finishes available. Imported from Spain by Stoeger Industries.
Price: Blue finish **$234.95**
Price: Satin chrome **$309.95**

Llama Super Comanche V Revolver
Similar to the Comanche except; large frame, 357 or 44 Mag., 4", 6" or 8½" barrel only; 6-shot cylinder; smooth, extra wide trigger; wide spur hammer; over-size walnut, target-style grips. Weight is 3 lbs., 2 ozs., over-all length is 11¾". Blue finish only.
Price: 44 Mag. **$334.95**
Price: 357 Mag. **$299.95**

MANURHIN MR 73 SPORT REVOLVER
Caliber: 357 Magnum, 6-shot.
Barrel: 5.25".
Weight: 37 oz. **Length:** 10.4" over-all.
Stocks: Checkered walnut.
Sights: Blade front, fully adjustable rear.
Features: Double action with adjustable trigger. High-polish blue finish, "Straw" colored hammer and trigger. Comes with sight adjusting tool. Imported from France by Manurhin International, Inc. Introduced 1984.
Price: **$730.00**

RG MODEL 23 REVOLVER
Caliber: 22 LR, 6 shot.
Barrel: 1¾" or 3⅜".
Weight: 16 oz. **Length:** 5⅛" over-all.
Stocks: Checkered plastic.
Sights: Fixed.
Features: Swing out cylinder with central ejector. From RG Industries.
Price: **$75.95**

RG MODEL 38S REVOLVER
Caliber: 38 Special, 6-shot.
Barrel: 3" or 4".
Weight: 32 oz. (3" bbl.). **Length:** 8¼" over-all.
Stocks: Checkered walnut or plastic.
Sights: Blade front, rear adjustable for windage.
Features: Swing out cylinder with spring ejector. From RG Industries.
Price: With plastic grips. **$124.95**
Price: With wood grips **$131.95**

RG MODEL 39 REVOLVER
Caliber: 32 S&W (6-shot) or 38 Special (5-shot).
Barrel: 2".
Weight: 21 oz. **Length:** 7" over-all.
Stocks: Checkered walnut.
Sights: Fixed.
Features: Swing out cylinder with ejector spring. Blue finish. From RG Industries.
Price: 32 S&W **$124.95**
Price: 38 Special **$127.95**

ROSSI MODEL 88 STAINLESS REVOLVER
Caliber: 38 Spec., 5-shot.
Barrel: 3".
Weight: 32 oz. **Length:** 8¾" over-all.
Stocks: Checkered wood, service-style.
Sights: Ramp front, square notch rear drift adjustable for windage.
Features: All metal parts except springs are of 440 stainless steel; matte finish; small frame for concealability. Introduced 1983. Imported from Brazil by Interarms.
Price: **$179.00**

ROSSI MODELS 68, 69 & 70 DA REVOLVERS
Caliber: 22 LR (M 70), 32 S & W (M 69), 38 Spec. (M 68).
Barrel: 3".
Weight: 22 oz.
Stocks: Checkered wood.
Sights: Ramp front, low profile adj. rear.
Features: All-steel frame. Thumb latch operated swing-out cylinder. Introduced 1978. Imported from Brazil by Interarms.
Price: 22, 32, or 38, blue **$139.00**
Price: As above, 38 Spec. only with 4" bbl. as M 31 . . . . **$139.00**
Price: Model 51 (6" bbl., 22 cal.) **$149.00**
Price: M68, M69, M70 in nickel **$144.00**

RG MODEL 14S REVOLVER
Caliber: 22 LR, 6-shot.
Barrel: 1¾" or 3".
Weight: 15 oz. **Length:** 5½" over-all.
Stocks: Checkered plastic.
Sights: Fixed.
Features: Pull-pin swing out cylinder. From RG Industries.
Price: **$58.00**

> Consult our Directory pages for the location of firms mentioned.

RG 38S

RG 39

Rossi Model 88 Stainless

Rossi Model 68

CAUTION: PRICES CHANGE. CHECK AT GUNSHOP.

RUGER SECURITY-SIX Model 117

Caliber: 357 Mag. (also fires 38 Spec.), 6-shot.
Barrel: 2¾″, 6″, or 4″ heavy barrel.
Weight: 33½ oz. (4″ bbl.) **Length:** 9¼″ (4″ bbl.) over-all.
Stocks: Hand checkered American walnut, semi-target style. Also available with over-size target-type or rubber grips.
Sights: Patridge-type front on ramp, white outline rear adj. for w. and e.
Features: Music wire coil springs throughout. Hardened steel construction. Integral ejector rod shroud and sighting rib. Can be disassembled using only a coin.
Price: 2¾″, 6″ and 4″ heavy barrel **$247.00**
Price: 4″ HB, 6″ with target grips, white outline rear sight, red ramp front.. **$266.00**

Ruger Security-Six

RUGER POLICE SERVICE-SIX 107, 108, 109, 707, 708

Caliber: 357 (Model 107, 707), 38 Spec. (Model 108, 708), 9mm (Model 109), 6-shot.
Barrel: 2¾″ or 4″.
Weight: 33½ oz. (4″ bbl.). **Length:** 9¼″ (4 bbl.) over-all.
Stocks: Checkered American walnut, semi-target style; rubber available.
Sights: Fixed, non-adjustable.
Features: Solid frame; barrel, rib and ejector rod housing combined in one unit. All steel construction Field strips without tools.
Price: Model 107 (357) 2¾″ and 4″............................. **$217.50**
Price: Model 108 (38) 4″.................................. **$217.50**
Price: Model 109 (9mm) 4″................................ **$236.50**
Price: Mod. 707 (357), Stainless, 4″, walnut or rubber grips **$239.50**
Price: Mod. 708 (38), Stainless, 4″, walnut or rubber grips.......... **$239.50**

Ruger Police Service-Six

RUGER SPEED-SIX Models 207, 208, 209, 737, 738, 739

Caliber: 357 (Model 207), 38 Spec. (Model 208), 9mm P (Model 209) 6-shot.
Barrel: 2¾″ or 4″.
Weight: 31 oz. (2¾″ bbl.). **Length:** 7¾″ over-all (2¾″ bbl.).
Stocks: Checkered walnut or checkered rubber with finger grooves.
Sights: Fixed, non-adjustable.
Features: Same basic mechanism as Security-Six. Hammer without spur available on special order. All steel construction. Music wire coil springs used throughout.
Price: Model 207 (357 Mag., 2¾″, 4″, walnut or rubber grips) **$221.50**
Price: Model 208 (38 Spec. only, 2¾″, walnut grips)............... **$221.50**
Price: Model 209 (9mm P, 2¾″, 4″, walnut grips).................. **$240.50**
Price: Mod. 737 (357 Mag., stainless, 2¾″, 4″, walnut or rubber grips) **$246.00**
Price: Mod. 738 (38 Spec. only, stainless, 2¾″, walnut grips) **$246.00**
Price: Model 739 (9mm P., stainless, 2¾″, walnut grips) **$261.00**

Ruger Speed-Six

RUGER STAINLESS SECURITY-SIX Model 717

Caliber: 357 Mag. (also fires 38 Spec.), 6-shot.
Barrel: 2¾″, 4″ or 6″.
Weight: 33 oz. (4 bbl.). **Length:** 9¼″ (4″ bbl.) over-all.
Stocks: Hand checkered American walnut or checkered rubber.
Sights: Patridge-type front, fully adj. rear.
Features: All metal parts except sights made of stainless steel. Sights are black alloy for maximum visibility. Same mechanism and features found in regular Security-Six.
Price: 2¾″, 6″ and 4″ heavy barrel **$270.50**
Price: 4″ HB, 6″ with checkered rubber grips, red ramp front, white outline rear sight **$290.00**

Ruger Security-Six 717

Ruger Redhawk

RUGER REDHAWK

Caliber: 357 Mag., 41 Mag., 44 Rem. Mag., 6-shot.
Barrel: 5½″, 7½″.
Weight: About 54 oz. (7½″ bbl.). **Length:** 13″ over-all.
Stocks: Square butt. American walnut.
Sights: Interchangeable Patridge-type front, rear adj. for w. & e.
Features: Stainless steel, brushed satin finish. Has a 9½″ sight radius. Introduced 1979.
Price: **$381.00**
Price: With Ruger stainless scope rings (44 Mag. only) **$408.50**

SMITH & WESSON M&P Model 10 REVOLVER
Caliber: 38 Special, 6 shot.
Barrel: 2″, 4″, 5″ or 6″.
Weight: 30½ oz. (4″ bbl.). **Length:** 9¼″ (4″ bbl.).
Stocks: Checkered walnut, Magna. Round or square butt.
Sights: Fixed, ⅛″ ramp front, square notch rear.
Price: Blued **$226.50**
Price: Nickeled **$245.00**

Smith & Wesson 38 M&P Heavy Barrel Model 10
Same as regular M&P except: 3″ or 4″ ribbed bbl. with ⅛″ ramp front sight, square rear, square butt, wgt. 34 oz.
Price: Blued **$226.50**
Price: Nickeled **$245.00**

S&W Model 10-H.B.

SMITH & WESSON 38 M&P AIRWEIGHT Model 12
Caliber: 38 Special, 6 shot.
Barrel: 2″ or 4″.
Weight: 18 oz. (2″ bbl.). **Length:** 6⅞″ over-all.
Stocks: Checkered walnut, Magna. Round or square butt.
Sights: Fixed, ⅛″ serrated ramp front, square notch rear.
Price: Blued **$299.50**
Price: Nickeled **$339.50**

SMITH & WESSON Model 13 H.B. M&P
Caliber: 357 and 38 Special, 6 shot.
Barrel: 3″ or 4″.
Weight: 34 oz. **Length:** 9¼″ over-all (4″ bbl.).
Stocks: Checkered walnut, service.
Sights: ⅛″ serrated ramp front, fixed square notch rear.
Features: Heavy barrel, K-frame, square butt.
Price: Blue, M-13 . . . . **$228.50**
Price: Nickel **$249.50**
Price: Model 65, as above in stainless steel **$259.00**

S&W Model 13

SMITH & WESSON COMBAT MASTERPIECE
Caliber: 38 Special (M15) or 22 LR (M18), 6 shot.
Barrel: 2″ or 4″ (M15) 4″ (M18).
Weight: Loaded, 22 36½ oz., 38 34 oz. **Length:** 9⅛″ (4″ bbl.).
Stocks: Checkered walnut, Magna. Grooved tangs and trigger.
Sights: Front, ⅛″ Baughman Quick Draw on ramp, micro click rear, adjustable for w. and e.
Price: Blued, M-15, 2″ or 4″ **$266.50**
Price: Nickel M-15, 2″ or 4″ **$287.00**
Price: Blued, M-18, 4″ (sq. butt, adj. sights) **$326.00**

S&W Model 19

SMITH & WESSON MODEL 17 K-22 MASTERPIECE
Caliber: 22 LR, 6-shot.
Barrel: 6″, 8⅜″.
Weight: 38½ oz. (6″ bbl.). **Length:** 11⅛″ over-all.
Stocks: Checkered walnut, service.
Sights: Patridge front, S&W micro. click rear adjustable for windage and elevation.
Features: Grooved tang and trigger. Polished blue finish.
Price: 6″ **$337.00**
Price: 8¾″ bbl. **$351.50**
Price: Model 48, as above in 22 Mag., 4″ or 6″ **$346.50**
Price: 8⅜″ bbl. **$363.00**

S&W Model 17

SMITH & WESSON 357 COMBAT MAGNUM Model 19
Caliber: 357 Magnum and 38 Special, 6 shot.
Barrel: 2½″, 4″, 6″.
Weight: 35 oz. **Length:** 9½″ (4″ bbl.).
Stocks: Checkered Goncalo Alves, target. Grooved tangs and trigger.
Sights: Front, ⅛″ Baughman Quick Draw on 2½″ or 4″ bbl., Patridge on 6″ bbl., micro click rear adjustable for w. and e.
Price: S&W Bright Blue or Nickel, adj. sights **$285.50**

SMITH & WESSON MODEL 24 44 SPECIAL
Caliber: 44 Special, 6-shot.
Barrel: 4″ or 6½″.
Weight: 41½ oz. (4″ bbl.). **Length:** 9½″ over-all (4″ bbl.).
Stocks: Checkered Goncalo Alves target-type.
Sights: Ramp front on 4″, Patridge front on 6½″; fully adjustable micrometer click rear.
Features: Limited production of 7,500 pieces. Built to the original specifications. Available only in S&W bright blue with grooved top strap and barrel rib. Reintroduced 1983.
Price: 4″ barrel **$358.50**
Price: 6½″ barrel **$387.00**

CAUTION: PRICES CHANGE. CHECK AT GUNSHOP.

SMITH & WESSON MODEL 25 REVOLVER
Caliber: 45 Colt, 6-shot.
Barrel: 4″, 6″, 8⅜″.
Weight: About 45 oz. **Length:** 11⅞″ over-all (6″ bbl.).
Stocks: Checkered Goncalo Alves, target-type.
Sights: ⅛″ S&W red ramp front, S&W micrometer click rear with white outline.
Features: Available in Bright Blue or nickel finish; target trigger, target hammer. Contact S&W for complete price list.
Price: 4″, 6″, blue or nickel $347.00
Price: 8⅜″, blue or nickel $359.50

S&W Model 25

SMITH & WESSON 357 MAGNUM M-27 REVOLVER
Caliber: 357 Magnum and 38 Special, 6 shot.
Barrel: 4″, 6″, 8⅜″.
Weight: 44 oz. (6″ bbl.). **Length:** 11¼″ (6″ bbl.).
Stocks: Checkered walnut, Magna. Grooved tangs and trigger.
Sights: Any S&W target front, micro click rear, adjustable for w. and e.
Price: S&W Bright Blue or Nickel, 4″, 6″. $327.00
Price: 8⅜″ bbl., sq. butt, target hammer, trigger, stocks $351.00

SMITH & WESSON HIGHWAY PATROLMAN Model 28
Caliber: 357 Magnum and 38 Special, 6 shot.
Barrel: 4″, 6″.
Weight: 44 oz. (6″ bbl.). **Length:** 11¼″ (6″ bbl.).
Stocks: Checkered walnut, Magna. Grooved tangs and trigger.
Sights: Front, ⅛″ Baughman Quick Draw, on plain ramp, micro click rear, adjustable for w. and e.
Price: S&W Satin Blue, sandblasted frame edging and barrel top ... $305.50
Price: With target stocks $327.00

S&W Model 29

SMITH & WESSON 44 MAGNUM Model 29 REVOLVER
Caliber: 44 Magnum, 44 Special or 44 Russian, 6 shot.
Barrel: 4″, 6″, 8⅜″, 10⅝″.
Weight: 47 oz. (6″ bbl.), 43 oz. (4″ bbl.). **Length:** 11⅞″ (6½″ bbl.).
Stocks: Oversize target type, checkered Goncalo Alves. Tangs and target trigger grooved, checkered target hammer.
Sights: ⅛″ red ramp front, micro click rear, adjustable for w. and e.
Features: Includes presentation case.
Price: S&W Bright Blue or Nickel 4″, 6″ $409.00
Price: 8⅜″ bbl., blue or nickel $423.50
Price: 10⅝″, blue only $423.50
Price: Model 629 (stainless steel), 4″, 6″ $472.50
Price: Model 629, 8⅜″ barrel $488.50

S&W Model 31

SMITH & WESSON 32 REGULATION POLICE Model 31
Caliber: 32 S&W Long, 6 shot.
Barrel: 2″, 3″.
Weight: 18¾ oz. (3″ bbl.). **Length:** 7½″ (3″ bbl.).
Stocks: Checkered walnut, Magna.
Sights: Fixed, ⅒″ serrated ramp front, square notch rear.
Features: Blued
Price: $276.00

SMITH & WESSON 1953 Model 34, 22/32 KIT GUN
Caliber: 22 LR, 6 shot.
Barrel: 2″, 4″.
Weight: 22½ oz. (4″ bbl.). **Length:** 8″ (4″ bbl. and round butt).
Stocks: Checkered walnut, round or square butt.
Sights: Front, ⅒″ serrated ramp, micro. click rear, adjustable for w. & e.
Price: Blued $271.00
Price: Nickeled $294.50
Price: Model 63, as above in stainless, 4″ $307.00

S&W Model 651

Smith & Wesson Model 650/651 Magnum Kit Gun
Similar to the Models 34 and 63 except chambered for the 22 WMR. Model 650 has 3″ barrel, round butt and fixed sights; Model 651 has 4″ barrel, square butt and adjustable sights. Both guns made of stainless steel. Introduced 1983.
Price: Model 650 .... $279.50
Price: Model 651 .... $307.00

SMITH & WESSON 38 CHIEFS SPECIAL & AIRWEIGHT
Caliber: 38 Special, 5 shot.
Barrel: 2″, 3″.
Weight: 19 oz. (2″ bbl.); 14 oz. (AIRWEIGHT). **Length:** 6½″ (2″ bbl. and round butt).
Stocks: Checkered walnut, Magna. Round or square butt.
Sights: Fixed, ⅒″ serrated ramp front, square notch rear.
Price: Blued, standard Model 36 .... $242.00
Price: As above, nickel $262.00
Price: Blued, Airweight Model 37 .... $274.50
Price: As above, nickel $310.50

Smith & Wesson 60 Chiefs Special Stainless
Same as Model 36 except: 2″ bbl. and round butt only.
Price: Stainless steel $304.00

SMITH & WESSON BODYGUARD MODEL 38
Caliber: 38 Special; 5 shot, double action revolver.
Barrel: 2″.
Weight: 14½ oz. **Length:** 6⅜″.
Stocks: Checkered walnut, Magna.
Sights: Fixed ⅒″ serrated ramp front, square notch rear.
Features: Alloy frame; integral hammer shroud.
Price: Blued $288.50
Price: Nickeled $326.00

S&W Model 38

Smith & Wesson Bodyguard Model 49 Revolver
Same as Model 38 except steel construction, weight 20½ oz.
Price: Blued $257.00
Price: Nickeled $280.00

SMITH & WESSON 41 MAGNUM Model 57 REVOLVER
Caliber: 41 Magnum, 6 shot.
Barrel: 4″, 6″ or 8⅜″.
Weight: 48 oz. (6″ bbl.). **Length:** 11⅜″ (6″ bbl.).
Stocks: Oversize target type checkered Goncalo Alves.
Sights: ⅛″ red ramp front, micro. click rear, adj. for w. and e.
Features: Includes presentation case.
Price: S&W Bright Blue or Nickel 4″, 6″ $347.00
Price: 8⅜″ bbl. $359.50

S&W Model 57

SMITH & WESSON MODEL 64 STAINLESS M&P
Caliber: 38 Special, 6-shot.
Barrel: 4″.
Weight: 30½ oz. **Length:** 9½″ over-all.
Stocks: Checkered walnut, service style.
Sights: Fixed, ⅛″ serrated ramp front, square notch rear.
Features: Satin finished stainless steel, square butt.
Price: $251.00

SMITH & WESSON MODEL 66 STAINLESS COMBAT MAGNUM
Caliber: 357 Magnum and 38 Special, 6-shot.
Barrel: 2½″, 4″, 6″.
Weight: 35 oz. **Length:** 9½″ over-all.
Stocks: Checkered Goncalo Alves target.
Sights: Front, ⅛″ Baughman Quick Draw on plain ramp, micro clock rear adj. for w. and e.
Features: Satin finish stainless steel, grooved trigger with adj. stop.
Price: $319.50

S&W Model 64-H.B.

SMITH & WESSON MODEL 67 K-38 STAINLESS COMBAT MASTERPIECE
Caliber: 38 Special, 6-shot.
Barrel: 4″.
Weight: 34 oz. (loaded). **Length:** 9⅛″ over-all.
Stocks: Checkered walnut, service style.
Sights: Front, ⅛″ Baughman Quick Draw on ramp, micro click rear adj. for w. and e.
Features: Stainless steel. Square butt frame with grooved tangs, grooved trigger with adj. stop.
Price: $313.00

SMITH & WESSON MODEL 586 Distinguished Combat Magnum
Caliber: 357 Magnum.
Barrel: 4″, 6″, both heavy.
Weight: 46 oz. (6″), 42 oz. (4″).
Stocks: Goncalo Alves target-type with speed loader cutaway.
Sights: Baughman red ramp front, S&W micrometer click rear (or fixed).
Features: Uses new L-frame, but takes all K-frame grips. Full length ejector rod shroud. Smooth combat-type trigger, semi-target type hammer. Trigger stop on 6″ models; 4″ models factory fitted with target hammer and trigger will have trigger stop. Also available in stainless as Model 686. Introduced 1981.
Price: Model 586 (blue only) $303.50
Price: Model 586, nickel $303.50
Price: Model 686 (stainless) $330.50
Price: Model 581 (fixed sight, blue), 4″ $239.00
Price: Model 581, nickel $262.00
Price: Model 681 (fixed sight, stainless) $276.00

S&W Model 586

SMITH & WESSON MODEL 547
Caliber: 9mm Parabellum
Barrel: 3″ or 4″ heavy.
Weight: 34 oz. (4″ barrel). **Length:** 9⅛″ over-all (4″ barrel).
Stocks: Checkered square butt Magna Service (4″), checkered walnut target, round butt (3″).
Sights: ⅛″ Serrated ramp front, fixed ⅛″ square notch rear.
Features: K-frame revolver uses special extractor system—no clips required. Has ¼″ half-spur hammer. Introduced 1981.
Price: Blue only $304.50

CAUTION: PRICES CHANGE. CHECK AT GUNSHOP.

TAURUS MODEL 66 REVOLVER
Caliber: 357 Magnum, 6-shot.
Barrel: 3″, 4″, 6″.
Weight: 35 ozs.
Stocks: Checkered walnut, target-type. Standard stocks on 3″.
Sights: Serrated ramp front, micro click rear adjustable for w. and e.
Features: Wide target-type hammer spur, floating firing pin, heavy barrel with shrouded ejector rod. Introduced 1978. From Taurus International.
Price: Blue, about $226.00
Price: Satin blue, about.. $226.00
Price: Model 65 (similar to M66 except has a fixed rear sight and ramp front), blue, about... $177.00
Price: Model 65, satin blue, about.............................. $188.00

Taurus Model 66

TAURUS MODEL 73 SPORT REVOLVER
Caliber: 32 S&W Long, 6-shot.
Barrel: 3″, heavy.
Weight: 22 oz. **Length:** 8¼″ over-all.
Stocks: Oversize target-type, checkered Brazilian walnut.
Sights: Ramp front, notch rear.
Features: Imported from Brazil by Taurus International.
Price: Blue, about $186.00
Price: Satin blue, about.. $198.00

TAURUS MODEL 80 STANDARD REVOLVER
Caliber: 38 Spec., 6-shot.
Barrel: 3″ or 4″.
Weight: 31 oz. (4″ bbl.). **Length:** 9¼″ over-all (4″ bbl.).
Stocks: Checkered Brazilian walnut.
Sights: Serrated ramp front, square notch rear.
Features: Imported from Brazil by Taurus International.
Price: Blue, about $170.00
Price: Satin blue, about.. $182.00

TAURUS MODEL 82 HEAVY BARREL REVOLVER
Caliber: 38 Spec., 6-shot.
Barrel: 3″ or 4″, heavy.
Weight: 33 oz. (4″ bbl.). **Length:** 9¼″ over-all (4″ bbl.).
Stocks: Checkered Brazilian walnut.
Sights: Serrated ramp front, square notch rear.
Features: Imported from Brazil by Taurus International.
Price: Blue, about $170.00
Price: Satin blue, about.. $182.00

TAURUS MODEL 83 REVOLVER
Caliber: 38 Spec., 6-shot.
Barrel: 4″ only, heavy.
Weight: 34½ oz.
Stocks: Over-size checkered walnut.
Sights: Ramp front, micro. click rear adj. for w. & e.
Features: Blue or nickel finish. Introduced 1977. Imported from Brazil by Taurus International.
Price: Blue, about $186.00
Price: Satin blue, about.. $198.00

Taurus Model 82

Dan Wesson 44 Magnum

TAURUS MODEL 85 REVOLVER
Caliber: 38 Spec., 5-shot.
Barrel: 3″.
Weight: 21 oz.
Stocks: Smooth walnut.
Sights: Ramp front, square notch rear.
Features: Blue or satin blue finish. Introduced 1980. Imported from Brazil by Taurus International.
Price: Blue, about $188.00
Price: Satin blue, about.. $201.00

DAN WESSON MODEL 41V & MODEL 44V
Caliber: 41 Mag., 44 Mag., six-shot.
Barrel: 4″, 6″, 8″, 10″; interchangeable.
Weight: 48 oz. (4″). **Length:** 12″ over-all (6″ bbl.).
Stocks: Smooth.
Sights: ⅛″ serrated front, white outline rear adjustable for windage and elevation.
Features: Available in blue or stainless steel. Smooth, wide trigger with adjustable over-travel; wide hammer spur. Available in Pistol Pac set also.
Price: 41 Mag., 4″, blue................................... $373.40
Price: As above except in stainless $416.05
Price: 44 Mag., 4″, blue................................... $373.40
Price: As above except in stainless $416.05

DAN WESSON MODEL 8-2 & MODEL 14-2
Caliber: 38 Special (Model 8-2); 357 (14-2), both 6-shot.
Barrel: 2½″, 4″, 6″, 8″; interchangeable.
Weight: 30 oz. (2½″). **Length:** 9¼″ over-all (4″ bbl.).
Stocks: Checkered, interchangeable.
Sights: ⅛″ serrated front, fixed rear.
Features: Interchangeable barrels and grips; smooth, wide trigger; wide hammer spur with short double action travel. Available in stainless or brite blue. Contact Dan Wesson for complete price list.
Price: Model 8-2, 2½″, blue $220.75
Price: As above except in stainless $253.65
Price: Model 14-2, 4″, blue.................................... $227.15
Price: As above except in stainless $259.20
Price: Model 714-2 Pistol Pac, stainless $430.65

Dan Wesson 9-2 & 15-2 Revolvers
Same as Models 8-2 and 14-2 except they have adjustable sight. Model 9-2 chambered for 38 Special, Model 15-2 for 357 Magnum. Available in blue or stainless. Contact Dan Wesson for complete price list.
Price: Model 9-2 or 15-2, 2½", blue **$272.50**
Price: As above except in stainless **$306.55**
Price: Model 15-2, 8", blue **$297.90**
Price: As above, with 15" barrel, blue **$365.25**

Dan Wesson Model 15-2

DAN WESSON MODEL 22 REVOLVER
Caliber: 22 LR, 22 Mag., six-shot.
Barrel: 2½", 4", 6", 8", 10"; interchangeable.
Weight: 36 oz. (2½"), 44 oz. (6"). **Length:** 9¼" over-all (4" barrel).
Stocks: Checkered; undercover, service or over-size target.
Sights: ⅛" serrated, interchangeable front, white outline rear adjustable for windage and elevation.
Features: Built on the same frame as the Dan Wesson 357; smooth, wide trigger with over-travel adjustment, wide spur hammer, with short double-action travel. Available in brite blue or stainless steel. Contact Dan Wesson for complete price list.
Price: 2½" bbl., blue **$272.50**
Price: As above, stainless **$306.55**
Price: With 4", vent. rib, blue **$300.85**
Price: As above, stainless **$335.15**
Price: Stainless Pistol Pac, 22 LR **$525.95**

Dan Wesson 22

HANDGUNS—SINGLE ACTION REVOLVERS

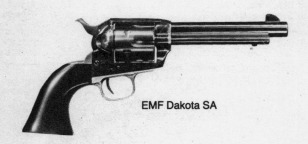

EMF Dakota SA

COLT NEW FRONTIER 22
Caliber: 22 LR, 6-shot.
Barrel: 4¾", 6", 7½".
Weight: 29½ oz. (4¾" bbl.). **Length:** 9⅝" over-all.
Stocks: Black composite rubber.
Sights: Ramp-style front, fully adjustable rear.
Features: Cross-bolt safety. Color case-hardened frame. Available in blue only. Re-introduced 1982.
Price: 4¾", blue **$283.50**
Price: 6", blue **$285.50**
Price: 7½", blue **$287.50**

DAKOTA SINGLE ACTION REVOLVERS
Caliber: 22 LR, 22 Mag., 357 Mag., 30 Carbine, 44-40, 45 Colt.
Barrel: 3½", 4⅝", 5½", 7½", 12", 16¼".
Weight: 45 oz. **Length:** 13" over-all (7½" bbl.).
Stocks: Smooth walnut.
Sights: Blade front, fixed rear.
Features: Colt-type hammer with firing pin, color case-hardened frame, blue barrel and cylinder, brass grip frame and trigger guard. Available in blue or nickel plated, plain or engraved. Imported by E.M.F.
Price: 22 LR, 30 Car., 357, 44-40, 45 L.C., 4⅝", 5½", 7½" **$295.00**
Price: 22 LR/22 Mag. Combo, 5½", 7½" **$330.00**
Price: 357, 44-40, 45, 12" **$330.00**
Price: 357, 44-40, 45, 3½" **$325.00**

F.I.E. TEXAS RANGER REVOLVER
Caliber: 22 LR, 22 Mag.
Barrel: 4¾", 7", 9",.
Weight: 31 oz. (4¾" bbl.). **Length:** 10" over-all.
Stocks: Stained hardwood.
Sights: Blade front, notch rear.
Features: Single-action, blue/black finish. Introduced 1983. Made in the U.S. by F.I.E.
Price: 22 LR, 4¾" **$69.95**
Price: As above, combo (22 LR/22 Mag.) **$84.95**
Price: 22 LR, 7" **$77.95**
Price: As above, combo (22 LR/22 Mag.) **$92.95**
Price: 22 LR, 9" **$84.95**
Price: As above, combo (22 LR/22 Mag.) **$99.95**

F.I.E. Texas Ranger

CAUTION: PRICES CHANGE. CHECK AT GUNSHOP.

F.I.E."HOMBRE" SINGLE ACTION REVOLVER
Caliber: 357 Mag., 44 Mag., 45 LC.
Barrel: 5½" or 7½".
Weight: 45 oz. (5½" bbl.).
Stocks: Smooth walnut with medallion.
Sights: Blade front, grooved topstrap (fixed) rear.
Features: Color case hardened frame. Bright blue finish. Super-smooth action.
Introduced 1979. Imported from West Germany by F.I.E. Corp.
Price: 357, 45 Colt **$179.95**
Price: 44 Mag. **$199.95**

F.I.E. Hombre

F.I.E. E15 BUFFALO SCOUT REVOLVER
Caliber: 22 LR/22 Mag., 6-shot.
Barrel: 4¾".
Weight: 32 oz. **Length:** 10" over-all.
Stocks: Black checkered nylon, walnut optional.
Sights: Blade front, fixed rear.
Features: Slide spring ejector. Blue, chrome, gold or blue with gold backstrap
and trigger guard models available.
Price: Blued, 22 LR, 4¾" **$59.95**
Price: Blue, 22 combo, 4¾" **$74.95**
Price: Chrome or blue/gold, 22 LR, 4¾" **$74.95**
Price: Chrome or blue/gold, combo, 4¾" **$89.95**
Price: Gold, 22 combo, 4¾" **$124.95**

FREEDOM ARMS 454 CASULL
Caliber: 454 Casull, 5-shot.
Barrel: 4¾", 7½", 10", 12".
Weight: 50 oz. **Length:** 14" over-all (7½" bbl.).
Stocks: Impregnated hardwood.
Sights: Blade front, notch or adjustable rear.
Features: All stainless steel construction; sliding bar safety system. Made in U.S.A.
Price: Fixed sight **$695.00**
Price: Adjustable sight **$795.00**

Freedom Arms 454 Casull

FREEDOM ARMS MINI REVOLVER
Caliber: 22 Short, Long, Long Rifle, 5-shot, 22 Mag., 4-shot.
Barrel: 1", 1¾", 3".
Weight: 4 oz. **Length:** 4" over-all.
Stocks: Black ebonite.
Sights: Blade front, notch rear.
Features: Made of stainless steel, simple take down; half-cock safety; floating
firing pin; cartridge rims recessed in cylinder. Comes in gun rug. Lifetime
warranty. Also available in percussion — see black powder section. From
Freedom Arms.
Price: 22 LR, 1" barrel **$105.35**
Price: 22 LR, 1¾" barrel **$105.35**
Price: 22 LR, 3" barrel **$118.70**
Price: 22 Mag., 1" barrel **$124.00**
Price: 22 Mag., 1¾" barrel **$124.00**
Price: 22 Mag., 3" barrel **$137.35**

Freedom Arms Mini Revolver

Freedom Arms Boot Gun
Similar to the Mini Revolver except has 3" barrel, weighs 5 oz. and is 5⅞"
over-all. Has over-size grips, floating firing pin. Made of stainless steel. Lifetime warranty. Comes in rectangular gun rug. Introduced 1982. From Freedom Arms.
Price: 22 LR **$118.70**
Price: 22 Mag. **$137.35**

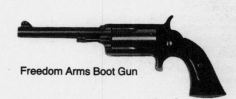
Freedom Arms Boot Gun

RUGER NEW MODEL SUPER BLACKHAWK STAINLESS
Caliber: 44 Magnum, 6-shot. Also fires 44 Spec.
Barrel: 7½" (6-groove, 20" twist), 10½".
Weight: 48 oz. (7½" bbl.) 51 oz. (10½" bbl.). **Length:** 13⅜" over-all (7½" bbl.).
Stocks: Genuine American walnut.
Sights: ⅛" ramp front, micro click rear adj. for w. and e.
Features: New Ruger interlocked mechanism, non-fluted cylinder, steel grip
and cylinder frame, square back trigger guard, wide serrated trigger and
wide spur hammer.
Price: **$325.00**

Ruger New Model Blackhawk

Ruger New Model 30 Carbine Blackhawk
Specifications similar to 44 Blackhawk. Fluted cylinder, round-back trigger
guard. Weight 44 oz., length 13⅛" over-all, 7½" barrel only.
Price: **$237.50**

Ruger Super Blackhawk KS 411 N

Ruger 357 Maximum

Ruger Super Single-Six

SEVILLE SINGLE ACTION REVOLVER
Caliber: 357 Mag., 357 Max./Super Mag., 375 USA Super Mag., 41 Mag., 44 Mag., 45 Colt, 454 Mag.
Barrel: 2½", 3½", 4⅝", 5½", 6½", 7½", 10½".
Weight: 52 oz. (4⅝", loaded)
Stocks: Smooth walnut, thumbrest, or Pachmayr.
Sights: Ramp front with red insert, fully adj. rear.
Features: Available in blue or stainless steel. Six-shot cylinder. From United Sporting Arms Inc.
Price: Blue. $325.00
Price: Blue with brass backstrap $320.00
Price: Stainless, all cals $375.00

Seville Stainless Super Mag
Similar to the standard Seville revolver except chambered for 357 Rem. Maximum, or 454 Magnum; 5½" or 7½" barrel only; grips of smooth walnut or Pachmayr rubber. Available only in stainless steel. Super Mag. and 454 Mag. in 7½" barrel only. Introduced 1983.
Price: 357 Maximum $400.00
Price: 454 Magnum $500.00

TANARMI S.A. REVOLVER MODEL TA22S LM
Caliber: 22 LR, 22 Mag., 6-shot.
Barrel: 4¾".
Weight: 32 oz. **Length:** 10" over-all.
Stocks: Walnut.
Sights: Blade front, rear adj. for w. & e.
Features: Manual hammer block safety; color hardened steel frame; brass backstrap and trigger guard. Imported from Italy by Excam.
Price: 22 LR/22 Mag. $103.00

Ruger New Model Super Blackhawk KS 411 N
Similar to the standard N.M. Super Blackhawk except has 10½" untapered bull barrel to provide extra weight; ejector rod and housing have been lengthened one inch to provide full-length ejection. Chambered only for 44 Mag.; target-type front and rear sights; smooth American walnut grips; weight is 54 oz. Introduced 1983.
Price: $325.00

RUGER NEW MODEL BLACKHAWK REVOLVER
Caliber: 357 or 41 Mag., 6-shot.
Barrel: 4⅝" or 6½", either caliber.
Weight: 42 oz. (6½" bbl). **Length:** 12¼" over-all (6½" bbl.).
Stocks: American walnut.
Sights: ⅛" ramp front, micro click rear adj. for w. and e.
Features: New Ruger interlocked mechanism, independent firing pin, hardened chrome-moly steel frame, music wire springs throughout.
Price: Blue, 357 . . . . $237.50
Price: Stainless steel (357) $307.50

Ruger New Model Blackhawk 357 Maximum
Similar to the standard N.M. Blackhawk except chambered for the 357 Maximum cartridge; available with either 7½" or 10½" bull barrel; weight with 7½" is 53 oz., with 10½" 55 oz.; over-all length with 10½" barrel is 16⅞". Introduced 1983. Anticipated engineering changes should be completed by mid-1984.
Price: $340.00

Ruger New Model 357/9mm Blackhawk
Same as the 357 Magnum except furnished with interchangeable cylinders for 9mm Parabellum and 357 Magnum cartridges.
Price: $260.00

RUGER NEW MODEL SUPER SINGLE-SIX CONVERTIBLE REVOLVER
Caliber: 22 S, L, LR, 6-shot. 22 Mag. in extra cylinder.
Barrel: 4⅝", 5½", 6½" or 9½" (6-groove).
Weight: 34½ oz. (6½" bbl.). **Length:** 11¹³⁄₁₆" over-all (6½" bbl.).
Stocks: Smooth American walnut.
Sights: Improved Patridge front on ramp, fully adj. rear protected by integral frame ribs.
Features: New Ruger "interlocked" mechanism, transfer bar ignition, gate-controlled loading, hardened chrome-moly steel frame, wide trigger, music wire springs throughout, independent firing pin.
Price: 4⅝", 5½", 6½", 9½" barrel $195.00
Price: 5½", 6½" bbl., stainless steel $265.00

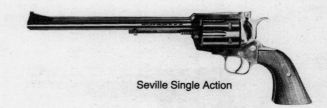

Seville Single Action

TANARMI SINGLE ACTION MODEL TA76
Same as TA22 models except blue backstrap and trigger guard.
Price: 22 LR, blue $59.00
Price: Combo, blue $75.50
Price: 22 LR, chrome $75.00
Price: Combo, chrome $89.00

CAUTION: PRICES CHANGE. CHECK AT GUNSHOP.

THE VIRGINIAN DRAGOON REVOLVER
Caliber: 44 Mag.
Barrel: 6″, 7½″, 8⅜″.
Weight: 50 oz. (6″ barrel). **Length:** 10″ over-all (6″ barrel).
Stocks: Smooth walnut.
Sights: Ramp-type Patridge front blade, micro. adj. target rear.
Features: Color case-hardened frame, spring-loaded floating firing pin, coil main spring. Firing pin is lock-fitted with a steel bushing. Introduced 1977. Made in the U.S. by Interarms Industries, Inc.
Price: 6″, 7½″, 8⅜″, blue. **$295.00**
Price: 44 Mag., 6″, 7½″, 8⅜″, stainless **$295.00**
Price: 44 Mag., 7½″, 8⅜″, 10½″ Sil. model **$425.00**

Virginian Dragoon

Virginian Dragoon Engraved Models
Same gun as the standard Dragoon except offered only in 44 Mag. 6″ or 7½″ barrel; choice of fluted or unfluted cylinder, stainless or blued. Hand-engraved frame, cylinder and barrel. Each gun comes in a felt-lined walnut presentation case. Introduced 1983.
Price: **$625.00**

Virginian Dragoon "Deputy" Model
Similar to the standard Dragoon except comes with traditional fixed sights, blue or stainless, in 357 (5″ barrel), 44 Mag. (6″ barrel). Introduced 1983.
Price: **$285.00**

VIRGINIAN 22 CONVERTIBLE REVOLVERS
Caliber: 22 LR, 22 Mag.
Barrel: 5½″.
Weight: 38 oz. **Length:** 10¾″ over-all.
Stocks: Smooth walnut.
Sights: Ramp-type Patridge front, open fully adjustable rear.
Features: Smaller version of the big-bore Dragoon revolvers; comes with both Long Rifle and Magnum cylinders, the latter unfluted; color case-hardened frame, rest blued. Introduced 1983. Made by Uberti; imported from Italy by Interarms.
Price: Blue, with two cylinders. **$219.00**
Price: Stainless with two cylinders **$249.00**

Virginian 22 Convertible

HANDGUNS—MISCELLANEOUS

ADVANTAGE ARMS 422 DERRINGER
Caliber: 22 LR, 22 Mag., 4-shot.
Barrel: 2½″.
Weight: 15 oz. **Length:** 4½″ over-all.
Stocks: Smooth walnut.
Sights: Fixed.
Features: Top break design with four barrels, double action trigger and rotating firing pin, spring loaded extractors. Nickel, blue or Q.P.Q. black finish. Introduced 1983. From Advantage Arms USA, Inc.
Price: 22 LR **$149.95**
Price: 22 Mag. **$159.95**

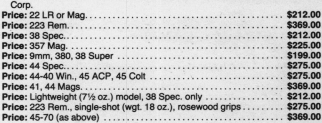

Advantage Arms 422

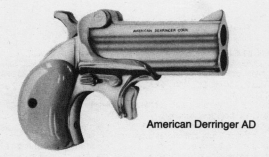

American Derringer AD

AMERICAN DERRINGER MODEL AD
Caliber: 22 LR, 22 Mag., 22 Hornet, 223 Rem., 30 Luger, 30-30 Win., 32 ACP, 38 Super, 380 ACP, 38 Spec., 9 × 18, 9mm Para., 357 Mag., 41 Mag., 44-40 Win., 44 Spec., 44 Mag., 45 Colt, 45 ACP.
Barrel: 3″.
Weight: 15½ oz. (38 Spec.). **Length:** 4.82″ over-all.
Stocks: Rosewood, Zebra wood.
Sights: Blade front.
Features: Made of stainless steel with high-polish or satin finish. Two shot capacity. Manual hammer block safety. Introduced 1980. Contact the factory for complete list of available calibers and prices. From American Derringer Corp.
Price: 22 LR or Mag. **$212.00**
Price: 223 Rem. **$369.00**
Price: 38 Spec. **$212.00**
Price: 357 Mag. **$225.00**
Price: 9mm, 380, 38 Super **$199.00**
Price: 44 Spec. **$275.00**
Price: 44-40 Win., 45 ACP, 45 Colt **$275.00**
Price: 41, 44 Mags. **$369.00**
Price: Lightweight (7½ oz.) model, 38 Spec. only **$212.00**
Price: 223 Rem., single-shot (wgt. 18 oz.), rosewood grips **$275.00**
Price: 45-70 (as above) **$369.00**

ARM TECH. DERRINGER
Caliber: 22 LR, 22 Mag., 4-shot.
Barrel: 2.6".
Weight: 19 ozs. **Length:** 4.6" over-all.
Stocks: Hard rubber or walnut, checkered or smooth.
Sights: Fixed, non-snagging.
Features: Four barrels with 90° rotating-indexing firing pin system. All stainless steel parts. Double-action only. Blued model available. Introduced 1983. From Armament Technologies Inc.
Price: Stainless, 22 LR, rubber grips $184.50
Price: As above, 22 Mag. $189.00
Price: Blued, 22 LR, walnut grips $174.50
Price: As above, 22 Mag. $179.00

HIGH STANDARD DERRINGER
Caliber: 22 LR, 22 Mag., 2 shot.
Barrel: 3½", over and under, rifled.
Weight: 11 oz. **Length:** 5" over-all.
Stocks: Smooth plastic.
Sights: Fixed, open.
Features: Hammerless, integral safety hammerblock, all steel unit is encased in a black, anodized alloy housing. Recessed chamber. Dual extraction. Top break, double action.
Price: Blue (M9194)... $135.00
Price: Blue (M9193), 22 LR $135.00
Price: Electroless nickel (M9420), 22 Mag....................... $175.00

LJUTIC LJ II PISTOL
Caliber: 22 Magnum.
Barrel: 2¾".
Stocks: Checkered walnut.
Sights: Fixed.
Features: Stainless steel; double action; ventilated rib; side-by-side barrels; positive on/off safety. Introduced 1981. From Ljutic Industries.
Price: $699.00

F.I.E. MODEL D-38 DERRINGER
Caliber: 38 Special.
Barrel: 3".
Weight: 14 oz.
Stocks: Checkered white nylon, walnut optional.
Sights: Fixed.
Features: Dyna-Chrome finish. Spur trigger. Tip-up barrel, extractors. Made in U.S. by F.I.E. Corp.
Price: With nylon grips $81.95
Price: With walnut grips $98.95

Ljutic Space Pistol

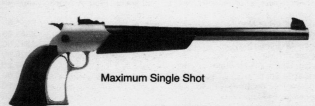

Maximum Single Shot

C. O. P. 357 MAGNUM
Caliber: 38/357 Mag., 4 shots.
Barrel: 3¼".
Weight: 28 oz. **Length:** 5.5" over-all.
Stocks: Checkered composition.
Sights: Open, fixed.
Features: Double-action, 4 barrels, made of stainless steel. Width is only one inch, height 4.1". From M & N Distributors.
Price: About $250.00
Price: In 22 Mag. $250.00
Price: In 22 LR (blued, aluminum frame)........................ $229.95

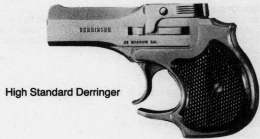

High Standard Derringer

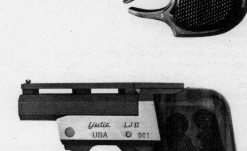

Ljutic LJ II Pistol

LJUTIC RECOILESS SPACE PISTOL
Caliber: 22 Mag., 357 Mag., 44 Mag., 308 Win.; single shot.
Barrel: 13½".
Weight: 5 lbs. (with scope).
Stocks: Walnut grip and fore-end.
Sights: Scope mounts furnished.
Features: Twist-bolt action; button trigger. From Ljutic Industries.
Price: $995.00

MAXIMUM SINGLE SHOT PISTOL
Caliber: 22 Hornet, 223 Rem., 22-250, 6mm BR, 6mm-223, 243, 250 Savage, 6.5mm-35, 7mm TCU, 7mm BR, 7mm-35, 7mm INT-R, 7mm-08, 30 Herrett, 308 Win., 357 Mag., 358 Win., 44 Mag.
Barrel: 10½", 14".
Weight: 61 oz. (10½" bbl.), 78 oz. (14" bbl.). **Length:** 15", 18½" over-all (with 10½" and 14" bbl., respectively).
Stocks: Smooth walnut stocks and fore-end.
Sights: Ramp front, fully adjustable open rear.
Features: Falling block action; drilled and tapped for most popular scope mounts; integral grip frame/receiver; adjustable trigger; Douglas barrel (interchangeable); Armoloy finish. Introduced 1983. Made in U.S. by M.O.A. Corp.
Price: Either barrel length...................................... $499.00
Price: Extra barrel $129.00
Price: Scope mount $39.00

CAUTION: PRICES CHANGE. CHECK AT GUNSHOP.

MERRILL SPORTSMAN'S SINGLE SHOT PISTOL

Caliber: 22 LR Sil., 22 Mag., 22 Hornet, 225 Win., 256 Win. Mag., 357 Mag., 357/44 B & D, 30-30 Win., 30 Herrett, 357 Herrett, 41 Mag., 44 Mag., 7mm Merrill, 30 Merrill, 7mm Rocket, 45-70.
Barrel: 9″ or 10¾″, semi-octagonal; .450″ wide vent. rib, matted to prevent glare; 14″ barrel in all except 22 cals.
Weight: About 54 oz. **Length:** 10½″ over-all (9″ bbl.)
Stocks: Smooth walnut with thumb and heel rest.
Sights: Front .125″ blade (.080″ blade optional); rear adj. for w. and e.
Features: Polished blue finish, hard chrome optional. Barrel is drilled and tapped for scope mounting. Cocking indicator visible from rear of gun. Has spring-loaded barrel lock, positive thumb safety. Trigger adjustable for weight of pull and over-travel. For complete price list contact Rock Pistol Mfg.
Price: 9″ barrel, about **$575.00**
Price: 10¾″, 22 Sil., about **$575.00**
Price: 10¾″ barrel, about **$575.00**
Price: 14″ barrel, about **$675.00**
Price: Extra barrel, 9″, 10¾″, about **$185.00**
Price: Extra 14″ bbl., about **$250.00**

Merrill Sportsman's Single Shot

Remington XP-100

REMINGTON MODEL XP-100 Bolt Action Pistol

Caliber: 221 Fireball, single shot.
Barrel: 10½″, ventilated rib.
Weight: 60 oz. **Length:** 16¾″.
Stock: Brown nylon one-piece, checkered grip with white spacers.
Sights: Fixed front, rear adj. for w. and e. Tapped for scope mount.
Features: Fits left or right hand, is shaped to fit fingers and heel of hand. Grooved trigger. Rotating thumb safety, cavity in fore-end permits insertion of up to five 38 cal., 130-gr. metal jacketed bullets to adjust weight and balance. Included is a black vinyl, zippered case.
Price: Including case **$349.00**

SEMMERLING LM-4 PISTOL

Caliber: 45 ACP.
Barrel: 3½″.
Weight: 24 oz. **Length:** 5.2″ over-all.
Stocks: Checkered black plastic.
Sights: Ramp front, fixed rear.
Features: Manually operated repeater. Over-all dimensions are 5.2″ x 3.7″ x 1″. Has a four-shot magazine capacity. Comes with manual, leather carrying case, spare stock screw and wrench. From Semmerling Corp.
Price: Complete **$894.00**
Price: Thin Version (blue sideplate instead of grips) **$894.00**

Semmerling LM-4

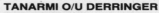

TANARMI O/U DERRINGER

Caliber: 38 Special.
Barrel: 3″.
Weight: 14 oz. **Length:** 4¾″ over-all.
Stocks: Checkered white nylon.
Sights: Fixed.
Features: Blue finish; tip-up barrel. Assembled in U.S. by Excam, Inc.
Price: **$75.00**

Thompson-Center Contender

THOMPSON-CENTER ARMS CONTENDER

Caliber: 221 Rem., 7mm T.C.U., 30-30 Win., 22 S, L, LR, 22 Mag., 22 Hornet, 256 Win., 6.5 T.C.U., 223 Rem., 30 & 357 Herrett, 357 Mag., 357 Rem. Max., also 222 Rem., 41 Mag., 44 Mag., 45 Long Colt, 45 Win. Mag., single shot.
Barrel: 10″, tapered octagon, bull barrel and vent. rib.
Weight: 43 oz. (10″ bbl.). **Length:** 13¼″ (10″ bbl.).
Stocks: Select walnut grip and fore-end, with thumb rest. Right or left hand.
Sights: Under cut blade ramp front, rear adj. for w. & e.
Features: Break open action with auto-safety. Single action only. Interchangeable bbls., both caliber (rim & centerfire), and length. Drilled and tapped for scope. Engraved frame. See T/C catalog for exact barrel/caliber availability.
Price: Blued (rimfire cals.) **$265.00**
Price: Blued (centerfire cals.). **$265.00**
Price: Extra bbls. (standard octagon) **$110.00**
Price: Bushnell Phantom scope base **$8.75**
Price: 357 and 44 Mag. vent. rib, internal choke bbl. **$125.00**

AKM Auto Rifle

AKM AUTO RIFLE
Caliber: 7.62x39, 30-shot magazine.
Barrel: 16.33″.
Weight: 6.4lbs. **Length:** 34.65″ over-all.
Stock: Laminated hardwood. Checkered composition pistol grip.
Sights: Protected post front, U-notch rear adjustable for elevation.
Features: Semi-auto only. Detachable box magazine. Cleaning kit, bayonet and scabbard, and sling available. Introduced to U.S. market 1982. Imported from Egypt by Gun South, Inc.
Price: Standard rifle. $995.00

Auto Ordnance 27 A-1

Auto-Ordnance 1927A-3 Thompson
A semi-auto only 22 caliber version of the 27A-1. Exact look-alike with alloy receiver. Weight is about 7 lbs., 16″ finned barrel, 10-, 30- and 50-shot magazines and drum. Introduced 1977. From Auto-Ordnance Corp.
Price: $519.95

AUTO-ORDNANCE MODEL 27 A-1 THOMPSON
Caliber: 45 ACP, 30-shot magazine.
Barrel: 16″.
Weight: 11½ lbs. **Length:** About 42″ over-all (Deluxe).
Stock: Walnut stock and vertical fore-end.
Sights: Blade front, open rear adj. for w.
Features: Re-creation of Thompson Model 1927. Semi-auto only. Deluxe model has finned barrel, adj. rear sight and compensator; Standard model has plain barrel and military sight. From Auto-Ordnance Corp.
Price: Deluxe $595.00
Price: Standard (horizontal fore-end) $575.00
Price: 1927A5 Pistol (M27A1 without stock; wgt. 7 lbs.) $556.00
Price: Lightweight model $469.95

BERETTA AR70 RIFLE
Caliber: 223, 30-shot magazine.
Barrel: 17¾″.
Weight: 8¼ lbs. **Length:** NA
Stock: Black high-impact plastic.
Sights: Blade front, diopter rear adjustable for windage and elevation.
Features: Matte black epoxy finish; easy take-down. Imported from Italy by Beretta U.S.A. Corp. Introduced 1984.
Price: $749.00

Consult our Directory pages for the location of firms mentioned.

BUSHMASTER AUTO RIFLE
Caliber: 223; 30-shot magazine
Barrel: 18½″.
Weight: 6¼ lbs. **Length:** 37.5″ over-all.
Stock: Rock maple
Sights: Protected post front adj. for elevation, protected quick-flip rear peep adj. for windage; short and long range.
Features: Steel alloy upper receiver with welded barrel assembly, AK-47-type gas system, aluminum lower receiver; silent sling and swivels; bayonet lug; one-piece welded steel alloy bolt carrier assembly. From Bushmaster Firearms.
Price: With maple stock $484.95
Price: With nylon-coated folding stock $494.95
Price: Matte electroless finish, maple stock $524.95
Price: As above, folding stock $534.95

Bushmaster Auto Rifle

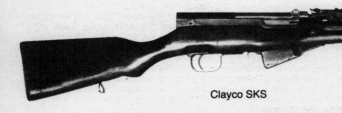

Clayco SKS

CLAYCO SKS CARBINE
Caliber: 7.62mm (M1943).
Barrel: 20.47″.
Weight: 8.84 lbs. **Length:** 40.16″ over-all.
Stock: Chinese Catalpa wood.
Sights: Hooded post front, tangent leaf rear.
Features: Chinese-made version of the Soviet SKS carbine. Has fixed, 10-round, double-row magazine. Comes with cleaning kit. Imported from China by Clayco Sports.
Price: $399.00

CAUTION: PRICES CHANGE. CHECK AT GUNSHOP.

CENTERFIRE RIFLES—MILITARY STYLE AUTOLOADERS

Colt AR-15 Sporter

COLT AR-15
Caliber: 223 Rem.
Barrel: 20".
Weight: 7½ lbs. **Length:** 38⅜" over-all.
Stock: Reinforced polycarbonate with buttstock stowage compartment.
Sights: Post front, rear adj. for w. and e.
Features: 5-round detachable box magazine, recoil pad, flash suppressor, sling swivels.
Price: **$599.95**

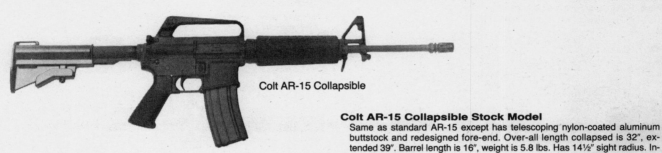

Colt AR-15 Collapsible

Colt AR-15 Collapsible Stock Model
Same as standard AR-15 except has telescoping nylon-coated aluminum buttstock and redesigned fore-end. Over-all length collapsed is 32", extended 39". Barrel length is 16", weight is 5.8 lbs. Has 14½" sight radius. Introduced 1978.
Price: **$659.95**

COMMANDO ARMS CARBINE
Caliber: 45 ACP.
Barrel: 16½".
Weight: 8 lbs. **Length:** 37" over-all.
Stock: Walnut buttstock.
Sights: Blade front, peep rear.
Features: Semi-auto only. Cocking handle on left side. Choice of magazines— 5, 20, 30 or 90 shot. From Commando Arms.
Price: Mark 9 or Mark 45, blue **$219.00**
Price: Nickel plated **$254.00**

DEMRO TAC-1M CARBINE
Caliber: 9mm (32-shot magazine), 45 ACP (30-shot magazine).
Barrel: 16⅞".
Weight: 7¾ lbs. **Length:** 35¾" over-all.
Stock: American walnut, removable.
Sights: Removable blade front, open rear adjustable for w. & e.
Features: Fires from open bolt. Thumb safety, integral muzzle brake. From Demro Products.
Price: **$523.25**
Price: With fitted attache case **$575.40**

Demro TAC-1M

Demro XF-7 Wasp Carbine
Similar to the TAC-1 Carbine except has collapsible buttstock, high impact synthetic fore-end and pistol grip. Has 5, 15 or 30-shot magazine (45 ACP) or 32-shot magazine (9mm).
Price: **$619.20**
Price: With fitted attache case **$685.60**

FN-LAR Paratrooper 308 Match 50-64
Similar to FN-LAR competition except with folding skeleton stock, shorter barrel, modified rear sight. Imported by Gun South, Inc.
Price: **$1,822.27**

FN-LAR Competition

FN-LAR COMPETITION AUTO
Caliber: 308 Win., 20-shot magazine.
Barrel: 21" (24" with flash hider).
Weight: 9 lbs., 7 oz. **Length:** 44½" over-all.
Stock: Black composition butt, fore-end and pistol grip.
Sights: Post front, aperture rear adj. for elevation, 200 to 600 meters.
Features: Has sling swivels, carrying handle, rubber recoil pad. Consecutively numbered pairs available at additional cost. Imported by Gun South, Inc.
Price: **$1,744.31**

FN 308 Model 50-63
Similar to the FN-LAR except has 18" barrel, skeleton-type folding buttstock, folding cocking handle. Introduced 1982. Imported from Belgium by Gun South, Inc. Distr., Inc.
. . . . **$2,016.79**

FNC Auto Rifle

FNC AUTO RIFLE
Caliber: 223 Rem.
Barrel: 18".
Weight: 9.61 lbs.
Stock: Synthetic stock.
Sights: Post front; flip-over aperture rear adj. for elevation.
Features: Updated version of FN-FAL in shortened carbine form. Has 30-shot box magazine, synthetic pistol grip, fore-end. Introduced 1981. Imported by Gun South, Inc.
Price: Standard model **$1,243.75**
Price: Paratrooper, with folding stock **$1,438.50**

FN-LAR Heavy Barrel 308 Match
Similar to FN-LAR competition except has wooden stock and fore-end, heavy barrel, folding metal bipod. Imported by Gun South, Inc.
Price: With wooden, stock **$2,310.77**
Price: With synthetic stock **$2,132.65**

FEDERAL XC-450 AUTO
Caliber: 45 ACP, 30-shot magazine.
Barrel: 16½".
Weight: 8½ lbs. **Length:** 34½" over-all.
Stock: Tubular steel.
Sights: Globe front, peep rear.
Features: Semi-automatic only; fires from closed bolt. All machined steel; Parkerized finish; quick take-down. Introduced 1984. From Wilkerson Firearms.
Price: **$586.98**
Price: XC-900 (9mm Para., 32-shot magazine, wgt. 8 lbs.) **$534.33**
Price: XC-220 (22 LR, 28-shot magazine, wgt. 7½ lbs.), illus.. . . . . . . **$349.95**

Federal XC-450

GALIL 308 SEMI-AUTO RIFLE
Caliber: 308 Win., 20-shot magazine.
Barrel: 21".
Weight: 8.7 lbs. **Length:** 41.3" over-all (stock extended).
Stock: Tube-type metal folding stock.
Sights: Post-type front, flip-type "L" rear.
Features: Gas operated, rotating bolt. Cocking handle, safety and magazine catch can be operated from either side. Introduced 1982. Imported from Israel by Magnum Research Inc.
Price: **$1,099.00**
Price: As above in 223 (18.1" bbl., 38.6" o.a.l.). **$999.00**

Galil Auto Rifle

HECKLER & KOCH HK-91 AUTO RIFLE
Caliber: 308 Win., 5- or 20-shot magazine.
Barrel: 17.71".
Weight: 9½ lbs. **Length:** 40¼" over-all.
Stock: Black high-impact plastic.
Sights: Post front, aperture rear adj. for w. and e.
Features: Delayed roller lock action. Sporting version of West German service rifle. Takes special H&K clamp scope mount. Imported from West Germany by Heckler & Koch, Inc.
Price: HK-91 A-2 with plastic stock. **$640.00**
Price: HK-91 A-3 with retractable metal stock **$699.00**
Price: HK-91 scope mount **$180.00**

Heckler & Koch HK-93 Auto Rifle
Similar to HK-93 except in 223 cal., 16.13" barrel, over-all length of 35½", weighs 7¾ lbs. Same stock, fore-end.
Price: HK-93 A-2 with plastic stock **$640.00**
Price: HK-93 A-3 with retractable metal stock **$699.00**

Heckler & Koch HK-91

HECKLER & KOCH HK-94 AUTO CARBINE
Caliber: 9mm Parabellum, 15-shot magazine.
Barrel: 16".
Weight: 6½ lbs. (fixed stock). **Length:** 34¾" over-all.
Stock: High-impact plastic butt and fore-end or retractable metal stock.
Sights: Hooded post front, aperture rear adjustable for windage and elevation.
Features: Delayed roller-locked action; accepts H&K quick-detachable scope mount. Introduced 1983. Imported from West Germany by Heckler & Koch.
Price: HK94-A2 (fixed stock) **$650.00**
Price: HK94-A3 (retractable metal stock) **$720.00**
Price: 30-shot magazine. **$25.00**
Price: Clamp to hold two magazines **$29.00**

CAUTION: PRICES CHANGE. CHECK AT GUNSHOP.

CENTERFIRE RIFLES—MILITARY STYLE AUTOLOADERS

Iver Johnson PM 30HB

IVER JOHNSON PM30HB CARBINE
Caliber: 30 U.S. Carbine, 5.7 MMJ.
Barrel: 18″ four-groove.
Weight: 6½ lbs. **Length:** 35½″ over-all.
Stock: Glossy-finished hardwood or walnut.
Sights: Click adj. peep rear.
Features: Gas operated semi-auto carbine. 15-shot detachable magazine.
Price: Blue finish, hardwood stock $203.00
Price: Stainless steel, walnut stock $253.00
Price: Blue finish, walnut stock $211.00

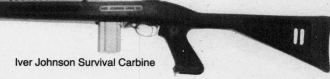

Iver Johnson Survival Carbine

Iver Johnson Survival Carbine
Similar to the stainless steel military carbine except has one-piece muzzle brake/flash hider, black DuPont Zytel stock with vertical pistol grip. Introduced 1983.
Price: $253.00
Price: With folding stock $297.00
Price: In blue steel $211.00
Price: As above with folding stock $250.00

Ruger Mini-14

RUGER MINI-14 RANCH RIFLE
Caliber: 222, 223 Rem., 5-shot detachable box magazine.
Barrel: 18½″.
Weight: 6.4 lbs. **Length:** 37¼″ over-all.
Stock: American hardwood, steel reinforced.
Sights: Ramp front, fully adj. rear.
Features: Fixed piston gas-operated, positive primary extraction. Ruger S100R scope rings included. 20-shot magazines available from Ruger dealers, 30-shot magazine available only to police departments and government agencies.
Price: $362.50
Price: As above except in stainless steel, 223-cal. only, no rings $375.00

Ruger Mini-4 Folding Stock

Ruger Mini-14 Folding Stock
Same as the Ranch Rifle except available only in 223 and has a folding stock, checkered high impact plastic verticle pistol grip. Over-all length with stock open is 37¾″, length closed is 27½″. Weight is about 7¾ lbs.
Price: Blued ordnance steel $409.50
Price: Stainless $454.00

SIG-AMT

SIG-AMT AUTO RIFLE
Caliber: 308 Win. (7.62mm NATO), 20-shot magazine.
Barrel: 18¾″.
Weight: 9½ lbs. **Length:** 39″ over-all.
Stock: Walnut butt and fore-end, black grooved synthetic pistol grip.
Sights: Adjustable post front, adjustable aperture rear.
Features: Roller-locked breech system with gas-assisted action; right-side cocking lever; loaded chamber indicator. No tools needed for take-down. Comes with bipod and winter trigger. Spare 5- and 10-shot magazines available. Imported from Switzerland by Osborne's Supplies. Introduced 1984.
Price: About. $2,500.00

SIG PE-57 AUTO RIFLE
Caliber: 7.5mm Swiss, 24-round box magazine.
Barrel: 23.8″, with flash suppressor.
Weight: 12.6 lbs. **Length:** 43.6″ over-all.
Stock: Black high-impact synthetic butt and pistol grip.
Sights: Folding hooded post front, folding click-adjustable aperture rear.
Features: Semi-automatic, gas-assisted delayed roller-lock action; bayonet lug, bipod, winter trigger, leather sling, maintenance kit, and 6-round magazine included; quick detachable scope mount optional. Imported from Switzerland by Osborne's Supplies. Introduced 1984.
Price: About. $2,500.00

SIG-StG 57 AUTO RIFLE
Caliber: 308 Win., 20-shot detachable box magazine.
Barrel: 18¾".
Weight: 9½ lbs. **Length:** 39" over-all.
Stock: Walnut stock and fore-end, composition vertical p.g.
Sights: Adj. post front, adj. aperture rear.
Features: Roller-lock breech, gas-assisted action; right-side cocking handle; loaded chamber indicator; no-tool take-down. Winter trigger (optional) allows firing with mittens. Spare parts, magazine, etc. available. From Mandall Shooting Supplies.
Price: $2,000.00

SPRINGFIELD ARMORY M1 GARAND RIFLE
Caliber: 30-06, 8-shot clip.
Barrel: 24".
Weight: 9½ lbs. **Length:** 43½" over-all.
Stock: Walnut, military.
Sights: Military square blade front, click adjustable peep rear.
Features: Commercially-made M-1 Garand duplicates the original service rifle. Introduced 1979. From Springfield Armory.
Price: Standard, about $560.00
Price: National Match, about $670.00
Price: Ultra Match, about $760.00

Springfield Armory M1A

SPRINGFIELD ARMORY M1A RIFLE
Caliber: 7.62mm Nato (308), 5-, 10- or 20-round box magazine.
Barrel: 25¹⁄₁₆" with flash suppressor, 22" without suppressor.
Weight: 8¾ lbs. **Length:** 44¼" over-all.
Stock: American walnut or birch with walnut colored heat-resistant fiberglass handguard. Matching walnut handguard available.

Sights: Military, square blade front, full click-adjustable aperture rear.
Features: Commercial equivalent of the U.S. M-14 service rifle with no provision for automatic firing. From Springfield Armory. Military accessories available including 3x-9x2 ART scope and mount.
Price: Standard M1A Rifle, about $650.00
Price: Match Grade, about $795.00
Price: Super Match (heavy Premium barrel), about $895.50
Price: M1A-A1 Assault Rifle, about $775.00

Springfield Armory BM-59

SPRINGFIELD ARMORY BM-59
Caliber: 7.62mm NATO (308 Win.); 20-round box magazine.
Barrel: 17.5".
Weight: 9¼ lbs. **Length:** 38.5" over-all.

Stock: Walnut, with trapped rubber butt pad.
Sights: Military square blade front, click adj. peep rear.
Features: Full military-dress Italian service rifle. Available in selective fire or semi-auto only. Refined version of the M-1 Garand. Accessories available include: folding alpine stock, muzzle brake/flash suppressor/grenade launcher combo, bipod, winter trigger, grenade launcher sights, bayonet, oiler. Extremely limited quantities. Introduced 1981.
Price: Standard Italian model, about $780.00
Price: Ital-Alpine model, about $940.00
Price: Alpine Paratrooper model, about $1,100.00
Price: Nigerian Mark IV model, about $875.00

STERLING MARK 6 CARBINE
Caliber: 9mm Parabellum, 34-shot magazine.
Barrel: 16.1".
Weight: 7½ lbs. **Length:** 35" over-all (stock extended), 27" folded.
Stock: Folding, metal skeleton.
Sights: Post front, flip-type peep rear.
Features: Semi-auto version of Sterling submachine gun. Comes with extra 8" display barrel. Black wrinkle finish paint on exterior. Blowback operation with floating firing pin. Imported from England by Lanchester U.S.A. Introduced 1983.
Price: About $595.00

Sterling Mark 6 Carbine

STEYR A.U.G. AUTOLOADING RIFLE
Caliber: 223 Rem.
Barrel: 16", 20", 24", interchangeable.
Weight: 7.2 lbs. (16" bbl.) **Length:** 27" over-all (16" bbl.).
Stock: Synthetic, green. One-piece moulding houses receiver group, hammer mechanism and magazine.
Sights: 1.5x scope only; scope and mount form the carrying handle.
Features: Semi-automatic, gas-operated action; can be converted to suit right or left-handed shooters, including ejection port. Transparent 30- or 40-shot magazines. Folding vertical front grip. Introduced 1983. Imported from Austria by Interarms.
Price: $1,160.00

Steyr A.U.G. Rifle

CAUTION: PRICES CHANGE. CHECK AT GUNSHOP.

Universal 1006 Carbine

UNIVERSAL 1003 AUTOLOADING CARBINE
Caliber: 30 M1, 5-shot magazine.
Barrel: 16", 18".
Weight: 5½ lbs. **Length:** 35½" over-all.
Stock: American hardwood stock inletted for "issue" sling and oiler, blued metal handguard.
Sights: Blade front with protective wings, adj. rear.
Features: Gas operated, cross lock safety. Receiver tapped for scope mounts.
Price: **$196.00**
Price: Model 1256 "Ferret" in 256 Win. **$219.00**

Universal Commemorative Model 1981 Carbine
Same basic specs as Model 1003 Carbine except comes with 5-, 15- and 30-shot magazines, Weaver scope and mount, bayonet and scabbard, brass belt buckle—all in a foam-fitted case. Stock is of select black walnut with inletted medallion. Metal parts are Parkerized. Introduced 1981.
Price: Complete **$650.00**

Universal Model 1006 Stainless Steel Carbine
Similar to the Model 1003 Carbine except made of stainless steel. Barrel length 16" or 18". Weighs 6 lbs., birch stock with satin finish walnut optional. Introduced 1982.
Price: **$235.00**

Universal 5000 Carbine

Universal Model 5000PT Carbine
Same as standard Model 1003 except comes with "Schmeisser-type paratrooper" folding stock. Barrel length 18". Over-all length open 36"; folded 26".
Price: Blue. **$235.00**
Price: As above with 16" bbl. (Model 5016). **$235.00**
Price: As above, stainless steel (Model 5006) **$281.00**

Universal Model 1005 SB Carbine
Same as Model 1003 except has "Super-Mirrored" blue finish, walnut Monte Carlo stock, deluxe barrel band. Also available finished in nickel (Model 1010N), 18K gold (Model 1015G), Raven Black Du Pont Teflon-S (Model 1020TB) or Camouflage Olive Teflon-S (Model 1025TCO).
Price: Model 1005SB **$218.50**
Price: Model 1010N. **$272.00**
Price: Model 1015G. **$304.50**
Price: Model 1020TB 1030 Teflon gray **$264.00**

> Consult our Directory pages for the location of firms mentioned.

UZI Carbine

UZI CARBINE
Caliber: 9mm Parabellum, 25-round magazine.
Barrel: 16.1".
Weight: 8½ lbs. **Length:** 24.2" (stock folded).
Stock: Folding metal stock.
Sights: Post-type front, "L" flip-type rear adj. for 100 meters and 200 meters.
Features: Adapted by Col. Uzi Gal to meet BATF regulations, this semi-auto has the same qualities as the famous submachine gun. Made by Israel Military Industries. Comes in molded Styrofoam case with sling, magazine and a short "display only" barrel. Exclusively imported from Israel by Action Arms Ltd. Introduced 1980.
Price: **$627.00**

Valmet M78 (NATO) Semi-Auto Rifle
Similar to M78 Standard rifle except is chambered for 7.62 x 51 NATO (308 Win.). Has straight 20-round box magazine, rubber recoil pad, folding carrying handle. Introduced 1981. Imported by Odin International. Also available as M78HV chambered for 223. Same price.
Price: **$725.00**

Valmet M78 Rifle

VALMET M78 STANDARD RIFLE
Caliber: 7.62 x 39.
Barrel: 24".
Weight: 10.5 lbs. **Length:** 43" over-all.
Stock: Birch buttstock, composition fore-end and pistol grip.
Sights: Hooded post front, open fully adj. rear with "night sight" blade.
Features: Semi-automatic only. Uses basic Kalishnikov action. Introduced 1982. Imported by Odin International.
Price: **$725.00**

CENTERFIRE RIFLES—MILITARY STYLE AUTOLOADERS

Valmet M-76

VALMET M-76 CARBINE
Caliber: 223, 15 or 30-shot magazine.
Barrel: 18".
Weight: About 8½ lbs. **Length:** 37¾" over-all.
Stock: Wood or folding metal type; composition fore-end.
Sights: Hooded adjustable post front, peep rear with luminous night sight.
Features: Semi-automatic only. Has sling swivels, flash supressor. Bayonet, cleaning kit, 30-shot magazine, scope adaptor cover optional. Imported from Finland by Valmet, Inc.
Price: Wood stock **$686.00**
Price: Folding stock **$873.00**

Weaver Nighthawk

WEAVER ARMS NIGHTHAWK
Caliber: 9mm Para., 25-shot magazine.
Barrel: 16.1".
Weight: 7 lbs. **Length:** 26½" (stock retracted).
Stock: Retractable metal frame.
Sights: Hooded blade front, adjustable peep V rear.
Features: Semi-auto fire only; fires from a closed bolt. Has 21" sight radius. Black nylon pistol grip and finger-groove front grip. Matte black finish. Introduced 1983. From Weaver Arms Corp.
Price: With black web sling **$525.00**

Wilkinson "Terry"

WILKINSON "TERRY" CARBINE
Caliber: 9mm Para., 30-shot magazine.
Barrel: 16³⁄₁₆".
Weight: 7 lbs. 2 oz. **Length:** 28½" over-all.
Stock: Maple stock and fore-end, grip is PVC plastic.
Sights: Williams adjustable.
Features: Closed breech, blow-back action. Bolt-type safety and magazine catch. Ejection port has spring operated cover. Receiver dovetailed for scope mount. Semi-auto only. Introduced 1977. From Wilkinson Arms.
Price: **$488.00**

CENTERFIRE RIFLES—SPORTING AUTOLOADERS

Browning Auto Rifle

Browning Magnum Auto Rifle
Same as the standard caliber model, except weighs 8⅜ lbs., 45" over-all, 24" bbl., 3-round mag. Cals. 7mm Mag., 300 Win. Mag.
Price: Grade I $547.95
Price: Grade III $1,160.00
Price: Grade IV $2,150.00

Browning Commemorative BAR
Similar to the standard BAR except has silver grey receiver with engraved and gold inlaid whitetail deer on the right side, a mule deer on the left; a gold-edged scroll banner frames "One of Six Hundred" on the left side, the numerical edition number replaces "One" on the right. Chambered only in 30-06. Fancy, highly figured walnut stock and fore-end. Introduced 1983.
Price: $3,550.00

BROWNING HIGH-POWER AUTO RIFLE
Caliber: 243, 270, 30-06, 308.
Barrel: 22" round tapered.
Weight: 7⅜ lbs. **Length:** 43" over-all.
Stock: French walnut p.g. stock (13⅝"x2"x1⅝") and fore-end, hand checkered.
Sights: Adj. folding-leaf rear, gold bead on hooded ramp front.
Features: Detachable 4-round magazine. Receiver tapped for scope mounts. Trigger pull 3½ lbs. Gold plated trigger on Grade IV. Imported from Belgium by Browning.
Price: Grade I $524.95
Price: Grade III $1,100.00
Price: Grade IV $2,090.00

CAUTION: PRICES CHANGE. CHECK AT GUNSHOP.

HECKLER & KOCH HK770 AUTO RIFLE

Caliber: 308 Win., 3-shot magazine.
Barrel: 19.6".
Weight: 7½ lbs. **Length:** 42.8" over-all.
Stock: European walnut. Checkered p.g. and fore-end.
Sights: Vertically adjustable blade front, open, fold-down rear adj. for w.
Features: Has the delayed roller-locked system and polygonal rifling. Magazine catch located at front of trigger guard. Receiver top is dovetailed to accept clamp-type scope mount. Imported from West Germany by Heckler & Koch, Inc.

Heckler & Koch HK770

Price: $560.00
Price: HK630, 223 Rem. $560.00
Price: HK940, 30-06 .... $580.00
Price: Scope mount with 1" rings $113.00

Heckler & Koch SL7

HECKLER & KOCH SL7 AUTO RIFLE

Caliber: 308 Win., 3-shot magazine.
Barrel: 17".
Weight: 8 lbs. **Length:** 39¾" over-all.

Stock: European walnut, oil finished.
Sights: Hooded post front, adjustable aperture rear.
Features: Delayed roller-locked action; polygon rifling; receiver is dovetailed for H&K quick-detachable scope mount. Introduced 1983. Imported from West Germany by Heckler & Koch.
Price: $500.00
Price: Model SL6 (as above except in 223 Rem.) $500.00
Price: Quick-detachable scope mount $113.00
Price: 10-shot magazine $24.00

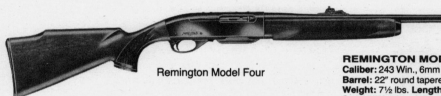

Remington Model Four

REMINGTON MODEL FOUR AUTO RIFLE

Caliber: 243 Win., 6mm Rem., 270 Win., 7mm Exp. Rem., 308 Win. and 30-06.
Barrel: 22" round tapered.
Weight: 7½ lbs. **Length:** 42" over-all.
Stock: Walnut, deluxe cut checkered p.g. and fore-end. Full cheekpiece, Monte Carlo.
Sights: Gold bead front sight on ramp; step rear sight with windage adj.
Features: Redesigned and improved version of the Model 742. Positive cross-bolt safety. Receiver tapped for scope mount. 4-shot clip mag. Has cartridge head medallion denoting caliber on bottom of receiver. Introduced 1981.
Price: $510.00
Price: Peerless Grade $2,345.00
Price: Premier Grade $4,832.00
Price: Premier Grade with gold inlays $7,247.00

Remington Model 7400 Auto Rifle

Similar to Model Four except does not have full cheekpiece Monte Carlo stock, has slightly different fore-end design, impressed checkering, no cartridge head medallion. Introduced 1981.
Price: $461.95

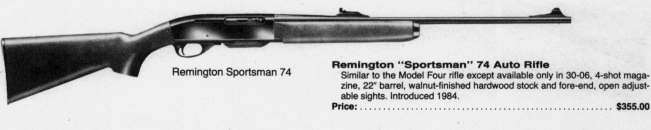

Remington Sportsman 74

Remington "Sportsman" 74 Auto Rifle

Similar to the Model Four rifle except available only in 30-06, 4-shot magazine, 22" barrel, walnut-finished hardwood stock and fore-end, open adjustable sights. Introduced 1984.
Price: $355.00

Ruger 44 Carbine

RUGER 44 AUTOLOADING CARBINE

Caliber: 44 Magnum, 4-shot tubular magazine.
Barrel: 18½" round tapered.
Weight: 5¾ lbs. **Length:** 36¾" over-all.
Stock: One-piece walnut p.g. stock (13⅜"x1⅝"x2¼").
Sights: ¹⁄₁₆" front, folding leaf rear sight adj. for e.
Features: Wide, curved trigger. Sliding cross-bolt safety. Receiver tapped for scope mount, unloading button.
Price: $332.00

Browning 1895

BROWNING MODEL 1895 LEVER ACTION RIFLE
Caliber: 30-06, 4-shot magazine.
Barrel: 24", round.
Weight: 8 lbs. **Length:** 42" over-all.
Stock: Straight grip walnut stock and fore-end with matte finish. High Grade has Grade III French walnut, fine checkering, high gloss finish.
Sights: Gold bead on elevated ramp front, buckhorn rear with elevator.
Features: Exact replica of John M. Browning's first successful box-magazine lever-action repeater. Top loading magazine, half-cock hammer safety. High Grade model has gold plated moose and grizzly on engraved and grey receiver. Introduced 1984.
Price: Grade I **$499.95**
Price: High Grade **$750.00**

Browning B-92

BROWNING B-92 LEVER ACTION
Caliber: 357 Mag., 44 Rem. Mag., 11-shot magazine.
Barrel: 20" round.
Weight: 5 lbs., 8 oz. **Length:** 37½" over-all.
Stock: Straight grip stock and classic fore-end in French walnut with high gloss finish. Steel, modified crescent buttplate. (12¾" x 2 " x 2⅞").
Sights: Post front, classic cloverleaf rear with notched elevation ramp. Sight radius 16⅝".
Features: Tubular magazine. Follows design of original Model 92 lever-action. Introduced 1979. Imported from Japan by Browning.
Price: **$324.95**

Browning BLR

BROWNING BLR LEVER ACTION RIFLE
Caliber: 22-250, 243, 257 Roberts, 7mm-08, 308 Win. or 358 Win. 4-shot detachable mag.
Barrel: 20" round tapered.
Weight: 6 lbs. 15 oz. **Length:** 39¾" over-all.
Stock: Checkered straight grip and fore-end, oil finished walnut.
Sights: Gold bead on hooded ramp front; low profile square notch adj. rear.
Features: Wide, grooved trigger; half-cock hammer safety. Receiver tapped for scope mount. Recoil pad installed. Imported from Japan by Browning.
Price: **$394.95**

Dixie Model 1873

DIXIE ENGRAVED MODEL 1873 RIFLE
Caliber: 44-40, 11-shot magazine.
Barrel: 20", round.
Weight: 7¾ lbs. **Length:** 39" over-all.
Stock: Walnut.
Sights: Blade front, adj. rear.
Features: Engraved and case hardened frame. Duplicate of Winchester 1873. Made in Italy. From Dixie Gun Works.
Price: **$550.00**
Price: Plain, blued carbine **$495.00**

Marlin 1894S

MARLIN 1894S LEVER ACTION CARBINE
Caliber: 44 Magnum, 10-shot tubular magazine
Barrel: 20" Micro-Grove®.
Weight: 6 lbs. **Length:** 37½".
Stock: American black walnut, straight grip and fore-end. Mar-Shield® finish.
Sights: Wide-Scan® hooded ramp front, semi-buckhorn folding rear adj. for w. & e.
Features: Hammer block safety. Receiver tapped for scope mount, offset hammer spur, solid top receiver sand blasted to prevent glare.
Price: **$280.95**

Marlin Model 1894CS Carbine
   Similar to the standard Model 1894S except chambered for 38 Special/357 Magnum with 9-shot magazine, 18½" barrel, hammer block safety, brass bead front sight. Introduced 1983.
Price: **$280.95**

CAUTION: PRICES CHANGE. CHECK AT GUNSHOP.

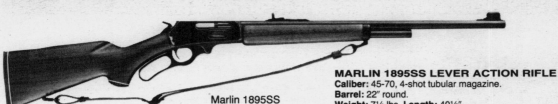

Marlin 1895SS

Marlin 30AS Lever Action Carbine
Same as the Marlin 336CS except: checkered walnut-finished hardwood p.g. stock, 30-30 only, 6-shot. Hammer block safety.
Price: **$240.95**

MARLIN 1894C CARBINE 357
Caliber: 357 Magnum, 9-shot tube magazine.
Barrel: 18½" Micro-Groove®.
Weight: 6 lbs. **Length:** 35½" over-all.
Stock: American black walnut, straight grip and fore-end.
Sights: Bead front, adjustable semi-buckhorn folding rear.
Features: Solid top receiver tapped for scope mount or receiver sight; offset hammer spur. Receiver top sandblasted to prevent glare.
Price: About **$272.95**

MARLIN 1895SS LEVER ACTION RIFLE
Caliber: 45-70, 4-shot tubular magazine.
Barrel: 22" round.
Weight: 7½ lbs. **Length:** 40½".
Stock: American black walnut, full pistol grip. Mar-Shield® finish; rubber butt-pad; q-d. swivels; leather carrying strap.
Sights: Bead front with Wide-Scan hood, semi-buckhorn folding rear adj. for w. and e.
Features: Hammer block safety. Solid receiver tapped for scope mounts or receiver sights, offset hammer spur.
Price: **$302.95**

MARLIN 336CS LEVER ACTION CARBINE
Caliber: 30-30 or 35 Rem., 6-shot tubular magazine
Barrel: 20" Micro-Groove®.
Weight: 7 lbs. **Length:** 38½".
Stock: Select American black walnut, capped p.g. with white line spacers. Mar-Shield® finish.
Sights: Ramp front with Wide-Scan™ hood, semi-buckhorn folding rear adj. for w. & e.
Features: Hammer block safety. Receiver tapped for scope mount, offset hammer spur; top of receiver sand blasted to prevent glare.
Price: Less scope **$266.95**

Marlin 336 ER

Marlin Model 336 Extra-Range Carbine
Similar to the standard Model 336CS except chambered for 307 Win. or 356 Win.; has new hammer block safety, rubber butt pad, 5-shot magazine. Comes with detachable sling swivels and branded leather sling. Introduced 1983.
Price: **$302.95**

Marlin 336 TS

Marlin 336TS Lever Action Carbine
Same as the 336CS except: straight stock; cal. 30-30 only. Squared finger lever, 18½" barrel, weight 6¾ lbs. Hammer block safety.
Price: **$266.95**

MARLIN 444SS LEVER ACTION SPORTER
Caliber: 444 Marlin, 4-shot tubular magazine
Barrel: 22" Micro-Groove®.
Weight: 7½ lbs. **Length:** 40½".
Stock: American black walnut, capped p.g. with white line spacers, rubber rifle butt pad. Mar-Shield® finish; q.d. swivels, leather carrying strap.
Sights: Hooded ramp front, folding semi-buckhorn rear adj. for w. & e.
Features: Hammer block safety. Receiver tapped for scope mount, offset hammer spur, leather sling with detachable swivels.
Price: **$302.95**

> Consult our directory pages for the location of firms mentioned.

NAVY ARMS HENRY CARBINE
Caliber: 44-40 or 44 rimfire.
Barrel: 21".
Weight: About 9 lbs. **Length:** About 39" over-all.
Stock: Oil stained American walnut.
Sights: Blade front, rear adj. for e.
Features: Reproduction of the original Henry carbine with brass frame and buttplate, rest blued. Will be produced in limited edition of 1,000 standard models, plus 50 engraved guns. Made in U.S. by Navy Arms.
Price: Standard **$500.00**
Price: Engraved **$1,500.00**

Navy Arms Henry

Mossberg 479 PCA

MOSSBERG 479 PCA LEVER ACTION RIFLE
Caliber: 30-30, 6-shot.
Barrel: 20″.
Weight: About 7 lbs. **Length:** 38½″ over-all.
Stock: Walnut-finish hardwood.
Sights: Bead on ramp front, adjustable open rear.
Features: Blue finish; hammer block safety and rebounding hammer. Trigger built into the cocking lever. Ejection port on right side of receiver. Re-introduced 1983.
Price: About **$190.00**

Remington Model Six

REMINGTON MODEL SIX SLIDE ACTION
Caliber: 6mm Rem., 243, 270, 308 Win., 30-06.
Barrel: 22″ round tapered.
Weight: 7½ lbs. **Length:** 42″ over-all.
Stock: Cut-checkered walnut p.g. and fore-end, Monte Carlo with full cheekpiece.
Sights: Gold bead front sight on matted ramp, open step adj. sporting rear.
Features: Redesigned and improved version of the Model 760. Has cartridge head medallion denoting caliber on bottom of receiver. Detachable 4-shot clip. Cross-bolt safety. Receiver tapped for scope mount. Introduced 1981.
Price: **$467.00**

Remington Model 7600

Remington Model 7600 Slide Action Rifle
Similar to Model Six except does not have Monte Carlo stock or cheekpiece no cartridge head medallion. Slightly different fore-end design. Impressed checkering. Introduced 1981.
Price: **$418.00**

Remington Sportsman 76

Remington "Sportsman" 76 Pump Rifle
Similar to the Model Six except available only in 30-06, 4-shot magazine, 22″ barrel, walnut-finished hardwood stock and fore-end, open adjustable sights. Introduced 1984.
Price: **$320.00**

Rossi Carbine

ROSSI SADDLE-RING CARBINE
Caliber: 38 Spec., 357 Mag., 44-40, 44 Mag., 10-shot magazine.
Barrel: 20″.
Weight: 5¾ lbs. **Length:** 37″ over-all.
Stock: Walnut.
Sights: Blade front, buckhorn rear.
Features: Re-creation of the famous lever-action carbine. Handles 38 and 357 interchangeably. Introduced 1978. Imported by Interarms.

Price: **$224.00**
Price: Blue, engraved **$279.00**
Price: 44-40 . . . . **$234.00**
Price: 44 Spec./44 Mag. **$239.00**

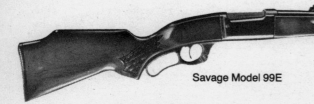

Savage Model 99E

SAVAGE 99E LEVER ACTION RIFLE
Caliber: 250 Savage, 300 Savage, 243 or 308 Win., 5-shot rotary magazine.
Barrel: 22″, chrome-moly steel.
Weight: 7 lbs. **Length:** 39¾″ over-all.
Stock: Walnut finished with checkered p.g.
Sights: Ramp front, adjustable ramp rear sight. Tapped for scope mounts.
Features: Grooved trigger, slide safety locks trigger and lever.
Price: **$343.00**

CAUTION: PRICES CHANGE. CHECK AT GUNSHOP.

Savage Model 99C

Savage 99C Lever Action Clip Rifle
Similar to M99E except: detachable staggered clip magazine with push-button ejection. Cocking indicator. Drilled and tapped for scope mounting. Cut checkering on Monte Carlo stock and fore-end. Wgt. about 6¾ lbs., 41¾" over-all with 22" bbl. Available in cals. 243, 308, 7mm-08 Rem.
Price: **$399.95**

Winchester 94 XTR Angle Eject

WINCHESTER MODEL 94 XTR ANGLE EJECT
Caliber: 307 Win., 356 Win., 375 Win., 6-shot magazine.
Barrel: 20".
Weight: 7 lbs. **Length:** 38⅝" over-all.
Stock: Monte Carlo-style American walnut with fine cut checkering. Satin finish.
Sights: Hooded ramp front, semi-buckhorn rear adjustable for w. & e.
Features: All external metal parts have Winchester's deep blue high polish finish. Rifling twist 1 in 12". Rubber recoil pad fitted to buttstock. Introduced 1983. Made under license by U.S. Repeating Arms Co.
Price: With scope rings and bases **$409.95**

Winchester 94 Angle Eject

WINCHESTER MODEL 94 ANGLE EJECT CARBINE
Caliber: 30-30, (12" twist). 444 Marlin (38" twist), 6-shot tubular magazine; 44 Rem. Mag./S&W Special, 45 Colt (38" twist), 11-shot magazine.
Barrel: 16", 20".
Weight: 6½ lbs. (30-30) **Length:** 37¾" over-all.
Stock: Straight grip walnut stock and fore-end.
Sights: Hooded blade front, semi-buckhorn rear. Drilled and tapped for receiver sight and scope mount.
Features: Solid frame, forged steel receiver; angle ejection, exposed rebounding hammer with automatic trigger-activated safety transfer bar. Introduced 1984.
Price: 30-30 . . . . **$234.95**
Price: 444 Marlin, 44 Rem. Mag./44 Spec., 45 Colt **$249.95**
Price: Trapper model (16" bbl., 30-30) **$234.95**

Winchester Model 94 Angle Eject Rifle, 7x30 Waters
Same as Model 94XTR Angle Eject except has 24" barrel, 7-shot magazine, over-all length of 41¾" and weight is 7 lbs. Barrel twist is 1-9½". Rubber butt pad instead of plastic. Introduced 1984.
Price: **$289.95**

Winchester 94 Crazy Horse

Winchester Model 94 Chief Crazy Horse Commemorative
Similar to the standard Model 94 except has Indian stock decorations of brass tacks and a medallion in the butt symbolizing the United Sioux Tribes. The names of the Sioux tribes are engraved on the color case-hardened receiver, along with a portrait and a buffalo hunting scene. Barrel is inscribed "Chief Crazy Horse." The crescent buttplate has a polished blue finish. All decorations are authenticated by the United Sioux Tribes of South Dakota, and the issue was approved by tribal chairmen of all eleven tribes. Royalties benefit the Sioux people. Limited edition of 19,999. Chambered for 38-55 Win. Introduced 1983.
Price: **$600.00**

Winchester Model 94XTR Angle Eject Carbine
Same as standard Model 94 except has high-grade finish on stock and fore-end with cut checkering on both. Metal has highly polished deep blue finish.
Price: **$269.95**

Winchester Wrangler II

Winchester Model 94 Wrangler II Angle Eject
Similar to the standard Model 94 except has a 16" barrel, hoop-type finger lever, roll-engraved Western scenes on receiver. Chambered for 38-55 Win. only. Weighs 6⅛ lbs. and is 33¾" o.a.l. Introduced 1983.
Price: **$269.95**

Alpha Custom

ALPHA CUSTOM BOLT ACTION RIFLE
Caliber: 243, 7mm-08, 308, 284, 25-284, 3-shot magazine.
Barrel: 21″ (284 and 25-284), 20″ all others.
Weight: About 6¼ lbs. **Length:** 39½″ over-all (20″ barrel).

Stock: Classic style California claro walnut, hand rubbed oil finish, hand check-ering; rosewood fore-end tip, rosewood or Niedner-type checkered steel grip cap; solid butt pad; swivel studs.
Sights: None furnished. Receiver drilled and tapped for scope mounting.
Features: Medium-length action with three-lug locking system and 60° bolt ro-tation; side safety; cocking indicator; aluminum bedding block system; steel or aluminum trigger guard/floorplate assembly; medium luster or dull matte bluing. Introduced 1984. From Alpha Arms, Inc.
Price: With hard case **$1,275.00**

Alpine Custom Grade

ALPINE BOLT ACTION RIFLE
Caliber: 22-250, 243 Win., 264 Win., 270, 30-06, 308, 308 Norma Mag., 7mm Rem Mag., 8mm, 300 Win. Mag., 5-shot magazine (3 for magnum).
Barrel: 23″ (std. cals.), 24″ (mag.).

Weight: 7½ lbs.
Stock: European walnut. Full p.g. and Monte Carlo; checkered p.g. and fore-end; rubber recoil pad; white line spacers; sling swivels.
Sights: Ramp front, open rear adj. for w. and e.
Features: Made by Firearms Co. Ltd. in England. Imported by Mandall Shoot-ing Supplies.
Price: Standard Grade **$375.00**
Price: Custom Grade (illus.) **$395.00**

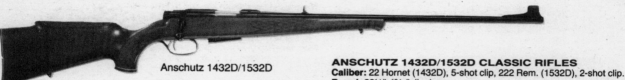

Anschutz 1432D/1532D

ANSCHUTZ 1432D/1532D Custom Rifles
Similar to the Classic models except have roll-over Monte Carlo cheekpiece, slim fore-end with Schnabel tip, Wundhammer palm swell on pistol grip, rosewood grip cap with white diamond insert. Skip-line checkering on grip and fore-end. Introduced 1982. Imported from Germany by PSI.
Price: 1432D (22 Hornet) **$650.00**
Price: 1532D (222 Rem.) **$650.00**

ANSCHUTZ 1432D/1532D CLASSIC RIFLES
Caliber: 22 Hornet (1432D), 5-shot clip, 222 Rem. (1532D), 2-shot clip.
Barrel: 23½″; ¹³⁄₁₆″ dia. heavy.
Weight: 7¾ lbs. **Length:** 42½″ over-all.
Stock: Select European walnut with checkered pistol grip and fore-end.
Sights: None furnished, drilled and tapped for scope mounting.
Features: Adjustable single stage trigger. Receiver drilled and tapped for scope mounting. Introduced 1982. Imported from Germany by PSI.
Price: 1432D (22 Hornet) **$607.00**
Price: 1532D (222 Rem.) **$607.00**

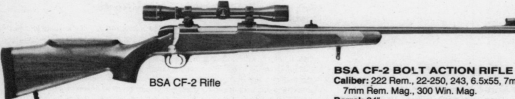

BSA CF-2 Rifle

BSA CF-2 BOLT ACTION RIFLE
Caliber: 222 Rem., 22-250, 243, 6.5x55, 7mm Mauser, 7x64, 270, 308, 30-06, 7mm Rem. Mag., 300 Win. Mag.
Barrel: 24″.
Weight: 7¾ lbs. **Length:** 45″ over-all.
Stock: European walnut with roll-over Monte Carlo, palm swell on right side of pistol grip, skip-line checkering. High gloss finish.
Sights: Open adjustable rear, hooded ramp front. Removable.
Features: Adjustable single trigger or optional double-set triggers, side safety, visible cocking indicator. Ventilated rubber recoil pad. North American-style stock has high gloss finish, European has oil. Introduced 1980. From Preci-sion Sports.
Price: Standard calibers, North American style **$525.00**
Price: Magnum calibers, North American style **$550.00**
Price: Double-set triggers, extra **$100.00**
Price: Heavy barrel, extra **$82.50**
Price: Standard calibers, European style **$575.00**
Price: Magnum calibers, European style **$600.00**

BSA CF-2 Stutzen Stock Rifle
Similar to the standard CF-2 except has improved bolt guide rib circlip and precision-ground striker; 20.5″ barrel; full-length Stutzen-style stock with contrasting Schnabel fore-end tip and grip cap. Available in 222, 6.5 x 55, 308 Win., 30-06, 270, 7 x 64. Measures 41.3″ over-all, weighs 7½ lbs. Intro-duced 1982. From Precision Sports.
Price: **$600.00**
Price: Double set triggers, add **$100.00**

CAUTION: PRICES CHANGE. CHECK AT GUNSHOP.

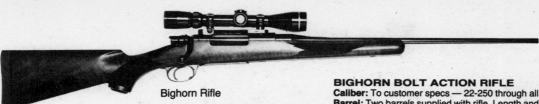

Bighorn Rifle

BERETTA 500 SERIES BOLT ACTION RIFLE
Caliber: 222, 223 (M500S); 243, 308 (M501SDL); 6.5x55, 270, 7x64, 7mm Rem. Mag., 30-06, 300 Win. Mag., 375 H&H (M502).
Barrel: 23.62″ to 24.41″.
Weight: 6.4 to 8.4 lbs. **Length:** NA.
Stock: Walnut, with oil finish, hand checkering.
Sights: Hooded blade front, open adjustable rear; none furnished on 502 which is drilled and tapped for scope mounting.
Features: Model 500 — short action; 501 — medium action; 502 — long action. All models have rubber butt pad. Imported from Italy by Beretta U.S.A. Corp. Introduced 1984.
Price: Model 500, 501, from.................................... $635.00
Price: Model 502, from....................................... $666.00

BIGHORN BOLT ACTION RIFLE
Caliber: To customer specs — 22-250 through all standard magnums.
Barrel: Two barrels supplied with rifle. Length and contour to customer specs.
Weight: About 6¾ lbs.
Stock: Standard grade has AA fancy claro walnut. Classic style.
Sights: None furnished. Drilled and tapped for scope mounting.
Features: Commercial Mauser action. Rifle comes with two easily interchangeable barrels, flush Pachmayr swivel sockets, black recoil pad. Available in several grades with many options. Introduced 1983. From Bighorn Rifles.
Price: With two barrels....................................... $2,495.00

Browning BBR Rifle

Browning BBR Limited Edition
Same as standard BBR except chambered only for 7mm Rem. Mag. Receiver is deeply engraved and highlighted with gold plated elk scenes. The high grade walnut stock has skip-line checkering with pearl borders and high gloss finish. Solid brass spacers are used at the recoil pad, grip cap and fore-end tip. Limited edition of 1,000 rifles. Introduced 1984.
Price: $1,395.00

BROWNING BBR BOLT ACTION RIFLE
Caliber: 25-06, 270, 30-06, 7mm Rem. Mag., 300 Win. Mag., 338 Win. Mag.
Barrel: 22″ medium sporter weight with recessed muzzle.
Weight: 8 lbs. **Length:** 44½″ over-all.
Stock: Select American walnut cut to lines of Monte Carlo sporter; full p.g. and high cheekpiece; 18 l.p.i. checkering. Recoil pad is standard on magnum calibers.
Features: Short throw (60°) bolt with fluted surface, 9 locking lugs, plunger-type ejector, adjustable trigger is grooved and gold plated. Hinged floorplate with detachable box magazine (4 rounds in standard cals, 3 in mags). Convenient slide safety on tang. Special anti-warp aluminum fore-end insert. Low profile swivel studs. Introduced 1978. Imported from Japan by Browning.
Price: $469.95

Browning BBR Short Action

Browning Short Action BBR
Similar to the standard BBR except has short action for 22-250, 243, 257 Roberts (22″ light barrel only), 7mm-08, 308 chamberings. Available with either 22″ light barrel or 24″ heavy barrel; weighs 7½ lbs. and 9½ lbs. respectively. Other specs essentially the same. Introduced 1983.
Price: Either barrel... $469.95

CHAMPLIN RIFLE
Caliber: All std. chamberings, including 458 Win. and 460 Wea. Many wildcats on request.
Barrel: Any length up to 26″ for octagon. Choice of round, straight taper octagon, or octagon with integral quarter rib, front sight ramp and sling swivel stud.
Weight: About 8 lbs. **Length:** 45″ over-all.
Stock: Hand inletted, shaped and finished. Checkered to customer specs. Select French, Circassian or claro walnut. Steel p.g. cap, trap buttplate or recoil pad.
Sights: Bead on ramp front, 3-leaf folding rear.
Features: Right or left hand Champlin action, tang safety or optional shroud safety, Canjar adj. trigger, hinged floorplate.
Price: From.. $5,400.00

Champlin

COLT SAUER GRAND AFRICAN
Caliber: 458 Win. Mag.
Barrel: 24″, round tapered.
Weight: 10½ lbs. **Length:** 44½″ over-all.
Stock: Solid African bubinga wood, cast-off M.C. with cheekpiece, contrasting rosewood fore-end and p.g. caps with white spacers. Checkered fore-end and p.g.
Sights: Ivory bead hooded ramp front, adj. sliding rear.
Price: $1,398.50

Colt Sauer Short Action Rifle
Same as standard rifle except chambered for 22-250, 243 and 308 Win. 24″ bbl., 43″ over-all. Weighs 7½ lbs. 3-shot magazine
Price: $1,256.95

Colt Sauer Rifle

COLT SAUER RIFLE
Caliber: 25-06, 270, 30-06, (std.), 7mm Rem. Mag., 300 Wea. Mag., 300 Win. Mag. (Magnum).
Barrel: 24″, round tapered.
Weight: 8 lbs. (std.). **Length:** 43¾″ over-all.

Stock: American walnut, cast-off M.C. design with cheekpiece. Fore-end tip and p.g. cap rosewood with white spacers. Hand checkering.
Sights: None furnished. Specially designed scope mounts for any popular make scope furnished.
Features: Unique barrel/receiver union, non-rotating bolt with cam-actuated locking lugs, tang-type safety locks sear. Detachable 3- and 4-shot magazines.
Price: Standard calibers $1,256.95
Price: Magnum calibers..................................... $1,299.50
Price: Grand Alaskan, 375 H&H $1,334.50

Du Biel Modern Classic

Du BIEL ARMS BOLT ACTION RIFLES
Caliber: Standard calibers 22-250 thru 458 Win. Mag. Selected wildcat calibers available.
Barrel: Selected weights and lengths. Douglas Premium
Weight: About 7½ lbs.
Stock: Five styles. Walnut, maple, laminates. Hand checkered.

Sights: None furnished. Receiver has integral milled bases.
Features: Basically a custom-made rifle. Left or right-hand models available. Five-lug locking mechanism; 36 degree bolt rotation; adjustable Canjar trigger; oil or epoxy stock finish; Presentation recoil pad; jeweled and chromed bolt body; sling swivel studs; lever latch or button floorplate release. All steel action and parts. Introduced 1978. From Du Biel Arms.
Price: Rollover Model, left or right-hand $2,500.00
Price: Thumbhole, left or right hand $2,500.00
Price: Classic, left or right hand $2,500.00
Price: Modern Classic, left or right hand..................... $2,500.00
Price: Thumbhole Mannlicher, left or right hand $2,500.00

Heym Model SR-20L

Heym SR-40 Bolt Action Rifle
Same as the SR-20 except has short action, chambered for 222 Rem., 223 Rem., 5.6x50 Mag. Over-all length of 44″, weight about 6¼ lbs., 24″ barrel. Carbine Mannlicher-style stock. Introduced 1984.
Price: $765.00
Price: Single set trigger, add ..'............................ $65.00

Heym SR-20, SR-40 Left Hand Rifles
All Heym bolt action rifles are available with true left-hand action and stock, in all calibers listed for the right-hand version, for an additional $160.00.

HEYM MODEL SR-20 BOLT ACTION RIFLES
Caliber: 5.6x57, 243, 6.5x55, 6.5x57, 270, 7x57, 7x64, 308, 30-06 (SR-20L); 9.3x62 (SR-20N) plus SR-20L cals.; SR-20G—6.5x68, 7mm Rem. Mag., 300 Win. Mag., 8x68S, 375H&H.
Barrel: 20½″ (SR-20L), 24″ (SR-20N), 26″ (SR-20G).
Weight: 7-8 lbs. depending upon model.
Stock: Dark European walnut, hand-checkered p.g. and fore-end. Oil finish. Recoil pad, rosewood grip cap. Monte Carlo-style. SR-20L has full Mannlicher-style stock, others have sporter-style with schnabel tip.
Sights: Silver bead ramp front, adj. folding leaf rear.
Features: Hinged floorplate, 3-position safety,. Receiver drilled and tapped for scope mounts. Adjustable trigger. Options available include double-set triggers, left-hand action and stock, Suhler claw mounts, deluxe engraving and stock carving. Imported from West Germany by Paul Jaeger, Inc.
Price: SR-20L $945.00
Price: SR-20N $835.00
Price: SR-20-G $880.00
Price: Single set trigger $65.00

Kimber Hornet Sporter

KIMBER MODEL 82 HORNET SPORTER
Caliber: 22 Hornet; 3-shot flush-fitting magazine.
Barrel: 22½″, 6 grooves; 1-in-14″ twist.
Weight: About 6¼ lbs. **Length:** 42″ over-all.
Stock: Three styles available. "Classic" is Claro walnut with plain, straight comb; "Cascade" has Monte Carlo comb with cheekpiece. "Custom Classic"

is of fancy select grade Claro walnut, ebony fore-end tip, Niedner-style buttplate. All have 18 lpi hand cut, borderless checkering, steel grip cap, checkered steel buttplate.
Sights: Hooded ramp front with bead, folding leaf rear (optional).
Features: All steel construction; twin rear horizontally opposed locking lugs; fully adjustable trigger; rocker-type safety. Receiver grooved for Kimber scope mounts. Introduced 1982.
Price: Classic stock, no sights................................ $618.00
Price: Cascade stock, no sights $668.00
Price: Custom Classic, no sights............................. $748.00
Price: Kimber scope mounts, from $45.00
Price: Open sights fitted (optional) $55.00

CAUTION: PRICES CHANGE. CHECK AT GUNSHOP.

Kimber Model 84

Kimber Model 82,84 Super America

Similar to the standard Model 82 except has the Classic stock only of specially selected, high-grade, California claro walnut, with Continental cheekpiece; borderless, full-coverage 22 lpi checkering; Niedner-type checkered steel buttplate; comes with quick-detachable, double lever scope mounts and barrel quarter-rib which has a folding leaf sight. Available in 22 Long Rifle, 22 Magnum, 22 Hornet, 223 Rem.

Price: 22 Long Rifle, less 4x scope **$950.00**
Price: 22 Mag., less scope **$1,023.00**
Price: 22 Hornet, less scope **$1,073.00**
Price: Model 84, 223 Rem. **$1,105.00**

KIMBER MODEL 84 223 SPORTER

Caliber: 223 Rem.; 5-shot magazine.
Barrel: 22½", 6 grooves; 1-in-12" twist.
Weight: About 6¼ lbs. **Length:** 42" over-all.
Stock: Three styles available. "Classic" is Claro walnut with plain, straight comb; "Cascade" has Monte Carlo comb with cheekpiece. "Custom Classic" is of fancy select grade Claro walnut, ebony fore-end tip, Niedner-style butt-plate. All have 18 lpi hand cut, borderless checkering, steel grip cap, checkered steel buttplate.
Sights: Hooded ramp front with bead, folding leaf rear (optional).
Features: All new Mauser-type head locking bolt action; steel trigger guard and hinged floorplate; Mauser-type extractor; fully adjustable trigger; chrome-moly barrel. Receiver grooved for scope mounting. Introduced 1984.
Price: Classic stock, no sights **$650.00**
Price: Cascade stock, no sights **$700.00**
Price: Custom Classic stock, no sights **$780.00**
Price: Kimber scope mounts, from **$45.00**
Price: Open sights fitted (optional) **$55.00**

Kleinguenther K-15 Insta-Fire

KRICO MODEL 600/700 BOLT ACTION RIFLE

Caliber: 308 Win. (Model 600), 30-06 (Model 700), 3-shot magazine.
Barrel: 23½".
Weight: 7 lbs. **Length:** 43½" over-all.
Stock: Select European walnut, European comb with cheekpiece; rosewood Schnabel fore-end tip; cut checkered grip and fore-end.
Sights: Blade on ramp front, open rear adjustable for windage.
Features: Butterknife bolt handle; single set trigger, optional match and double set available; engine-turned bolt; side safety; free floating barrel. Imported from West Germany by Krico North America.
Price: Model 600 or 700 . . . . **$1,049.50**

KLEINGUENTHER K-15 INSTA-FIRE RIFLE

Caliber: 243, 25-06, 270, 30-06, 308 Win., 7x57, 308 Norma Mag., 7mm Rem. Mag., 375 H&H, 257-270-300 Weath. Mag.
Barrel: 24" (Std.), 26" (Mag.).
Weight: 7 lbs., 12 oz. **Length:** 43½" over-all.
Stock: European walnut M.C. with 1" recoil pad. Left or right hand. Rosewood grip cap. Hand checkered. High luster or satin finish.
Sights: None furnished. Drilled and tapped for scope mounts. Iron sights optional.
Features: Ultra-fast lock/ignition time. Clip or feed from top of receiver. Guaranteed ½" 100 yd. groups. Many optional stock features available. Imported from Germany, assembled and accurized by Kleinguenther's.
Price: All calibers, choice of European or American walnut with oil finish. **$1,044.00**

Krico 640 Varmint

KRICO MODEL 640 VARMINT RIFLE

Caliber: 222 Rem., 4-shot magazine.
Barrel: 23.75".
Weight: 9.6 lbs. **Length:** 43½" over-all.
Stock: Select European walnut with high Monte Carlo comb, Wundhammer palm swell, rosewood fore-end tip; cut checkered grip and fore-end.
Sights: None furnished. Drilled and tapped for scope mounting.
Features: Free floating heavy bull barrel; double set trigger with optional match trigger available. Imported from West Germany by Krico North America.
Price: **$995.00**

KRICO MODEL 600/700L DELUXE BOLT ACTION

Caliber: 17 Rem., 222, 223, 22-250, 243, 308, 7x57, 7x64, 270, 30-06, 9.3x62, 8x68S, 7mm Rem. Mag., 300 Win. Mag., 9.3x64.
Barrel: 24" (26" in magnum calibers).
Weight: 7.5 lbs. **Length:** 44" over-all (24" barrel).
Stock: Traditional European style, select fancy walnut with rosewood Schnable fore-end, Bavarian cheekpiece, 28 lpi checkering.
Sights: Hooded front ramp, rear adjustable for windage.
Features: Butterknife bolt handle; gold plated single-set trigger; front sling swivel attached to barrel with ring; silent safety. Introduced 1983. Made in West Germany. Imported by Krico North America.
Price: Model 600, varmint calibers **$1,049.00**
Price: Model 600, standard calibers **$1,049.00**
Price: Model 700, magnum calibers **$1,049.00**

Krico Model 400

KRICO MODEL 400 BOLT ACTION RIFLE

Caliber: 22 Hornet, 5-shot magazine.
Barrel: 23.5".
Weight: 6.8 lbs. **Length:** 43" over-all.

Stock: Select European walnut, curved European comb with cheekpiece; solid rubber butt pad; cut checkered grip and fore-end.
Sights: Blade front on ramp, open rear adjustable for windage.
Features: Detachable box magazine; action has rear locking lugs, twin extractors. Available with single or optional match and double set trigger. Receiver grooved for scope mounts. Made in West Germany. Imported by Krico North America.
Price: **$649.00**
Price: Model 420 (as above except 19.5" bbl., full-length Mannlicher-style stock, double set trigger) **$749.50**

Krico Model 620/720

Krico Model 620/720 Bolt Action Rifle

Similar to the Model 600/700 except has 20.75″ barrel,. weighs 6.8 lbs., and has full-length Mannlicher-style stock with metal Schnabel fore-end tip; doubel set trigger with optional match trigger available. Receiver drilled and tapped for scope mounting. Imported from West Germany by Beeman; contact Beeman or Krico North America for information.

Price: Model 620 (308 Win.) **$992.00**
Price: Model 720 (270 Win.) **$899.00**
Price: Model 720 (30-06) **$995.00**

M-S Safari Varmint

M-S SAFARI ARMS VARMINT RIFLE

Caliber: Any standard centerfire; single shot.
Barrel: 24″, stainless
Weight: To customer specs.
Stock: Fiberglass, custom painted. Thumbhole or pistol grip style.
Sights: None furnished. Drilled and tapped for scope mounting.
Features: Electronic trigger; high-speed lock time; stainless steel action. Custom built to customer specs. From M-S Safari Arms.
Price: From **$1,145.00**

MARATHON SPORTSMAN BUSH & FIELD RIFLE

Caliber: 243, 308, 7x57, 30-06, 270, 7mm Rem. Mag., 300 Win. Mag.
Barrel: 24″.
Weight: 7.9 lbs. **Length:** 45″ over-all.
Stock: Select walnut with Monte Carlo and rubber recoil pad.
Sights: Bead front on ramp, open adjustable rear.
Features: Uses the Santa Barbara Mauser action. Triple thumb locking safety blocks trigger, firing pin and bolt. Blue finish. Also available as a kit requiring assembly, wood and metal finishing. Introduced 1984. Imported from Spain by Marathon Products.
Price: Finished **$379.49**
Price: Kit **$257.67**

Mark X Marquis Carbine

MARK X MARQUIS MANNLICHER-STYLE CARBINE

Caliber: 270, 7x57, 30-06, 308 Win.
Barrel: 20″.
Weight: 7½ lbs. **Length:** 40″ over-all.
Stock: Hand checkered European walnut.
Sights: Ramp front with removable hood; open rear adj. for w. and e.
Features: Quick detachable sling swivels; fully adj. trigger; blue steel fore-end cap; white line spacers at p.g. cap and buttplate. Mark X Mauser action. Imported from Yugoslavia by Interarms.
Price: With adj. trigger and sights **$430.00**

Interarms Mark X Alaskan

MARK X ALASKAN MAGNUM RIFLE

Caliber: 375 H&H, 458 Win Mag.; 3-shot magazine.
Barrel: 24″.
Weight: 8¼ lbs. **Length:** 44¾″ over-all.
Stock: Select walnut with crossbolt; hand checkered p.g. and fore-end; Monte Carlo; sling swivels.
Sights: Hooded ramp front; open rear adj. for w. & e.
Features: Hinged floorplate; right-hand thumb (tang) safety; adj. trigger. Imported from Yugoslavia by Interarms.
Price: **$460.00**

Parker-Hale 2100

PARKER-HALE MODEL 2100 MIDLAND RIFLE

Caliber: 22-250, 243, 6mm, 270, 6.5x55, 7x57, 7x64, 308, 30-06.
Barrel: 22″.
Weight: About 7 lbs. **Length:** 43″ over-all.
Stock: European walnut, cut-checkered pistol grip and fore-end; sling swivels.
Sights: Hooded post front, flip-up open rear.
Features: Mauser-type action has twin front locking lugs, rear safety lug, and claw extractor; hinged floorplate; adjustable single stage trigger; silent side safety. Imported from England by Precision Sports, Inc. Introduced 1984.
Price: **$299.00**
Price: Optional set trigger **$75.00**

CAUTION: PRICES CHANGE. CHECK AT GUNSHOP.

Parker-Hale 1200 Super

PARKER-HALE MODEL 1200 SUPER BOLT ACTION RIFLE
Caliber: 22-250, 243, 6mm, 270, 6.5x55, 7x57, 7x64, 308, 30-06.
Barrel: 24".
Weight: About 7½ lbs. **Length:** 44½" over-all.
Stock: European walnut, rosewood grip and fore-end tips, hand-cut checkering; roll-over cheekpiece; palm swell pistol grip; ventilated recoil pad; skipline checkering.
Sights: Hooded post front, open rear.
Features: Uses Mauser-style action with claw extractor; gold plated adjustable trigger; silent side safety locks trigger, sear and bolt; aluminum trigger guard. Imported from England by Precision Sports, Inc. Introduced 1984.
Price: $465.00
Price: Optional set trigger $75.00

Parker-Hale Model 1200 Super Clip Rifle
Same as the Model 1200 Super except has a detachable steel box magazine and steel trigger guard. Imported from England by Precision Sports, Inc. Introduced 1984.
Price: $495.00
Price: Optional set trigger $75.00

Parker-Hale 1000

Parker-Hale Model 1100M African Magnum
Similar to the Model 1000 Standard except has 24" barrel, 46" over-all length, weighs 9½ lbs., and is chambered for 375 H&H Magnum and 458 Win. Magnum. Has hooded post front sight, shallow V-notch rear, 180° flag safety (low 45° scope safety available). Specially lengthened steel magazine has hinged floorplate; heavily reinforced, glass bedded and weighted stock has a ventilated rubber recoil pad. Imported from England by Precision Sports, Inc. Introduced 1984.
Price: $695.00
Price: Optional set trigger $75.00

Parker-Hale Model 1000 Standard Rifle
Similar to the Model 1200 Super except has standard walnut Monte Carlo stock with satin varnish finish, no rosewood grip/fore-end caps; fitted with checkered buttplate, standard sling swivels. Imported from England by Precision Sports, Inc. Introduced 1984.
Price: $375.00
Price: Optional set trigger $75.00

Parker-Hale 81

PARKER-HALE MODEL 81 CLASSIC RIFLE
Caliber: 22-250, 243, 6mm Rem., 270, 6.5x55, 7x57, 7x64, 308, 30-06, 300 Win. Mag., 7mm Rem. Mag., 4-shot magazine.
Barrel: 24".
Weight: About 7¾ lbs. **Length:** 44½" over-all.
Stock: European walnut in classic style with oil finish, hand-cut checkering; palm swell pistol grip, rosewood grip cap.
Sights: None furnished. Drilled and tapped for open sights and scope mounting.
Features: Uses Mauser-style action; one-piece steel, Oberndorf-style trigger guard with hinged floorplate; rubber butt pad; quick-detachable sling swivels. Imported from England by Precision Sports, Inc. Introduced 1984.
Price: $550.00
Price: Optional set trigger $75.00

Parker-Hale Model 1100 Lightweight Rifle
Similar to the Model 81 Classic except has slim barrel profile, hollow bolt handle, alloy trigger guard/floorplate. The Monte Carlo stock has a Schnabel fore-end hand-cut checkering, swivel studs, palm swell pistol grip. Comes with hooded ramp front sight, open Williams rear adjustable for windage and elevation. Same calibers as Model 81. Over-all length is 43", weight 6½ lbs., with 22" barrel. Imported from England by Precision Sports, Inc. Introduced 1984.
Price: $450.00
Price: Optional set trigger $75.00

Remington 700 Classic

REMINGTON 700 "CLASSIC" RIFLE
Caliber: 22-250, 6mm Rem., 243, 250 Savage, 270, 30-06, 7mm Rem. Mag.
Barrel: 22" (6mm, 243, 270, 30-06), 24" (22-250, 250 Savage, 7mm Rem. Mag., 300 H&H).
Weight: About 7 lbs. **Length:** 43½" over-all (24" bbl.).
Stock: American walnut, 20 l.p.i. checkering on p.g. and fore-end. Classic styling. Satin finish.
Sights: No sights furnished. Receiver drilled and tapped for scope mounting.
Features: A "classic" version of the M700ADL with straight comb stock. Fitted with rubber butt pad on all but magnum caliber, which has a full recoil pad. Sling swivel studs installed.
Price: All cals. except 7mm Rem. Mag. $421.00
Price: 7mm Rem. Mag. $440.00

Consult our Directory pages for the location of firms mentioned.

Remington 700 ADL

REMINGTON 700 ADL BOLT ACTION RIFLE
Caliber: 222, 22-250, 6mm Rem., 243, 25-06, 270, 308 and 30-06.
Barrel: 22" or 24" round tapered.
Weight: 7 lbs. **Length:** 41½" to 43½".
Stock: Walnut, RKW finished p.g. stock with impressed checkering, Monte Carlo (13⅜"x1⅝"x2⅜").
Sights: Gold bead ramp front; removable, step-adj. rear with windage screw.
Features: Side safety, receiver tapped for scope mounts.
Price: **$395.00**
Price: 7mm Rem. Mag. **$413.00**

Remington Model Seven

REMINGTON MODEL SEVEN BOLT ACTION RIFLE
Caliber: 222 Rem., 223 Rem. (5-shot), 243, 7mm-08, 6mm, 308 (4-shot).
Barrel: 18½".
Weight: 6¼ lbs. **Length:** 37½" over-all.
Stock: Walnut, with modified Schnabel fore-end. Cut checkering.
Sights: Ramp front, adjustable open rear.
Features: New short action design; silent side safety; free-floated barrel except for single pressure point at fore-end tip. Introduced 1983.
Price: **$463.00**

Remington 700 BDL

Remington 700 BDL Bolt Action Rifle
Same as 700-ADL, except: also available in 223, 7mm-08 Rem.; skip-line checkering; black fore-end tip and p.g. cap, white line spacers. Matted receiver top, quick release floorplate. Hooded ramp front sight. Q.D. swivels and 1" sling.
Price: **$464.00**
Available also in 17 Rem., 7mm Rem. Mag. and 300 Win. Mag., 8mm Rem. Mag., calibers. 44½" over-all, weight 7½ lbs.
Price: **$482.00**
Price: Custom Grade I **$1,158.00**
Price: Custom Grade II **$2,105.00**
Price: Custom Grade III **$3,257.00**
Price: Custom Grade IV **$4,474.00**

Remington 700 BDL Varmint Special
Same as 700 BDL, except: 24" heavy bbl., 43½" over-all, wgt. 9 lbs. Cals. 222, 223, 22-250, 6mm Rem., 243, 25-06, 7mm-08 Rem. and 308. No sights.
Price: **$486.00**

Remington 700 Safari
Same as the 700 BDL except 375 H&H or 458 Win. Magnum calibers only. Hand checkered, oil finished stock with recoil pad installed. Delivery time is about five months.
Price: **$793.00**

Remington 700BDL Left Hand
Same as 700 BDL except: mirror-image left-hand action, stock. Available in 270, 30-06 only.
Price: **$501.00**
Price: 7mm Rem. Mag. **$520.00**

Remington Sportsman 78

Remington "Sportsman" 78 Bolt Action Rifle
Similar to the Model 700 except available only in 270 Win. or 30-06, 4-shot magazine, 22" barrel, straight comb walnut-finished hardwood stock. Open adjustable sights; weight about 7 lbs. Introduced 1984.
Price: **$300.00**

Ruger 77 Varmint

RUGER MODEL 77 VARMINT
Caliber: 22-250, 220 Swift, 243, 6mm, 25-06, 308.
Barrel: 24" heavy straight tapered, 26" in 220 swift.
Weight: Approx. 9 lbs. **Length:** Approx. 44" over-all.
Stock: American walnut, similar in style to Magnum Rifle.
Sights: Barrel drilled and tapped for target scope blocks. Integral scope mount bases in receiver.
Features: Ruger diagonal bedding system, Ruger steel 1" scope rings supplied. Fully adj. trigger. Barreled actions available in any of the standard calibers and barrel lengths.
Price: (Model 77V) **$393.00**

CAUTION: PRICES CHANGE. CHECK AT GUNSHOP.

Ruger International 77

RUGER 77 BOLT ACTION RIFLE

Caliber: 22-250, 6mm, 243, 308, 220 Swift (Short Stroke action); 270, 7x57, 257 Roberts, 280 Rem., 30-06, 25-06, 7mm Rem. Mag., 300 Win. Mag., 338 Win. Mag. (Magnum action).
Barrel: 22" round tapered (24" in 220 Swift and magnum action calibers).
Weight: 6¾ lbs. **Length:** 42" over-all.
Stock: Hand checkered American walnut (13¾"x1⅝"x2⅛"), p.g. cap, sling swivel studs and recoil pad.
Sights: Optional gold bead ramp front, folding leaf adj. rear, or scope rings.
Features: Integral scope mount bases, diagonal bedding system, hinged floor plate, adj. trigger, tang safety. Scope optional.

Ruger International Model 77 RSI Rifle
Same as the standard Model 77 except has 18½" barrel, full-length Mannlicher-style stock, with steel fore-end cap, loop-type sling swivel. Integral base receiver, open sights, Ruger 1" steel rings. Improved front sight. Available in 22-250, 250-3000, 243 or 308. Weighs 6 lbs., 4 oz. and uses the Ruger short action. Length over-all is 38½".
Price: **$480.00**

Price: With Ruger steel scope rings, no sights (77R) **$393.00**
Price: With rings and open sights (77RS) **$414.00**
Price: 458 Win. Mag. (77RS Tropical) **$496.50**
Price: Barreled action only all cals. except 458, open sights **$339.00**
Price: Barreled action, all cals. except 458, no sights **$319.00**
Price: Barreled action, 458, with open sights **$433.50**

Ruger 77 Ultra Light

Ruger Model 77 Ultra Light
Similar to the standard Model 77 except weighs only 6 lbs., chambered for 243, 270, 30-06, 257, 22-250, 250-3000 and 308; barrel tapped for target scope blocks; has 20" Ultra Light barrel. Ruger's steel 1" scope rings supplied. Introduced 1983.
Price: Model 77 RL **$455.00**

Ruger 77 Round Top

Ruger Model 77 Magnum Round Top
Same as Model 77 except: round top receiver, drilled and tapped for standard scope mounts, Open sights are standard equipment. Calibers 25-06, 270, 30-06 (22" barrel), 7mm Rem. Mag. (24" barrel).
Price: All cals. (Model 77ST) **$393.00**

Ruger Model 77 Magnum Rifle
Similar to Ruger 77 except: magnum-size action. Calibers 270, 7x57, 30-06 (5-shot), 7mm Rem. Mag., 300 Win., Mag., 338 Win. Mag., 243, 308 with 24" barrel. Weight about 7 lbs.
Price: Model 77 RS **$414.00**

Sako Classic Sporter

SAKO STANDARD SPORTER

Caliber: 17 Rem., 222, 223 (short action); 22-250, 220 Swift, 243, 308 (medium action); 25-06, 270, 30-06, 7mm Rem. Mag., 300 Win. Mag., 338 Win. Mag., 375 H&H Mag. (long action).
Barrel: 23" (222, 223, 243), 24" (other cals.).
Weight: 6¾ lbs. (short); 6¾ lbs. (med.); 8 lbs. (long).
Stock: Hand-checkered European walnut.
Sights: None furnished.
Features: Adj. trigger, hinged floorplate. 222 and 223 have short action, 243 and 22-250 have medium action, others are long action. Imported from Finland by Stoeger.
Price: Short action **$725.00**
Price: Medium action **$725.00**
Price: Long action **$741.95**
Price: Magnum cals. **$758.95**
Price: 375 H&H **$775.00**

Sako Safari Grade Bolt Action
Similar to the Standard Grade Sporter except available in long action, calibers 300 Win. Mag., 338 Win. Mag. or 375 H&H Mag. only. Stocked in French walnut, checkered 20 l.p.i., solid rubber butt pad; grip cap and fore-end tip; quarter-rib "express" rear sight, hooded ramp front. Front sling swivel band-mounted on barrel.
Price: **$1,995.00**

Sako Super Deluxe Sporter
Similar to Deluxe Sporter except has select European Walnut with high gloss finish and deep cut oak leaf carving. Metal has super high polish, deep blue finish.
Price: **$1,995.00**

Sako Classic Sporter
Similar to the Standard Sporter except: available in 17 Rem., 222, 223 (short action), 243, 308 (medium action) 270, 30-06 and 7mm Rem. Mag. (long action) only; straight-comb "classic-style" stock with oil finish; solid rubber recoil pad; recoil lug. No sights furnished—receiver drilled and tapped for scope mounting. Introduced 1980.
Price: 17 Rem., 222, 223 .... **$909.95**
Price: 243, 308 .... **$909.95**
Price: 270, 30-06, 7mm Rem. Mag. **$959.95**

Sako Finnsport 2700 Sporter
Similar to the Standard Sporter except has Monte Carlo stock design, different checkering, comes with scope mounts. Same calibers, actions as on Standard model. Weight, 6½ to 8 lbs. Introduced 1983.
Price: **$866.95**

Sako Carbine

Sako Carbine

Same action as the Standard Sporter except has full "Mannlicher" style stock, 20" barrel, weighs 7½ lbs., chambered for 222 Rem., 243, 270 and 30-06 only. Introduced 1977. From Stoeger.
Price: 243, 270, 30-06 only **$825.00**

Sako Heavy Barrel

Same as std. Super Sporter except has beavertail fore-end; available in 222, 223 (short action), 220 Swift, 22-250, 243, 308 (medium action). Weight from 8¼ to 8½ lbs. 5-shot magazine capacity.
Price: 222, 223 (short action) **$875.00**
Price: 22-250, 243, 308 (medium action) **$875.00**

Sako Deluxe Sporter

Same action as Standard Sporter except has select wood, rosewood p.g. cap and fore-end tip. Fine checkering on top surfaces of integral dovetail bases, bolt sleeve, bolt handle root and bolt knob. Vent. recoil pad, skip-line checkering, mirror finish bluing.
Price: 222 or 223 cals. **$995.00**
Price: 22-250, 243, 308 . . . . **$995.00**
Price: 25-06, 270, 30-06 . . . . **$995.00**
Price: 7mm Rem. Mag., 300 Win. Mag., 338 Mag., 375 H&H **$1,020.00**

> Consult our Directory pages for the location of firms mentioned.

Savage Model 110-V Varmint Rifle

Same as the Model 110-C except chambered only for 22-250, with heavy 26" barrel, special "varmint" stock. Introduced 1983.
Price: **$363.00**

Savage Model 110C

SAVAGE 110C BOLT ACTION RIFLE

Caliber: 22-250, 243, 270, 308, 30-06, 4-shot detachable box magazine, 300 Win. Mag., 7mm Rem. Mag. (3-shot).
Barrel: 22"; 24" in magnum calibers.
Weight: 7lbs. **Length:** 43" over-all.

Stock: Select walnut with Monte Carlo, skip-line cut checkered p.g. and fore-end. Swivel studs.
Sights: Removable ramp front, open rear adj. for w. & e.
Features: Tapped for scope mounting, free floating barrel, top tang safety, detachable clip magazine, rubber recoil pad on all calibers. Model 110CL (left-hand) in calibers 243, 270, 30-06, 308, 7mm Rem. Mag. only.
Price: Right hand 110C **$399.95**
Price: Left hand 110CL **$419.95**
Price: Right hand, mag. cals. **$399.95**
Price: Left hand, mag. cals. **$419.95**

Savage 110E

SAVAGE 110E BOLT ACTION RIFLE

Caliber: 270, 308, 30-06, 243, 7mm Rem. Mag., 4-shot.
Barrel: 22" round tapered.
Weight: 6¾ lbs. **Length:** 43" (22"barrel).
Stock: Walnut finished hardwood with Monte Carlo, checkered p.g. and fore-end, hard rubber buttplate.
Sights: Gold bead removable ramp front, step adj. rear.
Features: Top tang safety, receiver tapped for peep or scope sights.
Price: **$258.50**

Savage 340

SAVAGE 340 CLIP REPEATER

Caliber: 22 Hornet, 222 Rem., 223 (4-shot) and 30-30 (3-shot).
Barrel: 24" and 22" respectively.

Weight: About 6½ lbs. **Length:** 40"-42".
Stock: Walnut, Monte Carlo, checkered p.g. and fore-end.
Sights: Hooded ramp front, folding-leaf rear.
Features: Detachable clip magazine, sliding thumb safety, receiver tapped for scope mounts.
Price: **$236.00**

Shilen DGA Varmint

SHILEN DGA RIFLES

Caliber: All calibers.
Barrel: 24" (Sporter, #2 weight), 25" (Varminter, #5 weight).

Weight: 7½ lbs. (Sporter), 9 lbs., (Varminter).
Stock: Selected Claro walnut. Barrel and action hand bedded to stock with free-floated barrel, bedded action. Swivel studs installed.
Sights: None furnished. Drilled and tapped for scope mounting.
Features: Shilen Model DGA action, fully adjustable trigger with side safety. Stock finish is satin sheen epoxy. Barrel and action non-glare blue-black. From Shilen Rifles, Inc.
Price: Sporter or Varminter rifle, from **$1,400.00**

CAUTION: PRICES CHANGE. CHECK AT GUNSHOP.

Smith & Wesson Mountaineer

SMITH & WESSON M1500 MOUNTAINEER RIFLE
Caliber: 222, 223, 22-250, 243, 25-06, 270, 30-06, 308, 7mm Rem. Mag., 300 Win. Mag., 338 Win. Mag.
Barrel: 22" (24" in magnum calibers.).
Weight: 7½-7¾ lbs. **Length:** 42" over-all (42½" for 270, 30-06, 7mm).
Stock: American walnut with Monte Carlo comb and cheekpiece; 18-line-per-inch checkering on p.g. and fore-end.
Sights: Hooded ramp gold bead front, open round-notch rear adj. for w. & e. Drilled and tapped for scope mounts.
Features: Trigger guard and magazine box are a single unit with a hinged floorplate. Comes with q.d. swivel studs. Composition non-slip buttplate with white spacer. Magnum models have rubber recoil pad. Introduced 1979.
Price: Standard cals., no sights $361.95
Price: Magnum cals., no sights $377.95
Price: Standard cals., with sights $388.95
Price: Magnum cals., with sights $403.95

Smith & Wesson Model 1500 Deluxe Rifle
Similar to Standard model except comes without sights, has engine-turned bolt; floorplate has decorative scroll. Stock has skip-line checkering, pistol grip cap with inset S&W seal, white spacers. Sling, swivels and swivel posts are included. Magnum models have vent. recoil pad.
Price: Deluxe, std. cals. $434.95
Price: Deluxe, magnum cals. $450.95

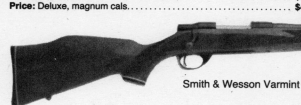

Smith & Wesson Varmint

Smith & Wesson Model 1500 Varmint Deluxe Rifle
Similar to the standard 1500 except has a 22" heavy barrel and fully adjustable trigger. Chambered for 222, 22-250 and 223. Weighs 9 lbs. 5 oz. Skip-line checkering, q.d. swivels. Introduced 1982.
Price: Blue. $456.95
Price: Parkerized, oil finished stock $469.95

Smith & Wesson Classic Hunter

Smith & Wesson Model 1700LS "Classic Hunter"
Similar to the standard Model 1500 except has classic-style stock with tapered fore-end and Schnabel tip, ribbon hand checkering, black rubber butt pad with black spacer; flush mounted sling swivels; removeable 5-shot magazine; jeweled bolt body with knurled bolt knob. Chambered only for 243, 270, 30-06. Introduced 1983.
Price: $493.95

Stevens Model 110-ES

STEVENS MODEL 110-ES BOLT ACTION RIFLE
Caliber: 243, 308, 30-06; 5-shot magazine.
Barrel: 22".
Weight: 7 lbs. **Length:** 43" over-all.
Stock: Walnut-finished hardwood with Monte Carlo; checkered p.g. and fore-end.
Sights: Removable ramp front, removable adjustable rear.
Features: Comes with 4x scope and mounts; hard rubber buttplate; top tang safety; free-floating barrel. Introduced 1981. From Savage Arms.
Price: Model 110-ES $323.00

Steyr-Mannlicher L

STEYR-MANNLICHER MODELS SL & L
Caliber: SL—222, 222 Rem. Mag., 223; SL Varmint—222; L—22-250, 6mm, 243, 308 Win.; L Varmint—22-250, 243, 308 Win.; L optional cal.—5.6x57.
Barrel: 20" (full stock); 23.6" (half stock).
Weight: 6 lbs. (full stock). **Length:** 38¼" (full stock).
Stock: Hand checkered walnut. Full Mannlicher or standard half-stock with Monte Carlo.
Sights: Ramp front, open U-notch rear.
Features: Choice of interchangeable single or double set triggers. Five-shot detachable "Makrolon" rotary magazine, 6 rear locking lugs. Drilled and tapped for scope mounts. Imported by Gun South, Inc.
Price: Full Stock $1,056.10
Price: Half-stock $998.94
Price: Optional caliber, add $73.56

Steyr-Mannlicher Varmint, Models SL and L
Similar to standard SL and L except chambered only for: 222 Rem. (SL), 22-250, 243, 308 and optional 5.6x57 (L). Has 26" heavy barrel, no sights (drilled and tapped for scope mounts). Choice of single or double-set triggers. Five-shot detachable magazine.
Price: $1,056.10
Price: Optional caliber, add $73.56
Price: Spare magazine $25.00

Steyr-Mannlicher Professional

Steyr-Mannlicher ML79 "Luxus"

Similar to Steyr-Mannlicher models L and M except has single-set trigger and detachable 3-shot steel magazine; 6-shot magazine optional. Same calibers as L and M. Oil finish or high gloss lacquer on stock.

Price: Full stock **$1,372.49**
Price: Half stock **$1,298.41**
Price: Optional cals., add **$68.77**
Price: Extra 3-shot magazine **$52.39**

STEYR-MANNLICHER MODEL M

Caliber: 7x64, 7x57, 25-06, 270, 30-06. Left-hand action cals.—7x64, 25-06, 270, 30-06. Optional cals.—6.5x57, 8x57JS, 9.3x62, 6.5x55, 7.5x55.
Barrel: 20″ (full stock); 23.6″ (half stock).
Weight: 6.8 lbs. to 7.5 lbs. **Length:** 39″ (full stock); 43″ (half stock).
Stock: Hand checkered walnut. Full Mannlicher or std. half stock with M.C. and rubber recoil pad.
Sights: Ramp front, open U-notch rear.
Features: Choice of interchangeable single or double set triggers. Detachable 5-shot rotary magazine. Drilled and tapped for scope mounting. Available as "Professional" model with parkerized finish and synthetic stock (right hand action only). Imported by Gun South, Inc.

Price: Full stock (carbine) **$1,056.10**
Price: Half stock (rifle) **$998.94**
Price: For left hand action add **$200.00**
Price: Professional model with iron sights **$897.82**

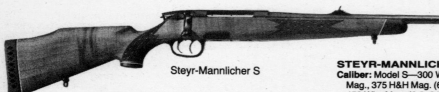

Steyr-Mannlicher S

TIKKA MODEL 55 DELUXE RIFLE

Caliber: 17 Rem., 222, 22-250, 6mm Rem., 243, 308
Barrel: 23″.
Weight: About 6½ lbs. **Length:** 41½″ over-all.
Stock: Hand checkered walnut with rosewood fore-end tip and grip cap.
Sights: Bead on ramp front, rear adjustable for windage and elevation.
Features: Detachable 3-shot magazine with 5- or 10-shot magazines available. Roll-over cheekpiece, palm swell in pistol grip. Adjustable trigger. Receiver dovetailed for scope mounting. Imported from Finland by Mandall and Armsport.

Price: **$650.00**
Price: QD scope mounts **$89.95**

TRADEWINDS HUSKY MODEL 5000 BOLT RIFLE

Caliber: 270, 30-06, 308, 243, 22-250.
Barrel: 23¾″.
Weight: 6 lbs. 11 oz.
Stock: Hand checkered European walnut, Monte Carlo, white line spacers on p.g. cap, fore-end tip and butt plate.
Sights: Fixed hooded front, adj. rear.
Features: Removable mag., full recessed bolt head, adj. trigger. Imported by Tradewinds.

Price: **$395.00**

STEYR-MANNLICHER MODELS S & S/T

Caliber: Model S—300 Win. Mag., 338 Win. Mag., 7mm Rem. Mag., 300 H&H Mag., 375 H&H Mag. (6.5x68, 8x68S, 9.3x64 optional); S/T—375 H&H Mag., 458 Win. Mag. (9.3x64 optional).
Barrel: 25.6″.
Weight: 8.4 lbs. (Model S). **Length:** 45″ over-all.
Stock: Half stock with M.C. and rubber recoil pad. Hand checkered walnut. Available with optional spare magazine inletted in butt.
Sights: Ramp front, U-notch rear.
Features: Choice of interchangeable single or double set triggers., detachable 4-shot magazine. Drilled and tapped for scope mounts. Imported by Gun South, Inc.

Price: Model S.. **$1,258.20**
Price: Model ST 375 H&H, 458 Win. Mag. **$1,332.27**

VOERE 2155, 2165 BOLT ACTION RIFLE

Caliber: 22-250, 270, 308, 243, 30-06, 7x64, 5.6x57, 6.5x55, 8x57 JRS, 7mm Rem. Mag., 300 Win. Mag., 8x68S, 9.3x62, 9.3x64, 6.5x68.
Stock: European walnut, hog-back style; checkered pistol grip and fore-end.
Sights: Ramp front, open adjustable rear.
Features: Mauser-type action with 5-shot detachable box magazine; double set or single trigger; drilled and tapped for scope mounting. Imported from Austria by L. Joseph Rahn. Introduced 1984.

Price: Standard calibers, single trigger **$423.00**
Price: As above, double set triggers........................... **$445.00**
Price: Magnum calibers, single trigger **$456.00**
Price: As above, double set triggers........................... **$475.00**
Price: Full-stock, single trigger **$551.00**
Price: As above, double set triggers........................... **$570.00**

Weatherby Vanguard VGX

Weatherby Vanguard VGL Rifle

Similar to the standard Vanguard except has a short action, chambered for 243 or 308 only, with 20″ barrel. Barrel and action have a non-glare blue finish. Guaranteed to shoot a 1½″ 3-shot group at 100 yards. Stock has a non-glare satin finish, hand checkering and a black butt pad with black spacer. Introduced 1984.

Price: **$389.00**

WEATHERBY VANGUARD VGX, VGS RIFLES

Caliber: 22-250, 25-06, 243, 270, and 30-06 (5-shot), 7mm Rem. and 300 Win. Mag. (3-shot).
Barrel: 24″ hammer forged.
Weight: 7⅞ lbs. **Length:** 44½″ over-all.
Stock: American walnut, p.g. cap and fore-end tip, hand inletted and checkered. 13½″ pull.
Sights: Optional, available at extra cost.
Features: Side safety, adj. trigger, hinged floorplate, receiver tapped for scope mounts. Imported from Japan by Weatherby.

Price: VGS **$389.95**
Price: VGX—deluxe wood, different checkering, ventilated recoil pad **$479.95**

CAUTION: PRICES CHANGE. CHECK AT GUNSHOP.

Weatherby Mark V

WEATHERBY MARK V BOLT ACTION RIFLE
Caliber: All Weatherby cals., 22-250 and 30-06
Barrel: 24" or 26" round tapered.
Weight: 6½-10½ lbs. **Length:** 43¼"-46½".
Stock: Walnut, Monte Carlo with cheekpiece, high luster finish, checkered p.g. and fore-end, recoil pad.
Sights: Optional (extra).
Features: Cocking indicator, adj. trigger, hinged floorplate, thumb safety, quick detachable sling swivels.

Weatherby Lazer Mark V Rifle
Same as standard Mark V except stock has extensive laser carving under cheekpiece, on butt, p.g. and fore-end. Introduced 1981.
Price: 22-250, 224 Wea., 24" bbl. $874.95
Price: As above, 26" bbl. $889.95
Price: 240 Wea. thru 300 Wea., 24" bbl. $894.95
Price: As above, 26" bbl. $914.95
Price: 340 Wea. $914.95
Price: 378 Wea. $1,069.95
Price: 460 Wea. $1,208.95

Price: Cals. 224 and 22-250, std. bbl. $749.95
Price: With 26" semi-target bbl. $764.95
Price: Cals. 240, 257, 270, 7mm, 30-06 and 300 (4" bbl.) $769.95
Price: With 26" No. 2 contour bbl. $789.95
Price: Cal. 340 (26" bbl.). $789.95
Price: Cal. 378 (26" bbl.). $944.95
Price: Cal. 460 (26" bbl.). $1,083.95

Weatherby Fibermark Rifle

Weatherby Fibermark Rifle
Same as the standard Mark V except the stock is of fiberglass; finished with a non-glare black wrinkle finish and black recoil pad; receiver and floorplate have low luster blue finish; fluted bolt has a satin finish. Currently available in right-hand model only, 24" or 26" barrel, 240 Weatherby Mag. through 340 Weatherby Mag. calibers. Introduced 1983.
Price: 240 W.M. through 300 W.M., 24" bbl. $869.95
Price: 240 W.M. through 340 W.M., 26" bbl. $889.95

Weatherby Mark V Rifle Left Hand
Available in all Weatherby calibers except 224 and 22-250 (and 26" No. 2 contour 300WM). Complete left handed action; stock with cheekpiece on right side. Prices are $15 higher than right hand models except the 378 and 460WM are unchanged.

Whitworth Express Rifle

Stock: Classic English Express rifle design of hand checkered, select European Walnut.
Sights: Three leaf open sight calibrated for 100, 200, 300 yards on ¼-rib, ramp front with removable hood (375, 458 only); other calibers have standard open sights.
Features: Solid rubber recoil pad, barrel mounted sling swivel, adjustable trigger, hinged floor plate, solid steel recoil cross bolt. Imported by Interarms.
Price: $490.00
Price: 375, 458, with express sights $590.00
Price: Mannlicher-style carbine, cals. 243, 270, 308, 7x57, 30-06 only, 20" bbl. $650.00

WHITWORTH EXPRESS RIFLE
Caliber: 22-250, 243, 25-06, 270, 7x57, 308, 30-06, 300 Win. Mag., 7mm Rem. Mag., 375 H&H, 458 Win. Mag.
Barrel: 24".
Weight: 7½-8 lbs. **Length:** 44".

Wichita Varmint Rifle

WICHITA VARMINT RIFLE
Caliber: 17 Rem. thru 308 Win., including 22 and 6mm PPC.
Barrel: 20⅛".
Weight: 9 lbs. **Length:** 40⅛" over-all.
Stock: AAA Fancy American walnut. Hand-rubbed finish, hand-checkered, 20 l.p.i. pattern. Hand-inletted, glass bedded steel grip cap, Pachmayr rubber recoil pad.
Sights: None. Drilled and tapped for scope mounts.
Features: Right or left-hand Wichita action with three locking lugs. Available as a single shot or repeater with 3-shot detachable magazine. Checkered bolt handle. Bolt is hand fitted, lapped and jeweled. Side thumb safety. Firing pin fall is ³⁄₁₆". Non-glare blue finish. Shipped in hard Protecto case. From Wichita Arms.
Price: Single shot $1,075.00
Price: With blind box magazine $1,205.00

WICHITA CLASSIC RIFLE
Caliber: 17 Rem. thru 308 Win., including 22 and 6mm PPC.
Barrel: 21⅛".
Weight: 8 lbs. **Length:** 41" over-all.
Stock: AAA Fancy American walnut. Hand-rubbed and checkered (20 l.p.i.). Hand-inletter, glass bedded, steel grip cap. Pachmayr rubber recoil pad.
Sights: None. Drilled and tapped for scope mounting.
Features: Available as single shot or repeater. Octagonal barrel and Wichita action, right or left-hand. Checkered bolt handle. Bolt is hand-fitted, lapped and jewelled. Adjustable Canjar trigger is set at 2 lbs. Side thumb safety. Firing pin fall is ³⁄₁₆". Non-glare blue finish. Shipped in hard Protecto case. From Wichita Arms.
Price: Single shot $1,725.00
Price: With blind box magazine $1,855.00

Winchester 70 XTR Sporter

WICHITA MAGNUM STAINLESS RIFLE
Caliber: From 270 Win. through 458 Win. Mag.
Barrel: 22″ or 24″.
Weight: 8½ lbs. **Length:** 44¾″ over-all (24″ barrel).
Stock: AAA fancy walnut; hand inletted; glass bedded; steel grip cap; Pachmayr rubber recoil pad.
Sights: None. Drilled and tapped for Burris scope mounts.
Features: Stainless steel barrel and action, round contour. Target grade barrel. Available as a single shot or with a blind magazine. Fully adj. trigger. Bolt is ⅞″ in diameter with recessed face. Hand rubbed stock finish, checkered 20 l.p.i. Shipped in a hard case. Introduced 1980. From Wichita Arms.
Price: Single shot $2,155.00
Price: With blind box magazine $2,285.00

Winchester 70 XTR Sporter Varmint Rifle
Same as 70 XTR Sporter Magnum except: 223, 22-250 and 243 only, no sights, 24″ heavy bbl., 44½″ over-all, 9¾ lbs. American walnut Monte Carlo stock with cheekpiece, black serrated buttplate, black fore-end tip, high luster finish.
Price: $479.95

WINCHESTER 70 XTR SPORTER MAGNUM
Caliber: 264 Win. Mag., 7mm Rem. Mag., 300 Win. Mag., 338 Win. Mag., 3-shot magazine.
Barrel: 24″.
Weight: 7¾ lbs. **Length:** 44½″ over-all.
Stock: American walnut with Monte Carlo cheekpiece. XTR checkering and satin finish.
Sights: Hooded ramp front, adjustable folding leaf rear.
Features: Three-position safety, detachable sling swivels, stainless steel magazine follower, rubber butt pad, epoxy bedded receiver recoil lug. Made under license by U.S. Repeating Arms Co.
Price: $479.95

Winchester Model 70 XTR Sporter
Same as the Model 70 XTR Sporter Magnum except available only in 270 Win. and 30-06, 5-shot magazine.
Price: $479.95

Winchester 70 XTR Express

WINCHESTER 70 XTR SUPER EXPRESS MAGNUM
Caliber: 375 H&H Mag., 458 Win. Mag., 3-shot magazine.
Barrel: 24″ (375), 22″ (458).
Weight: 8½ lbs.
Stock: American walnut with Monte Carlo cheekpiece. XTR wrap-around checkering and finish.
Sights: Hooded ramp front, open rear.
Features: Two steel crossbolts in stock for added strength. Front sling swivel mounted on barrel. Contoured rubber butt pad. Made under license by U.S. Repeating Arms Co.
Price: 375 H&H $739.95
Price: 458 Win $769.95

Winchester 70 Lightweight

WINCHESTER MODEL 70 LIGHTWEIGHT CARBINE
Caliber: 270, 30-06 (standard action); 22-250, 223, 243, 308 (short action), both 5-shot magazine.
Barrel: 20″.
Weight: 6¼ lbs. (std.), 6 lbs. (short). **Length:** 40½″ over-all (std.), 40″ (short).
Stock: American walnut with satin finish, deep-cut checkering.
Sights: None furnished. Drilled and tapped for scope mounting.
Features: Three position safety; stainless steel magazine follower; hinged floorplate; sling swivel studs. Introduced 1984.
Price: $349.95

Winchester 70 Featherweight

Winchester Model 70 XTR Featherweight
Available with standard action in 257 Roberts, 270 Win., 7mm Mauser, 30-06, short action in 22-250, 223, 243, 308; 22″ tapered Featherweight barrel; classic-style American walnut stock with Schnabel fore-end, wrap-around XTR checkering fashioned after early Model 70 custom rifle patterns. Red rubber butt pad with black spacer; sling swivel studs. Weighs 6¾ lbs. (standard action), 6½ lbs. (short action). Introduced 1984.
Price: $499.95

CAUTION: PRICES CHANGE. CHECK AT GUNSHOP.

H&R Model 171

HARRINGTON & RICHARDSON Model 171 Deluxe Cavalry Model Carbine
Caliber: 45-70 single shot.
Barrel: 22".
Weight: 7 lbs. **Length:** 41".
Stock: American walnut with saddle ring and bridle.
Sights: Blade front, barrel mounted leaf rear adj. for e.
Features: Replica of the 1873 Springfield Carbine. Blue-black finish. Deluxe version has engraved breech block, side lock & hammer.
Price: **$395.00**

H&R Model 158

HARRINGTON AND RICHARDSON 158 RIFLE
Caliber: 30-30, 22 Hornet, single shot.
Barrel: 22" round tapered.
Weight: 6 lbs. **Length:** 37".
Stock: Walnut finished hardwood stock and fore-end.
Sights: Blade front; folding adj. rear.
Features: Side lever break-open action with visible hammer. Easy takedown.
Price: **$109.50**

Harrington & Richardson Model 058 Combo Gun
    Same as Model 158, except fitted with accessory 20-ga. barrel (26", Mod.).
Price: 22 Hornet, or 30-30 Win., plus 20-ga. **$134.50**
Price: Model 258 (as above except nickel finish) 22 Hornet, 30-30, 357 Mag., 357 Max., 44 Mag. (with case) **$184.50**

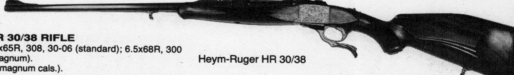

HEYM-RUGER Model HR 30/38 RIFLE
Caliber: 243, 6.5x57R, 7x64, 7x65R, 308, 30-06 (standard); 6.5x68R, 300 Win. Mag., 8x68S, 9.3x74R (magnum).
Barrel: 24" (standard cals.), 26" (magnum cals.).
Weight: 6½ to 7 lbs.
Stock: Dark European walnut, hand checkered p.g. and fore-end. Oil finish, recoil pad. Full Mannlicher-type or sporter-style with Schnabel fore-end, Bavarian cheekpiece.
Sights: Bead on ramp front, leaf rear.
Features: Ruger No. 1 action and safety, Canjar single-set trigger, hand-engraved animal motif. Options available include deluxe engraving and stock carving. Imported from West Germany by Paul Jaeger Inc.

Heym-Ruger HR 30/38

Price: HR-30N, round bbl., sporter stock, std. cals. **$1,995.00**
Price: HR-30G, as above except in mag. cals. **$1,995.00**
Price: HR-30L, round bbl., full stock, std. cals. **$2,110.00**
Price: For octagon barrel, add **$250.00**
Price: For sideplates with large hunting scenes, add **$640.00**

Ljutic Space Rifle

LJUTIC RECOILESS SPACE RIFLE
Caliber: 22-250, 30-30, 30-06, 308; single-shot.
Barrel: 24".
Weight: 8¾ lbs. **Length:** 44" over-all.
Stock: Walnut stock and fore-end.
Sights: Iron sights or scope mounts.
Features: Revolutionary design has anti-recoil mechanism. Twist-bolt action uses six moving parts. Scope and mounts extra. Introduced 1981. From Ljutic Industries.
Price: **$3,495.00**

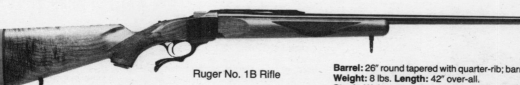

Ruger No. 1B Rifle

RUGER NO. 1B SINGLE SHOT
Caliber: 220 Swift, 22-250, 223, 243, 6mm Rem., 25-06, 257 Roberts, 270, 280, 30-06, 7mm Rem. Mag., 300 Win., 338 Win. Mag., 45-70, 458 Win. Mag., 375 H&H Mag.

Barrel: 26" round tapered with quarter-rib; barrel tapped for target scope block.
Weight: 8 lbs. **Length:** 42" over-all.
Stock: Walnut, two-piece, checkered p.g. and semi-beavertail fore-end.
Sights: None, 1" scope rings supplied for integral mounts.
Features: Under lever, hammerless falling block design has auto ejector, top tang safety. Standard Rifle 1B illus.
Price: **$405.00**
Price: Barreled action, blued only **$286.50**

Ruger No. 1 Light Sporter

Ruger No. 1 Light Sporter
Similar to the No. 1-B Standard Rifle except has lightweight 22" barrel, Alexander Henry style fore-end, adjustable folding leaf rear sight on quarter-rib, dovetailed ramp front with gold bead. Calibers 243, 30-06, 270 and 7x57. Weight about 7¼ lbs.
Price: No. 1-A.. $405.00

Ruger No. 1 Medium Sporter
Similar to the No. 1B Standard Rifle except has Alexander Henry style fore-end, adjustable folding leaf rear sight on quarter-rib, ramp front sight base and dovetail-type gold bead front sight. Calibers 7mm Rem. Mag., 338 Win. Mag., 300 Win. Mag., and 45-70 with 22" barrel. Weight about 8 lbs.
Price: No. 1-S.. $405.00

Ruger No. 1 International

Ruger No. 1 International
Similar to the No. 1-B Standard Rifle except has lightweight 20" barrel, full length Mannlicher-style fore-end with loop sling swivel, adjustable folding leaf rear sight on quarter rib, ramp front with gold bead. Calibers 243, 30-06, 270 and 7x57. Weight is about 7¼ lbs.
Price: No. 1-RSI.. $425.00

Ruger No. 1 Tropical Rifle
Similar to the No. 1-B Standard Rifle except has Alexander Henry fore-end, adjustable folding leaf rear sight on quarter-rib, ramp front with dovetail gold bead front, 24" heavy barrel. Calibers 375 H&H (weight about 8¼ lbs.) and 458 Win. Mag. (weight about 9 lbs.).
Price: No. 1-H.. $405.00

Ruger No. 1 Special Varminter
Similar to the No. 1-B Standard Rifle except has 24" heavy barrel. Semi-beavertail fore-end, barrel tapped for target scope block, with 1" Ruger scope rings. Calibers 22-250, 220 Swift, 223, 243, 25-06, 6mm, and 280 Rem. Weight about 9 lbs.
Price: No. 1-V.. $405.00

Ruger No. 3 Carbine

RUGER NO. 3 CARBINE SINGLE SHOT
Caliber: 223, 44 Magnum, 45-70.
Barrel: 22" round.
Weight: 7¼ lbs. **Length:** 38½".
Stock: American walnut, carbine-type.
Sights: Gold bead front, adj. folding leaf rear.
Features: Same action as No. 1 Rifle except different lever. Has auto ejector, top tang safety, adj. trigger. Drilled and tapped for Ruger bases and Ruger 1" rings.
Price: $284.00

NAVY ARMS ROLLING BLOCK RIFLE
Caliber: 45-70.
Barrel: 26½".
Stock: Walnut finished.
Sights: Fixed front, adj. rear.
Features: Reproduction of classic rolling block action. Available in Buffalo Rifle (octagonal bbl.) and Creedmore (half round, half octagonal bbl.) models. Made in U.S. by Navy Arms.
Price: 18", 26", 30" full octagon barrel $374.00
Price: Creedmore Model, 30" full octagon $399.00
Price: 30", half-round.. $379.00
Price: 26", half-round.. $374.00
Price: Half-round Creedmore.................................... $399.00

SHARPS "OLD RELIABLE" RIFLE
Caliber: 45-70, 45-120-3¼" Sharps.
Barrel: 28", full octagon, polished blue.
Weight: 9½ lbs. **Length:** 45" over-all.
Stock: Walnut with deluxe checkering at p.g. and fore-end.
Sights: Sporting blade front, folding leaf rear. Globe front, vernier rear optional at extra cost.
Features: Falling block, lever action. Color case-hardened hammer, buttplate and action with automatic safety. Available with engraved action for **$97.25** extra. From Shore.
Price: Old Reliable.. $377.50
Price: Sporter Rifle $362.50
Price: Military Carbine.. $345.00
Price: Sporter Carbine $362.50

Thompson/Center Single Shot

THOMPSON/CENTER SINGLE SHOT RIFLE
Caliber: 223 Rem., 22-250, 243 Win., 7mm Rem. Mag., 30-06.
Barrel: 23".
Weight: About 6¾ lbs. **Length:** 39½" over-all.
Stock: American black walnut, checkered p.g. and fore-end.
Sights: Blade on ramp front, open rear adj. for windage only.
Features: Break-open design with interchangeable barrels. Double-set or single-stage trigger function. Cross-bolt safety. Sights removable for scope mounting. Made in U.S. by T/C. Introduced 1983.
Price: $425.00
Price: Extra barrel $140.00

CAUTION: PRICES CHANGE. CHECK AT GUNSHOP.

ARMSPORT "EMPEROR" 4000 DOUBLE RIFLE
Caliber: 243, 270, 284, 7.65, 308, 30-06, 7mm Rem. Mag., 9.3, 300 H&H, 375 H&H; Shotgun barrels in 12, 16 or 20-ga.
Barrel: Shotgun barrel length and chokes to customer specs.
Stock: Dimensions to customer specs. Stock and fore-end of root walnut.
Sights: Rifle barrels have blade front with bead, leaf rear adj. for w.
Features: Receiver and sideplates engraved. Gun comes with extra set of barrels fitted to action. Packaged in a hand-made, fitted luggage-type leather case lined with Scotch loden cloth. Introduced 1978. From Armsport.
Price: Complete $16,300.00

> Consult our Directory pages for the location of firms mentioned.

ARMSPORT "EMPEROR" 4010 DOUBLE RIFLE
Side-by-side version of the Model 4000 over-under rifle. Available in 243, 270, 284, 7.65, 308, 30-06, 7mm Rem. Mag., 9.3, 300 H&H, 338 Win. and 375 H&H. Shotgun barrels in 16 or 20 ga., choice of length and choke. Comes in fitted luggage-type case.
Price: $12,750.00

BERETTA EXPRESS S689 DOUBLE RIFLE
Caliber: 9.3x74R, 375 H&H, 458 win. Mag.
Barrel: 23".
Weight: 7.7 lbs.
Stock: European walnut, checkered grip and fore-end.
Sights: Blade front on ramp, open V-notch rear.
Features: Boxlock action with silvered, engraved receiver; extractors on S689, ejectors on S689E; double triggers; solid butt pad. Imported from Italy by Beretta U.S.A. Corp. Introduced 1984.
Price: S689, 9.3x74R only $1,750.00
Price: SSO, 375 H&H, 458 Win. Mag. $7,500.00

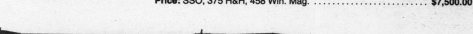

Browning Continental

BROWNING SUPERPOSED CONTINENTAL
Caliber/Gauge: 20 ga. x 20 ga. with extra 30-06x30-06 o/u barrel set.
Barrel: 20 ga.—26½" (Mod. & Full, 3" chambers), vent. rib, with medium raised German nickel silver sight bead. 30-06—24".
Weight: 6 lbs. 14 oz. (rifle barrels), 5 lbs. 14 oz. (shotgun barrels)
Stock: Select high grade American walnut with oil finish. Straight grip stock and Schnabel fore-end with 26 lpi hand checkering.
Sights: Rifle barrels have flat face gold bead front on matted ramp, folding leaf rear.
Features: Action is based on a specially engineered Superposed 20-ga. frame. Single selective trigger works on inertia; let-off is about 4½ lbs. Automatic selective ejectors. Manual top tang safety incorporated with barrel selector. Furnished with fitted luggage-type case. Introduced 1979. Imported from Belgium by Browning.
Price: $5,600.00

BROWNING EXPRESS RIFLE
Caliber: 270 or 30-06.
Barrel: 24".
Weight: About 6 lbs., 14 oz. **Length:** 41" over-all.
Stock: Select walnut with oil finish; straight grip, Schnabel fore-end; hand checkered to 25 lpi.
Sights: Gold bead on ramp front, adjustable folding leaf rear.
Features: Specially engineered Superposed action with reinforced breech face. Receiver hand engraved. Single selective trigger, auto. selective ejectors, manual safety. Comes in fitted luggage case. Imported from Belgium by Browning.
Price: Either caliber $3,925.00

Colt Sauer Drilling

COLT SAUER DRILLING
Caliber/Gauge: 12 ga., over 30-06, 12 ga. over 243.
Action: Top lever, cross bolt, box lock.
Barrel: 25" (Mod. & Full).
Weight: 8 lbs. **Length:** 41¾" over-all.
Stock: American walnut, oil finish. Checkered p.g. and fore-end. Black p.g. cap, recoil pad. 14¼"x2"x1½".
Sights: Blade front with brass bead, folding leaf rear.
Features: Cocking indicators, tang barrel selector, automatic sight positioner, set rifle trigger, side safety. Blue finish with bright receiver engraved with animal motifs and European-style scrollwork. Imported from West Germany by Colt.
Price: $4,227.95

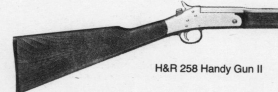

H&R 258 Handy Gun II

HARRINGTON & RICHARDSON 258 HANDY GUN II
Caliber/Gauge: 22 Hornet, 30-30 Win., 357 Mag., 357 Maximum, 44 Mag. with interchangeable 20-ga. 3" barrel.
Barrel: 22" (rifle), 22" (Mod.) shotgun.
Weight: About 6½ lbs. **Length:** 37" over-all.
Stock: American hardwood with walnut finish.
Sights: Bead front on shotgun; ramped blade front, adjustable folding leaf rear on rifle barrel.
Features: Interchangeable barrels. All metal parts have H&R Hard-Gard electroless matte nickel finish. Comes with heavy duck case. Introduced 1982.
Price: $184.50

DRILLINGS, COMBINATION GUNS, DOUBLE RIFLES

Heym 22S Combo

HEYM MODEL 22S SAFETY COMBO GUN
Caliber/Gauge: 16 or 20 ga. (2¾", 3") over 22 Hornet, 22 WMR, 222 Rem., 222 Rem. Mag., 223, 243 Win., 5.6x50R, 6.5x57R, 7x57R, 8x57 JRS.
Barrel: 24", solid rib.
Weight: About 5½ lbs.
Stock: Dark European walnut, hand-checkered p.g. and fore-end. Oil finish.
Sights: Silver bead ramp front, folding leaf rear.
Features: Tang mounted cocking slide, separate barrel selector, single set trigger. Base supplied for quick-detachable scope mounts. Patented rocker-weight system automatically uncocks gun if accidentally dropped or bumped hard. Imported from West Germany. Contact Heym for more data.
Price: Model 22S **$1,390.00**
Price: Model 22SZ takedown, add **$190.00**
Price: Scope mounts, add **$125.00**

Heym Model 37 Side Lock Drilling
Similar to Model 37 Double Rifle Drilling except has 12x12, 16x16 or 20x20 over 5.6x50R Mag., 5.6x57R, 6.5x57R, 7x57R, 7x65R, 8x57JRS, 9.3x74R, 222, 243, 270, 308 or 30-06. Rifle barrel is manually cocked and uncocked.
Price: Model 37 with border engraving **$5,190.00**
Price: As above with engraved hunting scenes.................. **$6,170.00**

HEYM MODEL 37B DOUBLE RIFLE DRILLING
Caliber/Gauge: 7x65R, 30-06, 8x57JRS, 9.3x74R; 20 ga. (3").
Barrel: 25" (shotgun barrel choked Full or Mod.).
Weight: About 8½ lbs. **Length:** 42" over-all.
Stock: Dark European walnut, hand-checkered p.g. and fore-end. Oil finish.
Sights: Silver bead front, folding leaf rear. Available with scope and Suhler claw mounts.
Features: Full side-lock construction. Greener-type crossbolt, double under-lugs, cocking indicators. Imported from West Germany by Paul Jaeger, Inc.
Price: Model 37 double rifle drilling **$6,860.00**
Price: Model 37 Deluxe (hunting scene engraving) from, ... **$7,840.00**

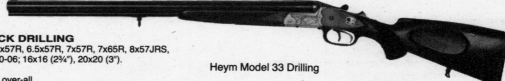

Heym Model 33 Drilling

HEYM MODEL 33 BOXLOCK DRILLING
Caliber/Gauge: 5.6x50R Mag., 5.6x57R, 6.5x57R, 7x57R, 7x65R, 8x57JRS, 9.3x74R, 222, 243, 270, 308, 30-06; 16x16 (2¾"), 20x20 (3").
Barrel: 25" (Full & Mod.).
Weight: About 6½ lbs. **Length:** 42" over-all.
Stock: Dark European walnut, checkered p.g. and fore-end; oil finish.
Sights: Silver bead front, folding leaf rear. Automatic sight positioner. Available with scope and Suhler claw mounts.
Features: Greener-type crossbolt and safety, double under-lugs. Double set triggers. Plastic or steel trigger guard. Engraving coverage varies with model. Imported from West Germany by Paul Jaeger Inc.
Price: Model 33, from....................................... **$3,350.00**

Heym Model 88B Double

HEYM MODEL 88B SIDE-BY-SIDE DOUBLE RIFLE
Caliber: 30-06, 8x57JRS, 300 Win. Mag., 9.3x74R, 375 H&H.
Barrel: 25".
Weight: 7½ lbs. (std. cals), 8½ lbs. (mag.) **Length:** 42" over-all.
Stock: Fancy French walnut, classic North American design.
Sights: Silver bead post on ramp front, fixed or 3-leaf express rear.
Features: Action has complete coverage hunting scene engraving. Available as boxlock or with q.d. sidelocks. Imported from West Germany by Paul Jaeger, Inc.
Price: Boxlock, from **$5,225.00**
Price: Sidelock, Model 88B-SS, from **$7,325.00**
Price: Disengageable ejectors, add **$190.00**
Price: Interchangeable barrels, add **$2,870.00**

Heym 55B/77B O/U

HEYM MODEL 55B/77B O/U DOUBLE RIFLE
Caliber: 7x65R, 308, 30-06, 8x57JRS, 9.3x74R; 375 H&H.
Barrel: 25"
Weight: About 8 lbs., depending upon caliber. **Length:** 42" over-all.
Stock: Dark European walnut, hand-checkered p.g. and fore-end. Oil finish.
Sights: Silver bead ramp front, open V-type rear.
Features: Boxlock or full sidelock; Kersten double crossbolt, cocking indicators; hand-engraved hunting scenes. Options available include interchangeable barrels, Zeiss scopes in claw mounts, deluxe engravings and stock carving, etc. Imported from West Germany by Paul Jaeger, Inc.
Price: Model 55B boxlock.................................... **$3,880.00**
Price: Model 55BSS sidelock................................. **$6,160.00**
Price: Interchangeable shotgun barrels **$1,715.00**

Heym Model 55BF/77BF O/U Combo Gun
Similar to Model 55B/77B o/u rifle except chambered for 12, 16 or 20 ga. (2¾" or 3") over 5.6x50R, 222 Rem., 5.6x57R, 243, 6.5x57R, 270, 7x57R, 7x65R, 308, 30-06, 8x57JRS, 9.3x74R, or 375 H&H. Has solid rib barrel. Available as boxlock or sidelock, with interchangeable shotgun and rifle barrels.
Price: Model 55BF boxlock................................... **$3,070.00**
Price: Model 55BFSS sidelock................................ **$5,350.00**

CAUTION: PRICES CHANGE. CHECK AT GUNSHOP.

DRILLINGS, COMBINATION GUNS, DOUBLE RIFLES

LEBEAU-COURALLY SIDELOCK DOUBLE RIFLE
Caliber: 8x57 JRS, 9.3x74R, 375 H&H, 458 Win.
Barrel: 23½" to 26".
Weight: 7 lbs., 8 oz. to 9 lbs., 8 oz.
Stock: Dimensions to customer specs. Best quality French walnut selected for maximum strength, pistol grip with cheekpiece, splinter or beavertail fore-end; steel grip cap.
Sights: Bead on ramp front, express rear on ¼-rib.
Features: Holland & Holland pattern sidelock with ejectors, chopper lump barrels; reinforced action with classic pattern; choice of numerous engraving patterns; can be furnished with scope in fitted claw mounts. Imported from Belgium by Wm. Larkin Moore.
Price: From **$17,900.00**

LEBEAU-COURALLY BOXLOCK DOUBLE RIFLE
Caliber: 8x57 JRS, 9.3x74R, 375 H&H, 458 Win.
Barrel: 23½" to 26".
Weight: 7 lbs., 8 oz. to 9 lbs., 8 oz.
Stock: Dimension to customer specs. Select French walnut, hand rubbed oil finish, pistol grip stock with cheekpiece, splinter or beavertail fore-end.
Sights: Bead on ramp front, express rear on ¼-rib.
Features: Anson & Deeley boxlock with ejectors and Purdey-type third fastener; choice of classic or rounded action; choice of numerous engraving patterns; can be furnished with scope in fitted claw mounts. Imported from Belgium by Wm. Larkin Moore.
Price: From **$9,000.00**

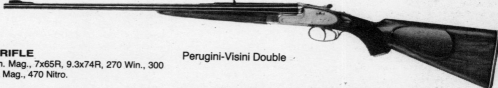

PERUGINI-VISINI DOUBLE RIFLE
Caliber: 22 Hornet, 30-06, 7mm Rem. Mag., 7x65R, 9.3x74R, 270 Win., 300 H&H, 338 Win., 375 H&H, 458 Win. Mag., 470 Nitro.
Barrel: 22"-26".
Weight: 7¼ to 8½ lbs., depending upon caliber. **Length:** 39½" over-all (22" bbl.).
Stock: Oil-finished walnut; checkered grip and fore-end; cheekpiece.
Sights: Bead on ramp front, express rear on ¼-rib.

Perugini-Visini Double

Features: True sidelock action with ejectors; sideplates are hand detachable; comes with leather trunk case. Introduced 1983. Imported from Italy by Wm. Larkin Moore.
Price: **$11,000.00**

PERUGINI-VISINI O/U DOUBLE RIFLE
Caliber: 7mm Rem. Mag., 7x65R, 9.3x74R, 270 Win., 338 Win. Mag., 375 H&H, 458 Win. Mag.
Barrel: 24".
Weight: 8 lbs. **Length:** 40½" over-all.
Stock: Oil-finished walnut; checkered grip and fore-end; cheekpiece, rubber recoil pad.
Sights: Bead on ramp front, express rear on ¼-rib; Swarovski scope and claw mounts optional.

Perugini-Visini O/U Double

Features: Boxlock action with ejectors; silvered receiver, rest blued; double triggers. Comes with trunk case. Deluxe engraving, better wood, etc. available. Introduced 1983. Imported from Italy by Wm. Larkin Moore.
Price: **$3,950.00**

PERUGINI-VISINI BOXLOCK DOUBLE RIFLE
Caliber: 7x65R, 7x57, 308, 9.3x74R, 375 H&H, 444 Marlin, 458 Win. Mag.
Barrel: 25".
Weight: 8 lbs. **Length:** 41½" over-all.
Stock: Oil-finished walnut; checkered grip and fore-end; cheekpiece; rubber recoil pad.
Sights: Bead on ramp front, express rear on ¼-rib.
Features: Boxlock action with ejectors; color case-hardened receiver; double triggers. Comes with trunk case. Introduced 1983. Imported from Italy by Wm. Larkin Moore.
Price: From **$2,950.00**

Perugini-Visini Boxlock Double

Savage Model 24-D

SAVAGE MODEL 24-D O/U
Caliber/Gauge: Top bbl. 22 S, L, LR or 22 Mag.; bottom bbl. 20 or 410 gauge.
Action: Bottom opening lever, low rebounding visible hammer, single trigger, barrel selector spur on hammer, separate extractors, color case-hardened frame.
Barrel: 24", separated barrels.
Weight: 6¾ lbs. **Length:** 40".
Stock: Walnut, checkered p.g. (14"x1½"x2½").
Sights: Ramp front, rear open adj. for e.
Features: Receiver grooved for scope mounting.
Price: **$195.50**

Savage Model 24-V
Similar to Model 24-D except: 22 Hornet, 222 Rem, or 30-30 and 20 ga., 223 or 357 Rem. Max. and 20 ga.; stronger receiver; color case-hardened frame; folding leaf rear sight; receiver tapped for scope.
Price: **$242.00**

Savage Model 24-F.G. O/U
Same as Model 24-D except: color case hardened frame, stock is walnut finished hardwood, no checkering or M.C.
Price: **$169.50**

DRILLINGS, COMBINATION GUNS, DOUBLE RIFLES

Savage Model 24-VS

Savage Model 24-VS Camper/Survival Shotgun
Similar to the standard Model 24-V except satin nickel finish, full-length, tung-oil finished stock and an accessory pistol grip stock. Chambered for 357 Rem. Max. over 20 gauge. Also available in 22 Long Rifle over 20 gauge as Model 24-CS. Introduced 1983.
Price: Model 24-VS $266.50
Price: Model 24-CS $208.00

Savage Model 24-C

SAVAGE MODEL 24-C O/U
Caliber/Gauge: Top bbl. 22 S, L, LR; bottom bbl. 20 gauge cyl. bore.
Action: Take-down, low rebounding visible hammer. Single trigger, barrel selector spur on hammer.
Barrel: 20″ separated barrels.
Weight: 5¾ lbs. **Length:** 35″ (taken down 20″).
Stock: Walnut finished hardwood, straight grip.
Sights: Ramp front, rear open adj. for e.
Features: Trap door butt holds one shotshell and ten 22 cartridges, comes with special carrying case. Measures 7″x22″ when in case.
Price: $189.50

Valmet 412S American Series
Similar to the 412K except better wood, finer checkering, palm swell on pistol grip, luminous sights, lighter weight, new fore-end latch spring mechanism and improved firing pin mechanism. Introduced 1984.
Price: 412S Combination Gun $879.00
Price: 412S Double Rifle with extractors $1,119.00
Price: As above but with ejectors $1,169.00

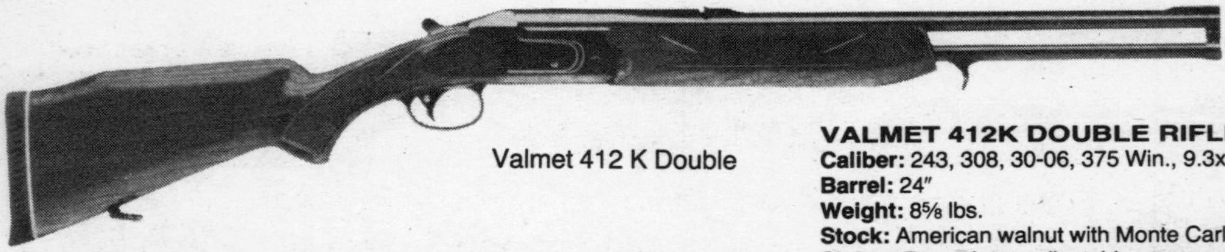

Valmet 412 K Double

VALMET 412K DOUBLE RIFLE
Caliber: 243, 308, 30-06, 375 Win., 9.3x74R.
Barrel: 24″
Weight: 8⅝ lbs.
Stock: American walnut with Monte Carlo style.
Sights: Ramp front, adjustable open rear.
Features: Barrel selector mounted in trigger. Cocking indicators in tang. Recoil pad. Valmet scope mounts available. Interchangeable barrels. Introduced 1980. Imported from Finland by Valmet.
Price: Extractors, 243, 308, 30-06 . . . . $1,069.00
Price: With ejectors, 375 Win., 9.3x74R $1,119.00
Price: Extra barrels, from $409.00
Price: Engraved model with full scroll $1,819.00
Price: Engraved with game scenes $2,569.00

VALMET 412KE COMBINATION GUN
Caliber/Gauge: 12 over 222, 223, 243, 308, 30-06.
Barrel: 24″ (Imp. & Mod.).
Weight: 7⅝ lbs.
Stock: American walnut, with recoil pad. Monte Carlo style. Standard measurements 14″x1⅜″x2″x2⅜″.
Sights: Blade front, flip-up-type open rear.
Features: Barrel selector on trigger. Hand checkered stock and fore-end. Barrels are screw-adjustable to change bullet point of impact. Barrels are interchangeable. Introduced 1980. Imported from Finland by Valmet.
Price: $834.00
Price: Extra barrels, from $409.00
Price: Engraved model with full scroll $1,579.00
Price: Engraved with game scenes $2,329.00

Winchester Double Xpress

WINCHESTER DOUBLE XPRESS O/U RIFLE
Caliber: 30-06/30-06, 9.3x74R/9.3x74R, 270/270, 257 Roberts/257 Roberts.
Barrel: 23½″.
Weight: 8½ lbs. **Length:** 39⅝″ over-all.
Stock: 2½″x1¹¹/₁₆″x14⅜″. Fancy American walnut with hand checkered pistol grip and fore-end, solid rubber butt pad.
Sights: Bead on ramp front, folding leaf rear on quarter-rib.
Features: Integral scope bases; q.d. sling swivels. Uses Model 101 action; receiver silvered and engraved, barrels blued. Comes with hard case. Introduced 1982. Imported from Japan by Winchester Group, Olin Corp.
Price: $2,995.00

WINCHESTER SUPER GRADE O/U COMBO
Caliber/Gauge: 12 ga. over 30-06.
Barrel: 25″. Shot barrel uses Winchoke system.
Weight: 8½ lbs. **Length:** 41¼″ over-all.
Stock: 2½″x1¾″x14″. Fancy American walnut with hand checkered pistol grip and fore-end; ventilated rubber recoil pad.
Sights: Bead front, folding leaf rear.
Features: Single selective mechanical trigger, combination barrel selector. Full length top barrel rib with integral scope bases. Uses Model 101 frame. Silvered and engraved receiver, blued barrels. Imported from Japan by Winchester Group, Olin Corp.
Price: $2,550.00

A. ZOLI RIFLE-SHOTGUN O/U COMBO
Caliber/Gauge: 12 ga./308 Win., 12 ga./222, 12 ga./30-06.
Barrel: Combo—24″; shotgun—28″ (Mod. & Full).
Weight: About 8 lbs. **Length:** 41″ over-all (24″ bbl.).
Stock: European walnut.
Sights: Blade front, flip-up rear.
Features: Available with German claw scope mounts on rifle/shotgun barrels. Comes with set of 12/12 (Mod. & Full) barrels. Imported from Italy by Mandall Shooting Supplies.
Price: With two barrel sets, without claw mounts $1,495.00
Price: With two barrel sets, scope and claw mounts $1,895.00

CAUTION: PRICES CHANGE. CHECK AT GUNSHOP.

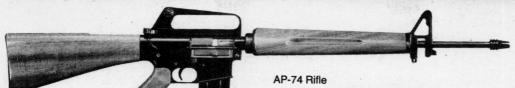

AP-74 Rifle

AP-74 AUTO RIFLE
Caliber: 22 LR, 32 ACP, 15 shot magazine.
Barrel: 20″ including flash reducer.
Weight: 6½ lbs. **Length:** 38½″ over-all.
Stock: Black plastic.
Sights: Ramp front, adj. peep rear.
Features: Pivotal take-down, easy disassembly. AR-15 look-alike. Sling and sling swivels included. Imported by EMF.
Price: $250.00
Price: With walnut stock and fore-end $275.00
Price: 32 ACP. $265.00
Price: With wood stock and fore-end $290.00

Anschutz Model 520/61

ANSCHUTZ DELUXE MODEL 520/61 AUTO
Caliber: 22 LR, 10-shot clip.
Barrel: 24″.
Weight: 6½ lbs. **Length:** 43″ over-all.
Stock: European hardwood; checkered pistol grip, Monte Carlo comb, beavertail fore-end.
Sights: Hooded ramp front, folding leaf rear.
Features: Rotary safety, empty shell deflector, single stage trigger. Receiver grooved for scope mounting. Introduced 1982. Imported from Germany by PSI.
Price: $234.00

Auto-Ordnance 1927A-3

AUTO-ORDNANCE MODEL 1927A-3
Caliber: 22 LR, 10, 30 or 50-shot magazine.
Barrel: 16″, finned.
Weight: About 7 lbs.
Stock: Walnut stock and fore-end.
Sights: Blade front, open rear adjustable for windage and elevation.
Features: Re-creation of the Thompson Model 1927, only in 22 Long Rifle. Alloy receiver, finned barrel.
Price: $519.85

BINGHAM PPS-50 CARBINE
Caliber: 22 LR, 50-shot drum.
Barrel: 16.1″.
Weight: 6½ lbs. **Length:** 33¾″ over-all.
Stock: Beechwood (standard), walnut optional.
Sights: Blade front, folding leaf rear.
Features: Semi-auto carbine with perforated barrel jacket. Standard model has blue finish with oil-finish wood. From Bingham Ltd.
Price: Standard $229.95
Price: Deluxe (blue with walnut stock) $249.95
Price: Duramil (chrome with walnut stock) $259.95

BINGHAM AK-22 CARBINE
Caliber: 22 LR, 15-shot magazine.
Barrel: 17¾″.
Weight: 6 lbs., 1 oz. **Length:** 35½″ over-all.
Stock: Beechwood (standard), walnut optional.
Sights: Hooded post front, open adjustable rear.
Features: Semi-auto rimfire version of the Soviet assault rifle. A 28-shot "Military Look-Alike" magazine optional. From Bingham Ltd.
Price: Standard $229.95
Price: Deluxe (walnut stock) $249.95

Browning Auto Rifle

BROWNING AUTOLOADING RIFLE
Caliber: 22 LR, 11-shot.
Barrel: 19¼″.
Weight: 4¾ lbs. **Length:** 37″ over-all.
Stock: Checkered select walnut (13¾″x1¹³⁄₁₆″x2⅝″) with p.g. and semi-beavertail fore-end.
Sights: Gold bead front, folding leaf rear.
Features: Engraved receiver is grooved for tip-off scope mount; cross-bolt safety; tubular magazine in buttstock; easy take down for carrying or storage. Imported from Japan by Browning.
Price: Grade I. $267.95
Price: Grade II $380.00
Price: Grade III $815.00
Price: Also available in Grade I, 22 S (16-shot) $267.95

Browning BAR-22

BROWNING BAR-22 AUTO RIFLE
Caliber: 22 LR only, 15-shot tube magazine.
Barrel: 20¼".
Weight: About 6¼ lbs. **Length:** 38¼" over-all.

Stock: French walnut. Cut checkering at p.g. and fore-end.
Sights: Gold bead front, folding leaf rear. Receiver grooved for scope mounting.
Features: Magazine tube latch locks closed from any position. Cross bolt safety in rear of trigger guard. Trigger pull about 5 lbs. Introduced 1977. Imported from Japan by Browning.
Price: Grade I **$244.95**
Price: Grade II **$349.95**

Charter AR-7 Explorer

CHARTER AR-7 EXPLORER CARBINE
Caliber: 22 LR, 8-shot clip.
Barrel: 16" alloy (steel-lined).
Weight: 2½ lbs. **Length:** 34½"/16½" stowed.
Stock: Moulded grey Cycloac, snap-on rubber butt pad.
Sights: Square blade front, aperture rear adj. for e.
Features: Take-down design stores bbl. and action in hollow stock. Light enough to float.
Price: Black or Silvertone finish **$107.00**

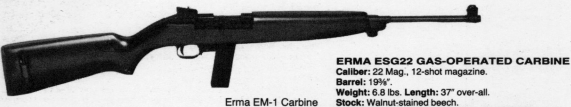

Erma EM-1 Carbine

ERMA ESG22 GAS-OPERATED CARBINE
Caliber: 22 Mag., 12-shot magazine.
Barrel: 19⅜".
Weight: 6.8 lbs. **Length:** 37" over-all.
Stock: Walnut-stained beech.
Sights: Military post front, peep rear adj. for w. & e.
Features: Locked breech, gas-operated action. Styled after M-1 Carbine. Comes with web sling and sling bar. Also available as standard blowback action. Receiver grooved for scope mounting. Introduced 1978. From Excam, Beeman.
Price: Gas. 22 Mag. (Excam) **$295.00**
Price: As above, from Beeman **$375.00**

Erma EM-1 Carbine
Similar to the ESG 22 except chambered for 22 LR, 15-shot magazine, 17¾" barrel, weight 5.9 lbs. and over-all length of 35¼", blowback action. Available from Excam, Beeman.
Price: EM-1 (Excam) **$195.00**
Price: EM-1 (Beeman) **$250.00**

F.I.E. Black Beauty

F.I.E. GR-8 BLACK BEAUTY AUTO RIFLE
Caliber: 22 LR, 14-shot tubular magazine.
Barrel: 19⅝".
Weight: 4 lbs. **Length:** 38½" over-all.
Stock: Moulded black nylon, checkered pistol grip and fore-end.
Sights: Blade on ramp front, adjustable open rear.
Features: Made mostly of moulded nylon; tube magazine housed in buttstock; top tang safety; receiver grooved for tip-off scope mounts. Imported from Brazil by F.I.E. Introduced 1984.
Price: **$89.95**

H&R Model 700 Auto

HARRINGTON & RICHARDSON Model 700 Auto Rifle
Caliber: 22 Mag., 5-shot clip.
Barrel: 22".
Weight: 6½ lbs. **Length:** 43¼" over-all.
Stock: Walnut, Monte Carlo, full p.g., composition buttplate.
Sights: Blade front, folding leaf rear.
Features: Drilled and tapped for scope mounting. 10-shot clip available. Made in U.S. by H&R.
Price: **$199.50**

H&R Model 700 Deluxe Rifle
Same as Model 700 except has select walnut stock with cheekpiece, checkered grip and fore-end, rubber rifle recoil pad. No iron sights; comes with H&R Model 432 4x, 1" tube scope, with base and rings.
Price: **$325.00**

CAUTION: PRICES CHANGE. CHECK AT GUNSHOP.

H&K Model 270 Auto

HECKLER & KOCH MODEL 300 AUTO RIFLE
Caliber: 22 Mag., 5-shot box mag.
Barrel: 19¾".
Weight: 5¾ lbs. **Length:** 39½" over-all.
Stock: European walnut, Monte Carlo with cheek rest; checkered p.g. and Schnabel fore-end.
Sights: Post front adj. for elevation, V-notch rear adj. for windage.
Features: Hexagon (polygonal) rifling, comes with sling swivels; straight blow-back inertia bolt action; single-stage trigger (3½-lb. pull). Clamp scope mount with 1" rings available at extra cost. Imported from West Germany by Heckler & Koch, Inc.
Price: HK300 .... $350.00
Price: Scope mount with 1" rings $113.00
Price: 15-shot magazine $24.00

HECKLER & KOCH HK270 AUTO RIFLE
Caliber: 22 LR, 5-shot magazine.
Barrel: 19¾".
Weight: 5.5 lbs. **Length:** 38.2" over-all.
Stock: European walnut.
Sights: Post front, diopter rear adjustable for windage and elevation.
Features: Straight blow-back action; 3½ lb. trigger pull. Extra 20-shot magazine available. Receiver grooved for scope mount. Introduced 1978. Imported from West Germany by Heckler & Koch.
Price: $250.00
Price: Scope mount, rings $65.10
Price: 20-shot magazine $24.00

Iver Johnson Trailblazer

IVER JOHNSON TRAILBLAZER RIFLE
Caliber: 22 LR, 10-shot magazine.
Barrel: 18½".
Weight: 5½ lbs. **Length:** 38" over-all.
Stock: American hardwood with checkered pistol grip and fore-end.
Sights: Bead front, open rear with elevator.
Features: Removable box magazine; receiver grooved for scope mounting. Stock is scaled for the junior shooter. Introduced 1984.
Price: $129.95

KASSNAR CONCORDE MODEL M-16
Caliber: 22 LR, 15-shot magazine.
Barrel: 19½", including flash hider/muzzle brake.
Weight: 6 lbs. **Length:** 38" over-all.
Stock: Mahogany, painted black.
Sights: Post front adjustable for elevation, peep rear adjustable for windage.
Features: Replica of AR-15 rifle. Comes with carrying sling. Imported from the Philippines by Kassnar.
Price: $139.00
Price: With collapsible buttstock as M-16R $149.00

Kassnar Concorde 20 P/S

KASSNAR CONCORDE MODEL 20 P/S RIFLE
Caliber: 22 Long Rifle, 15-shot magazine.
Barrel: 20".
Weight: 6 lbs. **Length:** 41" over-all.
Stock: Philippine mahogany with walnut finish.
Sights: Blade on ramp front, V-notch rear adjustable for elevation.
Features: Receiver grooved for scope mounting. Gun comes with 4x scope installed. Imported from the Philippines by Kassnar.
Price: $99.00
Price: Model 2000 (checkered stock, adj. rear sight) $109.00

Marlin Model 990

Consult our Directory pages for the location of firms mentioned.

MARLIN MODEL 990 SEMI-AUTO RIFLE
Caliber: 22 LR, 18-shot tubular magazine.
Barrel: 22" Micro-Groove®.
Weight: About 5½ lbs. **Length:** 40¾" over-all.
Stock: American black walnut, Monte Carlo style with fluted comb and full pistol grip; checkered p.g. and fore-end; white buttplate spacer; Mar-Shield® finish.
Sights: Ramp bead front with Wide-Scan™ hood, adjustable folding semi-buckhorn rear.
Features: Receiver grooved for tip-off mount; bolt hold-open device; cross-bolt safety. Introduced 1979.
Price: $130.95

MARLIN 70 AUTO
Caliber: 22 LR, 7-shot clip magazine.
Barrel: 18" (16-groove rifling).
Weight: 4½ lbs. **Length:** 36½" over-all.
Stock: Walnut-finished hardwood with Monte Carlo, full p.g.
Sights: Ramp front, adj. open rear. Receiver grooved for scope mount.
Features: Receiver top has serrated, non-glare finish; chrome plated trigger; cross-bolt safety; bolt hold-open; chrome plated magazine.
Price: Less scope $101.95

MARLIN MODEL 75C SEMI-AUTO RIFLE
Caliber: 22 LR, 14-shot tubular magazine.
Barrel: 18".
Weight: 5 lbs. **Length:** 36¾" over-all.
Stock: Walnut-finished hardwood; Monte Carlo with full p.g.
Sights: Ramp front, adj. open rear.
Features: Bolt hold-open device; cross-bolt safety; receiver grooved for scope mounting.
Price: $97.95

Marlin Model 995

MARLIN MODEL 995 SEMI-AUTO RIFLE
Caliber: 22 LR, 7-shot clip magazine
Barrel: 18″ Micro-Grove®.
Weight: 5½ lbs. **Length:** 36¾″ over-all.
Stock: American black walnut, Monte Carlo-style, with full pistol grip. Checkered p.g. and fore-end; white buttplate spacer; Mar-Shield® finish.
Sights: Ramp bead front with Wide-Scan hood; adjustable folding semi-buckhorn rear.
Features: Receiver grooved for tip-off scope mount; bolt hold-open device; cross-bolt safety. Introduced 1979.
Price: **$122.95**

Marlin Model 60

MARLIN 60 SEMI-AUTO RIFLE
Caliber: 22 LR, 18-shot tubular mag.
Barrel: 22″ round tapered.
Weight: About 5½ lbs. **Length:** 41″ over-all.
Stock: Walnut finished Monte Carlo.
Sights: Ramp front, open adj. rear.
Features: Matted receiver is grooved for tip-off mounts. Has new tube magazine closure system.
Price: Less scope **$101.95**

Mossberg 377 Plinkster

MOSSBERG 377 PLINKSTER AUTO RIFLE
Caliber: 22 LR, 15-shot tube magazine
Barrel: 20″ AC-KRO-GRUV.
Weight: 6¼ lbs. **Length:** 40″ over-all.
Stock: Straight line, moulded one-piece thumbhole.
Sights: No iron sights. Comes with 4x scope.
Features: Walnut texture stock finish, checkered fore-end. Tube magazine loads through port in buttstock. Has bolt hold-open.
Price: With 4x scope, about **$103.00**

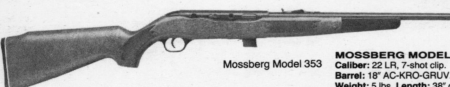

Mossberg Model 353

MOSSBERG MODEL 353 AUTO LOADING RIFLE
Caliber: 22 LR, 7-shot clip.
Barrel: 18″ AC-KRO-GRUV.
Weight: 5 lbs. **Length:** 38″ over-all.
Stock: Walnut, checkered at p.g. and fore-end. Black Tenite two-position fold-down fore-end.
Sights: Open step adj. U-notch rear, bead front on ramp.
Features: Sling swivels and web strap on left of stock, extension fore-end folds down for steady firing from prone position. Receiver grooved for scope mounting.
Price: About **$94.95**

MOSSBERG MODEL 380 AUTO RIFLE
Caliber: 22 LR, 15-shot tube magazine.
Barrel: 20″, tapered, with AC-KRO-GRUV.
Weight: About 5½ lbs. with scope.
Stock: Walnut-finished hardwood, with black non-slip buttplate.
Sights: Bead front, adj. open rear.
Features: Receiver grooved for scope mounting. Available with optional 4x scope, mount. Magazine feeds through buttstock. Introduced 1981.
Price: With open sights, about.................................. **$91.00**
Price: With 4x scope, about **$95.00**

Remington Nylon 66

REMINGTON NYLON 66MB AUTO RIFLE
Caliber: 22 LR, 14-shot tubular mag.
Barrel: 19⅝″ round tapered.
Weight: 4 lbs. **Length:** 38½″ over-all.
Stock: Moulded Mohawk Brown Nylon, checkered p.g. and fore-end.
Sights: Blade ramp front, adj. open rear.
Features: Top tang safety, double extractors, receiver grooved for tip-off mounts.
Price: **$137.00**

Remington Nylon 66BD Auto Rifle
Same as the Model 66MB except has black stock, barrel, and receiver cover. Black diamond-shape inlay in fore-end. Introduced 1978.
Price: **$137.00**

CAUTION: PRICES CHANGE. CHECK AT GUNSHOP.

Remington Model 552A

Remington Model 552BDL Deluxe Auto Rifle
Same as Model 552A except: Du Pont RKW finished walnut stock, checkered fore-end and capped p.g. stock. Blade ramp front and fully adj. rear sights.
Price: **$206.00**

REMINGTON 552A AUTOLOADING RIFLE
Caliber: 22 S (20), L (17) or LR (15) tubular mag.
Barrel: 21″ round tapered.
Weight: About 5¾ lbs. **Length:** 40″ over-all.
Stock: Full-size, walnut-finished hardwood.
Sights: Bead front, step open rear adj. for w. & e.
Features: Positive cross-bolt safety, receiver grooved for tip-off mount.
Price: **$182.00**

Ruger 10/22 Sporter

Ruger 10/22 Auto Sporter
Same as 10/22 Carbine except: Walnut stock with hand checkered p.g. and fore-end with straight buttplate, no bbl. band, has sling swivels.
Price: Model 10/22 SP **$163.00**

RUGER 10/22 AUTOLOADING CARBINE
Caliber: 22 LR, 10-shot rotary mag.
Barrel: 18½″ round tapered.
Weight: 5 lbs., 12 oz. **Length:** 36¾″ over-all.
Stock: Birch with p.g. and bbl. band.
Sights: Gold bead front, folding leaf rear adj. for e.
Features: Detachable rotary magazine fits flush into stock, cross-bolt safety, receiver tapped and grooved for scope blocks or tip-off mount. Scope base adapter furnished with each rifle.
Price: Model 10/22 RB **$134.50**

Stevens 987T

STEVENS MODEL 987T AUTO RIFLE
Caliber: 22 LR, 15-shot magazine.
Barrel: 20″.
Weight: About 5½ lbs. **Length:** 40½″ over-all.
Stock: Walnut finish with Monte Carlo; checkered pistol grip and fore-end.
Sights: Bead front, open adjustable rear.
Features: Top tang safety; metal parts blued. Comes with 4x scope and mount.
Price: Model 987T, with scope **$94.75**
Price: Model 987, without scope **$92.75**

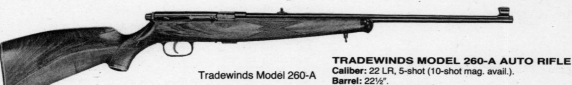

Tradewinds Model 260-A

TRADEWINDS MODEL 260-A AUTO RIFLE
Caliber: 22 LR, 5-shot (10-shot mag. avail.).
Barrel: 22½″.
Weight: 5¾ lbs. **Length:** 41½″.
Stock: Walnut, with hand checkered p.g. and fore-end.
Sights: Ramp front with hood, 3-leaf folding rear, receiver grooved for scope mount.
Features: Double extractors, sliding safety. Imported by Tradewinds.
Price: **$250.00**

Universal Leatherneck

UNIVERSAL 2200 LEATHERNECK CARBINE
Caliber: 22 LR, 10-shot.
Barrel: 18″.
Weight: 5½ lbs. **Length:** 35¾″ over-all.
Stock: Birch hardwood with lacquer finish.
Sights: Blade front, peep rear adj. for w. & e.
Features: Look-alike to the G.I. Carbine except in rimfire. Recoil operated. Metal parts satin-polish blue. Flip-type safety. Optional 30-shot magazine available. Receiver drilled and tapped for scope mounting. Introduced 1979. From Universal Firearms.
Price: **$227.00**

Voere 2115

VOERE MODEL 2115 AUTO RIFLE

Caliber: 22 LR, 8 or 15-shot magazine.
Barrel: 18.1″.
Weight: 5.75 lbs. **Length:** 37.7″ over-all.
Stock: Walnut-finished beechwood with cheekpiece; checkered pistol grip and fore-end.
Sights: Post front with hooded ramp, leaf rear.
Features: Clip-fed autoloader with single stage trigger, wing-type safety. Imported from Austria by L. Joseph Rahn. Introduced 1984.
Price: Model 2115 .... **$234.00**
Price: Model 2114S (as above except no cheekpiece, checkering or white line spacers at grip, buttplate) **$218.00**

Weatherby Mark XXII

WEATHERBY MARK XXII AUTO RIFLE, CLIP MODEL

Caliber: 22 LR only, 5- or 10-shot clip.
Barrel: 24″ round contoured.
Weight: 6 lbs. **Length:** 42¼″ over-all.
Stock: Walnut, Monte Carlo comb and cheekpiece, rosewood p.g. cap and fore-end tip. Skip-line checkering.
Sights: Gold bead ramp front, 3-leaf folding rear.
Features: Thumb operated tang safety. Single shot or semi-automatic side lever selector. Receiver grooved for tip-off scope mount. Single pin release for quick takedown.

Weatherby Mark XXII Tubular Model
Same as Mark XXII Clip Model except: 15-shot tubular magazine.
Price: **$349.95**

Price: **$339.95**
Price: Extra 5-shot clip **$8.00**
Price: Extra 10-shot clip **$10.00**

RIMFIRE RIFLES—LEVER & SLIDE ACTIONS

Browning BL-22

BROWNING BL-22 LEVER ACTION RIFLE

Caliber: 22 S(22), L(17) or LR(15). Tubular mag.
Barrel: 20″ round tapered.
Weight: 5 lbs. **Length:** 36¾″ over-all.
Stock: Walnut, 2-piece straight grip Western style.
Sights: Bead post front, folding-leaf rear.
Features: Short throw lever, ½-cock safety, receiver grooved for tip-off scope mounts. Imported from Japan by Browning.
Price: Grade I **$239.95**
Price: Grade II, engraved receiver, checkered grip and fore-end **$274.95**

Beeman/Erma EG722

BEEMAN/ERMA EG722 RIFLE

Caliber: 22 Short, Long, Long Rifle, 21, 17, 15 rounds.
Barrel: 18½″.
Weight: 5½ lbs. **Length:** 36½″ over-all.
Stock: Walnut-stained beechwood, grooved fore-end.
Sights: Hooded blade front, leaf rear adjustable for elevation.
Features: Blue finish; tubular magazine under barrel. Receiver grooved for scope mounting. Imported by Beeman. Introduced 1984.
Price: **$275.00**

ERMA EG73 LEVER ACTION CARBINE

Caliber: 22 Mag., 12-shot magazine.
Barrel: 19¼″.
Weight: 6 lbs. **Length:** 37⅜″ over-all.
Stock: Walnut-stained beech.
Sights: Hooded ramp front, buckhorn rear. Receiver grooved for scope mounting.
Features: Tubular magazine, side ejection. Introduced 1978. Imported by Excam.
Price: **$229.00**

CAUTION: PRICES CHANGE. CHECK AT GUNSHOP.

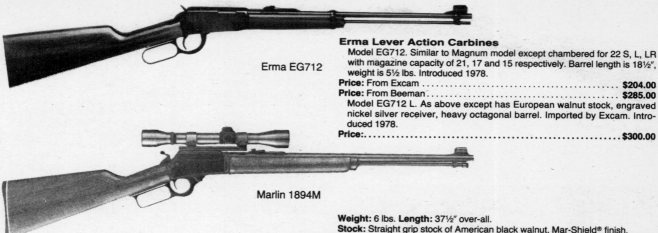

Erma EG712

Erma Lever Action Carbines
Model EG712. Similar to Magnum model except chambered for 22 S, L, LR with magazine capacity of 21, 17 and 15 respectively. Barrel length is 18½", weight is 5½ lbs. Introduced 1978.
Price: From Excam **$204.00**
Price: From Beeman **$285.00**
Model EG712 L. As above except has European walnut stock, engraved nickel silver receiver, heavy octagonal barrel. Imported by Excam. Introduced 1978.
Price: **$300.00**

Marlin 1894M

Weight: 6 lbs. **Length:** 37½" over-all.
Stock: Straight grip stock of American black walnut, Mar-Shield® finish.
Sights: Ramp front with brass bead, adjustable semi-buckhorn folding rear.
Features: Has new hammer block safety. Side-ejecting solid-top receiver tapped for scope mount or receiver sight; squared finger lever, reversible offset hammer spur for scope use. Scope shown is optional. Introduced 1983.
Price: **$280.95**

MARLIN MODEL 1894M CARBINE
Caliber: 22 Mag., 11-shot magazine.
Barrel: 20" Micro-Groove®.

Marlin Golden 39A

MARLIN GOLDEN 39A LEVER ACTION RIFLE
Caliber: 22 S(26), L(21), LR(19), tubular magazine.
Barrel: 24" Micro-Groove®.
Weight: 6½ lbs. **Length:** 40" over-all.
Stock: American black walnut with white line spacers at p.g. cap and buttplate; Mar-Shield® finish.
Sights: Bead ramp front with detachable "Wide-Scan"™ hood, folding rear semi-buckhorn adj. for w. and e.
Features: Take-down action, receiver tapped for scope mount (supplied), offset hammer spur.
Price: **$252.95**

MARLIN GOLDEN 39M CARBINE
Caliber: 22 S(21), L(16), LR(15), tubular magazine.
Barrel: 20" Micro-Grove®.
Weight: 6 lbs. **Length:** 36" over-all.
Stock: American black walnut, straight grip, white line buttplate spacer. Mar-Shield® finish.
Sights: "Wide-Scan"™ ramp front with hood, folding rear semi-buckhorn adj. for w. and e.
Features: Squared finger lever. Receiver tapped for scope mount (supplied) or receiver sight, offset hammer spur, take-down action.
Price: **$252.95**

Remington Model 572

REMINGTON 572 FIELDMASTER PUMP RIFLE
Caliber: 22 S(20), L(17) or LR(14). Tubular mag.
Barrel: 21" round tapered.
Weight: 5½ lbs. **Length:** 42" over-all.
Stock: Walnut-finished hardwood with p.g. and grooved slide handle.
Sights: Blade ramp front; sliding ramp rear adj. for w. & e.
Features: Cross-bolt safety, removing inner mag. tube converts rifle to single shot, receiver grooved for tip-off scope mount.
Price: **$189.00**
Price: Sling and swivels installed **$21.05**

Remington Model 572 BDL Deluxe
Same as the 572 except: p.g. cap, walnut stock with RKW finish, checkered grip and fore-end, ramp front and fully adj. rear sights.
Price: **$213.00**
Price: Sling and swivels installed **$21.05**

Consult our Directory pages for the location of firms mentioned.

ROSSI 62 SA PUMP RIFLE
Caliber: 22 S, L or LR, 22 Mag.
Barrel: 23", round or octagon.
Weight: 5¾ lbs. **Length:** 39¼" over-all.
Stock: Walnut, straight grip, grooved fore-end.
Sights: Fixed front, adj. rear.
Features: Capacity 20 Short, 16 Long or 14 Long Rifle. Quick takedown. Imported from Brazil by Interarms.
Price: Blue. **$149.00**
Price: Nickel. **$164.00**
Price: Blue, with octagon barrel. **$174.00**
Price: 22 Mag., as Model 59 .... **$184.00**

Rossi 62 SAC Carbine
Same as standard model except has 16¼" barrel. Magazine holds slightly fewer cartridges.
Price: Blue. **$149.00**
Price: Nickel. **$164.00**

RIMFIRE RIFLES—LEVER & SLIDE ACTIONS

Winchester 9422

Winchester 9422M XTR Lever Action Rifle
Same as the 9422 except chambered for 22 Mag. cartridge, has 11-round mag. capacity.

Price: **$309.95**

WINCHESTER 9422 XTR LEVER ACTION RIFLE
Caliber: 22 S(21), L(17), LR(15). Tubular mag.
Barrel: 20½″. (16″ twist).
Weight: 6¼ lbs. **Length:** 37⅛″ over-all.
Stock: American walnut, 2-piece, straight grip (no p.g.).
Sights: Hooded ramp front, adj. semi-buckhorn rear.
Features: Side ejection, receiver grooved for scope mounting, takedown action. Has XTR wood and metal finish. Made under license by U.S. Repeating Arms Co.

Price: **$309.95**

RIMFIRE RIFLES—BOLT ACTIONS & SINGLE SHOTS

Anschutz 1416/1516

Anschutz 1418D/1518D Deluxe Rifles
Similar to the 1416D/1516D rifles except has full length Mannlicher-style stock, shorter 19¾″ barrel. Weighs 5½ lbs. Stock has buffalo horn Schnabel tip. Double set trigger available on special order. Model 1418D chambered for 22 LR, 1518D for 22 Mag. Imported from Germany by PSI.

Price: 1418D **$490.00**
Price: 1518D **$499.00**

ANSCHUTZ DELUXE 1416/1516 RIFLES
Caliber: 22 LR (1416D), 5-shot clip, 22 Mag. (1516D), 4-shot clip.
Barrel: 22½″.
Weight: 6 lbs. **Length:** 41″ over-all.
Stock: European walnut; Monte Carlo with cheekpiece, Schnabel fore-end, checkered pistol grip and fore-end.
Sights: Hooded ramp front, folding leaf rear.
Features: Uses Model 1403 target rifle action. Adjustable single stage trigger. Receiver grooved for scope mounting. Imported from Germany by PSI.

Price: 1416D, 22 LR **$350.00**
Price: 1516D, 22 Mag. **$353.00**

Anschutz 1422/1522

Anschutz 1422D/1522D Custom Rifles
Similar to the Classic models except have roll-over Monte Carlo cheekpiece, slim fore-end with Schnabel tip, Wundhammer palm swell on pistol grip, rosewood grip cap with white diamond insert. Skip-line checkering on grip and fore-end. Introduced 1982. Imported from Germany by PSI.

Price: 1422D **$598.00**
Price: 1522D **$598.00**

ANSCHUTZ 1422D/1522D CLASSIC RIFLES
Caliber: 22 LR (1422D), 5-shot clip, 22 Mag. (1522D), 4-shot clip.
Barrel: 24″.
Weight: 7¼ lbs. **Length:** 43″ over-all.
Stock: Select European walnut; checkered pistol grip and fore-end.
Sights: Hooded ramp front, folding leaf rear.
Features: Uses Match 54 action. Adjustable single stage trigger. Receiver drilled and tapped for scope mounting. Introduced 1982. Imported from Germany by PSI.

Price: 1422D (22 LR) **$564.00**
Price: 1522D (22 Mag.) **$564.00**

Cabanas Varmint

CABANAS MASTER BOLT ACTION RIFLE
Caliber: 177, round ball or pellet; single shot.
Barrel: 19½″.
Weight: 8 lbs. **Length:** 45½″ over-all.
Stock: Walnut target-type with Monte Carlo.
Sights: Blade front, fully adjustable rear.
Features: Fires round ball or pellet with 22-cal. blank cartridge. Bolt action. Imported from Mexico by Mandall Shooting Supplies. Introduced 1984.

Price: **$149.95**
Price: Varmint model (21½″ barrel, 4½ lbs., 41″ o.a.l., varmint-type stock) **$109.95**

BINGHAM "BANTAM" BOLT ACTION
Caliber: 22 LR or 22 Mag., single shot.
Barrel: 18½″.
Weight: 3¼ lbs. **Length:** 34″ over-all.
Stock: Walnut finished hardwood.
Sights: Hooded ramp front, open adjustable rear.
Features: Classic-style stock, visual safe/fire indicator, manually cocked action. From Bingham Ltd.

Price: 22 LR or 22 Mag. **$119.95**

Cabanas Espronceda IV Bolt Action Rifle
Similar to the Leyre model except has full sporter stock, 18¾″ barrel, 40″ over-all length, weighs 5½ lbs.

Price: **$119.95**

CAUTION: PRICES CHANGE. CHECK AT GUNSHOP.

RIMFIRE RIFLES—BOLT ACTIONS & SINGLE SHOTS

Cabanas Master

Cabanas Leyre Bolt Action Rifle
Similar to Master model except 44" over-all, has sport/target stock.
Price: **$134.95**
Price: Model R83 (17" barrel, hardwood stock, 40" o.a.l.) **$79.95**
Price: Mini 82 Youth (16½" barrel, 33" o.a.l., 3½ lbs.) **$69.95**

Chipmunk Single Shot

CHIPMUNK SINGLE SHOT RIFLE
Caliber: 22, S, L, LR, or 22 Mag., single shot.
Barrel: 16⅛".
Weight: About 2½ lbs. **Length:** 30" over-all.
Stock: American walnut.
Sights: Post on ramp front, peep rear adj. for windage and elevation.
Features: Drilled and tapped for scope mounting using special Chipmunk base ($9.95). Made in U.S.A. Introduced 1982. From Chipmunk Mfg.
Price: **$119.95**
Price: Fully engraved Presentation Model with hand checkered fancy stock **$500.00**

Clayco Model 4

CLAYCO MODEL 4 BOLT ACTION RIFLE
Caliber: 22 LR, 5-shot clip.
Barrel: 24".
Weight: 5¾" lbs. **Length:** 42" over-all.
Stock: Hardwood with walnut finish.
Sights: Ramp front with bead, open rear adjustable for windage and elevation.
Features: Wing-type safety on rear of bolt. Receiver grooved for tip-off scope mount. Black composition buttplate and pistol grip cap. Introduced 1983. Imported from China by Clayco Sports Ltd.
Price: **$150.00**

H&R Model 865

HARRINGTON & RICHARDSON MODEL 865 RIFLE
Caliber: 22 S, L or LR. 5-shot clip mag.
Barrel: 22" round tapered.
Weight: 5 lbs. **Length:** 39" over-all.
Stock: Walnut finished hardwood with Monte Carlo and p.g.
Sights: Blade front, step adj. open rear.
Features: Cocking indicator, sliding side safety, receiver grooved for tip-off scope mounts.
Price: **$99.50**

HARRINGTON & RICHARDSON MODEL 750
Caliber: 22 S, L or LR, single shot.
Barrel: 22" round tapered.
Weight: 5 lbs. **Length:** 39" over-all.
Stock: Walnut finished hardwood with Monte Carlo comb and p.g.
Sights: Blade front, step adj. open rear.
Features: Double extractors, feed platform, cocking indicator, sliding side safety, receiver grooved for tip-off scope mount.
Price: **$89.50**

Kassnar Concorde 1400

KASSNAR CONCORDE M-1400 RIFLE
Caliber: 22 LR, 5-shot magazine.
Barrel: 23".
Weight: 7 lbs. **Length:** 41½" over-all.
Stock: Philippine mahogany, hand checkered.
Sights: Blade on ramp front, open rear adjustable for windage and elevation.
Features: Blued metal; twin locking locks. Imported by Kassnar.
Price: **$129.00**
Price: Model 14 P/S (no checkering, 4x scope installed) **$99.00**
Price: Model 1500 (22 Mag. version of M1400) **$149.00**

Kimber Model 82

KIMBER MODEL 82 BOLT ACTION RIFLE

Caliber: 22 LR, 22 Mag.; 5-shot detachable magazine (LR), 4-shot (Mag.).
Barrel: 22½"; 6-grooves; 1-in 16" twist.
Weight: About 6¼ lbs. **Length:** 42" over-all.
Stock: Three styles available. "Classic" is Claro walnut with plain, straight comb; "Cascade" has Monte Carlo comb with cheekpiece; "Custom Classic" is of fancy select grade Claro walnut, ebony fore-end tip, Niedner-style buttplate. All have 18 lpi hand cut, borderless checkering, steel grip cap, checkered steel buttplate.
Sights: Hooded ramp front with bead, folding leaf rear (optional).

Features: High quality, adult-sized, bolt action rifle. Barrel screwed into receiver; rocker-type silent safety; twin rear locking lugs. All steel construction. Fully adjustable trigger; receiver grooved for Kimber scope mounts. High polish blue. Barreled actions available. Made in U.S.A. Introduced 1979.
Price: 22 LR Classic stock, no sights $495.00
Price: As above, Cascade stock $545.00
Price: As above, Custom Classic $625.00
Price: 22 Mag Classic stock, no sights $568.00
Price: As above, Cascade stock $618.00
Price: As above, Custom Classic stock $698.00
Price: Extra 22 LR 5-shot clip $12.00
Price: Extra 22 LR 10-shot clip $13.50
Price: Extra 22 Mag. 4-shot clip. $15.00
Price: Kimber scope mounts, from $45.00
Price: Optional open sights fitted. $55.00

Kimber Super America

Kimber Model 82, 84 Super America

Similar to the standard Model 82 except has the Classic stock only of specially selected, high-grade, California claro walnut, with Continental cheekpiece; borderless, full-coverage 22 lpi checkering; Niedner-type checkered steel buttplate; comes with quick-detachable, double lever scope mounts and barrel quarter-rib which has a folding leaf sight. Available in 22 Long Rifle, 22 Magnum, 22 Hornet, 223 Rem.
Price: 22 Long Rifle, less 4x scope. $950.00
Price: 22 Mag., less scope. $1,023.00
Price: 22 Hornet, less scope. $1,073.00
Price: Model 84, 223 . . . . $1,105.00

Consult our Directory pages for the location of firms mentioned.

KLEINGUENTHER K-22 BOLT ACTION RIFLE

Caliber: 22 LR, 5-shot magazine.
Barrel: 21½".
Weight: 6½ lbs. **Length:** 40" over-all.
Stock: Walnut-stained beechwood; Monte Carlo; hand-cut checkering; sling swivels.
Sights: None furnished, drilled and tapped for scope mounting. Iron sights optional.
Features: Action has two forward locking lugs, 60° bolt lift; adjustable trigger (optional double set); silent safety locks sear, trigger and trigger lever. Will shoot into ½" or less at 50 yds. Imported from West Germany and accurized by Kleinguenther. Introduced 1984.
Price: $366.00
Price: For 22 Mag. add $99.00
Price: Double set trigger. $125.00

Krico 302

KRICO MODEL 304 BOLT ACTION RIFLE

Caliber: 22 LR, 5-shot magazine.
Barrel: 19.5".
Weight: 6 lbs. **Length:** 38½" over-all.
Stock: Select European walnut; full length Mannlicher-style with curved European comb and cheekpiece; cut checkered grip and fore-end.
Sights: Blade front on ramp, open rear adjustable for windage.
Features: Single or double set trigger; blued steel fore-end cap; detachable box magazine. Imported from West Germany by Krico North America.
Price: $549.50

KRICO MODEL 302 BOLT ACTION RIFLE

Caliber: 22 LR, 5-shot magazine.
Barrel: 23.5".
Weight: 6.5 lbs. **Length:** 43" over-all.
Stock: European walnut with straight American-style comb; cut checkered grip and fore-end.
Sights: Hooded blade front on ramp, open rear adjustable for windage.
Features: Dual extractors; single, match or double set triggers available; detachable box magazine. Imported from West Germany by Krico North America.
Price: $495.50

Krico 120M

KRICO MODEL 120M MILITARY TRAINER

Caliber: 22 LR, 5-shot magazine.
Barrel: 19½".
Weight: 6 lbs. **Length:** 36" over-all.
Stock: European hardwood.
Sights: Hooded blade front, tangent rear adjustable for elevation.
Features: Receiver grooved for scope mounting; adjustable trigger; polished blued metal, oil finish wood. Imported from West Germany by Morris Lawing. Introduced 1984.
Price: $249.00

CAUTION: PRICES CHANGE. CHECK AT GUNSHOP.

Marlin Model 780

MARATHON 22 LONG RIFLE BOLT ACTION
Caliber: 22 LR, single shot.
Barrel: 24".
Weight: 4.9 lbs. **Length:** 41½" over-all.
Stock: Select hardwood.
Sights: Bead front, step-adjustable open rear.
Features: Blued metal parts; receiver grooved for scope mounting. Also available as a kit, requiring assembly and metal and wood finishing. Introduced 1984. Imported from Spain by Marathon.
Price: Finished **$84.95**
Price: Kit **$59.95**

MARLIN 780 BOLT ACTION RIFLE
Caliber: 22 S, L, or LR; 7-shot clip magazine.
Barrel: 22" Micro-Groove.
Weight: 5½ lbs. **Length:** 41".
Stock: Monte Carlo American black walnut with checkered p.g. and fore-end. White line spacer at buttplate. Mar-Shield® finish.
Sights: "Wide-Scan"™ ramp front, folding semi-buckhorn rear adj. for w. & e.
Features: Gold plated trigger, receiver anti-glare serrated and grooved for tip-off scope mount.
Price: **$124.95**

Marlin 781 Bolt Action Rifle
Same as the Marlin 780 except: tubular magazine holds 25 Shorts, 19 Longs or 17 Long Rifle cartridges. Weight 6 lbs.
Price: **$129.95**

Marlin Model 783

Marlin 783 Bolt Action Rifle
Same as Marlin 782 except: Tubular magazine holds 12 rounds of 22 Rimfire Magnum ammunition.
Price: **$143.95**

Marlin 782 Bolt Action Rifle
Same as the Marlin 780 except: 22 Rimfire Magnum cal. only, weight about 6 lbs. Sling and swivels attached
Price: **$138.95**

Marlin 25 Bolt Action Repeater
Similar to Marlin 780, except: walnut finished p.g. stock, adjustable open rear sight, ramp front.
Price: **$101.95**

Marlin Model 25

Marlin Model 25M Bolt Action Rifle
Similar to the Model 25 except chambered for 22 Mag. Has 7-shot clip magazine, 22" Micro-Groove® barrel, walnut-finished hardwood stock. Introduced 1983.
Price: **$115.95**

Marlin 15Y Little Buckaroo

Marlin Model 15Y "Little Buckaroo" Rifle
Similar to the standard Model 15 rifle except is shorter and lighter. Buttstock, fore-end and barrel have been scaled down for young shooters. Barrel length is 16¼", over-all length is 33¼", and weight is 4¼ lbs. Comes with 4x15 scope and mount. Introduced 1984.
Price: With scope and mount................................... **$96.95**

MARLIN MODEL 15 BOLT ACTION RIFLE
Caliber: 22, S, L, LR, single shot.
Barrel: 22".
Weight: 5½ lbs. **Length:** 41" over-all.
Stock: Walnut-finished hardwood with Monte Carlo and full p.g.; Mar-Shield® finish.
Sights: Ramp front, adjustable open rear.
Features: Receiver grooved for tip-off scope mount; thumb safety; red cocking indicator.
Price: **$96.95**

Mossberg Model 341

MOSSBERG MODEL 341 RIFLE
Caliber: 22 S, L, LR, 7-shot clip.
Barrel: 24" AC-KRO-GRUV.
Weight: 6½ lbs. **Length:** 43½" over-all.
Stock: Walnut, checkered p.g. and fore-end, Monte Carlo and cheekpiece. Buttplate with white line spacer.
Sights: Bead front, U-notch rear adj. for w. and e.
Features: Sliding side safety, 8 groove rifling.
Price: About **$94.95**

Ruger 77/22

MOSSBERG MODEL 640K CHUCKSTER
Caliber: 22 Mag. 5-shot clip mag.
Barrel: 24" AC-KRO-GRUV.
Weight: 6¼ lbs. **Length:** 44¾" over-all.
Stock: Walnut, checkered p.g. and fore-end, Monte Carlo comb and cheekpiece.
Sights: Ramp front with bead, fully adj. leaf rear.
Features: Grooved trigger, sliding side safety, double extractors, receiver grooved for tip-off scope mounts and tapped for aperture rear sight.
Price: About **$104.00**

RUGER 77/22 RIMFIRE BOLT ACTION RIFLE
Caliber: 22 Long Rifle, 10-shot magazine.
Barrel: 20".
Weight: About 5¾ lbs. **Length:** 39¼" over-all.
Stock: Straight-grained American walnut.
Sights: Gold bead front, adjustable folding leaf rear.
Features: Mauser-type action uses Ruger's 10-shot rotary magazine; 3-position safety; simplified bolt stop; patented bolt locking system. Uses the dual-screw barrel attachment system of the 10/22 rifle. Integral scope mounting system with 1" Ruger rings. Announced 1983.
Price: **$275.00**

Stevens Model 35

STEVENS MODEL 35 BOLT ACTION RIFLE
Caliber: 22 LR or 22 Mag. (Model 35-M); detachable 5-shot clip.
Barrel: 22".
Weight: 4¾ lbs. **Length:** 41" over-all.
Stock: Walnut-finished hardwood.
Sights: Ramp front, step-adjustable open rear.
Features: Checkered pistol grip and fore-end. Receiver grooved for scope mounting. Introduced 1982. From Savage Arms.
Price: Model 35 . . . . **$94.00**
Price: Model 35-M **$97.50**
Price: Model 36 (22 LR, single shot) **$89.95**

Savage-Stevens 72

SAVAGE-STEVENS MODEL 89
Caliber: 22 LR, single shot.
Barrel: 18½".
Weight: 5 lbs. **Length:** 35" over-all.
Stock: Walnut finished hardwood.
Sights: Blade front, step adj. rear.
Features: Single-shot Martini-type breech block. Hammer must be cocked by hand independent of lever prior to firing. Automatic ejection. Satin black frame finish.
Price: **$80.50**

SAVAGE-STEVENS MODEL 72 CRACKSHOT
Caliber: 22 S, L, LR, single shot.
Barrel: 22" octagonal.
Weight: 4½ lbs. **Length:** 37" over-all.
Stock: Walnut, straight grip and fore-end.
Sights: Blade front, step adj. rear.
Features: Falling block action, color case hardened frame.
Price: **$131.00**

Springfield Armory M6

SPRINGFIELD ARMORY M6 SURVIVAL RIFLE
Caliber: 22 LR over 410 shotgun.
Barrel: 18".
Weight: 3½ lbs. **Length:** 31½" over-all.
Stock: Steel, folding, with magazine for nine 22 LR, four 410 cartridges.
Sights: Blade front, military aperture for 22; V-notch for 410.
Features: All metal construction. Designed for quick disassembly and minimum maintenance. Folds for compact storage. Introduced 1982. Made in U.S. by Springfield Armory.
Price: About **$136.00**

Voere 1007

VOERE MODEL 1007/1013 BOLT ACTION RIFLE
Caliber: 22 LR (M1007 Biathlon), 22 Mag. (M1013).
Barrel: 18".
Weight: About 5½ lbs. (M1007)
Stock: Oil-finished beechwood.
Sights: Hooded front, open adjustable rear.
Features: Single-stage trigger (M1013 available with double set). Military-look stock; sling swivels. Convertible to single shot. Imported from Austria by L. Joseph Rahn. Introduced 1984.
Price: 1007 Biathlon **$203.00**
Price: 1013 22 Mag. **$301.00**

CAUTION: PRICES CHANGE. CHECK AT GUNSHOP.

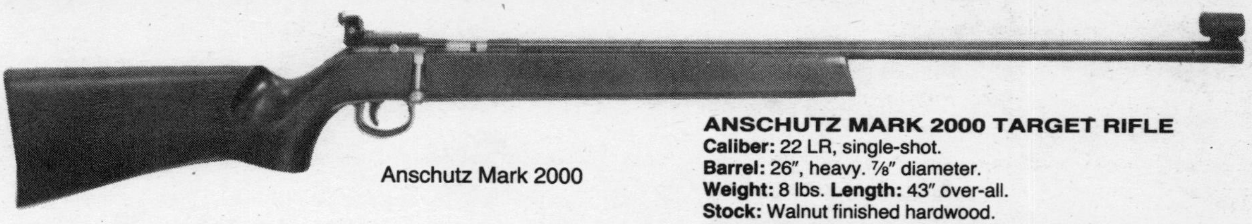

Anschutz Mark 2000

ANSCHUTZ MODEL 1403D MATCH RIFLE
Caliber: 22 LR only. Single shot.
Barrel: 26″ round (1¹¹⁄₁₆″ dia.)
Weight: 7¾ lbs. **Length:** 44″ over-all.
Stock: Walnut finished hardwood, cheekpiece, checkered p.g., beavertail fore-end, adj. buttplate.
Sights: None furnished.
Features: Sliding side safety, adj. single stage trigger, receiver grooved for Anschutz sights. Imported from West Germany by PSI.
Price: Without sights $379.00
Price: 1403DL (left hand) $401.00
Price: Match sight set $107.50

ANSCHUTZ MARK 2000 TARGET RIFLE
Caliber: 22 LR, single-shot.
Barrel: 26″, heavy. ⅞″ diameter.
Weight: 8 lbs. **Length:** 43″ over-all.
Stock: Walnut finished hardwood.
Sights: Globe front (insert-type), micro-click peep rear.
Features: Action similar to the Anschutz Model 1403D. Stock has thumb groove, Wundhammer swell p.g., adjustable hand stop and sling swivel. Imported from West Germany by PSI.
Price: Without sights $195.00
Price: Sight set $30.00

ANSCHUTZ MODEL 64-MS
Caliber: 22 LR, single shot.
Barrel: 21¾″, medium heavy, ⅞″ diameter.
Weight: 8 lbs. 1 oz. **Length:** 39½″ over-all.
Stock: Walnut-finished hardwood, silhouette-type.
Sights: None furnished. Receiver drilled and tapped for scope mounting.
Features: Designed for metallic silhouette competition. Stock has stippled checkering, contoured thumb groove with Wundhammer swell. Two-stage trigger is adj. for weight of pull, take-up, and over-travel. Slide safety locks sear and bolt. Introducted 1980. Imported from West Germany by PSI.
Price: $351.00

Anschutz 1813 Super Match

ANSCHUTZ 1811 MATCH RIFLE
Caliber: 22 LR. Single Shot.
Barrel: 27¼″ round (1″ dia.)
Weight: 11 lbs. **Length:** 46″ over-all.
Stock: French walnut, American prone style with Monte Carlo, cast-off cheekpiece, checkered p.g., beavertail fore-end with swivel rail and adj. swivel, adj. rubber buttplate.
Sights: None. Receiver grooved for Anschutz sights (extra). Scope blocks.
Features: Single stage adj. trigger, wing safety, short firing pin travel. Imported from West Germany by PSI.
Price: Right hand, no sights.................................. $792.00
Price: M1811-L (true left-hand action and stock) $872.00
Price: Anschutz Int'l. sight set $149.75

Anschutz 1813 Super Match Rifle
Same as the model 1811 except: International-type stock with adj. cheekpiece, adj. aluminum hook buttplate, weight 15½ lbs., 46″ over-all. Imported from West Germany by PSI.
Price: Right hand, no sights $1,165.00
Price: M1813-L (left-hand action and stock) $1,218.00

Anschutz Model 1810 Super Match II
Similar to the Super Match 1813 rifle except has a stock of European hardwood with tapered fore-end and deep receiver area. Hand and palm rests not included. Uses Match 54 action. Adjustable hook buttplate and cheekpiece. Sights not included. Introduced 1982. Imported from Germany by PSI.
Price: Right-hand.. $987.00
Price: Left-hand $1,086.00
Price: International sight set............................... $149.75
Price: Match sight set $107.50

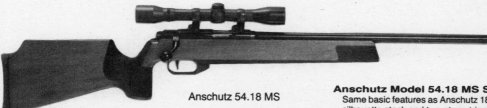

Anschutz 54.18 MS

ANSCHUTZ 1808ED SUPER RUNNING TARGET
Caliber: 22 LR, single shot.
Barrel: 23½″; ⅞″ diameter.
Weight: 9¼ lbs. **Length:** 42″ over-all.
Stock: European hardwood. Heavy beavertail fore-end, adjustable cheekpiece, buttplate, stippled pistol grip and fore-end.
Sights: None furnished. Receiver grooved for scope mounting.
Features: Uses Super Match 54 action. Adjustable trigger from 14 oz. to 3.5 lbs. Removable sectioned barrel weights. **Special Order Only.** Introduced 1982. Imported from Germany by PSI.
Price: Right-hand.. $777.00
Price: Left-hand, 1808EDL.................................... $864.00

Anschutz Model 54.18 MS Silhouette Rifle
Same basic features as Anschutz 1813 Super Match but with special metallic silhouette stock and two-stage trigger.
Price: $660.00
Price: Model 54.18 MSL (true left-hand version of above) $727.00

Anschutz 1807 Match Rifle
Same as the model 1811 except: 26″ bbl. (⅞″ dia.), weight 10 lbs. 44½″ over-all to conform to ISU requirements and also suitable for NRA matches.
Price: Right hand, no sights................................. $693.00
Price: M1807-L (true left-hand action and stock) $762.00
Price: Int'l sight set...................................... $149.75
Price: Match sight set $107.50

Anschutz 1827B Biathlon

Stock: Walnut-finished hardwood; cheekpiece, stippled pistol grip and fore-end.
Sights: Globe front specially designed for Biathlon shooting, micrometer rear with hinged snow cap.
Features: Uses Match 54 action and adjustable trigger; adjustable wooden buttplate, Biathlon butt hook, adjustable hand-stop rail. **Special Order Only.** Introduced 1982. Imported from Germany by PSI.
Price: Right-hand... $913.40
Price: Left-hand $1,041.70

ANSCHUTZ 1827B BIATHLON RIFLE
Caliber: 22 LR, 5-shot magazine.
Barrel: 21½".
Weight: 9 lbs. with sights. **Length:** 42½" over-all.

BSA CFT Target

BSA CFT TARGET RIFLE
Caliber: 308 Win. (7.62mm), single shot.
Barrel: 26.5".
Weight: 11 lbs. **Length:** 47.6" over-all.
Stock: Beechwood. Full target style with adjustable rubber buttplate, broad fore-end with full length hand-stop rail, rotating front sling swivel, palm swell pistol grip, and high cheekpiece.

Sights: Removable tunnel front with five elements; Parker aperture rear with choice of three base locations, fully adjustable for windage and elevation.
Features: Receiver bottom is flat for perfect bedding; top surface has a machined 19mm dovetail rail for scope mounting; fully adjustable trigger; full length guide rib on bolt, two locking lugs, recessed bolt face. Imported from England by Precision Sports, Inc. Introduced 1984.
Price: $950.00

BSA Martini Match

BSA MARTINI ISU MATCH RIFLE
Caliber: 22 LR, single shot.
Barrel: 28".
Weight: 10¾ lbs. **Length:** 43-44" over-all.
Stock: Match type French walnut butt and fore-end; flat cheekpiece, full p.g.; spacers are fitted to allow length adjustment to suit each shooting position; adj. buttplate.
Sights: Modified PH-1 Parker-Hale tunnel front, PH-25 aperture rear with aperture variations from .080" to .030".
Features: Fastest lock time of any commercial target rifle; designed to meet I.S.U. specs. for the Standard Rifle. Fully adjustable trigger (less than ½ lb. to 3½ lbs.). Mark V has heavier barrel, weighs 12¼ lbs. Imported from England by Freelands Scope Stands.
Price: I.S.U., Standard weight $950.00
Price: Mark V heavy bbl. $1,000.00

Beeman Mini-Match 2000

BEEMAN/FEINWERKBAU 2000 TARGET RIFLE
Caliber: 22 LR.
Barrel: 26¼"; 22" for Mini-Match.
Weight: 9 lbs. 12 oz. **Length:** 43¾" over-all (26¼" bbl.).
Stock: Standard match. Walnut with stippled p.g. and fore-end; walnut-stained birch for the Mini-Match.
Sights: Globe front with interchangeable inserts; micrometer match aperture rear.
Features: Meets ISU standard rifle specifications. Shortest lock time of any small bore rifle. Electronic or mechanical trigger, fully adjustable for weight, release point, length, lateral position, etc. Available in Standard and Mini-Match models. Introduced 1979. Imported from West Germany by Beeman.
Price: Model 2000 .... $795.00 to $925.00
Price: Mini-Match................................... $765.00 to $868.00

CAUTION: PRICES CHANGE. CHECK AT GUNSHOP.

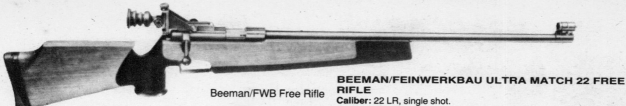

Beeman/FWB Free Rifle

BEEMAN/FEINWERKBAU ULTRA MATCH 22 FREE RIFLE
Caliber: 22 LR, single shot.
Barrel: 26.4".
Weight: 17 lbs. (with accessories).
Stock: Anatomically correct thumbhole stock of laminated wood.
Sights: Globe front with interchangeable inserts, micrometer match aperture rear.
Features: Fully adjustable mechanical or new electronic trigger; accessory rails for moveable weights and adjustable palm rest; adjustable cheekpiece and hooked buttplate. Right or left hand. Introduced 1983. Imported by Beeman.
Price: Right hand, electronic trigger **$1,595.00**
Price: As above, mechanical trigger **$1,400.00**
Price: Left hand, electronic trigger. **$1,695.00**
Price: As above, mechanical trigger **$1,400.00**

BEEMAN/WEIHRAUCH HW60 TARGET RIFLE
Caliber: 22 LR, single shot.
Barrel: 26.8".
Weight: 10.8 lbs. **Length:** 45.7" over-all.
Stock: Walnut with adjustable buttplate. Stippled p.g. and fore-end. Rail with adjustable swivel.
Sights: Hooded ramp front, match-type aperture rear.
Features: Adj. match trigger with push-button safety. Left-hand version also available. Introduced 1981. Imported from West Germany by Beeman.
Price: Right-hand. **$495.00**
Price: Left-hand **$545.00**

Finnish Lion Standard

FINNISH LION STANDARD TARGET RIFLE
Caliber: 22 LR, single-shot.
Barrel: 27⅝".
Weight: 10½ lbs. **Length:** 44⁹⁄₁₆" over-all.

Stock: French walnut, target style.
Sights: None furnished. Globe front, International micrometer rear available.
Features: Optional accessories: palm rest, hook buttplate, fore-end stop and swivel assembly, buttplate extension, 5 front sight aperture inserts, 3 rear sight apertures, Allen wrench. Adjustable trigger. Imported from Finland by Mandall Shooting Supplies.
Price: **$500.00**
Price: Thumbhole stock model **$695.00**
Price: Heavy barrel model (either stock) **$535.00**
Price: Sight set (front and rear) **$100.00**

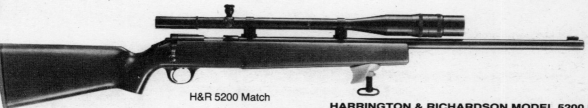

H&R 5200 Match

HARRINGTON & RICHARDSON MODEL 5200 RIFLE
Caliber: 22 LR, single shot.
Barrel: 28" target-weight with recessed muzzle.
Weight: 11 lbs. **Length:** 46" over-all.
Stock: American walnut; target-style with full length accessory rail, rubber butt pad. Comes with hand-stop.
Sights: None supplied. Receiver drilled and tapped for receiver sight, barrel for front sight.
Features: Fully adj. trigger (1.1 to 3.5 lbs.), heavy free-floating target weight barrel, "Fluid-Feed" loading platform, dual extractors. Polished blue-black metal finish. Introduced 1981. From Harrington & Richardson.
Price: **$350.00**

> Consult our Directory pages for the location of firms mentioned.

Krico 640S Match

KRICO MODEL 640S MATCH SPORTER
Caliber: 17 Rem., 222, 223, 22-250, 243, 308.
Barrel: 20", semi-bull.
Weight: 7.5 lbs.
Stock: French walnut with ventilated fore-end.
Sights: None furnished.
Features: Five-shot repeater with detachable box magazine. Available with single or double-set trigger. Imported from West Germany by Krico North America.
Price: 17 Rem., 222, 223 cals **$995.00**
Price: 22-250, 243, 308 cals **$995.00**
Price: Model 440S, 22 Hornet **$715.00**

Krico Model 650SS Sniper

KRICO MODEL 650SS SNIPER RIFLE
Caliber: 223, 308.
Barrel: 26″. Specially designed match bull barrel, matte blue finish, with muzzle brake/flash hider.
Weight: 9.6 lbs. **Length:** 44¾″ over-all.
Stock: Select walnut with oil finish. Spring-loaded, adj. cheekpiece, adjustable recoil pad. Standard model (640S) is without adjustable stock.
Sights: None furnished. Drilled and tapped for scope mounts.
Features: Match trigger with 10mm wide shoe; single standard or double set trigger available. All metal has matte blue finish. Bolt knob has 1¼″ diameter. Scope mounts available for special night-sight devices. Imported from West Germany by Krico North America.
Price: Without scope, mount **$1,298.50**
Price: Model 640S, as above but without moveable cheekpiece . . . **$1,049.50**

KRICO MODEL 340S (MS) SILHOUETTE RIFLE
Caliber: 22 Long Rifle, 5-shot clip.
Barrel: 21″, match quality.
Weight: 7.5 lbs. **Length:** 39.5″ over-all.
Stock: European walnut match-style designed for off-hand shooting. Suitable for right- or left-hand shooters. Stippled grip and fore-end.
Sights: None furnished. Receiver grooved for tip-off mounts.
Features: Free-floated heavy barrel; fully adjustable two-stage match trigger or double-set trigger. Meets NRA official MS rules. Introduced 1983. Imported by Krico North America.
Price: **$649.00**

Krico 340 Mini-Sniper

KRICO MODEL 340 MINI-SNIPER RIFLE
Caliber: 22 LR, 5-shot magazine.
Barrel: 21″.
Weight: 8 lbs. **Length:** 40″ over-all.
Stock: Select European walnut with high comb; stippled grip with palm swell, stippled ventilated fore-end.
Sights: None furnished. Receiver grooved for scope mounting.
Features: Free floating bull barrel with muzzle brake; large bolt knob; match quality single trigger; barrel and receiver have sandblast finish. Scaled down version of big-bore 640/650 rifles. Imported from West Germany by Krico North America.
Price: **$795.00**

M-S Safari Match

M-S SAFARI ARMS 1000 YARD MATCH RIFLE
Caliber: 30-338, 300 Win. Mag.; single shot.
Barrel: 28″, heavy.
Weight: 18½ lbs. with scope.
Stock: Fiberglass, custom painted to customer specs.
Sights: None furnished. Drilled and tapped for scope mounting.
Features: Sleeved stainless steel action, high-speed lock time. Fully adjustable prone stock. Electronic trigger. From M-S Safari Arms.
Price: **$2,045.00**

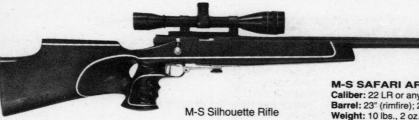

M-S Silhouette Rifle

M-S SAFARI ARMS SILHOUETTE RIFLE
Caliber: 22 LR or any standard centerfire cartridge; single shot.
Barrel: 23″ (rimfire); 24″ (centerfire). Fluted or smooth.
Weight: 10 lbs., 2 oz. (with scope).
Stock: Fiberglass, silhouette-design; custom painted.
Sights: None furnished. Drilled and tapped for scope mounting.
Features: Electronic trigger, stainless steel action, high-speed lock time. Custom built to customer specs. From M-S Safari Arms.
Price: 22 LR **$1,145.00**
Price: Centerfire, from **$1,145.00**

CAUTION: PRICES CHANGE. CHECK AT GUNSHOP.

COMPETITION RIFLES—CENTERFIRE & RIMFIRE

Mossberg 144

MOSSBERG MODEL 144 TARGET RIFLE
Caliber: 22 LR only. 7-shot clip.
Barrel: 27″ round (¹⁵⁄₁₆″ dia.)
Weight: About 8 lbs. **Length:** 43″ over-all.
Stock: Target-style walnut with high thick comb, cheekpiece, p.g., beavertail fore-end, adj. handstop and sling swivels.
Sights: Lyman 17A hooded front with inserts, Mossberg S331 receiver peep with ¼-minute clicks.
Features: Wide grooved trigger adj. for wgt. of pull, thumb safety, receiver grooved for scope mounting.
Price: About **$175.00**

Remington Model 40-XC

REMINGTON 40-XR RIMFIRE POSITION RIFLE
Caliber: 22 LR, single-shot.
Barrel: 24″, heavy target.
Weight: 10 lbs. **Length:** 43″ over-all.
Stock: Position-style with front swivel block on fore-end guide rail.
Sights: Drilled and tapped. Furnished with scope blocks.
Features: Meets all I.S.U. specifications. Deep fore-end, buttplate vertically adjustable, wide adjustable trigger.
Price: **$736.00**

REMINGTON 40-XC NAT'L MATCH COURSE RIFLE
Caliber: 7.62 NATO, 5-shot.
Barrel: 23¼″, stainless steel.
Weight: 10 lbs. without sights. **Length:** 42½″ over-all.
Stock: Walnut, position-style, with palm swell.
Sights: None furnished.
Features: Designed to meet the needs of competitive shooters firing the national match courses. Position-style stock, top loading clip slot magazine, anti-bind bolt and receiver, bright stainless steel barrel. Meets all I.S.U. Army Rifle specifications. Adjustable buttplate, adjustable trigger.
Price: **$1,113.00**

Remington Model 40-XB

REMINGTON 40-XB RANGEMASTER TARGET Centerfire
Caliber: 222 Rem., 22-250, 6mm Rem., 243, 25-06, 7mm Rem. Mag., 30-338 (30-7mm Rem. Mag.), 300 Win. Mag., 7.62 NATO (308 Win.), 30-06. Single shot.
Barrel: 27¼″ round (Stand. dia.—¾″, Hvy. dia.—⅞″)
Weight: Std.—9¼ lbs., Hvy.—11¼ lbs. **Length:** 47″.
Stock: American walnut with high comb and beavertail fore-end stop. Rubber non-slip buttplate.
Sights: None. Scope blocks installed.
Features: Adjustable trigger pull. Receiver drilled and tapped for sights.
Price: Standard s.s., stainless steel barrel **$937.00**
Price: Repeating model **$1,003.00**
Price: Extra for 2 oz. trigger **$110.00**

Remington Model 40XB-BR

SHILEN DGA BENCHREST SINGLE SHOT RIFLE
Caliber: 22, 22-250, 6x47, 308.
Barrel: Select/Match grade stainless. Choice of caliber, twist, chambering, contour or length shown in Shilen's catalog.
Weight: To customer specs.
Stock: Fiberglass. Choice of Classic or thumbhole pattern.
Sights: None furnished. Specify intended scope and mount.
Features: Fiberglass stocks are spray painted with acrylic enamel in choice of basic color. Comes with Benchrest trigger. Basically a custom-made rifle. From Shilen Rifles, Inc.
Price: From **$1,400.00**

REMINGTON MODEL 40XB-BR
Caliber: 22 BR Rem., 222 Rem., 223, 6mm x47, 6mm BR Rem., 7.62 NATO (308 Win.).
Barrel: 20″ (light varmint class), 26″ (heavy varmint class).
Weight: Light varmint class, 7¼ lbs., Heavy varmint class, 12 lbs. **Length:** 38″ (20″ bbl.), 44″ (26″ bbl.).
Stock: Select walnut.
Sights: None. Supplied with scope blocks.
Features: Unblued stainless steel barrel, trigger adj. from 1½ lbs. to 3½ lbs. Special 2 oz. trigger at extra cost. Scope and mounts extra.
Price: **$988.00**
Price: Extra for 2-oz. trigger **$110.00**

SAVAGE 110S, SILHOUETTE RIFLE

Caliber: 308 Win., 7mm-08 Rem., 5-shot.
Barrel: 22", heavy tapered.
Weight: 8 lbs., 10 oz. **Length:** 43" over-all.
Stock: Special Silhouette stock of select walnut. High fluted comb, Wundhammer swell, stippled p.g. and fore-end. Rubber recoil pad.
Sights: None. Receiver drilled and tapped for scope mounting.
Features: Receiver has satin blue finish to reduce glare. Barrel is free-floating. Top tang safety, internal magazine. Available in right-hand only. Introduced 1978.
Price: **$363.00**

Steyr-Mannlicher SSG Match

Same as Model SSG Marksman except has heavy barrel, match bolt, Walther target peep sights and adj. rail in fore-end to adj. sling travel. Weight is 11 lbs.
Price: Synthetic half stock.................................. **$1,334.00**
Price: Walnut half stock...................................... **$1,495.00**

Steyr SSG Marksman

STEYR-MANNLICHER SSG MARKSMAN

Caliber: 308 Win.
Barrel: 25.6".
Weight: 8.6 lbs. **Length:** 44.5" over-all.

Stock: Choice of ABS "Cycolac" synthetic half stock or walnut. Removable spacers in butt adjusts length of pull from 12¾" to 14".
Sights: Hooded blade front, folding leaf rear.
Features: Parkerized finish. Choice of interchangeable single or double set triggers. Detachable 5-shot rotary magazine (10-shot optional). Drilled and tapped for scope mounts. Imported from Austria by Gun South, Inc.
Price: Synthetic half stock **$873.17**
Price: Walnut half stock...................................... **$1,058.59**
Price: Optional 10-shot magazine............................... **$74.46**

Steyr UIT

STEYR-MANNLICHER MATCH UIT RIFLE

Caliber: 243 Win. or 308 Win., 10-shot magazine.
Barrel: 25.5".

Weight: 10.9 lbs. **Length:** 44.48" over-all.
Stock: Walnut with stippled grip and fore-end. Special UIT Match design.
Sights: Walther globe front, Walther peep rear.
Features: Double-pull trigger adjustable for let-off point, slack, weight of first-stage pull, release force and length; buttplate adjustable for height and length. Meets UIT specifications. Introduced 1984. Imported from Austria by Gun South, Inc.
Price: **$2,100.00**

Swiss K-31 Target

SWISS K-31 TARGET RIFLE

Caliber: 308 Win., 6-shot magazine.
Barrel: 26".

Weight: 9½ lbs. **Length:** 44" over-all.
Stock: Walnut.
Sights: Protected blade front, ladder-type adjustable rear.
Features: Refined version of the Schmidt-Rubin straight-pull rifle. Comes with sling and muzzle cap. Imported from Switzerland by Mandall Shooting Supplies.
Price: **$1,000.00**

Tanner Free Rifle

TANNER 300 METER FREE RIFLE

Caliber: 308 Win., 7.5 Swiss; single shot.
Barrel: 28.7".
Weight: 15 lbs. **Length:** 45.3" over-all.

Stock: Seasoned walnut, thumb-hole style, with accessory rail, palm rest, adjustable hook butt.
Sights: Globe front with interchangeable inserts, Tanner-design micrometer-diopter rear with adjustable aperture.
Features: Three-lug revolving-lock bolt design; adjustable set trigger; short firing pin travel; supplied with 300-meter test target. Imported from Switzerland by Osborne's Supplies. Introduced 1984.
Price: About... **$3,750.00**

CAUTION: PRICES CHANGE. CHECK AT GUNSHOP.

COMPETITION RIFLES—CENTERFIRE & RIMFIRE

Tanner UIT

TANNER STANDARD UIT RIFLE
Caliber: 308, 7.5mm Swiss, 10-shot.
Barrel: 25.8″.
Weight: 10.5 lbs. **Length:** 40.6″ over-all.
Stock: Match style of seasoned nutwood with accessory rail; coarsely stippled pistol grip; high cheekpiece; vented fore-end.
Sights: Globe front with interchangeable inserts, Tanner micrometer-diopter rear with adjustable aperture.
Features: Two locking lug revolving bolt encloses case head. Trigger adjustable from ½ to 6½ lbs.; match trigger optional. Comes with 300-meter test target. Imported from Switzerland by Osborne's. Introduced 1984.
Price: About **$3,600.00**

Consult our Directory pages for the location of firms mentioned.

TANNER 50 METER FREE RIFLE
Caliber: 22 LR; single shot.
Barrel: 27.7″.
Weight: 13.9 lbs. **Length:** 43.4″ over-all.
Stock: Seasoned nutwood with palm rest, accessory rail, adjustable hook buttplate.
Sights: Globe front with interchangeable inserts, Tanner micrometer-diopter rear with adjustable aperture.
Features: Bolt action with externally adjustable set trigger. Supplied with 50-meter test target. Imported from Switzerland by Osborne's Supplies. Introduced 1984.
Price: About **$3,125.00**

TIKKA MODEL 65 WILD BOAR RIFLE
Caliber: 7x64, 308, 30-06, 7mm Rem. Mag., 300 Win. Mag.; 5-shot detachable clip.
Barrel: 20½″.
Weight: About 7½ lbs. **Length:** 41″ over-all.
Stock: Hand checkered walnut; vent. rubber recoil pad.
Sights: Bead on post front, special ramp-type open rear.
Features: Adjustable trigger; palm swell in pistol grip. Sight system developed for low-light conditions. Imported from Finland by Mandall Shooting Supplies.
Price: **$595.00**

WALTHER U.I.T. SPECIAL
Caliber: 22 LR, single shot.
Barrel: 25½″.
Weight: 10 lbs., 3 oz. **Length:** 44¾″.
Stock: Walnut, adj. for length and drop; fore-end guide rail for sling or palm rest.
Sights: Globe-type front, fully adj. aperture rear.
Features: Conforms to both NRA and U.I.T. requirements. Fully adj. trigger. Left hand stock available on special order. Imported from Germany by Interarms.
Price: **$775.00**

WALTHER RUNNING BOAR MATCH RIFLE
Caliber: 22 LR, single shot.
Barrel: 23.6″.
Weight: 8 lbs. 5 oz. **Length:** 42″ over-all.
Stock: Walnut thumb-hole type. Fore-end and p.g. stippled.
Features: Especially designed for running boar competition. Receiver grooved to accept dovetail scope mounts. Adjustable cheekpiece and butt plate. 1.1 lb. trigger pull. Left hand stock available on special order. Imported from Germany by Interarms.
Price: **$750.00**

Walther Model U.I.T.-E Match Rifle
Similar to the U.I.T. Special model except has state-of-the-art electronic trigger. Introduced 1984.
Price: **$1,150.00**

Walther GX-1 Match Rifle
Same general specs as U.I.T. except has 25½″ barrel, over-all length of 44½″, weight of 15½ lbs. Stock is designed to provide every conceivable adjustment for individual preference and anatomical compatibility. Left-hand stock available on special order. Imported from Germany by Interarms.
Price: **$1,150.00**

Walther U.I.T. Match
Same specifications and features as standard U.I.T. Super rifle but has scope mount bases. Fore-end had new tapered profile, fully stippled. Imported from Germany by Interarms.
Price: **$850.00**

Wichita Silhouette

WICHITA SILHOUETTE RIFLE
Caliber: All standard calibers with maximum over-all cartridge length of 2.800″.
Barrel: 24″ free-floated Matchgrade.
Weight: About 9 lbs.
Stock: Metallic gray fiberthane with ventilated rubber recoil pad.
Sights: None furnished. Drilled and tapped for scope mounts.
Features: Legal for all NRA competitions. Single shot action. Fluted bolt, 2-oz. Canjar trigger; glass-bedded stock. Comes with hard case. Introduced 1983. From Wichita Arms.
Price: **$1,185.00**
Price: Left-hand **$1,285.00**

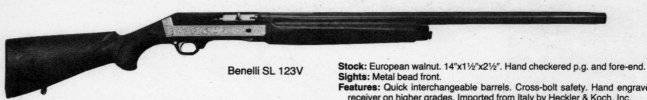

Benelli SL 123V

BENELLI AUTOLOADING SHOTGUN
Gauge: 12 ga. (5-shot, 3-shot plug furnished).
Barrel: 26″ (Skeet, Imp. Cyl., Mod.); 28″ (Full, Imp. Mod., Mod.). Vent. rib.
Weight: 6¾ lbs.

Stock: European walnut. 14″x1½″x2½″. Hand checkered p.g. and fore-end.
Sights: Metal bead front.
Features: Quick interchangeable barrels. Cross-bolt safety. Hand engraved receiver on higher grades. Imported from Italy by Heckler & Koch, Inc.
Price: Standard model, SL 121V **$449.00**
Price: Engraved, SL 123V **$525.00**
Price: Slug gun, 121V **$492.00**
Price: Model SL 201, 20 ga. **$453.00**
Price: Extra barrels **$236.00**

Beretta Model A-302

BERETTA A-302 AUTO SHOTGUN
Gauge: 12 or 20, 2¾″ or 3″.
Barrel: 12 ga. — 22″ (Slug); 26″ (Imp. Cyl., Skeet); 28″ (Mod., Full, Multi-choke); 30″ (Full, Full Trap); 20 ga. — 26″ (Imp. Cyl., Skeet); 28″ (Mod., Full).
Weight: About 6½ lbs. (20 ga.).

Stock: European walnut; hand checkered grip and fore-end.
Features: Gas-operated action, alloy receiver with scroll engraving; magazine cut-off, push-button safety. Multi-choke models come with four interchangeable screw-in choke tubes. Introduced 1983. Imported from Italy by Beretta U.S.A.
Price: 12 or 20 ga., standard chokes **$565.00**
Price: Multi-choke, 12 ga. only **$650.00**
Price: 12 ga. trap with Monte Carlo stock **$590.00**
Price: 12 or 20 ga. Skeet **$580.00**

Browning Auto-5

BROWNING AUTO-5 LIGHT 12 and 20
Gauge: 12, 20; 5-shot; 3-shot plug furnished; 2¾″ chamber.
Action: Recoil operated autoloader; takedown.
Barrel: 26″ (Skeet boring in 12 & 20 ga., Cyl., Imp. Cyl., Mod in 20 ga.); 28″ (Skeet in 12 ga., Mod., Full); 30″ (Full in 12 ga.); also available with 26″, 28″, 30″ and 32″ Invector (choke tube) barrel.

Weight: 12 ga. 7¼ lbs., 20 ga. 6⅜ lbs.
Stock: French walnut, hand checkered half-p.g. and fore-end. 14¼″ x 1⅝″ x 2½″.
Features: Receiver hand engraved with scroll designs and border. Double extractors, extra bbls. interchangeable without factory fitting; mag. cut-off; cross-bolt safety. Imported from Japan by Browning.
Price: Vent. rib only **$559.95**
Price: Extra barrels, vent. rib only **$175.00**
Price: Invector model **$589.95**

Browning Auto-5 Magnum 12
Same as Std. Auto-5 except chambered for 3″ magnum shells (also handles 2¾″ magnum and 2¾″ HV loads). 28″ Mod., Full; 30″ and 32″ (Full) bbls. Also available with Invector choke tubes. 14″x1⅝″x2½″ stock. Recoil pad. Wgt. 8¾ lbs.
Price: Vent. rib only **$569.95**
Price: Invector model **$599.95**

Browning Auto-5 Magnum 20
Same as Magnum 12 except barrels 28″ Full or Mod., or 26″ Full, Mod., Imp. Cyl. or Invector. With ventilated rib, 7½ lbs.
Price: **$569.95**
Price: Invector model **$599.95**

Browning A-5 Buck Special

Browning Auto-5 Light 12, 20 or 12 Buck Special
Same as A-5 Light model except: 24″ bbl. choked for slugs, gold bead front sight on contoured ramp, rear sight adj. for w.&e. Wgt. 12 ga., 7 lbs.; 20 ga., 6 lbs. 2 oz.; 3″ Mag. 12, 8¼ lbs. All Buck Specials are available with carrying sling, detachable swivels and swivel attachments for **$20.00** extra.
Price: **$569.95**
Price: 12 or 20 ga. Magnum **$584.95**

Browning Auto-5 Classic & Gold Classic
Same as the standard Auto-5 Light 12 with 28″ (Mod.) barrel. Classic edition has hunting and wildlife scenes engraved on the satin grey receiver, including a portrait of John M. Browning, and is limited to 5,000 guns. Also engraved is "Browning Classic. One of Five Thousand." The Gold Classic has a variation of the engraved scenes but with gold animals and portrait. Only 500 will be made, each numbered "1 of Five Hundred," etc. with "Browning Gold Classic."

Both editions have select, figured walnut, special checkering with carved border, and the semi-pistol grip stock. Scheduled for 1984 delivery. Introduced 1984.
Price: Auto-5 Classic **$1,200.00**
Price: Auto-5 Gold Classic **$6,500.00**

CAUTION: PRICES CHANGE. CHECK AT GUNSHOP.

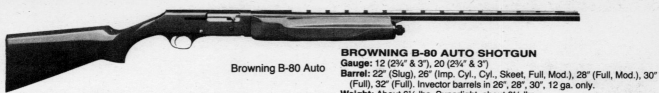

Browning B-80 Auto

COSMI AUTOMATIC SHOTGUN
Gauge: 12 or 20, 2¾" or 3" chamber.
Barrel: 22" to 35". Choke and length to customer specs.
Weight: 6¼ lbs. (20 ga.)
Stock: Length and style to customer specs. Exhibition grade walnut.
Features: Hand-made, essentially a custom gun. Recoil-operated auto with tip-up barrel. Made completely of stainless steel (lower receiver polished); magazine tube in buttstock holds 7 rounds. Comes with fitted leather case. Imported from Italy by Incor Inc.
Price: From $6,200.00

BROWNING B-80 AUTO SHOTGUN
Gauge: 12 (2¾" & 3"), 20 (2¾" & 3")
Barrel: 22" (Slug), 26" (Imp. Cyl., Cyl., Skeet, Full, Mod.), 28" (Full, Mod.), 30" (Full), 32" (Full). Invector barrels in 26", 28", 30", 12 ga. only.
Weight: About 6½ lbs. Superlight, about 6¼ lbs.
Stock: 14¼" x 1⅝" x 2½". Hand checkered French walnut. Solid black recoil pad.
Features: Vent. rib barrels have non-reflective rib; steel receiver with high-polish blue; cross-bolt safety; interchangeable barrels. Introduced 1981. Imported from Belgium by Browning.
Price: 12 or 20 ga., 2¾" or 3", vent. rib $559.95
Price: Buck Special, 12 or 20 ga., 2¾" or 3" $569.95
Price: Buck Special, with accessories (carrying strap, swivels) $589.95
Price: Extra barrels $175.95
Price: Invector 12 ga., vent. rib $589.95
Price: Extra Invector barrels $205.00

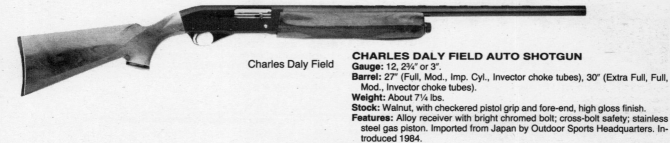

Charles Daly Field

CHARLES DALY FIELD AUTO SHOTGUN
Gauge: 12, 2¾" or 3".
Barrel: 27" (Full, Mod., Imp. Cyl., Invector choke tubes), 30" (Extra Full, Full, Mod., Invector choke tubes).
Weight: About 7¼ lbs.
Stock: Walnut, with checkered pistol grip and fore-end, high gloss finish.
Features: Alloy receiver with bright chromed bolt; cross-bolt safety; stainless steel gas piston. Imported from Japan by Outdoor Sports Headquarters. Introduced 1984.
Price: $374.95

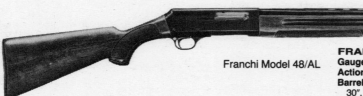

Franchi Model 48/AL

Franchi Slug Gun
Same as Standard automatic except 22" Cylinder bored plain barrel, adj. rifle-type sights, sling swivels.
Price: 12 or 20 ga., standard $394.95
Price: As above, Hunter grade $419.95
Price: Extra barrel $154.95

FRANCHI 48/AL AUTO SHOTGUN
Gauge: 12 or 20, 5-shot. 2¾" or 3" chamber.
Action: Recoil-operated automatic.
Barrel: 24" (Imp. Cyl. or Cyl.); 26" (Imp. Cyl. or Mod); 28" (Skeet, Mod. or Full); 30", 32" (Full). Interchangeable barrels.
Weight: 12 ga. 6¼ lbs., 20 ga. 5 lbs. 2 oz.
Stock: Epoxy-finished walnut, with cut-checkered pistol grip and fore-end.
Features: Chrome-lined bbl., easy takedown, 3-round plug provided. Ventilated rib barrel. Imported from Italy by F.I.E.
Price: Vent. rib 12, 20 . . . . $394.95
Price: Hunter model (engraved) $419.95
Price: 12 ga. Magnum $419.95
Price: Extra barrel $154.95

Ithaca Model 51A

Ithaca Model 51A Waterfowler
Same Standard Model 51 except has 3" chamber, 30" barrel, matte finish, sling and swivels.
Price: With vent rib $477.00
Price: As Turkey Gun, 26" barrel. $477.00

Ithaca Model 51A Supreme Skeet
Same gun as Model 51 Skeet with fancy American walnut stock, 26" (Skeet) barrel, 12 or 20 ga..
Price: $614.00

ITHACA MODEL 51A AUTOMATIC
Gauge: 12 or 20 ga., 2¾" chamber.
Action: Gas-operated, rotary bolt has three locking lugs. Takedown. Self-compensating for high or low base loads.
Barrel: Roto-Forged, 28" (Mod.). Extra barrels available. Raybar front sight.
Weight: About 7½ lbs.
Stock: 14"x1⅝"x2½". Hand checkered walnut, white spacers on p.g. and under recoil pad.
Features: Hand fitted, engraved receiver, 3 shot capacity, safety is reversible for left hand shooter.
Price: With vent, rib $477.00
Price: Presentation Series $1,658.00

Ithaca Model 51A Supreme Trap
Same gun as standard Model 51 with fancy American walnut trap stock, 30" (Full).
Price: $614.00
Price: With Monte Carlo stock $650.00

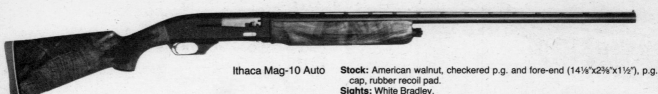

Ithaca Mag-10 Auto

Stock: American walnut, checkered p.g. and fore-end (14⅛"x2⅜"x1½"), p.g. cap, rubber recoil pad.
Sights: White Bradley.
Features: "Countercoil" gas system. Piston, cylinder, bolt, charging lever, action release and carrier made of stainless steel. ⅜" vent. rib. Reversible cross-bolt safety. Low recoil force. Supreme and Presentation models have full fancy claro American black walnut.

ITHACA MAG-10 GAS OPERATED SHOTGUN
Gauge: 10, 3½" chamber, 3-shot.
Barrel: 26", 28" (Full, Mod.), 32".
Weight: 11¼ lbs.

Price: Standard, plain barrel $670.00
Price: Deluxe, vent. rib $860.00
Price: Standard, vent. rib $730.00
Price: Supreme, vent. rib $995.00
Price: Presentation Series $1,727.00

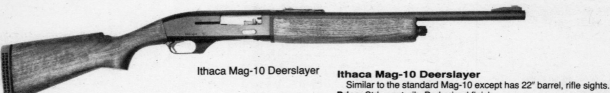

Ithaca Mag-10 Deerslayer

Ithaca Mag-10 Deerslayer
Similar to the standard Mag-10 except has 22" barrel, rifle sights.
Price: Std., vent. rib, Parkerized finish $730.00
Price: Deluxe, blue finsih $860.00
Price: Supreme grade $995.00

K.F.C. Model 250

Stock: 14⅛"x1½"x2½". American walnut, hand checkered p.g. and fore-end.
Features: Gas-operated, ventilated barrel rib. Has only 79 parts. Cross-bolt safety is reversible for left-handed shooters. Available with fixed or Tru-Choke interchangeable choke tube system. Introduced 1980. Imported from Japan by La Paloma Marketing.

KAWAGUCHIYA K.F.C. M-250 AUTO SHOTGUN
Gauge: 12, 2¾".
Barrel: 26" (Imp. Cyl.), 28" (Mod.), 30" (Full); or with Tru-Choke interchangeable choke tube system.
Weight: 7 lbs. **Length:** 48" over-all (28" barrel).

Price: Standard Grade $485.00
Price: Deluxe Grade (silvered, etched receiver). $520.00
Price: With Tru-Choke, Standard Grade $565.00
Price: As above, Deluxe Grade. $599.00

Kassnar/Churchill Auto

Stock: Select claro walnut with high gloss or matte finish, checkered pistol grip and fore-end; rosewood grip cap with white inlay.
Features: Stainless steel gas piston; cross-bolt safety; Standard model has anodized alloy receiver, Deluxe has etched and polished receiver. Imported from Japan by Kassnar. Introduced 1984.

KASSNAR/CHURCHILL GAS AUTO SHOTGUNS
Gauge: 12, 2¾" or 3".
Barrel: 20" (Slug); 26" (Imp. Cyl., Skeet); 28" (Mod., Full); 30" (Full); or with ICT choke tubes in 26", 27", 28", 30".
Weight: About 7½ lbs.

Price: Standard, fixed chokes $405.00
Price: Deluxe, fixed chokes $449.00
Price: Standard, ICT choke tubes. $435.00
Price: Deluxe, ICT choke tubes. $495.00
Price: Deerfield slug gun $419.00

Mossberg Model 5500

MOSSBERG 5500 AUTO SHOTGUN
Gauge: 12 only, 2¾" or 3" chamber.
Barrel: 18½" (Cyl.), 24" (Slugster), 26" (Imp. Cyl.), 28" (Mod.), 30" (Full, 2¾" or 3").
Weight: 7½ lbs. **Length:** 48" over-all (with 28" barrel).
Stock: 14"x1½"x2½". Walnut-finished hardwood.
Sights: Bead front.
Features: Safety located on top of receiver. Interchangeable barrels and ACCU-CHOKE choke tubes. Introduced 1983.
Price: About $340.00
Price: Slug gun, about. $291.00

CAUTION: PRICES CHANGE. CHECK AT GUNSHOP.

Remington Model 1100

REMINGTON MODEL 1100 AUTO
Gauge: 12, 3-shot plug furnished.
Action: Gas-operated autoloader.
Barrel: 26″ (Imp. Cyl.), 28″ (Mod., Full), 30″ Full in 12 ga. only.
Weight: 12 ga. 7½ lbs.
Stock: 14″x1½″x2½″ American Walnut, checkered p.g. and fore-end.
Features: Quickly interchangeable barrels within gauge. Matted receiver top with scroll work on both sides of receiver. Cross-bolt safety.
Price: **$463.00**
Price: With vent. rib **$507.00**
Price: Left hand model with vent. rib **$571.00**

Remington 1100 Magnum
Same as 1100 except: chambered for 3″ magnum loads. Available in 12 ga. (30″) or 20 ga. (28″) Mod. or Full, 14″x1½″x2½″ stock with recoil pad, Wgt. 7¾ lbs.
Price: With vent rib **$553.00**
Price: Left hand model with vent. rib **$619.00**

Remington 1100 Special Field

Remington 1100 "Special Field"
Similar to standard Model 1100 except comes with 21″ barrel only, choked Imp. Cyl., Mod., Full; 12 ga. weighs 7¼ lbs., LT-20 version 6½ lbs.; has straight-grip stock, shorter fore-end, both with cut checkering. Comes with vent rib only; matte finish receiver without engraving. Introduced 1983.
Price: **$535.00**

Remington 1100 Small Gauge
Same as 1100 except: 28 ga. 2¾″ (5-shot) or 410, 3″ (except Skeet, 2½″ 4-shot). 45½″ over-all. Available in 25″ bbl. (Full, Mod., or Imp. Cyl.) only.
Price: With vent. rib **$540.00**
Price: SA Skeet **$568.00**
Price: Tournament Skeet **$671.00**

Remington 1100 LT-20
Basically the same design as Model 1100, but with special weight-saving features that retain strength and dependability of the standard Model 1100.
Barrel: 28″ (Full, Mod.), 26″ (Imp. Cyl.).
Weight: 6½ lbs.
Price: **$463.00**
Price: With vent. rib **$507.00**
Price: LT-20 magnum **$553.00**
Price: LT-20 Deer Gun (20″ bbl.) **$507.00**
Price: LT-20 Ltd. has 23″ (Mod. or Imp. Cyl.) bbl., 1″ shorter stock . . . **$507.00**

Remington 1100D Tournament Auto
Same as 1100 Standard except: vent, rib, better wood, more extensive engraving.
Price: **$2,345.00**

Remington 1100 SA Skeet
Same as the 1100 except: 26″ bbl., special Skeet boring, vent. rib (high rib on LT-20), ivory bead front and metal bead middle sights. 14″x1½″x2½″ stock. 12, 20, 28, 410 ga. Wgt. 7½ lbs., cut checkering, walnut, new receiver scroll.
Price: 12 ga., Skeet SA **$555.00**
Price: 12 ga. Left hand model with vent. rib **$588.00**
Price: 28 & 410 ga., 25″ bbl. **$568.00**
Price: 20 ga. LT-20 Skeet SA **$555.00**
Price: Tournament Skeet (28, 410) **$671.00**
Price: Tournament Skeet (12 or 20) **$657.00**

Remington 1100F Premier Auto
Same as 1100D except: select wood, better engraving
Price: **$4,832.00**
Price: With gold inlay **$7,247.00**

Remington 1100 TA Trap

Remington 1100 TA Trap
Same as the standard 1100 except: recoil pad. 14⅜″x1⅜″x1¾″ stock. Right- or left-hand models. Wgt. 8¼ lbs. 12 ga. only. 30″ (Mod. Trap, Full) vent. rib bbl. Ivory bead front and white metal middle sight.
Price: **$567.00**
Price: With Monte Carlo stock **$577.00**
Price: 1100TA Trap, left hand **$600.00**
Price: With Monte Carlo stock **$600.00**
Price: Tournament Trap **$670.00**
Price: Tournament Trap with M.C. stock, better grade wood, different checkering, cut checkering **$680.00**

Remington 1100 Extra bbls. 12 and 20 ga.: Plain **$105.26** (20, 28 & 410, **$114.00**). Vent., rib 12 and 20 **$151.00** (20, 28 & 410, **$161.00**). Vent. rib Skeet **$171.00**. Vent. rib Trap **$162.00**. Deer bbl. **$125.00**. Available in the same gauges and chokes as shown on guns. **Prices are approximate.**

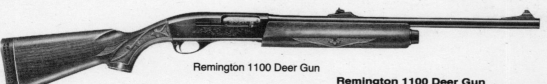

Remington 1100 Deer Gun

Remington 1100 Deer Gun
Same as 1100 except: 12 ga. only, 22″ bbl. (Imp. Cyl.), rifle sights adjustable for w. and e.; recoil pad with white spacer. Weight 7¼ lbs.
Price: **$507.00**
Price: Left-hand Deer Gun **$571.00**

S & W Model 1000 Auto

SMITH & WESSON MODEL 1000 AUTO
Gauge: 12, 2¾" or 3" chamber, 4-shot.
Action: Gas-operated autoloader.
Barrel: 26" (Skeet, Imp. Cyl.), 28" (Mod. Full). Also available with screw-in Multi-Choke tubes.
Weight: 7½ lbs. (28" bbl.). **Length:** 48" over-all (28" bbl.).
Stock: 14"x1½"x2⅜", American walnut.
Features: Interchangeable cross-bolt safety, vent. rib with front and middle beads, engraved alloy receiver, pressure compensator and floating piston for light recoil.
Price: **$507.00**
Price: Extra barrels (as listed above) **$151.95**
Price: Extra 22" barrel (Cyl. bore) with rifle sights **$125.95**
Price: With 3" chamber, 30" (Mod., Full) barrel.............. **$553.95**
Price: With Multi-Choke system **$534.95**
Price: Extra Multi-Choke barrel **$177.95**

Smith & Wesson Model 1000 20 Gauge & 20 Magnum
Similar to 12 ga. model except scaled down to weigh only 6½ lbs. Has self-cleaning gas system. Choice of four interchangeable barrels (26", Imp. Cyl. or Skeet, 28" Mod., Full) or Multi-Choke system which includes tubes for Imp. Cyl., Mod., Full.
Price: **$507.95**
Price: Extra barrels **$151.95**
Price: With 3" chamber, (Mod., Full).......................... **$553.95**
Price: With Multi-Choke system, ... **$534.95**

Smith & Wesson Model 1000 Trap Shotgun
Similar to the standard Model 1000 except has Monte Carlo trap stock, medium width stepped rib with white middle bead, Bradley front; integral wire shell catcher; specially tuned trigger; 30" Multi-Choke barrel with Full, Mod. and Imp. Mod. tubes. Steel receiver. Introduced 1983.
Price: **$605.95**

Smith & Wesson Model 1000 Waterfowler Auto
Similar to the standard Model 1000 except all exterior metal is Parkerized to reduce glare, bolt is black oxidized, stock has a dull oil finish. Comes with q.d. swivels and a padded, camouflaged sling. Available with 30" (Full) barrel with 3" chamber. Introduced 1982.
Price: **$580.95**
Price: Super 12 Waterfowler **$625.95**

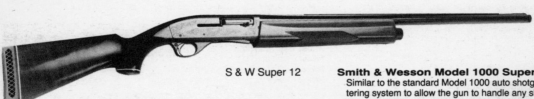

S & W Super 12

Smith & Wesson Model 1000 Super 12 Shotgun
Similar to the standard Model 1000 auto shotgun except has a new gas metering system to allow the gun to handle any shell from 3-inch mags to 1-oz. 2¾-inch field loads without changing the barrel. Super 12 barrels are not interchangeable with other Model 1000 guns, or vice versa. A longer magazine tube gives four-shot capability. In 12-gauge only, the Super 12 has a 3-inch chamber with choice of 26, 28 or 30-inch Multi-Choke barrel; also available in a Parkerized "Waterfowler" version with 28-inch Multi-Choke barrel.
Price: Super 12 .... **$598.95**
Price: Waterfowler **$625.95**
Price: Extra slug barrel, blue or Parkerized **$125.00**

> Consult our Directory pages for
> the location of firms mentioned.

S & W Model 1000 S

Smith & Wesson Model 1000S Super Skeet, 12 & 20
Similar to Model 1000 except has "recessed-type" Skeet choke with a compensator system to soften recoil and reduce muzzle jump. Stock has right-hand palm swell. Trigger is contoured (rounded) on right side; pull is 2½ to 3 lbs. Vent. rib has double sighting beads with a "Bright Point" fluorescent red front bead. Fore-end cap weights (included) of 1 and 2 oz. can be used to change balance. Select-grade walnut with oil finish. Barrel length is 25", weight 8¼ lbs., over-all length 45.7". Stock measures 14"x1½"x2½" with .08" cast-off at butt, .16" at toe.
Price: 12 ga. **$709.95**
Price: 20 ga. **$578.95**
Price: Super Skeet interchangeable barrel **$236.95**

Tradewinds Model H-170

TRADEWINDS H-170 AUTO SHOTGUN
Gauge: 12 only, 2¾" chamber.
Action: Recoil-operated automatic.
Barrel: 26", 28" (Mod.) and 28" (Full), chrome lined.
Weight: 7 lbs.
Stock: Select European walnut stock, p.g. and fore-end hand checkered.
Features: Light alloy receiver, 5-shot tubular magazine, ventilated rib. Imported from Italy by Tradewinds.
Price: **$395.00**

CAUTION: PRICES CHANGE. CHECK AT GUNSHOP.

SHOTGUNS—AUTOLOADERS

Weatherby Eighty-Two Auto

WEATHERBY EIGHTY-TWO AUTO
Gauge: 12 only, 2¾" and 3" chamber.
Barrel: 22" Slug (with sights), 26", 28", 30" with IMC (Integral Multi-Choke) tubes; 26" available with Mod., Imp. Cyl., Skeet, others with Full, Mod., Imp. Cyl.

Weight: 7½ lbs. **Length:** 48½" (28" bbl.).
Stock: Walnut, hand checkered p.g. and fore-end, rubber recoil pad.
Features: Gas operated autoloader with "Floating Piston." Cross-bolt safety, fluted bolt, gold plated trigger. Each gun comes with three flush fitting IMC choke tubes. Imported from Japan by Weatherby. Introduced 1982.
Price: $429.00
Price: Extra interchangeable barrel $186.00
Price: Extra IMC choke tubes $12.50

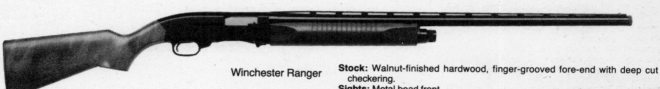

Winchester Ranger

WINCHESTER RANGER AUTO SHOTGUN
Gauge: 12 and 20, 2¾" chamber.
Barrel: 28" vent. rib with Winchoke tubes (Imp. Cyl., Mod., Full), or 28" plain barrel (Mod.).
Weight: 7 to 7¼ lbs. **Length:** 48⅝" over-all.

Stock: Walnut-finished hardwood, finger-grooved fore-end with deep cut checkering.
Sights: Metal bead front.
Features: Cross-bolt safety, front-locking rotating bolt, black serrated buttplate, gas-operated action. Made under license by U.S. Repeating Arms. Co.
Price: Vent. rib with Winchoke................................. $289.95
Price: Plain barrel $264.95
Price: Deer barrel combo $319.95
Price: Deer gun $284.95

SHOTGUNS—SLIDE ACTIONS

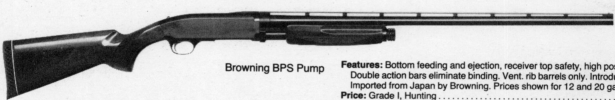

Browning BPS Pump

BROWNING BPS PUMP SHOTGUN
Gauge: 12 or 20 gauge, 3" chamber (2¾" in target guns), 5-shot magazine.
Barrel: 22", 24", 26", 28", 30", 32" (Imp. Cyl., Mod. or Full). Also available with Invector choke tubes, 12 or 20 ga.; Upland Special has 22" barrel with Invector tubes.
Weight: 7 lbs. 12 oz. (28" barrel). **Length:** 48¾" over-all (28" barrel).
Stock: 14¼"x1½"x2½". Select walnut, semi-beavertail fore-end, full p.g. stock.

Features: Bottom feeding and ejection, receiver top safety, high post vent. rib. Double action bars eliminate binding. Vent. rib barrels only. Introduced 1977. Imported from Japan by Browning. Prices shown for 12 and 20 gauge guns.
Price: Grade I, Hunting $374.95
Price: As above, with Invector chokes and Upland Special $404.95
Price: Grade I, Trap $394.95
Price: Invector Trap, vent. rib $424.95
Price: Extra Trap barrel..................................... $139.95
Price: As above, Invector chokes $169.95
Price: Extra hunting barrel.................................. $129.95
Price: As above, Invector chokes $159.95
Price: BPS, Buck Special, no accessories $399.95
Price: As above with accessories $419.95

Ithaca Model 37

ITHACA MODEL 37 FIELD GRADE
Gauge: 12, 20 (5-shot; 3-shot plug furnished).
Action: Slide; takedown; bottom ejection.
Barrel: 26", 28", 30" in 12 ga.; 26" or 28" in 20 ga. (Full, Mod. or Imp. Cyl.)
Weight: 12 ga. 6½ lbs., 20 ga. 5¾ lbs.
Stock: 14"x1⅝"x2⅝". Checkered hardwood p.g. stock and ring-tail fore-end.
Features: Ithaca Raybar front sight; decorated receiver, cross-bolt safety; action release for removing shells.
Price: Standard $292.00
Price: Standard Vent Rib $333.00
Price: Presentation Series $1,658.00

Ithaca Model 37 Deerslayer
Same as Model 37 except: 26" or 20" bbl. designed for rifled slugs; sporting rear sight, Raybar front sight: rear sight ramp grooved for Redfield long eye relief scope mount. 12, or 20 gauge. With checkered stock, beavertail fore-end and recoil pad.
Price: $385.00
Price: Super Deluxe model $435.00

Ithaca Model 37 Supreme
Same as Model 37 except: hand checkered fore-end and p.g. stock, Ithaca recoil pad and vent. rib. Model 37 Supreme also with Skeet (14"x1½"x2¼") or Trap (14½"x1½"x1⅞") stocks available at no extra charge. Other options available at extra charge.
Price: $650.00

Ithaca Model 37 Field Grade

Ithaca Model 37 Field Grade Magnum
Similar to the standard Model 37 Field Grade pump except has American hardwood stock, traditional "ring-tail" fore-end. Plain or vent. rib, 12 or 20 gauge, 3″ chamber only, interchangeable choke tubes. Raybar front sight. Introduced 1984.
Price: Vent. rib $367.00

Ithaca Model 37 Ultralite
Weighs five pounds. Same as standard Model 37 except 20 ga. comes only with 25″ vent. rib barrel choked Full, Mod. or Imp. Cyl.; 12 ga., 26″ barrel with same chokes as 20 ga. Has recoil pad, gold plated trigger, Sid Bell-designed grip cap. Also available as Ultra-Deerslayer with 20″ barrel, 20 ga. only.
Price: $435.00
Price: Deerslayer model $414.00

Ithaca Model 37 Magnum
Same as standard Model 37 except chambered for 3″ shells with resulting longer receiver. Stock dimensions are 14″x1⅞″x1½″. Grip cap has a Sid Bell-designed flying mallard on it. Has a recoil pad, vent. rib barrel with Raybar front sight. Available in 12 or 20 ga. with 30″ (Full), 28″ (Mod.) and 26″ (Imp. Cyl.) barrel. Weight about 7¼ lbs. Introduced 1978.
Price: $414.00

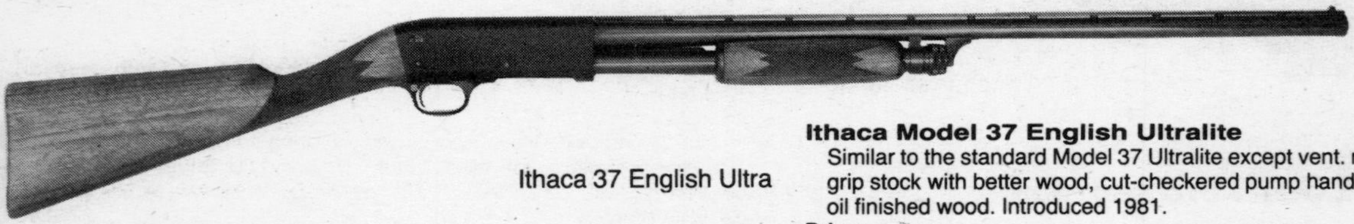

Ithaca 37 English Ultra

Ithaca Model 37 English Ultralite
Similar to the standard Model 37 Ultralite except vent. rib barrel has straight-grip stock with better wood, cut-checkered pump handle, grip area and butt, oil finished wood. Introduced 1981.
Price: $496.00

KASSNAR/CHURCHILL PUMP SHOTGUNS
Gauge: 12, 2¾″ or 3″ chamber.
Barrel: 20″ (Slug), 26″ (Imp. Cyl., Skeet), 28″ (Mod.), 30″ (Full), fixed chokes; 26″, 27″, 28″, 30″ for ICT choke tubes.
Weight: About 7½ lbs.
Stock: Select claro walnut with matte or high gloss finish, checkered pistol grip and fore-end, rosewood grip cap with inlay.
Features: Short stroke action with twin action bars; anodized aluminum receiver. Imported from Japan by Kassnar.
Price: With fixed chokes $389.00
Price: Deerfield slug gun $405.00
Price: With ICT choke tubes $419.00

KASSNAR/OMEGA PUMP SHOTGUNS
Gauge: 12, 2¾″ chamber.
Barrel: 20″, 26″ (Imp. Cyl.); 28″ (Mod.); 30″ (Full).
Weight: 6¾ lbs. (Slug) to 7½ lbs.
Stock: Stained hardwood.
Sights: Bead front; rifle-type on Deerfield Slug.
Features: Blued receiver; Damascened bolt; cross-bolt safety. Imported from the Philippines by Kassnar. Introduced 1984.
Price: Field $189.00
Price: Deerfield Slug $199.00

KASSNAR OMEGA SHOTGUN
Gauge: 12 only, 2¾″ chamber.
Barrel: 20″ (Imp. Cyl., Slug); 24″ (Slug); 26″ (Imp. Cyl.); 28″ (Mod.); 30″ (Full).
Weight: 7 lbs. **Length:** 48″ over-all (30″ bbl.).
Stock: Philippine mahogany.
Features: Checkered grip and fore-end; slug guns have ramp front, open rear sights. Imported from the Philippines by Kassnar.
Price: Riot or slug model $199.00
Price: Field model $189.00

> Consult our Directory pages for the location of firms mentioned.

Marlin Model 120

MARLIN 120 MAGNUM PUMP GUN
Gauge: 12 ga. (2¾″ or 3″ chamber) 5-shot; 3-shot plug furnished.
Action: Hammerless, side ejecting, slide action.

Barrel: 20″ slug, 26″ (Imp. Cyl.), 28″ (Mod.), 30″ (Full), with vent. rib or 38″ MXR plain.
Weight: 8 lbs. **Length:** 50½″ over-all (30″ bbl.).
Stock: 14″x1½″x2⅜″. Hand-checkered walnut, capped p.g., semi-beavertail fore-end. Mar-Shield® finish.
Features: Interchangeable bbls., slide lock release; large button cross-bolt safety.
Price: $369.95
Price: Extra barrels, about $107.95

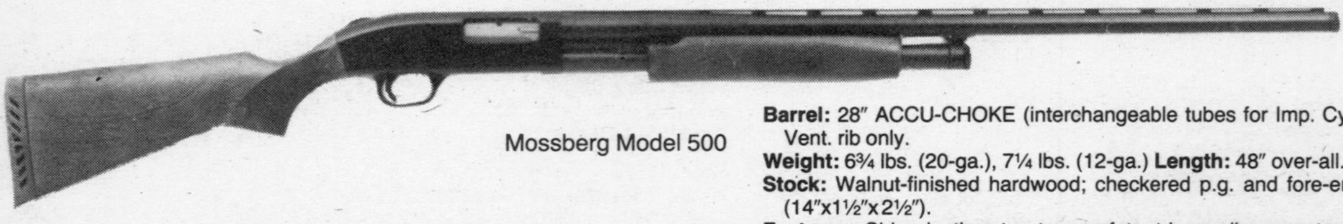

Mossberg Model 500

MOSSBERG MODEL 500 AGVD, CGVD
Gauge: 12, 20, 3″.
Action: Takedown.

Barrel: 28″ ACCU-CHOKE (interchangeable tubes for Imp. Cyl., Mod., Full). Vent. rib only.
Weight: 6¾ lbs. (20-ga.), 7¼ lbs. (12-ga.) **Length:** 48″ over-all.
Stock: Walnut-finished hardwood; checkered p.g. and fore-end; recoil pad. (14″x1½″x2½″).
Features: Side ejection; top tang safety; trigger disconnector prevents doubles. Easily interchangeable barrels within gauge.
Price: Vent rib, either gauge, about $206.00
Price: Extra barrels, from $24.95
Price: Youth model, 20 ga., 13″ buttstock, 25″ (Mod.), about $180.00

CAUTION: PRICES CHANGE. CHECK AT GUNSHOP.

Mossberg 500 AHT/AHTD

Mossberg Model 500AHT/AHTD

Same as Model 500 except 12 ga. only with extra-high Simmons Olympic-style free floating rib and built-up Monte Carlo trap-style stock. 30″ barrel (Full), 28″ ACCU-CHOKE with 3 interchangeable choke tubes (Mod., Imp. Mod., Full).
Price: With 30″ barrel, fixed choke .... **NA**
Price: With ACCU-CHOKE barrel, 28″ or 30″ .... **NA**

Mossberg Model 500EGV

Similar to Mossberg Model 500 except: 410 bore only, 26″ bbl. (Full); 2½″, 3″ shells; holds six 2¾″ or five 3″ shells. Walnut-finished stock with checkered p.g. and fore-end, fluted comb and recoil pad (14″x1¼″x2½″). Weight about 6 lbs., length over-all 45¾″.
Price: With vent. rib barrel .... **N.A.**

Mossberg Model 500ASG Slugster

Same as standard Mossberg Model 500 except has Slugster barrel with ramp front sight, open adj. folding-leaf rear, running deer scene etched on receiver. 12 ga.—18½″, 24″, 20-ga.—24″ bbl.
Price: .... **N.A.**

Remington Model 870

REMINGTON 870 WINGMASTER PUMP GUN

Gauge: 12, 20, (5-shot; 3-shot wood plug).
Action: Takedown, slide action
Barrel: 12, 20, ga., 26″ (Imp. Cyl.); 28″ (Mod. or Full); 12 ga., 30″ (Full).

Weight: 7 lbs., 12 ga. (7¾ lbs. with Vari-Weight plug); 6½ lbs., 20 ga.
Length: 48½″ over-all (28″ bbl.).
Stock: 14″x1⅝″x2½″. Checkered walnut, p.g.; fluted extension fore-end; fitted rubber recoil pad.
Features: Double action bars, crossbolt safety. Receiver machined from solid steel. Hand fitted action.
Price: Plain bbl. **$355.00**
Price: With vent. rib **$400.00**
Price: Left hand, vent. rib., 12 ga. only............................. **$446.00**
Price: Youth Gun, 21″ vent. rib, Imp. Cyl., Mod **$400.00**

Remington 870 Special Field

Remington Model 870 "Special Field"

Similar to the standard Model 870 except comes with 21″ barrel only, 3″ chamber, choked Imp. Cyl., Mod., Full; 12 ga. weighs 6¾ lbs., Ltwt. 20 weighs 6 lbs.; has straight-grip stock, shorter fore-end, both with cut checkering. Vent. rib barrel only. Introduced 1984.
Price: **$428.00**

Remington 870 Magnum

Same as the M870 except 3″ chamber, 12 ga. 30″ bbl. (Mod. or Full), 20 ga. 28″ bbl. (Mod. or Full). Recoil pad installed. Wgt., 12 ga. 8 lbs., 20 ga. 7½ lbs.
Price: With vent. rib **$400.00**
Price: Left hand model, vent. rib. bbl **$475.00**

Remington 870 Small Gauges

Exact copies of the large ga. Model 870, except that guns are offered in 28 and 410 ga. 25″ barrel (Full, Mod., Imp. Cyl.). D and F grade prices same as large ga. M870 prices.
Price: With vent. rib barrel **$422.37**

Remington 870F Premier

Same as M870, except select walnut, better engraving
Price: **$4,8320.00**
Price: With gold inlay **$7,247.00**

Remington Model 870 20 Ga. Lt. Wt.

Same as standard Model 870 except weighs 6 lbs.; 26″ (Imp. Cyl.), 28″ (Full, Mod.), 30″ (Full).
Price: Vent. rib barrel **$400.00**
Price: Magnum, vent. rib barrel **$400.00**

Remington 870 TA Trap

Remington 870 TA Trap

Same as the M870 except: 12 ga. only, 30″ (Mod., Full) vent. rib. bbl., ivory front and white metal middle beads. Special sear, hammer and trigger assy. 14⅜″x1½″x1⅞″ stock with recoil pad. Hand fitted action and parts. Wgt. 8 lbs.
Price: Model 870TA Trap **$429.00**
Price: TA Trap with Monte Carlo stock............................. **$440.00**

Remington Model 870 Competition Trap

Same as standard 870 except single shot, gas reduction system, select wood. Has 30″ (Full choke) vent. rib barrel
Price: **$675.00**

Remington 870 Extra Barrels

Plain $89.47; Vent. rib $135.53; Vent. rib Skeet $146.05; Vent. rib Trap $146.05; 34″ Trap $146.05. With rifle sights $117.11. Available in the same gauges and chokes as shown on guns. **Prices are approximate.**

Remington 870D Tournament

Same as 870 except: better walnut, hand checkering. Engraved receiver and bbl. Vent. rib. Stock dimensions to order.
Price: **$2,345.00**

SHOTGUNS—SLIDE ACTIONS

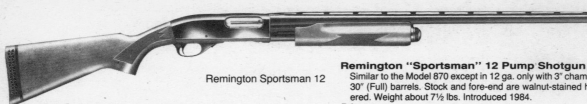

Remington Sportsman 12

Remington "Sportsman" 12 Pump Shotgun
Similar to the Model 870 except in 12 ga. only with 3″ chamber, 28″ (Mod.) or 30″ (Full) barrels. Stock and fore-end are walnut-stained hardwood, checkered. Weight about 7½ lbs. Introduced 1984.
Price: **$218.00**

Remington Model 870 Brushmaster Deluxe
Carbine version of the M870 with 20″ bbl. (Imp. Cyl.) for rifled slugs. 40½″ over-all, wgt. 6½ lbs. Recoil pad. Adj. rear, ramp front sights, 12 or 20 ga. Deluxe.
Price: **$378.00**
Price: Left-hand model **$422.00**

S & W Model 3000

SMITH & WESSON MODEL 3000 PUMP
Gauge: 12 or 20 ga., 3″ chamber.
Barrel: 22″ (Cyl.) with rifle sights, 26″ (Imp. Cyl.), 28″ (Mod.), 30″ (Full), vent. rib or plain. Also available with Multi-Choke system.
Weight: About 7½ lbs. **Length:** 48½″ over-all (28″ bbl.).
Stock: 14″x1⅜″x2¼″. American walnut
Features: Dual action bars for smooth functioning. Rubber recoil pad, steel receiver, chrome plated bolt. Cross-bolt safety reversible for left-handed shooters. Introduced 1980.
Price: With vent. rib barrel **$400.95**
Price: Extra vent. rib barrel **$135.95**
Price: Slug barrel with rifle sights **$110.95**
Price: With Multi-Choke system **$426.95**
Price: Extra Multi-Choke barrel **$161.95**

Smith & Wesson Model 3000 Waterfowler Pump
Similar to the standard Model 3000 except all exterior metal is Parkerized to reduce glare, bolt is black oxidized, stock has a dull oil finish. Comes with q.d. swivels and a padded, camouflaged sling. Available with 30″ (Full) barrel with 3″ chamber. Introduced 1982.
Price: **$426.95**
Price: With Multi-Choke barrel **$452.95**
Price: Slug gun **$360.95**

Stevens 67VR

Weight: 7 lbs. **Length:** 49½″ over-all (30″ bbl.).
Stock: Walnut-finished hardwood; checkered p.g. and slide handle. 14″x1½″x2½″.
Sights: Metal bead front.
Features: Grooved slide handle, top tang safety, steel receiver. From Savage Arms. Introduced 1981.
Price: Model 67 .... **$181.50**
Price: Model 67VR (vent. rib) **$191.50**
Price: Model 67 Slug Gun (21″ barrel, rifle sights) **$185.50**
Price: Model 67-T (with 3 choke tubes) **$189.50**
Price: Model 67-VRT (as above with vent. rib) **$211.50**

STEVENS MODEL 67 PUMP SHOTGUN
Gauge: 12, 20 (2¾″ & 3″), 410 (2½″ & 3″).
Barrel: 26″ (Full, 410 ga.), 28″ (Mod., Full), 30″ (Full, 12 ga.), or interchangeable choke tubes.

Weatherby Ninety-Two

Weight: About 7½ lbs. **Length:** 48⅛″ (28″ bbl.).
Stock: Walnut, hand checkered p.g. and fore-end, white line spacers at p.g. cap and recoil pad.
Features: Short stroke action, cross-bolt safety. Comes with three flush-fitting IMC choke tubes. Introduced 1982. Imported from Japan by Weatherby.
Price: **$339.95**
Price: Extra interchangeable bbls. **$149.00**
Price: Extra IMC choke tubes **$12.50**

WEATHERBY NINETY-TWO PUMP
Gauge: 12 only, 3″ chamber.
Action: Short stroke slide action.
Barrel: 22″ Slug (with sights), 26″, 28″, 30″ with IMC (Integral Multi-Choke) tubes; 26″ with Mod., Imp. Cyl., Skeet, others with Full, Mod., Imp. Cyl.

Winchester Ranger

Weight: 7 to 7¼ lbs. **Length:** 48⅝″ to 50⅝″ over-all.
Stock: Walnut finished hardwood with ribbed fore-end.
Sights: Metal bead front.
Features: Cross-bolt safety, black rubber butt pad, twin action slide bars, front-locking rotating bolt. Made under license by U.S. Repeating Arms Co.
Price: Plain barrel **$189.95**
Price: Vent. rib barrel, Winchoke **$219.95**
Price: Vent. rib. Mod. choke **$204.95**

WINCHESTER RANGER PUMP GUN
Gauge: 12 or 20, 3″ chamber, 4-shot magazine.
Barrel: 28″ vent rib or plain with Full, Mod., Imp. Cyl. Winchoke tubes, or 30″ plain.

CAUTION: PRICES CHANGE. CHECK AT GUNSHOP.

SHOTGUNS—SLIDE ACTIONS

Winchester Ranger Combination

Winchester Ranger Pump Gun Combination
Similar to the standard Ranger except comes with two barrels: 24⅛" (Cyl.) deer barrel with rifle-type sights and an interchangeable 28" vent. rib Winchoke barrel with Full, Mod. and Imp. Cyl. choke tubes. Available in 12 and 20 gauge 3" only, with recoil pad. Introduced 1983.
Price: With two barrels **$249.95**

Winchester 1300

Winchester Ranger Youth Pump Gun
Similar to the standard Ranger except chambered only for 3" 20 ga., 22" plain barrel with Winchoke tubes (Full, Mod., Imp. Cyl.) or 22" plain barrel with fixed Mod. choke. Weighs 6½ lbs., measures 41⅝" o.a.l. Stock has 13" pull length and gun comes with discount certificate for full-size stock. Introduced 1983. Made under license by U.S. Repeating Arms Co.
Price: Plain barrel, Winchoke. **$204.95**
Price: Plain barrel, Mod. choke **$189.95**

WINCHESTER MODEL 1300 FEATHERWEIGHT PUMP
Gauge: 12 and 20, 3" chamber, 5-shot capacity.
Barrel: 22", vent. rib, with Full, Mod., Imp. Cyl. Winchoke tubes.
Weight: 6⅜ lbs. **Length:** 42⅝" over-all.
Stock: American walnut, with deep cut checkering on pistol grip, traditional ribbed fore-end; high luster finish.
Sights: Metal bead front.
Features: Twin action slide bars; front-locking rotating bolt; roll-engraved receiver; blued, highly polished metal; cross-bolt safety with red indicator. Introduced 1984.
Price: 12 or 20 gauge **$299.95**

SHOTGUNS—OVER-UNDERS

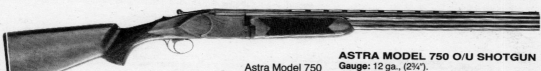

Astra Model 750

ASTRA MODEL 750 O/U SHOTGUN
Gauge: 12 ga., (2¾").
Barrel: 28" (Mod. & Full or Skeet & Skeet), 30" Trap (Mod. & Full).
Weight: 6½ lbs.
Stock: European walnut, hand-checkered p.g. and fore-end.
Features: Single selective trigger, scroll-engraved receiver, selective auto ejectors, vent. rib. Introduced 1980. From L. Joseph Rahn, Inc.
Price: **$735.00**
Price: With extractors only **$600.00**
Price: Trap or Skeet (M.C. stock and recoil pad.). **$850.00**

Astra Model 650 O/U Shotgun
Same as Model 750 except has double triggers.
Price: With extractors **$495.00**
Price: With ejectors **$630.00**

ARMSPORT MODEL 2500 O/U
Gauge: 12 or 20 ga.
Barrel: 26" (Imp. Cyl. & Mod.); 28" (Mod. & Full); vent. rib.
Weight: 8 lbs.
Stock: European walnut, hand checkered p.g. and fore-end.
Features: Single selective trigger, automatic ejectors, engraved receiver. Imported by Armsport.
Price: **$695.00**
Price: With extractors only **$595.00**

> Consult our Directory pages for the location of firms mentioned.

Beeman/Fabarm

BEEMAN/FABARM OVER-UNDER SHOTGUN
Gauge: 12, 2¾" chambers.
Barrel: 26½" (Skeet & Skeet), 29" (Full & Mod.).
Weight: About 7½ lbs. **Length:** 46" over-all.
Stock: Select walnut with cut-checkered grip and fore-end; Schnabel fore-end.
Sights: Luminous red bead front, white bead middle.
Features: Boxlock action with single selective trigger, automatic ejectors; chrome lined bores and chambers; silvered, engraved receiver. Skeet/Trap combo version has interchangeable barrels and comes with case. Imported from Italy by Beeman. Introduced 1984.
Price: Field **$695.00**
Price: Trap or Skeet **$795.00**
Price: Skeet/Trap Combo **$1,195.00**

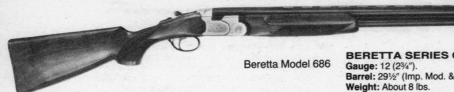

Beretta Model 686

BERETTA SO-3 O/U SHOTGUN
Gauge: 12 ga. (2¾" chambers).
Action: Back-action sidelock.
Barrel: 26", 27", 28", 29" or 30", chokes to customer specs.
Stock: Standard measurements—14⅛"x1⁷⁄₁₆"x2⅜". Straight "English" or p.g.-style. Hand checkered European walnut.
Features: SO-3—"English scroll" floral engraving on action body, sideplates and trigger guard. Stocked in select walnut. SO-3EL—as above, with full engraving coverage. Hand-detachable sideplates. SO-3EELL—as above with deluxe finish and finest full coverage engraving. Internal parts gold plated. Top lever is pierced and carved in relief with gold inlaid crown. Introduced 1977. Imported from Italy by Beretta U.S.A. Corp.

Price: SO-3	$6,245.00
Price: SO-3EL	$7,440.00
Price: SO-3EELL	$10,000.00

BERETTA SERIES 680 OVER-UNDER
Gauge: 12 (2¾").
Barrel: 29½" (Imp. Mod. & Full, Trap), 28" (Skeet & Skeet).
Weight: About 8 lbs.
Stock: Trap—14⅜"x1¼"x2⅛"; Skeet—14⅜"x1⅜"x2⁷⁄₁₆". European walnut with hand checkering.
Sights: Luminous front sight and center bead.
Features: Trap Monte Carlo stock has deluxe trap recoil pad, Skeet has smooth pad. Imported from Italy by Beretta U.S.A. Corp.

Price: Skeet or Trap gun	$1,580.00
Price: As above with fitted case	$1,580.00
Price: M686 Field gun (illus.)	$980.00
Price: M685 Field gun	$820.00
Price: M687EL, Field	$2,212.00
Price: M680 Single bbl. Trap, 32" or 34"	$1,580.00
Price: M680 Combo Trap O/U, with single bbl.	$2,200.00

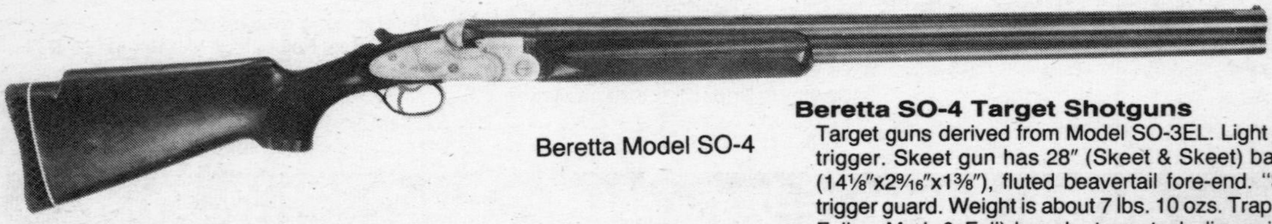

Beretta Model SO-4

Beretta SO-4 Target Shotguns
Target guns derived from Model SO-3EL. Light engraving coverage. Single trigger. Skeet gun has 28" (Skeet & Skeet) barrels, 10mm rib, p.g. stock (14⅛"x2⁹⁄₁₆"x1⅜"), fluted beavertail fore-end. "Skeet" is inlaid in gold into trigger guard. Weight is about 7 lbs. 10 ozs. Trap guns have 30" (Imp. Mod. & Full or Mod. & Full) barrels, trap stock dimensions, fitted recoil pad, fluted beavertail fore-end. Weight is about 7 lbs. 12 ozs. "Trap" is inlaid in gold into trigger guard. Special dimensions and features, within limits, may be ordered. Introduced 1977.

Price: Skeet	$7,285.00
Price: Trap	$7,285.00

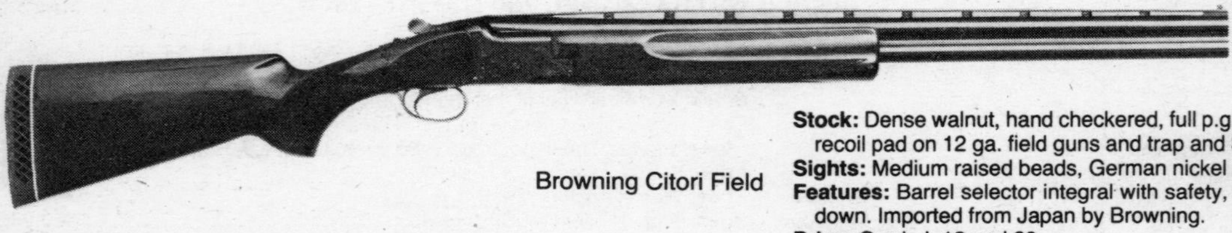

Browning Citori Field

BROWNING CITORI O/U SHOTGUN
Gauge: 12, 20, 28 and 410.
Barrel: 26", 28" (Mod. & Full, Imp. Cyl. & Mod.), in all gauges, 30" (Mod. & Full, Full & Full) in 12 ga. only. Also offered with Invector choke tubes.
Weight: 6 lbs. 8 oz. (26" 410) to 7 lbs. 13 oz. (30" 12-ga.).
Length: 43" over-all (26" bbl.).

Stock: Dense walnut, hand checkered, full p.g., beavertail fore-end. Field-type recoil pad on 12 ga. field guns and trap and Skeet models.
Sights: Medium raised beads, German nickel silver.
Features: Barrel selector integral with safety, auto ejectors, three-piece takedown. Imported from Japan by Browning.

Price: Grade I, 12 and 20	$775.00
Price: Grade I, 28 and 410	$800.00
Price: Grade V, 12 and 20	$1,960.00
Price: Grade V, 28 and 410	$1,960.00
Price: Grade VI, 12 and 20	$2,050.00
Price: Grade VI, 28 and 410, high post rib	$2,050.00
Price: Grade I. Invector	$802.00

Browning Citori Superlight

Browning Superlight Citori Over-Under
Similar to the standard Citori except availiable in 12, 20, 28 or 410 with 24", 26" barrels choked Imp. Cyl. & Mod. or 28" choked Mod. & Full. Has straight grip stock, Schnabel fore-end tip. Superlight 12 weighs 6 lbs. 9 oz. (26" barrels); Superlight 20, 5 lbs., 12 oz. (26" barrels). Introduced 1982.

Price: Grade I only, 12, 20, 28 or 410.	$800.00
Price: Grade VI	$2,050.00
Price: Grade I Invector	$835.00
Price: Grade I Invector, Upland Special (24" bbls.)	$835.00

Browning Citori O/U Skeet Models
Similar to standard Citori except: 26", 28" (Skeet & Skeet) only; stock dimensions of 14⅜"x1½"x2", fitted with Skeet-style recoil pad; conventional target rib and high post target rib.

Price: Grade I Invector (high post rib)	$895.00
Price: Grade I, 12 & 20 (high post rib)	$865.00
Price: Grade I, 28 & 410 (high post rib)	$900.00
Price: Grade V, all gauges (high post rib)	$2,095.00
Price: Grade VI, all gauges, (high post rib)	$2,150.00
Price: Four barrel Skeet set — 12, 20, 28, 410 barrels, with case, Grade I only	$2,900.00

Browning Citori O/U Trap Models
Similar to standard Citori except: 12 gauge only; 30", 32" (Full & Full, Imp. Mod. & Full, Mod. & Full), 34" single barrel in Combo Set (Full, Imp. Mod., Mod.), or Invector model; Monte Carlo cheekpiece (14⅜"x1⅜"x1⅜"x2"); fitted with trap-style recoil pad; conventional target rib and high post target rib.

Price: Grade I Invector (high post target rib)	$900.00
Price: Grade V Invector (high post target rib)	$2,130.00
Price: Grade V (high post rib)	$2,095.00
Price: Grade VI Invector (high post target rib)	$2,185.00
Price: Grade VI (high post target rib)	$2,150.00

CAUTION: PRICES CHANGE. CHECK AT GUNSHOP.

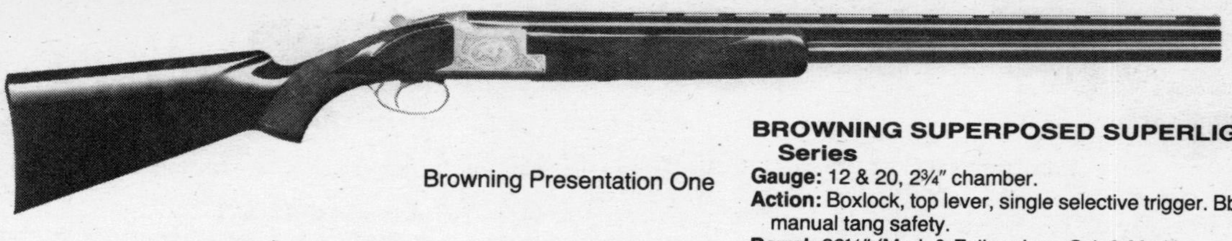

Browning Presentation One

Browning Limited Edition Waterfowl Superposed

Same specs as the Lightning Superposed. Available in 12 ga. only, 28″ (Mod. & Full). Limited to 500 guns, the edition number of each gun is inscribed in gold on the bottom of the receiver with "Black Duck" and its scientific name. Sides of receiver have two gold inlayed black ducks, bottom has two, and one on the trigger guard. Receiver is completely engraved and grayed. Stock and fore-end are highly figured dark French walnut with 24 lpi checkering, hand-oiled finish, checkered butt. Comes with form fitted, velvet-lined, black walnut case. Introduced 1983.
Price: **$8,000.00**
Price: Similar treatment as above except for the Pintail Duck Issue **$7,700.00**

Browning Presentation Superposed Magnum 12

Browning Superposed 3″ chambers; 30″ (Full & Full or Full & Mod.) barrels. Stock, 14¼″x1⅝″x2½″ with factory fitted recoil pad. Weight 8 lbs.
Price: From **$4,500.00**

Browning Superposed Classic & Gold Classic

Same as the standard Superposed 20-ga. with 26″ (Imp. Cyl. & Mod.) barrels except has an upland setting of bird dogs, pheasant and quail on the satin grey receiver. Gold Classic has the animals in inlaid gold. Straight grip stock and Schnabel fore-end are of select American walnut. Classic has pearl borders around the checkering and high gloss finish; Gold Classic has fine checkering and decorative carving with oil finish. Delivery scheduled for 1986. Introduced 1984.
Price: Superposed Classic **$2,500.00**
Price: Superposed Gold Classic **$8,800.00**

Browning Presentation Superposed Combinations

Standard and Lightning models are available with these factory fitted extra barrels: 12 and 20 ga., same gauge bbls.; 12 ga., 20 ga. bbls.; 20 ga., extra sets 28 and/or 410 gauge; 28 ga., extra 410 bbls. Extra barrels may be had in Lightning weights with Standard models and vice versa. Prices range from **$6,275.00** (12, 20 ga., one set extra bbls. same gauge) for the Presentation I Standard to about **$18,800.00** for the Presentation 4 grade in a 4-barrel matched set (12, 20, 28 and 410 gauges).

BROWNING SUPERPOSED SUPERLIGHT Presentation Series

Gauge: 12 & 20, 2¾″ chamber.
Action: Boxlock, top lever, single selective trigger. Bbl. selector combined with manual tang safety.
Barrel: 26½″ (Mod. & Full, or Imp. Cyl. & Mod.)
Weight: 6⅜ lbs., average
Stock: Straight grip (14¼″x1⅝″x2½″) hand checkered (fore-end and grip) select walnut.
Features: The Presentation Series is available in four grades and covers the Superposed line. Basically this gives the buyer a wide choice of engraving styles and designs and mechanical options which would place the gun in a "custom" bracket. Options are too numerous to list here and the reader is urged to obtain a copy of the latest Browning catalog for the complete listing. Series introduced 1977. Imported from Belgium by Browning.
Price: From **$4,560.00**

Browning Presentation Superposed Lightning Skeet

Same as Standard Superposed except: Special Skeet stock, fore-end; center and front ivory bead sights. Wgt. 6½-7¾ lbs.
Price: All gauges, from **$4,570.00**

Browning Presentation Superposed Lightning Trap 12

Same as Browning Lightning Superposed except: semi-beavertail fore-end and ivory sights; stock, 14⅜″x1⁷⁄₁₆″x1⅝″. 7¾ lbs. 30″ (Full & Full, Full & Imp. Mod. or Full & Mod.)
Price: From **$4,570.00**

Superposed Presentation Broadway Trap 12

Same as Browning Lightning Superposed except: ⅝″ wide vent. rib; stock, 14⅜″x1⁷⁄₁₆″x1⅝″. 30″ or 32″ (Imp. Mod., Full; Mod., Full; Full, Full). 8 lbs. with 32″ bbls.
Price: From **$4,680.00**

Browning Presentation Superposed All-Gauge Skeet Set

Consists of four matched sets of barrels in 12, 20, 28 and 410 ga. Available in either 26½″ or 28″ length. Each bbl. set has a ¼″ wide vent. rib with two ivory sight beads. Grade I receiver is hand engraved and stock and fore-end are checkered. Weight 7 lbs., 10 oz. (26½″ bbls.), 7 lbs., 12 oz. (28″ bbls.). **Contact Browning for prices.**

Caprinus Sweden

CAPRINUS SWEDEN OVER-UNDER SHOTGUN

Gauge: 12 only, 2¾″ chambers
Barrel: 28″, 30″ (interchangeable choke tubes—Cyl., Skeet, Imp. Cyl., Mod., Imp. Mod. and Full)
Weight: 6.8 lbs. (Game model).
Stock: 14″x1¾″x2⅛″ (Game model). High-grade walnut with rubber pad or checkered butt. Monte Carlo optional. Tru-oil or linseed oil finish.
Features: Made completely of stainless steel. Single selective trigger; barrel selector in front of the trigger; gas pressure activated auto. ejectors; firing pins set by top lever action; double safety system. Six standard choke tubes,

plus optional tubes to change point of impact. Imported from Sweden by Caprinus U.S.A. Introduced 1982.
Price: Skeet Special, from................................... **$5,500.00**
Price: Skeet Game, from..................................... **$5,800.00**
Price: Game, from **$5,800.00**
Price: Trap, from **$5,840.00**

Clayco Model 6

CLAYCO MODEL 6 OVER-UNDER SHOTGUN

Gauge: 12, 2¾″ chambers.
Barrel: 26″ (Imp. Cyl. & Mod.), 28″ (Mod. & Full).

Weight: 7 lbs. 15 oz. (26″ bbls.). **Length:** 43″ over-all (26″ bbls.).
Stock: 14¼″ x 1⅝″ x 2½″. Walnut finished hardwood. Checkered pistol grip and fore-end.
Features: Mechanical single trigger, automatic safety; ventilated rubber recoil pad. Scroll-engraved blued receiver. Ventilated top rib. Introduced 1983. Imported from China by Clayco Sports Ltd.
Price: **$295.00**

SHOTGUNS—OVER-UNDERS

Daly Diamond Grade

Charles Daly Diamond Trap Over-Under
Similar to the Diamond Grade except has competition vent. top and middle ribs, target trigger; oil-finished Monte Carlo stock. Available in 12 gauge, 30" (Full & Imp. Mod.).
Price: **$1,030.00**

CHARLES DALY DIAMOND GRADE OVER-UNDER
Gauge: 12 and 20.
Barrel: 27" (Full, Mod., Imp. Cyl. choke tubes); three tubes included.
Weight: 7 lbs.
Stock: Select extra-fancy European walnut, oil finish.
Features: Boxlock action with single selective competition trigger; silvered and engraved receiver; selective automatic ejectors; 22 lpi checkering on grip and fore-end. Imported from Italy by Outdoor Sports Headquarters. Introduced 1984.
Price: **$895.00**

Daly Diamond Trap

Charles Daly Presentation Grade Over-Under
Similar to the Diamond Grade except has dummy sideplates, better wood, finish, and extensive game scene engraving on the silvered receiver and sideplates.
Price: **$1,165.00**

Charles Daly Diamond Skeet Over-Under
Similar to the standard Diamond Grade except has oil-finished Skeet stock, competition vent. rib, target trigger. Available in 12 gauge only, 26" (Skeet & Skeet).
Price: **$1,030.00**

Charles Daly Superior II Over-Under
Similar to the Field II model except better wood, silvered receiver, more and better engraving. Same barrel lengths and chokes.
Price: **$674.00**

Daly Field III

CHARLES DALY FIELD III OVER-UNDER
Gauge: 12 or 20.
Barrel: 26" (Imp. Cyl. & Mod.), 28", 30" (Full & Mod.); vent. rib.
Weight: About 6¾ lbs.
Stock: Select European walnut, checkered pistol grip and fore-end.
Features: Single selective trigger; extractors only; blued and engraved frame; chrome lined bores. Imported from Italy by Outdoor Sports Headquarters. Introduced 1984.
Price: **$569.95**

ARMI FAMARS FIELD OVER-UNDER
Gauge: 12 (2¾"), 20 (3").
Barrel: 26", 28", 30" (Mod. & Full).
Weight: 6½ to 6¾ lbs.
Stock: 14½" x 1½" x 2½". European walnut.
Sights: Gold bead front.
Features: Boxlock action with single selective trigger; automatic selective trigger. Color case-hardened receiver with engraving. Imported from Italy by Mandall Shooting Supplies.
Price: **$750.00**

FRANCHI DIAMOND GRADE OVER-UNDER
Gauge: 12 ga. only, 2¾" chambers.
Barrel: 28" (Mod. & Full).
Weight: 6 lbs. 13 oz.
Stock: French walnut with cut checkered pistol grip and fore-end.
Features: Top tang safety, automatic ejectors, single selective trigger. Chrome plated bores. Decorative scroll on silvered receiver. Introduced 1982. Imported from Italy by F.I.E. Corp.
Price: Diamond Grade **$850.00**

EXEL SERIES 300 OVER-UNDER SHOTGUNS
Gauge: 12, 2¾" or 3" chambers.
Barrel: 28" (Full & Mod.), 29" (Full & Mod. or Full & Imp. Mod.).
Weight: 6½ to 8 lbs.
Stock: 14⅜" x 1⅜" x 2½" (Field), 14⅜" x 1½" x 1⅝" (Monte Carlo). European walnut with checkered grip and fore-end.
Features: Boxlock action with silvered and engraved finish; ventilated rib; full pistol grip stock; automatic selective ejectors. Made in Spain by Laurona; imported by Exel Arms of America. Introduced 1984.
Price: Model 301, 302 .... **$566.50**
Price: Model 303, 304 .... **$628.30**
Price: Model 305, 306 .... **$695.00**
Price: Model 307, 308 .... **$674.65**
Price: Model 309, 310 .... **$766.66**

Franchi Alcione SL Super Deluxe
Similar to the Falconet Super except has best quality hand engraved, silvered receiver, 24K gold plated trigger, elephant ivory bead front sight. Comes with luggage-type fitted case. Has 14K gold inlay on receiver. Same barrel and chokes as on Falconet Super. Introduced 1982.
Price: Alcione Super Deluxe................................. **$1,595.00**

Franchi Falconet Super

Franchi Falconet Super
Similar to the Diamond Grade except has a lightweight alloy receiver, single selective mechanical trigger with the barrel selector button on the trigger, and a rubber butt pad. Higher quality hand engraved receiver. Available in 12 ga. only, 27" (Imp. Cyl. & Mod.) or 28" (Mod. & Full) barrels. Translucent front sight bead. Introduced 1982.
Price: Falconet Super **$1,015.00**

CAUTION: PRICES CHANGE. CHECK AT GUNSHOP.

IGA Over-Under

IGA OVER-UNDER SHOTGUN
Gauge: 12, 20, 28 (2¾"), 410 (3").
Barrel: 26" (Full & Full, 410 only, Imp. Cyl. & Mod.), 28" (Mod. & Full).
Weight: 6¾ to 7 lbs.
Stock: 14½" x 1½" x 2½". Oil finished hardwood with checkered pistol grip and fore-end.
Features: Manual safety, double triggers, extractors only, ventilated top rib. Introduced 1983. Imported from Brazil by Stoeger Industries.
Price: Double triggers $417.00
Price: Single trigger $499.95

K.F.C. "FG" OVER-UNDER SHOTGUN
Gauge: 12 only (2¾").
Barrel: 26", 28" (Imp. Cyl. & Imp. Mod.); vent. rib.
Weight: About 6.8 lbs.
Stock: 14"x1½"x2⅜". High grade French walnut.
Sights: Sterling silver front bead.
Features: Selective single trigger, selective auto ejectors, non-automatic safety; chrome lined bores, chrome trigger. Introduced 1981. Imported from Japan by La Paloma Marketing.
Price: $748.00

HEYM MODEL 55/77 O/U SHOTGUN
Gauge: 12, 16, 20 ga. (2¾" or 3").
Barrel: 28" (Full & Mod.) standard; other lengths and chokes to customer specs.
Weight: 6¾-7½ lbs.
Stock: European walnut, hand-checkered p.g. and fore-end.
Features: Boxlock or full sidelock action; Kersten double cross bolt, double under lugs; cocking indicators. Arabesque or hunting engraving. Options include interchangeable barrels, front trigger that functions as a single non-selective trigger, deluxe engraving and stock carving. Imported from West Germany by Paul Jaeger, Inc.
Price: Model 55F or 77F boxlock $3,070.00
Price: Model 55FSS or 77FSS sidelock $5,350.00
Price: Interchangeable o/u rifle barrels $2,570.00
Price: Interchangeable rifle-shotgun barrels $1,715.00

K.F.C. OT-Skeet Shotguns
Skeet versions of FG model. Model E-1 has 26" or 28" (Skeet & Skeet) barrels with 13mm vent. rib, middle and front bead sights, gold colored wide trigger. Stock dimensions are 14"x1½"x2½". Plastic buttplate, push-button fore-end release. Weight is about 7½ lbs.
Price: E-1 .... $1,070.00
Price: E-2 .... $1,660.00

K.F.C. "FG" Standard

K.F.C. OT-Trap-E1 Shotgun
Trap version of FG over-under. Has 30" (Imp. Mod. & Full) barrels, 13mm vent. rib, bone white middle and front beads, scroll-engraved, blued receiver, wide gold-colored trigger. Stock dimensions are 14"x1¼"x1¼"x2"; high grade French walnut; rubber recoil pad; oil finish. Weight is about 7.9 lbs. Introduced 1981. From La Paloma Marketing.
Price: $1,070.00

K.F.C. OT-Trap-E2 Shotgun
Same as E-1 model except chromed receiver has high grade scroll engraving, super deluxe French walnut stock and fore-end.
Price: $1,660.00

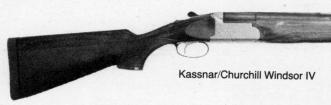

Kassnar/Churchill Windsor IV

KASSNAR/CHURCHILL WINDSOR OVER-UNDER SHOTGUNS
Gauge: 12, 20, 410, 3" chambers.
Barrel: 26" (Skeet & Skeet, Imp. Cyl. & Mod.), 28" (Mod. & Full), 30" (Mod. & Full, Full & Full), 12 ga.; 26" (Skeet & Skeet, Imp. Cyl. & Mod.), 28" (Mod. & Full) 20 ga.; 24", 26" (Full & Full), 410 ga.; or 27", 30" ICT choke tubes.
Stock: European walnut, checkered pistol grip.
Features: Boxlock action with silvered, engraved finish; single selective trigger; automatic ejectors on Windsor IV, extractors only on Windsor III. Imported from Italy by Kassnar. Introduced 1984.
Price: Windsor III, fixed chokes $629.00
Price: 12 or 20 ga. ICT choke tubes $689.00
Price: Windsor IV, fixed chokes $705.00
Price: 12 or 20 ga., ICT choke tubes $765.00

Kassnar/Churchill Regent Over-Under Shotguns
Similar to the Windsor Grade except better wood with oil finish, better engraving; available only in 12 or 20 gauge (2¾" chambers), 27" barrels, with ICT interchangeable choke tubes (Imp. Cyl., Mod., Full). Regent V has standard boxlock action, Regent VII has dummy sideplates. Introduced 1984.
Price: Regent V, 12 or 20 ga. $945.00
Price: Regent VII, 12 or 20 ga. $1,049.00

Kassnar/Churchill Regent Skeet

Kassnar/Churchill Regent Trap & Skeet
Similar to the Regent V except Trap has ventilated side rib, Monte Carlo stock, ventilated recoil pad. Oil finished wood, fine checkering, chrome bores. Weight is 8 lbs. Regent Skeet available in 12 or 20 ga., 26" (Skeet & Skeet); oil finished stock measures 14½", 1½" x 2⅜". Both guns have silvered and engraved receivers. Introduced 1984.
Price: Regent Trap (30" Imp. Mod. & Full) $975.00
Price: Regent Skeet, 12 or 20 ga. $975.00

KASSNAR/OMEGA OVER-UNDER SHOTGUN
Gauge: 410, 3".
Barrel: 24" (Full & Full).
Weight: 5½ lbs.
Stock: Checkered European walnut.
Features: Single trigger; automatic safety; ventilated rib. Imported from Italy by Kassnar. Introduced 1984.
Price: **$299.00**

LEBEAU-COURALLY BOSS MODEL O-U SHOTGUN
Gauge: 12 or 20 (std.), 28 (optional).
Barrel: 26" to 30"; choked to customer specs.
Weight: 5 lbs. 4 oz. (28-ga.) to 8 lbs. 4 oz. (12-ga.).
Stock: Dimensions to customer specs. Finest quality French walnut with very fine checkering with lace borders; straight or pistol grip stock, classic or splinter fore-end.
Features: Boss pattern sidelock ejector with low profile action; classic Boss sculpturing; double or single trigger; barrels normally furnished with ventilated rib. Imported from Belgium by Wm. Larkin Moore.
Price: From **$27,500.00**

Lanber Model 844

LANBER MODEL 844 OVER-UNDER
Gauge: 12, 2¾" or 3".
Barrel: 28" (Imp. Cyl. & Imp. Mod.), 30" (Mod. & Full).
Weight: About 7 lbs. **Length:** 44⅜" (28" bbl.).
Stock: 14¼" x 1⅝" x 2½". European walnut; checkered grip and fore-end.
Features: Single non-selective or selective trigger, double triggers on magnum model. Available with or without ejectors. Imported from Spain by Lanber Arms of America, and Exel Arms of America. Introduced 1981.
Price: Field, with selective trigger, extractors **$475.00**
Price: As above, 3" Mag., 844 MST **$499.00**

Lanber Model 2004 Over-Under
Same basic specifications as Model 844 except fitted with LanberChoke interchangeable choke tube system. Available in trap, Skeet, pigeon and field models; ejectors only; single selective trigger; no middle rib on target guns (2008, 2009). Imported from Spain by Lanber Arms of America and Exel Arms of America.
Price: Model 2004 . . . . **$698.00**
Price: Model 2008 . . . . **$859.00**
Price: Model 2009 (30" bbl., illus.) **$859.00**

Ljutic Bi-Gun

LJUTIC BI-GUN O/U SHOTGUN
Gauge: 12 ga only.
Barrel: 28" to 34"; choked to customer specs.
Weight: To customers specs.
Stock: To customer specs. Oil finish, hand checkered.
Features: Custom-made gun. Hollow-milled rib, choice of pull or release trigger, pushbutton opener in front of trigger guard. From Ljutic Industries.
Price: **$7,995.00**
Price: Bi-Gun Combo (interchangeable single barrel, two trigger guards, one for single trigger, one for doubles) **$12,995.00**
Price: Extra barrels with screw-in chokes or O/U barrel sets **$3,500.00**

Ljutic Four Barrel Skeet Set
Similar to Bi-Gun except comes with matched set of four 28" barrels in 12, 20, 28 and 410. Ljutic Paternator chokes and barrel are integral. Stock is to customer specs, of American or French walnut with fancy checkering.
Price: Four barrel set **$16,000.00**

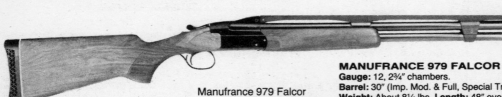

Manufrance 979 Falcor

MANUFRANCE 979 FALCOR COMPETITION TRAP
Gauge: 12, 2¾" chambers.
Barrel: 30" (Imp. Mod. & Full, Special Trap), chrome lined bores.
Weight: About 8¼ lbs. **Length:** 48" over-all.
Stock: Choice French walnut, hand checkered, hand-rubbed oil finish; smooth beavertail fore-end.
Sights: Ivory front bead in metal sleeve, middle ivory bead.
Features: Boxlock action with inertia-type trigger, top tang safety/barrel selector, special heavy-duty automatic ejectors, coil springs. Light alloy, ⁹⁄₁₆" wide, high-post rib. Each gun adjusted for point of impact. Imported from France by Armsource, Inc. Introduced 1984.
Price: **$1,860.00**

Manufrance 1985 Trap

Manufrance 1985 Falcor Trap Over-Under
Similar to the Competition Trap model except has standard vent. rib, middle rib, checkered grip and fore-end, luminous yellow front bead in metal sleeve, middle metal bead. Introduced 1984.
Price: **$1,000.00**
Price: Model 1987 Skeet, as above but with 27½" (Skeet & Skeet) barrels, smooth Skeet butt pad **$970.00**

CAUTION: PRICES CHANGE. CHECK AT GUNSHOP.

Manufrance 1977 Falcor

MANUFRANCE 1977 FALCOR PHEASANT GUN
Gauge: 12, 2¾" chambers.
Barrel: 27½" (Mod. & Full), chrome-lined bores.

Weight: About 7¼ lbs. **Length:** 44¼" over-all.
Stock: Choice French walnut, hand checkered grip and fore-end.
Sights: Metal bead front.
Features: Boxlock action with single trigger, top tang safety/barrel selector, automatic ejectors. Silver-gray finish and scroll engraving on receiver, top lever, trigger guard. Imported from France by Armsource, Inc. Introduced 1984.
Price: **$940.00**

Marocchi America

MAROCCHI AMERICA TARGET SHOTGUN
Gauge: 12 or 20, 2¾" chambers.
Barrel: 26" to 29" (Skeet), 27" to 32" (trap), 32" (trap mono, choice of top single or high rib under), 30" (over-under with extra 32" single).

Weight: 7¼ to 8 lbs.
Stock: Hand checkered select walnut with left or right-hand palm swell; choice of beavertail or Schnabel fore-end.
Features: Designed specifically for American target sports. Frame has medium engraving coverage with choice of three finishes. No extra charge for special stock dimensions or stock finish. Comes with fitted hard shell case. Custom engraving and inlays available. Introduced 1983. Imported from Italy by Marocchi U.S.A.
Price: From **$2,000.00**

Marocchi Contrast Cup

MAROCCINI O/U SHOTGUN
Gauge: 12 or 20 ga., 3".
Barrel: 28" (Mod. & Full); vent. top and middle ribs.
Weight: 7¾ lbs.
Stock: Walnut, hand checkered.
Features: Auto. safety; extractors; double triggers; engraved antique silver receiver. Imported from Italy by F.I.E.
Price: **$369.95**

MAROCCHI CONTRAST TARGET SHOTGUN
Gauge: 12 or 20 ga., 2¾" chambers.
Barrel: 26" to 29" (Skeet), 27" to 32" trap.
Weight: 7¼ to 8 lbs.
Stock: Select walnut with hand rubbed wax finish; hand checkered p.g. and fore-end; beavertail or Schnabel fore-end; grip has right or left palm swell.
Features: Lightly engraved frame on standard grade, or can be ordered with custom engraving and inlays in choice of three finishes. Optional different buttstock available. Gun comes with fitted hard shell case. Introduced 1983. Imported from Italy by Marocchi U.S.A.
Price: From **$2,000.00**

Navy Bird Hunter

NAVY ARMS MODEL 84 BIRD HUNTER O-U
Gauge: 12, 20; 3" chambers.
Barrel: 28" (Imp. Cyl. & Mod., Mod. & Full).
Weight: About 7½ lbs.
Stock: European walnut, checkered grip and fore-end.
Sights: Metal bead front.
Features: Boxlock action with double triggers; extractors only; silvered, engraved receiver; vented top and middle ribs. Imported from Italy by Navy Arms. Introduced 1984.
Price: About **$295.00**

ROTTWEIL OLYMPIA '72 SKEET SHOTGUN
Gauge: 12 ga. only.
Action: Boxlock.
Barrel: 27" (special Skeet choke), vent. rib. Chromed lined bores, flared chokes.
Weight: 7¼ lbs. **Length:** 44½" over-all.
Stock: French walnut, hand checkered, modified beavertail fore-end. Oil finish.
Sights: Metal bead front.
Features: Inertia-type trigger, interchangeable for any system. Frame and lock milled from steel block. Retracting firing pins are spring mounted. All coil springs. Selective single trigger. Action engraved. Extra barrels are available. Introduced 1976. Imported from West Germany by Dynamit Nobel.
Price: **$2,295.00**
Price: Trap model (Montreal) is similar to above except has 30" (Imp. Mod. & Full) bbl., weighs 8 lbs., 48½" over-all. **$2,295.00**

Rottweil Olympia '72

ROTTWEIL 72 AMERICAN SKEET
Gauge: 12, 2¾".
Barrel: 26¾" (Skeet & Skeet).
Weight: About 7½ lbs.
Stock: 14½" x 1⅜" x 1⅜" x ¼". Select French walnut with satin oil finish; hand checkered grip and fore-end; double ventilated recoil pad.
Sights: Plastic front in metal sleeve, center bead.
Features: Interchangeable trigger groups with coil springs; interchangeable buttstocks; special .433" ventilated rib; matte finish silvered receiver with light engraving. Introduced 1978. Imported from West Germany by Dynamit Nobel.
Price: **$2,295.00**

Rottweil American Trap

ROTTWEIL AMERICAN TRAP COMBO

Gauge: 12 ga. only.
Action: Boxlock
Barrel: Separated o/u, 32″ (Imp. Mod. & Full); single is 34″ (Full), both with high vent. rib.
Weight: 8½ lbs. (o/u and single)
Stock: Monte Carlo style, walnut, hand checkered and rubbed. Unfinished stocks available. Double vent. recoil pad. Choice of two dimensions.
Sights: Plastic front in metal sleeve, center bead.
Features: Interchangeable inertia-type trigger groups. Trigger groups available: single selective; double triggers;, release/pull; release/release selective. Receiver milled from block steel. Chokes are hand honed, test fired and reworked for flawless patterns. All coil springs, engraved action. Introduced 1977. Imported from West Germany by Dynamit Nobel.
Price: $2,850.00
Price: American Trap O/U (as above except only with o/u bbls.) . . . $2,295.00

ROTTWEIL AAT TRAP GUN

Gauge: 12, 2¾″.
Barrel: 32″ (Imp. Mod. & Full).
Weight: About 8 lbs.
Stock: 14½″x1⅜″x1⅜″x1⅞″. Monte Carlo style of selected French walnut with oil finish. Checkered fore-end and p.g.
Features: Has infinitely variable point of impact via special muzzle collar. Extra single lower barrels available—32″ (Imp. Mod.) or 34″ (Full). Special trigger groups—release/release or release/pull—also available. Introduced 1979. From Dynamit Nobel.
Price: With single lower barrel $2,295.00
Price: Combo (single and o/u barrels) $2,295.00
Price: Interchangeable trap trigger group $345.00

Rottweil Field Supreme

ROTTWEIL FIELD SUPREME O/U SHOTGUN

Gauge: 12 only.
Action: Boxlock.
Barrel: 28″ (Mod. & Full, Imp. Cyl. & Imp. Mod.), vent. rib.
Weight: 7¼ lbs. **Length:** 47″ over-all.
Stock: Select French walnut, hand checkered and rubbed. Checkered p.g. and fore-end, plastic buttplate. Unfinished stocks available.
Sights: Metal bead front.
Features: Removable single trigger assembly with button selector (same trigger options as on American Trap Combo); retracting spring mounted firing pins; engraved action. Extra barrels available. Imported from West Germany by Dynamit Nobel.
Price: $2,295.00
Price: Live Pigeon (28″ Mod. & Full) $2,295.00

Ruger Red Label

RUGER "RED LABEL" O/U SHOTGUN

Gauge: 20, 3″ chambers, 12, 2¾″ and 3″ chambers.
Barrel: 26″, (Skeet & Skeet, Imp. Cyl. & Mod., Full & Mod.) 12 and 20 ga.; 28″ (20 ga. only, Skeet & Skeet, Imp. Cyl. & Mod., Full & Mod.).
Weight: About 7 lbs. **Length:** 43″ (26″ barrels).
Stock: 14″x1½″x2½″. Straight grain American walnut. Checkered p.g. and fore-end, rubber recoil pad.
Features: Automatic safety/barrel selector, stainless steel trigger. Patented barrel side spacers may be removed if desired. 20 ga. introduced 1977; 12 ga. introduced 1982.
Price: About $798.00

Sile Sky Stalker

SILE SKY STALKER FOLDING SHOTGUN

Gauge: 410, 3″ chambers.
Barrel: 26″ (Full & Full or Mod. & Full), with vent. rib.
Weight: About 6 lbs.
Stock: Walnut with cut checkering and Schnabel fore-end.
Features: Gun folds in half for storage or carrying. Chrome lined bores; matte finished hard chrome finish on receiver. Introduced 1984. Imported by Sile.
Price: $199.95

TECHNI-MEC MODEL SPL 640 FOLDING O-U

Gauge: 12, 16, 20, 28, (2¾″) 410 (3″).
Barrel: 26″ (Mod. & Full).
Weight: 5½ lbs.
Stock: European walnut.
Features: Gun folds in half for storage, transportation. Chrome lined barrels; ventilated rib; photo-engraved silvered receiver. Imported from Italy by L. Joseph Rahn. Introduced 1984.
Price: Double triggers $240.00
Price: Single trigger $256.00

TECHNI-MEC MODEL SR 692 EM OVER-UNDER

Gauge: 12, 16, 20, 2¾″ or 3″.
Barrel: 26″, 28″, 30″ (Mod., Full, Imp. Cyl., Cyl.).
Weight: 6½ lbs.
Stock: 14½″ x 1½″ x 2½″. European walnut with checkered grip and fore-end.
Features: Boxlock action with dummy sideplates, fine game scene engraving; single selective trigger; automatic ejectors available. Imported from Italy by L. Joseph Rahn. Introduced 1984.
Price: $550.00

CAUTION: PRICES CHANGE. CHECK AT GUNSHOP.

VALMET MODEL 412K OVER-UNDER

Gauge: 12 or 20 ga. (2¾" or 3").
Barrel: 26" (Imp. Cyl. & Mod.), 28" (Mod. & Full), 30" (Mod. & Full); vent. rib.
Weight: About 7½ lbs.
Stock: American walnut. Standard dimensions-13⁹⁄₁₀"x1½"x2⅖". Checkered p.g. and fore-end.
Features: Model 412K is extractor (basic) model. Free interchangeability of barrels, stocks and fore-ends into KE (auto. ejector) model, double rifle model, combination gun, etc. Barrel selector in trigger; auto. top tang safety; barrel cocking indicators. Double triggers optional. Introduced 1980. Imported from Finland by Valmet.
Price: Model 412K (extractors), from **$749.00**
Price: Extra barrels from.......... **$409.00**
Price: Engraved model with full scroll.......... **$1,499.00**
Price: Engraved model with game scenes.......... **$2,249.00**

Valmet 412KE Target Series

Trap and Skeet versions of 412 gun. Auto. ejectors only; 12 ga., 2¾", 3" chambers, 30" barrels (Imp. & Full.—Trap, Skeet & Skeet—Skeet). 20 ga., 3" chambers. Trap stock measures 14³⁄₁₀"x1⅖"x1⅗"x2½"; Skeet stock measures 13⁹⁄₁₀"x1⅘"x2⅘"x1⅘". Trap weight 7⅝ lbs.: Skeet weight 7½ lbs. Non-automatic safety. Introduced 1980. Imported from Finland by Valmet.
Price: Trap **$749.00**
Price: Skeet **$749.00**

Valmet 412S American Series

Similar to the 412K except better wood, finer checkering, palm swell on pistol grip, luminous sights, lighter weight, new fore-end latch spring mechanism and improved firing pin mechandism. Introduced 1984.
Price: 412S with ejectors field, trap or Skeet **$799.00**

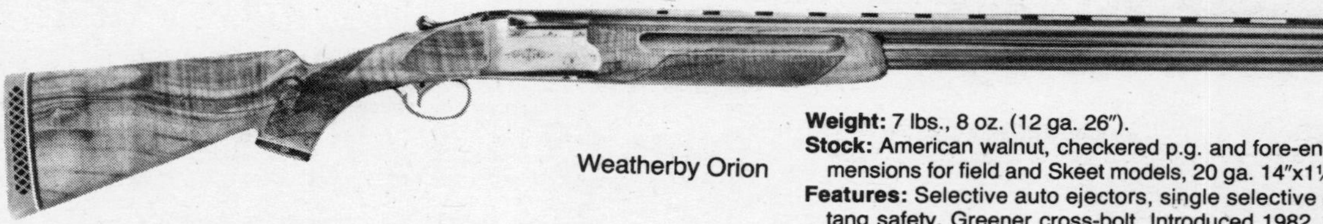

Weatherby Orion

WEATHERBY ORION O/U SHOTGUN

Gauge: 12 or 20 ga. (3" chambers; 2¾" on Trap gun).
Action: Boxlock (simulated side-lock).
Barrel: 12 ga. 30" (Full & Mod.), 28" (Full & Mod., Mod. & Imp. Cyl.), 26" (Mod. & Imp. Cyl., Skeet & Skeet); 20 ga. 28" (Full & Mod., Mod. & Imp. Cyl.), 26" (Mod. & Imp. Cyl., Skeet & Skeet).
Weight: 7 lbs., 8 oz. (12 ga. 26").
Stock: American walnut, checkered p.g. and fore-end. Rubber recoil pad. Dimensions for field and Skeet models, 20 ga. 14"x1½"x2½".
Features: Selective auto ejectors, single selective mechanical trigger. Top tang safety, Greener cross-bolt. Introduced 1982. Imported from Japan by Weatherby.
Price: 12 ga. Field, fixed choke **$769.95**
Price: Skeet, fixed choke **$809.00**
Price: 12 ga. Trap, fixed choke **$819.00**
Price: IMC Multi-Choke Field, 12 ga. **$799.00**
Price: IMC Multi-Choke Trap **$849.00**
Price: Extra IMC choke tubes **$12.50**

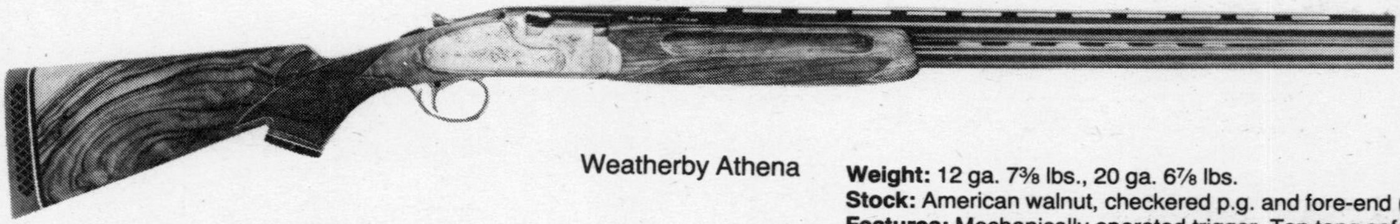

Weatherby Athena

WEATHERBY ATHENA O/U SHOTGUN

Gauge: 12 or 20 ga. (3" chambers; 2¾" on Trap gun).
Action: Boxlock (simulated side-lock) top lever break-open. Selective auto ejectors, single selective trigger (selector inside trigger guard).
Barrel: Fixed choke, 12 or 20 ga. — 26" (Mod. & Imp. Cyl., Skeet & Skeet), 28" (Mod. & Imp. Cyl., Full & Mod.), 30" (Full & Mod., Full & Imp. Mod.), 32" Trap (Full & Imp. Mod.). IMC Multi-Choke, 12 ga. only — 26" (Mod., Imp. Cyl., Skeet), 28" (Full, Mod., Imp. Cyl.), 30" (Full, Mod., Imp. Mod.).
Weight: 12 ga. 7⅜ lbs., 20 ga. 6⅞ lbs.
Stock: American walnut, checkered p.g. and fore-end (14¼"x1½"x2½").
Features: Mechanically operated trigger. Top tang safety, Greener cross-bolt, fully engraved receiver, recoil pad installed. IMC models furnished with three interchangeable flush-fitting choke tubes. Imported from Japan by Weatherby. Introduced 1982.
Price: 12 or 20 ga. Field, fixed choke **$1,149.95**
Price: Skeet.......... **$1,159,00**
Price: 12 ga. Trap Model.......... **$1,169.00**
Price: IMC Multi-Choke Field, 12 ga. **$1,179.00**
Price: IMC Multi-Choke Trap **$1,199.00**
Price: Extra IMC Choke tubes.......... **$12.50**

Winchester 501 Grand European

WINCHESTER MODEL 501 GRAND EUROPEAN O-U

Gauge: 12 ga. (Trap), 12 and 20 ga. (Skeet). 2¾" chambers.
Barrel: 27" (Skeet & Skeet), 30" (Imp. Mod. & Full), 32" (Imp. Mod. & Full).
Weight: 7½ lbs. (Skeet), 8½ lbs. (Trap) **Length:** 47⅛" over-all (30" barrel).
Stock: 14⅛"x1½"x2½" (Skeet). Full fancy walnut, hand-rubbed oil finish.
Features: Silvered, engraved receiver; engine-turned breech interior. Slide-button selector/safety, selective auto. ejectors. Chrome bores, tapered vent. rib. Trap gun has Monte Carlo or regular stock, recoil pad; Skeet gun has rosewood buttplate. Introduced 1981. Imported from Japan by Winchester Group, Olin Corp.
Price: Trap or Skeet.......... **$2,060.00**

Winchester 101 Diamond Grade Target Guns

Similar to the Model 101 except designed for trap and Skeet competition, with tapered and elevated rib, anatomically contoured trigger and internationally-dimensioned stock. Receiver has deep-etched diamond-pattern engraving. Skeet guns available in 12, 20, 28 and 410 with ventilated muzzles to reduce recoil. Trap guns in 12 ga. only; over-under, combination and single-barrel configurations in a variety of barrel lengths with Winchoke system. Straight or Monte Carlo stocks available. Introduced 1982. Imported from Japan by Winchester Group, Olin Corp.
Price: Trap, o/u, standard and Monte Carlo, 30", 32".......... **$1,730.00**
Price: Trap, single barrel, 32" or 34".......... **$1,840.00**
Price: Trap, o/u-single bbl. combo sets **$2,800.00**
Price: Skeet, 12 and 20.......... **$1,730.00**
Price: Skeet, 28 and 410.......... **$1,730.00**

Winchester Model 101 Waterfowl Winchoke

Same as Model 101 Field Grade except in 12 ga. only, 3" chambers, 32" barrels. Comes with four Winchoke tubes: Mod., Imp. Mod., Full, Extra-Full. Blued receiver with hand etching and engraving. Introduced 1981. Imported from Japan by Winchester Group, Olin Corp.
Price: **$1,355.00**

Winchester 101 Lightweight

WINCHESTER 101 WINCHOKE O/U FIELD GUN
Gauge: 12, or 20, 3″ chambers.
Action: Top lever, break open. Manual safety combined with bbl. selector at top of receiver tang.
Barrel: 27″, Winchoke interchangeable choke tubes.
Weight: 12 ga. 7 lbs. Others 6½ lbs. **Length:** 44¾″ over-all.
Stock: 14″x1½″x2½″. Checkered walnut p.g. and fore-end; fluted comb.
Features: Single selective trigger, auto ejectors. Hand engraved satin gray receiver. Comes with hard gun case. Imported from Japan by Winchester Group, Olin Corp.
Price: **$1,355.00**

Winchester 101 Pigeon Grade

Winchester Model 101 Pigeon Grade
Similar to the Model 101 Field except comes in three styles: Lightweight (12 or 28 ga., Mod. & Full, Mod. & Imp. Cyl., 28″), Lightweight-Winchoke (12 or 20 ga., six choke tubes for 12 ga., four for 20 ga., 27″), Featherweight (12 or 20 ga., Imp. Cyl. & Mod., 25½″), all with 3″ chambers. Vent. rib barrel with middle bead, fancy American walnut. Featherweight has English-style stock. Hard case included. Introduced 1983. Imported from Japan by Winchester Group, Olin Corp.
Price: Lightweight and Featherweight. **$1,575.00**
Price: Lightweight-Winchoke **$1,665.00**

Zanoletti 2000 Field

PIETRO ZANOLETTI MODEL 2000 FIELD O-U
Gauge: 12 only.
Barrel: 28″ (Mod. & Full).
Weight: 7 lbs.
Stock: European walnut, checkered grip and fore-end.
Sights: Gold bead front.
Features: Boxlock action with auto ejectors, double triggers; engraved receiver. Imported from Italy by Mandall Shooting Supplies. Introduced 1984.
Price: **$695.00**

Zoli Angel

A. ZOLI MODEL ANGEL FIELD GRADE O-U
Gauge: 12, 20.
Barrel: 26″, 28″, 30″ (Mod. & Full).
Weight: About 7½ lbs.
Stock: Straight grained walnut with checkered grip and fore-end.
Sights: Gold bead front.
Features: Boxlock action with single selective trigger, auto ejectors; extra-wide vent. top rib. Imported from Italy by Mandall Shooting Supplies.
Price: **$895.00**
Price: Condor model **$895.00**

Zoli Silver Snipe

ZOLI SILVER SNIPE O/U SHOTGUN
Gauge: 12, 20 (3″ chambers).
Action: Purdey-type double boxlock, crossbolt.
Barrel: 26″ (Imp. Cyl. & Mod.), 28″ (Mod. & Full), 30″, 12 only (Mod. & Full); 26″ Skeet (Skeet & Skeet), 30″ Trap (Full & Full).
Weight: 6½ lbs. (12 ga.).
Stock: Hand checkered p.g. and fore-end, European walnut.
Features: Auto. safety (exc. Trap and Skeet), vent rib, single trigger, chrome bores. Imported from Italy by Mandall Shooting Supplies.
Price: Field **$795.00**

A. ZOLI DELFINO S.P. O/U
Gauge: 12 or 20 (3″ chambers).
Barrel: 28″ (Mod. & Full); vent. rib.
Weight: 5½ lbs.
Stock: Walnut. Hand checkered p.g. and fore-end; cheekpiece.
Features: Color case hardened receiver with light engraving; chrome lined barrels; automatic sliding safety; double triggers; ejectors. From Mandall Shooting Supplies.
Price: **$795.00**

Zoli Golden Snipe O/U Shotgun
Same as Silver Snipe except selective auto. ejectors.
Price: Field **$895.00**

AYA MODEL XXV BL, SL DOUBLE
Gauge: 12, 20, 28, 410.
Barrel: 25″, chokes as specified.
Weight: 5 lbs., 2 oz. to 6 lbs., 8 oz.
Stock: 14½″x2¼″x1½″. European walnut. Straight grip stock with classic pistol grip, checkered butt.
Features: Boxlock (Model BL), sidelock (Model SL). Churchill rib, auto ejectors, double triggers (single available), color case-hardened action (coin-finish available). Imported from Spain by Wm. Larkin Moore & Co. and Precision Sports, Inc.
Price: BL, 12 ga., about **$1,995.00**
Price: BL, 20 ga., about **$1,995.00**
Price: SL, 12 ga., about **$3,295.00**
Price: SL, 20 ga., about **$3,295.00**
Price: SL, 28 or 410, about **$3,395.00**

ARMSPORT GOOSEGUN SIDE-BY-SIDE
Gauge: 10 ga. (3½″ chambers).
Barrel: 32″ (Full & Full). Solid matted rib.
Weight: 11 lbs.
Stock: European walnut, checkered p.g. and fore-end.
Features: Double triggers, vent. rubber recoil pad with white spacer. Imported by Armsport.
Price: **$595.00**

AyA Model XXVSL

ARMSPORT WESTERN DOUBLE
Gauge: 12 only (3″ chambers).
Barrel: 20″.
Weight: 6½ lbs.
Stock: European walnut, checkered p.g. and beavertail fore-end.
Sights: Metal front bead on matted solid rib.
Features: Exposed hammers. Imported by Armsport.
Price: **$500.00**

AYA MODEL 117 DOUBLE BARREL SHOTGUN
Gauge: 12 (2¾″), 20 (3″).
Action: Holland & Holland sidelock, Purdey treble bolting.
Barrel: 26″ (Imp. Cyl. & Mod.) 28″ (Mod. & Full).
Stock: 14½″x2⅜″x1½″. Select European walnut, hand checkered p.g. and beavertail fore-end.
Features: Single selective trigger, automatic ejectors, cocking indicators; concave barrel rib; hand-detachable lockplates; hand engraved action. Imported from Spain by Precision Sports, Inc.
Price: **$1,650.00**

AyA Model No. 2

AYA No. 1 Side-by-Side
Similar to the No. 2 except barrel lengths to customer specifications. Barrels are of chrome-nickel steel. Imported from Spain by Wm. Larkin Moore & Co. and Precision Sports, Inc.
Price: 12, 16, 20 ga., from **$4,895.00**
Price: 28 ga., from **$5,495.00**
Price: 410 ga., from **$5,495.00**

AYA No. 2 SIDE-BY-SIDE
Gauge: 12, 16, 20, 28, 410.
Barrel: 26″, 27″, 28″, choked to customer specs.
Weight: 5 lbs. 2 oz. to 7½ lbs.
Stock: 14½″x2¼″x1½″. European walnut. Straight grip stock, checkered butt, classic fore-end. Can be made to custom dimensions.
Features: Sidelock action with auto. ejectors, double triggers standard, single trigger optional. Hand-detachable locks. Color case-hardened action. Imported from Spain by Wm. Larkin Moore & Co. and Precision Sports, Inc.
Price: 12, 16, 20 ga., from **$2,175.00**
Price: 28 ga., from **$2,365.00**
Price: 410 ga., from **$2,365.00**

AYA No. 4 DELUXE SIDE-BY-SIDE
Gauge: 12, 20, 28 & 410.
Barrel: 26″, 27″, 28″ (Imp. Cyl. & Mod. or Mod. & Full).
Weight: 5 lbs. 2 oz. to 6½ lbs.
Stock: 14½″x2¼″x1½″. European walnut. Straight grip with checkered butt, classic fore-end.
Features: Boxlock action, color case-hardened, automatic ejectors, double triggers (single trigger available). Imported from Spain by William Larkin Moore & Co. and Precision Sports, Inc.
Price: 12, 16 ga., about **$2,195.00**
Price: 20 ga., about **$2,195.00**
Price: 28, 410 ga., about **$2,255.00**

AyA No. 4 Deluxe

AYA Model 56 Side-By-Side
Similar to the No. 1 except in 12, 16 or 20 ga. only, third fastener and side-clips; heavier weight in 12-ga.; available with raised, level or vent rib. Does not have hand-detachable locks. Imported from Spain by Wm. Larkin Moore & Co. and Precision Sports, Inc.
Price: About **$5,250.00**

BERNARDELLI SERIES S. UBERTO DOUBLES
Gauge: 12, 16, 20, 28; 2½″, 2¾″, or 3″ chambers.
Barrel: 25⅝″, 26¾″, 28″, 29⅛″ (Mod. & Full).
Weight: 6 to 6½ lbs.
Stock: 14⅛″ x 2⅝″ x 1⁹⁄₁₆″ standard dimensions. Select walnut with hand checkering.
Features: Anson & Deeley boxlock action with Purdey locks, choice of extractors or ejectors. Uberto 1 has color case hardened receiver, Uberto 2 and F.S. silvered and differ in amount and quality of engraving. Custom options available. Imported from Italy by Armes De Chasse and Quality Arms.
Price: S. Uberto 1 . . . . **$860.00**
Price: As above with ejectors **$970.00**
Price: S. Uberto 2 . . . . **$901.00**
Price: As above with ejectors **$1,010.00**
Price: S. Uberto F.S. **$1,054.00**
Price: As above with ejectors **$1,164.00**

> Consult our Directory pages for
> the location of firms mentioned.

Bernardelli Series Roma Shotguns
Similar to the Series S. Uberto models except with dummy sideplates to simulate sidelock action. Same gauges and specifications apply.
Price: Roma 3 . . . . **$944.00**
Price: As above with ejectors **$1,054.00**
Price: Roma 4 . . . . **$1,079.00**
Price: As above with ejectors **$1,188.00**
Price: Roma 6 . . . . **$1,316.00**
Price: As above with ejectors **$1,426.00**

BERNARDELLI LAS PALOMAS SIDE-BY-SIDE

Gauge: 12, 2¾".
Barrel: 28" (Mod. & Full), specially bored for pigeon shooting.
Weight: 7½ lbs.
Stock: 14½" x 1¼" x 1½", cast-off right ⅛" x 9/16". Select walnut.
Features: Reinforced Anson & Deeley action; single trigger with back position and special trigger guard; manual safety (auto. safety optional); beavertail fore-end, Australian pistol grip with shaped heel and palm swell; vent. recoil pad. Many optional features available. Imported from Italy by Armes De Chasse and Quality Arms. Introduced 1984.
Price: **$2,153.00**

Bernardelli System Holland H. Side-by-Side

Similar to the Las Palomas model with true sidelock action. Available in 12 gauge only, reinforced breech, three round Purdey locks, automatic ejectors, folding right trigger. Model VB Liscio has color case hardened receiver and sideplates with light engraving, VB and VB Tipo Lusso are silvered and engraved.
Price: VB Liscio.. **$4,743.00**
Price: VB.. **$5,496.00**
Price: VB Tipo Lusso.. **$6,432.00**

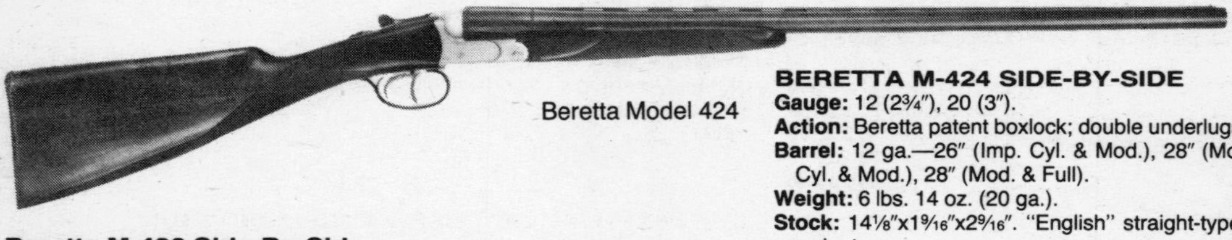

Beretta Model 424

BERETTA M-424 SIDE-BY-SIDE

Gauge: 12 (2¾"), 20 (3").
Action: Beretta patent boxlock; double underlugs and bolts.
Barrel: 12 ga.—26" (Imp. Cyl. & Mod.), 28" (Mod. & Full); 20 ga.—26" (Imp. Cyl. & Mod.), 28" (Mod. & Full).
Weight: 6 lbs. 14 oz. (20 ga.).
Stock: 14⅛"x1 9/16"x2 9/16". "English" straight-type, hand checkered European walnut.
Features: Coil springs throughout action; double triggers (front is hinged); automatic safety; extractors. Concave matted barrel rib. Introduced 1977. Imported by Beretta U.S.A. Corp.
Price: **$900.00**

Beretta M-426 Side-By-Side

Same as M-424 except action body is engraved; pistol grip stock; a silver pigeon is inlaid into top lever; single selective trigger; selective automatic ejectors. Introduced 1977. Imported by Beretta U.S.A. Corp.
Price: **$1,115.00**

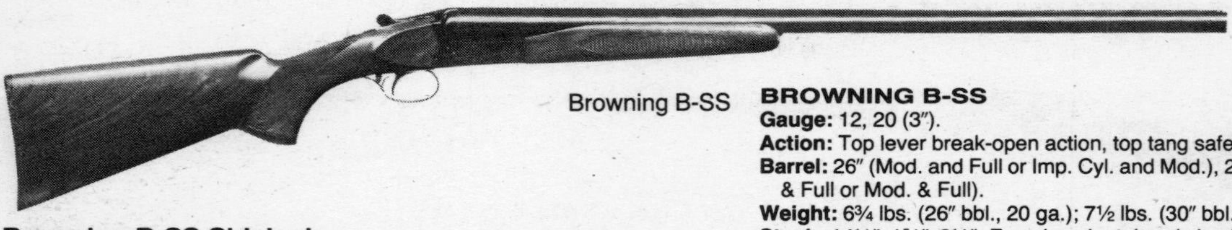

Browning B-SS

BROWNING B-SS

Gauge: 12, 20 (3").
Action: Top lever break-open action, top tang safety, single trigger.
Barrel: 26" (Mod. and Full or Imp. Cyl. and Mod.), 28" (Mod. and Full), 30" (Full & Full or Mod. & Full).
Weight: 6¾ lbs. (26" bbl., 20 ga.); 7½ lbs. (30" bbl., 12 ga.).
Stock: 14¼"x1⅝"x2½". French walnut, hand checkered. Full p.g., full beavertail fore-end.
Features: Automatic safety, automatic ejectors. Hand engraved receiver, mechanical single selective trigger with barrel selector in rear of trigger guard. Imported from Japan by Browning.
Price: Grade I, 12 or 20 ga.. **$760.00**

Browning B-SS Sidelock

Similar to the B-SS Sporter except gun is a true sidelock. Receiver, fore-end iron, trigger guard, top lever, and tang are all satin grey with rosettes and scroll work. Straight grip stock with checkered butt of French walnut. Double triggers, automatic safety and cocking indicator. Introduced 1984.
Price: 12 or 20 gauge **$1,500.00**

Browning B-SS Sporter

Browning B-SS Sporter

Similar to standard B-SS except has straight-grip stock and full beavertail fore-end with traditional oil finish. Introduced 1977.
Price: Grade I, 12 or 20 ga.. **$760.00**

Hermanos Model 150

CRUCELEGUI HERMANOS MODEL 150 DOUBLE

Gauge: 12 or 20 (2¾" chambers).
Action: Greener triple crossbolt.
Barrel: 20", 26", 28", 30", 32" (Cyl. & Cyl., Full & Full, Mod. & Full, Mod. & Imp. Cyl., Imp. Cyl. & Full, Mod. & Mod.).
Weight: 5 to 7¼ lbs.
Stock: Hand checkered walnut, beavertail fore-end.
Features: Exposed hammers; double triggers; color case hardened receiver; sling swivels; chrome lined bores. Imported from Spain by Mandall Shooting Supplies.
Price: **$349.95**
Price: Model 225 (hammerless version) **$349.95**

EXEL MODELS 201, 202, 203 DOUBLES

Gauge: 12, 2¾" chambers (M201, 202); 20, 3" chambers (M203).
Barrel: Model 201 — 28" (Full & Mod.); Model 202 — 26" (Imp. Cyl. & Mod.); Model 203 — 27" (Full & Mod.).
Weight: 6½-7 lbs.
Stock: 14⅜" x 1½" x 2½". Walnut, straight or full pistol grip.
Sights: Metal bead front.
Features: Boxlock action with color case hardened finish; double triggers; extractors only; high matted rib; hand checkered stock and fore-end. Made in Spain by Ugartechea; imported by Exel Arms of America.
Price: **$398.62**

Exel Models 204, 205, 206 Doubles

Similar to Models 201, 202, 203 except with silvered and engraved receiver, automatic selective ejectors, single or double triggers. Others specs are the same.
Price: **$608.14**

Exel Models 207, 208, 209, 210 Doubles

Similar to the Models 201, 202, 203 except full sidelock action. Models 207, 208, 209 in 12 ga., 2¾" chambers; 28" (Mod. & Full) for 207 and 208, 26" (Imp. Cyl. & Mod.) for 209, 20 ga., 3", 27" (Mod. & Full) for 210. Selective ejectors, trigger, stock and frame finish to customer specs.
Price: Model 207 .... **$593.66**
Price: Model 208, 209, 210 .... **$651.58**
Price: Models 211, 212, 213 (similar to above but with better wood, engraving).. **$3,100.00**

CAUTION: PRICES CHANGE. CHECK AT GUNSHOP.

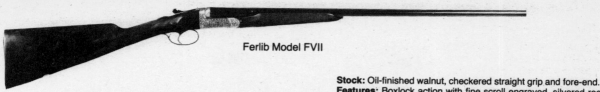

Ferlib Model FVII

FERLIB MODEL F VII DOUBLE SHOTGUN
Gauge: 12, 20, 28, 410.
Barrel: 25″ to 28″.
Weight: 5½ lbs. (20 ga.).

Stock: Oil-finished walnut, checkered straight grip and fore-end.
Features: Boxlock action with fine scroll engraved, silvered receiver. Double triggers standard. Introduced 1983. Imported from Italy by Wm. Larkin Moore.
Price: 12 or 20 ga. $3,300.00
Price: 28 or 410 ga. $3,600.00
Price: Extra for single trigger, beavertail fore-end $300.00

GIB Magnum

GIB 10 GAUGE MAGNUM SHOTGUN
Gauge: 10 ga. (3½″ chambers).
Action: Boxlock.
Barrel: 32″ (Full).

Weight: 10 lbs.
Stock: 14½″x1½″x2⅝″. European walnut, checkered at p.g. and fore-end.
Features: Double triggers; color hardened action, rest blued. Front and center metal beads on matted rib; ventilated rubber recoil pad. Fore-end release has positive Purdey-type mechanism. Imported from Spain by Mandall Shooting Supplies.
Price: $500.00

Garbi Model 51

GARBI MODEL 51 SIDE-BY-SIDE
Gauge: 12, 16, 20 (2¾″ chambers).
Barrel: 28″ (Mod. & Full).
Weight: 5½ to 6½ lbs.
Stock: Walnut, to customer specs.
Features: Boxlock action; hand-engraved receiver; hand-checkered stock and fore-end; double triggers; extractors. Introduced 1980. Imported from Spain by L. Joseph Rahn, Inc.
Price: Model 51A, 12 ga., extractors $515.00
Price: Model 51B, 12, 16, 20 ga., ejectors...................... $890.00

Garbi Model 60

Garbi Model 62
Similar to Model 60 except choked Mod. & Full, plain receiver with engraved border, demi-bloc barrels, gas exhaust valves, jointed triggers, extractors. Imported from Spain by L. Joseph Rahn.
Price: Model 62A, 12 ga., only.................................. $830.00
Price: Model 62B, 12, 16, 20 ga., ejectors $1,115.00

GARBI MODEL 60 SIDE-BY-SIDE
Gauge: 12, 16, 20 (2¾″ chambers).
Barrel: 26″, 28″, 30″; choked to customers specs.
Weight: 5½ to 6½ lbs.
Stock: Select walnut. Dimensions to customer specs.
Features: Sidelock action. Scroll engraving on receiver. Hand checkered stock. Double triggers. Extractors. Imported from Spain by L. Joseph Rahn, Inc.
Price: Model 60A, 12 ga. only $830.00
Price: With demi-bloc barrels and ejectors, 12, 16, 20 ga. $1,139.00

GARBI MODEL 100 DOUBLE
Gauge: 12, 16, 20.
Barrel: 26″, 28″, choked to customer specs.
Weight: 5½ to 7½ lbs.
Stock: 14½x2¼″x1½″. European walnut. Straight grip, checkered butt, classic fore-end.
Features: Sidelock action, automatic ejectors, double triggers standard. Color case-hardened action, coin finish optional. Single trigger; beavertail fore-end, etc. optional. Five other models are available. Imported from Spain by Wm. Larkin Moore.
Price: From $2,150.00

Garbi Model 103A, B Side-by-Side
Similar to the Garbi Model 100 except has Purdey-type fine scroll and rosette engraving. Better over-all quality than the Model 101. Model 103B has nickel-chrome steel barrels, H&H-type easy opening mechanism; other mechanical details remain the same. Imported from Spain by Wm. Larkin Moore.
Price: Model 103A $3,000.00
Price: Model 103B $3,900.00

Garbi Model Special Side-by-Side
Similar to the Garbi Model 100 except has best quality wood and metal work. Special game scene engraving with or without gold inlays, fancy figured walnut stock. Imported from Spain by Wm. Larkin Moore.
Price: From $4,200.00

Garbi Model 101 Side-by-Side
Similar to the Garbi Model 100 except is available with optional level, file-cut, Churchill or ventilated top rib, and in a 12-ga. pigeon or wildfowl gun. Has Continental-style floral and scroll engraving, select walnut stock. Better over-all quality than the Model 100. Imported from Spain by Wm. Larkin Moore.
Price: $3,000.00

CAUTION: PRICES CHANGE. CHECK AT GUNSHOP.

Garbi Model 200

Garbi Model 200 Side-by-Side
Similar to the Garbi Model 100 except has barrels of nickel-chrome steel, heavy duty locks, magnum proofed. Very fine continental-style floral and scroll engraving, well figured walnut stock. Other mechanical features remain the same. Imported from Spain by Wm. Larkin Moore.
Price: **$4,500.00**

Garbi Model 71

GARBI MODEL 71 DOUBLE
Gauge: 12, 16, 20.
Barrel: 26", 28", choked to customer specs.
Weight: 5 lbs., 15 oz. (20 ga.).
Stock: 14½x2¼"x1½". European walnut. Straight grip, checkered butt, classic fore-end.
Features: Sidelock action, automatic ejectors, double triggers standard. Color case-hardened action, coin finish optional. Five other models are available. Imported from Spain by L. Joseph Rahn.
Price: Model 71, from **$1,528.00**

GARBI MODEL 102 SHOTGUN
Gauge: 12, 16, 20.
Barrel: 12 ga.-25" to 30"; 16 & 20 ga.-25" to 28". Chokes as specified.
Weight: 20 ga.-5 lbs., 15 oz. to 6 lbs., 4 oz.
Stock: 14½"x2¼x1½"; select walnut.
Features: Holland pattern sidelock ejector with chopper lump barrels, Holland-type large scroll engraving. Double triggers (hinged front) std., non-selective single trigger available. Many options available. Imported from Spain by Wm. Larkin Moore.
Price: From **$3,000.00**

IGA Side-by-Side

Weight: 6¾ to 7 lbs.
Stock: 14½" x 1½" x 2½". Oil-finished hardwood. Checkered pistol grip and fore-end.
Features: Automatic safety, extractors only, solid matted barrel rib. Double triggers only. Introduced 1983. Imported from Brazil by Stoeger Industries.
Price: **$325.00**
Price: Coach Gun, 12 or 20 ga., 20" bbls. **$283.95**

IGA SIDE-BY-SIDE SHOTGUN
Gauge: 12, 20, 28 (2¾"), 410 (3").
Barrel: 26" (Full & Full, 410 only, Imp. Cyl. & Mod.), 28" (Mod. & Full).

Kassnar/Churchill Windsor

Barrel: 24" (Mod. & Full), 410 and 20 ga.; 26" (Imp. Cyl. & Mod., Mod. & Full); 28" (Mod. & Full, Skeet & Skeet — 28 ga.); 30" (Full & Full, Mod. & Full); 32" (Full & Full — 10 ga.).
Weight: About 7½ lbs. (12 ga.).
Stock: Hand checkered European walnut with rubber butt pad.
Features: Anson & Deeley boxlock action with silvered and engraved finish; automatic top tang safety; double triggers; beavertail fore-end. Windsor I with extractors only; Windsor II has selective automatic ejectors. Imported from Spain by Kassnar. Introduced 1984.
Price: Windor I, 10 ga. **$479.00**
Price: Windsor I, 12 through 410 ga. **$375.00**
Price: Windsor II, 12 or 20 ga. only **$495.00**

KASSNAR/CHURCHILL WINDSOR SIDE-BY-SIDE SHOTGUNS
Gauge: 10 (3½"), 12, 16, 20, 28, 410 (2¾" 16 ga., 3" others).

Kassnar/Churchill Regent

Kassnar/Churchill Regent Side-by-Side Shotguns
Similar to the Windsor Grade except fancy walnut, better checkering and engraving; tapered Churchill rib; 25" (Imp. Cyl. & Mod.) or 28" (Mod. & Full) barrels only; 12 or 20 ga., 2¾" only. Regent IV is boxlock; Regent VI is full sidelock, both with double triggers, automatic selective ejectors, straight English-style stock and splinter fore-end. Introduced 1984.
Price: Regent IV **$555.00**
Price: Regent IV, left-hand model **$645.00**
Price: Regent VI **$855.00**

KASSNAR/OMEGA SIDE-BY-SIDE SHOTGUNS
Gauge: 410, 3".
Barrel: 24" (Full & Full).
Weight: 5½ lbs.
Stock: Standard has checkered beechwood, Deluxe has walnut; both have semi-pistol grip.
Features: Blued barrels and receiver; top tang safety. Imported from Spain by Kassnar. Introduced 1984.
Price: Standard **$179.00**
Price: Deluxe **$199.00**

CAUTION: PRICES CHANGE. CHECK AT GUNSHOP.

Lebeau-Courally Sidelock

LEBEAU-COURALLY BOXLOCK SHOTGUN
Gauge: 12, 16, 20, 28.
Barrel: 26″ to 30″, choked to customer specs.
Weight: 6 lbs., 6 oz. to 8 lbs., 4 oz. (12 ga.).
Stock: Dimensions to customer specs. Select French walnut with hand rubbed oil finish, straight grip (p.g. optional), splinter fore-end (beavertail optional).
Features: Anson & Deeley boxlock with ejectors, Purdey-type fastener; choice of rounded action, with or without sideplates; choice of level rib, file cut or smooth; choice of numerous engraving patterns. Imported from Belgium by Wm. Larkin Moore.
Price: $7,500.00
Price: With sideplates $8,100.00

LEBEAU-COURALLY SIDELOCK SHOTGUN
Gauge: 12, 16, 20 (standard), 28 (optional).
Barrel: 26″ to 30″, choked to customer specs.
Weight: 6 lbs., 6 oz. to 8 lbs., 4 oz. (12 ga.)
Stock: Dimensions to customer specs. Best quality French walnut with hand rubbed oil finish, straight grip stock and checkered butt (std.), classic splinter fore-end.
Features: Holland & Holland pattern sidelock ejector double with chopper lump barrels; choice of classic or rounded action; concave or level rib, file cut or smooth; choice of numerous engraving patterns. Can be furnished with H&H type self-opening mechanism. Imported from Belgium by Wm. Larkin Moore.
Price: From $16,200.00

Manufrance 254 Robust

Manufrance 222 Robust Field Side-by-Side
Same as the Robust Deluxe model except has plain color case-hardened receiver. Available with 27½″ (Mod. & Full) or 20½″ (Imp. Cyl. & Imp. Cyl.), extractors only. Introduced 1984.
Price: $560.00

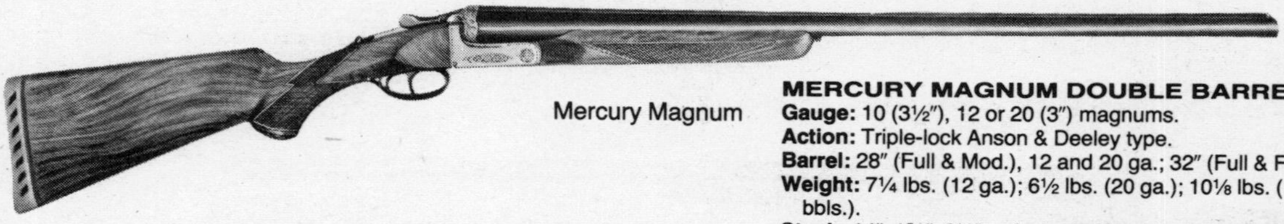

MANUFRANCE 254 ROBUST DELUXE DOUBLE
Gauge: 12, 2¾″ chambers.
Barrel: 27½″ (Mod. & Full), chrome-lined bores.
Weight: About 6½ lbs. **Length:** 44¼″ over-all.
Stock: Choice, dense French walnut with 21 lpi checkering; beavertail fore-end.
Features: Boxlock action with double triggers, automatic ejectors, top tang safety. Silver-gray finish and fine scroll engraving on receiver, top lever and trigger guard. Retractable sling in butt optional. Imported from France by Armsource, Inc. Introduced 1984.
Price: $760.00

Mercury Magnum

PARKER DHE SIDE-BY-SIDE SHOTGUN
Gauge: 20, 2¾″ or 3″ chambers.
Barrel: 26″ (Imp. Cyl. & Mod.), 28″ (Mod. & Full, 3″ chambers only).
Weight: About 6½ lbs.
Stock: American walnut, checkered grip and fore-end. Straight or pistol grip style.
Sights: Metal bead front.
Features: Reproduction of the original Parker DHE — all parts interchangeable with original. Double or single trigger; skeleton or hard rubber buttplate. Reproduced by Winchester in Japan, imported by Parker Gun. Introduced 1984.
Price .... NA

MERCURY MAGNUM DOUBLE BARREL SHOTGUN
Gauge: 10 (3½″), 12 or 20 (3″) magnums.
Action: Triple-lock Anson & Deeley type.
Barrel: 28″ (Full & Mod.), 12 and 20 ga.; 32″ (Full & Full), 10 ga.
Weight: 7¼ lbs. (12 ga.); 6½ lbs. (20 ga.); 10⅛ lbs. (10 ga.). **Length:** 45″ (28″ bbls.).
Stock: 14″x1⅝″x2¼″ walnut, checkered p.g. stock and beavertail fore-end, recoil pad.
Features: Double triggers, front hinged, auto safety, extractors; safety gas ports, engraved frame. Imported from Spain by Tradewinds.
Price: (12, 20 ga.) $295.00
Price: (10 ga.) $480.00

Piotti Model Monte Carlo Side-by-Side
Similar to the Piotti King No. 1 except has Purdey-style scroll and rosette engraving, no gold inlays, over-all workmanship not as finely detailed. Other mechanical specifications remain the same. Imported from Italy by Wm. Larkin Moore.
Price: $9,200.00

Piotti King No. 1

Piotti Model King EELL Side-by-Side
Similar to the Piotti King No. 1 except highest quality wood and metal work. Choice of either bulino game scene engraving or game scene engraving with gold inlays. Engraved and signed by a master engraver. Exhibition grade wood. Other mechanical specifications remain the same. Imported from Italy by Wm. Larkin Moore.
Price: $16,000.00

PIOTTI KING NO. 1 SIDE-BY-SIDE
Gauge: 12, 16, 20, 28, 410.
Barrel: 25″ to 30″ (12 ga.), 25″ to 28″ (16, 20, 28, 410). To customer specs. Chokes as specified.
Weight: 6½ lbs. to 8 lbs. (12 ga., to customer specs.)
Stock: Dimensions to customer specs. Finely figured walnut; straight grip with checkered butt with classic splinter fore-end and hand-rubbed oil finish standard. Pistol grip, beavertail fore-end, satin luster finish optional.
Features: Holland & Holland pattern sidelock action, auto. ejectors. Double trigger with front trigger hinged standard; non-selective single trigger optional. Coin finish standard; color case-hardened optional. Top rib: level, file cut standard; concave, ventilated optional. Very fine, full coverage scroll engraving with small floral bouquets, gold crown in top lever, name in gold, and gold crest in fore-end. Imported from Italy by Wm. Larkin Moore.
Price: $11,000.00

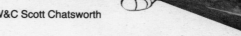

PIOTTI MODEL PIUMA SIDE-BY-SIDE

Gauge: 12, 16, 20, 28, 410.
Barrel: 25″ to 30″ (12 ga.), 25″ to 28″ (16, 20, 28, 410).
Weight: 5½ to 6¼ lbs. (20 ga.).
Stock: Dimensions to customer specs. Straight grip stock with checkered butt, classic splinter fore-end, hand rubbed oil finish are standard; pistol grip, beavertail fore-end, satin luster finish optional.
Features: Anson & Deeley boxlock ejector double with chopper lump barrels. Level, file-cut rib, light scroll and rosette engraving, scalloped frame. Double triggers with hinged front standard, single non-selective optional. Coin finish standard, color case hardened optional. Imported from Italy by Wm. Larkin Moore.
Price: $4,700.00

ROSSI "SQUIRE" DOUBLE BARREL

Gauge: 12, 20, 410 (3″ chambers).
Barrel: 12 — 28″ (Mod. & Full); 20 ga.—26″ (Imp. Cyl. & Mod.), 28″ (Mod. & Full); 410—26″ (Full & Full).
Weight: About 7½ lbs.
Stock: Walnut finished hardwood.
Features: Double triggers, raised matted rib, beavertail fore-end. Massive twin underlugs mesh with synchronized sliding bolts. Introduced 1978. Imported by Interarms.
Price: 12 or 20 ga. $274.00
Price: 410 .... $281.00

Piotti Model Lunik

Piotti Model Lunik Side-by-Side

Similar to the Piotti King No. 1 except better over-all quality. Has Renaissance-style large scroll engraving in relief, gold crown in top lever, gold name, and gold crest in fore-end. Best quality Holland & Holland-pattern sidelock ejector double with chopper lump (demi-bloc) barrels. Other mechanical specifications remain the same. Imported from Italy by Wm. Larkin Moore.
Price: $11,500.00

ROSSI OVERLAND DOUBLE BARREL

Gauge: 12, 20, 410 (3″ chambers).
Action: Sidelock with external hammers; Greener crossbolt.
Barrel: 12 ga., 20″ (Imp. Cyl., Mod.) 28″ (Mod. & Full), 20 ga., 20″, 26″ (Imp. Cyl. & Mod.), 410 ga., 26″ (Full & Full).
Weight: 6½ to 7 lbs.
Stock: Walnut p.g. with beavertail fore-end.
Features: Solid raised matted rib. Exposed hammers. Imported by Interarms.
Price: 12 or 20 .... $249.00
Price: 410 .... $256.00

Savage Fox B-SE

SAVAGE FOX MODEL B-SE DOUBLE

Gauge: 12, 20, 410 (20, 2¾″ and 3″; 410, 2½″ and 3″ shells).
Action: Hammerless, takedown; non-selective single trigger; auto. safety. Automatic ejectors.
Barrel: 12, 20 ga., 26″ (Imp. Cyl., Mod.); 12 ga. (Mod., Full); 410, 26″ (Full, Full). Vent. rib on all.
Weight: 12 ga. 7 lbs., 16 ga. 6¾ lbs., 20 ga. 6½ lbs., 410 ga. 6¼ lbs.
Stock: 14″x1½″x2½″. Walnut, checkered p.g. and beavertail fore-end.
Features: Decorated, case-hardened frame; white bead front and middle sights.
Price: $399.95

Savage-Stevens 311

SAVAGE-STEVENS MODEL 311 DOUBLE

Gauge: 12, 20, 410 (12, 20 and 410, 3″ chambers).
Action: Top lever, hammerless; double triggers, auto. top tang safety.
Barrel: 12, 20 ga. 26″ (Imp. Cyl., Mod.); 12 ga. 28″ (Mod., Full); 12 ga. 30″ (Mod., Full); 410 ga. 26″ (Full, Full).
Weight: 7-8 lbs. (30″ bbl.). **Length:** 45¾″ over-all.
Stock: 14″x1½″x2½″. Walnut finish, p.g., fluted comb.
Features: Box type frame, case-hardened finish.
Price: $262.50

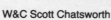

W&C SCOTT CHATSWORTH GRANDE LUXE DOUBLE

Gauge: 12, 16, 20, 28.
Barrel: 25″, 26″, 27″, 28″, 30″ (Imp. Cyl. & Mod., or to order); concave rib standard, Churchill or flat rib optional.
Weight: About 6½ lbs. (12 ga.).
Stock: 14¾″ x 1½″ x 2¼″, or made to customer specs. French walnut with 32 lpi checkering.
Features: Entirely hand fitted; boxlock action (sideplates optional); English scroll engraving; gold name plate shield in stock. Imported from England by L. Joseph Rahn and British Guns.
Price: 12 or 16 ga. $7,346.00
Price: 20 ga. $8,431.00
Price: 28 ga. $8,846.00

W&C Scott Chatsworth

W&C Scott Kinmount Game Gun

Similar to the Bowood DeLuxe Game Gun except less ornate engraving and wood work; checkered 20 lpi; other details essentially the same. Imported from England by L. Joseph Rahn and British Guns.
Price: 12 or 16 ga. $3,602.00
Price: 20 ga. $4,128.00
Price: 28 ga. $4,307.00

W&C Scott Bowood DeLuxe Game Gun

Similar to the Chatsworth Grande Luxe except less ornate metal and wood work; checkered 24 lpi at fore-end and pistol grip. Imported from England by L. Joseph Rahn and British Guns.
Price: 12 or 16 ga. $5,020.00
Price: 20 ga. $5,755.00
Price: 28 ga. $6,035.00

CAUTION: PRICES CHANGE. CHECK AT GUNSHOP.

SHOTGUNS—SIDE-BY-SIDES

VENTURA 66/66 XXV-SL DOUBLES
Gauge: 12 ga. (2¾″), 20 ga. (3″), 28 ga. (2¾″), 410 (3″)..
Action: H&H sidelock with double underlugs.
Barrel: 25″, 27½″, 30″ (12 ga. only), with chokes according to use.
Weight: 12 ga.—6½ lbs.; 28 ga.—5¾ lbs.
Stock: Select French walnut, hand checkered. Straight English or pistol grip stock, slender beavertail fore-end.
Features: Single selective or double triggers, auto. ejectors, gas escape valves, and intercepting safeties. Extensive hand engraving and finishing. Can be made to customer specs. Accessories, extra barrels also available. Imported by Ventura Imports.
Price: From . . . . **$1,100.00 to 1,396.00**

Ventura 66/66 XXV-SL

VENTURA 53/53XXV-BL DOUBLES
Gauge: 12 ga. (2¾″), 20 ga. (3″), 28 ga. (2¾″), 410 ga. (3″).
Action: Anson & Deeley with double underlugs.
Barrel: 25″, 27½″, 30″ (12 ga. only), with chokes according to use.
Weight: 12 ga.—6½ lbs.; 28 ga.—5½ lbs.
Stock: Select French walnut, hand checkered. Straight English or pistol grip stock with slender beavertail fore-end.
Features: Single selective or double triggers, auto ejectors, hand-engraved scalloped frames. Accessories also available. Imported by Ventura Imports.
Price: From . . . . **$736.00 to 996.00**

VENTURA MODEL 51 DOUBLE
Gauge: 12 ga. (2¾″), 20 ga. (3″).
Action: Anson & Deeley with double underlugs.
Barrel: 27½″, 30″ (12 ga. only) with chokes according to use.
Weight: 6 to 6½ lbs.
Stock: Select French walnut, hand checkered pistol grip stock with slender beavertail fore-end.
Features: Single selective trigger, auto ejectors, hand-engraved action. Leather trunk cases, wood cleaning rods and brass snap caps available. Imported by Ventura Imports.
Price: From **$696.00**

Ventura Model 51

Winchester Model 23

Winchester Model 23 XTR Lightweight
Similar to standard Pigeon Grade except has 25½″ barrels, English-style straight grip stock, thinner semi-beavertail fore-end. Available in 12 or 20 gauge (Imp. Cyl. & Mod.). Silver-gray frame has engraved bird scenes. Comes with hard case. Introduced 1981. Imported from Japan by Winchester Group, Olin Corp.
Price: **$1,435.00**

Winchester Model 23 Heavy Duck
Same basic features as the standard Model 23 Pigeon Grade except has plain, blued receiver, 30″ barrels choked Full and Extra Full, 3″ chambers. Comes with hard case. Introduced 1983.
Price: **$1,580.00**

WINCHESTER MODEL 23 PIGEON GRADE DOUBLE
Gauge: 12, 20, 3″ chambers.
Barrel: 26″, (Imp. Cyl. & Mod.), 28″ (Mod. & Full). Vent. rib.
Weight: 7 lbs. (12 ga.); 6½ lbs. (20 ga.). **Length:** 46¾″ over-all (28″ bbls.).
Stock: 14″x1½″x2½″ High grade American walnut, beavertail fore-end. Hand cut checkering.
Features: Mechanical trigger; tapered ventilated rib; selective ejectors. Receiver, top lever and trigger guard have silver gray satin finish and fine line scroll engraving. Introduced 1978. Imported from Japan by Winchester Group, Olin Corp.
Price: **$1,345.00**

Winchester Model 23 Pigeon Grade Winchoke
Same features as standard Model 23 Pigeon Grade except has 25½″ barrels with interchangeable Winchoke tubes. Six are supplied with 12 ga. (Skeet, Imp. Cyl., Mod., Imp. Mod., Full, Extra Full), four with 20 ga. (Skeet, Imp. Cyl., Mod., Full). Comes with hard case. Introduced 1983.
Price: **$1,475.00**

SHOTGUNS—BOLT ACTIONS

Marlin Model 55

MARLIN MODEL 55 GOOSE GUN BOLT ACTION
Gauge: 12 only, (3″ mag. or 2¾″).
Action: Bolt action, thumb safety, detachable 2-shot clip. Red cocking indicator.
Barrel: 36″, Full choke.
Weight: 8 lbs. **Length:** 57″ over-all.
Stock: Walnut-finished hardwood, p.g., ventilated recoil pad, leather strap & swivels. Mar-Shield® finish.
Features: Tapped for receiver sights. Swivels and leather carrying strap. Brass bead front sight, U-groove rear sight.
Price: **$160.95**

SHOTGUNS—BOLT ACTIONS

Mossberg 595/585

MOSSBERG 595/585 BOLT ACTION
Gauge: 12, 2¾" or 3" (M595), 12 or 20 ga., 2¾" or 3" (M585).
Barrel: 28" (C-LECT-CHOKE), 38" (Full, fixed, M595).
Weight: 7½ lbs. (12 ga.).
Stock: Walnut-finished hardwood, vent. recoil pad.
Sights: Bead front.
Features: Rotary safety at rear of bolt blocks trigger; 2-shot magazine. Introduced 1984.
Price: .... **NA**

MARLIN SUPERGOOSE 10 M5510
Gauge: 10, 3½" Magnum or 2⅞" regular, 2-shot clip.
Barrel: 34" (Full), bead front sight, U-groove rear sight.
Weight: About 10½ lbs. **Length:** 55½" over-all.
Stock: Extra long walnut-finished hardwood with p.g., Pachmayr vent. pad., white butt spacer; Mar-Shield® finish.
Features: Bolt action, removable 2-shot clip magazine. Positive thumb safety, red cocking indicator. Comes with quick-detachable swivels and leather carrying strap.
Price: **$263.95**

MOSSBERG MODEL 183K BOLT ACTION
Gauge: 410, 3-shot (3" chamber).
Action: Bolt; top-loading mag.; thumb safety.
Barrel: 25" with C-Lect-Choke.
Weight: 5¾ lbs. **Length:** 45¼" over-all.
Stock: Walnut finish, p.g., Monte Carlo comb., rubber recoil pad w/spacer.
Features: Moulded trigger guard with finger grooves, gold bead front sight.
Price: About **$102.00**

SHOTGUNS—SINGLE SHOTS

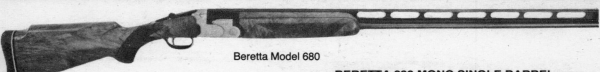

Beretta Model 680

FIE "C.B.C" SINGLE BARREL SHOTGUN
Gauge: 12, 20, 410 (3").
Barrel: 12 ga. & 20 ga. 28" (Full); 410 ga. (Full).
Weight: 6½ lbs.
Stock: Walnut stained hardwood, beavertail fore-end.
Sights: Metal bead front.
Features: Trigger guard button is pushed to open action. Exposed hammer, auto ejector, three-piece takedown. Imported from Brazil by F.I.E. Corp.
Price: **$74.95**
Price: Youth model **$79.95**

BERETTA 680 MONO SINGLE BARREL
Gauge: 12 only (2¾").
Barrel: 32", 34" (Full).
Weight: About 8 lbs.
Stock: 14⅜"x1⅜"x1⅝". Premium walnut with Monte Carlo, checkered p.g. and fore-end.
Features: Low profile boxlock action, auto ejector, manual safety. High rib, two sight beads, chrome lined bores. Ventilated recoil pad. Comes with fitted case. Imported from Italy by Beretta U.S.A. Corp.
Price: **$1,580.00**

Browning BT-99

FIE "S.O.B." SINGLE BARREL
Gauge: 12, 20, 410 (3").
Action: Button-break on trigger guard.
Barrel: 18½" (Cyl.).
Weight: 6½ lbs.
Stock: Walnut finished hardwood, full beavertail fore-end.
Features: Exposed hammer. Automatic ejector. Imported from Brazil by F.I.E. Corp.
Price: **$99.95**

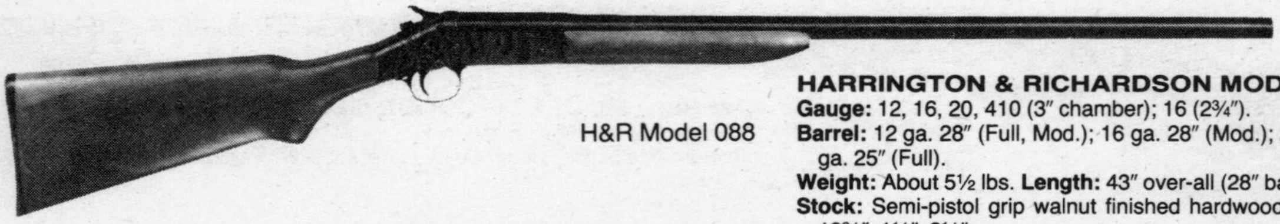

BROWNING BT-99 COMPETITION TRAP SPECIAL
Gauge: 12 gauge only (2¾").
Action: Top lever break-open, hammerless.
Barrel: 32" or 34" (Mod., Imp. Mod. or Full) with ¹¹⁄₃₂" wide high post floating vent. rib. Also comes with Invector choke tubes.
Weight: 8 lbs. (32" bbl.).
Stock: French walnut; hand checkered, full pistol grip, full beavertail fore-end; recoil pad. Trap dimensions with M.C. 14⅜"x1⅜"x1⅜"x2".
Sights: Ivory front and middle beads.
Features: Gold plated trigger with 3½-lb. pull, deluxe trap-style recoil pad, auto ejector, no safety. Also available in engraved Pigeon Grade. Imported from Japan by Browning.
Price: Grade I Competition **$724.95**
Price: Grade I Invector **$754.95**

H&R Model 088

HARRINGTON & RICHARDSON MODEL 088 DELUXE
Gauge: 12, 16, 20, 410 (3" chamber); 16 (2¾").
Barrel: 12 ga. 28" (Full, Mod.); 16 ga. 28" (Mod.); 20 ga. 26" (Full, Mod.); 410 ga. 25" (Full).
Weight: About 5½ lbs. **Length:** 43" over-all (28" barrel).
Stock: Semi-pistol grip walnut finished hardwood; semi-beavertail fore-end. 13¾"x1½"x2½".
Sights: Bead front.
Features: Color case-hardened frame, blued barrel.
Price: **$88.50**
Price: 12 ga., 20", 32" (Full) **$89.50**
Price: 12 ga., 36" (Full) **$92.50**

CAUTION: PRICES CHANGE. CHECK AT GUNSHOP.

H&R Model 176

H & R Model 176 Magnum
Similar to the Model 088 except in 10 gauge (3½″ chamber) only with 36″ (Full) barrel. Also available with 32″ (Full) barrel. All barrels specially designed for steel shot use. Special long fore-end and recoil pad.
Price: From **$116.50**

H & R Model 176 10 Ga. Slug Gun
Similar to standard Model 176 magnums except chambered for 10 ga. slugs. Ramp front sight, adjustable folding leaf rear sight, recoil pad, sling swivels. Has 28″ barrel (Cyl.), 3½″ chamber. Extra length magnum-type fore-end. Weighs 9¼ lbs. Introduced 1982.
Price: **$134.50**

H & R Model 162
Same as the 088 except 12 or 20 ga., 24″ Cyl. bored bbl., adj. folding leaf rear sight, blade front, 5½ lbs.; over-all 40″. Cross bolt safety; push-button action release.
Price: **$109.50**

ITHACA 5E GRADE SINGLE BARREL TRAP GUN
Gauge: 12 only.
Action: Top lever break open hammerless, dual locking lugs.
Barrel: 32″ or 34″, rampless vent. rib.
Stock: (14½″x1½″x1⅞″). Select walnut, checkered p.g. and beavertail fore-end, p.g. cap, recoil pad, Monte Carlo comb, cheekpiece. Cast-on, cast-off or extreme deviation from standard stock dimensions $100 extra. Reasonable deviation allowed without extra charge.
Features: Frame, top lever and trigger guard extensively engraved and gold inlaid. Gold name plate in stock.
Price: Custom made **$7,000.00**
Price: Dollar Grade. **$9,700.00**

KASSNAR/OMEGA FOLDING SHOTGUN
Gauge: 12, 16, 20, 28, 410, 2¾″, 3″ chamber.
Barrel: 410 — 26″ (Full); 12, 16, 20, 28 — 28″ (Full); 12 — 30″ (Full).
Stock: Standard has checkered beechwood, Deluxe has checkered walnut.
Sights: Metal bead front.
Features: Standard model has matte chrome receiver, bottom opening lever; Deluxe has blued receiver, top lever, vent. rib. Both guns fold for storage and transport. Imported from Italy by Kassnar. Introduced 1984.
Price: . . . . **NA**

Ljutic LTX Mono

Ljutic LTX Mono Gun
Similar to the standard Mono Gun except has exhibition quality wood, extra-fancy checkering pattern in 24 lpi, double recessed choking. Weight is about 8 lbs., extra light 33″ barrel; medium-height Olympic rib. Introduced 1984.
Price: **$4,995.00**
Price: With four screw-in choke tubes. **$5,595.00**

LJUTIC MONO GUN SINGLE BARREL
Gauge: 12 ga. only.
Barrel: 34″, choked to customer specs; hollow-milled rib, 35½″ sight plane.
Weight: Approx. 9 lbs.
Stock: To customer specs. Oil finish, hand checkered.
Features: Totally custom made. Pull or release trigger; removable trigger guard contains trigger and hammer mechanism; Ljutic pushbutton opener on front of trigger guard. From Ljutic Industries.
Price: **$3,495.00**
Price: With Olympic Rib, custom 32″ barrel **$3,695.00**
Price: As above with screw-in chokes. **$3,895.00**

Ljutic Space Gun

LJUTIC RECOILLESS SPACE GUN SHOTGUN
Gauge: 12 only, 2¾″ chamber.
Barrel: 30″ (Full).
Weight: 8½ lbs.
Stock: 14½″ to 15″ pull length; universal comb; medium or large p.g.
Sights: Choice of front sight or vent. rib model.
Features: Choice of pull or release button trigger; anti-recoil mechanism. Revolutionary new design. Introduced 1981. From Ljutic Industries.
Price: From **$3,495.00**

Savage-Stevens Model 94

SAVAGE-STEVENS MODEL 94 Single Barrel Gun
Gauge: 12, 16, 20, 410 (12, 20 and 410, 3″ chambers).
Action: Top lever break open; hammer; auto. ejector.
Barrel: 12 ga. 28″, 30″, 32″, 36″; 16, 20 ga. 28″; 410 ga. 26″. Full choke only.
Weight: About 6 lbs. **Length:** 42″ over-all (26″ bbl.).
Stock: 14″x1½″x2½″. Walnut finish.
Features: Color case-hardened frame, low rebounding hammer.
Price: 26″ to 32″ bbls. **$88.50**
Price: With 36″ bbl. **$95.00**

Stevens M94-Y Youth's Gun
Same as Model 94-C except: 26″ bbl., 20 ga. Mod. or 410 Full, 12½″ stock with recoil pad. Wgt. about 5½ lbs. 40½″ over-all.
Price: **$95.00**

SHOTGUNS—SINGLE SHOTS

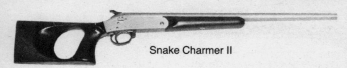

Snake Charmer II

SNAKE CHARMER II SHOTGUN
Gauge: 410, 3" chamber.
Barrel: 18⅛" (Cyl.).
Weight: 3½ lbs. **Length:** 28⅛" over-all.
Stock: Moulded high impact plastic, thumbhole type.
Sights: None.
Features: Redesigned positive safety mechanism. Measures 19" when taken apart. All stainless steel construction. Storage compartment in buttstock holds four spare rounds of 410. Reintroduced 1984. From Sporting Arms, Inc.
Price: About **$115.00**

Stevens 9478 Single

STEVENS 9478 SINGLE BARREL
Gauge: 10, 12, 20 or 410.
Barrel: 28" (Full), 30" (Full), 32" (Full), 36" (Full).
Weight: 6¼ lbs. (9½ lbs. for 10 ga.) **Length:** 42" to 52" over-all.
Stock: Walnut finished hardwood. 14"x1½"x2½".
Features: Bottom opening action "lever", manually cocked hammer, auto. ejection. Color case-hardened frame.
Price: 9478 .... **$84.95**
Price: 10 ga., 36" (Full) **$123.00**

SHOTGUNS—MILITARY & POLICE

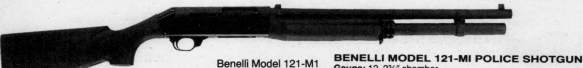

Benelli Model 121-M1

BENELLI MODEL 121-MI POLICE SHOTGUN
Gauge: 12, 2¾" chamber.
Barrel: 20" (Cyl.).
Weight: About 7½ lbs.
Stock: Oil-finished Beech.
Sights: Post front, buckhorn-type rear.
Features: All metal parts black Parkerized, including bolt; smooth, non-checkered stock, swivel stud on butt. Imported by Heckler & Koch.
Price: **$499.00**

FIE SPAS 12

FIE SPAS 12 PUMP/AUTO ASSAULT SHOTGUN
Gauge: 12, 2¾".
Barrel: 21½". Barrel threaded for SPAS choke tubes.
Weight: 9.6 lbs. **Length:** 31¾" (stock folded).
Stock: Folding, metal.
Sights: Blade front, aperture rear.
Features: Functions as pump or gas-operated auto. Has 9-shot magazine. Parkerized alloy receiver, chrome lined bore, resin pistol grip and pump handle. Made in Italy by Franchi. Introduced 1983. Imported by FIE Corp.
Price: **$599.95**
Price: Mod. or Full choke tube **$24.95**

Ithaca 37 Handgrip

ITHACA MODEL 37 M & P SHOTGUN
Gauge: 12, 2¾" chamber, 5-shot magazine.
Barrel: 18" (Cyl.), 20" (Cyl. or Full).
Weight: 6½ lbs.
Stock: Oil-finished walnut with grooved walnut pump handle.
Sights: Bead front.
Features: Metal parts are Parkerized or matte chrome. Available with vertical hand grip instead of full butt.
Price: 5-shot, Parkerized **$328.00**
Price: 8-shot, Parkerized **$343.00**
Price: 8-shot, chrome **$383.00**
Price: Handgrip stock, 5-shot.............................. **$351.00**
Price: Handgrip stock, 8-shot.............................. **$366.00**
Price: M&P II, Handgrip with buttstock.................... **$345.00**

Ithaca Model 37 M&P Handgrip
Compact, handgrip version of the 12 gauge Model 37 M&P. Choice of 5-shot, 18½" (Cyl.), or 8-shot 20" (Cyl.) barrel. Comes with sling and swivels. Introduced 1983.
Price: Blued, 5-shot, 18½" **$315.00**
Price: Parkerized, 5-shot, 18½".......................... **$351.00**
Price: Parkerized, 8-shot, 20" **$366.00**
Price: Chrome, 8-shot, 20" **$406.00**

Ithaca 37 DSPS

Ithaca Model 37 DSPS Shotgun

Law enforcement version of the Model 37 Deerslayer. Designed primarily for shooting rifled slugs but equally effective with buckshot. Available in either 5- or 8-shot models in blue, Parkerized or matte chrome finishes. Has 20" barrel with Full choke, oil-finished stock, adjustable rifle-type sights.
Price: Parkerized, 5-shot $363.00
Price: Blue, 5-shot $363.00
Price: Matte chrome, 8-shot $418.00
Price: Parkerized or blue, 8-shot $378.00
Price: With Handgrip and buttstock $380.00

Ithaca Model 37 LAPD

Similar to the Model 37 DSPS except comes with sling swivels, sling, rubber recoil pad. Rifle-type sights, checkered pistol grip stock, 5-shot magazine.
Price: $405.00

Ithaca Mag-10 Roadblocker

ITHACA MAG-10 ROADBLOCKER

Gauge: 10, 3½" chamber.
Barrel: 22" (Cyl.).
Weight: 10¾ lbs.
Stock: Walnut stock and fore-end, oil finish.
Sights: Bead front.
Features: Non-glare finish on metal parts. Uses Ithaca's Countercoil gas system. Rubber recoil pad. Vent. rib or plain barrel.
Price: Plain barrel $696.00
Price: Vent rib barrel $725.00

KASSNAR/OMEGA RIOT PUMP SHOTGUN

Gauge: 12, 2¾" chamber.
Barrel: 20" (Imp. Cyl.).
Weight: 7½ lbs.
Stock: European hardwood.
Sights: Metal bead front.
Features: Blued receiver, Damascened bolt; cross-bolt safety. Imported from the Philippines by Kassnar. Introduced 1984.
Price: $199.00

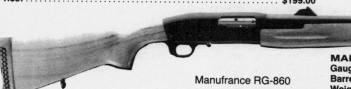

Manufrance RG-860

MANUFRANCE RG-860 POLICE SHOTGUN

Gauge: 12, 2¾" chamber.
Barrel: 20" (Cyl.).
Weight: 6⅛ lbs. Length: 41" over-all.
Stock: Walnut, with low-gloss finish, recoil pad.
Sights: Hooded ramp front, open rear.
Features: Matte black light alloy receiver; 7-shot magazine; interchangeable barrel; fitted with sling swivels. Imported from France by Armsource, Inc. Introduced 1984.
Price: $445.00

Mossberg 500

MOSSBERG MODEL 500 SECURITY SHOTGUNS

Gauge: 12, 20 (2¾"), 410 (3").
Barrel: 18½", 20" (Cyl.).
Weight: 5½ lbs. (410), 7 lbs. (12 ga.).
Stock: Walnut-finished hardwood.
Sights: Rifle-type front and rear or metal bead front.
Features: Available in 6- or 8-shot models. Top-mounted safety, double action slide bars, sling swivels, rubber recoil pad. Blue, Parkerized or electroless nickel finishes. Price list not complete—contact Mossberg for full list.
Price: 12 ga., 6-shot, 18½", blue, bead sight, about $178.95
Price: As above, Parkerized, about $215.00
Price: As above, nickel, about $240.00
Price: 12 ga., 8-shot, 20" Parkerized, rifle sights, about $218.00
Price: 20 ga., 6-shot, 18½", blue, bead sight, about $202.00
Price: Model 500 US, Parkerized finish, handguard, about $220.00
Price: Model 500 ATP, blued, bayonet lug, sling, about $245.00

Mossberg Cruiser Persuader Shotgun

Similar to the Model 500 Security guns except fitted with the "Cruiser" pistol grip. Grip and fore-end are solid black. Available in either blue or electroless nickel; 12 gauge only with 18½" (6-shot) or 20" (8-shot) barrel. Folding stock. Muzzle cut with "Muzzle Brake" slots to reduce recoil. Comes with extra long black web sling. Weight is 5¾ lb. (18½"), 6 lb. (20"). Over-all length is 28" with 18½" barrel.
Price: 6-shot, 18½", blue, about $200.00
Price: As above, nickel, about $240.00
Price: 8-shot, 20", blue, about $215.00
Price: As above, nickel, about $240.00

Mossberg 595 AP5

MOSSBERG 595 AP5 BOLT ACTION SHOTGUN

Gauge: 12 ga., 2¾" chamber.
Barrel: 18½".
Weight: 7½ lbs. Length: 38½" over-all.
Stock: Hardwood.
Sights: Bead front, open rear.
Features: Detachable 5-shot box magazine, rubber recoil pad, grooved fore-end. Comes with sling swivel studs. Introduced 1983.
Price: .... NA

Mossberg 5500 AP5

MOSSBERG 5500 AP5 GUARDIAN SHOTGUN

Gauge: 12, 2¾″ chamber.
Barrel: 18½″ (Cyl.).
Weight: 7½ lbs. **Length:** 38½″ over-all.
Stock: Hardwood.
Sights: Bead front.
Features: Matte blue finish, grooved fore-end. Also available with Cruiser pistol grip. Introduced 1983.
Price: .... **NA**

Remington 870 Police

REMINGTON MODEL 870P POLICE SHOTGUN

Gauge: 12, 2¾″ chamber.
Barrel: 18″, 20″ (Police Cyl.), 20″ (Imp. Cyl.).
Weight: About 7 lbs.
Stock: Lacquer-finished hardwood or folding stock.
Sights: Metal bead front or rifle sights.
Features: Solid steel receiver, double-action slide bars.
Price: Wood stock, 18″ or 20″, bead sight **$332.00**
Price: Wood stock, 20″, rifle sights **$357.00**

SILE TP8 POLICE/SURVIVAL SHOTGUN

Gauge: 12, 2¾″ chamber, 7-shot magazine.
Barrel: 19¾″.
Weight: 6¾ lbs. **Length:** 39½″ over-all with stock, 29½″ without.
Stock: Hollow, plastic coated, steel tube, plastic fore-end.
Sights: Bead on ramp front, open bar rear.
Features: Dual action bars, non-reflective electroless nickel finish. Stock holds spare ammunition or survival equipment. Rotating sling swivels. Hard chrome lined barrel. Introduced 1982. Imported from Italy by Sile.
Price: **$255.00**

Savage 69-R/69-RXL

SAVAGE MODEL 69-R/69-RXL PUMP SHOTGUN

Gauge: 12 only, 3″ chamber.
Barrel: M69-R — 18¼″ (Cyl.), M69-RXL — 20″ (Cyl.).
Weight: 6½ lbs. **Length:** 38″ over-all.
Stock: Hardwood, tung-oil finish.
Sights: Bead front.
Features: Top tang safety, 5-shot (69-R) or 7-shot (69-RXL). Stock has fluted comb and full pistol grip, ventilated rubber pad. QD swivel studs. Introduced 1982.
Price: Either model **$185.50**
Price: Model 69-N (satin nickel finish) **$258.00**

STEVENS MODEL 311-R GUARD GUN DOUBLE

Gauge: 12 or 20 ga.
Barrel: 18¼″ (Cyl. & Cyl.).
Weight: 6¾ lbs. **Length:** 35¼″ over-all.
Stock: Hardwood, tung-oil finish.
Sights: Bead front.
Features: Top tang safety, double triggers, color case-hardened frame, blue barrels. Ventilated rubber recoil pad. Introduced 1982.
Price: **$262.50**

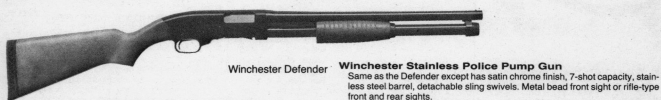

Winchester Defender

Winchester Stainless Police Pump Gun

Same as the Defender except has satin chrome finish, 7-shot capacity, stainless steel barrel, detachable sling swivels. Metal bead front sight or rifle-type front and rear sights.
Price: With bead front sight **$349.95**
Price: With rifle-type sights..................................... **$364.95**

WINCHESTER DEFENDER PUMP GUN

Gauge: 12, 20, 3″ chamber, 7-shot capacity.
Barrel: 18″ (Cyl.).
Weight: 6¾ lbs. **Length:** 38⅝″ over-all.
Stock: Walnut finished hardwood stock and ribbed fore-end.
Sights: Metal bead front.
Features: Cross-bolt safety, front-locking rotating bolt, twin action slide bars. Black rubber butt pad. Made under license by U.S. Repeating Arms Co.
Price: **$209.95**

Winchester "Stainless Marine" Pump Gun

Same as the Defender except has bright chrome finish, stainless-steel barrel, rifle-type sights only. Has special fore-end cap for easy cleaning and inspection.
Price: **$364.95**

Winchester Pistol Grip

Winchester Pistol Grip Pump Security Shotguns

Same as regular Security Series but with pistol grip and fore-end of high-impact resistant ABS plastic with non-glare black finish. Introduced 1984.
Price: Pistol Grip Defender (12 and 20 ga.) **$209.95**
Price: Pistol Grip Stainless Police Bead Sight **$309.95**
Price: As above with rifle sights................................ **$319.95**
Price: Pistol Grip Stainless Marine **$319.95**

CAUTION: PRICES CHANGE. CHECK AT GUNSHOP.

The following pages catalog the black powder arms currently available to U.S. shooters. These range from quite precise replicas of historically significant arms to totally new designs created expressly to give the black powder shooter the benefits of modern technology.

Most of the replicas are imported, and many are available from more than one source. Thus examples of a given model such as the 1860 Army revolver or Zouave rifle purchased from different importers may vary in price, finish and fitting. Most of them bear proof marks, indicating that they have been test fired in the proof house of their country of origin.

A list of the importers and the retail price range are included with the description for each model. Many local dealers handle more than one importer's products, giving the prospective buyer an opportunity to make his own judgment in selecting a black powder gun. Most importers have catalogs available free or at nominal cost, and some are well worth having for the useful information on black powder shooting they provide in addition to their detailed descriptions and specifications of the guns.

A number of special accessories are also available for the black powder shooter. These include replica powder flasks, bullet moulds, cappers and tools, as well as more modern devices to facilitate black powder cleaning and maintenance. Ornate presentation cases and even detachable shoulder stocks are also available for some black powder pistols from their importers. Again, dealers or the importers will have catalogs.

The black powder guns are arranged in four sections: Single Shot Pistols, Revolvers, Muskets & Rifles, and Shotguns. The guns within each section are arranged roughly by date of the original, with the oldest first. Thus the 1847 Walker replica leads off the revolver section, and flintlocks precede percussion arms in the other sections.

BLACK POWDER SINGLE SHOT PISTOLS—FLINT & PERCUSSION

Scottish Black Watch

BLACK WATCH SCOTCH PISTOL
Caliber: 577 (.550" round ball).
Barrel: 7", smoothbore.
Weight: 1½ lbs. **Length:** 12" over-all.
Stock: Brass.
Sights: None.
Features: Faithful reproduction of this military flintlock. From Dixie.
Price: **$135.00**

Dixie Charleville

CHARLEVILLE FLINTLOCK PISTOL
Caliber: 69, (.680" round ball).
Barrel: 7½".
Weight: 48 oz. **Length:** 13½" over-all.
Stock: Walnut.
Sights: None.
Features: Brass frame, polished steel barrel, iron belt hook, brass buttcap and backstrap. Replica of original 1777 pistol. Imported by Dixie.
Price: **$135.00**

CVA TOWER PISTOL
Caliber: 45.
Barrel: 9", octagon at breech, tapering to round at muzzle. Rifled.
Weight: 36 oz. **Length:** 15¼" over-all.
Stock: Selected hardwood.
Sights: None.
Features: Color case-hardened and engraved lock plate; early-style brass trigger; brass trigger guard, nose cap, thimbles, grip cap; blued barrel and ramrod. Introduced 1981.
Price: Complete, percussion **$104.95**
Price: Kit form, percussion **$73.95**
Price: Kit form, flintlock **$83.95**

HARPER'S FERRY 1806 PISTOL
Caliber: 54.
Barrel: 10".
Weight: 40 oz. **Length:** 16" over-all.
Stock: Walnut.
Sights: Fixed.
Features: Case hardened lock, brass mounted browned bbl. Replica of the first U.S. Gov't.-made flintlock pistol. Imported by Navy Arms, Dixie.
Price: .... **$135.00 to $165.00**

Dixie Queen Anne

DIXIE QUEEN ANNE FLINTLOCK PISTOL
Caliber: 50.
Barrel: 7½", smoothbore.
Stock: Walnut.
Sights: None.
Features: Browned steel barrel, fluted brass trigger guard, brass mask on butt. Lockplate left in the white. Made by Pedersoli in Italy. Introduced 1983. Imported by Dixie Gun Works.
Price: **$99.95**

Dixie Pennsylvania Pistol

Lyman Plains Pistol

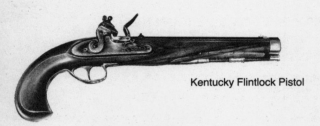

Kentucky Flintlock Pistol

Kentucky Percussion Pistol
Similar to flint version but percussion lock. Imported by The Armoury, Navy Arms, F.I.E., CVA, Armsport, Sile, Hopkins & Allen, Toledo Armas.
Price: About $120.00
Price: Brass barrel (Navy Arms) $136.75
Price: In kit form . . . . $35.95 to $102.00
Price: Single cased set (Navy Arms) $208.00
Price: Double cased set (Navy Arms) $335.00
Price: Brass bbl. single cased set (Navy Arms) $225.00
Price: Brass bbl., double cased set (Navy Arms) $370.00

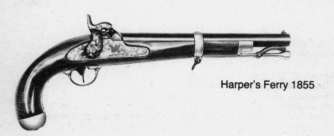

Harper's Ferry 1855

J & S Hawken Pistol

DIXIE PENNSYLVANIA PISTOL
Caliber: 44 (.430″ round ball).
Barrel: 10″ (⅞″ octagon).
Weight: 2½ lbs.
Stock: Walnut-stained hardwood.
Sights: Blade front, open rear drift-adj. for windage; brass.
Features: Available in flint or percussion. Brass trigger guard, thimbles, nose-cap, wedgeplates; high-lustre blue barrel. Imported from Italy by Dixie Gun Works.
Price: Flint, finished $119.95
Price: Percussion, finished $105.00
Price: Flint, kit $85.00
Price: Percussion, kit $72.50

LYMAN PLAINS PISTOL
Caliber: 50 or 54.
Barrel: 8″, 1-in-30″ twist, both calibers.
Weight: 50 oz. **Length:** 15″ over-all.
Stock: Walnut half-stock.
Sights: Blade front, square notch rear adj. for windage.
Features: Polished brass trigger guard and ramrod tip, color case-hardened coil spring lock, spring-loaded trigger, stainless steel nipple, blackened iron furniture. Hooked patent breech, detachable belt hook. Introduced 1981. From Lyman Products.
Price: Finished $129.95
Price: Kit $99.95

KENTUCKY FLINTLOCK PISTOL
Caliber: 44, 45.
Barrel: 10⅛″.
Weight: 32 oz. **Length:** 15½″ over-all.
Stock: Walnut.
Sights: Fixed.
Features: Specifications, including caliber, weight and length may vary with importer. Case hardened lock, blued bbl.; available also as brass bbl. flint Model 1821 ($136.75, Navy). Imported by Navy Arms, The Armoury, CVA (kit only), Hopkins & Allen, Sile.
Price: . . . . $40.95 to $142.00
Price: In kit form, from . . . . $90.00 to $112.00
Price: Brass barrel (Navy Arms) $153.00
Price: Single cased set (Navy Arms) $225.00
Price: Double cased set (Navy Arms) $370.00
Price: Brass bbl., single cased set (Navy Arms) $240.00
Price: Brass bbl., double cased set (Navy Arms) $400.00

CVA COLONIAL PISTOL
Caliber: 45.
Barrel: 6¾″, octagonal, rifled.
Length: 12¾″ over-all.
Stocks: Selected hardwood.
Features: Case hardened lock, brass furniture, fixed sights. Steel ramrod. Available in either flint or percussion. Imported by CVA.
Price: Percussion $73.95
Also available in kit form, either flint or percussion. Stock 95% inletted.
Price: Flint $62.95
Price: Percussion $49.95

HARPER'S FERRY MODEL 1855 PERCUSSION PISTOL
Caliber: 58.
Barrel: 11¾″, rifled.
Weight: 56 oz. **Length:** 18″ over-all.
Stock: Walnut.
Sights: Fixed.
Features: Case hardened lock and hammer; brass furniture; blued bbl. Shoulder stock available, priced at $35.00. Imported by Navy Arms and Dixie.
Price: $218.50
Price: From Dixie $135.00
Price: With detachable shoulder stock $263.50

J&S HAWKEN PERCUSSION PISTOL
Caliber: 50, uses 50-cal. mini; 54, uses 54-cal. mini.
Barrel: 9″.
Weight: 41 oz. **Length:** 14″ over-all.
Stock: European walnut with checkered grip.
Sights: Fixed.
Features: Blued steel barrel with swivel-type rammer, three-quarter stocked, adj. single set trigger, German silver furniture, scroll engraved lock. From Navy Arms.
Price: Finished, either cal. $200.00

CAUTION: PRICES CHANGE. CHECK AT GUNSHOP.

BLACK POWDER SINGLE SHOT PISTOLS—FLINT & PERCUSSION

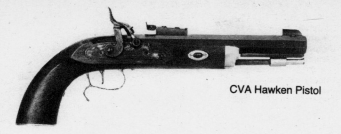

CVA Hawken Pistol

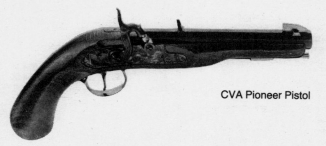

CVA Pioneer Pistol

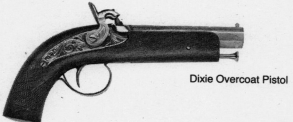

Dixie Overcoat Pistol

CVA HAWKEN PISTOL
Caliber: 50.
Barrel: 9¾", octagonal, 1" flats; rifled.
Weight: 50 oz. **Length:** 16½" over-all.
Stock: Select walnut.
Sights: Beaded blade front, fully adjustable rear.
Features: Hooked breech, early-style brass trigger. Color case-hardened lock plate; brass wedge plate, nose cap, ramrod thimbles, trigger guard, grip cap; blue barrel and sights.
Price: Finished, percussion **$111.95**
Price: Finished, flintlock **$121.95**
Price: Kit, percussion **$73.95**
Price: Kit, flintlock **$83.95**

CVA PIONEER PERCUSSION PISTOL
Caliber: 32.
Barrel: 7½" octagonal, ⅞" across flats.
Weight: 14 oz. **Length:** 13" over-all.
Stock: Hardwood.
Sights: Dovetailed brass blade front, fixed open rear.
Features: Color case-hardened and engraved lock plate, screw-adjustable sear engagement, V-type mainspring, brass trigger guard, thimble and ramrod tip, rest blued. Introduced 1984.
Price: Finished **$69.95**
Price: Kit **$59.95**

DIXIE OVERCOAT PISTOL
Caliber: 39.
Barrel: 4", smoothbore.
Weight: 13 oz. **Length:** 8" over-all.
Stock: Walnut-finished hardwood. Checkered p.g.
Sights: Bead front.
Features: Shoots .380" balls. Breech plug and engraved lock are burnished steel finish; barrel and trigger guard blued.
Price: Engraved model **$34.50**

BRITISH DRAGOON FLINT PISTOL
Caliber: .615".
Barrel: 12", polished steel.
Weight: 3 lbs., 2 oz. **Length:** 19" over-all.
Stock: Walnut, with brass furniture.
Features: Lockplate marked "Willets 1761." Brass trigger guard and butt cap. Made in U.S. by Navy Arms.
Price: **$475.00**
Price: Kit **$295.00**

PHILADELPHIA DERRINGER PERCUSSION PISTOL
Caliber: 45.
Barrel: 3⅛".
Weight: 14 oz. **Length:** 7" over-all.
Stock: Walnut, checkered grip.
Sights: Fixed.
Features: Engraved wedge holder and bbl. Also available in flintlock version (Armoury, $29.95). Imported by Sile (45-cal. only), CVA (45-cal. only), Navy Arms, Toledo Armas.
Price: .... **$18.37 to $131.00**
Price: Kit form (CVA, Navy Arms) **$98.50**

CVA MOUNTAIN PISTOL
Caliber: 45 or 50 cal.
Barrel: 9", octagon. 15⁄16" across flats.
Weight: 40 oz. **Length:** 14" over-all.
Stock: Select hardwood.
Sights: German silver blade front, fixed primitive rear.
Features: Engraved color case-hardened lock. Adjustable sear engagement. Fly and bridle. Hooked breech. Browned steel on finished pistol. German silver wedge plates. Stainless steel nipples. Hardwood ramrod. Belt hook optional. Introduced 1978. From CVA.
Price: 50-cal. only in finished form **$131.95**
Price: Kit form, percussion **$115.95**
Price: Kit form, flintlock **$115.95**

DIXIE LINCOLN DERRINGER
Caliber: 41.
Barrel: 2", 8 lands, 8 grooves.
Weight: 7 oz. **Length:** 5½" over-all.
Stock: Walnut finish, checkered.
Sights: Fixed.
Features: Authentic copy of the "Lincoln Derringer." Shoots .400" patched ball. German silver furniture includes trigger guard with pineapple finial, wedge plates, nose, wrist, side and teardrop inlays. All furniture, lockplate, hammer, and breech plug engraved. Imported from Italy by Dixie Gun Works.
Price: With wooden case **$159.95**
Price: Kit (not engraved) **$59.95**

Dixie Philadelphia

DIXIE PHILADELPHIA DERRINGER
Caliber: 41.
Barrel: 3½", octagon.
Weight: 8 oz. **Length:** 5½" over-all.
Stock: Walnut, checkered p.g.
Sights: Fixed.
Features: Barrel and lock are blued; brass furniture. From Dixie Gun Works.
Price: **$45.00**

BLACK POWDER SINGLE SHOT PISTOLS—FLINT & PERCUSSION

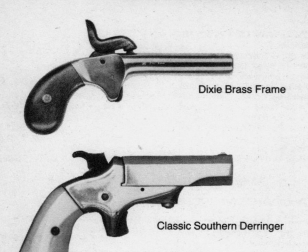

Dixie Brass Frame

Classic Southern Derringer

T.G.A. LIEGE DERRINGER
Caliber: .451″.
Barrel: 2⅜″.
Weight: 7 oz. **Length:** 6½″ over-all.
Stock: Walnut.
Sights: None.
Features: Removable round, rifled barrel. All metal parts case-hardened. Folding trigger. Introduced 1980. From Trail Guns Armory.
Price: Deluxe engraved model with case and flask $99.00

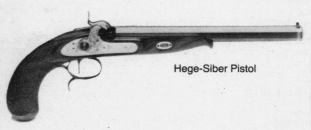

Dixie Screw Barrel

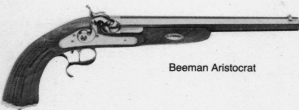

Hege-Siber Pistol

Beeman Aristocrat

Moore & Patrick Flint

DIXIE BRASS FRAME DERRINGER
Caliber: 41.
Barrel: 2½″.
Weight: 7 oz. **Length:** 5½″ over-all.
Stocks: Walnut.
Features: Brass frame, color case hardened hammer and trigger. Shoots .395″ round ball. Engraved model available. From Dixie Gun Works.
Price: Plain model $49.95
Price: Engraved model $59.95
Price: Kit form, plain model $37.50

CLASSIC ARMS SOUTHERN DERRINGER
Caliber: 44.
Barrel: 2½″.
Weight: 12 oz. **Length:** 5″ over-all.
Stock: White plastic.
Sights: Blade front.
Features: Percussion, uses .440″ round ball. Brass frame, steel barrel. Introduced 1982. Made in U.S. by Classic Arms Ltd.
Price: $84.95
Price: Kit $54.00

DIXIE ABILENE DERRINGER
Caliber: 41.
Barrel: 2½″, 6-groove rifling.
Weight: 8 oz. **Length:** 6½″ over-all.
Stocks: Walnut.
Features: All steel version of Dixie's brass-framed derringers. Blued barrel, color case hardened frame and hammer. Shoots .395″ patched ball. Comes with wood presentation case.
Price: $54.95
Price: Kit form $45.00

DIXIE SCREW BARREL PISTOL
Caliber: .445″.
Barrel: 2½″.
Weight: 8 oz. **Length:** 6½″ over-all.
Stocks: Walnut.
Features: Trigger folds down when hammer is cocked. Close copy of the originals once made in Belgium. Uses No. 11 percussion caps.
Price: $79.95

HEGE-SIBER PISTOL
Caliber: 33, 44.
Barrel: 10″.
Weight: 34 oz. **Length:** 15½″ over-all.
Stock: French walnut, cut-checkered grip.
Sights: Barleycorn front, micro adjustable rear.
Features: Reproduction of pistol made by Swiss watchmaker Jean Siber in the 1800s. Precise lock and set trigger give fast lock time. French Deluxe version (illus.) is engraved, has gold trim on blued barrel; English/British version has less ornate engraving, plum browned barrel, trigger guard. Imported by Beeman, 33-cal. only, Navy Arms, 33, 44 cals. Introduced 1984.
Price: French (Beeman) $1,495.00
Price: French, matched pair (Beeman). $2,750.00
Price: English (Beeman). $795.00
Price: French (Navy Arms) $1,120.00
Price: British (Navy Arms, ... $735.00
Price: French, matched pair (Navy Arms) $2,260.00

BEEMAN PB "ARISTOCRAT" PISTOL
Caliber: 36 or 44.
Barrel: 9″.
Weight: 38 oz. **Length:** 15¼″ over-all.
Stock: Select walnut with grooved grip.
Sights: Fixed post front.
Features: Set trigger; grip cap; plum brown barrel. Imported by Beeman. Introduced 1984.
Price: $360.00

MOORE & PATRICK FLINT DUELING PISTOL
Caliber: 45.
Barrel: 10″, rifled.
Weight: 32 oz. **Length:** 14½″ over-all.
Stock: European walnut, checkered.
Sights: Fixed.
Features: Engraved, silvered lock plate, blue barrel. German silver furniture. Imported from Italy by Dixie and Navy Arms.
Price: . . . . $200.00 to $225.00

CAUTION: PRICES CHANGE. CHECK AT GUNSHOP.

Le Page Dueling Pistol

F. Rochatte Pistol

John Manton Pistol

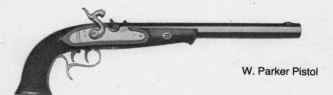

W. Parker Pistol

NAVY ARMS LE PAGE DUELING PISTOL
Caliber: 44.
Barrel: 9″, octagon.
Weight: 34 oz. **Length:** 15″ over-all.
Stock: European walnut.
Sights: Adjustable rear.
Features: Single set trigger. Silvered metal finish. From Navy Arms.
Price: **$275.00**
Price: Single cased set **$440.00**
Price: Double cased set **$725.00**

F. ROCHATTE PERCUSSION PISTOL
Caliber: 45, uses .440″ round ball.
Barrel: 10″.
Weight: 32 oz. **Length:** 16½″ over-all.
Stock: European walnut.
Sights: Dovetailed front and rear, adj. for windage.
Features: Single adj. trigger, highly polished lock and round barrel with top flat; all steel furniture. French-style finial on butt. From Navy Arms.
Price: Finished gun **$250.00**

JOHN MANTON MATCH PISTOL
Caliber: 45, uses .440″ round ball.
Barrel: 10″, rifled.
Weight: 36 oz. **Length:** 15½″ over-all.
Stock: European walnut; checkered grip.
Sights: Bead front.
Features: Highly polished steel barrel and lock, brass furniture. From Navy Arms.
Price: Finished gun **$225.00**

W. PARKER PERCUSSION PISTOL
Caliber: 45, uses .440″ round ball.
Barrel: 10″, rifled.
Weight: 40 oz. **Length:** 16″ over-all.
Stock: European walnut; checkered grip.
Sights: Dovetailed front and rear, adj. for windage.
Features: Fully adj. double set triggers, German silver furniture; lock engraved "London." From Navy Arms.
Price: Finished gun **$250.00**
Price: As above from Dixie, 11″ bbl. **$250.00**

H & A ENGLISH FLINTLOCK TARGET PISTOL
Caliber: 45.
Barrel: 10″.
Weight: 2 lbs. 4 oz. **Length:** 15″ over-all.
Stock: English walnut with checkered grip.
Sights: Fixed.
Features: Engraved lock in white, browned barrel, German silver furniture. Special roller bearing frizzen spring. Also available in percussion lock. From Hopkins & Allen.
Price: **$254.30**

H&A 1810 ENGLISH DUELING PISTOL
Caliber: 45.
Barrel: 11″.
Weight: 2 lbs., 5 oz. **Length:** 15″ over-all.
Stock: European walnut, checkered, with German silver inlays.
Sights: Fixed.
Features: Double set triggers, precision "match" barrel, silver plated furniture, browned barrel. Percussion lock only. From Hopkins & Allen.
Price: **$265.30**

H & A Target Boot

HOPKINS & ALLEN BOOT PISTOL
Caliber: 36 or 45.
Barrel: 6″.
Weight: 42 oz. **Length:** 13″ over-all.
Stock: Walnut.
Sights: Silver blade front; rear adj. for e.
Features: Under-hammer design. From Hopkins & Allen.
Price: **$71.50**
Price: Kit form **$55.20**
Price: Target version with wood fore-end, ramrod, hood front sight, elevator rear **$89.80**

CLASSIC ARMS ELGIN CUTLASS PISTOL
Caliber: 44 (.440″).
Barrel: 4¼″.
Weight: 21 oz. **Length:** 12″ over-all.
Stock: Walnut.
Sights: None.
Features: Replica of the pistol used by the U.S. Navy as a boarding weapon. Smoothbore barrel. Available as a kit or finished. Made in U.S. by Navy Arms.
Price: Kit **$78.50**
Price: Finished **$104.95**

Elgin Cutlass Pistol

Thompson/Center Patriot

THOMPSON/CENTER PATRIOT PERCUSSION PISTOL
Caliber: 36, 45.
Barrel: 9¼".
Weight: 36 oz. **Length:** 16" over-all.
Stock: Walnut.
Sights: Patridge-type. Rear adj. for w. and e.
Features: Hook breech system; double set triggers; coil mainspring. From Thompson/Center Arms.
Price: $185.00

Dixie Tornado Target

DIXIE TORNADO TARGET PISTOL
Caliber: 44 (.430" round ball).
Barrel: 10", octagonal, 1-in-22" twist.
Stock: Walnut, target-style. Left unfinished for custom fitting. Walnut fore-end.
Sights: Blade on ramp front, micro-type open rear adjustable for windage and elevation.
Features: Grip frame style of 1860 Colt revolver. Improved model of the Tingle and B.W. Southgate pistol. Trigger adjustable for pull. Frame, barrel, hammer and sights in the white, brass trigger guard. Comes with solid brass, walnut-handled cleaning rod with jag and nylon muzzle protector. Introduced 1983. From Dixie Gun Works.
Price: $145.00

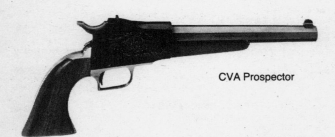

CVA Prospector

CVA PROSPECTOR SINGLE SHOT PERCUSSION PISTOL
Caliber: 44.
Barrel: 8½", octagonal.
Weight: 42 oz. **Length:** 12¾" over-all.
Stocks: One-piece walnut.
Sights: Blade front, hammer notch rear.
Features: Brass backstrap and trigger guard, rest blued. Frame engraved with two different scenes. Introduced 1984.
Price: Finished $81.95
Price: Kit $62.95

BLACK POWDER REVOLVERS

WALKER 1847 PERCUSSION REVOLVER
Caliber: 44, 6-shot.
Barrel: 9".
Weight: 72 oz. **Length:** 15½" over-all.
Stocks: Walnut.
Sights: Fixed.
Features: Case hardened frame, loading lever and hammer; iron backstrap; brass trigger guard; engraved cylinder. Imported by Sile, Navy Arms, Dixie, Armsport, Allen Fire Arms.
Price: . . . . $125.00 to $249.00
Price: Single cased set (Navy Arms) $264.00

Walker 1847

Allen 1st Dragoon

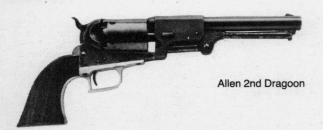

Allen 2nd Dragoon

ALLEN 1st MODEL DRAGOON
Caliber: 44.
Barrel: 7½", part round, part octagon.
Weight: 66 oz.
Stocks: One piece walnut.
Sights: German silver blade front, hammer notch rear.
Features: First model has oval bolt cuts in cylinder, square-back flared trigger guard, V-type mainspring, short trigger. Ranger and Indian scene on cylinder. Color cased frame, loading lever, plunger and hammer; blue barrel, cylinder, trigger and wedge. Polished brass backstrap and trigger guard. From Allen Fire Arms.
Price: $229.00

Allen 2nd Model Dragoon Revolver
Similar to the 1st Model except this model is distinguished by its rectangular bolt cuts in the cylinder, straight square-back trigger guard, short trigger and flat mainspring with roller in hammer.
Price: $229.00

CAUTION: PRICES CHANGE. CHECK AT GUNSHOP.

BLACK POWDER REVOLVERS

Dixie Third Dragoon

DIXIE THIRD MODEL DRAGOON
Caliber: 44 (.454″ round ball).
Barrel: 7⅜″.
Weight: 4 lbs., 2½ oz.
Stocks: One-piece walnut.
Sights: Brass pin front, hammer notch rear, or adjustable folding leaf rear.
Features: Cylinder engraved with Indian fight scene; steel backstrap with polished brass backstrap; color case-hardened steel frame, blue-black barrel. Imported by Dixie Gun Works.
Price: **$140.00**

Allen 3rd Model Dragoon Revolver
Similar to the 1st Model except has oval trigger guard, long trigger, flat mainspring and rectangular bolt cuts.
Price: **$225.00**
Price: With silver plated guard and backstrap or as Confederate Tucker & Sherrard **$239.00**

ALLEN BABY DRAGOON REVOLVER
Caliber: 31.
Barrel: 3″, 4″, 5″; 7 groove, RH twist.
Weight: About 21 oz.
Stocks: Varnished walnut.
Sights: Brass pin front, hammer notch rear.
Features: Unfluted cylinder with Ranger and Indian scene; cupped cylinder pin; no grease grooves; one safety pin on cylinder and slot in hammer face; straight (flat) mainspring. Silver backstrap and trigger guard. From Allen Fire Arms.
Price: **$199.00**

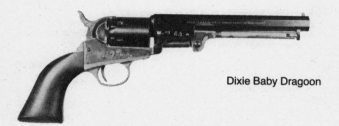

Dixie Baby Dragoon

BABY DRAGOON 1848 PERCUSSION REVOLVER
Caliber: 31, 5-shot.
Barrel: 4″, 5″, 6″.
Weight: 24 oz. (6″ bbl.). **Length:** 10½″ (6″ bbl.).
Stocks: Walnut.
Sights: Fixed.
Features: Case hardened frame; safety notches on hammer and safety pin in cylinder; engraved cylinder scene; octagonal bbl. Imported by Dixie (5″ only), Allen.
Price: About **$199.00**

Allen London 1851

ALLEN LONDON MODEL 1851 NAVY REVOLVER
Caliber: 36.
Barrel: 7½″, octagonal, 7 groove, LH twist.
Weight: 42 oz.
Stocks: One-piece varnished walnut.
Sights: Brass pin front, hammer notch rear.
Features: Faithful reproduction of the original gun. Color cased frame, loading lever, plunger, hammer and latch. Blue cylinder, trigger, barrel, screws, wedge. Silver plated brass backstrap and square-back trigger guard. Accessories available. From Allen Fire Arms.
Price: **$219.00**

Dixie 1851 Navy

1851 Squareback Navy 36
Same as standard Colt model except 36 cal. only, has earlier square-back trigger guard, nickel plated backstrap, color case hardened frame. From Lyman, Euroarms, Allen.
Price: **$209.00**
Price: Kit form **$119.95**
Price: Stainless steel (Allen) **$239.00**

1851 NAVY-SHERIFF
Same as 1851 Sheriff model except: 4″ barrel, fluted cylinder, belt ring in butt. Imported by Sile, Euroarms of America.
Price: .... **$50.00 to $114.95**

Allen 1861 Navy Percussion Revolver
Similar to 1851 Navy except has round 7½″ barrel, rounded trigger guard, German silver blade front sight, "creeping" loading lever.
Price: **$215.00**

ARMY 1851 PERCUSSION REVOLVER
Caliber: 44, 6-shot.
Barrel: 7½″.
Weight: 45 oz. **Length:** 13″ over-all.
Stocks: Walnut finish.
Sights: Fixed.
Features: 44 caliber version of the 1851 Navy. Imported by Sile, The Armoury.
Price: .... **$33.50 to $138.00**

NAVY MODEL 1851 PERCUSSION REVOLVER
Caliber: 36 or 44, 6-shot.
Barrel: 7½″.
Weight: 44 oz. **Length:** 13″ over-all.
Stocks: Walnut finish.
Sights: Post front, hammer notch rear.
Features: Brass backstrap and trigger guard; some have engraved cylinder with navy battle scene; case hardened frame, hammer, loading lever. Imported by Shore, (36 cal. only) The Armoury, Navy Arms, Allen, Dixie, (illus.) Euroarms of America, Sile, Armsport, Hopkins & Allen, CVA.
Price: Brass frame .... **$31.50 to $209.00**
Price: Steel frame .... **$40.95 to $140.95**
Price: Kit form .... **$30.95 to $93.00**
Price: Engraved model (Dixie) **$97.50**
Price: Also as "Hartford Pistol," Kit (Richard) ...... $59.95 Complete **$79.95**
Price: Also as "Hartford Dragoon Buntline" (Hopkins & Allen) **$166.95**
Price: Navy-Civilian model (Navy Arms) **$124.50**
Price: Single cased set, steel frame (Navy Arms) **$207.00**
Price: Double cased set, steel frame (Navy Arms) **$339.75**
Price: As above, civilian model (Navy Arms) **$212.00**
Price: Double cased set, civilian model (Navy Arms) **$350.00**
Price: Shoulder stock (Navy Arms) **$45.00**

CAUTION: PRICES CHANGE. CHECK AT GUNSHOP.

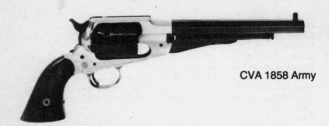

CVA 1858 Army

1851 SHERIFF MODEL PERCUSSION REVOLVER

Caliber: 36, 44, 6-shot.
Barrel: 5".
Weight: 40 oz. **Length:** 10½" over-all.
Stocks: Walnut.
Sights: Fixed.
Features: Brass backstrap and trigger guard; engraved navy scene; case hardened frame, hammer, loading lever. Available with brass frame from some importers at slightly lower prices. Imported by Allen, Sile, The Armoury.
Price: Steel frame . . . . **$41.95 to $110.00**
Price: Brass frame . . . . **$34.95 to $209.00**
Price: Kit, brass or steel frame (Sile) **$66.15**

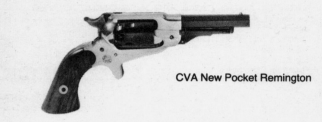

CVA New Pocket Remington

Dixie 1860 Army

CVA 1860 ARMY REVOLVER

Caliber: 44, 6-shot.
Barrel: 8" round.
Weight: 44 oz. **Length:** 13½" over-all.
Stocks: One-piece walnut.
Sights: Blade front, hammer-notch rear.
Features: Engraved cylinder, creeping-style loading lever, solid brass trigger guard, blued barrel. Introduced 1982. From CVA.
Price: Finished **$157.95**
Price: Kit **$121.95**

1861 NAVY MODEL REVOLVER

Caliber: 36, 44, 6-shot.
Barrel: 7½".
Weight: 2½ lbs. **Length:** 13" over-all.
Stocks: One piece smooth walnut.
Sights: Blade front, hammer notch rear.
Features: Shoots .380" ball. Case hardened frame, loading lever and hammer. Cut for shoulder stock. Non-fluted cylinder. From CVA (brass frame, 44-cal.), Navy Arms, Armsport, Euroarms of America, Allen.
Price: . . . . **$100.00 to $215.00**
Price: Blued steel backstrap, trigger guard (Navy Arms) **$142.00**
Price: With full fluted cyl. . . . . **$100.00 to $142.00**
Price: Single cased set (Navy Arms) **$230.00**
Price: Double cased set (Navy Arms) **$386.50**
Price: Kit form (CVA), steel frame **$114.95**
Price: Finished, 36 cal., steel frame (CVA) **$155.95**
Price: 44 cal. (CVA), brass frame **$99.95**
Price: 44 cal. kit (CVA), brass frame **$79.95**
Price: Stainless steel (Allen) **$245.00**

NEW MODEL 1858 ARMY PERCUSSION REVOLVER

Caliber: 36 or 44, 6-shot.
Barrel: 6½" or 8".
Weight: 40 oz. **Length:** 13½" over-all.
Stocks: Walnut.
Sights: Blade front, groove-in-frame rear.
Features: Replica of Remington Model 1858. Also available from some importers as Army Model Belt Revolver in 36 cal., shortened and lightened version of the 44. Target Model (Iver Johnson, Navy) has fully adj. target rear sight, target front, 36 or 44 ($74.95-$209.00). Imported by CVA, (as 1858 Remington Army), Dixie, Navy Arms, Hopkins & Allen, Iver Johnson, The Armoury, Shore (44 cal., 8" bbl. only), Euroarms of America (engraved, stainless and plain), Armsport, Sile, Allen.
Price: . . . . **$49.95 to $215.00**
Price: Single cased set (Navy Arms) **$225.00**
Price: Double cased set (Navy Arms) **$375.00**
Price: Kit form . . . . **$66.95 to $123.95**
Price: Nickel finish (Navy Arms) **$152.75**
Price: Single cased set (Navy Arms) **$240.00**
Price: Double cased set (Navy Arms) **$400.00**
Price: Stainless steel (Euroarms, Navy Arms, Sile, Allen) **$140.00 to $259.00**
Price: Target model (Sile, Euroarms, Navy Arms, Allen) . . **$95.95 to $185.00**

CVA Brass Frame 1858 Remington Army

Similar to the New Model 1858 Army except in 44 caliber only, 8" barrel, brass frame with blued trigger, cylinder, trigger guard, and barrel, color case-hardened hammer. Weighs 38 oz., 13" over-all. Introduced 1984.
Price: Finished **$119.95**
Price: Kit **$99.95**

CVA NEW MODEL POCKET REMINGTON

Caliber: 31.
Barrel: 4", octagonal.
Weight: 15½ oz. **Length:** 7½" over-all.
Stocks: Two-piece walnut.
Sights: Post front, grooved top-strap rear.
Features: Spur trigger, brass frame with blued barrel and cylinder. Available finished or in kit form. Introduced 1984.
Price: Finished **$80.95**
Price: Kit **$66.95**

1860 ARMY PERCUSSION REVOLVER

Caliber: 44, 6-shot.
Barrel: 8".
Weight: 40 oz. **Length:** 13⅝" over-all.
Stocks: Walnut.
Sights: Fixed.
Features: Engraved navy scene on cylinder; brass trigger guard; case hardened frame, loading lever and hammer. Some importers supply pistol cut for detachable shoulder stock, have accessory stock available. Imported by Navy Arms, Shore, The Armoury, Dixie (half-fluted cylinder, not roll engraved), Iver Johnson, Euroarms of America (engraved, stainless steel or burnished steel model), Armsport, Sile, Hopkins & Allen, Allen.
Price: . . . . **$44.95 to $219.00**
Price: Single cased set (Navy Arms) **$220.00**
Price: Double cased set (Navy Arms) **$365.00**
Price: 1861 Navy: Same as Army except 36 cal., 7½" bbl., wt. 41 oz., cut for stock; round cylinder (fluted avail.), from Navy **$142.00**
Price: Single cased set (Navy Arms) **$230.00**
Price: Double cased set (Navy Arms) **$386.50**
Price: Kit (Sile) **$134.95**
Price: Stainless steel (Euroarms, Allen) . . . . **$200.00 to $245.00**
Price: Brass frame (Allen) **$125.00**

ROGERS & SPENCER PERCUSSION REVOLVER

Caliber: 44.
Barrel: 7½".
Weight: 47 oz. **Length:** 13¾" over-all.
Stocks: Walnut.
Sights: Cone front, integral groove in frame for rear.
Features: Accurate reproduction of a Civil War design. Solid frame; extra large nipple cut-out on rear of cylinder; loading lever and cylinder easily removed for cleaning. Comes with six spare nipples and wrench/screwdriver. From Euroarms of America (engraved, burnished, target models), Navy Arms, Dixie, Sile.
Price: . . . . **$120.00 to $169.00**
Price: Nickel plated **$120.00**
Price: Kit version **$95.00**
Price: Target version **$200.00**

CAUTION: PRICES CHANGE. CHECK AT GUNSHOP.

BLACK POWDER REVOLVERS

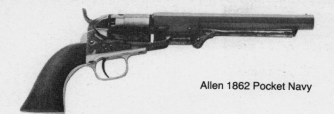

Allen 1862 Pocket Navy

NAVY ARMS 1862 LEECH & RIGDON REVOLVER
Caliber: .375".
Barrel: 7½".
Weight: 2 lbs., 10 oz. **Length:** 13½" over-all.
Stocks: Smooth walnut.
Sights: Fixed.
Features: Modern version of the famous Civil War revolver. Brass backstrap and trigger guard. Color case hardened frame. Copy of the Colt Navy but with round barrel. From Navy Arms.
Price: **$136.50**

Dixie Spiller & Burr

DIXIE "WYATT EARP" REVOLVER
Caliber: 44.
Barrel: 12" octagon.
Weight: 46 oz. **Length:** 18" over-all.
Stocks: Two piece walnut.
Sights: Fixed.
Features: Highly polished brass frame, backstrap and trigger guard; blued barrel and cylinder; case hardened hammer, trigger and loading lever. Navy-size shoulder stock ($45.00) will fit with minor fitting. From Dixie Gun Works.
Price: **$99.95**

Freedom Mini Percussion

Ruger Old Army

ALLEN 1862 POCKET NAVY PERCUSSION REVOLVER
Caliber: 36.
Barrel: 5½", octagonal, 7 groove, LH twist.
Weight: 27 oz.
Stocks: One piece varnished walnut.
Sights: Brass pin front, hammer notch rear.
Features: Rebated cylinder, hinged loading lever, silver plated backstrap and trigger guard, color cased frame, hammer, loading lever, plunger and latch, rest blued. Has original-type markings. From Allen Fire Arms.
Price: **$209.00**

1862 POCKET POLICE PERCUSSION REVOLVER
Caliber: 36, 5-shot.
Barrel: 5½", 7½".
Weight: 26 oz. **Length:** 12" (6½" bbl.).
Stocks: Walnut.
Sights: Fixed.
Features: Half-fluted and rebated cylinder; case hardened frame, loading lever and hammer; silver trigger guard and backstrap. Imported by Navy Arms (5½" only), Euroarms of America, Allen.
Price: .... **$198.00 to $209.00**
Price: Cased with accessories (Navy Arms) **$250.00**
Price: Stainless steel (Allen) **$235.00**

SPILLER & BURR REVOLVER
Caliber: 36 (.375" round ball).
Barrel: 7", octagon.
Weight: 2½ lbs. **Length:** 12½" over-all.
Stocks: Two-piece walnut.
Sights: Fixed.
Features: Reproduction of the C.S.A. revolver. Brass frame and trigger guard. Also available as a kit. From Dixie, Navy Arms.
Price: .... **$69.95 to $109.00**
Price: Kit form .... **$39.95 to $65.00**

FREEDOM ARMS PERCUSSION MINI REVOLVER
Caliber: 22, 5-shot.
Barrel: 1", 1¾", 3".
Weight: 4¾ oz. (1" bbl.).
Stocks: Simulated ebony, or rosewood (optional).
Sights: Fixed.
Features: Percussion version of the 22 RF gun. All stainless steel; spur trigger. Gun comes with leather carrying pouch, bullet setting tool, powder measure, 20 29-gr. bullets. Introduced 1983. From Freedom Arms.
Price: 1" barrel **$130.00**
Price: 1¾" barrel **$130.00**
Price: 3" barrel **$142.70**

GRISWOLD & GUNNISON PERCUSSION REVOLVER
Caliber: 36, 44, 6-shot.
Barrel: 7½".
Weight: 44 oz. (36 cal.). **Length:** 13" over-all.
Stocks: Walnut.
Sights: Fixed.
Features: Replica of famous Confederate pistol. Brass frame, backstrap and trigger guard; case hardened loading lever; rebated cylinder (44 cal. only). Imported by Navy Arms, Sile, Allen.
Price: **$169.00**
Price: As above from Sile (1851 Confederate) **$75.90**
Price: Kit (Navy Arms) **$76.75**
Price: Single cased set (Navy Arms) **$180.00**
Price: Double cased set (Navy Arms) **$288.00**
Price: Shoulder stock (Navy Arms) **$60.00**

RUGER 44 OLD ARMY PERCUSSION REVOLVER
Caliber: 44, 6-shot. Uses .457" dia. lead bullets.
Barrel: 7½" (6-groove, 16" twist).
Weight: 46 oz. **Length:** 13½" over-all.
Stocks: Smooth walnut.
Sights: Ramp front, rear adj. for w. and e.
Features: Stainless steel standard size nipples, chrome-moly steel cylinder and frame, same lockwork as in original Super Blackhawk. Also available in stainless steel in very limited quantities. Made in USA. From Sturm, Ruger & Co.
Price: Stainless steel (Model KBP-7) **$285.00**
Price: Blued steel (Model BP-7) **$216.50**

Dixie Brown Bess

DIXIE SECOND MODEL BROWN BESS
Caliber: 74.
Barrel: 41¾" smoothbore.
Weight: 9½ lbs. **Length:** 57¾".
Stock: Walnut-finished hardwood.
Sights: Fixed.
Features: All metal finished bright. Brass furniture. Lock marked "Tower" and has a crown with "GR" underneath. From Dixie Gun Works.
Price: $275.00
Price: Kit form $245.00

NAVY ARMS CHARLEVILLE MUSKET
Caliber: 69
Barrel: 44⅝".
Weight: 8¾ lbs. **Length:** 59⅜" over-all.
Stock: Walnut.
Sights: Blade front.
Features: Replica of Revolutionary War 1763 musket. Bright metal, walnut stock. From Navy Arms.
Price: Finished $400.00
Price: Kit $310.00

Navy Brown Bess

Weight: 9½ lbs. **Length:** 59" over-all.
Stock: Walnut.
Sights: Fixed.
Features: Polished barrel and lock with brass trigger guard and buttplate. Bayonet and scabbard available. From Navy Arms.
Price: Finished $450.00
Price: Kit $342.00
Price: Finished gun with maple stock $295.00

NAVY ARMS BROWN BESS MUSKET
Caliber: 75, uses .735" round ball.
Barrel: 42", smoothbore.

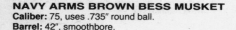

CVA Blunderbuss

Sights: None.
Features: Styled after 1700s British guns. Historically correct oval-shaped barrel. Engraved, color case hardened flintlock with screw-adjustable sear engagement and authentic V-type mainspring. Solid brass buttplate, ramrod thimbles, trigger, trigger guard, barrel and engraved sideplate. Introduced 1984.
Price: Finished $249.95
Price: Kit $209.95

CVA BLUNDERBUSS
Caliber: 69.
Barrel: 16", brass, tapered to flared muzzle.
Weight: 5 lbs., 5 oz. **Length:** 31½ oz.
Stock: Hardwood.

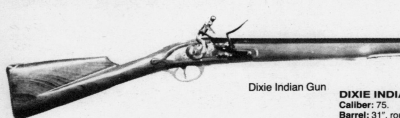

Dixie Indian Gun

DIXIE INDIAN GUN
Caliber: 75.
Barrel: 31", round tapered.
Weight: About 9 lbs. **Length:** 47" over-all.
Stock: Hardwood.
Sights: Blade front.
Features: Modified Brown Bess musket; brass furniture, browned lock and barrel. Lock is marked "GRICE 1762" with crown over "GR." Serpent-style sideplate. Introduced 1983.
Price: Complete $375.00
Price: As above, in kit form $360.00

CVA MOUNTAIN RIFLE
Caliber: 50.
Barrel: 32", octagon; ¹⁵⁄₁₆" across flats; 1-66" twist.
Weight: 7 lbs., 14 oz. **Length:** 48" over-all.
Stock: Select hardwood with cheekpiece.
Sights: German silver blade front, screw-adj. rear.
Features: Available in percussion or flintlock. Engraved lock with adj. sear engagement; hooked breech with two barrel tenons; rifled 1-in-66"; double set triggers; German silver patch box, tenon plates, pewter-type nosecap; browned iron furniture. From CVA.
Price: Kit, percussion $189.95
Price: Kit, flintlock $199.95
Price: Finished rifle, percussion $299.95
Price: Finished rifle, flintlock $299.95

CVA Big Bore Mountain Rifle
Similar to the standard Mountain Rifle except comes in 54 or 58 cal. only. Barrel flats measure 1" across. Stock does not have a patch box. Introduced 1980.
Price: 54 cal., percussion, complete rifle $309.95
Price: 54 cal., percussion, kit $220.95
Price: 58 cal. percussion, 1-72" twist, kit only $220.95

CAUTION: PRICES CHANGE. CHECK AT GUNSHOP.

BLACK POWDER MUSKETS & RIFLES

CVA Squirrel Rifle

CVA SQUIRREL RIFLE
Caliber: 32.
Barrel: 25″, octagonal; 11/16″ flats.
Weight: 5 lbs., 12 oz. **Length:** 40¾″ over-all.
Stock: Hardwood.
Sights: Beaded blade front, fully adjustable hunting-style rear.
Features: Available in right or left-hand versions. Color case-hardened lock plate, brass buttplate, trigger guard, wedge plates, thimbles; double-set triggers; hooked breech; authentic V-type mainspring. Introduced 1983. From CVA.
Price: Finished, percussion, right hand **$189.95**
Price: Finished, left hand **$199.95**
Price: Finished, flintlock **$199.95**
Price: Kit, percussion, right hand **$134.95**
Price: Kit, left hand **$144.95**
Price: Kit, flintlock **$144.95**

CVA KENTUCKY RIFLE
Caliber: 45 (.451″ bore).
Barrel: 33½″, rifled, octagon (⅞″ flats).
Length: 48″ over-all.
Stock: Select hardwood.
Sights: Brass Kentucky blade type front, dovetail open rear.
Features: Available in either flint or percussion. Stainless steel nipple included. From CVA.
Price: Percussion **$184.95**
Price: Flint **$194.95**
Price: Percussion Kit **$109.95**
Price: Flint Kit **$117.95**

H&A Plainsman Rifle

HOPKINS & ALLEN PLAINSMAN RIFLE
Caliber: 45.
Barrel: 37″.
Weight: 7½ lbs. **Length:** 53″ over-all.
Stock: Walnut.
Sights: Blade front, rear adjustable for w. & e.
Features: Double set triggers, blued barrel has 13/16″ flats, solid brass barrel rib, engraved percussion lockplate. From Hopkins & Allen.
Price: **$292.60**

Lyman Great Plains

TRYON RIFLE
Caliber: 50, 54 cal.
Barrel: 34″, octagon; 1-63″ twist.
Weight: 9 lbs. **Length:** 49″ over-all.
Stock: European walnut with steel furniture.
Sights: Blade front, fixed rear.
Features: Reproduction of an American plains rifle with double set triggers and back-action lock. Imported from Italy by Trail Guns Armory and Dixie.
Price: Percussion only **$350.00**
Price: From Dixie Gun Works **$299.00**
Price: Kit (Dixie) **$249.00**

LYMAN GREAT PLAINS RIFLE
Caliber: 50 or 54 cal.
Barrel: 32″, 1-66″ twist.
Weight: 9 lbs.
Stock: Walnut.
Sights: Steel blade front, buckhorn rear adj. for w. & e. and fixed notch primitive sight included.
Features: Blued steel furniture. Stainless steel nipple. Coil spring lock, Hawken-style trigger guard and double set triggers. Round thimbles recessed and sweated into rib. Steel wedge plates and toe plate. Introduced 1980. From Lyman.
Price: Percussion **$284.95**
Price: Flintlock **$294.95**
Price: Percussion Kit **$199.95**

Dixie Tennessee Rifle

PENNSYLVANIA HALF-STOCK PLAINS RIFLE
Caliber: 45 or 50.
Barrel: 32″ rifled, 15/16″ dia.
Weight: 8½ lbs.
Stock: Walnut.
Sights: Fixed.
Features: Available in flint or percussion. Blued lock and barrel, brass furniture. Offered complete or in kit form. From The Armoury.
Price: Flint **$235.00**
Price: Percussion **$210.00**

DIXIE TENNESSEE MOUNTAIN RIFLE
Caliber: 32 or 50.
Barrel: 41½″, 6-groove rifling, brown finish.
Length: 56″ over-all.
Stock: Walnut, oil finish; Kentucky-style.
Sights: Silver blade front, open buckhorn rear.
Features: Re-creation of the original mountain rifles. Early Schultz lock, interchangeable flint or percussion with vent plug or drum and nipple. Tumbler has fly. Double-set triggers. All metal parts browned. From Dixie.
Price: Flint or Percussion, finished rifle, 50 cal. **$250.00**
Price: Kit, 50 cal. **$195.00**
Price: Left-hand model, flint or perc. **$250.00**
Price: Left-hand kit, flint or perc., 50 cal. **$225.00**
Price: Squirrel Rifle (as above except in 32 cal. with 13/16″ barrel), flint or percussion **$295.00**
Price: Kit, 32 cal., flint or percussion **$255.00**

CAUTION: PRICES CHANGE. CHECK AT GUNSHOP.

BLACK POWDER MUSKETS & RIFLES

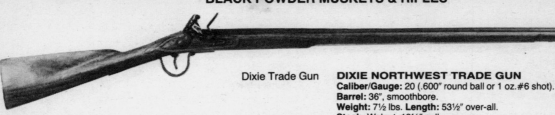

Dixie Trade Gun

DIXIE NORTHWEST TRADE GUN
Caliber/Gauge: 20 (.600″ round ball or 1 oz.#6 shot).
Barrel: 36″, smoothbore.
Weight: 7½ lbs. **Length:** 53½″ over-all.
Stock: Walnut, 13½″ pull.
Sights: Brass blade front only.
Features: Flintlock. Brass buttplate, serpentine sideplate; browned barrel, Wheeler flint lock, triggerguard; hickory ramrod with brass tip. From Dixie Gun Works.
Price: **$450.00**

ALAMO LONG RIFLE
Caliber: 38, 45, 50 cal.
Barrel: 35″.
Weight: 7½ lbs. **Length:** 51″ over-all.
Stock: European walnut.
Sights: Blade front, fixed rear.
Features: Double set trigger. Blued octagon barrel, bright lock, brass trigger guard, patch box, buttplate, thimbles. Has Alamo battle scene engraved on patch box. Imported from Italy by Trail Guns Armory.
Price: Percussion. **$265.00**
Price: Flintlock **$275.00**

Lyman Trade Rifle

Weight: 8¾ lbs. **Length:** 45″ over-all.
Stock: European walnut.
Sights: Blade front, open rear adj. for w. or optional fixed sights.
Features: Polished brass furniture with blue steel parts, stainless steel nipple. Hook breech, single trigger, coil spring percussion lock. Steel barrel rib and ramrod ferrules. Introduced 1979. From Lyman.
Price: Percussion. **$199.95**
Price: Kit, percussion **$149.95**
Price: Flintlock **$209.95**

LYMAN TRADE RIFLE
Caliber: 50 or 54.
Barrel: 28″ octagon, 1-48″ twist.

CVA Frontier

CVA FRONTIER RIFLE
Caliber: 45, 50.
Barrel: 28″, octagon; ${}^{15}/{}_{16}″$ flats, 1-66″ twist.
Weight: 6 lbs. 14 oz. **Length:** 44″ over-all.
Stock: American hardwood.
Sights: Brass blade front, fully adjustable hunting-style rear.
Features: Available in flint or percussion. Solid brass nosecap, trigger guard, buttplate, thimbles and wedge plates; blued barrel; color case-hardened lock and hammer. Double set triggers, patented breech plug bolster, V-type mainspring. Hooked breech. Introduced 1980.

Price: 50 cal., percussion, complete rifle **$204.95**
Price: Finished, left hand **$225.95**
Price: 50-Cal. flint, complete rifle **$214.95**
Price: 50 cal., percussion, kit **$149.95**
Price: Percussion kit, left hand **$167.95**
Price: 50 cal. flint, kit **$159.95**
Price: 45-cal. percussion kit **$157.95**

H&A Pa. Hawken

Weight: 7½ lbs. **Length:** 44″ over-all.
Stock: Walnut.
Sights: Blade front, open rear adjustable for windage.
Features: Single trigger, dual barrel wedges. Convertible ignition system. Brass patch box.
Price: With percussion lock **$199.50**
Price: Conversion kit (percussion to flint)....................... **$39.95**

HOPKINS & ALLEN PA. HAWKEN RIFLE
Caliber: 50.
Barrel: 29″.

KENTUCKY FLINTLOCK RIFLE
Caliber: 44 or 45.
Barrel: 35 ″.
Weight: 7lbs. **Length:** 50″ over-all.
Stock: Walnut stained, brass fittings.
Sights: Fixed.
Features: Available in Carbine model also, 28″ bbl. Some variations in detail, finish. Kits also available from some importers. Imported by Navy Arms, The Armoury, F.I.E., CVA, Armsport, Hopkins & Allen, Sile, Shore (45-cal. only).
Price: .... **$59.95 to $273.75**
Price: Kit form (CVA, Numrich, F.I.E., Sile) ...... **$72.95 to 189.95**
Price: Deluxe model, flint or percussion (Navy Arms, Sile), about ... **$400.00**
Price: As above, 50-cal. (Navy Arms) **$273.75**

Kentucky Percussion Rifle
Similar to flintlock except percussion lock. Finish and features vary with importer. Imported by Navy Arms, The Armoury, CVA, Hopkins & Allen, Armsport (rifle-shotgun combo), Shore, Sile.
Price: .... **$54.95 to 250.00**
Price: Kit form (Sile) **$169.95**
Price: Armsport combo **$295.00**
Price: Deluxe model (Navy Arms)............................. **$375.00**
Price: 50 cal. (Navy Arms) **$246.00**

CAUTION: PRICES CHANGE. CHECK AT GUNSHOP.

BLACK POWDER MUSKETS & RIFLES

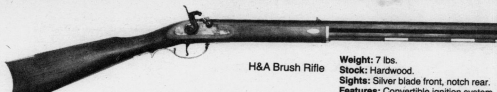

H&A Brush Rifle

HOPKINS & ALLEN BRUSH RIFLE
Caliber: 36 or 45.
Barrel: 25″, octagon, ¹⁵/₁₆″ flats.

Weight: 7 lbs.
Stock: Hardwood.
Sights: Silver blade front, notch rear.
Features: Convertible ignition system. Brass furniture. Introduced 1983.
Price: Percussion. **$189.00**
Price: Flint. **$200.10**
Price: Pre-assembled kit, percussion. **$129.00**
Price: As above, flint **$140.10**
Price: Kit, percussion. **$99.50**
Price: Kit, flint **$110.60**

H&A Heritage

HOPKINS & ALLEN BUGGY RIFLES
Caliber: 45.
Barrel: 20″, 25″ or 32″, octagonal.

Weight: 6½ lbs. **Length:** 37″ over-all.
Stock: American walnut.
Features: A short under-hammer rifle. Blued barrel and receiver, black plastic buttplate. All models available with straight or pistol grip stock.
Price: 45-cal. 20″ or 25″ bbl. **$208.47**
Price: Heritage, 36, 45, 50-cal. 32″ bbl. **$223.47**
Price: Deerstalker, 58-cal., 28″ bbl. **$239.30**
Price: Target, 45-cal., 32″ or 42″ bbl. **$229.60**

Kentuckian Rifle

KENTUCKIAN RIFLE & CARBINE
Caliber: 44.
Barrel: 35″ (Rifle), 27½″ (Carbine).

Weight: 7 lbs. (Rifle), 5½ lbs. (Carbine). **Length:** 51″ (Rifle) over-all, Carbine 43″.
Stock: Walnut stain.
Sights: Brass blade front, steel V-Ramp rear.
Features: Octagon bbl., case hardened and engraved lock plate. Brass furniture. Imported by Dixie.
Price: Rifle or carbine, flint **$185.00**
Price: As above, percussion **$175.00**

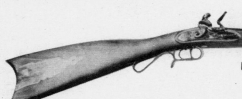

Dixie York County

YORK COUNTY RIFLE
Caliber: 45 (.445″ round ball).
Barrel: 36″, rifled, ⅞″ octagon, blue.

Weight: 7½ lbs. **Length:** 51½″ over-all.
Stock: Maple, one piece.
Sights: Blade front, V-notch rear, brass.
Features: Adjustable double-set triggers. Brass trigger guard, patchbox, buttplate, nosecap and sideplate. Case-hardened lockplate. From Dixie Gun Works.
Price: Percussion. **$210.00**
Price: Flint. **$215.00**
Price: Percussion Kit. **$149.00**
Price: Flint Kit **$160.00**

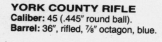

HATFIELD SQUIRREL RIFLE
Caliber: 32, 36, 45, 50.
Barrel: 39½″, octagon, 32″ on half-stock.
Weight: 8 lbs. (32 cal.).
Stock: American fancy maple fullstock.
Sights: Silver blade front, buckhorn rear
Features: Recreation of the traditional squirrel rifle. Available in flint or percussion with browned steel or brass trigger guard and buttplate. From Hatfield Rifle Works. Introduced 1983.
Price: Full-stock, flint. **$699.95**
Price: Full-stock, percussion **$599.95**
Price: Full-stock kit **$499.95**

Hatfield Squirrel Rifle

PECOS VALLEY HALF STOCK PENNSYLVANIA RIFLE
Caliber: 36, 45.
Barrel: 35½″; 1-in-48″ twist (36-cal.), 1-in-72″ twist (45-cal.).
Weight: About 6½ lbs. **Length:** 50½″ over-all.
Stock: Select grade maple with satin finish, 13½″ length of pull.
Sights: Silver blade, buckhorn rear.
Features: Durrs Egg percussion lock by L&R; Davis double set trigger; brass furniture. Made in U.S. by Pecos Valley Armory. Introduced 1984.
Price: **$399.00**

CAUTION: PRICES CHANGE. CHECK AT GUNSHOP.

CVA Pennsylvania

CVA PENNSYLVANIA LONG RIFLE
Caliber: 50.
Barrel: 40″, octagonal; ⅞″ flats.

Weight: 8 lbs., 3 ozs. **Length:** 55¾″ over-all.
Stock: Select walnut.
Sights: Brass blade front, fixed semi-buckhorn rear.
Features: Color case-hardened lock plate, brass buttplate, toe plate, patch-box, trigger guard, thimbles, nosecap; blued barrel, double-set triggers; authentic V-type mainspring. Introduced 1983. From CVA.
Price: Finished, percussion $289.95
Price: Finished, flintlock $299.95
Price: Kit, percussion $249.95
Price: Kit, flintlock $259.95

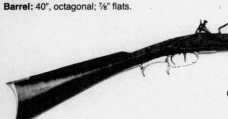

Ozark Taney County

OZARK MOUNTAIN TANEY COUNTY RIFLE
Caliber: 32, 36, 40.
Barrel: 36″.
Weight: 7½ lbs. **Length:** 53″ over-all.
Stock: American maple, fullstock design.
Sights: German silver blade front, full buckhorn rear.
Features: Available in flint or percussion, right or left hand; double set trigger.
Price: From $585.00

Ozark Mountain Muskrat Rifle
Same as the Taney County rifle except has maple half-stock. Available in right or left hand, flint or percussion.
Price: From $525.00

MOWREY ETHAN ALLEN SQUIRREL RIFLE
Caliber: 32, 36, or 45.
Barrel: 28″, 8-groove rifling, octagon, 1:60 twist.
Weight: 7½ lbs. **Length:** 43″ over-all.
Stock: Curly maple.
Sights: Open, fully adj.
Features: Box-lock action, cut-rifled barrel, hand-rubbed oil finish. Available with either brass or browned steel furniture, action. Made in U.S.
Price: Complete $328.00
Price: Kit $237.00

Mowrey Ethan Allen Plains Rifle
Similar to Squirrel Rifle except in 50 or 54 caliber, 32″ barrel, weighs 9½ lbs.
Price: Complete $328.00
Price: Kit $237.00

Thompson/Center Hawken

THOMPSON/CENTER HAWKEN RIFLE
Caliber: 45, 50 or 54.
Barrel: 28″ octagon, hooked breech.
Stock: American walnut.
Sights: Blade front, rear adj. for w. & e.
Features: Solid brass furniture, double set triggers, button rifled barrel, coil-type main spring. From Thompson/Center Arms.
Price: Percussion Model (45, 50 or 54 cal.) $270.00
Price: Flintlock model (45, 50, or 54 cal.) $282.50
Price: Percussion kit $195.00
Price: Flintlock kit $207.50

Thompson/Center Hawken Cougar
Similar to the standard T/C Hawken except stock is of highly figured walnut; all furniture—lock plate, hammer, triggers, trigger plate, trigger guard, fore-end cap, thimbles escutcheons, etc. are of stainless steel with matte finish. Replacing the patch box is a stainless steel medallion cast in deep relief depicting a crouching cougar. Internal parts, breech plug, tang, barrel, sights and under rib are ordnance steel. Barrel, sights and under rib are blued. Buttplate is solid brass, hard chromed to match the stainless parts. Limited production. Introduced 1982. From Thompson/Center Arms.
Price: $350.00

Thompson/Center Cherokee

THOMPSON/CENTER CHEROKEE RIFLE
Caliber: 32 or 45.
Barrel: 24″; 13/16″ across flats.
Weight: About 6 lbs.
Stock: American walnut. Same as Seneca except minus patch box, toe plate, fore-end cap.
Sights: Open hunting style; square notch rear fully adjustable for w. and e.
Features: Interchangeable barrels. Uses T/C Seneca breech, lock, triggers, sights and stock. Brass buttplate, trigger guard, fore-end escutcheons and lock plate screw bushing. Introduced 1984.
Price: 32 or 45 caliber $225.00
Price: Interchangeable 32 or 45-cal. barrel $105.00

> Consult our Directory pages for the location of firms mentioned.

CAUTION: PRICES CHANGE. CHECK AT GUNSHOP.

BLACK POWDER MUSKETS & RIFLES

T/C Renegade

THOMPSON/CENTER RENEGADE RIFLE
Caliber: 50 and 54 plus 56 cal., smoothbore.
Barrel: 26", 1" across the flats.
Weight: 8 lbs.
Stock: American walnut.
Sights: Open hunting (Patridge) style, fully adjustable for w. and e.
Features: Coil spring lock, double set triggers, blued steel trim.
Price: Percussion model... $225.00
Price: Flintlock model, 50 and 54 cal. only....................... $237.50
Price: Percussion kit... $175.00
Price: Flintlock kit.. $187.50

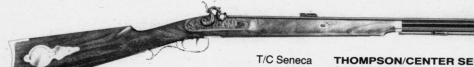

T/C Seneca

THOMPSON/CENTER SENECA RIFLE
Caliber: 36, 45.
Barrel: 27".
Weight: 6½ lbs.
Stock: American walnut.
Sights: Open hunting style, square notch rear fully adj. for w. and e.
Features: Coil spring lock, octagon bbl. measures ¹³/₁₆" across flats, brass stock furniture.
Price:... $270.00

Buffalo Hunter Rifle

BUFFALO HUNTER PERCUSSION RIFLE
Caliber: 58.
Barrel: 25½".
Weight: 8 lbs. **Length:** 41½" over-all.
Stock: Walnut finished, hand checkered, brass furniture.
Sights: Fixed.
Features: Designed for primitive weapons hunting. 20 ga. shotgun bbl. also available $90.00. Imported by Navy Arms, Dixie.
Price:.. $215.00 to $264.00

Ozark Hawken Rifle

OZARK MOUNTAIN HAWKEN RIFLE
Caliber: 50, 52, 54, 58.
Barrel: 34".
Weight: About 9½ lbs. **Length:** 50¼" over-all.
Stock: American maple; full and half-stock designs available.
Sights: Blade front, semi-buckhorn rear.
Features: Flint or percussion, right or left hand models (except in flintlock — right-hand only); browned steel furniture.
Price: From.. $675.00

Charles Daly Hawken

CHARLES DALY HAWKEN RIFLE
Caliber: 45, 50.
Barrel: 28" octagonal, ⅞" flats.
Weight: 7½ lbs. **Length:** 45½" over-all.
Stock: European hardwood.
Sights: Blade front, open fully adjustable rear.
Features: Color case-hardened lock uses coil springs; trigger guard, buttplate, fore-end cap, ferrules and ramrod fittings are polished brass. Left-hand model available in 50-cal. only. Imported by Outdoor Sports Headquarters. Introduced 1984.
Price: Right-hand, percussion.................................... $299.95
Price: Left-hand, percussion (50-cal. only)..................... $245.00
Price: Right-hand, flintlock..................................... $239.95
Price: Left-hand, flintlock (50-cal. only)...................... $278.95

BLACK POWDER MUSKETS & RIFLES

SILE HAWKEN HUNTER CARBINE
Caliber: 45, 50, 54.
Barrel: 22″, full octagon with hooked breech and hard chrome rifled or smooth bore.
Weight: 7 lbs. **Length:** 38″ over-all.
Stock: Walnut with checkered p.g. and fore-end, rubber recoil pad.
Sights: Blade front, fully adjustable open rear.
Features: Black oxidized brass hardware, engraved case hardened lock plate, sear fly and coil spring mechanism. Stainless steel nipple. Adjustable double set triggers. From Sile Dist.
Price: Percussion, rifle or carbine $261.00
Price: Flintlock $271.80

ARMOURY R140 HAWKIN RIFLE
Caliber: 45, 50 or 54.
Barrel: 29″.
Weight: 8¾ to 9 lbs. **Length:** 45¾″ over-all.
Stock: Walnut, with cheekpiece.
Sights: Dovetail front, fully adjustable rear.
Features: Octagon barrel, removable breech plug; double set triggers; blued barrel, brass stock fittings, color case hardened percussion lock. From Armsport, The Armoury, Sile (hard chrome bore).
Price: .... $175.00 to $282.00
Price: Kit .... $205.70 to $210.00

Navy Hawken Mark I

NAVY ARMS MARK I HAWKEN RIFLE
Caliber: 50 and 54.
Barrel: 26″.
Weight: 9 lbs. **Length:** 43″ over-all.
Stock: American walnut with cheek rest.
Sights: Blade front, adjustable Williams rear.
Features: Designed specifically for maxi-ball shooting. Double set triggers, blued barrel, polished brass furniture. Stainless steel chamber insert. Flint or percussion. Made in U.S. by Navy Arms.
Price: Finished, percussion, 50 or 54 .... $263.00
Price: As above, kit $175.95
Price: Finished, flintlock, 50 or 54 .... $275.00
Price: As above, kit $186.00

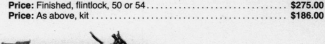

Kassnar Hawken

HAWKEN RIFLE
Caliber: 45, 50, 54 or 58.
Barrel: 28″, blued, 6-groove rifling.
Weight: 8¾ lbs. **Length:** 44″ over-all.
Stock: Walnut with cheekpiece.
Sights: Blade front, fully adj. rear.
Features: Coil mainspring, double set triggers, polished brass furniture. Also available with chrome plated bore or in flintlock model from Sile. Introduced 1977. From Kassnar, Sile, Dixie (45 or 50 only, walnut stock), Armsport, Toledo Armas, Shore and Hopkins & Allen, 50-cal. only.
Price: .... $175.00 to $252.95
Price: Hard chrome bore, Sile, about $238.95
Price: True left-hand rifle, percussion (Kassnar) $339.00

Armsport Hawken Rifle-Shotgun Combo
Similar to Hawken above except 50-cal. only, with 20 gauge shotgun barrel. From Armsport.
Price: $250.00

CVA HAWKEN RIFLE
Caliber: 50 or 54.
Barrel: 28″, octagon; 1″ across flats; 1-66″ twist.
Weight: 7 lbs. 15 oz. **Length:** 44″ over-all.
Stock: Select walnut.
Sights: Beaded blade front, fully adj. open rear.
Features: Fully adj. double set triggers; brass patch box, wedge plates, nose cap, thimbles, trigger guard and buttplate; blued barrel; color case-hardened, engraved lockplate. Percussion or flintlock. Hooked breech. Introduced 1981.
Price: Finished rifle, percussion $262.95
Price: Finished rifle, flintlock $272.95
Price: Kit, percussion $169.95
Price: Kit, flintlock $179.95

ITHACA-NAVY HAWKEN RIFLE
Caliber: 50 and 54.
Barrel: 32″ octagonal, 1-inch dia.
Weight: About 9 lbs.
Stock: Black walnut.
Sights: Blade front, rear adj. for w.
Features: Completely made in U.S. Hooked breech, 1⅞″ throw percussion lock. Attached twin thimbles and under-rib. German silver barrel key inlays, Hawken-style toe and buttplates, lock bolt inlays, barrel wedges, entry thimble, trigger guard, ramrod and cleaning jag, nipple and nipple wrench. American made. Introduced 1977. Made in U.S. by Navy Arms.
Price: Complete, percussion $460.00
Price: Kit, percussion $320.00
Price: Complete, flint $525.00
Price: Kit, flint $410.00

Dixie Wesson Rifle

DIXIE PERCUSSION WESSON RIFLE
Caliber: 50.
Barrel: 28″; 1⅛″ octagon, with false muzzle.
Length: 45″ over-all.
Stock: Hand checkered walnut.
Sights: Blade front, rear adj. for e.
Features: Adjustable double set triggers, color case hardened frame. Comes with loading rod and loading accessories. From Dixie Gun Works.
Price: With false muzzle $325.00

CAUTION: PRICES CHANGE. CHECK AT GUNSHOP.

Parker-Hale Whitworth

PARKER-HALE WHITWORTH MILITARY TARGET RIFLE
Caliber: 45.
Barrel: 36″.
Weight: 9¼ lbs. **Length:** 52½″ over-all.
Stock: Walnut. Checkered at wrist and fore-end.
Sights: Hooded post front, open step-adjustable rear.
Features: Faithful reproduction of the Whitworth rifle, only bored for 45-cal. Trigger has a detented lock, capable of being adjusted very finely without risk of the sear nose catching on the half-cock bent and damaging both parts. Introduced 1978. Imported from England by Navy Arms.
Price: **$575.00**

Parker-Hale 1853

PARKER-HALE ENFIELD 1853 MUSKET
Caliber: .577″.
Barrel: 39″, 3-groove cold-forged rifling.
Weight: About 9 lbs. **Length:** 55″ over-all.
Stock: Seasoned walnut.
Sights: Fixed front, rear step adj. for elevation.
Features: Three band musket made to original specs from original gauges. Solid brass stock furniture, color hardened lock plate, hammer; blued barrel, trigger. Imported from England by Navy Arms.
Price: **$475.00**

Parker-Hale 1861

PARKER-HALE ENFIELD 1861 CARBINE
Caliber: .577″.
Barrel: 24″.
Weight: 7½ lbs. **Length:** 40¼″ over-all.
Stock: Walnut.
Sights: Fixed front, adj. rear.
Features: Percussion muzzle loader, made to original 1861 English patterns. Imported from England by Navy Arms.
Price: **$335.00**

PARKER-HALE VOLUNTEER RIFLE
Caliber: .451″.
Barrel: 32″.
Weight: 9½ lbs. **Length:** 49″ over-all.
Stock: Walnut, checkered wrist and fore-end.
Sights: Globe front, adjustable ladder-type rear.
Features: Recreation of the type of gun issued to volunteer regiments during the 1860's. Rigby-pattern rifling, patent breech, detented lock. Stock is glass bedded for accuracy. Comes with comprehensive accessory/shooting kit. From Navy Arms.
Price: **$575.00**

NAVY ARMS 2-BAND ENFIELD 1858
Caliber: .577″ Minie, .575″ round ball.
Barrel: 33″.
Weight: 10 lbs. **Length:** 49″ over-all.
Stock: Walnut.
Sights: Folding leaf rear adjustable for elevation.
Features: Blued barrel, color case-hardened lock and hammer, polished brass buttplate, trigger guard, nose cap. From Navy Arms, Euroarms of America.
Price: **$360.00**

PARKER-HALE ENFIELD PATTERN 1858 NAVAL RIFLE
Caliber: .577″.
Barrel: 33″.
Weight: 8½ lbs. **Length:** 48½″ over-all.
Stock: European walnut.
Sights: Blade front, step adj. rear.
Features: Two-band Enfield percussion rifle with heavy barrel. 5-groove progressive depth rifling, solid brass furniture. All parts made exactly to original patterns. Imported from England by Navy Arms.
Price: **$435.00**

Navy Arms 3-Band Musket
Faithful reproduction of the Confederate-used rifle. Blued barrel, brass buttplate, trigger guard, nose cap. From Navy Arms.
Price: **$385.00**

London Armory 3-Band Enfield

LONDON ARMORY 3-BAND 1853 ENFIELD
Caliber: 58 (.577″ Minie, .575″ round ball, .580″ maxi ball).
Barrel: 39″.
Weight: 9½ lbs. **Length:** 54″ over-all.
Stock: European walnut.
Sights: Inverted "V" front, traditional Enfield folding ladder rear.
Features: Re-creation of the famed London Armory Company Pattern 1862 Enfield Musket. One-piece walnut stock, brass buttplate, trigger guard and nosecap. Lockplate marked "London Armoury Co." and with a British crown. Blued Baddeley barrel bands. From Dixie, Euroarms of America.
Price: .... **$285.00 to $315.00**

J. P. Murray Carbine

J.P. MURRAY ARTILLERY CARBINE
Caliber: 58 (.577" Minie).
Barrel: 23½".
Weight: 7 lbs., 9 oz. **Length:** 39" over-all.
Stock: Walnut.
Sights: Blade front, rear drift adj. for windage.
Features: Browned barrel, color case-hardened lock, blued swivel and band springs, polished brass buttplate, trigger guard, barrel bands. From Navy Arms.
Price: $263.00

ERMA-EXCAM GALLAGER CARBINE
Caliber: 54 (.540" ball).
Barrel: 22⅓".
Weight: 7¼ lbs. **Length:** 39" over-all.
Stock: European walnut.
Sights: Post front, rear adjustable for w. & e.
Features: Faithful reproduction of the 1860 breech-loading carbine. Made in West Germany. Imported by Excam. Introduced 1978.
Price: $325.00

U.S. M-1862 REMINGTON CONTRACT RIFLE
Caliber: 58.
Barrel: 33".
Weight: 9½ lbs. **Length:** 48½" over-all.
Stock: Walnut, brass furniture.
Sights: Blade front, folding 3-leaf rear.
Features: Re-creation of the 1862 military rifle. Each rifle furnished with two stainless steel nipples. From Euroarms of America.
Price: About $200.00

COOK & BROTHER CONFEDERATE CARBINE
Caliber: 58.
Barrel: 24".
Weight: 7½ lbs. **Length:** 40½" over-all.
Stock: Select walnut.
Features: Re-creation of the 1861 New Orleans-made artillery carbine. Color case-hardened lock, browned barrel. Buttplate, trigger guard, barrel bands, sling swivels and nosecap of polished brass. From Euroarms of America.
Price: $190.00

SHILOH NEW MODEL 1863 SHARPS RIFLE
Caliber: 54.
Barrel: 30", 1-in-48".
Weight: 8¾ lbs. **Length:** 47" over-all.
Stock: Black walnut, oil finish.
Sights: Blade front, rear leaf adj. for e.
Features: Duplicate of original percussion rifle. Receiver, sideplate, hammer, buttplate, patch box color hardened; barrel is blue-black. Twelve different models of the Sharps now available in many original chamberings. Made in U.S. by C. Sharps Arms Co.
Price: Sporting Rifle............................ $630.00
Price: Military Rifle.............................. $650.00

Shiloh New Model 1863 Sharps Carbine
Shortened, carbine version of the 1863 rifle. Caliber 54. Has 22" barrel, black walnut stock without patch box, single barrel band. Weighs 8 lbs., 12 oz., over-all length is 39⅛". Made in U.S. by C. Sharps Arms Co.
Price: $515.00

Dixie Sharps Rifle

Dixie Sharps Rifle
Similar to the Shiloh Sharps except has 28½" barrel, checkered half-stock fore-end and stock wrist, flat lockplate. Carbine-style case hardened buttplate. Imported from Italy by Dixie Gun Works.
Price: $349.95
Price: Military Carbine (22" barrel) $329.95

Dixie 1863 Musket

DIXIE 1863 SPRINGFIELD MUSKET
Caliber: 58 (.570" patched ball or .575" Minie).
Barrel: 50", rifled.
Stock: Walnut stained.
Sights: Blade front, adjustable ladder-type rear.
Features: Bright-finish lock, barrel, furniture. Reproduction of the last of the regulation muzzle loaders. Imported from Japan by Dixie Gun Works.
Price: Finished $265.00
Price: Kit $225.00

Navy 1863 Springfield

NAVY ARMS 1863 SPRINGFIELD
Caliber: 58, uses .575" mini-ball.
Barrel: 40", rifled.
Weight: 9½ lbs. **Length:** 56" over-all.
Stock: Walnut.
Sights: Open rear adj. for elevation.
Features: Full-size 3-band musket. Polished bright metal, including lock. From Navy Arms.
Price: Finished rifle $400.00
Price: Kit $310.00

BLACK POWDER MUSKETS & RIFLES

Dixie Zouave Rifle

ZOUAVE PERCUSSION RIFLE
Caliber: 58, 59.
Barrel: 32½".
Weight: 9½ lbs. **Length:** 48½" over-all.
Stock: Walnut finish, brass patch box and buttplate.
Sights: Fixed front, rear adj. for e.
Features: Some small details may vary with importers. Also available from Navy Arms as carbine, with 22" bbl. Extra 20 ga. shotgun bbl. $45.00. Imported by Navy Arms, Dixie.
Price: .... $87.95 to $265.00
Price: Deluxe Model (Navy Arms)................................ $400.00

Mississippi Model 1841 Percussion Rifle
Similar to Zouave Rifle but patterned after U.S. Model 1841. Imported by Navy Arms, Dixie.
Price: .... $225.00 to $275.00

KODIAK DOUBLE RIFLE
Caliber: 58x58, 50x50 and 58-cal./12 ga. optional.
Barrel: 28", 5 grooves, 1-in-48" twist.
Weight: 9½ lbs. **Length:** 43¼" over-all.
Stock: Czechoslovakian walnut, hand checkered.
Sights: Adjustable bead front, adjustable open rear.
Features: Hooked breech allows interchangeability of barrels. Comes with sling and swivels, adjustable powder measure, bullet mould and bullet starter. Engraved lock plates, top tang and trigger guard. Locks and top tang polished, rest blued. Imported from Italy by Trail Guns Armory, Inc.
Price: 58 cal. SxS $495.00
Price: 50 cal. SxS $495.00
Price: 50 cal. x 12 ga., 58x12................................ $495.00
Price: Spare barrels, 58 cal. SxS, 50 cal. SxS $294.25
Price: Spare barrels, 58x12 ga................................ $294.25
Price: Spare barrels, 12 ga. x 12 ga. $160.00

SHILOH SHARPS 1874 MILITARY RIFLE
Caliber: 45-70, 50-70.
Barrel: 30", Round.
Weight: 8¾ lbs.
Stock: American walnut.
Sights: Blade front, Lawrence-style open rear.
Features: Military-style fore-end with three barrel bands and 1¼" sling swivels. Color case-hardened receiver, buttplate and barrel bands, blued barrel. Recreation of the original Sharps rifles. Five other models in many original chamberings available. From C. Sharps Arms Co.
Price: 1874 Military Rifle...................................... $650.00
Price: 1874 Carbine... $515.00
Price: 1874 Business Rifle..................................... $590.00
Price: 1874 Sporting Rifle No. 1 .... $735.00
Price: 1874 Sporting Rifle No. 3 .... $630.00
Price: 1874 Long Range Express Sporting Rifle $790.00

Navy Mule Ear

NAVY ARMS MULE EAR SQUIRREL RIFLE
Caliber: 32, 36, 45.
Barrel: 26".
Weight: 5½ lbs.
Stock: Pennsylvania black walnut with satin finish.
Sights: Blade front, open adjustable rear.
Features: Mule ear action gives fast ignition; brass buttplate, trigger guard, fore-end cap, ramrod tip; color case-hardened lock. Made in U.S.A. by Navy Arms. Introduced 1984.
Price: Finished $185.00
Price: Kit $134.00

MAC Wolverine

Sights: Brass-bead front, adjustable folding leaf rear.
Features: New design uses straight-line ignition with #209 shotshell primer. Fires from an open bolt; has positive safety notch. Fully adjustable trigger. Introduced 1983. Made in U.S. by Michigan Arms Corp.
Price: Blue ordnance steel $398.00
Price: As above except in stainless steel....................... $595.00
Price: Friendship Special (select barrel, Lyman globe front, Williams target peep rear, adjustable recoil pad, custom stock, special breech block) $599.00

MAC WOLVERINE RIFLE
Caliber: 45, 50, 54.
Barrel: 26", octagon, 1" flats.
Weight: 7¾ lbs.
Stock: Choice of walnut, cherry or maple; soft recoil pad.

Morse/Navy Rifle

MORSE/NAVY RIFLE
Caliber: 45, 50 or 58.
Barrel: 26", octagonal.
Weight: 6 lbs. (45 cal.). **Length:** 41½" over-all.
Stock: American walnut, full p.g.
Sights: Blade front, open fixed rear.
Features: Brass action, trigger guard, ramrod pipes. Made in U.S. by Navy Arms.
Price: $167.00
Price: Kit $100.00

Sanftl Schuetzen Rifle

SANFTL SCHUETZEN PERCUSSION TARGET RIFLE
Caliber: 45 (.445" round ball).
Barrel: 29", ⅞" octagon.
Weight: 9 lbs. **Length:** 43" over-all.
Stock: Walnut, Schuetzen-style.
Sights: Open tunnel front post, peep rear adjustable for windage & elevation.
Features: True back-action lock with "backward" hammer; screw-in breech plug; buttplate, trigger guard and stock inlays are polished brass. Imported from Italy by Dixie Gun Works, Hopkins & Allen.
Price: **$595.00**

Navy Federal Target

NAVY SWISS FEDERAL TARGET RIFLE
Caliber: 45.
Barrel: 32".
Weight: 13¼ lbs. **Length:** 49½" over-all.
Stock: European walnut with hook buttplate, Schuetzen-style trigger guard.
Sights: Tunnel front, aperture rear adjustable for windage and elevation.
Features: Hand-built reproduction of 1800s target rifle; quick detachable, five-lever, double-set trigger, adjustable to 4 oz. Color case-hardened furniture. Imported from Italy by Navy Arms. Introduced 1984.
Price: **$795.00**
Price: Swiss-style palm rest **$35.00**

Navy Arms Cub

NAVY ARMS CUB 45 YOUTH RIFLE
Caliber: 45.
Barrel: 22" octagonal.
Weight: 4½ lbs. **Length:** 37" over-all.
Stock: American walnut with satin finish.
Sights: Blade front, open adjustable rear.
Features: Made for young or small shooters. Color case-hardened lock, polished brass furniture. Made in U.S.A. by Navy Arms.
Price: **$119.00**

BLACK POWDER SHOTGUNS

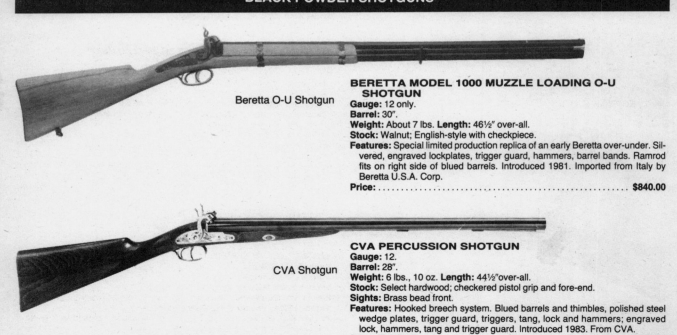

Beretta O-U Shotgun

BERETTA MODEL 1000 MUZZLE LOADING O-U SHOTGUN
Gauge: 12 only.
Barrel: 30".
Weight: About 7 lbs. **Length:** 46½" over-all.
Stock: Walnut; English-style with checkpiece.
Features: Special limited production replica of an early Beretta over-under. Silvered, engraved lockplates, trigger guard, hammers, barrel bands. Ramrod fits on right side of blued barrels. Introduced 1981. Imported from Italy by Beretta U.S.A. Corp.
Price: **$840.00**

CVA Shotgun

CVA PERCUSSION SHOTGUN
Gauge: 12.
Barrel: 28".
Weight: 6 lbs., 10 oz. **Length:** 44½"over-all.
Stock: Select hardwood; checkered pistol grip and fore-end.
Sights: Brass bead front.
Features: Hooked breech system. Blued barrels and thimbles, polished steel wedge plates, trigger guard, triggers, tang, lock and hammers; engraved lock, hammers, tang and trigger guard. Introduced 1983. From CVA.
Price: Finished **$259.95**
Price: Kit **$199.95**

CAUTION: PRICES CHANGE. CHECK AT GUNSHOP.

BLACK POWDER SHOTGUNS

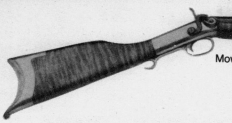

Mowrey A & T Shotgun

MOWREY A. & T. 12 GAUGE SHOTGUN
Gauge: 12 ga. only.
Barrel: 32″, octagon.
Weight: 8 lbs. **Length:** 48″ over-all.
Stock: Curly maple, oil finish, brass furniture.
Sights: Bead front.
Features: Available in percussion only. Steel or brass action. Uses standard 12 ga. wadding. Made by Mowrey.
Price: Complete **$328.00**
Price: Kit form. **$237.00**

SILE DELUXE DOUBLE BARREL SHOTGUN
Gauge: 12.
Barrel: 28″ (Cyl. & Cyl.); hooked breech, hard chrome lining.
Weight: 6 lbs. **Length:** 44½″ over-all.
Stock: Walnut, with checkered grip.
Features: Engraved, polished blue and color case-hardened hardware; locks are color case-hardened and engraved. Steel buttplate; brass bead front sight. From Sile.
Price: Percussion only **$299.00**
Price: Confederate Cavalry Model (shortened version of above model with 14″ bbl. 30½″ o.a.l., checkered stock, swivels, brass ramrod). **$299.00**

Sile Confederate Cavalry

Navy Classic Double

NAVY CLASSIC DOUBLE BARREL SHOTGUN
Gauge: 10, 12.
Barrel: 28″.
Weight: 7 lbs., 12 ozs. **Length:** 45″ over-all.
Stock: Walnut.
Features: Color case-hardened lock plates and hammers; hand checkered stock. Imported by Navy Arms.
Price: 12 ga. **$342.00**
Price: 10 ga. **$360.00**
Price: Kit, 12 ga. **$265.00**
Price: Kit, 10 ga. **$280.00**

Morse/Navy Shotgun

MORSE/NAVY SINGLE BARREL SHOTGUN
Gauge: 12 ga.
Barrel: 26″.
Weight: 5 lbs. **Length:** 41½″ over-all.
Stock: American walnut, full p.g.
Sights: Front bead
Features: Brass receiver, black buttplate. Made in U.S. by Navy Arms.
Price: **$167.00**
Price: Kit **$105.00**

TRAIL GUNS KODIAK 10 GAUGE DOUBLE
Gauge: 10.
Barrel: 20″, 30¾″ (Cyl. bore).
Weight: About 9 lbs. **Length:** 47⅛″ over-all.
Stock: Walnut, with cheek rest. Checkered wrist and fore-end.
Features: Chrome plated bores; engraved lockplates, brass bead front and middle sights; sling swivels. Introduced 1980. Imported from Italy by Trail Guns Armory.
Price: **$379.95**

Dixie Double Barrel

DOUBLE BARREL PERCUSSION SHOTGUN
Gauge: 12.
Barrel: 30″ (I.C.&Mod.).
Weight: 6¼ lbs. **Length:** 45″ over-all.
Stock: Hand checkered walnut, 14″ pull.
Features: Double triggers, light hand engraving. Details vary with importer. Imported by The Armoury, Dixie, Euroarms of America, Hopkins & Allen.
Price: Upland . . . . **$125.00 to $299.85**
Price: 12 ga. kit (Dixie, magnum) **$235.00**
Price: 10 ga. (Dixie, magnum) **$335.00**
Price: 10 ga. kit (Dixie, magnum) **$285.00**

Guns in this section are powered by: A) disposable CO_2 cylinders, B) hand-pumped compressed air released by trigger action, C) air compressed by a spring-powered piston released by trigger action. Calibers are generally 177 (BB or pellet) and 22 (ball or pellet); a few guns are made in 20 or 25 caliber. Pellet guns are usually rifled, those made for BB's only are smoothbore.

AIR MATCH MODEL 600 PISTOL
Caliber: 177, single shot.
Barrel: 8.8".
Weight: 32 oz. **Length:** 13.19" over-all.
Power: Single stroke pneumatic.
Stocks: Match-style with adjustable palm shelf.
Sights: Interchangeable post front, fully adjustable match rear with interchangeable blades.
Features: Velocity of 420 fps. Adjustable trigger with dry-fire option. Comes with fitted case. Available with three different grip styles, barrel weight, sight extension. Add $5.00 for left-hand models. Introduced 1984. Imported from Italy by Great Lakes Airguns, Kendall Arms.
Price: With adjustable grip **$394.50**
Price: With non-adjustable grip **$384.50**
Price: Non-adjustable grip (Kendall Arms) **$285.00**

Air Match 600

BSA SCORPION AIR PISTOL
Caliber: 177 or 22, single shot.
Barrel: 7⅞", rifled.
Weight: 3.6 lbs. **Length:** 15¾" over-all.
Power: Spring-air, barrel cocking.
Stock: Moulded black plastic contoured with thumbrest.
Sights: Interchangeable bead or blade front with hood, open rear adjustable for w. & e.
Features: Muzzle velocity of 510 fps (177) and 380 fps (22). Comes with pellets, oil, targets and steel target holder. Scope and mount optional. Introduced 1980. Imported from England by Precision Sports.
Price: 177 or 22 cal. **$119.95**
Price: 1.5x15 scope and mount **$59.95**

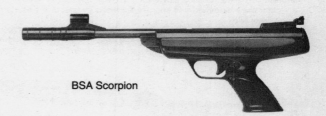
BSA Scorpion

BEEMAN/WEBLEY HURRICANE PISTOL
Caliber: 177 or 22, single shot.
Barrel: 8", rifled.
Weight: 2.4 lbs. **Length:** 11½" over-all.
Power: Spring piston.
Stocks: Thumbrest, checkered high-impact synthetic.
Sights: Hooded front, micro-click rear adj. for w. & e.
Features: Velocity of 470 fps (177-cal.). Single stroke cocking, adjustable trigger pull, manual safety. Rearward recoil like a firearm pistol. Steel piston and cylinder. Scope base included; 1.5x scope **$39.95** extra. Shoulder stock available. Introduced 1977. Imported from England. Imported by Beeman, available from Beeman and Great Lakes Airguns.
Price: **$129.95**

Beeman/Webley Hurricane

BEEMAN/WEBLEY TEMPEST AIR PISTOL
Caliber: 177 or 22, single shot.
Barrel: 6.75", rifled ordnance steel.
Weight: 32 oz. **Length:** 9" over-all.
Power: Spring piston.
Stocks: Checkered black epoxy with thumbrest.
Sights: Post front; rear has sliding leaf adjustable for w. and e.
Features: Adjustable trigger pull, manual safety. Velocity 470 fps (177 cal.). Steel piston in steel liner for maximum performance and durability. Unique rearward spring simulates firearm recoil. Shoulder stock available. Introduced 1979. Imported from England by Beeman, available from Beeman, Great Lakes Airguns.
Price: **$99.95**

BEEMAN/FAS MODEL 604 AIR PISTOL
Caliber: 177, single shot.
Barrel: 7.5", 10-groove rifled steel.
Weight: 2.3 lbs. **Length:** 11.3" over-all.
Power: Single stroke pneumatic.
Stocks: Anatomically shaped stippled walnut; small, medium, large sizes.
Sights: Adjustable.
Features: Top of receiver is cocking arm, requires 13 lbs. effort. Adjustable trigger may be dry-fired without fully cocking pistol. Imported from Italy by Beeman. Introduced 1984.
Price: . . . . **$495.00 to $525.00**

Beeman/Webley Tempest

CAUTION: PRICES CHANGE. CHECK AT GUNSHOP.

BEEMAN/WISCHO S-20 STANDARD
Caliber: 177, single shot.
Barrel: 7".
Weight: 2 lbs., 2 oz.
Power: Spring piston.
Stocks: Walnut.
Sights: Hooded front, open rear adj. for elevation.
Features: Stocks suitable for right or left-handed shooters; 450 fps; 24 oz. trigger pull. Introduced 1980. Imported by Beeman.
Price: $129.50

BEEMAN/FEINWERKBAU MODEL 2 CO² PISTOL
Caliber: 177, single shot
Barrel: 10.1".
Weight: 2.5 lbs. **Length:** 16¼" over-all.
Power: Special CO² cylinder.
Stocks: Stippled walnut with adjustable palm shelf.
Sights: Blade front with interchangeable inserts; open micro. click rear with adjustable notch width.
Features: Power adjustable from 360 fps to 525 fps. Fully adjustable trigger; three weights for balance and weight adjustments. Short-barrel Mini-2 model also available. Introduced 1983. Imported by Beeman.
Price: Right hand $575.00
Price: Left hand $615.00
Price: Mini-2, right hand $555.00
Price: Mini-2, left hand $585.00

BEEMAN/FEINWERKBAU FWB-65 MKII AIR PISTOL
Caliber: 177, single shot.
Barrel: 6.1"; fixed bbl. wgt. avail.
Weight: 42 oz. **Length:** 14.1" over-all.
Power: Spring, sidelever cocking.
Stocks: Walnut, stippled thumbrest; adjustable or fixed.
Sights: Front, interchangeable post element system, open rear, click adj. for w. & e. and for sighting notch width. Scope mount avail.
Features: New shorter barrel for better balance and control. Cocking effort 9 lbs. 2-stage trigger, 4 adjustments. Quiet firing, 525 fps. Programs instantly for recoil or recoilless operation. Permanently lubricated. Steel piston ring. Special switch converts trigger from 17.6 oz. pull to 42 oz. let-off. Imported by Beeman, available from Beeman, Great Lakes Airguns.
Price: Right-hand .... $495.00 to $555.00
Price: Left-hand .... $525.00 to $608.00
Price: Model 80 (Great Lakes Airguns), std. grip $570.00
Price: Model 65 Mk.I (7.5" bbl.) .... $485.00 to $575.00

BEEMAN/FEINWERKBAU MODEL 90 PISTOL
Caliber: 177, single shot.
Barrel: 7.5", 12-groove rifling.
Weight: 3.0 lbs. **Length:** 16.4" over-all.
Power: Spring piston, single stroke sidelever cocking.
Stocks: Stippled walnut with adjustable palm shelf.
Sights: Interchangeable blade front, fully adjustable open notch rear.
Features: Velocity of 475 to 525 fps. Has new adjustable electronic trigger. Recoilless action, metal piston ring and dual mainsprings. Cocking effort is 12 lbs. Introduced 1983. Imported by Beeman.
Price: .... $645.00 to $675.00

BEEMAN/WEIHRAUCH HW-70 AIR PISTOL
Caliber: 177, single shot.
Barrel: 6¼", rifled.
Weight: 38 oz. **Length:** 12¾" over-all.
Power: Spring, barrel cocking.
Stocks: Plastic, with thumbrest.
Sights: Hooded post front, square notch rear adj. for w. and e.
Features: Adj. trigger. 24-lb. cocking effort, 410 f.p.s. M.V.; automatic barrel safety. Imported by Beeman, available from Beeman, Great Lakes Airguns.
Price: From Beeman $115.00
Price: From Great Lakes Airguns $102.50

FWB Mini-2

FWB 65 Mk. II

BSF S-20

BEEMAN/WISCHO CM PISTOL
Caliber: 177, single shot.
Barrel: 7" rifled.
Weight: 45 oz. **Length:** 15.8" over-all.
Power: Spring piston barrel cocking.
Stocks: Walnut with thumbrest.
Sights: Bead front, rear adj. for e.
Features: Cocking effort of 17 lbs.; M.V. 450 f.p.s.; adj. trigger. Optional scope and mount available. Detachable aluminum stock optional. Available from Beeman.
Price: $159.50

Benjamin Series 130

BENJAMIN SUPER S. S. TARGET PISTOL SERIES 130
Caliber: BB, single shot.
Barrel: 8"; BB smoothbore; 22 and 177, rifled.
Weight: 2 lbs. **Length:** 11" over-all.
Power: Hand pumped.
Features: Bolt action; fingertip safety; adj. power.
Price: M130, BB $70.29

CAUTION: PRICES CHANGE. CHECK AT GUNSHOP.

Benjamin 232

CROSMAN MODEL 357 AIR PISTOL

Caliber: 177, 6-shot.
Barrel: 4″ (Model 357 Four), 6″ (Model 357 six), 8″ (Model 357 Eight); rifled steel.
Weight: 32 oz. (6″) **Length:** 11⅜″ over-all.
Power: CO_2 Powerlet.
Stocks: Checkered wood-grain plastic.
Sights: Ramp front, fully adjustable rear.
Features: Average 430 fps (Model 357 Six). Break-open barrel for easy loading. Single or double action. Vent rib barrel. Wide, smooth trigger. Two speed loaders come with each gun. Models Four and Six introduced 1983, Model Eight introduced 1984.
Price: 4″ or 6″, about $40.00
Price: 8″, about $60.00

Crosman 1322/1377

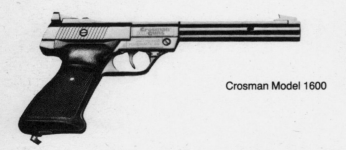

Crosman Model 1600

CROSMAN MARK II TARGET PISTOL

Caliber: 177 or BB.
Barrel: 7¼″, button rifled.
Weight: 44 oz. **Length:** 11⅛″ over-all.
Power: Crosman Powerlet CO_2 cylinder.
Features: New system provides same shot-to-shot velocity of 435-485 fps (pellets). Checkered thumbrest grips, right or left. Patridge front sight, rear adj. for w. & e. Adj. trigger.
Price: About $49.00

DAISY 179 SIX GUN

Caliber: BB, 12-shot.
Barrel: Steel lined, smoothbore.
Weight: NA **Length:** 11½″ over-all.
Power: Spring.
Features: Forced feed from under-barrel magazine. Single action, molded wood grained grips.
Price: About $23.00

BENJAMIN 232/237 SINGLE SHOT PISTOLS

Caliber: 177 and 22.
Weight: 32 oz. **Length:** 11¾″ over-all.
Power: Hand pumped.
Stocks: Walnut, with walnut pump handle.
Sights: Blade front, open adjustable rear.
Features: Bolt action; fingertip safety; adjustable power.
Price: Model 232 (22 cal.)....................................... $78.10
Price: Model 237 (177 cal.) $78.10

Crosman Model 357

CROSMAN MODEL 1322 AIR PISTOL

Caliber: 22, single shot.
Barrel: 8″, button rifled.
Weight: 37 oz. **Length:** 13⅝″.
Power: Hand pumped.
Sights: Blade front, rear adj. for w. and e.
Features: Moulded plastic grip, hand size pump forearm. Cross bolt safety. Also available in 177 Cal. as **Model 1377** (same price).
Price: About $45.00

CROSMAN 1600 BB PISTOL

Caliber: BB, 17-shot.
Barrel: 7¾″.
Weight: 29 oz. **Length:** 11⅜″ over-all.
Power: Standard CO_2.
Stocks: Contoured with thumbrest.
Sights: Patridge-type front, fully adj. rear.
Features: Gives about 80 shots per powerlet, slide-action safety, steel barrel, die-cast receiver. Introduced 1983.
Price: About $27.00

Crosman Mark II

Daisy Model 179

CAUTION: PRICES CHANGE. CHECK AT GUNSHOP.

DAISY MODEL 188 BB/PELLET PISTOL
Caliber: 177.
Barrel: 9.9".
Weight: 1.67 lbs. **Length:** 12" over-all.
Stocks: Die-cast metal; checkered with thumbrest.
Sights: Blade and ramp front, notched rear.
Features: Single shot for pellets, 24-shot for BBs. Spring action with under-barrel cocking lever. Grip and receiver of die-cast metal. Introduced 1979.
Price: About **$23.00**

Daisy Model 188

HAMMERLI "MASTER" CO₂ TARGET PISTOL
Caliber: 177, single shot.
Barrel: 6.4", 12-groove.
Weight: 38.4 oz. **Length:** 16" over-all.
Power: 12 gram cylinder.
Stocks: Plastic with thumbrest and checkering.
Sights: Ramp front, micro rear, click adj. Adj. sight radius from 11.1" to 13.0".
Features: Single shot, manual loading. Residual gas vented automatically. 5-way adj. trigger. Available from Mandall Shooting Supplies.
Price: **$495.00**

Consult our Directory pages for the location of firms mentioned.

Marksman Plainsman

MARKSMAN PLAINSMAN 1049 CO₂ PISTOL
Caliber: BB, 100-shot repeater.
Barrel: 5⅞", smooth.
Weight: 28 oz. **Length:** 9½" over-all.
Stocks: Simulated walnut with thumbrest.
Power: 8.5 or 12.5 gram CO₂ cylinders.
Features: Velocity of 400 fps. Three-position power switch. Auto. ammunition feed. Positive safety.
Price: **$32.95**

MARKSMAN #1010 REPEATER PISTOL
Caliber: 177, 20-shot repeater.
Barrel: 2½", smoothbore.
Weight: 24 oz. **Length:** 8¼".
Power: Spring
Features: Thumb safety. Uses BBs, darts or pellets. Repeats with BBs only.
Price: Matte black finish **$15.50**
Price: Model 1020 (as above except fires BBs only) **$15.50**

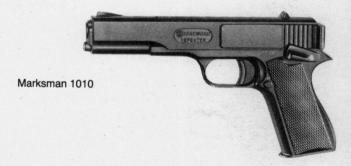

Marksman 1010

NORICA BLACK WIDOW AIR PISTOL
Caliber: 177, single shot.
Barrel: 7¾".
Weight: 3 lbs. **Length:** 15" over-all.
Power: Spring air, barrel cocking.
Stocks: Target-style of black high-impact plastic.
Sights: Hooded front, open adjustable rear.
Features: Velocity 395 fps. Side mounted automatic safety; receiver grooved for scope mounting. Imported from Spain by Kassnar.
Price: **$46.00**

Precise Minuteman Micron

PRECISE MINUTEMAN® MICRON AIR PISTOL
Caliber: 177, single shot.
Barrel: 6¼", rifled.
Weight: 28 oz. **Length:** 12½" over-all.
Power: Spring air, barrel cocking.
Stocks: Contoured plastic
Sights: Hooded front, fixed rear.
Features: Blue finish. Comes with 250 pellets. Introduced 1983. Imported by Precise International.
Price: **$20.00**

POWER LINE MODEL 1207 PISTOL
Caliber: BB, 60-shot magazine.
Barrel: 10½", smoothbore.
Weight: 34 oz. **Length:** 23⅛" over-all, with stock.
Power: CO₂ cartridge.
Stocks: Checkered plastic.
Sights: Blade and ramp front, adjustable open rear.
Features: Velocity of 420 fps. Model 1200 pistol with a detachable wire frame shoulder stock. Cross-bolt trigger block safety. From Daisy.
Price: About **$49.00**
Price: 1200 pistol without stock, about **$41.00**

CAUTION: PRICES CHANGE. CHECK AT GUNSHOP.

POWER LINE MATCH 777 PELLET PISTOL

Caliber: 177; single shot.
Barrel: 9.61″ rifled steel.
Weight: 49 oz. **Length:** 13½″ over-all.
Power: Sidelever, single pump pneumatic.
Stocks: Smooth hardwood, fully contoured; right or left hand.
Sights: Blade and ramp front, match-grade open rear with adj. width notch, micro. click adjustments.
Features: Adjustable trigger; manual cross-bolt safety. MV of 360 fps. Comes in foam-filled carrying case and complete cleaning kit, adjustment tool and pellets.
Price: About **$250.00**

Power Line 777

POWER LINE MODEL 790

Caliber: 177 cal. pellet, single-shot.
Barrel: 8½″, rifled steel.
Weight: 42 oz.
Power: 12 gram CO_2 cartridge.
Stocks: Simulated walnut, checkered. Thumbrest. Left or right hand.
Sights: Patridge front, fully adj. rear with micro. click windage adjustment.
Features: Pull-bolt action, cross-bolt safety. High-low power adjustment.
Price: About **$52.00**

Power LIne 780/790

POWER LINE 717 PELLET PISTOL

Caliber: 177, single shot.
Barrel: 9.61″.
Weight: 48 oz. **Length:** 13½″ over-all.
Stocks: Molded wood-grain plastic, with thumbrest.
Sights: Blade and ramp front, micro. adjustable notch rear.
Features: Single pump pneumatic pistol. Rifled brass barrel. Cross-bolt trigger block. Muzzle velocity 360 fps (177 cal.), 290 fps (22 cal.). From Daisy. Introduced 1979.
Price: Either model, about **$52.00**
Price: With detachable wire shoulder stock, about. **$65.00**

Power Line 717

POWER LINE CO_2 1200 CUSTOM TARGET PISTOL

Caliber: BB, 177.
Barrel: 10½″, smooth.
Weight: 30 oz. **Length:** 11¼″ over-all.
Power: Daisy CO_2 cylinder.
Stocks: Contoured, checkered moulded wood-grain plastic.
Sights: Blade ramp front, fully adj. square notch rear.
Features: 60-shot BB reservoir, gravity feed. Cross-bolt safety. Velocity of 420-450 fps for more than 100 shots.
Price: About **$37.00**

Precise RO-72

PRECISE/RO-72 BULLSEYE AIR PISTOL

Caliber: 177, single shot.
Barrel: 7¼″, rifled.
Weight: 35 oz.
Power: Spring air, barrel cocking.
Stock: Molded plastic with thumbrest.
Sights: Hooded front, micro. adj. open rear for w. and e.
Features: Four interchangeable front sights—triangle, bead, narrow post, wide post. Rear sight rotates to give four distinct sight pictures. Muzzle velocity 325 fps. Precise International, importer.
Price: **$40.00**

RWS Model 5G

RWS MODEL 5G AIR PISTOL

Caliber: 177, single shot.
Barrel: 7″.
Weight: 2¾ lbs. **Length:** 16″ over-all.
Power: Spring air, barrel cocking.
Stocks: Plastic, thumbrest design.
Sights: Tunnel front, micro click open rear.
Features: Velocity of 410 fps. Two-stage trigger with automatic safety. Imported from West Germany by Dynamit Nobel of America, also available from Great Lakes Airguns.
Price: **$125.00**

RWS MODEL 5GS AIR PISTOL

Same as the Model 5G except comes with 1.5×15 pistol scope with ramp-style mount, muzzle brake/weight. No open sights supplied. Introduced 1983.
Price: **$160.00**

CAUTION: PRICES CHANGE. CHECK AT GUNSHOP.

RWS MODEL 6M MATCH AIR PISTOL
Caliber: 177, single shot.
Barrel: 7".
Weight: 3 lbs. **Length:** 16" over-all.
Power: Spring air, barrel cocking.
Stocks: Walnut-finished hardwood with thumbrest.
Sights: Adjustable front, micro click open rear.
Features: Velocity of 410 fps. Recoilless double piston system, moveable barrel shroud to protect front sight during cocking. Imported from West Germany by Dynamit Nobel of America, also available from Great Lakes Airguns.
Price: **$220.00**

RWS Model 6M

RWS Model 10

RWS Model 10 Match Air Pistol
Refined version of the Model 6M. Has special adjustable match trigger, oil finished and stippled match grips, barrel weight. Also available in left-hand version, and with fitted case.
Price: Model 10 . . . . **$435.00**
Price: Model 10, left hand. **$460.00**
Price: Model 10, with case **$455.00**
Price: Model 10, left hand, with case **$475.00**

RECORD MODEL 3 AIR PISTOL
Caliber: 177, single shot.
Barrel: 5.25", rifled.
Weight: 1.9 lbs. **Length:** 11.42" over-all.
Power: Spring air, barrel cocking.
Stocks: Checkered plastic with thumbrest.
Sights: Hooded front, fully adjustable rear.
Features: Velocity of about 300 fps. Matte blue/black finish. Introduced 1983. Imported from West Germany by Great Lakes Airguns.
Price: **$39.95**

Record Model 3

RECORD MODEL 68 AIR PISTOL
Caliber: 177, single shot.
Barrel: 7", rifled.
Weight: 2.91 lbs. **Length:** 14.37" over-all.
Power: Spring air, barrel cocking.
Stocks: Checkered plastic with thumb rest.
Sights: Hooded front with square post, fully adjustable rear.
Features: Velocity of about 300 fps. Easily accessible trigger adjustment knob. Introduced 1983. Imported from West Germany by Great Lakes Airguns.
Price: **$64.50**

Record Model 68

RECORD "JUMBO" DELUXE AIR PISTOL
Caliber: 177, single shot.
Barrel: 6", rifled.
Weight: 1.9 lbs. **Length:** 7.25" over-all.
Power: Spring air, lever cocking.
Stocks: Smooth walnut.
Sights: Blade front, fully adjustable open rear.
Features: Thumb safety. Grip magazine compartment for extra pellet storage. Introduced 1983. Imported from West Germany by Great Lakes Airguns.
Price: **$66.50**

Record Jumbo

Sheridan Model HB

SHERIDAN MODEL HB PNEUMATIC PISTOL
Caliber: 5mm; single shot.
Barrel: 9⅜", rifled.
Weight: 36 oz. **Length:** 12" over-all.
Power: Underlever pneumatic pump.
Stocks: Checkered simulated walnut; fore-end is walnut.
Sights: Blade front, fully adjustable rear.
Features: "Controller-Power" feature allows velocity and range control by varying the number of pumps—3 to 10. Maximum velocity of 400 fps. Introduced 1982. From Sheridan Products.
Price: **$80.40**

CAUTION: PRICES CHANGE. CHECK AT GUNSHOP.

Sheridan Model EB

SHERIDAN MODEL EB CO₂ PISTOL
Caliber: 20 (5mm).
Barrel: 6½", rifled, rust proof.
Weight: 27 oz. **Length:** 9" over-all.
Power: 12 gram CO₂ cylinder.
Stocks: Checkered simulated walnut. Left- or right-handed.
Sights: Blade front, fully adjustable rear.
Features: Turn-bolt single-shot action. Gives about 40 shots at 400 fps per CO₂ cylinder.
Price: $60.35

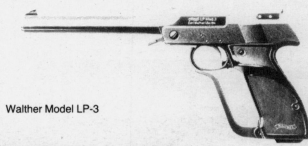

Walther Model LP-3

WALTHER MODEL LP-3
Caliber: 177, single shot.
Barrel: 9⅜", rifled.
Weight: 45½ oz. **Length:** 13³⁄₁₆" over-all.
Power: Compressed air, lever cocking.
Features: Recoilless operation, cocking in grip frame. Micro-click rear sight, adj. for w. & e., 4-way adj. trigger. Plastic thumbrest grips. Imported by Interarms.
Price: $350.00

Walther Model LP-3 Match Pistol
Same specifications as LP-3 except for grips, frame shape and weight. Has adjustable walnut grips to meet international shooting regulations. Imported by Interarms.
Price: $400.00

WISCHO BSF S-20 PISTOL
Caliber: 177, single shot.
Barrel: 7" rifled.
Weight: 45 oz. **Length:** 15.8" over-all.
Power: Spring piston barrel cocking.
Stocks: Walnut with thumbrest.
Sights: Bead front, rear adj. for e.
Features: Cocking effort of 17 lbs.; M.V. 450 f.p.s.; adj. trigger. Optional scope and mount available. Detachable aluminum stock optional. Available from Great Lakes Airguns.
Price: $145.00

WALTHER CP-2 CO₂ AIR PISTOL
Caliber: 177, single shot.
Barrel: 9".
Weight: 40 oz. **Length:** 14¾" over-all.
Power: CO₂.
Stocks: Full target type stippled wood with adjustable hand-shelf.
Sights: Target post front, fully adjustable target rear.
Features: Velocity of 520 fps. CO₂ powered; target-quality trigger; comes with adaptor for charging with standard CO₂ air tanks, case, and accessories. Introduced 1983. Imported from West Germany by Interarms.
Price: $600.00

Wischo BSF S-20

AIR GUNS—LONG GUNS

Anschutz Model 335

ANSCHUTZ MODEL 335 AIR RIFLE
Caliber: 177, single shot.
Barrel: 18½".
Weight: 7¼ lbs. **Length:** 43¼" over-all.
Power: Spring piston; barrel cocking.
Stock: European hardwood; checkered pistol grip.
Sights: Williams peep rear, Anschutz globe front.
Features: Specially designed for 10 meter "novice-expert" shooters. Adjustable two-stage trigger. Introduced 1982. Imported from Germany by PSI.
Price: Without sight $172.50
Price: Magnum model, no sights. $174.50
Price: Sight set $28.35

ANSCHUTZ MODEL 380 AIR RIFLE
Caliber: 177, single shot.
Barrel: 20¼".
Weight: 10.8 lbs. (including sights). **Length:** 42⅛" over-all.
Power: Spring piston; sidelever cocking.
Stock: European hardwood with stippled pistol grip and fore-end. Adjustable cheekpiece and rubber buttpad.
Sights: Globe front; match aperture rear.
Features: Recoilless and vibration free. Two-stage adjustable match trigger. Introduced 1982. Imported from Germany by PSI.
Price: With sights $867.00
Price: Left-hand, with sights. $892.00

> Consult our Directory pages for the location of firms mentioned.

CAUTION: PRICES CHANGE. CHECK AT GUNSHOP.

BSA Airsporter-S

BSA AIRSPORTER-S AIR RIFLE

Caliber: 177 or 22.
Barrel: 19.5", rifled.
Weight: 8 lbs. **Length:** 44.7" over-all.
Power: Spring air, underlever action.
Stock: Oil-finished walnut, high comb Monte Carlo cheekpiece.
Sights: Ramp front with interchangeable bead and blade, adjustable for height; tangent-type rear adj. for w. & e.
Features: Muzzle velocity of 825 fps (177) and 635 fps (22). Fully adj. trigger. Cylinder is a large diameter, one-piece impact extrusion. Scope and mount optional. Introduced 1980. Imported from England by Precision Sports.
Price: 177 or 22 cal. **$399.95**
Price: Standard Airsporter **$329.95**
Price: 4x20 scope and mount **$59.95**

ARROW PELLET RIFLE

Caliber: 177, single shot.
Barrel: 16½", rifled.
Weight: 6 lbs. **Length:** 39½" over-all.
Power: Spring piston; underlever.
Stock: Hardwood.
Sights: Adjustable hooded post front, open adjustable rear.
Features: Muzzle velocity of about 500 fps. Single pump required for shooting. Comes with sling swivels, has military look. Imported from China by Paragon Sales.
Price: **$89.50**

BSA AIRSPORTER-S COMMEMORATIVE

Commemorates BSA's 100-year anniversary in 1982. Similar to standard Airsporter-S except has a new cocking lever concealed in the fore-end, new hand-checkered Stutzen stock with Schnabel tip, grip cap. Comes with 4×40 scope and mount, leather sling and swivels, pile-lined case, BSA patch, shooting kit, and registration certificate. Only 1000 made. Introduced 1983.
Price: **$650.00**

BSA MERCURY AIR RIFLE

Caliber: 177 or 22, single shot.
Barrel: 18.5", rifled.
Weight: 7 lbs. **Length:** 43.5" over-all.
Power: Spring-air, barrel cocking.
Stock: European hardwood. Monte Carlo cheekpiece, ventilated butt pad.
Sights: Adjustable bead/blade front, tangent rear adj. for w. & e.
Features: Muzzle velocity of 700 fps (177) and 550 fps (22). Reversible "V" and "U" notch rear sight blade. Single stage match-type trigger, adj. for weight of pull and sear engagement. Scope and mount optional. Introduced 1980. Imported from England by Precision Sports.
Price: 177 or 22 cal. **$229.95**
Price: 4x20 scope and mount **$59.95**

BSA Mercury-S

BSA Mercury-S Air Rifle

Similar to the standard Mercury model except weighs 7¼ lbs., has European walnut stock with oil finish, checkered fore-end and pistol grip. Muzzle velocity of 825 fps (177), 635 fps (22). Introduced 1982. From Precision Sports.
Price: **$289.95**

BSA Meteor Super

BSA METEOR/METEOR SUPER AIR RIFLES

Caliber: 177 or 22, single shot.
Barrel: 18.5", rifled.
Weight: 6 lbs. **Length:** 42" over-all.
Power: Spring air, barrel cocking.
Stock: European hardwood.
Sights: Adj. bead/blade front, adj. tangent rear with reversible "U" and "V" notch blade.
Features: Muzzle velocity of 650 fps (177) and 500 fps (22). Aperture rear sight element supplied. Cylinder is dovetailed for scope mounting. Adjustable trigger mechanism. Meteor Super has M.C. cheekpiece, vent. rubber recoil pad. Introduced 1980. Imported from England by Precision Sports.
Price: Meteor **$129.95**
Price: Meteor Super **$139.95**

BSF MODEL 55D AIR RIFLE

Caliber: 177, single shot.
Barrel: 16", rifled.
Weight: 6.5 lbs. **Length:** 40.7" over-all.
Power: Spring-air, barrel cocking.
Stock: Walnut stained hardwood.
Sights: Hooded front, open rear adjustable for elevation.
Features: Velocity of 870 fps. Adjustable trigger, receiver grooved for scope. Rubber butt pad. Comes with Bushnell ¾" 4x air rifle scope installed. Imported from West Germany by Great Lakes Airguns.
Price: With scope. **$164.50**

BSF MODEL 55 SPECIAL AIR RIFLE

Caliber: 177, 22, single shot.
Barrel: 16.5", rifled.
Weight: 7.5 lbs. **Length:** 44.5" over-all.
Power: Spring air, barrel cocking.
Stock: Walnut-stained hardwood.
Sights: Hooded bead front, fully adjustable open rear.
Features: Velocity of 870-900 fps. Permanently attached barrel weight, rubber butt pad, blued metal. Introduced 1984. Imported from West Germany by Great Lakes Airguns.
Price: **$169.50**

BSF 55 Special

BSF Model S80

BSF MODEL S80 AIR RIFLE
Caliber: 177, single shot.
Barrel: 19½".
Weight: 8.5 lbs. **Length:** 44" over-all.
Power: Spring-air, barrel cocking.
Stock: Walnut-finished hardwood.
Sights: Hooded post front with bead, open fully adjustable rear.
Features: Velocity of 850 fps. Permanently attached barrel weight. Monte Carlo stock with rubber butt pad; adjustable trigger. Scope mount rail installed. Introduced 1984. Imported from West Germany by Great Lakes Airguns.
Price: **$198.50**

BSF MODEL S70 AIR RIFLE
Caliber: 177, single shot.
Barrel: 19", rifled.
Weight: 7 lbs. **Length:** 43¼" over-all.
Power: Spring-air, barrel cocking.
Stock: Walnut-stained hardwood.
Sights: Hooded bead front, open fully adjustable rear.
Features: Velocity about 850 fps. Scope mount base installed; rubber butt pad; blued metal. Imported from West Germany by Great Lakes Airguns.
Price: **$159.28**

BSF Model 35

BSF MODEL 35 AIR RIFLE
Caliber: 177, single shot.
Barrel: 16.75", rifled.
Weight: 4.5 lbs. **Length:** 39" over-all.
Power: Spring-air, barrel cocking.
Stock: Walnut-stained hardwood.
Sights: Hooded bead front, open rear adjustable for elevation.
Features: Velocity about 550 fps. Short, light rifle for young shooters. Plastic buttplate, blued metal. Imported from West Germany by Great Lakes Airguns.
Price: **$89.50**

BEEMAN/FEINWERKBAU 124/127 MAGNUM
Caliber: 177 (FWB-124); 22 (FWB-127); single shot.
Barrel: 18.3", 12-groove rifling.
Weight: 6.8 lbs. **Length:** 43½" over-all.
Power: Spring piston air; single stroke barrel cocking.
Stock: Walnut finished hardwood.
Sights: Tunnel front; click-adj. rear for w., slide-adj. for e.
Features: Velocity 680-820 fps, cocking effort of 18 lbs. Forged steel receiver; nylon non-drying piston and breech seals. Auto. safety, adj. trigger. Standard model has no checkering, cheekpiece. Deluxe has hand-checkerd p.g. and

Beeman FWB 124/127

fore-end, high comb cheekpiece, and buttplate with white spacer. Imported by Beeman, available from Beeman, Great Lakes Airguns (124 only).
Price: Standard model **$269.50**
Price: Deluxe model (illus.) **$299.50**

FWB 300-S Universal

BEEMAN/FEINWERKBAU 300-S "UNIVERSAL" MATCH
Caliber: 177, single shot.
Barrel: 19.9".
Weight: 10.2 lbs. (without barrel sleeve). **Length:** 43.3" over-all.
Power: Spring piston, single stroke sidelever.
Stock: Walnut, stippled p.g. and fore-end. Detachable cheekpieces (one std., high for scope use.) Adjustable buttplate, accessory rail. Buttplate and grip cap spacers included.
Sights: Two globe fronts with interchangeable inserts. Rear is match aperture with rubber eyecup and sight viser. Front and rear sights move as a single unit.

Features: Recoilless, vibration free. Grooved for scope mounts. Steel piston ring. Cocking effort about 9½ lbs. Barrel sleeve optional. Left-hand model available. Introduced 1978. Imported by Beeman.
Price: Right-hand **$789.50**
Price: Left-hand **$850.00**

FWB 300-S

BEEMAN/FEINWERKBAU 300-S SERIES MATCH RIFLE
Caliber: 177, single shot.
Barrel: 19.9", fixed solid with receiver.
Weight: Approx. 10 lbs. with optional bbl. sleeve. **Length:** 42.8" over-all.

Power: Single stroke sidelever, spring piston.
Stock: Match model—walnut, deep fore-end, adj. buttplate.
Sights: Globe front with interchangeable inserts. Click micro. adj. match aperture rear. Front and rear sights move as a single unit.
Features: Recoilless, vibration free. Five-way adjustable match trigger. Grooved for scope mounts. Permanent lubrication, steel piston ring. Cocking effort 9 lbs. Optional 10 oz. bbl. sleeve. Available from Beeman.
Price: Right hand **$698.50**
Price: Left hand **$749.50**

CAUTION: PRICES CHANGE. CHECK AT GUNSHOP.

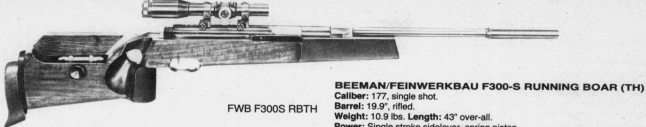

FWB F300S RBTH

BEEMAN/FEINWERKBAU MODEL 600 AIR RIFLE
Caliber: 177, single shot.
Barrel: NA.
Weight: NA. **Length:** NA.
Power: Single stroke pneumatic.
Stock: Special laminated hardwoods and hard rubber for stability.
Sights: Tunnel front with interchangeable inserts, click micrometer match aperture rear.
Features: Recoilless action; double supported barrel; special, short rifled area frees pellet from barrel faster so shooter's motion has minimum effect on accuracy. Fully adjustable match trigger. Trigger and sights blocked when loading latch is open. Imported by Beeman. Introduced 1984.
Price: About $800.00

BEEMAN/FEINWERKBAU F300-S RUNNING BOAR (TH)
Caliber: 177, single shot.
Barrel: 19.9", rifled.
Weight: 10.9 lbs. **Length:** 43" over-all.
Power: Single stroke sidelever, spring piston.
Stock: Walnut with adjustable buttplate, grip cap and comb. Designed for fixed and moving target use.
Sights: None furnished; grooved for optional scope.
Features: Recoilless, vibration free. Permanent lubrication and seals. Barrel stabilizer weight included. Crisp single-stage trigger. Available from Beeman.
Price: Right-hand $698.00
Price: Left-hand $760.00

FWB Mini-Match

BEEMAN/FEINWERKBAU 300-S MINI-MATCH
Caliber: 177, single shot.
Barrel: 17⅛".
Weight: 8.8 lbs. **Length:** 40" over-all.

Power: Spring piston, single stroke sidelever cocking.
Stock: Walnut. Stippled grip, adjustable buttplate. Scaled-down for youthful or slightly built shooters.
Sights: Globe front with interchangeable inserts, micro. adjustable rear. Front and rear sights move as a single unit.
Features: Recoilless, vibration free. Grooved for scope mounts. Steel piston ring. Cocking effort about 9½ lbs. Barrel sleeve optional. Left-hand model available. Introduced 1978. Imported by Beeman.
Price: Right-hand $649.50
Price: Left-hand $695.00

BEEMAN/WEBLEY VULCAN II DELUXE
Caliber: 177 or 22, single shot.
Barrel: 17", rifled.
Weight: 7.6 lbs. **Length:** 43.7" over-all.
Power: Spring piston air, barrel cocking.
Stock: Walnut. Cut checkering, rubber butt pad, checkpiece. Standard version has walnut-stained beech.
Sights: Hooded front, micrometer rear.

Webley Vulcan II

Features: Velocity of 830 fps (177), 675 fps (22). Single stage adjustable trigger; receiver grooved for scope mounting. Self-lubricating piston seal. Introduced 1983. Imported by Beeman.
Price: Standard $189.50
Price: Deluxe $229.50

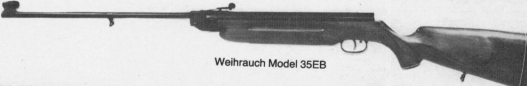

Weihrauch Model 35EB

BEEMAN HW 35L/35EB SPORTER RIFLES
Caliber: 177 (35L), 177 or 22 (35EB), single shot.
Barrel: 19½".
Weight: 8 lbs. **Length:** 43½" over-all (35L).
Power: Spring, barrel cocking.
Stock: Walnut finish with high comb, full pistol grip.
Sights: Globe front with five inserts, target micrometer rear with rubber eyecup.
Features: Fully adjustable trigger, manual safety. Thumb-release barrel latch. Model 35L has Bavarian cheekpiece stock, 35EB has walnut, American-style stock with cheekpiece, sling swivels, white spacers. Imported by Beeman, available from Beeman, Great Lakes Airguns.
Price: Model 35L $269.50
Price: Model 35EB $299.50

BEEMAN HW 55 TARGET RIFLES

Model:	55SM	55MM	55T
Caliber:	177	177	177
Barrel:	18½"	18½"	18½"
Length:	43½"	43½"	43½"
Wgt. lbs.:	7.8	7.8	7.8
Rear sight:	All aperture		
Front sight:	All with globe and 4 interchangeable inserts.		
Power:	All spring (barrel cocking). 660-700 fps.		
Price:	$369.50	$450.50	$449.50

Features: Trigger fully adj. and removable. Micrometer rear sight adj. for w. and e. on all. Pistol grip high comb stock with beavertail fore-end, walnut finish stock on 55SM. Walnut stock on 55MM, Tyrolean stock on 55T. Imported by Beeman.

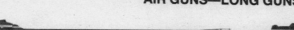

Beeman HW77

BEEMAN/HW77 AIR RIFLE
Caliber: 177 or 22, single shot.
Barrel: 18.5", 12-groove rifling.
Weight: 8.9 lbs. **Length:** 43.7" over-all.
Power: Spring-piston; underlever cocking.
Stock: Walnut-stained beech; rubber buttplate, cut checkering on grip; cheek-piece.
Sights: Blade front, open adjustable rear.
Features: Velocity 830 fps. Fixed-barrel with fully opening, direct loading breech. Extended underlever gives good cocking leverage. Adjustable trigger. Grooved for scope mounting. Imported by Beeman.
Price: Right-hand $359.50
Price: Left-hand $389.50

BEEMAN CARBINE MODEL C1
Caliber: 177, single shot.
Barrel: 14", 12-groove rifling.
Weight: 6¼ lbs. **Length:** 38" over-all.
Power: Spring-piston, barrel cocking.
Stock: Walnut-stained beechwood with rubber butt pad.
Sights: Blade front, rear click-adjustable for windage and elevation.
Features: Velocity 830 fps. Adjustable trigger. Receiver grooved for scope mounting. Imported by Beeman.
Price: $169.50

Beeman Falcon 1

BEEMAN FALCON 1 AIR RIFLE
Caliber: 177, single shot.
Barrel: 18", rifled.
Weight: 6.6 lbs. **Length:** 43" over-all.
Power: Spring-piston, barrel cocking.
Stock: Walnut-stained hardwood.
Sights: Tunnel front with interchangeable inserts; rear with rotating disc to give four sighting notches.
Features: Velocity 680 fps. Match-type adjustable trigger. Receiver grooved for scope mounting. Imported by Beeman.
Price: $139.95

Beeman Falcon 2 Air Rifle
Similar to the Falcon 1 except weighs 5.8 lbs., 41" over-all; front sight is hooded post on ramp, rear sight has two-way click adjustments. Adjustable trigger. Imported by Beeman.
Price: $109.95

Beeman Model R1

BEEMAN R1 AIR RIFLE
Caliber: 177 or 22, single shot.
Barrel: 19.6", 12-groove rifling.
Weight: 8.5 lbs. **Length:** 45.2" over-all.
Power: Spring-piston, barrel cocking.
Stock: Walnut-stained beech; cut checkered pistol grip Monte Carlo comb and cheekpiece; rubber butt pad.
Sights: Tunnel front with interchangeable inserts, open rear click adjustable for windage and elevation. Grooved for scope mounting.
Features: Velocity of 940 fps (177), 800 fps (22). Non-drying nylon piston and breech seals. Adjustable metal trigger. Right or left hand stock. Imported by Beeman.
Price: Right hand, 177 . . . . $329.50
Price: Left hand, 177 . . . . $359.50
Price: Right hand, 22 . . . . $329.50
Price: Left hand, 22 . . . . $359.50

BEEMAN R8 AIR RIFLE
Caliber: 177, single shot.
Barrel: 18.3".
Weight: 7.2 lbs. **Length:** 43.1" over-all.
Power: Barrel cocking, spring-piston.
Stock: Walnut with Monte Carlo cheekpiece; checkered pistol grip.
Sights: Globe front, fully adjustable rear; interchangeable inserts.
Features: Velocity of 735 fps. Nylon piston and breech seals. Adjustable match-grade, two-stage, grooved metal trigger. Rubber butt pad. Imported by Beeman.
Price: $229.50

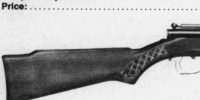

Beeman R7

Beeman R7 Air Rifle
Similar to the R8 model except has double-jointed cocking lever, match grade trigger block; velocity of 680-700 fps; barrel length 17"; weights 5.8 lbs. Imported by Beeman.
Price: $169.50

Benjamin Series 340

BENJAMIN SERIES 3100 SUPER REPEATER RIFLES
Caliber: BB, 100-shot; 22, 85-shot.
Barrel: 23", rifled or smoothbore.
Weight: 6¼ lbs. **Length:** 35" over-all.
Power: Hand pumped.
Features: Bolt action. Piggy back full view magazine. Bar V adj. rear sight. Walnut stock and pump handle.
Price: M3100, BB $92.60
Price: M3120, 22 rifled $92.60

BENJAMIN SERIES 340 AIR RIFLE
Caliber: 22 or 177, pellets or BB; single shot.
Barrel: 23", rifled and smoothbore.
Weight: 6 lbs. **Length:** 35" over-all.
Power: Hand pumped.
Features: Bolt action, walnut Monte Carlo stock and pump handle. Ramp-type front sight, adj. stepped leaf type rear. Push-pull safety.
Price: M340, BB $96.20
Price: M343, 22 . . . . $96.20
Price: M347, 177 . . . . $96.20

AIR GUNS—LONG GUNS

Crosman Model 84

CROSMAN MODEL 1 RIFLE
Caliber: 22, single shot.
Barrel: 19", rifled brass.
Weight: 5 lbs., 1 oz. **Length:** 39" over-all.
Power: Pneumatic, variable power.
Stock: Walnut stained American hardwood.
Sights: Blade front, Williams rear with micrometer click settings.
Features: Precision trigger mechanism for light, clean pull. Metal receiver grooved for scope mounting. Bolt action with cross-bolt safety. Muzzle velocities range from 365 fps (three pumps) to 625 fps (10 pumps). Introduced 1981.
Price: About $79.00

CROSMAN MODEL 84 CO₂ MATCH RIFLE
Caliber: 177, single shot.
Barrel: 18¼". Barrel has a shroud to give extra sight radius. Choice of blue, stainless steel or chrome.
Weight: 10.2 lbs. **Length:** 43" over-all.
Power: Refillable CO_2 cylinders.
Stock: Walnut; Olympic match design with stippled pistol grip and fore-end, adjustable buttplate and comb.
Sights: Match sights — globe front micrometer adjustable rear.
Features: A CO_2 pressure regulated rifle with adjustable velocity up to 720 fps. Each CO_2 cylinder has more than enough power to complete a 60-shot Olympic match course. Electric trigger adjustable from ½ oz. to 3 lbs. Each gun can be custom fitted to the shooter. Made in U.S.A. Introduced 1984.
Price: About $1,500.00

Crosman 2200 Magnum

CROSMAN MODEL 2200 MAGNUM AIR RIFLE
Caliber: 22, single-shot.
Barrel: 19", rifled steel.
Weight: 4 lbs., 13 oz. **Length:** 39¾" over-all.
Stock: Full-size, wood-grained plastic with checkered p.g. and fore-end.
Sights: Ramp front, open step-adjustable rear.
Features: Variable pump power—3 pumps give 395 fps, 6 pumps 530 fps, 10 pumps 620 fps (average). Full-size adult air rifle. Has white line spacers at pistol grip and buttplate. Introduced 1978.
Price: About $54.00

CROSMAN MODEL 788 BB SCOUT RIFLE
Caliber: 177, BB.
Barrel: 14", steel.
Weight: 2 lbs. 7 oz. **Length:** 31" over-all.
Stock: Wood-grained ABS plastic.
Sights: Blade on ramp front, open adj. rear.
Features: Variable pump power—3 pumps give MV of 330 fps, 6 pumps 437 fps, 10 pumps 470 fps (BBs, average). Steel barrel, cross-bolt safety. Introduced 1978.
Price: About $26.00

CROSMAN MODEL 66 POWERMASTER
Caliber: 177 (single shot) or BB
Barrel: 20", rifled, solid steel.
Weight: 3 lbs., 14 oz. **Length:** 38½" over-all.
Stock: Wood-grained plastic; checkered p.g. and fore-end.
Sights: Ramp front, fully adjustable open rear.
Features: Velocity about 675 fps. Bolt action, cross-bolt safety. Introduced 1983.
Price: About $40.00

Crosman Model 66

CROSMAN MODEL 6100 CHALLENGER RIFLE
Caliber: 177, single shot.
Weight: 7 lbs., 12 oz. **Length:** 46" over-all.
Power: Spring air, barrel cocking.
Stock: Stained hardwood with checkered pistol grip, rubber recoil pad.
Sights: Globe front, open fully adjustable rear.
Features: Average velocity 820 fps. Automatic safety, two-stage adjustable trigger. Receiver grooved for scope mounting. Introduced 1982. Imported from West Germany by Crosman Air Guns.
Price: About $202.25

Crosman 6100 Challenger

Crosman Model 781

CROSMAN MODEL 781 SINGLE PUMP
Caliber: 177, BB, 4-shot pellet clip, 195-shot BB magazine.
Barrel: 19½".
Weight: 2 lbs., 14 oz. **Length:** 35¾" over-all.
Power: Pneumatic, single pump.
Stock: Wood-grained plastic; checkered p.g. and fore-end.
Sights: Blade front, open adjustable rear.
Features: Velocity of 350-400 fps (pellets). Uses only one pump. Hidden BB reservoir holds 195 shots; pellets loaded via 4-shot clip. Introduced 1984.
Price: About $25.00

CAUTION: PRICES CHANGE. CHECK AT GUNSHOP.

Crosman 2100 Classic

CROSMAN MODEL 2100 CLASSIC AIR RIFLE
Caliber: 177 pellets or BBs, 180-shot BB magazine.
Barrel: 21", rifled.
Weight: 4 lbs., 13 oz. **Length:** 39¾" over-all.
Power: Pump-up, pneumatic.
Stock: Wood-grained checkered ABS plastic.
Features: Three pumps gives about 450 fps, 10 pumps about 700 fps. Cross-bolt safety; concealed reservoir holds over 180 BBs.
Price: About **$45.00**

Crosman Model 760

CROSMAN MODEL 760 PUMPMASTER
Caliber: 177 pellets or BB, 200 shot.
Barrel: 19½", rifled steel.
Weight: 4 lbs., 3 oz. **Length:** 35" over-all.
Power: Pneumatic, hand pump.
Features: Short stroke, power determined by number of strokes. Walnut finished plastic checkered stock and fore-end. Post front sight and adjustable rear sight. Cross-bolt safety. Introduced 1983.
Price: About **$30.00**

DAISY MODEL 850/851 PNEUMATIC RIFLE
Caliber: BB or 177, 100-shot BB reservoir.
Barrel: 20.8", rifled steel.
Weight: 4.3 lbs. **Length:** 33⅜" over-all.
Power: Single pump pneumatic.
Stock: Moulded plastic with woodgrain finish.
Sights: Ramp front, fully adjustable open rear.
Features: Shoots either BB's or pellets at 520 fps (BB) and 480 fps (pellet). Manual cross-bolt trigger block safety. Introduced 1981.
Price: About **$62.00**
Price: Model 851 (as above with wood stock and fore-end) **$80.00**

Daisy Model 850

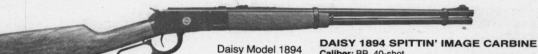

Daisy Model 1894

DAISY 1894 SPITTIN' IMAGE CARBINE
Caliber: BB, 40-shot.
Barrel: 17½", smoothbore.
Length: 38⅜" over-all.
Power: Spring.
Features: Cocks halfway on forward stroke of lever, halfway on return.
Price: About **$43.00**

Daisy Model 840

DAISY MODEL 840
Caliber: 177 pellet (single-shot) or BB (350-shot).
Barrel: 19", smoothbore, steel.
Weight: 3¼ lbs. **Length:** 37⅛" over-all.
Stock: Moulded wood-grain stock and fore-end.
Sights: Ramp front, open, adj. rear.
Features: Single pump pneumatic rifle. Muzzle velocity 325 fps (BB), 300 fps (pellet). Steel buttplate; straight pull bolt action; cross-bolt safety. Fore-end forms pump lever. Introduced 1978.
Price: About **$36.00**

Daisy Model 95

DAISY RIFLES

Model:	95	111	105
Caliber:	BB	BB	BB
Barrel:	18"	18"	13½"
Length:	35"	35"	30½"
Power:	Spring	Spring	Spring
Capacity:	700	700	450
Price: About	$30.00	$27.00	$24.00

Features: Model 95 stock and fore-end are wood; 105 and 111 have plastic stocks.

CAUTION: PRICES CHANGE. CHECK AT GUNSHOP.

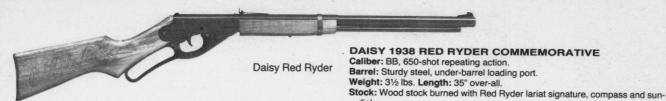

Daisy Red Ryder

ERMA ELG 10 AIR RIFLE
Caliber: 177, single shot.
Barrel: 17.7″, rifled.
Weight: 6.4 lbs. **Length:** 38.2″.
Power: Spring-piston, lever-action cocking.
Stock: Walnut-stained beechwood.
Sights: Hooded ramp post front, open rear adjustable for windage and elevation.
Features: Velocity to 550 fps. Sliding manual safety. Dummy magazine tube under barrel contains a brass cleaning rod. Imported by Beeman.
Price: **$279.50**

DAISY 1938 RED RYDER COMMEMORATIVE
Caliber: BB, 650-shot repeating action.
Barrel: Sturdy steel, under-barrel loading port.
Weight: 3½ lbs. **Length:** 35″ over-all.
Stock: Wood stock burned with Red Ryder lariat signature, compass and sundial.
Sights: Post front, adjustable V-slot rear.
Features: Wood fore-end. Saddle ring with leather thong. Lever cocking. Gravity feed. Controlled velocity. Commemorates one of Daisy's most popular guns, the Red Ryder of the 1940s and 1950s.
Price: About **$43.00**

El Gamo 126

EL GAMO 126 SUPER MATCH TARGET RIFLE
Caliber: 177, single shot.
Barrel: Match grade, precision rifled.
Weight: 10.6 lbs. **Length:** 43.8″ over-all.
Power: Single pump pneumatic.
Stock: Match-style, hardwood, with stippled grip and fore-end.
Sights: Hooded front with interchangeable elements, fully adjustable match rear.

Features: Velocity of 590 fps. Adjustable trigger; easy loading pellet port; adjustable butt pad. Introduced 1984. Imported from Spain by Daisy.
Price: About **$400.00**

MARATHON MODEL 100 AIR RIFLE
Caliber: 177, single shot.
Barrel: 17″, rifled.
Weight: 5.7 lbs. **Length:** 41″ over-all.
Stock: Walnut-stained hardwood with Monte Carlo cheekpiece.
Sights: Hooded post front, micro click open rear.
Features: Velocity of 525 fps. Automatic safety; receiver grooved for scope mounting. Introduced 1984. Imported from Spain by Marathon Products.
Price: **$69.95**

Marathon Model 200 Air Rifle
Similar to the Model 100 except has adjustable trigger, velocity of 640 fps, tunnel front sight with interchangeable inserts, buttplate with white line spacer, and over-all length of 41¾″. Available in 177 or 22 caliber. Introduced 1984.
Price: **$89.95**

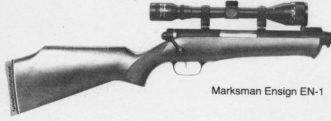

Marksman Ensign EN-1

MARKSMAN ENSIGN MODEL EN-1 AIR RIFLE
Caliber: 177 or 22, 2-shot repeater.
Barrel: 17½″.
Weight: 6½ lbs. **Length:** 41″ over-all.
Power: Compressed air cartridges.
Stock: Walnut on the Royale, walnut-stained beechwood on Elite.
Sights: Open, fully adjustable.
Features: Velocity of 1000 fps (177), 800 fps (22). Bolt action, uses pre-primed centerfire cartridges; recoilless action; fully adjustable 2-stage trigger. Interchangeable barrels available to switch calibers. Comes with a charging unit for the cartridges and 10 cartridges. Introduced 1984. Imported from England.
Price: Royale, about **$375.00**
Price: Elite, about.. **$335.00**

Marksman Model 1770

MARKSMAN MODEL #1770 AIR RIFLE
Caliber: 177, 25-shot repeater.
Barrel: 17″.
Weight: 5¾ lbs. **Length:** 42″ over-all.
Power: Spring air, barrel cocking.
Stock: Walnut-finished beechwood with Monte Carlo.
Sights: Hooded ramp front, micro adjustable rear.
Features: Velocity of 575 fps. Fully adjustable trigger. Magazine tube on top of action. Introduced 1984.
Price: With open sights................................... **$120.00**
Price: With 3-7 x 20 scope **$150.00**

CAUTION: PRICES CHANGE. CHECK AT GUNSHOP.

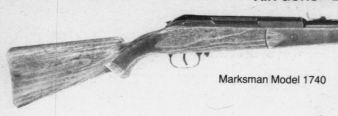

Marksman Model 1740

NORICA MODEL 73 AIR RIFLE
Caliber: 177 or 22, single shot.
Barrel: 18".
Weight: 6¼ lbs. **Length:** 41¾" over-all.
Power: Spring air, barrel cocking.
Sights: Hooded front with four interchangeable blades, open adjustable rear.
Features: Velocity 610 fps. Adult-size stock with full pistol grip; two-stage trigger; receiver grooved for scope mounting. Imported from Spain by Kassnar. Introduced 1984.
Price: **$64.00**

NORICA MODEL 80G AIR RIFLE
Caliber: 177 or 22, single shot.
Barrel: 18".
Weight: 7¼ lbs. **Length:** 43" over-all.
Power: Spring air, barrel cocking.
Stock: Monte Carlo competition-style.
Sights: Hooded front with four interchangeable blades, fully adjustable diopter rear on ramp.
Features: Velocity 610 fps. Adjustable trigger; target-type buttplate; blued metal. Imported from Spain by Kassnar. Introduced 1984.
Price: **$80.00**

POWER LINE MODEL 120 CADET RIFLE
Caliber: 177, single shot.
Barrel: 15.7", rifled.
Weight: 5.2 lbs. **Length:** 37.4" over-all.
Power: Spring air, barrel cocking.
Stock: Stained hardwood.
Sights: Hooded post front on ramp, open fully adjustable rear.
Features: Velocity of 650 fps. Lever-type automatic safety, blued steel receiver. Imported from Spain by Daisy. Introduced 1984.
Price: About **$69.00**

POWER LINE 880 PUMP-UP AIR GUN
Caliber: 177 pellets, BB.
Barrel: Smooth bore, steel.
Weight: 6 lbs. **Length:** 37¾" over-all.
Power: Spring air.
Stock: Wood grain moulded plastic.
Sights: Ramp front, open rear adj. for e.
Features: Crafted by Daisy. Variable power (velocity and range) increase with pump strokes. 10 strokes for maximum power. 100-shot BB magazine. Cross-bolt trigger safety. Positive cocking valve.
Price: About **$60.00**
Price: Model 980 (as above with hardwood stock and fore-end), about **$90.00**

POWER LINE MODEL 917/922
Caliber: 177 (917), 22 (922), 5-shot clip.
Barrel: 20.8". Decagon rifled brass barrel.
Weight: 5 lbs. **Length:** 37¾" over-all.
Stock: Moulded wood-grained plastic with checkered p.g. and fore-end.
Sights: Ramp front, full adj. open rear.
Features: Muzzle velocity from 285 fps. (two pumps) to 555 fps. (ten pumps). Straight pull bolt action. Separate buttplate and grip cap with white spacers. Introduced 1978.
Price: About **$64.00**
Price: Models 970/920 (as above with hardwood stock and fore-end), about **$100.00**

MARKSMAN 1740 AIR RIFLE
Caliber: 177 or 100-shot BB repeater.
Barrel: 15½", smoothbore.
Weight: 5 lbs., 1 oz. **Length:** 36½" over-all.
Power: Spring, barrel cocking.
Stock: Moulded high-impact ABS plastic.
Sights: Ramp front, open rear adj. for e.
Features: Automatic safety; fixed front, adj. rear sight; shoots 177 cal. BB's pellets and darts. Velocity about 475-500 fps.
Price: **$29.50**
Price: Model 1744 (as above with 4 x 15 scope) **$43.50**

NORICA BLACK WIDOW AIR RIFLE
Caliber: 177 or 22, single shot.
Barrel: 16½".
Weight: 5¼ lbs. **Length:** 37½" over-all.
Power: Spring air, barrel cocking.
Stock: Black stained hardwood.
Sights: Hooded front, open adjustable rear.
Features: Velocity 500 fps. Stocked for young shooters. Receiver grooved for scope mounting. Imported from Spain by Kassnar. Introduced 1984.
Price: **$49.00**

POWER LINE 881 PUMP-UP AIR GUN
Caliber: 177 pellets, BB.
Barrel: Decagon rifled.
Weight: 6 lbs. **Length:** 37¾" over-all.
Power: Spring air.
Stock: Wood grain moulded plastic with Monte Carlo cheekpiece.
Sights: Ramp front, step-adj. rear for e.
Features: Crafted by Daisy. Accurized version of Model 880. Checkered fore-end and p.g.
Price: About **$73.00**

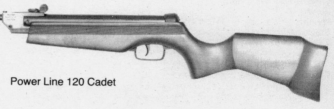

Power Line 120 Cadet

Power Line 880

Power Line Model 922

CAUTION: PRICES CHANGE. CHECK AT GUNSHOP.

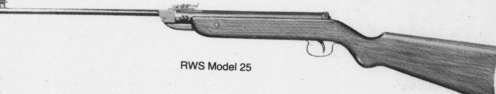

PRECISE MINUTEMAN® MAGNUM
Caliber: 177, single shot.
Barrel: 19.4", rifled.
Weight: 7¼ lbs. **Length:** 44" over-all.
Power: Spring, under-lever cocking.
Stock: Stained hardwood, with cheek rest.
Sights: Hooded front, open rear adj. for w. and e.
Features: Velocity of 575 fps. Blued finish. Receiver grooved for scope mounting. Precise International, importer.
Price: **$100.00**

Precise Minuteman

Precise Minuteman® Middleweight
Similar to the Minuteman Magnum except has 19" barrel, weighs 5½ lbs., has over-all length of 43". Velocity of 785 fps. Introduced 1983. Imported by Precise International.
Price: **$60.00**

Precise Minuteman® Medalist Air Rifle
Same as the Minuteman Middleweight except has ratchet-adjustable open rear sight, barrel lock/release to ease cocking. Introduced 1983. Imported by Precise International.
Price: **$65.00**

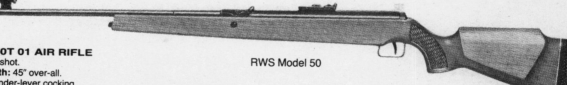

RWS MODEL 25 AIR RIFLE
Caliber: 177, single shot.
Weight: 5¼ lbs. **Length:** 38" over-all.
Power: Spring air, barrel cocking.
Stock: Walnut-finished hardwood.
Sights: Globe front, micro click open rear.
Features: Velocity of 541 fps. Two-stage trigger. Small dimensions for young shooters. Imported from West Germany by Dynamit Nobel of America.
Price: **$120.00**

RWS Model 25

RWS Model 27 Air Rifle
Similar to the Model 25 except has a fully adjustable two stage trigger, micro click rear sight with four-way blade, dovetail base for peep sight or scope mounting. Available in 177 or 22 caliber. Measures 42" over-all and weighs 6 lbs.
Price: 177 or 22 .... **$155.00**

RWS MODEL 50T 01 AIR RIFLE
Caliber: 177, single shot.
Weight: 8 lbs. **Length:** 45" over-all.
Power: Spring air, under-lever cocking.
Stock: Walnut-finished hardwood with cheekpiece, checkered grip, rubber butt pad.
Sights: Globe front, micro click open rear.
Features: Velocity of 750 fps. Automatic safety. Dovetail base for scope or peep sight mounting. Imported from West Germany by Dynamit Nobel of America.
Price: **$270.00**

RWS Model 50

RWS Model 35 Air Rifle
Similar to the Model 27 except slightly heavier and needs less cocking effort. Has hardwood stock with cheekpiece, checkered pistol grip, rubber butt pad. Globe front sight uses optional interchangeable inserts. Available in 177 or 22 caliber. Weighs 6½ lbs.
Price: **$185.00**

RWS Model 75

RWS MODEL 75T 01 MATCH AIR RIFLE
Caliber: 177, single shot.
Barrel: 19".
Weight: 11 lbs. **Length:** 43.7" over-all.
Power: Spring air, side-lever cocking.
Stock: Oil finished walnut with stippled grip, adjustable buttplate, accessory rail, Conforms to I.S.U. rules.
Sights: Globe front with 5 inserts, fully adjustable match peep rear.
Features: Velocity of 574 fps. Fully adjustable trigger. Model 75 HV has stippled fore-end, adjustable cheekpiece. Uses double opposing piston system for recoilless operation. Imported from West Germany by Dynamit Nobel of America.
Price: Model 75T 01 .... **$600.00**
Price: Model 75 HVT 01 .... **$695.00**
Price: Model 75T 01 left hand **$630.00**
Price: Model 75 HVT 01 left hand **$730.00**
Price: Model 75 UT 01 (adj. cheekpiece, buttplate, M82 sight) **$745.00**

Consult our Directory pages for the location of firms mentioned.

RWS Model 75KT 01 Running Boar Air Rifle
Similar to the Model 75 Match except has adjustable cheekpiece and buttplate, different stock, sandblasted barrel sleeve, detachable barrel weight, elevated-grip cocking lever, and a 240mm scope mount. Introduced 1983.
Price: **$730.00**

CAUTION: PRICES CHANGE. CHECK AT GUNSHOP.

RWS MODEL 45 AIR RIFLE

Caliber: 177 or 22, single shot.
Weight: 7¾ lbs. **Length:** 46″ over-all.
Power: Spring air, barrel cocking.
Stock: Walnut-finished hardwood with rubber recoil pad.
Sights: Globe front with interchangeable inserts, micro click open rear with four-way blade.
Features: Velocity of 820 fps (177 cal.), 689 fps (22 cal.). Dovetail base for either micrometer peep sight or scope mounting. Automatic safety. Imported from West Germany by Dynamit Nobel of America.
Price: 177 or 22 .... $210.00
Price: With deluxe walnut stock................................ $245.00

RWS Model 45S Air Rifle

Same as the standard Model 45 except comes without sights and has a 4×20 scope, ramp-type mount, muzzle brake/weight, sling and swivels. Introduced 1983.
Price: $250.00
Price: As above, without scope, mount, sling, swivels $200.00

SIG-HAMMERLI MILITARY LOOK 420

Caliber: 177 or 22, single shot.
Barrel: 19″, rifled.
Weight: About 7 lbs. **Length:** 44¼″ over-all.
Stock: Synthetic stock and handguard.
Sights: Open, fully adj.
Features: Side lever cocking; adjustable trigger; rifled steel barrel. Introduced 1977. Imported by Mandall Shooting Supplies.
Price: $295.00

SIG-Hammerli 403

SIG-HAMMERLI MODELS 401 & 403 AIR RIFLES

Caliber: 177, single shot.
Weight: 7.8 lbs. **Length:** 44″ over-all.
Power: Spring air, sidelever cocking.
Stock: Beechwood.
Sights: Globe front accepts interchangeable inserts; fully adj. open rear (Model 401) or match aperture rear (Model 403).
Features: Sidelever cocking effort of 20 lbs. Automatic safety. Model 403 has a 2-lb. barrel sleeve and adj. buttplate. Fully adj. trigger. Introduced 1980. Imported by Mandall Shooting Supplies, Great Lakes Airguns.
Price: Model 401 (Mandall) $379.00
Price: Model 403, target model (Mandall) $399.50
Price: Model 401 (Great Lakes Airguns) $174.50
Price: Model 403, target model (Great Lakes Airguns) $279.95

> Consult our Directory pages for the location of firms mentioned.

Sharp-Innova Rifle

SHARP-INNOVA AIR RIFLE

Caliber: 177 and 22, single shot.
Barrel: 19.5″, rifled.
Weight: 4.4 lbs. **Length:** 34.6″ over-all.
Power: Pneumatic, multi-stroke.
Stock: Mahogany.
Sights: Hooded front, adjustable aperture rear.

Features: Velocity of 960 fps with 8 pumps (177). Adjustable trigger. Receiver grooved for scope mount. Introduced 1983. Imported from Japan by Great Lakes Airguns.
Price: $129.50

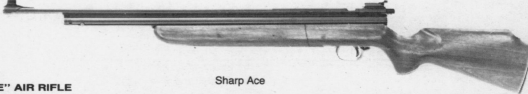

Sharp Ace

SHARP MODEL "ACE" AIR RIFLE

Caliber: 177, 22, single shot.
Weight: 6.3 lbs. **Length:** 38.4″ over-all.
Power: Pneumatic, multi-stroke.
Stock: Stained hardwood.
Sights: Hooded ramp front, fully adjustable peep rear.

Features: Velocity of 1019 fps (177-cal.), 892 fps (22-cal.). Receiver grooved for scope mounting. Turn-bolt action for loading. Introduced 1984. Imported from Japan by Great Lakes Airguns.
Price: $245.95

Sheridan CO_2

Power: Standard 12.5 gram CO_2 cylinder.
Stock: Walnut sporter.
Sights: Open, adj. for w. and e. Optional Sheridan-Williams 5D-SH receiver sight or Weaver D4 scope.
Features: Bolt action single shot, CO_2 powered. Velocity approx. 514 fps., manual thumb safety. Blue or Silver finish. Left-hand models avail. at same prices.
Price: CO_2 Blue Streak $88.95
Price: CO_2 Silver Streak $92.95
Price: CO_2 Blue Streak with receiver sight $105.75
Price: CO_2 Blue Streak with scope $121.95

SHERIDAN CO_2 AIR RIFLES

Caliber: 5mm (20 cal.), single shot.
Barrel: 18½″, rifled.
Weight: 6 lbs. **Length:** 37″ over-all.

Sheridan Blue Streak

SHERIDAN BLUE AND SILVER STREAK RIFLES
Caliber: 5mm (20 cal.), single shot.
Barrel: 18½", rifled.
Weight: 5 lbs. **Length:** 37" over-all.
Power: Hand pumped (swinging fore-end).
Features: Rustproof barrel and piston tube. Takedown. Thumb safety. Mannlicher type walnut stock. Left-hand models same price.
Price: Blue Streak **$101.55**
Price: Silver Streak **$105.40**

Sterling HR-81 Rifle

STERLING HR-81/HR-82 AIR RIFLE
Caliber: 177 or 22, single-shot.
Barrel: 19½".
Weight: 8½ lbs. **Length:** 31½" over-all.
Power: Spring air, (barrel cocking).
Stock: Stained hardwood, with checkpiece, checkered pistol grip.
Sights: Tunnel-type front with four interchangeable elements, open adjustable V-type rear.
Features: Velocity of 900 fps (177), 660 fps (22). Bolt action with easily accessible loading port; adjustable single-stage match trigger; rubber recoil pad. Integral scope mount rails. Scope and mount optional. Introduced 1983. Made in U.S.A. by Benjamin Air Rifle Co.
Price: HR-81 (177 cal.) **$229.00**
Price: HR-82 (22 cal.) **$238.00**

Walther LGV Special

WALTHER LGV SPECIAL
Caliber: 177, single shot.
Barrel: 16", rifled.
Weight: 10¼ lbs. **Length:** 41⅜" over-all.
Power: Spring air (barrel cocking).
Features: Micro. click adj. aperture receiver sight; Adj. trigger. Walnut match stock, adj. buttplate. Double piston provides vibration-free shooting. Easily operated bbl. latch. Removable heavy bbl. sleeve. 5-way adj. trigger. Imported from Germany by Interarms.
Price: **$500.00**

WALTHER LGR RIFLE
Caliber: 177, single-shot.
Barrel: 19½", rifled.
Weight: 10.2 lbs. **Length:** 44¼" over-all.
Power: Side lever cocking, compressed air.
Stock: French walnut.
Sights: Replaceable insert hooded front, Walther micro. adjustable rear.
Features: Recoilless operation. Trigger adj. for weight, pull and position. High comb stock with broad stippled fore-end and p.g. Imported from Germany by Interarms.
Price: **$625.00**

WALTHER LGR UNIVERSAL MATCH AIR RIFLE
Caliber: 177, single shot.
Barrel: 25.5".
Weight: 13 lbs. **Length:** 44¾" over-all.
Power: Spring air, barrel cocking.
Stock: Walnut match design with stippled grip and fore-end, adjustable cheekpiece, rubber butt pad.
Features: Has the same weight and contours as the Walther U.I.T. rimfire target rifle. Comes complete with sights, accessories and muzzle weight. Imported from West Germany by Interarms.
Price: **$725.00**

Weihrauch Model 80

WEIHRAUCH MODEL 80 AIR RIFLE
Caliber: 177, single shot.
Barrel: 19.5", rifled.
Weight: 8.82 lbs. **Length:** 45.28" over-all.
Power: Spring-air, barrel cocking.
Stock: Walnut stained hardwood.
Sights: Globe front, open rear adjustable for windage and elevation.
Features: Velocity of 900 fps. Adjustable trigger, checkered p.g., rubber butt pad. Imported from West Germany by Great Lakes Airguns.
Price: With iron sights **$299.50**

Walther LGR Match Air Rifle
Same basic specifications as standard LGR except has a high comb stock, sights are mounted on riser blocks. Introduced 1977.
Price: **$700.00**

CAUTION: PRICES CHANGE. CHECK AT GUNSHOP.

Chokes & Brakes

Baker Superior Choke Tubes

Stan Baker's Superior choke tubes can be installed only in single-barrel guns. The external diameter of the barrel is enlarged by swaging, allowing enough for reaming and threading to accept the screw-in WinChoke-style tube. Installation on a single-barrel gun without rib is **$85.00**; with vent rib, cost is **$110.00**. Prices are higher for target guns, so contact Baker for specifics. Price includes honing the bore. Extra choke tubes are **$15.95** each. One tube and wrench are provided. Baker also installs WinChoke tubes.

Briley Screw-In Chokes

Installation of these choke tubes requires that all traces of the original choking be removed, the barrel threaded internally with square threads and then the tubes are custom fitted to the specific barrel diameter. The tubes are thin and, therefore, made of stainless steel. Cost of installation for single-barrel guns (pumps, autos) runs **$75.00**; un-single target guns run **$150.00**; over-unders and side-by-sides cost **$150.00** per barrel. Prices include one choke tube and a wrench for disassembly. Extra tubes are **$40.00** each.

Briley also makes "Eccentric" choke tubes that allow horizontal or vertical movement of the pattern up to 11″. Add **$35.00** to the prices above. Installation available only from Briley.

Cellini Recoil Reducer

Designed for handgun and rifle applications, the Cellini Reducer is available as a removable factory-installed accessory. Over-all length is 2½″, weight is 3.5 ounces, and the unit must be installed by the maker. It is said to reduce muzzle jump to zero, even for automatic weapons. Cost starts at $150. Contact Cellini for full details.

Cutts Compensator

The Cutts Compensator is one of the oldest variable choke devices available. Manufactured by Lyman Gunsight Corporation, it is available with a steel body. A series of vents allows gas to escape upward and downward. For the 12-ga. Comp body, six fixed-choke tubes are available: the Spreader—popular with Skeet shooters; Improved Cylinder; Modified; Full; Superfull, and Magnum Full. Full, Modified and Spreader tubes are available for 12, or 20, and an Adjustable Tube, giving Full through Improved Cylinder chokes, is offered in 12, or 20 gauges. Cutts Compensator, complete with wrench, adaptor and any single tube **$63.35**; with adjustable tube **$80.80**. All single choke tubes **$17.50** each. No factory installation available.

Emsco Choke

E. M. Schacht of Waseca, Minn., offers the Emsco, a small diameter choke which features a precision curve rather than a taper behind the 1½″ choking area. 9 settings are available in this 5 oz. attachment. Its removable recoil sleeve can be furnished in dural if desired. Choice of three sight heights. For 12, 16 or 20 gauge. Price installed, **$29.95**. Not installed, **$18.50**.

Lyman CHOKE

The Lyman CHOKE is similar to the Cutts Comp in that it comes with fixed-choke tubes or an adjustable tube, with or without recoil chamber. The adjustable tube version sells for **$34.95** with recoil chamber, in 12 or 20 gauge. Lyman also offers Single-Choke tubes at **$17.50**. This device may be used with or without a recoil-reduction chamber; cost of the latter is **$7.95** extra. Available in 12 or 20 gauge only, no factory installation offered.

Mag-Na-Port

Electrical Discharge Machining works on any firearm except those having shrouded barrels. EDM is a metal erosion technique using carbon electrodes that control the area to be processed. The Mag-na-port venting process utilizes small trapezoidal openings to direct powder gases upward and outward to reduce recoil.

No effect is had on bluing or nickeling outside the Mag-na-port area so no refinishing is needed. Cost for the Mag-na-port treatment is **$49.00** for handguns, **$65.00** for rifles, plus transportation both ways, and **$2.00** for handling.

Poly-Choke

The Poly-Choke Co., manufacturers of the original adjustable shotgun choke, now offers two models in 12, 16, 20 and 28 gauge, the Deluxe Ventilated and the Deluxe Standard. Each provides 9 choke settings including Xtra-Full and Slug. The Ventilated model reduces 20% of a shotgun's recoil, the company claims, and is priced at **$52.25**. The Standard model is **$49.95**, postage not included.

Pro-Choke

Pro-Choke is a system of interchangeable choke tubes that can be installed in any single or double-barreled shotgun, including over-unders. The existing chokes are bored out, the muzzles over-bored and threaded for the tubes. A choice of three Pro-Choke tubes are supplied—Skeet, Imp. Cyl., Mod., Imp. Mod., or Full. Cost of the installation is **$179.95** for single-barrel guns, **$229.95** for doubles. Extra tubes cost **$40** each. Postage and handling charges are **$8.50**.

Pro-Port

A compound ellipsoid muzzle venting process similar to Mag-na-porting, only exclusively applied to shotguns. Like Mag-na-porting, this system reduces felt recoil, muzzle jump, and shooter fatigue. Very helpful for Trap doubles shooters. Pro-Port is a patented process and installation is available in both the U.S. and Canada. Cost for the Pro-Port process is **$110.00** for over-unders (both barrels); **$80.00** for only the bottom barrel; and **$65.00** for single barrel shotguns. Prices do not include shipping and handling.

Walker Choke Tubes

This interchangeable choke tube system uses an adaptor fitted to the barrel without swaging. Therefore, it can be fitted to any single-barreled gun. The choke tubes use the conical-parallel system as used on all factory-choked barrels. These tubes can be used in Winchester, Mossberg, Smith & Wesson, Weatherby, or similar barrels made for the standard screw-in choke system. Available for 10 gauge, 12, 16 and 20. Factory installation with choice of Standard Walker Choke tube is **$90.00**. A full range of constriction is available. Contact Walker Arms for more data.

CAUTION: PRICES CHANGE. CHECK AT GUNSHOP.

Micrometer Receiver Sights

BEEMAN/WEIHRAUCH MATCH APERTURE SIGHT
Micrometer ¼-minute click adjustment knobs with settings indicated on scales. Price **$69.95**

BEEMAN/FEINWERKBAU MATCH APERTURE SIGHTS
Locks into one of four eye-relief positions. Micrometer ¼-minute click adjustments; may be set to zero at any range. Extra windage scale visible beside eyeshade. Primarily for use at 5 to 20 meters. Price **$99.95**

BEEMAN SPORT APERTURE SIGHT
Positive click micrometer adjustments. Standard units with flush surface screwdriver adjustments. Deluxe version has target knobs.
Price: Standard **$32.98**
Price: Deluxe **$38.98**

BUEHLER
"Little Blue Peep" auxiliary rear sight used with Buehler scope mounts.
Price **$3.75**

FREELAND TUBE SIGHT
Uses Unertl 1" micrometer mounts. For 22-cal. target rifles, inc. 52 Win., 37, 40X Rem. and BSA Martini. Price **$123.00**

LYMAN No. 57
¼-min. clicks. Stayset knobs. Quick release slide, adjustable zero scales. Made for almost all modern rifles. Price **$45.95**

LYMAN No. 66
Fits close to the rear of flat-sided receivers, furnished with Stayset knobs. Quick release slide, ¼-min. adj. For most lever or slide action or flat-sided automatic rifles. Price **$45.95**

REDFIELD "PALMA" TARGET SIGHT
Windage and elevation adjustments are ¼-MOA and can be adjusted for "hard" or "soft" feel. Repeatability error limited to .001" per click. Windage latitude 36 MOA, elevation 60 MOA. Mounting arm has three positions, providing ample positioning latitude for other sighting aids such as variable diopter correction, adjustable filters. An insert in the sighting disc block accepts either the standard American sighting disc thread or the European 9.5mm × 1 metric thread. Elevation staff and the sighting disc block have dovetail construction for precise travel. Price **$209.95**

Williams FP-TK on XP-100.

Beeman Sport

Redfield Palma.

WILLIAMS FP
Internal click adjustments. Positive locks. For virtually all rifles, T/C Contender, Heckler & Koch HK-91, Ruger Mini-14, plus Win., Rem. and Ithaca shotguns. Price **$34.75**
With Twilight Aperture **$35.75**
With Target Knobs **$41.35**
With Target Knobs & Twilight Aperture **$42.35**
With Square Notched Blade **$36.55**
With Target Knobs & Square Notched Blade **$43.20**

WILLIAMS 5-D SIGHT
Low cost sight for shotguns, 22's and the more popular big game rifles. Adjustment for w. and e. Fits most guns without drilling or tapping. Also for Br. SMLE. Price **$19.75**
With Twilight Aperture **$20.75**
Extra Shotgun Aperture **$5.15**

WILLIAMS GUIDE
Receiver sight for .30 M1 Car., M1903A3 Springfield, Savage 24's, Savage-Anschutz rifles and Wby. XXII. Utilizes military dovetail; no drilling. Double-dovetail W. adj., sliding dovetail adj. for e. Price **$18.70**
With Twilight Aperture **$19.70**
With Open Sight Blade **$17.20**

Sporting Leaf and Open Sights

BINGHAM SPORTING RIFLE SIGHTS
All-steel sights are imported from Europe. Many styles of both front and rear sights available; random sampling listed here.
European express gold bead for European express ramp **$4.25**
European express ramp **$7.50**
Semi-buckhorn rear, with elevator **$6.50**
Rocky Mountain front, blue or bright **$3.95**
European 2-leaf folding express rear (V and U notch) **$12.50**

BINGHAM CLASSIC SIGHTS
All-steel sights for "classic" rifles. Rear sights only. This listing not complete; contact Bingham for full list.
Model 66 folding ladder-type **$19.95**
Model Saddle Ring Carbine (73, 92, 94, etc.) **$14.95**
Elevator, Winchester-type, early series (1876-WW II) **$4.95**

BURRIS SPORTING REAR SIGHT
Made of spring steel, supplied with multi-step elevator for coarse adjustments and notch plate with lock screw for finer adjustments. Price **$10.95**

LYMAN No. 16
Middle sight for barrel dovetail slot mounting. Folds flat when scope or peep sight is used. Sight notch plate adjustable for e. White triangle for quick aiming. 3 heights: A—.400" to .500", B—.345" to .445", C—.500" to .600".
Price **$9.95**

MARBLE FALSE BASE
New screw-on base for most rifles replaces factory base. ⅜" dovetail slot permits installation of any Marble rear sight. Can be had in sweat-on models also. Price **$4.50**

MARBLE CONTOUR RAMP
For late model Rem. 725, 740, 760, 742 rear sight mounting. ⁹⁄₁₆" between mounting screws. Price **$10.00**

MARBLE FOLDING LEAF
Flat-top or semi-buckhorn style. Folds down when scope or peep sights are used. Reversible plate gives choice of "U" or "V" notch. Adjustable for elevation. Price **$9.00**
Also available with both w. and e. adjustment **$10.50**

MARBLE SPORTING REAR
With white enamel diamond, gives choice of two "U" and two "V" notches of different sizes. Adjustment in height by means of double step elev,2a,2t,2o,2r
and sliding notch piece. For all rifles; screw or dovetail installation.
Price . . . . **$6.25-$10.50**

MILLET RIFLE SIGHT
Open, fully adjustable rear sight fits standard ⅜" dovetail cut in barrel. Choice of white outline or target rear blades, .360". Front with white or orange bar, .343", .400", .430", .460", .500", .540".
Price: Rear sight **$44.95**
Price: Front sight **$9.95**

MILLET RUGER 10/22 SIGHT COMBO
Replacement sight system for the 10/22 rifle has a fully adjustable open rear with deep notch and white outline or target blade. Combo set includes interchangeable white or orange bar front. Also fits Win. 77, 94, Rem. 740-760, 700 old model dovetail rear.
Price: Combo set **$73.95**
Price: Without quick-change front sight feature **$53.95**

WICHITA MULTI RANGE SIGHT SYSTEM
Designed for silhouette shooting. System allows you to adjust the rear sight to four repeatable range settings, once it is pre-set. Sight clicks to any of the settings by turning a serrated wheel. Front sight is adjustable for weather and light conditions with one adjustment. Specify gun when ordering.
Price: Rear sight **$69.95**
Front sight **$39.95**

WILLIAMS DOVETAIL OPEN SIGHT
Open rear sight with w. and e. adjustment. Furnished with "U" notch or choice of blades. Slips into dovetail and locks with gib lock. Heights from .281" to .531". Price with blade **$10.70**
Less Blade **$7.00**
Extra Blades **$3.70**

WILLIAMS GUIDE OPEN SIGHT
Open rear sight with w. and e. adjustment. Bases to fit most military and commercial barrels. Choice of square "U" or "V" notch blade, ³⁄₁₆", ¼", ⁵⁄₁₆", or ⅜" high. Price with blade **$12.90**
Extra blades, each **$3.70**
Price, less blade **$9.20**

Front Sights

LYMAN BLADE & DOVETAIL SIGHTS
Made with gold or ivory beads $\frac{1}{16}$" to $\frac{3}{32}$" wide and in varying heights for most military and commercial rifles. Price $6.95

MARBLE STANDARD
Ivory, red, or gold bead. For all American made rifles, $\frac{1}{16}$" wide bead with semi-flat face which does not reflect light. Specify type of rifle when ordering. Price $5.50

MARBLE-SHEARD "GOLD"
Shows up well even in darkest timber. Shows same color on different colored objects; sturdily built. Medium bead. Various models for different makes of rifles so specify type of rifle when ordering. Price. $6.90

MARBLE CONTOURED
Same contour and shape as Marble-Sheard but uses standard $\frac{1}{16}$" or $\frac{3}{32}$" bead, ivory, red or gold. Specify rifle type. Price $6.35

POLY-CHOKE
Rifle front sights available in six heights and two widths. Model A designed to be inserted into the barrel dovetail; Model B is for use with standard .350 ramp; both have standard $\frac{3}{8}$" dovetails. Gold or ivory color $\frac{1}{16}$" bead. Price $4.95

WILLIAMS GUIDE BEAD SIGHT
Fits all shotguns, $\frac{1}{8}$" ivory, red or gold bead. Screws into existing sight hole. Various thread sizes and shank lengths. Price. $3.65

Globe Target Front Sights

FREELAND SUPERIOR
Furnished with six 1" plastic apertures. Available in 4½"-6½" lengths. Made for any target rifle. Price $37.00
Price with 6 metal insert apertures $39.00
Price, front base $8.00

FREELAND TWIN SET
Two Freeland Superior or Junior Globe Front Sights, long or short, allow switching from 50 yd. to 100 yd. ranges and back again without changing rear sight adjustment. Sight adjustment compensation is built into the set; just interchange and you're "on" at either range. Set includes 6 plastic apertures. Price with 6 metal apertures $58.00

FREELAND MILITARY
Short model for use with high-powered rifles where sight must not extend beyond muzzle. Screw-on base; six plastic apertures. Price . . $35.00
Price with 6 metal apertures $39.00
Price, front base $8.00

LYMAN No. 17A
7 interchangeable inserts which include 4 apertures, one transparent amber and two posts .50" and .100" in width. Price $19.95

REDFIELD Nos. 63 and 64
For rifles specially stocked for scopes where metallic sights must be same height as scopes. Instantly detachable to permit use of scope. Two styles and heights of bases. Interchangeable inserts. No. 64 is ¼" higher. Price No. 63, ... $39.85
No. 64 . . . . $39.65

REDFIELD No. 65
1" long, $\frac{5}{8}$" diameter. Standard dovetail base with 7 aperture or post inserts which are not reversible. For any rifle having standard barrel slot. $\frac{13}{32}$" height from bottom of base to center of aperture. No. 65NB ($29.90) same as above with narrow base. Price $29.90

REDFIELD No. 66
Replaces entire removable front sight stud, locked in place by screw in front of barrel band. ¾" from bottom of base to center of aperture. For Spgfld. 1903. Price $33.90

REDFIELD No. 68
For Win. 52, heavy barrel, Sav. 19 and 33, and other rifles requiring high front sight. $\frac{17}{32}$" from bottom of base to center of aperture. Standard dovetail size only. Price $29.90

REDFIELD OLYMPIC FRONT
Detachable. 10 inserts—5 steel, sizes .090", .110", .120", .140", .150"; one post insert, size .100"; four celluloid, sizes .090", .110", .120", .140". For practically all rifles and with any type rear sight. Fits all standard Redfield, Lyman, or Fecker scope blocks. Price $59.85

REDFIELD INTERNATIONAL SMALLBORE FRONT
Similar to Olympic. Drop-in insertion of eared inserts. Outer sleeve prevents light leakage. Comes complete with 6 clear inserts and 6 skeleton inserts. Price $59.85

REDFIELD INTERNATIONAL BIG BORE
Same as International Match except tube only 2¼" long. For 30 cal. use. Price $55.80

Ramp Sights

JAEGER CUSTOM FRONT SIGHT RAMP
Banded style machined from bar stock. Front sights are interchangeable and slide into the ramp, lock with a set screw. Sights available are Silver Bead ($7.50), Sourdough Bead ($9.00), Silver Bead with Folding Night Sight ($20.00), and Reflective Bead (Raybar-type, $9.00).
Price: Ramp with set screw, wrenches $45.00
Price: Sight hood $3.90

LYMAN SCREW-ON RAMP AND SIGHT
Used with 8-40 screws but may also be brazed on. Heights from .10" to .350". Ramp without sight $11.95

MARBLE FRONT RAMPS
Available in either screw-on or sweat-on style. 5 heights; $\frac{3}{16}$", $\frac{5}{16}$", $\frac{3}{8}$", $\frac{7}{16}$", $\frac{9}{16}$". Standard $\frac{3}{8}$" dovetail slot. Price $11.35
Hoods for above ramps $2.50

WILLIAMS SHORTY RAMP
Companion to "Streamlined" ramp, about ½" shorter. Screw-on or sweat-on. It is furnished in $\frac{1}{8}$", $\frac{3}{16}$", $\frac{9}{32}$", and $\frac{3}{8}$" heights without hood only.
Price $9.20

WILLIAMS STREAMLINED RAMP
Hooded style in screw-on or sweat-on models. Furnished in $\frac{9}{16}$", $\frac{7}{16}$", $\frac{3}{8}$", $\frac{5}{16}$", $\frac{3}{16}$" heights. Price with hood $14.50
Price without hood $12.05

WILLIAMS SHOTGUN RAMP
Designed to elevate the front bead for slug shooting or for guns that shoot high. Diameters to fit most 12, 16, 20 ga. guns. Fastens by screwclamp, no drilling required. Price, with Williams gold bead $8.95
Price, without bead $6.60
Price, with Guide Bead $10.25

Handgun Sights

BINGHAM PISTOL SIGHTS
All-steel sights of various designs for Colt Government Model and Browning Hi-Power. Low profile "battle sights" (front and rear) for either Colt G.M. or Browning HP. Price $16.95
Combat sight set, low profile, white outline for Colt G.M., front and rear $21.95
National Match front sight, Colt G.M. $3.75
Camp Perry front sight, Colt G.M. $4.95

BO-MAR DE LUXE BMCS
Gives $\frac{3}{8}$" w. and e. adjustment at 50 yards on Colt Gov't 45, sight radius under 7". For GM and Commander models only. Uses existing dovetail slot. Has shield-type rear blade. Price $45.00

BO-MAR LOW PROFILE RIB & ACCURACY TUNER
Streamlined rib with front and rear sights; 7⅛" sight radius. Brings sight line closer to the bore than standard or extended sight and ramp. Weighs 5 oz. Made for Colt Gov't 45, Super 38, and Gold Cup 45 and 38. Price $64.00

BO-MAR COMBAT RIB
For S&W Model 19 revolver with 4" barrel. Sight radius 5¾"; weight 5½ oz. Price $55.00

BO-MAR FAST DRAW RIB
Streamlined full length rib with integral Bo-Mar micrometer sight and serrated fast draw sight. For Browning 9mm, S&W 39, Colt Commander 45, Super Auto and 9mm. Price $55.00

BO-MAR WINGED RIB
For S&W 4" and 6" length barrels—K-38, M10, HB 14 and 19. Weight for the 6" model is about 7¼ oz. Price. $63.00

BO-MAR COVER-UP RIB
Adj. rear sight, winged front guards. Fits right over revolver's original front sight. For S&W 4" M-10HB, M-13, M-58, M-64 & 65, Ruger 4" models SDA-34, SDA-84, SS-34, SS-84, GF-34, GF-84. Price. $60.00

C-MORE SIGHTS
Replacement front sight blades offered in two types and five styles. Made of DuPont Acetal, they come in a set of five high-contrast colors: blue, green, pink, red and yellow. Easy to install. Patridge style for Colt Python (all barrels), Ruger Super Blackhawk (7½"), Ruger Blackhawk (4⅝"); Ramp style for Python (all barrels), Blackhawk (4⅝"), Super Blackhawk (7½" and 10½"). From Mag-num Sales Ltd., Inc. Price, per set $14.95

MICRO
Click adjustable w. and e. rear with plain or undercut front sight in $\frac{1}{8}$" widths. Standard model available for 45, Super 38 or Commander autos. Low model for above pistols plus Colt Service Ace. Also for Ruger with 4¾" or 6" barrel. Price for sets. $35.00
Price with ramp front sight $43.00
Adjustable rear sight only $29.50
Front ramp only, with blade. $19.00

MICRO
All-steel replacement for Ruger single-action and double-action revolvers. Two styles: MR-44 for square front end of sight leaf. Price . . . $18.00

CAUTION: PRICES CHANGE. CHECK AT GUNSHOP.

MMC MODEL 84 SIGHT SYSTEM
Replacement sight system for Colt 1911 autos and Browning Hi-Power. Streamlined 1.94" long base covers the dovetail for a custom look. Ideally suited for PPC, metallic silhouette, bowling pin shooting. Contact MMC for details, full prices.

Complete rear sight	$69.00
Serrated ramp front	$8.80
Ramp Bar Cross front	$14.40

MMC "BAR CROSS" SIGHT SYSTEM
Provides a quick, clear sight picture in a variety of lighting conditions. Black oxide finish is non-reflective. Front sight has a horizontal white bar with vertical white bar, gives illusion of cross hair in poor light. Fixed rear comes with or without white outline. Various front blades available.

White outline rear sight	$19.05
Plain rear	$14.85
Ramp Bar Cross front	$13.65

MMC COMBAT DESIGN
Available specifically for Colt M1911 and descendants, High Standard autos, Ruger standard autos. Adaptable to other pistols. Some gunsmithing required. Not necessary to replace front sight. Contact MMC for complete details.

Price, less leaf	$28.75
Plain leaf	$8.55
White outline leaf	$12.55
With reflector beads, add	$2.50

MILLETT SERIES 100 SIGHTS
Replacement sights for revolvers and auto pistols. Positive click adjustments for windage and elevation. Designed for accuracy and ruggedness. Made to fit S&W, Colt, High Standard, Ruger, Dan Wesson, Browning, AMT Hardballer and Abilene handguns. Rear blades are available in white outline or positive black target. All steel construction and easy to install.

Price	$39.95 to $56.95

MILLETT MARK SERIES PISTOL SIGHTS
Mark I and Mark II replacement combat sights for government-type auto pistols. Mark I is high profile, Mark II low profile. Both have horizontal light deflectors.

Mark I, front and rear	$27.95
Mark II, front and rear	$39.95

MILLETT FRONT SIGHTS
All-steel replacement front sights with either white or orange bar. Easy to install. For Ruger Redhawk, Security-Six, Police-Six, Speed-Six, Colt Python, Dan Wesson 22 and 15-2. Price. $$10.95 to $12.95

MILLETT DUAL-CRIMP/STAKE-ON FRONT SIGHTS
Replacement front sights for automatic pistols. Dual-Crimp uses an all-steel two-point hollow rivet system. Available in eight heights and four styles. Stake-On sights have skirted base that covers the front sight pad. Easily installed with the Millett Installation Tool Set. Available in seven heights and four styles—Blaze Orange Bar, White Bar, Serrated Ramp, Plain Post. Price. $12.95

OMEGA OUTLINE SIGHT BLADES
Replacement rear sight blades for Colt and Ruger single action guns and the Interarms Virginian Dragoon. Standard Outline available in gold or white notch outline on blue metal. Price. $5.95

MILLETT DUAL-CRIMP/STAKE-ON FRONT SIGHT
Replacement front sight for automatic pistols. Dual-Crimp uses an all-steel two-point hollow rivet system. Available in eight heights and four styles. Stake-On sights have a skirted base that covers the front sight pad. Easily installed with the Millett Installation Tool Set. Available in seven heights and four styles—Blaze Orange Bar, White Bar, Serrated Ramp, Plain Post. Price. $12.95

OMEGA MAVERICK SIGHT BLADES
Replacement "peep-sight" blades for Colt, Ruger SAs, Virginian Dragoon. Three models available—No. 1, Plain, No. 2, Single Bar, No. 3 Double Bar Rangefinder. Price, each. $6.95

WICHITA SIGHT SYSTEMS
For 45 auto pistols. Target and Combat styles available. Designed by Ron Power. All-steel construction, click adjustable. Each sight has two traverse pins, a large hinge pin and two elevation return springs. Sight blade is serrated and mounted on an angle to deflect light. Patridge front for target, ramp front for combat. Both are legal for ISPC and NRA competitons.

Rear sight, target or combat	$49.50
Front sight, patridge or ramp	$8.95

WICHITA GRAND MASTER DELUXE RIBS
Ventilated rib has wings machined into it for better sight acquisition. Made of stainless steel, sights blued. Uses Wichita Multi-Range rear sight, adjustable front sight. Made for revolvers with 6" barrel.

Price: Model 301 (adj. sight K-frames with custom bbl. of 1.000"-1.032" dia., L and N frames with 1.062"-1.100" bbl.)	$129.95
Price: Model 302 (fixed-sight K-frames; M10, 65, 13 with 1.000" bbl. N-frame with 1.062" bbl.)	$129.95
Price: Model 303 (Model 29, 629 with factory bbl., adj. sight K, L, N frames)	$129.95
Price: Extra for white outline rear sight	$6.00

WICHITA COMBAT V RIBS
Designed by Ron Power, the ventilated rib has a lengthwise V-groove that emphasizes the front sight and reduces glare and distortion. Over-size rear sight blade for the click-adjustable sight. Made for Browning Hi-Power, Colt Commander, Govt. and Gold Cup models, Ruger Mark I, 4" S&W K-frames—models 10HB, 13, 64HB, 65, 58 with 4" barrel. From Wichita Arms Inc.

Price: With sights	$89.95
Price: Extra for white outline rear sight	$6.00

Sight Attachments

FREELAND LENS ADAPTER
Fits 1⅛" O.D. presciption ground lens to all standard tube and receiver sights for shooting without glasses. Price without lens. $44.00

Clear lens ground to prescription	$21.00
Yellow or green prescription lens	$21.00

MERIT ADAPTER FOR GLOBE FRONT SIGHTS
An Iris Shutter Disc with a special adapter for mounting in Lyman or Redfield globe front sights. Price. $42.00

MERIT IRIS SHUTTER DISC
Eleven clicks gives 12 different apertures. No. 3 and Master, primarily target types, 0.22" to .125"; No. 4, ½" dia. hunting type, .025" to .155". Available for all popular sights. The Master Disc, with flexible rubber light shield, is particularly adapted to extension, scope height, and tang sights. All Merit Deluxe models have internal click springs; are hand fitted to minimum tolerance.

Master Deluxe	$54.30
No. 4 Hunting Disc	$37.50

MERIT LENS DISC
Similar to Merit Iris Shutter (Model 3 or Master) but incorporates provision for mounting prescription lens integrally. Lens may be obtained locally from your optician. Sight disc is ⁷⁄₁₆" wide (Mod. 3), or ¾" wide (Master). Model 3 Deluxe. Price. $57.75

Master Deluxe	$67.50

MERIT OPTICAL ATTACHMENT
For revolver and pistol shooters, instantly attached by rubber suction cup to regular or shooting glasses. Any aperture .020" to .156". Price, Deluxe (swings aside). $54.75

WILLIAMS APERTURES
Standard thread, fits most sights. Regular series ⅜" to ½" O.D., .050" to .125" hole. "Twilight" series has white reflector ring. .093" to .125" inner hole. Price, regular series. $2.90 Twilight series $3.95
New wide open ⁵⁄₁₆" aperture for shotguns fits 5-D and Foolproof sights. Price. $5.15

Shotgun Sights

ACCURA-SITE
For shooting shotgun slugs. Three models to fit most shotguns—"A" for vent. rib barrels, "B" for solid ribs, "C" for plain barrels. Rear sight has windage and elevation provisions. Easily removed and replaced. Includes front and rear sights. Price. $25.95 to $27.95

FOR DOUBLE BARREL SHOTGUNS (PRESS FIT)
Marble 214—Ivory front bead, ¹¹⁄₆₄". . .$3.00; 215—same with .080" rear bead and reamers . . .$10.00. Marble 220—Bi-color (gold and ivory) front bead, ¹¹⁄₆₄" and .080" rear bead, with reamers . . .$11.50; Marble 221—front bead only . . .$4.40. Marble 223—Ivory rear .080". . .$2.80. Marble 224—Front sight reamer for 214-221 beads . . .$2.20; Marble 226—Rear sight reamer for 223. Price. $2.20

FOR SINGLE OR DB SHOTGUNS (SCREW-ON FIT)
Marble 217—Ivory front bead ¹¹⁄₆₄". . .$3.30; Marble 216 . . .$6.85; Marble 218—Bi-color front, ¹¹⁄₆₄". . .$4.80; Marble 219 . . .$8.40; Marble 223T—Ivory rear .080" Price. $4.50
Marble Bradley type sights 223BT—⅛", ⁵⁄₆₄" and ¹¹⁄₆₄" long. Gold, Ivory or Red bead. $3.10

MILLETT SHURSHOT SHOTGUN SIGHT
A sight system for shotguns with a ventilated rib. Rear sight attaches to the rib, front sight replaces the front bead. Front has an orange face, rear has two orange bars.

Price: Front and rear	$29.95
Price: As above, adjustable rear	$39.95

POLY-CHOKE
Replacement front sights in four styles—Xpert, Poly Bead, Xpert Mid Rib sights, and Bev-L-Block. Xpert Front available in 3x56, 6x48 thread, ³⁄₃₂" or ⁵⁄₃₂" shank length, gold, ivory ($2.00); or Sun Spot orange bead ($3.00); Poly Bead is standard replacement ⅛" bead, 3x56 or 6x48, short, medium, long shank ($1.50); Xpert Mid Rib in tapered carrier (ivory only) or 3x56 threaded shank (gold only), $2.00; Hi and Lo Blok sights with 6x48 thread, gold or ivory ($2.00) or Sun Spot Orange ($3.00).

SLUG SITE
A combination V-notch rear and bead front sight made of adhesive-backed formed metal approx. 7" over-all. May be mounted, removed and re-mounted as necessary, using new adhesive from the pack supplied. Price. $10.00

CAUTION: PRICES CHANGE. CHECK AT GUNSHOP.

Maker and Model	Magn.	Field at 100 Yds (feet)	Relative Brightness	Eye Relief (in.)	Length (in.)	Tube Diam. (in.)	W&E Adjustments	Weight (ozs.)	Price	Other Data
Aimpoint										
Mark III	0	—	—	—	6	—	Int.	12	219.95	Projects variable intensity aiming dot. Has potentiometer to give fixed dot intensity. Dot covers about 3" @ 100 meters. No parallax. Unlimited eye relief. 3x magnification lens, $94.95, 1.5-4x lens $135.95. Imported by Aimpoint USA, Inc.
American Import Co.										
Dickson 200[1]	4	19	13.7	3.5	11.5	¾	Int.	6	12.50	[1]Complete with mount for 22-cal. RF rifles. [2]Standard crosshair reticle, coated lenses. [3]Anodized finish. [4]Wide angle. [5]Super wide angle. [6]Post and crosshair, 3 post,, tapered post, crosshair and 4-post crosshair all available as options. 2, 3, apply to all models. [7]Complete with bridge mount.
Dickson 218 32mm	2½	32	164	3.7	12	1	Int.	9.3	47.95	
Dickson 220 32mm[2]	4	29	64	3.6	12	1	Int.	9.1	49.95	
Dickson 224 40mm	4	30	100	3.5	12½	1	Int.	10	54.95	
Dickson 226 40mm[3]	6	20	44.7	3.7	13	1	Int.	10	54.95	
Dickson 228 32mm[4]	4	37	64	3.3	12	1	Int.	10.5	73.95	
Dickson 230 40mm	4	37	100	3.8	12.4	1	Int.	12	78.95	
Dickson 231 40mm[4]	6	24½	44.5	3.8	12.4	1	Int.	12	81.00	
Dickson 232 32mm[4]	3-9	42-14	112.4-13	3.1-2.5	12.9	1	Int.	12	93.95	
Dickson 240 32mm	3-9	37-12.3	112-13	3	12.8	1	Int.	13.8	62.95	
Dickson 242 40mm	3.9	37-12.3	177-19.4	3	12.8	1	Int.	15.2	78.95	
Dickson 244 20mm	1½-5	46	177	4.3	11.3	1	Int.	10.3	67.95	
Dickson Pistol 250[7]	1½	15.3	100	11-16	8½	¾	Int.	6	19.95	
Apollo										
4x32 Compact	4	29	—	3.3	11.7	1	Int.	10	132.95	Rubber armored, water and fog proof. Comes with see through filter caps; ¼-minute click adjustments. Imported from Japan by Senno Corp.
3-9x40 Variable	3-9	35.3-13.2	—	3.3-3	12	1	Int.	14	159.95	
Bausch & Lomb										
3x-9x 40mm	3-9	36-12	267	3.2	13	1	Int.	17	339.95	Contact Bushnell for details.
4x 40 mm	4	28	150	3.2	12¾	1	Int.	14½	219.95	
Beeman										
Blue Ribbon 20[1]	1.5	14	150	11-16	8.3	¾	Int.	3.6	47.95	All scopes have 5-pt. reticle, all glass, fully coated lenses. [1]Pistol scope; cast mounts included. [2]Pistol scope; silhouette knobs. [3]Rubber armor coating; built-in double adj. mount, parallax-free setting. [4]Objective focus, built-in double-adj. mount; matte finish. [5]Objective focus. [6]Has 8 lenses; objective focus; milled mounts included. [7]Includes cast mounts. [8]Objective focus; silhouette knobs; matte finish. [9]Has 9 lenses; objective focus. Models RC-11, RC-12, RC-13, RC-16 are wide angle. All RC model scopes are rubber armored. Models RC-16, 17, 18 recommended for rimfire, airgun use; 10, 11, 12, 13, for centerfires. All have coated lenses, waterproof, nitrogen filled; ¼" click adjustments. Imported by Beeman.
Blue Ribbon 25[2]	2	19	150	10-24	9¹/₁₆	1	Int.	7.4	119.50	
SS-1[3]	2.5	30	61	3.25	5½	1	Int.	7	119.95	
SS-2[4]	3	34.5	74	3.5	6.8	1.38	Int.	13.6	189.50	
50R[5]	2.5	33	245	3.5	12	1	Int.	11.8	84.95	
35R[6]	3	25	67	2.5	11¼	¾	Int.	5.1	39.95	
30A[7]	4	21	21	2	10.2	¾	Int.	4.5	34.95	
Blue Ribbon 66R[8]	2-7	62-16	384-31	3	11.4	1	Int.	14.9	159.50	
45R[9]	3-7	26-12	67-9	2.5	10⅝	¾	Int.	6	65.95	
RC-10 4x32	4	29	96	3.3	11.7	1	Int.	10	119.95	
RC-11 4x40	4	38	150	3	12	1	Int.	11.5	149.95	
RC-12 3-9x32	3-9	43.5-15.0	172-20	3.3-3.0	12.2	1	Int.	13.5	159.95	
RC-13 3-9x40	3-9	43.5-15.0	265-29	3.3-3.0	12.2	1	Int.	14.5	169.95	
RC-16 3-9x40	3-9	43.5-15.0	265-29	3.3-3.0	12.2	1	Int.	15.5	189.95	
RC-17 4x32	4	29	96	3.3	11.7	1	Int.	12	139.95	
RC-18 3-9x32	3-9	35.3-13.2	172-20	3.3-3.0	12	1	Int.	14	165.95	
Burris										
4x Fullfield[1]	3.8	37	49	3¼	11¼	1	Int.	11	159.95	Dot reticle $10 extra. Target knobs $15 extra. ½-minute dot $10 extra. LER = Long Eye Relief—ideal for forward mounting on handguns. Plex or crosshair. Matte "Safari" finish avail. on 4x, 6x, 2-7x, 3-9x with Plex reticle, $10 extra. [1]3" dot $10 extra. [2]1"-3" dot $10 extra. [3]1"-3" dot $10 extra. [4]With parallax adjustment $135.95. [5]With parallax adjustment $142.95. [6]With parallax adjustment $151.95. [7]With parallax adjustment $158.95. Parallax adjustment adds 5 oz. to weight.
2x-7x Fullfield[2] HiLume	2.5-6.8	50-19	81-22	3¼	11⅞	1	Int.	14	213.95	
3x-9x Fullfield[3] HiLume	3.3-8.6	40-15	72-17.6	3¼	12¾	1	Int.	15	229.95	
2¾ Fullfield	2.7	53	49	3¼	10½	1	Int.	9	150.95	
6x Fullfield	5.8	24	36	3¼	13	1	Int.	12	172.95	
1¾-5x Fullfield HiLume	2.5-6.8	70-27	121-25	3¼	10¾	1	Int.	13	188.95	
4x-12x Fullfield	4.4-11.8	28-10½	—	3-3¼	15	1	Int.	18	263.95	
■ 6x-18x Fullfield	6.5-17.6	17-7.5	—	3-3¾	15.8	12	Int.	18.5	267.95	
■ 10x Fullfield	9.8	12½	—	3¼	15	1	Int.	15	224.95	
■ 12x Fullfield	11.8	11	—	3¼	15	1	Int.	15	231.95	
2x LER	1.7	21	—	10-24	8¾	1	Int.	6.8	117.95	
3x LER	2.7	17	—	10-20	8⅞	1	Int.	6.8	124.95	
4x LER[6]	3.7	11	—	10-22	9⅝	1	Int.	8.5	133.95	
5x LER[7]	4.5	8.7	—	12-22	10⅞	1	Int.	9.5	140.95	
7x IER	6.5	6.5	—	10-16	11¼	1	Int.	10	172.95	
10x IER	9.5	4	—	8-12	13.6	1	Int.	14	199.95	
1½x-4x LER	1.6-3.8	16-11	—	11-24	10½	1	Int.	11	213.95	
2x-7x Mini	2.5-6.9	32-14	—	3¾	9⅜	1	Int.	10.5	159.95	
4x Mini	3.6	24	—	3¾	8¼	1	Int.	7.8	116.95	
6x Mini	5.5	17	—	3¾	9	1	Int.	7.8	124.95	
3x-9x Mini	3.6-8.8	25-11	—	3¾	9⅞	1	Int.	11.5	168.95	
4-12x Mini	4.5-11.6	19-8	—	3¾	11.2	1	Int.	15	249.95	
Bushnell										
Scope Chief VI	4	37.3	150	3	12.3	1	Int.	12	159.95	All ScopeChief, Banner and Custom models come with Multi-X reticle, with or without BDC (bullet drop compensator) that eliminates holdover. Prismatic Rangefinder (PRF) on some models. Contact Bushnell for data on full line. Prices include BDC—deduct $5 if not wanted. Add $30 for PRF. BDC feature available in all Banner models, except 2.5x. [1]Wide angle. [2]Complete with mount rings. [3]Equipped with Wind Drift Compensator and Parallax-free adjustment. [4]Parallax focus adjustment. [5]Wide angle. [6]Wide angle. [7]Parallax focus adjustment. [8]Phantoms intended for handgun use. [9]Mount separate. [10]Has battery-powered, lighted reticle. [11]With mounts.
Scope Chief VI	4	29	96	3½	12	1	Int.	9.3	119.95	
Scope Chief VI	3-9	35-12.6	267-30	3½-3⅓	12.6	1	Int.	14.3	191.95	
Scope Chief VI	3-9	43-14.6	241-26.5	3	12.1	1	Int.	15.4	239.95	
Scope Chief VI	2½-8	45-14	247-96	3.7-3.3	11.2	1	Int.	12.1	169.95	
Scope Chief VI	1½-4½	73.7-24.5	267-30	3.5-3.5	9.6	1	Int.	9.5	159.95	
Scope Chief VI	4-12	29-10	150-17	3.2	13.5	1	Int.	17	234.95	
Centurion Handgun 4x32mm	4	10.2	96	10-20	8¾	1	Int.	9.3	169.95	
Custom 22	4	28.4	—	2½	10⁵/₁₆	⅞	Int.	5¼	41.95	
Custom 22	3-7	29-13.6	28-5	2¼-2½	10	⅞	Int.	6½	51.95	

CAUTION: PRICES CHANGE. CHECK AT GUNSHOP.

Maker and Model	Magn.	Field at 100 Yds (feet)	Relative Bright-ness	Eye Relief (in.)	Length (in.)	Tube Diam. (in.)	W&E Adjust-ments	Weight (ozs.)	Price	Other Data
Bushnell (cont'd.)										
Banner	2½	45	96	3½	10.9	1	Int.	8	86.95	
Banner 32mm	4	29	96	3½	12	1	Int.	10	100.95	
Banner 40mm	4	37⅓	150	3	12⅓	1	Int.	12	131.95	
Banner Lite-Site 4x[10]	4	28	150	3.3	12.9	1	Int.	11½	199.95	
Banner 40mm	6	19.5	67	3	13.5	1	Int.	11.5	109.95	
Banner[1]	6	19½	42	3	13½	1	Int.	10½	109.95	
Banner 22[2]	4	27.5	37.5	3	11⅝	1	Int.	8	64.95	
■ Banner Silhouette[3]	10	12	24	3	14½	1	Int.	14.6	167.95	
■ Banner	10	12	24	3	14½	1	Int.	14.6	167.95	
Banner[4]	1½-4	63-28	294-41	3½	10½	1	Int.	10.3	123.95	
Banner[5]	1¾-4½	71-27	216-33	3	10.2	1	Int.	11½	143.95	
Banner Lite-Site 3x-9x[10]	3.9	36-12	267	3.5-3.3	13.6	1	Int.	14	239.95	
Banner 32mm	3-9	39-13	171-19	3½	11.5	1	Int.	11	137.95	
Banner 38mm[6]	3-9	43-14.6	241-26½	3	12	1	Int.	14	160.95	
Banner 40mm	3-9	35-12.6	267-30	3½	13	1	Int.	13	180.95	
Banner[7]	4-12	29-10	150-17	3.2	13½	1	Int.	15½	163.95	
Magnum Phantom[8]	1.3	17	441	7-21	7.8	15⁄16	Int.	5½	71.95	
Magnum Phantom[9]	2½	9	100	8-21	9.7	15⁄16	Int.	6½	79.95	
Sportview	3-9	41.5-13.6	241-26.5	3	12.5	1	Int.	14	86.95	
Sportview	4	34.5	135	3	12.5	1	Int.	11.5	66.95	
Sportview 22	3-7	26-12	67.4-12.6	2.5	11.5	1	Int.	5.5	39.95	
Sportview 4x32mm	4	28	96	4	11.8	1	Int.	11.3	59.95	
Sportview 4x15mm[11]	4	17	21	2.3	10.2	⅞	Int.	6	13.95	
Colt										
AR-15 3x	3	40	—	—	6	—	Int.	—	$179.95	All Colt scopes come complete with mount and allow use of iron sights. Reflex sighting system provides a variable intensity red dot; battery oper-ated, batteries not included.
AR-15 4x	4	30	—	—	6	—	Int.	—	198.50	
Reflex Sight	1	—	—	—	7½	—	Int.	—	212.95	
Davis Optical										
Spot Shot 1½"	10,12 15,20 25,30	10-4	—	2	25	.75	Ext.	—	116.00	Focus by moving non-rotating obj. lens unit. Ext. mounts included. Recoil spring $4.50 extra.
Spot Shot 1¼"	10,12, 15,20	10.6	—	2	25	.75	Ext.	—	90.00	
Fontaine										
4x32 Wide Angle	4	38	64	3.0	11.8	1	Int.	10.0	104.45	Non-waterproof also available. Scopes listed have Jennison TCS with Optima system. Extra TCS drums $5.50 ea. Scopes with TCS also avail. Also with duplex reticle.
4 x 40 Wide Angle	4	38	100	3.0	12.0	1	Int.	11.6	127.00	
3-9 x 32 Wide Angle	3-9	43.5-15	114-12.8	3.3-3.0	12.2	1	Int.	12.0	156.20	
3-9 x 40 Wide Angle	3-9	43.5-15	177.3-19.6	3.3-3.0	12.2	1	Int.	12.5	175.40	
Jason										
860	4	29	64	3	11.8	1	Int.	9.2	50.00	Constantly centered reticles, ballbearing click stops, nitrogen filled tubes, coated lenses. 4-Post crosshair about $3.50 extra on models 860, 861, 864, 865.
861	3-9	35-13	112-12	3	12.7	1	Int.	10.9	76.00	
862	4	19	14	2	11	¾	Int.	5.5	13.50	
863C	3-7	23-10	43-8	3	11	¾	Int.	8.4	44.00	
865	3-9	35-13	177-19	3	13	1	Int.	12.2	80.00	
869	4	19	25	2	11.4	¾	Int.	6	23.00	
873	4	29	100	3	12.7	1	Int.	11.1	75.00	
875	3-9	35-13	177-19	3	13	1	Int.	12.2	80.00	
877	4	37	100	3	11.6	1	Int.	11.6	85.00	
878	3-9	42.5-13.6	112-12	2.7	12.7	1	Int.	12.7	110.00	
Kahles										
Helia Super 2.5 x 20[1]	2.5	50	64	3.25	9.8	1	Int.	12.6	279.00	[1]Lightweight model weighs 10.1 oz. [2]Light-weight—11.2 oz. [3]Lightweight—13 oz. [4]Light-weight—16 oz. [5]Lightweight—12.6 oz. [6]Light-weight—15.4 oz. [7]Lightweight—15.7 oz. [8]Lightweight—17.8 oz. [9]Calibrated for 7.62 NATO ammo, 100 to 800 meters. All scopes have constantly centered reticles except ZF69; all come with lens caps. 30mm rings available for Redfield, Burris, Leupold bases. Imported from Austria by Kahles of America. (Del-Sports, Inc.).
Helia Super 4 x 32[2]	4	30	60	3.25	11.6	1	Int.	15	319.00	
Helia 6 x 42[3]	6	21.1	49	3.25	12.8	1	Int.	17.5	349.00	
Helia 8 x 56[4]	8	15.6	49	3.25	14.8	1	Int.	23	389.00	
Helia 1.1-4.5 x 20[5]	1.1-4.5	72.2-27	328-18	3.25	10.8	30mm	Int.	15	369.00	
Helia 1.5-6 x 20[6]	1.5-6	55.6-19.5	784-49	3.25	12.8	30mm	Int.	20	399.00	
Helia 2.2-9 x 42[7]	2.2-9	36.1-13.5	364-21	3.25	13.7	30mm	Int.	20.3	449.00	
Helia 3-12 x 56[8]	3-12	27.1-10	347-21	3.25	15.6	30mm	Int.	24.8	499.00	
ZF69 Sniper[9]	6	22.5	49	3.25	12.2	26mm	Int.	16.8	499.00	
Kassnar										
2x-7x Wide Angle	2-7.	49-19	258-21	3-2.7	11	1	Int.	12.8	77.00	Other models avail., including ¾" and ⅞" tubes for 22-cal. rifles. Contact Kassnar for details. [1]Also in 3x-9x40—$71.00. [2]Also in 4x40—$57.00. [3]Also in 3x-9x40—$74.00.
3x-9x Wide Angle[1]	3-9	42-15	112-13	3-2.7	12.2	1	Int.	13	79.00	
4x32 Wide Angle[2]	4	36	64	3.5	12	1	Int.	9.2	57.00	
6x40 Wide Angle	6	24	44	3	12.8	1	Int.	12	66.00	
1.5-4x Std.	1.5-4	52-27	177-25	4.4-3	10	1	Int.	9.5	64.00	
2x-7x Std.	2-7	42-16	256-21	3.1-3	11	1	Int.	11	71.00	
3x-9x Std.[3]	3-9	36-13	112-13	3.1-3	12.2	1	Int.	13.5	72.00	
4x-12x40 Std.	4-12	27-9.6	100-11	3-2.7	13.5	1	Int.	16	111.00	
2.5x32 Std.	2.5	36	164	3.6	12	1	Int.	9.3	52.00	
Leatherwood										
ART II	3.0-8.8	31-12	—	3.5	13.9	1	Int.	42	675.00	
ART/MPC	3.0-8.7	31-12	—	3.7	14.1	1	Int.	33	349.50	
4x	4.1	27	—	4	12.25	1	Int.	12.3	125.00	
Leupold										
M8-2X EER[1]	1.8	22.0	—	12-24	8.1	1	Int.	6.8	150.55	Constantly centered reticles, choice of Duplex, tapered CPC, Leupold Dot, Crosshair and Dot. CPC and Dot reticles extra. [1]2x and 4x scope have from 12"-24" of eye relief and are suitable for handguns, top ejection arms and muzzle-loaders. [2]8x, 12x, 3x9, 3.5x10 and 6.5x20 come with Adjustable Objective. [3]Silhouette/Target scopes have 1-min divisions with ¼ min clicks, and Adjustable Objectives. 50-ft. Focus Adaptor available for indoor target ranges, $38.65. Sun-shade available for all Adjustable Objective scopes, $11.15. [4]Also available in matte finish for about $18.00 extra.
M8-2X EER Silver[1]	1.8	22.0	—	12-24	8.1	1	Int.	6.8	159.45	
M8-4X EER[1]	3.5	9.5	—	12-24	8.4	1	Int.	7.6	183.75	
M8-4X EER Target[1]	3.5	9.5	—	12-24	8.4	1	Int.	8.5	200.30	
M8-2.5X Compact	2.3	42	—	4.3	8.5	1	Int.	7.4	165.70	
M8-4X Compact	3.6	26.5	—	4.1	10.3	1	Int.	8.5	189.30	
6x Compact	5.7	16	—	3.9	10.7	1	Int.	8.5	193.15	
3-9x Compact	3.2-8.5	34.5-13.5	—	3.8-3.1	11	1	Int.	9.5	257.50	
3-9x Compact Sil.	3.2-8.5	34.5-13.5	—	3.8-3.1	11	1	Int.	9.5	293.20	
M8-4X[4]	3.6	28	—	4.4	11.4	1	Int.	8.8	189.25	

CAUTION: PRICES CHANGE. CHECK AT GUNSHOP.

HUNTING, TARGET ■ & VARMINT ■ SCOPES

Maker and Model	Magn.	Field at 100 Yds (feet)	Relative Bright-ness	Eye Relief (in.)	Length (in.)	Tube Diam. (in.)	W&E Adjust-ments	Weight (ozs.)	Price	Other Data
Leupold (cont'd.)										
M8-6X	5.9	18.0	—	4.3	11.4	1	Int.	9.9	**201.15**	
M8-8X[2]	7.8	14.5	—	4.0	12.5	1	Int.	13.0	**269.45**	
M8-12X[2]	11.6	9.2	—	4.2	13.0	1	Int.	13.5	**273.05**	
6.5 x 20 Target AO	6.5-19.2	14.8-5.7	—	5.3-3.7	14.2	1	Int.	16	**406.65**	
M8-12X Target[3]	11.6	9.2	—	4.2	13.0	1	Int.	14.5	**306.15**	
M8-24X[3]	24.0	4.7	—	3.2	13.6	1	Int.	14.5	**406.65**	
M8-36X[3]	36.0	3.2	—	3.4	13.9	1	Int.	15.5	**406.65**	
Vari-X-II 1X4	1.6-4.2	70.5-28.5	—	4.3-3.8	9.2	1	Int.	9.0	**231.55**	
Vari-X-II 2X7	2.5-6.6	44.0-19.0	—	4.1-3.7	10.7	1	Int.	10.4	**253.10**	
Vari-X-II 3X9[4]	3.5-9.0	32.0-13.5	—	4.1-3.7	12.3	1	Int.	13.1	**271.85**	
Vari-X-II 3X9[2]	3.5-9.0	32.0-13.5	—	4.1-3.7	12.3	1	Int.	14.5	**307.60**	
Vari-X-III 1.5X5	1.5-4.6	66.0-24.0	—	4.7-3.5	9.4	1	Int.	9.3	**267.35**	
Vari-X-III 2.5X8[4]	2.7-7.9	38.0-14.0	—	4.2-3.4	11.3	1	Int.	11.0	**301.65**	
Vari-X-III 3.5X10	3.4-9.9	29.5-10.5	—	4.6-3.6	12.4	1	Int.	13.0	**315.45**	
Vari-X-III 3.5X10[2]	3.4-9.9	29.5-10.5	—	4.6-3.6	12.4	1	Int.	14.4	**351.15**	
Vari-X-III 6.5X20[2]	6.5-19.2	14.8- 5.7	—	5.3-3.7	14.2	1	Int.	16	**373.60**	
Lyman										
Lyman 4x	4	30	—	3¼	12	1	Int.	10	**149.95**	Choice of standard CH, tapered post, or tapered post and CH reticles. All-weather reticle caps. All Lyman scopes have Perma-Center reticle which remains in optical center regardless of changes in w&e. Adj. for parallax. [1]⅛ or ¼ MOA clicks. [2]Non-rotating objective lens focusing. ¼ MOA click adjustments. [3]Standard crosswire, 4 Center-Range reticles. [4]Std. Fine, Extra Fine, 1 Min. Dot, ½-Min. Dot reticles. External adjustment knobs; hand lapped zero repeat w. and e. systems. Choice of 4 reticles.
2x-7x Variable	1.9-6.8	49-19	—	3¼	11⅝	1	Int.	10½	**169.95**	
3x-9x Variable	3-9	39-13	—	3¾-3¼	10½	1	Int.	14	**179.95**	
■ 20x LWBR[1]	20	5.5	—	2¼	17⅛	1	Int.	15¼	**199.75**	
■ 25x LWBR	25	4.8	—	3	17	1	Int.	19	**199.95**	
■ 35x LWBR	35	3.8	—	3	17	1	Int.	19	**299.95**	
Metallic Silhouette[3] 6x-SL	6.2	20	—	3¼	13⅞	1	Int.	14¼	**249.95**	
Metallic Silhouette[4] 8x-SL	8.1	14	—	3¼	14⅝	1	Int.	15¼	**259.95**	
Metallic Silhouette 10x-SL	10	12	—	3¼	15⅜	1	Int.	15¼	**269.95**	
Millet										
Cyclops 22 Reflex	—	—	—	5-12	6	—	Int.	5	**69.95**	Reflex sight needs no batteries. Polycarbonate tube. Comes with three interchangeable reticles and tip-off mounts. For rimfires, airguns, crossbows. Imported from England by Millet Sights.
RWS										
100 4x32	4	20	—	—	10⅞	¾	Int.	6	**33.00**	Air gun scopes. All have Dyna-Plex reticle. Imported from Japan by Dynamit Nobel of America.
200 3-7x-20	3-7	24-17	—	—	11¼	¾	Int.	6	**51.00**	
300 4x32	4	28	—	—	12¾	1	Int.	11	**81.00**	
400 2-7x32	2-7	56-17	—	—	12¾	1	Int.	12	**125.00**	
800 1.5x20	1.5	19	—	—	8¾	1	Int.	6½	**85.00**	
Redfield										
Illuminator Trad. 3-9x	2.9-8.7	33-11	—	3½	12¾	1	Int.	17	**359.20**	*Accutrac feature avail. on these scopes at extra cost. Traditionals have round lenses. 4-Plex reticle is standard. [1]"Magnum Proof." Specially designed for magnum and auto pistols. Uses "Double Dovetail" mounts. [2]Mounts solidly on receiver. CH or dot. 20x—$308.20, 24x—$317.65.
Illuminator Widefield 3-9x*	2.9-8.7	38-13	—	3½	12¾	1	Int.	17	**394.95**	
Tracker 4x	3.9	28.9	—	3½	11.02	1	Int.	9.8	**110.75**	
Tracker 2-7x	2.3-6.9	36.6-12.2	—	3½	12.20	1	Int.	11.6	**148.30**	
Tracker 3-9x	3.0-9.0	34.4-11.3	—	3½	14.96	1	Int.	13.4	**166.15**	
Traditional 4x¾"	4	24½	27	3½	9⅜	¾	Int.	—	**105.40**	
Traditional 2½x	2½	43	64	3½	10¼	1	Int.	8½	**146.50**	
Traditional 4x	4	28½	56	3½	11⅜	1	Int.	9¾	**164.40**	
Traditional 6x	6	19	—	3½	12½	1	Int.	11½	**193.00**	
Traditional 3x-9x* Royal	3-9	34-11	—	3½-4¼	12½	1	Int.	13	**285.95**	
Traditional 2x-7x*	2-7	42-14	207-23	3½	11¼	1	Int.	12	**225.15**	
Traditional 3x-9x*	3-9	34-11	163-18	3½	12½	1	Int.	13	**246.60**	
Traditional 8xMS	8	16.6	—	3-3¾	14⅛	1	Int.	17⅕	**251.95**	
Traditional 10xMS	10	12.6	—	3-3¾	14⅛	1	Int.	17½	**262.70**	
Traditional 12xMS	12.4	8.1	—	3-3¾	14⅛	1	Int.	17½	**277.00**	
Pistol Scopes										
4xMP	3.6	9	—	12-22	9¹¹⁄₁₆	1	Int.	11.1	**175.10**	
Traditional 4x-12x*	4-12	26-9	112-14	3½	13⅞	1	Int.	14	**343.15**	
Traditional 6x-18x*	6-18	18-6	50-6	3½	13¹⁵⁄₁₆	1	Int.	18	**382.45**	
Low Profile Scopes										
Widefield 2¾xLP	2¾	55½	69	3½	10½	1	Int.	8	**184.05**	
Widefield 4xLP	3.6	37½	84	3½	11½	1	Int.	10	**205.05**	
Widefield 6xLP	5.5	23	—	3½	12¾	1	Int.	11	**225.15**	
Widefield 1¾x5xLP	1¾-5	70-27	136-21	3½	10¾	1	Int.	11½	**255.54**	
Widefield 2x7xLP*	2-7	49-19	144-21	3½	11¾	1	Int.	13	**264.50**	
Widefield 3x-9xLP*	3-9	39-15	112-18	3½	12½	1	Int.	14	**309.15**	
Sanders										
Bisley 2½x20	2½	42	64	3	10¾	1	Int.	8¼	**48.50**	Alum. alloy tubes, ¼" adj. coated lenses. Five other scopes are offered; 6x45 at $68.50, 8x45 at $70.50, 2½x7x at $69.50, 3-9x33 at $72.50 and 3-9x40 at $78.50. Rubber lens covers (clear plastic) are $3.50. Write to Sanders for details. Choice of reticles in CH, PCH, 3-post.
Bisley 4x33	4	28	64	3	12	1	Int.	9	**52.50**	
Bisley 6x40	6	19	45	3	12½	1	Int.	9½	**56.50**	
Bisley 8x40	8	18	25	3¼	12½	1	Int.	9½	**62.50**	
Bisley 10x40	10	12½	16	2½	12½	1	Int.	10¼	**64.50**	
Bisley 5-13x40	5-13	29-10	64-9	3	14	1	Int.	14	**86.50**	
Schmidt & Bender										
Vari-M 1¼-4x20[2]	1¼-4	96-16	—	3¼	10.4	30mm	Int.	12.3	**378.00**	[1]With or without rail mount. [2]Without rail mount. Rail mount only. [4]Also in steel, **$314.00.** [5]Also in steel, **$343.00.** [6]Also in steel, **$375.00.** [7]Also in steel, **$429.00.** All have ⅓-minute adjustments. Imported from West Germany by Paul Jaeger, Inc.
Vari-M 1½-6x42[1]	1½-6	60-19.5	—	3¼	12.2	30mm	Int.	17.5	**451.00**	
Vari-M 2½-10x56[2]	2½-10	37.5-12	—	3¼	14.6	30mm	Int.	21.9	**529.00**	
Light Metal M[3,4] 1½x15	1½	90	—	3¼	10	—	Int.	12.3	**332.00**	
Light Metal M[3,5] 4x36	4	30	—	3¼	11.2	—	Int.	13.7	**362.00**	
Light Metal M[3,6] 6x42	6	21	—	3¼	13	—	Int.	16.9	**389.00**	
Light Metal M[3,7] 8x56	8	16.5	—	3¼	15	—	Int.	20.7	**438.00**	
Steel M12x42[2]	12	10.5	—	3¼	13	26mm	Int.	17.9	**402.00**	

HUNTING, TARGET ■ & VARMINT ■ SCOPES

Maker and Model	Magn.	Field at 100 Yds (feet)	Relative Bright-ness	Eye Relief (in.)	Length (in.)	Tube Diam. (in.)	W&E Adjust-ments	Weight (ozs.)	Price	Other Data
Shepherd										
3 x 9 40mm	3-9	43.5-15.0	—	3.3	13	1	Int.	13½	NA	Instant range finding and bullet drop compensating; choice of plain, range finding or bullet drop reticle by turning cover cap; built-in collimator. From Shepherd Scope Ltd.
Simmons										
1002 Rimfire[1]	4	23	—	3	11.5	¾	Int.	6	11.00	[1]With ring mount. [2]With ring mount. [3]With rings. [4]3-9x32; also avail. 3-9x40. [5]3-9x32; also avail. 3-9x40. [6]4x32; also avail. 4x40 as #1034. [7]3-9x32; also avail. 3-9x40 as #1038. [8]Avail. in brushed aluminum finish as #1052. [9]Avail. with silhouette knobs as #1085, in brushed aluminum as #1088. Max-Ilume Mono Tube models have dull finish, speed focus, rubber shock ring, Truplex reticle in all models. All scopes sealed, fog-proof, with constantly centered reticles. Imported from Japan by Simmons Outdoor Corp.
1004 Rimfire[2]	3-7	22.5-9.5	—	3	11	¾	Int.	8.4	44.50	
1007 Rimfire[3]	4	25	—	3	10	1	Int.	9	77.00	
1005 Waterproof	2½	46	—	3	11.5	1	Int.	9.3	63.50	
1006 Waterproof	4	29	—	—	12	1	Int.	9.1	52.50	
1010 Waterproof[4]	3-9	37-12.7	—	3-3¼	12.8	1	Int.	12.8	71.00	
1014 Waterproof	4-12	30-11	—	3-3¼	14	1	Int.	14.9	111.00	
1016 Waterproof	6-18	19-6.7	—	3-3¼	15.7	1	Int.	16.2	137.00	
1024 W.A.	4	37	—	3	11.8	1	Int.	10.5	82.50	
1025 W.A.	6	24.5	—	3	12.4	1	Int.	12	102.00	
1026 W.A.	1½-4½	86-28.9	—	3-3¼	10.6	1	Int.	13.2	110.50	
1027 W.A.	2-7	54.6-18.3	—	3-3¼	12	1	Int.	12.8	110.50	
1028 W.A.[5]	3-9	42-14	—	3-3¼	12.9	1	Int.	12.9	103.00	
1032 Mono Tube[6]	4	37	—	3	12.2	1	Int.	11.5	117.00	
1036 Mono Tube[7]	3-9	42-14	—	3-3¼	13.3	1	Int.	13	152.00	
1040 Mono Tube	2-7	54-18	—	3-3¼	13.1	1	Int.	12.9	155.00	
1049 Compact	2½	37	—	3	9.3	1	Int.	9.1	132.00	
1050 Compact[8]	4	22	—	3	9	1	Int.	9.1	132.00	
1053 Compact	1½-4½	86-28.9	—	3-3¼	10.6	1	Int.	9.1	180.00	
1054 Compact	3-9	40-14	—	3-3¼	10.5	1	Int.	10.5	170.00	
1063 Armored	4	37	—	3	12.4	1	Int.	16	132.00	
1064 Armored	3-9	42-14	—	3-3¼	12.3	1	Int.	17.6	145.00	
1030 Silhouette	4-12	31-11	—	3-3¼	14.1	1	Int.	17.8	148.50	
1031 Silhouette	6-18	22-7.8	—	3-3¼	15.8	1	Int.	19.1	171.50	
1070 Silhouette	6	20	—	3	12.9	1	Int.	15.2	120.00	
1071 Silhouette	12	11	—	3	13.4	1	Int.	16.3	127.00	
1072 Silhouette	24	5.8	—	3	17.7	1	Int.	18.7	150.00	
1073 Sil. Airgun	2-7	54.6-18.3	—	3-3¼	12.1	1	Int.	15.7	140.00	
1080 Handgun	2	18	—	10-20	7.1	1	Int.	8.1	87.50	
1084 Handgun[9]	4	9	—	10-20	8.7	1	Int.	9.5	139.00	
1091 Handgun	1½	15.3	—	10-20	8.5	¾	Int.	6	34.00	
Swarovski Habicht										
Nova 1.5x20	1.5	61	—	3⅛	9.6	1	Int.	12.7	330.00	All models offered in either steel or lightweight alloy tubes except 1.5x20, ZFM 6x42 and Cobras. Weights shown are for lightweight versions. Choice of nine constantly centered reticles. Eyepiece recoil mechanism and rubber ring shield to protect face. Cobra and ZFM also available in NATO Stanag 2324 mounts. Imported by Swarovski America Ltd.
Nova 4x32	4	33	—	3⅛	11.3	1	Int.	13	340.00	
Nova 6x42	6	23	—	3⅛	12.6	1	Int.	14	380.00	
Nova 8x56	8	17	—	3⅛	14.4	1	Int.	17	455.00	
Nova 1.5 6x42	1.5-6	61-21	—	3⅛	12.6	1	Int.	17	470.00	
Nova 2.2-9x42	2.2-9	39.5-15	—	3⅛	13.3	1	Int.	16.5	580.00	
Nova 3-12x56	3-12	30-11	—	3⅛	15.25	1	Int.	19	640.00	
ZFM 6x42	6	23	—	3⅛	12	1	Int.	18	535.00	
Cobra 1.5-14	1.5	50	—	3.9	7.87	1	Int.	10	325.00	
Cobra 3x14	3	21	—	3.9	8.75	1	Int.	11	340.00	
Swift										
600 4x15	4	16.2	—	2.4	11	¾	Int.	4.7	19.98	All Swift Mark I scopes, with the exception of the 4x15, have Quadraplex reticles and are fog-proof and waterproof. The 4x15 has crosshair reticle and is non-waterproof.
650 4x32	4	29	—	3½	12	1	Int.	9	68.00	
651 4x32 WA	4	37	—	3½	11¾	1	Int.	10½	76.50	
653 4x40 WA	4	35½	—	3¾	12¼	1	Int.	12	89.50	
654 3-9x32	3-9	35¾-12¾	—	3	12¾	1	Int.	13¾	92.50	
656 3-9x40 WA	3-9	42½-13½	—	2¾	12¾	1	Int.	14	105.00	
657 6x40	6	18	—	3¾	13	1	Int.	10	78.00	
658 1½-4½x32	1½-4½	55-22	—	3½	12	1	Int.	13	98.00	
Tasco										
1860 Tube Sight[1]	4	12½	14	3	32½	¾	Ext.	25	124.95	[1]Brass tube for many black powder guns. [2]Supercon®, fully coated lenses; waterproof, shockproof, fogproof; includes haze filter caps, lifetime warranty. [3]Trajectory-Range Finding scopes. [4]30/30 range finding reticle; rubber covered; built-in mounting rings. Also avail. in wide angle models. [5]Waterproof; anodized finish; ¼-min. click stops; R.F. reticle. [6]R.F. reticle, fully coated lenses; ¼-min. clicks; waterproof. [7]Integral mount for 22 RF, airguns with grooved receiver. Also avail. in brushed aluminum finish. [8]Adj., built-in mount; adj. rheostat, polarizer; ½-min. clicks. Avail. to fit Rem. 870, 1100, also with side mounts, in wide angle. [9]World Class Wide Angle®. Contact Tasco for complete list of models offered.
WA 4x40 Wide Angle[2,9]	4	36	100	3¼	12⅝	1	Int.	12½	124.95	
WA 3-9x40 Wide Angle[2,9]	3-9	43½-15	178-20	3¼	12⅝	1	Int.	11½	129.95	
WA 2.5x32 Wide Angle[2,9]	2.5	52	44	3¼	12	1	Int.	9½	149.95	
WA 2-7x32 Wide Angle[2,9]	2-7	56-17	256-21	3¼	11½	1	Int.	11½	109.95	
WA 1¾-5 x 20 Wide Angle[2,9]	1.75-5	72-24	131-16	3¼	10⅝	1	Int.	10¾	139.95	
RC 3-9 x 40 WA[2,4,9]	3-9	43½-15	178-20	3¼	—	1	Int.	12⅝	189.95	
RC 4 x 40 WA[2,4,9]	4	36	100	3¼	11⅞	1	Int.	11	169.95	
TR 3-9 x 32 TRF[3]	3-9	35-14	114-13	3¼	12	1	Int.	12	129.95	
TR 6-18 x 40 TRF[3]	6-18	16-5	44-5	3	16¼	1	Int.	16½	199.95	
W 4 x 32[5]	4	28	64	3¼	11¾	1	In.t	9½	64.95	
W 4-12 x 40[5]	4-12	29-9	100-11	3	13¾	1	Int.	15	159.95	
PM 4 x 18[6,7]	4	—	20	3	16¼	⅞	Int.	—	69.95	
BDIXCFV Battery Dot[8]	1	—	—	—	7½	—	Int.	10	199.95	
Thompson/Center										
Lobo 1½ x[1]	1.5	16	127	11-20	7¾	⅞	Int.	5	75.00	[1]May be used on light to medium recoil guns, including muzzleloaders. Coated lenses, nitrogen filled, lifetime warranty. [2]For heavy recoil guns. Nitrogen filled. Duplex reticle only. Target turrets avail. on 1½x, 3x models. Electra Dot illuminated reticle available in RP 2½x ($31 extra) and RP 3x ($36 extra).[3] Rifle scopes have Electra Dot reticle.
Lobo 3x[1]	3	9	49	11-20	9	⅞	Int.	6.3	80.00	
RP 1½ x[2]	1.5	28	177	11-20	7½	1	Int.	5.1	99.00	
RP 2½x[2]	2.5	15	64	11-20	8½	1	Int.	6.5	99.00	
RP 3x[2]	3	13	44	11-20	8¾	1	Int.	5.4	99.00	
RP 4x[2]	4	10	71	12-20	9¼	1	Int.	10.4	120.00	
TC 4x Rifle[3]	4	29	64	3.3	12⅞	1	Int.	12.3	120.00	
TC 3/9V Rifle[3]	3-9	35.3-13.2	177-19	3.3	12⅞	1	Int.	15.5	195.00	

CAUTION: PRICES CHANGE. CHECK AT GUNSHOP.

HUNTING, TARGET ■ & VARMINT ■ SCOPES

Maker and Model	Magn.	Field at 100 Yds (feet)	Relative Brightness	Eye Relief (in.)	Length (in.)	Tube Diam. (in.)	W&E Adjustments	Weight (ozs.)	Price	Other Data
Unertl										[1]Dural ¼ MOA click mounts. Hard coated lenses. Non-rotating objective lens focusing. [2]¼ MOA click mounts. [3]With target mounts. [4]With calibrated head. [5]Same as 1" Target but without objective lens focusing. [6]Price with ¼ MOA click mounts. [7]With new Posa mounts. [8]Range focus until near rear of tube. Price is with Posa mounts. Magnum clamp. With standard mounts and clamp ring $266.00.
■ 1" Target	6,8,10	16-10	17.6-6.25	2	21½	¾	Ext.	21	155.00	
■ 1¼" Target[1]	8,10,12,14	12-16	15.2-5	2	25	¾	Ext.	21	203.00	
■ 1½" Target	8,10,12,14 16,18,20	11.5-3.2	—	2¼	25½	¾	Ext.	31	230.00	
■ 2" Target[2]	8,10,12, 14,16,18, 24,30,36	8	22.6-2.5	2¼	26¼	1	Ext.	44	310.00	
■ Varmint, 1¼∞[3]	6,8,10,12	1-7	28-7.1	2½	19½	⅞	Ext.	26	204.00	
■ Ultra Varmint, 2"[4]	8,10 12,15	12.6-7	39.7-11	2½	24	1	Ext.	34	291.00	
■ Small Game[5]	4,6	25-17	19.4-8.4	2¼	18	¾	Ext.	16	120.00	
■ Vulture[6]	8 10	11.2 10.9	29 18½	3-4 —	15⅝ 16⅛	1	Ext.	15½	226.00	
■ Programmer 200[7]	8,10,12 14,16,18, 20,24,30,36	11.3-4	39-1.9	—	26½	1	Ext.	45	385.00	
■ BV-20[8]	20	8	4.4	4.4	17⅞	1	Ext.	21¼	278.00	
Weatherby										Lumiplex reticle in all models. Blue-black, non-glare finish.
Mark XXII	4	25	50	2.5-3.5	11¾	⅞	Int.	9.25	85.35	
Supreme 1¾-5x20	1.7-5	66.6-21.4	—	3.4	10.7	1	Int.	11	190.00	
Supreme 4x34	4	32	—	3.1	11⅛	1	Int.	9.6	190.00	
Supreme 2-7x34	2.1-6.8	59-16	—	3.4	11¼	1	Int.	10.4	240.00	
Supreme 4x44	3.9	32	—	3	12½	1	Int.	11.6	240.00	
Supreme 3-9x44	3.1-8.9	36-13	—	3.5	12.7	1	Int.	11.6	280.00	
Williams										TNT models
Twilight Crosshair	2½	32	64	3¾	11¼	1	Int.	8½	109.95	
Twilight Crosshair	4	29	64	3½	11¾	1	Int.	9½	118.50	
Twilight Crosshair	2-6	45-17	256-28	3	11½	1	Int.	11½	161.15	
Twilight Crosshair	3-9	36-13	161-18	3	12¾	1	Int.	13½	169.95	
Zeiss										All scopes have ¼-minute click-stop adjustments. Choice of Z-Plex or fine crosshair reticles. Rubber armored objective bell, rubber eyepiece ring. Lenses have T-Star coating for highest light transmission. Imported from West Germany by Carl Zeiss, Inc.
Diatal C 4x32	4	30	—	3.5	10.6	1	Int.	11.3	305.00	
Diatal C 6x32	6	20	—	3.5	10.6	1	Int.	11.3	340.00	
Diatal C 10x36	10	12	—	3.5	12.7	1	Int.	14.1	395.00	
Diavari C 3-9x36	3-9	36-13	—	3.5	11.2	1	Int.	15.2	540.00	

■ Signifies target and/or varmint scope. Hunting scopes in general are furnished with a choice of reticle—crosshairs, post with crosshairs, tapered or blunt post, or dot crosshairs, etc. The great majority of target and varmint scopes have medium or fine crosshairs but post or dot reticles may be ordered. W—Windage   E—Elevation   MOA—Minute of angle or 1" (approx.) at 100 yards, etc.

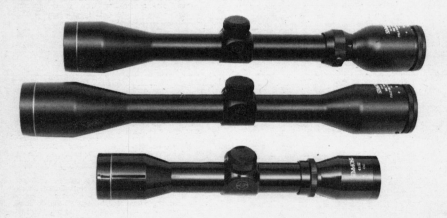

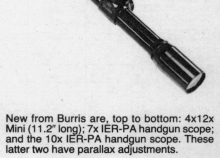

A relative newcomer to the riflescope field is Simmons Outdoor Corp. which has a line of quality scopes for nearly every need. Shown above, top to bottom: Model 1038 Mono-Tube Wide Angle 3-9x40; Model 1034 Mono-Tube Wide Angle 4x40; and the Model 1050 4x32 Compact.

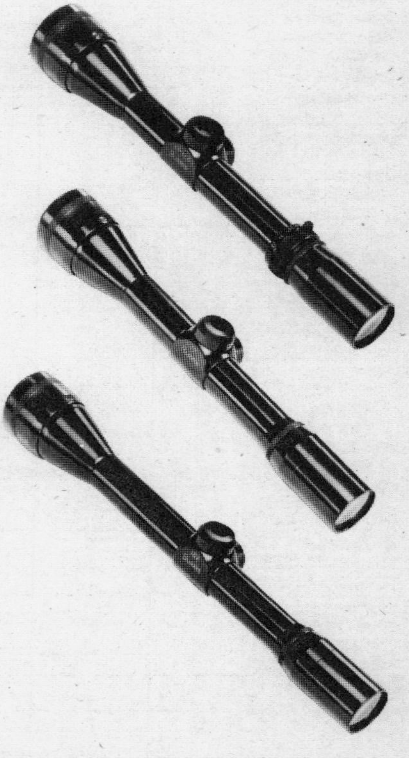

Thompson/Center now has a 3-9x scope (#8620) that uses a lighted reticle for low-light conditions. Called "Electra Dot," it's powered by a hearing aid battery giving up to 40 hours of service.

New from Burris are, top to bottom: 4x12x Mini (11.2" long); 7x IER-PA handgun scope; and the 10x IER-PA handgun scope. These latter two have parallax adjustments.

CAUTION: PRICES CHANGE. CHECK AT GUNSHOP.

SCOPE MOUNTS

Maker, Model, Type	Adjust.	Scopes	Price	Suitable for
B-Square				[1]Clamp-on, blue finish. Stainless finish $59.95. [2]For Bushnell Phantom only. [3]Blue finish; stainless finish $59.95. [4]For solid rib—requires drilling & tapping. [5]Clamp-on. [6]Clamp-on, blue; stainless finish $49.95. [7]Clamp-on, for Bushnell Phantom only; blue; stainless finish $49.95. [8]Requires drilling & tapping. [9]No gunsmithing, no sight removal; blue; stainless finish $59.95. [10]Clamp-on. [11]Also M600, 660. Partial listing of mounts shown here. Contact B-Square for more data.
Pistols				
Colt Python[1]	W&E	1″	$ 49.95	
Daisy 717/722 Champion[2]	No	1″	19.95	
Dan Wesson Clamp-On[3]	W&E	1″	49.95	
Dan Wesson Integral[4]	W&E	1″	39.95	
Hi-Standard Mono-Mount[5]	No	1″	39.95	
Hi-Standard Victor	W&E	1″	49.95	
Ruger 22 Auto Mono-Mount[6]	No	1″	39.95	
Ruger Single-Six[7]	No	1″	39.95	
T-C Contender	W&E	1″	49.95	
Sterling X-Caliber	W&E	1″	49.95	
Rifles				B-Square also has mounts for Aimpoint scopes to fit many popular military rifles, shotguns and handguns. Write them for a complete listing.
Mini-14[8]	W&E	1″	49.95	
Mini-14[9]	W&E	1″	49.95	
M-94 Side Mount	W&E	1″	49.95	
Ruger 77[10]	W&E	1″	49.95	
SMLE Side Mount	W only	1″	49.95	
T-C Single-Shot Rifle	W&E	1″	49.95	
Rem. Model Seven[11]	W&E	1″	39.95	
Military				
M1-A	W&E	1″	59.95	
AR-15/16	W&E	1″	49.95	
FN-LAR	W only	1″	149.95	
HK-91/93	W only	1″	49.95	
Valmet M71S	W&E	1″	129.95	
AK-47	W&E	1″	149.95	
Shotguns				
Rem. 870/1100	W&E	1″	59.95	
S&W 1000P	W&E	1″	59.95	
Beeman				All grooved receivers and scope bases on all known air rifles and 22-cal. rimfire rifles (½″ to ⅝″—6mm to 15mm). [1]Centerfire rifles. Scope detaches easily, returns to zero. [2]Designed specifically for Krico rifles. [3]Designed to fit rubber armor ridges of Beeman Rhinohide scopes. M87 for 11mm dovetail; M88 fits Weaver-style bases.
Double Adjustable	W&E	1″	$23.98	
Deluxe Ring Mounts	No	1″	19.98	
Professional Mounts	W&E	1″	79.50	
Professional Pivot[1]	W	1″	129.50	
Buehler[2]	W	1″	70.00	
Model 87[3]	No	—	18.98	
Model 88[3]	No	—	18.98	
Buehler				[1]Most popular models. [2]Most popular models. [3]Most popular models. [4]Sako dovetail receivers. [5]15 models. [6]No drilling & tapping. [7]Aircraft alloy, dyed blue or to match stainless; for Colt Diamondback, Python, Trooper, Ruger Blackhawk, Single-Six, Security-Six, S&W K-frame, Dan Wesson.
One Piece (T)[1]	W only	1″ split rings, 3 heights.	Complete—59.50	
		1″ split rings, 3 heights, engraved	Rings only—83.00	
		26mm, 2 heights	Rings only—43.25	
One Piece Micro Dial (T)[2]	W&E	1″ split rings.	Complete—73.50	
Two Piece (T)[3]	W only	1″ split rings.	Complete—59.50	
Two Piece Dovetail (T)[4]	W only	1″ split rings.	Complete—73.50	
One Piece Pistol (T)[5]	W only	1″ split rings.	Complete—59.50	
One Piece Pistol Stainless (T)[1]	W only	1″ split rings. Stainless steel	Complete—77.75	
One Piece Ruger Mini 14 (T)[6]	W only	1″ split rings.	Complete—73.50	
One Piece Pistol Model 83[6,7]	No	1″ split rings.	59.50	
One Piece Pistol Model 83 Stainless[6,7]	No	1″ split rings.	77.75	
Burris				[1]Most popular rifles. Universal, rings, mounts fit Burris, Universal, Redfield, Leupold and Browning bases. Comparable prices. [2]Browning Standard 22 Auto rifle. [3]Most popular rifles. [4]Grooved receivers. [5]Universal dovetail; accept Burris, Universal, Redfield, Leupold rings. For Dan Wesson, S&W, Virginian, Ruger Blackhawk, Win. 94. [6]Medium standard front, extension rear, per pair. Low standard front, extension rear, per pair.
Supreme One Piece (T)[1]	W only	1″ split rings, 3 heights.	25.95	
			1 piece-base—18.95	
Trumount Two Piece (T)	W only	1″ split rings, 3 heights.	2 piece base—16.95	
Browning Auto Mount[2]	No	¾″, 1″ split rings.	14.95	
Sight-Thru Mount[3]	No	1″ Split rings.	16.95	
Rings Mounts[4]	No	¾″, 1″ split rings.	¾″ rings—12.95	
			1″ rings—12.95	
L.E.R. Mount Bases[5]	No	1″ split rings.	16.95	
Extension Rings[6]	No	1″ scopes.	29.95	
Bushnell				[1]Most popular rifles. Includes windage adj. [2]V-block bottoms lock to chrome-moly studs seated into two 6-48 holes. Rem. XP-100. [3]Heavy loads in Colt, S&W, Ruger revolvers, Ruger Hawkeye. [4]M94 Win., center dovetail.
Detachable (T) mounts only[1]	W only	1″ split rings, uses Weaver base.	Rings—15.95	
22 mount	No	1″ only.	Rings— 7.95	
All Purpose[2]	No	Phantom.	17.95	
Rigid[3]	No	Phantom.	17.95	
94 Win.[4]	No	Phantom.	17.95	
Clearview				[1]All popular rifles including Sav. 99. Uses Weaver bases. [2]Allows use of open sights. [3]For 22 rimfire rifles, with grooved receivers or bases. [4]Fits 13 models. Broadest view area of the type. [5]Side mount for both M94 and M94-375 Big Bore.
Universal Rings (T)[1]	No	1″ split rings.	19.95	
Mod 101, & 336[2]	No	1″ split rings.	19.95	
Broad-View[4]	No	1″	19.95	
Model 22[3]	No	¾″, ⅞″, 1″	11.95	
94 Winchester[5]	No	1″	19.95	
Conetrol				[1]All popular rifles, including metric-drilled foreign guns. Price shown for base, two rings. Matte finish. [2]Gunnur grade has mirror-finished rings, satin-finish base. Price shown for base, two rings. [3]Custum grade has mirror-finished rings and mirror-finished, contoured base. Price shown for base, 2 rings. [4]Win. 94, Krag, older split-bridge Mannlicher-Schoenauer, Mini-14, M-1 Garand, etc. Prices same as above. [5]For guns with integral mounting provision, including Sako, BSA, Ithacagun, Ruger, H&K and many others. Also for grooved-receiver rimfires and air rifles. Prices same as above. [6]For XP-100, T/C Contender, Colt SAA, Ruger Blackhawk, S&W. [7]Sculptured 2-piece bases as found on fine custom rifles. Price shown is for base alone. Also available unfinished—$49.98.
Huntur[1]	W only	1″, 26mm, 26.5mm solid or split rings, 3 heights.	48.93	
Gunnur[2]	W only	1″, 26mm, 26.5mm solid or split rings, 3 heights.	59.91	
Custum[3]	W only	1″, 26mm, 26.5mm solid or split rings, 3 heights.	74.91	
One Piece Side Mount Base[4]	W only	1″, 26mm, 26.5mm solid or split rings, 3 heights.		
Daptar Bases[5]	W only	1″, 26mm, 26.5mm solid or split rings, 3 heights.		
Pistol Bases, 2 or 3-ring[6]	W only	1″ scopes.		
Fluted Bases[7]	W only	Standard Conetrol rings	74.97	

SCOPE MOUNTS

Maker, Model, Type	Adjust.	Scopes	Price	Suitable for
EAW				
Pivot[1]	W&E	1"/26mm	150.00	[1]Most popular magazine rifles. Optional 30mm. [2]For Sako; also for mounting Kahles ZF69 on Steyr SSG rifle. [3]For Kahles 30mm scope. Bases by Redfield, Leupold, Burris. Two heights. [4]Low, medium, high; fits Redfield, Leupold, Burris bases. [5]For Kahles 30mm scopes/Ruger 77 with integral bases. Imported by Paul Jaeger, Inc., Kahles of America (Del Sports, Inc.).
Slide On[2]	W only	1"/26mm	100.00	
Kahles[3]	W only	1"/26mm/30mm	50.00	
Kahles[4]	W only	1"/26mm	45.00	
Ruger 77R[5]	W only	30mm	75.00	
Griffin & Howe				
Standard Double Lever (S).	No	1" or 26mm split rings.	145.00	All popular models (Garand $175; Win. 94 $175). All rings $50. Top ejection $75.
Holden				
Wide Ironsighter[TS]	No	1" Split rings.	19.95	[1]Most popular rifles including Ruger Mini-14, H&R M700, and muzzleloaders. Rings have oval holes to permit use of iron sights. [2]For 1" dia. scopes. [3]For ¾" or ⅞" dia. scopes. [4]For 1" dia. extended eye relief scopes.
Ironsighter Center Fire[1]	No	1" Split rings.	19.95	
Ironsighter S-94	No	1" split rings	24.95	
Ironsighter 22 cal. rimfire				
Model #500[2]	No	1" Split rings.	10.95	
Model #600[3]	No	⅞" Split rings also fits ¾".	10.95	
Ironsighter Handguns[4]	No	1" Split rings.	21.95	
Jaeger				
QD, with windage (S)	W only	1", 3 heights.	190.00	All popular models. From Paul Jaeger, Inc.
Kimber				
Standard[1]	No	1", split rings	48.90	[1]High rings; low rings—**$45.00**; both only for Kimber rifles. [2]For Kimber rifles only. Also avail. for Mauser (FN,98) Rem. 700, 721, 722, 725, Win. M70, Mark X. [3]Vertically split rings; for Kimber and other popular CF rifles.
Double Lever[2]	No	1", split rings	69.00	
Non-Detachable[3]	No	1", split rings	48.00	
Kris Mounts				
Side-Saddle[1]	No	1", 26mm split rings.	11.98	[1]One-piece mount for Win. 94. [2]Most popular rifles and Ruger. [3]Blackhawk revolver. Mounts have oval hole to permit use of iron sights.
Two Piece (T)[2]	No	1", 26mm split rings.	7.98	
One Piece (T)[3]	No	1", 26mm split rings.	11.98	
Kwik-Site				
KS-See-Thru[1]	No	1"	18.95	[1]Most rifles. Allows use of iron sights. [2]22-cal. rifles with grooved receivers. Allows use of iron sights. [3]Model 94, 94 Big Bore. No drilling or tapping. [4]Most rifles. One-piece solid construction. Use on Weaver bases. 32mm obj. lens or larger. [5]Non-see-through model; for grooved receivers.
KS-22 See-Thru[2]	No	1"'	15.95	
KS-W94[3]	Yes	1"	32.95	
KSM Imperial[4]	No	1"	25.95	
KS-WEV	No	1"	19.95	
KS-WEV-HIGH	No	1"	19.95	
KS-T22 1"[5]	No	1" .	15.95	
Leatherwood				
M-1A, M-14	W only	ART II, ART/MPC (Weaver rings)	75.00	[1]Popular bolt actions. [2]With M-16 adaptor. [3]Adaptor base for H&K rail mounts.
AR-15, M-16	No	As above	17.95	
FN-FAL	No	As above	175.00	
SSG	No	As above	50.00	
One-piece Bridge[1]	No	As above	9.95	
Night Vision Adaptor[2]	No	Night vision scopes	37.50	
H&K Adaptor[3]	No	ART II, ART/MPC (Weaver rings)	59.95	
Leupold				
STD Bases (T)[1]	W only	One piece base (dovetail front, windage rear)	Base—19.25	[1]Most popular rifles. Also available in 2-piece version, same price. [2]Ruger revolvers, Thompson/Center Contender, S&W K&N Frame revolvers and Colt .45 "Gold Cup" N.M. Available with silver or blue finish. [3]Reversible extended front; regular rear rings, in two heights.
STD Handgun mounts[2] Base and two rings[2]	No	1"	49.25	
STD Rings		1" & 26mm, 3 ring heights interchangeable with other mounts of similar design.	1" rings—27.80 26mm rings—30.40	
Extension-Ring Sets[3]		1"	38.50	
Marlin				
One Piece QD (T)	No	1" split rings.	12.10	Most Marlin and Glenfield lever actions.
Millett				
Black Onyx Chaparral		1" Low, medium, high Engraved	26.95 39.95	Rem. 40X, 700, 722, 725, Ruger 77 (round top) Weatherby, etc. FN Mauser, FN Brownings, Colt 57, Interarms MkX, Parker-Hale, Sako (round receiver), many others.
Universal Two Piece Bases				
700 Series	W only	Two-piece bases	20.95	
FN Series	W only	Two-piece bases	20.95	
Numrich				
Side Mount	No	1" split rings.	7.95	M-1 carbine.
Pachmayr				
Lo-Swing (S)[1]	Yes	¾", ⅞", 1", 26mm solid or split loops.	65.00	[1]All popular rifles, including Ruger Mini-14, Browning BBR, Scope swings aside for instant use of iron sights. [2]Adjustable base. Win. 70, 88; Rem. 721, 722, 725, 740, 760; Mar. 336; Sav. 99, New Model for Colt Sauer.
Lo-Swing (T)[2]	Yes	¾", ⅞", 1", 26mm split rings.	65.00	
Redfield				
JR-SR(T)[1]	W only	¾", 1", 26mm.	JR—19.80-26.95 SR—23.95-51.85	[1]Low, med. & high, split rings. Reversible extension front rings for 1". 2-piece bases for Sako. Colt Sauer bases $63.90. [2]Split rings for grooved 22's. See-thru mounts $23.30. [3]Used with MP scopes for: S&W K or N frame. XP-100, Colt J or I frame. T/C Contender, Colt autos, black powder rifles.
Ring (T)[2]	No	¾" and 1".		
Double Dovetail MP[3]	No	1", split rings.	52.90	
S&K				
Insta-Mount (T) base only[1]	W only	Use S&K rings only.	18.00-81.00	[1]1903, A3, M1 Carbine, Lee Enfield #1, MK. III, #4, #5, M1917, M98 Mauser, FN Auto, AR-15, AR-180, M-14, M-1, Ger. K-43, Mini-14, M1-A, Krag, AKM, AK-47. [2]Most popular rifles already drilled and tapped. For "see through underneath" risers, add $10.00.
Conventional rings and bases[2]	W only	1" split rings.	40.00	
Sako				
QD Dovetail	W only	1" only. .	91.25	Sako, or any rifle using Sako action, 3 heights available, Stoeger, importer.

CAUTION: PRICES CHANGE. CHECK AT GUNSHOP.

SCOPE MOUNTS

Maker, Model, Type	Adjust.	Scopes	Price	Suitable for
Simmons				
1401	No	1"	8.00	Weaver-type bases. #1401 (low) also in high style
1406	No	1"	8.00	(#1403). #1406, 1408 for grooved receiver 22s.
1408	No	1"	8.00	Bases avail. for most popular rifles; one- and two-
1414	No	1"	19.00	piece styles.
Tasco				
790BA and 792BA series[1]	No	1", regular or high.	9.95	[1]Many popular rifles. Also in brushed aluminum. [2]For
794[2]	No	Split rings.	9.95	22s with grooved receivers. [3]Most popular rifles.
795 Quick Peep[3]	No	1" only.	9.95	[4]Most popular rifles. [5]"Quick Peep" 1" ring mount; fits
796[5]	No	1" only	9.95	all 22-cal. rifles with grooved receivers. [6]For Ruger
885 BK[8]	No	1" only	23.95	Mini-14; also in brushed aluminum. [7]Side mount for
895[7]	No	1" only	5.95	Win. 94. [8]Side mount rings and base for Win. 94 in
896[6]	No	1" only	39.95	30-30, 375 Win.
800L Series (with base)[4]	No	1" only.	13.95	
Thompson/Center				
Contender 9746[1]	No	T/C Lobo	8.75	[1]All Contenders except vent. rib. [2]T/C rail mount
Contender 9741[2]	No	2½, 4 RP	8.75	scopes; all Contenders except vent. rib. [3]All S&W K
Contender 7410	No	Bushnell Phantom 1.3, 2.5x	8.75	and Combat Masterpiece, Hi-Way Patrolman, Out-
S&W 9747[3]	No	Lobo or RP	8.75	doorsman, 22 Jet, 45 Target 1955. Requires drilling,
Ruger 9748[4]	No	Lobo or RP	8.75	tapping. [4]Blackhawk, Super Blackhawk, Super Sin-
Hawken 9749[5]	No	Lobo or RP	8.75	gle-Six. Requires drilling, tapping. [5]45 or 50 cal.; re-
Hawken/Renegade 9754[6]	No	Lobo or RP	8.75	places rear sight. [6]Rail mount scopes; 54-cal. Haw-
Cherokee/Seneca[7]	No	Lobo or RP	8.75	ken, 50, 54, 56-cal. Renegade. Replaces rear sight.
Unerti				[7]Cherokee 32 or 45 cal., Seneca 36 or 45 cal. Re-
Posa (T)[1]	Yes	¾", ⅞", 1" scopes.	Per set 63.00	places rear sight.
¼ Click (T)[2]	Yes	¾", 1" target scopes.	Per set 59.00	[1]Unerti target or varmint scopes. [2]Any with regular
Weaver				dovetail scope bases.
Detachable Mount (T & S)[1]	No	¾", ⅞", 1" 26mm	20.00	[1]Nearly all modern rifles. Extension rings, 1" $23.45.
Pivot Mount (T)[2]	No	1"	25.75	[2]Most modern big bore rifles. [3]22s with grooved re-
Tip-Off (T)[3]	No	¾", ⅞".	11.15	ceivers. [4]Same. Adapter for Lee Enfield—$9.65.
Tip-Off (T)[4]	No	1", two-piece.	20.00	[5]⅞"—$13.45. 1" See-Thru extension—$23.45. [6]Colt
See-Thru Mount[5]	No	1" Split rings and ⅞"-tip-off. Fits all top mounts.	20.00	Officer's Model, Python, Ruger B'hawk, Super B'hawk, Security Six, 22 Autos, Mini-14, Ruger Red-
Mount Base System[6]	No	1"	44.95	hawk, S&W N frames. No drilling or tapping. Also in stainless steel—$58.95.
Williams				
Offset (S)[1]	No	¾", ⅞", 1" 26mm solid, split or extension rings.	47.05	[1]Most rifles, Br. S.M.L.E. (round rec) $3.85 extra. [2]Same. [3]Most rifles including Win. 94 Big Bore.
QC (T)[2]	No	Same.	38.60	[4]Most rifles. [5]Many modern rifles. [6]Most popular ri-
QC (S)[3]	No	Same.	38.60	fles.
Low Sight-Thru[4]	No	1", ⅞", sleeves $1.80.	17.75	
Sight-Thru[5]	No	1", ⅞", sleeves $1.80.	17.75	
Streamline[6]	No	1" (bases form rings).	17.75	

(S)—Side Mount   (T)Top Mount   22mm—.866"   25.4mm = 1"1.024"   26.5mm = 1.045"   30mm = 1.81"

Williams SM-94-375 mount with 4x Guide Line scope on 94 Winchester 375 rifle.

Above—Weaver's mount and base products are now made by Omark Industries. Shown is their Integral 1" See-Thru mount. Below—Kimber Double Lever mounts fit Kimber and other popular rifles. Nondetachable versions also available.

EAW Quick Detachable mount on a pre-'64 Winchester Model 70, Schmidt & Bender 1½-6x scope. From Paul Jaeger.

CAUTION: PRICES CHANGE. CHECK AT GUNSHOP.

SPOTTING SCOPES

APOLLO 20 X 50 BOBCAT—50mm objective lens. Field of view at 1000 yds. is about 100 ft. Length 9.4″, weight 17.5 oz. Tripod socket.
Price:.. **$154.95**
Compact tripod, about **$20.00**

BAUSCH & LOMB DISCOVERER—15X to 60X zoom, 60mm objective. Constant focus throughout range. Field at 1000 yds. 40 ft (60X), 156 ft. (15X). Comes with lens caps. Length 17½″, wgt. 48½ oz.
Price:.. **$399.95**

BUSHNELL SPACEMASTER—60MM objective. Field at 1000 yds., 158′ to 37′. Relative brightness, 5.76. Wgt., 36 oz. Length closed, 11⅝″. prism focusing, without eyepiece.
Price:.. **$254.95**
15X, 20X, 40X and 60X eyepieces, each **$49.95**
22X wide angle eyepiece **$54.95**

BUSHNELL SPACEMASTER 45°—Same as above except: Wgt., 43 oz., length closed 13″. Eyepiece at 45°, without eyepiece.
Price:.. **$319.95**

BUSHNELL ZOOM SPACEMASTER—20X-45X zoom. 60mm objective. Field at 1000 yards 120′-72′. Relative brightness 9-1.7. Wgt. 36 oz., length 11⅝″.
Price:.. **$379.95**

BUSHNELL SENTRY®—50mm objective. Field at 1000 yards 120′-45′. Relative brightness 6.25. Wgt., 25½ oz., length 12⅝″, without eyepiece.
Price:.. **$139.95**
20X, 32X and 48X eyepieces, each **$44.95**

BUSHNELL ZOOM SPOTTER—40mm objective. 9X-30X var. power.
Price:.. **$99.95**

BUSHNELL COMPETITOR—40mm objective. Prismatic. Field at 1000 yards 140′. Minimum focus 33′. Length 12½″, weight 18½ oz.
Price:.. **$91.95**

BUSHNELL TROPHY—16X-36X zoom. Rubber armored, prismatic. 50mm objective. Field at 1000 yards 131′ to 90′. Minimum focus 20′ Length with caps 13⅝″, weight 38 oz.
Price:.. **$319.95**
With interchangeable eyepieces—20x, 32x, 48x **$244.95**

BUSHNELL—10x30mm hand telescope. Field 183 ft. at 1000 yards. Weight 11 ozs.; 10″ long. Tripod mount
Price:.. **$34.95**

DICKSON 270—20x to 60x variable, 60mm objective, achromatic coated objective lens, complete with metal table tripod with 5 vertical and horizontal adjustments. Turret type, 20x, 30x, 40x 60x
Price:.. **$249.95**

DICKSON 274A—20x to 60x variable zoom. 60mm achromatic coated objective lens, complete with adjustable metal table tripod.
Price:.. **$150.00**

DICKSON 274B—As above but with addition of 4 × 16 Finder Scope.
Price:.. **$161.95**

HUTSON CHROMATAR 60—63.4mm objective. 22.5X eyepiece at 45°. Wgt. 24 oz., 8″ over-all. 10½ foot field at 100 yards.
Price:.. **$119.00**
15X or 45X eyepieces, each **$22.00**

OPTEX MODEL 420—15x-60x-60 Zoom; 18″ overall; weighs 4 lbs. with folding tripod (included). From Southern Precision Instrument
Price:.. **$135.00**

OPTEX MODEL 421—15x-45x-50 Zoom; 18″ over-all; weighs 4 lbs. with folding tripod (included). From Southern Precision Instrument
Price:.. **$110.00**

OPTEX MODEL 422—8x-25x-30 Zoom. Armour coated; 18″ over-all; weighs 3 lbs. with tripod (included). From Southern Precision Instrument
Price:.. **$100.00**

OPTEX MODEL 423—Same as Model 422 except 12x-40x-40
Price:.. **$120.00**

REDFIELD 30x SPOTTER—60mm objective, 30x. Field of view 9.5 ft. at 100 yds. Uses catadioptric lens system. Length over-all is 7.5″, weight is 11.5 oz. Eye relief 0.5″.
Price:.. **$411.05**

SIMMONS 1210—50mm objective, 25x standard, 16, 20, 40, 48, 16-36x zoom eyepieces available. Field at 1000 yds. 22 ft. Length 12.2″, weight 32 oz. Comes with tripod, 3x finder scope with crosshair.
Price: About.. **$127.50**
Price: Fixed eyepieces **$39.95**
Price: Zoom eyepiece **$79.95**

SIMMONS 1215—50mm objective, 25x standard, 16, 20, 40, 48, 16-36x zoom eyepieces available. Field at 1000 yds. 22 ft. Length 12.2″, weight 48 oz. Comes with tripod, 3x finder scope with crosshair.
Price: About.. **$190.00**
Price: Fixed eyepieces **$39.95**
Price: Zoom eyepiece **$79.95**

SIMMONS 1220—60mm objective, 25x standard, 16, 20, 40, 48, 16-36x zoom eyepieces available. Field at 1000 yds. 22 ft. Length 13.8″, weight 44 oz. with tripod (included). Has 3x finder scope with crosshairs.
Price: About.. **$198.95**
Price: Fixed eyepieces **$39.95**
Price: Zoom eyepiece **$79.95**

SWAROVSKI HABICHT HAWK 30x75S TELESCOPE—75mm objective, 30X. Field at 1,000 yds. 90ft. Minimum, focusing distance 90 ft. Length: closed 13 in., extended 20½″. Weight: 47 oz. Precise recognition of smallest details even at dusk. Leather or rubber covered, with caps and carrying case.
Price:.. **$895.00**
Same as above with short range supplement. Minimum focusing distance 24 to 30 ft. **$935.00**

SWAROVSKI 25-40X75 TELESCOPE—75mm objective, variable power from 25x to 40x with a field of 98 ft. (25x) and 72 ft. (40x). Minimum focusing distance 66 ft. (26 ft. with close focus model). Length closed is 11″, extended 15.5″; weight 46 oz. Rubber covered.
Price: Standard **$880.00**
Price: Close focus model **910.00**

SWIFT TELEMASTER M841—60mm objective. 15X to 60X variable power. Field at 1000 yards 160 feet (15X) to 40 feet (60X). Wgt. 3.4 lbs. 17.6″ over-all.
Price:.. **$399.95**
Tripod for above...................................... **$79.95**
Photo adapter **$16.00**
Case for above **$57.00**

SWIFT M844A COMMANDO PRISMATIC SPOTTING SCOPE/ TELEPHOTO LENS, MK.II—60mm objective. Comes with 20X eyepiece; 15X, 30X, 40X, 50X, 60X available. Built-in sunshade. Field at 1000 yds. with 20X, 120 ft. Length 13.7″, wgt. 2.1 lbs.
Price:.. **$260.00**

SWIFT M847 SCANNER—50mm objective. Comes with 25x eyepiece; 20x, 30x, 35x eyepieces available. Field of view at 1000 yds. is 112 ft. (25x). Length 13.6″, weight 23 oz.
Price:.. **$139.50**
Each additional eyepiece.............................. **$27.50**
Tubular case.. **$25.00**
Tripod **$79.95**

SWIFT M700 SCOUT—9X-30X, 30mm spotting scope. Length 15½″, weighs 2.1 lbs. Field of 204 ft. (9X), 60 ft. (30X).
Price:.. **$87.00**

TASCO 31T SQUARE SPOTTING SCOPE—40mm objective. 12X and 20X. Field at 1000 yds. 185 ft. (12X) and 120 ft. (20X). Built-in tripod and swivel turret. Weight 29.5 oz. Length 8¼″.
Price:.. **$99.95**

TASCO 32T SQUARE SPOTTING SCOPE—50mm objective. 17X and 30X. Field at 1000 yds. 133 ft. (17X) and 89 ft. (30X). Built-in tripod and swivel turret. Weight 25.9 oz. Length 11½″.
Price:.. **$119.95**

TASCO 33T ZOOM SQUARE SPOTTING SCOPE—60mm objective. Prismatic. 20X to 45X. Field at 1000 yds. 104 ft. (20X) to 70 ft. (45X). With tripod and 45° angle swivel turret. Weight 52 oz. Length 15″.
Price:.. **$299.95**

TASCO 34T RUBBER COVERED SPOTTING SCOPE—50mm objective. 25X. Field at 1000 yds. 136 ft. With tripod and built-in tripod adapter. Weight 29.9 oz. Length 13¾″.
Price:.. **$199.95**

TASCO 21T SPOTTING SCOPE—40mm objective. 20X. Field at 1000 yds. 136 ft. With Tasco 8P tripod. Weight 18.2 oz. Length 12⅜″.
Price:.. **$109.95**

TASCO 26T SPOTTING SCOPE—50mm objective. 25X. Field at 1000 yds. 109 ft. With Tasco 8P tripod. Weight 23.6 oz. Length 13¾″.
Price:.. **$149.95**

TASCO 25T/25P RUBBER COVERED SPOTTING SCOPE—60mm objective. 25X. Field at 1000 yds. 94 ft. Prismatic. With Tasco 25P deluxe tripod, olive green to match rubber covering. Weight 38.3 oz. Length 11½″.
Price:.. **$509.95**

TASCO 34TZ RUBBER COVERED—50mm objective. 18-36X zoom. Comes with tripod and built-in tripod adapter. Weight 29.9 oz., length 13¾″.
Price:.. **$239.95**

UNERTL RIGHT ANGLE—63.5mm objective, 24X. Field at 100 yds., 7 ft. Relative brightness, 6.96. Eye relief, ½″. Wgt., 41 oz. Length closed, 19″. Push-pull and screw-focus eyepiece. 16X and 32X eyepieces **$35.00** each.
Price:.. **$242.00**

UNERTL STRAIGHT PRISMATIC—Same as Unertl Right Angle except: straight eyepiece and wgt. of 40 oz.
Price:.. **$205.00**

UNERTL 20X STRAIGHT PRISMATIC—54mm objective. 20X. Field at 100 yds., 8.5 ft. Relative brightness, 6.1. Eye relief, ½″. Wgt. 36 oz. Length closed, 13½″. Complete with lens covers.
Price:.. **$172.00**

UNERTL TEAM SCOPE—100mm objective. 15X, 24X, 32X eyepieces. Field at 100 yds. 13 to 7.5 ft. Relative brightness, 39.06 to 9.79. Eye relief, 2″ to 1½″. Weight 13 lbs. 29⅞″ overall. Metal tripod, yoke and wood carrying case furnished (total weight, 67 lbs.)
Price:.. **$900.00**

WEATHERBY—60mm objective, 20X-45X zoom
Price:.. **$323.95**
Tripod for above...................................... **$69.95**

PERIODICAL PUBLICATIONS

Airgun World
10 Sheet St., Windsor, Berks., SL4 1BG, England.£11.50 for 12 issues. Monthly magazine catering exclusively to the airgun enthusiast.

Alaska Magazine
Alaska Northwest Pub. Co., Box 4-EEE, Anchorage, AK 99509. $18.00 yr. Hunting, fishing and Life on the Last Frontier articles of Alaska and western Canada.

American Field†
222 W. Adams St., Chicago, IL. 60606. $18.00 yr. Field dogs and trials, occasional gun and hunting articles.

American Firearms Industry
Nat'l. Assn. of Federally Licensed Firearms Dealers, 2801 E. Oakland Park Blvd., Ft. Lauderdale, FL 33306. $20 yr. For firearms dealers & distributors.

American Handgunner*
591 Camino de la Reina, San Diego, CA 92108. $11.95 yr. Articles for handgun enthusiasts, collectors and hunters.

American Hunter (M)
Natl. Rifle Assn., 1600 Rhode Island Ave. N.W., Washington, DC 20036. $15.00 yr. Wide scope of hunting articles.

American Rifleman (M)
National Rifle Assn., 1600 Rhode Island Ave., N.W., Wash., DC 20036. $15.00 yr. Firearms articles of all kinds.

The American Shotgunner
P.O. Box 3351, Reno, NV 89505. $15.00 yr. Official publ. of the American Assn. of Shotgunning. Shooting, reloading, hunting, investment collecting, new used gun classifieds.

American West
Amer. West Publ. Co., 3033 No. Campbell, Tucson, AZ 85719. $15.00 yr.

AMI
New Fashion Media, Avenue Louis 60, B1050 Brussels, Belgium. Belg. Franc 325, 11 issues. Arms, shooting militaria information; French text.

Angler & Hunter
Ontario's Wildlife Magazine, P.O. Box 1541, Peterborough, Ont. K9J 7H7, Canada.

Arms Collecting (Q)
Museum Restoration Service P.O. Drawer 390, Bloomfield, Ont., Canada K0K IG0 and P.O. Box 70, Alexandria Bay, NY 13607. $10.00 yr. $27.50 3 yrs.

Austrialian Shooters' Journal
Sporting Shooter's Assn. of Australia, Box 1064 G.P.O., Adelaide, SA 5001, Australia. $20 yr. locally; $35 yr. overseas. Hunting and shooting articles.

The Backwoodsman Magazine
Rte. 8, Box 579, Livingston, TX 77351. $9.00 for 6 issues pr. yr.; sample copy $1. Subject incl. muzzle-loading, woodslore, trapping, homesteading, et al.

The Black Powder Report
The Buckskin Press, Inc., P.O. Box 789, Big Timber, MT 59011. $15.00 yr. Shooting, hunting, gun-building and restoration articles.

Black Powder Times*
P.O. Box 842, Mount Vernon, WA 98273. $10.00 for 6 issues. Magazine for blackpowder activities; test reports.

The Blade Magazine*
P.O. Box 22007, Chattanooga, TN 37422. $14.99 yr. Add $10 f. foreign subscription. A magazine for all enthusiasts of the edged blade.

The Buckskin Report
The Buckskin Press, P.O. Box 789, Big Timber, MT 59011. $18.00 yr. Articles for the blackpowder shooter.

Deer Unlimited*
P.O. Box 509, Clemson, SC 29631. $12.00 yr.

Deutsches Waffen Journal
Journal-Verlag Schwend GmbH, Postfach 100340, D7170 Schwäbisch Hall, Germany. DM71.00 yr. plus DM16.80 for postage. Antique and modern arms. German text.

Ducks Unlimited, Inc. (M)
1 Waterfowl Way at Gilmer, Long Grove, IL 60047

Enforcement Journal (Q)
Frank J. Schira, editor, Natl. Police Officers Assn., 609 West Main St., Louisville, KY 40202 $6.00 yr.

FFL Business News
Nat'l. Assn. of Federally Licensed Firearms Dealers, 2801 E. Oakland Pk. Blvd., Ft. Lauderdale, FL 33306. $6.00 yr. For firearms dealers & distributors.

The Field†
The Harmsworth Press Ltd., Carmelite House, London EC4Y OJA, England. $88.00 yr. Hunting and shooting articles, and all country sports.

Field & Stream
CBS Magazines, 1515 Broadway, New York, NY 10036. $11.94 yr. Articles on firearms plus hunting and fishing.

Fur-Fish-Game
A.R. Harding Pub. Co., 2878 E. Main St., Columbus, OH 43209. $8.00 yr. "Gun Rack" column by Don Zutz.

Gray's Sporting Journal
Gray's Sporting Journal Co., 205 Willow St., So. Hamilton, MA 01982. $23.50 per yr. f. 4 consecutive issues. Hunting and fishing journals.

Gun Owner(Q)
Gun Owners Inc., 1025 Front St., Suite 300, Sacramento, CA 95814. With membership $20 yr.; single copy $3. An outdoors magazine for sportsmen everywhere.

The Gun Report
World Wide Gun Report, Inc., Box 111, Aledo, IL 61231. $25.00 yr. For the antique gun collector.

The Gunrunner
Div. of Kexco Publ. Co. Ltd., Box 565, Lethbridge, Alb., Canada T1J 3Z4. $15.00 yr. Monthly newspaper, listing everything from antiques to artillery.

The Gun Gazette
P.O. Box 2685, Warner Robins, GA 31099. $10 yr. Extensive gun show listings, with articles on guns, knives and hunting.

Gun Week†
Hawkeye Publishing, Inc., P.O. Box 411, Station C, Buffalo NY 14209. $20.00 yr. U.S. and possessions; $24.00 yr. other countries. Tabloid paper on guns, hunting, shooting and collecting.

Gun World
Gallant Publishing Co., 34249 Camino Capistrano, Capistrano Beach, CA 92624. $14.00 yr. For the hunting, reloading and shooting enthusiast.

Guns & Ammo
Petersen Pub. Co., 8490 Sunset Blvd., Los Angeles, CA 90069. $11.94 yr. Guns, shooting, and technical articles.

Guns
Guns Magazine, 591 Camino de la Reina, San Diego, CA 92108. $14.95 yr. Articles for gun collectors, hunters and shooters.

Guns Review
Ravenhill Pub. Co. Ltd., Box 35, Standard House, Bonhill St., London E.C. 2A 4DA, England. £11.55 sterling (approx. U.S. $24) USA & Canada yr. For collectors and shooters.

Handloader*
Wolfe Pub. Co. Inc., Box 3030, Prescott, AZ 86302 $13.00 yr. The journal of ammunition reloading.

The IMAS Journal (M)
International Military Arms Society, P.O. Box 122, Williamstown, WV 26187. Military gun collecting articles.

INSIGHTS*
NRA, 1600 Rhode Island Ave. N.W., Washington, DC 20036. Editor Mary E. Shelsby. $5.00 yr. (6 issues). Plenty of details for the young target shooter.

International Shooting Sport*
International Shooting Union (UIT), Bavariaring 21, D-8000 Munich 2, Fed. Rep. of Germany. Europe: (Deutsche Mark) DM39.00 yr., p.p.; outside Europe: DM45.00. For the International target shooter.

The Journal of the Arms & Armour Society (M)
A.R.E. North (Secy.), Dept. of Metalwork, Victoria and Albert Museum, London, England. $16.00 yr. Articles for the historian and collector.

Journal of the Historical Breechloading Smallarms Assn.
Publ. annually, Imperial War Museum, Lambeth Road, London SE1 6HZ, England. $8.00 yr. Articles for the collector plus mailings of lecture transcripts, short articles on specific arms, reprints, newsletter, etc.; a surcharge is made f. airmail.

Knife World
Knife World Publications, P.O. Box 3395, Knoxville, TN 37917. $8.00 yr., $14.00 2 yrs. Published monthly f. knife enthusiasts and collectors. Articles on custom and factory knives; other knife related interests.

Law and Order
Law and Order Magazine, 5526 N. Elston Ave., Chicago, IL 60630. $12.00 yr. Articles on weapons for law enforcement, etc.

Man At Arms*
222 West Exchange St., Providence, RI 02903. $18.00 yr. The magazine of arms collecting-investing, with excellent brief articles for the collector of antique and modern firearms.

MAN/MAGNUM
S.A. Man (1982) (Pty) Ltd., P.O. Box 35204, Northway, Durban 4065, Rep. of South Africa. R19 f. 12 issues. Africa's only publication on hunting, shooting, firearms, bushcraft, knives, etc.

The Marlin Collector (M)
R.W. Paterson, 407 Lincoln Bldg., 44 Main St., Champaign, IL 61820.

Muzzle Blasts (M)
National Muzzle Loading Rifle Assn., P.O. Box 67, Friendship, IN 47021. $16.00 yr. For the black powder shooter.

Muzzleloader Magazine*
Rebel Publishing Co., Inc., Route 5, Box 347-M, Texarkana, TX 75501. $10.00 U.S., $12.00 foreign yr. The publication for black powder shooters.

National Defense (M)*
American Defense Preparedness Assn., Rosslyn Center, Suite 900, 1700 North Moore St., Arlington, VA 22209. $25.00 yr. Articles on military-related topics, including weapons, materials technology, management.

National Knife Collector (M)
Natl. Knife Coll. Assn., P.O. Box 21070, Chattanooga, TN 37421. Membership $15 yr, $40.00 International yr.

National Rifle Assn. Journal (British) (Q)
Natl. Rifle Assn. (BR.), Bisley Camp, Brookwood, Woking, Surrey, England. GU24, OPB. $14.00 inc. air postage.

National Wildlife*
Natl. Wildlife Fed., 1412 16th St. N.W., Washington, DC 20036. $10.50 yr. (6 issues); International Wildlife, 6 issues, $10.50 yr. Both, $17.50 yr., plus membership benefits. Write to this addr., attn.: Promotion Dept., for the proper information.

New Zealand Wildlife (Q)
New Zealand Deerstalkers Assoc. Inc., P.O. Box 6514, Wellington, N.Z. $13.00 (N.Z.). Hunting, shooting and firearms/game research articles.

North American Hunter* (M)
7901 Flying Cloud Dr., P.O. Box 35557, Minneapolis, MN 55435. $18.00 yr. (6 issues). Articles on North American game hunting.

Northwestern Sportsman
Box 1208, Big Timber, MT 59011. $10.00 yr.

Outdoor Life
Times Mirror Magazines, Inc., 380 Madison Ave., New York, NY 10017. $11.94 yr. Shooting columns by Jim Carmichel, and others.

Point Blank
Citizens Committee for the Right to Keep and Bear Arms (sent to contributors) Liberty Park, 12500 NE 10th Pl., Bellevue, WA 98005

The Police Marksman*
6000 E. Shirley Lane, Montgomery, AL 36117. $15.00 yr.

Police Times/Command (M)
1100 N.E. 125th St., No. Miami, FL 33161

Popular Mechanics
Hearst Corp., 224 W. 57th St., New York, NY 10019. $11.97 yr. Hunting, shooting and camping articles.

Precision Shooting
Precision Shooting, Inc., 37 Burnham St., East Hartford, CT 06108. $15.00 yr. Journal of the International Benchrest Shooters, National Benchrest Shooting Assn., and target shooting in general.

Rendezvous & Longrifles (M)
Canadian Black Powder Federation Newsletter, P.O. Box 2876, Postal Sta. "A", Moncton, N.B. E1C, 8T8, Canada. 6 issues per yr. w. $15.00 membership.

Rifle*
Wolfe Publishing Co. Inc., Box 3030, Prescott, AZ 86302. $13.00 yr. The magazine for shooters.

Rod & Rifle Magazine
Lithographic Serv. Ltd., P.O. Box 38-138, Petone, New Zealand. $25.00 yr. (6 issues) Hunting and shooting articles.

Safari* (M)
Safari Magazine, 5151 E. Broadway, Tucson, AZ 85711. $20 (6 times). Official journal of Safari Club International; the journal of big game htg.

Saga
Lexington Library, Inc., 355 Lexington Ave., New York, NY 10017. Currently annual. No subscription. $1.75 p. issue U.S.

Schweizer Waffen Magazin
OF Orell Füssli Zeitschriften, Postfach, CH-8036 Zürich, Switzerland. SF 105.00 (U.S. $46.70 air mail) f. 10 issues. Modern and antique arms. German text.

Second Amendment Reporter
Second Amendment Fdn., James Madison Bldg., 12500 NE 10th Pl., Bellevue, WA 98005. $15.00 yr. (non-contributors).

Shooting Industry
Publisher's Dev. Corp., 591 Camino de la Reina, Suite 200, San Diego, CA 92108. $25.00 yr. To the trade $12.50

Shooting Magazine
10 Sheet St., Windsor, Berks. SL4 1BG England. £11.50 for 12 issues. Monthly journal catering mainly to claypigeon shooters.

The Shooting Times & Country Magazine (England)†
10 Sheet St., Windsor, Berkshire SL4 1BG, England. $48.75 yr. (52 issues). Game shooting, wild fowling, hunting, game fishing and firearms articles.

Shooting Times
PJS Publications, News Plaza. P.O. Box 1790, Peoria, IL 60656. $15.00 yr. Guns, shooting, reloading; articles on every gun activity.

The Shotgun News‡
Snell Publishing Co., Box 669, Hastings, NE 68901. $15.00 yr.; all other countries $100.00 yr. Sample copy $3.00. Gun ads of all kinds.

Shotgun Sports
P.O. Box 340, Lake Havasu City, AZ 86403. $20. yr.

Shotgun West
2052 Broadway, Santa Monica, CA 90404. $8.50 yr. Trap, Skeet and international shooting, scores; articles, schedules.

The Sixgunner (M)
Handgun Hunters International, P.O. Box 357, MAG. Bloomingdale, OH 43910

The Skeet Shooting Review
National Skeet Shooting Assn., P.O. Box 28188, San Antonio, TX 78228. $15.00 yr. (Assn. membership of $20.00 includes mag.) Competition results, personality profiles of top Skeet shooters, how-to articles, technical, reloading information.

Soldier of Fortune
Subscription Dept., P.O. Box 310, Martinsville, NJ 08836. $26.00 yr. U.S., Can., Mex.; $33.00 all other countries surface.

Sporting Goods Business
Gralla Publications, 1515 Broadway, New York, NY 10036. Trade journal.

The Sporting Goods Dealer
1212 No. Lindbergh Blvd., St. Louis, Mo. 63132. $30.00 yr. The sporting goods trade journal.

Sporting Gun
Bretton Court, Bretton, Peterborough PE3 8DZ, England £15.00 (approx. U.S. $28.00) (airmail £24.00) yr. For the game and clay enthusiasts.

Sports Afield
The Hearst Corp., 250 W. 55th St., New York, NY 10019. $11.97 yr. Grits Gresham on firearms, ammunition and Thomas McIntyre, Lionel Atwill, Gerald Almy on hunting.

Sports Merchandiser
A W.R.C. Smith Publication, 1760 Peachtree Rd. NW, Atlanta, GA 30357. Trade Journal.

Survival Guide
McMullen Publishing, Inc., 2145 West La Palma Ave., Anaheim, CA 92801. 12 issues $20.98.

TACARMI
Via E. De Amicis, 25;20123 Milano, Italy. $33.00 yr. Antique and modern guns. (Italian text.).

Trap & Field
1100 Waterway Blvd., Indianapolis, IN 46202. $18.00 yr. Official publ. Amateur Trapshooting Assn. Scores, averages, trapshooting articles.

Turkey Call* (M)
Natl. Wild Turkey Federation, Inc., P.O. Box 530, Edgefield, SC 29824. $15.00 w. membership (6 issues p. yr.)

The U.S. Handgunner* (M)
U.S. Revolver Assn., 96 West Union St., Ashland, MA 01721. $5.00 yr. General handgun and competition articles. Bi-monthly sent to members.

Waterfowler's World*
P.O. Box 38306, Germantown, TN 38183. $12.00 yr.

The Weekly Bullet
Second Amendment Fdn., James Madison Bldg., 12500 NE 10th Pl., Bellevue, WA 98005. $35.00 yr.

Wisconsin Sportsman*
Wisconsin Sportsman, Inc., P.O. Box 2266, Oshkosh, WI 54903. $9.95.

*Published bi-monthly † Published weekly ‡ Published three times per month. All others are published monthly.
M = Membership requirements; write for details. Q = Published Quarterly.

Shooting Sports Booklets & Pamphlets

Basic Pistol Marksmanship—Textbook for basic courses in pistol shooting. 50¢[2]

Basic Rifle Marksmanship—Text for a basic course in shooting the rifle. 50¢[2]

The Cottontail Rabbit—56-page rundown on America's most popular hunting target. Where to find him, how to hunt him, how to help him. Bibliography included. $2 ea.[4]

The Elk—125-page report on the hunting and management of this game animal, more properly called *wapiti*. Extensive biblio. $2 ea.[4]

Fact Pact II—Authoritative and complete study on gun use and ownership. This is a valuable 102-page reference. $2 ea[1].

For The Young Hunter—A 32-page booklet giving fundamental information on the sport. 50¢ each.[4]

Free Films—Brochure listing outdoor movies available to sportsmen's clubs. Free[1]

Fundamentals of Claybird Shooting—A 39-page booklet explaining the basics of Skeet and trap in non-technical terms. Many diagrams. 25¢[5]

Game, Gunners and Biology—A thumbnail history of American wildlife conservation. $2 ea.[4]

Gray Fox and Squirrels—112-page paperbound illustrated book giving full rundown on the squirrel families named. Extensive bibliography. $2 ea.[4]

Hunting Dogs—An excellent primer on hunting dogs for the novice hunter. 50¢ ea.[4]

The Mallard—80-page semi-technical report on this popular duck. Life cycle, laws and management, hunting—even politics as they affect this bird—are covered. Bibliography. $2 ea.[4]

The Mourning Dove—Illustrated booklet includes life history, conservation and hunting of the mourning dove. $2[4]

NRA Air Gun Training Program—A "self-teaching" precision air rifle and pistol manual. $1[2]

NRA Hunter Safety & Conservation Program Instructor's Manual—Teaching outlined and sources of information for hunter safety and conservation instructor, including exercises and demonstrations. 50¢[2]

NRA Hunter Safety & Conservation Program Student Manual (Revised)—Textbook for use in creating safer hunting environment and explain hunter's involvement in wildlife conservation. 50¢[2]

NRA Illustrated International Shooting Handbook—18 major articles detailing shooting under ISU rules, training methods, etc. NRA, Washington, DC, 1964. $2.50 ea. ($1.50 to NRA members.)[2]

Principles of Game Management—A 25-page booklet surveying in popular manner such subjects as hunting regulations, predator control, game refuges and habitat restoration. Single copies free, 25¢ each in bulk[4]

The Ring-Necked Pheasant—Popular distillation of much of the technical literature on the "ringneck." 104-page paperbound book, appropriately illustrated. Bibliography included. $2 ea.[2]

Ruffed Grouse, by John Madson—108-page booklet on the life history, management and hunting of *Bonasa umbellus* in its numerous variations. Extensive biblio. $2[4]

Trap or Skeet Fundamentals—Handbooks explaining fundamentals of these two sports, complete with explicit diagrams to start beginners off right. Free[3]

The White-Tailed Deer—Interesting fact-filled booklet gives life history, conservation and hunting information on this popular game animal. $2[4]

[1]National Shooting Sports Foundation, Inc., 1075 Post Road, Riverside, CT 06878
[2]National Rifle Association of America, 1600 Rhode Island Ave., Washington, DC 20036

[3]Remington Arms Company, Dept. C, Bridgeport, CT. 06602
[4]Olin Corp., Conservation Dept., East Alton, IL 62024
[4]Winchester-Western, Shotgun Shooting Promotion, P.O. Box 30-275, New Haven, CT 06511

The Arms Library for

COLLECTOR · HUNTER · SHOOTER · OUTDOORSMAN

A selection of books—old, new and forthcoming—for everyone in the arms field, with a brief description by . . . JOE RILING

IMPORTANT NOTICE TO BOOK BUYERS

Books listed here may be bought from Ray Riling Arms Books Co., 114 Greenwood Ave., Box 135, Wyncote, PA 19095, phone 215/438-2456. Joe Riling, the proprietor, is the researcher and compiler of "The Arms Library" and a seller of gun books for over 30 years.

The Riling stock includes books classic and modern, many hard-to-find items, and many not obtainable elsewhere. These pages list a portion of the current stock. They offer prompt, complete service, with delayed shipments occurring only on out-of-print or out-of-stock books.

NOTICE FOR ALL CUSTOMERS: Remittance in U.S. funds must accompany all orders. For U.S. add $1.50 per book for postage and insurance. Minimum order $10.00. For U.P.S. add 50% to mailing costs.

All foreign countries add $2.00 per book for postage and handling, plus $3.30 per 10-lb. package or under for safe delivery by registered mail. Parcels not registered are sent at the "buyers risk."

Payments in excess of order or for "Backorders" are credited or fully refunded at request. Books "As-Ordered" are not returnable except by permission and a handling charge on these of $2.00 per book is deducted from refund or credit. Only Pennsylvania customers must include current sales tax.

A full variety of arms books are also available from Rutgers Book Center, 127 Raritan Ave., Highland Park, NJ 08904.

NEW BOOKS

(Alphabetically, no categories)

Advanced Wild Turkey Hunting & World Records, by Dave Harbour, Winchester Press, Piscataway, NJ, 1983. 264 pp., illus. $19.95.

The definitive book, written by an authority who has studied turkeys and turkey calling for over 40 years.

All-American Deer Hunter's Guide, edited by Jim Zumbo and Robert Elman, Winchester Press, Piscataway, NJ, 1983. 320 pp., illus. $29.95.

The most comprehensive, thorough book yet published on American deer hunting.

American Gunsmiths, by Frank M. Sellers, The Gun Room Press, Highland Park, NJ, 1983. 349 pp. $39.95.

A comprehensive listing of the American gun maker, patentee, gunsmith and entrepreneur.

American Primitive Knives 1770-1870, by G.B. Minnes, Museum Restoration Service, Ottawa, Canada, 1983. 112 pp., illus. $14.95.

Origins of the knives, outstanding specimens, structural details, etc.

Basic Gunsmithing, by John E. Traister, Tab Books, Inc., Blue Ridge Summit, PA, 1983. 288 pp., illus. Paper covers. $9.95.

An owner's guide to repairing, remodelling, cleaning, and restoring rifles, shotguns, and handguns.

Bear Hunting, by Jerry Meyer, Stackpole Books, Harrisburg, PA., 1983. 224 pp., illus. $14.95.

First complete guide on the how-to's of bear hunting. Information on every type of bear found in the U.S. and Canada.

The Best of Jack O'Connor, by Jack O'Connor, Amwell Press, Clinton, NJ, 1984. 192 pp., illus. $27.50.

A collection of Jack O'Connor's finest writings.

Big Game of North America, ecology and management, by Wildlife Management Institute, Stackpole Books, Harrisburg, PA, 1983. 512 pp., illus. $29.95.

An outstanding reference for professionals and students of wildlife management.

Bolt Action Rifles, Revised edition, by Frank de Haas, DBI Books, Inc., Northfield, IL, 1984. 448 pp., illus. Paper covers. $13.95.

A revised edition of the most definitive work on all major bolt action rifle designs.

Buckskins and Black Powder, by Ken Grissom, Winchester Press, Piscataway, NJ, 1983. 224 pp., illus. $15.95.

A mountain man's guide to muzzleloading.

The Cartridge Collector's Notebook, by Charles Yust, edited by Steve Fuller, Military Research Service, San Jose, CA, 1984. 128 pp. Paper covers. $10.95.

A compilation of cartridge articles published in the American Rifleman and Gun Digest, by Charles Yust, Jr., cartridge authority.

Churchill's Game Shooting, edited by Macdonald Hastings, Arms and Armour Press, London, England, 1979. 252 pp., illus. Paper covers. $15.00.

The standard textbook on the successful use of the shotgun.

Collector's Guide to Ames U.S. Contract Military Edged Weapons:1832-1906, by Ron Hickox, Ron Hickox, Brandon, FL, 1984. 50 pp., illus. Paper covers. $12.95.

Complete guide to U.S. military edged weapons made by the Ames Manufacturing Co.

Colonel Colt London, by Joseph G. Rosa, Arms and Armour Press, London, England, 1983. 218 pp., illus. $24.95.

The standard reference volume on the London activities of Samuel Colt.

The Complete Book of Target Shooting, by Wes Blair, Stackpole Books, Harrisburg, PA, 1984. 416 pp., illus. $24.95.

The encyclopedia of up-to-date shooting information.

The Complete Encyclopedia of Arms and Weapons, by Leonid Tarassuk and Claude Blair, Charles Scribner's Sons, New York, NY, 1983. 560 pp., illus. $41.50.

Describes armor, crossbows, swords, daggers, cannons, pistols, rifles, bayonets, etc. Comprehensive and arranged alphabetically.

The Complete Guide to Bowhunting Deer, by Chuck Adams, DBI Books, Inc., Northfield, IL, 1984. 256 pp., illus. Paper covers. $10.95.

Plenty on equipment, bows, sights, quivers, arrows, clothes, lures and scents, stands and blinds, etc.

The Complete Turkey Hunt, by William Morris Daskal, El-Bar Enterprises Publishers, New York, N.Y., 1982. 129 pp., illus. Paper covers. $7.95.

Covers every aspect of turkeys and turkey hunting, by an expert hunter.

Confessions of an Outdoor Maladroit, by Joel M. Vance, Amwell Press, Clinton, NJ, 1983. $20.00.

Anthology of some of the wildest, irreverent, and zany hunting tales ever.

Contemporary American Stockmakers, by Ron Toews, The Dove Press, Enid, OK, 1979. 216 pp., illus. $80.00.

The only reference book on its subject. Over 200 detailed photos of fine rifle stocking.

Covey Rises and Other Pleasures, by David H. Henderson, Amwell Press, Clinton, NJ, 1983. 155 pp., illus. $17.50.

A collection of essays and stories concerned with field sports.

Deer Hunter's Guide to Guns, Ammunition, and Equipment, by Edward A. Matunas, an Outdoor Life Book, distributed by Stackpole Books, Harrisburg, PA, 1983. 352 pp., illus. $24.95.

Where-to-hunt for North American deer. An authoritative guide that will help every deer hunter get maximum enjoyment and satisfaction from his sport.

Deer in Their World, by Erwin Bauer, Stackpole Books, Harrisburg, PA, 1984. 256 pp., illus. $29.95.

A showcase of more than 250 natural habitat deer photographs. Substantial natural history of North American deer.

The Duck Hunter's Book, edited by Lamar Underwood, Amwell Press, Clinton, NJ, 1983. 650 pp., illus. $25.00.

Anthology of the finest duck hunting stories.

Encyclopedia of Big Game Animals of Africa, by Pierre Fiorenza, Larousse and Co., Inc., New York, NY, 1983. $85.00.

Detailed information on the life and habitat of each species. 120 full-color photos.

The Fighting Rifle, Chuck Taylor, Paladin Press, Boulder, CO, 1983. 184 pp., illus. Paper covers. $12.95.

The difference between assault and battle rifles and auto and light machine guns.

Firearms of the American West, 1803-1865, by Louis A. Garavaglia and Charles G. Worman, University of New Mexico Press, Albuquerque, NM, 1983. 300 pp., illus. $35.00.

An encyclopedic study tracing the development of uses of firearms on the frontier during that period.

For Whom the Ducks Toll!, by Keith C. Russell, et al, Winchester Press, Piscataway, NJ, 1984. 288 pp., illus. Slipcased limited edition. $30.00.

A select gathering of memorable waterfowling tales by the author and 68 of his closest friends.

Frankonia Jagd Catalogues, Waffen-Frankonia, Wurzburg, Germany. Catalogs from this famous German sporting goods supplier. Rifles, shotguns, handguns, and accessories. Paper covers.

1980-81 ....$15.00
1982-83 ....$15.00
1983-84 ....$15.00

Game in the Desert Revisited, by Jack O'Connor. Amwell Press, Clinton, NJ, 1984. 306 pp., illus. $27.50.

Reprint of a Derrydale Press classic on hunting in the Southwest.

Game Warden: Chesapeake Assignment, by Wille J. Parker, Tidewater Publishers, Centreville, MD, 1983. 275 pp., illus. $14.95.

A book about the illegal hunting of waterfowl on the Chesapeake Bay.

Gas, Air, and Spring Guns of the World, by W.H.B. Smith, Arms and Armour Press, London, England, 1983. 288 pp., illus. Paper covers. $17.50.

The standard work of its kind, invaluable to serious students, gunsmiths, developers, and collectors.

The German Bayonet, by John Walter, Arms and Armour Press, London, England, 1982. 128 pp., illus. $19.95.

A comprehensive, illustrated history of the regulation patterns 1871-1945.

The German Rifle, by John Walter, Arms and Armour Press, London, England, 1982. 160 pp., illus. $16.95.

A comprehensive illustrated history of the standard bolt-action design, 1871-1945.

The Gun Collector's Handbook of Values, 1983-84, by C.E. Chapel, G.P. Putnam and Son, East Rutherford, NJ, 1984. 462 pp., illus. $19.95.

The 14th revised edition of the best-known price reference for collectors.

Gun Digest 1985, 39th edition, edited by Ken Warner, DBI Books, Inc., Northfield, IL, 1984. 472 pp., illus. Paper covers. $14.95.

The perennial best seller for firearms fans.

The Gun Digest Book of Autoloading Pistols, by Dean A. Grennell, DBI Books, Inc., Northfield, IL, 1983. 288 pp., illus. Paper covers. $10.95.

History, operating principles and firing techniques for rimfire, military/police, competition, hunting, assault autos. Value trends.

The Gun Digest Book of Combat Handgunnery, by Jack Lewis and Jack Mitchell, DBI Books, Inc., Northfield, IL, 1983. 288 pp., illus. Paper covers. $10.95.

From the basics to competition, training and exercises.

Gun Digest Book of Trap and Skeet Shooting, by Art Blatt, DBI Books, Inc., Northfield, IL, 1984. 288 pp., illus. Paper Covers. $10.95.

Valuable information for both beginner and seasoned shooter.

Guns and Ammo, 1985 Annual, edited by Craig Boddington, Peterson Publishing Co., Los Angeles, CA, 1984, 288 pp., illus. Paper covers. $6.95.

Annual catalog of sporting firearms and accessories along with articles for the gun enthusiasts.

Guns and Gunmaking Tools of Southern Appalachia, by John Rice Irwin, Schiffer Publishing Ltd., 1983. 118 pp., illus. Paper covers. $9.95.

The story of the Kentucky rifle.

Guns Illustrated 1985, 17th edition, edited by Harold A. Murtz, DBI Books, Inc., Northfield, IL, 1984. 344 pp., illus. Paper covers. $12.95.

Packed with timely interesting articles and solid field testing on a wide variety of firearms.

Gunsmith Kinks 2, by Bob Brownell, F. Brownell & Son, Publishers, Montezuma, Iowa, 1983. 496 pp., illus. $14.95.

An incredible collection of gunsmithing knowledge, shop kinks, new and old techniques, short-cuts and general know-how straight from those who do them best—the gunsmiths.

Handguns for Self Defence, by Gerry Gore, Macmillan South Africa, Johannesburg, South Africa, 1981. 164 pp., illus. Paper covers. $15.00.

Choosing the gun, basic skills, the draws, stopping power, etc.

Hit the White Part, by Massad Ayoob, Massad Ayoob, Concord, NH, 1982. 107 pp., illus. Paper covers. $7.95.

Second Chance, the art of bowling pin shooting.

Hodgdon Data Manual No. 24, Hodgdon Powder Co., Shawnee Mission, KS, 1984. 400 pp., illus. Paper covers. $10.95.

Has a new silhouette section and complete data on new H4350 powder.

Home Gunsmithing Digest, 3rd Edition, by Tommy L. Bish, DBI Books, Inc., Northfield, IL, 1984. 256 pp., illus. Paper covers. $10.95.

The know-how supplied by an expert.

How to Buy and Sell Used Guns, by John Traister, Stoeger Publishing Co., So. Hackensack, NJ, 1984. 192 pp., illus. Paper covers. $9.95.

A new guide to buying and selling guns.

The Hunter's World, by Charles F. Waterman, Winchester Press, Piscataway, NJ, 1983. 250 pp., illus. $29.95.

A classic. One of the most beautiful hunting books ever produced.

Hunting the Rocky Mountain Goat, by Duncan Gilchrist, Duncan Gilchrist, Hamilton, MT, 1983. 175 pp., illus. Paper covers. $10.95.

Hunting techniques for mountain goats and other alpine game. Tips on rifles for the high country.

Inscribed Union Swords, 1861-1865, by David V. Stroud, Pinecrest Publishing Co., Kilgore, TX, 1984. 192 pp., illus. Limited, numbered and signed edition. $27.50.

A definitive work on presentation swords.

Knives '85, edited by Ken Warner, DBI Books, Inc., Northfield, IL, 1984. 256 pp., illus. Paper covers. $10.95.

The annual "must" edition for the knife enthusiast.

Law Enforcement Bible, No. 2, edited by Det. Robert A. Scanlon, Stoeger Publishing Co., So. Hackensack, NJ, 1984. 368 pp., illus. Paper covers. $11.95.

World's standard law enforcement reference.

The Machine Gun: Book 2, by Col. George M. Chinn, USMC (Ret.), Bureau of Ordnance, Dept. of the Navy, 1952, reprinted by Col. Chinn, 1982. 236 pp., illus. Limited signed and numbered edition. $29.95.

History, evolution and development of manual, auto, and airborne repeating weapons by the Soviet Union and her satellites.

The Machine Gun: Book 3, by Col. George M. Chinn, USMC (Ret.), Bureau of Ordnance, Dept. of the Navy, 1951, reprinted by Col. Chinn. 1982. 717 pp., 407 illus. $49.95.

Development during WW II and the Korean conflict by the U.S. and their Allies of full-auto machine gun systems.

The Machine Gun: Book 4, by Col. George M. Chinn, USMC (Ret.), Bureau of Ordnance, Dept. of the Navy, 1955, reprinted by Col. Chinn, 1982. 662 pp., 415 illus. Signed and numbered edition. $49.95.

Graphs and schematic line drawings and mechanisms and their operation.

A Manual of Clayshooting, by Chris Cradock, Hippocrene Books, Inc., New York, NY, 1983. 192 pp., illus.

Covers everything from building a range to buying a shotgun, with lots of illustrations and diagrams.

Manual of Pistol and Revolver Cartridges, Volume 1, Centerfire and Metric Calibers, by Hans A. Erlmeier and Jakob H. Brandt, Journal-Verlag, Weisbaden, Germany, 1967. 271 pp., illus. $29.95.

Specifications for each cartridge cataloged tells bullet and case type with important case dimensions.

The Manufacture of Gunflints, by S.B.J. Skeetchly, Museum Restoration Service, Ottawa, Canada, 1984. 110 pp., illus. $24.95.

Reprint of an 1879 study of the manufacturing of gunflints in England.

Master Index to Handloader and Rifle Magazine, compiled by the staff of Wolfe Publishing Co., Prescott AZ, 1983. Unpaginated. Paper covers. $8.50.

Covers issues #1-#100 of the Handloader; issues #1-#84 of Rifle.

Military Ballistics, by C.L. Farrar and D.W. Leeming, Pergamon Press, Oxford, England, 1983. 200 pp., illus. Paper covers. $22.50.

Principles of ballistics, illustrated by reference of military applications.

Military Rifles of Japan, by Fred L. Honeycutt, Jr. and F. Patt Anthony, Julin Books, Lake Park, FL, 2nd edition, 1983. 206 pp., illus. $29.00.

Limited signed and numbered edition. Includes the early Murata period, markings, etc.

Mr. Single Shot's Gunsmithing Idea Book, by Frank DeHaas, Tab Books, Inc., Blue Ridge Summit, PA, 1983. 168 pp., illus. $18.95.

A must-have manual for anyone interested in collecting, repairing, or modifying single-shot rifles.

Modern Guns, Fred Adolph Catalog, reprinted by Armory Publications, Tacoma, WA, 1983. 67 pp., illus. Paper covers. $10.95.

Reprint of a scarce American gun catalog of the early 1900's.

More Stories of the Old Duck Hunters, by Gordon MacQuarrie, Willow Creek Press, Oshkosh, WI, 1983. 200 pp., illus. $15.00.

Collection of 18 treasured stories of The Old Duck Hunters originally published in major outdoor magazines of the 1930s and 40s.

More Than a Trophy, by Dennis Walrod, Stackpole Books, Harrisburg, PA, 1983. 256 pp., illus. Paper covers. $12.95.

Field dressing, skinning, quartering, and butchering to make the most of your valuable whitetail, blacktail, mule deer.

Murry Burnham's Hunting Secrets, by Murry Burnham with Russell Tinsley, Winchester Press, Piscataway, NJ, 1984. 244 pp., illus. $17.95

One of the great hunters of our time gives the reasons for his success in the field.

My Lost Wilderness: Tales of an Alaskan Woodsman, by Ralph Young, Winchester Press, Piscataway, NJ, 1983. 193 pp., illus. $15.95.

True tales of an Alaskan hunter, guide, fisherman, prospector, and backwoodsman.

The NRA Gunsmithing Guide—Updated, by Ken Raynor and Brad Fenton, National Rifle Association, Wash., D.C., 1984. 336 pp., illus. Paper covers. $15.95.

Material includes chapters and articles on all facets of the gunsmithing art.

New England Grouse Shooting, by William Harnden Foster, Willow Creek Press, Oshkosh, WI, 1983. 213 pp., illus. $45.00.

A new release of a classic book on grouse shooting.

The Official Guide to Gun Marks, by David Byron, The House of Collectibles, Inc., Orlando, FL, 1983. 247 pp., illus. Paper covers. $6.95.

The ultimate gun identification guide. Trademarks, proof marks, trade names and codes.

On Target for Successful Turkey Hunting, by Wayne Fears, Target Communications, Mequon, WI, 1983. 92 pp., illus. Paper covers. $5.95.

Professional turkey hunting advice.

Opening Shots and Parting Lines; the Best of Dickey's Wit, Wisdom, and Wild Tales for Sportsmen, by Charley Dickey, Winchester Press, Piscataway, NJ, 1983. 208 pp., illus. $14.95.

Selected by the writer who has entertained millions of readers in America's top sporting publications — 49 of his best pieces.

The Outdoor Life Bear Book, edited by Chet Fish, an Outdoor Life book, distributed by Stackpole Books, Harrisburg, PA, 1983. 352 pp., illus. $26.95.

All-time best personal accounts of terrifying attacks, exciting hunts, and intriguing natural history.

Outdoor Life Deer Hunter's Yearbook 1984, by contributors to Outdoor Life magazine, an Outdoor Life book distributed by Stackpole Books, Harrisburg, PA, 1983. 192 pp., illus. $16.95.

Up-to-date information on deer hunting techniques.

The Pinfire System, by Gene P. Smith and Chris C. Curtis, The Pinfire System, San Francisco, CA, 1983. 216 pp., illus. $35.00.

The first attempt to record the invention, development and use of pinfire cartridge arms and ammunition.

The Pistol Book, by John Walter, Arms and Armour Press, London, England, 1983. 176 pp., illus. $19.95.

A concise and copiously illustrated guide to the handguns available today.

The Pistols of Germany and Its Allies in Two World Wars, by Jan C. Still, Douglas, Alaska, 1983. 145 pp., illus. Paper covers. $12.95.

Military pistols of Imperial Germany and her World War I Allies and postwar military, paramilitary and police reworks.

Popular Sporting Rifle Cartridges, by Clay Harvey, DBI Books, Inc., Northfield, IL, 1984. 320 pp., illus. Paper covers. $12.95.

Provides the hunter/shooter with extensive information on most of the cartridges introduced during this century.

Professional Care and Finishing of Gun Metal, by John E. Traister, Tab Books, Inc., Blue Ridge Summit, PA, 1982. 303 pp., illus. Paper covers. $12.95.

Restore old and antique firearms into handsome workable possessions.

The Radom Pistol, by Robert J. Berger, Robert J. Berger, Milford, CT, 1981. 99 pp., illus. Paper covers. $10.00.

The complete story of the Vis or Radom pistols.

Ralf Coykendall's Duck Decoys and How to Rig Them, revised by Ralf Coykendall, Jr., Winchester Press, Piscataway, NJ, 1983. 128 pp., illus. slipcased. $21.95.

For every discriminating book collector and sportsman, a superb new edition of a long out-of-print classic.

Recreating the American Longrifle, by William Buchele, et al, George Shumway, Publisher, York, PA, 1983. 175 pp., illus. Paper covers. $20.00; cloth. $27.50.

Includes full-scale plans for building a Kentucky rifle.

The Rifleman's Rifle: Winchester's Model 70, 1936-63, by Roger C. Rule, Alliance Books, Inc., Northridge, CA, 1982. 368 pp., illus. $59.95.

The most complete reference book on the Model 70, with much fresh information on the Model 54 and the new Model 70.

Ruger Automatic Pistols and Single Action Revolvers, Book 3, by Hugo A. Lueders, Blacksmith Corp., Southport, CT, 1983. 95 pp., illus. Paper covers. $17.50.

A key reference for every Ruger enthusiast, collector and dealer.

Scottish Arms Makers, by Charles E. Whitelaw, Arms and Armour Press, London, England, 1982. 336 pp., illus. $29.95.

An important and basic addition to weapons reference literature.

Charles Sheldon Trilogy, by Charles Sheldon, Amwell Press, Clinton, NJ, 1983. 3 volumes in slipcase. "The Wilderness of the Upper Yukon," 363 pp., illus.; "The Wilderness of the North Pacific Coast Islands," 246 pp., illus.; "The Wilderness of Denali," 412 pp., illus. Deluxe edition. $205.00.

Custom-bound reprinting of Sheldon's classics, each signed and numbered by the author's son, William G. Sheldon.

Shooter's Bible, 1985, No. 76, edited by William Jerrett, Stoeger Publishing Co., So. Hackensack, NJ, 1984. 576 pp., illus. Paper covers. $12.95.

A standard firearms reference book for decades.

Skeeter Skelton on Handguns, Skeeter Skelton, PJS Publications, Peoria, IL, 1983. 122 pp., illus. $9.95.

Loaded with vintage Skeeter.

Skyline Pursuits, by John H. Batten, Amwell Press, Clinton, NJ, 1983. 318 pp., illus. Custom bound in slipcase. $125.00.

Possibly the most important work on high country hunting in the 20th century.

Small Arms of the World, 12th Edition, by W.H.B. Smith, revised by Edward C. Ezell, Stackpole Books, Harrisburg, PA, 1983. 1,024 pp., illus. $49.95.

An encyclopedia of global weapons — over 3,500 entries.

Spencer Repeating Firearms, by Roy M. Marcot, Northwood Heritage Press, Irvine, CA, 1984. 400 pp., illus. $45.00.

A detailed, reliable, exhaustive study covering Spencer repeating rifles and carbines, 1858-68, Roper repeating rifles and shotguns, 1866-1876, and Spencer slide action shotguns, 1871-1907.

The Sporting Shotgun: A User's Handbook, by Robin Marshall-Ball, Stonewall Press, Wash., DC, 1982. 176 pp., illus. $23.95.

An important international reference on shotgunning in North America and Europe, including Britain.

Street Survival Tactics for Armed Encounters, by Ronald J. Adams, et al, Calibre Press, Northbrook, IL, 1983. 403 pp., illus. $25.95.

Positive tactics to employ on the street to effectively use firearms to defeat assailants.

Successful Deer Hunting, by Sam Fadala, DBI Books, Inc., Northfield, IL, 1983. 288 pp., illus. Paper covers. $10.95.

Covers habitat, hunting techniques, guns and equipment.

Successful Turkey Hunting, by J. Wayne Fears, Target Communications, Corp., Mequon, WI, 1983. 92 pp., illus. Paper covers. $5.95.

How to be more successful and get more enjoyment from turkey hunting.

The Sword in the Age of Chivalry, by R. Ewar Oakeshott, Arms and Armour Press, London, England, 1982. 160 pp., illus. $32.50.

A classic work — the result of 25 years of research by an authority whose work is acknowledged by scholars all over the world.

Through the Brazilian Wilderness, by Theodore Roosevelt, Greenwood Press, Westport, CT, 1982. Reprinting of the original 1914 work. 370 pp., illus. $22.50.

An account of a zoogeographic reconnaissance through the Brazilian hinterland.

Turkey Hunting, Spring and Fall, by Doug Camp, Outdoor Skills Bookshelf, Nashville, TN, 1983. 165 pp., illus. Paper covers. $12.95.

Practical turkey hunting, calling, dressing and cooking, by a professional turkey hunting guide.

U.S. Enfield, by Ian Skennerton, Ian Skennerton, Margate, Australia, 1983. 190 pp., illus. $21.50.

Covers both the British pattern and the U.S. Model 1917 rifles.

U.S. Military Small Arms 1816-1865, by Robert M. Reilly, The Gun Room Press, Highland Park, NJ, 1983. 270 pp., illus. $35.00.

Covers every known type of primary and secondary martial firearms used by Federal Forces.

Where the Grizzly Walks, by Bill Schneider, The Mountain Press, Missoula, MT, 1983. 204 pp., illus. Paper covers. $8.95.

The survival of the grizzly is discussed by the author.

The Winchester Era, by David Madis, Art and Reference House, Brownsville, TX, 1984. 100 pp., illus. $14.95.

Story of the Winchester company, management, employees, etc.

Winchester Shotguns and Shotshells, by Ronald W. Stadt, Armory Publications, Tacoma, WA, 1984. Approx. 200 pp., illus. $29.50.

From the hammer double to the Model 59.

The Women's Guide to Handguns, by Jim Carmichel, Stoeger Publishing Co., So. Hackensack, NJ, 1984. 190 pp., illus. Paper covers. $8.95.

For women interested in learning how to select, buy, store, carry, care for and use a handgun.

You Can't Miss, by John Shaw and Michael Bane, John Shaw, Memphis, TN, 1983. 152 pp., illus. Paper covers. $9.95.

The secrets of a successful combat shooter tells how to better your defensive shooting skills.

ballistics *and* handloading

ABC's of Reloading, 2nd Edition, by Dean A. Grennell, DBI Books, Inc., Northfield, IL, 1980. 288 pp., illus. Paper covers. $9.95.

A natural, logical, thorough set of directions on how to prepare shotgun shells, rifle and pistol cases prior to reloading.

American Ammunition and Ballistics, by Edward A. Matunas, Winchester Press, Piscataway, NJ, 1979. 288 pp., illus. $18.95.

A complete reference book covering all presently made and much discontinued American rimfire, centerfire, and shotshell ammunition.

The Art of Bullet Casting from Handloader & Rifle Magazines 1966-1981, compiled by Dave Wolfe, Wolfe Publishing Co., Prescott, AZ, 1981. 258 pp., illus. Paper covers. Deluxe hardbound. $19.50.

Articles from "Handloader" and "Rifle" magazines by authors such as Jim Carmichel, John Wootters, and the late George Nonte.

Ballistic Science for the Law Enforcement Officer, by Charles G. Wilber, Ph.D., Charles C. Thomas, Springfield, IL, 1977. 309 pp., illus. $33.00.

A scientific study of the ballistics of civilian firearms.

Basic Handloading, by George C. Nonte, Jr., Outdoor Life Books, New York, NY, 1982. 192 pp., illus. Paper covers. $4.50.

How to produce high-quality ammunition using the safest, most efficient methods known.

The Bullet's Flight, by Franklin Mann, Wolfe Publishing Co., Inc., Prescott, AZ, 1980. 391 pp., illus. $22.00.

The ballistics of small arms. A reproduction of Harry Pope's personal copy of this classic with his marginal notes.

Cartridges of the World 4th Edition, by Frank C. Barnes, DBI Books, Inc., Northfield, IL. 352 pp., illus. Paper covers. $12.95.

Gives the history, dimensions, performance and physical characteristics for more than 1,000 different cartridges.

Cast Bullets, by Col. E. H. Harrison, A publication of the National Rifle Association of America, Washington, DC, 1979. 144 pp., illus. Paper covers. $12.95.

An authoritative guide to bullet casting techniques and ballistics.

Computer for Handloaders, by Homer Powley. A Slide rule plus 12 page instruction book for use in finding charge, most efficient powder and velocity for any modern centerfire rifle. $6.95.

Discover Swaging, by David Corbin, Stackpole Books, Harrisburg, PA, 1980. 288 pp., illus. $18.95.

A book for the serious rifle and handgun reloading enthusiast.

Firearms Identification, by Dr. J. H. Mathews, Charles C. Thomas, Springfield, IL, 1973 3 vol. set. A massive, carefully researched, authoritative work published as:

Vol. I **The Laboratory Examination of Small Arms** 400 pp., illus. $56.75.

Vol. II **Original Photographs and Other Illustrations of Handguns** 492 pp., illus. $56.75.

Vol. III **Data on Rifling Characteristics of Handguns and Rifles** 730 pp., illus. $88.00.

Firearms Investigation, Identification and Evidence, by J. S. Hatcher, Frank J. Jury and Jac Weller. Stackpole Books, Harrisburg, PA, 1977. 536 pp., illus. $26.95.

Reprint of the 1957 printing of this classic book on forensic ballistics. Indispensable for those interested in firearms identification and criminology.

Game Loads and Practical Ballistics for The American Hunter, by Bob Hagel, Alfred A. Knopf, NY, NY, 1978. 315 pp., illus., hardbound. $13.95.

Everything a hunter needs to know about ballistics and performance of commercial hunting loads.

The Gun Digest Black Powder Loading Manual, by Sam Fadala, DBI Books, Inc., Northfield, IL, 1982. 244 pp., illus. Paper covers. $9.95.

Covers 450 loads for 86 of the most popular black powder rifles, handguns and shotguns.

Handbook for Shooters and Reloaders, by P.O. Ackley, Salt Lake City, UT, 1970. *Vol. I,* 567 pp., illus. $12.50. *Vol. II,* a new printing with specific new material. 495 pp., illus. $9.95.

Handbook of Metallic Cartridge Reloading, by Edward Matunas, Winchester Press, Piscataway, NJ, 1981. 272 pp., illus. $18.95.

Up-do-date, comprehensive loading tables prepared by four major powder manufacturers.

Handloader's Digest, 9th Edition, edited by Ken Warner, DBI Books, Inc., Northfield, IL, 1982. 320 pp., illus. Paper covers. $10.95.

Latest edition of the book no handloader should be without.

Handloader's Digest Bullet and Powder Update, edited by Ken Warner, DBI Books, Inc., Northfield, IL, 1980. 128 pp., illus. Paper covers $5.95.

An update on the 8th ed. of "Handloader's Digest". Included is a round-up piece on new bullets, another on new primers and powders plus five shooters' reports on the various types of bullets.

Handloading, by Bill Davis, Jr., NRA Books, Wash., D.C., 1980. 400 pp., illus. Paper covers. $15.95.

A complete update and expansion of the NRA Handloader's Guide.

Handloading for Handgunners, by Geo. C. Nonte, DBI Books, Inc., Northfield, IL, 1978. 288 pp., illus. Paper covers. $9.95.

An expert tells the ins and outs of this specialized facet of reloading.

Handloading for Hunters, by Don Zutz, Winchester Press, Piscataway, NJ, 1977. 288 pp., illus. Paper covers. $11.95.

Precise mixes and loads for different types of game and for various hunting situations with rifle and shotgun.

The Home Guide to Cartridge Conversions, by Maj. George C. Nonte Jr., The Gun Room Press, Highland Park, NJ, 1976. 404 pp., illus. $19.95.

Revised and updated version of Nonte's definitive work on the alteration of cartridge cases for use in guns for which they were not intended.

Hornady Handbook of Cartridge Reloading, Hornady Mfg. Co., Grand Island, NE, 1981. 650 pp., illus. $12.95.

New edition of this famous reloading handbook. Latest loads, ballistic information, etc.

Lyman Cast Bullet Handbook, 3rd Edition, edited by C. Kenneth Ramage, Lyman Publications, Middlefield, CT, 1980. 416 pp., illus. Paper covers. $16.95.

Information on more than 5,000 tested cast bullet loads and 19 pages of trajectory and wind drift tables for cast bullets.

Lyman Black Powder Handbook, ed. by C. Kenneth Ramage, Lyman Products for Shooters, Middlefield, CT, 1975. 239 pp., illus. Paper covers $11.95.

The most comprehensive load information ever published for the modern black powder shooter.

Lyman Pistol & Revolver Handbook, edited by C. Kenneth Ramage, Lyman Publications, Middlefield, CT, 1978. 280 pp., illus. Paper covers. $11.95.

An extensive reference of load and trajectory data for the handgun.

Lyman Reloading Handbook No. 46, edited by C. Kenneth Ramage, Lyman Publications, Middlefield, CT, 1982. 300 pp., illus. $16.95.

A large and comprehensive book on reloading. Extensive list of loads for jacketed and cast bullets.

Lyman Shotshell Handbook, 2nd ed., edited by C. Kenneth Ramage, Lyman Gunsight Corp., Middlefield, CT, 1976. 288 pp., illus., paper covers. $11.95.

Devoted exclusively to shotshell reloading, this book considers: gauge, shell length, brand, case, loads, buckshot, etc. plus an excellent reference section. Some color illus.

Metallic Cartridge Reloading, edited by Robert S.L. Anderson, DBI Books, Inc., Northfield, IL, 1982. 320 pp., illus. Paper covers. $12.95.

A true reloading manual with a wealth of invaluable technical data provided by outstanding reloading experts. A must for any reloader. Extensive load tables.

Metallic Reloading Basics, edited by C. Kenneth Ramage, Lyman Publications, Middlefield, CT, 1976. 60 pp., illus. Paper covers. $1.95.

Provides the beginner with loading data on popular bullet weights within the most popular calibers.

Modern Handloading, by Maj. Geo. C. Nonte, Winchester Press, Piscataway, NJ, 1972. 416 pp., illus. $15.00.

Covers all aspects of metallic and shotshell ammunition loading, plus more loads than any book in print.

Nosler Reloading Manual Number Two, Nosler Bullets, Inc., Bend, OR, 1981. 308 pp., illus. $8.95.

Thorough coverage of powder data, specifically tailored to the well known Nosler partition and solid base bullets.

Pet Loads, by Ken Waters, Wolfe Publ. Co., Inc., Prescott, AZ, 1979. Unpaginated. In looseleaf form. $29.50.

A collection of the last 13 years' articles on more than 70 metallic cartridges. Most calibers featured with updated material.

Practical Handgun Ballistics, by Mason Williams, Charles C. Thomas, Publisher, Springfield, IL, 1980. 215 pp., illus. $19.50.

Factual information on the practical aspects of ammunition performance in revolvers and pistols.

Reloading for Shotgunners, edited by Robert S.L. Anderson, DBI Books, Inc., Northfield, IL, 1981. 224 pp., illus. Paper covers. $8.95.

Articles on wildcatting, slug reloading, patterning, skeet and trap loads, etc., as well as extensive reloading tables.

Sierra Bullets Reloading Manual, Second Edition, by Robert Hayden et al, The Leisure Group, Inc., Santa Fe Springs, CA, 1978. 700 pp., illus. Looseleaf binder. $16.95.

Includes all material in the original manual and its supplement updated, plus a new section on loads for competitive shooting.

Speer Reloading Manual Number 10, Omark Industries, Inc., Lewiston, ID, 1979, 560 pp., illus. Paper covers. $12.00.

Expanded version with facts, charts, photos, tables, loads and tips.

Why Not Load Your Own? by Col. T. Whelen, A. S. Barnes, New York, 1957, 4th ed., rev. 237 pp., illus, $10.95.

A basic reference on handloading, describing each step, materials and equipment. Loads for popular cartridges are given.

Yours Truly, Harvey Donaldson, by Harvey Donaldson, Wolfe Publ. Co., Inc., Prescott, AZ, 1980. 288 pp., illus. $19.50.

Reprint of the famous columns by Harvey Donaldson which appeared in "Handloader" from May 1966 through December 1972.

COLLECTORS

American Handguns & Their Makers, compiled by J.B. Roberts, Jr. and Ted Bryant, NRA Books, Wash., DC, 1981. 248 pp., illus. Paper covers. $11.95.

First in a series of manuals on gun collecting and the history of firearms manufacturing.

" . . . And Now Stainless", by Dave Ecker with Bob Zwirz, Charter Arms Corp., Bridgeport, CT, 1981. 165 pp., illus. $15.00.

The Charter Arms story. Covers all models to date.

Arms & Accoutrements of the Mounted Police 1873-1973, by Roger F. Phillips and Donald J. Klancher, Museum Restoration Service, Ont., Canada, 1982. 224 pp., illus. $49.95.

A definitive history of the revolvers, rifles, machine guns, cannons, ammunition, swords, etc. used by the NWMP, the RNWMP and the RCMP during the first 100 years of the Force.

Arms & Equipment of the Civil War, by Jack Coggins, Outlet Books, New York, NY, 1983. 160 pp., illus. $7.98.

Lavishly illustrated guide to the principal weapons and equipment of the Civil War used by the forces of the Blue and the Gray.

Arms Makers of Maryland, by Daniel D. Hartzler, George Shumway, York, PA, 1975. 200 pp., illus. $35.00.

A thorough study of the gunsmiths of Maryland who worked during the late 18th and early 19th centuries.

Ballard Rifles in the H.J. Nunnemacher Coll., by Eldon G. Wolff. Milwaukee Public Museum, Wisc., 2nd ed., 1961. Paper, 77 pp. plus 4 pp. of charts and 27 plates. $5.00.

A thoroughly authoritative work on all phases of the famous rifles, their parts, patent and manufacturing history.

Basic Documents on U.S. Marital Arms, commentary by Col. B. R. Lewis, reissue by Ray Riling, Phila., PA., 1956 and 1960. *Rifle Musket Model 1855.* The first issue rifle of musket caliber, a muzzle loader equipped with the Maynard Primer, 32 pp. $2.50. *Rifle Musket Model 1863.* The Typical Union muzzle-loader of the Civil War, 26 pp. $1.75. *Breech-Loading Rifle Musket Model 1866.* The first of our 50 caliber breechloading rifles, 12 pp. $1.75. *Remington Navy Rifle Model 1870.* A commercial type breech-loader made at Springfield, 16 pp. $1.75 *Lee Straight Pull Navy Rifle Model 1895.* A magazine cartridge arm of 6mm caliber. 23 pp. $3.00. *Breech-Loading Arms* (five models)-27 pp. $2.75. *Ward-Burton Rifle Musket 1871*-16 pp. $2.50. *U.S. Magazine Rifle and Carbine (cal. 30) Model 1892*(the Krag Rifle) 36 pp. $3.00.

British Military Pistols 1603-1888, by R.E. Brooker, Jr., The Gun Room Press, Highland Park, NJ, 1983. 139 pp., illus. $29.95.

Covers flintlock and percussion pistols plus cartridge revolvers up to the smokeless powder period.

The British Service Lee, Lee-Metford, and Lee-Enfield, by Ian Skennerton, Arms & Armour Press, London, England, 1982. 380 pp., illus. $32.50.

A very comprehensive and authoritative book on these famous military arms. A must for the Enfield collector.

California Gunsmiths 1846-1900, by Lawrence P. Sheldon, Far Far West Publ., Fair Oaks, CA, 1977. 289 pp., illus. $29.65.

A study of early California gunsmiths and the firearms they made.

Carbines of the Civil War, by John D. McAulay, Pioneer Press, Union City, TN, 1981. 123 pp., illus. Paper covers. $7.95.

A guide for the student and collector of the colorful arms used by the Federal cavalry.

Cartology Savalog, by Gerald Bernstein, Gerald Bernstein, St. Louis, MO, 1976. 177 pp., illus. Paper covers. $8.95.

An infinite variations catalog of small arms ammunition stamps.

The Cartridge Guide, by Ian V. Hogg, Stackpole Books, Harrisburg, PA, 1982. 160 pp., illus. $24.95.

The small arms ammunition identification manual.

Catalogue of the Enfield Pattern Room: British Rifles, Herbert Wooden, Her Majesty's Stationery Office, London, England, 1981. 80 pp., illus. Paper covers. $14.95.

The first exhaustive catalog of a specific section of the collection in the Pattern Room at the Royal Small Arms Factory at Enfield Lock.

Civil War Carbines, by A.F. Lustyik. World Wide Gun Report, Inc., Aledo, Ill, 1962. 63 pp., illus. Paper covers. $3.50.

Accurate, interesting summary of most carbines of the Civil War period, in booklet form, with numerous good illus.

Civil War Guns, by William B. Edwards, Castle Books, NY, 1976. 438 pp., illus. $15.00.

Describes and records the exciting and sometimes romantic history of forging weapons for war and heroism of the men who used them.

A Collector's Guide to Air Rifles, by Dennis E. Hiller, London, England, 1980. 170 pp., illus. Paper covers. $15.95.

Valuations, exploded diagrams and many other details of air rifles, old and new.

Colt Engraving, by R.L. Wilson, The Gun Room Press, Highland Park, NJ, 1982. 560 pp., illus. $69.95.

New and completely revised edition of the author's original work on finely engraved Colt firearms.

The Collector's Handbook of U.S. Cartridge Revolvers, 1856 to 1899, by W. Barlow Fors, Adams Press, Chicago, IL, 1973. 96 pp., illus. $10.95.

Concise coverage of brand names, patent listings, makers' history, and essentials of collecting.

Colt Firearms from 1836, by James E. Serven, new 8th edition, Stackpole Books, Harrisburg, PA, 1979. 398 pp., illus. $29.95. Deluxe ed. $49.95.

Excellent survey of the Colt company and its products. Updated with new SAA production chart and commemorative list.

The Colt Heritage, by R.L. Wilson, Simon & Schuster, 1979. 358 pp., illus. $50.00.

The official history of Colt firearms 1836 to the present.

Colt Pistols 1836-1976, by R.L. Wilson in association with R.E. Hable, Jackson Arms, Dallas, TX, 1976. 380 pp., illus. $100.00.

A magnificently illustrated book in full-color featuring Colt firearms from the famous Hable collection.

Colt's SAA Post War Models, George Garton, Gun Room Press, Highland Park, NJ, 1979. 166 pp., illus. $21.95.

Details all guns produced and their variations.

Colt's Variations of the Old Model Pocket Pistol, 1848 to 1872, by P.L. Shumaker. Borden Publishing, Co., Alhambra, CA, 1966, a reprint of the 1957 edition. 150 pp., illus. $8.95.

A useful tool for the Colt specialist and a welcome return of a popular source of information that had been long out-of-print.

Confederate Longarms and Pistols, "A Pictorial Study", by Richard Taylor Hill and Edward W. Anthony, Taylor Publishing Co., Dallas, TX, 1978. $29.95.

A reference work identifying over 175 Confederate arms through detailed photography, and a listing of information.

Contemporary Makers of Muzzleloading Firearms, by Robert Weil, Screenland Press, Burbank, CA, 1981. 300 pp., illus. $39.95.

Illustrates the work of over 30 different contemporary makers.

Early Indian Trade Guns: 1625-1775, by T.M. Hamilton, Museum of the Great Plains, Lawton, OK, 1968. 34 pp., illus. Paper covers. $7.95.

Detailed descriptions of subject arms, compiled from early records and from the study of remnants found in Indian country.

Fifteen Years in the Hawken Lode, by John D. Baird, The Gun Room Press, Highland Park, NJ, 1976. 120 pp., illus. $15.00.

A collection of thoughts and observations gained from many years of intensive study of the guns from the shop of the Hawken brothers.

Firearms in Colonial America: The Impact on History and Technology 1492-1792, by M.L. Brown, Smithsonian Institution Press, Wash., D.C., 1980. 449 pp., illus. $45.00.

An in-depth coverage of the history and technology of firearms in Colonial North America.

Firearms of the Confederacy, by Claud R. Fuller & Richard D. Steuart, Quarterman Publ., Inc., Lawrence, MA, 1977. 333 pp., illus. $25.00.

The shoulder arms, pistols and revolvers of the Confederate soldier, including the regular United States Models, the imported arms and those manufactured within the Confederacy.

The Firearms Price Guide, 2nd Edition, by D. Byron, Crown Publishers, New York, NY, 1981. 448 pp., illus. Paper covers. $9.95.

An essential guide for every collector and dealer.

Flayderman's Guide to Antique American Firearms . . . And Their Values, Third Edition, by Norm Flayderman, DBI Books, Inc., Northfield, IL, 1983. 624 pp., illus. Paper Covers. $18.95.

Updated and expanded third edition of this bible of the antique gun field.

The .45-70 Springfield, by Albert J. Frasca and Robert H. Hall, Springfield Publishing Co., Northridge, CA, 1980. 380 pp., illus. $39.95.

A carefully researched book on the trapdoor Springfield, including all experimental and very rare models.

The 45/70 Trapdoor Springfield Dixie Collection, compiled by Walter Crutcher and Paul Oglesby, Pioneer Press, Union City, TN, 1975. 600 pp., illus. Paper covers. $9.95.

An illustrated listing of the 45-70 Springfields in the Dixie Gun Works Collection. Little known details and technical information is given, plus current values.

Gun Collector's Digest, 3rd Edition, edited by Joseph J. Schroeder, DBI Books, Inc., Northfield, IL, 1981. 256 pp., illus. Paper covers. $9.95.

Excellent reading by some of the world's finest collector/writers. The best book on general gun collecting available.

Gun Traders Guide, 10th Edition, by Paul Wahl, Stoeger Publ. Co., S. Hackensack, NJ, 1983. 256 pp., illus. Paper covers. $10.95.

A fully illustrated and authoritative guide to identification of modern firearms with current market values.

The Gunsmiths and Gunmakers of Eastern Pennsylvania, by James B. Whisker and Roy Chandler, Old Bedford Village Press, Bedford, PA, 1982. 130 pp., illus. Limited, numbered edition. Paper covers. $17.50.

Locates over 2,000 gunsmiths practicing before 1900, with references and documentation.

The Gunsmiths and Gunmakers of Western Pennsylvania, by James B. Whisker and Vaughn E. Whisker, Old Bedford Village Press, Bedford, PA, 1982. 103 pp., illus. Limited, numbered and signed edition. Paper covers. $17.50.

Lists over 650 names of gunsmiths practicing before 1900.

Gunsmiths of Ohio—18th & 19th Centuries: Vol. I, Biographical Data, by Donald A. Hutslar, George Shumway, York, PA, 1973. 444 pp., illus. $35.00.

An important source book, full of information about the old-time gunsmiths of Ohio.

The Hand Cannons of Imperial Japan, 1543-1945, by Harry Derby, Harry Derby, Charlotte, NC, 1982. 300 pp., illus. $37.00.

Superb, comprehensive and definitive study of Japanese handguns beginning with the introduction of the matchlock in Japan and continuing into the post-WW II period.

The Hawken Rifle: Its Place in History, by Charles E. Hanson, Jr., The Fur Press, Chadron, NE, 1979. 104 pp., illus. Paper covers. $6.00.

A definitive work on this famous rifle.

Hawken Rifles, The Mountain Man's Choice, by John D. Baird, The Gun Room Press, Highland Park, NJ, 1976. 95 pp., illus. $15.00.

Covers the rifles developed for the Western fur trade. Numerous specimens are described and shown in photographs.

High Standard Automatic Pistols, 1932-1950, by Charles E. Petty, American Ordnance Publications, Charlotte, NC, 1976. 124 pp., illus. $12.95.

Describes and illustrates the early history of the company and many details of the various popular pistols. Includes dates and serial numbers.

Historical Hartford Hardware, by William W. Dalrymple, Colt Collector Press, Rapid City, SD, 1976. 42 pp., illus. Paper covers. $5.50.

Historically associated Colt revolvers.

A History of the Colt Revolver, by Charles T. Haven and Frank A. Belden, Outlet Books, New York, NY, 1978. 711 pp., illus. $25.00.

A giant of a book packed with information and pictures about the most cherished American revolver.

A History of the John M. Browning Semi-Automatic .22 Caliber Rifle, by Homer C. Tyler, Jefferson City, MO, 1982. 58 pp., illus. Paper covers. $10.00.

All models and variations are shown. Includes engraved guns.

The History and Development of Small Arms Ammunition, Vol. 1, by George A. Hoyem, Armory Publications, Tacoma, WA, 1981. 230 pp., illus. $27.50.

Describes and illustrates ammunition from military long arms—flintlock through rimfire.

The History and Development of Small Arms Ammunition, Vol. 2, by George A. Hoyem, Armory Publications, Tacoma, WA, 1982. 303 pp., illus. $34.50.

Small arms and ammunition of 31 nations and dominions covered in detail together for the first time.

History of Modern U.S. Military Small Arms Ammunition, Vol. 2, 1940-1945, by F.W. Hackley, W.M. Woodin and E.L. Scranton, The Gun Room Press, Highland Park, NJ, 1976. 300 pp., illus. $35.00.

A unique book covering the entire field of small arms ammunition developed during the critical World War II years.

The History of Winchester Firearms 1866-1980, edited by Duncan Barnes, et al, Winchester Press, Piscataway, NJ, 1980. 237 pp., illus. $24.95.

Specifications on all Winchester firearms. Background information on design, manufacture and use.

The Kentucky Rifle, by Merrill Lindsay, Arma Press, NY/the Historical Society of York County, York, PA, 1972. 100 pp., 81 large colored illustrations. $17.95.

Presents in precise detail and exact color 77 of the finest Kentucky rifles ever assembled in one place. Also describes the conditions which led to the development of this uniquely American arm.

Kentucky Rifles and Pistols 1756-1850, compiled by members of the Kentucky Rifle Association, Wash., DC, Golden Age Arms Co., Delaware, OH, 1976. 275 pp., illus. $29.50.

Profusely illustrated with more than 300 examples of rifles and pistols never before published.

Know Your Ruger Single Action Revolvers 1953-1963, by John C. Dougan, edited by John T. Amber, Blacksmith Corp., Southport, CT, 1981. 199 pp., illus. $35.00.

A definitive reference work for the Ruger revolvers produced in the period 1953-1963.

The Krag Rifle Story, by Franklin B. Mallory and Ludwig Olson, Springfield Research Service, Silver Spring, MD, 1979. 224 pp., illus. $20.00.

Covers both U.S. and European Krags. Gives a detailed description of U.S. Krag rifles and carbines and extensive data on sights, bayonets, serial numbers, etc.

Krag Rifles, by William S. Brophy, The Gun Room Press, Highland Park, NJ, 1980. 200 pp., illus. $29.95.

The first comprehensive work detailing the evolution and various models, both military and civilian.

The Krieghoff Parabellum, by Randall Gibson, Randall Gibson, Midland, TX, 1980. 280 pp., illus. $30.00.

A definitive work on the most desirable model Luger pistol.

Lever Action Magazine Rifles Derived from the Patents of Andrew Burgess, by Samuel L. Maxwell Sr., Samuel L. Maxwell, Bellevue, WA, 1976. 368 pp., illus. $29.95.

The complete story of a group of lever action magazine rifles collectively referred to as the Burgess/Morse, the Kennedy or the Whitney.

Manual of Pistol and Revolver Cartridges, Volume 2, Centerfire U.S. and British Calibers, by Hans A. Erlmeier and Jakob H. Brandt, Journal-Verlag, Weisbaden, Germany, 1981. 270 pp., illus. $35.00.

Catalog system allows cartridges to be traced either by caliber or alphabetically.

Mauser Bolt Rifles, by Ludwig Olson, F. Brownell & Son, Inc., Montezuma, IA, 1976. 364 pp., illus. $29.95.

The most complete, detailed, authoritative and comprehensive work ever done on Mauser bolt rifles.

The Metric FAL, by R. Blake Stevens and Jean E. Van Rutten, Collector Grade Publications, Toronto, Canada, 1981. 372 pp., illus. Paper covers. $50.00.

Volume three of the FAL series. The free world's right arm.

Miliary Pistols of Japan, by Fred L. Honeycutt, Jr., Julin Books, Lake Park, FL. 1982. 167 pp., illus. $24.00.

Covers every aspect of military pistol production in Japan through WWII.

Military Small Arms Ammunition of the World, 1945-1980, by Peter Labbett, Presidio Press, San Rafael, CA, 1980. 129 pp., illus. $18.95.

An up-to-date international guide to the correct identification of ammunition by caliber, type, and origin.

M1 Carbine, Design, Development and Production, by Larry Ruth, The Gun Room Press, Highland Park, NJ, 1983. 300 pp., illus. Paper covers. $17.95.

The complete history of one of the world's most famous and most produced military firearms.

Modern Guns Identification and Values, 3rd Edition, edited by Russell and Steve Quertermous, Collector Books, Paducah, KY, 1981. 432 pp., illus. Paper covers. $11.95.

A catalog of well over 20,000 guns with important identifying information and facts.

More Single Shot Rifles, by James C. Grant, The Gun Room Press, Highland, NJ, 1976. 324 pp., illus. $19.95.

Details the guns made by Frank Wesson, Milt Farrow, Holden, Borchardt, Stevens, Remington, Winchester, Ballard and Peabody-Martini.

The New England Gun, by Merrill Lindsay, David McKay Co., NY, 1976. 155 pp., illus. Paper covers, $12.50. Cloth, $20.00.

A study of more than 250 New England guns, powder horns, swords and polearms in an exhibition by the New Haven Colony Historical Society.

Simeon North: First Official Pistol Maker of the United States, by S. North and R. North, The Gun Room Press, Highland Park, NJ, 1972. 207 pp., illus. $9.95.

Reprint of the rare first edition.

The Northwest Gun, by Charles E. Hanson, Jr., Nebraska State Historical Society, Lincoln, NB, 1976. 85 pp., illus., paper covers. $6.

Number 2 in the Society's "Publications in Anthropology." Historical survey of rifles which figured in the fur trade and settlement of the Northwest.

The Official 1981 Price Guide to Antique and Modern Firearms, edited by Thomas E. Hudgeons, House of Collectibles, Inc., Orlando, FL, 1981. 450 pp., illus. Paper covers. $9.95.

Over 10,000 current collectors values for over 650 manufacturers of American and foreign made firearms.

The P-08 Parabellum Luger Automatic Pistol, edited by J. David McFarland, Desert Publications, Cornville, AZ, 1982. 20 pp., illus. Paper covers. $4.95.

Covers every facet of the Luger, plus a listing of all known Luger models.

Paterson Colt Pistol Variations, by R.L. Wilson and R. Phillips, Jackson Arms Co., Dallas, TX, 1979. 250 pp., illus. $35.00.

A tremendous book about the different models and barrel lengths in the Paterson Colt story.

Peacemaker Evolutions & Variations, by Keith A. Cochran, Colt Collectors Press, Rapid City, SD, 1975. 47 pp., illus. Paper covers. $10.00.

Corrects many inaccuracies found in other books on the Peacemaker and gives much new information regarding this famous arm.

The Pennsylvania-Kentucky Rifle, by Henry J. Kauffman, Crown Publishers, New York, NY 1981. 293 pp., illus. $9.98.

A colorful account of the history and gunsmiths who produced the first American rifle superior to those brought from the Old Country.

Pennsylvania Longrifles of Note, by George Shumway, George Shumway, Publisher, York, PA, 1977. 63 pp., illus. Paper covers. $6.95.

Illustrates and describes samples of guns from a number of Pennsylvania rifle-making schools.

The Plains Rifle, by Charles E. Hanson, Jr., The Gun Room Press, Highland Park, NJ, 1977. 171 pp., illus. $19.95.

Historical survey of popular civilian arms used on the American frontiers, their makers, and their owners.

The Rare and Valuable Antique Arms, by James E. Serven, Pioneer Press, Union City, TN, 1976. 106 pp., illus. Paper covers. $4.95.

A guide to the collector in deciding which direction his collecting should go, investment value, historic interest, mechanical ingenuity, high art or personal preference.

Reloading Tools, Sights and Telescopes for Single Shot Rifles, by Gerald O. Kelver, Brighton, CO, 1982. 163 pp., illus. Paper covers. $10.00.

A listing of most of the famous makers of reloading tools, sights and telescopes with a brief description of the products they manufactured.

Rifles in Colonial America, Vol. I, by George Shumway, George Shumway, Publisher, York, PA, 1980. 353 pp., illus. $49.50.

An extensive photographic study of American longrifles made in the late Colonial, Revolutionary, and post-Revolutionary periods.

Rifles in Colonial America, Vol. II, by George Shumway, George Shumway, Publisher, York, PA, 1980. 302 pp., illus. $49.50.

Final volume of this study of the early evolution of the rifle in America.

Ruger Rimfire Handguns 1949-1982, by J.C. Munnell, G.D.G.S. Inc., McKeesport, PA, 1982. 189 pp., illus. Paper covers. $12.00.

Updated edition with additional material on the semi-automatic pistols and the New Model revolvers.

Samuel Colt's New Model Pocket Pistols; The Story of the 1855 Root Model Revolver, by S. Gerald Keogh, S.G. Keogh, Ogden, UT, 1974. 31 pp., illus., paper covers. $5.00.

Collector's reference on various types of the titled arms, with descriptions, illustrations, and historical data.

Savage Automatic Pistols, by James R. Carr. Publ. by the author, St. Charles, Ill., 1967. A reprint. 129 pp., illus. with numerous photos. $20.00.

Collector's guide to Savage pistols, models 1907-1922, with features, production data, and pictures of each.

Sharps Firearms, by Frank Seller, Frank M. Seller, Denver, CO, 1982. 358 pp., illus. $39.95.

Traces the development of Sharps firearms with full range of guns made including all martial variations.

Small Arms of the Sea Services, by Robert H. Rankin. N. Flayderman & Co., New Milford, CT, 1972. 227 pp., illus. $14.50.

Encyclopedic reference to small arms of the U.S. Navy, Marines and Coast Guard. Covers edged weapons, handguns, long arms and others, from the beginnings.

Southern Derringers of the Mississippi Valley, by Turner Kirkland. Pioneer Press, Tenn., 1971. 80 pp., illus., paper covers. $2.00.

A guide for the collector, and a much-needed study.

The Standard Directory of Proof-Marks, ed. by R.A. Steindler, The John Olson Company, Paramus, NJ, 1976. 144 pp., illus. Paper covers. $5.95.

A comprehensive directory of the proof-marks of the world.

Still More Single Shot Rifles, by James J. Grant, Pioneer Press, Union City, TN, 1979. 211 pp., illus. $17.50.

A sequel to the author's classic works on single shot rifles.

The 36 Calibers of the Colt Single Action Army, by David M. Brown. Publ. by the author at Albuquerque, NM, new reprint 1971. 222 pp., well-illus. $65.00.

Edited by Bev Mann of *Guns Magazine.* This is an unusual approach to the many details of the Colt S.A. Army revolver. Halftone and line drawings of the same models make this of especial interest.

The Trapdoor Springfield, by M.D. Waite and B.D. Ernst, The Gun Room Press, Highland Park, NJ, 1983. 250 pp., illus. $29.95.

The first comprehensive book on the famous standard military rifle of the 1873-92 period.

Underhammer Guns, by H.C. Logan. Stackpole Books, Harrisburg, PA, 1965. 250 pp., illus. $10.00.

A full account of an unusual form of firearm dating back to flintlock days. Both American and foreign specimens are included.

U.S. Cartridges and Their Handguns, by Charles R. Suydam, Beinfeld Publ., Inc., No. Hollywood, CA, 1977. 200 pp., illus. Paper covers. $9.95.

The first book ever showing which gun used what cartridge. A must for the gun and cartridge collector.

The Virginia Manufactory of Arms, by Giles Cromwell, University Press of Virginia, Charlottesville, VA, 1975. 205 pp., illus. $29.95.

The only complete history of the Virginia Manufactory of Arms which produced muskets, pistols, swords, and cannon for the state's militia from 1802 through 1821.

Walther P-38 Pistol, by Maj. George Nonte, Desert Publications, Cornville, AZ, 1982. 100 pp., illus. Paper covers. $5.95.

Complete volume on one of the most famous handguns to come out of WWII. All models covered.

Walther Models PP and PPK, 1929-1945, by James L. Rankin, assisted by Gary Green, James L. Rankin, Coral Gables, FL, 1974. 142 pp., illus. $20.00.

Complete coverage on the subject as to finish, proof marks and Nazi Party inscriptions.

Walther Volume II, Engraved, Presentation and Standard Models, by James L. Rankin, J.L. Rankin, Coral Gables, FL, 1977. 112 pp., illus. $20.00.

The new Walther book on embellished versions and standard models. Has 88 photographs, including many color plates.

Walther, Volume III, 1908-1980, by James L. Rankin, Coral Gables, FL, 1981. 226 pp., illus. $24.50.

Covers all models of Walther handguns from 1908 to date, includes holsters, grips and magazines.

The Whitney Firearms, by Claud Fuller. Standard Publications, Huntington, W. Va., 1946. 334 pp., many plates and drawings. $30.00.

An authoritative history of all Whitney arms and their maker. Highly recommended. An exclusive with Ray Riling Arms Books Co.

The William M. Locke Collection, compiled by Robert B. Berryman, et al, The Antique Armory, Inc., East Point, GA, 1973. 541 pp., illus. $40.00.

A magnificently produced book illustrated with hundreds of photographs of guns from one of the finest collection of American firearms ever assembled.

The Winchester Book, by George Madis, Art & Reference House, Lancaster, TX, 1980. 638 pp., illus. $39.50.

A greatly enlarged edition of this most informative book on these prized American arms.

The Winchester Handbook, by George Madis, Art & Reference House, Lancaster, TX, 1982. 287 pp., illus. $19.95.

The complete line of Winchester guns, with dates of manufacture, serial numbers, etc.

Winchester—The Gun That Won the West, by H.F. Williamson. Combat Forces Press, Washington, D.C., 1952. Later eds. by Barnes, NY. 494 pp., profusely illus., paper covers. $20.00.

A scholarly and essential economic history of an honored arms company, but the early and modern arms introduced will satisfy all but the exacting collector.

The Robert Abels Collection of Bowie Type Knives of American Interest, by Robert Abels, Robert Abels, Hopewell Junction, NY, 1974. 20 pp., illus. Paper covers. $1.95.

A selection of American Bowie-type knives from the collection of Robert Abels.

American Axes, by Henry Kauffman, The Stephen Green Press, Brattleboro, VT, 1972. 200 pp., illus. $25.00.

A definitive work on the subject. Contains a roster of American axe makers, glossary and notes on the care and use of axes.

American Knives; The First History and Collector's Guide, by Harold L. Peterson, The Gun Room Press, Highland Park, NJ, 1980. 178 pp., illus. $15.00.

A reprint of this 1958 classic. Covers all types of American knives.

American Polearms 1526-1865, by Rodney Hilton Brown, H. Flayderman & Co., New Milford, CT, 1967. 198 pp., illus. $14.50.

The lance, halbred, spontoon, pike and naval boarding weapons used in the American military forces through the Civil War.

The American Sword, 1775-1945, by Harold L. Peterson, Ray Riling Arms Books, Co., Phila., PA, 1980. 286 pp. plus 60 pp. of illus. $29.95.

1977 reprint of a survey of swords worn by U.S. uniformed forces, plus the rare "American Silver Mounted Swords, (1700-1815)."

The Art of Blacksmithing, by Alex W. Bealer, Funk & Wagnalls, New York, NY, revised edition, 1976. 438 pp., illus. $16.95.

Required reading for anyone who makes knives or is seriously interested in the history of cutlery.

Basic Manual of Knife Fighting, by William L. Cassidy, Paladin Press, Boulder, CO, 1978. 41 pp., illus. Paper covers. $4.

A manual presenting the best techniques developed by the experts from 1930 to date.

The Best of Knife World, Volume I, edited by Knife World Publ., Knoxville, TN, 1980. 92 pp., illus. Pater covers. $3.95.

A collection of articles about knives. Reprinted from monthly issues of Knife World.

Blacksmithing for the Home Craftsman, by Joe Pehoski, Joe Pehoski, Washington, TX, 1973. 44 pp., illus. Paper covers. $3.50.

This informative book is chock-full of drawings and explains how to make your own forge.

Blades and Barrels, by H. Gordon Frost, Wallon Press, El Paso, TX, 1972. 298 pp., illus. $17.95.

The first full scale study about man's attempts to combine an edged weapon with a firearm.

Bowie Knives, by Robert Abels, Robert Abels, NY, 1960. 48 pp., illus. Paper covers. $3.00.

A booklet showing knives, tomahawks, related trade cards and advertisements.

Custom Knife...II, by John Davis Bates, Jr., and James Henry Schippers, Jr., Custom Knife Press, Memphis, TN, 1974. 112 pp., illus. $20.00.

The book of pocket knives and folding hunters. A guide to the 20th century makers' art.

The Cutlery Story: From Stone Age to Steel Age, by Lewis D. Bement, Custom Cutlery Co., Dalton, GA, 1972. 36 pp., illus. Paper covers. $3.50.

A classic booklet about the history, romance, and manufacture of cutlery from the earliest times to modern methods of manufacture.

Edge of the Anvil, by Jack Andrews, Rodale Press, Emmaus, PA, 1978. 224 pp., illus. Paper covers. $10.95.

A basic blacksmith book.

The Fighting Knife, by W.D. Randall, Jr. and Col. Rex Applegate, W.D. Randall, Orlando, FL, 1975. 60 pp., illus. Paper covers. $2.75.

Manual for the use of Randall-made fighting knives and similar types.

For Knife Lovers Only, by Harry K. McEvoy, Knife World Publ., Knoxville, TN, 1979. 67 pp., illus. Paper covers. $4.95.

A fascinating and unusual approach to the story of knives.

A Guide to Handmade Knives, edited by Mel Tappan, The Janus Press, Inc., Los Angeles, CA, 1977. No paper covers. Deluxe hardbound. $19.50.

The official directory of the Knifemakers Guild.

Gun Digest Book of Knives, 2nd Edition, by Jack Lewis and Roger Combs, DBI Books, Inc., Northfield, IL, 1982. 288 pp., illus. Paper covers. $10.95.

Covers the complete spectrum of the fascinating world of knives.

How to Make Knives, by Richard W. Barney & Robert W. Loveless, Beinfield Publ., Inc., No. Hollywood, CA, 1977. 178 pp., illus. $15.00.

A book filled with drawings, illustrations, diagrams, and 500 how-to-do-it photos.

How to Make Your Own Knives, by Jim Mayes, Everest House, New York, NY, 1978. 191 pp., illus. $7.95.

An illustrated step-by-step guide for the sportsman and home hobbyist.

Kentucky Knife Traders Manual No. 6, by R.B. Ritchie, Hindman, KY, 1980. 217 pp., illus. Paper covers. $10.00.

Guide for dealers, collectors and traders listing pocket knives and razor values.

The Knife Album Price Guide 1976 Edition, by Robert Mayes, Robert Mayes, Middlesboro, KY, 1976. 174 pp. Paper covers. $6.00.

The only book on identification and accurate pricing.

Knife Digest, Second Annual Edition, edited by William L. Cassidy, Knife Digest Publ. Co., Berkeley, CA, 1976. 178 pp., illus. $15.00.

The second annual edition of the internationally known book on blades.

Knife Throwing, Sport...Survival...Defense, by Blackie Collins, Knife World Publ., Knoxville, TN, 1979. 31 pp., illus. Paper covers. $3.00.

How to select a knife, how to make targets, how to determine range and how to survive with a knife.

Knife Throwing a Practical Guide, by Harry K. McEvoy, Charles E. Tuttle Co., Rutland, VT, 1973. 108 pp., illus. Paper covers. $3.95.

If you want to learn to throw a knife this is the "bible".

Knifecraft: A Comprehensive Step-by-Step Guide to the Art of Knifemaking, by Sid Latham, Stackpole Books, Harrisburg, PA, 1978. 224 pp., illus. $24.95.

An exhaustive volume taking both amateur and accomplished knifecrafter through all the steps in creating a knife.

Knifemakers of Old San Francisco, by Bernard R. Levine, Badger Books, San Francisco, CA, 1978. 240 pp., illus. $12.95.

The story about the knifemakers of San Francisco, the leading cutlers of the old West.

The Knife Makers Who Went West, by Harvey Platts, Longspeak Press, Longmont, CO, 1978. 200 pp., illus. $19.95.

Factual story of an important segment of the American cutlery industry. Primarily about Western knives and the Platts knife makers.

Knives and Knifemakers, by Sid Latham, Winchester Press, Piscataway, NJ, 1973. 152 pp., illus. $17.50.

Lists makers and suppliers of knife-making material and equipment.

Light But Efficient, by Albert N. Hardin, Jr. and Robert W. Hedden, Albert N. Hardin, Jr., Pennsauken, NJ, 1973. 103 pp., illus. $7.95.

A study of the M1880 Hunting and M1890 intrenching knives and scabbards.

Marble Knives and Axes, by Konrad F. Schreier, Jr., Beinfeld Publ., Inc., No. Hollywood, CA, 1978. 80 pp., illus. Paper covers. $5.95.

The first work ever on the knives and axes made by this famous old, still-in-business, manufacturer.

The Modern Blacksmith, by Alexander G. Weygers, Van Nostrand Reinhold Co., NY, 1977. 96 pp., illus. $10.95.

Shows how to forge objects out of steel. Use of basic techniques and tools.

Nathan Starr Arms Maker 1776-1845, by James E. Hicks, The Restoration Press, Phoenix, AZ, 1976. 166 pp., illus. $12.95.

Survey of the work of Nathan Starr of Middletown, CT, in producing edged weapons and pole arms for the U.S., 1799-1840, also some firearms.

Naval Swords, by P.G.W. Annis, Stackpole Books, Harrisburg, PA, 1970. 80 pp., illus. $5.50.

British and American naval edged weapons 1660-1815.

The Official 1981 Price Guide to Collector Knives, by James F. Parker and J. Bruce Voyles, House of Collectibles, Orlando, FL, 1981. 533 pp., illus. Paper covers. $9.95.

Buying and selling prices on collector pocket and sheath knives.

A Photographic Supplement of Confederate Swords with Addendum, by William A. Albaugh III, Moss Publications, Orange, VA, 1979. 259 pp., illus. $20.00.

A new updated edition of the classic work on Confederate edged weapons.

Pocket Knife Book 1 & 2—Price Guide, by Roy Ehrhardt, Heart of America Press, Kansas City, MO, 1974. 96 pp., illus. Spiral bound stiff paper covers. $6.95.

Reprints from the pocket knife sections of early manufacturers and sporting goods catalogs.

Pocket Knife Book 3—Price Guide, by Roy and Larry Ehrhardt, Heart of America Press, Kansas City, MO, 1974. Spiral bound stiff paper covers. $6.95.

Compiled from sections of various product sales catalogs of both Winchester and Marble Co. dating from the '20s and '30s.

The Pocketknife Manual, by Blackie Collins, Blackie Collins, Rock Hill, SC, 1976. 102 pp., illus. Paper covers. $5.50.

Building, repairing and refinishing pocketknives.

Practical Blacksmithing, edited by J. Richardson, Outlet Books, NY, 1978. four volumes in one, illus. $7.98.

A reprint of the extremely rare, bible of the blacksmith. Covers every aspect of working with iron and steel, from ancient uses to modern.

Rice's Trowel Bayonet, reprinted by Ray Riling Arms Books, Co., Phila., PA, 1968. 8 pp., illus. Paper covers. $3.00.

A facsimile reprint of a rare circular originally published by the U.S. Government in 1875 for the information of U.S. Troops.

The Samurai Sword, by John M. Yumoto, Charles E. Tuttle Co., Rutland, VT, 1958. 191 pp., illus. $11.00.

A must for anyone interested in Japanese blades, and the first book on this subject written in English.

Scottish Swords from the Battlefield at Culloden, by Lord Archibald Campbell, The Mowbray Co., Providence, RI, 1973. 63 pp., illus. $5.00.

A modern reprint of an exceedingly rare 1894 privately printed edition.

Secrets of Modern Knife Fighting, by David E. Steele, Phoenix Press, Arvada, CO, 1974. 149 pp., illus. $17.50.

Details every facet of employing the knife in combat, including underwater fighting.

Step-by-Step Knifemaking, by Davis Boye, Rodale Press, Emmous, PA, 1978. 288 pp., illus. $12.95.

Gives the fundamentals of knifemaking and shows how to make knives either as a hobby or as a business.

Swords and Other Edged Weapons, by Robert Wilkinson-Latham, Arco Publishing Co., New York, NY, 1978. 227 pp., illus. $8.95.

Traces the history of the "Queen of Weapons" from its earliest forms in the stone age to the military swords of the Twentieth century.

Tomahawks Illustrated, by Robert Kuck, Robert Kuck, New Knoxville, OH, 1977. 112 pp., illus. Paper covers. $8.50.

A pictorial record to provide a reference in selecting and evaluating tomahawks.

U.S. Military Knives, Bayonets and Machetes, Book III, by M. H. Cole, M.H. Cole, Birmingham, AL, 1979. 219 pp., illus. $23.00.

The most complete text ever written on U.S. military knives, bayonets, machetes and bolo's.

GENERAL

The Airgun Book, by John Walter, Stackpole Books, Harrisburg, PA, 1981. 320 pp., illus. $21.95.

Provides the airgun enthusiast with a much-needed basic book on his subject.

American Tools of Intrigue, by John Minnery & Jose Ramos, Desert Publications, Cornville, AZ, 1981. 128 pp., illus. Paper covers. $8.95.

Clandestine weapons which the Allies supplied to resistance fighters.

Bannerman Catalogue of Military Goods—1927, replica edition, DBI Books, Inc., Northfield, IL 1981. 384 pp., illus. Paper covers. $12.95.

Fascinating insights into one of the more colorful American arms merchants.

Black Powder Gun Digest, 3rd Edition, edited by Jack Lewis, DBI Books, Inc., Northfield, IL, 1982. 256 pp., illus. Paper covers. $10.95.

All new articles, expressly written for the black powder gun buff.

The Book of Shooting for Sport and Skill, edited by Frederick Wilkinson, Crown Publishers, Inc., New York, NY, 1980. 348 pp., illus. $19.95.

A comprehensive and practical encyclopedia of gunmanship by a squad of over twenty experts from both sides of the Atlantic.

Carbine; The Story of David Marshall "Carbine" Williams, by Ross E. Beard, Jr., The Sandlapper Store, Inc., Lexington, SC, 1977. 315 pp., illus. Deluxe limited edition, numbered and signed by the author and "Carbine". $25.

The story of the man who invented the M1 Carbine and holds 52 other firearms patents.

Colonial Frontier Guns, by T.M. Hamilton, The Fur Press, Chadron, NE, 1980. 176 pp., illus. Paper covers. $12.00.

French, Dutch, and English trade guns before 1780.

Colonial Riflemen in the American Revolution, by Joe D. Huddleston, George Shumway Publisher, York, PA, 1978. 70 pp., illus. $18.00.

This study traces the use of the longrifle in the Revolution for the purpose of evaluating what effects it had on the outcome.

The Complete Black Powder Handbook, by Sam Fadala, DBI Books, Inc. Northfield, IL, 1979. 288 pp., illus. Paper covers. $9.95.

Everything you want to know about black powder firearms and their shooting.

Complete Book of Shooting: Rifles, Shotguns, Handguns, by Jack O'Connor, Stackpole Books, Harrisburg, PA, 1983. 392 pp., illus. $24.95.

A thorough guide to each area of the sport, appealing to those with a new or ongoing interest in shooting.

The Complete Book of Thompson Patents, compiled by Don Thomas, The Gun Room Press, Highland Park, NJ, 1981. 482 pp., illus. Paper covers. $15.95.

From John Blish's breech closure patented in 1915 to Charles W. Robin's automatic sear release of 1947. Includes all other firearm patents granted to the developers of the famed "Tommy gun."

The Complete Book of Trick & Fancy Shooting, by Ernie Lind, The Citadel Press, Secaucus, NJ, 1977. 159 pp., illus. Paper covers. $6.00.

Step-by-step instructions for acquiring the whole range of shooting skills with rifle, pistol and shotgun.

The Complete Survival Guide, edited by Mark Thiffault, DBI Books, Inc., Northfield, IL, 1983. 256 pp., illus. Paper covers. $10.95.

Covers all aspects of survival from manmade and natural disasters—equipment, techniques, weapons, etc.

Dead Aim, by Lee Echols, Acme Printing Co., San Diego, CA, a reprint, 1972. 116 pp., illus. $9.95.

Nostalgic antics of hell-raising pistol shooters of the 1930's.

Eli Whitney and the Whitney Armory, by Merrill Lindsay, Arma Press, North Branford, CT, 1979. 95 pp., illus. Paper covers. $4.95. Cloth $9.95.

History of the Whitney Armory 1767-1862, with notes on how to identify Whitney flintlocks.

The Encyclopedia of Infantry Weapons of World War II, by Ian V. Hogg, Harper & Row, New York, NY, 1977. 192 pp., illus. $15.95.

A fully comprehensive and illustrated reference work including every major type of weapon used by every army in the world during World War II.

Encyclopedia of Modern Firearms, Vol. 1, compiled and publ. by Bob Brownell, Montezuma, IA, 1959. 1057 pp. plus index, illus. $50.00. Dist. by Bob Brownell, Montezuma, IA 50171.

Massive accumulation of basic information of nearly all modern arms pertaining to "parts and assembly". Replete with arms photographs, exploded drawings, manufacturers' lists of parts, etc.

The FP-45 Liberator Pistol, 1942-1945, by R.W. Koch, Research, Arcadia, CA, 1976. 116 pp., illus. $15.00.

A definitive work on this unique clandestine weapon.

Famous Guns & Gunners, by George E. Virgines, Leather Stocking Press, West Allis, WI, 1980. 113 pp., illus. $12.95.

Intriguing and fascinating tales of men of the West and their guns.

The German Sniper, 1914-1945, by Peter R. Senich, Paladin Press, Boulder, CO, 1982. 468 pp., illus. $49.95.

The development and application of Germany's sniping weapons systems and tactics traced from WW I through WW II.

Great Sporting Posters, by Sid Latham, Stackpole Books, Harrisburg, PA, 1980. 48 pp., illus. Paper covers. $14.95.

Twenty-three full-color reproductions of beautiful hunting and fishing poster art, mostly of the early 1900s.

Gun Digest Book of Metallic Silhouette Shooting, by Elgin Gates, DBI Books, Inc., Northfield, IL, 1979. 256 pp., illus. Paper covers. $8.95.

Examines all aspects of this fast growing sport including history, rules and meets.

Gun Digest Book of Holsters and Other Gun Leather, edited by Roger Combs, DBI Books, Inc., Northfield, IL, 1983. 256 pp., illus. Paper covers. $9.95.

An in-depth look at all facets of leather goods in conjunction with guns. Covers design, manufacture, uses, etc.

Gun Digest Book of Scopes and Mounts, by Bob Bell, DBI Books, Inc., Northfield, IL, 1983. 224 pp., illus. Paper covers. $9.95.

Traces the complete history, design, development of scopes and mounts from their beginnings to the current high-tech level of today. Covers the various uses and applications for the modern shooter/hunter.

Gun Talk, edited by Dave Moreton, Winchester Press, Piscataway, NJ, 1973. 256 pp., illus. $9.95.

A treasury of original writing by the top gun writers and editors in America. Practical advice about every aspect of the shooting sports.

The Gun That Made the Twenties Roar, by Wm. J. Helmer, rev. and enlarged by George C. Nonte, Jr., The Gun Room Press, Highland Park, NJ, 1977. Over 300 pp., illus. $16.95.

Historical account of John T. Thompson and his invention, the infamous "Tommy Gun."

The Gunfighter, Man or Myth? by Joseph G. Rosa, Oklahoma Press, Norman, OK, 1969. 229 pp., illus. (including weapons). Paper covers. $9.95.

A well-documented work on gunfights and gunfighters of the West and elsewhere. Great treat for all gunfighter buffs.

The Gunfighters, by Dale T. Schoenberger, The Caxton Printers, Ltd., Caldwell, ID, 1971. 207 pp., illus. $12.95.

Startling expose of our foremost Western folk heroes.

Guns of the Gunfighters, by the editors of Guns & Ammo, Crown Publishing Co., New York, NY, 1982. 50 pp., illus. Paper covers. $6.98.

A must for Western buffs and gun collectors alike.

The Gunsmith in Colonial Virginia, by Harold B. Gill, Jr., University Press of Virginia, Charlottesville, VA, 1975. 200 pp., illus. $11.95.

The role of the gunsmith in colonial Virginia from the first landing at Jamestown through the Revolution is examined, with special attention to those who lived and worked in Williamsburg.

Guns & Shooting: A Selected Bibliography, by Ray Riling, Ray Riling Arms Books Co., Phila., PA, 1982. 434 pp., illus. Limited, numbered edition. $75.00.

A limited edition of this superb bibliographical work, the only modern listing of books devoted to guns and shooting.

Gun Traders Guide 10th Edition, by Paul Wahl, Stoeger Publishing Co., So. Hackensack, NJ, 1983. 415 pp., illus. Paper covers. $10.95.

Illustrated guide to identification of modern firearms with current market values.

Hatcher's Notebook, by Maj. Gen. J. S. Hatcher. Stackpole Books, Harrisburg, Pa., 1952. 2nd ed. with four new chapters, 1957. 629 pp., illus. $19.95.

A dependable source of information for gunsmiths, ballisticians, historians, hunters, and collectors.

Home Guide to Muzzle Loaders, by George C. Nonte, Jr., Stackpole Books, Harrisburg, PA, 1982. 224 pp., illus. Paper covers. $14.95.

From the basics of muzzleloading, to the differences between the modern and replica muzzle loader, plus how to make one.

How to Make Practical Pistol Leather, by J. David McFarland, Desert Publications, Cornville, AZ. 1982. 68 pp., illus. Paper covers. $6.95.

A guide for designing and making holsters and accessories for law enforcement, security, survival and sporting use.

The Identification and Registration of Firearms, by Vaclav "Jack" Krcma, C. C. Thomas, Springfield, IL, 1971. 173 pp., illus. $21.50.

Analysis of problems and improved techniques of recording firearms data accurately.

Kill or Get Killed, by Col. Rex Applegate, new rev. and enlarged ed. Paladin Press, Boulder, CO, 1976. 421 pp., illus. $19.95.

For police and military forces. Last word on mob control.

The Law Enforcement Book of Weapons, Ammunition and Training Procedures, Handguns, Rifles and Shotguns, by Mason Williams, Charles C. Thomas, Publisher, Springfield, IL, 1977. 496 pp., illus. $35.00.

Data on firearms, firearm training, and ballistics.

Law Enforcement Handgun Digest, 3rd Edition, by Jack Lewis, DBI Books, Inc., Northfield, IL, 1980. 288 pp., illus. Paper covers. $9.95.

Covers such subjects as the philosophy of a firefight, SWAT, weapons, training, combat shooting, etc.

L'Incisione Delle Armi Sportive (Engraving of Sporting Arms), by Mario Abbiatico, Edizioni Artistiche Italiane, Famars, Brescia, Italy, 1983. 536 pp., illus. Italian text. $125.00.

An encyclopedia of Italian engraving on sporting arms, with 1,000 black and white and 200 full-color photos.

Lyman Muzzleloader's Handbook, 2nd Edition, edited by C. Kenneth Ramage, Lyman Publications, Middlefield, CT, 1982. 248 pp., illus. Paper covers. $11.95.

Hunting with rifles and shotguns, plus muzzle loading products.

Medicolegal Investigation of Gunshot Wounds, by Abdullah Fatteh, J.B. Lippincott Co., Phila., PA, 1977. 272 pp., illus. $27.50.

A much-needed work, clearly written and easily understood, dealing with all aspects of medicolegal investigation of gunshot wounds and deaths.

Military Small Arms of the 20th Century, 4th Edition, by Ian V. Hogg and John Weeks, DBI Books, Inc., Northfield, IL, 1981. 288 pp., illus. Paper covers. $12.95.

A comprehensive illustrated encyclopedia of the world's small-caliber firearms.

Modern Airweapon Shooting, by Bob Churchill & Granville Davis, David & Charles, London, England, 1981. 196 pp., illus. $20.00.

A comprehensive, illustrated study of all the relevant topics, from beginnings to world championship shooting.

Modern Gun Values, 4th Edition, by Jack Lewis, ed. by Harold A. Murtz, DBI Books, Inc., Northfield, IL, 1983. 400 pp., illus. Paper covers. $12.95.

An updated and expanded edition of the book that has become the standard for valuing modern firearms.

No Second Place Winner, by Wm. H. Jordan, publ. by the author, Shreveport, LA (Box 4072), 1962. 114 pp., illus. $10.00.

Guns and gear of the peace officer, ably discussed by a U.S. Border Patrolman for over 30 years, and a first-class shooter with handgun, rifle, etc.

Old Time Posters from the Great Sporting Days, Stackpole Books, Harrisburg, PA, 1982. 48 pp., illus. Paper covers. $19.95.

Quality reproductions of 22 fine sporting posters in full color. 11"x16".

Olympic Shooting, by Colonel Jim Crossman, NRA, Washington, DC, 1978. 136 pp., illus. $12.95.

The complete, authoritative history of U.S. participation in the Olympic shooting events from 1896 until the present.

The Practical Book of Guns, by Ken Warner, Winchester Press, Piscataway, NJ, 1978. 261 pp., illus. $14.95.

A book that delves into the important things about firearms and their use.

E.C. Prudhomme, Master Gun Engraver, A Retrospective Exhibition: 1946-1973, intro. by John T. Amber, The R.W. Norton Art Gallery, Shreveport, LA, 1973. 32 pp., illus., paper covers. $5.00.

Examples of master gun engraving by Jack Prudhomme.

The Quiet Killers II: Silencer Update, by J. David Truby, Paladin Press, Boulder, CO, 1979. 92 pp., illus. Paper covers. $8.00.

A unique and up-to-date addition to your silencer bookshelf.

Sam Colt: Genius, by Robt. F. Hudson, American Archives Publ. Co., Topsfield, MA, 1971. 160 pp., illus. Plastic spiral bound. $6.50.

Historical review of Colt's inventions, including facsimiles of patent papers and other Colt information.

The Shooter's Workbench, by John A. Mosher, Winchester Press, Piscataway, NJ, 1977. 256 pp., illus. $15.95.

Accessories the shooting sportsman can build for the range or shop, for transport and the field, and for the handloading bench.

Sporting Arms of the World, by Ray Bearse, Outdoor Life/Harper & Row, N.Y., 1977. 500 pp., illus. $15.95.

A mammoth, up-to-the-minute guide to the sporting world's favorite rifles, shotguns, handguns.

Survival Guns, by Mel Tappan, The Janus Press, Inc., Los Angeles, CA, 1976. 458 pp., illus. Paper covers. $9.95.

A guide to the selection, modification and use of firearms and related devices for defense, food gathering, etc. under survival conditions.

Thompson Guns 1921-1945, Anubis Press, Houston, TX, 1980. 215 pp., illus. Paper covers. $7.95.

Facsimile reprinting of five complete manuals on the Thompson submachine gun.

A Treasury of Outdoor Life, edited by William E. Rae, Stackpole Books, Harrisburg, PA, 1983. 520 pp., illus. $24.95.

The greatest hunting, fishing, and survival stories from America's favorite sportsman's magazine.

Triggernometry, by Eugene Cunningham. Caxton Printers Lt., Caldwell, ID, 1970. 441 pp., illus. $12.95.

A classic study of famous outlaws and lawmen of the West—their stature as human beings, their exploits and skills in handling firearms. A reprint.

Weapons of the American Revolution, and Accoutrements, by Warren Moore. A & W Books, NY, 1974. 225 pp., fine illus. $15.

Revolutionary era shoulder arms, pistols, edged weapons, and equipment are described and shown in fine drawings and photographs, some in color.

 Gunsmithing

The Art of Engraving, by James B. Meek, F. Brownell & Son, Montezuma, IA, 1973. 196 pp., illus. $24.95.

A complete, authoritative, imaginative and detailed study in training for gun engraving. The first book of its kind—and a great one.

Artistry in Arms, The R.W. Norton Gallery, Shreveport, LA., 1970. 42 pp., illus. Paper, $5.00.

The art of gunsmithing and engraving.

Building the Kentucky Pistol, by James R. Johnston, Golden Age Arms Co., Worthington, OH, 1974. 36 pp., illus. Paper covers. $4.00.

A step-by-step guide for building the Kentucky pistol. Illus. with full page line drawings.

Building the Kentucky Rifle, by J.R. Johnston. Golden Age Arms Co., Worthington, OH, 1972. 44 pp., illus. Paper covers. $5.00.

How to go about it, with text and drawings.

Checkering and Carving of Gun Stocks, by Monte Kennedy. Stackpole Books, Harrisburg, PA, 1962. 175 pp., illus. $27.95.

Rev., enlarged clothbound ed. of a much sought-after, dependable work.

Clyde Baker's Modern Gunsmithing, revised by John E. Traister, Stackpole Books, Harrisburg, PA, 1981. 530 pp., illus. $24.95.

A revision of the classic work on gunsmithing.

The Complete Rehabilitation of the Flintlock Rifle and Other Works, by T.B. Tyron. Limbo Library, Taos, NM, 1972. 112 pp., illus. Paper covers. $6.95.

A series of articles which first appeared in various issues of the *American Rifleman* in the 1930s.

Do-It-Yourself Gunsmithing, by Jim Carmichel, Outdoor Life-Harper & Row, New York, NY, 1977. 371 pp., illus. $16.95.

The author proves that home gunsmithing is relatively easy and highly satisfying.

Firearms Assembly 3: The NRA Guide to Rifle and Shotguns, NRA Books, Wash., D.C., 1980. 264 pp., illus. Paper covers. $11.50.

Text and illustrations explaining the takedown of 125 rifles and shotguns, domestic and foreign.

Firearms Assembly 4: The NRA Guide to Pistols and Revolvers, NRA Books, Wash., D.C., 1980. 253 pp., illus. Paper covers. $11.50.

Text and illustrations explaining the takedown of 124 pistol and revolver models, domestic and foreign.

Firearms Blueing and Browning, by R.H. Angier. Stackpole Books, Harrisburg, PA, 151 pp., illus. $12.95.

A useful, concise text on chemical coloring methods for the gunsmith and mechanic.

First Book of Gunsmithing, by John E. Traister, Stackpole Books, Harrisburg, PA, 1981. 192 pp., illus. $18.95.

Beginner's guide to gun care, repair and modification.

Gun Digest Book of Exploded Firearms Drawings, 3rd Edition edited by Harold A. Murtz, DBI Books, Inc., Northfield, IL, 1982. 480 pp., illus. Paper covers. $12.95.

Contains 470 isometric views of modern and collector's handguns and long guns, with parts lists. A must for the gunsmith or tinkerer.

Gun Digest Book of Riflesmithing, by Jack Mitchell, DBI Books, Inc., Northfield, IL, 1982. 256 pp., illus. Paper covers. $9.95.

The art and science of rifle gunsmithing. Covers tools, techniques, designs, finishing wood and metal, custom alterations.

Gunsmithing: The Tricks of the Trade, by J.B. Wood, DBI Books, Inc., Northfield, IL, 1982. 256 pp., illus. Paper covers. $9.95.

How to repair and replace broken gun parts using ordinary home workshop tools.

Gun Care and Repair, by Monte Burch, Winchester Press, Piscataway, NJ, 1978. 256 pp., illus. $15.95.

Everything the gun owner needs to know about home gunsmithing and firearms maintenance.

Gun Digest Book of Firearms Assembly/Disassembly Part I: Automatic Pistols, by J.B. Wood, DBI Books, Inc., Northfield, IL, 1979. 320 pp., illus. Paper covers. $10.95.

A thoroughly professional presentation on the art of pistol disassembly and reassembly. Covers most modern guns, popular older models, and some of the most complex pistols ever produced.

Gun Digest Book of Firearms Assembly/Disassembly Part II: Revolvers, by J. B. Wood, DBI Books, Inc., Northfield, IL, 1979. 320 pp., illus. Paper covers. $10.95.

How to properly dismantle and reassemble both the revolvers of today and of the past.

The Gun Digest Book of Firearms Assembly/Disassembly Part III: Rimfire Rifles, by J. B. Wood, DBI Books, Inc., Northfield, IL, 1980. 288 pp., illus. Paper covers. $9.95.

A most comprehensive, uniform, and professional presentation available for disassembling and reassembling most rimfire rifles.

The Gun Digest Book of Firearms Assembly/Disassembly Part IV: Centerfire Rifles, by J. B. Wood, DBI Books, Inc., Northfield, IL, 1980. 288 pp., illus. Paper covers. $9.95.

A professional presentation on the assembly and reassembly of centerfire rifles.

The Gun Digest Book of Firearms Assembly/Disassembly, Part V: Shotguns, by J.B. Wood, DBI Books, Inc., Northfield, IL, 1980. 288 pp., illus. Paper covers. $9.95.

A professional presentation on the complete disassembly and assembly of 26 of the most popular shotguns, new and old.

The Gun Digest Book of Firearms Assembly/Disassembly Part VI: Law Enforcement Weapons, by J.B. Wood, DBI Books, Inc., Northfield, IL, 1981. 288 pp., illus. Paper covers. $9.95.

Step-by-step instructions on how to completely dismantle and reassemble the most commonly used firearms found in law enforcement arsenals.

Gun Digest Book of Gunsmithing Tools and Their Uses, by John E. Traister, DBI Books, Inc., Northfield, IL, 1980. 256 pp., illus. Paper covers. $8.95.

The how, when and why of tools for amateur and professional gunsmiths and gun tinkerers.

The Gun Digest Book of Pistolsmithing, by Jack Mitchell, DBI Books, Inc., Northfield, IL, 1980. 288 pp., illus. Paper covers. $10.95.

An expert's guide to the operation of each of the handgun actions with all the major functions of pistolsmithing explained.

Gun Digest Review of Custom Guns, edited by Ken Warner, DBI Books, Inc., Northfield, IL, 1980. 256 pp., illus. Paper covers. $9.95.

An extensive look at the art of custom gun making. This book is a must for anyone considering the purchase of a custom firearm.

Gun Digest Book of Shotgun Gunsmithing, by Ralph Walker, DBI Books, Inc., Northfield, IL, 1983. 256 pp., illus. Paper covers. $9.95.

The principles and practices of repairing, individualizing and accurizing modern shotguns by one of the world's premier shotgun gunsmiths.

Gun Owner's Book of Care, Repair & Improvement, by Roy Dunlap, Outdoor Life-Harper & Row, NY, 1977. 336 pp., illus. $12.95.

A basic guide to repair and maintenance of guns, written for the average firearms owner.

Gunsmith Kinks, by F.R. (Bob) Brownell. F. Brownell & Son, Montezuma, I. 1st ed., 1969. 496 pp., well illus. $12.95.

A widely useful accumulation of shop kinks, short cuts, techniques and pertinent comments by practicing gunsmiths from all over the world.

Gunsmithing, by Roy F. Dunlap. Stackpole Books, Harrisburg, PA, 714 pp., illus. $27.95.

Comprehensive work on conventional techniques, incl. recent advances in the field. Valuable to rifle owners, shooters, and practicing gunsmiths.

Gunsmiths and Gunmakers of Vermont, by Warren R. Horn, The Horn Co., Burlington, VT, 1976. 76 pp., illus. Paper covers. $5.00.

A checklist for collectors, of over 200 craftsmen who lived and worked in Vermont up to and including 1900.

The Gunsmith's Manual, by J.P. Stelle and Wm.B. Harrison, The Gun Room Press, Highland Park, NJ, 1982. 376 pp., illus. $12.95.

For the gunsmith in all branches of the trade.

Gunstock Finishing and Care, by A. Donald Newell, Stackpole Books, Harrisburg, PA, 1982. 512 pp., illus. $22.95.

The most complete resource imaginable for finishing and refinishing gun wood.

Home Gun Care & Repair, by P.O. Ackley, Stackpole Books, Harrisburg, PA, 1969. 191 pp., illus. Paper covers. $6.95.

Basic reference for safe tinkering, fixing, and converting rifles, shotguns, handguns.

How to Build Your Own Wheellock Rifle or Pistol, by George Lauber, The John Olson Co., Paramus, NJ, 1976. Paper covers. $9.95.

Complete instructions on building these arms.

How to Build Your Own Flintlock Rifle or Pistol, by Georg Lauber, The John Olson Co., Paramus, NJ, 1976. Paper covers. $9.95.

The second in Mr. Lauber's three-volume series on the art and science of building muzzle-loading black powder firearms.

"How to Build Your Own Percussion Rifle or Pistol", by Georg Lauber, The John Olson Co., Paramus, NJ, 1976. Paper covers. $9.95.

The third and final volume of Lauber's set of books on the building of muzzle-loaders.

Learn Gunsmithing, by John Traister, Winchester Press, Piscataway, NJ, 1980. 202 pp., illus. $16.95.

The troubleshooting method of gunsmithing for the home gunsmith and professional alike.

Lock, Stock and Barrel, by R.H. McCrory. Publ. by author at Bellmore, NY, 1966. Paper covers. 122 pp., illus. $6.00.

A handy and useful work for the collector or the professional with many helpful procedures shown and described on antique gun repair.

The Modern Gunsmith, by James V. Howe, Bonanza Books, NY, 1982. 415; 424; 68 pp., illus. $14.95.

Two volumes and the supplement in one. The most authoritative work ever written on gunsmithing and gunmaking.

The Modern Kentucky Rifle, How to Build Your Own, by R.H. McCrory. McCrory, Wantagh, NY, 1961. 68 pp., illus., paper bound. $6.00.

A workshop manual on how to fabricate a flintlock rifle. Also some information on pistols and percussion locks.

Pistolsmithing, by George C. Nonte, Jr., Stackpole Books, Harrisburg, PA, 1974. 560 pp., illus. $27.95.

A single source reference to handgun maintainence, repair, and modification at home, unequaled in value.

Professional Gunsmithing, by W.J. Howe, Stackpole Books, Harrisburg, PA, 1968 reprinting. 526 pp., illus. $24.95.

Textbook on repair and alteration of firearms, with detailed notes on equipment and commercial gunshop operation.

Respectfully Yours H.M. Pope, compiled and edited by G.O. Kelver, Brighton, CO, 1976. 266 pp., illus. $16.50.

A compilation of letters from the files of the famous barrelmaker, Harry M. Pope.

The Trade Gun Sketchbook, by Charles E. Hanson, The Fur Press, Chadron, NB, 1979. 48 pp., illus. Paper covers. $4.00.

Complete full-size plans to build seven different trade guns from the Revolution to the Indian Wars and a two-thirds size for your son.

The Trade Rifle Sketchbook, by Charles E. Hanson, The Fur Press, Chadron, NB, 1979. 48 pp., illus. Paper covers. $4.00.

Includes full scale plans for ten rifles made for Indian and mountain men; from 1790 to 1860, plus plans for building three pistols.

Troubleshooting Your Rifle and Shotgun, by J.B. Wood, DBI Books, Inc., Northfield, IL, 1978. 192 pp., illus. Paper covers. $6.95.

A gunsmiths advice on how to keep your long guns shooting.

handguns

American Pistol and Revolver Design and Performance, by L. R. Wallack, Winchester Press, Piscataway, NJ, 1978. 224 pp., illus. $19.95.

How different types and models of pistols and revolvers work, from trigger pull to bullet impact.

American Police Handgun Training, by Charles R. Skillen and Mason Williams, Charles C. Thomas, Springfield, IL, 1980. 216 pp., illus. $17.50.

Deals comprehensively with all phases of current handgun training procedures in America.

Askins on Pistols and Revolvers, by Col. Charles Askins, NRA Books, Wash., D.C., 1980. 144 pp., illus. Paper covers. $8.95.

A book full of practical advice, shooting tips, technical analysis and stories of guns in action.

The Black Powder Handgun by Sam Fadala, DBI Books, Inc., Northfield, IL, 1981. 288 pp., illus. Paper covers. $9.95.

The author covers this oldtimer in all its forms: pistols and six-shooters in both small and large bore, target and hunting.

Blue Steel and Gun Leather, by John Bianchi, Beinfeld Publishing, Inc., No. Hollywood, CA, 1978. 200 pp., illus. $12.00.

A complete and comprehensive review of holster uses plus an examination of available products on today's market.

Browning Hi-Power Pistols, Desert Publications, Cornville, AZ, 1982. 20 pp., illus. Paper covers. $4.95.

Covers all facets of the various military and civilian models of this gun.

Colt Automatic Pistols, by Donald B. Bady, Borden Publ. Co., Alhambra, CA, 1974. 368 pp., illus. $16.95.

The rev. and enlarged ed. of a key work on a fascinating subject. Complete information on every automatic marked with Colt's name.

The Colt .45 Auto Pistol, compiled from U.S. War Dept. Technical Manuals, and reprinted by Desert Publications, Cornville, AZ, 1978. 80 pp., illus. Paper covers. $5.95.

Covers every facet of this famous pistol from mechanical training, manual of arms, disassembly, repair and replacement of parts.

Combat Handgun Shooting, by James D. Mason, Charles C. Thomas, Springfield, IL, 1976. 256 pp., illus. $27.50.

Discusses in detail the human as well as the mechanical aspects of shooting.

Combat Handguns, edited by Edward C. Ezell, Stackpole Books, Harrisburg, PA, 1980. 288 pp., illus. $19.95.

George Nonte's last great work, edited by Edward C. Ezell. A comprehensive reference volume offering full coverage of automatic handguns vs. revolvers, custom handguns, combat autoloaders and revolvers—domestic and foreign, and combat testing.

Combat Shooting for Police, by Paul B. Weston. Charles C. Thomas, Springfield, IL, 1967. A reprint. 194 pp., illus. $15.00.

First publ. in 1960 this popular self-teaching manual gives basic concepts of defensive fire in every position.

The Complete Book of Combat Handgunning, by Chuck Taylor, Desert Publications, Cornville, AZ, 1982. 168 pp., illus. Paper covers. $12.95.

Covers virtually every aspect of combat handgunning.

Defensive Handgun Effectiveness, by Carroll E. Peters, Carroll E. Peters, Manchester, TN, 1977. 198 pp., charts and graphs. $15.00.

A systematic approach to the design, evaluation and selection of ammunition for the defensive handgun.

The Defensive Use of the Handgun for the Novice, by Mason Williams, Charles C. Thomas, Publisher, Springfield, IL, 1980. 226 pp., illus. $15.00.

This book was developed for the home owner, housewife, elderly couple, and the woman who lives alone. Basic instruction for purchasing, loading and firing pistols and revolvers.

Flattops & Super Blackhawks, by H.W. Ross, Jr., H.W. Ross, Jr., Bridgeville, PA, 1979. 93 pp., illus. Paper covers. $9.95.

An expanded version of the author's book "Ruger Blackhawks" with an extra chapter on Super Blackhawks and the Mag-Na-Ports with serial numbers and approximate production dates.

Gun Digest Book of Single Action Revolvers, by Jack Lewis, DBI Books, Inc., Northfield, IL, 1982. 256 pp., illus. Paper covers. $9.95.

A fond, in-depth look at the venerable "wheelgun" from its earliest days through today's latest developments.

Hallock's .45 Auto Handbook, by Ken Hallock, The Mihan Co., Oklahoma City, OK, 1981. 178 pp., illus. Paper covers. $11.95.

For gunsmiths, dealers, collectors and serious hobbyists.

A Handbook on the Primary Identification of Revolvers & Semi-automatic Pistols, by John T. Millard, Charles C. Thomas, Springfield, IL, 1974. 156 pp., illus. $15.00.

A practical outline on the simple, basic phases of primary firearm identification with particular reference to revolvers and semi-automatic pistols.

Handguns of the World, by Edward C. Ezell, Stackpole Books, Harrisburg, PA., 1981. 704 pp., illus. $39.95.

Encyclopedia for identification and historical reference that will be appreciated by gun enthusiasts, collectors, hobbyists or professionals.

High Standard Automatic Pistols 1932-1950, by Charles E. Petty, American Ordnance Publ., Charlotte, NC, 1976. 124 pp., illus. $12.95.

A definitive source of information for the collector of High Standard pistols.

The Illustrated Book of Pistols, by Frederick Wilkinson, Hamlyn Publishing Group, Ltd. London, England, 1979. 192 pp., illus. $10.98.

A carefully researched study of the pistol's evolution and use in war and peace.

Japanese Hand Guns, by F.E. Leithe, Borden Publ. Co., Alhambra, CA, 1968. Unpaginated, well illus. $12.95.

Identification guide, covering models produced since the late 19th century. Brief text material gives history. descriptions, and markings.

Jeff Cooper on Handguns, by Jeff Cooper, Petersen Publishing Co., Los Angeles, CA, 1979. 96 pp., illus. Paper covers. $2.50.

An expert's guide to handgunning. Technical tips on actions, sights, loads, grips, and holsters.

Know Your 45 Auto Pistols—Models 1911 & A1, by E.J. Hoffschmidt, Blacksmith Corp., Southport, CT, 1974. 58 pp., illus. Paper covers. $5.95.

A concise history of the gun with a wide variety of types and copies.

Know Your Walther P.38 Pistols, by E.J. Hoffschmidt, Blacksmith Corp., Southport, CT, 1974. 77 pp., illus. Paper covers. $5.95. variations.

Covers the Walther models Armee, M.P., H.P., P.38—history and variations.

Know Your Walther P.P. & P.P.K. Pistols, by E.J. Hoffschmidt, Blacksmith Corp., Southport, CT, 1975. 87 pp., illus. Paper covers. $5.95.

A concise history of the guns with a guide to the variety and types.

The Luger Pistol (Pistole Parabellum), by F.A. Datig. Borden Publ. Co., Alhambra, CA, 1962. 328 pp., well illus. $13.95.

An enlarged, rev. ed. of an important reference on the arm, its history and development from 1893 to 1945.

Luger Variations, by Harry E. Jones, Harry E. Jones, Torrance, CA, 1975. 328 pp., 160 full page illus., many in color. $30.00.

A rev. ed. of the book known as "The Luger Collector's Bible".

Lugers at Random, by Charles Kenyon, Jr. Handgun Press, Chicago, IL. 1st ed., 1970. 416 pp., profusely illus. $20.00.

An impressive large side-opening book carrying throughout alternate facing-pages of descriptive text and clear photographs. A new boon to the Luger collector and/or shooter.

Mauser Pocket Pistols 1910-1946, by Roy G. Pender, Collectors Press, Houston, TX, 1971. 307 pp. $14.95.

Comprehensive work covering over 100 variations, including factory boxes and manuals. Over 300 photos. Limited, numbered ed.

The Mauser Self-Loading Pistol, by Belford & Dunlap, Borden Publ. Co., Alhambra, CA. Over 200 pp., 300 illus., large format. $13.50.

The long-awaited book on the "Broom Handles", covering their inception in 1894 to the end of production. Complete and in detail: pocket pistols, Chinese and Spanish copies, etc.

Modern American Centerfire Handguns, by Stanley W. T. Trzoniec, Winchester Press, Piscataway, NJ, 1981. 260 pp., illus. $24.95.

The most comprehensive reference on handguns in print.

The New Handbook of Handgunning, by Paul B. Weston, Charles C. Thomas, Publisher, Springfield, IL, 1980. 102 pp., illus. $15.00.

A step-by-step, how-to manual of handgun shooting.

The Pistol Guide, by George C. Nonte, Stoeger Publ. Co., So. Hackensack, NJ, 1980. 256 pp., illus. Paper covers. $8.95.

A unique and detailed examination of a very specialized type of gun: the autoloading pistol.

Pistol & Revolver Guide, 3rd Ed., by George C. Nonte, Stoeger Publ. Co., So. Hackensack, NJ, 1975. 224 pp., illus. Paper covers. $6.95.

The standard reference work on military and sporting handguns.

Pistols of the World, Revised Edition, by Ian V. Hogg and John Weeks, DBI Books, Inc., Northfield, IL, 1982. 306 pp., illus. $12.95.

A valuable reference for collectors and everyone interested in guns.

Pistol & Revolver Digest, 3rd Edition, by Dean A. Grennell, DBI Books, Inc., Northfield, IL, 1982. 288 pp., illus. Paper covers. $9.95.

The latest developments in handguns, shooting, ammunition, and accessories, with catalog.

Quick or Dead, by William L. Cassidy, Paladin Press, Boulder, CO, 1978. 178 pp., illus. $12.95.

Close-quarter combat firing, with particular reference to prominent twentieth-century British and American methods of instruction.

Report of Board on Tests of Revolvers and Automatic Pistols. From the *Annual Report* of the Chief of Ordnance, 1907. Reprinted by J.C. Tillinghast Marlow, NH, 1969. 34 pp., 7 plates, paper covers. $5.00.

A comparison of handguns, including Luger, Savage, Colt, Webley-Fosbery and other makes.

Revolver Guide, by George C. Nonte, Jr., Stoeger Publishing Co., So. Hackensack, NJ, 1980. 288 pp., illus. Paper covers. $8.95.

Fully illustrated guide to selecting, shooting, caring for and collecting revolvers of all types.

Target Pistol Shooting, by K.B. Hinchliffe, David and Charles, London, 1981. 235 pp., illus. $25.00.

A complete guide to target shooting designed to give the novice and expert guidance on the correct techniques for holding, aiming, and firing pistols.

10 Shots Quick, by Daniel K. Stern. Globe Printing Co., San Jose, CA, 1967. 153 pp., photos. $12.50.

History of Savage-made automatic pistols, models of 1903-1917, with descriptive data for shooters and collectors.

The Walther P-38 Pistol, by Maj. Geo. C. Nonte, Paladin Press, Boulder, CO, 1975. 90 pp., illus. Paper covers. $5.00.

Covers all facets of the gun—development, history, variations, technical data, practical use, rebuilding, repair and conversion.

The Walther Pistols 1930-1945, by Warren H. Buxton, Warren H. Buxton, Los Alamos, NM, 1978. 350 pp., illus. $29.95.

Volume I of a projected 4 volume series "The P.38 Pistol". The histories, evolutions, and variations of the Walther P.38 and its predecessors.

hunting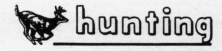

NORTH AMERICA

After Your Deer is Down, by Josef Fischl and Leonard Lee Rue, III, Winchester Press, Piscataway, NJ, 1981. 160 pp., illus. Paper covers. $10.95.

The care and handling of big game, with a bonus of venison recipes.

All About Deer in America, edited by Robert Elman, Winchester Press, Piscataway, NJ, 1976. 256 pp., illus. $15.95.

Twenty of America's great hunters share the secrets of their hunting success.

All About Small-game Hunting in America, edited by Russell Tinsley, Winchester Press, Piscataway, NJ, 1976. 308 pp., illus. $16.95.

Collected advice by the finest small-game experts in the country.

All About Varmint Hunting, by Nick Sisley, The Stone Wall Press, Inc., Wash., DC, 1982. 182 pp., illus. Paper covers. $8.95.

The most comprehensive up-to-date book on hunting common varmints found throughout North America.

All About Wildfowling in America, by Jerome Knap, Winchester Press, Piscataway, NJ, 1977. 256 pp., illus. $13.95.

More than a dozen top writers provide new and controversial ideas on how and where to hunt waterfowl successfully.

All Season Hunting, by Bob Gilsvik, Winchester Press, Piscataway, NJ, 1976. 256 pp., illus. $14.95.

A guide to early-season, late-season and winter hunting in America.

The Art of Hunting Big Game in North America, by Jack O'Connor, Random House, NY, 1978. 418 pp., illus. $17.95.

A revised and updated edition on technique, planning, skill, outfitting, etc.

The Best of Nash Buckingham, by Nash Buckingham, selected, edited and annotated by George Bird Evans, Winchester Press, Piscataway, NJ, 1973. 320 pp., illus. $17.95.

Thirty pieces that represent the very cream of Nash's output on his whole range of outdoor interests—upland shooting, duck hunting, even fishing.

Big Rack, Texas All-Time Largest Whitetails 1892-1975, by Robert Rogers, et al, Outdoor Worlds of Texas, Inc., 1980. 167 pp., illus. $19.95.

Pictures and stories of all classifications of Texas trophy whitetail deer.

Bird Hunting Know-How, by D.M. Duffey, Van Nostrand, Princeton, NJ, 1968. 192 pp., illus. $9.95.

Game-getting techniques and sound advice on all aspects of upland bird hunting, plus data on guns and loads.

Black Powder Hunting, by Sam Fadala, Stackpole Books, Harrisburg, PA, 1978. 192 pp., illus. $10.95.

The author demonstrates successful hunting methods using percussion firearms for both small and big game.

The Bobwhite Quail Book, Compiled by Lamar Underwood, Amwell Press, Clinton, NJ, 1981. 442 pp., illus. $25.00.

An anthology of the finest stories on Bobwhite quail ever assembled under one cover.

Bobwhite Quail Hunting, by Charley Dickey, printed for Stoeger Publ. Co., So. Hackensack, NH, 1974. 112 pp., illus., paper covers. $3.95.

Habits and habitats, techniques, gear, guns and dogs.

The Bobwhite Quail, Its Life and Management, by Walter Rosene. Rutgers University Press, New Brunswick, NJ. 1st ed., 1969. 418 pp., photographs, maps and color plates. $50.00.

An exhaustive study of an important species which has dimished under the impact of changing agricultural and forestry practices.

The Book of the Wild Turkey, by Lovett E. Williams, Jr., Winchester Press, Piscataway, NJ, 1981. 204 pp., illus. $21.95.

A definitive reference work on the wild turkey for hunter, game manager, conservationist, or amateur naturalist.

The Complete Book of Hunting, by Rober Elman, Abbeville Press, New York, NY, 1982. 320 pp., illus. $29.95.

A compendium of the world's game birds and animals, handloading, international hunting, etc.

The Complete Book of Deer Hunting, by Byron W. Dalrymple, Winchester Press, Piscataway, NJ, 1973. 247 pp., illus. $12.95.

Practical know-how information. Covers the 20-odd North American sub-species of deer.

The Complete Book of the Wild Turkey, by Roger M. Latham, Stackpole Books, Harrisburg, Pa., 1978. 228 pp., illus. $12.95.

A new revised edition of the classic on American wild turkey hunting.

The Complete Guide to Bird Dog Training, by John R. Falk, Winchester Press, Piscataway, NJ, 1976. 256 pp., illus. $16.95.

How to choose, raise, train, and care for a bird dog.

The Complete Guide to Game Care and Cookery, by Sam Fadala, DBI Books, Inc., Northfield, IL., 1981. 288 pp., illus. Paper covers. $9.95.

How to dress, preserve and prepare all kinds of game animals and birds.

Coveys and Singles: The Handbook of Quail Hunting, by Robert Gooch, A.S. Barnes, San Diego, CA, 1981. 196 pp., illus. $11.95.

The story of the quail in North America.

Death in the Silent Places, by Peter Hathaway Capstick, St. Martin's Press, New York, NY, 1981. 243 pp., illus. $13.95.

The author recalls the extraordinary careers of legendary hunters such as Corbett, Karamojo Bell, Stigand and others.

Deer Hunting, by R. Smith, Stackpole Books, Harrisburg, PA, 1978. 224 pp., illus. Paper covers. $10.95.

A professional guide leads the hunt for North America's most popular big game animal.

The Deer Book, edited by Lamar Underwood, Amwell Press, Clinton, NJ, 1982. 480 pp., illus. $25.00.

An anthology of the finest stories on North American deer ever assembled under one cover.

Deer Hunter's Yearbook, by the editors of Outdoor Life magazine, Stackpole Books, Harrisburg, PA, 1983. 192 pp., illus. $16.95.

A collection of the choicest stories on deer hunting published by the ever-popular Outdoor Life magazine.

The Desert Bighorn, edited by Gale Monson and Lowell Sumner, University of Arizona Press, Tucson, AZ, 1980. 392 pp., illus. $35.00.

Life history, ecology and management of the Desert Bighorn.

The Dove Shooter's Handbook, by Dan M. Russell, Winchester Press, Piscataway, NJ, 1974. 256 pp., illus. $12.95.

A complete guide to America's top game bird.

Dove Hunting, by Charley Dickey, Galahad Books, NY, 1976. 112 pp., illus. $6.00.

This indispensable guide for hunters deals with equipment, techniques, types of dove shooting, hunting dogs, etc.

Drummer in the Woods, by Burton L. Spiller, Stackpole Books, Harrisburg, PA, 1980. 240 pp., illus. $15.95.

Twenty-one wonderful stories on grouse shooting by "the Poet Laureate of Grouse".

The Duck Hunter's Handbook, by Bob Hinman, Winchester Press, Piscataway, NJ, 1974. 252 pp., illus. $14.95.

Down-to-earth, practical advice on bagging ducks and geese.

The Duck-Huntingest Gentlemen, by Keith C. Russell et al, Winchester Press, Piscataway, NJ, 1980. 284 pp., illus. $17.95.

A collection of stories on waterfowl hunting.

Ducks of the Mississippi Flyway, ed. by John McKane, North Star Press, St. Cloud, MN, 1969. 54 pp., illus. Paper covers. $6.95.

A duck hunter's reference. Full color paintings of some 30 species, plus descriptive text.

Expert Advice on Gun Dog Training, edited by David M. Duffey, Winchester Press, Piscataway, NJ, 1977. 256 pp., illus. $16.95.

Eleven top pros talk shop, revealing the techniques and philosophies that account for their consistent success.

A Gallery of Waterfowl and Upland Birds, by Gene Hill, with illustrations by David Maass, Pedersen Prints, Los Angeles, CA, 1978. 132 pp., illus. $44.95.

Gene Hill at his best. Liberally illustrated with fifty-one full-color reproductions of David Maass' finest paintings.

The Game Trophies of the World, edited and compiled by G. Kenneth Whitehead, Paul Parey, Hamburg, W. Germany. 215 pp., illus. Paper covers. $29.00.

Covers all the game trophies of the world using the Boone & Crockett method of scoring. Text in English, French and German.

Getting the Most out of Modern Waterfowling, by John O. Cartier, St. Martin's Press, NY, 1974. 396 pp., illus. $17.95.

The most comprehensive, up-to-date book on waterfowling imaginable.

Goose Hunting, by Charles L. Cadieux, A Stonewall Press Book, distributed by Winchester Press, Piscataway, NJ, 1979. 197 pp., illus. $16.95.

Great Whitetails of North America, by Robert Rogers, Texas Hunting Services, Corpus Christi, TX, 1981. 223 pp., illus. $24.95.

Pictures and stories of over 100 of the largest whitetail deer ever taken in North America.

Grizzly Country, by Andy Russell. A.A. Knopf, NYC, 1973, 302 pp., illus. $13.95.

Many-sided view of the grizzly bear and his world, by a noted guide, hunter and naturalist.

Grizzlies Don't Come Easy, by Ralph Young, Winchester Press, Piscataway, NJ, 1981. 200 pp., illus. $15.95.

The life story of a great woodsman who guided famous hunters such as O'Connor, Keith, Fitz, Page and others.

The Grizzly Book/The Bear Book, two volume set edited by Jack Samson, Amwell Press, Clinton, NJ, 1982. 304 pp.; 250 pp., illus. Slipcase. $37.50.

A delightful pair of anthologies. Stories by men such as O'Connor, Keith, Fitz, Page, and many others.

1984 Gun Digest Hunting Annual, edited by Robert S.L. Anderson, DBI Books, Inc., Northfield, IL, 1983. 224 pp., illus. Paper covers. $9.95.

The top writers in their fields of shooting and hunting give the reader technical and factual information on how to hunt, where, when, and more.

Grouse Magic, by Nick Sisley, Nick Sisley, Apollo, PA, 1981. 240 pp., illus. Limited edition, signed and numbered. Slipcase. $30.00.

A book that will enrich your appreciation for grouse hunting and all the aura that surrounds the sport.

Gun Digest Book of the Hunting Rifle, by Jack Lewis, DBI Books, Inc., Northfield, IL, 1983. 256 pp., illus. Paper covers. $10.95.

A thorough and knowledgeable account of today's hunting rifles.

Grouse and Woodcock, An Upland Hunter's Book, by Nick Sisley, Stackpole Books, Harrisburg, PA, 1980. 192 pp., illus. $13.95.

Latest field techniques for effective grouse and woodcock hunting.

Hal Swiggett on North American Deer, by Hal Swiggett, Jolex, Inc., Oakland, NJ, 1980. 272 pp., illus. Paper covers. $8.95.

Where and how to hunt all species of North American deer.

Handgun Hunting, by Maj. George C. Nonte, Jr. and Lee E. Jurras, Winchester Press, Piscataway, NJ, 1975. 245 pp., illus. $10.95.

A book with emphasis on the hunting of readily available game in the U.S. with the handgun.

Hard Hunting, by Patrick Shaughnessy and Diane Swingle, Winchester Press, Piscataway, NJ, 1978. 200 pp., illus. $15.95.

A couple explores a no-frills, low-cost, highly successful, adventurous approach to wilderness hunting.

The History of Wildfowling, by John Marchington, Adam and Charles Black, London, England, 1980. 288 pp., illus. $27.50.

Covers decoys, punting, and punt guns.

Horns in the High Country, by Andy Russell, Alfred A. Knofp, NY, 1973. 259 pp., illus. $15.50.

A many-sided view of wild sheep and their natural world.

How to Hunt, by Dave Bowring, Winchester Press, Piscataway, NJ, 1982. 208 pp., illus. Paper covers. $10.95; Cloth. $15.00.

A basic guide to hunting big game, small game, upland birds, and waterfowl.

The Hunter's Book of the Pronghorn Antelope, by Bert Popowski and Wilf E. Pyle, Winchester Press, Piscataway, NJ, 1982. 376 pp., illus. $16.95.

A comprehensive, copiously illustrated volume and a valuable guide for anyone interested in the pronghorn antelope.

A Hunter's Fireside Book, by Gene Hill, Winchester Press, Piscataway, NJ, 1972. 192 pp., illus. $14.95.

An outdoor book that will appeal to every person who spends time in the field—or who wishes he could.

The Hunter's Shooting Guide, by Jack O'Connor, Outdoor Life Books, New York, NY, 1982. 176 pp., illus. Paper covers. $4.50.

A classic covering rifles, cartridges, shooting techniques for shotguns/rifles/handguns.

Hunting the American Wild Turkey, by Dave Harbour, Stackpole Books, Harrisburg, PA, 1975. 256 pp., illus. $14.95.

The techniques and tactics of hunting North America's largest, and most popular, woodland game bird.

Hunting America's Game Animals and Birds, by Robert Elman and George Peper, Winchester Press, Piscataway, NJ, 1975. 368 pp., illus. $16.95.

A how-to, where-to, when-to guide—by 40 top experts—covering the continent's big, small, upland game and waterfowl.

Hunting America's Mule Deer, by Jim Zumbo, Winchester Press, Piscataway, NJ, 1981. 272 pp., illus. $16.95.

The best ways to hunt mule deer. The how, when, and where to hunt all seven sub-species.

Hunting Dog Know-How, by D.M. Duffey, Winchester Press, Piscataway, NJ, 1983. 208 pp., illus. Paper covers. $8.95.

Covers selection, breeds, and training of hunting dogs, problems in hunting and field trials.

Hunting Moments of Truth, by Eric Peper and Jim Rikhoff, Winchester Press, Piscataway, NJ, 1973. 208 pp., illus. $15.00.

The world's most experienced hunters recount 22 most memorable occasions.

Hunting and Stalking Deer Throughout the World, by Kenneth G. Whitehead, Batsford Books, London, 1982. 336 pp., illus. $35.00.

Comprehensive coverage of deer hunting areas on a country-by-country basis, dealing with every species in any given country.

Hunting Trophy Deer, by John Wootters, Winchester Press, Piscataway, NJ, 1983. 265 pp., illus. $12.95.

All the advice you need to succeed at bagging trophy deer.

Hunting the Uplands with Rifle and Shotgun, by Luther A. Anderson, Winchester Press, Piscataway, NJ, 1977. 224 pp., illus. $12.95.

Solid practical know-how to help make hunting deer and every major species of upland game bird easier and more satisfying.

Hunting Wild Turkeys in the Everglades, by Frank P. Harben, Harben Publishing Co., Safety Harbor, FL, 1983. 341 pp., illus. Paper covers. $8.95.

Describes techniques, ways and means of hunting this wary bird.

Hunting Whitetail Deer, by Robert E. Donovan, Winchester Press, Piscataway, NJ, 1978. 256 pp., illus. $15.95.

For beginners and experts alike, this book is the key to successful whitetail hunting.

Hunting the Woodlands for Small and Big Game, by Luther A. Anderson, A. S. Barnes & Co., New York, NY, 1980. 256 pp., illus. $12.00.

A comprehensive guide to hunting in the United States. Chapters on firearms, game itself, marksmanship, clothing and equipment.

In Search of the Wild Turkey, by Bob Gooch, Greatlakes Living Press, Ltd., Waukegan, IL, 1978. 182 pp., illus. $9.95.

A state-by-state guide to wild turkey hot spots, with tips on gear and methods for bagging your bird.

The Market Hunter, by David and Jim Kimball, Dillon Press Inc., Minneapolis, MN, 1968. 132 pp., illus. $10.00.

The market hunter, one of the "missing chapters" in American history, is brought to life in this book.

Matching the Gun to the Game, by Clair Rees, Winchester Press, Piscataway, NJ, 1982. 272 pp., illus. $26.95.

Covers selection and use of handguns, black-powder firearms for hunting, matching rifle type to the hunter, calibers for multiple use, tailoring factory loads to the game.

Mixed Bag, by Jim Rikhoff, National Rifle Association of America, Wash., DC, 1981. 284 pp., illus. Paper covers. $9.95.

Reminiscences of a master raconteur.

Modern Pheasant Hunting, by Steve Grooms, Stackpole Books, Harrisburg, PA, 1982. 224 pp., illus. $16.95.

New look at pheasants and hunters from an experienced hunter who respects this splendid gamebird.

Modern Turkey Hunting, by James F. Brady, Crown Publ., N.Y.C., NY, 1973. 160 pp., illus. $30.00.

A thorough guide to the habits, habitat, and methods of hunting America's largest game bird.

Modern Wildfowling, by Eric Begbie, Saiga Publishing Co., Ltd., Surrey, England, 1980. 171 pp., illus. $27.50.

History of wildfowling, guns and equipment.

More Grouse Feathers, by Burton L. Spiller. Crown Publ., NY, 1972. 238 pp., illus. $15.00.

Facsimile of the original Derrydale Press issue of 1938. Guns and dogs, the habits and shooting of grouse, woodcook, ducks, etc. Illus by Lynn Bogue Hunt.

Mostly Tailfeathers, by Gene Hill, Winchester Press, Piscataway, NJ, 1975. 192 pp., illus. $14.95.

An interesting, general book about bird hunting.

The Muzzleloading Hunter, by Rick Hacker, Winchester Press, Piscataway, NJ, 1981. 283 pp., illus. $19.95.

A comprehensive guide for the black powder sportsman.

The Nash Buckingham Library, compiled by Douglas C. Mauldin, Delta Arms Sporting Goods, Indianola, MS 1980. 7 volume set in slipcase. $150.00.

Seven outdoor hunting classics by Nash Buckingham, the 20th century's greatest sporting writer.

North American Big Game Hunting, by Byron W. Dalrymple, Winchester Press, Piscataway, NJ, 1974. 384 pp., illus. $15.00.

A comprehensive, practical guide, with individual chapters devoted to all native species.

North American Elk: Ecology and Management, edited by Jack Ward Thomas and Dale E. Toweill, Stackpole Books, Harrisburg, PA, 1982. 576 pp., illus. $39.95.

The definitive, exhaustive, classic work on the North American Elk.

The North American Waterfowler, by Paul S. Bernsen, Superior Publ. Co., Seattle, WA, 1972. 206 pp., Paper covers. $4.95.

The complete inside and outside story of duck and goose shooting. Big and colorful, illus. by Les Kouba.

The Old Pro Turkey Hunter, by Gene Nunnery, Gene Nunnery, Meridian, MS, 1980. 144 pp., illus. $12.95.

True facts and old tales of turkey hunters.

1001 Hunting Tips, by Robert Elman, Winchester Press, Piscataway, NJ, 1983. 544 pp., illus. Paper covers. $14.95.

New edition, updated and expanded. A complete course in big and small game hunting, wildfowling and hunting upland birds.

The Old Man's Boy Grows Older, by Robert Ruark, Holt, Rinehart and Winston, New York, NY, 1961. 302 pp., illus. $35.00.

A classic by a big-game hunter and world traveler.

One Man's Wilderness, by Warren Page, Holt, Rinehart and Winston, NY, 1973. 256 pp., illus. $30.00.

A world-known writer and veteran sportsman recounts the joys of a lifetime of global hunting.

The Outlaw Gunner, by Harry M. Walsh, Tidewater Publishers, Cambridge, MD, 1973. 178 pp., illus. $12.50.

A colorful story of market gunning in both its legal and illegal phases.

Pinnell and Talifson: Last of the Great Brown Bear Men, by Marvin H. Clark, Jr., Great Northwest Publishing and Distributing Co., Spokane, WA, 1980. 224 pp., illus. $20.00.

The story of these famous Alaskan guides and some of the record bears taken by them.

Practical Hunter's Dog Book, by John R. Falk, Winchester Press, Piscataway, NJ, 1971. 336 pp., illus. $11.95.

Helps to choose, train and enjoy your gun dog.

The Practical Hunter's Handbook, by Anthony J. Acerrano, Winchester Press, Piscataway, NJ, 1978. 224 pp., illus. Paper covers. $11.95.

How the time-pressed hunter can take advantage of every edge his hunting situation affords him.

The Practical Wildfowler, by John Marchington, Adam and Charles Black, London, England, 1977. 143 pp., illus. $21.95.

Advice on both the practical and ethical aspects of the sport.

Predator Caller's Companion, by Gerry Blair, Winchester Press, Piscataway, NJ, 1981. 280 pp., illus. $18.95.

Predator calling techniques and equipment for the hunter and trapper.

Ranch Life and the Hunting Trail, by Theodore Roosevelt, Readex Microprint Corp., Dearborn, MI. 1966 186 pp. With drawings by Frederic Remington. $15.00.

A facsimile reprint of the original 1899 Century Co., edition. One of the most fascinating books of the West of that day.

Records of Exotics, Volume 2, 1978 Edition, compiled by Thompson B. Temple, Thompson B. Temple, Ingram, TX, 1978. 243 pp., illus. $15.00.

Lists almost 1,000 of the top exotic trophies bagged in the U.S. Gives complete information on how to score.

Ringneck! Pheasants & Pheasant Hunting, by Ted Janes, Crown Publ., NY, 1975. 120 pp., illus. $8.95.

A thorough study of one of our more popular game birds.

Sheep and Sheep Hunting, by Jack O'Connor, Winchester Press, Piscataway, NJ, 1983. 320 pp., illus. Paper covers. $13.95.

Memorial edition of the definitive book on wild sheep hunting.

Shooting Pictures, by A.B. Frost, with 24 pp. of text by Chas. D. Lanier, Winchester Press, Piscataway, NJ, 1972. 12 color plates. Enclosed in a board portfolio. Ed. limited to 750 numbered copies. $200.00.

Frost's 12 superb 12" by 16" pictures have often been called the finest sporting prints published in the U.S. A facsimile of the 1895-6 edition printed on fine paper with superb color fidelity.

Shots at Mule Deer, by Rollo S. Robinson, Winchester Press, Piscataway, NJ, 1970. 209 pp., illus. $15.00.

Description, strategies for bagging it, the correct rifle and cartridge to use.

Small Game Hunting, by Tom Brakefield, J.B. Lippincott Co., Phila., PA, 1978. 244 pp., illus. $10.

Describes where, when, and how to hunt all major small game species from coast to coast.

Squirrels and Squirrel Hunting, by Bob Gooch. Tidewater Publ., Cambridge, MD, 1973. 148 pp., illus. $6.

A complete book for the squirrel hunter, beginner or old hand. Details methods of hunting, squirrel habitat, management, proper clothing, care of the kill, cleaning and cooking.

Strayed Shots and Frayed Lines, edited by John E. Howard, Amwell Press, Clinton, NJ, 1982. 425 pp., illus. $25.00.

Anthology of some of the finest, funniest stories on hunting and fishing ever asembled.

Successful Deer Hunting, by Sam Fadala, DBI Books, Inc., Northfield, IL, 1983. 288 pp., illus. Paper covers. $10.95.

Here's all the dope you'll need—where, why, when and how—to have a successful deer hunt.

Successful Waterfowling, by Zack Taylor, Crown, Publ., NY, 1974. 276 pp., illus. Paper covers. $15.95.

The definitive guide to new ways of hunting ducks and geese.

Timberdoodle, by Frank Woolner, Crown Publ., Inc., NY, 1974. 168 pp., illus. $15.95.

A thorough, practical guide to the American woodcock and to woodcock hunting.

Topflight; A Speed Index to Waterfowl, by J.A. Ruthven & Wm. Zimmerman, Moebius Prtg. Co., Milwaukee, WI, 1968. 112 pp. $8.95.

Rapid reference for specie identification. Marginal color band of book directs reader to proper section. 263 full color illustrations of body and feather configurations.

The Trophy Hunter, by Col. Allison, Stackpole Books, Harrisburg, 1981. 240 pp., illus. $24.95.

Action-packed tales of hunting big game trophies around the world—1860 to today.

Trouble With Bird Dogs . . . and What to do About Them, by George Bird Evans, Winchester Press, Piscataway, NJ, 1976. 288 pp., illus. $15.95.

How to custom-train your dog for specific kinds of hunting.

Turkey Hunting with Charlie Elliot, by Charles Elliot, David McKay Co., Inc., New York, NY 1979. 275 pp., illus. $14.95.

The old professor tells all about America's big-game bird.

Turkey Hunter's Guide, by Byron W. Dalrymple, et al, a publication of The National Rifle Association, Washington, DC, 1979. 96 pp., illus. Paper covers. $4.95.

Expert advice on turkey hunting hotspots, guns, guides, and calls.

The Whispering Wings of Autumn, by Gene Hill and Steve Smith, Amwell Press, Clinton, NJ, 1982. 192 pp., illus. $17.50.

A collection of both fact and fiction on two of North America's most famous game birds, the Ruffed Grouse and the Woodcock.

The Whitetail Deer Hunter's Handbook, by John Weiss, Winchester Press, Piscataway, NJ, 1979. 256 pp., illus. Paper covers. $11.95.

Wherever you live, whatever your level of experience, this brand-new handbook will make you a better deer hunter.

Whitetail: Fundamentals and Fine Points for the Hunter, by George Mattis, World Publ. Co. New York, NY, 1976. 273 pp., illus. $9.95.

A manual of shooting and trailing and an education in the private world of the deer.

Whitetail Hunting, by Jim Dawson, Stackpole Books, Harrisburg, PA, 1982. 224 pp., illus. $14.95.

New angles on hunting whitetail deer.

The Wild Sheep of the World, by Raul Valdez, Wild Sheep and Goat International, Mesilla, NM, 1983. 150 pp., illus. $40.00.

The first comprehensive survey of the world's wild sheep written by a zoologist.

The Wild Turkey Book, edited and with special commentary by J. Wayne Fears, Amwell Press, Clinton, NJ, 1982. 303 pp., illus. $22.50.

An anthology of the finest stories on wild turkey ever assembled under one cover.

The Wings of Dawn, by George Reiger, Stein and Day, New York, NY, 1980. 320 pp., illus. $29.95.

The complete book of North American waterfowling.

20 Great Trophy Hunts, by John O. Cartier, David McKay Co., Inc., New York, NY, 1981. 320 pp., illus. $22.50.

The cream of outstanding true-life hunting stories.

AFRICA/ASIA

African Rifles & Cartridges, by John Taylor. The Gun Room Press, Highland Park, NJ, 1977. 431 pp., illus. $21.95.

Experiences and opinions of a professional ivory hunter in Africa describing his knowledge of numerous arms and cartridges for big game. A reprint.

African Hunting and Adventure, by William Charles Baldwin, Books of Zimbabwe, Bulawayo, 1981. 451 pp., illus. $65.00.

Facsimile reprint of the scarce 1863 London edition. African hunting and adventure from Natal to the Zambesi.

Bell of Africa, by Walter (Karamojo) D. M. Bell, Neville Spearman, Suffolk, England, 1983. 236 pp., illus. $35.00.

Autobiography of the greatest elephant hunter of them all.

Big Game Hunting Around the World, by Bert Klineburger and Vernon W. Hurst, Exposition Press, Jericho, NY, 1969. 376 pp., illus. $30.00.

The first book that takes you on a safari all over the world.

Jim Corbett's India, edited by R. E. Hawkins, Oxford University Press, London, England, 1979. 250 pp., illus. $30.00.

A selection of stories from Jim Corbett's big game hunting books.

Death in the Long Grass, by Peter Hathaway Capstick, St. Martin's Press, New York, NY, 1977. 297 pp., illus. $13.95.

A big game hunter's adventures in the African bush.

The Elephant Hunters of the Lado, by Major W. Robert Foran, Amwell Press, Clinton, NJ, 1981. 311 pp., illus. Limited, numbered, and signed edition, in slipcase. $200.00.

From a previously unpublished manuscript by a famous "white hunter."

Elephant Hunting in East Equatorial Africa, by Arthur H. Neumann, Books of Zimbabwe, Bulawayo, 1982. 455 pp., illus. $85.00.

Facsimile reprint of the scarce 1898 London edition. An account of three years ivory hunting under Mount Kenya.

Green Hills of Africa, by Ernest Hemingway. Charles Scribner's Sons, NY, 1963. 285 pp., illus. Paper covers. $5.95.

A famous narrative of African big-game hunting, first published in 1935.

Horned Death, by John F. Burger. Standard Publications, Huntington, WV, 1947. 340 pp., illus. $175.00.

Hunting the African cape buffalo.

A Hunter's Wanderings in Africa, by F. C. Selous, Books of Zimbabwe, Bulawayo, 1981. 455 pp., illus. $85.00.

A facsimile reprint of the 1881 London edition. A narrative of nine years spent among the game of the interior of South Africa.

Hunting in Africa, by Bill Morkel, Howard Timmins, Publishers, Capetown, South Africa, 1980. 252 pp., illus. $25.00.

An invaluable guide for the inexperienced hunter contemplating a possible safari.

Hunting the Big Cats, two volume set, edited by Jim Rikhoff, Amwell Press, Clinton, NJ, 1981. Total of 808 pp., illustrated by Bob Kuhn. Limited, numbered, and signed edition. In slipcase. $175.00.

The most definitive work on hunting the world's largest wild cats ever compiled. A collection of 70 articles on hunting in Africa, Asia, North and South America.

Hunting on Safari in East and Southern Africa, by Aubrey Wynne-Jones, Macmillan South Africa, Johannesburg, S. Africa, 1980. 180 pp., illus. $42.50.

Every aspect of hunting in East and Southern Africa is covered, from the early planning stages of the hunt itself.

The Recollections of an Elephant Hunter 1864-1875, by William Finaughty, Books of Zimbabwe, Bulawayo, 1980. 244 pp., illus. $65.00.

Reprint of the scarce 1916 privately published edition. The early game hunting exploits of William Finaughty in Matabeleland and Nashonaland.

Tanzania Safari, by Brian Herne, Amwell Press, Clinton, NJ, 1982. 259 pp., illus. Limited, signed and numbered edition. Slipcase. $75.00.

The story of Tanzania and hunting safaris, professional hunters, and a little history, too.

The Wanderings of an Elephant Hunter, by W.D.M. Bell, Neville Spearman, Suffolk, England, 1981. 187 pp., illus. $35.00.

The greatest of elephant books by perhaps the greatest elephant hunter of all times, 'Karamojo' Bell.

The Accurate Rifle, by Warren Page, Winchester Press, Piscataway, NJ, 1973. 256 pp., illus. $15.95.

A masterly discussion. A must for the competitive shooter hoping to win, and highly useful to the practical hunter.

The AK-47 Assault Rifle, Desert Publications, Cornville, AZ, 1981. 150 pp., illus. Paper covers. $6.95.

Complete and practical technical information on the only weapon in history to be produced in an estimated 30,000,000 units.

American Rifle Design and Performance, by L.R. Wallack, Winchester Press, Piscataway, NJ, 1977. 288 pp., illus. $20.00.

An authoritative, comprehensive guide to how and why every kind of sporting rifle works.

The Bolt Action: A Design Analysis, by Stuart Otteson, edited by Ken Warner, Winchester Press, Piscataway, NJ, 1976. 320 pp., illus. Paper covers. $14.95; Cloth. $20.00.

Precise and in-depth descriptions, illustrations and comparisons of 16 bolt actions.

The Book of the Garand, by Maj.-Gen. J.S. Hatcher, The Gun Room Press, Highland Park, NJ, 1977. 292 pp., illus. $15.00.

A new printing of the standard reference work on the U.S. Army M1 rifle.

Carbines Cal. .30 M1, M1A1, M2 and M3, by D.B. McLean, Normount Armament Co., Wickenburg, AZ, 1964. 221 pp., well illus., paperbound. $7.95.

U.S. field manual reprints on these weapons, edited and reorganized.

The Commerical Mauser '98 Sporting Rifle, by Lester Womack, Womack Associates, Publishers, Prescott, AZ, 1980. 69 pp., illus. $20.00.

The first work on the sporting rifles made by the original Mauser plant in Oberndorf.

The Deer Rifle, by L.R. Wallack, Winchester Press, Piscataway, NJ, 1978. 256 pp., illus. $15.95.

Everything the deer hunter needs to know to select and use the arms and ammunition appropriate to his needs.

F.N.-F.A.L. Auto Rifles, Desert Publications, Cornville, AZ, 1981. 130 pp., illus. Paper covers. $6.95.

A definitive study of one of the free world's finest combat rifles.

The First Winchester, by John E. Parsons, Winchester Press, Piscataway, NJ, 1977. 207 pp., illus. $35.00.

The story of the 1866 repeating rifle.

A Forgotten Heritage; The Story of a People and the Early American Rifle, by Harry P. Davis, The Gun Room Press, Highland Park, NJ, 1976. 199 pp., illus. $9.95.

Reprint of a very scarce history, originally published in 1941, the Kentucky rifle and the people who used it.

The Golden Age of Single-Shot Rifles, by Edsall James, Pioneer Press, Union City, TN, 1975. 33 pp., illus. Paper covers. $2.75.

A detailed look at all of the fine, high quality sporting single-shot rifles that were once the favorite of target shooters.

The Gun Digest Book of the .22 Rimfire, by John Lachuk, DBI Books, Northfield, IL, 1978. 224 pp., illus. Paper covers. $7.95.

Everything you want to know about the .22 rimfire cartridge and the arms that use it.

Gun Digest Book of the Hunting Rifle, by Jack Lewis, DBI Books, Inc., Northfield, IL, 1983. 256 pp., illus. Paper covers. $10.95.

Covers all aspects of the hunting rifle—design, development, different types, uses, and more.

Know Your M1 Garand, by E. J. Hoffschmidt, Blacksmith Corp., Southport, CT, 1975, 84 pp., illus. Paper covers. $5.95.

Facts about America's most famous infantry weapon. Covers test and experimental models, Japanese and Italian copies, National Match models.

The M-14 Rifle, facsimile reprint of FM 23-8, Desert Publications, Cornville, AZ, 50 pp., illus. Paper $5.95.

In this well illustrated and informative reprint, the M-14 and M-14E2 are covered thoroughly.

The Modern Rifle, by Jim Carmichel, Winchester Press, Piscataway, NJ, 1975. 320 pp., illus. $15.95.

The most comprehensive, thorough, up-to-date book ever published on today's rifled sporting arms.

North American FALS, by R. Blake Stevens, Collector Grade Publications, Toronto, Canada, 1979. 166 pp., illus. Paper covers. $20.00.

NATO's search for a standard rifle.

100 Years of Shooters and Gunmakers of Single Shot Rifles, by Gerald O. Kelver, Brighton, CO, 1975. 212 pp., illus. Paper covers $10.00.

The Schuetzen rifle, targets and shooters, primers, match rifles, original loadings and much more. With chapters on famous gunsmiths like Harry Pope, Morgan L. Rood and others.

The '03 Springfields, by Clark S. Campbell, Ray Riling Arms Books Co., Phila., PA, 1978. 320 pp., illus. $29.95.

The most authoritative and definitive work on this famous U.S. rifle, the 1903 Springfield and its 30-06 cartridge.

The Pennsylvania Rifle, by Samuel E. Dyke, Sutter House, Lititz, PA, 1975. 61 pp., illus. Paper covers. $5.00.

History and development, from the hunting rifle of the Germans who settled the area. Contains a full listing of all known Lancaster, PA, gunsmiths from 1729 through 1815.

The Revolving Rifles, by Edsall James, Pioneer Press, Union City, TN, 1975. 23 pp., illus. Paper covers. $2.50.

Valuable information on revolving cylinder rifles, from the earliest matchlock forms to the latest models of Colt and Remington.

The Rifle Book, by Jack O'Connor, Random House, NY, 1978. 337 pp., illus. Paper covers. $10.95.

The complete book of small game, varmint and big game rifles.

Rifle Guide, by Robert A. Steindler, Stoeger Publishing Co., South Hackensack, NJ, 1978. 304 pp., illus. Paper covers. $7.95.

Complete, fully illustrated guide to selecting, shooting, caring for, and collecting rifles of all types.

Rifles AR15, M16, and M16A1, 5.56 mm, by D.B. McLean. Normount Armament Co., Wickenburg, AZ, 1968. Unpaginated, illus., paper covers. $8.95.

Descriptions, specifications and operation of subject models are set forth in text and picture.

Rifle Shooting as a Sport, by Bernd Klingner, A.S. Barnes and Co., Inc., San Diego, CA, 1980. 186 pp., illus. Paper covers. $15.00.

Basic principles, positions and techniques by an international expert.

Ned H. Roberts and the Schuetzen Rifle, edited by Gerald O. Kelver, Brighton, CO, 1982. 99 pp., illus. $10.00.

A compilation of the writings of Major Ned H. Roberts which appeared in various gun magazines.

The Ruger No. 1, by J.D. Clayton, edited by John T. Amber, Blacksmith Corp., Southport, CT, 1983. 200 pp., illus. $39.50.

Covers this famous rifle from original conception to current production.

Schuetzen Rifles, History and Loading, by Gerald O. Kelver, Gerald O. Kelver, Publisher, Brighton, CO, 1972. Illus. $7.50.

Reference work on these rifles, their bullets, loading, telescopic sights, accuracy, etc. A limited, numbered ed.

Single Shot Rifles and Actions, by Frank de Haas, ed. by John T. Amber, DBI Books, Northfield, IL, 1969. 352 pp., illus. $9.95.

The definitive book on over 60 single shot rifles and actions. Covers history, parts photos, design and construction, etc.

The Sporting Rifle and its Projectiles, by Lieut. James O Forsyth, The Buckskin Press, Big Timber, MT, 1978. 132 pp., illus. $10.00.

Facsimile reprint of the 1863 edition, one of the most authoritative books ever written on the muzzle-loading round ball sporting rifle.

The Springfield Rifle M1903, M1903A1, M1903A3, M1903A4, Desert Publications, Cornville, AZ, 1982. 100 pp., illus. Paper covers. $5.95.

Covers every aspect of disassembly and assembly, inspection, repair and maintenance.

The .22 Rifle, by Dave Petzal, Winchester Press, Piscataway, NJ, 1972. 244 pp., illus. $12.95.

All about the mechanics of the .22 rifle. How to choose the right one, how to choose a place to shoot, what makes a good shot, the basics of small-game hunting.

U.S. Rifle M14, from John Garand to the M21, by R. Blake Stevens, Collector Grade Publications, Toronto, Canada, 1983. 400 pp., illus. $34.95.

The complete history of the M14 rifle.

The American Shotgun, by David F. Butler, Lyman Publ., Middlefield, CT, 1973. 256 pp. illus. Paper covers. $11.95.

A comprehensive history of the American smoothbore's evolution from Colonial times to the present day.

American Shotgun Design and Performance, by L.R. Wallack, Winchester Press, Piscataway, NJ, 1977. 184 pp., illus. $16.95.

An expert lucidly recounts the history and development of American shotguns and explains how they work.

The Double Shotgun, by Don Zutz, Winchester Press, Piscataway, NJ, 1978. 288 pp., illus. $19.95.

The history and development of most classic of all sporting arms.

The Golden Age of Shotgunning, by Bob Hinman, Wolfe Publishing Co., Inc., Prescott, AZ, 1982. $17.95.

A valuable history of the late 1800s detailing that fabulous period of development in shotguns, shotshells and shotgunning.

How to be a Winner Shooting Skeet & Trap, by Tom Morton, Tom Morton, Knoxville, MD, 1974. 144 pp., illus. Paper covers. $8.95.

The author explains why championship shooting is more than a physical process.

L.C. Smith Shotguns, by Lt. Col. William S. Brophy, The Gun Room Press, Highland Park, NJ, 1979. 244 pp., illus. $29.95.

The first work on this very important American gun and manufacturing company.

The Mysteries of Shotgun Patterns, by George G. Oberfell and Charles E. Thompson, Oklahoma State University Press, Stillwater, OK, 1982. 164 pp., illus. Paper covers. $25.00.

Shotgun ballistics for the hunter in non-technical language, with information on improving effectiveness in the field.

The Parker Gun, by Larry L. Baer, The Gun Room Press, Highland Park, NJ, 1983. 240 pp., illus. $29.95.

The only comprehensive work on the subject of America's most famous shotgun.

Plans and Specifications of the L.C. Smith Shotgun, by Lt. Col. William S. Brophy, USAR Ret., F. Brownell & Son, Montezuma, IA, 1982. 247 pp., illus. $19.95.

The only collection ever assembled of all the drawings and engineering specifications on the incomparable and very collectable L.C. Smith shotgun.

The Police Shotgun Manual, by Robert H. Robinson, Charles C. Thomas, Springfield, IL 1973. 153 pp., illus. $17.50.

A complete study and analysis of the most versatile and effective weapon in the police arsenal.

Score Better at Skeet, by Fred Missildine, with Nick Karas. Winchester Press, NY 1972. 160 pp., illus. $10.00.

The long-awaited companion volume to *Score Better at Trap.*

Score Better at Trap, by Fred Missildine, Winchester Press, Piscataway, NJ, 1976. 159 pp., illus. $10.00.

An essential book for all trap shooters.

75 Years with the Shotgun, by C.T. (Buck) Buckman, Valley Publ., Fresno, CA, 1974. 141 pp., illus. $10.00.

An expert hunter and trapshooter shares experiences of a lifetime.

The Shotgun Book, by Jack O'Connor, Alfred A. Knopf, New York, NY, 2nd rev. ed., 1981. 341 pp., illus. Paper covers $9.95.

An indispensable book for every shotgunner containing authoritative information on every phase of the shotgun.

The Shotgun in Combat, by Tony Lesce, Desert Publications, Cornville, AZ, 1979. 148 pp., illus. Paper covers. $6.95.

A history of the shotgun and its use in combat.

Shotgun Digest, 2nd Edition, edited by Jack Lewis and Jack Mitchell, DBI Books, Inc., Northfield, IL 1980. 288 pp., illus. Paper covers. $9.95.

All-new look at shotguns by a double-barreled team of writers.

Shotgunners Guide, by Monte Burch, Winchester Press, Piscataway, NJ, 1980. 208 pp., illus. $18.95.

A basic book for the young and old who want to try shotgunning or who want to improve their skill.

Shotgunning: The Art and the Science, by Bob Brister, Winchester Press, Piscataway, NJ, 1976. 321 pp., illus. $15.95.

Hundreds of specific tips and truly novel techniques to improve the field and target shooting of every shotgunner.

Sure-Hit Shotgun Ways, by Francis E. Sell, Stackpole Books, Harrisburg, PA, 1967. 160 pp., illus. $15.00.

On guns, ballistics and quick skill methods.

Skeet Shooting with D. Lee Braun, edited by R. Campbell, Grosset & Dunlap, NY, 1967. 160 pp., illus. Paper covers $5.95.

Thorough instructions on the fine points of Skeet shooting.

Trapshooting with D. Lee Braun and the Remington Pros., ed. by R. Campbell. Remington Arms Co., Bridgeport, CT. 1969. 157 pp., well illus., Paper covers. $5.95.

America's masters of the scattergun give the secrets of professional marksmanship.

Wing & Shot, by R.G. Wehle, Country Press, 167. 190 pp., illus. $12.

Step-by-step account on how to train a fine shooting dog.

The World's Fighting Shotguns, by Thomas F. Swearengen, T. B. N. Enterprises, Alexandria, VA 1979. 500 pp., illus. $29.95.

The complete military and police reference work from the shotgun's inception to date, with up-to-date developments.

IMPORTANT NOTICE TO BOOK BUYERS

Books listed here may be bought from Ray Riling Arms Books Co., 114 Greenwood Ave., Box 135, Wyncote, PA 19095, phone 215/438-2456. Joe Riling, the proprietor, is the researcher and compiler of "The Arms Library" and a seller of gun books for over 30 years.

The Riling stock includes books classic and modern, many hard-to-find items, and many not obtainable elsewhere. These pages list a portion of the current stock. They offer prompt, complete service, with delayed shipments occurring only on out-of-print or out-of-stock books.

NOTICE FOR ALL CUSTOMERS: Remittance in U.S. funds must accompany all orders. For U.S. add $1.50 per book for postage and insurance. Minimum order $10.00. For U.P.S. add 50% to mailing costs.

All foreign countries add $2.00 per book for postage and handling, plus $3.30 per 10-lb. package or under for safe delivery by registered mail. Parcels not registered are sent at the "buyers risk."

Payments in excess of order or for "Backorders" are credited or fully refunded at request. Books "As-Ordered" are not returnable except by permission and a handling charge on these of $2.00 per book is deducted from refund or credit. Only Pennsylvania customers must include current sales tax.

A full variety of arms books are also available from Rutgers Book Center, 127 Raritan Ave., Highland Park, NJ 08904.

ARMS ASSOCIATIONS IN AMERICA AND ABROAD

UNITED STATES

ALABAMA

Alabama Gun Collectors Assn.
Dick Boyd, Secy., P.O. Box 5548, Tuscaloosa, AL 35405

ARIZONA

Arizona Arms Assn.,
Clay Fobes, Secy., P.O. Box 17061, Tucson, AZ 85731

CALIFORNIA

Calif. Hunters & Gun Owners Assoc.
V.H. Wacker, 2309 Cipriani Blvd., Belmont, CA 94002
Greater Calif. Arms & Collectors Assn.
Donald L. Bullock, 8291 Carburton St., Long Beach, CA 90808
Los Angeles Gun & Ctg. Collectors Assn.
F.H. Ruffra, 20810 Amie Ave., Apt. #9, Torrance, CA 90503

COLORADO

Pikes Peak Gun Collectors Guild
Charles Cell, 406 E. Uintah St., Colorado Springs, CO 80903

CONNECTICUT

Ye Conn. Gun Guild, Inc.
Robert L. Harris, P.O. Box 8, Cornwall Bridge, CT 06754

FLORIDA

Florida Gun Collectors Assn., Inc.
John D. Hammer, 5700 Mariner Dr., 304-W, Tampa, FL 33609
Tampa Bay Arms Collectors' Assn.
John Tuvell, 2461 — 67th Ave. S., St. Petersburg, FL 33712
Unified Sportsmen of Florida
P.O. Box 6565, Tallahassee, FL 32314

GEORGIA

Georgia Arms Collectors
Cecil W. Anderson, P.O. Box 218, Conley, GA 30027

HAWAII

Hawaii Historic Arms Assn.
John A. Bell, P.O. Box 1733, Honolulu, HI 96806

IDAHO

Idaho State Rifle and Pistol Assn.
Tom Price, 3631 Pineridge Dr., Coeur d'Alene, ID 83814

ILLINOIS

Fox Valley Arms Fellowship, Inc.
16 S. Bothwell St., Palatine, IL 60067
Illinois State Rifle Assn.
520 N. Michigan Ave., Room 615, Chicago, IL 60611
Illinois Gun Collectors Assn.
195 So. Schuyler Ave., Bradley, IL 60915

Little Fort Gun Collectors Assn.
David Linderholm, P.O. Box 8641, Waukegan, IL 60085
Mississippi Valley Gun & Cartridge Coll. Assn.
Lawrence Maynard, R.R. 2, Aledo, IL 61231
NIPDEA
c/o Phil Stanger, 1029 Castlewood Lane, Deerfield, IL 60015
Sauk Trail Gun Collectors
Gordell M. Matson, 3817-22 Ave., Moline, IL 61265
Wabash Valley Gun Collectors Assn., Inc.
Eberhard R. Gerbsch, 416 South St., Danville, IL 61832

INDIANA

Indiana Sportsmen's Council-Legislative
Maurice Latimer, P.O. Box 93, Bloomington, IN 47402
Indiana State Rifle & Pistol Assn.
Thos. Glancy, P.O. Box 552, Chesterton, IN 46304
Southern Indiana Gun Collectors Assn., Inc.
Harold M. McClary, 509 N. 3rd St., Boonville, IN 47601

IOWA

Central States Gun Collectors Assn.
Avery Giles, 1104 S. 1st Ave., Marshtown, IA 50158

KANSAS

Four State Collectors Assn.
M.G. Wilkinson, 915 E. 10th, Pittsburg, KS 66762
Kansas Cartridge Coll. Assn.
Bob Linder, Box 84, Plainville, KS 67663
Missouri Valley Arms Collectors Assn.
Chas. F. Samuel, Jr., Box 8204, Shawnee Mission, KS 66208

KENTUCKY

Kentuckiana Arms Coll. Assn.
Tony Wilson, Pres., Box 1776, Louisville, KY 40201
Kentucky Gun Collectors Assn., Inc.
Ruth Johnson, Box 64, Owensboro, KY 42302

LOUISIANA

Washitaw River Renegades
Sandra Rushing, P.O. Box 256, Main St., Grayson, LA 71435

MARYLAND

Baltimore Antique Arms Assn.
Stanley I. Kellert, E-30, 2600 Insulator Dr., Baltimore, MD 21230

MASSACHUSETTS

Bay Colony Weapons Collectors, Inc.
Ronald B. Santurjian, 47 Homer Rd., Belmont, MA 02178
Massachusetts Arms Collectors
John J. Callan, Jr., P.O. Box 1001, Worcester, MA 01613

MICHIGAN

Royal Oak Historical Arms Collectors, Inc.
Nancy Stein, 25487 Hereford, Huntington Woods, MI 48070

MINNESOTA

Minnesota Weapons Coll. Assn., Inc.
Box 662, Hopkins, MN 55343

MISSISSIPPI

Mississippi Gun Collectors Assn.
Mrs. Jack E. Swinney, P.O. Box 1332, Hattiesburg, MS 39401

MISSOURI

Mineral Belt Gun Coll. Assn.
D.F. Saunders, 1110 Cleveland Ave., Monett, MO 65708

MONTANA

Montana Arms Collectors Assn.
Lewis E. Yearout, 308 Riverview Dr. East, Great Falls, MT 59404
The Winchester Arms Coll. Assn.
Lewis E. Yearout, 308 Riverview Dr. East, Great Falls, MT 59404

NEW HAMPSHIRE

New Hampshire Arms Collectors, Inc.
Frank H. Galeucia, Rte. 28, Box 44, Windham, NH 03087

NEW JERSEY

Englishtown Benchrest Shooters Assn.
Tony Hidalgo, 6 Capp St., Carteret, NJ 07008
Experimental Ballistics Associates
Ed Yard, 110 Kensington, Trenton, NJ 08618
Jersey Shore Antique Arms Collectors
Joe Sisia, P.O. Box 100, Bayville, NJ 08721
New Jersey Arms Collectors Club, Inc.
Angus Laidlaw, 230 Valley Rd., Montclair, NJ 07042

NEW YORK

Empire State Arms Coll. Assn.
P.O. Box 2328, Rochester, NY 14623
Hudson-Mohawk Arms Collectors Assn., Inc.
Bennie S. Pisarz, 6 Lamberson St., Dolgeville, NY 13329
Iroquois Arms Collectors Assn.
Kenneth Keller, club secy., (Susan Keller, show secy.) 214 - 70th St., Niagara Falls, NY 14304
Mid-State Arms Coll. & Shooters Club
Jack Ackerman, 24 S. Mountain Terr., Binghamton, NY 13903

NORTH CAROLINA

Carolina Gun Collectors Assn.
Jerry Ledford, 3231 - 7th St. Dr. NE, Hickory, NC 28601

OHIO

Central Ohio Gun and Indian Relic Coll. Assn.
Coyt Stookey, 134 E. Ohio Ave., Washington C.H., OH 43160
Ohio Gun Collectors, Assn., Inc.
Drawer 24F, Cincinnati, OH 45224
The Stark Gun Collectors, Inc.
William I. Gann, 5666 Waynesburg Dr., Waynesburg, OH 44688

OKLAHOMA

Indian Territory Gun Collectors Assn.
P.O. Box 4491, Tulsa, OK 74159

OREGON

Oregon Cartridge Coll. Assn.
Richard D. King, 3228 N.W. 60th, Corvallis, OR 97330
Oregon Arms Coll. Assn., Inc.
Ted Dowd, P.O. Box 25103, Portland, OR 97225

PENNSYLVANIA

Presque Isle Gun Coll. Assn.
James Welch, 156 E. 37 St., Erie, PA 16504

SOUTH CAROLINA

Belton Gun Club, Inc.
J.K. Phillips, Route 1, Belton, SC 29627

SOUTH DAKOTA

Dakota Territory Gun Coll. Assn., Inc.
Curt Carter, Castlewood, SD 57223

TENNESSEE

Memphis Antique Weapons Assn.
Jan Clement, 1886 Lyndale #1, Memphis TN 38107
Smoky Mountain Gun Coll. Assn., Inc.
Hugh W. Yarbro, P.O. Box 286, Knoxville, TN 37901
Tennessee Gun Collectors Assn., Inc.
M.H. Parks, 3556 Pleasant Valley Rd., Nashville, TN 37204

TEXAS

Houston Gun Collectors Assn., Inc.
P.O. Box 741429, Houston, TX 77274
Texas State Rifle Assn.
P.O. Drawer 810809, Dallas, TX 75381-0809

UTAH

Utah Gun Collectors Assn.
Nick Davis, 5676 So. Meadow Lane #4, Ogden, UT 84403

WASHINGTON

Washington Arms Collectors, Inc.
J. Dennis Cook, P.O. Box 7335, Tacoma, WA 98407

WISCONSIN

Great Lakes Arms Coll. Assn., Inc.
Edward C. Warnke, 2913 Woodridge Lane, Waukesha, WI 53186
Wisconsin Gun Collectors Assn., Inc.
Lulita Zellmer, P.O. Box 181, Sussex, WI 53089

WYOMING

Wyoming Gun Collectors
Bob Funk, Box 1805, Riverton, WY 82501

NATIONAL ORGANIZATIONS

Amateur Trapshooting Assn.
P.O. Box 458, Vandalia, OH 45377
American Association of Shotgunning
P.O. Box 3351, Reno, NV 89505
American Defense Preparedness Assn.
Rosslyn Center, Suite 900, 1700 N. Moore St., Arlington, VA 22209
American Police Pistol & Rifle Assn.
1100 N.E. 125th St., No. Miami, FL 33161
American Single Shot Rifle Assn.
L.B. Thompson, 987 Jefferson Ave., Salem, OH 44460
American Society of Arms Collectors, Inc.
Robt. F. Rubendunst, 6550 Baywood Lane, Cincinnati, OH 45224
Armor & Arms Club
J.K. Watson, Jr., c/o Lord, Day & Lord, 25 Broadway, New York, NY 10004
Association of Firearm and Toolmark Examiners
Eugenia A. Bell, Secy., 7857 Esterel Dr., LaJolla, CA 92037
Boone & Crockett Club
205 South Patrick, Alexandria, VA 22314
Cast Bullet Assn., Inc.
Ralland J. Fortier, 14193 Van Doren Rd., Manassas, VA 22111
Citizens Committee for the Right to Keep and Bear Arms
Natl. Hq.: 12500 N.E. Tenth Pl., Bellevue, WA

98005
Deer Unlimited of America, Inc.
P.O. Box 509, Clemson, SC 29631
Ducks Unlimited, Inc.
One Waterfowl Way, Long Grove, IL 60047
Experimental Ballistics Associates
Ed Yard, 110 Kensington, Trenton, NJ 08618
Handgun Hunters International
J. D. Jones, Dir., P. O. Box 357 MAG, Bloomingdale, OH 43910
International Benchrest Shooters
Evelyn Richards, 411 N. Wilbur Ave. Sayre, PA 18840
International Cartridge Coll. Assn., Inc.
Victor v. B. Engel, 1211 Walnut St., Williamsport, PA 17701
International Handgun Metallic Silhouette Assoc.
Box 1609, Idaho Falls, ID 83401
International Military Arms Society
David M. Armstrong, P.O. Box 122, Williamstown, WV 26187
International Quail Foundation
P.O. Box 550, Edgefield, SC 29824-0550
Marlin Firearms Coll. Assn., Inc.
Dick Paterson, Secy., 407 Lincoln Bldg., 44 Main St., Champaign, IL 61820
Miniature Arms Collectors/Makers Society Ltd.
Joseph J. Macewicz, 104 White Sand Lane, Racine, WI 53402
National Assn. of Federally Licd. Firearms Dealers
Andrew Molchan, 2801 E. Oakland Park Blvd., Ft. Lauderdale, Fl 33306
National Automatic Pistol Collectors Assn.
Tom Knox, P.O. Box 15738, Tower Grove Station, St. Louis, MO 63163
National Bench Rest Shooters Assn., Inc.
Stella Buchtel, 5735 Sherwood Forest Dr., Akron, OH 44319
National Deer Hunter Assn.
1415 Fifth St. So., Hopkins, MN 55343
National Muzzle Loading Rifle Assn.
Box 67, Friendship, IN 47021
National Police Officers Assn. of America
Frank J. Schira, Ex. Dir., 609 West Main St., Louisville, KY 40202
National Reloading Mfrs. Assn., Inc.
4905 S.W. Griffith Dr., Suite 101, Beaverton, OR 97005
National Rifle Assn. of America
1600 Rhode Island Ave., N.W., Washington, DC 20036
National Shooting Sports Fdtn., Inc.
Arnold H. Rohlfing, Exec. Director, 1075 Post Rd., Riverside, Ct 06878
National Skeet Shooting Assn.
Ann Myers, Exec. Director, P.O. Box 28188, San Antonio, TX 78228
National Varmint Hunters Assn. (NVHA)
P.O. Box 17962, San Antonio, TX 78217
National Wild Turkey Federation, Inc.
P.O. Box 530, Edgefield, SC 29824
North American Hunting Club
7901 Flying Cloud Dr., P.O. Box 35557, Minneapolis, MN 55435
North-South Skirmish Assn., Inc.
T.E. Johnson, Jr., 9700 Royerton Dr., Richmond, VA 23228
Remington Society of America
Fritz Baehr, 3125 Fremont Ave., Boulder, CO 80302
Ruger Collector's Assn., Inc.
Nancy J. Padua, P.O. Box 211, Trumbull, CT 06611
SAAMI, Sporting Arms and Ammunition Manufacturers' Institute, Inc.
P.O. Box 218, Wallingford, CT 06492
Safari Club International
Holt Bodinson, 5151 E. Broadway, Suite 1680, Tucson, AZ 85711
Sako Collectors Assn., Inc.
Mims C. Reed, Pres., 313 Cooper Dr., Hurst, TX 76053
Second Amendment Foundation
James Madison Building, 12500 N.E. 10th Pl., Bellevue, WA 98005
Southern California Schuetzen Society
Thomas Trevor, 13621 Sherman Way, Van Nuys, CA 91405
U.S. Revolver Assn.
Chick Shuter, 96 West Union St., Ashland, MA 01721
Winchester Arms Collectors Assoc.
Lewis E. Yearout, 308 Riverview Dr., E., Great Falls, MT 59404
World Fast Draw Assn.
Bob Arganbright, 4704 Upshaw, Northwoods, MO 63121

AUSTRALIA

Sporting Shooters' Assn. of Australia Inc.
Mr. K. MacLaine, P.O. Box 210, Belgrave, Vict. 3160, Australia

CANADA

Alberta

Canadian Historical Arms Society
P.O. Box 901, Edmonton, Alb., Canada T5J 2L8

BRITISH COLUMBIA

B.C. Historical Arms Collectors
Ron Tyson, Box 80583, Burnaby, B.C. Canada V5H 3X9

NEW BRUNSWICK

Canadian Black Powder Federation
Mrs. Janet McConnell, P.O. Box 2876, Postal Sta. "A", Moncton, N.B. E1C 8T8, Can.

ONTARIO

Ajax Antique Arms Assn.
Monica A. Wright, P.O. Box 145, Millgrove, Ont., L0R 1V0, Canada
Glengarry Antique Arms - Tri-County
P.O. Box 122, R.R. #1, North Lancaster, Ont., K0C 1Z0, Canada
National Firearms Assn.
P.O. Box 4610 Sta. F, Ottawa, Ont., K1S 5H8 Canada
The Ontario Handgun Assn.
1711 McCowan Rd., Suite 205, Scarborough, Ont., M1S 2Y3, Canada
Oshawa Antique Gun Coll. Inc.
Monica A. Wright, P.O. Box 145, Millgrove, Ont., L0R 1V0, Canada

EUROPE

ENGLAND

Arms and Armour Society of London
A.R.E. North. Dept. of Metalwork, Victoria & Albert Museum, South Kensington, London SW7 2RL
British Cartridge Collectors Club
Peter F. McGowan, 15 Fuller St., Ruddington, Nottingham
Historical Breechloading Smallarms Assn.
D.J. Penn, M.A., Imperial War Museum, Lambeth Rd., London SE1 6HZ, England. Journal and newsletter are $8 a yr. seamail; surcharge for airmail
National Rifle Assn. (British)
Bisley Camp, Brookwood, Woking, Surrey, GU24 OPB, England

FRANCE

Syndicat National de l'Arquebuserie du Commerce de l'Arme Historique
B.P. No 3, 78110 Le Vesient, France

GERMANY (WEST)

Deutscher Schützenbund
Lahnstrasse, 6200 Wiesbaden-Klarenthal, West Germany

NEW ZEALAND

New Zealand Deerstalkers Assn.
Mr. Shelby Grant, P.O. Box 6514, Wellington, New Zealand

SOUTH AFRICA

Historical Firearms Soc. of South Africa
P.O. Box 145, 7725 Newlands, Republic of South Africa
South African Reloaders Assn.
Box 27128, Sunnyside, Pretoria 0132, South Africa

Directory of the Arms Trade

AMMUNITION (Commercial)

BBM Corp., 221 Interstate Dr., West Springfield, MA 01089/413-737-3118 (45 ACP shotshell)

Bingham Ltd., 1775-C Wilwat Dr., Norcross, GA 30093

Cascade Cartridge Inc., (See Omark)

Dynamit Nobel of America, Inc., 105 Stonehurst Court, Northvale, NJ 07647/201-767-1660(RWS)

Eley-Kynoch, ICI-America, Wilmington, DE 19897/302-575-3000

Estate Cartridge Inc., P.O. Box 3702, Conroe, TX 77305 (shotshell)

Federal Cartridge Co., 2700 Foshay Tower, Minneapolis, MN 55402/612-333-8255

Frontier Cartridge Division-Hornady Mfg. Co., Box 1848, Grand Island, NE 68801/308-382-1390

Hansen Cartridge Co., 246 Old Post Rd., Southport, CT 06490/203-259-5454

ICI-America, Wilmington, DE 19897/302-575-3000(Eley-Kynoch)

Midway Arms, Inc., 7450 Old Hwy. 40 West, Columbia, MO 65201/314-445-9521

Omark Industries, Box 856, Lewiston, ID 83501

Precision Prods. of Wash., Inc., N. 311 Walnut Rd., Spokane, WA 99206/509-928-0604 (Exammo)

RWS, (See Dynamit Nobel of America)

Remington Arms Co., 939 Barnum Ave., P. O. Box #1939, Bridgeport, CT 06601

Service Armament, 689 Bergen Blvd., Ridgefield, NJ 07657

Super Vel, FPC, Inc., Hamilton Rd., Rt. 2, P. O. Box 1398, Fond du Lac, WI 54935/414-921-2652

Ten-X Mfg., 2410 East Foxfarm Rd., Cheynne, WY 82001

United States Ammunition Co. (USAC), 1476A Thorne Rd., Tacoma, WA 98421/206-627-8700

Weatherby's, 2781 E. Firestone Blvd., South Gate, CA 90280

Winchester, Shamrock St., East Alton, IL 62024

AMMUNITION (Custom)

Beal's Bullets, 170 W. Marshall Rd., Lansdowne, PA 19050/215-259-1200 (Auto Mag Specialists)

Bell's Gun & Sport Shop, 3309-19 Mannheim Rd., Franklin Park, IL 60131

Brass Extrusion Labs. Ltd., 800 W. Maple Lane, Bensenville, IL 60106

C.W. Cartridge Co., 71 Hackensack St., Wood-Ridge, NJ 07075 (201-438-5111)

Russell Campbell Custom Loaded Ammo, 219 Leisure Dr., San Antonio, TX 78201/512-735-1183

Colorado Sutler Ammunition, 7538 E. Fremont Dr., Englewood, CO 80112/303-771-3363

Crown City Arms, P.O. Box 1126, Cortland, NY 13045/607-753-8238

Cumberland Arms Rt. 1, Shafer Rd., Blantons Chapel, Manchester, TN 37355

Denali Bullet Co., P.O. Box 82217, Fairbanks, AK 99701/907-479-8227

Eagle Cap Custom Bullets, P.O. Box 659, Enterprise, OR 97828/503-426-4282

E.W. Ellis Sport Shop, RFD 1, Box 315, Corinth, NY 12822

Ellwood Epps Northern Ltd., 210 Worthington St. W., North Bay, Ont. PIB 3B4, Canada

Estate Cartridge Inc., P.O. Box 3702, Conroe, TX 77305/409-539-9144 (shotshell)

Jack First Distributors, Inc., 44633 Sierra Hwy., Lancaster, CA 93534/805-945-6981

Ramon B. Gonzalez, P.O. Box 370, Monticello, NY 12701/914-794-4515

R.H. Keeler, 817 "N" St., Port Angeles, WA 98362/206-457-4702

KTW Inc., 710 Foster Park Rd., Lorain, OH 44053 216/233-6919 (bullets)

Dean Lincoln, Custom Tackle & Ammo, P.O. Box 1886, Farmington, NM 87401/505-632-3539

Lindsley Arms Cartridge Co., Inc., P.O. Box 5738, Lake Worth, FL 33466/305-968-1678 (inq. S.A.S.E.)

Lomont Precision Bullets, 4236 West 700 South, Poneto, IN 46781/219-694-6792 (custom cast bullets only)

McConnellstown Reloading & Cast Bullets, Inc., R.D. 3, Box 40, Huntingdon, PA 16652/814-627-5402

Numrich Arms Corp., 203 Broadway, W. Hurley, NY 12491

Olsen Development Lab., 307 Conestoga Way #37, Edgeville, PA 19403/215-631-1716 (Invicta)

Pearl Armory, Revenden Springs, AR 72460

Robert Pomeroy, Morison Ave., Corinth, ME 04427/207-285-7721 (custom shells)

Precision Ammo Co., P.O. Box 63, Garnerville, NY 10923/914-947-2720

Precision Prods. of Wash., Inc., N. 311 Walnut Rd., Spokane, WA 99206/509-928-0604 (Exammo)

Anthony F. Sailer-Ammunition, 707 W. Third St., P. O. Box L, Owen, WI 54460/715-229-2516

Sanders Cust. Gun Serv., 2358 Tyler Lane, Louisville, KY 40205

Senica Run, Inc., P.O. Box 3032, Greeley, CO 80633

George W. Spence, 115 Locust St., Steele, MO 63877/314-695-4926 (boxer-primed cartridges)

The 3-D Company, Box J, Main St., Doniphan, NE 68832/402-845-2285 (re-loaded police ammo)

Zero Ammunition Co., Inc., P.O. Box 1188, Cullman, AL 35055/205-739-1606

AMMUNITION (Foreign)

Beeman Inc., 47-GDD Paul Drive, San Rafael, CA 94903/415-472-7121

Dynamit Nobel of America, Inc., 105 Stonehurst Court, Northvale, NJ 07647/210-767-1660(RWS, Geco, Rottweil)

Fiocchi of America, Inc., 1308 Chase, Springfield, MO 65803/417-864-6970

Hansen Cartridge Co., 246 Old Post Rd., Southport, CT 06490/203-259-5454

Norma, (See Outdoor Sports Headquarters, Inc.)

Hirtenberger Patronen-, Zündhütchen- & Metallwarenfabrik, A.G., Leobersdorfer Str. 33, A2552 Hirtenberg, Austria

Paul Jaeger, Inc., 211 Leedom St., Jenkintown, PA 19046/215-884-6920 (RWS centerfire ammo)

Kendall International Arms, Inc., 501 East North, Carlisle, KY 40311/606-289-7336 (Lapua)

Lapua (See Kendall International, Inc.)

Outdoor Sports HQ, Inc., 967 Watertower Lane, Dayton, OH 45449/513-865-5855 (Norma)

PMC (See Patton and Morgan Corp.)

Patton and Morgan Corp., 5900 Wilshire Blvd., Suite 1400, Los Angeles, CA 90036/213-938-0143 (PMC ammo)

RWS (Rheinische-Westfälische Sprengstoff) [See Dynamit Nobel of America; Paul Jaeger, Inc.]

AMMUNITION COMPONENTS—BULLETS, POWDER, PRIMERS

Accurate Arms Co., Inc., (Propellents Div.), Rt. 1, Box 167, McEwen, TN, 37101/615-729-5301 (powders)

Alberts Corp., 519 E. 19th St., Paterson, NJ 07514/201-684-7583 (swaged bullets)

Ammo-O-Mart Ltd., P.O. Box 125, Hawkesbury, Ont., Canada K6A 2R8/613-632-9300 (Nobel powder)

Austin Powder Co. (See Red Diamond Dist. Co.)

Ballistic Prods., Inc., Box 488, 2105 Shaughnessy Circle, Long Lake, MN 55356

Ballistic Research Industries (BRI), 6000 B Soquel Ave., Santa Cruz, CA 95062/408-476-7981 (12-ga. Sabo shotgun slug)

Barnes Bullets, P.O. Box 215, American Fork, UT 84003/801-756-4222

Bell's Gun & Sport Shop, 3309-19 Mannheim Rd., Franklin Pk., IL 60131

Bitterroot Bullet Co., Box 412, Lewiston, ID 83501/208-743-5635 (Coin or stamps) f.50¢ U.S.; 75¢ Can. & Mex.; intl. $3.00 and #10 SASE for lit.

B.E.L.L., Brass Extrusion Laboratories, Ltd., 800 W. Maple Lane, Bensenville, IL 60106

Milton Brynin, 214 E. Third St., Mount Vernon, NY 10550/914-664-1311 (cast bull.)

CCI, (See: Omark Industries)

CheVron Bullets, R.R. 1, Ottawa, IL 61350/815-433-2471

Kenneth E. Clark, 18738 Highway 99, Madera, CA 93637/209-674-6016 (Bullets)

Denali Bullet Co., P.O. Box 82217, Fairbanks, AK 99701/907-479-8227 (bullets)

Division Lead, 7742 W. 61 Pl., Summit, IL 60502

DuPont, Explosives Dept., Wilmington, DE 19898

Dynamit Nobel of America, Inc., 105 Stonehurst Court, Northvale, NJ 07647/201-767-1660 (RWS percussion caps)

Eagle Cap Custom Bullets, P.O. Box 659, Enterprise, OR 97828/503-426-4282

Elk Mountain Shooters Supply Inc., 1719 Marie, Pasco, WA 99301 (Alaskan bullets)

Farmer Bros., 1102 N. Washington, Eldora, IA 50627/515-858-3651 (Lage wad)

Federal Cartridge Co., 2700 Foshay Tower, Minneapolis, MN 55402/612-333-8255 (nickel cases)

Forty Five Ranch Enterprises, 119 S. Main, Miami, OK 74354/918-542-9307

Glaser Safety Slug, 711 Somerset Lane, P.O. Box 8223, Forest City, CA 94404

Godfrey Reloading Supply, Hi-Way 67-111, Brighton, IL 62012 (cast bullets)

Lynn Godfrey, (See: Elk Mtn. Shooters Supply)

GOEX, Inc., Belin Plant, Moosic, PA 18507/717-457-6724 (black powder)

Green Bay Bullets, P.O. Box 10446, 1486 Servais St., Green Bay, WI 54307-54304/414-469-2992 (cast lead bullets)

GTM Co., George T. Mahaney, 15915B E. Main St., La Puente, CA 91744 (all brass shotshells)

Hardin Specialty Distr., P. O. Box 338, Radcliff, KY 40160/502-351-6649 (empty, primed cases)

Hepplers Gun Shop, 6000 B Soquel Ave., Santa Cruz, CA 95062/408-475-1235 (BRI 12-ga. slug)

Hercules Inc., Hercules Plaza, Wilmington, DE 19894 (smokeless powder)

Hodgdon Powder Co. Inc., P.O. Box 2905, Shawnee Mission, KS 66201/913-362-5410

Hornady Mfg. Co., Box 1848, Grand Island, NE 68802/308-382-1390

Kendall International Arms, Inc., 501 East North, Carlisle, KY 40311/606-289-7336 (Lapua bull.)

NORMA (See Outdoor Sports Headquarters, Inc.)

N.E. House Co., 195 West High St., E. Hampton, CT 06424/203-267-2133 (zinc bases in 30, 38, 44 and 45-cal. only)

Jaro Manuf., P.O. Box 6125, 206 E. Shaw, Pasadena, TX 77506/713-472-0471 (bullets)

L.L.F. Die Shop, 1281 Highway 99 North, Eugene, OR 97402/503-688-5753

Lage Uniwad Co., 1102 Washington St., Eldora, IA 50627/515-858-3651

Ljutic Ind., Inc., Box 2117, Yakima, WA 98902 (Mono-wads)

Lomont Precision Bullets, 4236 West 700 South, Poneto, IN 46781/219-694-6792 (custom cast bullets)

Lyman Products Corp., Rte. 147, Middlefield, CT 06455

Michael's Antiques, Box 233, Copiague, L.I., NY 11726 (Balle Blondeau)

Miller Trading Co., 20 S. Front St., Wilmington, NC 28401/919-762-7107 (bullets)

Nosler Bullets, P.O. Box 688, Beaverton, OR 97005

Ohio Shooters Supply, 7532 Tyler Blvd., Mentor, OH 44060 (cast bullets)

Omark Industries, Box 856, Lewiston, ID 83501/208-746-2351

The Oster Group, 50 Sims Ave., Providence, RI 02909 (alloys f. casting bull.)

Outdoor Sports Headquarters, Inc., 967 Watertower Lane, Dayton, OH 45449/513-865-5855 (Norma powder)

Pyrodex, See: Hodgdon Powder Co., Inc. (black powder substitute)

Robert Pomeroy, Morison Ave., East Corinth, ME 04427/207-285-7721 (empty cases)

Red Diamond Distributing Co., 1304 Snowdon Dr., Knoxville, TN 37912 (black powder)

Remington-Peters, 939 Barnum Ave., P.O. Box #1939, Bridgeport, CT 06601

S&S Precision Bullets, 22965 La Cadena, Laguna Hills, CA 92653/714-768-6836 (linotype cast bull.)

Sierra Bullets Inc., 10532 So. Painter Ave., Santa Fe Springs, CA 90670

Speer Products, Box 856, Lewiston, ID 83501

C.H. Stocking, Rte. 3, Box 195, Hutchinson, MN 55350 (17 cal. bullet jackets)

Supreme Products Co., 1830 S. California Ave., Monrovia, CA 91016/800-423-7159/818-357-5395 (rubber bullets)

Taracorp Industries, 16th & Cleveland Blvd., Granite City, IL 62040/618-451-4524 (Lawrence Brand lead shot)

Taylor Bullets, P.O. Box 21254, San Antonio, TX 78221 (cast)

Vitt & Boos, 2178 Nichols Ave., Stratford, CT 06497/203-375-6859 (Aerodynamic shotgun slug, 12-ga. only)

Winchester, Shamrock St., East Alton, IL 62024

Worthy Products, Inc., Box 88 Main St., Chippewa Bay, NY 13623/315-324-5450 (slug loads)

Zero Bullet Co. Inc., P.O. Box 1188, Cullman, AL 35055/205-739-1606

ANTIQUE ARMS DEALERS

Beeman Inc., 47 Paul Dr., San Rafael, CA 94903/415-472-7121 (airguns only)

Wm. Boggs, 1243 Grandview Ave., Columbus, OH 43212

Dave Chicoine, d/b/a Liberty A.S.P., 19 Key St., Eastport, ME 04631/207-853-2327

Ed's Gun House, Rte. 1, Minnesota City, MN 55959/507-689-2925

Ellwood Epps Northern Ltd., 210 Worthington St. W., North Bay, Ont. P1B 3B4 Canada

William Fagan, 126 Belleview, Mount Clemens, MI 48043/313-465-4637

Jack First Distributors, Inc., 44633 Sierra Hwy., Lancaster, CA 93534/805-945-6981

N. Flayderman & Co., Squash Hollow, New Milford, CT 06776/203-354-5567

Fulmer's Antique Firearms, Chet Fulmer, P.O. Box 792, Detroit Lakes, MN 56501/218-847-7712

Garcia National Gun Traders, Inc., 225 S.W. 22nd Ave., Miami, FL 33135

Herb Glass, Bullville, NY 10915/914-361-3021

James Goergen, Rte. 2, Box 182BB, Austin, MN 55912/507-433-9280

Griffin's Guns & Antiques, R.R. 4, Peterborough, Ont., Canada K9J 6X5/705-748-3220

The Gun Shop, 6497 Pearl Rd., Parma Heights (Cleveland), OH 44130/216-884-7476

Hansen & Company, 244 Old Post Rd., Southport, CT 06490/203-259-7337

Holbrook Antique Militaria, 4050 S.W. 98th Ave., Miami, FL 33165/305-223-6500

Jackson Arms, 6209 Hillcrest Ave., Dallas, TX 75205/214-521-9929

Lever Arms Serv. Ltd., 572 Howe St., Vancouver, B.C., Canada V6C 2E3/604-685-6913

Lone Pine Trading Post, Jct. Highways 61 and 248, Minnesota City, MN 55959/507-689-2922

Charles W. Moore, R.D. #1, Box 276, Schenevus, NY 12155/607-278-5721

Museum of Historical Arms, 1038 Alton Rd., Miami Beach, FL 33139/305-672-7480 (ctlg $5)

New Orleans Arms Co., 5001 Treasure St., New Orleans, LA 70186/504-944-3371

O.K. Hardware, Westgate Shopping Center, Great Falls, MT 59404

Old Western Scrounger, 3509 Carlson Blvd., El Cerrito, CA 94530/415-527-3872 (write for list; $2)

Pioneer Guns, 5228 Montgomery, (Cincinnati) Norwood, OH 45212/513-631-4871

Pony Express Sport Shop, Inc., 17460 Ventura Blvd., Encino, CA 91316/213-788-0123

Martin B. Retting, Inc., 11029 Washington, Culver City, CA 90230/213-837-6111

Ridge Guncraft, Inc., 125 E. Tyrone Rd., Oak Ridge, TN 37830/615-483-4024

San Francisco Gun Exch., 124 Second St., San Francisco, CA 94105/415-982-6097

Santa Ana Gunroom, P.O. Box 1777, Santa Ana, CA 92701/714-541-3035

Ward & Van Valkenburg, 114-32nd Ave. N., Fargo, ND 58102

M.C. Wiest, 125 E. Tyrone Rd., Oak Ridge, TN 37830/615-483-4024

J. David Yale, Ltd., 2618 Conowingo Rd., Bel Air, MD 21014/301-838-9479

Lewis Yearout, 308 Riverview Dr. E., Great Falls, MT 59404

BOOKS (ARMS), Publishers and Dealers

Armory Publications, P.O. Box 44372, Tacoma, WA 98444/206-531-4632

Arms & Armour Press, 2-6 Hampstead High Street, London NW3 1QQ, England

Beeman Inc., 47 Paul Dr., San Rafael, CA 94903/415-472-7121 (airguns)

Blacksmith Corp., P.O. Box 424, Southport, CT 06490/203-367-4041

Blacktail Mountain Books, 42 First Ave. West, Kalispell, MT 59901/406-257-5573

DBI Books, Inc., One Northfield Plaza, Northfield, IL 60093/312-441-7010

Dove Press, P.O. Box 3882, Enid, OK 73702/405-234-4347

Fortress Publications Inc., P.O. Box 241, Stoney Creek, Ont. L8G 3X9, Canada/416-662-3505

Guncraft Books, Div. of Ridge Guncraft, Inc., 125 E. Tyrone Rd., Oak Ridge, TN 37830/615-483-4024

Gunnerman Books, P.O. Box 4292, Auburn Heights, MI 48057/313-879-2779

Handgun Press, 5832 S. Green, Chicago, IL 60621

Jackson Arms, 6209 Hillcrest Ave., Dallas, TX 75205

Long Survival Publications, 718 Lincoln Ave., P.O. Box 163, Wamego, KS 66547/913-456-7384

Lyman, Route 147, Middlefield, CT 06455

Paladin Press, Box 1307, Boulder, CO 80306

Personal Firearms Record Book Co., P.O. Box 2800, Santa Fe, NM 87501/505-983-2381

Petersen Publishing Co., 84990 Sunset Blvd., Los Angeles, CA 99069

Gerald Pettinger Arms Books, Route 2, Russell, IA 50238/515-535-2239

Ray Riling Arms Books Co., 114 Greenwood Ave., Box 135, Wyncote, PA 19095/215-438-2456

Rutgers Book Center, Mark Aziz, 127 Raritan Ave., Highland Park, NJ 08904/201-545-4344

Stackpole Books, Cameron & Kelker Sts., Telegraph Press Bldg., Harrisburg, PA 17105

Stoeger Publishing Co., 55 Ruta Court, South Hackensack, NJ 07606

Ken Trotman, 2-6 Hampstead High St., London, NW3, 1QQ, England

Winchester Press, 220 Old New Brunswick Rd., Piscataway, NJ 08854/201-981-0820

Wolfe Publishing Co., Inc., Box 30-30, Prescott, AZ 86302/602-445-7810

BULLET & CASE LUBRICANTS

Chopie Mfg. Inc., 700 Copeland Ave., La Crosse, WI 54601/608-784-0926 (Black-Solve)

Clenzoil Corp., P.O. Box 1226, Sta. C, Canton, OH 44708/216-833-9758

Cooper-Woodward, Box 972, Riverside, CA 92502/714-688-2127 (Perfect Lube)

Corbin Mfg. & Supply Inc., P.O. Box 2659, White City, OR 97503/503-826-5211

Green Bay Bullets, 1486 Servais St., Green Bay, WI 54304/414-469-2992 (EZE-Size case lube)

Gussert Bullet & Cartridge Co., Inc., P.O. Box 3945, Green Bay, WI 54303 (Super Lube)

Hodgdon Powder Co., Inc., P.O. Box 2905, Shawnee Mission, KS 66201/913-362-5410

Javelina Products, Box 337, San Bernardino, CA 92402/714-882-5847 (Alox beeswax)

Jet-Aer Corp., 100 Sixth Ave., Paterson, NJ 07524

LeClear Industries, 1126 Donald Ave., Royal Oak, MI 48073/313-588-1025

Lyman Products Corp., Rte. 147, Middlefield, CT. 06455 (Size-Ezy)

Marmel Prods., P.O. Box 97, Utica, MI 48087/313-731-8029 (Marvellube, Marvelux)

Micro Ammunition Co., P.O. Box 117, Mesilla Park, NM 88047/505-522-2674 (Micro-Lube)

Mirror Lube, American Speclty. Lubricants, P.O. Box 693, San Juan Capistrano, CA 92693/714-496-1098

M&N Bullet Lube, P.O. Box 495, 151 N.E. Jefferson St., Madras, OR 97741/503-475-2992

Northeast Industrial, Inc., P.O. Box 249, 405 N. Canyon Blvd., Canyon City, OR 97820/503-575-2513 (Ten X-Lube; NEI mold prep)

Pacific Tool Co., P.O. Box 2048, Ordnance Plant Rd., Grand Island, NE 68801/308-384-2308

RCBS, Inc., Box 1919, Oroville, CA 95965

SAECO Rel, 2207 Border Ave., Torrance, CA 90501/213-320-6973

Shooters Accessory Supply (SAS) (See Corbin Mfg. & Supply)

Tamarack Prods., Inc., P.O. Box 224, Barrington, IL 60010/312-526-9333 (Bullet lube)

Testing Systems, American Gas & Chemical Co., Ltd., 220 Pegasus Ave., Northvale, NJ 07647/201-767-7300

BULLET SWAGE DIES AND TOOLS

C-H Tool & Die Corp., 106 N. Harding St., Owen, WI 54460/715-229-2146

Lester Coats, 416 Simpson St., North Bend, OR 97459/503-756-6995 (lead wire core cutter)

Corbin Mfg. & Supply Inc., P.O. Box 2659, White City, OR 97503/503-826-5211

Hollywood, Whitney Sales Inc., P.O. Box 875, Reseda, CA 91335

Huntington Die Specialties, P.O. Box 991, Oroville, CA 95965/916-534-1210

Independent Machine & Gun Shop, 1416 N. Hayes, Pocatello, ID 83201/208-232-1264 (TNT bullet dies)

L.L.F. Die Shop, 1281 Highway 99 North, Eugene, OR 97402/503-688-5753

Rorschach Precision Products, P.O. Box 1613, Irving, TX 75060/214-254-2762

SAS Dies, (See Corbin Mfg. & Supply)

Sport Flite Mfg., Inc., 2520 Industrial Row, Troy, MI 48084/313-280-0648

TNT (See Ind. Mach. & Gun Shop)

CARTRIDGES FOR COLLECTORS

AD Hominem, R.R. 3, Orillia, Ont., Canada L3V 6H3/705-689-5303

Cameron's, 16690 W. 11th Ave., Golden CO 80401/303-279-7365

Centrefire Sports Dunedin, P.O. Box 1293, 41 Dowling St., Dunedin, New Zealand

Chas. E. Duffy, Williams Lane, West Hurley, NY 12419

Tom M. Dunn, 1342 So. Poplar, Casper, WY 82601/307-237-3207

Ellwood Epps (Orillia) Ltd., Hwy. 11 North, Orillia, Ont. L3V 6H3, Canada/705-689-5333

Jack First Distributors, Inc., 44633 Sierra Hwy., Lancaster, CA 93534/805-945-6981

"Gramps" Antique Cartridges, Box 341, Washago, Ont., Canada L0K 2B0

Hansen Cartridge Co., 246 Old Post Rd., Southport, CT 06490/203-259-5454

Idaho Ammunition Service, 410 21st Ave., Lewiston, ID 83501

San Francisco Gun Exchange, 124 Second St., San Francisco, CA 94105/415-982-6097

Ernest Tichy, 365 So. Moore, Lakewood, CO 80226

James C. Tillinghast, Box 405, Hancock, NH 03449/603-525-6615 (list $1)

Lewis Yearout, 308 Riverview Dr. E., Great Falls, MT 59404

CASES, CABINETS AND RACKS—GUN

Alco Carrying Cases, 601 W. 26th St., New York, NY 10001/212-675-5820 (aluminum)

Bob Allen Sportswear, 214 S.W. Jackson, Des Moines, IA 50315/515-283-1988/800-247-8048 (carrying)

Allen Co., Inc., 640 Compton St., Broomfield, CO 80020/303-469-1857

Art Jewel Ltd., 421A Irmen Dr., Addison, IL 60101/312-628-6220

Assault Systems of St. Louis, 869 Horan, St. Louis, MO 63026/314-343-3575 (canvas carrying case)

Beeman Precision Arms, Inc., 47-GDD Paul Dr., San Rafael, CA 94903/415-472-7121

Morton Booth Co., Box 123, Joplin, MO 64801

Boyt Co., Div. of Welsh Sportg. Gds., Box 1108, Iowa Falls, IA 50126

Brenik, Inc., 925 W. Chicago Ave., Chicago, IL 60622

Browning, Rt. 4, Box 624-B, Arnold, MO 63010

Cap-Lex Gun Cases, Capitol Plastics of Ohio, Inc., 333 Van Camp Rd., Bowling Green, OH 43402

Challanger Mfg. Corp., 30 South St., Mt. Vernon, NY 10550/914-664-7134

Dara-Nes Inc., see: Nesci

Dart Mfg. Co., 4012 Bronze Way, Dallas, TX 75237/214-333-4221

Detroit-Armor Corp., 2233 No. Palmer Dr., Schaumburg, IL 60195/312-397-4070 (Saf-Gard steel gun safe)

Doskocil Mfg. Co., Inc., P.O. Box 1246, Arlington, TX 75010/817-467-5116 (Gun Guard carrying)

East-Tenn Mills, Inc., 3112 Industrial Dr., Skyline Industrial Park, Johnson City, TN 37601/615-928-7186 (gun socks)

Ellwood Epps (Orillia) Ltd., R.R. 3, Hwy, 11 North, Orillia, Ont. L3V 6H3, Canada/705-689-5333 (custom gun cases)

Norbert Ertel, P.O. Box 1150, Des Plaines, IL 60018/312-825-2315 (cust. gun cases)

Flambeau Plastics Corp., 801 Lynn, Baraboo, WI 53913

Fort Knox Security Products, 1051 N. Industrial Park Rd., Orem, UT 84057/801-224-7233 (safes)

Gun-Ho Case Mfg. Co., 110 East 10th St., St. Paul, MN 55101

Hansen Cartridge Co., 246 Old Post Rd., Southport, CT 06490/203-259-5454

Harbor House Gun Cabinets, 12508 Center St., South Gate, CA 90280

Marvin Huey Gun Cases, Box 98, Reed's Spring, MO 65737/417-538-4233 (handbuilt leather cases)

Jumbo Sports Prods., P.O. Box 280-Airport Rd., Frederick, MD 21701

Kalispel Metal Prods. (KMP), P.O. Box 267, Cusick, WA 99119/509-445-1121 (aluminum boxes)

Kane Products Inc., 5572 Brecksville Rd., Cleveland, OH 44131/216-524-9962 (GunChaps)

Kolpin Mfg., Inc., Box 231, Berlin, WI 54923/414-361-0400

Marble Arms Corp., 420 Industrial Park, Gladstone, MI 49837/906-428-3710

Bill McGuire, 1600 No. Eastmont Ave., East Wenatchee, WA 98801 (custom cases)

Merchandise Brokers, P.O. Box 491, Lilburn, GA 30247/404-923-0015 (GunSlinger portable rack)

Nesci Enterprises, Inc., P.O. Box 119, Summit St., East Hampton, CT 06424/203-267-2588 (firearms security chests)

Nortex Industrial Fan Co., 2821 Main St., Dallas TX 75226/214-748-1157 (automobile gun rack)

Paul-Reed, Inc., P.O. Box 227, Charlevoix, MI 49720

Penguin Industries, Inc., Airport Industrial Mall, Coatesville, PA 19320/215-384-6000

Precise, 3 Chestnut, Suffern, NY 10901

Protecto Plastics, Div. of Penquin Ind., Airport Industrial Mall, Coatesville, PA 19320/215-384-6000 (carrying cases)

Provo Steel & Supply Co., P.O. Box 977, Provo, UT 84601 (steel gun cases)

Randall Manufacturing, 7965 San Fernando Rd., Sun Valley, CA 91352/213-875-2045

Red Head Brand Corp., 4949 Joseph Hardin Dr., Dallas, TX 75236/214-333-4141

Richland Arms Co., 321 W. Adrian, Blissfield, MI 49228

Saf-T-Case Mfg. Co., Inc., P.O. Box 5472, Irving, TX 75062

San Angelo Co. Inc., P.O. Drawer 5820, San Angelo, TX 76902/915-655-7126

Buddy Schoellkopf, 4949 Joseph Hardin Dr., Dallas, TX 75236/214-333-2121

Se-Cur-All Cabinet Co., K-Prods., P.O. Box 2052, Michigan City, IN 46360/219-872-7957

Security Gun Chest, (See Tread Corp.)

Stearns Mfg. Co., P.O. Box 1498, St. Cloud, MN 56301

Stowline Inc., 811 So. 1st Kent, WA 98031/206-852-9200 (vaults)

Tread Corp., P.O. Box 13207, Roanoke, VA 24032/703-982-6881 (security gun chest)

Trik Truk, P.O. Box 3760, Kent, WA 98301 (P.U. truck cases)

Weather Shield Sports Equipm. Inc., Rte. #3, Petoskey Rd., Charlevoix, MI 49720

Wilson Case Co., P.O. Box 953, Hastings, NE 68901/402-463-2893 (cases)

Woodstream Corp., Box 327, Lititz, PA 17543

CHOKE DEVICES, RECOIL ABSORBERS & RECOIL PADS

Action Products Inc., 22 N. Mulberry St., Hagerstown, MD 21740/301-797-1414 (rec. shock eliminator)

Arms Ingenuity Co., Box 1; 51 Canal St., Weatogue, CT 06089/203-658-5624 (Jet-Away)

Stan Baker, 5303 Roosevelt Way NE, Seattle, WA 98105/206-522-4575 (shotgun)

Briley Mfg. Co., 1085-A Gessner, Houston, TX 77055/713-932-6995 (choke tubes)

C&H Research, 115 Sunnyside Dr., Lewis, KS 67552/316-324-5445 (Mercury recoil suppressor)

Vito Cellini, Francesca Inc., 3115 Old Ranch Rd., San Antonio, TX 78217/512-826-2584 (recoil reducer; muzzle brake)

Defense Technology Associates, 3333 Midway Dr., Suite 104, San Diego, CA 92110/619-223-5339 (Muzzle-Mizer rec. abs.)

Diverter Arms, Inc., P.O. Box 22084, Houston, TX 77027 (shotgun diverter)

Edwards Recoil Reducer, 269 Herbert St., Alton, IL 62002/618-462-3257

Emsco Variable Shotgun Chokes, 101 Second Ave., S.E., Waseca, MN 56093/507-835-1779

Griggs Recreational Prods. Inc., P.O. Box 324, Twin Bridges, MT 59754/406-684-5202 (recoil director)

La Paloma Marketing, 4500 E. Speedway Blvd., Suite 93, Tucson, AZ 85712/602-881-4750 (Action rec. shock eliminator)

Lyman Products Corp., Rte. 147, Middlefield, CT. 06455 (Cutts Comp.)

MBM Enterprises, Rt. 4, Box 265, 715 E. 46th St., Stillwater, OK 70474/405-377-0296 (Counter-Coil rec. abs.)

Mag-na-port International, Inc., 41302 Executive Drive, Mt. Clemens, MI 48045/313-469-6727 (muzzle-brake system)

Mag-Na-Port of Canada, 1861 Burrows Ave., Winnipeg, Manitoba R2X 2V6, Canada

Don Mitchell Corp., 1800 Talbott Way, Anaheim, CA 92805/714-634-1131 (muzzle brakes)

Multi-Gauge Enterprises, 433 W. Foothill Blvd., Monrovia, CA 91016/818-357-6117/358-4549 (screw-in chokes)

Pachmayr Gun Works, Inc., 1220 So. Grand Ave., Los Angeles, CA 90015/213-748-7271 (recoil pads)

P.A.S.T. Corp., 210 Park Ave., P.O. Box 7372, Columbia, MO 65205/314-449-7278 (recoil reducer shield)

Poly-Choke Div., Marble Arms, 420 Industrial Park, Gladstone, MI 49837/906-428-3710

Pro-Choke, Inc., 4201 Oak Circle #32, Boca Raton, FL 33431/305-392-7170

Pro-Port Ltd., 41302 Executive Dr., Mt. Clemens, MI 48045/313-469-7323

Purbaugh, see: Multi-Gauge Enterprises

Supreme Products Co., 1830 S. California Ave., Monrovia, CA 91016/800-423-7159/818-357-5395 (recoil pads)

CHRONOGRAPHS AND PRESSURE TOOLS

B-Square Co., Box 11281, Ft. Worth, TX 76110/800-433-2909

Custom Chronograph Co., Box 1061, Brewster, WA 98812/509-689-2004

Diverter Arms, Inc., P.O. Box 22084, Houston, TX 77027 (press. tool)

Oehler Research, P.O. Box 9135, Austin, TX 78756

Telepacific Electronics Co., Inc., P.O. Box 1329, San Marcos, CA 92069/714-744-4415

Tepeco, P.O. Box 919, Silver City, NM 88062/505-388-2070 (Tepeco Speed-Meter)

M. York, 5508 Griffith Rd., Gaithersburg, MD 20760/301-253-4217 (press. tool)

CLEANING & REFINISHING SUPPLIES

A 'n A Co., Box 571, King of Prussia, PA 19406 (Valet shotgun cleaner)

Armite Labs., 1845 Randolph St., Los Angeles, CA 90001/213-587-7744 (pen oiler)

Armoloy Co. of Ft. Worth, 204 E. Daggett St., Ft Worth, TX 76104/817-461-0051

Beeman Inc., 47 Paul Dr., San Rafael, CA 94903/415-472-7121

Belltown, Ltd., P.O. Box 74, Route 37, Sherman, CT 06784/203-354-5750 (gun clg. cloth kit)

Birchwood-Casey, 7900 Fuller Rd., Eden Prairie, MN 55344/612-927-7933

Blue and Gray Prods., Inc., R.D. #6, Box 362, Wellsboro, PA 16901/717-724-1383

Break-Free, a Div. of San/Bar Corp., 9999 Muirlands Blvd., Irvine, CA 92714/714-855-9911

Jim Brobst, 299 Poplar St., Hamburg, PA 19526/215-562-2103 (J-B Bore Cleaning Compound)

GB Prods. Dept. H & R, Inc., Industrial Rowe, Gardner, MA 01440

Browning Arms, Rt. 4, Box 624-B, Arnold, MO 63010

J.M. Bucheimer Co., P.O. Box 280, Airport Rd., Frederick, MD 21701/301-662-5101

Burnishine Prod. Co., 8140 N. Ridgeway, Skokie, IL 60076/312-583-1810 (Stock Glaze)

Call 'N, Inc., 1615 Bartlett Rd., Memphis, TN 38134/901-372-1682 (Gunskin)

Chem-Pak, Inc., 11 Oates Ave., P.O. Box 1685, Winchester, VA 22601/703-667-1341 (Gun-Savr.protect. & lubricant)

Chopie Mfg. Inc., 700 Copeland Ave., La Crosse, WI 54601/608-784-0926 (Black-Solve)

Clenzoil Corp., Box 1226, Sta. C, Canton, OH 44708/216-833-9758

Clover Mfg. Co., 139 Woodward Ave., Norwalk, Ct. 06856/800-243-6492 (Clover compound)

J. Dewey Mfg. Co., 186 Skyview Dr., Southbury, CT 06488/203-264-3064 (one-piece gun clg. rod)

Diah Engineering Co., 5177 Haskell St., La Canada, CA 91011/213-625-2184 (barrel lubricant)

Dri-Slide, Inc., 411 N. Darling, Fremont, MI 49412/616-924-3950

Forty-Five Ranch Enterpr., 119 S. Main St., Miami, OK 74354/918-542-9307

Frank C. Hoppe Div., Penguin Ind., Inc., Airport Industrial Mall, Coatesville, PA 19320/215-384-6000

Ken Jantz Supply, Rt. 1, Sulphur, OK 73086/405-622-3790

Jet-Aer Corp., 100 Sixth Ave., Paterson, NJ 07524 (blues & oils)

Kellog's Professional Prods., Inc., P.O. Box 1201, Sandusky, OH 44870

K.W. Kleinendorst, R.D. #1, Box 113B, Hop Bottom, PA 18824/717-289-4687 (rifle clg. cables)

Terry K. Kopp, Highway 13, Lexington, MO 64067/816-259-2636 (stock rubbing compound; rust preventative grease)

LPS Chemical Prods., Holt Lloyd Corp., 4647 Hugh Howell Rd., Tucker, GA 30048/404-934-7800

LaPaloma Marketing, Inc., 4500 E. Speedway Blvd., Suite 93, Tucson, AZ 85712/602-881-4750 (Amer-Lene solution)

Mark Lee, 2333 Emerson Ave. No., Minneapolis, MN 55411/612-521-0673 (rust blue solution)

LEM Gun Spec., Box 31, College Park, GA 30337/404-761-9054 (Lewis Lead Remover)

Liquid Wrench, Box 10628, Charlotte, NC 28201 (pen. oil)

Lynx Line Gun Prods. Div., Protective Coatings, Inc., 20626 Fenkell Ave., Detroit, MI 48223/313-255-6032

MJL Industries, P.O. Box 122, McHenry, IL 60050/815-344-1040 (Rust Free)

Marble Arms Co., 420 Industrial Park, Gladstone, MI 49837/906-428-3710

Marksman Inc., P.O. Box 598, Chesterland, OH 44026/216-729-9392 (bore cleaner & conditioner)

Micro Sight Co., 242 Harbor Blvd., Belmont, CA 94002/415-591-0769 (bedding)

Mirror-Lube, American Speclty. Lubricants, P.O. Box 693, San Juan Capistrano, CA 92693/714-496-1098

Mount Labs, Inc., see: LaPaloma Marketing, Inc.

New Method Mfg. Co., P.O. Box 175, Bradford, PA 16701/814-362-6611 (gun blue; Minute Man gun care)

Northern Instruments, Inc., 6680 North Highway 49, Lino Lake, MN 55014 (Stor-Safe rust preventer)
Numrich Arms Co., West Hurley, NY 12491 (44-40 gun blue)
Old World Oil Products, 3827 Queen Ave. No., Minneapolis, MN 55412
Omark Industries, Box 856, Lewiston, ID 83501
Original Mink Oil, Inc., P.O. Box 20191, 10652 N.E. Holman, Portland, OR 97220/503-255-2814
Outers Laboratories; see: Omark Industries
RBS Industries Corp., 1312 Washington Ave., St. Louis, MO 63103/314-241-8564 (Miracle All Purpose polishing cloth)
Reardon Prod., 103 W. Market St., Morrison, IL 61270 (Dry-Lube)
Rice Protective Gun Coatings, 235-30th St., West Palm Beach, FL 33407/305-845-2383
Richards Classic Oil Finish, John Richards, Rt. 2, Box 325, Bedford, KY 40006/502-255-7222 (gunstock oil, wax)
Rig Products, 87 Coney Island Dr., Sparks, NV 89431/703-331-5666
Rusteprufe Labs., Rte. 5, Sparta, WI 54656/608-269-4144
Rust Guardit; see: Schwab Industries
San/Bar Corp., Break-Free Div., 9999 Muirlands Blvd, Irvine, CA 92714/714-855-9911
Saunders Sptg. Gds., 338 Somerset, No. Plainfield, NJ 07060 (Sav-Bore)
Schultea's Gun String 67 Burress, Houston, TX 77022 (pocket-size rifle cleaning kit)
Schwab Industries, Inc., P.O. Box 1269, Sequim, WA 98382/206-683-2944 (Rust Guardit)
Secoa Technologies, Inc., see: West Coast Secoa
Service Armament, 689 Bergen Blvd., Ridgefield, NJ 07657 (Parker-Hale)
Silicote Corp., Box 359, Oshkosh, WI 54901 (Silicone cloths)
Silver Dollar Guns, P.O. Box 475, 10 Frances St., Franklin, NH 03235/603-934-3292 (Silicone oil)
TDP Industries, Inc., 603 Airport Blvd., Doylestown, PA 18901/215-345-8687
Taylor & Robbins, Box 164, Rixford, PA 16745 (Throat Saver)
Testing Systems, American Gas & Chemical Co., Ltd., 220 Pegasus Ave., Northgate, NJ 07647/201-767-7300 (gun lube)
Texas Platers Supply Co., 2453 W. Five Mile Parkway, Dallas, TX 75233 (plating kit)
Totally Dependable Products; See: TDP
Treso Inc., P.O. Box 4640, Pagosa Springs, CO 81157/303-264-2295 (mfg. Durango Gun Rod)
C. S. Van Gorden, 1815 Main St., Bloomer, WI 54724/715-568-2612 (Van's Instant Blue)
WD-40 Co., P.O. Box 80607, San Diego, CA 92138-9021/619-275-1400
West Coast Secoa, 3915 U S Hwy 98S, Lakeland, FL 33801 (Teflon coatings)
Williams Gun Sight, 7389 Lapeer Rd., Davison, MI 48423 (finish kit)
Winslow Arms Inc., P.O. Box 783, Camden, SC 29020 (refinishing kit)
Wisconsin Platers Supply Co., (See Texas Platers Supply Co.)
Woodstream Corp., P.O. Box 327, Lititz, PA 17543 (Mask)
Zip Aerosol Prods., 21320 Deering Court, Canoga Park, CA 91304

CUSTOM GUNSMITHS

Ahlman's Inc., R.R. 1, Box 20, Morristown, MN 55052/507-685-4244
Don Allen Inc., R.R. 4, Northfield, MN 55057/507-645-9216
American Custom Gunmakers Guild, 3507 Red Oak Lane, Plainview, TX 79072/806-293-9042
Amrine's Gun Shop, 937 Luna Ave., Ojai, CA 93023
Andy's Gun Shop, A. Fleury, Burke, NY 12917
Antique Arms Co., D. F. Saunders, 1110 Cleveland Ave., Monett, MO 65708/417-235-6501 (Hawken copies)
R. J. Anton, 874 Olympic Dr., Waterloo, IA 50701/319-233-3666
Armament Gunsmithing Co., Inc., 525 Route 22, Hillside, NJ 07205/201-686-0960
John & Mary Armbrust, John's Gun Shop, 823 S. Union St., Mishawaka, IN 46544/219-255-0973
Armurier Hiptmayer, P.O. Box 136, Eastman, Que. JOE 1P0, Canada/514-297-2492
Armuriers Liegeois-Artisans Reunis "ALAR," rue Masset 27, 4300 Ans, Belgium
Atkinson Gun Co., P.O. Box 512, Prescott, AZ 86301
Ed von Atzigen, The Custom Shop, 890 Cochrane Crescent, Peterborough, Ont., K9H 5N3 Canada/705-742-6693
Creighton Audette, 19 Highland Circle, Springfield, VT 05156/802-885-2331
Richard W. Baber, Hanson's Gun Center, 1440 N. Hancock Ave., Colorado Springs, CO 80903/303-634-4220
Bain and Davis Sptg. Gds., 307 E. Valley Blvd., San Gabriel, CA 91776/213-573-4241
Les Baer, Sr., The Gun Shop, 1725 Minesite Rd., Allentown, PA 18103/215-398-2362 (rifles)
Stan Baker, 5303 Roosevelt Way NE, Seattle, WA 98105/206-522-4575 (shotgun specialist)
Joe J. Balickie, Rte. 2, Box 56-G, Apex, NC 27502/919-362-5185
Barta's Gunsmithing, 10231 US Hwy., #10, Cato, WI 54206/414-732-4472
George Beitzinger, 116-20 Atlantic Ave., Richmond Hill, NY 11419/212-846-2753
Bell's Custom Shop, David Norin, 3319 Mannheim Rd., Franklin Park, IL 60131/312-678-1900 (handguns)
Bennett Gun Works, 561 Delaware Ave., Delmar, NY 12054/518-439-1862
Gordon Bess, 708 River St., Canon City, CO 81212/303-275-1073
Al Biesen, 5021 Rosewood, Spokane, WA 99208/509-328-9340
Roger Biesen, W. 2039 Sinto Ave., Spokane, WA 99201
Billingsley & Brownell, Box 25, Dayton, WY 82836/307-655-9344 (cust. rifles)
Bob's Gun & Tackle Shop, 746 Granby St., Norfolk, VA 23510/804-627-8311
Boone Mountain Trading Post, 118 Sunrise Rd., Saint Marys, PA 15857/814-834-4879
Victor Bortugno, Atlantic & Pacific Arms Co., 4859 Virginia Beach Blvd., Virginia Beach, VA 23462
Charles Boswell (Gunmakers), Div. of Saxon Arms Ltd., P.O. Box 968, Lambeth, Ont. NOL 1S0 Canada/519-681-6482
Art Bourne, (See Guncraft)
Kent Bowerly, 1213 Behshel Hts. Rd., Kelso, WA 98626/206-636-2859

Larry D. Brace, 771 Blackfoot Ave., Eugene, OR 97404/503-688-1278
Breckheimers, Rte. 69-A, Parish, NY 13131
Lenard M. Brownell, (See Billingsley & Brownell)
Buckhorn Gunsmithing, Larry Matthews, 341 W. 17th St. Coquille, OR 97423/503-396-5998
Ted Buckland, 361 Flagler Rd., Nordland, WA 98358/206-385-2142 (ML)
David Budin, Main St., Margaretville, NY 12455/914-568-4103
George Bunch, 7735 Garrison Rd., Hyattsville, MD 20784
Ida I. Burgess, Sam's Gun Shop, 25 Squam Rd., Rockport, MA 01966/617-546-6839 (bluing repairs)
Leo Bustani, P.O. Box 8125, W. Palm Beach, FL 33407
Cache La Poudre Rifleworks, 168 No. College Ave., Ft. Collins, CO 80524/303-482-6913 (cust. ML)
Cameron's Guns, 16690 W. 11th Ave., Golden, CO 80401
Lou Camilli, 4700 Oahu Dr. N.E., Albuquerque, NM 87111/505-293-5259 (ML)
Dick Campbell, 1198 Finn Ave., Littleton, CO 80124/303-799-0145
Ralph L. Carter, Carter's Gun Shop, 225 G St., Penrose, CO 81240/303-372-6240
R. MacDonald Champlin, P.O. Box 693, Manchester, NH 03105/603-622-1420 (ML rifles and pistols)
Mark Chanlynn, Bighorn Trading Co., 1704-14th St., Boulder, CO 80302
Dave Chicoine, d/b/a Liberty A.S.P., 19 Key St., Eastport, ME 04631/207-853-2327
Claude Christopher, 1606 Berkley Rd., Greenville, NC 27834/919-756-0872 (ML)
Classic Arms Corp., P.O. Box 8, Palo Alto, CA 94302/415-321-7243
John Edward Clark, R.R. #4, Tottenham, Ont. L0G 1W0 Canada/416-936-2131 (ML)
Kenneth E. Clark, 18738 Highway 99, Madera, CA 93637/209-674-6016
John Corry, 628 Martin Lane, Deerfield, IL 60015/312-541-6250 (English doubles & repairs)
Raymond A. Cover, Rt. 1, Box 101A, Mineral Point, MO 63660/314-749-3783
Crest Carving Co., 14849 Dillow St., Westminster, CA 92683
Crocker, 1510 - 42nd St., Los Alamos, NM 87544 (rifles)
J. Lynn Crook, Rt. 7, Box 119-A, Lebanon, TN 37087/615-449-1930
Philip R. Crouthamel, 513 E. Baltimore, E. Lansdowne, PA 19050/215-623-5685
Cumberland Knife & Gun Works, 5661 Bragg Blvd., Fayetteville, NC 28303/919-867-0009 (ML)
The Custom Gun Guild, 5091-F Buford Hwy., Doraville, GA 30340/404-455-0346
Dahl's Custom Stocks, Rt. 4, Box 558, Lake Geneva, WI 53147/414-248-2464
Dahl's Gunshop, 6947 King Ave., Route 4, Billings, MT 59106/406-656-6132
Homer L. Dangler, Box 254, Addison, MI 49220/517-547-6745 (Kentucky rifles; brochure $3)
Jack Dever, 8520 N.W. 90, Oklahoma City, OK 73132/405-721-6393
R. H. Devereaux, D. D. Custom Rifles, 475 Trucky St., St. Igance, MI 49781/906-643-8625
Dominic DiStefano, 4303 Friar Lane, Colorado Springs, CO 80907
Dixon Muzzleloading Shop, Inc., RD #1, Box 175, Kempton, PA 19529/215-756-6271 (ML)
William Dixon, Buckhorn Gun Works, Rt. 4 Box 200, Rapid City, SD 57701/605-787-6289
Charles Duffy, Williams Lane, W. Hurley, NY 12491
David R. Dunlop, Rte. 1, Box 199, Rolla, ND 58367
D. W. Firearms, D. Wayne Schlumbaum, 1821 - 200th S.W., Alderwood Manor, WA 98036
Jere Eggleston, 400 Saluda Ave., Columbia, SC 29205/803-799-3402
Elko Arms, Dr. L. Kortz, 28 rue Ecole Moderne, B-7400 Soignies, H.T., Belgium
Bob Emmons, 238 Robson Rd., Grafton, OH 44044/216-458-5890
Bill English, 4411 S.W. 100th, Seattle, WA 98146/206-932-7345
Englishtown Sporting Goods, Inc., Donald J. Maxham, 38 Main St. Englishtown, NJ 07726/201-446-7717
Armas ERBI, S. coop., Avda. Eulogio Estarta, Elgoibar (Guipuzcoa), Spain
Ken Eyster, Heritage Gunsmiths Inc., 6441 Bishop Rd., Centerburg, OH 43011/614-625-6131
Andy Fautheree, P.O. Box 863, Pagosa Springs, CO 81147/303-264-2892 (cust. ML)
Ted Fellowes, Beaver Lodge, 9245-16th Ave., S.W., Seattle, WA 98106/206-763-1698 (muzzleloaders)
Jack First Distributors Inc., 44633 Sierra Highway, Lancaster, CA 93534/805-945-6981
Clyde E. Fischer, P.O. Box 1437, Three Rivers, TX 78071/512-786-4125
Marshall F. Fish, Rt. 22 North, Westport, NY 12993/518-962-4897
Jerry A. Fisher, 1244-4th Ave. West, Kalispell, MT 59901/406-755-7093
Flynn's Cust. Guns, P.O. Box 7461, Alexandria, LA 71306/318-445-7130
John Fordham, Box 9 Dial Star Rt., P.O. Box 1093, Blue Ridge, GA 30513/404-632-3602
Larry L. Forster, Box 212, Gwinner, ND 58040/701-678-2475
Jay Frazier, S.R. Box 8644, Bird Creek, AK 99540/903-653-8302
Freeland's Scope Stands, 3737—14th Ave., Rock Island, IL 61201/309-788-7449
Fredrick Gun Shop, 10 Elson Drive, Riverside, RI 02915/401-433-2805
Frontier Arms, Inc., 420 E. Riding Club Rd., Cheyenne, WY 82001
Frontier Shop & Gallery, The Depot, Main St., (Box 1805), Riverton, WY 82501/307-856-4498
Fuller Gunshop, Cooper Landing, AK 99572
Karl J. Furr, 76 East 350 No., Orem, UT 84057/801-225-2603
Garcia Natl. Gun Traders, Inc., 225 S.W. 22nd Ave., Miami, FL 33135
Jim Garrett, 2820 East NaniLoa Circle, Salt Lake City, UT 84117/801-277-6930
Gentry's Bozeman Gunsmith, David O. Gentry, 2010 No. 7th, Bozeman, MT 59715/406-586-1405 (cust. Montana Mtn. Rifle)
Gentry's Bluing & Guns Shop, Box 984, Belgrade,MT 59714
Edwin Gillman, R.R. 6, Box 195, Hanover, PA 17331/717-632-1662
Gilman-Mayfield, 1552 N. 1st, Fresno, CA 93703/209-237-2500
Dale Goens, Box 224, Cedar Crest, NM 87008
Dave Goode, 14906 Robinwood St., Lansing, MI 48906/517-321-5392
A. R. Goode, 12845 Catoctin Furnace Rd., Thurmont, MD 21788/301-271-2228
Goodling's Gunsmithing, R.D. #1, Box 1097, Spring Grove, PA 17362/717-225-3350

Gordie's Gun Shop, Gordon Mulholland, 1401 Fulton St., Streator, IL 61364/815-672-7202

Charles E. Grace, 10144 Elk Lake Rd., Williamsburg, MI 49690/616-264-9483

Roger M. Green, 315 S. 2nd St., P.O. Box 984, Glenrock, WY 82637/307-436-9804

Griffin & Howe, 589 Broadway, New York, NY 10012/212-966-5323

H. L. "Pete" Grisel, 61912 Skyline View Dr., Bend, OR 97701/503-389-2649 (rifles)

Karl Guenther, 43-32 160th St., Flushing, NY 11372/212-461-7325

Gun City, 504 East Main Ave., Bismarck, ND 58501/701-223-2304

Guncraft, Inc., 117 W. Pipeline, Hurst, TX 76053/817-268-2887

Guncraft (Kamloops) Ltd., 127 Victoria St., Kamloops, B.C. V2C 1Z4, Canada/604-374-2151

Guncraft (Kelowna) Ltd., 1771 Harvey Ave., Kelowna, B.C. V1Y 6G4, Canada/604-860-8977

The Gunshop, R.D. Wallace, 320 Overland Rd., Prescott, AZ 86301

The Gun Works, Joe Williams, 236 Main St., Springfield, OR 97477/503-741-4118 (ML)

H-S Precision, Inc., 112 N. Summit, Prescott, AZ 85302/602-445-0607

Paul Haberly, 2364 N. Neva, Chicago, IL 60635/312-889-1114

Martin Hagn, Herzogstandweg 41, 8113 Kochel a. See, W. Germany (s.s. actions & rifles)

Fritz Hallberg, The Outdoorsman, P.O. Box 339, Ontario, OR 97914/503-889-3135

Charles E. Hammans, P.O. Box 788, Stuttgart, AR 72160/501-673-1388

Dick Hanson, Hanson's Gun Center, 1440 No. Hancock, Colorado Springs, CO 80903/303-634-4220

Harkrader's Cust. Gun Shop, 825 Radford St., Christiansburg, VA 24073

Rob't W. Hart & Son Inc., 401 Montgomery St., Nescopeck, PA 18635/717-752-3481 (actions, stocks)

Hartmann & Weiss KG, Rahlstedter Str. 139, 2000 Hamburg 73, W. Germany

Hubert J. Hecht, Waffen-Hecht, 724-K St., Sacramento, CA 95814/916-448-1177

Edw. O. Hefti, 300 Fairview, College Station, TX 77840/409-696-4959

Stephen Heilmann, P.O. Box 657, Grass Valley, CA 95945/916-272-8758

Iver Henriksen, 1211 So. 2nd St. W., Missoula, MT 59801

Wm. Hobaugh, The Rifle Shop, Box M, Philipsburg, MT 59858/406-859-3515

Richard Hodgson, 5589 Arapahoe, Unit 104, Boulder, CO 80301

George Hoenig, 6521 Morton Dr., Boise, ID 83705/208-375-1116

Dick Holland, 422 N.E. 6th St., Newport, OR 97365/503-265-7556

Hollingsworth's Guns, Route 1, Box 55B, Alvaton, KY 42122/502-842-3580

Hollis Gun Shop, 917 Rex St., Carlsbad, NM 88220/505-835-3782

Bill Holmes, Rt. 2, Box 242, Fayetteville, AR 72701/501-521-8958

Al Hunkeler, Buckskin Machine Works, 3235 So. 358th St., Auburn, WA 98001/206-927-5412 (ML)

Huntington's, P.O. Box 991, Oroville, CA 95965/916-534-1210

Hyper-Single Precision SS Rifles, 520 E. Beaver, Jenks, OK 74037/918-299-2391

Independent Machine & Gun Shop, 1416 N. Hayes, Pocatello, ID 83201

Paul Jaeger, Inc. 211 Leedom St., Jenkintown, PA 19046/215-884-6920

R. L. Jamison, Jr., Route 4, Box 200, Moses Lake, WA 98837/206-762-2659

J. J. Jenkins Ent. Inc., 375 Pine Ave. No. 25, Goleta, CA 93017/805-967-1366

Jerry's Gun Shop, 9220 Ogden Ave., Brookfield, IL 60513/312-485-5200

Neal G. Johnson, Gunsmithing Inc., 111 Marvin Dr., Hampton, VA 23666/804-838-8091

Peter S. Johnson, The Orvis Co., Inc., Manchester, VT 05254/802-362-3622

Joseph & Associates, 4810 Riverbend Rd., Boulder, CO 80301/303-332-6720

Jos. Jurjevic, Gunshop, 605 Main St., Marble Falls, TX 78654/512-693-3012

Ken's Gun Specialties, K. Hunnell, Box 241, Lakeview, AR 72642/501-431-5606

Kennedy Gun Shop, Rte. 12, Box 21, Clarksville, TN 37040/615-647-6043

Monty Kennedy, P.O. Box 214, Kalispell, MT 59901/406-857-3596

Kennon's Custom Rifles, 5408 Biffle, Stone Mtn., GA 30088/404-469-9339

Stanley Kenvin, 5 Lakeville Lane, Plainview, NY 11803/516-931-0321

Kesselring Gun Shop, 400 Pacific Hiway No., Burlington, WA 98233/206-724-3113

Benjamin Kilham, Kilham & Co., Main St., Box 37, Lyme, NH 03768/603-795-4112

Don Klein Custom Guns, P.O. Box 277, Camp Douglas, WI 54618/608-427-6948

K. W. Kleinendorst, R.D. #1, Box 113B, Hop Bottom, PA 18824/717-289-4687

Terry K. Kopp, Highway 13, Lexington, MO 64067/816-259-2636

J. Korzinek, R.D. #2, Box 73, Canton, PA 17724/717-673-8512 (riflesmith) (broch. $1.50)

L & W Casting Co., 5014 Freeman Rd. E., Puyallup, WA 98371

Sam Lair, 520 E. Beaver, Jenks, OK 74037/918-299-2391 (single shots)

Maynard Lambert, Kamas, UT 84036

Harry Lawson Co., 3328 N. Richey Blvd., Tucson, AZ 85716/602-326-1117

John G. Lawson, (The Sight Shop), 1802 E. Columbia, Tacoma, WA 98404/206-474-5465

Mark Lee, 2333 Emerson Ave., N., Minneapolis, MN 55411/612-521-0673

Bill Leeper, (See Guncraft)

LeFever Arms Co. Inc., R.D. #1, Box 31, Lee Center, NY 13363/315-337-6722

Leland Firearms Co., 13 Mountain Ave., Llewellyn Park, West Orange, NJ 07052/201-964-7500 (shotguns)

Lenz Firearms Co., 310 River Rd., Eugene, OR 97404/503-689-6900

Al Lind, 7821—76th Ave. S.W., Tacoma, WA 98498/206-584-6363

Max J. Lindauer, R.R. 2, Box 27, Washington, MO 63090

Robt. L. Lindsay, J & B Enterprises, 9416 Emory Grove Rd., P.O. Box 805, Gaithersburg, MD 20877/301-948-2941 (services only)

Ljutic Ind., Box 2117, Yakima, WA 98904 (shotguns)

Llanerch Gun Shop, 2800 Township Line, Upper Darby, PA 19082/215-789-5462

James W. Lofland, 2275 Larkin Rd., Boothwyn, PA 19061/215-485-0391 (SS rifles)

London Guns, 1528—20th St., Santa Monica, CA 90404/213-828-8486

McCann's Muzzle-Gun Works, Tom McCann, 200 Federal City Rd., Pennington, NJ 08534/609-737-1707 (ML)

John I. McCann, 2911 N. 5th Ave., Coeur d'Alene, ID 83814/208-667-3919

McCormick's Gun Bluing Service, 609 N.E. 104th Ave., Vancouver, WA 98664/206-256-0579

Stan McFarland, 2221 Idella Ct., Grand Junction, CO 81506/303-243-4704 (cust. rifles)

Bill McGuire, 1600 N. Eastmont Ave., East Wenatchee, WA 98801

Harold E. MacFarland, Route #4, Box 1249, Cottonwood, AZ 86326/602-634-5320

Nick Makinson, R.R. #3, Komoka, Ont. N0L 1R0 Canada/519-471-5462 (English guns; repairs & renovations)

Frank E. Malin, Charles Boswell (Gunmakers), Divs. of Saxon Arms Ltd., P.O. Box 968, Lambeth, Ont. N0L 1S0, Canada/519-681-6482

Monte Mandarino, 136 Fifth Ave. West, Kalispell, MT 59901/406-257-6208 (Penn. rifles)

Lowell Manley, 3684 Pine St., Deckerville, MI 48427/313-376-3665

Dale Marfell, 107 N. State St., Litchfield, IL 62056/217-327-3832

Marquart Precision Co., P.O. Box 1740, Prescott, AZ 86302/602-445-5646

Marsh Al's, 3341 W. Peoria Ave., Suite 401, Phoenix, AZ 85029/602-939-0464

Elwyn H. Martin, Martin's Gun Shop, 937 S. Sheridan Blvd., Lakewood, CO 80226/303-922-2184

Mashburn Arms & Sporting Goods Co., Inc., 1218 N. Pennsylvania, Oklahoma City, OK 73107/405-236-5151

Seely Masker, Custom Rifles, 261 Washington Ave., Pleasantville, NY 10570/914-769-2627

E. K. Matsuoka, 2801 Kinohou Place, Honolulu HI 96822/808-988-3008

Geo. E. Matthews & Son Inc., 10224 S. Paramount Blvd., Downey, CA 90241

Maurer Arms, 2154-16th St., Akron, OH 44314/216-745-6864 (muzzleloaders)

John E. Maxson, Box 332, Dumas, TX 79029/806-935-5990 (high grade rifles)

Miller Arms, Inc., Dean E. Miller, P.O. Box 260, St. Onge, SD 57779/605-578-1790

Miller Custom Rifles, 655 Dutton Ave., San Leandro, CA 94577/415-568-2447

Miller Gun Works, S. A. Miller, P.O. Box 7326, Tamuning, Guam 96911

David Miller Co., 3131 E. Greenlee Rd., Tucson, AZ 85716/602-326-3117 (classic rifles)

Earl Milliron, 1249 N.E. 166th Ave., Portland, OR 97230/503-252-3725

Wm. Larkin Moore & Co., 31360 Via Colinas, Suite 109, Westlake Village, CA 91360/213-889-4160

Mitch Moschetti, P.O. Box 27065, Cromwell, CT 06416/203-632-2308

Mountain Bear Rifle Works, Inc., Wm. Scott Bickett, 100-B Ruritan Rd., Sterling, VA 22170/703-430-0420

Larry Mrock, R.F.D. 3, Box 207, Woodhill-Hooksett Rd., Bow, NH 03301/603-224-4096 (broch. $3)

Newman Gunshop, 119 Miller Rd., Agency, IA 52530/515-937-5775

Paul R. Nickels, Interwest Gun Service, P.O. Box 243, 52 N. 100 W., Providence, UT 84332/801-753-4260

Ted Nicklas, 5504 Hegel Rd., Goodrich, MI 48438/313-797-4493

William J. Nittler, 290 More Drive, Boulder Creek, CA 95006/408-338-3376 (shotgun repairs)

Jim Norman, Custom Gunstocks, 11230 Calenda Rd., San Diego, CA 92127/619-487-4173

Nu-Line Guns, 1053 Caulks Hill Rd., Harvester, MO 63303/314-441-4500

O'Brien Rifle Co., 324 Tropicana No. 128, Las Vegas, NV 89109/702-736-6082 (17-cal. Rifles)

Vic Olson, 5002 Countryside Dr., Imperial, MO 63052/314-296-8086

The Orvis Co., Inc., Peter S. Johnson, Manchester, VT 05254/802-362-3622

Maurice Ottmar, Box 657, 113 East Fir, Coulee City, WA 99115/509-632-5717

Pachmayr Gun Works, 1220 S. Grand Ave., Los Angeles, CA 90015

Paterson Gunsmithing, 438 Main St., Paterson, NJ 07501/201-345-4100

C. R. Pedersen & Son, 2717 S. Pere Marquette, Ludington, MI 49431/616-843-2061

John Pell, 410 College Ave., Trinidad, CO 81082/303-846-9406

A. W. Peterson Gun Shop, 1693 Old Hwy. 441, Mt. Dora, FL 32757 (ML rifles, also)

Eugene T. Plante, Gene's Custom Guns, 3890 Hill Ave., P.O. Box 10534, White Bear Lake, MN 55110/612-429-5105

R. Neal Rice, 5152 Newton, Denver, CO 80221

Ridge Guncraft, Inc., 125 E. Tyrone Rd., Oak Ridge, TN 37830/615-483-4024

Rifle Ranch, Jim Wilkinson, Rte. 10, 3301 Willow Creek Rd., Prescott, AZ 86301/602-778-7501

Rifle Shop, Box M, Philipsburg, MT 59858

Wm. A. Roberts Jr., Rte. 4, Box 75, Athens, AL 35611/205-232-7027 (ML)

Bob Rogers Guns, P.O. Box 305, Franklin Grove, IL 61031/815-456-2685

Carl Roth, 4728 Pine Ridge Ave., Cheyenne, WY 82001/307-634-3958 (rust bluing)

Royal Arms, 1210 Bert Costa, El Cajon, CA 92020/619-448-5466

R.P.S. Gunshop, 11 So. Haskell, Central Point, OR 97502/503-664-5010

Murray F. Ruffino, c/o Neal G. Johnson, 111 Marvin Dr., Hampton, VA 23666/804-838-8091

Rush's Old Colonial Forge, 106 Wiltshire Rd., Baltimore, MD 21221 (Ky.-Pa. rifles)

Russell's Rifle Shop, Route 5, Box 92, Georgetown, TX 78626/512-778-5338 (gunsmith services)

Sanders Custom Gun Serv., 2358 Tyler Lane, Louisville, KY 40205

Sandy's Custom Gunshop, Rte. #1, Box 20, Rockport, IL 62370/217-437-4241

Saratoga Arms Co., 1752 N. Pleasantview Rd., Pottstown, PA 19464/215-323-8326

Roy V. Schaefer, 965 W. Hilliard Lane, Eugene, OR 97404/503-688-4333

SGW, Inc. (formerly Schuetzen Gun Works), 624 Old Pacific Hwy. S.E., Olympia, WA 98503/206-456-3471

Schumaker's Gun Shop, Rte. 4, Box 500, Colville, WA 99114/509-684-4848

Schwartz Custom Guns, 9621 Coleman Rd., Haslett, MI 48840/517-339-8939

David W. Schwartz Custom Guns, 2505 Waller St., Eau Claire, WI 54701/715-832-1735

Schwarz's Gun Shop, 41-15th St., Wellsburg, WV 26070/304-737-0533

Butch Searcy, 5801 Stevenson Dr., Farmington, NM 87401

Shane's Gunsmithing, P.O. Box 321, Hwy. 51 So., Minocqua, WI 54548/715-356-9631

Shaw's, Finest in Guns, 9447 W. Lilac Rd., Escondito, CA 92025/619-728-7070

George H. Sheldon, P.O. Box 475, Franklin, NH 03235 (45 autos only)

Lynn Shelton Custom Rifles, 1516 Sherry Court, Elk City, OK 73644/405-225-0372

Shell Shack, 113 E. Main, Laurel, MT 59044

Shilen Rifles, Inc., 205 Metro Park Blvd., Ennis, TX 75119/214-875-5318

Harold H. Shockley, 204 E. Farmington Rd., Hanna City, IL 61536/309-565-4524 (hot bluing & plating)

Shootin' Shop, Inc., 225 Main St., Springfield, OR 97477/503-747-0175

Walter Shultz, 1752 N. Pleasantview Rd., Pottstown, PA 19464

Silver Dollar Guns, P.O. Box 475, 10 Frances St., Franklin, NH 03235/603-934-3292 (45 autos only)

Simmons Gun Spec., 700 So. Rogers Rd., Olathe, KS 66062/913-782-3131

Simms Hardware Co., 2801 J St., Sacramento, CA 95816/916-442-3800

Steve Sklany, 566 Birch Grove Dr., Kalispell, MT 59901/406-755-4527 (Ferguson rifle)

Jerome F. Slezak, 1290 Marlowe, Lakewood (Cleveland), OH 44107/216-221-1668

John Smith, 912 Lincoln, Carpentersville, IL 60110

Snapp's Gunshop, 6911 E. Washington Rd., Clare, MI 48617/517-386-9226

Fred D. Speiser, 2229 Dearborn, Missoula, MT 59801/406-549-8133

Sport Service Center, 2364 N. Neva, Chicago, IL 60635

Sportsman's Bailiwick, 5306 Broadway, San Santonio, TX 78209/512-824-9649

Sportsmen's Equip. Co., 915 W. Washington, San Diego, CA 92103/619-296-1501

Sportsmen's Exchange & Western Gun Traders, Inc., P.O. Box 111, 560 S. "C" St., Oxnard, CA 93032/805-483-1917

Jess L. Stark, Stark Mach. Co., 12051 Stroud, Houston, TX 77072/713-498-5882

Ken Starnes, Rt. 1, Box 269, Scroggins, TX 75480/214-365-2312

Keith Stegall, Box 696, Gunnison, CO 81230

Victor W. Strawbridge, 6 Pineview Dr., Dover Point, Dover, NH 03820/603-742-0013

W. C. Strutz, Rifle Barrels, Inc., P.O. Box 611, Eagle River, WI 54521/715-479-4766

Suter's House of Guns, 332 N. Tejon, Colorado Springs, CO 80902/303-635-1475

A. D. Swenson's 45 Shop, P.O. Box 606, Fallbrook, CA 92028

T-P Shop, 212 E. Houghton, West Branch, MI 48661

Talmage Ent., 43197 E. Whittier, Hemet, CA 92344/714-927-2397

Taylor & Robbins, Box 164, Rixford, PA 16745

James A. Tertin, c/o Gander Mountain, P.O. Box 128 - Hwy. W, Wilmot, WI 53192/414-862-2344

Larry A. Thompson, Larry's Gun Shop, 521 E. Lake Ave., Watsonville, CA 95076/408-724-5328

Gordon A. Tibbitts, 1378 Lakewood Circle, Salt Lake City, UT 84117/801-272-4126

Daniel Titus, 872 Penn St., Bryn Mawr, PA 19010/215-525-8829

Tom's Gunshop, Tom Gillman, 4435 Central, Hot Springs, AR 71913/501-624-3856

Todd Trefts, 1290 Story Mill Rd., Bozeman, MT 59715/406-586-6003

Trinko's Gun Serv., 1406 E. Main, Watertown, WI 53094

Dennis A. "Doc" Ulrich, 2511 S. 57th Ave., Cicero, IL 60650

Brent Umberger, Sportsman's Haven, R.R. 4, Cambridge, OH 43725

Upper Missouri Trading Co., Inc., Box 181, Crofton, MO 68730

Chas. VanDyke Gunsmith Service, 201 Gatewood Cir. W., Burleson, TX 76028/817-295-7373 (shotgun & recoil pad specialist)

Milton Van Epps, Rt. 69-A, Parish, NY 13131/313-625-7498

Gil Van Horn, P.O. Box 207, Llano, CA 93544

Vic's Gun Refinishing, 6 Pineview Dr., Dover, NH 03820/603-742-0013

Walker Arms Co., Rt. 2, Box 73, Selma, AL 36701

Walker Arms Co., 127 N. Main St., Joplin, MO 64801

R. D. Wallace, 320 Overland Rd., Prescott, AZ 86301/602-445-0568

R. A. Wardrop, Box 245, 409 E. Marble St., Mechanicsburg, PA 17055

Weatherby's, 2781 Firestone Blvd., South Gate, CA 90280/213-569-7186

Weaver Arms Co., P.O. Box 8, Dexter, MO 63841/314-568-3800 (ambidextrous bolt action)

J. S. Weeks & Son, 4748 Bailey Rd., Dimondale, MI 48821 (custom rifles)

Terry Werth, 1203 Woodlawn Rd., Lincoln, IL 62656/217-732-3870

Charles Westbrook, 80 Park Creek Ct., Roswell, GA 30076

Jerry Wetherbee, 63470 Hamehook Rd., Bend, OR 97701/503-389-6080 (ML)

Cecil Weems, P.O. Box 657, Mineral Wells, TX 76067/817-325-1462

Wells Sport Store, Fred Wells, 110 N. Summit St., Prescott, AZ 86301/602-445-3655

R. A. Wells, 3452 N. 1st Ave., Racine, WI 53403/414-639-5223

Terry Werth, 123 Lincoln Ave., Lincoln, IL 62656/217-732-9314

Robert G. West, 27211 Huey Lane, Eugene, OR 97402/503-689-6610

Western Gunstocks Mfg. Co., 550 Valencia School Rd., Aptos, CA 95003

Whitefish Sportsman, Pete Forthofer, 711 Spokane Ave., Whitefish, MT 59937/406-862-7252

Duane Wiebe, P.O. Box 497, Lotus, CA 95651/916-626-6240

M. Wiest & Son, 125 E. Tyrone Rd., Oak Ridge, TN 37830/615-483-4024

Dave Wills, 2776 Brevard Ave., Montgomery, AL 36109/205-272-8446

Williams Gun Sight Co., 7389 Lapeer Rd., Davison, MI 48423

Bob Williams, P.O. Box 143, Boonsboro, MD 21713

Williamson-Pate Gunsmith Service, 117 W. Pipeline, Hurst, TX 76053/817-268-2887

Thomas E. Wilson, 644 Spruce St., Boulder, CO 80302 (restorations)

Robert M. Winter, P.O. Box 484, Menno, SD 57045/605-387-5322

Lester Womack, 512 Westwood Dr., Prescott, AZ 86301/602-778-9624

J. David Yale, Ltd., 2618 Conowingo Rd., Bel Air, MD 21014/301-838-9479 (ML work)

Mike Yee, 4732-46th Ave. S.W., Seattle, WA 98116/206-935-3682

York County Gun Works, RR 4, Tottenham, Ont., LOG 1WO Canada (muzzleloaders)

Russ Zeeryp, 1601 Foard Dr., Lynn Ross Manor, Morristown, TN 37814

CUSTOM METALSMITHS

Billingsley & Brownell, Box 25, Dayton, WY 82836/307-655-9344

Ted Blackburn, 85 E., 700 South, Springville, UT 84663/801-489-7341 (precision metalwork; steel trigger guard)

Gregg Boeke, Rte. 2, Cresco, IA 52136/319-547-3746

Larry D. Brace, 771 Blackfoot Ave., Eugene, OR 97404/503,688-1278

Tom Burgess, 180 McMannamy Draw, Kalispell, MT 59901/406-755-4110

Dave Cook, 5831-26th Lane, Brampton, MI 49837/906-428-1235

Ken Eyster Heritage Gunsmiths Inc., 6441 Bishop Rd., Centerburg, OH 43011/614-625-43031

Phil Fischer, 7333 N.E. Glisan, Portland, OR 97213/503-255-5678

Geo. M. Fullmer, 2499 Mavis St., Oakland, CA 94601/415-533-4193 (precise chambering—300 cals.)

Roger M. Green, P.O. Box 984, 315 S. 2nd St., Glenrock, WY 82637/307-436-9804

Harkrader's Custom Gun Shop, 825 Radford St., Christiansburg, VA 24073

Stephen Heilmann, P.O. Box 657, Grass Valley, CA 95945/916-272-8758

Huntington's, P.O. Box 991, Oroville, CA 95965

Paul Jaeger, Inc., 211 Leedom St., Jenkintown, PA 19046/215-884-6920

Ken Jantz, Rt. 1, Sulphur, OK 73086/405-622-3790

Benjamin Kilham, Kilham & Co., Main St., Box 37, Lyme, NH 03768/603-795-4112

Terry K. Kopp, Highway 13, Lexington, MO 64067/816-259-2636

Ron Lampert, Rt. 1, Box 61, Guthrie, MN 56461/218-854-7345

Mark Lee, 2333 Emerson Ave., N., Minneapolis, MN 55411/612-521-0673

Bruce A. Nettestad, Rt. 1, Box 140, Pelican Rapids, MN 56572/218-863-4301

Precise Chambering Co., 2499 Mavis St., Oakland, CA 94601/415-533-4193

Dave Talley, Rt. 4, Box 366, Leesville, SC 29070/803-532-2700

Herman Waldron, Box 475, Pomeroy, WA 99347/509-843-1404

R. D. Wallace/The Gun Shop, 320 Overland Rd., Prescott, AZ 86301/602-445-0568

Edward S. Welty, R.D. 2, Box 25, Cheswick, PA 15024

Terry Werth, 1203 Woodlawn Rd., Lincoln, IL 62656/217-732-3870

John Westrom, Precise Firearm Finishing, 25 N.W. 44th Ave., Des Moines, IA 50313/515-288-8680

Dick Willis, 141 Shady Creek Rd., Rochester, NY 14623

DECOYS

Carry-Lite, Inc., 5203 W. Clinton Ave., Milwaukee, WI 53223

Ted Devlet's Custom Purveyors, P.O. Box 886, Fort Lee, NJ 07024/201-886-0196

Flambeau Plastics Corp., P.O. Box 97, Middlefield, OH 44062/216-632-1631

G & H Decoy Mfg. Co., P.O. Box 1208, Henryetta, OK 74437/918-652-3314

Penn's Woods Products, Inc., 19 W. Pittsburgh St., Delmont, PA 15626/412-468-8311

Tex Wirtz Ent., Inc., 1925 Hubbard St., Chicago, IL 60622

Woodstream Corp., P.O. Box 327, Lititz, PA 17543

ENGRAVERS, ENGRAVING TOOLS

Abominable Engineering, P.O. Box 1904, Flagstaff, AZ 86002/602-779-3025

John J. Adams, P.O. Box 167, Corinth, VT 05039/802-439-5904

Aurum Etchings, P.O. Box 401059, Garland, TX 75040/214-276-8551 (acid engraving)

Paolo Barbetti, c/o Stan's Gunshop, 53103 Roosevelt Way N.E., Seattle, WA 98105/206-522-4575

Robert Barnard, P.O. Box 93, Fordyce, AR 71742/501-352-5861

Billy R. Bates, 2905 Lynnwood Circle S.W., Decatur, AL 35603/205-355-3690

Joseph C. Bayer, 439 Sunset Ave., Sunset Hill Griggstown, RD 1, Princeton, NJ 08540/201-359-7283

Angelo Bee, 10703 Irondale Ave., Chatsworth, CA 91311/213-882-1567

Sid Bell Originals Inc., R.D. 2, Box 219, Tully, NY 13159/607-842-6431

Weldon Bledsoe, 6812 Park Place Dr., Fort Worth, TX 76118/817-589-1704

Rudolph V. Bochenski, 318 Sweet Ave., Buffalo, NY 14212/716-897-5148

Carl Bleile, Box 11464, Cincinnati, OH 45211/513-662-0802

C. Roger Bleile, Box 5112, Cincinnati, OH 45205/513-251-0249

Erich Boessler, Gun Engraving Intl., Am Vogeltal 3, 8732 Münnerstadt, W. Germany/9733-9443

Henry "Hank" Bonham, 218 Franklin Ave., Seaside Heights, NJ 08751

Boone Trading Co., 562 Coyote Rd., Brinnon, WA 98320/206-796-4330 (ivory, scrimshaw tools)

Bryan Bridges, 6350 E. Paseo San Andres, Tucson, AZ 85710

Frank Brgoch, 1580 So. 1500 East, Bountiful, UT 84010/801-295-1885

Dennis B. Brooker, RR #3, Indianola IA 50125/515-961-8200

Burgess Vibrocrafters (BVI), Rt. 83, Grayslake, IL 60030

Byron Burgess, 1941 Nancy, Los Osos, CA 93402/805-528-3349

Brian V. Cannavaro, Gun City U.S.A., 573 Murfreesboro Rd., Nashville, TN 37210/615-256-6127

Winston Churchill, Twenty Mile Stream Rd., RFD Box 29B, Proctorsville, VT 05153/802-226-7772

Ron Collings, See: John Corry

John Corry, 628 Martin Lane, Deerfield, IL 60015/312-541-6250

Crocker Engraving, 1510 - 42nd St., Los Alamos, NM 87544

W. Daniel Cullity, 209 Old County Rd., East Sandwich, MA 02537/617-888-1147

Art A. Darakis, RD #2, Box 350, Fredericksburg, OH 44627/216-695-4271

Tim Davis, 230 S. Main St., Eldorado, OH 45321/513-273-4611

James R. DeMunck, 3012 English Rd., Rochester, NY 14616/716-225-0626 (SASE)

C. Gregory Dixon, RD 1, Box 175, Kempton, PA 19529/215-756-6271

Howard M. Dove, 52 Brook Rd., Enfield, CT 06082/203-749-9403

Michael W. Dubber, 3107 E. Mulberry, Evansville, IN 47714/812-476-4036

Henri Dumoulin & Fils, rue du Tilleul 16, B-4411 Milmoret (Herstal), Belgium

Ken Eyster, Heritage Gunsmiths Inc., 6441 Bishop Rd., Centerburg, OH 43011/614-625-6131

John Fanzoi, P.O. Box 25, Ferlach, Austria 9170

Jacqueline Favre, 3111 So. Valley View Blvd., Suite B-214, Las Vegas, NV 89102/702-876-6278

Armi FERLIB, 46 Via Costa, 25063 Gardone V.T. (Brescia), Italy

L. R. Fliger, 3616 78th Ave. N., Brooklyn Park, MN 55443/612-566-3808

The Firarms Engravers Guild of America, Robert Evans, Secy., 332 Vine St., Oregon City, OR 97045

Henry Frank, 210 Meadow Rd., Box 984, Whitefish, MT 59937/406-862-2681
Leonard Francolini, 56 Morgan Rd., Canton, CT 06019/203-693-2529
J. R. French, 2633 Quail Valley, Irving TX 75060
GRS Corp., P.O. Box 748, 900 Overland St., Emporia, KS 66801/316-343-1084 (Gravermeister tool)
Donald Glaser, 1520 West St., Emporia, KS 66801
Eric Gold, Box 1904, Flagstaff, AZ 86002
Howard V. Grant, P.O. Box 396, Lac Du Flambeau, WI 54538/715-588-3586
Griffin & Howe, 589 Broadway, New York, NY 10012/212-966-5323
The Gunshop, R. D. Wallace, 320 Overland Rd., Prescott, AZ 86301/602-445-0568
Gurney Engraving Method Ltd., 11440 Kingsway Ave., Edmonton, Alberta, Canada T5G 0X4/403-451-4097
Hand Engravers Supply Co., P.O. Box 3001, Overlook Branch, Dayton, OH 45431/513-426-6762
Jack O. Harwood, 1191 S. Pendlebury Lane, Blackfoot, ID 83221/208-785-5468
Frank E. Hendricks, Master Engravers, Inc., P.O. Box 95, Bergheim, TX 78004/512-336-2665
Neil Hermsen, 505 Pepperidge Rd., Lewisville, NC 27023/919-945-9304
Heidemarie Hiptmayer, R.R. 112, #750, P.O. Box 136, Eastman, Que. J0E 1PO, Canada/514-297-2492
Ken Hunt, c/o Hunting World, Inc., 16 E. 53rd St., New York, NY 10022/212-755-3400
Jim Hurst, 4537 S. Irvington Ave., Tulsa, OK 74135/918-627-5460
Ken Hurst/Firearm Engraving Co., P.O. Box 249, Route 501, Rustburg, VA 24588/804-332-6440
Ralph W. Ingle, #4 Missing Link, Rossville, GA 30741/404-866-5589 (color broch. $3)
Paul Jaeger, Inc., 211 Leedom, Jenkintown, PA 19046/215-884-6920
Ken Jantz Supply, Rt. 1, Sulphur, OK 73086/405-622-3790 (tools)
Bill Johns, 1113 Nightingale, McAllen, TX 78501/512-682-2971
Ann N. Jordan, 733 Santa Lucia, Los Osos, CA 93402/805-528-7398 (scrimshaw)
Joseph, 301 E. 6th St., P.O. Box 638, Joseph, OR 97846/503-432-3585
Steven Kamyk, 9 Grandview Dr., Westfield, MA 01085/413-568-0457
T. J. Kaye, P.O. Box 4, Telegraph, TX 76883
Lance Kelly, 1824 Royal Palm Dr., Edgewater, FL 32032/904-423-4933
Jim Kelso, Rt. 1, Box 5300, Worcester, VT 05682/802-229-4254
Kleinguenther's, P.O. Box 1261, Seguin, TX 78155
E. J. Koevenig, Engraving Service, P.O. Box 55, Hill City, SD 57745/605-574-2239
John Kudlas, 622-14th St. S.E., Rochester, MN 55901/507-288-5579
Ben Lane, Jr., 2118 Lipscomb St., Amarillo, TX 79109/806-372-3771
Beth Lane, Pontiac Gun Co., 815 N. Ladd, Pontiac, IL 61764/815-842-2402
Herb Larsen, 35276 Rockwell Dr., Abbotsford, B.C. V2S 4N4, Canada/604-853-5151
Terry Lazette, 142 N. Laurens Dr., Bolivar, OH 44612/216-874-4403
Franz Letschnig, Master-Engraver, 210 Chemin Marieville, Richelieu, P. Queb. J3L 3V8, Canada/514-658-5616
W. Neal Lewis, 9 Bowers Dr., Newnan, GA 30263/404-251-3045
Frank Lindsay, 1326 Tenth Ave., Holdrege, NE 68949/308-995-4623
Steve Lindsay, P.O. Box 1413, Kearney, NE 68847/308-236-7885
London Guns, 1528-20th St., Santa Monica, CA 90404/213-828-8486
Ed. J. Machu, Jr., Sportsman's Bailiwick, 5306 Broadway, San Antonio, TX 78209
Harvey McBurnette, Rt. 4, Box 337, Piedmont, AL 36272
Lynton S.M. McKenzie, 6940 N. Alvernon Way, Tucson, AZ 85718/602-299-5090
Wm. H. Mains, 3111 S. Valley View Blvd., Suite B-214, Las Vegas, NV 89102/702-876-6278
Robert E. Maki, P.O. Box 947, Northbrook, IL 60062/312-724-8238
George Marek, P.O. Box 213, Westfield, MA 01086/413-568-5957
Rudy Marek, Rt. 1, Box 1A, Banks, OR 97106
S. A. Miller, Miller Gun Works, P.O. Box 7326, Tamuning, Guam 96911
Cecil J. Mills, 2265 Sepulveda Way, Torrance, Ca 90501/213-328-8088
Frank Mittermeier, 3577 E. Tremont Ave., New York, NY 10465
Mitch Moschetti, P.O. Box 27065, Denver, CO 80227/303-936-1184
Gary K. Nelson, 975 Terrace Dr., Oakdale, CA 95361/209-847-4590
NgraveR Co., 879 Raymond Hill Rd., Oakdale, CT 06370/203-848-8031 (engr. tool)
New Orleans Jewelers Supply, 206 Chartres St., New Orleans, LA 70130/504-523-3839 (engr. tool)
Hans Obiltschnig, 12. November St. 7, 9170 Ferlach, Austria
Oker's Engraving, 365 Bell Rd., Bellford Mtn. Hts., P.O. Box 126, Shawnee, CO 80475/303-838-6042
Gale Overbey, 612 Azalea Ave., Richmond, VA 23227
Pachmayr Gun Works, Inc., 1220 S. Grand Ave., Los Angeles, CA 90015/213-748-7271
Rex Pedersen, C. R. Pedersen & Son, 2717 S. Pere Marquette, Ludington, MI 49431/616-843-2061
Marcello Pedini, 5 No. Jefferson Ave., Catskill, NY 12414/518-943-5257
Paul R. Piquette, 40 Royalton St., Chicopee, MA 01020/413-592-1057
Arthur Pitetti, Hawk Hollow Rd., Denver, NY 12421
Eugene T. Plante, Gene's Custom Guns, 3890 Hill Ave., P.O. Box 10534, White Bear Lake, MN 55110/612-429-5105
Jeremy W. Potts, 912 Poplar St., Denver, CO 80220/303-355-5462
Wayne E. Potts, 912 Poplar St., Denver, CO 80220/303-355-5462
Ed Pranger, 1414-7th St., Anacortes, WA 98221/206-293-3488
E. C. Prudhomme, 513 Ricou-Brewster Bldg., Shreveport, LA 71101/318-425-8421
Puccinelli Design, 114 Gazania Ct., Novato, CA 94947/415-892-7977
Martin Rabeno, Spook Hollow Trading Co., Box 37F, RD #1, Ellenville, NY 12428/914-647-4567
Wayne Reno, P.O. Box 1983, Englewood, CO 80150/303-985-5447
Jim Riggs, 206 Azalea, Boerne, TX 78006/512-249-8567 (handguns)
J. J. Roberts, 166 Manassas Dr., Manassas Park, VA 22111/703-361-4513
Hans Rohner, P.O. Box 2038, Niwot, CO 80544/303-652-2659
John R. Rohner, Sunshine Canyon, Boulder, CO 80302/303-444-3841
Bob Rosser, 162 Ramsey Dr., Albertville, AL 35950/205-878-5388

Richard D. Roy, 87 Lincoln Way, Windsor, CT 06095/203-688-0304
Joe Rundell, 6198 Frances Rd., Clio, MI 48420/313-687-0559
Robert P. Runge, 94 Grove St., Ilion, NY 13357/315-894-3036
Shaw-Leibowitz, Rt. 1, Box 421, New Cumberland, WV 26047/304-564-3108 (etchers)
Shaw's "Finest In Guns," 9447 W. Lilac Rd., Escondido, CA 92025/619-728-7070
George Sherwood, Box 735, Winchester, OR 97495/503-672-3159
Ben Shostle, The Gun Room, 1201 Burlington Dr., Muncie, IN 47302/317-282-9073
W. P. Sinclair, 36 South St., Warminster, Wiltsh. BA12 8DZ, England
Ron Skaggs, 508 W. Central, Princeton, IL 61536/815-872-1661
Mark A. Smith, 200 N. 9th, Sinclair, WY 82334/307-324-7929
Russell J. Smith, Box 595, So. Yarmouth, MA 02664/617-398-0845
R. Spinale, 3415 Oakdale Ave., Lorain, OH 44055/216-246-5344
Ray Swan, 885 French Rd., Cheektowaga, NY 14227/716-668-3430
Robt. Swartley, 2800 Pine St., Napa, CA 94559
George W. Thiewes, 1846 Allen Lane, St. Charles, IL 60174/312-584-1383
Denise Thirion, Box 408, Graton, CA 95444/707-829-1876
Anthony Tuscano, 1473 Felton Rd., South Euclid, OH 44121
Robert B. Valade, 931-3rd. Ave., Seaside, OR 97138/503-738-7672
John Vest, 6715 Shasta Way, Klamath Falls, OR 97603/503-884-5585
Ray Viramontez, 4348 Newberry Ct., Dayton, OH 45432/513-426-6762
Louis Vrancken, 30-rue sur le bois, 4531 Argenteau (Liege), Belgium
Vernon G. Wagoner, 2325 E. Encanto, Mesa, AZ 85203/602-835-1307
R. D. Wallace/The Gun Shop, 320 Overland Rd., Prescott, AZ 86301/602-445-0568
Terry Wallace, 385 San Marino, Vallejo, CA 94590
Floyd E. Warren, 1273 State Rt. 305 N.E., Cortland, OH 44410/216-637-3429
Kenneth W. Warren, Mountain States Engraving, P.O. Box 4631, Scottsdale, AZ 85261/602-991-5035
David W. Weber, 1712 East 5th, North Platte, NE 69101/308-534-2525
Rachel Wells, 110 N. Summit St., Prescott, AZ 86301/602-445-3655
Sam Welch, Box 2152, Kodiak, AK 99615/907-486-5085
Claus Willig, c/o Paul Jaeger, Inc., 211 Leedom St., Jenkintown, PA 19046
Mel Wood, Star Route, Box 364, Elgin, AZ 85611/602-455-5541

GAME CALLS

Black Duck, 1737 Davis Ave., Whiting, IN 46394/219-659-2997
Burnham Bros., Box 669, 912 Main St., Marble Falls, TX 78654/512-693-3112
Call'N, Inc., 1615 Bartlett Rd., Memphis, TN 38134/901-372-1682
Faulk's, 616 18th St., Lake Charles, LA 70601
Lohman Mfg. Co., P.O. Box 220, Neosho, MO 64850/417-451-4438
Mallardtone Game Calls, 2901 16th St., Moline, IL 61265/309-762-8089
Phil. S. Olt Co., Box 550, Pekin, IL 61554/309-348-3633
Penn's Woods Products, Inc., 19 W. Pittsburgh St., Delmont, PA 15626
Scotch Game Call Co., Inc., 60 Main St., Oakfield, NY 14125
Johnny Stewart Game Calls, Box 7954, Waco, TX 76710/817-772-3261
Sure-Shot Game Calls, Inc., P.O. Box 816, Groves, TX 77619
Thomas Game Calls, P.O. Box 336, Winnsboro, TX 75494
Weems Wild Calls, P.O. Box 7261, Ft. Worth, TX 76111/817-531-1051
Tex Wirtz Ent., Inc., 1925 W. Hubbard St., Chicago, IL 60622

GUNMAKERS, FERLACH, AUSTRIA

Ludwig Borovnik, Dollichgasse 14, A-9170
Johann Fanzoj, Griesgasse 1, A-9170
Wilfried Glanznig, Werkstr. 9, A-9170
Josef Hambrusch, Gartengasse 2, A-9170
Karl Hauptmann, Bahnhofstr. 5, A-9170
Gottfried Juch, Pfarrhofgasse 2, A-9170
Josef Just, Hauptplatz 18, A-9170
Jakob Koschat, 12.-November-Str. 2, A-9170
Johann Michelitsch, 12.-November-Str. 2, A-9170
Josef Orasche, Lastenstr. 5, A-9170
Komm.-Rat A. Sch. Outschar, Josef-Orgis-Gasse 23, A-9170
Valentin Rosenzopf's Erbe, Griesgasse 2, A-9170
Helmut Scheiring-Düsel, 10.-Oktober-Str. 8, A-9170
R. Franz Schmid, Freibacherstr. 10, A-9170
Anton Sodia, Unterferlach 39, A-9170
Vinzenz Urbas, Neubaugasse 6, A-9170
Benedikt Winkler, Postgasse 1, A-9170
Josef Winkler, Neubaugasse 1, A-9170

GUN PARTS, U.S. AND FOREIGN

Badger Shooter's Supply, 106 So. Harding, Owen, WI 54460/715-229-2101
Behlert Custom Guns, Inc., Box 227, Monmouth Junction, NJ 08852/201-329-2284 (handgun parts)
Dave Chicoine, d/b/a Liberty A.S.P., 19 Key St., Eastport, ME 04631/207-853-2327 (S&W only; ctlg. $5)
Philip R. Crouthamel, 513 E. Baltimore, E. Lansdowne, PA 19050/215-623-5685
Charles E. Duffy, Williams Lane, West Hurley, NY 12491
Christian Magazines, P.O. Box 184, Avoca, PA 18641
Federal Ordnance Inc., 1443 Potrero Ave., So. El Monte, CA 91733/213-350-4161
Jack First Distributors Inc., 44633 Sierra Highway, Lancaster, CA 93534/805-945-6981
Gun City, 504 E. Main, Bismarck, ND 58501/701-223-2304 (magazines, gun parts)
Gun-Tec, P.O. Box 8125, W. Palm Beach, FL 33407 (Win. mag. tubing; Win. 92 conversion parts)
Hansen & Co., 244 Old Post Rd., Southport, CT 06490/203-259-7337
Hunter's Haven, Zero Prince St., Alexandria, VA 22314
Walter H. Lodewick, 2816 N.E. Halsey, Portland, OR 97232/503-284-2554 (Winchester parts)

Marsh Al's, 3341 W. Peoria Ave., Suite 401, Phoenix, AZ 85029/602-939-0464 (Contender rifle)

Michigan Armament Marketing, Inc., 135 Sumner, Lake Elsinore, CA 92330/714-674-5750 (handgun parts; magazines)

Morgan Arms Co., Inc., 2999 So. Highland Dr., Las Vegas, NV 89109/702-737-5247 (MK-I kit)

Numrich Arms Co., West Hurley, NY 12491

Pacific Intl. Merch. Corp., 2215 "J" St., Sacramento, CA 95816/916-446-2737 (Vega 45 Colt mag.)

Potomac Arms Corp. (See Hunter's Haven)

Pre-64 Winchester Parts Co., P.O. Box 8125, West Palm Beach, FL 33407 (send stamped env. w. requ. list)

Martin B. Retting, Inc., 11029 Washington Blvd., Culver City, CA 90230/213-837-6111

Rock Island Armory, Inc., 111 E. Exchange St., Geneseo, IL 61254/309-944-2109

Royal Ordnance Works Ltd., P.O. Box 3245, Wilson, NC 27893/919-237-0515

Sarco, Inc., 323 Union St., Stirling, NJ 07980

Sherwood Intl. Export Corp., 18714 Parthenia St., Northridge, CA 91324

Simms, 2801 J St., Sacramento, CA 95816/916-442-3800

Clifford L. Smires, R.D. 1, Box 100, Columbus, NJ 08022/609-298-3158 (Mauser rifle parts)

Springfield Sporters Inc., R.D. 1, Penn Run, PA 15765/412-254-2626

Triple-K Mfg. Co., 568-6th Ave., San Diego, CA 92101/619-232-2066 (magazines, gun parts)

GUNS (Foreign)

Abercrombie & Fitch, 2302 Maxwell Lane, Houston, TX 77023 (Ferlib)

Action Arms, P.O. Box 9573, Philadelphia, PA 19124/215-744-0100

American Arms Inc., P.O. Box 27163, Salt Lake City, UT 84127/801-972-5006

Anschutz (See PSI)

AYA (Aguirre y Aranzabal) See IGI Domino or Wm. L. Moore (Spanish shotguns)

Armoury Inc., Rte. 202, New Preston, CT 06777

Armes de Chasse, 3000 Valley Forge Circle, Suite 1051, King of Prussia, PA 19046/215-783-6133 (Merkel)

Armsource Inc., 6 Donald Dr., Orinda, CA 94563/415-254-2767 (Manufrance)

Armsport, Inc., 3590 N.W. 49th St., Miami, FL 33142/305-635-7850

Armurier Liegeois-Artisans Reunis (A.L.A.R.), 27, rue Lambert Masset, 4300 Ans, Belgium

Baikal International, 12 Fairview Terrace, Paramus, NJ 07652/201-845-8710 (Russian shotguns)

Pedro Arrizabalaga, Eibar, Spain

Beeman, Inc., 47-GDD Paul Dr., San Rafael, CA 94903/415-472-7121 (FWB, Weihrauch, FAS, Unique firearms)

Benelli Armi, S.p.A., via della Staziona 50, 61029 Urbino, Italy

Beretta U.S.A., 17601 Indian Head Highway, Accokeek, MD 20607/301-283-2191

Bingham Ltd., 1775-C Wilwat Dr., Norcross, GA 30093/404-448-1440

M. Braun, 32, rue Notre-Dame, 2240 Luxemburg, Luxemburg (all types)

Britarms/Berdan (Gunmakers Ltd.), See: Action Arms

British Guns, P.O. Box 1924, Corvallis, OR 97339/503-752-5886 (Agent for W.&C. Scott)

Bretton, 21 Rue Clement Forissier, 42-St. Etienne, France

Browning (Gen. Offices), Rt. 1, Morgan, UT 84050/801-876-2711

Browning, (parts & service), Rt. 4, Box 624-B, Arnold, MO 63010/314-287-6800

Caprinus U.S.A., Inc., 100 Prospect St., Stamford, CT 06901/203-359-3773 (stainl. steel shotguns)

Century Arms Co., 3-5 Federal St., St. Albans, VT 05478

Champlin Firearms, Inc., Box 3191, Enid, OK 73701

Ets. Chapuis, 42380 St. Bonnet-le-Chateau, France (See R. Painter)

Christopher & Associates, 5636 San Fernando Rd., Glendale, CA 91202/213-725-7221 (SAM 180 rifle)

Clayco Sports Ltd., 625 W. Crawford, Clay Center, KS 67432/913-632-2180

Conco Arms, P.O. Box 159, Emmaus, PA 18049/215-967-5477 (Larona)

Connecticut Valley Arms Co., 5988 Peachtree Corners, East, Norcross, GA 30092 (CVA)

Walter Craig, Inc., Box 927, Selma, AL 36701/205-875-7989

Creighton & Warren, P.O. Box 15723, Nashville, TN 37215 (Krieghoff combination guns)

Diana Import, 842 Vallejo St., San Francisco, CA 94133

Charles Daly (See Outdoor Sports HQ)

Dikar s. Coop. (See Connecticut Valley Arms Co.)

Dixie Gun Works, Inc., Hwy 51, South, Union City, TN 38261/901-885-0561 ("Kentucky" rifles)

Dynamit Nobel of America, Inc., 105 Stonehurst Court, Northvale, NJ 07647/201-767-1660 (Rottweil)

E.M.F. Co. Inc. (Early & Modern Firearms), 1900 E. Warner Ave. 1-D, Santa Ana, CA 92705/714-966-0202

Ernest Dumoulin-Deleye, see: Midwest Gun Sport

Henri Dumoulin & Fils, rue du Tilleul 16, B-4411 Milmort (Herstal), Belgium

Peter Dyson Ltd., 29-31 Church St., Honley, Huddersfield, Yorkshire HD7 2AH, England (accessories f. antique gun collectors)

Elko Arms, 28 rue Ecole Moderne, 7400 Soignes, Belgium

Euroarms of American, Inc., P.O. Box 3277, 1501 Lenoir Dr., Winchester, VA 22601/703-661-1863 (ML)

Excam Inc., 4480 E. 11 Ave., P.O. Box 3483, Hialeah, FL 33013

Exel Arms of America, 14 Main St., Gardner, MA 01440/617-632-5008

Famars, Abbiatico & Salvinelli, Via Cinelli 29, Gardone V.T. (Brescia), Italy 25063

J. Fanzoj, P.O. Box 25, Ferlach, Austria 9170

Armi FERLIB, 46 Via Costa, 25063 Gardone V.T. (Brescia), Italy

Fiocchi of America, Inc., 1308 W. Chase, Springfield, MO 65803/417-864-6970 (Antonio Zoli)

Firearms Imp. & Exp. Corp., (F.I.E.), P.O. Box 4866, Hialeah Lakes, Hialeah, FL 33014/305-685-5966

Flaig's Inc., Babcock Blvd. & Thompson Rd., Millvale, PA 15209/412-821-1717

Auguste Francotte & Cie, S.A., 61 Mont St. Martin, 4000 Liege, Belgium

Frankonia Jagd, Hofmann & Co., Postfach 6780, D-8700 Wurzburg 1, West Germany

Freeland's Scope Stands, Inc., 3737 14th Ave., Rock Island, IL 61201/309-788-7449

Renato Gamba, S.p.A., Gardone V.T. (Brescia), Italy (See Steyr Daimler Puch of America Corp.)

Armas Garbi, Urki #12, Eibar (Guipuzcoa) Spain (shotguns, See W. L. Moore)

Gastinne Renette, P.O. Box 3395, College Sta.; 225 Industrial Dr., Fredericksburg, VA 22401/703-898-1524

George Granger, 66 Cours Fauriel, 42 St. Etienne, France

Gun South, Dept. Steyr, Box 6607, 7605 Eastwood Mall, Birmingham, AL 35210/800-821-3021

Heckler & Koch Inc., 14601 Lee Rd., Chantilly, VA 22021/703-631-2800

A. D. Heller, Inc., Box 56, 2322 Grand Ave., Baldwin, NY 11510/516-868-6300

Heym, Friedr. Wilh., see: Paul Jaeger, Inc.

HOWCO Dist. Inc., 122 Lafayette Ave., Laurel, MD 20707/301-953-3301

Hunting World, 16 E. 53rd St., New York, NY 10022

IGI Domino Corp., 200 Madison Ave., New York, NY 10016/212-889-4889 (Breda)

Incor, Inc., P.O. Box 132, Addison, TX 75001/214-931-3500 (Cosmi auto shotg.)

Interarmco, See Interarms (Walther)

Interarms Ltd., 10 Prince St., Alexandria, VA 22313 (Mauser, Valmet M-62/S)

Italguns, Via Voltabo, 20090 Cusago (Milano), Italy

Paul Jaeger Inc., 211 Leedom St., Jenkintown, PA 19046/215-884-6920 (Heym)

Jenkins Imports Corp., 462 Stanford Pl., Santa Barbara, CA 93111/805-967-5092 (Gebrüder Merkel)

Kassnar Imports, 5480 Linglestown Rd., Harrisburg, PA 17110

Kawaguchiya Firearms, c/o La Paloma Marketing, 4500 E. Speedway Blvd., Suite 93, Tucson, AZ 85712/602-881-4750

Kendall International, Inc., 501 East North, Carlisle, KY 40311/606-289-7336

Kimel Industries, Box 335, Matthews, NC 28105/704-821-7663

Kleinguenther's, P.O. Box 1261, Seguin, TX 78155

Knight & Knight, 302 Ponce de Leon Blvd., St. Augustine, FL 32084/904-829-9671 (Bernardelli shotguns)

Krico-North America, P.O. Box 266, Bolton, Ont. LOP 1AO, Canada/416-880-5267

L. A. Distributors, 4 Centre Market Pl., New York, NY 10013

Lanber Arms of America, Inc., 377 Logan St., Adrian, MI 49221/517-263-7444 (Spanish o-u shotguns)

Lanchester U.S.A., Inc., P.O. Box 47332, Dallas, TX 75247/214-688-0073 (Sterling)

La Paloma Marketing, 4500 E. Speedway Blvd., Suite 93, Tucson, AZ 85712/602-881-4750 (K.F.C. shotguns)

Morris Lawing, 150 Garland Court, Charlotte, NC 28202/704-375-1740

Leland Firearms Co., 13 Mountain Ave., Llewellyn Park, West Orange, NJ 07052/201-325-3379 (Spanish shotguns)

Liberty Arms Organization, Box 306, Montrose, CA 91020/213-248-0618

Llama (See Stoeger)

MRE Dist. Inc., 19 So. Bayles Ave., Pt. Washington, NY 11050/516-944-8200 (IGI Domino)

Magnum Research, Inc., 2825 Anthony Lane So., Minneapolis, MN 55418/612-781-3446 (Israeli Galil)

Mandall Shtg. Suppl. 7150 East 4th St., Scottsdale, AZ 85252/602-945-2553

Mannlicher (See Steyr Daimler Puch of Amer.)

Manu-Arm, B.P. No. 8, Veauche 42340, France

Manufrance, See: Arms Source, Inc.

Manurhin International, Inc., 631 So. Washington St., Alexandria, VA 22314/703-836-8886

Marocchi USA Inc., 5939 W. 66th St., Bedford Park, IL 60638

Marathon Products Inc., 1331 Silas Deane Highway, Wethersfield, CT 06109/203/563-0222

Mauser-Werke Oberndorf, P. O. Box 1349, 7238 Oberndorf/Neckar, West Germany

Mendi s. coop. (See Connecticut Valley Arms Co.)

Merkuria, FTC, Argentinska 38, 17005 Prague 7, Czechoslovakia (BRNO)

Midwest Gun Sport, Belgian HQ, 1942 OakWood View Dr., Verona, WI 53593/608-845-7447 (E. Dumoulin-Deleye)

Mitchell Arms Corp., 116 East 16th St., Costa Mesa, CA 92627/714-548-7701 (Uberti pistols)

Wm. Larkin Moore & Co., 31360 Via Colinas, Suite 109, Westlake Village, CA 91360/213-889-4160 (AYA, Garbi, Ferlib, Piotti, Lightwood Perugini Visini)

Navy Arms Co., 689 Bergen Blvd., Ridgefield, NJ 07657

O&L Guns Inc., P.O. Box 1146, Seminole, TX 79360/915-758-2933 (Wolverine rifle)

Odin International, Ltd., 818 Slaters Lane, Alexandria, VA 22314/703-339 8005 (Valmet/military types; CETME; Zastava)

Osborne Shooting Supplies, P.O. Box 408, Cheboygan, MI 49721/616-625-9626 (Hammerli; Tanner rifles)

Outdoor Sports Headquarters, Inc., 967 Watertower Lane, Dayton, OH 45449/513-865-5855 (Charles Daly shotguns)

P.M. Air Services, Ltd., P.O. Box 1573, Costa Mesa, CA 92626

PSI, Inc., P.O. Box 1776, Westfield, MA 01086/413-562-2989 (Anschutz)

Pachmayr Gun Works, 1220 S. Grand Ave., Los Angeles, CA 90015

Pacific Intl. Merch. Corp., 2215 "J" St., Sacramento, CA 95816/916-446-2737

Painter Co., 2901 Oakhurst Ave., Austin, TX 78703/512-474-2824 (Chapuis)

The Parker Gun, Div. of Reagent Chemical & Research, Inc., 1201 N. Watson Rd., Suite 224, Arlington, TX 76011/817-649-8781

Parker-Hale, Bisleyworks, Golden Hillock Rd., Sparbrook, Birmingham B11 2PZ, England

Perazzi U.S.A. Inc., 206 S. George St., Rome, NY 13440/315-337-8566

Precise, 3 Chestnut, Suffern, NY 10901

Precision Sports, P.O. Box 219, 123 Lake St., Ithaca, NY 14850/607-273-2993 (BSA CF rifle; AYA side-by-side shotgun)

Puccinelli Co., 114 Gazania Ct., Novato, CA 94947/415-892-7977 (I.A.B., Rizzini, Bernardelli shotguns of Italy)

Quality Arms, Inc., Box 19477, Houston, TX 77224/713-870-8377 (Bernardelli shotguns)

Quantetics Corp., Imp.-Exp. Div., 582 Somerset St. W., Ottawa, Ont. K1R 5K2 Canada/613-237-0242 (Unique pistols-Can. only)
RG Industries, Inc., 2485 N.W. 20th St., Miami, FL 33142/305-635-5311 (Erma)
L. Joseph Rahn, Inc., 104 W. Main St., Manchester, MI 48158/313-428-9290 (Garbi, Astra shotguns)
Ravizza Caccia Pesca Sport, s.p.a., Via Volta 60, 20090 Cusago, Italy
Richland Arms Co., 321 W. Adrian St., Blissfield, MI 49228
F. lli Rizzini, 25060 Magno di Gardone V.T., (Bs.) Italy
Rottweil, (See Dynamit Nobel of America)
Sarco, Inc., 323 Union St., Stirling, NJ 07980/201-647-3800
Savage Industries, Inc., Springdale Rd., Westfield, MA 01085/413-562-2361
Thad Scott, P.O. Box 412, Indianola, MS 38751 (Perugini Visini; Bertuzzi s/s dble. shotguns)
Security Arms Co., (See Heckler & Koch)
Service Armament, 689 Bergen Blvd., Ridgefield, NJ 07657 (Greener Harpoon Gun)
Sherwood Intl. Export Corp., 18714 Parthenia St., Northridge, CA 91324
Shore Galleries, Inc., 3318 W. Devon Ave., Chicago, IL 60645
Shotguns of Ulm, P.O. Box 253, Millitown, NJ 08850/201-297-0573
Sile Distributors, 7 Centre Market Pl., New York, NY 10013/212-925-4111
Simmons Gun Specialties, Inc., 700 S. Rogers Rd., Olathe, KS 66062/913-782-3131
Sloan's Sprtg. Goods, Inc., 10 South St., Ridgefield, CT 06877
Franz Sodia Jagdgewehrfabrik, Schulhausgasse 14, 9170 Ferlach, (Kärnten) Austria
Steyr-Daimler-Puch, Gun South, Inc., Box 6607, 7605 Eastwood Mall, Birmingham, AL 35210/800-821-3021 (rifles)
Stoeger Industries, 55 Ruta Ct., S. Hackensack, NJ 07606/201-440-2700
Taurus International Mfg. Inc., P.O. Box 558567, Ludlam Br., Miami, FL 33155/305-662-2529
Thomas & Barrett, North Frost Center, 1250 Northeast Loop 410, Suite 200, San Antonio, TX 78209/512-826-0943
Toledo Armas, S.A., 302 Ponce de Leon Blvd., St. Augustine, FL 32084/904-829-9671
Tradewinds, Inc., P.O. Box 1191, Tacoma, WA 98401
Uberti, Aldo & Co., Via G. Carducci 41 or 39, Ponte Zanano (Brescia), Italy
Ignacio Ugartechea, Apartado 21, Eibar, Spain
Valmet Sporting Arms Div., 7 Westchester Plaza, Elmsford, NY 10523/914-347-4440 (sporting types)
Valor of Florida Corp., P.O. Box 10116, Hialeah, FL 33010/305-633-0127 (Valmet)
Ventura Imports, P.O. Box 2782, Seal Beach, CA 90740 (European shotguns)
Verney-Carron, B.P. 72, 54 Boulevard Thiers, 42002 St. Etienne Cedex, France
Perugini Visini & Co. s.r.l., Via Camprelle, 126, 25080 Nuvolera (Bs.), Italy
Waffen-Frankonia, see: Frankonia Jagd
Weatherby's, 2781 Firestone Blvd., So. Gate, CA 90280/213-569-7186
Winchester, Olin Corp., 120 Long Ridge Rd., Stamford, CT 06904
Fabio Zanotti di Stefano, Via XXV Aprile 1, 25063 Gardone V.T. (Brescia) Italy
Zavodi Crvena Zastava, 29 Novembra St., No. 12, Belgrade, Yugosl.
Antonio Zoli & Co., See: Fiocchi of America, Inc.

GUNS & GUN PARTS, REPLICA AND ANTIQUE

Antique Gun Parts, Inc., 1118 S. Braddock Ave., Pittsburgh, PA 15218/412-241-1811 (ML)
Armoury Inc., Rte. 202, New Preston, CT 06777
Artistic Arms, Inc., Box 23, Hoagland, IN 46745 (Sharps-Borchardt replica)
Beeman Precisions Arms, Inc., 47-GDD Paul Dr., San Rafael, CA 94903/415-472-7121
Bob's Place, Box 283J, Clinton, IA 52732 (obsolete Winchester parts only)
Dave Chicoine, d/b/a Liberty A.S.P., 19 Key St., Eastport, ME 04631/207-853-2327(S&W only; ctlg. $5)
Collector's Armoury, Inc., 800 Slaters Lane, Alexandria, VA 22314/703-339-8005
Dixie Gun Works, Inc., Hwy 51, South, Union City, TN 38261/901-885-0561
Federal Ordnance Inc., 1443 Portrero Ave., So. El Monte, CA 91733/213-350-4161
Jack First Distributors, Inc., 44633 Sierra Hwy., Lancaster, CA 93534/805-945-6981
Fred Goodwin, Goodwin's Gun Shop, Sherman Mills, ME 04776/207-365-4451 (antique guns & parts)
Hansen & Co., 244 Old Post Rd., Southport, CT 06490/203-259-7337
Terry H. Kopp, Highway 13, Lexington, MO 64067/816-259-2636 (restoration & pts. 1890 & 1906 Winch.)
The House of Muskets, Inc., 120 N. Pagosa Blvd., Pagosa Springs, CO 81147/303-264-2295 (ML guns)
Log Cabin Sport Shop, 8010 Lafayette Rd., Lodi, OH 44254/216-948-1082 (ctlg. $30)
Edw. E. Lucas, 32 Garfield Ave., East Brunswick, NJ 08816/201-251-5526 (45/70 Springfield parts; some Sharps, Spencer parts)
Lyman Products Corp., Middlefield, CT 06455
Tommy Munsch Gunsmithing, Rt. 2, Box 248, Little Falls, MN 56345/612-632-5835 (parts list $1.50; oth. inq. SASE)
Numrich Arms Co., West Hurley, NY 12491
Replica Models, Inc., 800 Slaters Lane, Alexandria, VA 22314/703-339-8005
S&S Firearms, 88-21 Aubrey Ave., Glendale, NY 11385/212-497-1100
Sarco, Inc., 323 Union St., Stirling, NJ 07980/201-647-3800
C. H. Stoppler, 1426 Walton Ave., New York, NY 10452 (miniature guns)
Upper Missouri Trading Co., Box 191, Crofton, NE 68730/402-388-4844
C. H. Weisz, Box 311, Arlington, VA 22210/703-243-9161
W. H. Wescombe, P.O. Box 488, Glencoe, CA 95232 (Rem. R.B. parts)

GUNS (Pellet)

Barnett International, Inc., P.O. Box 934, 1967 Gunn Highway,Odessa, FL 33556/920-2241
Beeman Precision Airguns, 47 Paul Dr., San Rafael, CA 94903/415-472-7121

Benjamin Air Rifle Co., 1525 So. 8th St., Louis, MO 63104
Crosman Airguns, 980 Turk Hill Rd., Fairport, NY 14450/716-223-6000
Daisy Mfg. Co., Rogers, AR 72756 (also Feinwerkbau)
Dynamit Nobel of America, Inc., 105 Stonehurst Ct., Northvale, NJ 07647/201-767-1660 (Dianawerk)
Great Lakes Airguns, 6175 So. Park Ave., Hamburg, NY 14075/716-648-6666
Harrington & Richardson Arms Co., Industrial Rowe, Gardner, MA 01440 (Webley)
Gil Hebard Guns, Box 1, Knoxville, IL 61448
Interarms, 10 Prince, Alexandria, VA 22313 (Walther)
Kendall International Inc., 501 East North, Carlisle, KY 40311/606-289-7336 (Italian Airmatch)
Mandall Shooting Supplies, Inc., P.O. Box 2327, Scottsdale, AZ 85251/602-945-2553 (Cabanas line)
Marathon Products Inc., 1331 Silas Deane Highway, Wethersfield, CT 06109/203-563-0222
Marksman Products, see: S/R Industries
Paragon Sales & Services, Inc., P.O. Box 2022, Joliet, IL 60434/815-725-9212
Phoenix Arms Co., Little London Rd., Horam, Nr. Heathfield, East Sussex TN21 OBJ, England (Jackal)
Power Line (See Daisy Mfg. Co.)
Precise, 3 Chestnut, Suffern, NY 10901
Precision Sports, P.O. Box 219, 123 Lake St., Ithaca, NY 14850/607-273-2993 (B.S.A.)
S/R Industries, Inc., 2133 Dominguez St., P.O. Box 2983, Torrance, CA 90509/213-320-8004 (Marksman)
Service Armament, 689 Bergen Blvd., Ridgefield, NJ 07657 (Webley)
Sheridan Products, Inc., 3205 Sheridan, Racine, WI 53403
Smith & Wesson, 2100 Roosevelt Ave., Springfield, MA 01104
Target Airgun Supply, 11552 Knott St., Suite 2, Garden Grove, CA 92641/714-892-4473

GUNS, SURPLUS—PARTS AND AMMUNITION

Can Am Enterprises, Fruitland, Ont. LOR ILO, Canada/416-643-4357 (Enfield rifles)
Century Arms, Inc., 3-5 Federal St., St. Albans, VT 05478
Walter Craig, Inc., Box 927, Selma, AL 36701/205-875-7989
Eastern Firearms Co., 790 S. Arroyo Pkwy., Pasadena, CA 91105
J. M. Emringer, Armurier, 3A, rue de Bettembourg, L-3346 Leudelange, Grand-Duchy of Luxemburg
Garcia National Gun Traders, 225 S.W. 22nd, Miami, FL 33135
Hansen Cartridge Co., 246 Old Post Rd., Southport, CT 06490/203-259-5424
Lever Arms Serv. Ltd., 572 Howe St., Vancouver, B.C., Canada V6C 2E3/604-685-6913
Paragon Sales & Services, Inc., P.O. Box 2022, Joliet, IL 60434 (ammunition)
Sarco, Inc., 323 Union St., Stirling, NJ 07980/201-647-3800
Service Armament Co., 689 Bergen Blvd., Ridgefield, NJ 07657
Sherwood Intl. Export Corp., 18714 Parthenia St., Northridge, CA 91324
Springfield Sporters Inc., R.D. 1, Penn Run, PA 15765/412-254-2626

GUNS, U.S.-made

AMT (Arcadia Machine & Tool), 536 N. Vincent Ave., Covina, CA 91722/213-915-7803
Accuracy Systems, Inc., 15203 N. Cave Creek Rd., Phoenix, AZ 85032/602-971-1991
Advantage Arms USA, Inc., 840 Hampden Ave., St. Paul, MN 55114/612-644-5197
Allen Fire Arms Co., 1107 Pen Rd., Santa Fe, NM 87501/505-983-1961 (ML)
Alpha Arms, Inc., 12923 Valley Branch, Dallas, TX 75234/214-243-8124
American Arms (Eagle 380 auto pistol), See: Wilkerson Firearms Corp.
American Derringer Corp., 127 N. Lacy Dr., Waco, TX 76705/817-799-9111
ArmaLite, 118 E. 16th St., Costa Mesa, CA 92627
Armament Systems and Procedures, Inc., Box 356, Appleton, WI 54912/414-731-8893 (ASP pistol)
Arminex, 7882 E. Gray Rd., Scottsdale Airpark, Scottsdale, AZ 85260/800-TRI-FIRE (Excalibur s.a. pistol)
Arm Tech, Armament Technologies Inc., 240 Sargent Dr., New Haven, CT 06511/203-562-2543 (22-cal. derringers)
Arnett Guns (See Gary DelSignore Weaponry)
Artistic Arms, Inc.,Box 23, Hoagland, IN 46745 (Sharps-Borchardt)
Artistic Firearms Corp., John Otteman, 4005 Hecker Pass Hwy., Gilroy, CA 95020/408-842-4278 (A.F.C. Comm. Rife 1881-1981)
Auto Nine Corp., see: FTL Marketing Corp.
Auto-Ordnance Corp., Box ZG, West Hurley, NY 12491
Barrett Firearms Mfg. Co. Inc., 312 S. Church St., Murfreesboro, TN 37130/615-896-2938 (Light Fifty)
Bighorn Rifle Co., P.O. Box 215, American Fork, UT 84003/801-756-4222
Bogun Inc., 15125 Garfield Ave., P.O. Box 740, Paramount, CA 90723/213-531-2211 (conv. rifle/shotgun)
Bren Ten (See Dornaus & Dixon Ent.)
Brown Precision Co., P.O. Box 270W; 7786 Molinos Ave., Los Molinos, CA 96055/916-384-2506 (High Country rifle)
Browning (Gen. Offices), Rt. 1, Morgan, UT 84050/801-876-2711
Browning (Parts & Service), Rt. 4, Box 624-B, Arnold, MO 63010/314-287-6800
Bushmaster Firearms Co., 803 Forest Ave., Portland ME 04103/207-775-3324 (police handgun)
CB Arms, Inc., 65 Hathaway Court, Pittsburgh, PA 15235/412-795-4621 (Double Deuce h'gun)
Challanger Mfg. Corp., 118 Pearl St., Mt. Vernon, NY 10550 (Hopkins & Allen)
Champlin Firearms, Inc., Box 3191, Enid, OK 73701
Charter Arms Corp., 430 Sniffens Ln., Stratford, CT 06497
Chipmunk Manufacturing Inc., 114 E. Jackson, Medford, OR 97501/503-664-5722 (22 S.S. rifle)
Classic Arms, 815-22nd St., Union City, NJ 08757/201-863-1493
Colt Firearms, P.O. Box 1868, Hartford, CT 06102/203-236-6311
Commando Arms, Inc., Box 10214, Knoxville, TN 37919

Coonan Arms, Inc., 830 Hampden Ave., St. Paul, MN 55114/612-646-6672 (357 Mag. Autom.)
Crown City Arms, P.O. Box 1126, Cortland, NY 13045/607-753-8238 (45 auto handgun)
Cumberland Arms, Rt. 1, Shafer Rd., Blanton Chapel, Manchester, TN 37355
Davis Industries, 13748 Arapahoe Pl., Chino, CA 91710/714-591-4727 (derringer)
Leonard Day & Co., P.O. Box 723, East Hampton, MA 01027/413-527-7990 (ML)
Gary DelSignore Weaponry, 3675 Cottonwood, Cedar City, UT 84720/801-586-2505 (Arnett Guns)
Demro Products Inc., 372 Progress Dr., Manchester, CT 06040/203-649-4444 (Wasp, Tac guns)
Detonics Mfg. Corp., 2500 Seattle Tower, Third & University, Seattle, WA 98101/206-747-2100 (auto pistol)
Dornaus & Dixon Enterprises, Inc., 15896 Manufacture Lane, Huntingdon Beach, CA 92649/714-891-5090
DuBiel Arms Co., 1724 Baker Rd., Sherman, TX 75090/214-893-7313
El Dorado Arms, 35 Gilpin Ave., Happauge, NY 11787/516-234-0212
Excalibur (See Arminex)
FTL Marketing Corp., 12521-3 Oxnard St., No. Hollywood, CA 91601/213-985-2946
Falling Block Works, P.O. Box 3087, Fairfax, VA 22038/703-476-0043
Federal Eng. Corp., 3161 N. Elston Ave., Chicago, IL 60618 (XC-220 carbine)
Firearms Imp. & Exp. Corp., P.O. Box 4866, Hialeah Lakes, Hialeah, FL 33014/305-685-5966 (FIE)
Frankford Arsenal, Inc., 1047 NE 43d Court, Ft. Lauderdale, FL 33334/305-566-8690 (XM-177 carbine)
Fraser Firearms Corp., 34575 Commerce Rd., Fraser, MI 48026/313-293-9545
Freedom Arms Co., Freedom, WY 83120 (mini revolver, Casull rev.)
Golden Age Arms Co., 14 W. Winter St., Delaware, OH 43015
HJS Industries, Inc., P.O. Box 4351, Brownsville, TX 78520/512-542-3340 (22 4-bbl.; 38 S&W SS derringers)
Harrington & Richardson, Industrial Rowe, Gardner, MA 01440
Hatfield Rifle Works, 2028 Frederick Ave., St. Joseph, MO 64501/816-279-8688 (squirrel rifle)
Hawken Armory, P.O. Box 2604, Hot Springs, AR 71901/501-268-8296 (ML)
A.D. Heller, Inc., Box 268, Grand Ave., Baldwin, NY 11510
High Standard Sporting Firearms, 31 Prestige Park Circle, East Hartford, CT 06108
Holmes Firearms Corp., Rte. 6, Box 242, Fayetteville, AR 72701
Hopkins & Allen Arms, 3 Ethel Ave., P.O. Box 217, Hawthorne, NJ 07507/201-427-1165 (ML)
Hyper-Single Precision SS Rifles, 520 E. Beaver, Jenks, OK 74037/918-299-2391
Interdynamic of America, Inc., 1190 Southwest 128th St., Miami, FL 33186/305-232-2158
Ithaca Gun Co., Ithaca, NY 14850
Iver Johnson, 2202 Redmond Rd., Jacksonville, AR 72076/501-982-9491
Jennings Firearms, 4510 Carter Ct., Chino, CA 91710/714-591-3921
KK Arms Co., Karl Kash, Star Route, Box 671, Kerrville, TX 78028/512-257-4441 (handgun)
Kimber of Oregon, Inc., 9039 S.E. Jannsen Rd., Clackamas, OR 97015/503-656-1704
Kimel Industries, Box 335, Matthews, NC 28105/704-821-7663
L.A.R. Manufacturing Co., 4133 West Farm Rd., West Jordan, UT 84084/801-255-7106 (Grizzly Win Mag pistol)
Ljutic Ind., Inc., P.O. Box 2117, 918 N. 5th Ave., Yakima, WA 98902/509-248-0476 (Mono-Gun)
Lone Star Armaments, Inc., 1701 No. Greenville Ave., Suite 202, Richardson, TX 75081 (semi-auto pistols)
M & N Distributors, 23535 Telo St., Torrance, CA 90505/213-530-9000 (Budischowsky)
MS Safari Arms, P.O. Box 23370, Phoenix, AZ 85062/602-269-7283
Magnum Sales, Subs. of Mag-na-port, 41302 Executive Drive, Mt. Clemens, MI 48045/313-469-7534
Marlin Firearms Co., 100 Kenna Drive, New Haven, CT 06473
Matteson Firearms Inc., Otsego Rd., Canajoharie, NY 13317/607-264-3744 (SS rifles)
Merrill Pistol, see: Rock Pistol Mfg.
Michigan Armament, Marketing Inc., 135 Sumner Ave., Lake Elsinore, CA 92330/714-674-5750 (pistols)
Michigan Arms Corp., 363 Elmwood, Troy, MI 48083/313-583-1518 (ML)
Mitchell Arms of California, Inc., 1800 Talbott Way, Anaheim, CA 92805/714-634-1131 (AR-50 survival rifle)
The M.O.A. Corp., 110 Front St., Dayton, OH 45402/513-223-6401 (Maximum pistol)
O.F. Mossberg & Sons, Inc., 7 Grasso St., No. Haven, CT 06473
Mowrey Gun Works, Box 38, Iowa Park, TX 76367
Navy Arms Co., 689 Bergen Blvd., Ridgefield, NJ 07657
North American Arms, P.O. Box 280, Spanish Fork, UT 84660/801-798-9893
North Georgia Armament, 5265 Jimmy Carter Blvd., Suite 1442, Norcross, GA 30093/404-446-3504
Numrich Arms Corp., W. Hurley, NY 12491
ODI, Inc., 124A Greenwood Ave., Midland Park, NJ 07432/201-444-4557
Oregon Trail Riflesmiths, Inc., P.O. Box 45212, Boise, ID 83711/208-336-8631 (ML)
Ozark Mountain Arms, Inc., P.O. Box 397, 141 Byrne St., Ashdown, AR 71822/501-989-2345 (ML)
Pecos Valley Armory, 1022 So. Canyon, Carlsbad, NM 88220/505-887-6023 (ML)
Phillips & Bailey, Inc., P.O. Box 219253, Houston, TX 77218/713-392-0207 (357/9 Ultra, rev. conv.)
Power Custom, Inc., P.O. Box 1604, Independence, MO 64055 (Power Custom Combat handgun)
Provider Arms, Inc., 261 Haglund Dr., Chesterton, IN 46304/219-879-5590 (ML Predator rifle)
R.B. Industries, Ltd. (See Fraser Firearms Corp.)
R G Industries, 2485 N.W. 20th St., Miami, FL 33142/305-635-5311
Randall Manufacturing, 7965 San Fernando Rd., Sun Valley, CA 91352/213-875-2045
Raven Arms, 1300 Bixby Dr., Industry, CA 91745/213-961-2511 (P-25 pistols)
Remington Arms Co., 939 Barnum Ave., P.O. Box #1939, Bridgeport, CT 06601
Rock Pistol Mfg., Inc., 150 Viking, Brea, CA 92621/714-990-2444 (Merrill pistol)
Ruger (See Sturm, Ruger & Co.)
Savage Industries, Inc., Springdale Rd., Westfield, MA 01085/413-562-2361
Sceptre, Inc., P.O. Box 1282, Marietta, GA 30061/404-428-5513
Semmerling Corp., P.O. Box 400, Newton, MA 02160
Serrifile, Inc., P.O. Box 508, Littlerock, CA 93543/805-945-0713 (derringer; single shot)
C. Sharps Arms Co., Inc., P.O. Box 885, Big Timber, MT 59011/406-932-4353
Shepherd & Turpin Dist. Co., P.O. Box 40, Washington, UT 84780/801-635-2001
Shiloh Products, 181 Plauderville Ave., Garfield, NJ 07026 (Sharps)
The Silhouette, 1409 Benton, Box 1509, Idaho Falls, ID 83401/208-529-5313 (Wichita International pistol)
Six Enterprises, 6564 Hidden Creek Dr., Dan Jose, CA 95120/408-268-8296 (Timberliner rifle)
Smith & Wesson, Inc., 2100 Roosevelt Ave., Springfield, MA 01101
Sokolovsky Corp., Box 70113, Sunnyvale, CA 94086/408-738-1935 (45 Automaster pistol)
Sporting Arms, Inc., 12923 Valley Branch, Dallas, TX 75234/214-243-8124 (Snake Charmer II shotgun)
Springfield Armory, 111 E. Exchange St., Geneseo, IL 61254
SSK Industries, Rt. 1, Della Dr., Bloomingdale, OH 43910/614-264-0176
Steel City Arms, Inc., 1883 Main St., Pittsburgh, PA 15215/412-784-9400 (d.a. "Double Deuce" pistol)
Sterling Arms Corp., 211 Grand St., Lockport, NY 14094/716-434-6631
Sturm, Ruger & Co., Southport, CT 06490
Tennessee Valley Arms, P.O. Box 2022, Union City, TN 38261/901-885-4456
Texas Gun & Machine Co., P.O. Box 2837, Texas City, TX 77590/713-945-0070 (Texas rifles)
Texas Longhorn Arms, Inc., P. O. Box 703, Richmond, TX 77469/713-341-0775 (S.A. sixgun)
Thompson-Center Arms, Box 2405, Rochester, NH 03867
Trail Guns Armory, 1634 E. Main St., League City, TX 77573 (muzzleloaders)
Trapper Gun, Inc., 18717 E. 14 Mile Rd., Fraser, MI 48026/313-792-0133 (handguns)
United Sporting Arms, Inc, 2021 E. 14th St., Tucson, AZ 85719/602-623-4001 (handguns)
U.S. Repeating Arms Co., P.O. Box 30-300, New Haven, CT 06511/203-789-5000
Universal Firearms, 3740 E. 10th Ct., Hialeah, FL 33013
Weatherby's, 2781 E. Firestone Blvd., South Gate, CA 90280
Weaver Arms Corp., 344 No. Vinewood St., Escondido, CA 92026/714-745-4342
WSI, P.O. Box 66, Youngstown, OH 44501/216-743-9666 (9mm Viking)
Dan Wesson Arms, 293 So. Main St., Monson, MA 01057
Wichita Arms, 444 Ellis, Wichita, KS 67211/316-265-0661
Wildey, 28 Old Route 7, Brookfield, CT 06804/203-775-4261
Wildey Firearms, 299 Washington St., Newburgh, NY 12550/1-800-243-GUNS
Wilkerson Firearms Corp., 6531 Westminster Blvd., Westminster, CA 92683/714-891-1441 (Eagle 380 d.a. auto)
Wilkinson Arms, Rte. #2, Box 2166, Parma, ID 83660/208-722-6771
Winchester, (See U.S. Repeating Arms)

GUNSMITHS, CUSTOM (see Custom Gunsmiths)

GUNSMITHS, HANDGUN (see Pistolsmiths)

GUNSMITH SCHOOLS

Colorado School of Trades, 1575 Hoyt, Lakewood, CO 80215/303-233-4697
Lassen Community College, P.O. Box 3000, Hiway 139, Susanville, CA 96130/916-257-6161
Modern Gun Repair School, 2538 No. 8th St., Phoenix, AZ 85006/602-990-8346 (home study)
Montgomery Technical College, P.O. Drawer 487, Troy, NC 27371/919-572-3691
Murray State College, Gunsmithing Program, Tishomingo, OK 73460/405-371-2371
North American School of Firearms, Curriculum Development Ctr., 4401 Birch St., Newport Beach, CA 92663/714-546-7360 (correspondence)
North American School of Firearms, Education Service Center, Oak & Pawnee St., Scranton, PA 18515/717-342-7701
Penn. Gunsmith School, 812 Ohio River Blvd., Avalon, Pittsburgh, PA 15202/412-766-1812
Pine Technical Institute, 1100 Fourth St., Pine City, MN 55063/612-629-6764
Police Sciences Institute, 4401 Birch St., Newport Beach, CA 92660/714-546-7360 (General Law Enforcement Course)
Shenandoah School of Gunsmithing, P.O. Box 300, Bentonville, VA 22610/703-743-5494
Southeastern Community College, Gunsmithing Dept., Drawer F, West Burlington, IA 52655/319-752-2731
Trinidad State Junior College, 600 Prospect, Trinidad, CO 81082/303-846-5621
Yavapai College, 1100 East Sheldon St., Prescott, AZ 86301/602-445-7300

GUNSMITH SUPPLIES, TOOLS, SERVICES

Acoustic Trap Co., 34 Bay Ridge Ave., Brooklyn, NY 11220/212-745-9311 (test bullet trap)

Albright Prod. Co., P. O. Box 1144, Portola, CA 96122 (trap buttplates)

Alley Supply Co., Carson Valley Industrial Park, P.O. Box 848, Gardnerville, NV 89410/702-782-3800 (JET line lathes, mills, etc.)

Ametek, Hunter Spring Div., One Spring Ave., Hatfield, PA 19440/215-822-2971 (trigger gauge)

Anderson Mfg. Co., Union Gap Sta., P.O. Box 3120, Yakima, WA 98903/509-453-2349 (tang safe)

Answer Stocking Systems, 113 N. 2nd St., Whitewater, WI 53190/414-473-4848 (urethane hammers, vice jaws, etc.)

Armite Labs., 1845 Randolph St., Los Angeles, CA 90001/213-587-7744 (pen oiler)

B-Square Co., Box 11281, Ft. Worth, TX 76110/800-433-2909

Jim Baiar, 490 Halfmoon Rd., Columbia Falls, MT 59912 (hex screws)

Behlert Custom Guns, Inc., Box 227, Monmouth Junction, NJ 08852/201-329-2284

Dennis M. Bellm Gunsmithing, Inc., dba P.O. Ackley Rifle Barrels, 2376 S. Redwood Rd., Salt Lake City, UT 84119/801-974-0697 (rifles only)

Al Biesen, W. 2039 Sinto Ave., Spokane, WA 99201 (grip caps, buttplates)

Roger Biesen, 5021 W. Rosewood, Spokane, WA 99208/509-328-9340 (grip caps, buttplates)

Billingsley & Brownell, Box 25, Dayton, Wy 82836/307-655-9344 (cust. grip caps, bolt handle, etc.)

Blue Ridge Machine and Tool, P.O. Box 536, Hurricane, WV 25526/304-562-3538 (machinery, tools, shop suppl.)

Bonanza Sports Mfg. Co., 412 Western Ave., Faribault, MN 55021/507-332-7153

Briganti Custom Gun-Smithing, P.O. Box 56, 475-Route 32, Highland Mills, NY 10930/914-928-9816 (cold rust bluing, hand polishing, metal work)

Brookstone Co., 125 Vose Farm Rd., Peterborough, NH 03458

Brownell's, Inc., Rt. 2, Box 1, Montezuma, IA 50171/515-623-5401

Lenard M. Brownell (See Billingsley & Brownell)

W.E. Brownell Co. Checkering Tools, 3356 Moraga Place, San Diego, CA 92117/619-276-6146

Burgess Vibrocrafters, Inc. (BVI), Rte. 83, Grayslake, IL 60030

M.H. Canjar, 500 E. 45th Denver, CO 80216/303-623-5777 (triggers, etc.)

Chapman Mfg. Co., P.O. Box 250, Rte. 17 at Saw Mill Rd., Durham, CT 06422/203-349-9228

Chase Chemical Corp., 3527 Smallman St., Pittsburgh, PA 15201/412-681-6544 (Chubb Multigauge for shotguns)

Chicago Wheel & Mfg. Co., 1101 W. Monroe St., Chicago, IL 60607/312-226-8155 (Handee grinders)

Dave Chicoine, d/b/a Liberty A.S.P., 19 Key St., Eastport, ME 04631/207-853-2327 (spl. S&W tools)

Classic Arms Corp., P.O. Box 8, Palo Alto, CA 94302/415-321-7243 (floorplates, grip caps)

Clover Mfg. Co., 139 Woodward Ave., Norwalk, CT 06856/800-243 6492 (Clover compound)

Clymer Mfg. Co., Inc., 14241 W. 11 Mile Rd., Oak Park, MI 48237/313-541-5533 (reamers)

Dave Cook, 720 Hancock Ave., Hancock, MI 49930 (metalsmithing only)

Dayton-Traister Co., 9322-900th West, P.O. Box 593, Oak Harbor, WA 98277/206-675-5375 (triggers)

Dem-Bart Checkering Tools, Inc., 6807 Hiway #2, Snohomish, WA 98290/206-568-7356

Dremel Mfg. Co., 4915-21st St., Racine, WI 53406 (grinders)

Chas. E. Duffy, Williams Lane, West Hurley, NY 12491

Peter Dyson Ltd., 29-31 Church St., Honley, Huddersfield, Yorksh. HD7 2AH, England (accessories f. antique gun coll.)

Edmund Scientific Co., 101 E. Glouster Pike, Barrington, NJ 08007

Emco-Lux, 2050 Fairwood Ave., P.O. Box 07861, Columbus, OH 43207/614-445-8328

Jack First Distributors, Inc., 44633 Sierra Hwy., Lancaster, CA 93534/805-945-6981

Forster Products, Inc., 82 E. Lanark Ave., Lanark, IL 61046/815-493-6360

Francis Tool Co., (f'ly Keith Francis Inc.), P.O. Box 7861, Eugene, OR 97401/503-746-4831 (reamers)

G. R. S. Corp., P.O. Box 748, 900 Overlander St., Emporia, KS 66801/316-343-1084 (Gravermeister; Grave Max tools)

Gilmore Pattern Works, P.O. Box 50084, Tulsa, OK 74150/918-245-9627 (Wagner safe-T-planer)

Glendo Corp., P.O. Box 1153, Emporia, KS 66801/316-343-1084 (Accu-Finish tool)

Grace Metal Prod., 115 Ames St., Elk Rapids, MI 49629 (screw drivers, drifts)

Gunline Tools, Box 478, Placentia, CA 92670/714-528-5252

Gun-Tec, P.O. Box 8125, W. Palm Beach, Fl 33407

Half Moon Rifle Shop, 490 Halfmoon Rd., Columbia Falls, MT 59912/406-892-4409 (hex screws)

Henriksen Tool Co., Inc., P.O. Box 668, Phoenix, OR 97535/503-535-2309 (reamers)

Huey Gun Cases (Marvin Huey), Box 98, Reed's Spring, MO 65737/417-538-4233 (high grade English ebony tools)

Ken Jantz Supply, Rt. 1, Sulphur, OK 73086/405-622-3790

Jeffredo Gunsight Co., 1629 Via Monserate, Fallbrook, CA 92028 (trap buttplate)

K&D Grinding Co., P.O. Box 1766, Alexandria, LA 71301/318-487-0823 (cust. tools f. pistolsmiths)

Kasenit Co., Inc., 3 King St., Mahwah, NJ 07430/201-529-3663 (surface hrdng. comp.)

Terry K. Kopp, Highway 13, Lexington, MO 64067/816-259-2636 (stock rubbing compound; rust preventive grease)

J. Korzinek, RD#2, Box 73, Canton, PA 17724/717-673-8512 (stainl. steel bluing; broch. $1.50)

John G. Lawson, (The Sight Shop) 1802 E. Columbia Ave., Tacoma, WA 98404/206-474-5465

Lea Mfg. Co., 237 E. Aurora St., Waterbury, CT 06720/203-753-5116

Lock's Phila. Gun Exch., 6700 Rowland Ave., Philadelphia, PA 19149/215-332-6225

Longbranch Gun Bluing Co., 2455 Jacaranda Lane, Los Osos, CA 93402/805-528-1792

McIntrye Tools, P.O. Box 491/State Road #1144, Troy, NC 27371/919-572-2603 (shotgun bbl. facing tool)

Michaels of Oregon Co., P.O. Box 13010, Portland, OR 97213/503-255-6890

Viggo Miller, P.O. Box 4181, Omaha, NE 68104 (trigger attachment)

Miller Single Trigger Mfg. Co., R.D. 1, Box 99, Millersburg, PA 17061/717-692-3704

Frank Mittermeier, 3577 E. Tremont, New York, NY 10465

Moderntools, 1671 W. McNab Rd., Ft. Lauderdale, FL 33309/305-979-3900

N&J Sales Co., Lime Kiln Rd., Northford, CT 06472/203-484-0247 (screwdrivers)

Karl A. Neise, Inc., 1671 W. McNab Rd., Ft. Lauderdale, FL 33309/305-979-3900

Palmgren Steel Prods., Chicago Tool & Engineering Co., 8383 South Chicago Ave., Chicago, IL 60617/312-721-9675 (vises, etc.)

Panavise Prods., Inc., 2850 E. 29th St., Long Beach, CA 90806/213-595-7621

C.R. Pedersen & Son, 2717 S. Pere Marquette, Ludington, MI 49431/616-843-2061

Pilkington Gun Co., P.O. Box 1296, Mukogee, OK 74401/918-683-9418 (Q.D. scope mt.)

Richland Arms Co., 321 W. Adrian St., Blissfield, MI 49228

Riley's Inc., 121 No. Main St., P.O. Box 139, Avilla, IN 46710/219-897-2351 (Niedner buttplates, grip caps)

Roto/Carve, 6509 Indian Hills Rd., Minneapolis, MN 55435/800-533-8988 (tool)

A.G. Russell Co., 1705 Hiway 71 North, Springdale, AR 72764/501-751-7341 (Arkansas oilstones)

Schaffner Mfg. Co., Emsworth, Pittsburgh, PA 15202 (polishing kits)

SGW, Inc. (formerly Schuetzen Gun Works), 624 Old Pacific Hwy, S.E. Olympia, WA 98503/206-456-3471

Shaw's, 9447 W. Lilac Rd., Escondido, CA 92025/619-728-7070

L.S. Starrett Co., 121 Crescent St., Athol, MA 01331/617-249-3551

Texas Platers Supply Co., 2453 W. Five Mile Parkway, Dallas, TX 75233 (plating kit)

Timney Mfg. Inc., 3106 W. Thomas Rd., Phoenix, AZ 85017/602-269-6937

Stan de Treville, Box 33021, San Diego, CA 92103/619-298-3393 (checkering patterns)

Turner Co., Div. Cleanweld Prods., Inc., 821 Park Ave., Sycamore, IL 60178/815-895-4545

Twin City Steel Treating Co., Inc. 1114 S. 3rd, Minneapolis, MN 55415/612-332-4849 (heat treating)

Walker Arms Co., Rt. 2, Box 73, Hwy. 80 W, Selma, AL 36701/205-872-6231 (tools)

Will-Burt Co., 169 So. Main, Orrville, OH 44667 (vises)

Williams Gun Sight Co., 7389 Lapeer Rd., Davison, MI 48423

Wilson Arms Co., 63 Leetes Island Rd., Branford, CT 06405/203-488-7297

Wisconsin Platers Supply Co. (See Texas Platers)

W.C. Wolff Co., P.O. Box 232, Ardmore, PA 19003/215-647-1880 (springs)

Woodcraft Supply Corp., 313 Montvale, Woburn, MA 01801

HANDGUN ACCESSORIES

Assault Accessories, P.O. Box 8994 CRB, Tucson, AZ 85738/602-791-7860 (pistol shoulder stocks)

Baramie Corp., 6250 E. 7 Mile Rd., Detroit, MI 48234 (Hip-Grip)

Bar-Sto Precision Machine, 13377 Sullivan Rd., Twentynine Palms, CA 92277/619-367-2747

Behlert Custom Guns, Inc., Box 227, Monmouth Junction, NJ 08852/201-329-2284

Bingham Ltd., 1775-C Wilwat Dr., Norcross, GA 30093 (magazines)

C'Arco, P.O. Box 308, Highland, CA 92346 (Ransom Rest)

Central Specialties Co., 6030 Northwest Hwy., Chicago, IL 60631/312-774-5000 (trigger lock)

Dave Chicoine, d/b/a Liberty A.S.P., 19 Key St., Eastport, ME 04631/207-853-2327 (shims f. S&W revs.)

D&E Magazines Mfg., P.O. Box 4876, Sylmar, CA 91342 (clips)

Doskocil Mfg. Co., Inc, P.O. Box 1246, Arlington, TX 75010/817-467-5116 (Gun Guard cases)

Essex Arms, Box 345, Island Pond, VT 05846/802-723-4313 (45 Auto frames)

Frielich Police Equipment, 396 Broome St., New York, NY 10013/212-254-3045 (cases)

R. S. Frielich, 211 East 21st St., New York, NY 10010/212-777-4477 (cases)

Terry K. Kopp, Highway 13, Lexington, MO 64067/816-259-2636

Lee's Red Ramps, 7252 E. Ave. U-3, Littlerock, CA 93543/805-944-4487 (ramp insert kits; spring kits)

Lee Precision Inc., 4275 Hwy. U, Hartford, WI 53027 (pistol rest holders)

Kent Lomont, 4236 West 700 South, Poneto, IN 46781 (Auto Mag only)

Lone Star Gunleather, 1301 Brushy Bend Dr., Round Rock, TX 78664/512-255-1805

Los Gatos Grip & Specialty Co., P.O. Box 1850, Los Gatos, CA 95030 (custom-made)

Mascot rib sight (See Travis R. Strahan)

No-Sho Mfg. Co., 10727 Glenfield Ct., Houston, TX 77096/713-723-0966

Harry Owen (See Sport Specialties)

Pachmayr, 1220 S. Grand, Los Angeles, CA 90015 (cases)

Pacific Intl. Mchdsg. Corp., 2215 "J" St., Sacramento, CA 95818/916-446-2737 (Vega 45 Colt comb. mag.)

Poly-Choke Div., Marble Arms Corp., 420 Industrial Park, Gladstone, MI 49837/906-428-3710 (handgun ribs)

Randall Manufacturing, 7965 San Fernando Rd. Sun Valley, CA 91352/213-875-2045 (magazines, carrying rugs)

Sile Distributors, 7 Centre Market Pl., New York, NY 10013

Sport Specialties, (Harry Owen), Box 5337, Hacienda Hts., CA 91745/213-968-5806 (.22 rimfire adapters; .22 insert bbls. f. T/C Contender, autom. pistols)

Sportsmen's Equipment Co., 415 W. Washington, San Diego, CA 92103/619-296-1501

Travis R. Strahan, Rt. 7,Townsend Circle, Ringgold, GA 30736/404-937-4495 (Mascot rib sights)
Turkey Creek Enterprises, Rt. 1, Box 10, Red Oak, CA 74563/918-754-2884 (wood handgun cases)
Melvin Tyler, 1326 W. Britton, Oklahoma City, OK 73114/800-654-8415 (grip adaptor)
Whitney Sales, P.O. Box 875, Reseda, CA 91335/818-345-4212

HANDGUN GRIPS

Ajax Custom Grips, Inc., 12229 Cox Lane, Dallas, TX 75234/214-241-6302
Art Jewel Enterprises Ltd., 421A Irmen Dr., Addison, IL 60101/312-628-6220
Beeman Inc., 47 Paul Dr., San Rafael, CA 94903/415-472-7121 (airguns only)
Bingham Ltd., 1775-C Wilwat Dr., Norcross, GA 30093
Boone Trading Co., Inc., 562 Coyote Rd., Brinnon, WA 98320/206-796-4330 (ivory, custom)
Dave Chicoine, d/b/a Liberty A.S.P., 19 Key St., Eastport, ME 04631/207-853-2327 (orig. S&W 1855-1950)
Fitz Pistol Grip Co., Box 171, Douglas City, CA 96024
Gateway Shooters' Supply, Inc., 10145-103rd St., Jacksonville, FL 32210/904-778-2323 (Rogers grips)
The Gunshop, R.D. Wallace, 320 Overland Rd., Prescott, AZ 86301
Herrett's , Box 741, Twin Falls, ID 83301
Hogue Combat Grips, P.O. Box 2038, Atascadero, CA 93423/805-466-6266 (Monogrip)
Paul Jones Munitions Systems, (See Fitz Co.)
Russ Maloni, 40 Sigman Lane, Elma, NY 14059/716-652-7131
Millett Industries, 16131 Gothard St., Huntington Beach, CA 92647/714-842-5575 (custom)
Monogrip, (See Hogue)
Monte Kristo Pistol Grip Co., Box 171, Douglas City, CA 96024/916-778-3136
Mustang Custom Pistol Grips, see: Supreme Products Co.
Pachmayr Gun Works, Inc., 1220 S. Grand Ave., Los Angeles, CA 90015/213-748-7271
Robert H. Newell, 55 Coyote, Los Alamos, NM 87544/505-662-7135 (custom stocks)
Rogers Grips (See Gateway Shooters' Supply)
A. Jack Rosenberg & Sons, 12229 Cox Lane, Dallas, TX 75234/214-241-6302 (Ajax)
Royal Ordnance Works Ltd., P.O. Box 3254, Wilson, NC 27893/919-237-0515
Russwood Custom Pistol Grips, 40 Sigman Lane, Elma, NY 14059/716-652-7131 (cust. exotic woods)
Jean St. Henri, 6525 Dume Dr., Malibu, CA 90265 (custom)
Sile Dist., 7 Centre Market Pl., New York, NY 10013/212-925-4111
Sports Inc., P.O. Box 683, Park Ridge, IL 60068/312-825-8952 (Franzite)
Supreme Products Co., 1830 S. California Ave., Monrovia, CA 91016/800-423-7159/818-357-5359

HEARING PROTECTORS

AO Safety Prods., Div. of American Optical Corp., 14 Mechanic St., Southbridge, MA 01550/617-765-9711 (ear valves, ear muffs)
Bausch & Lomb, 635 St. Paul St., Rochester, NY 14602
David Clark Co., Inc., 360 Franklin St., Worcester, MA 01604
Norton Co., see: Siebe
Safety Direct, 23 Snider Way, Sparks, NV 89431/702-354-4451 (Silencio)
Siebe Norton, Inc., 16624 Edwards Rd., Cerritos, CA 90701/213-926-0545 (Lee Sonic ear valve)
Smith & Wesson, 2100 Roosevelt Ave., Springfield, MA 01101
Willson Safety Prods. Div., P.O. Box 622, Reading, PA 19603 (Ray-O-Vac)

HOLSTERS & LEATHER GOODS

Active Leather Corp., 36-29 Vernon Blvd., Long Island City, NY 11106
Alessi Custom Concealment Holsters, 2465 Niagara Falls Blvd., Tonawanda, NY 14150/716-691-5615
American Sales & Mfg. Co., P.O. Box 677, Laredo, TX 78040/512-723-6893
Andy Anderson, P.O. Box 225, North Hollywood, CA 91603/213-877-2401 (Gunfighter Custom Holsters)
Armament Systems & Procedures, Inc., P.O. Box 356, Appleton, WI 54912/414-731-8893 (ASP)
Beeman Inc., 47-GDD Paul Dr., San Rafael, CA 94903/415-472-7121
Bianchi International Inc., 100 Calle Cortez, Temecula, CA 92390/714-676-5621
Ted Blocker's Custom Holsters, Box 821, Rosemead, CA 91770/213-442-5772 (shop: 4945 Santa Anita Ave., Temple City, CA 91780)
Edward H. Bohlin, 931 N. Highland Ave., Hollywood, CA 90038/213-463-4888
Bo-Mar Tool & Mfg. Co., Rt. 12, Box 405, Longview, TX 75605/214-759-4784
Boyt Co., Div. of Welch Sptg., Box 1108, Iowa Falls, IA 51026
Brauer Bros. Mfg. Co., 2012 Washington Ave., St. Louis, MO 63103/314-231-2864
Browning, Rt. 4, Box 624-B, Arnold, MO 63010
J.M. Bucheimer Co., P.O. Box 280, Airport Rd., Frederick, MD 21701/301-662-5101
Buffalo Leather Goods, Inc., P.O. Box 4, 417 W. Main, Magnolia, AR 71753/501-234-6367
Cathey Enterprises, Inc., 9516 Neils Thompson Dr., Suite 116, Austin, TX 78758/512-837-7150
Cattle Baron Leather Co., P.O. Box 100724, San Antonio, TX 78201
Chace Leather Prods., Longhorn Div., 507 Alden St., Fall River, MA 02722/617-678-7556
Cobra Ltd., 1865 New Highway, Farmingdale, NY 11735/516-752-8544
Colt, P.O. Box 1868, Hartford, CT 06102/203-236-6311
Daisy Mfg. Co., Rogers, AR 72756
Davis Leather Co., G. Wm. Davis, P.O. Box 446, Arcadia, CA 91006/213-445-3872

Eugene DeMayo & Sons, Inc., 2795 Third Ave., Bronx, NY 10455/212-665-7075
Ellwood Epps Northern Ltd., 210 Worthington St. W., North Bay, Ont. P1B 3B4, Canada (custom made)
GALCO Gun Leather, 4311 W. Van Buren, Phoenix, AZ 85043/602-233-0596
Gunfighter (See Anderson)
Ernie Hill Speed Leather, 3128 S. Extension Rd., Mesa, AZ 85202
Hoyt Holster Co., Inc., P.O. Box 69, Coupeville, WA 98239/206-678-6640
Don Hume, Box 351, Miami, OK 74354/918-542-6604
The Hunter Corp., 3300 W. 71st Ave., Westminster, CO 80030/303-427-4626
John's Custom Leather, 525 S. Liberty St., Blairsville, PA 15717/412-459-6802
Jumbo Sports Prods., P.O. Box 280, Airport Rd., Frederick, MD 21701
Kirkpatrick Leather Co., P.O. Box 3150, Laredo, TX 89041/512-723-6631
Kolpin Mfg. Inc., P.O. Box 231, Berlin, WI 54923/414-361-0400
Morris Lawing, 150 Garland Ct., Charlotte, NC 28202/704-375-1740
George Lawrence Co., 306 S. W. First Ave., Portland, OR 97204/503-228-8244
Liberty Organization Inc., P.O. Box 306, Montrose, CA 91020/213-248-0618
Lone Star Gunleather, 1301 Brushy Bend Dr., Round Rock, TX 78664/512-255-1805
Mixson Leathercraft, Inc., 1950 W. 84th St., Hialeah, FL 33014/305-820-5190 (police leather products)
Nordac Mfg. Corp., Rt 12, Box 124, Fredericksburg, VA 22405/703-752-2552
Kenneth L. Null-Custom Concealment Holsters, R.D. #5, Box 197, Hanover, PA 17331 (See Seventrees)
Arvo Ojala, 3960 S.E. 1st, Gresham, OR 97030
Old West Reproductions, R. M. Bachman, 1840 Stag Lane, Kalispell, MT 59901/406-755-6902 (ctlg. $2)
Pioneer Prods., P.O. Box G, Magnolia, AR 71753/501-234-1566
Pony Express Sport Shop Inc., 17460 Ventura Blvd., Encino, CA 91316/213-788-0123
Red Head Brand Corp., 4949 Joseph Hardin Dr., Dallas, TX 75236/214-333-4141
Red River Outfitters, P.O. Box 241, Tujunga, CA 91042/213-352-0177
Rogers Holsters Co., Inc., 1736 St. Johns Bluff Rd., Jacksonville, FL 32216/904-641-9434
Roy's Custom Leather Goods, Hwy. 1325 & Rawhide Rd., P.O. Box G, Magnolia, AR 71753/501-234-1566
Safariland Leather Products, 1941 So. Walker Ave., Monrovia, CA 91016/213-357-7902
Safety Speed Holster, Inc., 910 So. Vail, Montebello, CA 90640/213-723-4140
Buddy Schoellkopf Products, Inc., 4949 Joseph Hardin Dr., TX 75236/214-333-2121
Seventrees Systems Ltd., R.D. 5, Box 197, Hanover, PA 17331/717-632-6873 (See Null)
Sile Distr., 7 Centre Market Pl., New York NY 10013/212-925-4111
Smith & Wesson, 2100 Roosevelt Ave., Springfield, MA 01101
Milt Sparks, Box 187, Idaho City, ID 83631/208-392-6695 (broch. $2)
Robert A. Strong Co., 105 Maplewood Ave., Gloucester, MA 01930/617-281-3300
Torel, Inc., 1053 N. South St., P.O. Box 592, Yoakum, TX 77995/512-293-2341 (gun slings)
Triple-K Mfg. Co., 568 Sixth Ave., San Diego, CA 92101/619-232-2066
Viking Leathercraft, Inc., P.O. Box 2030, 2248-2 Main St., Chula Vista, CA 92012/619-429-8050
Whitco, Box 1712, Brownsville, TX 78520 (Hide-A-Way)
Wildlife Leather, P.O. Box 339, Merrick, NY 11566/516-379-3440 (lea. gds. w. outdoor themes)
Wyman Corp., P.O. Box 8644, Salt Lake City, UT 84104/801-359-0368 (Cannon Packer f. rifle, shotgun)

HUNTING AND CAMP GEAR, CLOTHING, ETC.

Bob Allen Sportswear, P.O. Box 477, Des Moines, IA 50302/800-247-8048
Eddie Bauer, 15010 NE 36th St., Redmond, WA 98052
L. L. Bean, Freeport, ME 04032
Bear Archery, R.R. 4, 4600 Southwest 41st Blvd., Gainesville, FL 32601/904-376-2327 (Himalayan backpack)
Bernzomatic Corp., 740 Driving Pk. Ave., Rochester, NY 14613 (stoves & lanterns)
Big Beam, Teledyne Co., 290 E. Prairie St., Crystal Lake, IL 60014 (lamp)
Big Buck, Brazell Mfg. & Distr. Co., 5645 S. Waterbury Way, Suite #202, Salt Lake City, UT 84121/801-272-4471
Browning, Rte. 1, Morgan, UT 84050
Camp Trails, P.O. Box 23155, Phoenix, AZ 85063/602-272-9401 (packs only)
Camp-Ways, 12915 S. Spring St., Los Angeles, CA 90061/213-532-0910
Challanger Mfg. Co., Box 550, Jamaica, NY 11431 (glow safe)
Chippewa Shoe Co., 925 First Ave., Chippewa Falls, WI 54729/715-723-5571 (boots)
Coleman Co., Inc., 250 N. St. Francis, Wichita, KS 67201
Converse Rubber Co., 55 Fordham Rd., Wilmington, MA 01887 (boots)
Danner Shoe Mfg. Co., P.O. Box 22204, Portland, OR 97222/503-653-2920 (boots)
DEER-ME Prod. Co., Box 34, Anoka, MN 55303/612-421-8971 (tree steps)
Dunham Co., P.O. Box 813, Brattleboro, VT 05301/802-254-2316 (boots)
Durango Boot, see: Georgia/Northlake
Frankonia Jagd, Hofmann & Co., Postfach 6780, D-8700 Wurzburg 1, West Germany
Freeman Ind., Inc., 100 Marblehead Rd., Tuckahoe, NY 10707 (Trak-Kit)
French Dressing Inc., 15 Palmer Heights, Burlington, VT 05401/802-658-1434 (boots)
Game-Winner, Inc., 2690 Cumberland Parkway, Suite 440, Atlanta, GA 30339/404-434-9210 (camouflage suits; orange vests)
Gander Mountain, Inc., P.O. Box 248, Hwy. "W", Wilmot, WI 53192/414-862-2331
Georgia Boot Div., U.S. Industry, 1810 Columbia Ave., Franklin, TN 37064/615-794-1556
Georgia/Northlake Boot Co., P.O. Box 10, Franklin, TN 37064/615-794-1556 (Durango)

Gokeys, 84 So. Wabasha, St. Paul, MN 55107/612-292-3933
Gun Club Sportswear, Box 477, Des Moines, IA 50302
Gun-Ho Case Mfg. Co., 110 E. 10th St., St. Paul, MN 55101
Joseph M. Herman Shoe Co., Inc., 114 Union St., Millis, MA 02054/617-376-2601 (boots)
Himalayan Industries, Inc., P.O. Box 7465, Pine Bluff, AR 71611/501-534-6411
Bob Hinman Outfitters, 1217 W. Glen, Peoria, IL 61614
Hunting World, 16 E. 53rd St., New York, NY 10022
Jung Shoe Mfg. Co., 620 S. 8th St., Sheboygan, WI 53081/414-458-3483 (boots)
Kap Outdoors, 1704 Locust St., Philadelphia, PA 19103/215-723-3449 (clothing)
Kelty Pack, Inc., 9281 Borden Ave., Sun Valley, CA 91352/213-768-1922
La Crosse Rubber Mills Co., P.O. Box 1328, La Crosse, WI 54601/608-782-3020 (boots)
Langenberg Hat Co., P.O. Box 1860, Washington, MO 63090/314-239-1860
Peter Limmer & Sons Inc., Box 66, Intervale, NH 03845 (boots)
Marathon Rubber Prods. Co. Inc., 510 Sherman St., Wausau, WI 54401/715-845-6255 (rain gear)
Marble Arms Corp., 420 Industrial Park, Gladstone, MI 49837
Nimrod & Wayfarer Trailers, 500 Ford Blvd., Hamilton, OH 45011
The Orvis Co., Manchester, VT 05254/802-362-3622 (fishing gear; clothing)
PGB Assoc., 310 E. 46th St., Suite 3E, New York, NY 10017/212-867-9560
Prime Leather Finishes Co., 205 S. Second St., Milwaukee, WI 53204 (leath. waterproofer/ Boot n' Saddle Soap)
Quabaug Rubber Co./Vibram U.S.A., 17 School St. N. Brookfield, MA 01535/617-867-7731 (boots)
Quoddy Moccasins, Div. R. G. Barry Corp., 67 Minot Ave., Auburn, ME 04210/207-784-3555
Ranger Mfg. Co., Inc., P.O. Box 3676, Augusta, GA 30904
Ranger Rubber Co., 1100 E. Main St., Endicott, NY 13760/607-757-4260 (boots)
Red Ball, P.O. Box 3200, Manchester, NH 03105/603-669-0708 (boots)
Red Head Brand Corp., 4949 Joseph Hardin Dr., Dallas, TX 75236/214-333-4141
Red Wing Shoe Co., Rte 2, Red Wing, MN 55066
Refrigiwear, Inc., 71 Inip Dr., Inwood, Long Island, NY 11696
Reliance Prod. Ltd., 1830 Dublin Ave., Winnipeg 21, Man. R3H 0H3 Can. (tent peg)
W. R. Russell Moccasin Co., 285 S.W. Franklin, Berlin, WI 54923
Safarliand Hunting Corp., P.O. Box NN, McLean, VA 22101/703-356-0622 (camouflage rain gear)
Safesport Mfg. Co., 1100 West 45th Ave., Denver, CO 80211/303-433-6506
Saf-T-Bak, see: Kap Outdoors
Servus Rubber Co., 1136 2nd St., Rock Island, IL 61201 (footwear)
The Ski Hut-Trailwise, 1615 University Ave., P.O. Box 309, Berkeley, CA 94710
Spruce Creek Sportswear, see: Kap Outdoors
Stearns Mfg. Co., P.O. Box 1498, St. Cloud, MN 56301
Sterno Inc., 300 Park Ave., New York, NY 10022 (camp stoves)
Teledyne Co., Big Beam, 290 E. Prairie St., Crystal Lake, IL 60014
10-X Mfg. Products Group, 2828 Forest Lane, Suite 1107, Dallas, TX 75234/214-243-4016
Thermos Div., KST Co., Norwich, CT 06361 (Pop Tent)
Norm Thompson, 1805 N.W. Thurman St., Portland, OR 97209
Trim Unlimited, 2111 Glen Forest, Plano, TX 75023/214-596-5059 (electric boat)
Utica Duxbak Corp., 1745 S. Acoma St., Denver, CO 80223/303-778-0324
Waffen-Frankonia, see: Frankonia Jagd
Walker Shoe Co., P.O. Box 1167, Asheboro, NC 27203-1167/919-625-1380 (boots)
Weinbrenner Shoe Corp., Polk St., Merrill, WI 54452
Wenzel Co., 1280 Research Blvd., St. Louis, MO 63132
Wolverine Boots & Shoes Div., Wolverine World Wide, 9341 Courtland Dr., Rockford, MI 49351/616-866-1561 (footwear)
Woods Inc., 90 River St., P.O. Box 407, Ogdensburg, NY 13669/315-393-3520
Woodstream Corp., Box 327, Lititz, PA 17543 (Hunter Seat)
Woolrich Woolen Mills, Mill St., Woolrich, PA 17779/717-769-6464
Yankee Mechanics, RFD No. 1, Concord, NH 03301/603-225-3181 (hand winches)

KNIVES AND KNIFEMAKER'S SUPPLIES—FACTORY and MAIL ORDER

Alcas Cutlery Corp., Olean, NY 14760/716-372-3111 (Cutco)
Atlanta Cutlery, Box 839, Conyers, GA 30207/404-922-3700 (mail order, supplies)
Bali-Song, see: Pacific Cutlery Corp.
L. L. Bean, 386 Main St., Freeport, ME 04032/207-865-3111 (mail order)
Benchmark Knives, P.O. Box 2089, Gastonia, NC 28052/704-867-1307
Crosman Blades™, The Coleman Co., 250 N. St. Francis, Wichita, KS 67201
Boker, The Cooper Group, P.O. Box 728, Apex, NC 27502/919-362-7510
Bowen Knife Co., Box 1929, Waycross, GA 31501/912-287-1200
Browning, Rt. 1, Morgan, UT 84050/801-876-2711
Buck Knives, Inc., P.O. Box 1267; 1900 Weld Blvd., El Cajon, CA 92022/619-449-1100 or 800-854-2557
Camillus Cutlery Co., 52-54 W. Genesee St., Camillus, NY 13031/315-672-8111 (Sword Brand)
W. R. Case & Sons Cutlery Co., 20 Russell Blvd., Bradford, PA 16701/814-368-4123
Charter Arms Corp., 430 Sniffens Lane, Stratford, CT 06497/203-377-8080 (Skatchet)
Chicago Cutlery Co., 5420 N. County Rd. 18, P.O. Box 9494, Minneapolis, MN 55440/612-533-0472
Collins Brothers Div. (belt-buckle knife), See Bowen Knife Co.
Colonial Knife Co., P.O. Box 3327, Providence, RI 02909/401-421-1600 (Master Brand)
Custom Knifemaker's Supply, P.O. Box 308, Emory, TX 75440/214-473-3330

Custom Purveyors, Ted Devlet's, P.O. Box 886, Fort Lee, NJ 07024/201-886-0196 (mail order)
Dixie Gun Works, Inc., P.O. Box 130, Union City, TN 38261/901-885-0700 (supplies)
Eze-Lap Diamond Prods., Box 2229, 15164 Weststate St., Westminster, CA 92683/714-847-1555 (knife sharpeners)
Gerber Legendary Blades, 14200 S.W. 72nd St., Portland, OR 99223/503-639-6161
Golden Age Arms Co., 14 W. Winter St., Delaware, OH 43015/614-369-6513 (supplies)
Gutmann Cutlery Co., Inc., 900 S. Columbus Ave., Mt. Vernon, NY 10550/914-699-4044
H & B Forge Co., Rte. 2, Box 24, Shiloh, OH 44878/419-896-3435 (throwing knives, tomahawks)
Russell Harrington Cutlery, Inc., Subs. of Hyde Mfg. Co., 44 River St., Southbridge, MA 01550/617-764-4371 (Dexter, Green River Works)
J. A. Henckels Zwillingswerk, Inc., 9 Skyline Dr., Hawthorne, NY 10532/914-592-7370
Imperial Knife Associated Companies, 1776 Broadway, New York, NY 10019/212-757-1814
Indian Ridge Traders, Box 869, Royal Oak, MI 48068/313-399-6034 (mostly blades)
J.A. Blades, Inc., an affiliate of E. Christoper Firearms Co., 128 & Ferry Street, Miamitown, OH 45041/513-353-1321 (supplies)
Ken Jantz Supply, Rt. 1, Sulphur, OK 73086/405-622-3790 (supplies)
Jet-Aer Corp., 100 Sixth Ave., Paterson, NJ 07524/201-278-8300
KA-BAR Cutlery Inc., 5777 Grant Ave., Cleveland, OH 44105/216-271-4000
KA-BAR Knives, Collectors Division, 434 No. 9th St., Olean, NY 14760/716-372-5611
Keene Corp., Cutting Serv. Div., 1569 Tower Grove Ave., St. Louis, MO 63110/314-771-1550
Kershaw Cutlery Co., 6024 Jean Rd., Suite D, Lake Oswego, OR 97034/503-636-0111
Knife and Gun Supplies, P.O. Box 13522, Arlington, TX 76013/817-261-0569
Koval Knives, P.O. Box 14130, Columbus, OH 43214/614-888-6486 (supplies)
Lamson & Goodnow Mfg. Co., 45 Conway St., Shelburne Falls, MA 03170/413-625-6331
Lansky Sharpeners, P.O. Box 800, Buffalo, NY 14221/716-634-6333 (sharpening devices)
Al Mar Knives, Inc., P.O. Box 1626, 5755 SW Jean Rd., Suite 101, Lake Oswego, OR 97034/503-635-9229
Matthews Cutlery, P.O. Box 33095, Decatur, GA 30033/404-636-7923 (mail order)
R. Murphy Co., Inc., 13 Groton-Harvard Rd., Ayer, MA 01432/617-772-3481 (StaySharp)
Nordic Knives, 1643-C-Z Copenhagen Dr., Solvang, CA 93463 (mail order)
Normark Corp., 1710 E. 78th St., Minneapolis, MN 55423/612-869-3291
Ontario Knife Co., Subs. of Servotronics, Inc., P.O. Box 145, Franklinville, NY 14737/716-676-5527 (Old Hickory)
Pacific Cutlery Corp., 3039 Roswell St., Los Angeles, CA 90085/213-258-7021 (Bali-Song)
Parker Cutlery, 6928 Lee Highway, Chattanooga, TN 37415/615-894-1782
Plaza Cutlery Inc., 3333 Bristol, #161, South Coast Plaza, Costa Mesa, CA 92626/714-549-3932 (mail order)
Queen Cutlery Co., P.O. Box 500, Franklinville, NY 14737/617-676-5540
R & C Knives and Such, P.O. Box 32631, San Jose, CA 95152/408-923-5728 (mail order; ctlg. $2)
Randall-Made Knives, Box 1988, Orlando, FL 32802/305-855-8075 (ctlg. $1)
Rigid Knives, P.O. Box 816, Hwy. 290E, Lake Hamilton, AR 71951/501-525-1377
A. G. Russell Co., 1705 Hiwy. 71 No., Springdale, AR 72764/501-751-7341
Bob Sanders, 2358 Tyler Lane, Louisville, KY 40205 (Bahco steel)
San Diego Knives, P.O. Box 326, Lakeside, CA 92040/714-561-5900 (mail order)
Schrade Cutlery Corp., 1776 Broadway, New York, NY 10019/212-757-1814
Sheffield Knifemakers Supply, P.O. Box 141, Deland, FL 32720/904-734-7884
Smith & Wesson, 2100 Roosevelt Ave., Springfield, MA 01101/413-781-8300
Jesse W. Smith Saddlery, E. 3024 Sprague, Spokane, WA 99201 (sheathmakers)
Swiss Army Knives, Inc., P.O. Box 846, Shelton, CT 06484/203-929-6391 (Victorinox; folding)
Tekna, 1075 Old County Rd., Belmont, CA 94002/415-592-4070
Thompson/Center, P.O. Box 2405, Rochester, NH 03867/603-332-2394
Tommer-Bordein Corp., 220 N. River St., Delano, MN 55328/612-972-3901
Tru-Balance Knife Co., 2155 Tremont Blvd., N.W., Grand Rapids, MI 49504/616-453-3679
Utica Cutlery Co., 820 Noyes St., Utica, NY 13503/315-733-4663 (Kutmaster)
Valor Corp., 5555 N.W. 36th Ave., Miami, FL 33142
Washington Forge, Inc., Englishtown, NJ 07727/201-446-7777 (Carriage House)
Wenoka Cutlery, P.O. Box 8238, West Palm Beach, FL 33407/305-845-6155
Western Cutlery Co., 1800 Pike Rd., Longmont, CO 80501/303-772-5900 (Westmark)
Walt Whinnery, Walts Cust. Leather, 1947 Meadow Creek Dr., Louisville, KY 40281/502-458-4351 (sheathmaker)
J. Wolfe's Knife Works, Box 1056, Larkspur, CA 94939 (supplies)
Wyoming Knife Co., 209 Commerce Dr. #2, Ft. Collins, CO 80524/303-224-3454

LABELS, BOXES, CARTRIDGE HOLDERS

Milton Brynin, 214 E. Third St., Mount Vernon, NY 10710/914-667-6549 (cartridge box labels)
E-Z Loader, Del Rey Products, P.O. Box 91561, Los Angeles, CA 90009
Peterson Label Co., P.O. Box 186, 23 Sullivan Dr., Redding Ridge, CT 06876/203-938-2349 (cartridge box labels; Targ-Dots)

LOAD TESTING and PRODUCT TESTING, (CHRONOGRAPHING, BALLISTIC STUDIES)

Hutton Rifle Ranch, P.O. Box 31868, Tucson, AZ 85751/602-748-2788
Kent Lomont, 4236 West 700 South, Poneto, IN 45781/219-694-6792 (handguns, handgun ammunition)
Plum City Ballistics Range, Norman E. Johnson, Rte. 1, Box 29A, Plum City, WI 54761/715-647-2539
Russell's Rifle Shop,' Rte. 5, Box 92, Georgetown, TX 78626/512-778-5338 (load testing and chronographing to 300 yds.)
John M. Tovey, 4710 - 104th Lane NE, Circle Pines, MN 55014/612-786-7268
H. P. White Laboratory, Inc., 3114 Scarboro Rd., Street, MD 21154/301-838-6550

MISCELLANEOUS

Action, Mauser-style only, Crandell Tool & Machine Co., 1540 N. Mitchell St., Cadillac, MI 49601/616-775-5562
Action, Single Shot, Miller Arms, Inc., P.O. Box 260, St. Onge, SD 57779 (de-Haas-Miller)
Activator, B.M.F. Activator, Inc., 3705 Broadway, Houston, TX 77017/713-645-6726
Adapters, Sage Industries, P.O. Box 2248, Hemet, CA 92342/714-925-1006 (12-ga. shotgun; 38 S&W blank)
Archery, Bear, R.R. 4, 4600 Southwest 41st Blvd., Gainesville, FL 32601/904-376-2327
Arms Restoration, J. J. Jenkins Ent. Inc., 375 Pine Ave. No. 25, Goleta, CA 93017/805-967-1366
Assault Rifle Accessories, Cherokee Gun Accessories, 830 Woodside Rd., Redwood City, CA 94061
Assault Rifle Accessories, Choate Machine & Tool Corp., P.O. Box 218, Bald Knob, AR 72010 (folding stocks)
Assault Rifle Accessories, Feather Enterprises, 2500 Central Ave., Boulder, CO 80301
Assault Rifle Accessories, R&R Enterprises, Box 385, Jefferson, SD 57038 (folding stock)
Assault Rifle Accessories, Ram-Line, Inc., 406 Violet St., Golden, CO 80401/303-279-0886 (folding stock)
Barrel Band Swivels, Phil Judd, 83 E. Park St., Butte, MT 59701
Bedding Kit, Fenwal, Inc., Resins Systems Div., 400 Main St., Ashland, MA 01721
Belt Buckles, Adina Silversmiths Corp., P.O. Box 348, 3195 Tucker Rd., Cornwell Heights, PA 19020/215-639-7246
Belt Buckles, Bergamot Brass Works, 820 Wisconsin St., Delavan, WI 53115/414-728-5572
Belt Buckles, Just Brass Inc., 121 Henry St., P.O. Box 112, Freeport, NY 11520/516-379-3434 (ctlg. $2)
Belt Buckles, Sports Style Associates, 148 Hendrickson Ave., Lynbrook, NY 11563/516-599-5080
Belt Buckles, Pilgrim Pewter Inc., R.D. 2, Tully, NY 13159/607-842-6431
Benchrest & Accuracy Shooters Equipment, Bob Pease Accuracy, P.O. Box 787, Zipp Road, New Braunfels, TX 78130/512-625-1342
Blowgun, PAC Outfitters, P.O. Box 56, Mulvane, KS 67110/316-777-4909
Bootdryers, Baekgaard Ltd., 1855 Janke Dr., Northbrook, IL 60062
Breech Plug Wrench, Swaine Machine, 195 O'Connell, Providence, RI 02905
Bulletproof Clothing, EMGO USA Ltd., 115 E. 57th St., Suite 1430, New York NY 10022/212-772-3444
Cannons, South Bend Replicas Ind., 61650 Oak Rd., S. Bend, IN 44614/219-289-4500 (ctlg. $5)
Cartridge Adapters, Sport Specialties, Harry Owen, Box 5337, Hacienda Hts., CA 91745/213-968-5806 (ctlg. $3)
Case Gauge, Plum City Ballistics Range, Rte. 1, Box 29A, Plum City, WI 54761/715-647-2539
Cased, high-grade English tools, Marvin Huey Gun Cases, Box 98, Reed's Spring, MO 65737/417-538-4233 (ebony, horn, ivory handles)
Cherry Converter, Amimex Inc., 2660 John Montgomery Dr., Suite #3, San Jose, CA 95148/408-923-1720 (shotguns)
Clips, D&E Magazines Mfg., P.O. Box 4876, Sylmar, CA 91342 (handgun and rifle)
CO2 Cartridges, Nittan U.S.A. Inc., 4901 Morena Blvd., Suite 307, San Diego, CA 92117/714-272-6113
Crossbows, Barnett International, 1967 Gunn Highway, Odessa, FL 33552/813-920-2241
Deer Drag, D&H Prods. Co., Inc., P.O. Box 22, Glenshaw, PA 15116/412-443-2190
Defendor, Ralide, Inc., P.O. Box 131, Athens, TN 37303/615-745-3525
Dryer, Thermo-Electric, Golden-Rod, Buenger Enterprises, Box 5286, Oxnard, CA 93030/805-985-0541
E-Z Loader, Del Rey Prod., P.O. Box 91561, Los Angeles, CA 90009/213-823-04494 (f. 22-cal. rifles)
Ear-Valve, Norton Co., Siebe Norton, 16624 Edwards Rd., Cerritos, CA 90701/213-926-0545 (Lee-Sonic)
Embossed Leather Belts, Wallets, Wildlife Leather, P.O. Box 339, Merrick, NY 11566/516-379-3440 (outdoor themes)
Farrsight, Farr Studio, 1231 Robinhood Rd., Greenville, TN 37743
Flares, Colt Industries, P.O. Box 1868, Hartford, CT 06102
Flares, Smith & Wesson Chemical Co., 2399 Forman Rd., Rock Creek, OH 44084
Frontier Outfitters, Red River Outfitters, P.O. Box 241, Tujunga, CA 91042/213-352-0177 (frontier, western, military Americana clothing)
Game Hoist, Cam Gear Ind., P.O. Box 1002, Kalispell, MT 59901 (Sportsmaster 500 pocket hoist)
Game Hoist, Precise, 3 Chestnut, Suffern, NY 10901
Game Scent, Buck Stop Lure Co., Inc., 3015 Grow Rd. N.W., R. #1, Stanton, MI 48888/517-762-5091
Game Scent, Pete Rickard, Inc., Rte. 1, Cobleskill, NY 12043/518-234-2731 (Indian Buck lure)

Game Scent, Safariland Hunting Corp., P.O. Box NN, McLean, VA 22101/703-356-0622 (buck lure)
Gargoyles, Pro-tec Inc., 11108 Northrup Way, Bellevue, WA 98004/306-828-6595
Gas Pistol, Penguin Ind., Inc., Airport Industrial Mall, Coatesville, PA 19320/215-384-6000
Grip Caps, Classic Arms Corp., P.O. Box 8, Palo Alto, CA 94301/415-321-7243
Grip Caps, Knickerbocker Enterprises, 16199 S. Maple Ln. Rd., Oregon City, OR 97045
Grip Caps, Philip D. Letiecq, AQ 18 Wagon Box Rd., P.O. Box 251, Story, WY 82842/307-683-2817
Gun Bedding Kit, Fenwal, Inc., Resins System Div., 400 Main St., Ashland, MA 01721/617-881-2000
Gun Jewelry, Sid Bell Originals, R.D. 2, Box 219, Tully, NY 13159/607-842-6431
Gun Jewelry, Pilgrim Pewter Inc., R.D. 2, Tully, NY 13159/607-842-6431
Gun Jewelry, Al Popper, 614 Turnpike St., Stoughton, MA 02072/617-344-2036
Gun Jewelry, Sports Style Assoc., 148 Hendricks Ave., Lynbrook, NY 11563
Gun photographer, Mustafa Bilal, 727 Belleview Ave. East, Suite 103, Seattle, WA 98102/206-322-5449
Gun photographer, Art Carter, 818 Baffin Bay Rd., Columbia, SC 29210/803-772-2148
Gun photographer, John Hanusin, 3306 Commercial, Northbrook, IL 60062/312-564-2706
Gun photographer, Int. Photographic Assoc., Inc., 4500 E. Speedway, Suite 90, Tucson, AZ 85712
Gun photographer, Charles Semmer, 7885 Cyd Dr., Denver, CO 80221/303-429-6947
Gun photographer, Jim Weyer, 224½ Huron St., Toledo, OH 43604/419-241-5454
Gun photographer, Steve White, 1920 Raymond Dr., Northbrook, IL 60062/312-564-2720
Gun Sling, Kwikfire, Wayne Prods. Co., P.O. Box 247, Camp Hill, PA 17011
Gun Sling, La Paloma Marketing, 4500 E. Speedway Blvd., Suite 93, Tucson, AZ 85712/602-881-4750 (Pro-sling system)
Gun Slings, Torel, Inc., 1053 N. South St., Yoakum, TX 77995
Hand Exerciser, Action Products, Inc., 22 No. Mulberry St., Hagerstown, MD 21740/301-797-1414
Horsepac, Yellowstone Wilderness Supply, P.O. 129, West Yellowstone, MT 59758/406-646-7613
Hugger Hooks, Roman Products, Inc., 4363 Loveland St., Golden, CO 80403/303-279-6959
Insert Chambers, GTM Co., Geo. T. Mahaney, 15915B E. Main St., La Puente, CA 91744 (shotguns only)
Insect Repellent, Armor, Div. of Buck Stop, Inc., 3015 Grow Rd., Stanton, MI 48888
Insert Barrels and Cartridge Adapters, Sport Specialties, Harry Owen, Box 5337, Hacienda Hts., CA 91745/213-968-5806 (ctlg. $3)
Kentucky Rifle Drawings, New England Historic Designs, P.O. Box 171, Concord, NH 03301/603-224-2096
Knife Sharpeners, Lansky Sharpeners, P.O. Box 800, Buffalo, NY 14221/716-634-6333
Light Load, Jacob & Tiffin Inc., P.O. Box 547, Clanton, AL 35045
Locks, Gun, Bor-Lok Prods., 105 5th St., Arbuckle, CA 95912
Locks, Gun, Master Lock Co., 2600 N. 32nd St., Milwaukee, WI 53245
Magazines, Mitchell Arms of California, Inc., 1800 Talbot Way, Anaheim, 92805/714-634-1131 (stainless steel)
Magazines, Ram-Line, Inc., 406 Violet St., Golden, CO 80401/303-279-0886
Miniature Cannons, Karl J. Furr, 76 East, 350 North, Orem, UT 84057/801-225-2603 (replicas)
Miniature Guns, Charles H. Stoppler, 5 Minerva Place, New York, NY 10468
Monte Carlo Pad, Frank A. Hoppe Div., Penguin Ind., Airport Industrial Mall, Coatesville, PA 19320/215-384-6000
Muzzle Rest, Meadow Industries, P.O. Box 450, Marlton, NJ 08053/609-953-0922
Muzzle-Top, Allen Assoc., Box 532, Glenside, PA 19038 (plastic gun muzzle cap)
Old Gun Industry Art, Hansen & Co., 244 Old Post Rd., Southport, CT 06490/203-259-7337
Patterning Data, Whits Shooting Stuff, P.O. Box 1340, Cody, WY 82414
Pell Remover, A. Edw. Terpening, 838 E. Darlington Rd., Tarpon Springs, FL 33589
Powderhorns, Kirk Olson, Ft. Woolsey Guns, P.O. Box 2122, Prescott, AZ 86302/602-778-3035
Powderhorns, Tennessee Valley Mfg., P.O. Box 1125, Corinth, MS 38834
Powderhorns, Thomas F. White, 5801 Westchester Ct., Worthington, OH 43085/614-888-0128
Practice Ammunition, Hoffman New Ideas Inc., 821 Northmoor Rd., Lake Forest, IL 60045/312-234-4075
Pressure Testg. Machine, M. York, 5508 Griffith Rd., Gaithersburg, MD 20760/301-253-4217
Ram-Line accessories, Chesco, Inc., 406 Violet St., Golden, CO 80401/303-279-0886
Ransom Handgun Rests, C'Arco, P.O. Box 308, Highland, CA 92346
Reloader's Record Book, Reloaders Paper Supply, Don Doerkson, P.O. Box 550, Hines, OR 97738
Rifle Magazines, Butler Creek Corp., Box GG, Jackson Hole, WY 83001/307-733-3599 (30-rd. Mini-14)
Rifle Magazines, Condor Mfg. Co., 418 W. Magnolia Ave., Glendale, CA 91204/213-240-1745 (25-rd. 22-cal.)
Rifle Magazines, Miller Gun Works, P.O. Box 7326, Tamuning, Guam 96911 (30-cal. M1 15&30-round)
Rifle Slings, Bianchi International, 100 Calle Cortez, Temecula, CA 92390/714-676-5621
Rifle Slings, Chace Leather Prods., Longhorn Div., 507 Alden St., Fall River, MA 02722/617-678-7556
Rifle Slings, John's Cust. Leather, 525 S. Liberty St., Blairsville, PA 15717/412-459-6802

Rifle Slings, Kirkpatrick Leather Co., P.O. Box 3150, Laredo, TX 78041/512-723-6631

RIG, NRA Scoring Plug, Rig Products, 87 Coney Island Dr., Sparks, NV 89431/702-331-5666

Rubber Cheekpiece, W. H. Lodewick, 2816 N.E. Halsey, Portland, OR 97232/503-284-2554

Saddle Rings, Studs, Fred Goodwin, Sherman Mills, ME 04776

Safeties, William E. Harper, The Great 870 Co., P.O. Box 6309. El Monte, CA 91734/213-579-3077 (f. Rem. 870P)

Safeties, Williams Gun Sight Co., 7389 Lapeer Rd., Davison, MI 48423

Safety Slug, Glaser Safety Slug, 711 Somerset Lane, P.O. Box 8223, Forest City, CA 94404

Salute Cannons, Naval Co., R.D. 2, 4747 Cold Spring Creamery Rd., Doylestown, PA 18901

Sav-Bore, Saunders Sptg. Gds., 338 Somerset St., N. Plainfield, NJ 07060

Scrimshaw Engraving, C. Milton Barringer, 217-2nd Isle N., Port Richey, FL 33568/813-868-3777

Sharpening Stones, A. G. Russell Co., 1705 Hiway 71 North, Springdale, AR 72764/501-751-7341 (Arkansas Oilstones)

Shell Catcher, Auto Strip Pak, 419 W. Magnolia Ave., Glendale, CA 91204/213-240-1745

Shell Shrinker Mfg. Co., P.O. Box 462, Fillmore, CA 93015

Shooter's Porta Bench, Centrum Products Co., 443 Century, S.W., Grand Rapids, MI 49503/616-454-9424

Shooters Rubber Stamps, Craft Haven, 828 N. 70th, Lincoln, NE 68505/402-466-5739

Shooting Coats, 10-X Products Group, 2828 Forest Lane, Suite 1107, Dallas, TX 75234/214-243-4016

Shooting Glasses, Willson Safety Prods. Division, P.O. Box 622, Reading, PA 19603

Shotgun Barrel, Pennsylvania Arms Co., Box 128, Duryea, PA 18642/717-457-0845 (rifled)

Shotgun bore, Custom Shootg. Prods., 8505 K St., Omaha, NE 68127

Shotgun Case Accessories, AC Enterprises, 507 N. Broad St., Edenton, NC 27932 (British-made Charlton)

Shotgun Converter, Amimex Inc., 2660 John Montgomery Dr., Suite #3, San Jose, CA 95148/408-923-1720

Shotgun Ribs, Poly-Choke Div., Marble Arms Corp., 420 Industrial Park, Gladstone, MI 49837/906-428-3710

Shotgun/riot, Combat Weapons, 1265 Balsam St., Lakewood, CO 80215

Shotgun Sight, bi-ocular, Trius Prod., Box 25, Cleves, OH 45002

Shotshell Adapter, PC Co., 5942 Secor Rd., Toledo, OH 43623/419-472-6222 (Plummer 410 converter)

Snap Caps, Edwards Recoil Reducer, 269 Herbert St., Alton, IL 62002/618-462-3257

Sportsman's Chair, Ted Devlet's Custom Purveyors, P.O. Box 886, Fort Lee, NJ 07024/201-886-0196

Springfield Safety Pin, B-Square Co., P.O. Box 11281, Ft. Worth, TX 76110/800-433-2909

Springs, W. C. Wolff Co., Box 232, Ardmore, PA 19003/215-647-1880

Stock pad, variable, Meadow Industries, P.O. Box 450, Marlton, NJ 08053/609-953-0922

Supersound, Edmund Scientific Co., 101 E. Gloucester Pike, Barrington, NJ 08007 (safety device)

Swivels, Michaels, P.O. Box 13010, Portland, OR 97213/503-255-6890

Swivels, Sile Dist., 7 Centre Market Pl., New York, NY 10013/212-925-4111

Swivels, Williams Gun Sight Co., 7389 Lapeer Rd., Davison, MI 48423

Tomahawks, H&B Forge Co., Rt. 2, Shiloh, OH 44878/419-896-2075

Tree Stand, Advanced Hunting Equipment Inc., P.O. Box 1277, Cumming, GA 30130/404-887-1171 (tree lounge)

Tree Stand, Climbing, Amacker Prods., P.O. Box 1432; 602 Kimbrough Dr., Tallulah, LA 71282/318-574-4903

Trophies, Blackinton & Co., P.O. Box 1300, Attleboro Falls, MA 02763

Trophies, F. H. Noble & Co., 888 Tower Rd., Mundelein, IL 60060

Warning Signs, Delta Ltd., P.O. Box 777, Mt. Ida, AR 71957

World Hunting Info., Jack Atcheson & Sons, Inc., 3210 Ottawa St., Butte, MT 59701

World Hunting Info., J/b adventures & Safaris, Inc., 800 E. Girard, Suite 603, Denver, CO 80231/303-696-0261

World Hunting Info., Wayne Preston, Inc., 3444 Northhaven Rd., Dallas, TX 75229/214-358-4477

MUZZLE-LOADING GUNS, BARRELS or EQUIPMENT

Luther Adkins, Box 281, Shelbyville, IN 46176/317-392-3795 (breech plugs)

Allen Fire Arms Co., 1107 Pen Rd., Santa Fe, NM 87501/505-983-1961

Anderson Mfg. Co., Union Gap Sta. P.O. Box 3120, Yakima, WA 98903/509-453-2349 (Flame-N-Go fusil; Accra-Shot)

Armoury, Inc., Rte. 202, New Preston, CT 06777

Arm Tech, Armament Technologies Inc., 240 Sargent Dr., New Haven, CT 06511/203-562-2543 (22-cal. derringers)

Beaver Lodge, 9245 16th Ave. S.W., Seattle, WA 98106/206-763-1698

Beeman Precision Arms, Inc., 47-GDD Paul Dr., San Rafael, CA 94903/415-472-7121

Blackhawk East, C2274 POB, Loves Park, IL 61131/815-633-7784 (black powder)

Blackhawk Mtn., 1337 Delmar Parkway, Aurora, CO 80010/303-366-3659 (black powder)

Blackhawk West, Box 285, Hiawatha, KS 66434 (blck powder)

Blue and Gray Prods., Inc. RD #6, Box 362, Wellsboro, PA 16901/717-724-1383

Jim Brobst, 299 Poplar St., Hamburg, PA 19526/215-562-2103 (ML rifle bbls.)

Ted Buckland, 361 Flagler Rd., Nordland, WA 98358/206-385-2142 (custom only)

G. S. Bunch, 7735 Garrison, Hyattsville, MD 20784/301-577-6598 (flask repair)

Butler Creek Corp., Box GG, Jackson Hole, WY 83001/307-733-3599 (poly & maxi patch)

C.N.S. Co., P.O. Box 238, Mohegan Lake, NY 10547

Cache La Poudre Rifleworks, 168 N. College, Ft. Collins, CO 80521/303-482-6913 (custom muzzleloaders)

Challanger Mfg. Co., 118 Pearl St., Mt. Vernon, NY 10550

R. MacDonald Champlin, P.O. Box 693, Manchester, NH 03105/603-622-1420 (custom muzzleloaders)

Chopie Mfg. Inc., 700 Copeland Ave., LaCrosse, WI 54601/608-784-0926 (nipple wrenches)

Connecticut Valley Arms Co. (CVA), 5988 Peachtree, East, Norcross, GA 30092 (kits also)

Earl T. Cureton, Rte. 2, Box 388, Willoughby Rd., Bulls Gap, TN 37711/615-235-2854 (powder horns)

Leonard Day & Co., P.O. Box 723, East Hampton, MA 01027/413-527-7990

Dixie Gun Works, Inc., P.O. Box 130, Union City, TN 38261

Dixon Muzzleloading Shop, Inc., RD #1, Box 175, Kempton, PA 19529/215-756-6271

EMF Co., Inc., 1900 E. Warner Ave. 1-D, Santa Ana, CA 92705/714-966-0202

Euroarms of America, Inc., P.O. Box 3277, 1501 Lenoir Dr., Winchester, VA 22601/703-662-1863

Excam, Inc., 4480 E. 11th Ave., Hialeah, FL 33012

Andy Fautheree, P.O. Box 863, Pagosa Springs, CO 81147/303-264-2892 (cust. ML)

Ted Fellowes, Beaver Lodge, 9245 16th Ave. S.W., Seattle, WA 98106/206-763-1698

Firearms Imp. & Exp. Corp., (F.I.E.), P.O. Box 4866, Hialeah Lakes, FL 33014/305-685-5966

Marshall F. Fish, Rt. 22 N., Westport, NY 12993/518-962-4897 (antique ML repairs)

The Flintlock Muzzle Loading Gun Shop, 1238 "G" So. Beach Blvd., Anaheim, CA 92804/714-821-6655

C. R. & D. E. Getz, Box 88, Beavertown, PA 17813 (barrels)

GOEX, Inc., Belin Plant, Moosic, PA 18507/717-457-6724 (black powder)

Golden Age Arms Co., 14 W. Winter St., Delaware, OH 43015 (ctlg. $2.50)

A. R. Goode, 12845 Catoctin Furnace Rd., Thurmont, MD 21788/301-271-2228 (ML rifle bbls.)

Green Mountain Rifle Barrel Co., Inc., RFD 1, Box 184, Center Ossipee, NH 03814/603-539-7721

Guncraft Inc., 117 W. Pipeline, Hurst, TX 76053/817-268-2887

The Gun Works, 236 Main St., Springfield, OR 97477/503-741-4118 (supplies)

Hatfield Rifle Works, 2028 Frederick Ave., St. Joseph, MO 64501/816-279-8688 (squirrel rifle)

Hawken Armory, P.O. Box 2604, Hot Springs, AR 71901/501-268-8296

Hopkins & Allen, 3 Ethel Ave., P.O. Box 217, Hawthorne, NJ 07507/201-427-1165

The House of Muskets, Inc., 120 N. Pagosa Blvd., Pagosa Springs, CO 81147/303-264-2295 (ML bbls. & supplies)

JJJJ Ranch, Wm. Large, Rte. 1, State Route 243, Ironton, OH 45638/614-532-5298

Jerry's Gun Shop, 9220 Odgen Ave., Brookfield, IL 60513/312-485-5200

Kern's Gun Shop, 319 E. Main St., Ligonier, PA 15658/412-238-7651 (ctlg. $1.50)

LaChute Ltd., Box 48B, Masury, OH 44438/216-448-2236 (powder additive)

Les' Gun Shop (Les Bauska), 105-9th West, P.O. Box 511, Kalispell, MT 59901/406-755-2635

Lever Arms Serv. Ltd., 572 Howe St., Vancouver, BC V6C 2E3, Canada

Log Cabin Sport Shop, 8010 Lafayette Rd., Lodi, OH 44254/216-948-1082 (ctlg. $3)

Lyman Products Corp., Rte. 147, Middlefield, CT 06455

McCann's Muzzle-Gun Works, 200 Federal City Rd., Pennington, NJ 08534/609-737-1707

McKenzie River Arms, P.O. Box 766, Springfield, OR 97477

McKeown's Sporting Arms, R.R. 4, Pekin, IL 61554/309-347-3559 (E-Z load rev. stand)

Mike Marsh, 6 Stanford Rd., Dronfield Woodhouse, Nr. Sheffield S18 SQJ, England (accessories)

Maurer Arms, 2154-16th St., Akron, OH 44314/216-745-6864 (cust. muzzleloaders)

Michigan Arms Corp., 363 Elmwood, Troy, MI 48083/313-583-1518

Mountain State Muzzleloading Supplies, Inc., Box 154-1, State Rt. 14 at Boaz, Williamstown, WV 26187/304-375-7842

Mowrey Gun Works, FM 368, Box 28, Iowa Park, TX 76367/817-592-2331

Muzzleloaders Etc., Jim Westberg, 9907 Lyndale Ave. S., Bloomington, MN 55420/612-884-1161

Numrich Corp., W. Hurley, NY 12491 (powder flasks)

Kirk Olson, Ft. Woolsey Guns, P.O. Box 2122, Prescott, AZ 86302/602-778-3035 (powderhorns)

Ox-Yoke Originals, 130 Griffin Rd., West Suffield, CT 06093/203-668-5110 (dry lubr. patches)

Ozark Mountain Arms Inc., P.O. Box 397, 141 Byrne St., Ashdown, AR 71822/501-989-2345 (rifles)

Orrin L. Parsons, Jr., Central Maine Muzzle-Loading & Gunsmithing, RFD #1, Box 787, Madison, ME 04950

Pecos Valley Armory, 1022 So. Canyon, Carlsbad, NM 88220/505-887-6023

A. W. Peterson Gun Shop, 1693 Old Hwy. 441 N., Mt. Dora, FL 32757 (ML guns)

Phyl-Mac, 609 N.E. 104th Ave., Vancouver, WA 98664/206-256-0579 (cust. charger)

Provider Arms, Inc., 261 Haglund Rd., Chesterton, IN 46304/219-879-5590 (Predator rifle)

Richland Arms, 321 W. Adrian St., Blissfield, MI 49228

Rush's Old Colonial Forge, 106 Wiltshire Rd., Baltimore, MD 21221

Salish House, Inc., P.O. Box 383, Lakeside, MT 55922/406-844-3625

H. M. Schoeller, 569 So. Braddock Ave., Pittsburgh, PA 15221

Shiloh Products, 181 Plauderville Ave., Garfield, NJ 07026 (4-cavity mould)

Shore Galleries, Inc., 3318 W. Devon Ave., Chicago, IL 60645/312-676-2900

Sile Distributors, 7 Centre Market Pl., New York, NY 10013/213-925-4111

C. E. Siler Locks, 7 Acton Woods Rd., Candler, NC 28715/704-667-2376 (flint locks)
C. Sharps Arms Co., Inc., P.O. Box 885, Big Timber, MT 59011/406-932-4353
Ken Steggles, see: Mike Marsh
The Swampfire Shop, 1693 Old Hwy. 441 N., Mt. Dora, FL 32757/904-383-0595
Tennessee Valley Arms, P.O. Box 2022, Union City, TN 38261/901-885-4456
Tennessee Valley Mfg., P.O. Box 1125, Corinth, MS 38834 (powderhorns)
Ten-Ring Precision, Inc., 1449 Blue Crest Lane, San Antonio, TX 78232/512-494-3063
Traditions, Inc., 2813 Turnpike, Coventry, CT 06238/203-649-6324 (guns, kits, accessories)
Treso Inc., P.O. Box 4640, Pagosa Springs, CO 81157 (accessories)
Upper Missouri Trading Co., Box 191, Crofton, NE 68730/402-388-4844
R. Watts, 826 Springdale Rd., Atlanta, GA 30306 (ML rifles)
J. S. Weeks & Son, 4748 Bailey Rd., Dimondale, MI 48821/517-636-0591 (supplies)
W. H. Wescomb, P.O. Box 488, Glencoe, CA 95232/209-293-7010 (parts)
Thos. F. White, 5801 Westchester Ct., Worthington OH 43085/614-888-0128 (powder horn)
Williamson-Pate Gunsmith Serv., 117 W. Pipeline, Hurst, TX 76053/817-268-2887
Winchester Sutler, Siler Route, Box 393-E, Winchester, VA 22601/703-888-3595 (haversacks)
York County Gun Works, R.R. #4, Tottenham, Ont. LOG 1WO, Canada (locks)

PISTOLSMITHS

Allen Assoc., Box 532, Glenside, PA 19038 (speed-cock lever for 45 ACP)
Armament Gunsmithing Co., Inc., 525 Route 22, Hillside, NJ 07205/201-686-0960
Les Baer, Sr., The Gun Shop, 1725 Minesite Rd., Allentown, PA 18103/215-398-2362 (accurizing 45 autos; cust. XP100s; T/C Cont.; rev.)
Bain and Davis Sptg. Gds., 307 E. Valley Blvd., San Gabriel, CA 91776/213-573-4241
Lee Baker, 7252 East Ave. U-3, Littlerock, CA 93543/805-944-4487 (cust. blue)
Bar-Sto Precision Machine, 73377 Sullivan Rd., Twentynine Palms, CA 92277/619-367-2747(S.S. bbls. f. 45 ACP)
Behlert Custom Guns, Inc., Box 227, Monmouth Junction, NJ 08852/201-329-2284 (short actions)
Bell's Custom Shop, 3319 Mannheim Rd., Franklin Park, IL 60131/312-678-1900/312-678-1900
F. Bob Chow, Gun Shop, Inc., 3185 Mission, San Francisco, CA 94110/415-282-8358
Brown Custom Guns, Inc., Steven N. Brown, 8810 Rocky Ridge Rd., Indianapolis, IN 46217/317-881-2771 aft. 5 PM
Dick Campbell, 1198 Finn Ave., Littleton, CO 80124/303-799-0145 (PPC guns; custom)
Dave Chicoine, d/b/a Liberty A.S.P., 19 Key St., Eastport, ME 04631/207-853-2327 (rep. & rest. of early S&W prods.)
J. E. Clark, Rte. 2, Box 22A, Keithville, LA 71047
Davis Co., 2793 Del Monte St., West Sacramento, CA 95691/916-372-6789
Day Arms Corp., 2412 S.W. Loop 410, San Antonio, TX 78227/512-674-5220
Dominic DiStefano, 4303 Friar Lane, Colorado Springs, CO 80907/303-599-3366 (accurizing)
Dan Dwyer, 915 W. Washington, San Diego, CA 92103/619-296-1501
Ken Eversull Gunsmith, Inc., P.O. Box 1766, Alexandria, LA 71301/318-487-0823
Jack First Distributors, Inc., 44633 Sierra Hwy., Lancaster, CA 93534/805-945-6981
John Fordham, Box 9 Dial Star Rte., P.O. Box 1093, Blue Ridge, GA 30513/404-632-3602
Giles' 45 Shop, 8614 Tarpon Springs Rd., Odessa, FL 33556/813-920-5366
The Gunshop, R. D. Wallace, 320 Overland Rd., Prescott, AZ 86301
Gil Hebard Guns, Box 1, Knoxville, IL 61448
Paul Jaeger, Inc., 211 Leedom St., Jenkintown, PA 19046/215-884-6920
J. D. Jones, Rt. 1, Della Dr., Bloomingdale, OH 43910/614-264-0176
L. E. Jurras & Assoc., P.O. Box 680, Washington, IN 47501/812-254-7698
Kart Sptg. Arms Corp., 1190 Old Country Rd., Riverhead, NY 11901/516-727-2719 (handgun conversions)
Benjamin Kilham, Kilham & Co., Main St., Box 37, Lyme, NH 03768/603-795-4112
Terry K. Kopp, Highway 13, Lexington, MO 64067/816-259-2636 (rebblg., conversions)
John G. Lawson, The Sight Shop, 1802 E. Columbia Ave., Tacoma, WA 98404/206-474-5465
Lenz Firearms Co., 310 River Rd., Eugene, OR 97404/503-689-6900
Kent Lomont, 4236 West South, Poneto, IN 46781/219-694-6792 (Auto Mag only)
Mag-na-port International, Inc., 41302 Executive Drive, Mt. Clemens, MI 48045/313-469-6727
Robert A. McGrew, 3315 Michigan Ave., Colorado Springs, CO 80910/303-636-1940
Rudolf Marent, 9711 Tiltree, Houston, TX 77075/713-946-7028 (Hammerli)
Robert L. Nassenstein, 4304 - 6th Ave., Tacoma, WA 98406/206-752-3107 (accurizing, custom 45 parts)
Nu-Line Guns, 1053 Caulks Hill Rd., Harvester, MO 63303/314-441-4501
Pachmayr Gun Works, 1220 S. Grand Ave., Los Angeles, CA 90015
Bob Rogers Gunsmithing, P.O. Box 305, Franklin Grove, IL 61031/815-456-2685 (custom)
SSK Industries (See: J. D. Jones)
L. W. Seecamp Co., Inc., Box 255, New Haven, CT 06502/203-877-3429 (DA Colt auto conversions)
Hank Shows, dba The Best, 1078 Alice Ave., Ukiah, CA 95482/707-462-9060
Silver Dollar Guns, P.O. Box 475, 10 Frances St., Franklin, NH 03235/603-934-3292 (45 ACP)

Spokhandguns Inc., Vern D. Ewer, East 1911 Sprague Ave., Spokane, WA 99202/509-325-3992
Sportsmens Equipmt. Co., 915 W. Washington, San Diego, CA 92103/619-296-1501 (specialty limiting trigger motion in autos)
Irving O. Stone, Jr., 73377 Sullivan Rd., Twentynine Palms, CA 92277/619-367-2747
Victor W. Strawbridge, 6 Pineview Dr., Dover Pt., Dover, NH 03820
A. D. Swenson's 45 Shop, P.O. Box 606, Fallbrook, CA 92028
Trapper Gun, 18717 East 14 Mile Rd., Fraser, MI 48026/313-792-0134
Dennis A. "Doc" Ulrich, 2511 S. 57th Ave., Cicero, IL 60650
Vic's Gun Refinishing, 6 Pineview Dr., Dover, NH 03820/603-742-0013
Walters Industries, 6226 Park Lane, Dallas, TX 75225/214-691-5150

REBORING AND RERIFLING

P.O. Ackley (See Dennis M. Bellm Gunsmithing, Inc.)
Atkinson Gun Co., P.O. Box 512, Prescott, AZ 86301
Dennis M. Bellm Gunsmithing Inc., 2376 So. Redwood Rd., Salt Lake City, UT 84119/801-974-0697 (price list $3 rifle only)
Dave Chicoine, d/b/a Liberty A.S.P., 19 Key St., Eastport, ME 04631/207-853-2327 (reline handgun bbls.)
H-S Precision, Inc., 112 N. Summit, Prescott, AZ 85302/602-445-0607
Terry K. Kopp, Highway 13, Lexington, MO 64067/816-259-2636 (Invis-A-Line bbl.; relining)
Les' Gun Shop, (Les Bauska), 105-9th West, P.O. Box 511, Kalispell, MT 59901/406-755-2635
Nu-Line Guns, 1053 Caulks Hill Rd., Harvester, MO 63303/314-441-4500 (handguns)
Redman's Gun Shop, R.R. 1, Box 330A, Omak, WA 98841/509-826-5512
SGW, Inc. (formerly Schuetzen Gun Works), 624 Old Pacific Hwy. S.E., Olympia, WA 98503/206-456-3471
Sharon Gun Specialties, 14587 Peaceful Valley Rd., Sonora, CA 95370
Siegrist Gun Shop, 8752 Turtle Rd., Whittemore, MI 48770/517-873-3929
Snapp's Gunshop, 6911 E. Washington Rd., Clare, MI 48617
J. W. Van Patten, P.O. Box 145, Foster Hill, Milford, PA 18337/717-296-7069
Robt. G. West, 27211 Huey Lane, Eugene, OR 97402/503-689-6610

RELOADING TOOLS AND ACCESSORIES

Advance Car Mover Co., Inc., P.O. Box 1181, 112 N. Outagamie St., Appleton, WI 54911/414-734-1878 (bottom pour lead casting ladles)
Accessory Specialty Co., 2711 So. 84th St., West Allis, WI 53227/414-545-0879 (Reload-a-stand)
Advanced Precision Prods. Co., 5183 Flintrock Dr., Westerville, OH 43081/614-895-0560 (case super luber)
American Wad Co., P&P Tool, 125 W. Market St., Morrison, IL 61270/815-772-7618 (12-ga. shot wad)
Anderson Mfg. Co., R.R.1, Royal, IA 51357/712-933-5542 (Shotshell Trimmers)
C'Arco, P.O. Box 308, Highland, CA 92346/714-862-8311 (Ransom "Grand Master" progr. loader)
Creighton Audette, 19 Highland Circle, Springfield, VT 05156/802-885-2331 (Universal Case Selection gauge)
B-Square Eng. Co., Box 11281, Ft. Worth, TX 76110/800-433-2909
Ballistic Prods., P.O. Box 488, 2105 Shaughnessy Circle, Long Lake, MN 55356/612-473-1550
Ballistic Research Industries (BRI), 600 B Soquel Ave., Santa Cruz, CA 95062/408-476-7981 (shotgun slug)
Bear Machine Co., 2110 1st Natl. Tower, Akron, OH 44308/216-253-4039
Belding & Mull, P.O. Box 428, 100 N. 4th St., Philipsburg, PA 16866/814-342-0607
Berdon Machine Co., Box 483, Hobart, WA 98025/206-392-1866 (metallic press)
Blackhawk East, Dowman Greene, C2274 POB, Loves Park, IL 61131/815-633-7784
Blackhawk Mtn., Richard Miller, 1337 Delmar Parkway, Aurora, CO 80010/303-366-3659
Blackhawk West, R. L. Hough, Box 285, Hiawatha, KS 66434/303-366-3659
Bonanza Sports, Inc., 412 Western Ave., Faribault, MN 55021/507-332-7153
Gene Bowlin, Rt. 1, Box 890, Snyder, TX 79549/915-573-2323 (arbor press)
Brown Precision Co., P.O. Box 270W, 7786 Molinos Ave., Los Molinos, CA 96055/916-384-2506 (Little Wiggler)
C-H Tool & Die Corp., 106 N. Harding St., Owen, WI 54460/715-229-2146
Camdex, Inc., 2228 Fourteen Mile Rd., Warren, MI 48092/313-977-1620
Carbide Die & Mfg. Co., Inc., 15615 E. Arrow Hwy., Irwindale, CA 91706/213-337-2518
Carter Gun Works, 2211 Jefferson Pk. Ave., Charlottesville, VA 22903
Cascade Cartridge, Inc., (See: Omark)
Cascade Shooters, 60916 McMullin Dr., Bend, OR 97702/503-389-5872 (bull. seating depth gauge)
Central Products f. Shooters, 435 Route 18, East Brunswick, NJ 08816 (neck turning tool)
Chevron Case Master, R.R. 1, Ottawa, IL 61350
Lester Coats, 416 Simpson St., No. Bend, OR 97459/503-756-6995 (core cutter)
Container Development Corp., 424 Montgomery St., Watertown, WI 53094
Continental Kite & Key Co., (CONKKO) P.O. Box 40, Broomall, PA 19008/215-353-0711 (primer pocket cleaner)
Cooper-Woodward, Box 972, Riverside, CA 92502/714-688-2127 (Perfect Lube)
Corbin Mfg. & Supply Inc., P.O. Box 2659, White City, OR 97503/503-826-5211
Custom Products, RD #1, Box 483A, Saegertown, PA 16443/814-763-2769 (decapping tool, dies, etc.)
J. Dewey Mfg. Co., 186 Skyview Dr., Southbury, CT 06488/203-264-3064

Dillon Precision Prods., Inc., 7755 E. Gelding Dr., Suite 106, Scottsdale, AZ 85260/602-948-8009
Diverter Arms, Inc., P.O. Box 22084, Houston, TX 77027 (bullet puller)
Division Lead Co., 7742 W. 61st Pl., Summit, IL 60502
Eagle Products Co., 1520 Adelia Ave., So. El Monte, CA 91733
Edmisten Co. Inc., P.O. Box 1293, Hwy 105, Boone, NC 28607/704-264-1490 (I-Dent-A Handloader's Log)
Efemes Enterprises, P.O. Box 122M, Bay Shore, NY 11706 (Berdan decapper)
W. H. English, 4411 S. W. 100th, Seattle, WA 98146 (Paktool)
Farmer Bros., 1102 N. Washington, Eldora, IA 50627/515-858-3651 (Lage)
Fitz, Box 171, Douglas City, CA 96024 (Fitz Flipper)
Flambeau Plastics Corp., P.O. Box 97 Middlefield, OH 44062/216-632-1631
Forster Products Inc., 82 E. Lanark Ave., Lanark IL 61046/815-493-6360
Francis Tool Co., P.O. Box 7861, Eugene, OR 97401/503-746-4831 (powder measure)
Freechec' (See: Paco)
Geo. M. Fullmer, 2499 Mavis St., Oakland, CA 94601/415-533-4193 (seating die)
Gene's Gun Shop, Rt. 1, Box 890, Snyder, TX 79549/915-573-2323 (arbor press)
Gopher Shooter's Supply, Box 278, Faribault, MN 55021
Hart Products, Rob W. Hart & Son Inc., 401 Montgomery St., Nescopeck, PA 18635
Hensley & Gibbs, P.O. Box 10, Murphy, OR 97533/503-862-2341 (bullet moulds)
Richard Hoch, The Gun Shop, 62778 Spring Creek Rd., Montrose, CO 81401/303-249-3625 (custom Schuetzen bullet moulds)
Hoffman New Ideas Inc., 821 Northmoor Rd., Lake Forest, IL 60045/312-234-4075 (spl. gallery load press)
Hollywood Reloading, (See Whitney Sales)
Hornady Mfg. Co., P.O. Box 1848, Grand Island, NE 68802/308-382-1390
Hulme see: Marshall Enterprises (Star case feeder)
Huntington, P.O. Box 991, Oroville, CA 95965/916-534-1210 (Compact Press)
Independent Mach. & Gun Shop, 1416 N. Hayes, Pocatello, ID 83201/208-232-1264
Javelina Products, Box 337, San Bernardino, CA 92402 (Alox beeswax)
Neil Jones, RD #1, Box 483A, Saegertown, PA 16433/814-763-2769 (decapping tool, dies)
Paul Jones Munitions Systems (See Fitz Co.)
Kexplore, P.O. Box 22084, Houston, TX 77027/713-789-6943
Kuharsky Bros. (See Modern Industries)
Lage Uniwad Co., 1102 N. Washington St., Eldora, IA 50627 (Universal Shotshell Wad)
Lee Custom Engineering, Inc. (See Mequon Reloading Corp.)
Lee Precision, Inc., 4275 Hwy. U, Hartford, WI 53027/414-673-3075
L. L. F. Die Shop, 1281 Highway 99 N., Eugene, OR 97402/503-688-5753
Dean Lincoln, Custom Tackle & Ammo, P.O. Box 1886, Farmington, NM 87401 (mould)
Ljutic Industries, 918 N. 5th Ave., Yakima, WA 98902/505-632-3539
Lock's Phila. Gun Exch., 6700 Rowland, Philadelphia, PA 19149/215-332-6225
Lyman Products Corp., Rte. 147, Middlefield, CT 06455
McKillen & Heyer Inc., 37603 Arlington Dr., Box 627, Willoughby, OH 44094/216-942-2491 (case gauge)
Paul McLean, 2670 Lakeshore Blvd., W., Toronto, Ont. M8V 1G8 Canada/416-259-3060 (Universal Cartridge Holder)
MEC, Inc. (See Mayville Eng. Co.)
MTM Molded Prod., 8000 Obco Ct., P.O. Box 14117, Dayton, OH 45414/513-890-7461
Magma Eng. Co., P.O. Box 881, Chandler, AZ 85224
Marmel Prods., P.O. Box 97, Utica, MI 48087/313-731-8029 (Marvelube, Marvelux)
Marquart Precision Co., P.O. Box 1740, Prescott, AZ 86302/602-445-5646 (precision case-neck turning tool)
Marshall Enterprises, 792 Canyon Rd., Redwood City, CA 94062/415-365-1230 (Hulme autom. case feeder f. Star rel.)
Mayville Eng. Co., 715 South St., Mayville, WI 53050/414-387-4500 (shotshell loader)
Mequon Reloading Corp., P.O. Box 253, Mequon, WI 53092/414-673-3060
Merit Gun Slight Co., P.O. Box 995, Sequim, WA 98382/206-683-6127
Multi-Scale Charge Ltd., 55 Maitland St., #310, Toronto, Ont. M4Y 1C9 Canada//416-967-5305
Normington Co., Box 6, Rathdrum, ID 83858 (powder baffles)
NorthEast Industrial Inc., N.E.I., P.O. Box 249, 405 N. Canyon Blvd., Canyon City, OR 97828/503-575-2513 (bullet mould)
J. Northcote, Box 5158, Hacienda Heights, CA 91745/213-968-5806 (hollow pointer)
Ohaus Scale, (See RCBS)
Omark Industries, Box 856, Lewiston, ID 83501/208-746-2351
P&P Tool Co., 125 W. Market St., Morrison, IL 61270/815-772-7618 (12-ga. shot wad)
Pacific Tool Co., P.O. Box 2048, Ordnance Plant Rd., Grand Island, NE 68801/308-384-2308
Paco, Box 17211, Tucson, AZ 85731 (Freechec' tool for gas checks)
Pak-Tool Co., 4411 S.W. 100th, Seattle, WA 98146
Pem's Manufacturing Co., 5063 Waterloo Rd., Atwater, OH 44201/216-947-2202 (pedestal cranks, primer pocket cleaner)
Pitzer Tool Mfg. Co., Rt. 1, Box 50, Winterset, IA 50273/515-462-4268 (bullet lubricator & sizer)
Plum City Ballistics Range, Norman E. Johnson, Rte. 1, Box 29A, Plum City, WI 54761/715-647-2539
Ponsness-Warren, Inc., P.O. Box 8, Rathdrum, ID 83858/208-687-1331
Marian Powley, Petra Lane, R.R.1, Eldridge, IA 52748/319-285-9214
Precise Alloys Inc., 406 Hillside Ave., New Hyde Park, NY 11040/516-354-8860 (chilled lead shot; bullet wire)
Quinetics Corp., P.O. Box 29007, San Antonio, TX 78229/516-684-8561 (kinetic bullet puller)

RCBS, Inc., Box 1919, Oroville, CA 95965/916-533-5191
Redding Inc., 114 Starr Rd., Cortland, NY 13045
Reloaders Equipment Co., 4680 High St., Ecorse, MI 48229 (bullet puller)
Reloaders Paper Supply, Don Doerksen, P.O. Box 550, Hines, OR 97738 (reloader's record book)
Rifle Ranch, Rte. 10, 3301 Willow Creek Rd., Prescott, AZ 86301/602-778-7501
Rochester Lead Works, 76 Anderson Ave., Rochester, NY 14607/716-442-8500 (leadwire)
Rorschach Precision Prods., P.O. Box 1613, Irving, TX 75060/214-254-9762 (carboloy bull. dies)
Rotex Mfg. Co. (See Texan)
SAECO Rel. 2207 Border Ave., Torrance, CA 90501/213-320-6973
SSK Industries, Rt. 1, Della Drive, Bloomingdale, OH 43910/614-264-0176 (primer tool)
Sandia Die & Cartridge Co., Rte. 5, Box 5400, Albuquerque, NM 87123/505-298-5729
Shannon Associates, P.O. Box 32737, Oklahoma City, OK 73123
Shiloh Products, 181 Plauderville Ave., Garfield, NJ 07026 (4-cavity bullet mould)
Shooters Accessory Supply, (See Corbin Mfg. & Supply)
Sil's Gun Prod., 490 Sylvan Dr., Washington, PA 15301 (K-spinner)
Jerry Simmons, 715 Middlebury St., Goshen, IN 46526/219-533-8546 (Pope de- & recapper)
J. A. Somers Co., P.O. Box 49751, Los Angeles, CA 90049 (Jasco)
Sport Flite Mfg., Inc., 2520 Industrial Row, Troy, MI 48084/313-280-0648 (swaging dies)
Star Machine Works, 418 10th Ave., San Diego, CA 92101/619-232-3216
TEK Ind., Inc., 2320 Robinson St., Colorado Springs, CO 80904/303-630-1295 (Vibra Tek Brass Polisher & Medium, Vibra Brite Rouge)
T&T Products, Inc., 6330 Hwy. 14 East, Rochester, MN 55901 (Meyer shotgun slugs)
Texan Reloaders, Inc., 444 So. Cips St., Watseka, IL 60970/815-432-5065
Trico Plastics, 590 S. Vincent Ave., Azusa, CA 91702
Tru Square Metal Products, P.O. Box 585, Auburn, WA 98002/206-833-2310 (Thumler's tumbler case polishers; Ultra Vibe 18)
WAMADET, Silver Springs, Goodleigh, Barnstaple, Devon, England
Walker Mfg. Inc., 8296 So. Channel, Harsen's Island, MI 48028 (Berdan decapper)
Wammes Guns Inc., 236 N. Hayes St., Bellefontaine, OH 43311 (Jim's powder baffles)
Weatherby, Inc., 2781 Firestone Blvd., South Gate, CA 90280/213-569-7186
Weaver Arms Corp., 344 No. Vinewood St., Escondido, CA 92025/714-745-4342 (progr. loader)
Webster Scale Mfg. Co., P.O. Box 188, Sebring, FL 33870/813-385-6362
Whits Shooting Stuff, P.O. Box 1340, Cody, WY 82414
Whitney Sales, P.O. 875, Reseda, CA 91335/818-345-4212 (Hollywood)
L. E. Wilson, Inc. P.O. Box 324, 404 Pioneer Ave., Cashmere, WA 98815/509-782-1328
Zenith Enterprises, 5781 Flagler Rd., Nordland, WA 98358/206-385-2142

RESTS—BENCH, PORTABLE, ETC.

A&A Design & Manufacturing, 361 SW "K" St., Grants Pass, OR 97526/503-474-1026 (Tour de Force bench rest)
B-Square Co., P.O. Box 11281, Ft. Worth, TX 76109/800-433-2909 (handgun)
Jim Brobst, 299 Poplar St., Hamburg, PA 19526/215-562-2103 (bench rest pedestal)
Bullseye Shooting Bench, 6100 - 40th St. Vancouver, WA 98661/206-694-6141 (portable)
C'Arco, P.O. Box 2043, San Bernardino, CA 92401 (Ransom handgun rest)
Centrum Products Co., 443 Century S.W., Grand Rapids, MI 49503/616-454-9424 (Porta Bench)
Cravener's Gun Shop, 1627 - 5th Ave., Ford City, PA 16226/412-763-8312 (portable)
Decker Shooting Products, 1729 Laguna Ave., Schofield, WI 54476 (rifle rests)
The Gun Case, 11035 Maplefield, El Monte, CA 91733
Joe Hall's Shooting Products, Inc., 443 Wells Rd., Doylestown, PA 18901/215-345-6354 (adj. portable)
Harris Engineering, Inc., Barlow, KY 42024/502-334-3633 (bipods)
Rob. W. Hart & Son, 401 Montgomery St., Nescopeck, PA 18635
Tony Hidalgo, 12701 S.W. 9th Place, Davie, FL 33325 (adj. shooting seat)
Hoppe's Div., Penguin Industries, Inc., Airport Industrial Mall, Coatesville, PA 19320/251-384-6000 (bench rests and bags)
North Star Devices, Inc., P.O. Box 2095, North St. Paul, MN 55109 (Gun Slinger)
Progressive Prods., Inc., P.O. Box 67, Holmen, WI 54636/608-526-3345 (Sandbagger rifle rest)
Rec. Prods. Res., Inc., 158 Franklin Ave., Ridgewood, NJ 07450 (Butts Bipod)
Suter's, Inc., House of Guns, 332 N. Tejon, Colorado Springs, CO 80902/303-635-1475
Tuller & Co., Basil Tuller 29 Germania, Galeton, PA 16922/814-435-2442 (Protektor sandbags)
Turkey Creek Enterprises, Rt. 1, Box 10, Red Oak, OK 74563/918-754-2884 (portable shooting rest)
Wichita Arms, 444 Ellis, Wichita, KS 67211/316-265-06612

RIFLE BARREL MAKERS

P.O. Ackley Rifle Barrels (See Dennis M. Bellm Gunsmithing Inc.)
Luther Adkins, P.O. Box 281, Shelbyville, IN 46176/317-392-3795
Atkinson Gun Co., P.O. Box 512, Prescott, AZ 86301
Jim Baiar, 490 Halfmoon Rd., Columbia Falls, MT 59912/406-892-4409
Bauska Rifle Barrels, Inc., 105-9th Ave. West, Kalispell, MT 59901/406-755-2635

Dennis M. Bellm Gunsmithing Inc., 2376 So. Redwood Rd., Salt Lake City, UT 84119/801-974-0697; price list $3 (new rifle bbls., incl. special & obsolete)

Leo Bustani, P.O. Box 8125, West Palm Beach, FL 33407/305-622-2710 (Win.92 take-down; Trapper 357-44 mag. bbls.)

Ralph L. Carter, Carter's Gun Shop, 225 G St., Penrose, CO 81240/303-372-6240

Charles P. Donnelly & Son, Siskiyou Gun Works, 405 Kubli Rd., Grants Pass, OR 97526/503-846-6604

Douglas Barrels, Inc., 5504 Big Tyler Rd., Charleston, WV 25312/304-776-1341

Douglas Jackalope Gun & Sport Shop, Inc., 1048 S. 5th St., Douglas, WY 82633/307-358-3854

Federal Firearms Co., Inc., P.O. Box 145, Thoms Run Rd., Oakdale, PA 15071/412-221-0300

C. R. & D. E. Getz, Box 88, Beavertown, PA 17813

A. R. Goode, 12845 Catoctin Furnace Rd., Thurmont, MD 21788/301-271-2228

Half Moon Rifle Shop, 490 Halfmoon Rd., Columbia Falls, MT 59912/406-892-4409

H-S Precision, Inc., 112 N. Summit, Prescott, AZ 85302/602-445-0607

Hart Rifle Barrels, Inc., RD 2, Lafayette, NY 13084/315-677-9841

H&H Barrels Works, Inc., 1520 S.W. 5th Ave., Ocala, FL 32674/904-351-4200

Wm. H. Hobaugh, The Rifle Shop, Box M, Philipsburg, MT 59858/406-859-3515

Huntington Precision Arms Inc., David R. Huntington, 670 So. 300 West, Heber City, UT 84032/801-654-2953

Terry K. Kopp, Highway 13, Lexington, MO 64067/816-259-2636 (22-cal. blanks)

Les' Gun Shop, (Les Bauska), 105-9th West, P.O. Box 511, Kalispell, MT 59901/406-755-2635

Marquart Precision Co., P.O. Box 1740, Prescott, AZ 86302/602-445-5646

Matco, Inc., Box 349, 126 E. Main St., No. Manchester, IN 46962/219-982-8282

McMillan Rifle Barrel U.S. International, 3604 Old College Rd., Bryan, TX 77801/409-846-3990

Nu-Line Guns, 1053 Caulks Hill Rd., Harvester, MO 63303/314-441-4500

Numrich Arms, W. Hurley, NY 12491

John T. Pell Octagon Barrels, (KOGOT), 410 College Ave., Trinidad, CO 81083/303-846-9406

Pennsylvania Arms Co., Box 128, Duryea, PA 18642/717-457-0845 (rifled shotgun bbl. only)

Sanders Cust. Gun Serv., 2358 Tyler Lane, Louisville, KY 40205

SGW, Inc., D. A. Schuetz, 624 Old Pacific Hwy. S.E., Olympia, WA 98503/206-456-3471

Sharon Gun Specialties, 14587 Peaceful Valley Rd., Sonora, CA 95370/209-532-4139

E. R. Shaw, Inc., Prestley & Thoms Run Rd., Bridgeville, PA 15017/412-221-3636

Shilen Rifles, Inc., 205 Metro Park Blvd., Ennis, TX 75119/214-875-5318

W. C. Strutz, Rifle Barrels, Inc., P.O. Box 611, Eagle River, WI 54521/715-479-4766

Titus Barrel & Gun Co., R.F.D. #1, Box 23, Heber City, UT 84032

Bob Williams, P.O. Box 143, Boonsboro, MD 21713

Wilson Arms, 63 Leetes Island Rd., Branford, CT 06405/203-488-7297

SCOPES, MOUNTS, ACCESSORIES, OPTICAL EQUIPMENT

Aimpoint U.S.A., 201 Elden St., Suite 103, Herndon, VA 22070/703-471-6828 (electronic sight)

The American Import Co., 1167 Mission, San Francisco, CA 94103/415-863-1506

Anderson Mfg. Co., Union Gap Sta. P.O. Box 3120, Yakima, WA 98903/509-453-2349 (lens cap)

Apollo Optics (See Senno Corp.)

Armsport, Inc., 3590 N.W. 49th St., Miami, FL 33122/305-635-7850

Armson, Inc., P.O. Box 2130, Farmington Hills, MI 48018/313-478-2577 (O.E.G.)

B-Square Co., Box 11281, Ft. Worth, TX 76109/800-433-2909 (Mini-14 mount)

Bausch & Lomb Inc., 1400 Goodman St., Rochester, NY 14602/716-338-6000

Beeman Inc., 47-GDD Paul Dr., San Rafael, CA 94903/415-472-7121

Bennett, 561 Delaware, Delmar, NY 12054/518-439-1862 (mounting wrench)

Billingsley & Brownell, Box 25, Dayton, WY 82836/307-655-9344 (cust. mounts)

Lenard M. Brownell (See Billingsley & Brownell)

Browning Arms, Rt. 4, Box 624-B, Arnold, MO 63010

Buehler Scope Mounts, 17 Orinda Highway, Orinda, CA 94563/415-254-3201

Burris Co. Inc., 331 E. 8th St., Box 1747, Greeley, CO 80631/303-356-1670

Bushnell Optical Co., 2828 E. Foothill Blvd., Pasadena, CA 91107

Butler Creek Corp., Box GG, Jackson Hole, WY 83001/307-733-3599 (lens caps)

Chesco, Inc., 406 Violet St., Golden, CO 80401/303-279-0886 (Ram-Line see thru mt. f. Mini 14)

Kenneth Clark, 18738 Highway 99, Madera, CA 93637/209-674-6016

Clearview Mfg. Co., Inc. 20821 Grand River Ave., Detroit, MI 48219/313-535-0033 (mounts)

Colt Firearms, P.O. Box 1868, Hartford CT 06102/203-236-6311

Compass Instr. & Optical Co., Inc., 104 E. 25th St., New York, NY 10010

Conetrol Scope Mounts, Hwy 123 South, Seguin, TX 78155

D&H Prods. Co., Inc., P. O. Box 22, Glenshaw, PA 15116/412-443-2190 (lens covers)

Davis Optical Co., P.O. Box 6, Winchester, IN 47934/317-584-5311

Del-Sports Inc., Main St., Margaretville, NY 12455/914-586-4103 (Kahles scopes; EAW mts.)

Dickson (See American Import Co.)

Eder Instrument Co., 5115 N. Ravenswood, Chicago, IL 60640 (borescope)

Flaig's, Babcock Blvd., Millvale, PA 15209

Fontaine Ind., Inc., 11552 Knott St., Suite 2, Garden Grove, CA 92641/714-892-4473

Freeland's Scope Stands, Inc., 3737 14th, Rock Island, IL 61201/309-788-7449

Griffin & Howe, Inc., 589 Broadway, New York, NY 10012/212-966-5323

H&H Assoc., P.O. Box 447, Strathmore, CA 93267 (target adj. knobs)

Heckler & Koch, Inc., 14601 Lee Rd., Chantilly, VA 22021/703-631-2800

H.J. Hermann Leather Co., Rt. 1, Skiatook, OK 74070 (lens caps)

J.B. Holden Co., 295 W. Pearl, Plymouth, MI 48170/313-455- 4850

The Hutson Corp., 105 Century Dr., No., Mansfield, TX 76063/817-477-3421

Import Scope Repair Co., P.O. Box 2633, Durango, CO 81301/303-247-1422

Interarms, 10 Prince St., Alexandria, VA 22313

Paul Jaeger, Inc., 211 Leedom St., Jenkintown, PA 19046/215-884-6920 (Schmidt & Bender; EAW mts., Noble)

Jason Empire Inc., 9200 Cody, P.O. Box 14930, Overland Park, KS 66214/913-888-0220

Jennison TCS (See Fontaine Ind., Inc.)

Kahles of America, Div. of Del-Sports, Inc., Main St., Margaretville, NY 12455/914-586-4103

Kris Mounts, 108 Lehigh St., Johnstown, PA 15905

Kuharsky Bros. (See Mondern Industries)

Kwik-Site, 5555 Treadwell, Wayne, MI 48185/313-326-1500 (rings, mounts only)

Leatherwood Enterprises, Suite 4B The Mall, P.O. Box 111, Stephenville, TX 76401/817-968-2719

T.K. Lee, 2830 S. 19th St., Off. #4, Birmingham, AL 35209/205-871-6065 (reticles)

E. Leitz, Inc., Rockleigh, NJ 07647

Leupold & Stevens Inc., P.O. Box 688, Beaverton, OR 97075/503-646-9171

Jake Levin and Son, Inc., 9200 Cody, Overland Park, KS 66214

W.H. Lodewick, 2816 N.E. Halsey, Portland, OR 97232/503-284-2554 (scope safeties)

Lyman Products Corp., Route 147, Middlefield, CT. 06455

Mandall Shooting Supplies, 7150 E. 4th St., Scottsdale, AZ 85252

Marble Arms Co., 420 Industrial Park, Gladstone, MI 49837/906-428-3710

Marlin Firearms Co., 100 Kenna Dr., New Haven, CO 06473

Robert Medaris, P.O. Box 309, Mira Loma, CA 91752/714-685-5666 (side mount f. H&K 91 & 93)

Millet Industries, 16131 Gothard St., Huntington Beach, CA 92647/714-842-5575 (mounts)

O.F. Mossberg & Sons, Inc., 7 Grasso Ave., North Haven, CT 06473

Nite-Site, Inc., P.O. Box O, Rosemount, MN 55068/612-890-7631

Numrich Arms, West Hurley, NY 12491

Nydar, (See Swain Nelson Co.)

Orchard Park Enterprise, P.O. Box 563, Orchard Park, NY 14127/716-662-2255 (Saddleproof mount)

Oriental Optical Co., 605 E. Walnut St., Pasadena, CA 91101/213-792-1252 (scope & binocular repairs)

PEM's Mfg. Co., 5063 Waterloo Rd., Atwater, OH 44201/216-947-2202 (rings, mounts)

Pachmayr Gun Works, 1220 S. Grand Ave., Los Angeles, CA 90015/213-748-7271

Pilkington Gun Co., P.O. Box 1296, Muskogee, OK 74401/918-693-9418 (Q. D. mt.)

Pioneer & Co., Marine & Optical Div., 216 Haddon Ave. Suite 522, Westmont, NJ 08108 (German Steiner binoculars)

Precise, 3 Chestnut, Suffern, NY 10901

Ranging, Inc., 90 Lincoln Rd. North, East Rochester, NY 14445/716-385-1250

Ray-O-Vac, Willson Prod. Div., P.O. Box 622, Reading, PA 19603 (shooting glasses)

Redfield Gun Sight Co., 5800 E. Jewell Ave., Denver, CO 80222/303-757-6411

S & K Mfg. Co., Box 247, Pittsfield, PA 16340/814-563-7803 (Insta-Mount)

SSK Industries, Rt. 1, Della Dr., Bloomingdale, OH 43910/614-264-0176 (bases)

Sanders Cust. Gun Serv., 2358 Tyler Lane, Louisville, KY 40205 (MSW)

Schmidt & Bender, see: Paul Jaeger, Inc.

Senno Corp., 505 E. 3d, P.O. Box 3506, Spokane, WA 99220/800-541-5689

Shepherd Scope Ltd., R.R. #1, P.O. Box 23, Waterloo, NE 68069/402-779-2424 (autom. range finding scope)

Sherwood Intl. Export Corp., 18714 Parthenia St., Northridge, CA 91324 (mounts)

W.H. Siebert, 22720 S.E. 56th Pl., Issaquah, WA 98027

Simmons Outdoor Corp., 8893 SW 129 Terrace, Miami, FL 33176/305-252-0477

Singlepoint (See Normark)

Southern Precision Inst. Co., 3419 E. Commerce St., San Antonio, TX 78219

Spacetron Inc., Box 84, Broadview, IL 60155(bore lamp)

Stoeger Industries, 55 Ruta Ct., S. Hackensack, NJ 07606/201-440-2700

Supreme Lens Covers, Box GG, Jackson Hole, WY 83001 (lens caps)

Swain Nelson Co., Box 45, 92 Park Dr., Glenview, IL 60025 (shotgun sight)

Swarovski Optik,Div. of Swarovski America Ltd., One Kenny Dr., Cranston, RI 02920/401-463-6400

Swift Instruments, Inc., 952 Dorchester Ave., Boston, MA 02125

Tasco, 7600 N.W. 26th St., Miami, FL 33122/305-591-3670

Ted's Sight Aligner, Box 1073, Scottsdale, AZ 85252

Tele Optics, 5514 W. Lawrence Ave., Chicago, IL 60630/312-283-7757 (repair services only)

Thompson-Center Arms, P.O. Box 2405, Rochester, NH 03867 (handgun scope)

Tradewinds, Inc., Box 1191, Tacoma, WA 98401

John Unertl Optical Co., 3551-5 East St., Pittsburgh, PA 15214

United Binocular Co., 9043 S. Western Ave., Chicago, IL 60620

Vissing (See Supreme Lens Covers)

Wasp Shooting Systems, Box 241, Lakeview, AR 72642/501-431-5606 (mtg. system f. Ruger Mini-14 only)

Weatherby's, 2781 Firestone, South Gate, CA 90280/213-569-7186

W.R. Weaver, Omark Industries, Box 856, Lewiston, ID 83501 (mounts & bases only)

Wide View Scope Mount Corp., 26110 Michigan Ave., Inkster, MI 48141

Williams Gun Sight Co., 7389 Lapeer Rd., Davison, MI 48423

Boyd Williams Inc., 8701-14 Mile Rd. (M-57),Cedar Springs, MI 49319 (BR)
Willrich Precision Instrument Co., 95 Cenar Lane, Englewood, NJ 07631/201-567-1411 (borescope)
Carl Zeiss Inc.,Consumer Prods. Div., Box 2010, 1015 Commerce St., Petersburg, VA 23803/804-861-0033

SIGHTS, METALLIC

Accura-Site Co., Inc., P.O. Box 114, Neenah, WI 54956/414-722-0039
B-Square Eng. Co., Box 11281, Ft. Worth, TX 76110/800-433-2909
Beeman Inc., 47 Paul Dr., San Rafael, CA 94903/415-472-7121 (airguns only)
Behlert Custom Sights, Inc., Box 227, Monmouth Junction, NJ 08852/201-329-2284
Bingham Ltd., 1775-C Wilwat Dr., Norcross, GA 30093/404-448-1440
Bo-Mar Tool & Mfg. Co., Rt. 12, Box 405, Longview, TX 75605
Buehler Scope Mounts, 17 Orinda Highway, Orinda, CA 94563/415-254-3201
Andy Fautheree, P.O. Box 863, Pagosa Springs, CO 81147/303-264-2892 ("Calif. Sight" f. ML)
Freeland's Scope Stands, Inc., 3734-14th Ave., Rock Island, IL 61201/309-788-7449
Paul T. Haberly, 2364 N. Neva, Chicago, IL 60635
Paul Jaeger, Inc., 211 Leedom St., Jenkintown, PA 19046/215-884-6920
Lee's Red Ramps, 7252 E. Ave. U-3, Littlerock, CA 93543/805-944-4487 (white outline rear sight)
James W. Lofland, 2275 Larkin Rd., Boothwyn, PA 19061/215-485-0391
Lyman Products Corp., Rte. 147, Middlefield, CT 06455
Mag-na-port International, Inc., 41302 Executive Drive, Mt. Clemens, MI 48045/313-469-6727
Marble Arms Corp., 420 Industrial Park, Gladstone, MI 49837/906-428-3710
Merit Gunsight Co., P.O. Box 995, Sequim, WA 98382/206-683-6127
Micro Sight Co., 242 Harbor Blvd., Belmont, CA 94002/415-591-0769
Millet Industries, 16131 Gothard St., Huntington Beach, CA 92647/714-842-5575
Miniature Machine Co., 210 E. Poplar, Deming, NM 88030/505-546-2151 (MMC)
Omega Sights, 41302 Executive Drive, Mt. Clemens, MI 48045/313-469-6727
C.R. Pedersen & Son, 2717 S. Pere Marquette, Ludington, MI 49431/616-843-2061
PEM's Manufacturing Co., 5063 Waterloo Rd., Atwater, OH 44201/216-947-2202
Poly Choke Div., Marble Arms Corp., 420 Industrial Park, Gladstone, MI 49837/906-428-3710
Redfield Gun Sight Co., 5800 E. Jewell St., Denver, CO 80222
S&M Tang Sights, P.O. Box 1338, West Babylon, NY 11704/516-226-4057
Schwarz's Gun Shop, 41-15th St., Wellsburg, WV 26070
Simmons Gun Specialties, Inc., 700 S. Rodgers Rd., Olathe, KS 66062/913-782-3131
Slug Site Co., Whitetail Wilds, Lake Hubert, MN 56469/218-963-4617
Sport Service Center, 2364 N. Neva, Chicago, IL60635/312-889-1114
Tradewinds, Inc., Box 1191, Tacoma, WA 98401
Wichita Arms, 444 Ellis, Wichita, KS 67211/316-265-0661
Williams Gun Sight Co., 7389 Lapeer Rd., Davison, MI 48423

STOCKS (Commercial and Custom)

Accuracy Products, 9004 Oriole Trail, Wonder Lake, IL 60097
Advanced Stocking Systems, see: Answer Stocking Systems
Ahlman's Inc., R.R. 1, Box 20, Morristown, MN 55052
Don Allen Inc., R.R. 4, Northfield, MN 55057/507-645-9216 (blanks)
Answer Stocking Systems, 113 N. 2nd St., Whitewater, WI 53190/414-473-4848 (synthetic f. shotguns)
R.J. Anton, 874 Olympic Dr., Waterloo, IA 50701/319-233-3666
Creighton Audette, 19 Highland Circle, Springfield, VT 05156/802-885-2331 (custom)
Jim Baiar, 490 Halfmoon Rd., Columbia Falls, MT 599123
Joe J. Balickie, Custom Stocks, Rte. 2, Box 56-G, Apex, NC 27502/919-362-5185
Bartas Gunsmithing, 10231 U.S.H.#10, Cato, WI 54206/414-732-4472
Donald Bartlett, 16111 S.E. 229th Pl., Kent, WA 98031/206-630-2190 (cust.)
Beeman Inc., 47 Paul Dr., San Rafael, CA 94903/415-472-7121 (airguns only)
Al Biesen, West 2039 Sinto Ave., Spokane, WA 99201
Roger Biesen, 5021 W. Rosewood, Spokane, WA 99208/509-328-9340
Stephen L. Billeb, Box 219, Philipsburg, MT 59858/406-859-3919
Billingsley & Brownell, Box 25, Dayton, WY 82836/307-655-9344 (cust.)
E.C. Bishop & Son Inc., 119 Main St., Box 7, Warsaw MO 65355/816-438-5121
Gregg Boeke, Rte. 2, Cresco, IA 52136/319-547-3746
John M. Boltin, 2008 Havens Dr., North Myrtle Beach, SC 29582/803-272-6581
Kent Bowerly, 1213 Behshel Hts. Rd., Kelso, WA, 98626/206-636-2859 (custom)
Larry D. Brace, 771 Blackfoot Ave., Eugene, OR 97404/503-688-1278 (custom)
Garnet D. Brawley, P.O. Box 668, Prescott, AZ 86301/602-445-4768 (cust.)
Brown Precision Co., P.O. Box 270W; 7786 Molinos Ave., Los Molinos, CA 96055/916-384-2506
Lenard M. Brownell, (See Billingsley & Brownell)
Jack Burres, 10333 San Fernando Road, Pacoima, CA 91331 (English, Claro, Bastogne Paradox walnut blanks only)
Calico Hardwoods, Inc., 1648 Airport Blvd., Windsor, CA 95492/707-546-4045 (blanks)
Dick Campbell, 1198 Finn Ave., Littleton, CO 80124/303-799-0145 (custom)
Shane Caywood, 321 Hwy. 51 So., Minocqua, WI 54548/715-356-9631 (cust.)
Claude Christopher, 1606 Berkley Rd., Greenville, NC 27834/919-756-0872 (rifles)
Winston Churchill, Twenty Mile Stream Rd., Rt. 1, Box 29B, Proctorsville, VT 05153
Reggie Cubriel, 15502 Purple Sage, San Antonio, TX 78255/512-695-8401 (cust. stockm.)

Bill Curtis, 4919 S. Spade, Murray, UT 84107/801-262-8413
Dahl's Custom Stocks, Rt. 4, Box 558, Lake Geneva, WI 53147/414-248-2464 (Martin Dahl)
Sterling Davenport, 9611 E. Walnut Tree Dr., Tucson, AZ 85715/602-749-5590 (custom)
Jack Dever, 8520 N.W. 90, Oklahoma City, OK 73132/405-721-6393
Charles De Veto, 1087 Irene Rd., Lyndhurst, OH 44124/216-442-3188
Bill Dowtin, 3919 E. Thrush Lane, Flagstaff, AZ 86001/602-779-1898 (Calif. Engl., black walnut blanks only)
David R. Dunlop, Rte. 1, Box 199, Rolla, ND 58367
D'Arcy A. Echols, 1309 Riverview Ave., Colorado Springs, CO 81601/303-945-0465 (custom)
Jere Eggleston, 400 Saluda Ave., Columbia, SC 29205/803-799-3402 (cust.)
Bob Emmons, 238 Robson Road, Grafton, OH 44044 (custom)
Englishtown Sporting Goods Co., Inc., Donald J. Maxham, 38 Main St., Englishtown, NJ 07726/201-446-7717 (custom)
Ken Eyster Heritage Gunsmiths Inc., 6441 Bishop Rd., Centerburg, OH 43011/614-625-6131 (cust.)
Reinhart Fajen, Box 338, Warsaw, MO 65355/816-438-5111
Ted Fellowes, Beaver Lodge, 9245 16th Ave. S.W., Seattle WA 98106/206-763-1698
Phil Fischer, 7333 N.E. Glisan, Portland, OR 97213/503-255-5678 (cust.)
Clyde E. Fischer, P.O. Box 1437, Three Rivers, TX 78071/512-786-4125 (Texas Mesquite)
Jerry A. Fisher, 1244-4th Ave. W., Kalispell, MT 59901/406-755-7093
Flaig's Lodge, Millvale, PA 15209
Donald E. Folks. 205 W. Lincoln St., Pontiac, IL 61764/815-844-7901 (custom trap, Skeet, livebird stocks)
Larry L Forster, Box 212, Gwinner, ND 58040/701-678-2475
Frank's Custom Rifles, 10420 E. Rusty Spur, Tucson, AZ 85749/602-749-4563
Freeland's Scope Stands, Inc., 3737 14th Ave., Rock Island, IL 61201/309-788-7449
Game Haven Gunstocks, 13750 Shire Rd., Wolverine, MI 49799/615-525-8257 (Kevlar riflestocks)
Jim Garrett, 2820 East NaniLoa Circle, Salt Lake City, UT 84117/801-227-6930 (fiberglass)
Dale Goens, Box 224, Cedar Crest, NM 87008
Gordie's Gun Shop, Gordon Mulholland, 1401 Fulton St., Streator, IL 61364/815-672-7202 (cust.)
Gary Goudy, 263 Hedge Rd., Menlo Park, CA 94025/415-322-1338 (cust.)
Gould's Myrtlewood, 341 W. 17th St., Coquille, OR 97423/503-396-5998 (gun blanks)
Charles E. Grace, 10144 Elk Lake Rd., Williamsburg, MI 49690/616-264-9483
Karl Guenther, 43-32 160th St., Flushing, NY 11372/212-461-7325
Guncraft, Inc., 117 W. Pipeline, Hurst, TX 76053/817-268-2887
The Gunshop, R.D. Wallace, 320 Overland Rd., Prescott, AZ 86301 (custom)
Half Moon Rifle Shop, 490 Halfmoon Rd., Columbia Falls, MT 59912
Rick J. Halstead, 1100 W. Polk Ave., Lovington, NM 88260
Harper's Custom Stocks, 928 Lombrano St., San Antonio, TX 78207/512-732-5780
Hayes Gunstock Service Co., 914 E. Turner St., Clearwater, FL 33516
Hubert J. Hecht, Waffen-Hecht, 724-K St., Sacramento, CA 95814/916-448-1177
Edward O. Hefti, 300 Fairview, College Station, TX 77840/409-696-4959
Warren Heydenberk, P.O. Box 339, Richlandtown, PA 18955/215-536-0798 (custom)
Doug Hill, 4518 Skyline Place, Enid, OK 73701/405-242-4455 (cust.)
Klaus Hiptmayer, P.O. Box 136, Eastman, Que., J0E 1P0 Canada/514-297-2492
Richard Hodgson, 5589 Arapahoe, Unit 104, Boulder, CO 80301
Hoenig & Rodman, 6521 Morton Dr., Boise, ID 83705/208-375-1116 (stock duplicating machine)
George Hoenig, 6521 Morton Dr., Boise, ID 83705/208-375-1116
Hollis Gun Shop, 917 Rex St., Carlsbad, NM 88220
Paul Jaeger, Inc., 211 Leedom St., Jenkintown, PA 19046/215-884-6920
Johnson Wood Products, I.D. Johnson & Sons, Rte. #1, Strawberry Point, IA 52076/319-933-4930 (blanks)
David Kartak, SRS Box 3042, South Beach, OR 97366/503-867-4951 (custom)
Monty Kennedy, P.O. Box 214, Kalispell, MT59901/406-857-3596
Stanley Kenvin, 5 Lakeville Lane, Plainview, NY 11803/516-931-0321 (custom)
Don Klein, P.O. Box 277, Camp Douglas, WI 54618/608-427-6948
LeFever Arms Co., Inc., R.D.#1, Box 31, Lee Center, NY 13363/315-337-6422
Lenz Firearms Co., 310 River Rd., Eugene, OR 97404/503-689-6900
Philip D. Letiecq, AQ, 18 Wagon Box Rd., P.O. Box 251, Story, WY 82842/307-683-2817
Al Lind, 7821 76th Ave. S. W., Tacoma, WA 98498/206-584-6361 (cust. stockm.)
Ron Long, 81 Delta St., Denver, CO 80221
Earl K. Matsuoka, 2801 Kinohou Pl., P.O. Box 61129, Honolulu, HI 96822/808-988-3008 (cust.)
John I. McCann, 2911 N. 5th St., Coeur d'Alene, ID 83814/208-667-3919
Bill McGuire, 1600 N. Eastmont Ave., East Wenatchee, WA 98801
Gale McMillan, 28638 N. 42 St., Box 7870-Cave Creek Stage, Phoenix, AZ 85020/602-585-4684
Maurer Arms, Carl R. Maurer, 2154-16th St., Akron, OH 44314/216-745-6864
John E. Maxson, Box 332, Dumas, TX 79029/806-935-5990 (custom)
R. M. Mercer, 216 S. Whitewater Ave., Jefferson, WI 53549/414-674-3839 (custom)
Robt. U. Milhoan & Son, Rt. 3, Elizabeth, WV 26143
Miller Arms, Inc., D. E. Miller, P.O. Box 260, St. Onge, SD 57779/605-578-1790
Earl Milliron Custom Guns & Stocks, 1249 N.E. 166th Ave., Portland, OR 97230/503-252-3725
Bill Monell, Red Mill Road, Pine Bush, NY 12566/914-744-3021 (custom)
Ted Nicklas, 5504 Hegel Rd., Goodrich, MI 48438/313-797-4493 (custom)
Paul R. Nickels, Interwest Gun Service, P.O. Box 243, Providence, UT 84332/801/753-4260

Oakley and Merkley, Box 2446, Sacramento, CA 95811 (blanks)
Jim Norman, Custom Gunstocks, 11230 Calenda Road, San Diego, CA 92127/619-487-4173
Maurice Ottmar, Box 657, 113 E. Fir, Coulee City, WA 99115/509-632-5717 (cust.)
Pachmayr Gun Works, 1220 S. Grand Ave., Los Angeles, CA 90015 (blanks and custom jobs)
Paulsen Gunstocks, Rte. 71, Box 11, Chinook, MT 59523/406-357-3403 (blanks)
Rely-A Outfitters Corp., P.O. Box 697, Saratoga Springs, NY 12866/518-584-6964 (Rely-A gunstock)
R. Neal Rice, 5152 Newton, Denver, CO 80221
Carl Roth, Jr., 4728 Pineridge Ave., Cheyenne, WY 82001/309-634-3958
Matt Row, Lock, Stock 'N Barrel, 8972 East Huntington Dr., San Gabriel, CA 91775/818-287-0051
Royal Arms, 1210 Bert Costa, El Cajon, CA 92020/619-448-5466
Sage International Ltd., 1856 Star Batt Dr., Rochester, MI 48063/313-852-8733 (telescoping shotgun stock)
Sanders Cust. Gun Serv., 2358 Tyler Lane, Louisville, KY 40205 (blanks)
Saratoga Arms Co., 1752 N. Pleasantview RD., Pottstown, PA 19464/215-323-8386
Roy Schaefer, 965 W. Hilliard Lane, Eugene, OR 97404/503-688-43333 (blanks)
Schwartz Custom Guns, 9621 Coleman Rd., Haslett, MI 48840/517-339-8939
David W. Schwartz, 2505 Waller St., Eau Claire, WI 54701/715-832-1735 (custom)
Shaw's, The Finest in Guns, 9447 W. Lilac Rd., Escondido, CA 92025/619-728-7070
Dan A. Sherk, 1311-105th Ave., Dawson Creek, B.C. V1G 2L9, Canada/604-782-3720 (custom)
Hank Shows, The Best,1078 Alice Ave., Ukiah, CA 95482/707-462-9060
Walter Shultz, 1752 N. Pleasantview Rd., Pottstown, PA 19464
Sile Dist., 7 Centre Market Pl., New York, NY 10013/213-925-4111 (shotgun stocks)
Six Enterprises, 6564 Hidden Creek Dr., San Jose, CA 95120/408-268-8296 (fiberglass)
Ed Sowers, 8331 DeCelis Pl., Sepulveda, CA 91343/818-893-1233 (custom hydro-coil gunstocks)
Fred D. Speiser, 2229 Dearborn, Missoula, MT 59801/406-549-8133
Sport Service Center, 2364 N. Neva, Chicago, IL 60635/312-889-1114 (custom)
Sportsmen's Equip. Co., 915 W. Washington, San Diego, CA 92103/714-296-1501 (carbine conversions)
Keith Stegall, Box 696, Gunnison, CO 81230
Stinehour Rifles, Box 84, Cragsmoor, NY 12420/914-647-4163
Surf N' Sea, Inc., 62-595 Kam Hwy., Box 268, Haleiwa, HI 96712 (custom gunstocks blanks)
Talmage Enterpr., 43197 E. Whittier, Hemet, CA 92344/714-927-2397
James C. Tucker, 205 Trinity St., Woodland, CA 95695/916-662-3109 (cust.)
Brent L. Umberger, Sportsman's Haven, R.R. 4, Cambridge, OH 43725
Milton van Epps, Rt. 69-A, Parish, NY 13131
Gil Van Horn, P.O. Box 207, Llano, CA 93544
John Vest, 6715 Shasta Way, Klamath Falls, OR 97603/503-884-5585 (classic rifles)
Weatherby's, 2781 Firestone, South Gate, CA 90280/213-569-7186
Cecil Weems, P.O. Box 657, Mineral Wells, TX 76067/817-325-1462
Frank R. Wells, 10420 E. Rusty Spur, Tucson, AZ 85749/602-749-4563 (custom stocks)
Terry Werth, 123 Lincoln Ave., Lincoln, IL 62656/217-732-9314 (custom)
Western Gunstocks Mfg. Co., 550 Valencia School Rd., Aptos, CA 95003
Duane Wiebe, P.O. Box 497, Lotus, CA 95651
Bob Williams, P.O. Box 143, Boonsboro, MD 21713
Williamson-Pate Gunsmith Service, 117 W. Pipeline, Hurst, TX 76053/817-268-2887
Jim Windish, 2510 Dawn Dr., Alexandria, VA 22306/703-765-1994 (walnut blanks)
Dave Wills, 2776 Brevard Ave., Montgomery, AL 36109/305-272-8446
Robert M. Winter, P.O. Box 484, Menno, SD 57045/605-387-5322
Mike Yee, 4732-46th Ave. S.W., Seattle, WA 98116/206-935-3682
Russell R. Zeryp, 1601 Foard Dr., Lynn Ross Manor, Morristown, TN 37814

TARGETS, BULLET & CLAYBIRD TRAPS

Beeman Inc., 47-GDD Paul Dr., San Rafael, CA 94903/415-472-7121 (airgun targets, silhouettes and traps)
Bulletboard Target Systems Laminations Corp., Box 469, Neenah, WI 54956/414-725-8368
Caswell Equipment Co., Inc., 1221 Marshall St. N.E., Minneapolis, MN 55413/612-379-2000 (target carriers; commercial shooting ranges)
J.G. Dapkus Co., P.O. Box 180, Cromwell, CT 06416/203-632-2308 (live bulls-eye targets)
Data-Targ, (See Rocky Mountain Target Co.)
Detroit-Armor Corp., Detroit Bullet Trap Div., 2233 N. Palmer Dr., Schaumburg, IL 60195/312-397-4070
Electro Ballistic Lab., 616 Junipero Serva Blvd., Stanford, CA 94305 (Electronic Trap Boy)
Ellwood Epps Northern Ltd., 210 Worthington St., W., North Bay, Ont. P1B 3B4, Canada (hand traps)
Hunterjohn, P.O. Box 477, St. Louis, MO 63166 (shotgun patterning target)
Jaro Manuf., 206 E. Shaw, Pasadena, TX 77506/713-472-0417 (paper targets)
Laminations Corp. ("Bullettrap"), Box 469, Neenah, WI 54956/414-725-8368
Laporte S.A., B.P. 212, 06603 Antibes, France (claybird traps)
MCM (Mathalienne de Construction Mecanique), Box 18, 17160 Matha, France (claybird traps)
Millard F. Lerch, Box 163, 10842 Front St., Mokena, IL 60448 (bullet target)
National Target Co., 4960 Wyaconda Rd., Rockville, MD 20852
Outers Laboratories, Div. of Omark Industries, Rte. 2, Onalaska, WI 54650/608-783-1515 (claybird traps)

Peterson Label Co., P.O. Box 186, 23 Sullivan Dr., Redding Ridge, CT 06876/203-938-2349 (paste-ons; Targ-Dots)
Recreation Prods. Res. Inc., 158 Franklin Ave., Ridgewood, NJ 07450 (Butts Bullet trap)
Remington Arms Co., Bridgeport, CT 06602 (claybird traps)
Reproductions West, Box 6765, Burbank, CA 91510 (silhouette targets)
Rocky Mountain Target Co., P.O. Box 700, Black Hawk, SD 57718/605-787-5946 (Data-Targ)
Sheridan Products, Inc., 3205 Sheridan, Racine, WI 54303 (traps)
South West Metallic Silhouettes, Rt. 7, Box 82, Abilene, TX 79605/915-928-4463
Trius Prod., Box 25, Cleves, OH 45002/513-914-5682 (claybird, can thrower)
U.S. Repeating Arms Co., P.O. Box 30-300, New Haven, CT 06511/203-789-5000 (claybird traps)
Winchester, Olin Corp., 120 Long Ridge Rd., Stamford, CT 06904

TAXIDERMY

Jack Atcheson & Sons, Inc., 3210 Ottawa St., Butte, MT. 59701
Dough's Taxidermy Studio, Doug Domedion, 2027 Lockport-Olcott Rd., Burt, NY 14028/716-625-8377 (deer head specialist)
Jonas Bros., Inc., 1037 Broadway, Denver, CO 80203 (catlg. $2)
Kulis Freeze-Dry Taxidermy, 725 Broadway Ave., Bedford, OH 44146
Mark D. Parker, 1233 Sherman Dr., Longmont, CO 80501/303-772-0214

TRAP & SKEET SHOOTERS EQUIP.

D&H Prods. Co., Inc., P.O. Box 22, Glenshaw, PA 15116/412-443-2190 (snap shell)
Griggs Recreational Prods. Inc., 200 S. Main, Twin Bridges, MT 59754/406-684-5202 (recoil redirector)
Ken Eyster Heritage Gunsmiths, Inc., 6441 Bishop Rd., Centerburg, OH 43011/614-625-6131 (shotgun competition choking)
LaPorte S.A., B.P. 212, Pont de la Brague, 06603 Antibes, France (traps, claybird)
MCM (Mathalienne de Construction de Mecanique), P.O. Box 18, 17160 Matha, France (claybird traps)
Wm. J. Mittler, 290 Moore Dr., Boulder Creek, CA 95006 (shotgun choke specialist)
Multi-Gauge Enterprises, 433 W. Foothill Blvd., Monrovia, CA 91061/213-358-4549; 357-6117 (shotgun specialists)
William J. Nittler, 290 Moore Dr., Boulder Creek, CA 95006/408-338-3376 (shotgun barrel repairs)
Outers Laboratories, Div. of Omark Industries, Route 2, Onalaska, WI 54650/608-783-1515 (trap, claybird)
Purbaugh & Sons (See Multi-Gauge) (shotgun barrel inserts)
Remington Arms Co., P.O. Box 1939, Bridgeport, Ct. 06601 (trap, claybird)
Super Pigeon Co., P.O. Box 428, Princeton, MN 55371 (claybird target)
Daniel Titus, Shooting Specialties, 872 Penn St., Bryn Mawr, PA 19010/215-525-8829 (hullbag)
Trius Products, Box 25, Cleves, OH 45002/513-941-5682 (can thrower; trap, claybird)
Winchester-Western, New Haven, CT 06504 (trap, claybird)

TRIGGERS, RELATED EQUIP.

Ametek, Hunter Spring Div., One Spring Ave., Hatfield, PA 19440/215-822-2971 (trigger gauge)
NOC, Cadillac Industrial Park, 1610 Corwin St., Cadillac, MI 49601/616-775-3425 (triggers)
M.H. Canjar Co., 500 E. 45th Ave., Denver, CO 80216/303-623-5777 (triggers)
Central Specialties Co., 6030 Northwest Hwy., Chicago,IL 60631/312-774-5000 (trigger lock)
Custom Products, Neil A. Jones, RD #1, Box 483A, Saegertown, PA 16433/814-763-2769 (trigger guard)
Dayton-Traister Co., 9322-900th West, P.O. Box 593, Oak Harbor, WA 98277/206-675-5375 (triggers)
Electronic Trigger Systems, 4124 Thrushwood Lane, Minnetonka, MN 55345/612-935-7829
Flaig's, Babcock Blvd. & Thompson Run Rd., Millvale, PA 15209 (trigger shoes)
Bill Holmes, Rt. 2, Box 242, Fayetteville, AR 72701/501-521-8958 (trigger release)
Neil A. Jones, see: Custom Products
Mad River Metalcraft Inc., 1524 Winding Trail, Springfield, OH 45503/513-399-0948 (bolt shroud safety)
Michaels of Oregon Co., P.O. Box 13010, Portland, OR 97213/503-255-6890 (trigger guards)
Miller Single Trigger Mfg. Co., R.D. 1, Box 99, Millersburg, PA 17061/717-692-3704
Viggo Miller, P.O. Box 4181, Omaha, NB 68104 (trigger attachment)
Bruce A. Nettestad, Rt. 1, Box 140, Pelican Rapids, MN 56572/218-863-4301 (trigger guards)
Ohaus Corp., 29 Hanover Rd., Florham Park, NJ 07932 (trigger pull gauge)
Pachmayr Gun Works, 1220 S. Grand Ave., Los Angeles, CA 90015 (trigger shoe)
Pacific Tool Co., P.O. Box 2048, Ordnance Plant Rd., Grand Island, NE 68801 (trigger shoe)
Richland Arms Co., 321 W. Adrian St., Blissfield, MI 49228 (trigger pull gauge)
Sport Service Center, 2364 N. Neva, Chicago, IL 60635 (release triggers)
Timney Mfg. Co., 3106 W. Thomas Rd., Suite 1104, Phoenix, AZ 85017/602-269-6937 (triggers)
Melvin Tyler, 1326 W. Britton Rd., Oklahoma City, OK 73114/800-654-8415 (trigger shoe)
Williams Gun Sight Co., 7389 Lapeer Rd., Davison, MI 48423 (trigger shoe)

Highlights of This Issue

There are reasons why this Sgt. York has a Luger. See page **6**.

Intended to excel in the smoke and clamor of the last Big War, the Enfield didn't. See page **76**.

A rifle resurrected from an African past does the job in Georgia today. See page **61**.

There is fun in those rule-beating rigs that win. See page **39**.

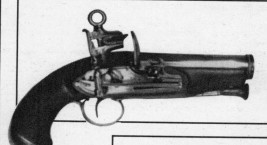
This small delight has a miquelet lock, of which much more may be learned on page **20**.

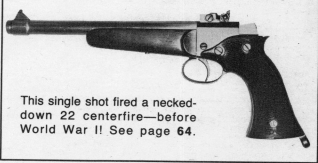
This single shot fired a necked-down 22 centerfire—before World War I! See page **64**.

Highlights of This Issue Con't.

Big bores and even bigger than that are sensible on big bears. See page **28**.

The grand man of guns, John M. Browning, seen here from a scholarly and Canadian perspective. Page **195**.

There have been several deans in the tough school of gunsmithing and P.O. Ackley is one. See page **46**.

New shotguns are getting to be real all-around guns. Page **193**.

Ever thought of a Grand Slam on turkeys? Dwain Bland has. See page **12**.

Double rifles work both ways. See page **129**.